Twentieth-Century Literary Criticism

Guide to Gale Literary Criticism Series

When you need to review criticism of literary works, these are the Gale series to use:

If the author's death date is: **You should turn to:**

After Dec. 31, 1959
(or author is still living)

CONTEMPORARY LITERARY CRITICISM

for example: Jorge Luis Borges, Anthony Burgess,
William Faulkner, Mary Gordon,
Ernest Hemingway, Iris Murdoch

1900 through 1959

TWENTIETH-CENTURY LITERARY CRITICISM

for example: Willa Cather, F. Scott Fitzgerald,
Henry James, Mark Twain, Virginia Woolf

1800 through 1899

NINETEENTH-CENTURY LITERATURE CRITICISM

for example: Fyodor Dostoevsky, Nathaniel Hawthorne,
George Sand, William Wordsworth

1400 through 1799

LITERATURE CRITICISM FROM 1400 TO 1800
(excluding Shakespeare)

for example: Anne Bradstreet, Daniel Defoe,
Alexander Pope, François Rabelais,
Jonathan Swift, Phillis Wheatley

SHAKESPEAREAN CRITICISM

Shakespeare's plays and poetry

Antiquity through 1399   *CLASSICAL AND MEDIEVAL LITERATURE CRITICISM*

for example: Dante, Homer, Plato, Sophocles, Vergil,
the Beowulf Poet

Gale also publishes related criticism series:

CHILDREN'S LITERATURE REVIEW

This series covers authors of all eras who have written for the
preschool through high school audience.

SHORT STORY CRITICISM

This series covers the major short fiction writers of all
nationalities and periods of literary history.

POETRY CRITICISM

This series covers poets of all nationalities and periods of literary
history.

ISSN 0276-8178

Volume 39

Twentieth-Century Literary Criticism

**Excerpts from Criticism of the
Works of Novelists, Poets, Playwrights,
Short Story Writers, and Other Creative Writers
Who Died between 1900 and 1960,
from the First Published Critical Appraisals
to Current Evaluations**

Paula Kepos
Editor

Laurie DiMauro
Michael W. Jones
David Kmenta
Marie Lazzari
Thomas Ligotti
Joann Prosyniuk
David Segal
Associate Editors

Gale Research Inc. · DETROIT · LONDON

STAFF

Paula Kepos, *Editor*

Laurie DiMauro, Michael W. Jones, David Kmenta, Marie Lazzari,
Thomas Ligotti, Joann Prosyniuk, David Segal, *Associate Editors*

Ian A. Goodhall, Tina Grant, Alan Hedblad, Grace Jeromski, Andrew
M. Kalasky, Ronald S. Nixon, James Poniewozik, Mark Swartz, Debra
A. Wells, *Assistant Editors*

Jeanne A. Gough, *Permissions & Production Manager*

Linda M. Pugliese, *Production Supervisor*
Maureen Puhl, Jennifer VanSickle, *Editorial Associates*
Donna Craft, Lorna Mabunda, Paul Lewon, Camille Robinson, *Editorial
Assistants*

Victoria B. Cariappa, *Research Manager*
Paula Cutcher-Jackson, Judy L. Gale, Maureen Richards, *Editorial
Associates*
Jennifer Brostrom, Robin Lupa, Mary Beth McElmeel, *Editorial
Assistants*

Sandra C. Davis, *Permissions Supervisor (Text)*
Josephine M. Keene, Kimberly F. Smilay, *Permissions Associates*
Maria L. Franklin, Michele Lonoconus, Shalice Shah, Rebecca A. Stanko,
Permissions Assistants

Patricia A. Seefelt, *Permissions Supervisor (Pictures)*
Margaret A. Chamberlain, *Permissions Associate*
Pamela A. Hayes, Keith Reed, *Permissions Assistants*

Mary Beth Trimper, *Production Manager*
Mary Winterhalter, *External Production Assistant*

Arthur Chartow, *Art Director*
C. J. Jonik, *Keyliner*

Copyright © 1991
Gale Research Inc.
835 Penobscot Building
Detroit, MI 48226-4094

Library of Congress Catalog Card Number 76-46132
ISBN 0-8103-2421-0
ISSN 0276-8178

Printed in the United States of America

Published simultaneously in the United Kingdom
by Gale Research International Limited
(An affiliated company of Gale Research Inc.)

Contents

Preface   vii

Acknowledgments   xi

Preface

Since its inception more than ten years ago, *Twentieth-Century Literary Criticism* has been purchased and used by nearly 10,000 school, public, and college or university libraries. *TCLC* has covered over 500 authors, representing 58 nationalities, and more than 25,000 titles. No other reference source has surveyed the critical response to twentieth-century authors and literature as thoroughly as *TCLC*. In the words of one reviewer, "there is nothing comparable available." *TCLC* "is a gold mine of information—dates, pseudonyms, biographical information, and criticism from books and periodicals—which many libraries would have difficulty assembling on their own."

Scope of the Series

TCLC is designed to serve as an introduction to authors who died between 1900 and 1960 and to the most significant interpretations of these authors' works. The great poets, novelists, short story writers, playwrights, and philosophers of this period are frequently studied in high school and college literature courses. In organizing and excerpting the vast amount of critical material written on these authors, *TCLC* helps students develop valuable insight into literary history, promotes a better understanding of the texts, and sparks ideas for papers and assignments. Each entry in *TCLC* presents a comprehensive survey of an author's career or an individual work of literature and provides the user with a multiplicity of interpretations and assessments. Such variety allows students to pursue their own interests; furthermore, it fosters an awareness that literature is dynamic and responsive to many different opinions.

Every fourth volume of *TCLC* is devoted to literary topics that cannot be covered under the author approach used in the rest of the series. Such topics include literary movements, prominent themes in twentieth-century literature, literary reaction to political and historical events, significant eras in literary history, prominent literary anniversaries, and the literatures of cultures that are often overlooked by English-speaking readers.

TCLC is designed as a companion series to Gale's *Contemporary Literary Criticism,* which reprints commentary on authors now living or who have died since 1960. Because of the different periods under consideration, there is no duplication of material between *CLC* and *TCLC*. For additional information about *CLC* and Gale's other criticism titles, users should consult the Guide to Gale Literary Criticism Series preceding the title page in this volume.

Coverage

Each volume of *TCLC* is carefully compiled to present:

- criticism of authors, or literary topics, representing a variety of genres and nationalities

- both major and lesser-known writers and literary works of the period

- 14-16 authors or 4-6 topics per volume

- individual entries that survey critical response to each author's work or each topic in literary history, including early criticism to reflect initial reactions; later criticism to represent any rise or decline in reputation; and current retrospective analyses.

Organization of This Book

An author entry consists of the following elements: author heading, biographical and critical introduction, list of principal works, excerpts of criticism (each preceded by an annotation and followed by a bibliographic citation), and a bibliography of further reading.

- The **author heading** consists of the name under which the author most commonly wrote, followed by birth and death dates. If an author wrote consistently under a pseudonym, the pseudonym will be listed in the author heading and the real name given in parentheses on the first line of the biographical and critical introduction. Also located at the beginning of the introduction to the author entry are any name variations under which an author wrote, including transliterated forms for authors whose languages use nonroman alphabets.

- The **biographical and critical introduction** outlines the author's life and career, as well as the critical issues surrounding his or her work. References are provided to past volumes of *TCLC* and to other biographical and critical reference series published by Gale, including *Short Story Criticism, Children's Literature Review, Contemporary Authors, Dictionary of Literary Biography,* and *Something about the Author.*

- Most *TCLC* entries include **portraits** of the author. Many entries also contain reproductions of materials pertinent to an author's career, including manuscript pages, title pages, dust jackets, letters, and drawings, as well as photographs of important people, places, and events in an author's life.

- The **list of principal works** is chronological by date of first book publication and identifies the genre of each work. In the case of foreign authors with both foreign-language publications and English translations, the title and date of the first English-language edition are given in brackets. Unless otherwise indicated, dramas are dated by first performance, not first publication.

- **Criticism** is arranged chronologically in each author entry to provide a perspective on changes in critical evaluation over the years. All titles of works by the author featured in the entry are printed in boldface type to enable the user to easily locate discussion of particular works. Also for purposes of easier identification, the critic's name and the publication date of the essay are given at the beginning of each piece of criticism. Unsigned criticism is preceded by the title of the journal in which it appeared. Some of the excerpts in *TCLC* also contain translated material. Unless otherwise noted, translations in brackets are by the editors; translations in parentheses or continuous with the text are by the critic. Publication information (such as publisher names and book prices) and parenthetical numerical references (such as footnotes or page and line references to specific editions of works) have been deleted at the editors' discretion to provide smoother reading of the text.

- Critical excerpts are prefaced by **annotations** providing the reader with information about both the critic and the criticism that follows. Included are the critic's reputation, individual approach to literary criticism, and particular expertise in an author's works. Also noted are the relative importance of a work of criticism, the scope of the excerpt, and the growth of critical controversy or changes in critical trends regarding an author. In some cases, these annotations cross-reference excerpts by critics who discuss each other's commentary.

- A complete **bibliographic citation** designed to facilitate location of the original essay or book follows each piece of criticism.

- An annotated list of **further reading** appearing at the end of each author entry suggests secondary sources on the author. In some cases it includes essays for which the editors could not obtain reprint rights.

Cumulative Indexes

- Each volume of *TCLC* contains a cumulative **author index** listing all authors who have appeared in the following Gale series: *Contemporary Literary Criticism, Twentieth-Century Literary Criticism, Nineteenth-Century Literature Criticism, Literature Criticism from 1400 to 1800,* and *Classical and Medieval Literature Criticism.* Topic entries devoted to a single author, such as the entry on James Joyce's *Ulysses* in *TCLC* 26, are listed in this index. Also included are cross-references to the Gale series *Poetry Criticism, Short Story Criticism, Children's Literature Review, Authors in the News, Contemporary Authors, Contemporary Authors Autobiography Series, Dictionary of Literary Biography, Concise Dictionary of American Literary Biography, Something about the Author, Something about the Author Autobiography Series,* and *Yesterday's Authors of Books for Children.* Useful for locating authors within the various series, this index is particularly valuable for those authors who are identified by a certain period but who, because of their death dates, are placed in another, or for those authors whose careers span two periods. For example, F. Scott Fitzgerald is found in *TCLC,* yet a writer often associated with him, Ernest Hemingway, is found in *CLC.*

- Each *TCLC* volume includes a cumulative **nationality index** which lists all authors who have appeared in *TCLC* volumes, arranged alphabetically under their respective nationalities, as well as Topics volume entries devoted to particular national literatures.

- Each new volume in Gale's Literary Criticism Series includes a cumulative **topic index,** which lists all literary topics treated in *NCLC, TCLC, LC 1400-1800,* and the *CLC* Yearbook.

- Each new volume of *TCLC,* with the exception of the Topics volumes, contains a **title index** listing the titles of all literary works discussed in the volume. The first volume of *TCLC* published each year contains an index listing all titles discussed in the series since its inception. Titles discussed in the Topics volume entries are not included in the *TCLC* cumulative index.

A Note to the Reader

When writing papers, students who quote directly from any volume in Gale's Literary Criticism Series may use the following general forms to footnote reprinted criticism. The first example pertains to material drawn from periodicals, the second to material reprinted from books.

[1] T. S. Eliot, "John Donne," *The Nation and the Athenaeum,* 33 (9 June 1923), 321-32; excerpted and reprinted in *Literature Criticism from 1400 to 1800,* Vol. 10, ed. James E. Person, Jr. (Detroit: Gale Research, 1989), pp. 28-9.

[2] Clara G. Stillman, *Samuel Butler: A Mid-Victorian Modern* (Viking Press, 1932); excerpted and reprinted in *Twentieth-Century Literary Criticism,* Vol. 33, ed. Paula Kepos (Detroit: Gale Research, 1989), pp. 43-5.

Suggestions Are Welcome

In response to suggestions, several features have been added to *TCLC* since the series began, including annotations to excerpted criticism, a cumulative index to authors in all Gale literary criticism series, entries devoted to criticism on a single work by a major author, more extensive illustrations, and a title index listing all literary works discussed in the series since its inception.

Readers who wish to suggest authors or topics to appear in future volumes, or who have other suggestions, are cordially invited to write the editors.

Acknowledgments

The editors wish to thank the copyright holders of the excerpted criticism included in this volume, the permissions managers of many book and magazine publishing companies for assisting us in securing reprint rights, and Anthony Bogucki for assistance with copyright research. We are also grateful to the staffs of the Detroit Public Library, Wayne State University Purdy/Kresge Library Complex, and the University of Michigan Libraries for making their resources available to us. Following is a list of the copyright holders who have granted us permission to reprint material in this volume of *TCLC*. Every effort has been made to trace copyright, but if omissions have been made, please let us know.

COPYRIGHTED EXCERPTS IN *TCLC*, VOLUME 39, WERE REPRINTED FROM THE FOLLOWING PERIODICALS:

American Literary Realism 1870-1910, v. 20, Fall, 1987. Copyright © 1987 by McFarland & Company, Inc. Reprinted by permission of the publisher.—*American Quarterly,* v. XX, Summer, 1968 for "Jack London's 'The Call of the Wild' " by Raymond Benoit. Copyright 1968, American Studies Association. Reprinted by permission of the publisher and author.—*Ball State University Forum,* v. XXI, Autumn, 1980. © 1980 Ball State University. Reprinted by permission of the publisher.—*Forum for Modern Language Studies,* v. XVII, October, 1981 for "Don Segundo Sombra and Machismo" by Peter R. Beardsell. Copyright © 1981 by *Forum for Modern Language Studies* and the author. Reprinted by permission of the publisher and the author.—*Genre,* v. XII, Fall, 1979 for "Very Like a Whale: The Comical-Tragical Illusions of 'The Good Soldier' " by David Eggenschwiler. © copyright 1979 by the University of Oklahoma. Reprinted by permission of the University of Oklahoma and the author.—*Great Plains Quarterly,* v. 7, Summer, 1987. Reprinted by permission of the publisher.—*Jack London Newsletter,* v. 2, September-December, 1969 for "Jack London's Naturalism: The Example of 'The Call of the Wild' " by Earl J. Wilcox; v. 4, September-December, 1971 for "Naturalism in the Works of Jack London" by Mary Kay Dodson; v. 7, May-August, 1974 for "A Syllabus for the 20th Century: Jack London's 'The Call of the Wild' " by Jonathan H. Spinner; v. 11, January-April, 1978 for " 'Call of the Wild'—Jack London's Catharsis" by Andrew Flink. Reprinted by permission of the respective authors.—*Journal of American Studies,* v. 20, December, 1986. © Cambridge University Press 1986. Reprinted with the permission of Cambridge University Press.—*Jump Cut,* n. 15, July, 1977. © 1977 by *Jump Cut.* Reprinted by permission of the publisher.—*Kansas Quarterly,* v. 1, Summer, 1969 for " 'Babbitt' as Situational Satire" by Helen B. Petrullo. © copyright 1969 by the *Kansas Quarterly.* Reprinted by permission of the publisher and the author.—*The Leo Baeck Institute of Jews from Germany Yearbook,* London, v. X, 1965. © Leo Baeck Institute 1965. Reprinted by permission of Dr. Arnold Paucker.—*The Markham Review,* v. 8, Fall, 1978. © Wagner College 1978. Reprinted by permission of the publisher.—*The Michigan Academician,* v. VIII, Winter, 1976. Copyright © The Michigan Academy of Science, Arts, and Letters, 1976. Reprinted by permission of the publisher.—*Modern Fiction Studies,* v. 9, Spring, 1963. Copyright © 1963 by Purdue Research Foundation, West Lafayette, IN 47907. All rights reserved. Reprinted with permission.—*Mosaic: A Journal for the Comparative Study of Literature and Ideas,* v. XII, Summer, 1979. © *Mosaic* 1979. Acknowledgment of previous publication is herewith made.—*The Nation,* New York, v. 214, May 22, 1972. Copyright 1972 *The Nation* magazine/The Nation Company, Inc. Reprinted by permission of the publisher.—*The New Republic,* v. LXXXII, March 20, 1935 for "Spirit of the Pampas" by Malcolm Cowley. Copyright 1935 The New Republic, Inc. Renewed 1963 by Malcolm Cowley. Reprinted by permission of the author.—*New York Herald Tribune Books,* April 6, 1930. Copyright 1930, renewed 1958 I.H.T. Corporation. Reprinted by permission of the publisher.—*The New York Review of Books,* v. 13, December 18, 1969. Copyright © 1969 Nyrev, Inc. Reprinted with permission from *The New York Review of Books.*—*The New York Times Book Review,* December 12, 1920; August 26, 1923. Copyright 1920, 1923 by The New York Times Company. Both reprinted by permission of the publisher.—*North Dakota Quarterly,* v. 40, Winter, 1972. Copyright 1972 by The University of North Dakota. Reprinted by permission of the publisher.—*The Ontario Review,* n. 11, Fall-Winter, 1979-80. Copyright © 1979 by The Ontario Review, Inc. Reprinted by permission of the publisher.—*Renascence,* v. XXXVII, Summer, 1985. © copyright, 1985, Marquette University Press. Reprinted by permission of the publisher.—*Satire Newsletter,* v. IV, Fall, 1966 for " 'Babbitt': Satiric Realism in Form and Content" by Philip Allan Friedman. Reprinted by permission of the publisher and the author.—*The Sewanee Review,* v. 88, Fall, 1980. © 1980 by The University of the South. Reprinted by permission of *The Sewanee Review.*—*Victorian Poetry,* v. 10, Spring, 1972. Reprinted by permission of the publisher.—*West Virginia University Philological Papers,* v. 33, 1987. Reprinted by permission of the publisher.

ford University Press, Inc.—Walcutt, Charles Child. From *Man's Changing Mask: Modes and Methods of Characterization in Fiction.* University of Minnesota Press, 1966. Copyright © 1966 by the University of Minnesota. All rights reserved. Reprinted by permission of the publisher.—Watson, Charles N., Jr. From *The Novels of Jack London: A Reappraisal.* The University of Wisconsin Press, 1983. Copyright © 1983 The Board of Regents of the University of Wisconsin System. All rights reserved. Reprinted by permission of the publisher.—Wellek, René. From "Walter Benjamin's Literary Criticism in His Marxist Phase," in *The Personality of the Critic.* Edited by Joseph P. Strelka. The Pennsylvania State University Press, 1973. Copyright © 1973, The Pennsylvania State University Press, University Park, PA. All rights reserved. Reproduced by permission of the publisher.—Wolin, Richard. From *Walter Benjamin: An Anesthetic of Redemption.* Columbia University Press, 1982. Copyright © 1982 Columbia University Press. All rights reserved. Used by permission of the publisher.

PHOTOGRAPHS AND ILLUSTRATIONS APPEARING IN *TCLC,* VOLUME 39, WERE RECEIVED FROM THE FOLLOWING SOURCES:

Suhrkamp Verlag: **p. 20;** Ernst Rowahlt Verlag; Photograph by Jaseha Stone: **p. 44;** Courtesy of Cleveland Public Library: **p. 87;** Courtesy of Cecil Goldbeck: **p. 120;** Courtesy of Jeanne Foster: **p. 136;** Courtesy of the Estate of Carl Van Vechten, Joseph Solomon, Executor: **p. 199;** Courtesy of Harcourt Brace Jovanovich, Inc.: **p. 211;** AP/Wide World Photos: **p. 227;** Copyright © 1977 by Seymour Linden: **p. 274;** Alexander Turnbull Library, Wellington, New Zealand: **p. 299;** Photograph by Ida Baker: **p. 317.**

Walter Benjamin

1892-1940

German philosopher, critic, essayist, and cultural theorist.

One of the most influential thinkers of the period between the First and Second World Wars, Benjamin is best known for his works of cultural criticism and his insightful studies of language and literature. Addressing such issues as the social function of the arts, the metaphysical implications of language, and the history of society as it is affected by technology, Benjamin's works are considered challenging and controversial texts that resist classification and invite critical debate, leading Julian Roberts to characterize Benjamin as a "highly respected enigma."

Born in Berlin to affluent Jewish parents, Benjamin received an elite, progressive education. In 1912 he began his postsecondary studies at the University of Freiburg and became a member of the popular German Youth Movement, which denounced modern society and advocated an ethical code based on such traditional values as heroism, nationalism, and the preservation of racial purity. One of the movement's strongest speakers, Benjamin represented a radical branch whose largely Jewish membership, rather than promoting a unified struggle for ethical improvement of society, stressed the spiritual refinement of the individual. Becoming disenchanted with the demand for consensus within the Youth Movement, even within the radical faction to which he belonged, Benjamin discontinued his involvement in 1914.

During World War I, Benjamin studied philosophy at universities in Munich and Berlin, and completed his doctorate in 1919 at the University of Bern in Switzerland. His dissertation on German Romantic art criticism, *Der Begriff der Kunstkritik in der deutschen Romantik*, considered the nature of art, literature, and criticism, concerns that persisted throughout his career. After graduation, Benjamin published reviews and articles in German periodicals, most notably his essay *Goethes "Wahlverwandschaften"* (*Goethe's "Elective Affinities"*) and wrote *Der Ursprung des deutschen Trauerspiels* (*The Origin of German Tragic Drama*), a study intended to fulfill an application requirement for a teaching position at the University of Frankfurt. The university rejected the work in 1925, one professor finding it an "incomprehensible morass"; most critics cite this incident as a turning point in Benjamin's career. Unable to continue his research and writing under the sponsorship of a university, he was compelled to free-lance during a period of financial difficulty for most Germans and in an atmosphere of increasing hostility towards Jews. During his years in Berlin, Benjamin established a friendship with the German dramatist Bertolt Brecht, whose plays he admired for their avant-garde presentation of communist philosophy. Attracted to the ideology and revolutionary nature of communism, bolshevism, and Marxism, Benjamin became a prominent figure in leftist circles, while refusing to be recognized as a member of any political party.

With Adolf Hitler's rise to power in 1933, Benjamin went

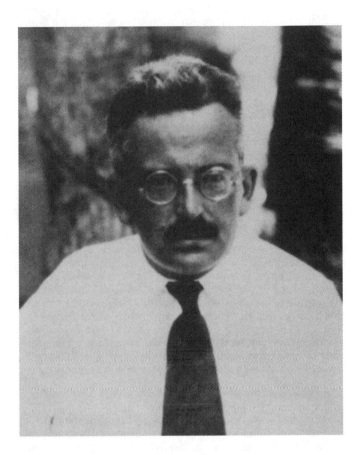

into exile. Living intermittently in Paris and Denmark, he published essays and reviews under pseudonyms in German journals. In 1935 Benjamin began contributing essays to the *Zeitschrift für Sozialforschung,* the publication of the Institute for Social Research, whose primary advocates, Theodor Adorno and Max Horkheimer, offered him a generous annual stipend. While his interest in documenting and interpreting cultural phenomena was pertinent to the Institute's goal of effecting social change through intellectual enlightenment, Adorno considered many of Benjamin's writings more politically pragmatic than theoretical, and their ensuing debate over the acceptability of Benjamin's works became known as the Benjamin-Adorno dispute. Despite the attempts of several of his colleagues to persuade him to leave Europe, Benjamin settled in Paris in 1939. After the German invasion of France in 1940, however, he resolved to relocate to the United States. That autumn, he and a small group of refugees were apprehended in their attempt to leave Europe, whereupon Benjamin committed suicide.

Benjamin's works may be divided into three categories: autobiographical writings and familiar essays, literary criticism, and philosophical essays. In the autobiographical *Berliner Kindheit um Neunzehnhundert* Benjamin evaluates the effects of the political and religious attitudes prevalent in turn-of-the-century Germany on his childhood experiences. *Einbahnstrasse (One-Way Street)* consists of aphoristic, reflective essays that comment on modern society through the examination of commonplace events in everyday life and the observation of the dynamics of city life. More complex in both style and content, Benjamin's literary criticism often both interprets a work of literature and theorizes on the nature of criticism, language, and translation. In *Goethe's "Elective Affinities,"* for example, Benjamin not only discusses Goethe's understanding of myth as displayed in *Elective Affinities,* but also uses his discussion of the novel to emphasize his own rejection of biographical criticism and to suggest his theory on the degeneration of language in modern society. Similarly complex is the methodology of his philosophical writings. *The Origin of German Tragic Drama,* considered one of Benjamin's most important works, analyzes allegory in the German baroque drama, or *Trauerspiel,* and the ways in which it informs aesthetic theory. While literary in nature, the essay is praised primarily for its philosophical examination of the function of *Trauerspiel* as stoic commentary on material transience. In "Das Kunstwerk im Zeitalter seiner technischen Reproduzierbarkeit" ("The Work of Art in the Age of Mechanical Reproduction") Benjamin discusses the relationship between art and technology. Defining his concept of "aura" as a quality of uniqueness and authenticity specific to a work of art, Benjamin contends that the ability to reproduce art mechanically (in photographs and film) diminishes the "aura" of art, freeing it from the "fabric of tradition" and changing its nature from aesthetic to political. Benjamin also focused specifically on the philosophy of history in several highly regarded essays later in his career.

Characterized by most critics as convoluted and problematic, Benjamin's works incorporate aspects of several ideologies, but the depth of Benjamin's commitment to any one of them remains controversial. Some critics, particularly René Wellek and Julian Roberts, find that Benjamin's career represents a gradual adoption of the principles of Marxism. The issue of Benjamin's commitment to Marxism centers on his espousal of dialectical materialism, the Marxist worldview that defines attitudes and ideas as the result of material conditions and emphasizes the power struggle between classes in society, which produces a constant process of change known as the "dialectic." Wellek and Roberts argue that Benjamin became dedicated to this philosophy and to Marxism during the last decade of his life. Wellek states that "Marxist themes—the alienation of man, 'reification,' the work of art as commodity—permeate his later work," while Roberts has described Benjamin as a "revolutionary specialist."

In opposition to the view of Benjamin as a Marxist, some commentators emphasize the importance of spiritual values in Benjamin's work. Prominent among these critics are Gershom Scholem and Hannah Arendt, who focus their criticism on Benjamin's commitment to Judaism. Scholem characterizes Benjamin as a "metaphysical genius" and dismisses Marxism as a passing interest resulting from his friendship with Brecht. Scholem also believed that Benjamin's works on the philosophy of language, with their references to sacred texts, as in his "Die Aufgabe des Übersetzers" ("The Task of the Translator"), indicate the strong influence that the ideas of messianism and spiritual redemption had on his critical thinking. Arendt argues that Benjamin believed language to be imbued with public values and that this belief is a manifestation of his espousal of Zionism, which for him was a form of protest against the oppression Jews endured in European society, much in the same way as his interest in Marxism was a reaction to an oppressive social structure.

Several commentators maintain that the resistance of Benjamin's work to categorization reflects his absolute refusal to confine himself to a single ideology. Adorno believed his colleague's position to be that of a nonconformist whose interest in cultural phenomena supplanted the conventional approaches to philosophy. Critics generally regard Benjamin as an original, perceptive, and important thinker. Concerning his sometimes contradictory and obscure writings, Bernd Witte suggests that "the esoteric itself needs to be comprehended as a constitutive element of Benjamin's thought."

PRINCIPAL WORKS

Der Begriff der Kunstkritik in der deutschen Romantik (criticism) 1920
Goethes "Wahlverwandtschaften" (essay) 1924-25
Einbahnstrasse (aphorisms) 1928
　[*One-Way Street,* published in *One-Way Street, and Other Writings,* 1979]
Der Ursprung des deutschen Trauerspiels (criticism) 1928
　[*The Origin of German Tragic Drama,* 1977]
Kleine Geschichte der Photographie (essay) 1931
　[*A Short History of Photography,* 1972]
Das Kunstwerk im Zeitalter seiner technischen Reproduzierbarkeit (essay) 1936
　[*The Work of Art in the Age of Mechanical Reproduction,* 1968]
Über den Begriff der Geschichte (criticism) 1942
　[*Theses on the Philosophy of History,* 1968]
Berliner Kindheit um Neunzehnhundert (memoirs) 1950
Schriften. 2 vols. (essays, addresses, and letters) 1955
Zentralpark (aphorisms) 1955
　[*Central Park* published in journal *New German Critique,* 1985]
Illuminationen: Ausgewählte Schriften (essays) 1961
　[*Illuminations,* 1968]
Zur Kritik der Gewalt und andere Aufsätze (essays) 1965
　[*Critique of Violence, and Other Essays,* 1978]
Briefe. 2 vols. (letters) 1966
Versuche über Brecht (criticism) 1966
　[*Understanding Brecht,* 1973]
Charles Baudelaire: Ein Lyriker im Zeitalter des Hochkapitalismus (essays) 1969
　[*Charles Baudelaire: A Lyric Poet in the Era of High Capitalism,* 1973]
Gesammelte Schriften. 6 vols. (essays, criticism, and letters) 1972-88
Reflections: Essays, Aphorisms, Autobiographical Writings (essays and aphorisms) 1978
Briefwechsel, 1933-40 (letters) 1980
　[*The Correspondence of Walter Benjamin and Gershom Scholem, 1932-1940,* 1989]

Moskauer Tagebuch (diary) 1980
[*Moscow Diary,* 1986]

Gershom Scholem   (lecture date 1964)

[*A German-born Jewish scholar, Scholem was the author of over five hundred books and articles. Much of his work concerns the Cabala, the traditional system of Jewish mysticism, and Scholem is generally credited with raising the study of the Cabala from a state of disreputability to what the* London Times *has called "a position of central importance" in Jewish thought. In the following excerpt from the transcript of a lecture first delivered in 1964, Scholem offers an appreciative discussion of Benjamin's philosophical and theological principles, emphasizing the importance of Judaism in his critical thought.*]

In the years that have passed since the publication of his **Schriften,** a good deal has been written about Benjamin, much of it silly or petty. He had too strong an element of the enigmatic and unfathomable in his mental makeup not to provoke that sort of thing. And his critics' misunderstandings would surely have been a source of amusement to him who even in his brightest hours never abandoned the esoteric thinker's stance. As Adorno said very aptly about him, "What Benjamin said and wrote sounded as if born of mystery, yet its force derived from cogency." The peculiar aura of authority emanating from his thought, though never explicitly invoked, tended to incite contradiction, while the rejection of any systematic approach in all his work published after 1922—a rejection that he himself proclaimed boldly from the hoardings—screened the center of his personality from the view of many.

That center can be clearly defined: Benjamin was a philosopher. He was one through all the phases and in all the fields of his activity. On the face of it he wrote mostly about subjects of literature and art, sometimes also about topics on the borderline between literature and politics, but only rarely about matters conventionally considered and accepted as themes of pure philosophy. Yet in all these domains he derives his impulse from the philosopher's experience. Philosophical experience of the world and its reality—that is how we can sum up the meaning of the term *metaphysics,* and that is certainly the sense in which it is used by Benjamin. He was a metaphysician; indeed, I would say, a metaphysician pure and simple. But it was borne in on him that in his generation the genius of a pure metaphysician could express itself more readily in other spheres, any other sphere rather than in those traditionally assigned to metaphysics, and this was precisely one of the experiences that helped to mold his distinctive individuality and originality. He was attracted more and more—in a fashion strangely reminiscent of Simmel, with whom otherwise he had little in common—by subjects which would seem to have little or no bearing on metaphysics. It is a special mark of his genius that under his gaze every one of these subjects discloses a dignity, a philosophic aura of its own which he sets out to describe.

His metaphysical genius flowed from the quality of his relevant experience, its abounding richness pregnant with symbolism. It was this latter aspect of his experience, I believe, which invests many of his most luminous statements with the character of the occult. Nor is this surprising. Benjamin was a man to whom occult experiences were not foreign. Rarely though—if ever—do they appear in his work in their immediate unprocessed form. (This is presumably why he was able to recapture the occult character of Proust's decisive experience with unsurpassed precision.) In his personal life, incidentally, this trait found expression in an almost uncanny graphological gift of which I witnessed a good many instances. (Later on he tended to conceal this gift.)

Even where he takes up controversial topics of literary and general history or politics as his starting point, the metaphysician's eye penetrates deep below the surface, and reveals in the objects of his discourse fresh layers bathed in a light of strange radiance. In his earlier works he seems to describe the configuration of such layers as if writing under dictation, while later on this immediacy gives way to an increasingly precise understanding of the tension and the dialectic motion astir in his subjects. He proceeds from the simplest elements, and entirely unexpected vistas open themselves up to him; the hidden inner life of his subjects is manifest to him. His discursive thinking commands great trenchancy, as displayed, for instance, in his first book, on the concept of art criticism among the early German romantics. In most of his work, however, this discursive element of strict conceptual exposition takes second place to a descriptive method by which he seeks to let his experience speak. It is this descriptive method which seems so strangely to open his subjects up to him, and which invests even short papers and essays of his with a character at the same time fragmentary and final.

To say that Benjamin is a difficult author would be an understatement. His major works demand an unusual degree of concentration from the reader. His thought was greatly compressed and inexorable in the often excessive brevity of exposition. Accordingly, his works—if I may say so—need to be meditated upon. At the same time they are written in a masterly prose of rare incandescence. His essay on **Goethe's "Elective Affinities"** [**Goethes "Wahlverwandtschaften"**], which moved Hofmannsthal to enthusiasm, combines in a manner unique in aesthetics the highest elevation of style with the deepest thought. The same applies to the last section of his book on the *Trauerspiel.* By contrast many of his smaller and smallest pieces—especially the essays in *Die Literarische Welt, Die Gesellschaft,* and *Frankfurter Zeitung*—are written with a gusto and facility of expression that seem to veil the profundity of interpretation. As his masterpiece in this genre I would rate the essay on Gottfried Keller, although others—for instance those on Johann Peter Hebel, Paul Scheerbart, Robert Walser, Nikolai Leskov, and Max Kommerell—come close to it. No wonder that the combination came off, sprang into life spontaneously as it were, where he was able to pay homage. (pp. 177-79)

His metaphysical genius dominates his writings, from the unpublished **"Metaphysics of Youth,"** which he wrote in 1913 at the age of twenty-one, to the **Theses on the Philosophy of History** of 1940, his latest extant piece of writing. It is manifested especially in two spheres that increasingly interpenetrate in his work: the philosophy of language and the philosophy of history. The one bent led to a growing preoccupation with literary critical analysis, the other similarly to social-critical analysis. But throughout it was always the philosopher speaking, unambiguous, an unmistakable voice. For about ten years he upheld the concept of the philosophic system as the form proper to philosophy, after which he himself was groping. Kant exerted a lasting influence on him, even where—as in the recently published **"Program of the Coming Philosophy"**—he passionately challenges the validity of the experience expressed in that philosophy. He expected that an experience of infinitely greater richness would still have to be fitted into what was basically Kant's frame of reference, however great the necessary modifications. But this ideal of the system, reflecting the traditional canons of philosophy, was corroded and eventually destroyed in his mind by a skepticism that stemmed in equal proportions from his study of neo-Kantian systems and from his own specific experience.

Margarete Susman has referred to an "exodus from philosophy" said to have occurred in Germany after World War I and to have ushered in a completely new mode of thinking. What she meant, to judge from her examples, was the tendency to turn from idealism to existentialism and theology. Few men can have provided more drastic an illustration of this exodus than Walter Benjamin, who forsook systematic philosophy to dedicate himself to the task of commenting on the great works, a task which at that time—with his prime interests still belonging to theology—he considered preliminary to commenting on sacred texts. This goal, though clearly envisaged, he never reached; the provisional, halfway stage remained the ever-changing and yet enduring field for his productivity, and the form of his philosophy was determined by the method of commentary. After the liquidation of the driving force of system, a dialectic unfolds in his commentaries that seeks to record the intrinsic movement of each object of contemplation at its specific historical locus. True, everything is still viewed from one common angle of vision here, but the separate pieces can no longer cohere into a unified system, which in his eyes became increasingly suspect of brutality.

The themes of most of his papers now become those of literary criticism, different though Benjamin's writings in this field are from the customary ingredients of that genre. Only rarely are his analyses and reflections literary in the conventional sense of being concerned with the structure and value of an important work. They are almost invariably philosophical probings of their specific and in particular their historical aura, to use a concept that often recurs in his writings, seen from many different angles. Each of his pieces outlines, as it were, an entire philosophy of its subject. Clearly, having set himself the task of interpreting and plumbing the depths of the great works of literature—in his eyes, incidentally, greatness did not always coincide with public fame—the philosopher did not surrender to the methods of literary history he had come to recognize as more than dubious, but worked all the time with the inheritance of the philosophical inspiration that never deserted him. He was at his most inspired where he felt the appeal of a kindred impulse or an inspiration close to his own—nowhere more so than in the cases of Marcel Proust and Franz Kafka to whose world he devoted years of intense exploration, of impassioned reliving and detached rethinking. In such cases there were virtually no limits to

the overflowing metaphysical richness at his command in recapturing the unique historical situation that he saw reflected in these works, its very uniqueness manifesting complete universality. It is nearly always this combination of historical cum philosophical insight with a wide-awake and highly articulate awareness of artistic values that turns his essays—and sometimes the shortest among them in particular—into true masterpieces. What was the anatomy of the imagination of "his" authors—though in fact he was theirs, possessed rather than self-possessed—and how was the mainspring of their imagination connected in each case with the characteristic tension of the historical and social ambience that determined their production? These were the questions that fascinated him.

To Benjamin, mystics and satirists, humanists and lyricists, scholars and monomaniacs are equally worthy of philosophical study in depth. As he proceeds he is liable without warning to switch from the profane to the theological approach, for he has a precise feel for the outline of theological substance even when it seems dissolved altogether in the world of the wholly temporal. And even where he thinks that he can successfully avail himself of the materialist method, he does not close his eyes to what he has perceived with the utmost clarity. For all his renunciation of system, his thought, presented as that of a fragmentarian, yet retains a systematic tendency. He used to say that each great work needed its own epistemology just as it had its own metaphysics. This constructive tendency in his mode of thinking—constructive even where applied to destructive facts or phenomena—also conditions his style. Meticulously pointed, shining with a contemplative luster that refuses the slightest concession to the fashionable expressionist prose of those years, this style is deeply embedded in the processes of a mind striving after order and cohesion. Benjamin's "texts" really are what the word says: "woven tissues." Although in his youth he was in close personal contact with the rising expressionism which celebrated its first triumphs in Berlin at that time, he never surrendered to it. In his best works the German language has achieved a perfection that takes the reader's breath away. It owes this perfection to the rare achievement of blending highest abstraction with sensuous richness and presentation in the round, and thus bears the hallmark of his notion of metaphysical knowledge. In a wonderful fashion his language, without abandoning depth of insight, closely and snugly fits the subject it covers and at the same time strives in competition with the subject's own language from which it keeps its precise distance. I know very few authors of this century whose writings include a comparable number of pages of sheer perfection. The tension between the language of Benjamin's analyses or interpretations and the texts on which they are based is often stupendous. The reader—if I may use a mathematical simile—finds himself between two transfinite classes reciprocally related, though not by a one-to-one correspondence. The perfection of language in Goethe's *Elective Affinities* or in Karl Kraus's polemical pages is matched in Benjamin's treatment of those works by the new beauty of the interpreter's language, which seems to descend from the language of a recording angel. Small wonder, then, that Hofmannsthal was overwhelmed by the long essay on [*Goethe's "Elective Affinities"*]; small wonder, too, that Kraus, while acknowledging that the essay devoted to him was "well meant," did not understand a word of it. (pp. 180-83)

Benjamin undoubtedly had his quirks. I have sometimes been asked whether his attitude toward Judaism was not perhaps one of those quirks to which he clung with all his obstinacy. But this is not the case. On May 25, 1925, shortly after the world of Marxist dialectic had first appeared in his field of vision, he said in a letter that two crucial experiences lay still ahead of him: contact with Marxist politics (he still thought little of the theory of Marxism at the time) and with Hebrew. This statement provides a key to the understanding of Benjamin, for these are precisely the two experiences that never came his way. It is a deeply and authentically revealing statement in a matter where my own personal experience, which in any case is scarcely communicable in a convincing way, might be found inconclusive.

When we inquire after the Jewish element in this man and his production, it is entirely in character with Walter Benjamin's contrariness and complexity that the Jewishness of which he was intensely aware as the root of his being, and often also as the ultimate destination of his thought, should be present only in overtones in the bulk of his work, though admittedly in very conspicuous places, for instance in the prospectus for the projected journal *Angelus Novus,* or in the **Theses on the Philosophy of History,** his last work. But there is much more behind it.

In the years of withdrawn study and preparation during World War I and immediately afterward, the phenomenon of Judaism occupied him a great deal, and he read sporadically but widely about the subject. When I told him in 1916 that *Philosophy of History or Reflections on Tradition* (*Philosophie der Geschichte, oder über die Tradition*)—a large four-volume work on the *kabbalah* by Franz Joseph Molitor, a pupil of Franz von Baader—published sixty to eighty years earlier, was surprisingly still available at the publishers', this was one of the first works on Judaism which he acquired. For many years it occupied a place of honor in his library. In Franz Rosenzweig's *Star of Redemption*—the most original work of Jewish theology of our generation, of which Benjamin, on the evidence of many of his own writings, was an avid reader—as well as in the kabbalist writings, he experienced that profound attachment of genuine Jewish theological thinking to the medium of language that became so marked a feature of his own work. In letters and conversations, he returned time after time to Jewish issues, and while going out of his way to emphasize his own factual ignorance, he would yet quite often approach them with his relentless intensity and delve into problems of Judaism as a matter that concerned him personally and fundamentally. Many a letter of his stands as a curious testimony to this interest. (pp. 191-2)

Benjamin's "theological thinking"—a marked tendency of his early years that impressed itself on all who came into close contact with him at the time—took its bearings (instinctively, I almost added) from Jewish concepts. Christian ideas never held any attraction for him. Indeed, he had an undisguised distaste for the type of neo-Catholicism which, at the time, was much in vogue among Jewish intellectuals in Germany and France.

Two categories above all, and especially in their Jewish versions, assume a central place in his writings: on the one hand Revelation, the idea of the Torah and of sacred texts in general, and on the other hand the messianic idea and

Redemption. Their significance as regulative ideas governing his thought cannot be overrated.

Over and over again one meets in his writings, often indeed in the most unexpected places, instances of a preoccupation with the problem of sacred texts, for instance in most of his papers on the philosophy of language, in the essay **"The Task of the Translator"** in the book on German tragic drama (*Trauerspiel*), but also in his remarks about the verbal imagination of children, when he says that "sentences formed in play by a child out of words [given in advance] are more akin to the language of sacred texts than to the colloquial language of the grown-ups." For many years he considered the confrontation with the sacred texts of Hebrew tradition as the crucial literary experience of which he stood in need to come really into his own. (p. 193)

[For] years Benjamin sought to go all the way to Judaism which, he hoped, would offer scope for the homecoming of his innermost intentions. Around 1930 he abandoned that hope as unrealizable in *his* life; yet echoes of fundamental Jewish concepts continued all the time to reverberate in his writings, now stamped with the seal of the Marxist dialectic. Thus he brings to light the Jewish element in Karl Kraus even at the stage of ultimate estrangement, when he identifies the "Jewish certainty" that "the world was the scene for the sanctification of the name" as the root cause of the contrasting attitudes to language of Karl Kraus and Stefan George; or he will base his analysis of the world of Franz Kafka on the categories of the *halakhah* and *haggadah.*

In addition, an apocalyptic element of destructiveness is preserved in the metamorphosis undergone in his writing by the messianic idea, which continues to play a potent part in his thought. The noble and positive power of destruction—too long (in his view) denied due recognition thanks to the one-sided, undialectic, and dilettantish apotheosis of "creativity"—now becomes an aspect of redemption, related to the immanence of the world, acted out in the history of human labor. A new concept of *subversiveness* now appears in his writings frequently and in the most surprising contexts, and illuminates for him patterns of profound meaning behind the phenomena he studies. There are few important works of his during that period where this concept does not play a central part, avowed or hidden, in inspiring his analyses, as for instance in the most characteristic essay **"Der destruktive Charakter,"** or in the great essays on Kraus, Proust, and Kafka. He developed an extremely accurate and sensitive feeling for the subversive elements in the *oeuvre* of great authors. Even in authors whose picture of the world exhibits mostly reactionary traits he heard the subterranean rumblings of revolution, and generally he was keenly aware of what he called "the strange interplay between reactionary theory and revolutionary practice." The secularization of Jewish apocalyptic doctrine is plain for all to see and nowhere denies its origin. The talmudic image of the angels created anew each moment in countless hosts, only to be destroyed and return into naught after having raised their voices before God, unites his earlier with his later writings. It appears at the end of his announcement of the projected journal *Angelus Novus,* which was never to materialize. This was in 1922, at the height of his theological period. It appears again at the end of his seemingly materialist essay of 1931 on Karl Kraus, which ushers in his later production with a Marxist bugle call. Yet, those ever new angels—one of them he found in Paul Klee's painting *Angelus Novus,* which he owned and deeply loved—bear the features of the angels of judgment as well as destruction. Their "quickly fading voice" proclaims the anticipation of the apocalypse in history—and it was this that mattered to him.

Jewish inspiration pure and simple, with no adjustment even to the terminology of the materialist dialectic, dominates Benjamin's tireless striving after an understanding of Kafka, whose writings he studied from the first with passionate involvement. This tendency is manifest above all in the great essay of 1934 to which Bertolt Brecht responded with the charge that "it was aiding and abetting Jewish fascism." It reveals itself also in his formidable letter of 1938, in which he sketched a new portrait of Kafka that he intended to execute in a book if a publisher could be found. The concepts of justice, of the study of Scripture and of exegesis are here consciously introduced and developed as Jewish concepts. "Study"—we read here—"is the gate of justice. And yet Kafka dared not attach to study those promises that tradition held out for the study of the Torah. His acolytes are beadles, but they have lost the house of prayer; his scholars are disciples, but they have lost the scripture." Equally far removed from Max Brod's optimistic interpretation of Kafka and from the existentialist interpretation which has been the fashion in recent years, Benjamin perceived the negative inversion to which the Jewish categories are subjected in Kafka's world; there the teaching no longer conveys a positive message, but offers only an absolutely Utopian—and therefore as yet undefinable—promise of a postcontemporary world. We are left nothing but the procedures of a "Law" that can no longer be deciphered. These procedures became the central feature of Kafka's vision. Benjamin knew that in Kafka we possess the *theologia negativa* of a Judaism not a whit less intense for having lost the Revelation as a positive message.

Benjamin, who was aware of a close affinity with this author—Proust and Kafka were probably the authors truly familiar to him at the deepest level—saw in the exegetic passages so often presented by Kafka the crystalization of Torah tradition mirrored in itself. The twelve lines on the interpretation of *Don Quixote* he considered to be the most perfect extant piece of Kafka's writing. Benjamin's commentaries on Brecht, among which the one on the "Legend of the Origin of the Book of T'ao teh Ching on Laotse's Way into the Emigration" is perhaps most outstanding, represent the ultimate form assumed by the commentary in Benjamin's hands. He fully realized that he was embarking on a problematic venture when he put this form in the service of interpreting revolutionary rather than archaic and authoritative texts. Indeed, these commentaries display a rare and pathetic helplessness—disconcerting in a mind of Benjamin's sovereign power—that is entirely absent from his interpretation of other texts. And yet, it is obvious that he had made up his mind—even if the price was high—not to forgo the explosive force which he more than any Jewish contemporary had rediscovered in the mysterious life of the commentary as a decisive religious category.

Among the Jewish categories which he introduced as such

and upheld to the last is the messianic idea; nothing is wider of the mark than the notion that he took it over from Ernst Bloch, though the two met on common Jewish ground. Another is the idea of remembrance. The last paragraph in Benjamin's work that can be chronologically placed, representing a *confessio in extremis* as it were, reads—all the more strikingly for being part of a quasi-Marxist text on historical time—like an apotheosis of Judaism: "The soothsayers who found out from time what it had in store for them certainly did not experience time as either homogeneous or empty. Anyone who keeps this in mind will perhaps get an idea of how past times were experienced in remembrance, namely in just the same way. We know that the Jews were prohibited from investigating the future. The Torah and the prayers instruct them in remembrance, however. This stripped the future of its magic, to which all those succumb who turn to the soothsayers for enlightenment. This does not imply, however, that for the Jews the future turned into homogeneous, empty time. For every second of time was the street gate through which the Messiah might enter."

The Judaism encompassed in this description was the goal which Walter Benjamin approached asymptotically throughout his life, without ever attaining it. Yet it may be stated that his deepest intuition, in the spheres of creation and destruction alike, sprang from the very center of that Judaism; and this statement about Benjamin, the thinker, loses nothing of its dialectic range by the fact that it is also about a life often beset by the dread shadows of loneliness, consumed in longing for fellowship, though it be the apocalyptic fellowship of revolution; by the fact that it illuminates the story of that burning, pining life with a deep radiance. (pp. 194-97)

Gershom Scholem, "Walter Benjamin," in his On Jews and Judaism in Crisis: Selected Essays, *edited by Werner J. Dannhauser, Schocken Books, 1976, pp. 172-97.*

Theodor W. Adorno (essay date 1967)

[*Adorno was a German philosopher and critic best known for his contributions as a member of Germany's Institute for Social Research, a privately funded center for Marxist studies. Often collaborating with his colleague Max Horkheimer, Adorno authored influential essays and articles on the nature of critical theory and popular culture. In the following essay, he discusses Benjamin's ideology and critical reputation.*]

The name of the philosopher who took his life while fleeing Hitler's executioners has, in the more than twenty years since then, acquired a certain nimbus, despite the esoteric character of his early writings and the fragmentary nature of his later ones. The fascination of the person and of his work allowed no alternative other than that of magnetic attraction or horrified rejection. Everything which fell under the scrutiny of his words was transformed, as though it had become radioactive. His capacity for continually bringing out new aspects, not by exploding conventions through criticism, but rather by organizing himself so as to be able to relate to his subject-matter in a way that seemed beyond all convention—this capacity can hardly be adequately described by the concept of 'originality'. None of the ideas which flowed from his inexhaustible reserve ever pretended to be mere inspiration. Benjamin, who as subject actually lived all the 'originary' experiences that official contemporary philosophy merely talks about, seemed at the same time utterly detached from them. Nothing was more foreign to him, and above all to his flair for instantaneous, definitive formulations, than what is traditionally associated with spontaneity and ebullience. The impression he left was not of someone who created truth or who attained it through conceptual power; rather, in citing it, he seemed to have transformed himself into a supreme instrument of knowledge on which the latter had left its mark. He had nothing of the philosopher in the traditional sense. His own contribution to his work was not anything 'vital' or 'organic'; the metaphor of the creator is thoroughly inappropriate for him. The subjectivity of his thought shrank to its own specific difference; the idiosyncratic moment of his mind, its singularity—something which, according to conventional philosophical mores, would have been held for contingent, ephemeral, utterly worthless—legitimized itself by giving his thought its compelling character. The thesis that where knowledge is concerned the most individual is the most general, suits him perfectly. Had all analogies drawn from physics not become profoundly suspect in an age which has been characterized by the radical divergence of social and scientific consciousness, his intellectual energy might well be described as a kind of mental atomic fission. His insistence dissolved the insoluble; he grasped the essential precisely when walls of sheer facticity sealed off illusive essences. To speak in terms of formulae, he was impelled to break the bonds of a logic which covers over the particular with the universal or merely abstracts the universal from the particular. He sought to comprehend the essence where it did not permit itself to be distilled by automatic operation or reveal itself to dubious intuition, by subjecting it to methodic conjecture within a configuration of individually opaque elements. The rebus is the model of his philosophy.

The deliberate digressiveness of his thought, however, is matched by its gentle irresistibility. This resides neither in magical effects, which were not foreign to him, nor in an 'objectivity', denoting the disappearance of the subject in those constellations. It stems rather from a quality which intellectual departmentalization otherwise reserves for art, but which sheds all semblance when transposed into the realm of theory and assumes incomparable dignity— the promise of happiness. Everything that Benjamin said or wrote sounded as if thought, instead of rejecting the promises of fairy tales and children's books with its usual disgraceful 'maturity', took them so literally that real fulfilment itself was now within sight of knowledge. In his philosophical topography, renunciation is totally repudiated. Anyone who was drawn to him was bound to feel like the child who catches a glimpse of the lighted Christmas tree through a crack in the closed door. But the light, as one of reason, also promised truth itself, not its powerless shadow. If Benjamin's thought was not creation *ex nihilo,* it had the generosity of abundance; it sought to make good everything, all the pleasure prohibited by adjustment and self-preservation, pleasure which is both sensual and intellectual. In his essay on Proust, a writer for whom he felt the strongest of affinities, Benjamin defined the desire for happiness as the basic motif; one would scarcely be misled in suspecting this to be the origin of a passion which produced two of the most perfect translations in

German—those of *A l'ombre des jeunes filles en fleurs* and of *Le côté de Guermantes.* However, just as in Proust the desire for happiness acquires profundity only through the onerous weight of the novel of disillusion, which is fatally completed in *La Recherche du temps perdu,* in Benjamin the devotion to happiness which has been denied is won only through a regretful sorrow, the like of which is as rare in the history of philosophy as the utopia of cloudless days. His relation to Kafka is no less intimate than that to Proust. Kafka's remark, that there is infinite hope except for us, could have served as the motto of Benjamin's metaphysics, had he ever deigned to write one, and it is no accident that at the centre of his most elaborate theoretical work, **The Origin of German Tragic Drama, (Ursprung des deutschen Trauerspiels)** there is the construction of 'sorrow' ['Trauer'] as the last self-negating, self-transcending allegory, that of Redemption. Subjectivity, plunging into the abyss of significances, 'becomes the ceremonial guarantee of the miracle because it announces divine action itself'. In all his phases, Benjamin conceived the downfall of the subject and the salvation of man as inseparable. That defines the macrocosmic arc, the microcosmic figures of which drew his devoted concern.

Because what distinguishes his philosophy is its kind of concretion. Just as his thought sought again and again to free itself of all impulse to classify, the prime image of all hope for him is the name, of things and of men, and it is this that his reflection seeks to reconstruct. In this respect he seems to converge with the general intellectual current which protested against idealism and epistemology, demanding 'the things themselves' instead of their conceptual form, and which found an academically respectable expression in phenomenology and the ontological schools stemming from it. But the decisive differences between philosophers have always consisted in nuances; what is most bitterly irreconcilable is that which is similar but which thrives on different centres; and Benjamin's relation to today's accepted ideologies of the 'concrete' is no different. He saw through them as the mere mask of conceptual thinking at its wits end, just as he also rejected the existential-ontological concept of history as the mere distillate left after the substance of the historical dialectic had been boiled away. The later Nietzsche's critical insight that truth is not identical with a timeless *universal,* but rather that it is solely the historical which yields the figure of the absolute, became, perhaps without his knowing it, the canon of his practice. The programme is formulated in a note to his fragmentary main work, that 'in any case the eternal is more like lace trimmings on a dress than like an idea'. By this he in no way intended the innocuous illustration of concepts through colourful historical objects as Simmel did when he depicted his primitive metaphysics of form and life in the cup-handle, the actor, Venice. Rather, his desperate striving to break out of the prison of cultural conformism was directed at constellations of historical entities which do not remain simply interchangeable examples for ideas but which in their uniqueness constitute the ideas themselves as historical.

This brought him the reputation of an essayist. Until today his nimbus has remained that of the sophisticated 'literator', as he himself, with antiquarian coquetry, would have put it. In view of his wily aim in opposing the shopworn themes and jargon of philosophy—the latter he habitually termed 'procurer language'—it would be easy enough to dismiss the cliché of 'essayist' as a mere misunderstanding. But the recourse to 'misunderstandings' as a means of explaining the effect of intellectual phenomena does not lead very far. It presupposes that there is an intrinsic substance, often simply equated with the author's intention, which exists independently of its historical fate; such a substance is in principle hardly identifiable and this is all the more so with an author as complex and as fragmentary as Benjamin. Misunderstandings are the medium in which the noncommunicable is communicated. The provocative assertion that an essay on the Paris Arcades is of greater interest philosophically than are ponderous observations on the Being of beings is more attuned to the meaning of his work than the quest for that unchanging, self-identical conceptual skeleton which he relegated to the dustbin. Moreover, by not respecting the boundary between the man of letters and the philosopher, he turned empirical necessity into 'intelligible'—in the Kantian sense—virtue. To their disgrace the universities refused him, while the antiquarian in him felt itself drawn to academic life in much the same ironic manner as Kafka felt drawn to insurance companies. The perfidious reproach of being 'too intelligent' haunted him throughout his life; an Existentialist overlord had the effrontery to defame him as being 'touched by demons', as though the suffering of a person dominated and estranged by the mind should be considered his metaphysical death sentence, merely because it disturbs the all-too-lively I-Thou relationship. In fact, however, he shrank before every act of violence against words; ingenuity was fundamentally alien to him. The true reason that he aroused hatred was that, inevitably and without any polemical intention, his glance revealed the ordinary world in the eclipse which is its permanent light. At the same time, the incommensurable quality of his nature, undaunted by every tactic and incapable of indulging in the social games of the Republic of Intellects, permitted him to earn his living as an essayist, on his own and unprotected. That greatly developed the agility of his profound mind. He learned how to convict the prodigious and ponderous claims of the *prima philosophia* of their hollowness, with a silent chuckle. All of his utterances are equally near the centre. The articles scattered throughout the *Literarische Welt* and the *Frankfurter Zeitung* are hardly less indicative of his stubborn intention than are the books and longer studies in the *Zeitschrift für Sozialforschung.* The maxim in **One-Way Street** which asserts that today all decisive blows are struck left-handedly, was one he followed himself, yet without ever sacrificing the truth even in the slightest. Even his most precious literary *jeux* [games] serve as studies for a genre, the masterwork, which he nevertheless thoroughly mistrusted.

The essay as form consists in the ability to regard historical moments, manifestations of the objective spirit, 'culture', as though they were natural. Benjamin could do this as no one else. The totality of his thought is characterized by what may be called 'natural history'. He was drawn to the petrified, frozen or obsolete elements of civilization, to everything in it devoid of domestic vitality no less irresistibly than is the collector to fossils or to the plant in the herbarium. Small glass balls containing a landscape upon which snow fell when shook were among his favourite objects. The French word for still-life, *nature morte,* could be written above the portals of his philosophical dungeons. The Hegelian concept of 'second nature', as the reification

of self-estranged human relations, and also the Marxian category of 'commodity fetishism' occupy key positions in Benjamin's work. He is driven not merely to awaken congealed life in petrified objects—as in allegory—but also to scrutinize living things so that they present themselves as being ancient, 'ur-historical' and abruptly release their significance. Philosophy appropriates the fetishization of commodities for itself: everything must metamorphose into a thing in order to break the catastrophic spell of things. Benjamin's thought is so saturated with culture as its natural object that it swears loyalty to reification instead of flatly rejecting it. This is the origin of Benjamin's tendency to cede his intellectual power to objects diametrically opposed to it, the most extreme example of which was his study on **The Work of Art in the Era of Mechanical Reproduction.** The glance of his philosophy is Medusan. If the concept of myth, as the antipode to reconciliation, occupies a central position in it, especially during its openly theological phase, then everything, and especially the ephemeral, becomes in his own thought mythical. His critique of the domination of nature, programmatically stated in the last piece of **One-Way Street,** negates and transcends the ontological dualism of myth and reconciliation; reconciliation is that of myth itself. In the course of such criticism the concept of myth becomes secularized. Fate, which begins as the guilt of the living, becomes that of society: 'So long as one beggar remains, there is still myth'. Thus, Benjamin's philosophy, which once sought to conjure up 'essences' directly, as in his **'Critique of Force',** moved ever more decisively towards dialectics. The latter did not intrude from without on a thought which was inherently static, nor was it the product of mere development, but was rather anticipated in the *quid pro quo* between the most rigid and the most dynamic elements in his thought during all of its phases. His conception of 'dialectics at a standstill' emerged with increasing clarity.

The reconciliation of myth is the theme of Benjamin's philosophy. But, as in good musical variations, this theme rarely states itself openly; instead, it remains hidden and shifts the burden of its legitimation to Jewish mysticism, to which Benjamin was introduced in his youth by his friend, Gershom Scholem, the distinguished student of the *cabbala.* It is difficult to say to what extent he was influenced by the neo-platonic and antinomian-messianic tradition. There is much to indicate that Benjamin—who hardly ever showed his cards and who was motivated by a deeply seated opposition to thought of the shoot-from-the-hip variety, to 'free floating' intelligentsia—made use of the popular mystic technique of pseudo-epigraphy—never, to be sure, disclosing the texts, in order thus to outwit truth, which he suspected of being no longer accessible to autonomous reflection. In any case, his notion of the sacred text was derived from the cabbala. For him philosophy consisted essentially in commentary and criticism, and language as the crystallization of the 'name' took priority over its function as a bearer of meaning and even of expression. The concern of philosophy with previously existent, codified doctrines is less foreign to its great tradition than Benjamin might have believed. Crucial writings or passages of Aristotle and Leibniz, Kant and Hegel, are 'critiques' not merely in the implicit sense of works which deal with problems already posed but rather as specific confrontations. It was only after they had banded together to form their own discipline and had begun to lose touch with their own thought that philosophers all deemed it necessary to cover themselves by beginning before the creation of the world, or, if at all possible, to incorporate it into the system. Benjamin maintained a determined Alexandrinism in the face of this trend and thereby provoked all fundamentalist furies. He transposed the idea of the sacred text into the sphere of enlightenment, into which, according to Scholem, Jewish mysticism itself tends to culminate dialectically. His 'essayism' consists in treating profane texts as though they were sacred. This does not mean that he clung to theological relics or, as the religious socialists, endowed the profane with transcendent significance. Rather, he looked to radical, defenceless profanation as the only chance for the theological heritage which squandered itself in profanity. The key to the picture puzzles is lost. They must, as a baroque poem about melancholy says, 'speak themselves'. The procedure resembles Thorstein Veblen's quip, that he studied foreign languages by staring at each word until he knew what it meant. The analogy with Kafka is unmistakable. But he distinguishes himself from the older Prague writer, who even at times of the most extreme negativity retains an element of the rural, epic tradition, through the far more pronounced moment of urbanity which serves as a contrast to the archaic, and through the resistance to demonic regression acquired by his thought through its affinity to enlightenment, a regression which often leaves Kakfa unable to distinguish between the *deus absconditus* and the devil. During his mature period, Benjamin was able to give himself over fully to socially critical insights without there being the slightest mental residue, and still without having to ban even one of his impulses. Exegetical power became the ability to see through the manifestations and utterances of bourgeois culture as hieroglyphs of its darkest secret—as ideologies. He spoke occasionally of the 'materialist toxins' that he had to add to his thought so that it might survive. Among the illusions that he renounced in order not to concede the necessity of renunciation, was that of the monadological, self-contained character of his own reflection, which he measured tirelessly and without flinching at the pain of objectification against the overwhelming trend of the collective. But he so utterly assimilated the foreign element to his own experience that the latter improved as a result.

Ascetic forces counterbalanced an imaginative power kindled ever anew by each object. This helped Benjamin to develop a philosophy directed against philosophy. It can well be described in terms of the categories which it does not use. A conception of them emerges if one examines his idiosyncratic distaste for words like 'personality'. From the very start his thought protested against the false claim that man and the human mind are self-constitutive and that an absolute originates in them. The incisiveness of this kind of reaction ought not to be confused with modern religious movements that attempt, in the sphere of philosophic reflection, to make of man the creature to which total social dependency has already degraded him independently of their efforts. His target is not an allegedly over-inflated subjectivism but rather the notion of a subjective dimension itself. Between myth and reconciliation, the poles of his philosophy, the subject evaporates. Before his Medusan glance, man turns into the stage on which an objective process unfolds. For this reason Benjamin's philosophy is no less a source of terror than a promise of happiness. Just as the domain of myth is ruled by multiplicity

and ambiguity and not subjectivity, the unequivocal character of reconciliation—conceived after the model of the 'name'—is the contrary of human autonomy. He reduces this autonomy to a moment of transition in a dialectical process, as with the tragic hero, and the reconciliation of men with the creation has as its condition the dissolution of all self-posited human existence. According to an oral statement, Benjamin accepted the 'self' solely as something mystical and not as metaphysical-epistemological, as 'substantiality'. Inwardness for him is not merely the seat of torpor and melancholic complacency; it is also the phantasma which distorts the potential image of man—he always contrasts it to the physical, external things. Thus, one will search his writings in vain for a concept like autonomy; yet others, such as totality, life, system, from the sphere of subjective metaphysics, are equally absent. What he praised in Karl Kraus, a writer as different from Benjamin in all other respects as possible, was one of his own traits—inhumanity against the deception of 'the universally human'; Kraus, it may be added, did not take kindly to this praise. The categories which Benjamin rejected, however, are those which compromise the essential ideology of society. From time immemorial, the masters have used such categories to set themselves up as God. As a critic of force, Benjamin as it were revokes the unity of the subject to mythic turmoil in order to comprehend such unity as itself being only a natural condition; with his philosophy of language oriented on the cabbala, Benjamin saw subjective unity as scribbling of the Name. That links his materialistic period with his theological one. He viewed the modern world as archaic not in order to conserve the traces of a purportedly eternal truth but rather to escape the trance-like captivity of bourgeois immanence. He sees his task not in reconstructing the totality of bourgeois society but rather in examining its blinded, nature-bound and diffuse elements under a microscope. His micrological and fragmentary method therefore never entirely integrated the idea of universal mediation, which in Hegel as in Marx produces the totality. He never wavered in his fundamental conviction that the smallest cell of observed reality offsets the rest of the world. To interpret phenomena materialistically meant for him not so much to elucidate them as products of the social whole but rather to relate them directly, in their isolated singularity, to material tendencies and social struggles. Benjamin thus sought to avoid the dangers of estrangement and reification, which threaten to transform all observation of capitalism as a system itself into a system. Motifs of the young Hegel, whom he hardly would have known, are prominent; in dialectical materialism, too, he sensed what Hegel called 'positivity', and opposed it in his way. In its close contact with material which was close at hand, in its affinity to that which is, his thought, despite all its strangeness and acumen, was always accompanied by a characteristic unconscious element, by a moment of naïveté. This naïveté enabled him at times to sympathize with groups in power-politics which, as he well knew, would have liquidated his own substance, unregimented intellectual experience. But also towards them he cunningly adopted the role of an exegete, as though one had only to interpret the objective spirit to satisfy its demands and to comprehend its horror in order to eliminate it. He preferred to supply heteronomy with speculative theories than to abandon speculation.

Politics and metaphysics, theology and materialism, myth and modernity, non-intentional matter and extravagant speculation—all the streets of Benjamin's city-tableau converge in the plan of the Paris book as in their Etoile. But he would never have agreed to use this project, destined for him *a priori,* as it were, to present a coherent exposition of his philosophy. Just as the conception arose out of a concrete occasion, it never in all the years that followed relinquished the form of a monograph. **'Dream Kitsch,'** an article which appeared in the *Neue Rundschau,* was concerned with the shocklike flashes of obsolete elements from the nineteenth century in surrealism. The material point of departure was provided by a magazine article on the Paris arcades, which he and Franz Hessel planned to write. He clung to the title of the arcades article long after a plan had crystallized according to which extreme physiognomic traits of the nineteenth century were to be handled in a manner similar to that used in dealing with the Baroque in the book on the tragic drama. Out of these traits he intended to construe the idea of the epoch in terms of an ur-history of modernity. This 'history' was not designed to uncover archaic rudiments in the recent past, but rather to define the idea of newness, of the 'latest thing', as itself an archaic pattern.

> The form of the new means of production, which in the beginning was still dominated by the old form . . . has its correlative within the collective mind in images in which the new mingles with the old. These images embody desires, and in them the collective seeks both to transcend and to transfigure the unfinished character of the social product and the deficiencies in the order of social production. The images also display the emphatic effort to set oneself apart from the obsolete, which, however, means from the recent past. These tendencies guide the image-producing imagination, which received its initial impulse from the new, back to the ancient past. Dreams, in which every epoch sees the images of that which is to succeed it, now show the coming age mingled with elements of ur-history—that is to say, of a classless society. The experiences of this society, stored in the unconscious of the collective, join with the new to produce the utopia which has left its trace in a thousand configurations of life, from lasting buildings to the most fleeting fashions.

Such images, however, were for Benjamin much more important than Jung's archetypes of the collective unconscious; he thought of them as objective crystallizations of the historical dynamic and gave them the name of 'dialectical images'. A magnificently improvised theory of the gambler provided their model: they were to decipher historically-philosophically the phantasmagoria of the nineteenth century as the figure of hell. The original layer of the **Arcades** project, from about 1928, was then covered over by a second, materialist one, perhaps because the determination of the nineteenth century as hell became untenable with the rise of the Third Reich, perhaps because the thought of hell tended to lead in a political direction entirely different from that which Benjamin saw implied in the strategic role which Haussmann's boulevards were to play; but above all, probably because he happened to come across a forgotten work, written in prison by Auguste Blanqui, *L'éternité par les astres,* which, in accents of absolute despair, anticipates Nietzsche's theory of the eternal return. The second phase of the **Arcades** plan is documented in the memorandum, dating from 1935, entitled **'Paris, Capital of the Nineteenth Century'**. This relates certain key figures of the epoch to categories of the world of images. Its subject-matter was supposed to consist of Fourier and Daguerre, of Grandville and Louis Philippe, of Baudelaire and Haussmann; instead it dealt with themes like fashions and *nouveauté,* fairs and cast-iron construction, the collector, the *flaneur,* prostitution. A passage on Grandville bears witness to the extreme excitement with which the interpretation was charged:

> World's Fairs erect a commodity universe. Grandville's phantasies endow the universe with commodity-character. They modernize it. Saturn's ring becomes a cast-iron balcony on which the inhabitants of Saturn take a breath of air in the evening. . . . Fashion prescribes the ritual which determines how the fetish will be honoured, Grandville extends fashion's authority to the objects of everyday use as well as to the cosmos. By pursuing fashion to its extremes he reveals its nature. It stands in opposition to the organic. It couples the living body with the inorganic world. In the living it sees the prerogatives of the corpse. Fetishism, which succumbs to the sex appeal of the inorganic, is its vital nerve. The commodity cult puts it to good use.

Considerations of this sort led to the planned chapter on Baudelaire. Benjamin detached it from the larger project in order to make a shorter, three-part book; a large section of it appeared in the 1939-40 issue of the *Zeitschrift für Sozialforschung* as the article entitled, **'On Some Motifs of Baudelaire'**. It is one of the few texts of the **Arcades** complex which he was able to complete. A second consists of the theses, **On the Concept of History,** which summarize, so to speak, the epistemological considerations which developed together with the **Arcades** project. Thousands of pages of this project have been preserved, studies of individual subjects which were hidden during the occupation of Paris. The whole, however, can hardly be reconstructed. Benjamin's intention was to eliminate all overt commentary and to have the meanings emerge solely through a shocking montage of the material. His aim was not merely for philosophy to catch up to surrealism, but for it to become surrealistic. In **One-Way Street** he wrote that citations from his works were like highwaymen, who suddenly descend on the reader to rob him of his convictions. He meant this literally. The culmination of his antisubjectivism, his major work was to consist solely of citations. Only seldom are there interpretations noted which could not be integrated into the Baudelaire study or the theses **On the Concept of History,** and there is no canon to indicate how the audacious venture of a philosophy purified of argument might be carried out, or even how the citations might be meaningfully ordered. His philosophy of fragmentation remained itself fragmentary, the victim, perhaps, of a method, the feasibility of which in the medium of thought must remain an open question.

The method, however, cannot be separated from the content. Benjamin's ideal of knowledge did not stop at the reproduction of what already is. He mistrusted all limitations placed on the realm of possible knowledge, the pride of modern philosophy in its illusionless maturity, for in it he sensed a plot to sabotage the claim of happiness, the attempt to strengthen a situation which tolerates only what is more of the interminable same; he sensed the presence of myth itself. The utopian motif in him, however, is paired with his antiromanticism. He remained uncorrupted by all apparently similar attempts, such as Max

Scheler's, to grasp transcendence through natural reason, as though the limiting process of the enlightenment could be revoked and one could simply reinstate the theologically grounded philosophies of the past. For this reason from its very inception his thought protected itself from the 'success' of unbroken cohesion by making the fragmentary its guiding principle. In order to achieve his aim he chose to remain completely outside of the manifest tradition of philosophy. Despite its great culture, the elements of that tradition enter his labyrinth scattered, submerged, obliquely. His incommensurability lies in the inordinate ability to give himself over to his object. By permitting thought to get, as it were, too close to its object, the object becomes as foreign as an everyday, familiar thing under a microscope. To interpret his lack of system and of a closed theoretical foundation as sufficient reason to align him with the representatives of 'intuition', eidetic or otherwise—and he was often misunderstood in this way, even by friends—is to overlook what is best in him. It is not his glance as such which lays claim to the unmediated possession of the absolute; rather his manner of seeing, the entire perspective is altered. The technique of enlargement brings the rigid in motion and the dynamic to rest. His preference in the *Arcades* for small or shabby objects like dust and plush is a complement of this technique, drawn as it is to everything that has slipped through the conventional conceptual net or to things which have been esteemed too trivial by the prevailing spirit for it to have left any traces other than those of hasty judgement. Benjamin, the dialectician of the imagination, which he defined as 'extrapolation at its most minute', sought, like Hegel, 'to observe the thing as it is, in and for itself'; that is, he refused to accept as ineluctable the threshold between consciousness and the thing-in-itself. But the distance of such observation has been shifted. Not because, as in Hegel, subject and object are ultimately developed as being identical, but rather because the subjective intention is seen to be extinguished in the object, Benjamin's thought is not content with intentions. The thoughts press close to its object, seek to touch it, smell it, taste it and so thereby transform itself. Through this secondary sensuousness, they hope to penetrate down to the veins of gold which no classificatory procedure can reach, and at the same time avoid succumbing to the contingency of blind intuition. The radical reduction of the distance of the object also establishes the relation to potential praxis which later guided Benjamin's thinking. What confronts experience in the *déjà vu* as opaque and without objectivity, what Proust hoped to gain for poetic reconstruction through involuntary memory, Benjamin sought to recapture and elevate to truth through the concept. He charged it with accomplishing what is otherwise reserved for nonconceptual experience. He strove to give thought the density of experience without having it therefore lose any of its stringency.

The utopia of knowledge, however, has utopia as its content. Benjamin called it 'the unreality of despair'. Philosophy condenses into experience so that it may have hope. But hope appears only in fragmented form. Benjamin overexposes the objects for the sake of the hidden contours which one day, in the state of reconciliation, will become evident, but in so doing he reveals the chasm separating that day and life as it is. The price of hope is life: 'Nature is messianic in its eternal and total transience', and happiness, according to a late fragment which risks everything, is its 'intrinsic rhythm'. Hence, the core of Benjamin's phi-

losophy is the idea of the salvation of the dead as the restitution of distorted life through the consummation of its own reification down to the inorganic level. 'Only for the sake of the hopeless are we given hope', is the conclusion of the study of *Goethe's "Elective Affinities."* In the paradox of the impossible possibility, mysticism and enlightenment are joined for the last time in him. He overcame the dream without betraying it and making himself an accomplice in that on which the philosophers have always agreed: that it shall not be. The character of the picture puzzle, as which he himself described the aphorisms in *One-Way Street* and which distinguished everything he ever wrote, originates in that paradox. It was nothing other than the explication and elucidation of this paradox, with the only means which philosophy has at its disposal, concepts, that drove Benjamin to immerse himself without reserve in the world of multiplicity. (pp. 229-41)

> *Theodor W. Adorno, "A Portrait of Walter Benjamin," in his* Prisms, *translated by Samuel Weber and Shierry Weber, 1967. Reprint by the MIT Press, 1981, pp. 227-41.*

Hannah Arendt   (essay date 1968)

[*A German-born American philosopher and literary critic, Arendt ranks among the most important political thinkers of the twentieth century. In her many works she considered central issues of the times—war, revolution, political power, violence, and anti-Semitism—with originality and insight. In her seminal* The Origins of Totalitarianism *(1951) and the controversial* Eichmann in Jerusalem *(1963), she examined the phenomenon of totalitarianism, illuminating the disintegration of social life and human personality that permitted its ascendance. Perceiving the political thinker as a "truth-teller" who counters the lies of politicians, Arendt sought through her writings to expand the realm of human freedom and resist tyranny. In the following excerpt, she emphasizes the fragmentary nature of Benjamin's writings as the poetic expression of his coming to terms with the dissipation of cultural tradition.*]

[Posthumous] fame, uncommercial and unprofitable, has now come in Germany to the name and work of Walter Benjamin, a German-Jewish writer who was known, but not famous, as contributor to magazines and literary sections of newspapers for less than ten years prior to Hitler's seizure of power and his own emigration. There were few who still knew his name when he chose death in those early fall days of 1940 which for many of his origin and generation marked the darkest moment of the war—the fall of France, the threat to England, the still intact Hitler-Stalin pact whose most feared consequence at that moment was the close co-operation of the two most powerful secret police forces in Europe. Fifteen years later a two-volume edition of his writings was published in Germany and brought him almost immediately a *succès d'estime* that went far beyond the recognition among the few which he had known in his life. And since mere reputation, however high, as it rests on the judgment of the best, is never enough for writers and artists to make a living that only fame, the testimony of a multitude which need not be astronomical in size, can guarantee, one is doubly tempted to say (with Cicero), *Si vivi vicissent qui morte vicerunt*—

how different everything would have been "if they had been victorious in life who have won victory in death."

Posthumous fame is too odd a thing to be blamed upon the blindness of the world or the corruption of a literary milieu. Nor can it be said that it is the bitter reward of those who were ahead of their time—as though history were a race track on which some contenders run so swiftly that they simply disappear from the spectator's range of vision. On the contrary, posthumous fame is usually preceded by the highest recognition among one's peers. When Kafka died in 1924, his few published books had not sold more than a couple of hundred copies, but his literary friends and the few readers who had almost accidentally stumbled on the short prose pieces (none of the novels was as yet published) knew beyond doubt that he was one of the masters of modern prose. Walter Benjamin had won such recognition early, and not only among those whose names at that time were still unknown, such as Gerhard Scholem, the friend of his youth, and Theodor Wiesengrund Adorno, his first and only disciple, who together are responsible for the posthumous edition of his works and letters. Immediate, instinctive, one is tempted to say, recognition came from Hugo von Hofmannsthal, who published Benjamin's essay on *Goethe's "Elective Affinities"* in 1924, and from Bertolt Brecht who upon receiving the news of Benjamin's death is reported to have said that this was the first real loss Hitler had caused to German literature. We cannot know if there is such a thing as altogether unappreciated genius, or whether it is the daydream of those who are not geniuses; but we can be reasonably sure that posthumous fame will not be their lot.

Fame is a social phenomenon; *ad gloriam non est satis unius opinio* (as Seneca remarked wisely and pedantically), "for fame the opinion of one is not enough," although it is enough for friendship and love. And no society can properly function without classification, without an arrangement of things and men in classes and prescribed types. This necessary classification is the basis for all social discrimination, and discrimination, present opinion to the contrary notwithstanding, is no less a constituent element of the social realm than equality is a constituent element of the political. The point is that in society everybody must answer the question of *what* he is—as distinct from the question of *who* he is—which his role is and his function, and the answer of course can never be: I am unique, not because of the implicit arrogance but because the answer would be meaningless. In the case of Benjamin the trouble (if such it was) can be diagnosed in retrospect with great precision; when Hofmannsthal had read the long essay on Goethe by the completely unknown author, he called it *"schlechthin unvergleichlich"* ("absolutely incomparable"), and the trouble was that he was literally right, it could not be compared with anything else in existing literature. The trouble with everything Benjamin wrote was that it always turned out to be *sui generis*.

Posthumous fame seems, then, to be the lot of the unclassifiable ones, that is, those whose work neither fits the existing order nor introduces a new genre that lends itself to future classification. Innumerable attempts to write à la Kafka, all of them dismal failures, have only served to emphasize Kafka's uniqueness, that absolute originality which can be traced to no predecessor and suffers no followers. This is what society can least come to terms with

and upon which it will always be very reluctant to bestow its seal of approval. To put it bluntly, it would be as misleading today to recommend Walter Benjamin as a literary critic and essayist as it would have been misleading to recommend Kafka in 1924 as a short-story writer and novelist. To describe adequately his work and him as an author within our usual framework of reference, one would have to make a great many negative statements, such as: his erudition was great, but he was no scholar; his subject matter comprised texts and their interpretation, but he was no philologist; he was greatly attracted not by religion but by theology and the theological type of interpretation for which the text itself is sacred, but he was no theologian and he was not particularly interested in the Bible; he was a born writer, but his greatest ambition was to produce a work consisting entirely of quotations; he was the first German to translate Proust (together with Franz Hessel) and St.-John Perse, and before that he had translated Baudelaire's *Tableaux Parisiens,* but he was no translator; he reviewed books and wrote a number of essays on living and dead writers, but he was no literary critic; he wrote a book about the German baroque and left behind a huge unfinished study of the French nineteenth century, but he was no historian, literary or otherwise; I shall try to show that he thought poetically, but he was neither a poet nor a philosopher. (pp. 153-56)

Insofar as the past has been transmitted as tradition, it possesses authority; insofar as authority presents itself historically, it becomes tradition. Walter Benjamin knew that the break in tradition and the loss of authority which occurred in his life-time were irreparable, and he concluded that he had to discover new ways of dealing with the past. In this he became a master when he discovered that the transmissibility of the past had been replaced by its citability and that in place of its authority there had arisen a strange power to settle down, piecemeal, in the present and to deprive it of "peace of mind," the mindless peace of complacency. "Quotations in my works are like robbers by the roadside who make an armed attack and relieve an idler of his convictions." This discovery of the modern function of quotations, according to Benjamin, who exemplified it by Karl Kraus, was born out of despair—not the despair of a past that refuses "to throw its light on the future" and lets the human mind "wander in darkness" as in Tocqueville, but out of the despair of the present and the desire to destroy it; hence their power is "not the strength to preserve but to cleanse, to tear out of context, to destroy." Still, the discoverers and lovers of this destructive power originally were inspired by an entirely different intention, the intention to preserve; and only because they did not let themselves be fooled by the professional "preservers" all around them did they finally discover that the destructive power of quotations was "the only one which still contains the hope that something from this period will survive—for no other reason than that it was torn out of it." In this form of "thought fragments," quotations have the double task of interrupting the flow of the presentation with "transcendent force" and at the same time of concentrating within themselves that which is presented. As to their weight in Benjamin's writings, quotations are comparable only to the very dissimilar Biblical citations which so often replace the immanent consistency of argumentation in medieval treatises. (pp. 193-94)

[Collecting] was Benjamin's central passion. It started early with what he himself called his "bibliomania" but soon extended into something far more characteristic, not so much of the person as of his work: the collecting of quotations. (Not that he ever stopped collecting books. Shortly before the fall of France he seriously considered exchanging his edition of the Collected Works of Kafka, which had recently appeared in five volumes, for a few first editions of Kafka's early writings—an undertaking which naturally was bound to remain incomprehensible to any nonbibliophile.) The "inner need to own a library" asserted itself around 1916, at the time when Benjamin turned in his studies to Romanticism as the "last movement that once more saved tradition." That a certain destructive force was active even in this passion for the past, so characteristic of heirs and latecomers, Benjamin did not discover until much later, when he had already lost his faith in tradition and in the indestructibility of the world. (This will be discussed presently.) In those days, encouraged by Scholem, he still believed that his own estrangement from tradition was probably due to his Jewishness and that there might be a way back for him as there was for his friend, who was preparing to emigrate to Jerusalem. (As early as 1920, when he was not yet seriously beset by financial worries, he thought of learning Hebrew.) He never went as far on this road as did Kafka, who after all his efforts stated bluntly that he had no use for anything Jewish except the Hasidic tales which Buber had just prepared for modern usage—"into everything else I just drift, and another current of air carries me away again." Was he, then, despite all doubts, to go back to the German or European past and help with the tradition of its literature?

Presumably this is the form in which the problem presented itself to him in the early twenties, before he turned to Marxism. That is when he chose the German Baroque Age as a subject for his *Habilitation* thesis, a choice that is very characteristic of the ambiguity of this entire, still unresolved cluster of problems. For in the German literary and poetic tradition the Baroque has, with the exception of the great church chorales of the time, never really been alive. Goethe rightly said that when he was eighteen years old, German literature was no older. And Benjamin's choice, baroque in a double sense, has an exact counterpart in Scholem's strange decision to approach Judaism via the Cabala, that is, that part of Hebrew literature which is untransmitted and untransmissible in terms of Jewish tradition, in which it has always had the odor of something downright disreputable. Nothing showed more clearly—so one is inclined to say today—that there was no such thing as a "return" either to the German or the European or the Jewish tradition than the choice of these fields of study. It was an implicit admission that the past spoke directly only through things that had not been handed down, whose seeming closeness to the present was thus due precisely to their exotic character, which ruled out all claims to a binding authority. Obligative truths were replaced by what was in some sense significant or interesting, and this of course meant—as no one knew better than Benjamin—that the "consistence of truth . . . has been lost." Outstanding among the properties that formed this "consistence of truth" was, at least for Benjamin, whose early philosophical interest was theologically inspired, that truth concerned a secret and that the revelation of this secret had authority. Truth, so Benjamin said shortly before he became fully aware of the irreparable break in tradition and the loss of authority, is not "an unveiling which destroys the secret, but the revelation which does it justice." Once this truth had come into the human world at the appropriate moment in history—be it as the Greek *a-letheia*, visually perceptible to the eyes of the mind and comprehended by us as "un-concealment" ("*Unverborgenheit*"—Heidegger), or as the acoustically perceptible word of God as we know it from the European religions of revelation—it was this "consistence" peculiar to it which made it tangible, as it were, so that it could be handed down by tradition. Tradition transforms truth into wisdom, and wisdom is the consistence of transmissible truth. In other words, even if truth should appear in our world, it could not lead to wisdom, because it would no longer have the characteristics which it could acquire only through universal recognition of its validity. Benjamin discusses these matters in connection with Kafka and says that of course "Kafka was far from being the first to face this situation. Many had accommodated themselves to it, adhering to truth or whatever they regarded as truth at any given time and, with a more or less heavy heart, forgoing its transmissibility. Kafka's real genius was that he tried something entirely new: he sacrificed truth for the sake of clinging to the transmissibility." He did so by making decisive changes in traditional parables or inventing new ones in traditional style; however, these "do not modestly lie at the feet of the doctrine," as do the haggadic tales in the Talmud, but "unexpectedly raise a heavy claw" against it. Even Kafka's reaching down to the sea bottom of the past had this peculiar duality of wanting to preserve and wanting to destroy. He wanted to preserve it even though it was not truth, if only for the sake of this "new beauty in what is vanishing" (see Benjamin's essay on Leskov); and he knew, on the other hand, that there is no more effective way to break the spell of tradition than to cut out the "rich and strange," coral and pearls, from what had been handed down in one solid piece.

Benjamin exemplified this ambiguity of gesture in regard to the past by analyzing the collector's passion which was his own. Collecting springs from a variety of motives which are not easily understood. As Benjamin was probably the first to emphasize, collecting is the passion of children, for whom things are not yet commodities and are not valued according to their usefulness, and it is also the hobby of the rich, who own enough not to need anything useful and hence can afford to make "the transfiguration of objects" their business. In this they must of necessity discover the beautiful, which needs "disinterested delight" (Kant) to be recognized. At any rate, a collected object possesses only an amateur value and no use value whatsoever. (Benjamin was not yet aware of the fact that collecting can also be an eminently sound and often highly profitable form of investment.) And inasmuch as collecting can fasten on any category of objects (not just art objects, which are in any case removed from the everyday world of use objects because they are "good" for nothing) and thus, as it were, redeem the object as a thing since it now is no longer a means to an end but has its intrinsic worth, Benjamin could understand the collector's passion as an attitude akin to that of the revolutionary. Like the revolutionary, the collector "dreams his way not only into a remote or bygone world, but at the same time into a better one in which, to be sure, people are not provided with what they need any more than they are in the everyday world, but in which things are liberated from the drudgery of usefulness." Collecting is the redemption of things which is to complement the redemption of man. Even the reading of his books is something questionable to a true bibliophile: " 'And you have read all these?' Anatole France is said to have been asked by an admirer of his library. 'Not one-tenth of them. I don't suppose you use your Sèvres china every day?' " (**"Unpacking My Library"**). (In Benjamin's library there were collections of rare children's books and of books by mentally deranged authors; since he was interested neither in child psychology nor in psychiatry, these books, like many others among his treasures, literally were not good for anything, serving neither to divert nor to instruct.) Closely connected with this is the fetish character which Benjamin explicitly claimed for collected objects. The value of genuineness which is decisive for the collector as well as for the market determined by him has replaced the "cult value" and is its secularization.

These reflections, like so much else in Benjamin, have something of the ingeniously brilliant which is not characteristic of his essential insights, which are, for the most part, quite down-to-earth. Still, they are striking examples of the *flânerie* in his thinking, of the way his mind worked, when he, like the *flâneur* in the city, entrusted himself to chance as a guide on his intellectual journeys of exploration. Just as strolling through the treasures of the past is the inheritor's luxurious privilege, so is the "collector's attitude, in the highest sense, the attitude of the heir" (**"Unpacking My Library"**) who, by taking possession of things—and "ownership is the most profound relationship that one can have to objects"—establishes himself in the past, so as to achieve, undistrubed by the present, "a renewal of the old world." And since this "deepest urge" in the collector has no public significance whatsoever but results in a strictly private hobby, everything "that is said from the angle of the true collector" is bound to appear as "whimsical" as the typically Jean Paulian vision of one of those writers "who write books not because they are poor, but because they are dissatisfied with the books which they could buy but don't like." Upon closer examination, however, this whimsicality has some noteworthy and not so harmless peculiarities. There is, for one thing, the gesture, so significant of an era of public darkness, with which the collector not only withdraws from the public into the privacy of his four walls but takes along with him all kinds of treasures that once were public property to decorate them. (This, of course, is not today's collector, who gets hold of whatever has or, in his estimate, will have a market value or can enhance his social status, but the collector who, like Benjamin, seeks strange things that are considered valueless.) Also, in his passion for the past for its own sake, born of his contempt for the present as such and therefore rather heedless of objective quality, there already appears a disturbing factor to announce that tradition may be the last thing to guide him and traditional values by no means be as safe in his hands as one might have assumed at first glance.

For tradition puts the past in order, not just chronologically but first of all systematically in that it separates the positive from the negative, the orthodox from the heretical, that which is obligatory and relevant from the mass of irrelevant or merely interesting opinions and data. The collector's passion, on the other hand, is not only unsystematic but borders on the chaotic, not so much because

it is a passion as because it is not primarily kindled by the quality of the object—something that is classifiable—but is inflamed by its "genuineness," its uniqueness, something that defies any systematic classification. Therefore, while tradition discriminates, the collector levels all differences; and this leveling—so that "the positive and the negative . . . predilection and rejection are here closely contiguous"—takes place even if the collector has made tradition itself his special field and carefully eliminated everything not recognized by it. Against tradition the collector pits the criterion of genuineness; to the authoritative he opposes the sign of origin. To express this way of thinking in theoretical terms: he replaces content with pure originality or authenticity, something that only French Existentialism established as a quality *per se* detached from all specific characteristics. If one carries this way of thinking to its logical conclusion, the result is a strange inversion of the original collector's drive: "The genuine picture may be old, but the genuine thought is new. It is of the present. This present may be meager, granted. But no matter what it is like, one must firmly take it by the horns to be able to consult the past. It is the bull whose blood must fill the pit if the shades of the departed are to appear at its edge." Out of this present when it has been sacrificed for the invocation of the past arises then "the deadly impact of thought" which is directed against tradition and the authority of the past.

Thus the heir and preserver unexpectedly turns into a destroyer. "The true, greatly misunderstood passion of the collector is always anarchistic, destructive. For this is its dialectics: to combine with loyalty to an object, to individual items, to things sheltered in his care, a stubborn subversive protest against the typical, the classifiable." The collector destroys the context in which his object once was only part of a greater, living entity, and since only the uniquely genuine will do for him he must cleanse the chosen object of everything that is typical about it. The figure of the collector, as old-fashioned as that of the *flâneur,* could assume such eminently modern features in Benjamin because history itself—that is, the break in tradition which took place at the beginning of this century—had already relieved him of this task of destruction and he only needed to bend down, as it were, to select his precious fragments from the pile of debris. In other words, the things themselves offered, particularly to a man who firmly faced the present, an aspect which had previously been discoverable only from the collector's whimsical perspective.

I do not know when Benjamin discovered the remarkable coincidence of his old-fashioned inclinations with the realities of the times; it must have been in the mid-twenties, when he began the serious study of Kafka, only to discover shortly thereafter in Brecht the poet who was most at home in this century. I do not mean to assert that Benjamin shifted his emphasis from the collecting of books to the collecting of quotations (exclusive with him) overnight or even within one year, although there is some evidence in the letters of a conscious shifting of emphasis. At any rate, nothing was more characteristic of him in the thirties than the little notebooks with black covers which he always carried with him and in which he tirelessly entered in the form of quotations what daily living and reading netted him in the way of "pearls" and "coral." On occasion he read from them aloud, showed them around like items from a choice and precious collection. And in this collection, which by then was anything but whimsical, it was easy to find next to an obscure love poem from the eighteenth century the latest newspaper item, next to Goecking's "Der erste Schnee" a report from Vienna dated Summer 1939, saying that the local gas company had "stopped supplying gas to Jews. The gas consumption of the Jewish population involved a loss for the gas company, since the biggest consumers were the ones who did not pay their bills. The Jews used the gas especially for committing suicide." Here indeed the shades of the departed were invoked only from the sacrificial pit of the present.

The close affinity between the break in tradition and the seemingly whimsical figure of the collector who gathers his fragments and scraps from the debris of the past is perhaps best illustrated by the fact, astonishing only at first glance, that there probably was no period before ours in which old and ancient things, many of them long forgotten by tradition, have become general educational material which is handed to schoolboys everywhere in hundreds of thousands of copies. This amazing revival, particularly of classical culture, which since the forties has been especially noticeable in relatively traditionless America, began in Europe in the twenties. There it was initiated by those who were most aware of the irreparability of the break in tradition—thus in Germany, and not only there, first and foremost by Martin Heidegger, whose extraordinary, and extraordinarily early, success in the twenties was essentially due to a "listening to the tradition that does not give itself up to the past but thinks of the present." Without realizing it, Benjamin actually had more in common with Heidegger's remarkable sense for living eyes and living bones that had sea-changed into pearls and coral, and as such could be saved and lifted into the present only by doing violence to their context in interpreting them with "the deadly impact" of new thoughts, than he did with the dialectical subtleties of his Marxist friends. For just as the above-cited closing sentence from the Goethe essay sounds as though Kafka had written it, the following words from a letter to Hofmannsthal dated 1924 make one think of some of Heidegger's essays written in the forties and fifties: "The conviction which guides me in my literary attempts . . . [is] that each truth has its home, its ancestral palace, in language, that this palace was built with the oldest *logoi,* and that to a truth thus founded the insights of the sciences will remain inferior for as long as they make do here and there in the area of language like nomads, as it were, in the conviction of the sign character of language which produces the irresponsible arbitrariness of their terminology." In the spirit of Benjamin's early work on the philosophy of language, words are "the opposite of all communication directed toward the outside," just as truth is "the death of intention." Anyone who seeks truth fares like the man in the fable about the veiled picture at Saïs: "this is caused not by some mysterious monstrousness of the content to be unveiled but by the nature of truth before which even the purest fire of searching is extinguished as though under water."

From the Goethe essay on, quotations are at the center of every work of Benjamin's. This very fact distinguishes his writings from scholarly works of all kinds in which it is the function of quotations to verify and document opinions, wherefore they can safely be relegated to the Notes. This is out of the question in Benjamin. When he was working on his study of German tragedy, he boasted of a collection of "over 600 quotations very systematically and clearly arranged"; like the later notebooks, this collection was not an accumulation of excerpts intended to facilitate the writing of the study but constituted the main work, with the writing as something secondary. The main work consisted in tearing fragments out of their context and arranging them afresh in such a way that they illustrated one another and were able to prove their *raison d'être* in a free-floating state, as it were. It definitely was a sort of surrealistic montage. Benjamin's ideal of producing a work consisting entirely of quotations, one that was mounted so masterfully that it could dispense with any accompanying text, may strike one as whimsical in the extreme and self-destructive to boot, but it was not, any more than were the contemporaneous surrealistic experiments which arose from similar impulses. To the extent that an accompanying text by the author proved unavoidable, it was a matter of fashioning it in such a way as to preserve "the intention of such investigations," namely, "to plumb the depths of language and thought . . . by drilling rather than excavating," so as not to ruin everything with explanations that seek to provide a causal or systematic connection. In so doing Benjamin was quite aware that this new method of "drilling" resulted in a certain "forcing of insights . . . whose inelegant pedantry, however, is preferable to today's almost universal habit of falsifying them"; it was equally clear to him that this method was bound to be "the cause of certain obscurities." What mattered to him above all was to avoid anything that might be reminiscent of empathy, as though a given subject of investigation had a message in readiness which easily communicated itself, or could be communicated, to the reader or spectator: *"No poem is intended for the reader, no picture for the beholder, no symphony for the listener"* (**"The Task of the Translator"**; italics added).

This sentence, written quite early, could serve as motto for all of Benjamin's literary criticism. It should not be misunderstood as another dadaist affront of an audience that even then had already become quite used to all sorts of merely capricious shock effects and "put-ons." Benjamin deals here with thought things, particularly those of a linguistic nature, which, according to him, "retain their meaning, possibly their best significance, if they are not *a priori* applied exclusively to man. For example, one could speak of an unforgettable life or moment even if all men had forgotten them. If the nature of such a life or moment required that it not be forgotten, that predicate would not contain a falsehood but merely a claim that is not being fulfilled by men, and perhaps also a reference to a realm in which it *is* fulfilled: God's remembrance." Benjamin later gave up this theological background but not the theory and not his method of drilling to obtain the essential in the form of quotations—as one obtains water by drilling for it from a source concealed in the depths of the earth. This method is like the modern equivalent of ritual invocations, and the spirits that now arise invariably are those spiritual essences from a past that have suffered the Shakespearean "sea-change" from living eyes to pearls, from living bones to coral. For Benjamin to quote is to name, and naming rather than speaking, the word rather than the sentence, brings truth to light. As one may read in the preface to the ***Origin of German Tragic Drama,*** Benjamin regarded truth as an exclusively acoustical phenomenon: "Not Plato but Adam," who gave things their names, was to him the "father of philosophy." Hence tradition was the form in which these name-giving words were transmitted; it too was an essentially acoustical phenomenon. He felt himself so akin to Kafka precisely because the latter, current misinterpretations notwithstanding, had "no farsightedness or 'prophetic vision,'" but listened to tradition, and "he who listens hard does not see" (**"Max Brod's Book on Kafka"**).

There are good reasons why Benjamin's philosophical interest from the outset concentrated on the philosophy of language, and why finally naming through quoting became for him the only possible and appropriate way of dealing with the past without the aid of tradition. Any period to which its own past has become as questionable as it has to us must eventually come up against the phenomenon of language, for in it the past is contained ineradicably, thwarting all attempts to get rid of it once and for all. The Greek *polis* will continue to exist at the bottom of our political existence—that is, at the bottom of the sea—for as long as we use the word "politics." This is what the semanticists, who with good reason attack language as the one bulwark behind which the past hides—its confusion, as they say—fail to understand. They are absolutely right: in the final analysis all problems are linguistic problems; they simply do not know the implications of what they are saying.

But Benjamin, who could not yet have read Wittgenstein, let alone his successors, knew a great deal about these very things, because from the beginning the problem of truth had presented itself to him as a "revelation . . . which must be heard, that is, which lies in the metaphysically acoustical sphere." To him, therefore, language was by no means primarily the gift of speech which distinguishes man from other living beings, but, on the contrary, "the world essence . . . from which speech arises," which incidentally comes quite close to Heidegger's position that "man can speak only insofar as he is the sayer." Thus there is "a language of truth, the tensionless and even silent depository of the ultimate secrets which all thought is concerned with" (**"The Task of the Translator"**), and this is "the true language" whose existence we assume unthinkingly as soon as we translate from one language into another. That is why Benjamin places at the center of his essay **"The Task of the Translator"** the astonishing quotation from Mallarmé in which the spoken languages in their multiplicity and diversity suffocate, as it were, by virtue of their Babel-like tumult, the *"immortelle parole"* ["immortal word"], which cannot even be thought, since "thinking is writing without implement or whispers, silently," and thus prevent the voice of truth from being heard on earth with the force of material, tangible evidence. Whatever theoretical revisions Benjamin may subsequently have made in these theological-metaphysical convictions, his basic approach, decisive for all his literary studies, remained unchanged: not to investigate the utilitarian or communicative functions of linguistic creations, but to understand them in their crystallized and thus ultimately fragmentary form as intentionless and noncommunicative utterances of a "world essence." What else does this mean than that he understood language as an essentially poetic phenomenon? And this is precisely what the last sentence of the Mallarmé aphorism, which he does not quote, says in unequivocal clarity: *"Seulement, sachons n'existerait pas le vers: lui, philosophiquement re-*

munère le défaut des langues, complément supérieur"—all this were true if poetry did not exist, the poem that philosophically makes good the defect of languages, is their superior complement. All of which says no more, though in a slightly more complex way, than what I mentioned before—namely, that we are dealing here with something which may not be unique but is certainly extremely rare: the gift of *thinking poetically.* (pp. 194-205)

> *Hannah Arendt, "Walter Benjamin: 1892-1940," in* Men in Dark Times, *translated by Harry Zohn, Harcourt Brace Jovanovich, 1968, pp. 153-206.*

Frank Kermode   (essay date 1969)

[*Kermode is an English critic whose career combines modern critical methods with expert traditional scholarship. For Kermode, a work of art has no single fixed meaning, but a multiplicity of possible interpretations; the best of modern writing, he feels, is constructed so that it invites a variety of interpretations, all of which depend upon the sensibility of the reader. True or "classic" literature, to Kermode, is thus a constantly reinterpreted living text, "complex and indeterminate enough to allow us our necessary pluralities." In the following excerpt, he offers a favorable review of* Illuminations, *focusing on the artistic qualities in Benjamin's literary criticism.*]

Reviewers of [*Illuminations*] are likely to be oppressed by two considerations, first that they have taken on something exceptionally important, and secondly that they have taken on something unusually difficult. The first appearance in English of a writer who is the subject of such high claims amply justifies the first sentiment, and the idiosyncracy of his method as well as the complexity of his historical situation excuses the second. (p. 30)

One might as well begin with literary criticism. There is a longish piece on Kafka. It starts off with a story about Potemkin, but this only sounds like a leisurely belletristic overture. *Stories,* as we shall see, are crucial to Benjamin. Soon he is discoursing intelligently about the ugly sexy women in Kafka, and about the beauty of the guilty. Good but not amazing, it sounds like capable commentary; but Benjamin distinguished between commentary and criticism, the latter being the higher activity and concerned, not with the communication to readers of *information,* here italicized as a word with special senses to be discussed later, but with, to be less vague than one sounds, the intuition of essences. Then, arising out of some remarks on *Amerika,* this passage occurs:

> Kafka's entire work constitutes a code of gestures which surely had no definite symbolic meaning for the author at the outset; rather, the author tried to derive such a meaning from them in everchanging contexts and experimental groupings. . . . The greater Kafka's mastery became, the more frequently did he eschew adapting these gestures to common situations or explaining them. . . . Each gesture is an event—one might even say, a drama—in itself. . . . Like El Greco, Kafka tears open the sky behind each gesture; but as with El Greco . . . the gesture remains the decisive thing. . . . He divests the human gesture of its traditional supports and then has a subject for reflection without end.

This condensed version perforce leaves out the supporting examples. The reader will supply them: the hunched backs, the raised hands, all those postures and movements which, in Kafka, import familiar behavior into a context which alters or strips it of usual meanings. Thus we know it is wrong to think of the novels as if they were analogous to dreams. Benjamin is saying why. Kafka "took all conceivable precautions against the interpretation of his writings," which is why explications and allegorizings, psycholanalytic or theological, are always wrong. He made *stories;* he dealt in primordial experience, which is why

> his novels are set in a swamp world. In his works created things appear at the stage which Bachofen has termed the hetaeric stage. The fact that it is now forgotten does not mean that it does not extend into the present. . . . An experience deeper than that of an average person can make contact with it.

But of course it cannot be interpreted in another language. Like all the literature of wisdom (wisdom being truth in its epic aspect) it expresses itself as story, a lost art. Kafka's world is not ours, if only because "his gestures of terror are given scope by the marvelous *margin* which the catastrophe will not grant us." Hence his wisdom, traditional though in decay; hence also his "radiant serenity," his acceptance of a world without hope for us, who have no source of serenity.

Benjamin, as one sees from this, is not a critic who goes in for "close analysis." He isn't even, on this evidence, the master of any great range of critical strategies. He is not noisily prophetic or apocalyptic; certainly he sees Kafka as providing a relevant wisdom, but he does not pretend that Kafka was needed to show the world what was already obvious, that it was on the brink of a disaster. On the other hand it must be said that he chooses his illustrations with extraordinary skill and insight. The code of gestures is a brilliant notion; the analogy with El Greco—one of many such rapid allusions to painting and sculpture—has terrific assurance and point. But it is doubtful whether these advantages alone would guarantee Benjamin the now widely endorsed opinion that he is pre-eminent among twentieth-century critics. And if we try to describe the quality which does vindicate that opinion I doubt if, at this stage, we shall come up with anything much more illuminating than *certainty.*

The centrality of Kafka is a public concept, but most ways of stating it simply seem intolerably vulgar and imprecise after Benjamin, who knows the author in his essence, and has exactly the means, nothing beyond or short of necessity, to show it forth. You hardly feel that you have been reading criticism; this is not because the method is eclectic or "impressionist," but because it requires the kind of response we are accustomed to give to works of art. This is the quality Miss Arendt [see excerpt above] is trying to describe when she talks about the *poetic* nature of his thought. Benjamin's is, however, a poetic of accuracy, not of vague suggestion. And this is why he really is a great critic. The fact that his primary critical operations had methodological by-products which he employed, with great ingenuity and taste, in the construction of literary and cultural theories is interesting but less important; what counts here is the *art* of criticism.

Before I get on to those secondary matters I had better

give a further example of the primary. On the evidence of this book, the second author of whom Benjamin speaks with unequalled authority is Proust, who figures largely not only in the essay devoted to him but also in the longest and most elaborate of the studies, the one on Baudelaire, who, for Benjamin, was Proust's evangelist.

Baudelaire, as we all know, invented for art the modern city—*l'immonde cité*—and its crowds. Benjamin subjects this commonplace to extraordinary processes of elaboration and refinement. For him the city is not only the locus of our complex modern isolation, it is also the source of modern *shock.* Its gestures are all productive of, or protective against, shock: switching, inserting, pressing, snapping; the exchange and avoidance of glances; the barrage of incomplete and discontinuous impressions. (This aspect of metropolitan life, incidentally, fascinated Conrad. Benjamin would have been very good on Conrad, but he lived in Paris and chose Poe.)

What is destroyed by this continuous discontuity is a quality Benjamin calls *aura*. This is variously described and apprehended. It is, for example, the quality of the unique work of art, handed down by a tradition, a quality lost in mechanical reproduction.

> That which withers in the age of mechanical reproduction is the aura of the work of art. This is a symptomatic process whose significance points beyond the realm of art. . . . The technique of reproduction detaches the reproduced object from the domain of tradition. By making many reproductions it substitutes a plurality of copies for a unique existence. And in permitting the reproduction to meet the beholder or listener in his own particular situation, it reactivates the object reproduced. These two processes lead to a tremendous shattering of tradition which is the obverse of the contemporary crisis and renewal of mankind.

Another great enemy of aura is the movie camera; the film, assaulting the senses in an almost tactile way by violent and discontinuous cutting, is the great agent of shock. Benjamin does not fail to relate these effects to those of the assembly line on unskilled workers.

> In a film, perception in the form of shocks was established as a formal principle. That which determines the rhythm of production on a conveyor belt is the basis of the rhythm of reception in the film.

And he goes on to cite Marx. But primarily he is concerned to say something about the essential Baudelaire and the essential Proust.

How, then, do aura and shock concern Proust? Proust, like Kafka, discovered, though at great cost, a way of preserving wisdom and telling stories (stories, the receptacles of wisdom, of experience with its auras) in the modern city. Fantastically devoted to "information" (the enemy of wisdom and story) he lived in the world of conscious memory but nevertheless retained access to the *mémoire involontaire,* where everything has aura. "To perceive the aura of an object we look at [? for] means to invest it with the ability to look at us in return." Thus Proust was able to find what was lost in the midst of things that had "lost their ability to look." And for Benjamin all that is left of "tradition" in our world is a store of discrete, fragmentary deposits like those attained by the Proustian involuntary memory.

No summary can convey much of the richness of these insights, nor of the high skill with which the controlling ideas are manipulated. Writing of Proust alone, Benjamin is content with a simpler brilliance; but he adds greatly to our knowledge of Proustian essences. He chooses an anecdote, matches it with one of his own; speaks aphoristically of Proust's defining the structure of the society by a "physiology of chatter"; asks whether it is not "the quintessence of experience to learn many things which apparently could be told in a very few words" but actually require an enormous mimicry of the society and its language. "Proust's most accurate, most convincing insights fasten on their objects as insects fasten on leaves, blossoms, branches, betraying nothing of their existence until a leap, a beating of wings, a vault, show the startled observer that some incalculable individual life has imperceptibly crept into an alien world." So keen is Proust's sense of concealment that he even mimics the concealment practiced by the class he is describing, its silence as to its economic foundation. A consequence is that the greatness of Proust's work "will remain inaccessible until this class has revealed its most pronounced features in the final struggle."

That last doctrinally adhesive observation is of a sort that occasionally occurs in Benjamin's work, but has to take its place with quite other kinds. The essay ends astonishingly with a meditation on Proust's psychogenic asthma as source and condition of his art: "Proust's syntax rhythmically and step by step reproduces his fear of suffocating." Thus begins the concluding passage, as accurate, as original, and as free from critical or ideological vulgarity, as the essay on Kafka.

Now it must be already clear that Benjamin uses some terms—"aura," "shock," "experience," "story," for instance—in a special sense; and they do indeed form a substructure which lies as it were between the criticism itself and the Marxist foundation on which his thinking, officially but as all admit precariously, rests. This is to be inferred from the criticism, but is also the material of some extracritical speculation, Benjamin's own informed inferences; I put it this way because it is so important to see the "poetry" of the criticism as primary, and because it will help us to see why Benjamin is a finer critic than Lukács, who is for the most part a critic last not first.

Yet it is precisely this extremely characteristic and independent layer of doctrine that has made it difficult for critics who know Benjamin's cultural milieu to convey their sense of his greatness. Miss Arendt calls him a kind of poet, but her superb essay is colored, I think, by a sense that Benjamin is somehow, considered as an intellectual, a little irresponsible. Mr. Alter [see Further Reading] rightly observes that Benjamin's mind normally operates "quite outside the prefabricated structures of Marxist theory," and properly regards this as distinguishing his work from that of Lukács or Goldmann. But even so there is always a feeling that Benjamin's individuality must be expressed by showing how he deviates from one or another philosophical norm. Thus Miss Arendt, for all her resourcefulness, seems secretly puzzled that he can be so good: in linking the Marxist "superstructure" to Baudelaire's *"correspondances"* he is showing himself the most peculiar Marxist who ever lived; his central image of the

flâneur—the nineteenth-century gentleman-stroller, connoisseur of metropolitan curiosities—is very un-Marxist, etc. Just so Adorno criticized him for using the relation of sub- and superstructure as metaphor rather than as fact. Instead of system there is, to everybody's surprise, poetry: they ask for a stone and are given bread.

Benjamin, we remind ourselves, aspired to literary criticism; he wanted to be the chief German literary critic. Like good poets, good literary critics need to have a lot in their heads, but it need not be systematic; and there is no need to be surprised that Benjamin at his best uses Marxist as well as Hasidic knowledge as elements of a system imposed by the criticism more or less *ad hoc*. . . . And in between the criticism and the big systems falls his own body of systematic inference.

A knowledge of Benjamin's secondary preoccupations will prevent the objection that he is too often merely paradoxical. For example, in his essay on translation he proposes a doctrine of inutility. Translation is not a means of conveying information; all good translations of a particular text, taken together, constitute an attempt to reveal some hypothetical *ur*-language underlying that in which the original was written; every translation is in a sense a contribution to the restoration of an ideal never wholly knowable. He even says that a translation is linguistically more definitive than an original, since it can no longer be displaced by a secondary rendering; but that is a flourish, and the basic insight (founded on no more than the observation that we really always assume a text *can* be translated) is a Mallarméan sense that the imperfection of languages, as revealed in their plurality, implies an ideal, *l'immortelle parole* ["the immortal word"], to the discovery of which each translation contributes.

It follows that the translator ought not to try for a version that sounds original in his own language, but rather that he should let the original taint his version deeply. This, in its expression, sounds rather dandyish, rather *épatant* ["shocking"]. Its implications are, however, serious; Benjamin would have approved of "Homage to Sextus Propertius" and, presumably, of Zukofsky's Catullus. And its rationale is also serious. "Information" is the enemy of art, inutility the necessary condition of the essential act of criticism, as Benjamin conceives it, which is at the farthest possible remove from reviewing or textbook writing, being more like the action of the involuntary memory, a *recherche* of the only possible kind into *le temps perdu*. Benjamin speaks thus of translation for the same reason that he abjures the close examination of the existential flurry of the "words on the page." He is interested in what does not render itself visible, whether it is language, a poem, or a Proustian memory.

In the great essay on Leskov he adumbrates a theory of story consistent with these assumptions. The art of story ends in modern times, ends, in fact, with the invention of the novel. Story belongs to a time before the machine devalued human experience; being the communication of experience as authenticated counsel; it belongs to wisdom, which is truth in its epic aspect. The decay of story and of wisdom is a "concomitant symptom of the secular productive forces of history." The novel has nothing to do with wisdom. It belongs to print, to a world in which the teller is not impressing his aura on the tale, is "himself uncounseled," and offers not a guide to the perplexed but mere perplexity. Information, which is absent from story, is critical to the novel; and the great novelists, Kafka and Proust, as we saw, achieve that greatness by finding ways to convert the novel into story, information into wisdom.

There follows a passage which might serve as a crucial instance of Benjamin's genius. Story, he says, belongs to a world in which death is familiar, a part of daily life. Now we have tidied death out of our houses and the novel is obliged, in conveying something of the "meaning of life," to provide it. Hence the extreme importance of the ends of novels, and the manner in which we regard characters as people in whose experience of death we intend to share; for if they do not actually die they suffer a figurative death at the end of the book. "This stranger's fate, by virtue of the flame which consumes it, yields us the warmth which we never draw from our own fate."

"Incomparable" is a word that has attached to Benjamin; it may be coolly applied to these few paragraphs on the eschatology of the novel. And it must not be forgotten that all such speculations are solidly supported by work on *novels.* So too with the "probes" about technology and aura; so with almost all the more speculative material. It may have elements borrowed from more formal thinkers (the theory of the novel owes something to Lukács's early book on the subject) but the force is generated by contact with texts. Thus the most McLuhanish piece in the book, *The Work of Art in the Age of Mechanical Reproduction,* is ostensibly an independent study of how certain superstructural changes had become visible "only today," half a century after the corresponding changes in the economic base. These changes alter the whole character and political bearing of art. The great single difference is reproducibility, with the attendant loss of aura. The old notion of art is now Fascist, because concepts such as creativity, genius, eternal value, mystery "lead to a processing of data in the Fascist sense." So Benjamin, in this essay, wishes to replace them with others that are more concordant with revolutionary demands.

Yet for all this half-willing radicalism, the concept of aura still belongs to his study of prerevolutionary art, an art that seeks to recover wisdom, an art associated with the sacred ritual from which mechanical reproduction will deliver it into the realm of politics.

Whenever Benjamin develops his ideas beyond their heuristic utility he arrives, naturally enough, at some such political position, so that his pronouncements can on occasion be rather remote from his critical practice. One such is the famous observation, made with Marinetti in mind, that Fascism aestheticizes politics while Communism politicizes art. We reach ideological base here, and also in some of the *Theses on the Philosophy of History,* in which he emerges, under the duress of a mode of thought that must often have been uncongenial, as an abolitionist. The art of the past is a set of trophies celebrating the victory of the few over the many. "There is no document of civilization which is not at the same time a document of barbarism," he wrote shortly before his death in 1940. "Barbarism taints also the manner in which it was transmitted from one owner to another [though this transmission he earlier associates with aura]. A historical materialist therefore dissociates himself from it as far as possible." Yet the Theses also associate this materialism with a kind of muted Messianism. We are thus reminded that the

Jews, forbidden to investigate the future, were instructed in remembrance of things past. Instruction in remembrance (though the world is full of "information") is his serious project: to give, without ignoring the modern intellect, without minimizing the shocks of modern reality, a human structure, so far as it may be had, to the "time of now."

The dilemma is clear enough, and in 1940 Benjamin must have experienced it with tragic fullness. The "politicization" of art, which the situation required, marks the end of the historical process in which barbarism assisted at the creation of those virtually sacral essences which it was his special gift to divine. His major essays take cognizance of the shock as well as of the aura. He believed both that the material of great criticism was being destroyed, and that it ought to be destroyed. In wanting to be a great literary critic he discovered that he could only be the last great literary critic, and in explaining *that,* he explained certain aspects of the modern with an authority that thirty years of unpredictable change have not vitiated. And although some may think him unlucky, deviant, others will regard him as one of the norms by which fortune and correctness need to be judged. (pp. 30-3)

Frank Kermode, "The Incomparable Benjamin" in The New York Review of Books, *Vol. 13, No. 11, December 18, 1969, pp. 30-3.*

Fredric Jameson (essay date 1972)

[*Jameson is considered America's most prominent Marxist critic of the twentieth century. While his literary studies have focused on the works of Jean-Paul Sartre, Jameson has written prolifically on the political aspects of mass culture and on the ideologies of such noted critics and philosophers as Theodor Adorno, Ernst Bloch, Herbert Marcuse, and Walter Benjamin. His seminal study* Marxism and Form *argues that literature achieves significance as a symbolic portrayal of a society's beliefs and conventions. In the following excerpt from that work, Jameson examines Benjamin's use of allegory and his distinction between the narrative conventions of the story and the novel.*]

Every feeling is attached to an a priori object, and the presentation of the latter is the phenomenology of the former.

Ursprung des deutschen Trauerspiels

So the melancholy that speaks from the pages of Benjamin's essays—private depressions, professional discouragement, the dejection of the outsider, distress in the face of a political and historical nightmare—searches the past for an adequate object, for some emblem or image at which, as in religious meditation, the mind can stare itself out, in which it can find momentary, if only aesthetic, relief. It finds it: in the Germany of the Thirty Years' War, in the Paris "capital of the nineteenth century." For they are both—the Baroque and the modern—in their very essence allegorical, and they match the thought process of the theorist of allegory, which, disembodied intention searching for some external object into which to take shape, is itself already allegorical *avant la lettre.*

Indeed, it seems to me that Walter Benjamin's thought is

best grasped as an allegorical one, as a set of parallel, discontinuous levels of meditation which are not without resemblance to that ultimate model of allegorical composition described by Dante when he speaks in his letter to Can Grande della Scala of the four dimensions of his poem: the literal (his hero's adventures in the afterworld), the moral (the ultimate fate of his soul), the allegorical (in which his encounters resume one aspect or another of the life of Christ), and the anagogical (where his own drama foreshadows the progress of the human race itself toward the Last Judgment). It will not be hard to adapt this scheme to twentieth-century realities, if for literal we simply read psychological, retaining the second, moral level as such; if for the dominant archetypal pattern of the life of Christ we substitute religion in the broadest sense of the religion of art, seeing the Incarnation now as the incarnation of meaning in language; if finally, replacing theology with politics, we make of Dante's eschatology an earthly one, where the human race finds its salvation not in eternity, but in history itself.

Benjamin's work seems to me to be marked by a painful straining toward a psychic wholeness or unity of experience which the historical situation threatens to shatter at every turn. A vision of a world of ruins and fragments, an ancient chaos of whatever nature on the point of overwhelming consciousness—these are some of the images that seem to recur, either in Benjamin himself or in your own mind as you read him. The idea of wholeness or unity is of course not original with him. How many modern philosophers have described the "damaged existence" we lead in modern society, the psychological impairment caused by the division of labor and by specialization, the general alienation and dehumanization of modern life in all its aspects? Yet for the most part these analyses remain abstract; through them there speaks the resignation of the intellectual specialist to his own maimed present, the dream of wholeness, where it persists, attaching itself to someone else's future. Benjamin is unique among these thinkers in that he wants to save his own life as well: hence the peculiar fascination of his writings, incomparable not only in their dialectical intelligence, nor even in the poetic sensibility they express, but above all, perhaps, in the manner in which the autobiographical part of his mind finds symbolic satisfaction in the shape of ideas abstractly, in objective guises, expressed.

Psychologically, the drive toward unity takes the form of an obsession with the past and with memory. Genuine memory determines "whether the individual can have a picture of himself, whether he can master his own experience." "Every passion borders on chaos, but the passion of the collector borders on the chaos of memory" (and it was in the image of the collector that Benjamin found one of his most comfortable identities). "Memory forges the chain of tradition that passes events on from generation to generation." Strange reflections, these—strange subjects of reflection for a Marxist (one thinks of Sartre's acid comment on his orthodox Marxist contemporaries: "materialism is the subjectivity of those who are ashamed of their own subjectivity"). Yet Benjamin kept faith with Proust, whom he translated, long after his own discovery of Communism; like Proust, he saw in his favorite poet Baudelaire an analogous obsession with reminiscence and involuntary memory; and in the fragmentary evocation of his own childhood called ***Berliner Kindheit um 1900*** he

Benjamin during a 1938 visit with Bertolt Brecht in Denmark.

too began the task of recovering his own existence with short essayistic sketches, records of dreams, of isolated impressions and experiences, which he was however unable to carry to the greater writer's ultimate narrative unity.

He was perhaps more conscious of what prevents us from assimilating our life experience than of the form such a perfected life would take—fascinated, for example, with Freud's distinction between unconscious memory and the conscious act of recollection, the latter being for Freud basically a way of destroying or eradicating what the former was designed to preserve: "consciousness appears in the system of perception *in place* of the memory traces . . . consciousness and the leaving behind of a memory trace are within the same system mutually incompatible." For Freud, the function of consciousness is the defense of the organism against shocks from the external environment. In this sense traumas, hysterical repetitions, dreams are ways in which the incompletely assimilated shock attempts to make its way through to consciousness and hence to ultimate appeasement. In Benjamin's hands, this idea becomes an instrument of historical description, a way of showing how in modern society, perhaps on account of the increasing number of shocks of all kinds to which the organism is now subjected, these defense mechanisms are no longer personal ones: a whole series of mechanical substitutes intervenes between consciousness and its objects, shielding us perhaps, yet at the same time depriving us of any way of assimilating what happens to us or of transforming our sensations into any genuinely personal experience. Thus, to give only one example, the newspaper acts as a shock absorber for the jolts of novelty, numbing us to events that might perhaps otherwise overwhelm us, but at the same time rendering them neutral and impersonal, transforming them into something that by definition has no common denominator with our private existences.

Experience is moreover socially conditioned in that it depends on a certain rhythm of recurrences and similarities in events which are properly cultural in origin. Thus even in Proust and Baudelaire, who lived in relatively fragmented societies, ritualistic devices, often unconscious, are primary elements in the construction of form: we recognize them in the "vie antérieure" ["previous life"] and the correspondences of Baudelaire, in the ceremonies of salon life in Proust. And where the modern writer tries to create a perpetual present—as in Kafka—the mystery inherent in the events seems to result not so much from their novelty as from the feeling that they have merely been forgotten, that they are in some sense "familiar," in the haunting significance which Baudelaire lent that word. Yet as society increasingly decays, such rhythms of experience are less and less available.

At this point, however, psychological description seems to pass over insensibly into *moral* judgment, into a vision of the reconciliation of past and present which is somehow an ethical one. But for the Western reader the whole ethical dimension of Benjamin's work is likely to be perplexing, incorporating as it does a kind of ethical psychology which, codified by Goethe, has become traditional in Germany and deeply rooted in the German language, but for which we have no equivalent, except in such cultural transplants as the works of Erik Erikson. This *Lebensweisheit* ["worldly wisdom"] is indeed a kind of halfway house between the classical idea of a fixed human nature, with its psychology of the humors, passions, sins, or character types; and the modern idea of pure historicity, of the determining influence of the situation or environment. As a compromise in the domain of the individual personality, it is not unlike the compromise of Hegel in the realm of history itself. Where for the latter a general meaning was immanent within the particular moment of history, for Goethe, in some sense, the overall goal of the personality and of its development is built into the particular emotion in question, or latent in the particular stage in the individual's growth. For the system is based on a vision of the full development of the personality (a writer like Gide, deeply influenced by Goethe, gives but a pale and narcissistic reflection of this ethic, which expressed middle-class individualism at the moment of its historic triumph); it neither aims to break the personality upon some purely external standard of discipline, as is the case with Christianity, nor to abandon it to the meaningless accidents of empirical psychology, as is the case with most modern ethics, but rather sees the individual psychological experience as something which includes within itself seeds of its own development, something in which ethical growth is inherent as a kind of interiorized Providence. So, for example, Goethe's *Orphic Words,* or the closing lines of *Wilhelm Mei-*

ster: "You make me think of Saul, the son of Kish, who went forth to seek his father's asses and found, instead, a kingdom!"

It is, however, characteristic of Benjamin that in his most complete expression of this Goethean ethic, the long essay on *Goethe's "Elective Affinities"*, he should lay more stress on the dangers that menace the personality than on the picture of its ultimate development. For this essay, which speaks the language of Goethean life-psychology, is at the same time a critique of the reactionary forces in German society which made that psychology their own; working with the concept of myth, it is at the same time an attack on the obscurantist ideologies which made the notion of myth their rallying cry. In this, the polemic posture of Benjamin can be instructive for those of us who, undialectically, are tempted simply to reject the concept of myth altogether, on account of the ideological uses to which it is ordinarily put; for whom this concept, like related ones of magic or charisma, seems not to aim at a rational analysis of the irrational but rather at a consecration of it through language.

But for Benjamin *Elective Affinities* may be considered a mythical work, on condition we understand myth as that element from which the work seeks to free itself: as some earlier chaos of instinctual forces, inchoate, natural, pre-individualistic, as that which is destructive of genuine individuality, that which consciousness must overcome if it is to attain any real autonomy of its own, if it is to accede to any properly human level of existence. Is it farfetched to see in this opposition between mythical forces and the individual spirit a disguised expression of Benjamin's thoughts about past and present, an image of the way in which a remembering consciousness masters its past and brings to light what would otherwise be lost in the prehistory of the organism? Nor should we forget that the essay on *Goethe's "Elective Affinities"* is itself a way of recovering the past, this time a cultural past, one given over to the dark mythical forces of a proto-Fascist tradition.

Benjamin's dialectical skill can be seen in the way this idea of myth is expressed through attention to the form of Goethe's novel, no doubt one of the most eccentric of Western literature in its combination of an eighteenth-century ceremoniousness with symbols of a strangely artificial, allegorical quality: objects which appear in the blankness of the nonvisual narrative style as though isolated against a void, as though fateful with a kind of geometrical meaning; the cautiously selected detail of landscape, too symmetrical not to have significance; analogies, such as the chemical one that gives the novel its title, too amply developed not to be emblematic. The reader is of course familiar with symbolism everywhere in the modern novel; but in general the symbolism is built into the work, like a sheet of instructions supplied inside the box along with the puzzle pieces. Here we feel the burden of guilt laid upon us as readers, in our lack of what strikes us almost as a culturally inherited mode of thinking, accessible only to those who are that culture's members; and no doubt the Goethean system does project itself in some such way, in its claim to universality.

It is the originality of Benjamin to have cut across the sterile opposition between the arbitrary interpretations of the symbol on the one hand, and the blank failure to see what it means on the other: *Elective Affinities* is to be read not as a novel by a symbolic writer, but as a novel *about* symbolism. If objects of a symbolic nature loom large in this work, it is not because they were chosen to underline the theme of adultery in some decorative manner, but rather because the real underlying subject is precisely the surrender to the power of symbols of people who have lost their autonomy as human beings. "When people sink to this level, even the life of apparently lifeless things grows strong. Gundolf quite rightly underlined the crucial role of objects in this story. Yet the intrusion of the thinglike into human life is precisely a criterion of the mythical universe." We are required to read these symbolic objects to the second power: not so much directly to decipher in them a one-to-one meaning, as to sense that of which the very fact of symbolism is itself symptomatic.

And as with the objects, so also with the characters. It has for example often been remarked that the figure of Ottilie, the saintlike young woman around whom the drama turns, is somehow rendered in a different fashion from the other, more empirically drawn and psychologically realistic characters. For Benjamin, however, this is not so much a flaw or an inconsistency, as a clue: Ottilie is not reality but appearance, and it is this that the rather external and visual mode of characterization conveys.

> It is clear that these Goethean characters come before us not so much as figures shaped from external models, nor wholly imaginary in their invention, but rather entranced somehow, as though under a spell. Hence a kind of obscurity about them which is foreign to purely visual images and which is comprehensible only for the reader who grasps their essence as pure appearance. For appearance is in this work not so much presented as a theme as it is rather implicit in the very nature and mode of the presentation itself.

This moral dimension of Benjamin's work, like that of Goethe's own, clearly represents an uneasy balance, a transitional moment between the psychological on the one hand, and the aesthetic or the historical on the other. The mind cannot long be satisfied with this purely ethical description of the events of the book as the triumph of fateful, mythical forces; it strains for historical and social explanation, and at length Benjamin himself is forced to express the conclusion "that the writer shrouds in silence: namely, that passion loses all its rights, under the laws of genuine human morality, when it seeks to make a pact with wealthy middle-class security." But in Benjamin's work, this inevitable slippage of morality into history and politics, characteristic of all modern thought, is mediated by *aesthetics,* is revealed by attention to the qualities of the work of art, just as the above conclusion was articulated by the analysis of those aspects of *Elective Affinities* that might best be described as allegorical rather than symbolic.

For in one sense Benjamin's life work can be seen as a kind of vast museum, a passionate collection, of all shapes and varieties of allegorical objects; and his most substantial work centers on that enormous studio of allegorical decoration which is the Baroque.

The Origins, not so much of German tragedy (*Tragödie*), as of German *Trauerspiel:* this distinction, for which English has no equivalent, is crucial to Benjamin's interpretation. For "tragedy," which he limits to ancient Greece as

a phenomenon, is a sacrificial drama in which the hero is offered up to the gods for atonement. *Trauerspiel,* on the other hand, which encompasses the Baroque generally, Elizabethans and Calderon as well as the seventeenth-century German playwrights, is something that might best be initially characterized as a pageant: a funereal pageant—so might the word be most adequately rendered.

As a form *Trauerspiel* reflects the baroque vision of history as chronicle, as the relentless turning of the wheel of fortune, a ceaseless succession across the stage of the world's mighty: princes, popes, empresses in their splendid costumes, courtiers, masqueraders, and poisoners—a dance of death produced with all the finery of a Renaissance triumph. For chronicle is not yet historicity in the modern sense:

> No matter how deeply the baroque intention penetrates the detail of history, its microscopic analysis never ceases to search painstakingly for political calculation in a substance seen as pure intrigue. Baroque drama knows historical events only as the depraved activity of conspirators. Not a breath of genuine revolutionary conviction in any of the countless rebels who appear before the baroque sovereign, himself immobilized in the posture of a Christian martyr. Discontent—such is the classic motive for action.

And such historical time, mere succession without development, is in reality secretly spatial, and takes the court (and the stage) as its privileged spatial embodiment.

At first glance, it would appear that this vision of life as chronicle in **The Origin of German Tragic Drama,** a pre-Marxist work, is accounted for in an idealistic and Weberian manner: as Lutherans, Benjamin says, the German baroque playwrights knew a world in which belief was utterly separate from works, in which not even the Calvinistic preordained harmony intervenes to restore a little meaning to the succession of empty acts that make up human life, the world thus remaining as a body without a soul, as the shell of an object divested of any visible function. Yet it remains at the least an open question whether this intellectual and metaphysical position *causes* the psychological experience that is at the heart of baroque tragedy, or whether it is not itself merely one of the various expressions, relatively abstract, through which an acute and concrete emotion tries to manifest itself. For the key to the latter is the enigmatic central figure of the prince himself, halfway between a tyrant justly assassinated and a martyr suffering his passion. Interpreted allegorically, he stands as the embodiment of melancholy in a stricken world, and Hamlet is his most complete expression. This interpretation of the funereal pageant as a basic expression of pathological melancholy has the advantage of accounting both for form and content at the same time.

For content, that is, in the sense of the characters' motivations:

> The indecision of the prince is nothing but saturnine *acedia.* The influence of Saturn makes people "apathetic, indecisive, slow." The tyrant falls on account of the sluggishness of his emotions. In the same fashion, the character of the courtier is marked by faithlessness—another trait of the predominance of Saturn. The courtier's mind, as portrayed in these tragedies, is fluctuation itself: be-

trayal is his very element. It is to be attributed neither to hastiness of composition nor to insufficient
characterization that the parasites in these plays
scarcely need any time for reflection at all before
betraying their lords and going over to the enemy.
Rather, the lack of character evident in their actions, partly conscious Machiavellianism to be
sure, reflects an inconsolable, despondent surrender to an impenetrable conjunction of baleful constellations, a conjunction that seems to have taken
on a massive, almost thinglike cast. Crown, royal
purple, scepter, all are in the last analysis the properties of the tragedy of fate, and they carry with
them an aura of destiny to which the courtier is the
first to submit, as to some portent of disaster. His
faithlessness to his fellow men corresponds to the
deeper, more contemplative faith he keeps with
these material emblems.

Once again Benjamin's sensitivity is for those moments in
which human beings find themselves given over into the
power of things; and the familiar content of baroque tragedy (that melancholy which we recognize from *Hamlet,*
those vices of melancholy—lust, treason, sadism—so predominant in the lesser Elizabethans, in Webster for instance) veers about slowly into a question of *form,* into the
problem of objects, which is to say of allegory itself. For
allegory is precisely the dominant mode of expression of
a world in which things have been for whatever reason utterly sundered from meanings, from spirit, from genuine
human existence.

And in the light of this new examination of the Baroque
from the point of view of form rather than of content, little
by little the brooding melancholy figure at the center of
the play himself alters in focus, the hero of the funereal
pageant little by little becomes transformed into the baroque playwright himself, the allegorist par excellence, in
Benjamin's terminology the *Grübler:* that superstitious,
overparticular reader of omens who returns in a more nervous, modern guise in the hysterical heroes of Poe and
Baudelaire. "Allegories are in the realm of thoughts what
ruins are in the realm of things"; and it is clear that Benjamin is himself foremost among these depressed and hyper-
conscious visionaries who people his pages.

> Once the object has beneath the brooding look of
> Melancholy become allegorical, once life has
> flowed out of it, the object itself remains behind,
> dead, yet preserved for all eternity; it lies before the
> allegorist, given over to him utterly, for good or ill.
> In other words, the object itself is henceforth inca-
> pable of projecting any meaning on its own; it can
> only take on that meaning which the allegorist
> wishes to lend it. He instills it with his own mean-
> ing, himself descends to inhabit it: and this must be
> understood not psychologically but in an ontologi-
> cal sense. In his hands the thing in question be-
> comes something else, speaks of something else, be-
> comes for him the key to some realm of hidden
> knowledge, as whose emblem he honors it. This is
> what constitutes the nature of allegory as script.

Script rather than language, the letter rather than the spirit; these are the fragments into which the baroque world
shatters, strangely legible signs and emblems nagging at
the too curious mind, a procession moving slowly across
a stage, laden with occult significance. In this sense, for the
first time it seems to me that allegory is restored to us—
not as a Gothic monstrosity of purely historical interest,

or, as in C. S. Lewis, a sign of the medieval health of the
essentially religious spirit, but rather as a pathology with
which in the modern world we are only too familiar. The
tendency of our own criticism has been to exalt symbol at
the expense of allegory (even though the privileged objects
proposed by that criticism—English Mannerism and
Dante—are more properly allegorical in nature; in this as
in other aspects of his sensibility Benjamin has much in
common with a writer like T. S. Eliot). The preference for
symbolism is perhaps more the expression of a value rather than a description of existing poetic phenomena: for the
distinction between symbol and allegory is that between
a complete reconciliation between object and spirit and a
mere will to such reconciliation. The usefulness of Benjamin's analysis lies however in his insistence on a temporal
distinction as well: the symbol is the instantaneous, the
lyrical, the single moment in time; and this temporal limitation perhaps expresses the historical impossibility in the
modern world for genuine reconciliation to endure in
time, for it to be anything more than a lyrical, accidental
present. Allegory is, on the contrary, the privileged mode
of our own life in time, a clumsy deciphering of meaning
from moment to moment, the painful attempt to restore
a continuity to heterogeneous, disconnected instants.

> Where the symbol as it fades shows the face of Na-
> ture in the light of salvation, in allegory it is the *fa-
> cies hippocratica* of history that lies like a frozen
> landscape before the eye of the beholder. History
> in everything that it has of the unseasonable, pain-
> ful, abortive, expresses itself in that face—nay rath-
> er in that death's-head. And while it may be true
> that such an allegorical mode is utterly lacking in
> any "symbolic" freedom of expression, in any clas-
> sical harmony of feature, in anything human—
> what is expressed here portentously in the form of
> a riddle is not only the nature of human life in gen-
> eral, but also the biographical historicity of the in-
> dividual in its most natural and organically cor-
> rupted form. This—the baroque, earthbound expo-
> sition of history as the story of the world's suffer-
> ing—is the very essence of allegorical perception;
> history takes on meaning only in the stations of its
> agony and decay. The amount of meaning is in
> exact proportion to the presence of death and the
> power of decay, since death is that which traces the
> jagged line between Physis and meaning.

And what marks baroque allegory holds true for the allegory of modern times, for Baudelaire as well: only in the
latter it is interiorized. "Baroque allegory saw the corpse
from the outside only. Baudelaire sees it from within." Or
again:

> Commemoration [*Andenken*] is the secularized
> version of the adoration of holy relics. . . . Com-
> memoration is the complement to experience. In
> commemoration there finds expression the increas-
> ing alienation of human beings, who take invento-
> ries of their past as of lifeless merchandise. In the
> nineteenth century allegory abandons the outside
> world, only to colonize the inner. Relics come from
> the corpse, commemoration from the dead occur-
> rences of the past which are euphemistically known
> as experience.

Yet in these late essays on modern literature a new preoccupation appears, which signals Benjamin's passage from
the predominantly aesthetic to the *historical* and *political*
dimension. This is the attention to the machine and to me-

chanical inventions, which characteristically first appears in the realm of aesthetics itself in the study of the movies (*The Reproducible Work of Art*) and is only later extended to the study of history in general (as in the essay **"Paris, Capital of the Nineteenth Century,"** in which the feeling of life in this period is conveyed by a description of the new objects and inventions characteristic of it: the commercial passageways, the use of cast iron, the Daguerreotype and the panorama, the great expositions, advertising). Yet it is important to point out that however materialistic such an approach to history may seem, nothing is farther from Marxism than the stress on invention and technique as the primary cause of historical change. Indeed, it seems to me that such theories (of the kind which regard the steam engine as the cause of the Industrial Revolution, and which have recently been rehearsed yet again, in streamlined modernistic form, in the works of Marshall McLuhan) function as a substitute for Marxist historiography in the way they offer a feeling of concreteness comparable to economic subject matter, at the same time that they dispense with any consideration of the human factors of classes and of the social organization of production.

Benjamin's fascination with the role of inventions in history seems to me most comprehensible in psychological or aesthetic terms. If we follow, for instance, his meditation on the role of the passerby and the crowd in Baudelaire, we find that after the evocation of Baudelaire's physical and stylistic characteristics, after the discussion of shock and organic defenses outlined earlier in this essay, the inner logic of Benjamin's material leads him to mechanical inventions:

> Comfort isolates. And at the same time it shifts its possessor deeper into the power of physical mechanisms. With the invention of matches around the middle of the century, there begins a whole series of novelties which have in common the replacement of a complicated set of operations with a single stroke of the hand. This development goes on in many different spheres at the same time: it is evident, among other instances, in the telephone, where in place of the continuous movement with which the crank of the older model had to be turned a single lifting of the receiver now suffices. Among the various gestures of sliding a mechanism home, depositing a token, or triggering an apparatus, that of "snapping" the photograph was particularly consequential. Pressing the finger once is enough to freeze an event for unlimited time. The apparatus lends the instant a posthumous shock, so to speak. And beside tactile experiences of this kind we find optical ones as well, such as the classified ads in a newspaper, or even the traffic in a big city. To move through the latter involves a whole series of shocks and collisions. At dangerous intersections, impulses crisscross the pedestrian like charges in a battery. Baudelaire describes the man who plunges into the crowd as a reservoir of electrical energy. Thereupon he calls him, thus singling out the experience of shock, "a *kaleidoscope* endowed with consciousness."

And Benjamin goes on to complete this catalogue with a description of the worker and his psychological subjection to the operation of the machine in the factory. Yet it seems to me that beyond the value of this passage as an analysis of the psychological effect of machinery, it has for Benjamin a secondary intention, it satisfies a psychological re-

quirement which is perhaps in some ways even deeper and more important than the official intellectual one; and that is to serve as a concrete embodiment for the state of mind of Baudelaire. The essay, indeed, begins with a relatively disembodied psychological state: the poet faced with the new condition of language in modern times, faced with the debasement of journalism, faced, as the inhabitant of a great city, with the increasing shocks and perceptual numbness of daily urban living. These phenomena are intensely familiar to Benjamin, but somehow he seems to feel them as insufficiently "rendered": he cannot possess them spiritually, he cannot express them adequately, until he finds some sharper and more concrete physical image in which to embody them. The machine, the list of inventions, is precisely such an image; and it will be clear to the reader that we consider such a passage, in appearance a historical analysis, as in reality an exercise in allegorical meditation, in the locating of some fitting emblem in which to anchor the peculiar and nervous modern state of mind which was Benjamin's subject matter.

For this reason the preoccupation with machines and inventions in Benjamin does not lead to a theory of historical causality; rather, it finds its completion elsewhere, in a theory of the modern object, in the notion of "aura." Aura for Benjamin is the equivalent in the modern world, where it still persists, of what anthropologists call the "sacred" in primitive societies; it is to the world of things what "mystery" is to the world of human events, what "charisma" is to the world of human beings. In a secularized universe it is perhaps easier to locate at the moment of its disappearance, the cause of which lies in general technical invention, the replacement of human perception with those substitutes for and mechanical extensions of perception which are machines. Thus it is easy to see how in the movies, in the "reproducible work of art," that aura which originally resulted from the physical presence of actors in the here and now of the theater is short-circuited by the new technical advance (and then replaced, in genuine Freudian symptom-formation, by the attempt to endow the stars with a new kind of personal aura of their own off the screen).

Yet in the world of objects, this intensity of physical presence which constitutes the aura of something can perhaps best be expressed by the image of the look, the intelligence returned: "The experience of aura is based on the transposition of a social reaction onto the relationship of the lifeless or of nature to man. The person we look at, the person who believes himself looked at, looks back at us in return. To experience the aura of a phenomenon means to endow it with the power to look back in return."

And elsewhere he defines aura thus: "The single, unrepeatable experience of distance, no matter how close it may be. While resting on a summer afternoon, to follow the outline of a mountain against the horizon, or of a branch that casts its shadow on the viewer, means to breathe the aura of the mountain, of the branch." Aura is thus in a sense the opposite of allegorical perception, in that in it a mysterious wholeness of objects becomes visible. And where the broken fragments of allegory represented a thing-world of destructive forces in which human autonomy was drowned, the objects of aura stand perhaps as the setting of a kind of Utopia, a Utopian present, not shorn of the past but having absorbed it, a kind of plenitude of existence in the world of things, if only for the briefest instant. Yet this Utopian component of Benjamin's thought, put to flight as it is by the mechanized present of history, is available to the thinker only in a simpler cultural past.

Thus it is his one evocation of a nonallegorical art, his essay on Nikolai Leskov, **"The Teller of Tales,"** which is perhaps his masterpiece. As with actors confronted with the technical advance of the reproducible work of art, so also with the tale in the face of modern communications systems, and in particular the newspaper. The function of the newspapers is to absorb the shocks of novelty, and by numbing the organism to them to dull their intensity. Yet the tale, always constructed around some novelty, was designed, on the contrary, to preserve its force; whereas the mechanical form "exhausts" ever-increasing quantities of new material, the older word-of-mouth communication is essentially characterized as that which recommends itself to memory. Its reproducibility is not mechanical, but natural to consciousness; indeed, that which allows the story to be remembered, to seem "memorable," is at the same time the means of its assimilation to the personal experience of the listeners.

It is instructive to compare Benjamin's analysis of the tale (and of its implied distinction from the novel) with that of Sartre, so similar in some ways, and yet so different in its ultimate emphasis. For both, the two forms are opposed not only in their social origins (the tale springing from collective life, the novel from middle-class solitude) and in their raw materials (the tale using what everyone can recognize as common experience, the novel that which is uncommon and highly individualistic), but also and primarily in their relationship to death and to eternity. Benjamin quotes Valéry: "It is almost as though the disappearance of the idea of eternity were related to the increasing distaste for any kind of work of long duration in time." Concurrent with the disappearance of the genuine story is the increasing concealment of death and dying in our society; for the authority of the story ultimately derives from the authority of death, which lends every event an absolute uniqueness. "A man who died at the age of thirty-five is at every point in his life a man who is going to die at the age of thirty-five": so Benjamin describes our apprehension of characters in the tale, in antipsychological fashion, as the simplified representatives of their own destinies. But what appeals to his sensitivity to the archaic is precisely what Sartre condemns as inauthentic: namely the violence to genuine lived human experience, which never in the freedom of its own present feels itself as fate, for which fate and destiny are always characteristic of other people's experience, seen from the outside as something closed and thinglike. For this reason Sartre opposes the tale (it is true that he is thinking of the well-made story of the late nineteenth century, which catered to a middle-class audience, rather than of the relatively anonymous folk product with which Benjamin is concerned) to the novel, whose task is precisely to render this open experience of consciousness in the present, of freedom, rather than the optical illusion of fate.

There can be no doubt that this opposition corresponds to a historical experience: the older tale, indeed the classical nineteenth-century novel as well, expressed a social life in which the individual was presented with single-shot, irreparable choices and opportunities, in which he had to play everything on a single roll of the dice, in which his life did therefore properly tend to take on the appearance of fate or destiny, of a story that can be told. Whereas in the modern world (which is to say, in Western Europe and the United States), economic prosperity is such that nothing is ever really irrevocable in this sense: hence the philosophy of freedom, hence the modernistic literature of consciousness of which Sartre is here a theorist; hence also the decay of plot, for where nothing is irrevocable (in the absence of death in Benjamin's sense) there is no story to tell either, there is only a series of experiences of equal weight whose order is indiscriminately reversible.

Benjamin is as aware as Sartre of the way in which the tale, with its appearance of destiny, does violence to our lived experience in the present; but for him it does justice to our experience of the past. Its "inauthenticity" is to be seen as a mode of commemoration, so that it does not really matter any longer whether the young man dead in his prime was aware of his own lived experience as fate. For us, henceforth remembering him, he will always be, at the various stages of his life, one about to become this destiny, and the tale thus gives us "the hope of warming our own chilly existence upon a death about which we read."

The tale is not only a psychological mode of relating to the past, of commemorating it: for Benjamin it is also a mode of contact with a vanished form of social and historical existence, and it is in this correlation between the activity of storytelling and the concrete form of a certain historically determinate mode of production that Benjamin can serve as a model of Marxist literary criticism at its most revealing. The twin sources of storytelling find their archaic embodiment in

> the settled cultivator on the one hand and the seafaring merchant on the other. Both forms of life have in fact produced their own characteristic type of storyteller. . . . A genuine extension of the possibilities of storytelling to its greatest historical range is, however, not possible without the most thoroughgoing fusion of the two archaic types. Such a fusion was realized during the Middle Ages in the associations and guilds of the artisans. The sedentary master and the wandering apprentice worked together in the same room; indeed, every master had himself been a wandering apprentice before settling down at home or in some foreign city. If peasants and sailors were the inventors of storytelling, the guild system proved to be the place of its highest development. In it the lore of distance, as the traveler brought it back, combined with that lore of the past that most fully reveals its riches to the stay-at-home.

The tale is thus the product of an artisanal culture, a handmade product like a cobbler's shoe or a pot; and like such a handmade object, "the touch of the storyteller clings to it like the trace of the potter's hand on the glazed surface."

In his ultimate statement of the relationship of literature to politics, Benjamin seems to have tried to bring to bear on the problems of the present this method, which had known success in dealing with the objects of the past. Yet the transposition is not without its difficulties, and Benjamin's conclusions remain problematical, particularly in his unresolved, ambiguous attitude toward modern industrial civilization, which seems to have fascinated him as much as it depressed him. The problem of propaganda in art can be solved, he maintains, by attention, not so much to the content of the work of art, as to its form: a progressive work of art is one which utilizes the most advanced artistic techniques, one in which, therefore, the artist lives his activity as a technician, and through this technical work finds a unity of purpose with the industrial worker. "The solidarity of the specialist with the proletariat . . . can never be anything but a mediated one." This Communist "politization of art," which he opposed to the Fascist "aesthetization of the machine," was designed to harness to the cause of revolution that modernism to which other Marxist critics (Lukács, for instance) were hostile. And there can be no doubt that Benjamin first came to a radical politics through his experience as a specialist: through his growing awareness, within the domain of his own literary activity, of the crucial influence exerted on the work of art by changes in the public and developments in technique, in short by history itself. But although in the realm of culture the historian can no doubt show a parallelism between specific technical advances in a given art and the general development of the economy as a whole, it is difficult to see how a technically advanced and difficult work of art can have anything but a "mediated" effect politically. Benjamin was of course fortunate in the artistic example which lay before him: for he illustrates his thesis with the epic theater of Brecht, perhaps indeed the only modern artistic innovation that *has* had direct and revolutionary political impact. But even here the situation is ambiguous: an astute critic has pointed out the secret relationship between Benjamin's fondness for Brecht on the one hand and "his lifelong fascination with children's books" on the other (children's books: hieroglyphs: simplified allegorical emblems and riddles). Thus, where we thought to emerge into the historical present, in reality we plunge again into the distant past of psychological obsession.

But if nostalgia as a political motivation is most frequently associated with Fascism, there is no reason why a nostalgia conscious of itself, a lucid and remorseless dissatisfaction with the present on the grounds of some remembered plenitude, cannot furnish as adequate a revolutionary stimulus as any other: the example of Benjamin is there to prove it. He himself, however, preferred to contemplate his destiny in terms of religious imagery, as in the following paragraph of the ***Geschichtsphilosophische Thesen,*** according to Gershom Scholem the last he ever wrote:

> Surely Time was felt neither as empty nor as homogeneous by the soothsayers who inquired after what it hid in its womb. Whoever keeps this in mind is in a position to grasp just how past time is experienced in commemoration: in precisely the same way. As is well known, the Jews were forbidden to search into the future. On the contrary, the Torah and the act of prayer instruct them in commemoration of the past. So for them the future, to which the clientele of soothsayers remains in thrall, is divested of its sacred power. Yet it does not for all that become simply empty and homogeneous time in their eyes. For every second of the future bears within it that little door through which Messiah may enter.

Angelus novus: Benjamin's favorite image of the angel that exists only to sing its hymn of praise before the face of God, to give voice, and then at once to vanish back into uncreated nothingness. So at its most poignant Benjamin's

experience of time: a present of language on the threshold of the future, honoring it by averted eyes in meditation on the past. (pp. 60-83)

> Fredric Jameson, "Versions of a Marxist Hermeneutic: Walter Benjamin; or, Nostalgia," in his Marxism and Form: Twentieth-Century Dialectical Theories of Literature, *Princeton University Press, 1972, pp. 60-83.*

René Wellek   (essay date 1973)

[*Wellek is an Austrian-born American critic. His* History of Modern Criticism *(1955-86) is a major, comprehensive study of the literary critics of the last three centuries. Wellek's critical method, as demonstrated in* A History *and outlined in his* Theory of Literature *(1949), is one of describing, analyzing, and evaluating a work solely in terms of the problems it poses for itself and how the writer solves them. For Wellek, biographical, historical, and psychological background pertaining to a work of literature is incidental. In the following excerpt, he focuses on concerns manifested in Benjamin's literary criticism—such as the alienation of man and the work of art as commodity—that indicate his allegiance with Marxism.*]

[It] is impossible to ignore Benjamin's commitment to Marxism and Communism, to consider it merely an effort at self-deception, or to ascribe it to the "baneful, and in some respects, disastrous influence of Bertolt Brecht" as his friend Gershom Scholem did. Benjamin not only had political sympathies for Communism, comprehensible in the years of the rise and triumph of Nazism, but he definitely adopted the central doctrines of dialectical materialism, proclaimed them, and applied them as a critical standard to friend and foe. He constantly repeated his allegiance to some basic Marxist views: the precedence of Being before Consciousness, the derivation of the superstructure from the substructure, the concept of triadic evolution, the rejection of relativistic historicism in favor of a contemporary judgment of the past, and particularly the view of the class struggle as the key to history and the diagnosis of capitalism as a world of alienation which led to the "reification" (*Verdinglichung*) of all human relations and the fetishism of things. Also on a concrete issue Benjamin agreed with Communist literary politics. In a lecture in Paris he proclaims the duty of the writer to side with the proletariat and produce work with a purpose (*Tendenz*). He argues that correct political tendency includes literary quality. Literary quality is guaranteed by the invention of new techniques for which Benjamin cites Sergey Tretyakov's reportage *Vyzov*, which describes his experiences and his active share in the total collectivization of Russian agriculture. A new relationship of author and reader is envisaged: the author should become a producer, a worker. Benjamin recommends the "factography," "the social command" of the first Five-Year Plan with assigned tasks for writing. The commitment could not be clearer. (Ironically, Tretyakov became a victim of the purges.)

In his article on Eduard Fuchs, the well-known author of histories of manners, of erotic art, and of caricature, Benjamin endorses Engels's view that there is no "independent history of art and thought" and in a complete reversal of his previous position, . . . Benjamin recommends the study of the reception, the post-history of writer. Dialectical historiography sacrifices contemplation, the epic element in history. "It pries the age loose from the factual continuity of history: it depicts the experience of history for us now, not the eternal image of the past, and puts this experience of history to work today." Benjamin also endorses "the manly recognition that art can have its rebirth only after the economic and political victory of the proletariat."

The same ideas recur in earlier and later pronouncements. Thus in a review of Werner Hegemann's *Das steinerne Berlin* (1930) Hegemann is chided for being merely "critical" of the conditions of the city. He does not properly "unmask the concrete constellations of a historical moment" as only "the dialectical insight (*Blick*) penetrates into the interior of history." Similarly, in a harsh review of Theodor Haecker's *Vergil: Vater des Abendlandes* (1932) Haecker is taken to task for asking the dilettantish question "What is Virgil to us?" instead of giving a "history of the reception and interpretation of Virgil's poetry." Haecker, Benjamin argues, believes wrongly in man in general and does not question the barbarous conditions to which present-day humanism is tied. Benjamin also rejects a moralistic interpretation of history which he finds incompatible with materialism. In a discussion of French surrealism (1929) Benjamin commends the surrealists for their effort to procure the "forces of intoxication (*Rausch*)" for the revolution. He praises the role of the revolutionary intelligentsia in breaking the intellectual dominance of the bourgeoisie but chides them for failing to establish contact with the revolutionary masses. This is a task which cannot be accomplished "contemplatively": the writer must become a revolutionary: an essential part of his function might even be the interruption of his "artist's career."

Much of this has little to do with literary criticism: it is ideology and, in the context of the times, a commitment to a struggle with pen and ink against Nazism. It should, however, be recapitulated, as it has been doubted and as, in the correspondence with his friend Gershom Scholem in Jerusalem, Benjamin often sounds apologetic. In a letter he speaks of Communism as "the lesser evil," a "much lesser evil [in comparison to Nazism] that it has to be approved in every practical, fruitful form." Earlier, before Hitler's seizure of power, he pleaded with Scholem not to "restrain him from displaying the red flag" in the west of Berlin; even though he knows that his writings are "counterrevolutionary" from a party point of view he wants at least "to make them completely unpalatable to the Right." In a letter to the Swiss critic Max Rychner Benjamin pleads for an understanding of his turn to materialism by his distaste for the scholarship of the George circle, for Gundolf and Ernst Bertram, which is only less than his distaste for conventional idealistic literary scholarship of the type represented by Emil Ermatinger and Oskar Walzel. A review of *Philosophie der Literaturwissenschaft* (1930), edited by Ermatinger, expressly declares his distaste for the sacred slogans: "creativity, empathy, *Zeitentbundenheit, Nachschöpfung, Miterleben,* illusion, and *Kunstgenuss,*" for the whole eclecticism and Alexandrianism of official German literary scholarship. The attitude of the materialist seems more fruitful in human terms and in scholarship.

To turn now to Benjamin's actual literary criticism one could say that the central topic of all his later writings was an attempt to construe a scheme of the history of art in the nineteenth century: the paper ***Das Kunstwerk im Zeitalter seiner technischen Reproduzierbarkeit*** (1934) puts it in the most general terms with emphasis on the role of photography and the film. As an avowed Marxist Benjamin welcomes the spread of works of art to all manner and conditions of men, the ease of their reproduction, and the rise of the new media; he seems, almost like Marshall McLuhan, to predict the end of the Gutenberg era, the end of contemplative reading and viewing, "the liquidation of the traditional value in the cultural heritage." He welcomes the new possibilities of an imaginary museum, the museum without walls, later celebrated in Malraux's *Voices of Silence.* Clearly, however, Benjamin's attitude is ambivalent: he also deplores the destruction of what he calls the "aura," the halo around a work of art, the detachment of art from cult and myth. It is an elegy to the past of art and of his own former concept of art which had centered on myth and the mythical as the acme of art and truth.

The central idea of this paper informs also the other projects, fragments, and essays. **"Paris, the Capital of the 19th Century"** offers Baudelaire as the exemplary poet in revolt against bourgeois society, as the poet who abandoned the aura, lost the halo in the mud, and did not bother to pick it up: a sketch in *spleen* which is central to Benjamin's interpretation. Baudelaire is seen as the first poet of the city who experiences it as an outsider, an alienated man who goes through the crowd indifferently as a stroller (*flaneur*). Baudelaire's main poetic method is that of allegory, which according to Benjamin means "reification," a reduction to thing, a dispersion in time, a destruction of the world into fragments and ruins. Unlike baroque allegory Baudelaire's shows "traces of resentment in order to destroy the harmonious forms of this world." It also means empathy for the inorganic, the dead, the unnatural, for minerals and jewels. What in the book on German tragedy was viewed with sympathy has now become a symptom of capitalist "reification," of man's surrender to things, to commodity economy. Baudelaire stands at the point when the bourgeoisie withdrew its mandate from the poet: when he became not only a Bohemian but an outcast, a Cain, a conspirator and mystifier and somehow also a defiant hero of Modernism, which Benjamin contrasts with the resignation of Romanticism. Baudelaire's poetry exemplifies the process of the decay of "experience" (*Erfahrung*), of a genuine relationship which, in Baudelaire, is replaced by the experience of shock in the crowd. Time disintegrates in Baudelaire; the poet seeks prehistory, reminiscence, but fails: even Spring has lost its odor. He succumbs to "spleen" in which there is no "aura." The world ceases to respond: eyes do not answer any more as in the early poem "Correspondances" where the forest of symbols returned "familiar looks."

All this and much more amounts to a fine characterization of Baudelaire as a poet and type in his time, but one wonders how the laboriously accumulated information on social conditions and details gleaned from hundreds of books can do more than give picturesque concretization to the Paris of Baudelaire's time, while attempts to make this knowledge bear directly on an interpretation of Baudelaire's text often become strained, far-fetched, and even definitely mistaken. Much is made, for instance, of Baudelaire's mystifying habits, his sudden reversals which are said to parallel the shiftiness of Napoleon III, who "almost overnight changed from protectionism to free trade." Nor can one see how Baudelaire can be called a "conspirator" whose strategy was the sudden shock, the flash, the *putsch,* in order to draw a parallel to Blanqui. "Blanqui's deed was the sister of Baudelaire's dream" seems to me a conclusion in no way justified by Baudelaire's overt or even latent attitudes. Nor can I see why the shock experience of the stroller in the crowd has anything to do with the shock of the worker handling an object on the conveyor belt or why this experience is, in turn, parallel to the jerky movements of the gambler who is in servitude to chance. Baudelaire, Benjamin admits, was no gambler. Nor can I see that the decay of the aura is, otherwise than chronologically, connected with the rise of photography which, in Benjamin's account, brought something inhuman, reified into art. Benjamin argues that "to experience the aura of any appearance means to lend it the ability to return your glance." This is possible only in poetry and painting; photography prevents such a return. Still, Benjamin can consider the "destruction of the aura" a merit of photography; the work of art becomes impersonal, the result of a moment of the click of the camera, a "collective formation" (*Gebilde*). But it is hard to see why Baudelaire figures so centrally in such a story. Actually if one studies his writings on aesthetics he will appear as a good romantic who believes in "constructive imagination," a term ultimately derived from Coleridge. In spite of many vacillations Baudelaire hoped for the reconciliation between man and nature. He said, like a good romantic: "Art is to create a suggestive magic containing at one and the same time the object and the subject, the external world and the artist himself."

Benjamin's interpretation, while often illuminating of the poet's attitude and social situation, seems to me mistaken if one analyzes his thought and position in the tradition of poetry. Adorno in a letter objected to the manuscript submitted by Benjamin that his "dialectics lack mediation." "The tendency predominates," he argued, "to relate the pragmatic contents of Baudelaire immediately to neighboring traits of the social history of the time." Adorno concluded that the work is "situated at the crossroads of magic and positivism" and rejected it for publication in the *Zeitschrift für Sozialforschung.* Benjamin, who as a refugee in Paris was financially dependent on Adorno's support, rewrote the piece without, however, substantially changing its tenor. The new version was published under the title **"Über einige Motive bei Baudelaire"** (1938).

Proust was an early love of Benjamin and Benjamin was one of Proust's first translators into German. In the Baudelaire essay Proust is seen as the man who tried synthetically to reconstruct the original experience available to the poet. The involuntary memory of Proust is, however, left to chance: to the tasting of the madeleine. It is thus, as an earlier essay on Proust (1934) suggests, nearer to forgetting than remembering. In Proust's involuntary memory only that is available which had not been experienced (*erlebt*). The experience of eternity in Proust, Benjamin argues, is neither Platonic nor Utopian but "ecstatic," an "eternal restoration of the original, the first happiness." But Benjamin misses in Proust the heroic defiance he

found in Baudelaire, though he admires his merciless criticism of French high society and approves his defense of sexual inversion.

Proust is worked into the general scheme of the decay of the aura. I cannot see that Benjamin even tried to fit Kafka into it. Brecht, as Benjamin reports, complained that his essays had isolated Kafka's work and had even "encouraged Jewish fascism." Benjamin rejects both the psychoanalytical and the theological interpretation of Kafka, particularly Max Brod's view of Kafka as a saint or a man on the way to sainthood. He also objects to a theological reading of *The Castle* which ignores the repulsive and terrifying aspects of the upper world, the alleged "realm of grace." He sees no grounds for claims of Kafka as a prophet or even the keeper of some special wisdom. Kafka, Benjamin argues, fails to change fiction into doctrine. Kafka is rather an inventor of parables who combines the "greatest mysteriousness with the greatest simplicity." Benjamin admires Kafka's serenity and purity but sees his work as a personal and artistic shipwreck. Kafka's world is not mythic, and not prophetic. It rather harks back to the oldest prehistoric world, to that of fairy tales, of German folklore where children, fools, and animals, the lamb-cat, Odradek, the flat, starry-shaped, spool-like creature, and Gregor Samsa, the beetle, escape from the swamp world. Benjamin concludes by quoting a poem about a hunchbacked hobgoblin: "Pray for the little hunchback too." It is Kafka's prayer for himself, the spiritual cripple in the world of fathers and officials; a prayer for all the lowly and innocent, the childlike and the foolish.

Both Proust and Kafka come late in the history of fiction. They do not tell stories, according to Benjamin. In an essay on the Russian novelist and short-story writer Nikolay Leskov (1936) Benjamin sketched a history of fiction which fits in with his overall scheme of the atrophy of experience and the decline of wisdom illustrated by Proust's and Kafka's desperate attempts to recapture them. The teller of a story, Benjamin explains, gave advice, dispensed wisdom, was personally involved in the telling, but gave no explanation of the story. The spread of information demanded explanation and hence the death of story telling. Benjamin associates the art of story telling with the world of artisans: it is a craft like theirs. He then elaborates the contrast between story and novel: the novel does not come from oral tradition as the tale does. It is told by an individual and read in solitude. A novel searches for the meaning of life while a story conveys a moral. A novel concludes, while a story asks "How does it go on?" Benjamin quotes a saying of Moritz Heimann to the effect that "a man who dies at the age of 35 is at every point of his life a man who dies at the age of 35" in order to modify it by saying that a man who dies at 35 will appear to *remembrance* at every point of his life as a man who died at the age of 35. The novel is seen as an experience of death. "What draws the reader to the novel is the hope of warming his shivering life with a death he reads about." Oddly enough, a few pages before we are told that "death is the sanction that the story-teller can tell. He has borrowed his authority from death." Even if one can think of ways of reconciling these contradictions one can quote many counter-examples, not only of comic or humorous novels and stories, and one could easily reverse Benjamin's distinction between the novel and the story. Many novels do not conclude (not even with death). They also allow us to ask "How does it go on?" (think of *War and Peace*), while, on the contrary, most stories (Chekhov excepted) conclude, make a point, draw a moral, as Benjamin himself said before.

Also, the further reflections on the survival of the fairy tale in the story and the idea that the fairy tale is not a remnant of the myth but rather a revolt against it seem highly doubtful. Benjamin is thinking of rogues and fools who defy or cheat the powers of the mythic world. Leskov's characters are interpreted as fitting into this scheme. They magically escaped the early world (as Kafka's good people did). They are the righteous and have a maternal touch. Benjamin's one example, however, the hero of the story "Kotin the Provider and Platonida," is strangely misinterpreted. Benjamin speaks of him as a "hermaphrodite." For twelve years his mother raised him as a girl. "His male and female organs matured simultaneously" and his bisexuality "becomes the symbol of the God-Man." I have read the story attentively and cannot find a trace of Benjamin's view in the text: the only support is the fact that the mother of Kotin, left destitute after the death of her husband, seeks employment as a servant in a nunnery and, out of necessity, pretends that her baby is a girl rather than a boy. She leaves the nunnery when the boy is twelve, changes his clothes, and puts him into a boys' school. There is no suggestion of bisexuality or hermaphroditism and not a word about the God-Man. I am at a loss to imagine how Benjamin could have misread this harmless story so flagrantly. Nor can I find anything in the story "The Alexandrite" which would prove the mystical as inherent in the nature of the story-teller. A gem engraver in Prague, a weird figure out of E. T. A. Hoffmann, interprets the stone's changing color from green to red as an allegory of the reign of Alexander II: from early hope to the blood of the assassination. It seems to me sheer fancy to see some connection between "soul, hand, and eye" in this story, to find mysterious support for the role of gesture and craft in the art of story telling, and to conclude: "the story teller is the figure in which the righteous man encounters himself." On occasion I confess I do not understand the workings of Benjamin's mind, particularly in this essay which has been considered his masterpiece.

The distinction between story and novel is of course a valid one: as early as 1930 in a review of Döblin's *Alexanderplatz* Benjamin uses the contrast between Döblin's ambition of writing an epic where montage and documents (a la Dos Passos) would replace the formulas of the old epic with Gide's *Counterfeiters,* a "pure," written, bookish novel, turned inward, elaborately reflected in Gide's own *Journal of the Counterfeiters.* Benjamin, however, denied that Döblin succeeded in his intention: his novel remains a *Bildungsroman,* bourgeois in the German tradition.

The only writer of the new proletarian dispensation whom Benjamin admired was Bertolt Brecht. Benjamin seems to have considered himself an expounder and commentator of Brecht's, abdicating any effort at criticism. The account of Brecht's *Dreigroschenroman* is mainly descriptive. It concludes that "satire is always a materialistic art" and that it becomes "dialectical" in Brecht's hands. The paper **"What Is Epic Theater?"** (1939) is a straightforward exposition of Brecht's theories without any comment except two historical remarks: that Brecht's techniques descend from medieval mysteries via the Baroque, and that Strindberg must not be identified with romantic irony, which lacks Brecht's doctrinal aim. The accounts of first performances of *Die Mutter* (1932) and of *Furcht und Elend des Dritten Reiches* (in Paris, May 1938) are merely approving reportage. The remark that German émigré actors playing an SA man or a judge of the people's court are faced with a different task from that of a kind-hearted man playing Iago, supports Brecht's view that empathy is the wrong method of acting. The comments on some of Brecht's poems try "to bring out the political contents of purely lyrical passages" but do not seem to me to go beyond the obvious. But the introductory reflections show that Benjamin thought of a commentary as "assuming the classicity of a text" and of Brecht as the new classic. Benjamin certainly uses Brecht's political lyrics which, he says, combine consciousness and activism, to condemn the poetry of Erich Kästner as "left-wing melancholia."

Further, Karl Kraus, who had appealed to Benjamin because of his attacks on journalism and his concern with the language, is ultimately condemned for his lack of understanding of economics and his social program which to Benjamin seemed to recommend only a return to the old bourgeoisie. Kraus, as early as 1931, appears as the last bourgeois, defending the phantom of the unpolitical or "natural" man. Kraus's later defense of the Dollfusz regime shocked Benjamin deeply but could hardly have surprised him. He saw in Kraus a new Timon (Kraus's favorite play of Shakespeare) who "jeeringly distributes the acquisitions of his life among his false friends."

We are back to politics. Politics in a wide sense dominates the later writings of Benjamin as it dominated his life. Marxist ideas—the alienation of man, "reification," the work of art as commodity—permeate his later work. I am not qualified to decide whether Benjamin's application of these ideas is orthodox Marxism. Both Adorno and Scholem thought that it was not. Still, it was, it seems to me, Marxism in the sense expounded in Lukács's *History and Class Consciousness.* There alienation and reification appear, for the first time, as central concerns of Marxist theory, and appear as identical terms. Lukács's book was denounced by Zinoviev at the fifth Congress of the Third International in 1924, and it was attacked as "idealistic" by the Soviet philosopher, A. M. Deborin. Lukács himself in the 1967 preface to the new edition condemned the identification of alienation and reification as a "fundamental and gross error." I suspect that Scholem was right when he predicted that within the Communist party Benjamin would soon have been "unmasked as a typical counterrevolutionary and bourgeois." But this would have been an even sillier label than that of orthodox Marxist. Benjamin had obviously transcended both these parties in his best criticism: in the essay on the *Elective Affinities,* in the book on German tragedy, and in the essays on Proust, Kafka, Leskov, and Baudelaire, not to speak of the many scattered articles and reviews which make him, almost incognito, what he wanted to be—"the first German critic" of his time. (pp. 169-77)

René Wellek, "Walter Benjamin's Literary Criticism in his Marxist Phase," in The Personality of the Critic, edited by Joseph P. Strelka, The Pennsylvania State University Press, 1973, pp. 168-78.

Richard Kazis   (essay date 1977)

[*Kazis is an American political writer whose works often center on the effects of new technologies on society. In the following excerpt, he discusses Benjamin's views on capitalism and the film industry as expressed in* The Work of Art in the Age of Mechanical Reproduction.]

Benjamin was an essayist: his insight came in short blasts. He planned to write a long work on 19th-century Paris but was never able to concentrate his efforts. He had an eye for the fragmentary, an almost gnostic appreciation of the secrets that can be gleaned from each small detail. Ernest Bloch, . . . a friend of Benjamin's, noted Benjamin's eye "for the marginal . . . for the impinging and unaccustomed, unschematic particularity which does not 'fit in' and therefore deserves a quite special and incisive attention." His favorite exhibit at one museum was two grains of wheat upon which had been painstakingly inscribed the *Shema Yisroel,* the one-line affirmation of the Jew's faith in God, the essence of an entire religion on the tiniest of entities. It was the seemingly insignificant that, for Benjamin, was the most significant; each fragment of actual, demonstrable reality—physical and social reality—contained implicit in it the key to a much broader understanding. Benjamin's sensibility was akin to that of a photographer: his eye focused on the moment, on the wonder of appearance as it is now and shall never be again, on the uniqueness of the historical present.

This sensibility derived from Benjamin's early fascination with Jewish mysticism, and it informed his intellectual and critical method throughout his life, even after he turned to Marxism. Benjamin differed with Georg Lukács, one of Marxism's most important aesthetic critics, over the question of method. Lukács stressed the importance of the description of the totality of the societal process; he believed that only by a portrayal of the totality can art reflect class antagonisms and reveal the progressive tendencies of history. For Lukács, the novel was the art form of the modern era. Benjamin proceeded from a different point. He saw his investigations as a kind of drilling, of plumbing the depths. He once wrote, "I tell Brecht that penetrating into depth is my way of travelling to the antipodes." If Lukács constructed his totality horizontally, Benjamin chose vertical coordinates. Benjamin felt that the task of the proletariat and the task of the revolutionary intellectual was "to make the continuum of history explode." The intellectual—the historical materialist—should reveal the significance of the present historical instant, should analyze the explosive convergence of past and future in the presence of the now so that it can be transformed.

It should not be construed that Benjamin's method was a static one: the historical materialist method, as he saw it, specifically involved an understanding and analysis of the dialectical tension of past and future in the present. To plumb the depths meant for Benjamin to explore dynamic interrelations; to focus on fragments meant to relate those fragments to the broader social reality. Benjamin understood that the social fabric is a complex weave, that "the rigid, isolated object (work, novel, book) is of no use whatsoever. It must be inserted into the context of living social relations." For Benjamin, not only must art be evaluated in terms of its depiction of the social reality of class antagonisms (as Lukács suggested): art must also be analyzed

in terms of its technique, in terms of its position within the literary production relations of a given era. Benjamin admired his friend Brecht's demand that intellectuals "not supply the production apparatus without, within the limits of the possible, changing that apparatus in the direction of socialism." The form of art had to be changed as well as the content. Benjamin saw that it is not enough, for example, simply to make people aware of human misery: photography can "make human misery an object of consumption" and can even turn "the struggle against misery into an object of consumption." Art must not stand above and outside the context of living social relations, an almost sacred trust as envisioned by Lukács. Benjamin wanted to see the barriers of competence, the distinctions between artist and audience, broken down. He wanted to see new form and new conceptualizations of the role of art and artist. "What we must demand from the photographer is the ability to put such a caption beneath his picture as will rescue it from the ravages of modishness and confer upon it a revolutionary use value."

Benjamin was intensely aware of the cultural crisis of interwar Germany that accompanied the rise of fascism. He saw how literature too was undergoing a profound crisis. In 1934, in an address delivered to the Institute for the Study of Fascism in Paris, Benjamin declared, "We are in the midst of a vast process in which literary forms are being melted down, a process in which many of the contrasts in terms of which we have been accustomed to think may lose their meaning." The implication of these changes for Benjamin was that artists could no longer afford to stand above the social struggle and look down: artists had to choose sides. Benjamin saw that art was not innocent, that every artist living in those years had to choose between the fascist aestheticization of politics and the communist politicization of art. The Italian Futurists were able to avoid political realities by understanding war as an aesthetic phenomenon, as a new architecture, as a symphony—as anything but the horror and the political event it is. In reaction to the growing support of fascism by artists like the Futurists, Benjamin developed his own contribution to the theory of art. In the preface to his 1936 essay *The Work of Art in the Age of Mechanical Reproduction,* Benjamin writes that the concepts he introduces in that essay "differ from the more familiar terms in that they are completely useless for the purposes of Fascism. They are, on the other hand, useful for the formulation of revolutionary demands in the politics of art."

In the body of the essay, Benjamin explores the interrelationship of art and the history of technological development under capitalism; he deals specifically with film as the art form for modern times. Film fascinated Benjamin in the same way that newspapers and photography did. They are all forms of mass communications made possible by the advent of mechanical reproduction, of technologies that allow the reproduction of a word, a picture or a scene so that it becomes accessible to a wide audience. The mode of artistic production and communication in a given era is determined in large part by the level of technological development at the time. At the same time, the mode of production and communication plays a large role in determining the relation between the working class and bourgeois society. Benjamin, in this essay, outlines the modern development in this way. The introduction of the technology of lithography, which enabled many copies to be printed from the same master plate, increased the potential of the lithograph to reach a mass audience. Once lithography had been perfected, the illustrated newspaper was the logical next step. The development of photography by the late 1800s further accelerated the speed of production, and it was only a matter of time and technology before film, the next step in the progression toward more exact representation in mass communications, evolved to its maturity.

What are the effects and significance of these new art forms? Benjamin understood and lauded the potential democratization of the communications media and the arts implicit in advances in mechanical reproduction. A work of art that once could only be seen by the wealthy in a museum or gallery could be reproduced at little cost and made accessible to many more people. The advent of inexpensive illustrated newspapers meant that current events had become the business of the masses. Film allows an event or a performance to be recorded and be available for countless audiences to see. Mechanical reproduction makes possible the involvement of the masses in culture and politics; it makes possible mass culture and mass politics.

In *The Work of Art in the Age of Mechanical Reproduction,* Benjamin analyzes how mechanical reproduction destroys the uniqueness and authenticity, the "aura" as he labelled it, of the work of art. The withering of aura in the age of mechanical reproduction is inevitable. And, in many respects, it is a good thing: if the mystique of the "original" is broken down, if the work of art is torn from the "fabric of tradition" of which it was a part, then it loses its false importance. "For the first time in world history, mechanical reproduction emancipates the work of art from its parasitical dependence on ritual." The value of the work of art no longer stems from its ritualistic cult value, whether it be a magical cult, religious cult or secularized cult like the cult of beauty. Authenticity is no longer a relevant criterion for evaluating artistic production. In photography, for example, it makes no sense to ask for the "authentic" print.

The effect of this withering of the aura is significant: "instead of being based on ritual," Benjamin notes, the function of art "begins to be based on another practice—politics." What this means is that art for art's sake, the theologizing of art, is rejected for artistic production that serves a purpose, that stands in direct relation to the political struggles of the time. Art and media begin to merge. When the distance (we could call it the mystification, though Benjamin does not use that word) between artist and society is lessened (and this is what accompanies the loss of aura), then the false distinctions between the social roles of artists and educators are negated. Benjamin explains, "By the absolute emphasis on its exhibition value as opposed to an ahistorical cult value, the work of art becomes a creation with entirely new functions, among which the one we are conscious of, the artistic function, later may be recognized as incidental." And he adds: "This much is certain: today, photography and the film are the most serviceable exemplifications of this new function."

For Benjamin, the withering of the aura is the result of two developments unique to films: the new relationship between actor and audience and the mass nature of the medium. In the theater, the actor responds to and adjusts to the audience. Each performance is different: there is a subtle interaction, a unique experience of relation between actor and audience. In film, there is no audience for the performance; there is only the camera. In fact, the actor's performance is not one performance but rather a series of performances. A film is an ordering of multiple fragments, a series of scenes shot in order of expedience rather than in logical or temporal order. The actor is put in the paradoxical situation of operating with his/her whole living person while being robbed of the aura that is tied to his/her presence. The actor is present to the camera, not to the audience; as a result, "the audience's identification with the actor is really an identification with the camera."

The importance of this, in Benjamin's opinion, is the distancing it forces on the audience: the filmgoer more easily takes on the role of critic, for there is no personal contact with the actor to influence judgments. The film viewer becomes a tester, almost a back-seat director. Benjamin even compares the film shot to a vocational aptitude test, describing both as examples of "segmental performances of the individual . . . taken before a committee of experts." This audience attitude is radically different from the audience attitude that appreciates the work of art for its cult value and that bows to the mystery and ritual power of the unique work. Benjamin states clearly, "This testing approach is not the approach to which cult values may be exposed." With the development of film, Benjamin argues, the audience no longer stands in awe of the work of art. The very nature of art is transformed, and it is transformed in a way that encourages—at least potentially—the removal of film from "the realm of the 'beautiful semblance' which, so far, had been taken to be the only sphere where art could thrive."

The actor's function is radically altered as well. The film can record reality, can document what is. This makes it possible for everyone to participate, as an actor, in the creation of the work of art. In many early Russian films, the people were themselves and they were collectively the "star" of the film. Benjamin explains that some of these players "are not actors in our sense but people who portray *themselves*—and primarily in their own work process." The distinctions that normally are considered important in art are blurred and even exploded by means of mechanical reproduction on film. The actor/audience distinction, the art/communications media distinction, the artist/public distinction—all are broken down. For Benjamin, the most revolutionary contribution of film is "the promotion of a revolutionary criticism of traditional concepts of art."

Even the art/science distinction no longer holds. Benjamin writes, "Of a screened behavior item which is neatly brought out in a certain situation, like the muscle of a body, it is difficult to say what is more fascinating, its artistic value or its value for science." Film can open up our own world for us, capture the significance of the insignificant moment, and consciously explore a space. Film has "burst this prison world asunder by the dynamite of a tenth of a second." Film has a potentially revolutionary use value in that it enables us to explore and understand our world and our historical situation: "the film, on the one hand, extends our comprehension of the necessities which rule our lives; on the other hand it manages to assure us of an immense and unexpected field of action."

When we all become actors, when the passivity of the awed art viewer is given up, then the potential for self-motivated creative and political activity increases. Film and other forms of mechanical reproduction further the possibility of such radical changes of mindset by the way they change the reaction of the masses toward art. Unlike paintings and sculptures, which are placed in museums for the contemplation of the few, film presents an object for simultaneous collective experience. Everyone is an expert: enjoyment and criticism are intimately fused. The masses, just as when illustrated newspapers were introduced, have the potential to know, and that leads inevitably to the potential to act.

The reader should not assume that Benjamin was pollyanna-ish about the future, that he saw the process of revolutionary mass culture as inevitable simply because of the nature of the film audience. On the contrary, Benjamin was all too painfully aware that film was not being used in a revolutionary way under capitalism and that the potential inherent in the medium might never be fully utilized. Throughout this article, Benjamin notes how false consciousness is maintained. Reactionary critics continue to read cult values and ritual elements into film in their efforts to class the film among the "arts." Benjamin mentions Franz Werfel, who once stated that film would be a great art form if only it didn't have to copy the exterior world. The very dominance of the cinema by capital (in Benjamin's day as well as in our own era of communications conglomerates) hides and subverts the revolutionary use value of film. The artist is made into a cult figure: a new ritual is created and sustained. The masses are influenced to reestablish and maintain the false distinctions between actor and audience, between artist and public. A false aura is created, an artificial build-up of the "personality." For Benjamin, "the spell of the personality" is "the phony spell of the commodity." The nature of film production under capitalism attempts to mystify the audience further. In contrast to the early Russian tendency to have the masses as the "star" of films, "capitalistic exploitation of the film denies consideration to man's legitimate claim on being reproduced." Instead of allowing the masses to participate—to act in and upon their own historical situation—the system of film production and distribution under capitalism forces the masses back into the passive role of spectator. Benjamin saw the film industry "trying hard to spur the interest of the masses through illusion-promoting spectacles and dubious speculations," to spur the interest of the masses toward illusion while denying them access to participation in those spectacles that would reflect their true interests.

Benjamin finishes the essay with an analysis of the way in which fascism uses the film medium for its own purposes and the ways in which the film medium lends itself to such use. Benjamin argues that under capitalism, the mechanical reproduction of reality onto film not only is *not* progressive, but it is dangerous. This is due, in part, to the very nature of film. Before the painting, Benjamin notes, "the spectator can abandon himself to his associations. Before the movie frame he cannot do so. No sooner has his eye grasped a scene than it is already changed." The film draws the viewer along. As Duhamel is quoted, "I can no longer think what I want to think. My thoughts have been replaced by moving images." For this reason, the propaganda value of film is great, greater than that of a painting or another more static art form that invites the spectator to contemplation. The Nazis knew this well: Leni Riefenstahl's films are cases in point. The films are awesome, inspiring, even "artful," yet they try to sweep the spectator along in a mystified passion for the cult of Fuhrer and Fatherland.

The film is the art and communications medium for modern times, Benjamin claims. He writes in a footnote, "The film is the art form that is in keeping with the increased threat to his life which modern man (sic) has to face." Further, film is the only medium which can reproduce the masses and bring them face to face with themselves. "Mass movements are usually discernible more clearly by a camera than by the naked eye. . . . The image received by the eye cannot be enlarged the way a negative is enlarged. This means that mass movements, including war, constitute a form of human behavior which particularly favors mechancial equipment." The struggle for the allegiance of the masses, the central political struggle of our times, cannot help but revolve around the use and abuse of the film medium.

Culture, communications, art—they constitute a single battleground where, Benjamin argues, fascism and communism have no choice—given the increasing formation of masses, the historical development of capitalism in the 1930s and the technological development of art to that time—but to fight. Fascism introduces aesthetics into political life as a way of giving the masses "a chance to express themselves" instead of a chance to claim their "right to change property relations." Communism responds by politicizing art, by demystifying the production, the distribution, the form and the content of art in an attempt to make art serve the cause of the masses and not vice versa. (pp. 23-5)

Benjamin's view of history was that of a pessimist, a person whose messianic hopes depended upon a miraculous, cataclysmic revolt of the masses. In his historical analysis, he consciously attempted to be a Marxist: he tried, as he himself acknowledged, to develop an historical materialist critique of art and culture. In his world view and his conception of human history, though, Benjamin differed significantly from Marx. Marx, a product of Enlightenment optimism, saw history as a progression, an inevitable passage through historical epochs leading to the triumph of justice and humanity in the triumph of the proletariat. Benjamin, living in a very different era, was less convinced. With less faith in rationality and a more developed understanding—and fear—of the nature and possible uses of art and the communications media, Benjamin always feared the worst. He, too, yearned for the ascendance of the proletariat and, in his own way, worked toward that goal, but ultimately his hope was a messianic hope for an end to history. Marx saw revolutions as the "locomotives" of history; Benjamin saw revolutions as the pulling of the "emergency brake," as the miraculous rescue of a world gone out of control. "The tradition of the oppressed teaches us that the 'state of emergency' in which we live is not the exception, but the rule. We must attain to a conception of history that is in keeping with this insight." For Benjamin, material progress was *not* the godsend too many social democrats and Marxists believed it to be; for Benjamin, modern history has been the record of the overpowering of tradition by conformism. The only hope had to be, and for Benjamin it was, an anti-historical messianism.

Much of Benjamin's popularity today may in fact be attributable to his pessimism and lack of faith in the future. We, like Benjamin, sense ourselves as living in a time of crisis, and we see that crisis as permanent, as increasing in its complexity and potential danger until, somehow, it is finally resolved. Progress, growth, development—these words have all taken on negative value since the mid-60s. It becomes harder and harder to retain Marx's positiveness and optimism, and it becomes easier to understand the world view and belief system of one who, like us all, was witness to the destruction and violence of fascism. With his affinity for Kafka and Karl Kraus, for the lost souls and the street life, Benjamin seems closer to the temperament and outlook of many who experienced the cultural revolution of the '60s than does the patrician Lukács or the strident Marx. Even Benjamin's essay style, his fragmentary observations and writings, makes him seem more modern. System building, as in the work of Marx or Freud or Einstein, is a thing of the past: the glut of information in modern society makes the quick, the fragmentary, the sharp insight far more accessible than the tome or the well-constructed totality.

This propensity for detail, for the "signposts" and "cultural wealth" of contemporary society, have also made Benjamin popular with those interested in semiology, the study of signs. The French editor of a collection of Benjamin's essays proclaimed him "the least known precursor of semiology." Whether the relation was linear or not, there are many shared concerns between Benjamin and semiologists. To "read" the values of a society through its artistic production, to drill through an item in order to place it in its larger societal context, to work almost as an archeologist would—Benjamin's method in his unfinished study of 19th century Paris is very similar to the style and goal of a writer like Roland Barthes in the short pieces collected in *Mythologies*. Barthes writes, "In a single day, how many really non-signifying fields do we cross? Very few, sometimes none. Here I am before the sea; it is true that it bears no message. But on the beach, what material for semiology! Flags, slogans, signals, sign-boards, clothes, suntan even, which are so many messages to me."

Benjamin studied these "ideas-in-form," these "signifying fields"; they were the details that, properly understood, properly placed in context, revealed great insights into the dominant ideology and its development. Benjamin looked at the architecture and street plan of Paris, at gambling, at photography; he tied their development to a broad analysis of the "era of high capitalism." Parallel quotations from both Barthes and Benjamin reveal their affinity. Benjamin writes, "Historicism rightly culminates in universal history. . . . Materialist historiography, on the other hand, is based on a constructive principle. Thinking involves not only the flow of thoughts, but their arrest as well." Barthes notes, "by treating 'collective presentations' as sign-systems, one might hope to . . . account in *detail* for the mystification which transforms petit-bourgeois culture into a universal nature."

Benjamin's popularity is on the rise, and many who have never heard of him by name are aware of the arguments he advanced. Current trends in both political and avant-garde cinema reflect concerns similar to those of Benjamin's. . . . It is remarkable that 40 years ago, only eight years after the first talkie, a German cultural critic interested primarily in literature could have been so perceptive about the nature of the film medium under capitalism that the implications of his ideas are only now being investigated fully. (p. 25)

Richard Kazis, "Benjamin's Age of Mechanical Reproduction," in Jump Cut, *No. 15, July, 1977, pp. 23-5.*

George Steiner   (essay date 1977)

[*Steiner is a French-born American critic, poet, and fiction writer. He has described his approach to literary criticism as "a kind of continuous inquiry into and conjecture about the relations between literature and society, between poetic value and humane conduct." A central concern of his critical thought is whether or not literature can survive the barbarism of the modern world, particularly in view of the Holocaust. Steiner has written, "We now know that a man can read Goethe or Rilke in the evening, that he can play Bach or Schubert and go to his day's work at Auschwitz in the morning." Steiner's work encompasses a wide range of subjects, including social and literary criticism, linguistics, philosophy, and chess. Though some commentators have found fault with his occasionally exuberant prose style, Steiner is generally regarded as a perceptive and extremely erudite critic. In the following excerpt he examines* The Origin of German Tragic Drama.]

For Benjamin, as for every German thinker after Herder, the word *Ursprung* is resonant. It signifies not only 'source', 'fount', 'origin', but also that primal leap (*Sprung*) into being which at once reveals and determines the unfolding structure, the central dynamics of form in an organic or spiritual phenomenon. Benjamin is at pains to show that the Aristotelian and neo-classical elements in the baroque theatre of Lutheran and Counter-Reformation Germany are deceptive, indeed immaterial. The true *Ursprung* is to be found in the intricate energies, visionary habits and political-doctrinal emblem-code of the baroque. German literary theory and scholarship, with its strong classicizing bias, has misread or simply neglected this compaction. From this oversight and misinterpretation derives the attempt to make of the baroque *Trauerspiel* a bastard or ancillary version of eighteenth-century tragedy. Nothing, according to Benjamin, could be more erroneous.

Tragödie and *Trauerspiel* are radically distinct, in metaphysical foundation and executive genre. Tragedy is grounded in myth. It acts out a rite of heroic sacrifice. In its fulfilment of this sacrificial-transcendent design, tragedy endows the hero with the realization that he is ethically in advance of the gods, that his sufferance of good and evil, of fortune and desolation, has projected him into a category beyond the comprehension of the essentially 'innocent' though materially omnipotent deities (Artemis' flight from the dying Hippolytus, Dionysus' myopia exceeding the blindness of Pentheus). This realization compels the tragic hero to silence, and here Benjamin is strongly influenced by Rosenzweig's concept of the 'meta-ethical' condition of tragic man.

The *Trauerspiel,* on the contrary, is not rooted in myth but in history. Historicity, with every implication of political-social texture and reference, generates both content and style. Feeling himself dragged towards the abyss of damnation, a damnation registered in a profoundly carnal sense, the baroque dramatist, allegorist, historiographer, and the personages he animates, cling fervently to the world. The *Trauerspiel* is counter-transcendental; it celebrates the immanence of existence even where this existence is passed in torment. It is emphatically 'mundane', earth-bound, corporeal. It is not the tragic hero who occupies the centre of the stage, but the Janus-faced composite of tyrant and martyr, of the Sovereign who incarnates the mystery of absolute will and of its victim (so often himself). Royal purple and the carmine of blood mingle in the same emblematic persona.

Behind this fusion stands the *exemplum* of Christ's kingship and crucifixion. Baroque drama is inherently emblematic-allegoric, as Greek tragedy never is, precisely because it postulates the dual presence, the twofold organizing pivot of Christ's nature—part god, part man, and overwhelmingly of this world. If the German baroque theatre has antecedents, these must be located not in the classics, but in the medieval misreading of classical-Senecan fragments and in the obsessive 'physicality' of the mystery cycles. It is in the Senecan obsession with loud agony and in the medieval-Christological insistence on the mortification of the flesh, especially where the flesh is merely the momentary husk of divine or sanctified spirit, that baroque stagecraft has its roots.

Drawing on Nietzsche's critique of Socrates, Benjamin differentiates the silences of tragedy from the torrential prolixity of the *Trauerspiel.* The Socratic dialogue, with its ironies and pathos, with its agonistic play of stroke and parry, with, above all, its declared trust in the capacity of language to image, elucidate and preserve reality, is the very opposite of tragic silence. As the end of the *Symposium* demonstrates, the discourse of the Socratic dialectic operates beyond the confines of either tragedy or comedy. It is purely dramatic. And it is from this dramatization of the word, says Benjamin, that stems the teeming, figurative, polarized rhetoric of the baroque playwrights.

These antinomies of transcendence and immanence of myth and history, of heroism and tyranny or martyrdom, of silence and loquacity, lead Benjamin to his fundamental distinction between tragedy and *Trauer.* Tragic feelings, in the sense assigned to them by Aristotle's *Poetics* and Nietzsche's *Birth of Tragedy,* are experienced by the spectator. They refine, enrich and bring into tensed equilibrium the inchoate muddle or incipience of the spectator's emotions. But fundamentally, tragedy does not require an audience. Its space is inwardness and the viewer aimed at is 'the hidden god'. *Trauer,* on the other hand, signifies sorrow, lament, the ceremonies and memorabilia of grief. Lament and ceremonial demand audience. Literally and in spirit, the *Trauerspiel* is a 'play of sorrow', a 'playing at and displaying of human wretchedness'. *Spiel* compounds, as it does in its English equivalent, the two meanings: game and stage-performance, the ludic and the mimetic-histrionic. Tragedy posits an aesthetic of reticence; the 'sorrow-play' is emphatically ostentatious, gestural,

and hyperbolic. It identifies the earth with the stage in the notion of the *theatrum mundi* (a conceit to which Shakespeare gives local stress when he plays on the word 'globe'). It sees in historical events, in architecture, in the collateral edifice of the human body and of the body politick, properties for a grievous pageant. The Dance of Death depicted in sixteenth and seventeenth-century art and ritual, is the crowning episode of the game or play of lamentation. Hence the striking affinities between the *Trauerspiel* of the German baroque and the puppet-theatre, a relation which the much greater finesse and visionary elegance of Spanish baroque drama internalizes (the puppet-play shown on the actual stage as an ironic or pathetic simulacrum of the main plot). Prince and puppet are impelled by the same frozen violence.

Having expounded this cardinal distinction between the tragic and the sorrowful, Benjamin proceeds to dependent topics. But his advance is oblique and digressive. It entails a running polemic against idealist and academic underestimates of the baroque. It considers, in passing, the affinities and contrasts between the *Trauerspiel,* various modes of authentic tragedy, and such specifically German genres as the eighteenth and nineteenth-century *Schicksalsdrama* or 'melodrama of fate'. Throughout his treatise, moreover, Benjamin wants to demonstrate the epistemological categories and methods of analysis which he has postulated in the philosophic prologue. As a result, the process of argument is sometimes elusive. But there are, at the same time, developments of great brilliance.

Relating the immanence of the baroque, its tortured worldliness, to the microcosm of the court, Benjamin elaborates the dominant role of the *Intrigant,* the courtier whose intimacy with the tyrant or royal victim makes of him the key witness and also the weaver of murderous plots. In baroque drama, more than in any other, 'plot' is both the cat's-cradle of incidents and the conspiracy that breeds disaster. Cain was the first courtier, because fratricide had made him homeless. All 'intriguers' after him have been the rootless creatures of their own devices. Via a series of acute comparisons, Benjamin measures the limitations of the German achievement: it can neither add to the *Intrigant* the compassionate magic of comedy which produces a Polonius and even, to a certain extent, an Iago; nor can it rival the poetry, the delicacy of felt motive which characterize the court and martyr-plays of Lope de Vega and Calderón. The dramas of Gryphius, of Lohenstein, of Martin Opitz, remain trapped in their special vortex of brutal sadness and allegory.

This vortex is best understood when one looks at the tropes, rhetorical and pictorial figures, and emblem-literature of the period. Among these 'Melencolia' and her attributes are essential. Working outward from Dürer's famous engraving, Benjamin offers an inspired diagnosis of the theory and embodiments of saturnine melancholy in the baroque world. He points to the cultivation of private and public *tristesse* so symptomatic of political and philosophic postures in the seventeenth-century. He relates it to the physiology of humours. He traces the irrational but perfectly congruent network which knits blackness in the individual soul or complexion to planetary maleficence, to bile and, above all, to that proximity of literal hell which haunts baroque reflexes. Benjamin shows how it is in its figuration of 'world-sadness', of *acedia*—that final boredom of the spirit—that baroque thought and art achieve their truest depths.

Allegory and emblem had begun to be studied seriously before Benjamin. Nevertheless, his contribution is at once solid and original. It draws on, it is exactly contemporaneous with Erwin Panofsky's and Fritz Saxl's monograph on Dürer's 'Melencolia, I' published in 1923. Benjamin was among the very first to recognize the seminal power of what was to become the Warburg Institute approach to renaissance and baroque art and symbolism. He sought personal contact with the Warburg group, but Panofsky's response to the *Ursprung* (did he read it?) was dismissive. This marks, I think, the most ominous moment in Walter Benjamin's career. It is the Aby Warburg group, first in Germany and later at the Warburg Institute in London, which would have afforded Benjamin a genuine intellectual, psychological home, not the Horkheimer-Adorno Institute for Research in the Social Sciences with which his relations were to prove so ambivalent and, during his life time, sterile. Panofsky could have rescued Benjamin from isolation; an invitation to London might have averted his early death.

Having sketched the history of allegory and the inner conventions of the allegoric code (with frequent reference to his own previous dissertation on romantic typologies of art), Benjamin proceeds to the emblematic devices, sayings, mottoes, *sententiae* and stock metaphors in baroque drama. These provide a natural transition to baroque language-theory. It is as a philosopher of language (a *Sprachphilosoph*), a species entirely different from, in fact antithetical to what Anglo-American usage identifies as 'linguistic philosophers', as a metaphysician of metaphor and translation as was Coleridge, that Benjamin accomplished his best work. Already by 1924, as the essay on [*Goethe's "Elective Affinities"*] shows, Benjamin had few rivals in degree of linguistic penetration and none who could mediate more subtly between a text and the speculative instruments of interpretation. His reflexions on the differences between the baroque concept of the written word (the 'hieroglyph') and the spoken are, therefore, profoundly instructive. Benjamin connects the strong cesura in the seventeenth-century alexandrine with the baroque instinct towards a segmented yet also equilibrated structure of statement. His hints towards a linguistic analysis of baroque theatrical utterance, of the way in which a pronouncement exercises an immediate, palpable fatality over speaker and hearer—almost every locution being, in essence, either curse or invocation—are pioneering. Here, more than anywhere else in the book, Benjamin is master of his ground.

The *Ursprung* closes with an almost mystically-intense apprehension of the ubiquity of evil in baroque sensibility. It suggests, in a vein which is unmistakably personal, that only allegory, in that it makes substance totally significant, totally representative of ulterior meanings and, therefore, 'unreal' in itself, can render bearable an authentic perception of the infernal. Through allegory, the Angel, who in Paul Klee's depiction, *Angelus Novus,* plays so obsessive a part in Benjamin's inner existence, can look into the deeps.

There remains the gnomic foreword. It can best be conceived of as in three movements. The first is methodological. Benjamin is working consciously in the current of

Schleiermacher and Dilthey, though he seeks to add something specifically private (the 'kabbalistic'). He is trying to determine and to instance, at precisely the same moment, the modes of intellection and argument proper to aesthetic-historical discourse. It is from this simultaneity that the difficulty springs: to determine by more or less normal types of definitional and sequential usage, and to exemplify, to act out at the same time that which is being determined. It is not only that Benjamin is trapped in the hermeneutic circle—the use of the part to define the whole whose own definition governs the status of the part—but, like Heidegger, he welcomes this circularity, perceiving in it the characteristic intimacy which binds object to interpretation and interpretation to object in the humanities. What Benjamin polemicizes against is the unworried dissociation between scholarly-critical styles of analysis and the privileged, irreducibly autonomous objects of such analysis, a dissociation that is particularly damaging in respect of works of art and letters. Category will locate and classify form, but form generates category. Being itself composed of language, the poem or play must elicit from its interpreter, who is working in and with words, a co-active, formally and substantively cognate, indeed mirroring response. Benjamin is striving to make clear, in what he says and in the manner of his saying, in just what ways the critical text, the translation of the life of the meditated object into the secondary 'meta-life' of the commentary, is a profoundly responsive and therefore responsible, mimetic act. The true critic-understander, the reader whose reading underwrites the continued life of the page before him, enacts his perceptions, creating an elucidatory, enhancing counter-statement to the primary text ('counter-statement' is Kenneth Burke's word, and there is in English-language literary theory and criticism no one closer to Benjamin's model).

In the case of German baroque drama, with its singular fabric of emblem and hyperbole, with its inauthentic relations to antique tragedy and the later neo-classical ideal, such reflective re-enactment demands a very particular, highly self-conscious idiom and argumentative proceeding (cf. Coleridge on *Venus and Adonis* in the *Biographia Literaria*). It will detour: 'Methode ist Umweg. Darstellung als Umweg . . . ' ['Method is detour. Representation as detour . . . ']. It will examine but also embody the authority of quotation, the many ways in which a quotation energizes or subverts the analytic context. And it is at this point that Benjamin refers most cogently to theology, to the pluralistic relations between canonic quote and commentary in the Hebraic and Christian traditions. But Benjamin's hermeneutic of and by citation also has its contemporary flavour: it is very obviously akin to the collage and montage-aesthetic in the poetry of Ezra Pound and T. S. Eliot, and in the prose of Joyce—all of whom are producing major works at exactly the same date as Benjamin's *Ursprung.*

The commentary will, moreover, have a fragmentary, possibly aphoristic tenor. It will not flinch from a built-in incompletion and abruptness of statement. Benjamin is reacting against the orotund inflation and magisterial, often bullying comprehensiveness of German academic-official rhetoric. It may be that he had in mind, though largely at a hearsay level, the riddling concision, the deliberate inadequacy of certain Talmudic exegetes. But again, the implicit notion is one that was in vogue: following on Lichtenberg and Nietzsche, Wittgenstein too was finding an aphoristic, 'leaping' style of philosophic discourse, whereas Kafka, yet another precise contemporary, was composing laconic, mysteriously unfinished parables.

Thirdly, Benjamin pleads, though in a voice muted by concurrent hopes of academic acceptance, for the rights of the esoteric. It is not only his material—the neglected plays and emblem-collections of the German seventeenth century—that is esoteric; it is his critical task. How could it be otherwise? How could the empathic decipherment of many-layered texts in an idiom long-forgot, pretend to perfect clarity? In this context opaqueness and inwardness of semantic arrangement are a manifest of honesty. No doubt, this plea reflects very strong traits in Benjamin's personality, traits which find expression in his love of the arcane, in his pretense to kabbalism, in the condensations and bracketings that mark his own prose. But once more, we are also dealing with a motif of the moment. The esoteric is a decisive symptom throughout the modernist movement, whether in Yeats's mature poetry, in *Ulysses,* in the *Tractatus* or in the abstract art and music of the 1920s. Benjamin's hermeticism represents a bias in himself and in the atmosphere of the day.

The second movement of the foreword is epistemological, and loses most readers. Benjamin was not, in any technical sense, a philosopher. Like other lyric thinkers, he chose from philosophy those metaphors, dramas of argument and intimations of systematic totality—whether Platonic, Leibnizian or Crocean—which best served, or rather which most suggestively dignified and complicated his own purpose. (Later on, in the **Historical-Philosophical Theses,** he was to use Marx in just this innocently-exploitative way.)

In the proem to the **Ursprung,** this source for a source, it is Plato, Leibniz and Croce who are enlisted. The questions posed by Benjamin are more or less traditional and lucid. How can there be a general and generalizing treatment of artistic-literary objects which are, by definition, unique? Is it possible to escape historical relativism or the vacant dogmatics of historicism while, at the same time, being faithful to the temporal specificity, even unrecapturability of one's documents? Can the interpreter interpret 'outside' his own self and moment? Affirmative answers depend on 'the rescue of phenomena' (the Kantian echo is explicit) and on 'the representation of Ideas'—in which term the capital letter is standard German usage but also figurative of Benjamin's purpose.

Combining a Platonic metaphor or mythography of 'Ideas' with a language-realism which does, for once, carry genuine kabbalistic overtones, Benjamin affirms that 'an Idea' is that moment in the substance and being of a word (*im Wesen des Wortes,* a phrase which is uncannily Heideggerian), in which this word has become, and performs as, a symbol. It is this capacity, this existentially potentialized capacity of language to symbolize as well as to become itself symbolic, which enables a critical-philosophic discourse to uncover 'Ideas'. Why 'Ideas'? Because it is 'ideally-ideationally' that discrete, fully autonomous objects—like baroque plays or renaissance paintings—enter into mutual compaction, into significant fusion without thereby losing their identity. The relevant paradigm is that of Leibniz's monads—independent, perfectly separate units which nevertheless and, indeed, necessarily enter into combinatorial, harmonic groupings and interactions. Thus the singular 'finds salvation', i.e. realizes its potential of full meaning, in the monadic plurality or, more precisely, in the representative manifold—the symbol, the icon, the declarative emblem—of 'Ideas'.

Such rescue and salvation, says Benjamin, is Platonic. The 'Idea' 'contains a picture of the world' specific to yet wholly transcending the particulars that have found lodging in it. It is in Croce's theory of the 'universal singularity' of linked cultural phenomena, of historical crystallizations such as the baroque, that Benjamin finds an application of his Platonic-Leibnizian scheme to actual cultural-textual material. But the allusions to Croce are only fleeting, and do little to clarify what is, so evidently, an acutely suggestive (consider the aphorism: 'Truth is the death of purpose'), but also incomplete and esoteric blueprint. The irate bafflement of the first academic readers is not surprising, and could not really have surprised Benjamin whose pride in difficulty was poignant.

Part three of the introduction is straightforward. Benjamin makes ritual, though perfectly valid, gestures towards the intrinsic interest of his chosen topic, and towards the neglect and misconceptions it has long endured. The time is ripe for revaluation: Franz Werfel's version of the *Trojan Women* (1915) and the Expressionist movement throughout the arts, give to the baroque theatre a fresh immediacy. As during the crises of the Thirty Years' War and its aftermath, so in Weimar Germany the extremities of political tension and economic misère are reflected in art and critical discussion. Having drawn the analogy, Benjamin closes with hints towards a recursive theory of culture: eras of decline resemble each other not only in their vices but also in their strange climate of rhetorical and aesthetic vehemence (the ambience of the **Ursprung** is sometimes that of Spengler). Thus a study of the baroque is no mere antiquarian, archival hobby: it mirrors, it anticipates and helps grasp the dark present. (pp. 15-24)

> *George Steiner, in an introduction to* The Origin of German Tragic Drama *by Walter Benjamin, translated by John Osborne, NLB, 1977, pp. 7-24.*

Ted Solotaroff   (essay date 1978)

[*Solotaroff is an American educator, editor, and critic. In the following excerpt, he finds Benjamin's concern over the decline of storytelling to be unfounded.*]

Walter Benjamin, in his magisterial essay **"The Storyteller,"** argued that the art of storytelling was dying out, that it was being superseded by the modern media of information and by the story's younger and more topical relative, the novel. There are reasons to believe that, writing in 1935, Benjamin was gloomily prophetic, but there are other reasons . . . to believe his prognosis was premature. Or even wrong. (p. 147)

Benjamin's use of the term "story" corresponds more closely to what we would call a "tale": i.e., it has its roots in the oral tradition, its favorite domicile was the hearth or the workroom, its archetypal artists were the peasant, the seafarer, the artisan; for "it combined the lore of faraway places, such as a much-traveled man brings home, with the lore of the past, as it best reveals itself to natives of a place." Thus its favorite province was not the here and now but the more philosophical there and then. For its principal distinguishing feature, in Benjamin's view, was its heuristic value. It dramatized a moral, practical instruction, or illustrated a proverb or maxim. In other words, the tale was spun into a useful fabric, one that provided counsel for its audience, "counsel" being understood, as Benjamin puts it, less as "an answer to a question than a proposal concerning the continuation [and significance] of a story which is just unfolding." And because such stories were typically drawn from the ways of the world, from shared or readily communicable experience, their counsel becomes "the epic side of truth," namely wisdom, which, like storytelling itself, Benjamin believes is dying out.

As I understand Benjamin, then, the story is less an evolving art form than a continuing if fading cultural resource: a vehicle for communicating and passing on the wisdom of the race by evoking "astonishment and thoughtfulness." Though open to individual embellishment, its nature is to be repeatable; hence the narrative line is clear and coherent: it introduces a situation, complicates it, and then resolves it. Like, say, Gogol's "The Overcoat" it does not depend upon psychological explanation for its coherence, its psychology is characteristically simple, uninflected, and it withholds explanation, part of its art, to allow the listener or reader to grasp its import by means of his own imagination and insight. Further, it is the lack of dependency on psychological nuance that contributes to, in Benjamin's lovely phrase, the "chaste compactness" of the story and enables it to be remembered and retold.

This "chaste compactness" is achieved by the craft with which a storyteller like Hawthorne hews to the main lines of a person's character, tracing them through situations that test and illuminate them, thereby casting a glow on the manners, mores, and attitudes of the tribe, animated by a man's life process flowing through them. Benjamin frequently relates the story to "natural history," the disparate, variable, mutable ingredients and events of the world which nonetheless draw ineluctably if fortuitously on to a predetermined end, which is, of course, death.

The storyteller is conversant most of all with fate and mortality. His art—layer upon layer of transparent incidents moving both indeterminately (suspense) and inexorably toward a fixed ending—is derived from his feeling for natural history. Indeed the older the storyteller, whether historically or personally, the more likely he is to identify his vision of life with nature and the "great inscrutable course of the world," and hence the more conversant he will be in communion with the transitory and mortal. But whether he is as early as Herodotus or as late as Nikolai Leskov, the nineteenth-century Russian writer whom Benjamin uses as his principal touchstone and source of examples, the signature of the true storyteller is found in the movement of his tale toward *completeness,* the sense it leaves of an earned definitiveness of experience, however open its meaning to speculation and mystery. In a remarkable passage, Benjamin associates death and storytelling as follows:

> It is characteristic that not only a man's knowledge or wisdom, but above all his real life—and this is the stuff that stories are made of—first assumes transmissible form at the moment of his death. Just

as a sequence of images is set in motion inside a man as his life comes to an end—unfolding the views of himself under which he has encountered himself without being aware of it—suddenly in his expressions and looks the unforgettable emerges and imparts to everything that concerned him that authority which even the poorest wretch in dying possesses for the living around him. This authority is at the very source of the story.

Part of Benjamin's explanation for the decline of storytelling is that death and its revelations have been pushed from the realm of domestic, lived fact to the periphery of our awareness by the ways in which we isolate ourselves from the dying and the dead. The point is typical of Benjamin's approach to the problem of the story. He does not concern himself with the arguments, familiar by 1935, that the conventions of plot are falsified by the random, provisional, indeterminate aspects of reality, that the freestanding, solid, explicable characters, more or less bereft of an unconscious, are belied by psychology as well as by our own inner life, that fiction with a moral in tow or designed to illustrate a maxim is immediately suspect of simplifying experience and subverting art. Since virtually all didactic fiction today is a form of propaganda for authoritarian systems, the form is doubly dubious. Of course, Benjamin would say he is talking about "counsel," not thought control. And he would attribute the decline of counsel and wisdom to the fallen value of experience itself, whether of the person or the community or the race, its supersession by the bewilderment of man in the face of his incessantly changing society, of a world that has gotten out of hand and has passed beyond the human scale of understanding and judgment. Hence the story is dying because of the incommunicability and incommensurability of being-in-the-world. He points out that the men returning from the First World War were silent rather than full of stories, and the novels that were later produced were "anything but experience that goes from mouth to mouth." What they communicated instead was mostly the enormity of modern warfare, the overwhelmment of the person. As he puts it,

> A generation that had gone to school on a horse-drawn street car now stood under the open sky in a countryside in which nothing remained unchanged but the clouds, and beneath these clouds, in a field of force of destructive torrents and explosions, was the tiny, fragile, human body.

What are we to say fifty years further along in the acceleration of history, which hardly requires war to reduce persons to random social particles? The mass society does that very readily, while its culture further undermines the communicability of experience by its various modes of pseudo communication, the more pseudo the better, as the TV ratings testify. Benjamin, who died in 1940, did not live to see his military image expand across the social spectrum, but he was already well aware of the media of information as a conquering adversary of the story. The product of the up-and-doing middle class with its preference for the factual and the explicable, the daily flood of information, works directly against the function and value of the traditional story. Though drawing upon the ways of the world, Benjamin's storyteller is indifferent to the verifiability of his account and offers no explanations for life in the there and then. Like man himself, the imaginative interest on which his story does depend has diminished to the meagerness of the "news story." (pp. 148-52)

The media are not the only lethal impediments and adversaries to Benjamin's notion of the story. There is also the novel. It departs from the story at its very outset, its roots being not in the oral tradition but in the printed word. The effect of this medium is, typically, to distance the writer from his audience: Instead of a man among men, who "takes what he tells from experience—his own or that reported by others . . . and in turn makes it the experience of those who are listening to the tale," the novelist keeps his narrative to himself and has to be his own audience until he is finished. Anyone who has successfully told a story to a circle of people and then, encouraged by his performance and their responsiveness, has tried to write it is aware of how the spontaneity and intimacy of the oral turns into the self-consciousness and loneliness of the written. It is partly this difference that Benjamin has in mind when he goes on to write about the novelist in what seems to be a rather arbitrary and extreme way:

> The novelist has isolated himself. The birthplace of the novel is the solitary individual, who is no longer able to express himself by giving examples of his most important concerns, is himself uncounseled, and cannot counsel others. To write a novel means to carry the incommensurable to extremes in the representation of human life. In the midst of life's fullness, and through the representation of this fullness, the novel gives evidence of the profound perplexity of the living.

Defoe? Fielding? Or, even more notably, Dickens?—the writer whose novels took their place at the hearthside of countless Victorian households, who was so much the counselor of his society, whose fullness of presented life was so securely organized and intuitively understood that it provided his readers with intelligence rather than bewilderment: Benjamin's storyteller with endless staying power. (pp. 153-54)

For Benjamin the "short story"—a term he uses only once—is less a development of the traditional story than another example of the various abbreviations of the forms and processes of the past by the modern means of productivity. Rather than carrying on the craft of the tale, the short story is, to his mind, an abbreviated novel. In any case, he writes about the story as though Chekhov, Mann, Kafka did not exist, though he also wrote perhaps the best single essay on Kafka and was, I suspect, haunted by him. He even begins his essay with a story about Potemkin, who was once undergoing one of his paralyzing depressions and paralyzing the state as well. A petty clerk, Shuvalkin, deciding to attack the problem directly, entered Potemkin's room with a sheaf of documents, and emerged triumphantly with them signed, only to discover they had been signed "Shulvalkin . . . Shuvalkin . . . Shuvalkin." The story, Benjamin writes, "is like a herald racing two hundred years ahead of Kafka's work. The enigma which beclouds it is Kafka's enigma." He uses several other stories to illustrate the range of the doomed transactions of Kafka's cosmically burdened characters with the world and its authorities, but he deals with Kafka as not so much a storyteller as the creator of a theater in which, like the classical Chinese, happenings are reduced to gestures, though in Kafka's case generally incongruous, enigmatic, confused, or futile ones.

But certainly Kafka was a storyteller of the there and then, and there is probably no better illustration of Benjamin's favorite kind of story, in which the elements of myth and fairy tale interpenetrate the natural, than "Metamorphosis." To be sure, Kafka is without counsel and there is no more perfect witness than his protagonists to the profound perplexity of the living in the midst of life's fullness, no author who has carried the incommensurable to a further extreme. And yet Kafka was full of stories, and even parables, myths, and fables.

I agree with Benjamin about the human usefulness he finds to be the story's defining ingredient, but I believe that it can be conveyed by other means than the counsels of the there and then. The contemporary short story is typically concerned with the here and now, particularly in cultures like ours, in which the new, the perplexing, the ominous, the random constitute our central universal. It is no accident that the storytellers of the there and then are today largely found in Latin America, where the past still flows through and shapes the present, often tragically so. I believe that the usefulness of the contemporary American story lies precisely in its fight in behalf of the human scale of experience and its communication against the forces that seek to diminish and trivialize it. I find that most stories that interest me accept the incommensurability of experience and struggle against it to make sense of the otherwise senseless, to locate the possibilities of coherence (in both senses of the term) in the otherwise incoherent flux of a society whose members are dazed by its mutability and by the babbling of its media about this "event," that "trend," which flatters our knowingness while impoverishing our understanding. (pp. 155-57)

> *Ted Solotaroff, "The Telling Story," in his A Few Good Voices in My Head: Occasional Pieces on Writing, Editing, and Reading My Contemporaries, Harper & Row, Publishers, 1987, pp. 147-65.*

Peter Demetz (essay date 1978)

[*Demetz is a Czechoslovakian-born American educator and critic. In the following excerpt, he offers an overview of Benjamin's writings, suggesting a chronological approach as the best way to understand his works.*]

I would suggest that the reader first approach those of Benjamin's writings that can loosely be termed autobiographical, including the ironic self-exploration in **"The Destructive Character,"** and then proceed to a group of early writings in which a systematic and metaphysical orientation predominates. In consonance with his intellectual development, we would, in the next step, deal with a third cluster of essays in which Benjamin moved to the speculative left or tried to formulate what he thought he had learned from Bertolt Brecht; and once we had learned something about his Marxist commitments, we might feel better prepared to deal with those particularly difficult texts in which, to the despair of partisan interpreters, spiritual and materialist ideas appear in cryptic configurations. In these (as, for example, the Paris précis) the failure of the systematic thinker constitutes the true triumph of the master of hermeneutics who, in "reading" the things of the world as if they were sacred texts, suddenly decodes the overwhelming forces of human history.

Benjamin's ***Berlin Chronicle,*** a relatively late text

sketched during his first stay (1932) in Ibiza, Spain, and never published while he lived, looks back in many important passages upon his early childhood experiences and upon the emotional vicissitudes of the thinker as a young man of the idealist *jeunesse dorée* ["golden youth"]. He himself suggests how we should read the text; the *Chronicle,* precisely because it explicates the nature of memory by testing its powers, is a far more restless and profound text than his ***Berlin Childhood Around the Turn of the Century,*** in which individual memories are neatly ordered in a static if not mannered way. In the ***Berlin Chronicle,*** his intimate childhood and the city of his youth emerge luminously: the shaft of light under his bedroom door revealing the consoling presence of his parents nearby, the first experience of a threatening thunderstorm over the city, the smell of perspiration in the classroom, the confusions of puberty, the pale whore in the blue sailor-suit dominating (as in an Antonioni movie) his recurrent dreams, the famous Romanische Café as well as the more modest Princess Café, where he wrote his first essays on a marble table-top. The details are vivid and precise, but Benjamin is not satisfied with the informative splinter: he wants to explore the process of remembering itself—unfolding, dredging up—and to analyze the particular movement of his thoughts that gives shape to the materials and isolates the illuminating significance of what is close to the center of his sensibilities. We are, as readers, involved in a Proustian exercise in creating a past by using the finest snares of consciousness; to remember, Benjamin writes, is to "open the fan of memory," but he who starts to open the fan "never comes to the end of its segments; no image satisfies him, for he has seen that it can be unfolded and only in its folds does the truth reside: that image, that taste, that touch for whose sake all this has been unfurled and dissected; and now remembrance advances from small to smallest details, from the smallest to the infinitesimal, while that which it encounters in these microcosms grows ever mightier." Memory is the "capability of endlessly interpolating." In an extended image (implying an allusion to Schliemann and his discovery of Troy), Benjamin praises the writer as an archeologist who is never satisfied with the first stroke of the spade and returns again and again to the same place to dig deeper and deeper.

Benjamin himself is aware that his memories are characterized by a remarkable absence of people, and he tells us of a sudden epiphany that revealed to him in what way modern cities take their revenge upon the many claims human beings make upon one another. Memory ruled by the city does not show encounters and visits, but, rather, the scenes in which we encounter ourselves or others, and such an insight betrays an entire syndrome of Benjamin's ideas about life in the modern world: his concern with the "thingness" of the cities, the only places of historical experience in industrial civilizations; his obsession (shared by the French Surrealists) with walking the streets and boulevards; his fundamental urge to rearrange everything lived by fixing it on maps, in graphic schemes, spatial order. In his imagination, as in that of Rainer Maria Rilke, space rules over time; his "topographical consciousness" shapes experience in architectonic patterns, in neighborhoods, and in particular in urban districts the borders of which have to be crossed in trembling and sweet fear. The ***Berlin Chronicle*** is a misnomer, because it actually offers a map of coexistent apartments, meeting places, elegant salons,

shabby hotel rooms, skating rinks, and tennis courts; social distinctions are expressed in terms of different urban landscapes in which the rich and the poor are enclosed without knowing one another; and certain streets, dividing the red-light districts around the railway station from the quarters of the *haute bourgeoisie,* are ontological thresholds on which the young man likes to dwell, tasting the terrible and magic moments of confronting a totally "other" life or the "edge of the void," the whores being "the household goddesses of [a] cult of nothingness." Benjamin always looked for threshold experiences, and not only in a private way. As a young man he may have loitered near the railway stations to face another way of living that radically negated all his personal values of absolute purity, and as a philosopher he continued moving toward thresholds of speculative potentialities, tasting, confronting, exploring, without really caring to cross over into a total commitment to the "other" once and for all. His early fascination with the other world of the red lights may be emblematic of the most secret bents of his mind.

One-Way Street was originally planned to be a highly personal record of observations, aphorisms, dreams, and prose epigrams assembled from 1924 to 1928 for a few intimate friends; the title suggests, in its urban metaphor, the fortunate turn of a street that opens onto a striking view of an entire new panorama, and indicates to readers that they should confront each of the little pieces as an abruptly illuminating moment of modern experience—intimate, literary, and political. The **"Imperial Panorama,"** Benjamin's diagnosis of German inflation, was possibly the first piece, to which others were added. It is a first-rate document, in which his private shock (often articulated in terms of his incipient Marxism) and the social dissolution of the age closely correspond. He wrote these observations from the double perspective of the reluctant bourgeois son who had been living on the financial resources of his father (the capitalist), and the revolutionary Marxist who was beginning to grasp, from his conversations with Asja Lacis and his readings of Georg Lukács, in what way middle-class stability, now seemingly destroyed forever, had caused the unstable fate of the less privileged. He rightly observes how inflationary pressures make money the destructive center of all interests, and yet he sounds very much like the disappointed middle-class idealist in the German Romantic tradition when he deplores the loss of communal warmth in human relationships, the disappearing feeling for a free and well-rounded personality, and the new dearth of productive conversation, due to the sudden predominance of the question of the cash nexus. But it is difficult to separate Benjamin the social commentator from the moralist in the French tradition; his brief and lucid observations on the fragility of feelings between men and women forcefully remind me of Stendhal's *De l'amour,* and he is particularly impressive when he fiercely comments on the analogies between books and prostitutes (variations of a leitmotif), discusses the insecurities of the modern writer, or playfully works out rules for writing bad books. Looking far into the future, he demands new forms of publications that would be more easily accessible, in an industrial mass society, to people averse to the "universal gesture of the book," and he speculates, as a pioneer in the semiotic tradition, about the literary and technological changes effected by new modes of print, advertising, and the developing cinema. As if in passing, and yet with astonishing foresight, he approaches problems that today dominate our changing awareness of literature and the media in the age of concrete poetry, Marshall McLuhan, and Jacques Derrida. (pp. xv-xix)

In the essays written during and immediately after the years of World War I, Benjamin wants to confront central questions about the order of the universe. He speaks of these writings as contributions to a new "metaphysical" philosophy and does not conceal his systematic interest in providing inclusive answers; the form of the essay may indicate some of his hesitations, yet it is always our knowledge of the entire *kosmos*—of God, man, and things—that is at stake. In a fragment about the essential tasks of (his) philosophy, Benjamin shows himself deeply impressed by Kant's epistemological fervor, but sharply contrasts a genuine philosophy, "conscious of time and eternity," with the Enlightenment, which unfortunately admitted to scrutiny only knowledge of the lowest kind (elsewhere he speaks of the "hollow" and the "flat" concerns of the Enlightenment). What he seeks is a theory dealing with higher knowledge that is not limited by mathematical and mechanical norms of certainty, but sustained by a new turn to language, which alone communicates what we philosophically know.

Benjamin's essay **"On the Mimetic Faculty,"** with its sudden shifts of attention and compressed arguments of astonishing range and illuminating suggestions, energetically seeks to close the gap between the universe of things and the world of signs, a gap widened by modern linguistics. It is man's mimetic faculty in the widest sense that brings together what seems split and divided; the wholeness of the universe is sustained, Benjamin suggests, by "natural correspondences" that in turn stimulate and challenge man to respond by creating analogies, similarities, something that is akin. Man's mimetic responses have their own history; and although Benjamin is inclined to believe in a distinct weakening of some forms of the mimetic force, he introduces the concept of a "nonsensuous similarity" that operates beyond the evidence of the senses. Astrology, dancing, and the onomatopoeic element in speech reveal the oldest forms of man's capabilities, but "nonsensuous similarity" (or in more recent parlance, a paradoxical nonsensuous iconicity of the sign, I would suspect) continues to reside in speech as well as in writing and guarantees wholeness and unity; "it is nonsensuous similarity that establishes the ties not only between the spoken and the signified but also between the written and the signified, and equally between the spoken and the written." Implicit in these arguments are two of Benjamin's most essential ideas—his belief that language is far from being a conventional system of signs (an idea further developed in his essay on language) and his hermeneutic urge to read and understand "texts" that are not texts at all. The ancients may have been "reading" the torn guts of animals, starry skies, dances, runes, and hieroglyphs, and Benjamin, in an age without magic, continues to "read" things, cities, and social institutions as if they were sacred texts.

His essay **"On Language as Such and on the Language of Man"** (written in 1916) clearly offers a central attempt to reestablish a metaphysical view of the word, in which the overwhelming power of language spoken and heard puts forth a truth that was hidden before; and whatever Marxists may say about his allegiances, here the enemy of the

Enlightenment has his place between gnostic traditions and Martin Heidegger. Quoting, against Kant, the German Romantics Hamann and Friedrich M. Müller, Benjamin separates his own ideas from a "bourgeois" (i.e., commonplace) and a "mystical" philosophy of language; the bourgeois theory unfortunately holds that language consists of mere conventional signs that are not necessarily related to Being, and the mystical view falsely identifies words with the essence of things. In his own view, the being of a richly layered world, as divine creation, remains separate from language, yet cannot but commune "in" rather than "through" it. Language, far from being a mere instrument, lives as a glorious medium of being; all creation participates in an infinite process of communication (communion), and even the inarticulate plant speaks in the idiom of its fragrance. "There is no event or thing in either animate or inanimate nature that does not in some way partake of language, for it is in the nature of all to communicate their mental meanings. . . . We cannot imagine a total absence of language in anything."

Following the gnostic tradition, Benjamin looks for his cue in biblical texts, and after a halfhearted attempt at reconciling the two creation narratives of the Old Testament, he develops his ideas from a close reading of Genesis 1, for he feels that the recurrent rhythm of "Let there be," "He made," and "He named" clearly indicates a striking relationship of creation to language. The hierarchies of the world and the order of language, or, rather, "words," intimately correspond: although the word of God is of absolute and active power, in man's realm the word is more limited, and it is "soundless" in the "silent magic of things." Man's dignity consists in mirroring God's absolute and creative word in "names" on the threshold between finite and infinite language; the names he gives to and receives from others may be but a reflection (*Abbild*) of the divine Word, but name giving sustains man's closeness to God's creative energies and defines his particular mode of being; "of all beings man is the only one who himself names his own kind, as he is the only one whom God did not name." To name is man's particular fate; he alone among the created beings (as Rilke and Hölderlin would confirm) responds to the silent language of things by "translating" their speechless communication. Thus "translation," in a complex meaning, acquires a central ontological importance because the communication of the lower strata of creation has to be translated (that is, elevated and made pellucid) to the higher orders. The speechless word of the things or the silent speech on the lowest level is translated by man into the "naming word" (*nennendes Wort*), the language of the anthropological stratum, and finally offered to God, who, in His word of creation (*schaffendes Wort*) guarantees the legitimacy of the translation, because it is He who has created the silent word of things as well as that of translating man. "Translating" means solving a task that God has given to man alone; and such a task would be impossible to fulfill "were not the name-language of man and the nameless one of things related in God, released from the same creative word, which in things became the communication of matter in magic community, and in man the language of knowledge and name in blissful mind." We are in a universe structured by the presence or absence of "linguistic" articulation, and all the levels of creation (articulate and inarticulate) are alien and yet intimately related to one another by the potentialities of the "name" (not less powerful than in Gertrude Stein's godless theory of poetry).

Benjamin's **"Theologico-Political Fragment"** (written 1920-21), a striking statement of the Messianism prevalent in his thought for a long time, connects his early meditations about language, knowledge, and the world with his **"Critique of Violence"** (1921), in which his experience of changing German society in the age of the Spartakus uprisings and his readings of Sorel's anarchist theories combine with his unshaken belief in a postlapsarian world crying for sudden eschatological change. In his **"Fragment,"** he wants to cope, at least by suggestion, with the seeming incompatibility of the profane (or historical) and the Messianic (or divine) order; and he bravely demands that a new philosophy of history (his own) try to relate the distinct forces in some way to one another. These forces do not move in a consonant rhythm, and yet, "if one arrow points to the goal toward which the profane dynamic acts, and another marks the direction of Messianic intensity, then certainly the quest of free humanity for happiness runs counter to the Messianic direction; but just as a force can, through acting, increase another that is acting in the opposite direction, so the order of the profane assists, through being profane, the coming of the Messianic Kingdom." Benjamin suggests that in the profane urge for being happy the most tender coming of the divine order announces itself, and we are left with hope in fragile and painful abeyance.

Benjamin's fragment **"Fate and Character,"** like many of his earlier essays, compresses far-reaching suggestions into a few pages, and it would be foolish to separate the strains of anthropology, autobiographical implication, and genre criticism too neatly. It is an impressive and tortuous example of how Benjamin brings together and divides again in a new and radical way what more traditional minds have related in superficial fashion. His concern with guilt, the law, and the gods, and his separation of the moral and the divine order, indicate that (though questions of characterology and the poetic predominate) we are still moving in a universe of metaphysical consistence. In the early passages, the fragment suggests why Benjamin, in search of a sign system of human experience, is far less ashamed of his intense interest in graphology (of which he was a gifted practitioner), chiromancy, and physiognomy than his critics. Later he argues that our concepts of fate and character have been mistaken, because we put these concepts in the wrong contexts—ethics and religion. But fate relates to guilt and misfortune (rather than to happiness, which would be a way of escaping fate) and belongs therefore to the world of the law, which is but a relic of the demonic stage in human development; and it is in tragedy that the genius of man first arises above the "mist of guilt"—not, as Hegel and his many disciples would suggest, restoring the disturbed order of the universe, but manifesting human resistance "by shaking up [the] tormented world." Similarly, the concept of character should be removed from the realm of ethics and related to "nature in man"; and if tragedy seeks to go beyond the "guilt context of the living," comedy shows character (for instance, in Molière's plays) "like a sun, in the brilliance of its single trait, which allows no other to remain visible in its proximity." We do not judge in moral terms but feel "high amusement," and far from presenting to us a monstrous puppet that is totally unfree, comedy—with its

commitment to an emancipated physiognomy—introduces a new age of the genius of humanity.

The **"Critique of Violence"** hides its paradoxes and disturbing self-subversion in a deceptively tight structure of arguments in which, as if he were a lawyer or a legal philosopher, Benjamin proposes to develop, with an almost merciless power of deduction, a close sequence of professional distinctions; and yet, on the later pages of the essay, the entire system of initial reasoning, if not an entire world of preliminary values, is pushed aside, and the expert lawyer changes into an enthusiastic chiliast who rhapsodically praises the violence of divine intervention, which will put a sudden end to our lives of insufficiency and dearth (the essay subverts its own fundaments in order to enact something of the ontological "break" in which the old world is abruptly transformed into a new). As in his other essays of the time (1916-21), Benjamin first wants to separate his own philosophical perspective from that of other traditional approaches, and in a technical argument of high sophistication he reviews the manner in which the "natural law" and the "positive law" have been dealing with the problems of violence. He shows that the one conceives of violence as a product of unchangeable nature, whereas the other deals with violence as a result of historical becoming (*Gewordenheit*). Both, however, are constantly concerned with the close interrelationships of means and ends within the legal system, and both fail to ask the question (central to his own interest) of how certain means of violence might be paradoxically justified totally outside the law. Benjamin surveys the legal implications of strikes, wars, and capital punishment and concludes that all violence in the human realm functions so that it is either constituting or sustaining the law (*rechtssetzend/rechtserhaltend*); and in a passage certain to challenge the liberal reader, he suggests that legal institutions forgetful of the latent presence of violence inevitably decay, that parliaments (ignoring the dignity of violence) err in trying to reach compromises, and that anarchists and Bolsheviks are right in fiercely attacking parliamentary systems. Fortunately, there is still a private sphere in which a "cultured heart," politesse, and trust in our fellow beings may come to subjective but nonviolent accords.

But here we are suddenly elevated from the profane to the mythical and divine orders, and violence, of a more radical kind, turns into an eschatological necessity. Not only is it difficult, Benjamin asserts, to think about solving any problems in the human world in a nonviolent way, but it is completely inconceivable that man's salvation from all historical modes of existence should ever occur without violence. We are compelled to postulate another kind of violence, one that operates outside the realm of legal principles, violence not as a means of legality but as a manifestation of Olympian power: "Niobe's arrogance calls down fate upon itself not because her arrogance offends against the law but because it challenges fate—to a fight in which fate must triumph, and can bring to light a law only in its triumph." Yet in his thirst for purity, plenitude, and otherness, Benjamin again relegates the violence of myth or the "manifestation of the Gods" to a dubious state of wordliness, because even mythical violence cannot finally escape an involvement with, or, rather, a definition of, profane legalities. True otherness is only in God, who asserts himself in a third and absolute type of violence completely alien to the order of profanity and myth; "if mythical violence is lawmaking, divine violence is law-destroying; if the former sets boundaries, the latter boundlessly destroys them; if mythical violence brings at once guilt and retribution, divine power only expiates; if the former threatens, the latter strikes; if the former is bloody, the latter is lethal without spilling blood." The anarchist mystic Benjamin sees the coming of the Messiah as abrupt, sudden, destructive, ending all human history and its barrenness by freeing pure, glorious, divine violence from contagion with myth or the regions below. Once again we have moved through all the strata of creation, but Benjamin does not tell us how we are to *live* after God's violent lightning has struck, when a timeless and crystalline space of terrible perfection, as in paradise, surrounds us again.

We cannot speak about anybody's Marxism in a general and abstract way any more, and to approach productively those of Benjamin's essays in which Marxist ideas predominate is to define the particular implications of these ideas and to describe their specific function in an individual moment of Central European politics and intellectual history. Whatever can be said about Benjamin as melancholy Marxist, I would stress above all that he, in his rather unobtrusive way, sided with those artists and critics on the radical left who were arguing against the growing traditionalism of the Soviet establishment and, often in close combat with the defenders of an ossifying party line, continued to believe that Marxists should not participate in construing a totally closed world, but should spontaneously respond to new technological changes in contemporary civilization. There are few indications that Benjamin, who was a secretive and studious man, often attended political mass meetings or marched under red banners through the streets of Berlin. His Marxism was a library affair (more Lenin and Trotsky than Marx, and more early Lukács than Engels), and the challenging way in which he speaks of Surrealism, Sergei Tretiakov, and Bertolt Brecht suggests that he was, in the concrete context of the late twenties and thirties, attracted by the impressive power of the Communist Party and inclined toward increasing opposition to the Stalinists, the dogma of Socialist Realism (after 1934), and the revolutionary decree from above. (pp. xx-xxviii)

I would include Benjamin's essay **"Surrealism,"** originally published as three installments in *Die Literarische Welt* in the late winter of 1929, among his most cryptic and important texts. Written from the distance of the German observer at a time of growing conflicts within the French Surrealist group, the essay offers a panoramic view of what the Surrealist poets had done since 1919 and, perhaps more essentially, reveals personal ideas that were to obsess Benjamin for the rest of his life. A consciousness in crisis seizes on the crisis of a poetic movement to define itself; and it is important to see how Benjamin characterizes the pressing problems of a "humanist concept of freedom" for one disenchanted with "eternal discussions" and longing for vital decisions to go beyond the alternatives of the "anarchist *fronde*" (close to his sensibilities) and "revolutionary discipline" (demanded by the organized Communists). He describes how the Surrealists have exploded traditional poetry from within by pushing the idea of "poetic life" to the utter limits of the possible; inevitably they have reached a tortuous moment of transition in which the heroic period of Surrealism, or the intimate years of the "inspiring wave of dreams," have to give way to a public

struggle for power, political commitment, and involvement with revolutionary action. Yet the key concept of the "profane illumination," which emerges here to characterize Surrealist vision, suggests Benjamin's own way of unveiling, in his materialist hermeneutics, how history resides in some of the things of the world and institutions of society; and by attributing to the Surrealists the virtue of "seeing" and "freeing" revolutionary energies in things nearly obsolete, Benjamin describes what he is actually going to do in his later essays on Paris and French society. The Surrealists (who may not always have been equal to their task) have discovered revolutionary forces in particular objects and everyday use (e.g., the first iron constructions, early photographs, dresses almost out of fashion); André Breton and his beloved Nadja change into revolutionary resolution, if not action, what others have felt in uncertain and frustrated moods when taking a trip in a sad railway carriage or looking, from a new apartment, out through the window and the rain. But Benjamin does not want to tolerate any irrational romantic, or intoxicating element in that secularized epiphany or the overwhelming moment of "profane illumination"; in spite of his hashish experiments (or, rather, because of them), he asserts that it is not productive to accentuate the mystical element in the mystery of discovering hidden forces and meanings, "for histrionic or fanatical stress on the mysterious side of the mysterious takes us no further; we penetrate the mystery only to the degree that we recognize it in the everyday world, by virtue of a dialectical optic that perceives the everyday as impenetrable, the impenetrable as everyday." There are few lines in which Benjamin reveals the intent of his late writings more clearly and openly. (pp. xxx-xxxii)

In his lecture **"The Author as Producer,"** given at the Paris Institute for the Study of Fascism (1934), Benjamin concentrates on important questions often discussed with Brecht; and I wonder how the functionaries responded to his nostalgic memories of the Soviet "Left Front," or *Levyi Front,* group (he did delete a long Trotsky quotation from his manuscript). The lecture begins in good Brechtian fashion by separating the "bourgeois entertainer" (Brecht would have said the "culinary" writer) from the progressive artist who has thrown his lot in with the revolutionary proletariat, but Benjamin does not want to accept the traditional idea that the correct tendency alone assures the quality of the text. Trying to redefine the old problem of content/form in a dialectical way, he rightly argues that it is insufficient to analyze "a book, work, or novel" independently of social relationships, and, dexterously shifting to his central question, he suggests that the question about the work and the social structure should be revised; instead of asking how a work of art relates "to" modes of production, we should ask how it operates "within" them (he is thinking of modes of property as well as of technology). Like the *Levyi Front* writers and Brecht since the late twenties, Benjamin demands that left-wing writing use the technological advances in the media, and he praises Sergei Tretiakov as a true "operative" (not merely "informational") author who energetically seized on new technologies and forms of expression, joined the peasant communes in the Russian countryside, organized *st'engazety* (newspapers on the walls), and brought radio and movies to the villages. Benjamin's image of the Soviet press may be rather romantic, but what he really wants is a radical democratization of cultural life, based on the potentialities of the mass media; he hopes (as does Herbert Marcuse later) that these new forms would not be easily absorbed by the capitalist apparatus of production/distribution, but would instead revolutionize the apparatus itself (a rather optimistic idea, if we remind ourselves of the experiments of the Italian futurists, allied with the Fascists, or of Leni Riefenstahl's experimental movies in praise of the butchers on the right). Benjamin finds little consolation in the German writing of his time; expressionists and activists, from Heinrich Mann to Alfred Döblin, have wanted "spiritual transformation" rather than "technical innovation," and even the *Neue Sachlichkeit* (New Objectivity) of the mid-twenties, with all its striking interest in photography and reportage techniques, has delivered its goods to the capitalist culture machinery, rather than change it. Yet we should not ignore the beginnings of a countermovement: "the revolutionary strength of Dada" tested the authenticity of art, John Heartfield used photo montage to teach the working people, and Bertolt Brecht, above all in plays like *The Measures Taken* (*Die Massnahme*), created the new paradigms of a theater obstinately refusing to be absorbed by capitalist society. Brecht (whose *Threepenny Novel* Benjamin vastly overrates) emerges as the master of what artists and the arts should do; his epic theater constitutes a model of production able to teach other producers what to produce and, by requiring a different kind of theatrical apparatus, transforms the old cultural institutions in a revolutionary way. There is much tragic irony in Benjamin's last stand as a theoretician of "operative" literature. He demands a new, open, and experimental Marxist art in the manner of Tretiakov and Brecht exactly at the moment when, in the Soviet Union, Karl Radek is attacking James Joyce, and eager Party functionaries are declaring that nineteenth-century traditions are the best way to the future. (pp. xxxiii-xxxv)

The Austrian Marxist Ernst Fischer once suggested that Benjamin contributed much to an interpretation of capitalism but little to changing the world, and added that his philosophy, sustained by utter loneliness, rather than by the concerns of the masses, particularly attracts those intellectuals who restlessly search for a better world and yet shy away from the grubbier commitments of a practical kind. Benjamin was tempted at times to say that in the age of Hitler, his brand of Communism was the "lesser evil" (May 6, 1934) and to picture himself as a shipwrecked mariner who had little choice. Whatever his motivation, he substantially participated in developing a sophisticated Marxist theory of history, society, and culture, and by at least sketching a systematic apologia for Mallarmé, Dada, and the Surrealists on Marxist grounds, he substantially aided the artists and critics of the independent left who were (and are) engaged in ever-renewed conflicts with orthodox party functionaries hiding their power games behind clichés about progressive realism (if the Eurocommunists develop a theory of culture, Benjamin will be one of their saints). Yet these are issues surviving from the early thirties, and it would be wrong, I think, to define Benjamin's importance to us solely in terms of a political anachronism, however resilient. He has more to offer to his readers now, and we should not disregard those of his essential concerns that go far beyond the agenda of his own day. In articulating his vision of language, Benjamin soon developed a strong interest in a theory of the sign and renewed semiotic tradition (which in Germany went back to the mid-eighteenth century). His romantic opposition

to the idea that the meaning of the sign was mere convention pushed him on to courageous speculations about the sign and the mimetic urge of mankind, and his later interest in the technology of the new media forcefully widened his thinking about signs to include problems of book production, graphic experiments, and advertising. He has few equals in restoring semiotics to our attention.

I wonder whether it would be possible to listen to Benjamin in a musical rather than a literary way, and to concentrate, as if his individual writings were fragments of an inclusive score, on the thematic orchestration of his ideas and arguments. His ultimate secret, I believe, is that he works with a few intimate leitmotifs that fascinate him throughout his life, regardless of the particular stage of his ideological transformations. The name and the sign, divine violence and mundane discipline, the threshold and the city, the *flâneur* and the archeologist of culture—these are a few of his elemental *topoi* and recurrent figures, absent occasionally, submerged perhaps for a while, yet never totally absent from his ken. Perhaps the best way to approach Benjamin's writings would be to imitate his willingness to keep the sensibilities open to the sober and profane illuminations that come to people who quietly and attentively walk through the astonishing streets of a foreign city. It is not a matter of reducing distances but of keeping them, and in confronting Benjamin, we should not try to diminish or explain away what is strange, difficult, and a productive provocation. It is precisely his fine and fierce otherness that is going to change our thought. (pp. xli-xliii)

> *Peter Demetz, in an introduction to* Reflections: Essays, Aphorisms, Autobiographical Writings *by Walter Benjamin, edited by Peter Demetz, translated by Edmund Jephcott, Harcourt Brace Jovanovich, 1978, pp. vii-xliii.*

Susan Sontag   (essay date 1978)

[*Sontag is among the most influential of contemporary American critics. Treating a wide variety of aesthetic concerns, her critical writings are informed by the belief that the act of interpretation unavoidably distorts the significance of a work. "The aim of all commentary on art," she has written, "should be to make works of art—and, by analogy, our own experience—more, rather than less, real to us. The function of criticism should be to show how it is what it is,* even, *that it is what it is, rather than to show what it means." In the following excerpt, she examines Benjamin's major works, finding them to be characterized by a melancholic temperament.*]

[Walter Benjamin] was what the French call *un triste*. In his youth he seemed marked by "a profound sadness," [Gershom] Scholem wrote. He thought of himself as a melancholic, disdaining modern psychological labels and invoking the traditional astrological one: "I came into the world under the sign of Saturn—the star of the slowest revolution, the planet of detours and delays. . . ." His major projects, the book published in 1928 on the German baroque drama (the *Trauerspiel;* literally, sorrow-play) and his never completed **"Paris, Capital of the Nineteenth Century,"** cannot be fully understood unless one grasps how much they rely on a theory of melancholy.

Benjamin projected himself, his temperament, into all his major subjects, and his temperament determined what he chose to write about. It was what he saw in subjects, such as the seventeenth-century baroque plays (which dramatize different facets of "Saturnine acedia") and the writers about whose work he wrote most brilliantly—Baudelaire, Proust, Kafka, Karl Kraus. He even found the Saturnine element in Goethe. For, despite the polemic in his great (still untranslated) essay on *Goethe's "Elective Affinities"* against interpreting a writer's work by his life, he did make selective use of the life in his deepest meditations on texts: information that disclosed the melancholic, the solitary. (Thus, he describes Proust's "loneliness which pulls the world down into its vortex"; explains how Kafka, like Klee, was "essentially solitary"; cites Robert Walser's "horror of success in life.") One cannot use the life to interpret the work. But one can use the work to interpret the life.

Two short books of reminiscences of his Berlin childhood and student years, written in the early 1930s and unpublished in his lifetime, contain Benjamin's most explicit self-portrait. To the nascent melancholic, in school and on walks with his mother, "solitude appeared to me as the only fit state of man." Benjamin does not mean solitude in a room—he was often sick as a child—but solitude in the great metropolis, the busyness of the idle stroller, free to daydream, observe, ponder, cruise. The mind who was to attach much of the nineteenth century's sensibility to the figure of the *flâneur,* personified by that superbly self-aware melancholic Baudelaire, spun much of his own sensibility out of his phantasmagorical, shrewd, subtle relation to cities. The street, the passage, the arcade, the labyrinth are recurrent themes in his literary essays and, notably, in the projected book on nineteenth-century Paris, as well as in his travel pieces and reminiscences. (Robert Walser, for whom walking was the center of his reclusive life and marvelous books, is a writer to whom one particularly wishes Benjamin had devoted a longer essay.) The only book of a discreetly autobiographical nature published in his lifetime was titled *One-Way Street.* Reminiscences of self are reminiscences of a place, and how he positions himself in it, navigates around it.

"Not to find one's way about in a city is of little interest," begins his still untranslated *A Berlin Childhood Around the Turn of the Century.* "But to lose one's way in a city, as one loses one's way in a forest, requires practice. . . . I learned this art late in life: it fulfilled the dreams whose first traces were the labyrinths on the blotters of my exercise books." This passage also occurs in *A Berlin Chronicle,* after Benjamin suggests how much practice it took to get lost, given an original sense of "impotence before the city." His goal is to be a competent street-map reader who knows how to stray. And to locate himself, with imaginary maps. Elsewhere in *Berlin Chronicle* Benjamin relates that for years he had played with the idea of mapping his life. For this map, which he imagined as gray, he had devised a colorful system of signs that "clearly marked in the houses of my friends and girl friends, the assembly halls of various collectives, from the 'debating chambers' of the Youth Movement to the gathering places of the Communist youth, the hotel and brothel rooms that I knew for one night, the decisive benches in the Tiergarten, the ways to different schools and the graves that I saw filled, the sites of prestigious cafés whose long-forgotten names daily

crossed our lips." Once, waiting for someone in the Café des Deux Magots in Paris, he relates, he managed to draw a diagram of his life: it was like a labyrinth, in which each important relationship figures as "an entrance to the maze."

The recurrent metaphors of maps and diagrams, memories and dreams, labyrinths and arcades, vistas and panoramas, evoke a certain vision of cities as well as a certain kind of life. Paris, Benjamin writes, "taught me the art of straying." The revelation of the city's true nature came not in Berlin but in Paris, where he stayed frequently throughout the Weimar years, and lived as a refugee from 1933 until his suicide while trying to escape from France in 1940—more exactly, the Paris reimagined in the Surrealist narratives (Breton's *Nadja,* Aragon's *Le paysan de Paris*). With these metaphors, he is indicating a general problem about orientation, and erecting a standard of difficulty and complexity. (A labyrinth is a place where one gets lost.) He is also suggesting a notion about the forbidden, and how to gain access to it: through an act of the mind that is the same as a physical act. "Whole networks of streets were opened up under the auspices of prostitution," he writes in *Berlin Chronicle,* which begins by invoking an Ariadne, the whore who leads this son of rich parents for the first time across "the threshold of class." The metaphor of the labyrinth also suggests Benjamin's idea of obstacles thrown up by his own temperament.

The influence of Saturn makes people "apathetic, indecisive, slow," he writes in *The Origin of German Trauerspiel* (1928). Slowness is one characteristic of the melancholic temperament. Blundering is another, from noticing too many possibilities, from not noticing one's lack of practical sense. And stubbornness, from the longing to be superior—on one's own terms. Benjamin recalls his stubbornness during childhood walks with his mother, who would turn insignificant items of conduct into tests of his aptitude for practical life, thereby reinforcing what was inept ("my inability even today to make a cup of coffee") and dreamily recalcitrant in his nature. "My habit of seeming slower, more maladroit, more stupid than I am, had its origin in such walks, and has the great attendant danger of making me think myself quicker, more dexterous, and shrewder than I am." And from this stubbornness comes, "above all, a gaze that appears to see not a third of what it takes in."

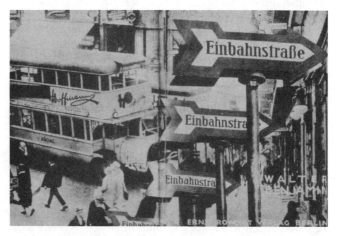

Dust jacket of Einbahnstraße (One-Way Street).

One-Way Street distills the experiences of the writer and lover (it is dedicated to Asja Lacis, who "cut it through the author"), experiences that can be guessed at in the opening words on the writer's situation, which sound the theme of revolutionary moralism, and the final **"To the Planetarium,"** a paean to the technological wooing of nature and to sexual ecstasy. Benjamin could write about himself more directly when he started from memories, not contemporary experiences; when he writes about himself as a child. At that distance, childhood, he can survey his life as a space that can be mapped. The candor and the surge of painful feelings in ***Berlin Childhood*** and ***Berlin Chronicle*** become possible precisely because Benjamin has adopted a completely digested, analytical way of relating the past. It evokes events for the reactions to the events, places for the emotions one has deposited in the places, other people for the encounter with oneself, feelings and behavior for intimations of future passions and failures contained in them. Fantasies of monsters loose in the large apartment while his parents entertain their friends prefigure his revulsion against his class; the dream of being allowed to sleep as long as he wants, instead of having to get up early to go to school, will be fulfilled when—after his book on the *Trauerspiel* failed to qualify him for a university lectureship—he realizes that "his hopes of a position and a secure livelihood had always been in vain"; his way of walking with his mother, "with pedantic care" keeping one step behind her, prefigures his "sabotage of real social existence."

Benjamin regards everything he chooses to recall in his past as prophetic of the future, because the work of memory (reading oneself backward, he called it) collapses time. There is no chronological ordering of his reminiscences, for which he disavows the name of autobiography, because time is irrelevant. ("Autobiography has to do with time, with sequence and what makes up the continuous flow of life," he writes in ***Berlin Chronicle.*** "Here, I am talking of a space, of moments and discontinuities.") Benjamin, the translator of Proust, wrote fragments of an opus that could be called *A la recherche des espaces perdus.* Memory, the staging of the past, turns the flow of events into tableaux. Benjamin is not trying to recover his past but to understand it: to condense it into its spatial forms, its premonitory structures.

For the baroque dramatists, he writes in ***The Origin of German Trauerspiel,*** "chronological movement is grasped and analyzed in a spatial image." The book on the *Trauerspiel* is not only Benjamin's first account of what it means to convert time into space; it is where he explains most clearly what feeling underlies this move. Awash in melancholic awareness of "the disconsolate chronicle of world history," a process of incessant decay, the baroque dramatists seek to escape from history and restore the "timelessness" of paradise. The seventeenth-century baroque sensibility had a "panoramatic" conception of history: "history merges into the setting." In ***Berlin Childhood*** and ***Berlin Chronicle,*** Benjamin merges his life into a setting. The successor to the baroque stage set is the Surrealist city: the metaphysical landscape in whose dreamlike spaces people have "a brief, shadowy existence," like the nineteen-year-old poet whose suicide, the great sorrow of Benjamin's student years, is condensed in the memory of rooms that the dead friend inhabited.

Benjamin's recurrent themes are, characteristically, means of spatializing the world: for example, his notion of ideas and experiences as ruins. To understand something is to understand its topography, to know how to chart it. And to know how to get lost.

For the character born under the sign of Saturn, time is the medium of constraint, inadequacy, repetition, mere fulfillment. In time, one is only what one is: what one has always been. In space, one can be another person. Benjamin's poor sense of direction and inability to read a street map become his love of travel and his mastery of the art of straying. Time does not give one much leeway: it thrusts us forward from behind, blows us through the narrow funnel of the present into the future. But space is broad, teeming with possibilities, positions, intersections, passages, detours, U-turns, dead ends, one-way streets. Too many possibilities, indeed. Since the Saturnine temperament is slow, prone to indecisiveness, sometimes one has to cut one's way through with a knife. Sometimes one ends by turning the knife against oneself.

The mark of the Saturnine temperament is the self-conscious and unforgiving relation to the self, which can never be taken for granted. The self is a text—it has to be deciphered. (Hence, this is an apt temperament for intellectuals.) The self is a project, something to be built. (Hence, this is an apt temperament for artists and martyrs, those who court "the purity and beauty of a failure," as Benjamin says of Kafka.) And the process of building a self and its works is always too slow. One is always in arrears to oneself.

Things appear at a distance, come forward slowly. In ***Berlin Childhood,*** he speaks of his "propensity for seeing everything I care about approach me from far away"—the way, often ill as a child, he imagined the hours approaching his sickbed. "This is perhaps the origin of what others call patience in me, but which in truth does not resemble any virtue." (Of course, others did experience it as patience, as a virtue. Scholem has described him as "the most patient human being I ever came to know.")

But something like patience is needed for the melancholic's labors of decipherment. Proust, as Benjamin notes, was excited by "the secret language of the salons"; Benjamin was drawn to more compact codes. He collected emblem books, liked to make up anagrams, played with pseudonyms. His taste for pseudonyms well antedates his need as a German-Jewish refugee, who from 1933 to 1936 continued to publish reviews in German magazines under the name of Detlev Holz, the name he used to sign the last book to appear in his lifetime, ***Deutsche Menschen,*** published in Switzerland in 1936. In the amazing text written in Ibiza in 1933, ***"Agesilaus Santander,"*** Benjamin speaks of his fantasy of having a secret name; the name of this text—which turns on the figure in the Klee drawing he owned, "Angelus Novus"—is, as Scholem has pointed out, an anagram of *Der Angelus Santanas.* He was an "uncanny" graphologist, Scholem reports, though "later on he tended to conceal his gift."

Dissimulation, secretiveness appear a necessity to the melancholic. He has complex, often veiled relations with others. These feelings of superiority, of inadequacy, of baffled feeling, of not being able to get what one wants, or even name it properly (or consistently) to oneself—these can be, it is felt they ought to be, masked by friendliness, or the most scrupulous manipulation. Using a word that was also applied to Kafka by those who knew him, Scholem speaks of "the almost Chinese courtesy" that characterized Benjamin's relations with people. But one is not surprised to learn, of the man who could justify Proust's "invectives against friendship," that Benjamin could also drop friends brutally, as he did his comrades from the Youth Movement, when they no longer interested him. Nor is one surprised to learn that this fastidious, intransigent, fiercely serious man could also flatter people he probably did not think his equals, that he could let himself be "baited" (his own word) and condescended to by Brecht on his visits to Denmark. This prince of the intellectual life could also be a courtier.

Benjamin analyzed both roles in *The Origin of German Trauerspiel* by the theory of melancholy. One characteristic of the Saturnine temperament is slowness: "The tyrant falls on account of the sluggishness of his emotions." "Another trait of the predominance of Saturn," says Benjamin, is "faithlessness." This is represented by the character of the courtier in baroque drama, whose mind is "fluctuation itself." The manipulativeness of the courtier is partly a "lack of character"; partly it "reflects an inconsolable, despondent surrender to an impenetrable conjunction of baleful constellations [that] seem to have taken on a massive, almost thing-like cast." Only someone identifying with this sense of historical catastrophe, this degree of despondency, would have explained why the courtier is not to be despised. His faithlessness to his fellow men, Benjamin says, corresponds to the "deeper, more contemplative faith" he keeps with material emblems.

What Benjamin describes could be understood as simple pathology: the tendency of the melancholic temperament to project its inner torpor outward, as the immutability of misfortune, which is experienced as "massive, almost thing-like." But his argument is more daring: he perceives that the deep transactions between the melancholic and the world always take place with things (rather than with people); and that these are genuine transactions, which reveal meaning. Precisely because the melancholy character is haunted by death, it is melancholics who best know how to read the world. Or, rather, it is the world which yields itself to the melancholic's scrutiny, as it does to no one else's. The more lifeless things are, the more potent and ingenious can be the mind which contemplates them.

If this melancholy temperament is faithless to people, it has good reason to be faithful to things. Fidelity lies in accumulating things—which appear, mostly, in the form of fragments or ruins. ("It is common practice in baroque literature to pile up fragments incessantly," Benjamin writes.) Both the baroque and Surrealism, sensibilities with which Benjamin felt a strong affinity, see reality as things. Benjamin describes the baroque as a world of things (emblems, ruins) and spatialized ideas ("Allegories are, in the realm of thought, what ruins are in the realm of things"). The genius of Surrealism was to generalize with ebullient candor the baroque cult of ruins; to perceive that the nihilistic energies of the modern era make everything a ruin or fragment—and therefore collectible. A world whose past has become (by definition) obsolete, and whose present churns out instant antiques, invites custodians, decoders, and collectors.

As one kind of collector himself, Benjamin remained faithful to things—as things. According to Scholem, building his library, which included many first editions and rare books, was "his most enduring personal passion." Inert in the face of thing-like disaster, the melancholy temperament is galvanized by the passions aroused by privileged objects. Benjamin's books were not only for use, professional tools; they were contemplative objects, stimuli for reverie. His library evokes "memories of the cities in which I found so many things: Riga, Naples, Munich, Danzig, Moscow, Florence, Basel, Paris . . . memories of the rooms where these books had been housed. . . . " Bookhunting, like the sexual hunt, adds to the geography of pleasure—another reason for strolling about in the world. In collecting, Benjamin experienced what in himself was clever, successful, shrewd, unabashedly passionate. "Collectors are people with a tactical instinct"—like courtiers.

Apart from first editions and baroque emblem books, Benjamin specialized in children's books and books written by the mad. "The great works which meant so much to him," reports Scholem, "were placed in bizarre patterns next to the most out-of-the-way writings and oddities." The odd arrangement of the library is like the strategy of Benjamin's work, in which a Surrealist-inspired eye for the treasures of meaning in the ephemeral, discredited, and neglected worked in tandem with his loyalty to the traditional canon of learned taste.

He liked finding things where nobody was looking. He drew from the obscure, disdained German baroque drama elements of the modern (that is to say, his own) sensibility: the taste for allegory, Surrealist shock effects, discontinuous utterance, the sense of historical catastrophe. "These stones were the bread of my imagination," he wrote about Marseilles—the most recalcitrant of cities to that imagination, even when helped by a dose of hashish. Many expected references are absent in Benjamin's work—he didn't like to read what everybody was reading. He preferred the doctrine of the four temperaments as a psychological theory to Freud. He preferred being a communist, or trying to be one, without reading Marx. This man who read virtually everything, and had spent fifteen years sympathizing with revolutionary communism, had barely looked into Marx until the late 1930s. (He was reading *Capital* on his visit to Brecht in Denmark in the summer of 1938.)

His sense of strategy was one of his points of identification with Kafka, a kindred would-be tactician, who "took precautions against the interpretation of his writing." The whole point of the Kafka stories, Benjamin argues, is that they have *no* definite, symbolic meaning. And he was fascinated by the very different, un-Jewish sense of ruse practiced by Brecht, the anti-Kafka of his imagination. (Predictably, Brecht disliked Benjamin's great essay on Kafka intensely.) Brecht, with the little wooden donkey near his desk from whose neck hung the sign "I, too, must understand it," represented for Benjamin, an admirer of esoteric religious texts, the possibly more potent ruse of reducing complexity, of making everything clear. Benjamin's "masochistic" (the word is Siegfried Kracauer's) relation to Brecht, which most of his friends deplored, shows the extent to which he was fascinated by this possibility.

Benjamin's propensity is to go against the usual interpretation. "All the decisive blows are struck left-handed," as he says in *One-Way Street.* Precisely because he saw that "all human knowledge takes the form of interpretation," he understood the importance of being against interpretation wherever it is obvious. His most common strategy is to drain symbolism out of some things, like the Kafka stories or *Goethe's "Elective Affinities"* (texts where everybody agrees it is there), and pour it into others, where nobody suspects its existence (such as the German baroque plays, which he reads as allegories of historical pessimism). "Each book is a tactic," he wrote. In a letter to a friend, he claimed for his writings, only partly facetiously, forty-nine levels of meaning. For moderns as much as for cabalists, nothing is straightforward. Everything is—at the least—difficult. "Ambiguity displaces authenticity in all things," he wrote in *One-Way Street.* What is most foreign to Benjamin is anything like ingenuousness: "the 'unclouded,' 'innocent' eye has become a lie."

Much of the originality of Benjamin's arguments owes to his microscopic gaze (as his friend and disciple Theodor Adorno called it), combined with his indefatigable command over theoretical perspectives. "It was the small things that attracted him most," writes Scholem. He loved old toys, postage stamps, picture postcards, and such playful miniaturizations of reality as the winter world inside a glass globe that snows when it is shaken. His own handwriting was almost microscopic, and his never realized ambition, Scholem reports, was to get a hundred lines on a sheet of paper. (The ambition was realized by Robert Walser, who used to transcribe the manuscripts of his stories and novels as micrograms, in a truly microscopic script.) Scholem relates that when he visited Benjamin in Paris in August 1927 (the first time the two friends had seen each other since Scholem emigrated to Palestine in 1923), Benjamin dragged him to an exhibit of Jewish ritual objects at the Musée Cluny to show him "two grains of wheat on which a kindred soul had inscribed the complete Shema Israel."

To miniaturize is to make portable—the ideal form of possessing things for a wanderer, or a refugee. Benjamin, of course, was both a wanderer, on the move, and a collector, weighed down by things; that is, passions. To miniaturize is to conceal. Benjamin was drawn to the extremely small as he was to whatever had to be deciphered: emblems, anagrams, handwriting. To miniaturize means to make useless. For what is so grotesquely reduced is, in a sense, liberated from its meaning—its tininess being the outstanding thing about it. It is both a whole (that is, complete) and a fragment (so tiny, the wrong scale). It becomes an object of disinterested contemplation or reverie. Love of the small is a child's emotion, one colonized by Surrealism. The Paris of the Surrealists is "a little world," Benjamin observes; so is the photograph, which Surrealist taste discovered as an enigmatic, even perverse, rather than a merely intelligible or beautiful, object, and about which Benjamin wrote with such originality. The melancholic always feels threatened by the dominion of the thing-like, but Surrealist taste mocks these terrors. Surrealism's great gift to sensibility was to make melancholy cheerful.

"The only pleasure the melancholic permits himself, and it is a powerful one, is allegory," Benjamin wrote in *The Origin of German Trauerspiel.* Indeed, he asserted, allegory is the way of reading the world typical of melancholics, and quoted Baudelaire: "Everything for me becomes Allegory." The process which extracts meaning from the petrified and insignificant, allegory, is the characteristic method of the German baroque drama and of Baudelaire, Benjamin's major subjects; and, transmuted into philosophical argument and the micrological analysis of things, the method Benjamin practiced himself.

The melancholic sees the world itself become a thing: refuge, solace, enchantment. Shortly before his death, Benjamin was planning an essay about miniaturization as a device of fantasy. It seems to have been a continuation of an old plan to write on Goethe's "The New Melusina" (in *Wilhelm Meister*), which is about a man who falls in love with a woman who is actually a tiny person, temporarily granted normal size, and unknowingly carries around with him a box containing the miniature kingdom of which she is the princess. In Goethe's tale, the world is reduced to a collectible thing, an object, in the most literal sense.

Like the box in Goethe's tale, a book is not only a fragment of the world but itself a little world. The book is a miniaturization of the world, which the reader inhabits. In *Berlin Chronicle,* Benjamin evokes his childhood rapture: "You did not read books through; you dwelt, abided between their lines." To reading, the delirium of the child, was eventually added writing, the obsession of the adult. The most praiseworthy way of acquiring books is by writing them, Benjamin remarks in an essay called **"Unpacking My Library."** And the best way to understand them is also to enter their space: one never really understands a book unless one copies it, he says in *One-Way Street,* as one never understands a landscape from an airplane but only by walking through it.

"The amount of meaning is in exact proportion to the presence of death and the power of decay," Benjamin writes in the *Trauerspiel* book. This is what makes it possible to find meaning in one's own life, in "the dead occurrences of the past which are euphemistically known as experience." Only because the past is dead is one able to read it. Only because history is fetishized in physical objects can one understand it. Only because the book is a world can one enter it. The book for him was another space in which to stroll. For the character born under the sign of Saturn, the true impulse when one is being looked at is to cast down one's eyes, look in a corner. Better, one can lower one's head to one's notebook. Or put one's head behind the wall of a book.

It is characteristic of the Saturnine temperament to blame its undertow of inwardness on the will. Convinced that the will is weak, the melancholic may make extravagant efforts to develop it. If these efforts are successful, the resulting hypertrophy of will usually takes the form of a compulsive devotion to work. Thus Baudelaire, who suffered constantly from "acedia, the malady of monks," ended many letters and his *Intimate Journals* with the most impassioned pledges to work more, to work uninterruptedly, to do nothing but work. (Despair over "every defeat of the will"—Baudelaire's phrase again—is a characteristic complaint of modern artists and intellectuals, particularly of those who are both.) One is condemned to work; otherwise, one might not do anything at all. Even the dreaminess of the melancholic temperament is harnessed to work, and the melancholic may try to cultivate phantasmagorical states, like dreams, or seek the access to concentrated states of attention offered by drugs. Surrealism simply puts a positive accent on what Baudelaire experienced so negatively: it does not deplore the guttering of volition but raises it to an ideal, proposing that dream states may be relied on to furnish all the material needed for work.

Benjamin, always working, always trying to work more, speculated a good deal on the writer's daily existence. *One-Way Street* has several sections which offer recipes for work: the best conditions, timing, utensils. Part of the impetus for the large correspondence he conducted was to chronicle, report on, confirm the existence of work. His instincts as a collector served him well. Learning was a form of collecting, as in the quotations and excerpts from daily reading which Benjamin accumulated in notebooks that he carried everywhere and from which he would read aloud to friends. Thinking was also a form of collecting, at least in its preliminary stages. He conscientiously logged stray ideas; developed mini-essays in letters to friends; rewrote plans for future projects; noted his dreams (several are recounted in *One-Way Street*); kept numbered lists of all the books he read. (Scholem recalls seeing, on his second and last visit to Benjamin in Paris, in 1938, a notebook of current reading in which Marx's *Eighteenth Brumaire* is listed as No. 1649.)

How does the melancholic become a hero of will? Through the fact that work can become like a drug, a compulsion. ("Thinking which is an eminent narcotic," he wrote in the essay on Surrealism.) In fact, melancholics make the best addicts, for the true addictive experience is always a solitary one. The hashish sessions of the late 1920s, supervised by a doctor friend, were prudent stunts, not acts of self-surrender; material for the writer, not escape from the exactions of the will. (Benjamin considered the book he wanted to write on hashish one of his most important projects.)

The need to be solitary—along with bitterness over one's loneliness—is characteristic of the melancholic. To get work done, one must be solitary—or, at least, not bound to any permanent relationship. Benjamin's negative feelings about marriage are clear in the essay on *Goethe's "Elective Affinities."* His heroes—Kierkegaard, Baudelaire, Proust, Kafka, Kraus—never married; and Scholem reports that Benjamin came to regard his own marriage (he was married in 1917, estranged from his wife after 1921, and divorced in 1930) "as fatal to himself." The world of nature, and of natural relationships, is perceived by the melancholic temperament as less than seductive. The self-portrait in *Berlin Childhood* and *Berlin Chronicle* is of a wholly alienated son; as husband and father (he had a son, born in 1918, who emigrated to England with Benjamin's ex-wife in the mid-1930s), he appears to have simply not known what to do with these relationships. For the melancholic, the natural, in the form of family ties, introduces the falsely subjective, the sentimental; it is a drain on the will, on one's independence; on one's freedom to concentrate on work. It also presents a challenge to one's humanity to which the melancholic knows, in advance, he will be inadequate.

The style of work of the melancholic is immersion, total concentration. Either one is immersed, or attention floats away. As a writer, Benjamin was capable of extraordinary concentration. He was able to research and write *The Origin of German Trauerspiel* in two years; some of it, he

boasts in *Berlin Chronicle,* was written in long evenings at a café, sitting close to a jazz band. But although Benjamin wrote prolifically—in some periods turning out work every week for the German literary papers and magazines—it proved impossible for him to write a normal-sized book again. In a letter in 1935, Benjamin speaks of "the Saturnine pace" of writing *Paris, Capital of the Nineteenth Century,* which he had begun in 1927 and thought could be finished in two years. His characteristic form remained the essay. The melancholic's intensity and exhaustiveness of attention set natural limits to the length at which Benjamin could develop his ideas. His major essays seem to end just in time, before they self-destruct.

His sentences do not seem to be generated in the usual way; they do not entail. Each sentence is written as if it were the first, or the last. ("A writer must stop and restart with every new sentence," he says in the Prologue to *The Origin of German Trauerspiel.*) Mental and historical processes are rendered as conceptual tableaux; ideas are transcribed in extremis and the intellectual perspectives are vertiginous. His style of thinking and writing, incorrectly called aphoristic, might better be called freeze-frame baroque. This style was torture to execute. It was as if each sentence had to say everything, before the inward gaze of total concentration dissolved the subject before his eyes. Benjamin was probably not exaggerating when he told Adorno that each idea in his book on Baudelaire and nineteenth-century Paris "had to be wrested away from a realm in which madness lies."

Something like the dread of being stopped prematurely lies behind these sentences as saturated with ideas as the surface of a baroque painting is jammed with movement. In a letter to Adorno in 1935, Benjamin describes his transports when he first read Aragon's *Le paysan de Paris,* the book that inspired *Paris, Capital of the Nineteenth Century:* "I would never read more than two or three pages in bed of an evening because the pounding of my heart was so loud that I had to let the book fall from my hands. What a warning!" Cardiac failure is the metaphoric limit of Benjamin's exertions and passions. (He suffered from a heart ailment.) And cardiac sufficiency is a metaphor he offers for the writer's achievement. In the essay in praise of Karl Kraus, Benjamin writes:

> If style is the power to move freely in the length and breadth of linguistic thinking without falling into banality, it is attained chiefly by the cardiac strength of great thoughts, which drives the blood of language through the capillaries of syntax into the remotest limbs.

Thinking, writing are ultimately questions of stamina. The melancholic, who feels he lacks will, may feel that he needs all the destructive energies he can muster.

"Truth resists being projected into the realm of knowledge," Benjamin writes in *The Origin of German Trauerspiel.* His dense prose registers that resistance, and leaves no space for attacking those who distribute lies. Benjamin considered polemic beneath the dignity of a truly philosophical style, and sought instead what he called "the fullness of concentrated positivity"—the essay on *Goethe's "Elective Affinities,"* with its devastating refutation of the critic and Goethe biographer Friedrich Gundolf, being the one exception to this rule among his major writings. But his awareness of the ethical utility of polemic made him appreciate that one-man Viennese public institution, Karl Kraus, a writer whose facility, stridency, love of the aphoristic, and indefatigable polemic energies make him so unlike Benjamin.

The essay on Kraus is Benjamin's most passionate and perverse defense of the life of the mind. "The perfidious reproach of being 'too intelligent' haunted him throughout his life," Adorno has written. Benjamin defended himself against this philistine defamation by bravely raising the standard of the "inhumanity" of the intellect, when it is properly—that is, ethically—employed. "The life of letters is existence under the aegis of mere mind as prostitution is existence under the aegis of mere sexuality," he wrote. This is to celebrate both prostitution (as Kraus did, because mere sexuality was sexuality in a pure state) and the life of letters, as Benjamin did, using the unlikely figure of Kraus, because of "the genuine and demonic function of mere mind, to be a disturber of the peace." The ethical task of the modern writer is to be not a creator but a destroyer—a destroyer of shallow inwardness, the consoling notion of the universally human, dilettantish creativity, and empty phrases.

The writer as scourge and destroyer, portrayed in the figure of Kraus, he sketched with concision and even greater boldness in the allegorical **"The Destructive Character,"** also written in 1931. Scholem has written that the first of several times Benjamin contemplated suicide was in the summer of 1931. The second time was the following summer, when he wrote **"Agesilaus Santander."** The Apollonian scourge whom Benjamin calls the destructive character

> is always blithely at work . . . has few needs . . . has no interest in being understood . . . is young and cheerful . . . and feels not that life is worth living but that suicide is not worth the trouble.

It is a kind of conjuration, an attempt by Benjamin to draw the destructive elements of his Saturnine character outward—so that they are not self-destructive.

Benjamin is not referring just to his own destructiveness. He thought that there was a peculiarly modern temptation to suicide. In **"The Paris of the Second Empire in Baudelaire,"** he wrote:

> The resistance which modernity offers to the natural productive élan of a person is out of proportion to his strength. It is understandable if a person grows tired and takes refuge in death. Modernity must be under the sign of suicide, an act which seals a heroic will. . . . It is *the* achievement of modernity in the realm of passions. . . .

Suicide is understood as a response of the heroic will to the defeat of the will. The only way to avoid suicide, Benjamin suggests, is to be beyond heroism, beyond efforts of the will. The destructive character cannot feel trapped, because "he sees ways everywhere." Cheerfully engaged in reducing what exists to rubble, he "positions himself at the crossroads."

Benjamin's portrait of the destructive character would evoke a kind of Siegfried of the mind—a high-spirited, childlike brute under the protection of the gods—had this apocalyptic pessimism not been qualified by the irony always within the range of the Saturnine temperament.

Irony is the positive name which the melancholic gives to his solitude, his asocial choices. In **One-Way Street** Benjamin hailed the irony that allows individuals to assert the right to lead lives independent of the community as "the most European of all accomplishments," and observed that it had completely deserted Germany. Benjamin's taste for the ironic and the self-aware put him off most of recent German culture: he detested Wagner, despised Heidegger, and scorned the frenetic vanguard movements of Weimar Germany such as Expressionism.

Passionately, but also ironically, Benjamin placed himself at the crossroads. It was important for him to keep his many "positions" open: the theological, the Surrealist/aesthetic, the communist. One position corrects another; he needed them all. Decisions, of course, tended to spoil the balance of these positions, vacillation kept everything in place. The reason he gave for his delay in leaving France, when he last saw Adorno in early 1938, was that "there are still positions here to defend."

Benjamin thought the freelance intellectual was a dying species anyway, made no less obsolete by capitalist society than by revolutionary communism; indeed, he felt that he was living in a time in which everything valuable was the last of its kind. He thought Surrealism was the last intelligent moment of the European intelligentsia, an appropriately destructive, nihilistic kind of intelligence. In his essay on Kraus, Benjamin asks rhetorically: Does Kraus stand on the frontier of a new age? "Alas, by no means. For he stands on the threshold of the Last Judgment." Benjamin is thinking of himself. At the Last Judgment, the Last Intellectual—that Saturnine hero of modern culture, with his ruins, his defiant visions, his reveries, his unquenchable gloom, his downcast eyes—will explain that he took many "positions" and defended the life of the mind to the end, as righteously and inhumanly as he could. (pp. 110-34)

> *Susan Sontag, "Under the Sign of Saturn," in her* Under the Sign of Saturn, *Farrar, Straus and Giroux, 1980, pp. 109-34.*

Richard Wolin   (essay date 1982)

[*In the following excerpt, Wolin comments on the originality of Benjamin's thought, especially as it is displayed in his works concerning the philosophy of history.*]

The posthumous fate of Benjamin's lifework confirms his own conviction that every product of culture experiences an autonomous post-history by virtue of which it transcends its determinate point of origin, his belief that, "The work is the death-mask of the conception." Since the republication of his works began in the 1950s, concerted attempts have been launched from all sides to categorize his thinking according to a variety of rubrics—literary, theological, Marxist—all of which merit partial validity, but none of which captures the truth in its entirety. For Benjamin was all of these things and none of them. His *oeuvre* does not present itself as a harmonious synthesis of the aforementioned tendencies, nor does it remain consistent with any of these taken individually. Instead, it takes on the form of a series of contradictions, a network of discontinuous extremes—in no uncertain terms, it assumes the form of a *ruin*. The words Benjamin used to summarize his feelings toward Kafka in a letter to Scholem could just as well have been employed to describe his own work: "To do justice to the figure of Kafka in its purity and peculiar beauty, one must never lose sight of one thing: it is the purity and beauty of a failure." Yet, to speak of the "failure" of Benjamin's work means the following: that it was precisely in terms of his incapacity to unite the extremes of his thought, in his unwillingness to subordinate the materialist side to the theological or vice versa, that the enigmatic character, the majesty (yes, ruins too can be majestic), the moment of his thought that remains living resides. Insofar as he refused to close prematurely the gap between these two dimensions, he escaped the fate of being merely one more in a long line of Marxist or theological thinkers. His theoretical strivings perpetually transcended the staleness of academic convention as well as all heteronomous methodological imperatives which seek to level the being-in-itself of things to standards which are posited abstractly by the knowing subject. In this way he sought to maintain a fundamental, almost precategorical allegiance to things themselves and their truth. It was, however, the insights of the philosopher to which Benjamin's own work in all its phases inexorably drew near. His concerns were not those of a philosopher in the traditional sense; rather, the question which ceaselessly animated his writings was what form philosophy must take in an age in which systematic philosophy has become impossible. Thus, he sought to latch on to those phenomena which had somehow miraculously escaped the all-enveloping web of social integration—childhood memories, drug experiences; above all, however, literary texts—and thereby emancipate the utopian potential that lay embedded therein. Like no philosopher before him, Benjamin elected to operate at a far remove from the so-called "great questions" of philosophy and to attempt nevertheless to force the most apparently ephemeral and insignificant phenomena to yield knowledge equivalent in stature to the most sublime metaphysical truth. (pp. 251-52)

The significance of "extremes" for Benjamin's thinking cannot be overestimated, not only in the more blatant sense of the antinomy between materialism and theology which dominated his work after 1925, but also in his very choice of objects of philosophical investigation. *Trauerspiel* and surrealism, arcades and Kafka, are all rather unlikely topics of philosophical study which nevertheless occupied center stage in Benjamin's work. For Benjamin, who interpreted the continuum of history as being homogeneous and mythical, as a pageant in which the rulers incessantly asserted and reasserted their stranglehold over the oppressed—a sort of *List der Vernunft* stood on its head—the counterimages to "natural history" were to be sought in those figures and traces which history had subjected to scorn, derision, or the oblivion of forgetting. For Benjamin, the eternal, the significant, indeed resembled more closely the "ruffles of a dress than an idea." It was the malcontents and maladapted of history—Baudelaire, Proust, Kafka—with whom he identified so profoundly and whose truths he struggled to immortalize in face of the transient nature of historical memory. From the excrescences and extremes of historical life, he sought to cull what was of lasting value for humanity; and thus in his own small way contribute to the process of resurrecting the dead and forgotten which would only be completed with the coming of the Messiah. Once the extremes have been gathered, wrenched from their original historical

context—be it in the case of an individual lifework or a determinate historical epoch such as seventeenth-century Germany or nineteenth-century France—the goal was not to seek their average or common denominator, which would merely depotentiate them, but merely to set them in the liberating context of a philosophically informed configuration; and by virtue of the idea to which this configuration gave rise, the extremes would accede to their own inherent meaning (their "origin") and thereby stand *redeemed.* (p. 253)

[I] would like to focus more closely on Benjamin's philosophy of history, especially on its implications for the traditions of Marxism and critical theory. Both traditions have in various ways already staked claims to his theoretical legacy. At the same time, I wish to proceed with the clear understanding that whereas these two traditions present extremely fruitful avenues along which his work might be pursued in the future, the sheer breadth—and imaginative force of his thought would preclude any attempt at wholesale assimilation within either of these theoretical currents. (pp. 253-54)

Benjamin's attitude towards the doctrines of historical materialism was neither consistent nor unequivocal. Altogether he displayed three different theoretical relations to Marxism. The first was embodied in the theory of Dialectical Images as articulated in the Arcades Exposé of 1935. There he sought to capture through the prism of Baudelaire's poetry the commingling of old and new forms of life in mid-nineteenth-century Paris in order to show how the "new" of the modern incessantly reverts to the always-the-same of myth:

> Novelty is a quality which does not depend on the use-value of the commodity. It is the source of the illusion which belongs inalienably to the images which the collective unconsciousness engenders. It is the quintessence of false consciousness, of which fashion is the tireless agent. This illusion of novelty is reflected, like one mirror in another, in the illusion of infinite sameness.

In his formulation of the concept of Dialectical Images, however, Benjamin attempted to envision a utopian dimension which compelled him to rely on the highly questionable Jungian conception of the "collective unconscious"; a reliance for which, as we have seen, Adorno sternly took him to task. Also, Benjamin's idea of Dialectical Images betrayed a strong indebtedness to the surrealist emphasis on the utopian value of dreams. As he contends at one important point in his argument, "The utilization of dream-elements in waking is a textbook example of dialectical thought." It is not too difficult to see from this remark that Benjamin's understanding of dialectics differed significantly from not only the traditional idealist and materialist versions, but every other existing version as well. The conception of historical materialism that served as the basis for his *Passagenarbeit* remained characteristically nonconformist and fanciful. Whereas this conception paved the way for discoveries and insights which would have certainly remained imperceptible from a traditional Marxist standpoint, it nevertheless seems reasonable to conjecture that Benjamin, even when he believed himself to be dutifully following in the footsteps of the historical materialist legacy, was in fact engaged in something quite different and unique.

This judgment is reconfirmed in the case of the second phase of Benjamin's development as a Marxist critic, in which he operated most narrowly in accordance with Brechtian principles. Under Brecht's guidance he temporarily relinquished the theory of Dialectical Images (many of whose aspects, such as shock, montage, etc., he had rediscovered in Brecht's theory of epic theater), and began concentrating intensively on more immediate political concerns centering around questions of aesthetic reception. The fruits of these labors were essays such as **"The Author as Producer"** and *The Work of Art in the Age of Mechanical Reproduction,* in which Benjamin argued for the definitive *Aufhebung* [termination] of autonomous culture and the necessity for the refunctioning of the bourgeois apparatus of cultural production along engaged, revolutionary lines. For the Benjamin of this period the power of "technique" in and of itself was deemed a sufficient indicator not only of "political tendency" but also of "aesthetic quality." Benjamin believed he could identify preliminary examples of the successful realization of this new aesthetics of commitment in Brecht's epic theater, Soviet journalism, and certain tendencies in the field of film, which, insofar as it was the most thoroughly technological of all the arts, was therefore considered the most "revolutionary." Yet, one must insist on the paradoxical fact that Benjamin's relevance for historical materialism is not to be discovered in those works where he considered himself to be operating most consistently according to Marxist convictions. The epistemological basis of both **"The Author as Producer"** and *The Work of Art* essay is a technological determinism, which is adopted from Marx's specification of the relationship between forces and relations of production in the Preface to the *Contribution to the Critique of Political Economy.* Benjamin sought to establish the absolute primacy of the forces of *aesthetic* production in the same way Marx attempted to do so for the forces of *economic* production. His efforts in this direction are thus vitiated by an extremely uncritical and reductionist reliance on orthodox Marxist dogmas. In this way he fell behind, in his rush to ensure immediate political relevance for his theory, the Western Marxism of Lukács and Korsch—not to mention that of critical theory—who had exposed those dogmas back in the early twenties. Hence, the Brechtian side of Benjamin's Janus-face demanded a sacrifice of theoretical integrity for the sake of political efficacy—a sacrifice from which no theory emerges unscathed. And despite all voluble, pseudo-radical clamor to the contrary, practice derives from theory, not vice versa.

Benjamin's earlier theory and certain aspects of his later materialist theory of experience serve as an important corrective to this tendency to elevate the political significance of art above all other moments. In his early work Benjamin attempted to show how genuine works of art displayed an autonomous post-history or afterlife, such that their truths refused to exhaust themselves in their own or successive epochs, and thus demanded critical interpretation anew with each passing generation. Works of art that possess an exclusively political significance, however, would prove devoid of that autonomy which differentiates them from mere life in general. By surrendering that element of autonomy, works of art would exhaust themselves in the here and now of the immediate present—in the language of reception aesthetics, the moment of their "effect"—and afterward become matters of indifference—as has proven the case with the great majority of so-called

committed works of art to date. Adorno has commented on this state of affairs as follows:

> The feigning of a true politics in the here and now, the freezing of historical relations which nowhere seem ready to melt, oblige the mind to go where it need not degrade itself. Today, every phenomenon of culture, even a model of integrity, is liable to be suffocated in the cultivation of kitsch. Yet paradoxically in the same epoch it is to works of art that has fallen the burden of wordlessly asserting what is barred to politics. . . . This is not a time for political art, but politics has migrated into autonomous art, and nowhere more so than where it appears to be politically dead.

These remarks remain even more relevant today. For with the dissolution of the attempt by the twentieth-century avant garde to merge art and life practice—an attempt initially motivated by a salutory revulsion against the complacency of *l'art pour l'art* in a world which begged for change—there has emerged with the phenomenon of postmodernism a new variety of aesthetic complacency, in which the distance between art and material life has been dissipated in an art which retains the anti-aesthetic trappings of authentic modernism but none of the substance. That is, what has transpired in the transition from modernism to postmodernism has been the *recuperation of the radical intentions* of modernism in an art which, though it formally takes its bearings from the modernism of the pre-World War II period, remains fully compatible with the marketing prerequisites of the culture industry. Thus, the destruction of the hiatus between art and life—which for the avant garde was synonymous with transferring the radical aesthetic values of modern art to the domain of everyday life itself—has taken place but *in reverse:* rather than having been aesthetically transfigured, material life has actually *absorbed* the radical promise of modernism, which in the guise of postmodernism becomes indistinguishable from fashion. As one critic [Jürgen Habermas] has recently observed: "When the containers of an autonomously developed cultural sphere are shattered, the contents get dispersed. Nothing remains from a desublimated meaning or a destructured form; an emancipatory effect does not follow." Ultimately then, the "dispersion" of autonomous culture within the heteronomous world of administered culture means a regression behind *l'art pour l'art,* which still preserved, despite and because of its asocial posture, a potential for otherness and negation in the very act of formally distancing itself from the functional imperatives of commodity society in general. For this reason society today would have more to fear from a radically articulated, de-aestheticized autonomous art than it would from a thoroughly culinary and ornamental postmodernism or a committed art staged for a bourgeois public sphere which has in effect become imaginary and mythical.

At the same time, upon closer scrutiny, the "dialectic of technique" embraced by Benjamin was itself hardly immune from metaphysical rudiments—a fact noted by Brecht in his diaries and which led to his negative assessment of *The Work of Art* essay. For in truth the structure of that essay is governed by two contrasting impulses, one speculative, the other materialist, and there is virtually no attempt made to link the two sides. The first part of the essay presents Benjamin's theory of the artistic aura, a phenomenon which has its origins in magical practices and doctrines. It is the aura which gives traditional works of art—be they religious or autonomous—a supernatural, transcendent quality, whose esoteric truth content is accessible only to elites (priests or connoisseurs). To be sure, up to this point in Benjamin's analysis there is little that would distinguish his essay as a genuinely materialist study and much to suggest that he had merely carried over motifs from his theological period and attempted to fit them into a materialist framework. On the other hand, the second half of the study consists of an unqualified endorsement of de-auraticized, mechanically reproduced arts such as film, with the last vestiges of speculative sentiment having been thoroughly purged. Somehow it is assumed—though the precise nature of the link is never specified—that the esoteric promise that is stored in the aura will be redeemed exoterically by mechanically reproduced art; a premise which suggests that there exists an essential *continuity* between these two species of art, and that the emancipatory potential of mechanically reproduced art is somehow dependent on its capacity to make good the utopian claims of auratic art. The interlacing of speculative and materialist motifs in the essay is thus much more thoroughgoing than it would appear initially—which suggests how little even in his most explicitly materialist studies Benjamin's thought was capable of parting definitively with metaphysical principles. When Scholem pointed out the glaring contradiction between the two parts of the essay to Benjamin in the late 1930s, he could only respond: "The philosophical unity you deem lacking between the two parts of my essay will be more effectively provided by the revolution than by me."

Hence, Benjamin's relationship to historical materialism was constantly fraught with tension, but at the same time it was precisely *because of* the "experimental" nature of this relationship rather than despite it that many of his essays in materialist criticism of the 1930s—especially the works on Leskov, Proust, Fuchs, and the second Baudelaire study—stand out as models which in many ways have yet to be surpassed. Marxism for Benjamin was therefore never a creed to be adopted *in toto,* but a way of thinking which represented an indispensable corrective to his earlier criticism, a vital confrontation with the idea that all facts of life are simultaneously sociohistorical facts, and that whoever elects to ignore this truth is living a life of illusion. Thus, while there is no reason to question the essential sincerity of his commitment to materialist principles of research, one finds nevertheless scattered throughout his letters and papers remarks such as the following, which point to the fundamental insufficiency of the Marxist world view taken by itself and the inevitable need to enhance it with a "metaphysical orientation":

> I have found the strongest propaganda imaginable for a materialist perspective not in the form of communist brochures, but rather in the "representative" works which have emerged in my field—literary history and criticism—from the bourgeois camp in the last twenty years. I have had as little to do with what has been produced in the academic ranks as with the monuments which a Gundolf or an [Ernst] Bertram have erected; and in order to separate myself early and clearly vis-à-vis the loathsome odes of this official and unofficial bustle [*Betrieb*], I did not find Marxist ways of thinking necessary—these I became acquainted with only

later—rather this I owe to the basic metaphysical orientation of my research.

Nowhere was the problematical character of his attitude toward the standpoint of historical materialism more evident than in the *Theses on the Philosophy of History,* his last extant writing and an autobiographical statement which itself represented the consummate "Dialectical Image" of his late thinking in its entirety: for in these Theses he located his own thought in a monadic, shock-charged Dialectic at a Standstill, in which the ultimate boundaries were established by the extremes of Marxism and theology. The *Theses* were originally intended to serve as the "theoretical armature" to the second Baudelaire essay, as Benjamin remarks to Horkheimer in a letter of February 1940; but as the accompanying notes and drafts demonstrate, what Benjamin had ultimately planned was a much more intricate and developed critique of the idea of "progress" in general—in both its Enlightenment and materialist variants. As was often the case with his more intimate, meta-theoretical reflections, Benjamin had no intention of publishing the *Theses:* "They would open the gate wide for enthusiastic misunderstanding." Nevertheless, their overwhelming significance for understanding his work as a whole is illustrated by his remark that they were something he had "kept to himself for twenty years."

It is above all, the first Thesis—the by now famous parable about the chess-playing "puppet in Turkish attire"—which represents the ultimate allegorical confession by Benjamin concerning his own theoretical relationship to the twin extremes of Marxism and theology:

> The story is told of an automaton constructed in such a way that it could play a winning game of chess, answering each move of an opponent with a countermove. A puppet in Turkish attire and with a hookah in its mouth sat before a chessboard placed on a large table. A system of mirrors created the illusion that this table was transparent on all sides. Actually, a little hunchback who was an expert chess player sat inside and guided the puppet's hand by means of strings. One can imagine a philosophical counterpart to this device. The puppet called "historical materialism" is to win all the time. It can easily be a match for anyone if it enlists the services of theology, which today, as we know, is wizened and has to keep out of sight.

The imagery of Benjamin's metaphor is highly revealing. According to this imagery, in order for the puppet "historical materialism" to be victorious it must enlist the services of theology—the little hunchback who is charged with the *ultimate* responsibility of pulling the strings and thus dictating the movements of the historical materialist "puppet." By way of this parable Benjamin seeks to call attention to the fact that historical materialism—especially in face of its manifest failure to meet the threat of fascism in the 1930s—remains in and of itself incapable of providing humanity with the full range of wisdom and understanding necessary to surmount the realm of historical necessity. This explicit return to the Messianic philosophy of history of his early work— . . . the content of the *Theses,* though more detailed, is nearly identical with that of the "Theologico-Political Fragment" of the early 1920s—signifies not a hasty appeal, made in an hour of historical despair, to a suprahistorical redeemer, but instead an acknowledgement of the fact that in its reliance on the Enlightenment myth of historical progress, historical materialism has remained a prisoner of the same logic it wanted to transcend. For in its Panglossian trust in the *historical necessity of socialism,* it has neglected the *negative, dark, and destructive side of the revolutionary process,* a side which evaporates in the forever optimistic prognosis concerning the imminent demise of the capitalist system. It is Benjamin's conviction therefore that Marxism has been lulled and seduced into a false sense of security based on the erroneous assumption that the forces of history are on its side; and thus he seeks to mobilize, in opposition to this fatal historical naïveté, the elements of distrust and pessimism, the powers of *"revolutionary nihilism,"* for the side of the revolutionary struggle. For this is an enemy whose diabolical nature it would be impossible to *over*-estimate. And thus in the fragments and sketches for the **Theses** Benjamin provides the following reflections on the relationship between destruction, history, and redemption:

> The destructive powers release those which lie in the idea of redemption.
>
> Three moments must be made to penetrate the foundations of the materialist view of history: the discontinuity of historical time; the destructive power of the working class; the tradition of the oppressed.
>
> The destructive or critical element in historiography receives its validity in the explosion of historical continuity. Authentic historiography does not select its object carelessly. It does not grasp it, it explodes it from the historical continuum. This destructive element in historiography must be understood as a reaction to a moment of danger which threatens equally the recipient of tradition *as well as* what is handed down [*dem Überlieferten*]. . . . In authentic historiography the redemptive impulse is as strong as the destructive impulse.

Benjamin's relevance for a nondogmatic and critical understanding of historical materialism therefore lies neither in the 1935 version of the theory of Dialectical Images nor in his advocacy of a technologically advanced, committed art, but instead in the "materialist theory of experience" whose consummate expression is the 1940 *Theses on the Philosophy of History.* The theory of Dialectical Images advanced here has renounced the mistaken tendency of the Arcades Exposé to view the Dialectical Image as a "dream" and returned to the original, authentic version of the theory as elaborated in *One-Way Street.* Moreover, in the materialist theory of experience developed in the late 1930s Benjamin had come round to correcting a crucial misconception of his Brechtian period, insofar as he now realized that for any materialist understanding of culture that seeks to be of value, it is essential to recognize that the contents of tradition contain a utopian claim, a *promesse de bonheur* ["promise of happiness"], and are not therefore something to be negated abstractly in a surfeit of revolutionary zeal. Thus, in the *Theses on the Philosophy of History* and related studies Benjamin reversed this earlier one-sided judgment against tradition. He realized that the erosion of the last remnants of tradition with the onslaught of rationalization and the capitalist fetishization of *nouveauté* ["novelty"] resulted in the catastrophic destruction of unrenewable meaning potentials;

meaning potentials that had been sedimented in the "great" works of culture, but also in the not so great—the forgotten allegories of the baroque era, Baudelaire's lyric versification of urbanism, and the stories, dances, and songs that for ages represented the mainstays of a vital popular culture. In these fragile relics of tradition the collective desires of unfree humanity found expression in the hope that one day some future generation would redeem the promises of a better life that it had been denied. As Benjamin states in a passage that is crucial for understanding his later materialist theory of experience:

> The past carries with it a temporal index by which it is referred to redemption. There is a secret agreement between past generations and the present one. Our coming was expected on earth. Like every generation that preceded us, we have been endowed with a *weak* Messianic power, a power to which the past has a claim. That claim cannot be settled cheaply.

It is precisely the *temporal index of redemption* encoded in the products of tradition, in which the guarantee of our "secret agreement" with past generations has been inscribed, that Benjamin sought to resuscitate and preserve in his final writings. As the nightmare of German fascism threatened to efface all remnants of tradition from the face of the earth, his task became more urgent and his tone all the more exhortatory—culminating in the apocalyptic pitch of the *Geschichtsphilosophische Thesen.* The powers of *redemptive criticism* were needed once again. Benjamin therefore sought to transpose his earlier esoteric theory of experience into an immanent, historical setting. He saw his mission as a historical materialist as one of redeeming endangered semantic potentials from the fate of oblivion that seemed ready at any moment to descend on them once and for all. It was the task of historical materialism to blast "now-times"—moments of a "Messianic cessation of happening"—out of the homogeneous and profane continuum of history; which meant "a revolutionary chance in the fight for the oppressed past"—"blasting a specific life out of the era or a specific work out of the lifework." "Cultural history" (Ranke, Dilthey, etc.) knows history only as the history of the victors, as progress in domination and oppression. Benjamin's theory of now-times seeks to break with this conception of progress in order to establish a *unique* relation to the past—i.e., one in which the rare and endangered images of redeemed life are separated out from the historical flow of eternal recurrence and allowed to shine forth on their own. For it is precisely in such now-times that the key to the redemption of the *historical past in its entirety* is enciphered. As Benjamin observes: "To be sure, only a redeemed humanity receives the fullness of its past—which is to say that only for a redeemed humanity has its past become citable in all its moments. Each moment it has lived becomes a citation *à l'ordre du jour*—and that day is Judgment Day."

For the later Benjamin, then, the concept of redemption, so paramount for his early work, has once again become central. In **"Some Motifs in Baudelaire"** it was the *correspondances* of Baudelaire's poetry that provided indications of how to recapture a long repressed *auratic* relation to nature. In **"The Storyteller"** the fluid continuum of experience characteristic of the world of the story was contrasted with the fragmented nature of experience in advanced industrial societies. And in the ***Theses on the Phi-***

losophy of History the task of the historical materialist becomes that of redeeming now-times from the oblivion of forgetting that incessantly threatens them. In these essays Benjamin no longer speaks of the *Aufhebung* of traditional bourgeois culture, an idea he entertained in **The Work of Art** essay and his commentaries on Brecht; rather it is the effort to preserve and render exoteric the secret utopian potential embedded in traditional works of culture that Benjamin views as the preeminent task of materialist criticism. The esoteric phraseology of his earlier conception of redemptive criticism has been cast aside in favor of a quasi-Marxian vocabulary, but in essence the two approaches are parallel. Nor could one say unequivocally that his later exercises in materialist criticism were possessed of a less abstruse or hermetic structure than his earlier studies of *Elective Affinities* or *Trauerspiel*. The materialist writings too were composed for a very select audience. The theme that unites these later studies in materialist criticism is the idea of *remembrance* (*Gedächtnis, Eingedenken*). For in face of the boundless and irrepressible triumph of the forces of rationalization in the modern era and the concomitant destruction of all traces of premodern, traditional life, Benjamin's great fear was that along with all remnants of tradition the all-important index of redemption which the past provides would also fall victim to the oblivion of forgetting—resulting in the most hollow and defective civilization imaginable, a civilization without origins, without memory. It was precisely the danger of this brave new world without tradition that he sought to counteract through the employment of the method of *"rettende Kritik"* in a new historical and exoteric context. For it is in the increasingly remote recesses of past life that the secret of redemption is inscribed. In 1940, Benjamin expresses this insight as follows:

> We know the Jews were prohibited from investigating the future. The Torah and the prayers instruct them in remembrance, however. This stripped the future of its magic, to which all those succumb who turn to soothsayers for enlightenment. This does not imply, however, that for the Jews the future turned into empty homogeneous time. For every second of time was the strait gate through which the Messiah might enter.

I would like to suggest that Benjamin's relevance for historical materialism is to be found in this late attempt to secularize the notion of redemptive criticism. His relevance lies precisely in the *reverential* attitude he assumes toward tradition, a position which to be sure stands in sharp contrast to most Marxist accounts. Benjamin's appreciation of the contents of tradition, his deep fears concerning the irretrievable decay of the semantic potentials embodied therein, serves therefore as a decisive corrective to the customary *devaluation* of the meaning of tradition characteristic of Marxist doctrines. That denigration of tradition echoes clearly in the standard Marxian dichotomy between "history" and "prehistory," which implies that all history before the advent of socialism would stand convicted of insubstantiality. One might go a step further. Perhaps the central conviction of revolutionaries from Robespierre to Lenin and beyond—that the idea of revolution implies the necessity to recast totally *all* elements of tradition (which are all, by definition, contaminated by the deficiencies of the *ancien régime*)—has been responsible for the totalitarian excesses which today seem inseparable from the very concept of "revolution."

While the idea of socialism as representing a decisive *break* with the historical past is certainly one that Benjamin would endorse, in the usual Marxist accounts the contents of tradition seem less dialectically preserved in the process of *Aufhebung* than merely *cancelled* and *suppressed*. The Marxist disdain for tradition is also evident in the unreflective employment of the method of ideology critique, in which cultural expressions are deemed illusory and valueless in and of themselves, mere epiphenomenal reflections of the economic infrastructure. Benjamin realized, however, that the lore of tradition stakes claims that the present can choose to ignore, but from which it will never be able to escape—for there is already too much of the past in us, and thus to deny the past is to deny part of ourselves. By such an understanding, he refutes these views. His studies in redemptive criticism demonstrate that the cultural remnants of tradition are in no way reducible to the status of epiphenomena, but contain a *promesse de bonheur* which future generations must preserve and redeem. (pp. 254-65)

I began these . . . remarks by speaking of the inconsummate character of Benjamin's lifework. The failures of his life however—his failure to habilitate, the failure of his work to get the reception it deserved among his contemporaries, his failure to complete his *Hauptwerk* on the Paris Arcades—were largely circumstantial in nature. There is also the admittedly ambivalent resolution of his general philosophical project itself: the attempt to combine the methods of materialism and metaphysics, to force the absolute to step forth from an unmediated constellation of material elements. The pre-Marxist **Trauerspiel** book exemplifies Benjamin's greatest achievement in this direction; one, however, whose idealist basis seemed incompatible with a truly exoteric, generalizable theory of experience. It was ultimately the weight of historical circumstances which compelled him to abandon this approach and seek a theory of knowledge that was consistent with materialist principles. Yet, in its traditional, scientistic versions, Marxism was diametrically opposed to the very substance of Benjamin's theoretical inclinations. Benjamin wished to downplay his originality, the initial genius he had shown as a literary critic, for the sake of more pressing political concerns, or at least to assimilate that originality to these concerns. It was, to be sure, a form of self-sacrifice, a self-sacrifice through which he sought at the same time to gain meaning for his life. Yet, this transformation of methodological focus also entailed a tacit and on occasion lethal subordination of theory to practice, a subordination which led to the problematical character of many of his later works. Yet, to desire for him to have lived or written in any other way would be to attempt to evade the real historical problems with which he found himself confronted. In *Negative Dialectics* Adorno has, in a polemical spirit, raised the by no means otiose question as to whether it would still be possible to write poetry in good conscience after Auschwitz. In a somewhat analogous manner, Benjamin came to view the critic's preoccupation with the ethereal realm of belles lettres as morally irresponsible in face of the impending threat of fascism. The philosophy of history penetrated the heart of his self-understanding as a theorist.

There is at the same time an "unaccountable" dimension of Benjamin's thinking which reveals great affinities with the concept of freedom. It is that aspect of his thought that is "nameless," that aspect which defies all traditional rubrics of intellectual categorization. A cursory glance at his writings of the 1930s would testify to the difficulties of assimilating his views in any organic way to the traditional concepts of Marxism. The same claim could easily be made for his speculations concerning the theory of knowledge or the realm of theology. In all these fields Benjamin's convictions remained staunchly heterodox. There is, to be sure, an ever-present danger in a mode of thought that is so thoroughly sui generis, a danger that originality and fancy will themselves turn into fetishes. Yet, Benjamin prevented his thinking from tumbling into sheer arbitrariness or solipsism insofar as he simultaneously displayed a profound *veneration* for the authority vested in tradition; a veneration, however, in which tradition is not treated as a power before which one must submit blindly, but as a now-time which enters into a unique relation to the present. The magical quality of his writing lies in the fact that the semantic potentials of tradition reappear not as something merely "transmitted," but as something transfigured and thus *actualized*. As Adorno has observed, "Everything which fell under the scrutiny of his words was transformed, as though it had become radioactive."

A longing for happiness was the profound desire animating the entirety of his work: "Everything Benjamin said or wrote sounded as if thought, instead of rejecting the promises of fairy tales and children's books with its usual disgraceful 'maturity,' took them so literally that real fulfillment itself was now within sight of knowledge" [see Adorno excerpt dated 1967]. As Benjamin once wrote in his essay on Proust: "Cocteau recognized what really should have been the major concern of all readers of Proust. . . . He recognized Proust's blind, senseless, frenzied quest for happiness"—words which one could apply equally to his own writing. The more happiness seemingly withdrew from immediate reach, the more fervently he renewed his quest. Benjamin's thought exhibited a unique sensibility for those objects and texts which through their sheer uselessness, their "intentionlessness," display a great affinity with the idea of emancipation; a world which would transcend the distortion of a society of universal being-for-other, in which things would be allowed to express their own inherent meanings, their being-for-self. As such his essays attain an exemplary status; they are models which because of their uniqueness can never be duplicated. They possess a fragile, autonomous existence, whose secret can never be divined by way of imitation, but only in an effort of concentration on the part of the reader that equals them in rigor. As with any truth worthy of the name, the understanding of the truth content of his thought must never be "an unveiling which destroys the secret, but a revelation which does it justice." The attempt to furnish an image of the absolute consistent with the Enlightenment principle of rational autonomy presented itself as a central concern to philosophers and men of letters in the age of German classicism. It was this very antinomy which preoccupied the lifework of Walter Benjamin, "Whose genius united the insight of the Metaphysician, the interpretative power of the Critic, and the erudition of the Scholar" [Gershom Scholem, *Major Trends in Jewish Mysticism*]. Today, the ruins of this lifework still radiate more brilliantly than the triumphs of other men and women. He was to be sure "A l'écart de tous les courants" ["Outside the main currents"]. (pp. 272-74)

Richard Wolin, in his Walter Benjamin: An Aesthetic of Redemption, *Columbia University Press, 1982, 316 p.*

Peter Szondi   (essay date 1986)

[*Szondi was a prominent German critic whose writings explore the role of history in literature. In the following essay, he discusses Benjamin's city portraits.*]

It was perhaps no accident that Benjamin reflected upon ways of describing cities in 1929, the year that lies midway between his city portraits and his reminiscences of Berlin. For his remarks bear precisely on the difference between portraits of cities by foreigners and those by natives. Seeking to explain why the latter are so much less common than the former, Benjamin wrote:

> The superficial cause [is that] the exotic, the picturesque has an effect only upon the foreigner. To portray a city, a native must have other, deeper motives—motives of one who travels into the past instead of into the distance. A native's book about his city will always be related to memoirs; the writer has not spent his childhood there in vain.

It is natural to look at Benjamin's city portraits in the light of this assertion. Their contours might thus become more sharply delineated and reveal whether in this observation, which appeared in a book review, Benjamin is not in essence writing about his own works. Is he not looking back critically at his descriptions of Naples (1925), Moscow (1927), and Marseilles (1929) and forward to his projected book *A Berlin Childhood Around Nineteen Hundred?* In this perspective, two things become clear. While Benjamin's characterization exactly fits the book on Berlin that he intended to write at the time, his judgment regarding portraits of foreign cities hardly applies to those he had already produced. The motives underlying them scarcely differ from those that marked the book of reminiscences—in no way could the terms "superficial" and "profound" be used to classify Benjamin's own descriptions. It appears, rather, that in his portraits of foreign cities he wished to demonstrate the superficiality of a distinction made on the basis of the author's birthplace. It is evident also that although his remark elucidates the city portraits, it requires elucidation in turn. This commentary is provided by his own city portraits.

Anyone who describes his own city must travel into the past instead of into the distance. One might ask why this journey is necessary at all, why the native cannot remain in the present. *A Berlin Childhood Around Nineteen Hundred* suggests in its very title that the answer is to be found in the thesis of the kinship of such books with memoirs. At the same time, it shows that the journey into the past, too, is a journey into the distance. For without distance there can be no description, except that of mere journalism. The portrait of one's own city is torn from this lower realm by the adult's painful separation from the scenes of his childhood. The city is still there, but that early period lies irrecoverably within it; this is a paradox that sharpens not only our pain but also our perception. Gone, therefore, is our familiarity with streets and houses, although they may still surround us; we see them with a doubly alien view: with the view of the child we no longer are, and with the view of the child to whom the city was not yet familiar.

Benjamin's Berlin book is proof of the constitutive role of distance. In this respect, it is like Gottfried Keller's *Der grüne Heinrich,* which was written not in Zurich but abroad; like *Buddenbrooks,* which was written in Italy; and like the novel of Dublin, which could be written only on the Continent because its author believed that absence is the highest degree of presence. So, too, Flaubert found himself at the foot of an Egyptian pyramid when he conceived the name Bovary, which was to stand as a monument to the petty narrowness of the French provinces.

All the same, *A Berlin Childhood* differs in one crucial respect from all other works whose mainspring is memory, and thus also from the book to which it stands the closest and which Benjamin translated into German: Proust's *Remembrance of Things Past* (*A la recherche du temps perdu*). For Benjamin's work is devoted not so much to memory itself as to one of its special gifts, which is captured in a sentence from his *One-Way Street:* "Like ultraviolet rays, memory points out to everyone in the book of life writing which, invisibly, glossed the text as prophecy." The adult's glance does not yearn to merge with the child's glance. It is directed toward those moments when the future first announced itself to the child. In *A Berlin Childhood* Benjamin writes of "the shock with which a word startles us like a forgotten muff in our room. Just as the latter allows us to infer that some unknown woman has been there, so certain words or pauses allow us to detect the presence of that invisible stranger, the future, who left them behind with us." Everywhere in the city, in the streets and parks, the Berlin book is on the trail of such shocks, the memories of which are preserved by the child until the adult can decipher them. Thus the Tiergarten is not merely a playground but also the place where the child "first grasped, never to forget it, what only later came [to him] as a word: love." Unlike Proust, Benjamin does not flee the future. On the contrary, he deliberately seeks it out in the emotional turmoil of certain childhood experiences, where it went, as it were, into hibernation, whereas upon entering the present it passes into its grave. His "lost time" is not the past but the future. His backward glance is on the shattered utopia that can kindle "the spark of hope" only "in the past." Benjamin, who in the years approaching the Third Reich could neither close his eyes to reality nor give up the promise of a time worthy of humanity, welded a paradoxical bond of hope and despair. It is only in this light that we can understand his plan for a "Prehistory of the Moderns"; and the same may be said of his anthology of letters *German Men,* on the origins of the German bourgeoisie, which—no less paradoxically— appeared as Noah's ark to the socialist driven out of Germany.

The remark quoted at the beginning of this essay was made at the expense of foreign cities. How little Benjamin's city portraits display the qualitative difference he notes can be seen from the very first sentence of his early text on the Russian metropolis: "Quicker than Moscow itself one learns to see Berlin from Moscow." This new perspective on his own city is the most tangible of Benjamin's gains from his stay in Russia. Things foreign do not lure the visitor into self-forgetfulness; he does not become intoxicated by the picturesque and exotic but rather sees his own life, sees himself with an estranged vision. The effect of a journey into the distance is no different from that of a journey into the past, which is likewise a journey into the

distance. Still, it is only because Benjamin goes still further that he can write on foreign cities. While he explores them, the same forces are at work that will later lead him to embark on the journey into his own childhood. From Benjamin's first impressions of Moscow, we learn that to the newcomer the city is a labyrinth; and the Berlin book begins with the sentence: "Not to find one's way about in a city is no great thing. But to get lost in a city, as one gets lost in the woods, requires practice." A foreign city fulfills this strange wish more easily than does one's own. But why this wish? Benjamin once described the labyrinth as the home of the tarrier and said it is the "right path for one who, in any event, always arrives early enough at his destination." The labyrinth is thus in space what memory—which seeks hints of the future in the past—is in time. For the path whose milestones are the shocks of which he speaks ought confidently to choose hope as its destination; it will never reach it and so will never be proved false.

In *One-Way Street* Benjamin writes of one's first glimpse of a village or city in the countryside; this is "so incomparable and so irrecoverable" because "in it distance resonates in the closest bond with nearness. Habit has not yet done its work." The glance that the adult casts on his childhood is determined not least by the wish to escape from the ordinary. The journey, however, is not into something entirely different; it is into that time when the habitual was not yet habitual, into the experiences of the for-the-first-time. "Once we have begun to find our way about a place, that earliest image can never reappear." This earliest image, which is a promise, comes to the adult not only from early childhood but also from distant cities.

There is yet another factor that links the description of these cities with the Berlin book. The foreign surroundings do not just replace the distance of childhood for the adult; they turn him into a child again. Many passages in Benjamin's writings evince this feeling. Of San Gimignano, we read that the town "does not look as if one could ever succeed in approaching it. But once one does, one is drawn into its lap and is unable to concentrate on oneself because of the humming of crickets and the shouting of children." Here the children's real screaming illustrates the process intended by the metaphor, but it simultaneously interrupts this process as well. The conclusion of the section on Moscow's transport system, in contrast, is more straightforward. There he describes the low sledges that afford no downwards view but only "a tender and rapid skimming along stones and by people and horses," and he remarks that on them "one feels like a child gliding through the house on a stool." That this is more than a chance association is shown by an observation at the beginning of the description of Moscow: "The childhood stage starts right upon arrival. On the thick glazed ice of these streets walking must be learned anew." The intensity of the melancholy happiness accompanying these sentences, however, is not yet explicitly expressed. It is first revealed in the page of *A Berlin Childhood* that later provided a commentary on the passage. There the adult writes of the child's set of reading boxes:

> The longing that it awakens in me proves how much a part of my childhood it was. What I am really seeking in it is the latter itself: my entire childhood, as it lay in the grasp with which the hand slid the letters along the ledge on which they were lined up. The hand can still dream of this

grasp, but can never awake and execute the gesture. In like manner, many an individual may dream of how he learned to walk. But that is of no help to him. He can walk now, but never again learn to walk.

The repetition of the "for-the-first-time," the return to the earliest image: both of these experiences seemed to be lost forever, but they still exist in the shelter of foreign lands.

Benjamin's descriptions of foreign cities thus derive from impulses that are no less personal than those underlying *A Berlin Childhood.* This does not mean, however, that he was insensitive to foreign reality. Indeed, a foreign city can fulfill its secret task of turning the visitor into a child only if it appears as exotic and as picturesque as the child's own city once appeared to him. When abroad, Benjamin surrenders with astonishment and curiosity to all the impressions streaming in upon him, like a child standing wide-eyed in a labyrinth he cannot fully compass. The images he offers the reader could hardly be richer, more colorful, or more precise. And yet, *what* he experiences seems just as relevant to his "Search for Lost Time" as the way in which he experiences it. Unlike Proust's search, Benjamin's is borne along by historical and sociological impulses. He is seeking a way out of sclerotic late bourgeois society, enslaved to the principle of individualism, back to the lost origins of society itself. The protest that the young Hegel and Hölderlin raised against "positivity" in the name of life becomes audible again in Benjamin. This accounts for his participation in the German Youth Movement, as his essay on **"Student Life"** attests.

From this point of view, the links between Benjamin's portraits of such different cities as Naples and Moscow become evident. In the South—in Marseilles, Naples, and San Gimignano—he encountered a collective life which had not yet become alienated from its origins (and which was the very opposite of the isolation he coldly describes at the beginning of the section on **"The North Sea"**). In the Soviet Union of 1929, on the other hand, he was able to observe a society in the process of formation. All the same, archaic and revolutionary seemed more closely related than the usual distinction between conservative and progressive would have it. And here he was not thinking solely of that idea of primitive communism which the Russia of the 1930s, already becoming a police state, betrayed with a positivity that mocked dialectical theory. The old in Naples and the new in Moscow are linked by more than just the fact that "To exist is a collective matter," as the following lines on Naples make clear:

> The architecture is as porous as [the] stone. Structures and activities merge in courtyards, arcades, and staircases. Enough room is left free everywhere to allow unforeseen constellations to form. The definitive, the sharply etched, is avoided. No situation seems to be conceived to stay forever just as it is; no shape asserts its "thus and no different." This is how architecture, that most concise and persuasive component of a community's rhythm, comes into being here.

This picture stands in bold contrast to the meticulousness characteristic of the North. Benjamin notes, for example, that the typical house in Bergen "still has strict boundaries." At the same time, the Naples portrait finds its analogy in the movement into which everything in Moscow has been plunged. Benjamin describes in detail the programmed "Remonte," which likewise did not tolerate anything definitive and which, as it were, stretched life out "on the laboratory table." "In this dominant passion there lies as much naive will to do good as boundless curiosity and playfulness. Little is more decisive in Russia today. The country is mobilized day and night. . . . " Private life, which had scarcely been allowed to develop in the South, has been "abolished" by bolshevism. There is a strange similarity in Benjamin's descriptions of the apartment houses in Moscow and in Naples. Once again, the children form the noisy background. They fill the streets and courtyards in countless hordes, as if they did not belong to individual families. The adult whose lonely youth was spent in a villa, as a "prisoner" of Berlin's old West End, seems to cast a longing glance at the community these children enjoy. And it is not only the children who are childish here. The Russians, Benjamin says, are constantly playing, no matter what the situation. "If a scene for a film is being shot on the street, passersby forget where they are going and why, tag along for hours, and then arrive in a state of bewilderment at their offices." It is only the last word of the sentence that reminds the reader that it is adults, not children, who are being described. And since even the adults are like children, it becomes necessary to call upon Lenin's authority for that astonishing maxim, "time is money."

Benjamin returned from his trip "with at best mixed feelings," as Friedrich Podszus reports in his biographical sketch. Reading Benjamin's description of early Soviet Russia, we can sense his suspicion that this dynamism would turn into stasis and the freedom into terror. In particular, the display of images of Lenin seems to have intensified Benjamin's suspicion, and the last section of his essay is devoted to the cult that was growing up around them. "In corners and niches consecrated to Lenin, they appear as busts; in the larger clubs, as bronze statues or reliefs; in offices, as life-size half-length portraits; in kitchens, laundry rooms, and storerooms as small photographs." An even clearer indication of Benjamin's premonition of the threat to the living inherent in the new positivity of the dead image is his observation that babies are called "Oktjabr" ("October") "from the moment they are able to point to Lenin's picture." No less revealing is the metaphor in the final sentence describing the market on the Sucharewkaja: "Since the selling of icons is considered part of the stationery and picture business, [the] stalls with icons tend to be located near paper goods stands, so that everywhere they are flanked by pictures of Lenin, like a prisoner between two policemen."

It is metaphor that makes Benjamin's city portraits what they are. Not only is it the source of their magic and, in a very precise sense, their status as poetic writing. The very purpose of these texts, to convey the experience of alienation and of being a foreigner, is first accomplished through the medium of language, which here is a language of images. The quest for lost time and for what takes its place is no less bound to language than the attempt to take possession of what one has already found. Name and image are the two poles of this field of force. In the labyrinth of the foreign city "every single step . . . is taken on named ground. And where one of these names happens to fall, fantasy constructs an entire quarter in next to no time. This will long defy subsequent reality, obstinately implanting itself therein, like brittle glass walls." While one is waiting for reality, it is preceded by its name, which functions as its surrogate. The name, however, creates its own reality. The competition between the two always ends, to be sure, with the victory of objective reality, but this is very often a Pyrrhic victory: its name is disillusion. Many pages of Proust's novel are devoted to this same theme, which already appears in the romantic writers and which is revived by Benjamin.

The counterpart of this theme is the process by which reality becomes an image. "Finding words for what lies before one's eyes—how hard that can be! But when they do come they strike against reality with little hammers until they have knocked the image out of it, as out of a copper plate." Thus begins Benjamin's description of San Gimignano, which, not without reason, is dedicated to the memory of the author of the *Lord Chandos Letter* (von Hofmannsthal) and written in the year of his death. The potential field in which reality oscillates between name and image requires a separation; it requires the distance of time or of space. For the ordinary has long since absorbed its name and dispelled expectation; it will never again be transformed into an image. But whoever voyages into his past finds that reality and name constantly break apart again. It may be that the name has outlived the reality and now takes its place in memory as its phantom; it may be that in those "for-the-first-time" experiences the name was there before the reality was experienced; or that the experience was there before it received a name, so that it remained there without being understood, like the prophetic writing that invisibly glosses the text in the book of one's life. Whether he described the Berlin of his childhood or some foreign city, the consciousness of this separation rarely ever left Benjamin. It is difficult to say, though, if this was more a source of joy or of pain to him. In any case, it is only against this background that we can understand the following episode from his voyage on **"The North Sea"**:

> In the evening, heart heavy as lead, full of anxiety, on the deck. For a long time I follow the play of the gulls. . . . The sun has long since gone down, and in the East it is very dark. The ship travels southwards. Some brightness is left in the West. What now happened to the birds—or to myself?—that occurred by virtue of the spot that I, so domineeringly, so lonely, selected for myself in my melancholy in the middle of the quarterdeck. All of a sudden there were two flights of gulls, one to the East, one to the West, left and right, so entirely different that the name gull fell away from them.

Melancholy sees only the dark side of everything. The tension between name and reality, which is the origin of poetry, is only experienced painfully, as the distance separating man from things. The experience that Benjamin reports, without reflecting upon it, breaks through this pain. The chiaroscuro of the sky tears reality asunder and abolishes the identity that made naming possible in the first place. The gulls' name falls away from them; they are now only themselves, but as such they are perhaps closer to man than if he possessed them by virtue of knowing their name.

These remarks do not yet adequately convey the meaning of this experience, which also brings to light the inverse of that which gives rise to metaphor in Proust as well as in Benjamin. Here the name falls away from the gulls because the sky divides them into groups, and the difference becomes greater than that which unites them, while in metaphor, two different things cease to be identical to themselves because they are superimposed through an analogy discovered by the writer. As Proust himself came to realize, metaphor aided him in his search for lost time. Like the experience with the madeleine, metaphor should lift man beyond temporality through the bond it creates between a moment in the present and a moment in the past. In Benjamin also, simile can assist memory when it seeks tokens of the future in the past. In such instances, the two members of the simile are related as a text that one actually experiences is related to its prophetic commentary, which is first deciphered by memory. We may take as an example the "Nibbling Child" of **One-Way Street,** who becomes the first-person narrator of **A Berlin Childhood;** "his hand," we read, slipped through "the crack of the barely opened cupboard like a lover through the night." Yet, in Benjamin metaphor is no more restricted to a single function than it is in Proust; on the contrary, it serves as a rule for the descriptive process itself. Benjamin seems to have shared Proust's view that the enumeration of objects in a description can never lead to truth and that truth first appears at the moment when the author takes two different objects and reveals their essence by linking them in a metaphor based on a common property.

The only thing that seems foreign to Benjamin's intentions here is the mention of "essence"; for his frequent use of metaphor and simile in portraying foreign cities derives from other grounds. The language of images makes it possible to understand unfamiliar things without their ceasing to be unfamiliar. Simile brings distant things near while at the same time freezing them in an image protected from the ravaging force of habit. Metaphor helps Benjamin to paint his city portraits as miniatures, much like his preferred form, the fragment. Moreover, in their linking of nearness and distance, in their withdrawn existence, such miniatures resemble those favorite objects of Benjamin's: glass globes in which snow falls on a landscape. His figurative language evinces supreme artistic understanding. Benjamin was a master in the creation of twofold definitions by the use of images: "What is sentimentality if not the flagging wing of feeling, which settles down anywhere at all because it can go on no further, and what, then, its opposite, if not this tireless movement, which so wisely holds itself back [and] settles down on no experience or memory, but rather remains hovering, grazing one after the other."

Benjamin is often dissatisfied with simple metaphors, and so he creates entire compositions with them, as in his description of Notre Dame de la Garde in Marseilles or in his evocation of the conflict between that city and its surrounding landscape. As each new image carries the comparison further, the danger grows that the bridge might not reach the other bank, and yet the link between the two banks becomes stronger with each new span. Sometimes, too, the image does not leave the language unaffected. Thus, Benjamin writes of Bergen; "Just as the inhabitants of remote mountain villages intermarry to the point of sickliness and death, so the staircases and corners of the houses have become intertwined." The new images are what make the comparison evident, although they themselves become possible only as a result of the comparison.

Sometimes Benjamin resorts to the metaphoric conditional tense, which in its suggestion of experiment betrays the whole playful awareness and fragility of the metaphor. For example: "If this sea is the Campagna, then Bergen lies in the Sabine Hills." Despite such artistry, Benjamin never uses figurative language without real commitment. Indeed, it is largely responsible for an effect aptly characterized by T. W. Adorno: "What Benjamin said and wrote sounds as if it derived from a secret. But its power comes from its obviousness."

Neither the secret nor the obviousness would be possible if it were true, as Hugo Friedrich asserts, that "the fundamental vocation of metaphor lies not in recognizing existing similarities but rather in inventing nonexistent ones." Metaphor's achievement lies beyond this alternative. It is not concerned, of course, with what is at hand, but neither is it interested in inventing similarities; it seeks, rather, to find them. Metaphor originates in the belief that the world is built up of correspondences that can and should be recognized. In his description of Weimar, Benjamin writes that "In the Goethe-Schiller Archives the staircases, drawing rooms, display cases and reading rooms are white. . . . The manuscripts are bedded down like patients in hospitals. And yet, the longer one exposes oneself to this harsh light, the more one believes that he discerns a reason, unconscious of itself, underlying such institutions." The metaphorist's glance proves to be that of the theologian's. Benjamin is a student of the baroque emblematists, whom he treats in his work on *The Origin of Tragic Drama.* And what is true of them is equally true of himself: that which seems to be artistry and was once learned from books is nothing less than the exegesis of the Creation.

The city portraits are products of the years between 1925 and 1930; *A Berlin Childhood* was written after 1930. Anyone familiar with Benjamin's biography and works will grasp the significance of these dates. From the period before 1925, we may mention an essay he wrote at the age of twenty-two on Hölderlin, a work that would have marked a new epoch in the study of that poet had it become known at the time. (The essay was first published in 1955.) Then came the great study on *Goethe's "Elective Affinities"* (1924) along with the major work on German baroque drama (1923-25), with which Benjamin vainly sought to qualify as a university lecturer at Frankfurt. It was only after Benjamin was obliged to give up the prospect of an academic career (his mind having been judged to be insufficiently academic) that he became a man of letters and a journalist. To earn a living, he began to write the articles for newspapers and journals that today contribute as much to his reputation as does his scholarly work. It is among these that we find the city portraits. Nothing earlier in his life had hinted at this activity, as becomes clear, for example, in reading a letter written in his student days in Bern (22 October 1917), in which he told Gershom Scholem of his plans for the future. It would thus appear that it was the university, whose representatives rejected him, which was responsible for Benjamin's becoming the kind of writer it suspected him of being.

The fact that Benjamin wrote no more city portraits in the period after 1933 can likewise be explained by the date in question. At that time a story was circulating in the emigrant community about a Jew who planned to emigrate to Uruguay; when his friends in Paris seemed astonished that he wanted to go so far away, he retorted: "Far from where?" With the loss of one's homeland the notion of distance also disappears. If everything is foreign, then that tension between distance and nearness from which the city portraits draw their life cannot exist. The emigrant's travels are not the kind one looks back upon; his map has no focal point around which foreign lands assume a fixed configuration. After he had finished his book of reminiscences about Berlin, Benjamin did, it is true, devote the last ten years of his life to a work on Paris, the city in which he had long felt at home. This work, however, has nothing in common with the earlier city portraits. Benjamin had frequently written about Paris even while he was still living in Germany, but he had never tried to capture the city's traits in a miniature ("too near," he remarked in a note reporting a dream about Paris). The path he entered on in Paris in search of Paris was thus the same one that—in the remark quoted at the start of this essay—he urged upon whoever undertakes to write about his native city; a journey into the past. The projected book, a montage of historical texts presented as if the city were writing its own memoirs, was to be called *Paris, Capital of the Nineteenth Century.* (pp. 133-43)

> *Peter Szondi, "Walter Benjamin's 'City Portraits',"* in his *On Textual Understanding and Other Essays, translated by Harvey Mendelsohn, University of Minnesota Press, 1986, pp. 133-43.*

Helga Geyer-Ryan   (essay date 1988)

[*In the following essay, Geyer-Ryan examines the implicit modernism of Benjamin's views of history and literature.*]

Throughout Benjamin's work between 1920 and 1940 there runs one major preoccupation: the sketching of a modernist theory of history. Closely linked to this are Benjamin's explorations of how human subjectivity might be reconstructed in a way which would meet the demands of cultural modernism without at the same time dissolving the capacity for political action. Thus his texts contain the basic elements for a new theory of the subject and a new theory of history; and, since history is itself a text, they also include a new hermeneutics of reading and writing.

As a modernist philosopher of history, Benjamin called into question such notions of traditional historical discourse as continuity, development, process, progress and organism. As a modernist theoretician of historiography, he was critical of traditional narrative with its rosary-like chain of cause-and-event stories. Inspired by the practice of the literary avant-garde, he developed his own theory of textual production or signification, which was based on the principle of fragmentation and montage: the central features of Benjamin's own texts are thus the quotation, the thesis, the fragment, the arrangement and the compilation.

It was the vision of nineteenth-century Paris, with its refracted and ruptured archaeology, which provided Benjamin with the material imagery out of which he strove to fashion his new conceptions. Paris was both the epitome of capitalism and a wellspring of the forces which opposed it, and as such it represented for him a mythological microcosm of modern times. Above all, Paris inspired Benjamin with its catalytic fusion of what he saw as the two most advanced developments in twentieth-century politics and culture: Marxism and Surrealism. In Benjamin's writing the two movements enrich and transform each other. The abstract language of Marxist theory becomes more concrete and sensually perceptible by being infused with the images of mythology (*Bilderschrift*). As Benjamin says:

> There is a central problem of historical materialism and it is about time it was recognized: that is, whether the Marxist understanding of history is only possible at the cost of reducing the concrete presence of history before our eyes. Or: how is it possible to enhance this concrete presence of history and to combine it with the application of Marxist methods? The first stage will be to adapt the montage principle in history; that means to erect the large constructions from the smallest, precisely and pointedly manufactured units.

At the same time the tendentially ahistorical mythologisation of Paris in avant-garde writing is revealed as a phantasm unless it is demystified by underpinning it with historical and political awareness. In this respect Benjamin explicitly sets his *Passagenwerk* apart from Aragon's *Paysan de Paris:*

> Whereas Aragon stays within the realm of dream, the aim in this case is to find the constellation of awakening. Whilst in Aragon there remains an element of impressionism—the mythology—and this impressionism is to be held responsible for the many formless philosophemes in the book, in this case it is a question of dissolving mythology into the realm of history. Of course, this can only happen by awakening an as yet unconscious knowledge of what has been.

The concept of dream and awakening are of crucial importance in Benjamin's writing. Dream is the juncture of the imagery of physical concreteness and exuberant materialism with the structures of desire. But this dreamworld is furnished by objects which in capitalism are necessarily commodities, and consequently the structures of desire are made up of desire and fear (*Angst*) at once. In contrast, awakening is the moment where the spell or illusion of reconciling a desire for fulfilment with a structure of exploitation and alienation can be broken. In this dream, under the spell of capitalism, desire and objects of fulfilment are authentic and distorted at the same time. The task of the new historian is to set free the forces and drives of authentic liberation without giving up a materially better life and the more refined structures of desire which go with it.

Benjamin's starting point is to 'read' Paris. He says: 'The topos of Nature's book shows that it is possible to read reality like a text. So this will be done here with the reality of the nineteenth century.' Benjamin's reading of nineteenth-century Paris constitutes the deciphering of the primal landscape (*Urlandschaft*) of twentieth-century capitalism and mass psychology. It is only better-informed later generations who will be able to look at the past in such a way as to produce a reading of it which illuminates the present like a flash of lightning. Conversely, Benjamin's specific reading of Paris can only come about at a historical moment where a fusion between Marxism and

Surrealism is possible and where such an *idiosyncratic* reading is vital for the politics of Benjamin's own time.

> It is not the case that the past sheds its light on the present or the present its light on the past, but the image is that in which, what has been, enters into a constellation with the 'Now' [*Jetzt*] in a sudden flash. In other words: the image is dialectics at a standstill [. . .]. The image read, i.e. the image in the 'Now' of the potential realization is most clearly marked by that critical and dangerous momentum, the basis of all reading.

And, even more important: 'the historical index of the images not only tells us that they belong to a certain time, above all it tells us that only at a certain time do they become readable'.

Thus we can detect two important implications for his philosophy of history. Firstly, to read the *world* in order to find out about history means that history becomes spatialised. The transformation of a temporal concept into a spatial one implies that a view of time as process or progression has been supplanted by a sense of time having stopped, of history having come to an end. This radical shift of perspective becomes a dominant theme of cultural production during the period opening around the turn of the century and culminating in the First World War and the proletarian revolutions which grew out of it. Secondly, to *read* the world assumes that history is seen as a text, as an artefact, as something constructed, the encoding and interpretation of which are always to be understood as socially and ideologically conditioned.

Both of these ideas, the spatialisation of time and history as text, emerged from the historical constellation from within which Benjamin began to write, and of which he was acutely aware from the beginning. With the First World War, history as *bourgeois* history, hitherto legitimised and sustained by the notion of 'progress', did indeed come to an end. Imperialism stood fully unmasked at last. At the same time an alternative force, whose political perspective opened up a whole new way of writing history, had seized power successfully in Russia. Nevertheless, after the defeat of the proletarian revolutions in Europe, the ruling classes reinforced their hegemony by satisfying certain demands for social and political reform. The Social Democrats increased their influence, but paid the high price of adapting themselves ever more to bourgeois modes of thought and action, a development facilitated by a deterministic interpretation of Marx's theory since the Second International.

Marx's analysis of capitalism had established on a theoretical level the proposition that capitalism necessarily produces the forces of its own destruction. But what he did not say was whether those counter-forces would inevitably triumph before capitalism had the chance to turn its own particular collapse into a universal catastrophe. It was on just such an assumption of inevitable triumph, however, that the social-democratic theory rested: the unconsidered supposition that the decline of capitalism would mean the ineluctable progress of socialism. This in turn made it possible to evolve the theory of the peaceful, because automatic, transformation of capitalism into socialism; a theory designed (not necessarily consciously) to still the desire to fight actively against bourgeois imperialism.

One social formation where this problem was perceived and tackled with increasing idiosyncrasy was the cultural avant-garde. Not only had bourgeois culture done nothing by 1914 to abolish ossified patterns of life, to eradicate social injustice and to prevent the First World War, but some artists had greeted and glorified that bloody spectacle in which a morally bankrupt capitalism flagrantly betrayed the humanist values to which it had hitherto claimed to subscribe. The reason for what looked like art's submission to the interests of the ruling class, and its function as a means of ideologically shoring up a crumbling society, was found in art's separation from life: by defining and institutionalising art as autonomous, bourgeois society had rendered it ineffectual. Thus the attempt to reintegrate art and life, to aestheticise life, in other words, was the common aim of avant-garde movements such as Dadaism, Futurism and Surrealism. It is the aim summed up in Breton's phrase 'practiquer la poésie' ['to practice poetry']. This reintegration was not, however, meant to take place within the existing society. Rather, the aesthetic way of perceiving and producing reality was seen as a means of changing society: a society dominated on all levels by abstraction, instrumentalism and technical rationality, and by an ideal of progress which concentrated wholly on the development of science and technology in order to maximise exploitation and profit.

Drastically oversimplified as it is, this outline of the situation around the time of the First World War needs to be borne in mind for a proper understanding of the historical and cultural trends which informed and shaped Benjamin's writings from 1920 to 1940. His whole *oeuvre* centres upon the same dominant issues, constantly weaving them together into the complex texture of his conception of history. Benjamin's idea of the pregnant or charged moment of historical recognition, whereby one can find condensed in a work a whole life, and in a life a whole epoch, applies equally to his own texts. Whichever of them we might select for closer analysis, and however remote it might seem at first sight from his main interests, it will turn out in the end to be one point in a magnetic field: a unit complete in its own specific thematic purpose, but directed at the same time towards a more fundamental and comprehensive concern which exists only in the total formation of its different units.

In this respect Benjamin's *Theses on the Philosophy of History,* written shortly before his death in 1940 and (significantly) not meant to be published, are only the very tip of the iceberg. This becomes clear when we recognise that the themes treated here recur in the *Passagenwerk,* his most ambitious intellectual project. Benjamin's *Theses* are dictated by the drive to rewrite history from the perspective not of the victors of history, i.e. the ruling classes, but of their victims. Such an alternative reconstruction of the past does not mean, however, just another version of traditional historicism, a mere chronicle of past events and great figures supposedly unconnected with the present, though in fact, of course, shaped by the historian's conscious or unconscious alliance with the ruling class. On the contrary. The writing of an oppositional history is doubly rooted in the social formation of the writer's own time. On the one hand only an alliance with the victims of, and potential liberators from, social and political oppression in the present can provide the vanishing-point towards which the counter-history is projected. And on the

other hand, this salvaged history, wrenched from the grasp of collective amnesia, is necessary for the abolition of the status quo, because, as Benjamin puts it, each generation has been vested with the messianic power to redeem all those who suffered in the past.

This rewriting of history is not an easy task, and it is constantly threatened by failure. There are three main reasons for this. The first is that the witnesses of the other history are continually disappearing. They are only to be found in what the dominant process of history has secreted as waste, as the superseded and outmoded which can thus, by definition, have no function within the 'advancing' capitalist order. Once free of its use-value, this waste has once again the potential to indicate a counterfactual history. For what is left is a pure form—pure because it is defunct—into which new meaning can be deposited, an activity performed by the artist, the historian and the collector alike. 'Anything which you know won't be existing much longer becomes an image', says Benjamin with reference to Baudelaire's way of finding material for his urban poetry, and he draws the comparison between the artist of the capitalist city and the ragman:

> The poets find the refuse of society on their street and derive their heroic subject from this very refuse. This means that a common type is, as it were, superimposed upon their illustrious type. This new type is permeated by the features of the rag picker with whom Baudelaire repeatedly concerned himself. One year before he wrote 'Le vin des chiffoniers' he published a prose presentation of the figure: 'Here we have a man who has to gather the day's refuse in the capital city. Everything that the big city threw away, everything it lost, everything it despised, everything it crushed underfoot, he catalogues and collects. He collates the annals of intemperance, the stockpile of waste. He sorts things out and makes a wise choice; he collects, like a miser guarding a treasure, the refuse which will assume the shape of useful or gratifying objects between the jaws of the goddess of Industry.'

The loss of that which is outmoded is the loss of the dream material, the very stuff of mythological and symbolic resonance. For what is disappearing are those objects of our own past, in which the connection between technology and mythology had been created. Such a connection can only be achieved by children, says Benjamin.

> Task of childhood: to bring the new world into the realm of the symbolic. The child can do what an adult is totally incapable of doing: recognise the new once again. Railway engines already have the character of symbols for us because we saw them in our childhood. For our children cars—of which we ourselves see only the new, elegant, slick side—have this character [. . .] for every truly new natural formation [*Naturgestalt*]—and basically, technology is one such—there are corresponding new images. Each generation of children discovers these new images to incorporate them into mankind's treasury of images.

So the second point is that this disappearance of the objective material of a counter-history is paralleled by an ever-increasing loss of experience on the part of the subject. Experience depends upon the capacity of personal memory to interrelate the biographical past and present. For Benjamin, biographical memory and historical memory are analogous procedures, and one cannot exist without the other. From this follows the third factor jeopardising the project. I have said that the medium in which the epistemological moment, the flash-like identity of subject and object, transpires, is for Benjamin no longer the language of theory but the language of images; but the mimetic powers are constantly being eroded and reduced by the demands of instrumental rationality, the philosophical backbone of capitalist technology.

These three points outline the material conditions for an alternative production of historical meaning. Benjamin's central stress on the mimetic and the imaginative as basic factors in changing the world of the status quo links him directly with surrealism and has also given rise to various attempts to claim him as a Judaic religious thinker. But what Benjamin found in the imagery of the Messiah or in the ecstatic moment of what he emphatically defines as *'profane illumination'*, are precisely the emotional and pictorial foundations of sensuous perception, of an alternative way of seeing, in short: of creativity.

Until then the mimetic and imaginative faculties had not been made productive for scientific, political and historical practice, but had survived mainly in areas where inspiration, vision and revelation as elements of mystical discourse paraphrased the moment of recognition. As these fields of application were themselves concerned with the production of imaginative material, especially in religion or art, the general validity of the mimetic faculty for all kinds of epistemological activity had been overlooked. But if we recall, for instance, that Kekule, the founder of organic chemistry, had visualised the structure of the benzine ring while dreaming of a snake swallowing its own tail, it may not be altogether fanciful to consider whether the mimetic—the aesthetic—might indeed be the general organon in which theory and practice are linked.

Modern psychology still speaks of the 'desirable and proper mystery which surrounds the creative act', and adds modestly but significantly: 'the best that can be said is that certain uniformities do seem to characterise highly original scientists and artists'. Even today we have only taken the very first steps towards establishing a psychology of the imagination, which neuro-physiologists do not hesitate to define as 'the highest level of mental experience', its processes inextricably bound up with those of 'the lower level of sensuous experience, imagery, hallucination and memory'.

I am quoting this not least because it points up the remarkable insights of Benjamin and the Surrealists nearly forty years before the quoted essay was written. Imagination, hallucination and memory are the key categories deployed by them in order to grasp a framework of epistemological production which is by definition aesthetic because it is always mimetic. In the epistemological process correspondences are discovered between objects which hitherto had appeared unconnected. Benjamin's key witnesses on this point are Baudelaire, Proust, Aragon and Breton's *Nadja*. We develop these faculties only because nature itself is full of correspondences. Therefore the Surrealists, for instance, gave accounts of everyday life in the confidence that its aesthetic character made any artistic procedure superfluous. *Le hasard objectif* ('objectified chance') is an aesthetic feature of reality. It is only because correspondences exist between past and present that we can bring

the two together, both on the personal biographical level and on the communal plane of history. Only in this way can true experience, that is, the investment of otherwise inert and isolated fragments with meaning, be achieved. It is precisely at this stage that Benjamin brings the philogenetic and the ontogenetic to the point of conflation. For authentic experience is always the salvaging of something in danger of being forgotten or repressed: the ever-vanishing traces of the historically defeated who did not write history, or the engrams of the unconscious described by Freud in *Beyond the Pleasure Principle* and by Proust as the content of the *mémoire involontaire;* especially when the chances of finding the right mimetic object for reactivating those fading traces are so slight and fleeting.

But for Benjamin it is not only the difficulty of still finding the right corresponding objects. The modern individual has also undergone a process of psychological reconstruction whereby unconscious engrams are increasingly less encoded. In mass society, especially in the cities, the main psychological stimulus is shock, but in order to avoid trauma the consciousness is continually on guard to protect itself against such an unforeseen flooding by high rates of impulse. According to Freud the psychic energy of conscious events disappears without trace. *Mémoire involontaire* and *mémoire volontaire*— memory and consciousness—are mutually exclusive. Thus Benjamin argues: 'Experience is indeed a matter of tradition, in collective existence as well as in private life. It is less the product of facts firmly anchored in memory than of a convergence in memory of accumulated and frequently unconscious data.' But the more people are exposed to shocks, the less material is laid down in the *mémoire involontaire* as the reservoir of authentic emotional and sensuous experience. People in capitalist mass society find it more and more difficult to make sense of their own lives as a result of the impoverishment of their store of mimetic material and emotional energy. The shattering of the matter of memory into disconnected episodes and events, out of which the individual desperately strives to distil real experience, is epitomised in Baudelaire's notion of 'spleen'. Spleen is the condition produced by the running wild of isolated happenings which can find no place in the context of a personal—or social—history which would render them meaningful.

Experience, understood as the reactivation of memory through its fusion with the present, is thus endangered by two factors. Firstly there is the diminishing possibility of accumulating unconscious data, which through correspondent structures would conflate and deepen the existing engrams or traces of memory in the cortex, as John Eccles has argued:

> The engram postulate accords well with the experience of remembered imagery. By far the most vivid memories are evoked by some closely similar experience. Here the new, evolving spatio-temporal pattern must tend to correspond closely to the old, congealed pattern: the impulses of the new pattern flow into a channel of the old and trigger its replaying.

The second factor is the total randomness of the principle by which one finds the object or situation which might trigger the old memory. For Benjamin this, too, is due to radically changed patterns of perception in modern society. Through the separation of private and public interest and the consequent atomised existence of the individual, public matter can no longer be assimilated so readily to the personal life. As Benjamin observes:

> According to Proust, it is a matter of chance whether an individual forms an image of himself, whether he can take hold of his experience. It is by no means inevitable to be dependent on chance in this matter. Man's inner concerns do not have their inescapably private character by nature. They do so only when he is increasingly unable to assimilate the data of the world around him by way of experience.

This is the reason for the disappearance of true story-telling, the oldest form of communication. In contrast with the modern mass media, in story-telling

> It is not the object of the story to convey a happening per se, which is the purpose of information; rather, it embeds it in the life of the storyteller in order to pass it on as experience to those listening. It thus bears the marks of the storyteller as much as the earthen vessel bears the marks of the potter's hand.

What appears in the marks of the story-teller and the potter's hand is Benjamin's concept of the aura. The aura is that emanation surrounding something, in which the most subjective, that which can only be perceived through an identification triggered by the senses, converges with the factual. We really can speak of the *unio mystica,* the inextricable blending of 'the nearest and the most remote': 'Experience of the aura thus rests on the transposition of a response common in human relationships to the relationship between the inanimate or natural object and man . . . To perceive the aura of an object we look at means to invest it with the ability to look at us in turn.'

It is the aura of Combray, the village which is so poignantly recalled by Proust's narrator in *Du côté du chez Swann,* which appears in Proust's *mémoire involontaire,* in contrast to the merely factual Combray of the reflexive, discursive *mémoire volontaire.* From here we can see introspectively the connection between the outmoded and the aura. But beyond the utterly private acts of memory of the private gentleman Proust, the most authentic experience, the strongest aura is evoked in the coincidence of private and collective experience. The calendar, with its public feast-days, provides a concept of time whereby such coincidences are socially organised. But until such time as a new calendar might be conceptualised, capable of really preserving individual memory through the collective memory of a liberated society, it is necessary to sustain a memory of history instilled with the desire for liberation. The struggle to conserve that alternative memory of history can be compared to the difficulty of evoking the *mémoire involontaire.* The conscious, discursive memory of fact, void of sensuous re-enactment and tending to stifle any experience truly pregnant with subjectivity—that is, with unconscious, mimetic, imaginative material—functions in the same way as the official bourgeois writing of history. Furthermore, both the paradigm of historicism and the paradigm of progress are closed to the possibility of imparting meaning to the collective memory. For historicism there is no link between past and present. For progress neither past nor present really exists, because they are perceived highly selectively and always as transitional: time there is empty. But apart from that, in the official version of history the sheer facticity of things seems to acquire the self-evidence of the necessary and ineluctable. The once-existing possibility of alternative paths of collective action disappears.

But how can the repressed and the forgotten be restored? As regards the perceiving subject, new ways of seeing have to be activated. As regards the object, the refuse and detritus of history have to be examined for their alternative potential. Benjamin twice gives the same example of the kind of fresh historical vision that needs to be acquired and, significantly enough, they are spatial scenarios. It is not alien to the perceiving subject, but has been superseded by automatised, functional modes of perception. The non-automatised mode of vision existed in the past at the point of learning something. Once that process is finished, however, the attitude towards the object is almost fixed forever. Benjamin uses the image of the city in order to clarify these different ways of relating to history. In **'Städtebilder'** he speaks about his experience of orientation in Moscow. At first the city was a phantasm created by the imagination around the names of streets, squares and buildings. This creation resists reality for a long time, unyielding. Then, in the clash between imagination and reality, the city becomes a labyrinth and the visitor falls victim to innumerable topographical traps. Now the city resists identification, it tries to mask itself, escapes and hatches plots. But finally the abstract schemes of maps will carry off the victory, and the vivid, sensuous encounter between man and city will be buried beneath a concept which is purely functional. And in ***One-Way Street*** Benjamin says:

> What renders the very first sight of a village or town in the landscape so incomparable and irresistible is the fact that it combines distance in strong connection with closeness. Habit has not yet done its job. Once we start to get our bearings the landscape disappears all at once like the front of a house when we enter it. . . . Once we start to know the place that former image can never be restored.

In order to reacquire that estranged vision, the mimetic and imaginative faculties must be developed and expanded through practice. The use of intoxicating drugs like opium or marijuana and the state of dreaming are only extreme forms of such practice, which can be pursued likewise in ordinary everyday activities such as reading, thinking, solitude or the strolling of the *flâneur* in the city. All these activities imply the discharge of consciousness. This intensified state of imaginative perception will then be able to recognise in certain outmoded objects and constellations those 'dialectical images' which can release material for an alternative, counterfactual history. The moment of recognition when the object 'opens its eyes beneath the gaze of the historian' is Benjamin's *profane Erleuchtung* ('profane illumination'). These moments are rare; they occur suddenly and fleetingly, like flashes of lightning.

The objects which are able to provide 'dialectical images' for an alternative historical signification are, on the one hand, the relics of an objectively scattered totality; and on the other, the fragments which the historian blasts out of what appears to be a coherent totality of historical meaning. What Benjamin recognises as the essence of modernist artistic production, the deconstruction of questionable totalities and the remounting of the fragments into artefacts, the meaning of which has no resemblance to their former function, is again fully applicable to the practice of the historian himself. The destruction of the organic artwork and its replacement by a form of art based on the montage principle is systematised in Benjamin's theory of allegory. The theory of allegory, the result of Benjamin's position as a modernist, but demonstrated fully in terms of the baroque drama, provides a general theory of the production of textual meaning.

If we deconstruct Benjamin's concept of allegory we find the following determinants, which describe the main aspects of textual production and reception:

> 1. The allegorist breaks an element out of its normal context. By doing so he isolates it, deprives it of its original function and meaning. An allegory is therefore a fragment in contrast to the organic symbol. As Benjamin puts it: with allegory 'the false illusion of totality is extinguished'.

> 2. The allegorist re-assembles his fragments and creates a new meaning. This sort of meaning is constructed and derives in no way from the original context of the fragment.

> 3. Benjamin interprets the allegoric procedure as an expression of melancholy. Under the eyes of the melancholic (the one who turns his back on life and social activity, thus interrupting the coherence of his own totality of existence) objects are stunned. They lose the capacity to communicate meaning.

The relation between allegory and melancholy leads to a further point:

> 4. Allegory represents history as decay. It exposes the image of a fragmented, paralysed history in the form of a frozen primal landscape.

The comparison of the organic and non-organic text on the level of production shows the convergence between allegory and what is known as montage. While the 'classicist' (which I use as shorthand for the organically or symbolically producing artist) respects the traditional meaning of his material and tries to create a new totality in accordance with it, the avant-gardist kills off his material by blasting it out of its context, and mounts the fragments anew, regardless of their tradition. The classicist tries to cover the fact that his product is constructed, and wants to create a second nature. The avant-gardist exposes the materiality and technicality of his work, thus stressing its character as an artefact.

In so far as the avant-gardist assembles his work out of fragments, destroying the category of totality, montage can be seen as the basic principle of all modernist texts. This has consequences for the mode of reception too. In the organic work every part received its ultimate meaning through its relation to the whole. In contrast, the non-organic work releases its parts into utter freedom from the whole. They can be read individually or in groups and they make perfect sense in themselves.

The montage principle as a mode of alternative historiography exactly reflects the decline of bourgeois history. Historicism and the theory of progress are both organic concepts of history. The different epochs, which 'are all equally near to God', as the historicist Ranke put it, are seen as mature, fully developed totalities closed off against each other. The notion of progress underlies the concept of evolution, which is likewise based on the image of an organic body still developing towards its final mature state. But after the First World War the function of these concepts is concentrated exclusively on the affirmative aspect of ideological constructs. Objectively the history of the bourgeoisie has fallen apart into isolated fragments. The once totalising force of its signification as progressive, humane and ascendant over feudal society has turned openly into mechanisms of domination and exploitation at all costs. A whole mode of history has come to an end, and this is widely reflected in cultural production during the opening decades of the twentieth century.

History has been transformed into a space where all its fragments are stored in chaotic disorder. What finally lurks beneath the veneer of history as progress is history as continuous catastrophe. Hence Benjamin's famous angel of history:

> His face is turned towards the past. Where we perceive a chain of events, he sees one single catastrophe which keeps piling wreckage upon wreckage and hurls it in front of his feet. The angel would like to stay, awaken the dead, and make whole what had been smashed. But a storm is blowing from Paradise; it has got caught in his wings with such violence that the angel can no longer close them. This storm irresistibly propels him into the future to which his back is turned, while the pile of debris before him grows skyward. This storm is what we call progress.

In the angel we see the allegorist, the melancholic who is paralysed in the face of the catastrophic destruction of the world and its meaning. But for the dialectical historian and those who are interested with him in the reconstruction of an alternative world, it is precisely the wreckage, the debris out of which the new foundations can be constructed.

For Benjamin the treasure-house of such historical debris was the city: Berlin, where he grew up, but especially Paris, where he lived for a long time and which was for him the capital of the nineteenth century. We can see now that the centrepiece of his theory of textual production, the allegoresis, is completely determined by the ever-accelerating wastage of commodities and their contextual structures, which could best be experienced in the metropolis. But it is also to be found in that marginal literature and art which was never appropriated by the official canon of high culture; and indeed it can be discerned in high culture itself once the deconstruction of bourgeois modes of interpretation has opened up the possibility of alternative ways of reading. It is contained likewise in objects salvaged from oblivion by the collector—Benjamin himself being an avid collector of books, especially children's books. If we recall that the German word for 'to read' is *lesen,* which is directly related to the Latin word *legere,* meaning 'to collect', we can see the close connection between textual reception/production and the collecting of vanishing items. Benjamin's ultimate aim is 'lesen, was niemals geschrieben wurde' ('to read what has never been written').

In this paradox we find the essence of his methodology. Firstly there is the conflation of the two meanings of *lesen.* When Benjamin says 'History is a text of images', those images can be products of the imagination and they can be concrete objects, both not written in the strict sense of the word. And secondly, there is the endeavour to read in a way which destroys the text in question as a written document of its *own* time. To read a text from the past in the light of a present perspective, dissolves our notion of 'the original', of the 'genetic'. At the same time the idea of correspondences, which makes possible the charging of the past with a *Jetztzeit* ["now-time"] constructed by the concern to emancipate society from repression, prevents such historiography from total arbitrariness or relativism. The concept of correspondences is at once the link between different periods and the avoidance of another powerful holistic and organic conception of history in the service of bourgeois society: Nietzsche's theory of eternal recurrence. In his collection of aphorisms entitled **Central Park** Benjamin states:

> As far as the idea of eternal recurrence is concerned, what is important is the fact that the bourgeoisie no longer dared to face the development of the productive relations which they themselves had initiated. The theory of Zarathustra and the motto embroidered on the cushion-cover—'Rest but a quarter of an hour'—are complementary.
>
> (pp. 66-79)

Helga Geyer-Ryan, "Counterfactual Artefacts: Walter Benjamin's Philosophy of History," in Visions and Blueprints: Avant-Garde Culture and Radical Politics in Early Twentieth-Century Europe, *edited by Edward Timms and Peter Collier, Manchester University Press, 1988, pp. 66-79.*

FURTHER READING

Abbas, Ackbar. "Walter Benjamin's Collector: The Fate of Modern Experience." *New Literary History* 20, No. 1 (Autumn 1988): 217-37.
　　Discusses Benjamin's characterization of the collector, its metaphoric function, and its relation to the protagonists in novels by Flaubert, Proust, Conrad, and others.

Alter, Robert. "Walter Benjamin: The Aura of the Past." In his *Defenses of the Imagination: Jewish Writers and Modern Historical Crisis,* pp. 47-66. Philadelphia: The Jewish Publication Society of America, 1977.
　　Challenges critical estimates of Benjamin as excessively nostalgic and socially disengaged, maintaining that his concept of the "aura of the past" is life-affirming and hopeful. Originally published in *Commentary* Vol. 48, No. 3 (September 1969): 86-93.

Belmore, H. W. "Some Recollections of Walter Benjamin." *German Life and Letters* XXVIII, No. 2 (January 1975): 119-27.
　　Discusses the influence of Benjamin's personality on his criticism, concluding that had he been "more open to people and the world, he might have brought out what lay in him of intellectual power and originality, and have become a great critic."

Benjamin, Andrew, ed. *The Problems of Modernity: Adorno and Benjamin.* London: Routledge, 1989, 220 p.
　　Includes the following essays on Benjamin: "Benjamin's *Flâneur* and the Problem of Realism," by John Rignall; "Tradition and Experience: Walter Benjamin's 'Some Motifs in Baudelaire'," by Andrew Benjamin; "The Invisible *Flâneuse:* Women and the Literature of Modernity," by Janet Wolff; and "On Some Jewish Motifs in Benjamin," by Irving Wohlfarth.

Berger, John. "Walter Benjamin." In *The Look of Things: Essays by John Berger,* edited by Nikos Stangos, pp. 87-93. New York: The Viking Press, 1971.
　　Examines the contradictory nature of Benjamin's writings.

Birkerts, Sven. "Walter Benjamin." In his *An Artificial Wilderness: Essays on 20th-Century Literature,* pp. 287-303. New York: William Morrow and Company, 1987.
　　Analyzes the figure of the flâneur as a symbol of the subtle complexities of Benjamin's character and works.

Brooks, Peter. "The Storyteller." *Yale Journal of Criticism* 1, No. 1 (Fall 1987): 21-38.
　　Discusses the nature of oral and written narration, especially as presented in Benjamin's essay "The Storyteller."

Bruck, Jan. "Beckett, Benjamin and the Modern Crisis in Communication." *New German Critique,* No. 26 (Spring-Summer 1982): 159-71.
　　Contrasts attitudes expressed in the works of Samuel Beckett and Benjamin towards the perceived loss of traditional art forms and values that signalled literary modernism.

Buck-Morss, Susan. *The Origin of Negative Dialectics: Theodor W. Adorno, Walter Benjamin, and the Frankfurt Institute.* New York: The Free Press, 1977, 335 p.
　　Examines the philosophical theories of Theodor Adorno and Benjamin, focusing on clarifying Adorno's concept of "negative dialectics."

———. *The Dialectics of Seeing: Walter Benjamin's "Arcades" Project.* Cambridge, Mass.: The MIT Press, 1989.
　　Speculates on the content and significance of Benjamin's unfinished *Arcades* project.

Colloquia Germanica: Perspectives on Walter Benjamin 12, No. 3 (1979): 193-300.
　　Special issue dedicated to topics, structure, and aesthetic theory in Benjamin's works. Includes articles in English by Stephen Eric Bronner, David Bathrick, and Heinz Puppe as well as a bibliographic checklist by Peter Beicken and Jay F. Bodine.

Cowan, Bainard. "Walter Benjamin's Theory of Allegory." *New German Critique,* No. 22 (Winter 1981): 109-22.
　　Explores the literary implications of Benjamin's theory of allegory, stating that "Benjamin achieves the first really significant definition of allegory since Dante by casting it in cultural and ontological terms."

de Man, Paul. " 'Conclusions': Walter Benjamin's 'The Task of the Translator'." *Yale French Studies* 69 (1985): 25-46.
　　Edited transcript of a lecture given by de Man in which Benjamin's theories on the nature of translation are discussed.

Eagleton, Terry. *Walter Benjamin: or, Towards a Revolutionary Criticism.* London: NLB, 1981, 187 p.

Study designed to clarify Benjamin's commitment to Marxism and refute the opinion that his political viewpoints were a "tolerable eccentricity."

Gilman, Richard. "Successful Failure." *The New Republic* 159, No. 24 (14 December 1968): 27-9.

Review of *Illuminations.* Gilman praises the impartiality of Benjamin's methods and concludes that he "did his quiet, marvelous, difficult work and left it to the future to determine, as it always does, what 'success' is and where it may be found."

Habermas, Jürgen. "Walter Benjamin: Consciousness-Raising or Rescuing Critique." In his *Philosophical-Political Profiles,* translated by Frederick G. Lawrence, pp. 129-63. Cambridge, Mass.: The MIT Press, 1983.

1972 essay examining Benjamin's theories of history and experience as they pertain to his role as a cultural critic, characterizing him as one "whose work is destined for disparate effective histories."

Hartman, Geoffrey H. "The Sacred Jungle 2: Walter Benjamin." In his *Criticism in the Wilderness: The Study of Literature Today,* pp. 63-85. New Haven: Yale University Press, 1980.

Offers close readings of Benjamin's essays on Baudelaire and Kafka, and on the philosophy of history, in a work that traces the development of cultural and literary criticism.

Higonnet, Anne; Higonnet, Margaret; and Higonnet, Patrice. "Façades: Walter Benjamin's Paris." *Critical Inquiry* 10, No. 3 (March 1984): 391-419.

Focuses on the essay "Paris, Capital of the Nineteenth Century" and analyzes the technique of and philosophy behind Benjamin's unfinished *Arcades* project. The critics suggest applications to various cultural phenomena of the nineteenth century.

Jacobs, Carol. "Walter Benjamin: Image of Proust." In her *The Dissimulating Harmony: The Image of Interpretation in Nietzche, Rilke, Artaud, and Benjamin,* pp. 87-110. Baltimore: The Johns Hopkins University Press, 1978.

Discusses Benjamin's essay "Towards the Image of Proust" as an innovative examination of "the relationship between life and image and what this relation implies about the possibility of interpretative judgment."

Jay, Martin. *The Dialectical Imagination: A History of the Frankfurt School and the Institute of Social Research, 1923-1950.* Boston: Little, Brown and Company, 1973, 382 p.

Appraises the social and theoretical contributions of Adorno, Horkheimer, Benjamin, and others active in the Frankfurt School and the Institute for Social Research.

Jennings, Michael W. *Dialectical Images: Walter Benjamin's Theory of Literary Criticism.* Ithaca: Cornell University Press, 1987, 233 p.

Examines Benjamin's "philosophy of history and language, his understanding of a truth content resident in the work of art, [and] his critical methodology" as developed in his essays on French and German literature.

Josipovici, Gabriel. "Walter Benjamin, 1892-1940." In his *The Lessons of Modernism, and Other Essays,* pp. 51-63. London: Macmillan, 1977.

Offers a general discussion of Benjamin's major ideas.

Lunn, Eugene. *Marxism and Modernism: An Historical Study of Lukács, Brecht, Benjamin, and Adorno.* Berkeley: University of California Press, 1982.

Discusses the works of Benjamin, Adorno, Brecht, and Lukács, studying "the historical sources and many-sided contours of [the] political-aesthetic 'encounter' " of Marxism and modernism.

Masuzawa, Tomoko. "Tracing the Figure of Redemption: Walter Benjamin's Physiognomy of Modernity." *Modern Language Notes* 100, No. 3 (April 1985): 514-36.

Analyzes recurring biblical references in Benjamin's theory of language as represented in various essays.

Nägele, Rainer, ed. *Benjamin's Ground: New Readings of Walter Benjamin.* Detroit: Wayne State University Press, 1988, 190 p.

Collection of essays by Rainer Nägele, David E. Wellbery, Timothy Bahti, Rodolphe Gasché, Beryl Schlossman, Avital Ronell, and Werner Hamacher, concerning structural, linguistic, and thematic issues in Benjamin's writings.

New German Critique: Special Walter Benjamin Issue, No. 17 (Spring 1979): 1-208.

Includes critical assessments by Jürgen Habermas, Peter Uwe Hohendahl, Irving Wohlfarth, and others, as well as a bibliography of secondary literature on Benjamin by Gary Smith.

Norris, Christopher. "Image and Parable: Readings of Walter Benjamin." *Philosophy and Literature* 7, No. 1 (April 1983): 15-31.

Analyzes major studies of Benjamin in a discussion of the ways in which Benjamin's writings necessitate a variety of interpretive strategies.

Radnoti, Sandor. "The Early Aesthetics of Walter Benjamin." *International Journal of Sociology* VII, No. 1 (Spring 1977): 76-123.

Examines *Goethe's "Elective Affinities"* and *Origins of the German Tragic Drama* as representative of the developmental stage of Benjamin's doctrine of art.

Ridless, Robin. "Walter Benjamin: The Changing of the Superstructure." In her *Ideology and Art: Theories of Mass Culture from Walter Benjamin to Umberto Eco.* New York: Peter Lang, 1984, 232 p.

Introduces Benjamin as a precursor of mass culture critics, focusing on his ideas in *The Work of Art in the Age of Mechanical Reproduction* and "The Author as Producer."

Ridley, Hugh. "Walter Benjamin—Towards a New Marxist Aesthetic." In *Weimar Germany: Writers and Politics,* edited by A. F. Bance, pp. 168-83. Edinburgh: Scottish Academic Press, 1982.

Views *The Work of Art in the Age of Mechanical Reproduction* and "The Author as Producer" as forming "an unmistakable part of the legacy of Weimar."

Roberts, Julian. *Walter Benjamin.* Atlantic Highlands, N. J.: Humanities Press, 1983, 250 p.

Full-length study of Benjamin's life and career, focusing on his commitment to Marxism.

Rosen, Charles. "The Ruins of Walter Benjamin" and "The

Origins of Walter Benjamin." *The New York Review of Books* XXIV, Nos. 17, 18 (27 October 1977; 10 November 1977): 31-40; 30-8.

Two-part review of *Origin of the German Tragic Drama*, characterizing Benjamin's works as esoteric and unteachable yet significant texts of cultural history.

Smith, Gary, ed. *On Walter Benjamin: Critical Essays and Recollections.* Cambridge, Mass.: The MIT Press, 1988, 400 p.

Collection intended as a definitive source of English criticism on the major issues in Benjamin's works.

Solmi, Renato. "Walter Benjamin: An Introduction." *The Denver Quarterly* 12, No. 1 (Spring 1977): 259-70.

Discusses Benjamin's major works, attempting to clarify their main theories and significance.

Vine, Richard. "The Beatification of Walter Benjamin." *The New Criterion* 8, No. 10 (June 1990): 37-48.

Offers an unfavorable estimate of Benjamin and his works, arguing that his "liberality is nothing other than the workings of a ruthlessly coercive agenda, just as [his] highly selective 'pluralism' turns out to be a thinly veiled disdain for the real aspirations of the vast majority of the earth's citizens."

Wellek, René. "The Early Literary Criticism of Walter Benjamin." *Rice University Studies* 57, No. 4 (Fall 1971): 123-34.

Outlines the content and significance of Benjamin's early, less recognized works.

Wohlfarth, Irving. "The Politics of Prose and the Art of Awakening: Walter Benjamin's Version of a German Romantic Motif." In *Glyph* 7, edited by Samuel Weber, pp. 131-48. Baltimore: The Johns Hopkins University Press, 1980.

Argues that Benjamin did not intend to "relive the Romantic dream—the dream of a synthesis of waking and dreaming—but, unlike the deconstructors, who 'solicit' it, he continues, in 'citing' it, to visualize the awakening as its prosaic telos."

Charles Waddell Chesnutt

1858-1932

American short story writer, novelist, essayist, journalist, and biographer.

For further information about Chesnutt's career, see *TCLC,* Volume 5.

Chesnutt was the first black American fiction writer to receive critical and popular attention from the predominantly white literary establishment and readership of his age. He is especially noted for short stories in which he conveyed implicit denunciations of slavery while appealing to readers of Plantation School fiction, nostalgic stories of the antebellum South by white authors. Chesnutt also wrote overtly didactic short stories and novels with racial themes, advocating in particular the cause of mixed-race Americans, but the unpopularity of these preceptive works virtually ended Chesnutt's literary career.

Chesnutt was born in Cleveland, Ohio, to free parents of mixed racial heritage, and raised in Fayetteville, North Carolina. An excellent student, at the age of fourteen he became a pupil-teacher at the State Normal School for black students. He taught elsewhere in North and South Carolina before returning to Fayetteville in 1877 to become assistant principal, and then principal, at the State Normal School. In 1878 he married; seeking more profitable employment to support his growing family, he worked briefly as a reporter for a New York newspaper before settling his family in Cleveland in 1884 and taking a job as a clerk and stenographer in the legal department of a railway company. Stimulated to study law, Chesnutt passed the Ohio bar exam in 1887 and founded a stenographic court reporting service which proved successful. Although he was light-complected enough to "pass" in white society, Chesnutt never denied his black ancestry and furthermore was unwilling to accept the elitism of the nascent black and mulatto middle class becoming established in the North. Subject to the inequities that befell those of mixed race, he was repudiated by many blacks as well as by whites.

Throughout his life Chesnutt considered his pursuit of a literary career to be a means of both making a living and presenting racial issues from the point of view of a black person. After a few short stories and sketches appeared in local periodicals, his story "The Goophered Grapevine" was published in the *Atlantic Monthly* in 1887. Similar in structure to the Uncle Remus stories of Joel Chandler Harris, "The Goophered Grapevine" begins and ends with a frame narrative. A white northern couple who have moved to the South encounter Julius McAdoo, a former slave, who regales them with a "conjure tale," or supernatural folktale. An adept raconteur, McAdoo tells the story to entertain the northerners and to influence a decision they are contemplating. Claiming that the vineyard on the plantation that the couple wishes to buy is under a dangerous "goopher," or magic spell, McAdoo hopes to persuade them not to buy; this would allow McAdoo to continue living on the abandoned plantation and profiting from his illicit manufacture of wine. Although the northerners disbelieve the tale of magic, they enjoy the tale-telling and offer McAdoo employment. Similarly, each subsequent conjure story influences the couple in a way that benefits McAdoo. Capitalizing on a vogue for southern local color fiction, Houghton Mifflin published *The Conjure Woman* in 1899. The success of the volume contributed to the decision to bring out a second collection, *The Wife of His Youth, and Other Stories of the Color Line,* including stories exploring the divided racial identity of mixed-blood Americans and the impassable racial barriers that prevent blacks from participating fully in the social, economic, and political life of the United States. This collection was less favorably received than Chesnutt's first, drawing criticism for focusing on racial issues that were commonly considered too sensitive for fictional exposition. Three subsequent novels, *The House behind the Cedars, The Marrow of Tradition,* and *The Colonel's Dream,* deal at length with such controversial themes as "passing" in white society, miscegenation, and proposed solutions to the racial problems of the South. The novels were unsuccessful financially and have been evaluated by critics as less accomplished artistically than the short stories. Chesnutt encountered increasing difficulties in finding publishers, and although he wrote several novels after *The Colo-*

nel's Dream, these works remain unpublished. While he continued to publish short stories in periodicals, as well as nonfiction essays addressing racial issues, he returned to his court reporting business in 1902, devoting much of his time to it thereafter. His 1928 award of the Spingarn Medal by the National Association for the Advancement of Colored People was largely due to his literary achievements of several decades earlier. He died in 1932.

With Chesnutt's conjure stories, American readers were presented for the first time with authentic black folk culture. In these works, folktale motifs of magic and the traditional African folk figure of the trickster are cast against a background of the antebellum South. Often the stories are tragic, illustrating the injustice and cruelty of the slave system. The framing device, which consists of the white narrator's commentary on each story and placed it in a postbellum setting, rendered the protest elements of the stories less explicit and therefore, some critics contend, more acceptable to Chesnutt's white readers. The uncompromising racial themes of his second collection and his published novels are presented within no such propitiating format, and critics maintain that in his novels Chesnutt further sacrificed literary artistry to the urgency of his message. Nevertheless, these works are acclaimed for addressing the pressing social problems of race relations in the United States. As the first American author to explore the range of black experience in his fiction, Chesnutt stands at the forefront of an entire generation of black realist authors.

(See also *Contemporary Authors,* Vols. 106 and 125, and *Dictionary of Literary Biography,* Vols. 12 and 50.)

PRINCIPAL WORKS

The Conjure Woman   (short stories)   1899
Frederick Douglass   (biography)   1899
The Wife of His Youth, and Other Stories of the Color Line
   (short stories)   1899
The House behind the Cedars   (novel)   1900
The Marrow of Tradition   (novel)   1901
The Colonel's Dream   (novel)   1905
The Short Fiction of Charles W. Chesnutt   (short stories)
   1974; revised edition, 1981

W. D. Howells   (essay date 1901)

[*Howells was the chief progenitor of American Realism and the most influential American literary critic during the late nineteenth century. Through Realism, a theory central to his fiction and criticism, Howells sought to disperse "the conventional acceptations by which men live on easy terms with themselves" that they might "examine the grounds of their social and moral opinions." To accomplish this, according to Howells, the writer must strive to record detailed impressions of everyday life, endowing characters with believable motives and avoiding authorial comment in the narrative. In addition to writing perceptive critical studies on the works of Henry James and Mark Twain, Howells reviewed three generations of international literature, promoting the works of*

Emile Zola, Bernard Shaw, Henrik Ibsen, Emily Dickinson, and other important authors. In the following excerpt, Howells reviews The Marrow of Tradition.]

Mr. Chesnutt, it seems to me, has lost literary quality in acquiring literary quantity, and though his book, ***The Marrow of Tradition,*** is of the same strong material as his earlier books, it is less simple throughout, and therefore less excellent in manner. At his worst, he is no worse than the higher average of the ordinary novelist, but he ought always to be very much better, for he began better, and he is of that race which has, first of all, to get rid of the cakewalk, if it will not suffer from a smile far more blighting than any frown. He is fighting a battle, and it is not for him to pick up the cheap graces and poses of the jouster. He does, indeed, cast them all from him when he gets down to his work, and in the dramatic climaxes and closes of his story he shortens his weapons and deals his blows so absolutely without flourish that I have nothing but admiration for him. ***The Marrow of Tradition,*** like everything else he has written, has to do with the relations of the blacks and whites, and in that republic of letters where all men are free and equal he stands up for his own people with a courage which has more justice than mercy in it. The book is, in fact, bitter, bitter. There is no reason in history why it should not be so, if wrong is to be repaid with hate, and yet it would be better if it was not so bitter. I am not saying that he is so inartistic as to play the advocate; whatever his minor foibles may be, he is an artist whom his stepbrother Americans may well be proud of; but while he recognizes pretty well all the facts in the case, he is too clearly of a judgment that is made up. One cannot blame him for that; what would one be one's self? If the tables could once be turned, and it could be that it was the black race which violently and lastingly triumphed in the bloody revolution at Wilmington, North Carolina, a few years ago, what would not we excuse to the white man who made the atrocity the argument of his fiction?

Mr. Chesnutt goes far back of the historic event in his novel, and shows us the sources of the cataclysm which swept away a legal government and perpetuated an insurrection, but he does not paint the blacks all good, or the whites all bad. He paints them as slavery made them on both sides, and if in the very end he gives the moral victory to the blacks—if he suffers the daughter of the black wife to have pity on her father's daughter by his white wife, and while her own child lies dead from a shot fired in the revolt, gives her husband's skill to save the life of her sister's child—it cannot be said that either his æsthetics or ethics are false. Those who would question either must allow, at least, that the negroes have had the greater practice in forgiveness, and that there are many probabilities to favor his interpretation of the fact. No one who reads the book can deny that the case is presented with great power, or fail to recognize in the writer a portent of the sort of negro equality against which no series of hangings and burnings will finally avail. (pp. 882-83)

W. D. Howells, *"A Psychological Counter-Current in Recent Fiction,"* in The North American Review, *Vol. 173, No. 6, December, 1901, pp. 872-88.*

Robert Bone (essay date 1975)

[*Bone is an American critic and educator with special interest in African-American literature and in Shakespeare. Bone has said of himself: "A white man and critic of black literature, I try to demonstrate by the quality of my work that scholarship is not the same thing as identity." He is the author of the informative critical histories* The Negro Novel in America *(1958) and* Down Home: A History of Afro-American Short Fiction from Its Beginnings to the Harlem Renaissance. *In the following excerpt from the last-named work, Bone discusses the* Conjure Woman *stories as satiric works written in opposition to the Plantation School of southern literature, and in particular as a response to the Uncle Remus stories of Joel Chandler Harris.*]

Paul Dunbar's undoing was his willingness to fulfill the expectations of the white world. Charles Chesnutt, a man of tougher moral fiber, was uncompromising in his opposition to anything that threatened his essential dignity. From the outset he refused to lie in the Procrustean bed prepared for him by partisans of the Plantation School. In a letter to George Washington Cable, he denounced the current literary portraiture of Negroes: ". . . their chief virtues have been their dog-like fidelity to their old masters, for whom they have been willing to sacrifice almost life itself. Such characters exist. . . . But I can't write about those people, or rather I won't write about them."

In rejecting the myth of the faithful black retainer, Chesnutt was striking at the heart of Southern pastoral. For the pastoral ideal, according to Empson, assumes "a proper or beautiful relation between rich and poor" [*Some Versions of Pastoral,* 1935]. If the master-servant relation is portrayed as other than idyllic, the effect is antipastoral. Chesnutt's antipastoral intentions are most explicit in a story called **"The Passing of Grandison,"** which is best described as a loyalty tale turned inside out. Here Chesnutt pushes the stereotype of the loyal slave to the point of absurdity, whereupon the tale, yielding to ironic pressure, is transformed into mock-pastoral.

Chesnutt's masterpiece of antipastoral is *The Conjure Woman.* Set in rural North Carolina, and dealing ostensibly with grape cultivation, this book of stories is designed to expose the serpent in the Southern garden. It constitutes, in fact, a devastating parody of Southern pastoral. Arcadia lies in ruins in the aftermath of civil war. Hence the images of dilapidation and decay that permeate these tales. The author's aim is to force us to confront the destruction of the Garden, ponder its fundamental cause, and trace it in the end to chattel slavery, the fatal flaw in the *ancien régime.*

Enough has perhaps been said to indicate that Chesnutt's art is rooted in antithesis and opposition. If the Plantation School inclines toward pastoral, he employs the counter-genre. If white audiences object to mulatto characters, he devotes a whole volume to stories of the color line. Nor is Chesnutt's contrariety exclusively a racial stance. In **"The Wife of His Youth"** and **"A Matter of Principle,"** he satirizes the color prejudices of the Negro middle class. In **"The Web of Circumstance"** he challenges the Washington formula of education and property as a panacea for racial ills. Chesnutt chose, in short, to work against the grain.

This cantankerous streak is the mark of a born satirist. A gift for satire was in fact Chesnutt's major contribution to Afro-American letters. Drawing on the satirical resources of the black folktale, he founded a tradition that descends through Langston Hughes and George Schuyler to William Melvin Kelley and Ishmael Reed. As a writer of satirical tales, Chesnutt was by far the most accomplished literary artist of the Age of Washington. His chef d'oeuvre, *The Conjure Woman,* is a tart confection of sly derision and purgatorial laughter. Unmatched for subtlety, sophistication, and depth of moral vision, this book is the most important product of the black imagination prior to the First World War. (pp. 74-5)

Chesnutt's first book of stories [*The Conjure Woman*] could not have been conceived without the prototype of the Uncle Remus tales. He himself acknowledges as much in [**"Superstitions and Folk-lore of the South,"** *Modern Culture,* May 1901]:

> Mr. Harris, in his Uncle Remus stories, has, with fine literary discrimination, collected and put into pleasing and enduring form, the plantation stories which dealt with animal lore, but so little attention has been paid to those dealing with so-called conjuration, that they seem in a fair way to disappear, without leaving a trace behind.

In retrospect, however, Chesnutt draws a sharp distinction between the Uncle Remus stories and his own conjure tales. In an essay published a year or two before his death, he discusses the genesis of his conjure stories:

> They are sometimes referred to as folk tales, but while they employ much of the universal machinery of wonder stories, especially the metamorphosis, with one exception, that of the first story, **"The Goophered Grapevine,"** of which the norm was a folk tale, the stories are the fruit of my own imagination, in which respect they differ from the Uncle Remus stories which are avowedly folk tales.

This crucial distinction, which ostensibly concerns the use of folk material, in fact reflects a difference of esthetic creeds. Harris, operating from a set of assumptions that might be described as representational or naturalistic, strives to preserve the authenticity of black folktales by leaving them "uncooked." Chesnutt, whose working assumptions are Coleridgean, stresses the primacy of the imagination and improvises freely on his folk materials. It is true, in short, that *The Conjure Woman* is based on an authentic body of plantation lore that deals with witchcraft and conjuration. But Chesnutt is correct to insist that his primary interest in this material is literary, not ethnological.

Chesnutt is in debt to Harris, but only for the outer trappings of his art. The Uncle Remus books consist of a narrative frame and a set of "inside" stories; *The Conjure Woman* has a similar design. Harris employs the venerable Uncle Remus as his narrator; Chesnutt, a similar figure named Uncle Julius. Both narrators recount a series of plantation legends in Negro dialect to a white audience. These resemblances, however, are superficial. Certain forms are employed by Harris in the service of a pastoral ideal. But Chesnutt takes these neutral forms and fills them with the demythologizing spirit of antipastoral.

The truth is that Chesnutt used Harris as a protective

mask. His strategy, in the face of a racist culture unwilling to accept him on his own terms, was to present himself in the guise of the harmless and familiar. He was able to appropriate a literary form made popular by Harris and infuse it with a content that was not only strikingly original, but profoundly subversive of the smiling face of slavery put forward in the Harris books. Against great cultural odds he managed to pursue his own artistic ends, which were not the concealment, but precisely the exposure of the cruelties and injustices of chattel slavery.

The Conjure Woman consists of seven stories, bound together by a common principle of plot construction, a common cast of characters, and a common theme. In each story there is an outside plot, narrated in standard English by a white Northerner, and an inside plot, narrated in Negro dialect by Uncle Julius. Typically an action is undertaken in the outside plot (frequently a carriage drive), in the course of which an occasion arises for the telling of a conjure tale. This inside story, told by Uncle Julius, contains at its core some act of metamorphosis, such as the transformation of a slave into a tree, a man into a mule, or a child into a bird.

The plan of the book, then, is anything but simple, as several critics have mistakenly averred. On the contrary, it is a rather intricate affair, based on the sophisticated device of the parallel plot. It cannot be too heavily stressed that Chesnutt, at a time when most Negro writers were still learning to tell a simple story, was constructing plots within plots, and compelling his readers to respond to complex analogies. Nor was this a matter of mere virtuosity. The function of the outside plot is to provide a clue to the meaning of the metamorphosis, and thereby to control our reading of the fable.

Chesnutt confronts us in *The Conjure Woman* with two radically divergent fictive worlds. That of the outside story is the world of actuality, the domain of the ordinary and the commonplace. It is preeminently a world of *economics:* of crop rotation, improvements to the land, and projects for increasing revenue. Its spiritual qualities, as embodied in the white narrator (a gentleman farmer, transplanted to Patesville from his native Ohio), include a naïve faith in rationality, and a dogged skepticism toward anything that smacks of magic or conjuration. It is the world, in short, of capitalist enterprise as it invades the Reconstruction South.

The inside story represents the realm of the imagination, the domain of the wonderful and marvelous. It is a fairy-tale universe of grotesque transformations and Gothic horrors. Its gruesome violence reminds us of its kinship with the black folktale. The world of the conjure tale confronts us not with the present but the past; not with realism but romanticism; not with reason but emotion; not with calculation but accident. The central values of this world are not progressive but traditional. *The Conjure Woman* thus projects the crucial tensions of the nation in the decades following the Civil War.

The book is designed, with its movement from the husk to the kernel, to lead us toward the fabulous and fanciful. The white narrator, and to a lesser extent his wife, represent what Wallace Stevens calls "the world without imagination." Their civilization, lacking in imagination except where it came to making money, did not hesitate to trade

in human flesh. Their lack of moral vision, even after Emancipation, continues to insulate them from comprehending the enormity of this historic crime. It is the function of the black storyteller, drawing on the imaginative resources of his folk tradition, to arouse the white man from his moral lethargy. Such were the politics of the imagination, as Chesnutt conceived of them in 1899.

The relation of Uncle Julius to his white employers is emblematic of the artist-audience relation. The black story-teller functions as a kind of proxy for Chesnutt, while John and Annie serve as stand-ins for Chesnutt's white audience. The impact of the conjure tale on its auditors is thus as much a part of Chesnutt's meaning as the tale itself. What John and Annie understand or fail to understand is often the dramatic center of the story. In Chesnutt's parable, the art of fiction serves as a corrective to the moral vision. John and Annie are the see-ers; chattel slavery the thing seen. Julius is the intermediary, or artist, who supplies the means of superior sight, or insight.

The role of the black writer, as Chesnutt conceives of it, is conveyed through the metaphor of conjuration. For Julius is a kind of conjurer, who works his roots and plies his magic through the art of storytelling. The point is that he succeeds in manipulating his white audience, in ways both small and large. He thus provides a model of how to conjure or bewitch the white folks. Through the medium of fiction, Chesnutt proposes to create a moral revolution, by enlarging the white man's sympathies and sharpening his moral vision.

The instrument of improved vision is the metamorphosis found at the center of each conjure tale. But why should a mere conjurer's trick—an alteration in the shape of things—enable us to see them better? Because fiction is concerned with the truth that lies beyond the form. It alters forms, in order to reveal essences. The artist will not suffer us to live in a world of surfaces; he insists on probing for a deeper reality. It is the reality of chattel slavery that interests Chesnutt, and he employs a series of brilliant transformations in exposing it to view.

The concept of metamorphosis is crucial to the thematic unity of *The Conjure Woman.* Beginning with a theory of the imagination, Chesnutt extends its working principle to the spheres of morality and politics. At the core of each conjure tale is a transformation that reveals some essential truth concerning slavery times. But the magical power of fiction as wielded by Uncle Julius is immediately felt in the hearts of his white listeners. There a moral transformation begins to occur. Projected on the historical plane, this transformation constitutes the Reconstruction. For Chesnutt understands that white Americans as well as black were in need of moral reconstruction after the Emancipation.

So much for the book's general design; we must now examine certain of the stories in detail. The basis of selection is somewhat arbitrary, for all but one of the seven stories that comprise *The Conjure Woman* are achievements of the first rank. [In a footnote, Bone writes: " **'Hot-Foot Hannibal,'** it seems to me, falls victim to the author's sentimental tendencies".] Limitations of space, however, preclude a full discussion of six conjure tales. Perhaps four will serve to illustrate the possibilities inherent in the form, as well as indicate, without belaboring the point, the stature of the book as a work of art.

"The Goophered Grapevine" is the most widely anthologized of Chesnutt's conjure tales. Since it is the opening story, it bears the burden of setting forth the basic situation and launching most of the principal themes. John, the white narrator, and Annie, his wife, have come to Patesville from Ohio in search of a tract of land suitable for cultivating grapes. As they survey a ruined plantation with an eye to its purchase they come upon an elderly Negro enjoying a hatful of scuppernong grapes. In response to their queries concerning the history of the vineyard, he tells them a tale of slavery times.

This very vineyard, Julius explains, was "goophered" by a conjure woman in the days before the war. To prevent his slaves from stealing grapes, Mars Dugal' hired Aunt Peggy to cast a powerful spell on his vineyard. According to the terms of the goopher, any slave who ate the grapes would be certain to die within a year. The goopher worked entirely to the satisfaction of old master, who was heard to remark to his overseer that "fifteen hund'ed gallon er wine wuz monst'us good intrus' on de ten dollars he laid out on de vimya'd."

When a newly purchased slave eats the grapes in ignorance of their magical properties, Aunt Peggy is persuaded to suspend the power of the conjure. If Henry will anoint his bald head every spring with the sap of the pruned vines, he will escape the consequences of his misdeed. Through the workings of this new conjure, Henry comes to share the properties of a grape plant, his life rhythms tied to the seasonal changes of the vines. When the plant sends forth its leaves and tendrils in the spring, Henry's hair grows thick and he is young and spry again. When the leaves fall and the grapes shrivel in the autumn, he becomes bowed and rheumatic; his hair falls out; and his physical strength declines.

Mars Dugal', who was never known to let a dollar slip by him in the dark, takes advantage of the situation to do some shrewd slave-trading. For five seasons he sells Henry in the spring and buys him back at a lower price in the fall, realizing a profit of a thousand dollars on each complete transaction. All goes well until a strange Yankee appears on the plantation. This high-pressure salesman bedazzles Mars Dugal' with promises of greater productivity if he will invest in a new wine press and adopt the latest methods of scientific farming. He persuades old master to push the vines beyond their limits, and in the end they are destroyed, along with Henry, who is linked symbolically to their fate.

What is the meaning of Chesnutt's fable, with its magical transformation of a black slave into a grape plant? Beneath the comic surface of the tale is a lesson in the economics of slavery. The slaves were in fact worth more in the spring, with the growing season still to come; in the fall prices declined, for an owner was responsible for supporting his slaves through the unproductive winter season. These fluctuations in price underscore the slave's status as *commodity;* his helpless dependence on the impersonal forces of the market. The target of Chesnutt's satire is the dehumanizing system that reduced the black man to the level of the crops that he was forced to cultivate.

"The Goophered Grapevine" is concerned with the moral dangers of a market economy abandoned to the trade in human flesh. Through the figure of Mars Dugal', Chesnutt satirizes a capitalist culture obsessed with a good return on its investment. But the institution of chattel slavery, operating within the capitalist ethos, produced an historical disaster. The story of Mars Dugal' and the Yankee swindler is a parable of greed. Slavery was a case of pruning the branches too close to the vine. Through a desire for excess profits and a total ruthlessness toward its black labor force, the white South brought about its own destruction.

The moral atmosphere of slavery, as Chesnutt re-creates it, is one of mutual deception, slyness, and intrigue. It is a world of masking jokers in which everyone—white and black alike—is trying to outsmart or swindle everybody else. It is in short the world of Brer Rabbit, where the devil takes the hindmost and the height of folly is to trust your neighbor. A secondary theme, which will reverberate throughout **The Conjure Woman,** is the deceitfulness of appearances and the necessity of a certain skepticism where human motives are concerned. Thus the white narrator discovers that Julius has been exercising squatter's rights on the ruined plantation and deriving a substantial profit from the goophered grapevine.

"Sis' Becky's Pickaninny" is a moving tribute to the sorrow songs. It is a celebration of the slave imagination which produced the spirituals and, by converting suffering to sorrow, enabled an oppressed people to survive. Sis' Becky is a field hand who is callously traded by her master, Colonel Pendleton, for a prize racehorse. Her infant son, Little Mose, is not a part of the bargain, and so the slave mother and her child suffer the agonies of separation when she is removed to the next county. In the end they are reunited, but not until the devious maneuvers of a conjure woman trick the white folks into canceling the trade.

The center of the fable consists of two metamorphoses performed by Aunt Peggy, the plantation conjure woman. She transforms little Mose into a hummingbird, then a mockingbird, and sends him on each occasion to pay a visit to his mother. Sis' Becky hears the birds humming or singing and imagines them to be her son. Her heart is thereby comforted and fortified against despair. The birds are emblematic of the black man's musical imagination. Music did not alter the slave's external circumstances, but it did offer consolation to his wounded spirit. Which is why, after all, his songs are called *spirituals.*

Human slavery, Chesnutt seems to imply, is a crime against human love. But behind the crime is a failure of imagination. Colonel Pendleton and his associates are portrayed as men of no imagination who cannot distinguish between trading in horses and trading in human beings. They represent a culture exclusively concerned with cash values. Men of prosaic and utilitarian temper, they hold in contempt the superstitions of their Negro slaves. The blacks, however, with their belief in magic, conjuration, and the like, are seen to possess in ample measure the saving quality of imagination.

The outside story corroborates this reading of the fable. At the outset the narrator's wife, Annie, is suffering a deep depression. Eventually she is aroused from "her settled melancholy" by hearing Julius' conjure tale. The art of storytelling is thus presented as a balm to the sick soul.

Annie's mysterious malaise is cured only when she listens to a tale about a conjure woman, who is a symbol of the artist, or maker of metamorphoses. As the story unfolds, it becomes clear that Annie's ailment is likewise emblematic: it represents the inability of her society to take what Coleridge has called the esemplastic power seriously. Bourgeois civilization, in short, suffers from a contempt for the imagination.

Exemplary of this malaise is her husband's attitude toward Julius and his rabbit foot: "Your people will never rise in the world until they throw off these childish superstitions and learn to live by the light of reason and common sense. How absurd to imagine that the forefoot of a poor dead rabbit, with which he timorously felt his way along through a life surrounded by snares and pitfalls, beset by enemies on every hand, can promote happiness or success, or ward off failure or misfortune!"

We need only be reminded of Chesnutt's admiration for the Uncle Remus books to scrutinize a passage concerning rabbits with extraordinary care. It was the Negro slave, after all, who "timorously felt his way along through a life surrounded by snares and pitfalls, beset by enemies on every hand. . . . " If Brer Fox, like Colonel Pendleton and the white narrator, is a symbol of power without imagination, Brer Rabbit, like Sis' Becky and Uncle Julius, is a symbol of the imagination without power, which sometimes manages to turn the tables, but always enables its possessor to endure.

Julius remarks toward the end of the story that "Ef Sis' Becky had had a rabbit foot, she nebber would a' went th'oo all dis trouble." We are to understand, however, that she had a good luck charm or fetish all along. Her rabbit foot was the power of imagination that enabled her to transform a hummingbird or mockingbird into her lost child. It is no accident, then, that John should discover a rabbit foot among his wife's effects, shortly after her condition takes a permanent turn for the better. As for Julius, his rabbit foot is his power as a storyteller: it is that which has kept him out of trouble with the white folks for more than forty years.

"The Conjurer's Revenge" is the subtlest and most difficult of Chesnutt's conjure tales. Designedly so, for the author means to place the burden of interpretation squarely on the reader, and thereby to compel the active involvement of his imagination. The inside story is based on two metamorphoses. Having offended a conjure man, a slave named Primus is turned into a mule. On his deathbed the conjure man relents, and determines to restore him to his human form. Unfortunately he dies before the second transformation is complete, and Primus is left permanently crippled by a club foot. Unfinished metamorphosis is thus the dominant conception of the story.

Muledom is developed as the metaphorical equivalent of slavery. From the first the mule is linked to the black man as a beast of burden. Julius remarks, for example, "eve'y time I cuts a mule wid a hick'ry, 'pears ter me mos' lackly I's cuttin' some er my own relations." Now let the metaphor expand: slavery is itself an act of conjuration, for it attempts, in effect, to turn a man into a mule. That is the point of the comical sequence in which Primus, turned mule, raids a tobacco patch, gets drunk on fermenting wine, and attacks a man who is courting his former sweet-

heart. A social system may change a man into a beast of burden, but his human traits will nonetheless persist.

In Chesnutt's fable, the man who conjured Primus into muledom undergoes a conversion to Christianity. Overcome by remorse, he hopes to atone for the harm that he has done by turning the mule back into a man. It is not so easy, however, to wipe the slate clean. Once a man has been a mule, he bears the scars of that condition in the form of a club foot. His Reconstruction, so to speak, is incomplete. Slavery has left the black man psychologically handicapped in his situation as a freedman. Chesnutt's unfinished metamorphosis, on its primary level of meaning, is an emblem of the unfinished business of American democracy.

Meanwhile the outside story is concerned with another kind of unfinished metamorphosis. As the story opens, it is a dull Sunday, and Julius' white employer seeks amusement in "the impossible career of the blonde heroine of a rudimentary novel." Exasperated, he throws the book aside and welcomes the diversion of a conjure tale. His wife too has been bored, but for once she is not amused by Julius' narrative: "That story does not appeal to me, Uncle Julius, and is not up to your usual mark. It isn't pathetic, it has no moral that I can discover, and I can't see why you should tell it. In fact, it seems to me like nonsense."

What follows is a brilliant defense of the art of fiction. Through a strategy and style deliberately evocative of Cervantes, Chesnutt establishes his theme: the deceitfulness of appearances. Whether it is a question of horse trading, or the apparent rising and setting of the sun, sense impressions are not to be trusted. It is the special virtue of fiction, precisely by manipulating appearances, to lead us to a deeper truth. But for this mode of knowledge to be viable, it is necessary that the reader see beyond the surfaces of things. Annie has failed to penetrate the surface of Julius' fable. The force of the tale is therefore lost on her and she must suffer, like all literal-minded men, the doom of nonsense.

Fiction is a joint enterprise: that is Chesnutt's essential point. It can succeed only by engaging the reader in an act of imaginative collaboration. If the reader fails to do his part, the metamorphosis will be incomplete. That is the secondary meaning of Primus' club foot. The conjure-man, or artist, initiates the transformation, but if the reader refuses to participate, the tale will limp along to a sorry conclusion. Something akin to Chesnutt's theme is expressed in Robert Frost's "The Grindstone," when the poet remarks of his own honings and sharpenings, "I was for leaving something to the whetter."

"The Gray Wolf's Ha'nt" explores the relationship of the imagination to the moral life. In this cautionary tale of a man who is turned into a wolf, Chesnutt warns us of the bestiality that must ensue if we neglect the proper uses of imagination. His ultimate reference is the crime of human bondage, for it was a mammoth failure of imagination on the white man's part that made possible the cruelties of chattel slavery. The story may thus be seen as a deeper probing of themes set forth in **"The Conjurer's Revenge."** There a white woman's failure to penetrate the meaning of a conjure tale brings upon her head the doom of nonsense. Here a similar failure of imagination calls down upon a black slave the doom of wolfishness.

Dan, who is annoyed by a free Negro's unwelcome attentions to his wife, accidentally kills the man with his fist. Unhappily, the victim is the son of a conjurer, and despite Dan's efforts to protect himself with a life-charm, the father takes a terrible revenge. He turns his son's slayer into a gray wolf and his wife into a black cat. By persuading Dan that the cat is a witch, he lures him into slaying his own spouse. The wolf, having discovered the conjure man's treachery, attacks and kills him, but not before he pronounces an incantation that will fix the charm forever: "Wolf you is en wolf you stays / All de rest er yo' bawn days."

Of what does Dan's "wolfishness" consist? He commits three murders, and on each occasion acts precipitately, on the basis of appearances alone. His tragic flaw is an inability to penetrate the various disguises in which evil may present itself. Like Othello, he falls prey to a satanic figure who manipulates appearances and tempts him into murdering his own wife. At bottom his crimes represent a failure of imagination, for that is the faculty by which we move beyond appearance to a deeper truth. Lacking in imagination, man declines to the level of a beast. Properly employed, the imagination is a "life-charm" which protects its possessor from every kind of evil, injury, or harm.

In customary fashion, Chesnutt controls the meaning of his fable through a set of clues embedded in the narrative frame. The outside story begins and ends in a Gothic atmosphere evocative of Poe and Hawthrone. A certain tract of land, according to Uncle Julius, is haunted by a howling wolf. Like the Southland which it represents, this haunted ground has been the witness of unutterable crimes. Maule's curse, or something like it, lies upon the land. These Gothic devices point the way to Chesnutt's wider philosophical concerns. For the Gothic mode is essentially a means of penetrating mere appearances and striking to the heart of things.

These concerns are made explicit in a passage of philosophy read by the white narrator to his wife. The passage is concerned with the problem of essence and existence, and the difficulty of deducing essence from the shifting appearances of things. The abstract language of philosophy at once gives way to the concrete imagery of fiction: "Some one was coming up the lane; at least, a huge faded cotton umbrella was making progress toward the house, and beneath it a pair of nether extremities in trousers was discernible." From these outward manifestations we are to deduce the essence of Julius. It is Chesnutt's playful way of suggesting that in the fable which ensues we must penetrate to the essence of slavery, whatever the disguises that it may assume.

One such disguise confronts us in the inside story. When the conjurer determines to revenge himself on Dan, he begins with an act of demonic possession: "So dis conjuh man 'mence' by gwine up ter Dan's cabin eve'y night, en takin' Dan out in his sleep en ridin' 'im roun' de roads en fiels ober de rough groun'." What is slavery, Chesnutt invites us to perceive, but a form of witchcraft in which one man takes possession of the body of another and uses it for his own purposes? Through such brilliant transforma-

tions Chesnutt forces us to look at a familiar evil with fresh eyes.

That slavery is Chesnutt's ultimate concern is apparent from a passage toward the end of Julius' tale: "Mars Dugal' tuk on a heap 'bout losin' two er his bes' han's in one day, en ole missis 'lowed it wuz a jedgment on 'im fer sump'n he'd done. But dat fall de craps wuz monst'us big, so Mars Dugal' say de Lawd had temper' de win' ter de sho'n ram, en make up ter 'im fer w'at he had los'." The nameless crime that Mars Dugal' has committed is of course the crime of holding slaves. What was involved, as in the case of Dan's murders, was a failure of empathy. To temper the wind to the shorn ram is to be capable of empathy, or the imaginative projection of one's consciousness into that of another being.

The great testimonial to empathy in English literature is Laurence Sterne's *A Sentimental Journey* (1768). It is Sterne's ruined maiden, Maria, who observes that "God tempers the wind . . . to the shorn lamb." Through this allusion, Chesnutt alerts us to a major source of inspiration for *The Conjure Woman.* We can imagine the shock of recognition as he read of Sterne's journey to Paris and his trip to the Bastille, discovered his parable of the captive starling, and finally perused the words: "Disguise thyself as thou wilt, still, Slavery! said I, still thou art a bitter draught! And though thousands in all ages have been made to drink of thee, thou art no less bitter on that account."

"The Gray Wolf 's Ha'nt" is Chesnutt's finest conjure tale; in it he comes closest to defining his essential theme. His intent throughout *The Conjure Woman* is to penetrate the disguises of the demon, Slavery. His assumption is that evil presents itself to men in the guise of innocence. The Plantation School, for example, was concerned entirely with the innocent surfaces of slavery. But the Brer Rabbit tales, which formed so crucial a part of Chesnutt's heritage, penetrated to the essence of the crime. Like the anonymous creators of the slave tales, Chesnutt was determined to strike through the mask. In pursuing this objective he developed a technique that made him an impressive master of the short-story form. (pp. 79-93)

> *Robert Bone, "Charles Chesnutt," in his* Down Home: A History of Afro-American Short Fiction from Its Beginnings to the End of the Harlem Renaissance, *G. P. Putnam's Sons, 1975, pp. 74-105.*

Addison Gayle, Jr.   (essay date 1975)

[Gayle is an American educator, critic, and biographer best known as the editor of The Black Aesthetic *(1971), a collection of essays by prominent black literary figures and artists, in which he stated that "the serious black artist of today is at war with American society." Refuting the contention that black art can be judged by white aesthetic standards, Gayle calls for a black aesthetic for judging creative works by blacks, contending that "The question for the black critic today is not how beautiful is a melody, a play, a poem, or a novel, but how much more beautiful has the poem, melody, play, or novel made the life of a single black man? How far has the work gone in transforming an American Negro into an*

African-American or a black man? The Black Aesthetic then . . . is a corrective—a means of helping black people out of the polluted mainstream of Americanism." In the following excerpt, Gayle considers Chesnutt's advocacy of the special needs and rights of the mulatto as the primary objective of his fiction.]

Of the three major black novelists between 1900 and 1920, [Paul Laurence] Dunbar is least able to regard black people as other than the stereotypes and images created in the minds of Euro-Americans. At this point, he was one with Booker T. Washington, believing also that most Blacks were minstrels, still, for all their new-found freedom, feeble-minded children lost without the parental guidance of the master race. Dunbar's reputation, nevertheless, is salvaged by the fact that other novelists, more confused about black humanity than he, will attempt in more sophisticated fashion to build upon his example.

This is not altogether true of his contemporary, Charles Waddell Chesnutt. The mulatto schoolteacher and law clerk, turned writer of fiction, dealt with the stereotypes of the time in some of his short fiction; for the most part, however, he created foils to the stereotypes of Page, Harris, and Dixon. The narrator in *The Conjure Woman* (1899), Uncle Julius McAdoo, is a fictional contradiction, an answer even to Harris's Uncle Remus. Julius fulfills the role of the darky entertainer, amusing the Yankees come South with humorous tales of ante-bellum times. This first dissimulating Black in African-American fiction performs this role, however, in order to secure personal gain for himself and his relatives. In each of the seven stories, he is revealed as being more akin to the "darky trickster" of the African literary tradition than the stereotype of the "darky entertainer." In his second volume of short stories, *The Wife of His Youth, and Other Stories of the Color Line* (1899), Chesnutt steps back from full endorsement of the stereotypes of the literature of his white contemporaries. One of these, that of the "tragic mulatto," has its genesis in the nineteenth century and was promulgated in the fiction of Harris, Page, and Dixon alike. Mythology held that the mulatto possessing a mixture of the blood of both races was a hybrid creature, whose character traits were determined by the dominant strain of blood. Blacks and whites held different ideas concerning genetic dominance. Evidence of a minimal amount of white blood meant for Blacks that the mulatto was closer to the Anglo-Saxon than his darker brothers. For whites, the mulatto was a freak of nature; admixture of white blood, dominated by the black, caused them to veer toward criminality, deception, and arrogance; they resembled nothing so much as players in a theater of the damned.

Chesnutt's view of the mulatto was twofold. There were, admittedly, such people as depicted in the works of white writers—arrogant, deceitful, and pretentious—who set themselves off as a race apart. Yet, there were others who were not damned because of an admixture of blood, but rather because of the oppressive nature of the society in which they lived. This dual view led him to counteract the southern imagists on the one hand, on the other, closer to the world envisioned by [William Wells] Brown and [Frank] Webb—closer, that is, to arguing anew the values of assimilationism based upon caste and class. "The races," he argued, "will be quite as effectively amalgamated by lightening the Negroes as they would be by darkening the whites." The major objective of his fiction, therefore, is to plead the case of the mulatto before his white audience, to seek not so much to create new images, but to counteract those prevalent in the literature of his day, to sanction the divisions to which Dunbar and Washington adhered. *The House behind the Cedars* (1900) is his first attempt in long fiction to achieve this task.

Initially entitled *Rena Walden,* the novel was designed as a character study of the heroine—Rena Walden. In commenting upon the mulatto characters found in the fiction of Albion Tourgée, Chesnutt differentiates between his and those of his white contemporaries: "In the fiction of Judge Tourgée, cultivated white Negroes are always bewailing their fate and cursing the drop of black blood which 'taints'—I hate the word, it implies corruption—their otherwise pure race." Rena Walden, though a cultivated "white Negro," is "a young woman fighting for love and opportunity against the ranked forces of society, against immemorial tradition, against pride of family and of race." The plan for the novel, based upon the distinction between Rena Walden and her contemporaries in the fiction of the day, was ingenious.

Take an illegitimate child, offspring of "a wealthy cultured white man" and a "free colored woman," who "in Louisiana or the West Indies . . . would have been called a quadroon or more loosely a creole; in North Carolina where fine distinctions were not the rule in matters of color, she was sufficiently differentiated when described as a bright mulatto." Upon this family arrangement build a plausible plot. At the behest of her brother John, Rena is encouraged to "pass" into the white race. She adopts a new name, Rena Warwick, is educated by her brother who, having passed previously, has achieved status and success. The mulatto becomes engaged to George Tryon, scion of a respectable southern family.

Upon receiving a telegram informing her of the illness of her mother, Rena returns to the home of her birth. A few days later, Tryon arrives in town on family business; through chance he discovers her presence and after an investigation into her parentage finds out that she is not white but Black. In light of the discovery, Chesnutt editorializes, attacks the argument that black blood leads to corruption: "Had they [Rena and John] possessed the sneaking, cringing, treacherous character traditionally ascribed to people of mixed blood—the character which the blessed institutions of a free slave-holding republic had been well adapted to foster among them; had they been selfish enough to sacrifice to their ambition the mother who gave them birth, society would have been placated or hum-bugged, and the voyage of their life might have been one of unbroken smoothness." A strong moral sense, coupled with devotion to her mother, prevented Rena from taking precautions against discovery by Tryon. Far from being deceptive, she had attempted on occasion to inform him of her true racial status. In Chesnutt's view that she tried to disclose the facts, that she did not undertake strenuous precautions against discovery, leads her to undergo the fate of the "tragic mulatto."

Rejected by Tryon, she receives a position as a schoolmistress to black students and becomes the target of Jeff Wain, a mulatto. Wain measures up to the mulatto image prevalent in white fiction, and Rena's appraisal of him equals the author's: "Her clear eye, when once set to take

Wain's measure, soon fathomed his shallow, selfish soul, and detected, or at least divined, behind his mask of good nature a lurking brutality which filled her with vague distrust. . . . " Wain is joined in his pursuit of Rena by Tryon. The latter, having surrendered all ideas of marriage, desires the mulatto as a mistress. Her opposition to the intentions of both Wain and Tryon enables Chesnutt to drive home the major thesis of the novel: the mental breakdown later sustained by Rena, and her death thereof, occurs not because of immorality on her part, but instead because she is morally superior to those for whom purity of blood is indicative of human worth. Her guiding principle is purity of sex—not purity of race—and when she dies in the arms of black Frank, a committed, though secret, lover, her death is attributable in part to the fact that she remained true to her womanhood, that she opposed the ethics of a society wherein values of the color line are more highly regarded than those founded upon virtue and morality.

Though Rena Walden is the central character of the novel, Molly Walden, her mother, is important in any understanding of the color-phobia among Blacks, persisting still, in this, the early part of the twentieth century. Unlike her daughter, she glorifies in her caste position, though she is not fair enough to pass for white. Happiness, along with prestige and status, are found in her role as a mulatto and her select membership in the "blue-veined society," a group composed of Blacks so fair that the blood in their veins is clearly visible through their skin. Molly is representative of those Blacks, who use pigmentation as a means of carving a special niche for themselves, who seek status based upon nothing more tangible than proximity, in terms of color, to whites. Lacking education, competence, and strength of character, her only sense of herself as a human being comes from the knowledge that though "she was not the rose, she had at least been near the rose."

Chesnutt remains sympathetic to the class of which Molly is an apt representative. Such people, he knows, are counterfeit human beings, living lives of fantasy, yet the fault, in part, is attributable to the society in which they live. Unable to achieve the impossible—to become white—they were forced to construct their own world, in an attempt to distinguish themselves from oppressed Blacks. They resembled nothing so much as Pied Pipers, following the lead of the black mythologists who, true to the ethic of Social Darwinism, postulated the thesis that man in mutated form represented an improvement, culturally and morally, over the old species. Not yet so stately as the rose, the Molly Waldens were grateful for their near approximation.

The House behind the Cedars is sentimental, overly propagandistic, and badly plotted. Nevertheless, as the first novel by an African-American to deal with the ramifications of caste upon whites and Blacks, it is an important novel. Chesnutt's personal views are suspect; yet, he maintains a certain objectivity in his treatment of his characters. Each receives a certain amount of sympathy, even Wain, arrogant, pompous, unprincipled, and immoral, is proven to be no more than an adequate metaphor for the society which created him. Chesnutt's plea, in his first novel, unlike that of Dunbar in *The Sport of the Gods,* is that fate can and must be altered. Change the society and "the tragic mulatto" will have no reason for existence, a

nation torn by questions of color and caste no necessity for being. If the fall of Rome be attributable to corruption and decadence, the fall of America will be attributable to tradition erected upon the disseradatum of color and caste. *The House behind the Cedars* is a protest novel, one designed to rouse the conscience of those who determine the actions of men and events.

The Marrow of Tradition, Chesnutt's second novel, appeared in 1901. Dixon's *The Leopard's Spots: A Romance of the White Man's Burden* (1865-1900) appeared one year later, and the attitude of both men toward their subject matter bears comparison. Both centered their attention upon the changing African-American, upon the transformation undergone since the days of slavery. *The Leopard's Spots* argued as its main thesis that change for Blacks was no change at all; despite manumission and attempts at reconstruction, they remained inferior beings, still hewers of wood and drawers of water. For Dixon the images from preslavery days remained outstanding. Chesnutt accepted Dixon's argument in the main. Real-life examples could be found of the images and stereotypes of which Dixon was so enamored. To be sure, Blacks existed who were true to the image of "hat-in-hand servitors, uncles, aunties, and mammies." Yet Chesnutt protested accepting these as metaphors of the race. They were nonrepresentative, specific examples of types, not general paradigms of an entire race. Having envisioned the New Negro before his birth was announced in the nineteen twenties, in contrasting Blacks of pre-slavery times with those of the Reconstruction years, he averred that the New Negro differed markedly from the old.

His assumptions on this score led him to set objectives for himself in his second novel, difficult of attainment. In an attempt to contrast Blacks before and during the Reconstruction years, he chose to analyze the social structure of a small town, Wilmington, South Carolina, scene of a race riot in 1898, and to use the town as a metaphor for the entire South during the period of Reconstruction. In *The House behind the Cedars,* he had sought to analyze the character of Rena Walden; in his second novel, the attempt to analyze an entire community means that he must deal with too many disparate elements and individuals. The result is a badly plotted, loosely organized novel, lacking central focus. The novel is replete with conflicts. There is romantic entanglement dramatized in the quest of two young men for the hand of a woman whose guardian is one of the town's leading men; there is murder and suspense, involving the framing of a black man for a crime committed by a white. Three of the town's most powerful men engage in activities designed to disenfranchise African-Americans and an attempt is made to steal the rightful inheritance of the mulatto wife of the town's leading Black. Finally, there is the vendetta which rages between the town's two extremists—the militant angry Black, Josh Green, and the onetime slave trader, now prosperous politician, Ed McBane.

A full-scale novel might have been structured around either of these conflicts. Thrown together in the same novel they cause confusion and disorganization, bringing to mind *The Garies and Their Friends.* For Webb's novel, beset with similar difficulties, succeeded better in presenting important portraits of individuals than a comprehensive analysis of a society in transition. *The Marrow of Tra-*

dition succeeds on much the same level. Its strength lies in the contrast between old and new images of black men. Chesnutt, in this single novel, presents the stereotype and its opposite side by side, and thus, for the first time in a black novel, balance in terms of black images is achieved.

His treatment of white characters makes the point equally as well as his treatment of black ones. Knowing that the Euro-Americans do not constitute a homogeneous grouping, he depicts a wide range of characters: the onetime overseer and slave tender, George McBane; Major Carteret, representing the old aristocracy rising to power during Reconstruction; Delamere, kindly old ex-slave master; and young Ellis, white liberal. The animosity between white man and white man is shown in Chesnutt's discussion of the attitudes of Carteret and his associates to McBane, one which places the white man on almost equal plane with the Black. McBane, who affronted the aristocratic sensibilities of Carteret because of crudeness and vulgarity, was " . . . a product of the democratic idea operating upon the poor white man, the descendant of the indentured bondservant and the socially unfit." For a man of Carteret's standing, to rub shoulders with "an illiterate and vulgar white man of no ancestry" was surpassed only by having similar contact with Blacks.

The aristocracy is as divided upon the subjects of Blacks as they are upon other things. The elder Delamere, depicted by Chesnutt as "an old-fashioned gentleman whose ideals not even slavery had been able to spoil . . . " is not only favorable to black enterprise but also takes an interest in "their [Blacks] achievement." This attitude is dramatized in the old man's relationship to his black ward, Sandy Campbell. Mrs. Ochiltree, a wealthy old dowager, is murdered by Delamere's son Tom, who is in need of money to pay off gambling debts. Tom, who committed the murder disguised as a Negro, wore the costume belonging to Campbell. Delamere, however, refuses to accept the fact of Campbell's guilt, and when forced to choose between loyalty to his son and devotion to truth and justice, chooses the latter. He is not, however, romanticized by Chesnutt. His perceptions of Blacks are distorted by tradition. His dogmatic assertion of his ward's innocence rests upon the belief that " . . . My Negroes . . . were well raised and well behaved."

Ellis, "son of a whig and non-slaveholder," displays the ambivalence concerning black men peculiar to liberals from that day to this. Favorably disposed toward Blacks, he is unable to adhere to his own principles, hold fast to his own convictions. The race riot which results from the machinations of Carteret and McBane force Ellis to reveal his true character: "In his heart he could not defend the deeds of this day. The petty annoyances which the whites had felt at the spectacle of a few Negroes in office; the not unnatural resentment of a proud people at what had seemed to them a presumptuous freedom of speech and lack of deference on the part of their inferiors—these things, which he knew were to be made the excuse for overturning the city government, he realized full well were no sort of justification for the wholesale murder or other horrors which might well ensue before the day was done. He could not approve the acts of his own people; neither could he, to a Negro, condemn them. Hence, he was silent."

Chesnutt is equally successful in dramatizing differences among black people. There were, in actuality, he readily admits, such characters as Pip, Nigger Jim, Aunt Mamie, and Uncle Tom, yet there were others whose views ranged in political and social matters from ultraconservative to strident militant. He paid obeisance to the stereotypes of old in the characterizations of Mammy Jane and her nephew, Jerry. Jane's actions and attitudes make her an apt metaphor for the "loyal darky." Listen to her comments to a young nurse, hired to help care for the Carteret child: "Look a here gal . . . I wants you ter understan' dat you got ter take good keer er dis chile; fer I nussed his mammy dere, an his gran'manny befo' im, and you is got a priv'lege dat mos lackly you don' 'preciate. I wants you to 'member, in yo incomins and outgoins, dat I got my eye on you, and am gwine ter see dat you does yo wo'k right."

The major contrast between one black character and another, however, is dramatized in the roles of the militant, Josh Green, and the conservative, Adam Miller. Green, representative of the lower classes, is the first such character in African-American fiction, and despite a sympathetic portrayal, Chesnutt is not always comfortable with the image. Men like Green, potential anarchists, are warnings of the Götterdämmerung to come if no *modus vivendi* can be worked out between the Adam Millers and the Major Carterets. Green and McBane symbolize the poles of white-black anarchy in the novel, and their conflict mirrors that between the forces of radicalism and conservatism in the town. Unable to portray Green as a race patriot, therefore, Chesnutt attributes his militancy, in part, to anger engendered by the murder of his father at the hands of the Ku Klux Klan, led by McBane: " . . . he wuz boss, he wuz de head man, an tol' de res w'at ter do. . . . " Green is prepared to " . . . die a vi'lent death in a quarrel wid a wite man. . . . "

Green and McBane represent the forces of irreconciliation pronounced in the town of Wellington. Centuries of antagonism between Blacks and whites have resulted in a vendetta between the two. This vendetta is the marrow of tradition, and if tradition continues unchanged, the smoldering fires of mistrust, hatred, and discontent will explode in conflagration marked by violence. Having created the characters of McBane and Green, Chesnutt moves beyond the optimism of his contemporaries, of Dunbar and Griggs, and envisions the world in terms of the coming apocalypse. He is, however, more moralist than cynic, though unable to maintain the moral vision throughout the novel. The apocalypse need not come. The tradition that produced Green and McBane is the tradition that also produced Adam Miller and the older Delamere. Miller serves the author in this respect as a *deus ex machina,* one, who, in the best of the Washington tradition, having survived adversity, can walk the hot coals of contention, overcoming antagonism with strength and intelligence.

He is the offspring of industrious stock. His father, an ex-slave, purchased his own freedom and achieved prosperity as a tradesman. He educated his son, who becomes a renowned man of medicine, a doctor respected everywhere except in his own town, in the best universities of America and Europe. Like Clotel, Miller is mulatto, and like Mr. Walters, ambitious and capable. But above all, though he is proud of his Anglo-Saxon heritage, he has no ambitions to enter the white race. He is closer in this respect to the characters of the novels of Jessie Fauset than to those of

James Weldon Johnson or those in Chesnutt's *The House behind the Cedars.* He is the image of the new man, representative of a special group of black men, those more fortunate in terms of education and material accomplishments than others. He is well-equipped for the role of race missionary and upon him falls the duty of uplifting his people. As a doctor, he attempts to do this by improving the health care of Blacks in the town.

He is, however, no egalitarian, and an important facet of his character is revealed in his evaluation of lower-class Blacks. He finds them at times to be good-natured, free and uninhibited, when not under the scrutinizing eyes of whites, a people capable of atavistic, sensual pleasure. On the other hand ". . . personally, and apart from the mere matter of racial sympathy, these people were just as offensive to him as to the whites. . . ." In such areas as public transportation, Miller welcomes classifications leading to barriers: "Surely if a classification of passengers on trains was at all desirable, it might be made upon some more logical and considerate basis than a mere arbitrary, tactless, and, by the very nature of things, brutal drawing of a color line."

Thus Chesnutt's argument for fair treatment of his major character is not that he is a black man, but a special kind of black man. The rebuffs which he suffers simply points out the severity of oppression, highlighting the adherence to tradition. When asked by a fellow doctor to observe an operation to be performed upon the daughter of the Major, Miller is refused. Discovered in the seating compartment of a train with the same companion, he is made to move to the dirty, smelly quarters reserved for Blacks. His wife, half-sister to the wife of Carteret, is cheated out of her inheritance, and his son is a victim of the race riot. Despite all of this, he remains a man of reason and compassion, a striking contradiction to Josh Green, the saving grace for Blacks and whites alike, metaphor of a special group within the American body politic, deserving of better treatment than other members of the race.

Chesnutt's attempt to drive home this point, however, weakens the character of Miller, making him, in the final analysis, not a special man, but one who has more in common with saints than with men. The attempt to prove Miller's dedication to peace and love rings hollow and false during the events which transpire after the race riot. Miller's own son is murdered by the rioters; he, himself, is badly mishandled. The hospital he had built is reduced to rubble. Many members of his class, personal friends, either lose their lives or flee their homes and property. Despite this, when called upon to save the life of the son of Carteret, the prime force behind the riot, Miller does so, though not without rendering a moral verdict: "There Major Carteret . . . there lies a specimen of your handiwork: There lies my only child, laid low by a stray bullet in this riot which you and your paper have fomented: struck down as much by your hand as though you had held the weapon with which his life was taken."

The contrast between Green and Miller is pronounced. A white man caused the death of Miller's son, even as a white man caused the death of Green's father. Chesnutt, however, because of his own middle-class bias, has little difficulty in unveiling the anger, unmasking the hatred, and ascribing motives of revenge to his lower-class character. Such characteristics must not be a part of the makeup of special men, for it is this that separates them from the lower class; they are capable of forgiveness and love in face of the most blatant provocation. Thus, Miller saves the life of the son of the man responsible for the murder of his own, while Josh Green violently murders the object of his hatred, Ed McBane.

Middle-class bias aside, Chesnutt is forced to face the reality of the weakness of Miller's position. Non-violence and turn the other cheek were philosophies incapable of producing change in the early part of the twentieth century. Factual evidence was not difficult to come by: There were such riots as that which took place at Wilmington, North Carolina (1899), upon which the novel was based; there was the successful disenfranchisement of Blacks; there were the resurgent lawlessness and indiscriminate violence of the Ku Klux Klan. These facts combine to make Miller's advocacy of the politics of peace and harmony appear forced and ludicrous: "Try as we may to build up the race in the essentials of good citizenship and win the good opinion of the best people, some black scoundrel comes along, and by a single criminal act . . . neutralizes the effect of a year's work." When compared to the sentiments expressed by McBane, those shared by the majority of the whites in the town, Miller's remarks are not only ludicrous but ironic as well: "Burn the nigger. . . . We seem to have the right nigger, but whether we have or not, burn a nigger. . . . The example would be all the more powerful if we got the wrong one. It would serve notice on the niggers that we shall hold the whole race responsible for the misdeeds of each individual."

Though favorably disposed toward Miller, in Green, Chesnutt has come closest to creating the image of the New Negro. Green, the revolutionary, is closer than the conservative Miller to twentieth-century man, more representative of those imbued with concern for improvement of the human condition. Anger and bitterness, at first derived from personal treatment, soon become a creative force, one which seeks to limit oppression by utilizing the tools of the oppressor. Violence becomes, for Green, a cathartic force; it is the barrier to man's ambitions enacted at the expense of others, the hour hand upon the clock of human endurance which the oppressor must not push forward. Compare the sentiments of Green on the night of the riot with those previously stated by Miller, and Green, despite Chesnutt, is the image of modern black man: "De w'ite folks are killin de niggers, an' we an' gwine ter stan' up an' be shot down like dogs. Deres two niggers in dis town ter eve'y w'ite man, an' ef we've got ter be kilt, we'll take some w'ite folks long wid us. . . ."

Still Miller's is the last word, his sentiments those with which the black middle class finds accord, those championed by black men from that day to this: "My advice is not heroic, but I think it is wise. In this riot we are placed as we should be in a war; we have no territory, no base of supplies, no organization, no outside sympathy—we stand in the position of a race, in a case like this, without money and without friends. Our time will come,—the time when we can command respect for our rights, but it is not yet in sight. Give it up boys, and wait. Good may come of this, after all." The black middle class has always opted for *supposed* wisdom instead of heroism.

By focusing upon situations and events, and presenting contrasts between one character and another, Chesnutt, in

The Marrow of Tradition and *The House behind the Cedars,* attempted to analyze the social consequences of heritage and history upon the individual. The new naturalism was still in its infancy, yet Chesnutt had already moved beyond its major premise, that the environment in which men live directs and controls their lives. There were, for him, factors equally as important—history and tradition; these were less difficult to confront and to change. Both novels, therefore, are historical, in the sense that the characters of each are always in conflict with the past. When he looked at the American society through the eyes of a black novelist, Chesnutt saw men engaged in a futile battle to alter the course of history and tradition. His conclusions, in the main, are not encouraging. Society and environment are conducive to change. Tradition, due to human failure, is not. Man's inability, therefore, to free himself from tradition and to learn from history were major factors in his inability to produce the humane social order. Like Du Bois, Chesnutt demanded that his age leap across the barriers erected by history and tradition, and by burying the old gods of irrelevance—hatred, prejudice, enmity—move forward to create a better world.

He is at one and the same time pessimist and optimist; and yet, despite this, he is more idealistic than his contemporaries. His horizons are higher, his belief in the ability of men and institutions to change, stronger than that of Washington, who appeared more cynic than believer, or than that of Dunbar, who held few such beliefs in regard to either men or institutions. Unlike Delany, Chesnutt cannot foresee a new world ushered in upon the shoulders of revolution, yet in his better moments, he might pray for a society in which the "talented tenth," having dramatized by example the true worth of black men, might bring about substantive change in the black condition. He believed that the human condition might be changed if the negative values derived from old traditions were destroyed. Without such fundamental changes, the future was bleak for Black and white alike. Despite technical deficiencies, *The Marrow of Tradition* is Chesnutt's best effort in long fiction. Unlike Dunbar, he did not shirk from warfare with the imagists, did not agree totally to the proposition that the stock characters of the Plantation school of literature were adequate representatives of a people who had survived numerous holocausts throughout their history. He was inhibited by time and age from developing a sensibility that bordered upon egalitarianism; he could not truthfully adhere to the democratic ideal. As aristocratic in intention as his white contemporaries, like Webb and Brown he did not oppose categorization, sought not the destruction of class stratification, but only those based upon race and caste. His portrait of Adam Miller, like that of Josh Green, will transcend the ages—Green, no less than Blake, doomed to oblivion until the nineteen seventies. Yet, the very manifestation of the Greens in the modern era, their resurgence in life and literature after the tumultuous sixties, says something about the clarity of Chesnutt's vision concerning the future. His major thesis from one novel to another is that the failure to confront history and tradition means to make obsolete such representative black men as Adam Miller. That Richard Wright, forty years later, would conclude that such circumstances mandated the creation of Bigger Thomas, cast in the mold of Josh Green, is already to speak of the Adam Millers, in fiction, if not in fact, as relics of a bygone era. (pp. 46-58)

Addison Gayle, Jr., "The Souls of Black Folk," in his The Way of the New World: The Black Novel in America, *Anchor Press, 1975, pp. 25-58.*

Arlene A. Elder   (essay date 1978)

[*In the following excerpt, Elder maintains that in* The Wife of His Youth, and Other Stories of the Color Line, *Chesnutt turned from the folkloric basis of the* Conjure Woman *stories toward social realism in the portrayal of the social, economic, and political situation of black Americans.*]

Chesnutt's short story **"The Wife of His Youth"** appeared in the July 1898 volume of the *Atlantic* and aroused a great deal of favorable comment. Public interest in this tale, plus the response to *The Conjure Woman,* led Chesnutt boldly to suggest a second volume of stories to his publishers.

On December 8, 1900, he wrote to Houghton Mifflin to report that he was in the process of arranging the order of these new stories and remarked that Walter Page had suggested the name *The Wife of His Youth, and Other Stories of the Color Line* for the forthcoming volume. "I have not been able to think of any better title," Chesnutt admitted.

> I would like to hope that the stories, while written by depicting life as it is in certain aspects that no one has ever before attempted to adequately describe, throws a little light upon the great problem on which the stories are strung; for the backbone of this volume is not a character, like Uncle Julius in *The Conjure Woman,* but a subject as indicated in the title—the Color Line.

This subject was a pressing one for Chesnutt; he commented in 1901, "My friend, Mr. Howells, who has said many nice things about my writings . . . has remarked several times that there is no color line in literature. On that point I take issue with him. I am pretty fairly convinced that the color line runs everywhere so far as the United States is concerned."

The Wife of His Youth pulls Chesnutt from the imaginative flights of folklore to a grounding in social realism. His concern, as he indicated to Page, is not with the Black artist/magician, but with the day-by-day social, economic, and political problems facing African-Americans, especially those like himself, fair enough to pass for white or to be ranked among the elite of Black society, where, ironically, personal worth was also judged by skin color. Propaganda is not his predominant voice in this volume, however; and while these stories are not folktales, Chesnutt is still attempting to fulfill the highest purpose of art, to convey meanings through an imaginative and truthful presentation of life. In this quest, he moves away from both the stereotypes of Dunbar and the southern apologists and the counterstereotypes of his Black predecessors.

Chesnutt's characters, like [Sutton E.] Grigg's, are primarily from the middle or upper levels of Black society. Sounding very much like Griggs, indeed, he satirizes the Blue Vein Society in the lead story, **"The Wife of His Youth,"** as an organization whose "purpose was to establish and maintain correct social standards among a people whose social condition presented almost unlimited room for improvement." In some degree at least, this group might correspond to the Cleveland Social Circle, which the Chesnutts were asked to join after they had lived in that city for several years. Chesnutt's daughter reports that this "little club had been organized in 1869 by a group of young colored people who wanted to promote social intercourse and cultural activities among the better educated people of color. This was a very exclusive organization—membership in it was the *sine qua non* of social standing." In Chesnutt's tale, "by accident, combined perhaps with some natural affinity, the society consisted of individuals who were, generally speaking, more white than black. Some envious outsider made the suggestion that no one was eligible for membership who was not white enough to show blue veins." Like J. McHenry Jones's Black aristocrats in *Hearts of Gold,* "the Blue Veins did not allow that any such requirement existed for admission to their circle, but, on the contrary, declared that character and culture were the only things considered; and that if most of their members were light-colored, it was because such persons, as a rule, had had better opportunities to qualify themselves for membership."

The next story, **"Her Virginia Mammy,"** opens on a scene at a dancing class similar, no doubt, to the ones that the Chesnutts attended in Cleveland. Miss Hohlfelder's first "colored class" was made up of

> people whom she would have passed on the street without a second glance, and among them were several whom she had known by sight for years, but had never dreamed of as being colored people. Their manners were good, they dressed quietly and as a rule with good taste, avoiding rather than choosing bright colors and striking combinations. . . . Among them . . . there were lawyers and doctors, teachers, telegraph operators, clerks, milliners and dressmakers, students at the local college and scientific school, and even a member of the legislature.

One class member indicates that, unlike Grigg's southern Black leaders, those in the North wish to put as much distance as possible between themselves and the masses of their people. Mr. Solomon Sadler explains,

> "The more advanced of us are not numerous enough to make the fine distinctions that are possible among white people; and of course as we rise in life we can't get entirely away from our brothers and our sisters and our cousins, who don't always keep abreast of us. We do, however, draw certain lines of character and manners and occupation. You see the sort of people we are. Of course we have no prejudice against color, and we regard all labor as honorable, provided a man does the best he can. But we must have standards that will give our people something to aspire to."

Chesnutt presents this pompous speech satirically. Like Grigg's Black "aristocrats" in *Overshadowed,* Sadler and his friends are aping white standards of behavior, while congratulating themselves for providing role models for less fortunate Blacks. Chesnutt good-naturedly pokes fun at this self-deception; he shared very little of it himself.

Chesnutt was clearly troubled by the "talented tenth" mentality by the time he undertook *The Wife of His Youth;* this theme provides the fabric of the title story and is woven throughout the book. His fourth story, **"A Mat-** **ter of Principle,"** offers a particularly incisive, if broadly humorous, look at the snobbishness evident in the Black middle class. From Mr. Cicero Clayton's first speech at the monthly meeting of the Blue Vein Society, advocating "a clearer conception of the brotherhood of man," to his final comeuppance for his own prejudices, Chesnutt starkly outlines his personal absurdities in order to bring those of his class into sharp focus.

Mr. Clayton is a racist. He resents the fact that whites have classified him with all other African-Americans, regardless of his light skin and social position, and has developed his plan for fighting back. "If we are not accepted as white," he announces, "we can at any rate make it clear that we object to being called black. Our protest cannot fail in time to impress itself upon the better class of white people; for the Anglo-Saxon race loves justice, and will eventually do it, where it does not conflict with their own interests." Chesnutt cannot allow this final bit of stupidity to pass unremarked and observes quietly to the reader, "Whether or not the fact that Mr. Clayton meant no sarcasm, and was conscious of no inconsistency in this eulogy, tended to establish the racial identity that he claimed may safely be left to the discerning reader."

Clayton's actions are consistent with his prejudices; he refuses to associate with Blacks whose skin is notably darker than his own. Moreover, he goes out of his way to enhance his non-Negroid appearance by emphasizing its Latin American cast, growing a Vandyke beard and waxing the ends of his mustache.

One serious consequence of such prejudice is a severe limitation of social contacts for the younger members of his class. Mr. Clayton's interest in the tale is to acquire a proper husband for his daughter, whose choice of mates is severely restricted by the group's exaggerated evaluation of her white blood. Miss Clayton and her friends "would not marry black men, and except in rare instances white men would not marry them. They were therefore restricted for a choice to the young men of their own complexion. But these, unfortunately for the girls, had a wider choice." Unlike the color-conscious Viola Martin, Mrs. Seabright, and Miss Letitia of Grigg's books, Chesnutt's discriminating middle class has no political strategy in mind. Purely and simply, it has accepted the white society's standards of beauty and worth.

Chesnutt's view of these people is clearly a comic one. When Clayton's own prejudice leads him into a complicated series of mistakes that prevents his daughter from meeting a congressman whom Clayton deemed worthy of her, Chesnutt laments, tongue in cheek, "Such luck is enough to disgust a man with trying to do right and live up to his principles." At the end of his tale, Clayton is still mouthing his meaningless cant; and while Chesnutt's treatment of him and his circle is humorous, the author's hopelessness about changing middle-class Black prejudices is evident in the cyclic structure of the story. Experience teaches nothing here.

Clearly, Chesnutt's stance in a number of tales in *The Wife of His Youth* is satiric rather than tragic. **"Uncle Wellington's Wives,"** for instance, tackles with humorous detachment the long-standing taboo against Black/white sexual relations. A more seriously developed undertone in the story, however, connects this theme of sexual liberation with the turn-of-the-century migration of Blacks to the North in hope of economic and political freedom.

With something akin to Dunbar's mistrust of urban ways, Chesnutt shifts from his light tone to one of dark foreboding once Wellington heads north. From the very beginning of his protagonist's movement away from the South, images of darkness, loneliness, and death predominate:

> He went around to the dark side of the train, and climbed into a second-class car, where he shrank into the darkest corner and turned his face away from the dim light of the single dirty lamp. There were no passengers in the car except one or two sleeping negroes, who had got on at some other station, and a white man who had gone into the car to smoke, accompanied by a gigantic bloodhound . . . as the train rattled through the outskirts of the town, he saw gleaming in the moonlight the white headstones of the colored cemetery where his only daughter had been buried several years before.

The journey to the city is infused with malevolent images that transform the story's previously easy tone. Wellington's sexual transgression there makes him swallow the bitter fruit of northern racism and opens his eyes to the impotency of unskilled Blacks.

Nevertheless, Wellington himself is essentially a figure of fun, as illustrated in the following account of his mental circumlocutions as he struggles to convince himself that he is justified in stealing his first wife's savings:

> The lawyer had told him that his wife's property was his own; in taking it he was therefore only exercising his lawful right. But at the point of breaking open the chest, it occurred to him that he was taking this money in order to get away from Aunt Milly, and that he justified his desertion of her by the lawyer's opinion that she was not his lawful wife. If she was not his wife, then he had no right to take the money; if she was his wife, he had no right to desert her, and would certainly have no right to marry another woman. His scheme was about to go to shipwreck on this rock, when another idea occurred to him.

> "De lawyer say dat in one sense er de word de ole 'oman is my wife, an' in anudder sense er de word she ain't my wife. Ef I goes ter de Norf an' marry a w'ite 'oman, I ain't commit no brigamy, 'caze in dat sense er de word she ain't my wife; but ef I takes dis money, I ain't stealin' it, 'caze in dat sense er de word she is my wife. Dat 'splains all de trouble away."

In addition . . . the chastened Wellington is treated to a homecoming that reestablishes this atmosphere of traditional humor and dilutes Chesnutt's naturalistic social commentary. It is apparent that the writer simply did not know what kind of tale he wished to write here, and his inconsistencies are its most striking feature.

There is only one story in this collection that presents a cunning Black like Uncle Julius; appropriately, **"The Passing of Grandison"** is also the only story set during slavery times. Once again, Chesnutt scrutinizes social standards, this time white society's. The word *principle* takes on satiric significance because of its frequent and careless use. The story begins with reference to the trial of a white man accused and convicted of helping a slave escape to Canada. After the trial, Dick Owens, a white "youth of about twenty-two, intelligent, handsome, and amiable, but extremely indolent, in a graceful and gentlemanly way," confesses "that while my principles were against the prisoner, my sympathies were on his side. . . . But father and the rest of them stood on the principle of the thing, and told the judge so, and the fellow was sentenced to three years in the penitentiary." The principle at issue here is, of course, the same as in Clayton's tale—the superiority of the white culture and the necessity of laws that ensure its survival. When the young woman whom Dick wishes to marry asserts that she considers the convicted man heroic and observes, pointedly, "I could love a man who would take such chances for the sake of others," he decides to aid in the escape of Grandison, one of his father's slaves. Romantic love, true to the popular tradition, is a fair substitute for principles.

Chesnutt engages in a number of ironic dialogues between this servant and the colonel, intended to reveal the master's complacent self-deception. Grandison is consistently cunning, perceptive, and, like the trickster heroes, successfully deceitful. The following amusing example is representative:

> "I should just like to know, Grandison," says the colonel, "whether you don't think yourself a great deal better off than those poor free negroes down by the plank road, with no kind master to look after them and no mistress to give them medicine when they're sick and—and—"

> "Well, I sh'd jes' reckon I is better off, suh, dan dem low-down free niggers, suh! Ef anybody ax 'em who dey b'long ter, dey has ter say nobody, er e'se lie erbout it. Anybody ax me who I b'long ter, I ain't got no 'casion ter be shame' ter tell 'em, no, suh, 'deed I ain', suh!"

> The colonel was beaming. This was true gratitude, and his feudal heart thrilled at such appreciative homage. What cold-blooded, heartless monsters they were who would break up this blissful relationship of kindly protection on the one hand, of wise subordination and loyal dependence on the other! The colonel always became indignant at the mere thought of such wickedness.

Aware that the old man is afraid that he will run away when he accompanies Dick Owen on a trip to the North, Grandison assures him that he would risk striking a white man rather than allow himself to be stolen from slavery. The colonel is so pleased by such loyalty that he promises the servant,

> ". . . if you please your master Dick, he'll buy you a present, and a string of beads for Betty to wear when you and she get married in the fall."

> "Thanky, marster, thanky, suh," replied Grandison, oozing gratitude at every pore; "you is a good marster, to be sho', suh; yas, 'deed you is. . . . "

> "All right, Grandison, you may go now. You needn't work anymore today, and here's a piece of tobacco for you off my own plug."

> "Thanky, marster, thanky, marster! You is de bes' marster any nigger ever had in dis worl'." And Grandison bowed and scraped and disappeared

round the corner, his jaws closing around a large section of the colonel's best tobacco.

Dick's repeated attempts to lose Grandison in the North, stratagems that give the slave every opportunity to escape to Canada, all go for nought. As he promised, Grandison proves "loyal." The young southerner finally is placed in the ridiculous position of having to hire kidnappers to steal his servant from him. Within a short time after Owen's return home, however, Grandison shows up and gravely reports to the colonel about his ordeal. Outraged and astonished at "the depths of depravity the human heart is capable of," the colonel reports proudly that "Grandison escaped, and, keeping his back steadily to the North Star, made his way, after suffering incredible hardships, back to the old plantation, back to his master, his friends, and his home. Why it's as good as one of Scott's novels! Mr. Simms or some other one of our Southern authors ought to write it up."

Like Ellison's Trueblood in *Invisible Man,* Grandison is valued and rewarded because he reinforces white notions of superiority: "His fame spread throughout the county, and the colonel gave him a permanent place among the house servants, where he could always have him conveniently at hand to relate his adventures to admiring visitors." However, "one Monday morning Grandison was missing. And not only Grandison, but his wife, Betty the maid; his mother, Aunt Eunice; his father, Uncle Ike; his brothers, Tom and John, and his little sister Elsie, were likewise absent from the plantation."

Clearly, Grandison returned from the North temporarily, to rescue his family from slavery's "blessings." His "passing" is not only his movement from the South to the North, from slavery to freedom, but also his successful pretense. He "passes" as a loyal, humble slave to ensure his family's passage out of bondage, an action reflecting the psychological freedom of Blacks presented in the slave narratives. Although its humor is satiric, then, this story is closer in tone to those in *The Conjure Woman* than most others in this volume.

Another story that conjures up the atmosphere and spirit of the Uncle Julius tales is **"Cicely's Dream,"** a piece about portents and dreams that go "by contraries." Unlike **"The Bouquet,"** a sentimental and predictable companion piece that also examines the ironies of relationships between white schoolmarms and their adoring, imitative Black pupils, **"Cicely's Dream"** is richly compelling. Its opening scenes create a fertile, southern Eden, which has nourished the girl whose "bare feet seemed to spurn the earth as they struck it" and whose "eyes were dreamy with vague yearnings." This dreamlike, pastoral atmosphere is maintained throughout the story, despite the sudden intrusion of the mysterious young man, the healing of whose physical and psychic wounds becomes Cicely's vocation, until Chesnutt shatters the mood with an improbable recognition scene at the end. The story finally fails because of this intrusion of the sentimental formula. Nevertheless, it remains an evocative blending of the real and the imaginative, of dream states and levels of consciousness.

A very different sort of tale, **"The Sheriff's Children"** deserves attention because of its probing examination of the ironies of miscegenation and the light that it might throw upon Chesnutt's self-image. He sets this tragic tale in a spot very different from the lush natural environment in which Cicely had grown to womanhood. Troy is a semiurban settlement symbolic of the stagnant, impoverished lives of southern poor whites. "If a traveler, accustomed to the bustling life of cities, could have ridden through Troy on a summer day," he observes,

> he might easily have fancied himself in a deserted village. Around him he would have seen weather-beaten houses, innocent of paint, the shingled roofs in many instances covered with a rich growth of moss. Here and there he would have met a razor-backed hog lazily rooting his way along the principal thoroughfare; and more than once he would probably have had to disturb the slumbers of some yellow dog dozing away the hours in the ardent sunshine, and reluctantly yielding up his place in the middle of the dusty road.

The farm folk who come to town on Saturday are Faulknerian: "bearded men in straw hats and blue homespun shirts, and butternut trousers of great amplitude of material and vagueness of outline; women in homespun frocks and slat-bonnets, with faces as expressionless as the dreary sandhills which gave them a meagre sustenance."

This story of a young mulatto accused of killing one of the town's leading white citizens foreshadows the concerns that Chesnutt will express at greater length in *The Marrow of Tradition.* Of the members of the lynch mob that immediately forms outside the jail, Chesnutt explains, "They had some vague notions of the majesty of the law and the rights of the citizen, but in the passion of the moment these sunk into oblivion; a white man had been killed by a negro." The writer's interest is equally divided between the dangerous and endangered young Black and the sheriff whose duty is to safeguard the prisoner. The latter is a man out of place in his community, "far above the average in wealth, education, and social position," who "had graduated at the State University at Chapel Hill, and had kept up some acquaintance with current literature and advanced thought." He "had traveled some in his youth, and was looked up to in the county as an authority on all subjects connected with the outer world."

After facing down and dispersing the mob, the sheriff is startled to find himself confronting a gun in the hands of the prisoner. Despite his superior intelligence and education, it is clear from his response to this situation that the sheriff, too, is limited by stereotypes: "The sheriff mentally cursed his own carelessness for allowing him to be caught in such a predicament. He had not expected anything of the kind. He had relied on the negro's cowardice and subordination in the presence of an armed white man as a matter of course." When he lamely tries to convince the young man to trust in the course of justice, the prisoner only laughs sarcastically at this empty phrase and assures the sheriff that he is well aware of the consequences of southern "justice" for Blacks.

The life-and-death relationship between the helpless lawman and his armed prisoner becomes doubly ironic when the young man reveals himself to be the sheriff's son. In the past, despite his relative enlightenment, the sheriff had behaved according to the accepted mores of his race and class. The prisoner's mother was a slave whom he had callously sold to a speculator: "He had been sorry for it many a time since. It had been the old story of debts, mortgages, and bad crops. He had quarreled with the mother. The price offered for her and her child had been unusually large, and he had yielded to the combination of anger and pecuniary stress."

Informed of their real relationship, the older man gasps, "Good God . . . you would not murder your own father?" Chesnutt uses the son's response to what the sheriff, no doubt, considered a rhetorical question in order to vent some of the anger and ambivalence that he must have felt about his own heritage:

> "My father?" replied the mulatto. "It were well enough for me to claim the relationship, but it comes with poor grace from you to ask anything by reason of it. What father's duty have you ever performed for me? Did you give me your name, or even your protection? Other white men gave their colored sons freedom and money, and sent them to the free States. *You* sold *me* to the rice swamps."

Chesnutt explains, "The Sheriff was conscientious; his conscience had merely been warped by his environment."

This melodramatic, but generally effective, revelation scene is violently and abruptly ended by a shot fired from the passage behind the prisoner, wounding him in the arm and causing him to drop his gun. Coincidentally, it was fired by Polly, the sheriff's daughter, who arrived at the very moment that her half-brother had decided that he would have to kill his father for his own safety. After this close escape, the sheriff begins to brood about the errors of his life and determines to make up for the years of neglect by doing everything in his power to discover the real criminal in the murder of which his son stands accused. This reversal, which is not completely believable, is followed by Chesnutt's melodramatically ending his tale by having the wounded mulatto commit suicide by tearing the bandage from his arm and bleeding to death.

While such an ending underscores the futility of the son's life and the self-deception of the father's tardy plans for postponed justice, it seems facile and ineffective. As a matter of fact, although **"The Sheriff's Children"** is an attempt at social realism, the story is most successful as allegory. It is significant that the white child, Polly, attempted to kill the Black in order to preserve the white father/sheriff, the symbol of society's traditions and codes, just as the white father had, in his own way, exploited and killed the Black slave mother. The sheriff's dream for his son, his plan to make up to him for the death of his mother and the son's degradation, is completely incongruous in this pattern of social and racial conflict; on the allegorical level, then, the only possible outcome would have been the death of the Black man.

Although **"The Sheriff's Children"** is a stark and harsh reminder of the tangled web of miscegenation, the most despairing story in this collection is **"The Web of Circumstance,"** a tale that rivals Dunbar's *Sport of the Gods* for naturalistic gloom. It concerns the thwarted dream of Ben, a self-confident, talented, and ambitious blacksmith, to rise by his own hard work and frugality in southern society. He lectures other Blacks about saving their money rather than wasting it on entertainments that profit the whites and points out the foolishness of their building churches rather than building homes for themselves. The white men who hear Ben's remarks agree with him and

even go so far as to echo Booker T. Washington's beliefs by asserting, "Yo'r people will never be respected till they've got property." Ben brags to his "good-looking yellow wife," "I paid Majah Ransom de intrus' on de mortgage dis mawnin' an' a hund'ed dollahs besides, an' I spec's ter hab de balance ready by de fust of nex' Jiniwary; an' den we won't owe nobody a cent. I tell yer dere ain' nothing' like propputy ter made a pusson feel like a man."

However, Chesnutt never fully accepted Washington's belief that acquiring property would solve most of the Blacks' problems in the South. The fragility of such a scheme is obvious when Ben is accused of the theft of a buggy whip, and his well-known philosophy of acquiring property is used to convict him. The prosecuting attorney ironically labels him

> "a man of dangerous character, a surly impudent fellow; a man whose views on property are prejudicial to the welfare of society, and who has been heard to assert that half the property which is owned in this country has been stolen, and that, if justice were done, the white people ought to divide up the land with the negroes; in other words, a negro nihilist, a communist, a secret devotee of Tom Paine and Voltaire, a pupil of the anarchist propaganda, which, if not checked by the stern hand of the law, will fasten its insidious fangs on our social system, and drag it down to ruin."

The actual thief is another Black who covets Ben's possessions, especially his "good-looking yellow wife." In the same corrupt southern court in which Ben is tried, a white man convicted of manslaughter is given a brief admonition and sentenced to one year in the penitentiary; a well-connected, young clerk guilty of forgery is sentenced to six months in the county jail and fined one hundred dollars; and Ben, for supposedly stealing a buggy whip, is given "the light sentence of imprisonment for five years in the penitentiary at hard labor." Like his predecessors, Chesnutt feels the need to establish the veracity of such incongruities and explains in a footnote that "there are no degrees of larceny in North Carolina, and the penalty for any offense lies in the discretion of the judge, to the limit of twenty years."

As in all naturalistic fiction, the fortunes of the main character rapidly deteriorate after his first slip. The formerly hopeful, ambitious dreamer steels himself against emotion as he hears his sentence read: "There was one flash of despair, and then nothing but a stoney blank, behind which he masked his real feelings, whatever they were."

To explain such a stoic response, Chesnutt returns to his belief in environmental and hereditary determinism: "Human character is a compound of tendencies inherited and habits acquired," he insists.

> In the anxiety, the fear of disgrace, spoke the nineteenth century civilization with which Ben Davis had been more or less closely in touch during twenty years of slavery and fifteen years of freedom. In the stolidity with which he received this sentence for a crime which he had not committed spoke who knows what trait of inherited savagery? For stoicism is a savage virtue.

Ben's retreat to "primitive" psychological methods of coping with life is hardly a failing, however, in a "sophisticated" society corrupt as that of the nineteenth-century

South. After five years' slavery in the convict camps, Ben's life is ended as abruptly and meaninglessly as his dreams of prosperity and social status.

Apparently aware that his audience's response to his hopeless, ironic twist at the end of this story would probably be negative, Chesnutt indulges in what was to become a pattern for closing his books. He ends with an uplifting, hopeful, but ultimately empty, paean to God's justice:

> Some time, we are told, when the cycle of years has rolled around there is to be another golden age, when all men will dwell together in love and harmony, and when peace and righteousness shall prevail for a thousand years. God speed the day, and let not the shining thread of hope become so enmeshed in the web of circumstance that we lose sight of it; but give us here and there, and now and then, some little foretaste of this golden age, that we may the more patiently and hopefully await its coming.

At the close of a book revealing the racist delusions and impossible dreams of Black people, Chesnutt can only assert the importance of maintaining pipe dreams. Perhaps he is merely providing the kind of ending that he knew the public demanded; or, as a mulatto who had climbed the ladder of success at least a few rungs, he might sincerely have been looking forward to a "golden age" of social justice for his brothers. It is certainly true that a cheerful optimism was as inherent a part of his personality as melancholy was of Dunbar's. Nevertheless, the ending of **"The Web of Circumstance"** does not develop naturally from the implications of its plot and, as the final note to *The Wife of His Youth,* is inappropriate and ineffective. (pp. 163-74)

> *Arlene A. Elder, "Charles Waddell Chesnutt: Art or Assimilation," in her* The "Hindered Hand": Cultural Implications of Early African-American Fiction, *Greenwood Press, 1978, pp. 147-97.*

Ladell Payne   (essay date 1978)

[*Payne is an American educator and critic. In the following excerpt, he discusses Chesnutt's didactic purpose in writing the novels* The House behind the Cedars *and* The Marrow of Tradition, *and considers the works representative of southern literary traditions.*]

Three years before he left North Carolina [where he was raised and attended school], seven years before the **"Goophered Grapevine"** appeared in the *Atlantic Monthly,* a decade before his first novel, Charles Waddell Chesnutt wrote in his journal:

> May 29, 1880
> I think I must write a book. . . . Fifteen years of life in the South, in one of the most eventful eras of its history, among a people whose life is rich in the elements of romance, under conditions calculated to stir one's soul to the very depths—I think there is here a fund of experience, a supply of material, which a skillful pen could work up with tremendous effect. Besides, if I do write, I shall write for a purpose, a high, holy purpose, and this will inspire me to greater effort. The object of my writings would be not so much the elevation of the col-

> ored people as the elevation of the whites—for I consider the unjust spirit of caste which is so insidious as to pervade a whole nation, and so powerful as to subject a whole race and all connected with it to scorn and social ostracism—I consider this a barrier to the moral progress of the American people.

This statement could well have been Chesnutt's literary manifesto. Certainly he uses southern Negro folk materials from the antebellum plantation South for his conjure stories. Like his fellow North Carolinian, Thomas Wolfe, Chesnutt used the town where he grew up as the thinly disguised location for his fiction. But it is in his novels that Chesnutt deals most explicitly and most characteristically with the evils of caste. And it is two of his novels that I wish to examine in some detail to suggest the extent to which Chesnutt is not only a black man from the South who wrote novels, but also a southern novelist. These are *The House behind the Cedars,* his first and most popular novel, and *The Marrow of Tradition,* his most forthright presentation of the racial problem in the South and the book which finally cost him his readership.

Set in "Patesville" (Fayetteville), North Carolina, *The House behind the Cedars* tells the story of John and Rena Walden, children of "a free colored woman" named "Molly Walden—her rightful name, for her parents were free-born and legally married." Like Faulkner's Sam Fathers, Molly is a mixture of black, white, and Indian strains. Years before the Civil War, she becomes the mistress of a distinguished gentleman who gives her a small house behind a cedar hedge, a store of gold pieces, and the promise of future provision in a will "which never came to light." A few years before the Civil War, young John Walden, the Caucasian-featured son of this union, decides that he will "pass." He is taken in as office boy by Judge Archibald Straight, who allows him to read law secretly out of friendship for John's dead father. At eighteen John leaves Molly and his seven-year-old sister and goes off to seek his fortune. As the novel opens, John has been away ten years and is returning incognito to Patesville. He is now John Warwick, a South Carolina gentleman. Escaping service in the Confederate Army in some vague way, made wealthy by a wife he married during the social upheaval after the war, he has established a genteel law practice in Clarence (Charleston), South Carolina. John's wife has recently died and he is left with an infant son. He returns to Patesville to persuade the now seventeen-year-old Rena to join him in South Carolina. She agrees, and after a brief stint at a finishing school, appears in Clarence as Rowena Warwick. There she is quickly wooed by and betrothed to George Tryon, a North Carolina gentleman. Before they can be married, however, Rena returns to Patesville to care for her sick mother. By coincidence, Tryon also appears in Patesville and discovers Rena's true identity. Although Tryon does not expose the Warwick deception, he cancels the wedding. Rena decides to enter the nineteenth-century North Carolina equivalent of a nunnery. She renounces the vanity of the white world and devotes herself as a teacher to improving the Negro race. Burying herself in a small rural school, which, unknown to her, is near the Tryon family estate, Rena finds herself pursued on the one hand by George Tryon and on the other by a lecherous mulatto school superintendent. Fleeing them both, Rena is overcome by nervous exhaustion and dies.

The most important thematic element that Chesnutt's first novel shares with many other southern novels, both earlier and later, is the protagonist's movement from innocence to knowledge and its effect upon the character's sense of identity. Of course, a protagonist's loss of innocence and concomitant discovery of himself is a novelistic concern which goes back at least as far as *Joseph Andrews* in the English tradition. In our national fiction, we have a multitude of American Adams seeking to regain the Garden of Eden. The southern writer seems almost unable to write without creating protagonists, usually in their youth, who first lose their innocence and then, characteristically, find themselves. Twain's Huck Finn; Faulkner's Ike McCaslin, Lucius Priest, Thomas Sutpen, and Chick Mallison; Capote's Joel Knox; Wolfe's Eugene Gant and George Webber; McCullers's Mick Kelley; Warren's Willie Stark; Styron's Nat Turner—the list seems almost endless. A recent reviewer states the case: "Perhaps it has something to do with the old Southern blend of agrarian idealism and the 18th century romance with the noble savage. Or maybe it is just all that ambling through the tall grass. In any case, Southern writers have had a particular weakness for seeing a beauty and naked truth through the eye of the innocent."

Of course, the nature of a protagonist's innocence and the terms of the identity he achieves vary. The innocence lost by Thomas Sutpen when he decides to define himself as a slave-owning gentleman because he learns that he is considered white trash is not the same as either the innocence of Eugene Gant looking for a lost lane back to his cosmic self or that of almost any of Flannery O'Connor's tortured figures fighting to escape their spiritual identity in the eyes of God.

To Chesnutt, as to almost all black writers northern or southern, achieving personal identity is inextricably interwoven with racial caste. For John Walden to have an identity in *The House behind the Cedars,* he (like Thomas Sutpen) must become a southern white gentleman. And like Sutpen, Walden gets his idea of what a white gentleman must be indirectly. For although Walden's father did not give him a gentleman's family name, he did (like David Copperfield's father) leave him a gentlemanly library: "Fielding's complete works, in fine print, set in double columns; a set of Bulwer's novels; a collection of everything that Walter Scott—the literary idol of the South—had ever written," in addition to the Bible, Shakespeare, Milton, and Bunyan. It is through his reading that John loses his innocence and gains knowledge. When Willie Stark learns of evil, Warren baptizes him in liquor. When Mr. Head ("The Artificial Nigger") discovers his pride, O'Connor says that he also recognized his share in the guilt of original sin. Chesnutt follows a similar impulse and describes Walden's transformation in biblical terms. "When he had read all the books—indeed, long before he had read all of them—he too had tasted of the fruit of the Tree of Knowledge: contentment took its flight, and happiness lay far beyond the sphere where he was born. The blood of his white fathers, the heirs of the ages, cried out for its own, and after the manner of that blood set about getting the object of its desire."

Without name or estate, young Walden turns to the law as a profession which will provide him with upward mobility in the antebellum South. When he approaches Judge Straight and tells him that he wants to become a lawyer, the old judge—who, as his name suggests, represents the aristocratic South at its best—is (like Walden himself) much more concerned with John's race than with his illegitimate birth. Their confrontation defines both what Walden is and must remain as a Negro and why becoming a white gentleman is his only means of attaining an acceptable identity as a man.

> "You are aware, of course, that you are a Negro?"
>
> "I am white," replied the lad, turning back his sleeve and holding out his arm, "and I am free, as all my people were before me."
>
> ". . . You are black," he said, "and you are not free. You cannot travel without your papers; you cannot secure accommodations at an inn; you could not vote, if you were of age; you cannot be out after nine o'clock without a permit. If a white man struck you, you could not return the blow, and you could not testify against him in a court of justice. You are black, my lad, and you are not free."

Judge Straight violates the customs of his caste and allows John to use his library so long as no one else knows about it. He further advises John to go to South Carolina, because his race, if questioned, could be decided legally "by reputation, by reception into society, and by [the] exercise of the privileges of the white man, as well as by admixture of blood. John follows Straight's advice and, despite his sister's disappointment and subsequent death, is at the novel's end living as a wealthy white South Carolina lawyer-gentleman in "the land of his father where, he conceived, he had an inalienable birth right."

Unlike her brother, Rena Walden suffers from no problems of knowing who she is, at least initially. A dutiful daughter, she accepts her life with her mother in the house behind the cedars, vaguely hoping in some indefinite way that she will be able to teach, now that the Yankees have started schools for both poor whites and blacks. When John offers her the chance to join him in South Carolina, however, and their mother acquiesces, she readily accepts.

The life which Rena and John leave, though socially repressed, is humanly rich. Like Dickens's Pip, they leave the reality of loving friends and family and enter an artificial society. Chesnutt suggests early in the novel that they are entering a fantasy world when black John Walden becomes white John Warwick, an identity borrowed not from the world of fact but from the world of romantic fiction. "From Bulwer's novel, he had read the story of Warwick the King-maker, and upon leaving home had chosen it for his own. He was a new man, but he had the blood of an old race, and he would select for his own one of its worthy names." Similarly, Rena Walden becomes Rowena Warwick, after the heroine of *Ivanhoe.* She makes her entrance into society on the day of the Clarence Social Club's annual tournament. Like Rena's new name, the tournament is borrowed directly from Scott's *Ivanhoe* and serves both as an emblem of and an ironic commentary on the white South. Chesnutt tells us with a straight face that during the month preceding the tournament, the local bookseller had sold his entire stock of *Ivanhoe* (some five copies) and had ordered seven copies more. With the "best people" in the grandstand, and the poor whites and Negroes in the bleachers, masquerading knights in colorful costumes of gilded cloth, paper, and cardboard prepare to attack wooden blocks with their swords and pierce iron rings with their wooden lances. It is, as John Warwick says with unconscious irony, "the renaissance of chivalry." But it is not a renaissance of historic chivalry (whatever that was); it is a late nineteenth-century South Carolina adaptation of Scott's early nineteenth-century romanticized fiction. And it is a renaissance, again as John Warwick says, which substitutes cardboard costumes for the discomfort of armor, which retains the formality of lists and knights and prancing steeds but eliminates the possibility of physical risk. It is, like the worst aspects of southern chivalry, a picturesque but bloodless display. George Tryon, in a performance worthy of a gilded Black Knight or cardboard Wilfred of Ivanhoe, wins the tourney and names Rowena Warwick as Queen of Love and Beauty at the post-tourney ball. The entire episode recalls the tournament at Ashby-de-la-Zouche in many ways. Scott's tournament was between the conquering Normans and the oppressed but worthy Saxons. It is the Saxon Lady Rowena who is named Queen of Honor and Love by Ivanhoe. In South Carolina, all identify themselves with the Saxons; actually, however, Rowena is more nearly analogous to the Jewess Rebecca. Like Rebecca, she loses both the man she loves and a proper place in society because of her race. In Scott's novel, the wedding of Lady Rowena and Ivanhoe is attended by both highborn Normans and Saxons, thus marking "the marriage of two individuals as a pledge of the future peace and harmony betwixt two races, which, since that period, had been so completely mingled, that the distinction has become wholly invisible" (*Ivanhoe*, chapter 44). Of course no such resolution occurs in nineteenth-century South Carolina, although the eradication of racial distinctions is Chesnutt's aim. The irony he conveys through his chivalric parallels is that despite the influence of Scott upon the old South, white southerners were blind to the applicability of the attack upon racial discrimination implicit in *Ivanhoe*.

John Warwick consistently accepts and defends the values of the South Carolina pseudo-renaissance. He states without conscious irony that the Clarence tourney is superior to the tournaments of the older times. "The spirit of a thing, after all, is what counts; and what is lacking here?" By extension, of course, he is defending his new identity as a white southern gentleman. Never throughout the novel does he question this identity or the values it embodies. Rena, on the other hand, while dazzled by the glamour of her new role as Queen of Love and Beauty and sincerely in love with her new knight-errant, never blindly accepts either the reality of white society or her new identity within it. On the evening of the grand ball she still recalls her life in Patesville. "Of the two, the present was more of a dream, the past was the more vivid reality." Her conversation with her brother after the ball suggests the differences in their perceptions. They both recognize that the tournament and ball are fantasy, but they differ as to the nature of reality. John suggests that reality is his life as a southern gentleman. "And now, sister . . . now that the masquerade is over, let us to sleep, and to-morrow take up the serious business of life." Rena, however, says, "It is a dream . . . only a dream. I am Cinderella before the clock has struck." Just as her earlier remarks suggested that her Patesville past was real and the present a dream, so this remark reveals not an awakening to a tomorrow as a South Carolina lady, but a reversion to her former lower

state. Similarly, it is not John but Rena who feels that her fiancé must be told about her past. And although she equivocates and does not tell Tryon directly, she does ask him if he would still love her were she the mulatto nurse of John's son. It is Rena who unquestioningly returns to Patesville to care for her sick mother only a few days before the scheduled wedding. And it is Rena who gains the undeniable knowledge that she cannot be white when George Tryon discovers the truth of her racial past. After this catastrophe John Warwick tries to persuade his sister to return with him to South Carolina, because even though Tryon will not now marry Rena, he is a "gentleman" and will be silent. As he has done consistently, John accepts a position based on appearances. Rena prefers her knowledge: " 'The law, you said, made us white; but not the law, nor even love can conquer prejudice. . . . I am not sorry that I tried it. It opened my eyes, and I would rather die of knowledge than live in ignorance. . . . I shall never marry any man, and I'll not leave mother again. God is against it; I'll stay with my own people'."

One question Rena must address is, "Who are my people?" The answer is not simple. Rejected as Tryon's wife, she cannot accept him on any other terms. Nor can she ever "again become quite the Rena Walden who had left the house behind the cedars no more than a year and a half before." As Rena Walden, she could have unquestioningly accepted the social values of mulatto society, values which are demonstrated during a mulatto dance party whose borrowed snobbery as well as music parallels that of the white Ball of Love and Beauty. Even though Rena attends the dance, she yearns for George Tryon. She decides that "one must stoop in order that one may lift others." Now neither black nor white, Rena decides to leave her mother and Patesville to teach Negro children who clearly are her intellectual and social inferiors. Her "desire to be of service to her rediscovered people" soon becomes a "discouraging sense of the insignificance of any part she could perform towards the education of three million people with a school term of two months a year." Her idealism frustrated, Rena finds herself pursued both by Jefferson Wain, a mulatto whose intentions are clearly lecherous, and by George Tryon, who does not seem clearly to know his own intentions. Rena can accept neither. Nor can she be rescued by Frank Fowler, the totally faithful, devoted, former slave who dearly loves her. Rena dies of physical exhaustion caused by her flight from both Wain and Tryon. But her physical death is merely an emblem of her destruction as a human being, the result of the painfully acquired knowledge which prevents her from being white and her own inner being which will not allow her to be anything else.

The end of man is knowledge, Robert Penn Warren tells us, but we do not know whether knowledge will save or destroy us. John Walden is transformed by knowledge into John Warwick, an identity he unquestioningly values despite both the destruction of his sister and his knowledge that at least one white gentleman shares his secret. Rena Walden is ultimately destroyed by knowledge. Trapped between two worlds, her knowledge of who and what she is prevents her from belonging to either. As John's role-playing and Rena's melodramatic death suggest, neither alternative is very attractive.

The convolutions of plot and large numbers of characters

Chesnutt in his study.

almost preclude an adequate synopsis of Chesnutt's *The Marrow of Tradition.* This novel presents the racial situation through the linked experiences of two half-sisters, their friends and families during the 1898 race riot in Wilmington, North Carolina. The elder sister is Olivia Merkell Carteret, the white daughter of Samuel and Elizabeth Merkell. She is married to Major Carteret, scion of "one of the oldest and proudest" families in the state. Hopelessly impoverished by the war, Carteret restores the family fortune through his marriage to Olivia. He is now the publisher of the leading newspaper in the state and a noted champion of white supremacy.

The younger sister is Janet Miller, the mulatto daughter of Samuel Merkell and his wife's maid, Julia. Although the documents proving it were destroyed at Merkell's death, Janet's father and mother were legally married. Cheated of her inheritance, Janet is as legitimate an heir in all respects as Olivia. The sisters look enough alike to be twins and are often mistaken for each other. Janet is married to Dr. William Miller, the mulatto son of a free Negro sufficiently affluent to send his son North to medical school. Dr. Miller has returned to the South to build a Negro hospital on the site of a plantation mansion destroyed in the Civil War. He, Janet, and their one son live

in the old mansion lost by the Carteret family after the war.

As the novel opens, Olivia has just given birth to a boy, the long awaited Carteret son and heir. When the novel closes, the Miller son has been killed in the race riot fomented by Carteret's newspaper; the Carteret son lies near death and can be saved by an operation which only Miller is in a position to perform. There is a melodramatic confrontation between the Carterets and the Millers in which Major Carteret begs the doctor and Olivia begs Janet for the life of their son. Emblematic of Chesnutt's attitude toward the entire racial mess are a young doctor's words to Miller as he heads up the stairs to operate on his wife's nephew: "There's time enough, but none to spare."

Caught up in the racial tragedy of Wellington are characters who represent the full range of southern life. There are white aristocratic gentlemen of the old school and their scapegrace heirs, white trash bigots, ineffectual white moderates, Jewish merchants, and visiting northerners. There are Aunt Jemimas and Uncle Toms, new Negroes male and female whose anger and frustration are a potential source of danger within the community, and black retainers of real dignity who are in every sense themselves southern gentlefolk. There are a few middle-class blacks, educated men who have become doctors and lawyers. Like the characters in a Dickens novel, all of these figures are touched by the social forces which control the novel, all of them are caught up in the catastrophe of the race riot.

As Robert Bone has pointed out in *The Negro Novel in America,* Chesnutt and other early black writers adopted the melodramatic plot from the popular literature of their day. It is the plot of the Scotts, the Hardys, the Dickenses, and the Bulwers gone to seed. It is also the plot, planted and germinating, of southern writers to come, of the Faulkners, the Warrens, the Styrons, the McCullerses. We tend to overlook the melodramatic, the sentimental, the coincidental in many white southern writers because these qualities are overlaid with poetic rhetoric, with the symbolic. In the highly melodramatic *All the King's Men,* for example, Jack Burden's story turns on solving the mystery of his parentage. Consider the number of chance meetings in Faulkner's *Light in August,* or, better yet, the number of guns throughout Faulkner which have failed to go off at point-blank range. More to the point, Robert N. Farnsworth [in his introduction to a 1969 edition of the novel (see Further Reading)] has commented on the similarity between Chesnutt's "family tragedy, marked by alienation of sisters due to racial bigotry" in *The Marrow of Tradition* and Faulkner's Sutpen family tragedy in *Absalom, Absalom!* In both the "alienation within the family is microcosmic. It symbolizes the bitter and unnatural gulf between black and white men and women who have a blood kinship which their cultural situation will not permit them to recognize." Although Farnsworth does not say so, Major Carteret's return to a devastated South and bankrupt state, his exchange of his family name for Olivia's family wealth, and his longing for a son are all genteel manifestations of the same impulse which drove Colonel Sutpen to try to restore the ruined Sutpen's Hundred, to breed a son with either Rosa Coldfield or Millie Jones, and, finally, to accept a semisuicidal death. The symbolism implicit in the new Negro hospital on the site of a ruined antebellum mansion, or the black doctor residing in the old Carteret mansion, or the black sibling cheated of an inheritance is clearly of a kind with the more complex, thoroughgoing symbolism developed by Faulkner or Warren or Styron.

It is not, however, simply the use of melodramatic plots or occasional symbols which suggests Chesnutt's kinship with white southern authors, especially those of this century. A number of ideas, motifs, and themes are explicitly present in *The Marrow of Tradition* which are the stock in trade of numerous southern novelists, early and later. A concern with the past is one of these. As C. Hugh Holman notes in *The Immoderate Past: The Southern Writer and History,* the southern imagination has been focused on history for almost two hundred years. Early writers such as William Gilmore Sims wrote Sir Walter Scott-like novels to show that the past teaches lessons which can be applied to contemporary lives. Chesnutt's references to *Ivanhoe* in *The House behind the Cedars,* as well as his use of an actual historical episode—the riot at Wilmington—as the central event in *The Marrow of Tradition* suggest a rather deliberate self-identification with the Scott-Sims literary school. Although hardly Sims-like in approach, later writers such as Wolfe, Faulkner, Warren, and Styron also share this early concern with the relationship between time past, present, and future. Chesnutt's interest is im-

plicit in the way he uses the flashback into the past to explain the events in time present. It is suggested symbolically by the presence of the carved font, "which had come from England in the reign of King Charles the Martyr," in which the Carteret baby is baptized. It is further suggested in the moving of the family tombstones but not bodies when the Poindexter place is sold to become the site of a Negro hospital. But Chesnutt also states his concern explicitly. When Dr. Miller sees the continuing anger of black Josh Green over his parents' mistreatment by the KKK, Chesnutt says: "He realized, too, for a moment, the continuity of life, how inseparably the present is woven with the past, how certainly the future will be but the outcome of the present." Not only does this passage generally recall the obsession with time expressed by any number of southern white novelists, it specifically suggests Jack Burden's web theory of life and his realization that he can have no present or future without an understanding of the past. Senile Aunt Polly Ochiltree, one of the most bigoted of the Carteret family retainers, represents a false attitude toward the past. When she sees new construction where the Poindexter mansion once stood, she thinks it is the destroyed past being restored rather than something new being built to benefit the future. When she is corrected, however, she exclaims: "Hugh Poindexter has sold the graves of his ancestors to a negro." Significantly enough, one of the graves has been opened and there is nothing left of the ancestor except a little dust. Only the tombstones, the symbol of the dead past, have been transferred to the white cemetery. A proper understanding of the past and present is specifically attributed to Rena Walden in *The House behind the Cedars.* "To her sensitive spirit to-day was born of yesterday, tomorrow would be but the offspring of to-day." Certainly it is Rena who is unable to deny her past, who must try to go home again, to return to her mother. It is John who says, characteristically enough, "Let the dead past bury its dead."

Rena, like Faulkner's Lena Grove, intuitively gains her understanding of time and the attitude toward life such an understanding implies. It is not a matter she has reasoned through. Along with Faulkner and many other latter-day southern romantics, Chesnutt feels that the human heart is the source of both man's glory and his misery. It is clearly superior to human reason. At one point in *The Marrow of Tradition* he comments: "We speak of the mysteries of inanimate nature. The workings of the human heart are the profoundest mystery of the universe. One moment they make us despair of our kind, and the next we see in them the reflection of the divine image." When he describes Janet Miller's attitude toward her white half-sister, Chesnutt tells us her feelings are mixed. Like Charles Bon waiting for his father, Colonel Sutpen, to acknowledge him, she yearns "for a kind word, a nod, a smile, the least thing that imagination might have twisted into a recognition of the tie between them. . . . When the heart speaks, reason falls into the background, and Janet would have worshiped this sister, even afar off, had she received even the slightest encouragement." Instead, she is—again like Charles Bon—spurned. When at the novel's end Olivia Carteret is forced to acknowledge Janet in order to get Dr. Miller to help save her son's life, Janet spurns the recognition as being too tardy. Janet allows her husband to try to save young Carteret not because he is the son of her sister but because, even as a woman who has been terribly wronged, she can feel sympathy for another human being, even the woman who has wronged her.

Throughout the novel Dr. Miller follows reason, Josh Green emotion. Miller is the highly educated physician who represses his feelings in order to be allowed to heal his people and care for his family. Josh Green is a laborer of great strength, a noble savage of violence waiting to revenge himself on those who have injured him and his parents. When the riot starts, Green asks Miller to lead a band of Negroes in resisting the whites. Miller refuses because the blacks are hopelessly outnumbered and can only be destroyed. He denies himself the satisfaction of the defiant gesture so that he may continue his work. Even though he is convinced that he is acting wisely, he also feels both shame and envy. As he leads the band away, the more impetuous Green says, "Come along, boys! . . . I'd rather be a dead nigger any day dan a live dog!" As Farnsworth has pointed out, this dramatization of the conflict between the rational desire to survive and the emotional desire for revenge suggests some of the conflict within Chesnutt himself: his mind is with Miller, his emotional impulses are with Green.

Chesnutt includes other truths of the heart which are familiar to students of southern literature. Despite the evil of the southern caste system, despite the forces which act upon him, man lives with free will in a moral universe. In *The House behind the Cedars,* Chesnutt frequently emphasizes that Molly Walden was a free agent and was responsible for her actions. Mink Snopes would recognize a figure very much like his "Old Moster" in Chesnutt's reference to "God, or Fate, or whatever one may choose to call the Power that holds the destinies of man in the hollow of his hand." Willie Stark would agree with Chesnutt's authorial comment that "selfishness is the most constant of human motives." Judith Sutpen would understand Chesnutt's feeling that "we are all puppets in the hand of Fate, and seldom see the strings that move us." Jack Burden and Cass Mastern would both respond to Chesnutt's simile: "As a stone dropped into a pool of water sets in motion a series of concentric circles which disturb the whole mass in varying degree, so Mrs. Ochiltree's enigmatic remark had started in her niece's mind a disturbing train of thought." Ike McCaslin would sympathize with gentlemanly old Mr. Delamere's resumé of slavery: "We thought to overrule God's laws, and we enslaved these people for our greed, and sought to escape the man stealer's curse by laying to our souls the flattering unction that we were making of barbarous negroes civilized and Christian men." Any number of latter-day Southern writers would endorse Chesnutt's judgment and prophecy that "Sins, like chickens, come home to roost. The South paid a fearful price for the wrong of negro slavery: in some form or another it will doubtless reap the fruits of [segregation and disenfranchisement]." And surely Faulkner's "They endured" captures poetically the ideas Chesnutt expresses much more prosaically in the mind of Dr. Miller:

> Was it not, after all, a wise provision of nature that had given to a race, destined to a long servitude and a slow emergence therefrom, a cheerfulness of spirit which enabled them to catch pleasure on the wing, and endure with equanimity the ills that seemed inevitable? The ability to live and thrive under adverse circumstances is the surest guaranty of the fu-

ture. The race which at the last shall inherit the earth—the residuary legatee of civilization—will be the race which remains longest upon it.

Chesnutt clearly is not among the great writers of the South. His plots are weak, not because they are melodramatic, but because the melodrama is so transparent; his characterizations are inadequate, not because they are stereotypes, but because they are bloodless stereotypes; his "message" lacks impact, not because it is trite, but because it is not embodied within the mythos of his story. His diction is wooden, his dialogue unrealistic, his effects strained. But he is clearly a southern writer. Not only is his subject matter southern, his interests and impulses are southern. His message is racial tolerance. His deepest concern is with an individual's attempt to achieve identity after the old order has been destroyed and before the new one has yet been clearly defined. He sees man as a morally free agent confronting forces and impulses that he cannot control. While he lacks a sense of either the truly comic or the truly tragic which informs the writings of his literary betters, Chesnutt also lacks despair. His work, in the words of Saunders Redding, "is fed by the same roots sunk into the same cultural soil" as the writings of his white southern colleagues. Not a great novelist, Chesnutt was a great southerner; he belongs within the southern literary tradition. (pp. 11-25)

> Ladell Payne, "Trunk and Branch: Charles Waddell Chesnutt, 1858-1932," in his Black Novelists and the Southern Literary Tradition, *The University of Georgia Press, 1981, pp. 9-25.*

William L. Andrews   (essay date 1980)

[*In the following excerpt, Andrews offers an extended analysis of Chesnutt's last published short story, "Baxter's Procrustes."*]

During the climactic years of Charles Chesnutt's literary career, he wrought only one sustained and unmixed success in fiction—**"Baxter's Procrustes."** For a long time this story has been singled out for both its aesthetic excellences and its distance from the social and moral concerns that usually predominate in Chesnutt's writing. Some critics have suggested a causal relationship between these two factors, a conclusion which encourages speculation that Chesnutt's divorcing himself from the race problem in **"Baxter's Procrustes"** allowed the sometime propagandist to concentrate without distraction on his art. However, a close look at both the thematic drift of the story and the parallels between its contents and the author's social and literary experience before its publication urges a different judgment of the artfulness of **"Baxter's Procrustes."** Internal evidence in the story argues that it is much more than simply a "bagatelle," as Vernon Loggins has called it [*The Negro Author in America,* 1931], or a clever critique of manners. The story synthesizes more gracefully and tellingly than Chesnutt would ever do again some of the racial, aesthetic, and personal concerns which, though germane to his purpose and development as an Afro-American writer, had eluded his prior attempts to incorporate them into a single imaginative statement.

Sometime in 1902, Chesnutt was denied membership in

the Cleveland, Ohio, Rowfant Club, an upper-class male social club distinguished by its fondness for books and book collecting. Presumably race prejudice was the cause. For a man who had left the South some twenty years earlier to escape such discrimination, this rebuff must have seemed a humiliating irony. It is not surprising, therefore, to find Chesnutt penning a tale two years later which mocks an organization of bibliophiles, the fictional equivalent of the Rowfant Club. The spoof of the Rowfanters is thoroughgoing and trenchant, indicating Chesnutt's minute knowledge of the Club's more vulnerable idiosyncrasies. **"Baxter's Procrustes"** begins with a comic inventory of the "Bodleian" club's collection of literary memorabilia—"a paperweight which once belonged to Goethe, a lead pencil used by Emerson, an autograph letter of Matthew Arnold, and a chip from a tree felled by Mr. Gladstone." The recitation of the Bodleians' eccentricities extends through another anticlimactic description of the club's pipe collection and its most "solemn" ceremony, an annual procession of Bodleians "all smoking furiously" through their clubhouse before concluding with a presidential address "on the virtues of nicotine." After these preliminary comic exaggerations of the Rowfanters' idiosyncrasies, Chesnutt gets down to the basic satiric business of the story—exposing the self-deluding dollar-consciousness of these supposedly discriminating lovers and collectors of literature.

The Bodleians' standard by which to judge the worth of a book is revealed early in the story. The greatest emphasis is laid upon "the qualities that make a book valuable in the eyes of collectors," which, as the narrator of the story explains, are "fine and curious bindings," "handmade linen papers," "uncut or deckle edges," "wide margins and limited editions." "The matter of contents," he confesses, merits "a less important consideration." The Bodleians' misplaced reverence for books as a practical investment is further attested when the narrator remarks that the most desirable books at the club's auctions have been uncut copies of elaborately tooled and crafted works of club members. Into this collection of genteel philistines masquerading as men of genuine literary culture comes an enigmatic figure named Baxter who contrives a hoax to prove to what absurd lengths the Bodleians will go to acquire sound "literary" investments. Having been solicited to enter a sealed and, by Bodleian logic, thereby supremely valuable copy of one of his own compositions, the *Procrustes,* into the club's auction, Baxter stuns his fellow Bodleians when they inadvertently discover that the handsome book for which they have bid such large sums has not a word printed on any of its expensive pages. The joke, of course, is on the bookmen, whose acquisitive instincts blind them to the true value of literature. By extending the story's logic, one can see that metaphorically speaking, **"Baxter's Procrustes"** attacks anyone who judges a book or a person by appearance without regard to intrinsic worth. Thus Chesnutt had his revenge on the prejudices, both social and literary, of the Rowfanters.

Revenge, however, may be too strong a word to describe Chesnutt's feelings in this affair. Deflating the social pretensions of exclusive snob societies, whether white (as in **"Baxter's Procrustes"**) or black (as in **"A Matter of Principle"**), engaged a certain droll irony in Chesnutt, not the caustic sort that flashes in some of the southern protest stories. One senses that Chesnutt's response to the Row-

fanters was much the same as his ambivalent view of the Blue Veins: some of them were his friends and their eccentricities his own, though he could see the absurdities and traps to which those eccentricities could lead. Consequently, in 1910 Chesnutt would authorize and accept a second nomination for membership in the Rowfant Club with a comment revelatory of his characteristically mixed feelings. The nomination, he reported to a friend, "went through all right, and I anticipate considerable pleasure from the company of gentlemen with whom I am at last found worthy to associate." The gentle sarcasm here belies Chesnutt's sincere desire to be a member of the Rowfant Club. In 1904 he would do nothing publicly to jeopardize his chances; that his satiric targets in **"Baxter's Procrustes"** were not offended by his treatment of them amply testifies to the carefulness with which he managed his irony. But privately a less politic and more sharp-tongued Chesnutt allowed himself the pleasure of an ironic riposte at his supposed betters, at men who, like the "purse-proud aristocrats" of his youth in North Carolina, thought him socially unworthy of their association because of his racial background. In **"Baxter's Procrustes"** the satiric underthrust is deftly made but well concealed indeed, a tribute to Chesnutt's ability to hold, at least in the space of short fiction, the emotional equipoise of detachment and involvement which his brand of irony demanded.

Still, the success with which **"Baxter's Procrustes"** transmutes painful private experience into art should not be measured solely by the story's relationship to the Rowfant Club affair. The time and circumstances of Chesnutt's career when **"Baxter's Procrustes"** appeared suggest that the biographical significance of this sally at bookmen may not be completely accounted for by noting its connection to what was, by the time of the story's publication, a two-year-old social slight. In the winter of 1904 when **"Baxter's Procrustes"** was written, Chesnutt could not only look back on a promising social opportunity stymied by some of the Rowfanters' social prejudice. He could also reflect on a frustrated, short-lived literary career, the dream of his life at one time, shattered apparently on the altar of public opinion. He had tried writing serious, socially corrective and informative novels, and they had been largely ignored by the average bookbuyer. He had tried to serve up a blander fictional fare in his nonracial romances, but none of them had been able to get past an editor. Meanwhile the years since his literary heyday were rapidly slipping by, squandering in the process his hard-earned literary fame. When one returns to **"Baxter's Procrustes"** with these facts in mind and notices that a major function of the exposé is to uncover the specious standards and prejudices of the Bodleian reviewers of the *Procrustes,* one begins to suspect that **"Baxter's Procrustes"** was to Chesnutt what "Bartleby, the Scrivener" may have been to Melville, an understated reproof to a wrong-headed literary audience.

If so, Chesnutt was wise to do his admonishing in a literary form and with a brand of satire which he knew well from past experience in writing about tricksters, hoaxes, and the ironies of self-deception. One reason why **"Baxter's Procrustes"** epitomizes Chesnutt's work in the short story is that it revives and refines some of the most distinctive satiric techniques of his conjure and color line stories. Describing Chesnutt's last *Atlantic* story as one in which a hoax is perpetrated on a group of self-assured but self-deluded gentlemen helps to place **"Baxter's Procrustes"** in a tradition which embraces such works as **"The Conjurer's Revenge," "A Matter of Principle,"** and **"The Passing of Grandison."** In each of these earlier stories an ostensibly innocuous but unexpectedly cunning subordinate—a handyman, an office assistant, and a slave—exposes the prejudices of his patron and supposed superior, by playing false roles and manipulating illusory situations so as to capitalize upon his superior's inability to look below the surfaces of things. The trickster triumphs simply by allowing the deceived to deceive themselves. Thus at the end of such diverse stories as **"Baxter's Procrustes," "A Matter of Principle,"** or **"The Passing of Grandison,"** the reader learns a good deal about deception though (and probably because) the duped does not. Similar to its predecessors, **"Baxter's Procrustes"** uses an irony mixed with pathos to elicit from the reader an Horatian smile of amusement at the follies of men. The reader is encouraged to laugh, but not too loudly or too long, for, like Chesnutt, his feeling of superiority to the Bodleians' investment-consciousness or the Blue Veins' social exclusivism will be tempered by a poignant recognition of his own sympathies with the now-questionable "principles" of these "best people" of American and Afro-American society.

What marks **"Baxter's Procrustes"** as an advancement over its forebears in Chesnutt's fiction is its attention to the character of the confidence man himself. Usually hardly more than a device or an authorial mouthpiece, the hoaxer in **"Baxter's Procrustes"** is characterized in almost as much detail as the hoaxed. Chesnutt seems at pains to individualize his hoaxer, even to the point of hinting at his past, his personal circumstances, his motives, and his "philosophy" of life. Apparently Chesnutt wanted his reader to pay as much attention to the hoaxer as to the effect of his hoax. The reason for this attempt to establish a bond of sympathy between Baxter and the reader becomes clearer as one examines the character of Baxter. For this is no ordinary hoaxer, not merely an instrument by which Chesnutt took his mocking revenge on the delusions of the socially pretentious and the racially "superior." Baxter is Chesnutt's most elaborate self-dramatization, the most transparent and close-fitting of the many masks the author assumed in his fiction. Baxter's satirical purpose derives from Chesnutt's apparent presentation of his own artistic situation in 1904 through that of Baxter, an unsuccessful author who is patronized, summarized, and categorized by an ignorant, commercially minded, pseudo-literary readership.

Chesnutt does not project a complete self-portrait through Baxter, but the points of resemblance are striking enough to establish a parallel. While Chesnutt was not a graduate of Harvard (though his son was) as Baxter is said to be, he was, like Baxter, a very "scholarly" man, one who "had traveled extensively" and "had read widely." Aside from their ages (Baxter is said to be thirty-five) and marital status (Baxter is single) Chesnutt and Baxter coincide in general appearance and temperament. Described by Jones, the narrator of the story, as a gray-eyed, fair-skinned, curly-haired fellow, Baxter resembles his creator. Baxter has a winning personality but is prone to stand aloof from others, a trait which often distinguished Chesnutt. The kind of "mild cynicism" which Jones attributes to Baxter crops up in Chesnutt's private writing more than his public work, but from the beginning of his literary career,

Chesnutt acknowledged that "my position, my surroundings, are not such as to make me take a humorous view of life. They rather tend the other way." That tendency "the other way" is dramatized in Baxter's exploitation of the Bodleians. Chesnutt lends Baxter something of the pose he assumed socially, that of the man of "genial" temper, dignified mien, and "occasional flashes of humor." But behind this sunny demeanor Baxter like Chesnutt plays false to the type-cast role his peers would like him to play. Baxter holds in reserve a cynical view of the individual's chances against oppressive social forces, a theme Chesnutt often advanced in his gloomier stories. The implied source of Baxter's cynicism and the basic theme of his "philosophy of life" disclose the particular ways in which this character speaks for his creator.

Here is Jones's summary of Baxter's "philosophy":

> Society was the Procrustes which, like the Greek bandit of old, caught every man born into the world, and endeavored to fit him to some preconceived standard, generally to the one for which he was least adapted. The world was full of men and women who were merely square pegs in round holes, and *vice versa*. Most marriages were unhappy because the contracting parties were not properly mated. Religion was mostly superstition, science for the most part sciolism, popular education merely a means of forcing the stupid and repressing the bright, so that all the youth of the rising generation might conform to the same dull, dead level of democratic mediocrity. Life would soon become so monotonously uniform and so uniformly monotonous as to be scarce worth the living.

It is not necessary to claim for Chesnutt all of these opinions. It is not even necessarily true that Baxter holds them all, given Jones's soon-to-be-demonstrated lack of reliability as a reader, much less an interpreter, of Baxter's writing. One need only discern the basic theme of Baxter's philosophy of life to recognize its relevance to Chesnutt's situation in 1904.

To Baxter, the experience of life is the experience of frustration. In the most general sense, "society," like the mythic giant Procrustes, forces everyone to conform to its own biases, without regard to the individual's abilities or ambitions. As a result all are compelled to know their places, though square pegs may be thrust into round holes for the sake of "democratic mediocrity." Baxter has a special vantage point from which to make such pronouncements. Something of a litterateur in the Bodleian Club, he is suspected by Jones of having been "an unsuccessful author." Baxter often exhibits his disdain for the mediocre democratic mass by denigrating "the vulgar popularity" which "modern literature," toward which he shows "profound contempt," obsessively solicits. On the other hand, he can "always" be heard speaking "in terms of such unmeasured pity for the slaves of the pen who were dependent upon the whim of an undiscriminating public for recognition and livelihood." Having hypothesized that Baxter's mild cynicism stems from "some bitter experience—some disappointment in love or ambition"—Jones cites Baxter's frequent remarks on the frustrations of the literary life to support his contention that his fellow clubman is actually an unappreciated literary artist.

First of all, it is not hard to see the special applicability of Baxter's view of life to Chesnutt's private experience as a person of color often frustrated in his social and economic ambitions by the "preconceived standards" of procrustean white society. The Procrustes myth had been on Chesnutt's mind at least since 1901, when Dr. Miller used it in *The Marrow of Tradition* to define the black man's incongruous social predicament. "It was a veritable bed of Procrustes, this standard which the whites had set for the negroes," Miller decides. "Those who grew above it must have their heads cut off, figuratively speaking,—must be forced back to the level assigned to their race; those who fell beneath the standard set had their necks stretched, literally enough, as the ghastly record in the daily papers gave conclusive evidence."

Nor is the judgment of life as inevitably frustrating for the aspiring individual, irrespective of race, foreign to Chesnutt's work during the climactic years of his career. One may argue, in fact, that as the author became more thwarted in his efforts to win a readership and a serious hearing for himself, his fiction registered his pessimism about overcoming his frustrations in progressively more and more despairing plots. Thus among the Waldens of *The House behind the Cedars,* John breaks out of the role and prospects to which society has relegated him, but his sister fails. In *The Marrow of Tradition* Miller, another of Chesnutt's frustrated men of high aspiration, cannot halt the take-over of his town by the Carteret cabal, though still there remains the hope of amelioration through the survival of the doctor. By the time of *The Colonel's Dream,* however, the defeat of the man of high ideals is virtually total; the hero of the novel collides with the New South racial standards and, defeated and disillusioned, leaves the region altogether. Both chronologically and ideologically, Baxter stands between the heroes of Chesnutt's last two novels, Dr. Miller and Colonel French, who embody respectively Chesnutt's idea of the fate of the black moderate and the white reformer in the South. Baxter inherits Miller's "procrustean philosophy" and anticipates French's "bitter experiences" in both "love and ambition." But his primary significance lies in the way he symbolizes his creator's most privately felt frustration—the frustration of the literary man of purpose in a country which appeared to admire only mediocrity and the ability to arouse "vulgar popularity." Through his hoaxing alter ego Chesnutt exposes the whims of the "undiscriminating public" for whom he had played "the slave of the pen" (a doubly degrading epithet for Chesnutt to apply to himself) in exchange for the "recognition" which he had sought for so long.

A large portion of **"Baxter's Procrustes"** recounts the deliberations of the committee charged by the Bodleian Club to review Baxter's book. As a member of the committee, Jones provides a curious commentary on the attitudes which govern the evaluation of the book by such supposedly "cultured" and "literary" men. In Jones's reluctance to "spoil" the market value of his uncut copy of the *Procrustes* by opening it, Chesnutt gibes at the misplaced priorities of the Rowfanters. But by describing the subsequent deceptions which the reviewers use to hide the fact that they have not read the book, Chesnutt hinted that the perversion of the critical function beyond the foibles of the Rowfanters was also his concern.

Consider the critical method by which the Bodleian reviewers reach their judgments of the *Procrustes.* They are united from the beginning in their refusal to spoil the copy by reading the text. To Jones, hearsay will do, so he courts "some other source" for his information about the book. What is his concept of the responsibility of the book reviewer vis-à-vis the book and his audience? Jones replies, "I supposed upon the theory that the appreciation of any book review would depend more or less upon the degree to which it reflected the opinion of those to whom the review should be presented." In more direct language, Jones believes a book reviewer will be most "appreciated" and safest when he holds up the mirror to the audience instead of the book—when he tells his audience what it wants to hear about the book in question. Thompson, another member of the reviewing committee, likes the ad hominem approach to book reviewing. " 'By knowing Baxter we are able to appreciate the book,' " he declares, thus implying that prior opinions of the author are a sure guide to the value of his work. Thompson's comrades in literary deception all operate on the same premise. Moreover, they prefer to gauge the value of the *Procrustes* by its conformity to their own weltanschauungen. Unwilling to discover what the philosophical "view of life" might actually be in the *Procrustes,* Davis, the third reviewer, ascribes to the poem his own indiscriminate genteel optimism. In his mind a good book is ipso facto an uplifting one. The view of life in the *Procrustes* will, according to Davis, "help us to fit our shoulders for the heavy burden of life, by bringing to our realization those profound truths of philosophy which find hope in despair and pleasure in pain." Thus criticism in the hands of the Bodleian reviewers descends to the level of validating popular shibboleths. Baxter is welcomed into the "literary fraternity" as an inspiration to all, for he has (apparently) endorsed the complacent and contradictory "truths of philosophy" by which the genteel reading community lives.

The encomia proliferate at the conclusion of the story until Jones resoundingly summarizes the reviewers' sentiments with a final unconscious irony: "This work, which might be said to represent all that the Bodleian stood for, was in itself sufficient to justify the club's existence." Almost immediately thereafter, the *Procrustes* is revealed to be a hollow sham. In the consternation that follows, the club's misplaced commercial priorities are exposed, but so are the reviewers and their critical priorities. Baxter is not the only one who has "sold" the Bodleians. They have been duped by a group of irresponsible, closed-minded, uninformed critics who, due to prejudice and self-aggrandizement, fail to perform their intellectual duties. Consequently, if **"Baxter's Procrustes"** warns against judging a book by its cover, it is equally cautionary about judging books or authors by their critical reception.

Applying biographical criticism to **"Baxter's Procrustes"** raises provocative questions about the extent of Chesnutt's half-concealed purposes in this story and about the seriousness with which the story should be taken as an exposé of either genteel bookmen like the Rowfanters or a clubby, genteel reviewing establishment as a whole. When studied against the background of Chesnutt's own career as an "unsuccessful author," the several levels of fatuity and pretense exposed in the story seem to interlock into a single satiric structure which is designed to peel away the social, economic, and aesthetic myths the cultured classes of Chesnutt's day lived by. But whether **"Baxter's Procrustes"** should be interpreted more specifically as an ironic allegory of Chesnutt's private literary career requires some reservation, some consideration of outside supporting evidence for such a reading.

A look at some of the reviews of Chesnutt's novels will unearth frauds like Jones or Thompson or Davis of the Bodleians, reviewers who sometimes openly admitted that they had not read Chesnutt's work, who resorted to extra-literary sources on which to base their judgments of him, who pandered to the sectional or racial prejudices of their audience, and who denied Chesnutt their endorsement because he seemed too bitter and not facile enough to perceive "hope in despair and pleasure in pain." But this is not the issue. What is—and what is impossible to ascertain—is whether this sort of review became in Chesnutt's mind representative or indicative of the general response of the white literary critical establishment in America. If one could discover Chesnutt's blanket estimate of the critics' handling of his major works, then one could anatomize **"Baxter's Procrustes"** for its correspondence to some stated opinion from Chesnutt on the subject of the aspiring writer versus the entrenched literati. Unfortunately, no such categorical statement survives in Chesnutt's papers. Typically, the author's comments during his career are limited to individual reviewers who seemed to him fair or unfair; the critical corps in toto he did not judge. Late in his life Chesnutt spoke on occasion of the curtailment and frustrations of his literary career, analyzing some of the causes and contributing factors behind his lack of popular success. Among the factors he cited were inauspicious timing, an unprepared public, and adverse social trends. He did not include short-sighted or hypocritical reviewers and critics.

Just how seriously or how systematically **"Baxter's Procrustes"** should be read as a statement of recrimination or as a key to the author's frame of mind in 1904, therefore, is probably impossible to determine. As in the case of the relationship of "Bartleby, the Scrivener" to Melville's situation at the close of his active literary career, **"Baxter's Procrustes"** offers many tantalizing hints about its author's private frustrations, his self-concept, and his view of the literary life after his own full-time literary career had been cut short. But as in many of Chesnutt's best stories, after a careful reading of **"Baxter's Procrustes,"** one still imagines the author and his intention standing just a little apart from the reader, the enigmatic smile of Baxter reinforcing the author's reticence toward the reader. What remains indisputable is the excellence of the story itself as comedy of manners and multi-layered satire. Jones is easily Chesnutt's most effectively conceived unconscious ironist, more complex and completely developed than the "John" prototypes of the conjure stories, less patently ridiculous than similarly duped figures like Colonel Owens in **"The Passing of Grandison"** or Cicero Clayton in **"A Matter of Principle."** The pace of **"Baxter's Procrustes"** is disarmingly even, with none of the abrupt shifts of tone and scene which often obtrude into Chesnutt's earlier short stories. And the conclusion of the story—not the climactic moment of exposure of the hoax, but the narrator's deadpan recitation of its aftermath in which the *Procrustes* is auctioned for "the highest price ever brought by a single volume published by the club"—this too is a wise and telling ironic stroke. In virtually every respect, therefore, Chesnutt made **"Baxter's Procrustes"** his most magisterial adaptation of the structure, the character types, and the ironic mode and tone of his often-experimented-with "hoax story." The subject matter of **"Baxter's Procrustes,"** so laden with hints at the author's unfulfilled private ambitions, tends to pull reader appreciation away from the fact of its craftsmanship. Still, the story is ultimately distinguished less for its ambiguity, which was not a thematic virtue Chesnutt studied, than for its artfulness, which was something Chesnutt wished to be appreciated for from the beginning of his writing career. This is a limited artfulness, to be sure. **"Baxter's Procrustes"** certainly epitomizes Chesnutt's hoax stories, but it is still a formula story, the final product of something Chesnutt had been evolving for almost two decades. Nevertheless, **"Baxter's Procrustes"** brought Chesnutt's short story career to a singular and indentifiable point of fruition. It showcases all that Chesnutt could do well in his most accomplished and controlled area of literary expression, the short story. (pp. 209-21)

> *William L. Andrews, in his* The Literary Career of Charles W. Chesnutt, *Louisiana State University Press, 1980, pp. 209-221.*

Sylvia Lyons Render (essay date 1980)

[*Render is an American educator and critic with special interest in Afro-American literature. In the following excerpt, she examines the depiction of character in Chesnutt's fiction.*]

> "The proper study of mankind is man"; and, while a power of description . . . of . . . the beauties of nature . . . is a valuable possession for an author; yet the power to understand human nature, to depict the passions of the human heart,—its loves, its hates; its joys, its sorrows; its ambitions, its disappointments; its strivings after the infinite,—toward a higher life, and the inevitable opposition which it finds in [the] "house of clay," which binds it down to earth—this is a far more valuable accomplishment, and to master it requires a correspondingly larger amount of observation and study.
> —*Charles W. Chesnutt*

Chesnutt was aware of the significance of character in imaginative writing before he met the established authors and critics who offered him advice. In an undated statement of his literary theory, **"The Writing of a Novel,"** he rated character as "perhaps the most important element in a work of creative imagination" and "good character [as the] highest product of the creative imagination. . . . There are characters in fiction which [*sic*] are more immortal than the names of those who wrote them." Chesnutt evidently knew of no blacks so portrayed when he began reading critically. Accepting the Spingarn Medal in 1928, he recalled:

> I observed, as soon as I was capable of intelligent observation, that the Negro in fiction had become standardized, and that there were very few kinds of Negroes. There was the bad Negro, as most of them were, who either broke the law or made himself obnoxious to the white people by demanding his rights or protesting against his wrongs; the good Negro who loved old "Massa" and preserved the same attitude toward his children as they had taken to him, that of a simple and childlike deference and respect—the good old Uncle and Mammy types; and the modern "white man's nigger," as we call

him, who, as teacher or preacher or politician or
whatever you will,

Crooks the pregnant hinges of the knee,
    Where thrift may follow fawning.

Then there was the wastrel type, who squandered
his substance in riotous living, and the minstrel
type, who tried to keep the white folks in a good
humor by his capers and antics.

During the time Chesnutt was concentrating on writing
fiction (c. 1885-1905), prevailing scholarly and popular
opinion of blacks was at an all-time low, influenced not
only by social evolutionary theories but also by fundamentalist religious dogma. Belief was widespread that the
Negro, whether created or evolved, was the most inferior
of races; that even the possibility of his equality with
whites was eons away; that God never intended the black
to have equal power with the white man. Despite the aridity and hostility of such a social climate, Chesnutt believed,
as he declared later in his literary manifesto, **"Post-
Bellum—Pre-Harlem,"** that "a body of twelve million
people, struggling upward slowly but surely from a lowly
estate, must present all along the line of its advancement
many situations full of dramatic interest, ranging from
farce to tragedy, with many admirable types worthy of de-
lineation.

Though Chesnutt must have been more inclined to portray in his fiction strong, self-respecting, and aspiring
Afro-Americans, as a realist he had to treat all types. His
tendency to delineate more upper class whites, whether
aristocrats or *nouveaux riches,* may be attributable to their
prominence and power; a similar emphasis upon Afro-
Americans of all classes is doubtlessly due to his greater
concern for all of them and his deep-seated resentment
both of their treatment in real life and their limited portrayal in American fiction. Moreover, as a "voluntary"
Negro, Chesnutt devoted special attention to mulattoes
"by depicting life as it is in certain aspects that no one has
ever before attempted to adequately describe." As a consequence his fiction had increased possibilities for novelty
and drama.

In portraying slaves, Chesnutt only suggests the idyllic
plantation life characteristic of Page, Harris, Allen, Edwards, Smith, Stuart, and Dunbar. He also reveals "the
darker side of slavery—the old master's extravagance and
overbearing haughtiness, the young gentleman's reckless
dissipation . . . the hopeless degradation of the poorer
whites, the slaves . . . bullied by overseer or frightened by
the prospect of being transferred to the lower South." Further, Chesnutt frequently makes such disclosures more
dispassionately than does Cable or Tourgée. While dis-
agreeing with Page and Dixon, who held that the Negro
could not survive as a free agent in American society and
that the freedman was the chief cause of Reconstruction
ills, he remains completely realistic in showing that any
ostensibly black man (Ben Davis in **"The Web of Circumstance"** and Dr. Miller in *The Marrow of Tradition,* for
example) who has the same qualities and qualifications as
his successful white counterpart cannot, because of ob-
struction by whites, realize the American Dream.

Unlike Tourgée, Chesnutt does not find that education
will assure racial amity in community or personal relations. Further, he does not try to balance the social rejec-

tion of Negroes by whites, as depicted in Dixon's novels,
by total personal interracial acceptance in his own writings. (Howells goes beyond Chesnutt to permit, in *An Imperative Duty,* intermarriage among the upper classes.) On
the whole, Chesnutt's advocacy of the Afro-American
cause seldom extends to the extreme of ideality of character or situation. He pictured people as he saw them in everyday affairs. By stripping away the facade of the stereotype, he reveals characters with universally recognizable
flaws. In his delineations, many types previously serving
only as vehicles of moral messages or of single qualities
achieve the complexity which denotes human personality.
Consequently, Chesnutt's black characters—regardless of
their color, class, or economic condition—are clearly imbued with a humanity and worth conspicuously absent in
depictions of Afro-Americans by most other writers of the
age.

Chesnutt lets his fictional blacks express their own
thoughts and feelings rather than reflect the attitudes of
whites. Such treatment is very different from that of
Thomas Nelson Page. Indeed, Chesnutt is so objective in
his handling of white characters, even in racially mixed
situations, that he was assumed to be a Caucasian until his
racial identity was publicized in 1899. But even after that
revelation, most contemporary critics found his novels to
be fair. While regretting that *The Marrow of Tradition* has
"more justice than mercy in it," Howells [see excerpt
dated 1901] admitted that Chesnutt does not "play the
advocate . . . he does not paint the blacks all good, or the
whites all bad. He paints them as slavery made them on
both sides, and if in the very end he gives the victory to
the blacks . . . it cannot be said that either his aesthetics
or ethics are false." In short, Chesnutt strove to treat all
characters as "real, live, natural human [beings] and not
[as] the creations of the books." He recognized that elemental human drives and emotions know no lines of caste
or color. His characters react as individuals to situations
which they themselves create or into which they are
thrust.

These situations reflect both the universals of human experience and special problems which bedeviled Americans,
North and South, during Chesnutt's lifetime. Moreover,
the perspective of the Afro-American character was unusual for that time.

Instead of individualizing the mean planters and brutal
overseers who appear in the Uncle Julius tales and other
fiction, Chesnutt stereotypes such characters; they are
more important for providing insights into conditions to
which the slaves had to adjust or avoid than they are as
persons. Most of the wealthy plantation owners are
strong-willed, self-serving, short-tempered, and sometimes dishonest. Their overseers ape them crudely. Colonel Pendleton in **"Sis' Becky's Pickaninny"** is obviously
more interested in horseflesh than in human beings. He
prefers to bet on and buy horses rather than prevent the
separation of a slave family, two of whom he owns initially. Moreover, he does not have the courage to tell the
young slave mother whose husband is now gone that she
is being sold away from her child forever. Unfeeling Mars
Jeems in **"Mars Jeems's Nightmare"** not only underfeeds
and overworks his slaves but also denies them recreational
activities after hours.

Chesnutt's capsulized description of Primus in **"The Con-**

jurer's Revenge," on the other hand, shows how unobtrusively the author transcends a stereotype in the case of the characterization of the happy-go-lucky slave, to create an individual to be reckoned with:

> "Dis yer Primus wuz de livelies' han' on de place, alluz a-dancin', en drinkin', en runnin' roun', en singin', en pickin' de banjo [end of stereotype]; 'cep'n' once in a w'ile w'en he'd 'low he wa'nt treated right 'bout sump'n ernudder, he'd git so sulky en stubborn dat de w'ite folks could n' ha'dly do nuffin wid'im.

> "It wuz 'gin' de rules fer any er de han's ter go 'way fum de plantation at night; but Primus did n' min' de rules, en went w'en he felt lack it; en de w'ite folks purten' lack dey did n' know it, fer Primus was dange'ous w'en he got in dem stubborn spells, en dey'd ruther not fool wid 'im."

Uncle Julius McAdoo, the actual spinner of the Uncle Julius tales, is an excellent example of a stereotype elaborated into an enriching, thought-provoking ambiguity. An illiterate former slave fieldhand who has lived on or near the McAdoo plantation all of his life, Uncle Julius seems as limited as his circumscribed life would suggest. He appears to hold himself in low esteem, as when in **"The Goophered Grapevine"** he offers to explain to John and Miss Annie how the scuppernong vines came to be conjured " 'ef you en young miss dere doan' min' lis' nin' ter a ole nigger run on a minute er two w'ile you er restin'." According to John, the narrator, through whose eyes "the venerable looking man" is presented,

> his curiously undeveloped nature was subject to moods which were almost childish in their variableness. . . . His way of looking at the past seemed very strange to us; his view of certain sides of life was essentially different from ours. . . . While he mentioned with a warm appreciation the acts of kindness which those in authority had shown to him and his people, he would speak of a cruel deed, not with the indignation of one accustomed to quick feeling and spontaneous expression, but with a furtive disapproval which suggested to us a doubt in his own mind as to whether he had a right to think or to feel, and presented to us the curious psychological spectacle of a mind enslaved long after the shackles had been struck off from the limbs of its possessor.

Although, as in **"The Conjurer's Revenge,"** Uncle Julius sharply rebukes a young black student for saying that the earth revolves around the sun when Uncle Julius "sees de yeath stan'in' still all de time," he believes strongly in signs, goophering, spells, and ghosts. Besides his apparent belief in all the marvelous events he recounts in the tales, in **"The Gray Wolf's Ha'nt"** Uncle Julius gets wet rather than risk having bad luck by coming up on his employers' porch with an umbrella up, and matter-of-factly attributes the balking of the horse in **"Hot-Foot Hannibal"** to the ability of gray horses to see ghosts on Friday afternoons. Again, he becomes almost an apologist for slavery at times. He declares in **"Sis' Becky's Pickaninny"** that he "had a good marster befo' de wah." He also holds that "Mars Jeems" in **"Mars Jeems's Nightmare"** " 'wuz de marster, en had a right ter do ez he please'. . . .' "

Uncle Julius obviously has some of the qualities of the stereotypic contented slave and superstitious Negro whose abysmal ignorance and inability to reason abstractly are taken for granted. However, these seeming limitations are otherwise belied, for Uncle Julius understands cause-and-effect relationships. In **"A Deep Sleeper"** he observes that he is not solely responsible for his inability to read. In **"Mars Jeems's Nightmare"** he suggests to his employers that many of the admitted shortcomings of the freedmen are traceable to their prior servitude; therefore whites, who have had advantages longer, should " 'make some 'lowance.' " Similarly, by recounting **"A Victim of Heredity,"** he convinces Miss Annie that since the conditions of slavery provided "some excuse" for the slaves to steal "chickens and other little things to eat," whites should be lenient about such thievery for a while. All those conditions and more are suggested in Uncle Julius's recollection in **"Mars Jeems's Nightmare"** that " 'dey wuz no use in libbin' at all ef you ha' ter lib roun' Mars Jeems.' "

Uncle Julius also makes fleeting but unmistakable references to his better judgment and insight by observing in **"Lonesome Ben"** that " 'Mars Dugal' said dis yer clay wouldn' make good brick, but I knowed better' " and declaring in **"A Deep Sleeper"** that " 'Ole Miss wuz a mighty smart woman, but she didn' know ev'ything' " when she said, " 'One nigger man [should be] de same as ernudder . . . ' " when a slave girl chose a husband. He demonstrates a like ability to understand and meet the needs of whites by lending Miss Annie his rabbit foot in **"Sis' Becky's Pickaninny,"** and by choosing to reveal the tragic outcome of a lovers' quarrel in **"Hot-Foot Hannibal"** shortly after Mabel and young Malcolm Murchison break their engagement. More often in the thirteen tales, Julius exercises his persuasive powers on John directly or indirectly through his wife for his own benefit.

This evidence that Uncle Julius, despite his disadvantaged position, repeatedly outmaneuvers John demands further assessment of the character. That the white employers can be so easily hoodwinked becomes more believable with the realization that they are newcomers to the South, a region which was then quite different from the rest of the country. Perhaps Patesville is Uncle Julius's briarpatch and he is operating like Uncle Remus's Br'er Rabbit, a carry-over from African folklore which symbolized the ability of the weak to triumph over the powerful. In such case John is not privy to all of Uncle Julius's thoughts and methods. John acknowledges their differences in point of view, but perhaps does not fully realize its import. In **"The Goophered Grapevine"** John, believing himself liberal in his attitude toward blacks, is unaware that his finding the shrewdness in Uncle Julius's eyes "not altogether African" is racist.

Uncle Julius, then, emerges as a clever character, wise in the ways of his world and of people anywhere, whose motherwit has enabled him to develop a means of coping in a hostile environment. He remains an intriguing enigma, an excellent subject for speculation, but forever beyond final explanation because Chesnutt provides no ultimate clues. Uncle Julius never divulges what he is thinking. The reader, whose perception is colored by his own experiences, must evaluate Julius solely on the basis of John's limited report and interpretation of his actions. In this respect the freedman provides an example of *Quashee,* a Jamaican term which describes a behavior pattern once attributed to the slaves, the most essential element of which is an "evasive, indefinable, somewhat disguised and ambiguous quality."

Uncle Julius lends himself admirably to Chesnutt's planned first step in opening, through literature, the way for Afro-Americans to take their rightful place in the American culture. Here, in trying to make a positive introduction of blacks to the predominantly white reading public, Chesnutt offers a character of a familiar type, not offensive enough either to threaten whites or insult blacks. If a reader is only entertained by the tales, Chesnutt's social purpose, if not promoted, is not hindered. If, on the other hand, the reader looks beneath the surface, he will have to see slavery and its aftermath from a black perspective which at least makes a strong appeal to his sense of fair play.

In addition to stereotypes, Chesnutt depicts seeming stereotypes who turn out to be exceptional characters, and others who are uncommon in literature. Both because he knew that stories treating stereotypes were more likely to be published and that some people did fit those patterns, Chesnutt gave more attention to such characters, black and white, at the beginning of his writing career than he did after he gained some recognition as an author. However, many of his early characters who seem stereotypical are, in fact, more complex.

The most striking of the unstereotypical characters is freeborn Aun' Peggy. Slaveowner and slave alike seek and follow her advice to solve difficult problems. In **"The Goophered Grapevine,"** Mars Dugal' pays Aun' Peggy handsomely in advance to goopher his grapevine so that the slaves will stop stealing the grapes. Moreover, in **"Hot-Foot Hannibal"** this same plantation owner fears even to upbraid Aun' Peggy for selling to Chloe and Jeff the doll with which they have conjured Hannibal, although the master has expressly forbidden such practices on his place. Admonishing Solomon in **"Mars Jeems's Nightmare,"** Aun' Peggy not only demonstrates her power but declares herself " 'wusser'n de patteroles. . . . W'en you is foolin' wid a cunjuh 'oman lack me, you got ter min' yo' P's en Q's er dey'll be trouble sho' 'nuff.' "

Chesnutt apparently found slavery so distasteful as an institution both to ex-slaves actually and to himself abstractly that he could not bring himself to feature a contented slave in his fiction. He states editorially in **The House behind the Cedars** that "no Negro, save in books, ever refused freedom; many of them ran frightful risks to achieve it." Grandison, a young adult slave owned by Kentucky Colonel Owens, is permitted to accompany his young master, indolent Dick Owens, to Boston because Colonel Owens thinks that Grandison will not try to run away. Feigning a Sambo attitude, Grandison has reassured the Colonel that

> "I is better off, suh, dan dem low-down free niggers, suh! Ef anybody ax 'em who dey b'longs ter, dey has ter say nobody, er e'se lie erbout it. Anybody ax me who I b'long ter, I ain' got no 'casion ter be sham' ter tell 'em, no, suh, 'deed I ain', suh!"

In turn, the Colonel contrasts Grandison's good life as a slave with living in Canada, where the woods are full of wild beasts, where the weather is frigid half the time, and the inhabitants equally inhospitable to "runaway niggers." Grandison, in the manner of a model slave, seems to be properly impressed. Dick, hopeful of winning his quixotic sweetheart by letting Grandison escape while away from home, provides many opportunities, but the slave forthrightly resists all temptation. Even after Dick, in desperation, has him kidnapped and held on the Canadian side of Niagara Falls, Grandison shows up at the Kentucky plantation a month later "ragged and travel-stained, bowed with weariness and upon his face a haggard look that told of hardship and privation." The reason for this exemplary behavior becomes apparent at the end of the story, when Grandison, his family, and his junesey (sweetheart) escape to Canada via the underground railroad.

Sandy Campbell (he and Uncle Julius are the only freedmen dignified by surnames), the body servant of old Mr. Delamere in **The Marrow of Tradition,** also has a multifaceted personality embracing the worshipful servant, man of integrity and pride, and the comic and superstitious Negro. Old Mr. Delamere describes him as "a gentleman in ebony." The extent of Sandy's devotion to the elder Delamere is shown by his decision to be lynched or sentenced to die for a robbery-murder the old man's grandson has committed rather than inflict the probably fatal pain of disclosure upon the ailing Delamere. (pp. 58-66)

Sandy is not idealized throughout the novel, however. He has picked up some of his employer's Chesterfieldian elegance, but betrays lack of taste in his best clothes, an incongruous combination of an outmoded long blue coat with brass buttons and a stylish pair of bright plaid trousers. While his long association with the Delamere family gives him the strength to rebuke young Tom for calling him a darkey to his face, it also makes him snobbish enough to disdain the new generation of blacks. In the same manner he considers the Methodist Church, of which he is a pillar, better than the Baptist connection. Crushed by the disgrace of being turned out of church for having allegedly participated in a cakewalk and being too proud to confess a sin he has not committed, Sandy begins to seek solace in alcohol. (pp. 66-7)

On the other hand, Mammy Jane in **The Marrow of Tradition** and old Peter in **The Colonel's Dream** are mainly stereotypes of the worshipful servants who are also freed persons. They recall through the haze of years "the good old days" popularized by Thomas Nelson Page. (The accuracy of their recollection, however, becomes questionable upon the revelation that after Emancipation their former owners maintained no active interest in their well-being.) Peter, in the meantime, has suffered great hardship. Jerry Letlow, Mammy Jane's grandson and Major Carteret's office "boy," is a comic fawner who goes to any length to " 'stan' in wid de Angry-Saxon race.' " Significantly, all three suffer sudden violent death because of their devotion to or dependency upon whites.

The most conditioned, genuinely Uncle Tomish of Chesnutt's characters is the diminutive Plato in **The House behind the Cedars,** whose thoughts mirror his attitude:

> Mars Geo'ge [Tryon] was white and rich, and could do anything. Plato was proud of the fact that he had once belonged to Mars Geo'ge. He could not conceive of any one so powerful as Mars Geo'ge, unless it might be God, of whom Plato had heard more or less, and even here the comparison might

not be quite fair to Mars Geo'ge, for Mars Geo'ge was the younger of the two.

Another youth in *The House behind the Cedars* calls no man master, not even for money. Little Dodie Carteret's young brown-skin nurse, trained at Dr. Miller's hospital, is contemptuous of subservient Negroes; work for her is a matter of business. Finally, in *The Marrow of Tradition,* brawny stevedore Josh Green beats almost to death a "dago" who calls him "a damn lowdown nigger." When, while dressing his wounds, Dr. Miller suggests that he be more forgiving, Josh retorts in part:

> " . . . It 'pears ter me dat dis fergitfulniss an' fer-givniss is mighty one-sided. De w'ite folks don' fer-give nothin' de niggers does. . . . De niggers is be'n train' ter fergiveniss; an' fer fear dey might fer-git how ter fergive, de w'ite folks gives 'em so-methin' new ev'y now an' den, ter practice on. A w'ite man kin do w'at he wants ter a nigger, but de minute de nigger gits back at 'im, up goes de nigger, an' don' come down tell somebody cuts 'im down. If a nigger gits a' office, er de race 'pears ter be prosperin' too much, de w'ite folks up an' kills a few, so dat de res' kin keep on fergivin' an' bein' thankful dat dey're lef' alive."

Despite the dehumanizing conditions suggested by Green's declaration, Chesnutt's Afro-American charac-ters manage to retain their humanity. Though at the time blacks were popularly considered incapable of feeling deeply, these characters display all the emotions with the same intensity expressed by other races and classes of peo-ple. Blacks as well as whites evince physical and ethical heroism in the face of certain disaster; both are also base. Chesnutt describes the corrupting effects of power and privilege, and a corresponding absence of *noblesse oblige.*

A major example of heroism is that of Josh Green in *The Marrow of Tradition.* Ever since his early childhood, when he had seen his father lynched and his mother crazed by the attendant horror, the angry black giant had planned to wreak vengeance on the one member of the Ku Klux Klan mob whose mask fell off and revealed his iden-tity. On the night of the riot Josh rallies a group of Afro-Americans to defend the Negro hospital. When it is set ablaze by whites, he leads the men out into a hail of bullets which do not stop him until he—preferring to " 'be a dead nigger any day dan a live dog!' "—smilingly buries his knife in Captain McBane's heart.

Many of Chesnutt's characters, including Josh, are com-pelled by stronger emotional forces to take less spectacular but equally significant steps. Though Josh had been burn-ing with the desire to avenge his father's death for many years, his actions were controlled by love for his mother. As her sole source of support, he has put off courting cer-tain death by attacking McBane until after his mother has died. Tom Taylor, who since childhood has planned a sim-ilar fate for the murderer of his father in **"The Doll,"** is likewise constrained to delay the doubly fatal slash be-cause of his higher duty to live for his little girl.

Mis' Molly Walden in *The House behind the Cedars,* Mrs. Harper in **"Her Virginia Mammy,"** Mrs. Janet Miller in *The Marrow of Tradition,* Mrs. Cartwright in **"The Kiss,"** and Miss Laura Treadwell in *The Colonel's Dream* are among other Chesnutt characters moved to sacrificial, sometimes ennobling, acts of love.

In *The House behind the Cedars,* dark-brown Frank Fow-ler, the son of a freedman who is now an enterprising coo-per, would gladly have given his life for Rena Walden. Like a chivalrous knight of the Middle Ages he loves and serves, hoping only to "win her friendship, and convince her of his humble devotion." He had saved Rena from drowning when she was small; through the years he has performed chores and run errands cheerfully for her and Mis' Molly. After Rena joins John, Frank finds a job in the Clarence area so that he may worship Rena from afar without divulging her background. Later, alarmed by hav-ing his poor opinion of Wain confirmed, Frank drives his mule and "kyart" down to Sampson County to check on Rena's well-being. Consequently, under bizarre circum-stances, he is able to fulfill his promise: " 'Ef you ever wan-ter come home, and can't git back no other way, jes' let *me* know, and I'll take my mule and my kyart an' fetch you back, ef it's from de een' er de worl'.' "

Unfortunately, neither George Tryon nor Jeff Wain dis-plays such nobility of character in his pursuit of Rena Walden. George Tryon reacts in an entirely different way after he becomes aware of his fiancée's ethnic identity. Ini-tially he conducts himself as a kind aristocrat, becoming almost literally a knight in shining armor while seeking the favor of Rowena, whom he chooses as the Queen of Love and Beauty during the Clarence Social Club annual tournament. However, when shortly before their wedding he finds out accidentally what Rena thinks he already knows—that she is of mixed blood—his feelings vacillate from longing to loathing and back again. At times he attri-butes to Rena all the undesirable traits ever assigned to Af-rican and Afro-American women. At other times he con-siders trying to prove that she is white or, if this is impossi-ble, of taking her away with him to live elsewhere. It is sig-nificant that he breaks the engagement and never again mentions marriage as a prerequisite for their living togeth-er. Later, when he finds that Rena is teaching in the vicini-ty of the Tryon estate, he proposes in a letter that they have a clandestine meeting at the same time he is half-heartedly courting a young white lady. Upon receiving Rena's unequivocal response that she wishes only to be let alone and forgotten, Tryon arranges to accost her on the road through the woods that she customarily takes on her way home from school. Her flight from him there fires him to follow her to Patesville, where her death terminates Tryon's harassment.

Mulatto Jeff Wain, toward whom Rena is never more than friendly, exposes his villainous nature by pursuing her too. He conceals his marital status when, as chairman of the school committee, he asks Rena to teach in his home com-munity. Wain later reveals himself as so dishonest, domi-neering, and cruel that his wife has left him. Misled by his vanity into thinking that Rena's avoiding all his advances is coyness, he avails himself of every opportunity to be in her presence. Once, when he contrives for the two of them to be alone momentarily, he tries to embrace her, but is rejected. On the same day that Tryon has posted himself to surprise Rena, Wain approaches the same path through the woods with an identical intention. Like Tryon, he last sees the frantic Rena disappearing in the underbrush. (pp. 67-70)

Chesnutt's Afro-American characters, especially males, fare much worse than comparative white characters. The disparity is even more noticeable when blacks run afoul of any element of the white power structure. It can be argued that Tobe in **"Tobe's Tribulations,"** Ben in **"Lonesome Ben,"** Uncle Wellington in **"Uncle Wellington's Wives,"** and Rufus Green in **"The Partners"** might never have been successful, even under ideal conditions, because of basic character defects. However, the same correlation between success or failure and dominant personality traits is not apparent in the fortunes of significant black and white characters who are contrasted in various Chesnutt stories. Black Dr. Miller and white Major Carteret in *The Marrow of Tradition* are both highly reputable young professionals devoted to their families. Using money inherited from his ex-slave father, European-trained Miller has already built a hospital and founded a school of nursing for his fellow blacks. However, he attends all who seek his services, even returning to the home of the Carterets to save their baby's life after once having been refused admittance to consult with the specialist who had invited him on the case. The enterprising Carteret, whose wealthy aristocrat family had gradually become impoverished, found his ownership of the local newspaper profitable enough to invest his wife's patrimony in business ventures which he hoped would enable his son to take a place in the world commensurate with the dignity of his ancestors. Perhaps this desire, as well as Carteret's obvious race prejudice, facilitated his political alliance with the less scrupulous General Belmont and Captain McBane. Urged by them, he misuses his influence as a publisher-editor finally to precipitate "wholesale murder and arson" which he cannot control. Miller, though blameless, loses his little son, some of his friends, the hospital, and some community support. On the other hand, Carteret's family and future are as secure at the end of the novel as at the beginning. In **"Walter Knox's Record"** neophyte Knox (white) makes an error in judgment which he is able to rectify without great penalty. In **"The Averted Strike"** Walker (black) is able to keep his well-deserved promotion to foreman without a major disruption at the factory only because he rescues the owner's daughter and a friend from a fiery death. In **"Dave's Neckliss,"** Dave is almost an ideal slave, and model freedman Ben Davis in **"The Web of Circumstance"** has built up a successful business and accumulated some property through honesty, industry, and thrift. But both, morally blameless, die young of unnatural causes. In *The Marrow of Tradition* young aristocrat Tom Delamere, having incurred gambling debts beyond his ability to pay, robs his old Aunt Polly and causes her death. He lives on, though less affluently.

Dr. Miller appraises the general situation very well in *The Marrow of Tradition:*

> It was a veritable bed of Procrustes, this standard which the whites had set for the negroes. Those who grew above it must have their heads cut off, figuratively speaking,—must be forced back to the level assigned to their race; those who fell beneath the standard set had their necks stretched, literally enough, as the ghastly record in the daily papers gave conclusive evidence.

Even white Colonel French in *The Colonel's Dream,* whose motives are unquestionable, suffers for siding with blacks when he thinks fair play demands it. After having been roundly defeated by reactionary forces, he—unlike Dr. Miller—chooses not to remain in the South. Even Miss Laura's appeal, " 'But, oh, Henry, if all of those who love justice and practise humanity should go away, what would become of us?' " does not change his mind.

That future looks bleak with men like General Belmont in *The Marrow of Tradition* and William Fetters in *The Colonel's Dream* amorally wielding financial and political power. After twenty years of endeavor Fetters has more money than he knows what to do with and reflects,

> There had been a time when these old aristocrats could speak, and the earth trembled, but that day was over. In this age money talked, and he had known how to get money, and how to use it to get more. There were a dozen civil suits pending against him in the court house there, and he knew in advance that he should win them every one, without directly paying any juryman a dollar.

Marked by restraint, indirection, and elusiveness, William Fetters is outstanding as a character. Though this able opportunist influences every community action in *The Colonel's Dream,* he appears only in the last third of the novel, and then Colonel French seeks him out. Fetters is so sure of his power and his influence is so pervasive that he remains in the background, quietly manipulating the strings which control the movements of his human puppets.

The most formidable of Chesnutt's villains, Fetters has the anonymity of a twentieth-century crime-syndicate man. As the forerunner of a certain type of unscrupulous politician or "God-father" of our day, his evil is so monstrous that it does not need the reinforcement of surface appearance to impress itself upon the reader. Yet Fetters is not just a simple personification of vice, as in the English morality plays, though the name *Fetters*—and McBane and Letlow as well—indicates immediately the concept of these characters which Chesnutt intends to convey.

The forcefulness of Fetters's character is also implicit in the imagery which Chesnutt uses as an additional descriptive device:

> Clarendon was decaying. Fetters was the parasite which, by sending out its roots toward rich and poor alike, struck at both extremes of society, and was choking the life of the town like a rank and deadly vine.

(pp. 70-3)

Whites as well as blacks were adversely affected by such men. In *The Marrow of Tradition* the power structure, represented by Carteret, Belmont, and McBane (the Unholy Three), cynically uses the masses to increase its political clout. The chilling potential of its influence is reflected also in the reaction of the blue-collar whites to slanted news items and editorials at the time the Delameres' servant Sandy is almost lynched for the robbery-murder of Mrs. Ochiltree and again when the riot occurs. In *The Colonel's Dream* William Fetters's convict-lease workers are white as well as black, although all his textile mill hands are white. When Colonel French visits the Excelsior Cotton Mills he sees the small unpainted company houses: "In the open doorways, through which the flies swarmed in and out, grown men, some old, some still in the prime of life, were lounging, pipe in mouth, while old women puttered about the yards. . . . Dirty babies were tumbling about the cabins." All the children from six years up and women through middle age were on their twelve-to-sixteen-hour shifts at the mills.

Even given their subordinate position as women in American society as a whole, Chesnutt's female Afro-American characters seem not to suffer defeat as often or as completely as their male counterparts. One reason is that they, more able psychologically than black men to acknowledge their vulnerability as the most potentially dangerous part of a minority group, react more often than they challenge outright. However, none of Chesnutt's black female characters meekly accept misfortune as their due. Further, they sometimes employ unorthodox tactics, both less risky and more likely to succeed than confrontation. In most cases, however, they persist; and if they do not prevail in situations of conflict, their adversaries pay dearly for victory.

'Liza Jane in **"The Wife of His Youth,"** for example, is completely self-motivated and direct in her long search for her husband, Sam. On the other hand, Dasdy in **"How Dasdy Came Through"** uses a subterfuge requiring only a few moments to embarrass her rival publicly for the attention of the straying 'Dolphus. Though powerless, both the concubine Cicely in **"The Sheriff's Children"** and Viney in *The Colonel's Dream* remonstrate with their owners. For the extreme punishment meted out to their slaves, both men later suffer greatly, Malcolm Murchison for twenty-five years because Viney pretends to be unable to speak and therefore incapable of revealing the location of a large sum of money left for her former master-paramour.

The most consistently successful tactic is goophering or conjuration, as employed by slave Phillis and free Aun' Peggy. In **"The Marked Tree"** Phillis avenges the selling and subsequent killing of her son Isham by causing the death of the family and all kin of her owner, Marse Aleck Spencer. In almost all the Uncle Julius tales, Aun' Peggy safely "wuks her roots" to correct conditions, often caused by injustice, as manifested in **"Sis' Becky's Pickaninny,"** **"Mars Jeems's Nightmare,"** and **"A Victim of Heredity."**

Chesnutt's fictional mulatto children usually have white fathers and mothers with more or less Negro blood. Except in **"Her Virginia Mammy,"** the fathers' negligence causes hardship for their dependents. The Anglo-Saxon begetter of John and Rena Walden in *The House behind the Cedars* dies without making adequate provision for his children. As a result, John, unable to overcome the double handicap of racial identity and genteel poverty in his hometown, finds success elsewhere as a white man and unwittingly sets in motion the train of events which is climaxed by Rena's death. Although in *The Marrow of Tradition* Sam Merkell makes a will in which he reveals his secret marriage to his housekeeper, Julia Brown, and his fatherhood of Janet, who becomes Dr. Miller's wife, he never publicly acknowledges this family. Upon his death Mrs. Polly Ochiltree, sister of his first wife, suppresses the will and drives the mother and child from the home which is rightfully theirs.

The mothers, though less derelict in their duties, are not role models. Mis' Molly has many paradoxical qualities, whose sum evokes pity rather than admiration: continued allegiance to a dead white "protector" who made no provision for the contingency of his early demise; fading beau-

ty; color prejudice derived from a white society which ignores her existence; great love for her children, which is in turn giving and demanding—especially of Rena; some degree of refinement; and illiteracy. The less aggressive Julia Merkell seems incapable of demanding and getting her just due. Unable to withstand Mrs. Ochiltree's continuing persecution and an unfortunate marriage, Julia succumbs during Janet's childhood.

Nevertheless, none of these and other mulatto children born of such mésalliances in Chesnutt's fiction is tragic or pathetic in the manner popularized by Cable. In a letter to him Chesnutt expressed distaste for fictional folk who are ashamed of their Negro blood and therefore lack proper self-esteem. Such abasement is certainly not true of the now educated and prosperous Mrs. Janet Miller, who since childhood has hoped for some sign of recognition from her half sister, Mrs. Olivia Carteret, simply because they are kin. However, when extremity drives Olivia to acknowledge the relationship and even to disclose its legality, the black woman—having suffered too much in the meantime—rejects the overtures. Mulatto Tom, the sheriff's son, goes further by committing suicide after trying to kill his father, who belatedly wishes to help him.

Reacting in another way, John Walden in *The House behind the Cedars* coldly reasons that if his ethnic identity is going to impede his progress, especially his desire to become an attorney, he will leave home and "pass." This is not difficult since he has "all the features of a white man." Walden is not ashamed of his mixed ancestry, but resents the barriers erected by race prejudice. Within a decade he has married well and become a successful lawyer and landowner. Nevertheless, he has been unable either to overcome loneliness for his own kind or to bridge the gulf, caused by his masquerade, between him and his closest white friends. During a surprise visit to his mother and sister, Warwick (as he is now known among his white associates) prevails upon Mis' Molly to let his sister Rena come to live with him. His love for the girl is obvious; moreover, his desire for her to have a better life must be overwhelming, for bringing her into his home greatly increases the danger of exposure which would result inevitably in disgrace, ostracism, and financial ruin for himself and his little son. Even after Tryon is privy to their secret, John tries to persuade Rena to come back to his household, to move with him and his little son Albert to the North or West, or at least to let him send her to school in the North. Though she refuses, he still holds himself responsible for her future and gives neighbor Frank Fowler a mule and cart in appreciation of his help during John's enforced absence.

John Walden / Warwick, who demands reader respect if not admiration, is shown almost exclusively in relationship with his mother and sister, particularly Rena, and with other characters who touch their lives. Rena, on the other hand, serves as the center of *The House behind the Cedars,* interacting with all the main characters and evoking a positive response from all who come in contact with her. Emerging both as Chesnutt's most completely portrayed and most ideal character, Rena Walden / Rowena Warwick is unique in nineteenth-century American literature as a mulatto who "passes." If she has a flaw, it is her seeming flawlessness by the standards of late nineteenth-century fiction. Even so, although her basic nature remains essentially unchanged, she grows in stature during a tragic round trip from a southern black middle-class society to a southern white upper-class society, a few hundred miles—yet worlds—apart.

Rena's physical beauty, in the classical Greek tradition, reflects her beauty of spirit. John Walden / Warwick, returning to Patesville after a ten-year absence, does not immediately recognize as his sister the "strikingly handsome" young woman with the "admirably proportioned" figure (the local white physician, Dr. Green, finds it "something on the Greek order"), "abundant hair, of a dark and glossy brown . . . plaited and coiled above an ivory column that rose straight from a pair of gently sloping shoulders. . . ." George Tryon considers Rowena, his fiancée, "the most beautiful white woman on earth," and his mother later discerns about Rena

> . . . an air of real refinement . . . not merely of a fine nature, but of contact with cultured people; a certain reserve of speech and manner quite inconsistent with Mrs. Tryon's experience of colored women . . . a fine, pure spirit, born out of place.

At the outset Rena is typical of sheltered middle-class colored girls in the South around the turn of the century: docile, intelligent, morally upright, and naïve to a fault. Perhaps because of the circumstances which inclined the Waldens to live somewhat apart from their neighbors, the young woman is serious-minded and introspective rather than frivolous like Alice Clayton in **"A Matter of Principle"** or effervescent like Graciella Treadwell in *The Colonel's Dream.* Rena's love for "weak creatures . . . kittens and puppies . . . shiftless poor white, half-witted or hungry Negro" is constant; moreover, her little nephew in Clarence and her pupils in Sampson County also thrive under her care and supervision.

In true southern style, Rena lacks her brother's avid interest in books and his daring initiative. Her ambition is to marry or to teach. She tells him once, "A man may make a new place for himself—a woman is born and bound to hers." In the beginning she also easily defers to authority figures in her life, such as Mis' Molly, John, Tryon, and Wain, within the proper bounds of their respective relationships. She takes no active part in making the decision which takes her to South Carolina; she follows her brother's advice in not making a clean breast of their ethnic identity to Tryon; and, diffident about her abilities as a teacher, agrees to accept the position down in Sampson County only after Wain, as chairman of the school board, assures her of his active support.

Rena is as happy for her brother's sake as for her own that she wins complete acceptance in Clarence. Unlike John, she keeps in touch with her mother, rushing to her bedside immediately when she finds out about Mis' Molly's illness, despite the higher risk of disclosure now that she has promised to marry Tryon. Later, she similarly places the welfare of her pupils above her own, for instead of going home to avoid a nervous breakdown, she attempts to finish the school term.

Further, by the time Rowena and George become engaged, after a most proper courtship, she is so in love that she cannot envision life without him. Her total emotional involvement with this man is suggested by her collapse when he summarily spurns her, by her sleeping dreams of

George as her beloved, by her fear of heartbreak or surrender should he treat her as of old, by her subsequent resolve never to marry, and by her indifference to a seemingly eligible suitor such as Jeff Wain. But a spirit like hers will not countenance bitterness, recrimination, or compromise.

For one thing, outright rejection by Tryon forces Rena to identify with black people and to become more understanding of their plight. Further, throughout her sojourn she has had grave doubts about the ethics of "passing." Recognizing the great need for Afro-American advancement, she decides to devote her life to the cause. Ultimately, however, Rena is alone. Just as her invisible blackness bars her from the whites, her manifest whiteness and air of good breeding set her apart from the blacks. Thus the temptation to fall back into the old ways—to walk in her mother's footsteps—must be great when George tries a different approach. However, disillusionment, with its accompanying pain, gives Rena a degree of self-awareness, personal esteem, and emotional independence which enables her to reject Tryon's improper overtures even if she cannot obliterate his image from her heart.

Rena Walden emerges from her trials in the black and white worlds as an admirable rather than an heroic figure. Because of her trusting nature and her sheltered life, she never becomes sophisticated enough to ward off male aggression. Nevertheless, she does not withdraw from life; once aware of her own vulnerability and man's culpability, she employs ethical tactics in losing battles while winning moral victories.

Rena Walden / Rowena Warwick overshadows all of Chesnutt's other female characters; their portrayal is either more limited or their characters less noble. Laura Treadwell and her niece Graciella in *The Colonel's Dream* deserve mention both as personalities and as symbols of the Old and the New South. Also in reduced circumstances, Miss Laura is unmatched in service to and sacrifice for her mother and niece. To supplement their meager income she gives music lessons to the daughter of the prosperous Negro barber, William Nichols. Nor has self-denial soured the gentility and sweetness which prompt Colonel French to declare, just before proposing, that verses from Proverbs 31 describe her:

> Who can find a virtuous woman? For her price is far above rubies. The heart of her husband doth safely trust in her. She will do him good and not evil all the days of her life. Strength and honour are her clothing, and she shall rejoice in time to come.

French is convinced that she can meet all his needs and function effectively as his wife and Phil's mother anywhere. But Laura Treadwell, more realistic, knows that she cannot make the radical adjustment necessary, especially in her views on race relations. Neither she nor French countenances social acceptance, of course; except for the family who used to be Treadwell slaves, Laura has been so conditioned as to automatically place Negroes in a world apart in which they should be treated fairly. In deference to local mores and her personal inclinations, she avoids all but necessary association with them in a properly stratified relationship. Thus, when French asks her to accompany him to the Negro school, she cannot accept spontaneously—even to please him. Later, when French proposes to build a library for all the townspeople, she suggests gently that "the white people wouldn't wish to handle the same books."

Laura's nearly seventeen-year-old niece is oblivious to such matters. A typically ingenuous, impulsive, self-centered teenager whose unruly brown hair suggests her spirit, Graciella loves faithful but impecunious Ben Dudley. However, she will not become engaged unless he can promise to take her to New York, the center of culture and excitement. Mistakenly believing that Colonel French is interested in marrying her, Graciella opportunistically breaks off with Ben. The basic fineness of her nature begins to manifest itself when she overhears French propose to her aunt. She is further chastened by rebuffs from young Dudley, but persists both in helping and becoming reconciled with him when he is in jail charged with shooting Barclay Fetters and seemingly less likely than ever to satisfy Graciella's desire to escape poverty and the South. That her emancipation on the race issue has also begun is evidenced in her immediate rejoinder, upon hearing that Uncle Peter's coffin has been removed from the French cemetery plot that, " 'it was a shame! . . . Peter was a good old nigger, and it wouldn't have done anybody any harm to leave him there. I'd rather be buried beside old Peter than near any of the poor white trash that dug him up—so there!' "

Chesnutt's characters speak for themselves—the blacks more eloquently than the whites as a whole, though it is evident that certain white characters are delineated better than some black ones. This difference is due in part to the author's identification with Afro-Americans, which gave him "an accuracy and insight not to be obtained by an outsider." He was also greatly concerned about the plight of Afro-Americans in life and in literature, and recognized the influence of one upon the other.

The manner in which he structured and presented his characters suggests that he was aware of the subtle and pervasive influence of the stereotype and would agree with Joseph Boskin in "Sambo: The National Jester in the Popular Culture" [in *The Great Fear: Race in the Mind of America*, Gary B. Nash and Richard Weiss, eds., 1970], that "stereotypes are often so powerful that they can be dislodged only after a series of assaults on them." The impact upon the American public (not just American readers) of derogatory stereotypes of Afro-Americans is incalculable. In 1890, for example, the Negro freedman was described [by Henry Clay Lukens, "American Literary Comedians," quoted in Wade H. Hall, *The Smiling Phoenix: Southern Humor from 1865 to 1914, 1965*] as "one of the liveliest and strongest forces in our varicolored national caricature!" He was exaggerated beyond recognition as a human being. Most often he became a comic animal. Since writing was his chief means of refuting such subtle psychological conditioning, Chesnutt sought through characterization not only to create viable images but also to show the fallaciousness of all existing stereotypes of Afro-Americans. At the same time he tried to improve the literary image of the blacks in the national mind, to show that circumstances rather than color are the major determinants of character, and to encourage people to see one another as individuals. He felt that he would make substantial progress toward his ultimate goal of a better way of life for all U.S. citizens if he could get the American public

to realize that black and white alike are persons and that all are clothed in the frail garb of humanity. (pp. 73-80)

Sylvia Lyons Render, in her Charles W. Chesnutt, *Twayne Publishers, 1980, pp. 58-80.*

John F. Callahan (essay date 1988)

[*Callahan is an American educator and critic. In the following excerpt, he considers the* Conjure Woman *stories as an African-American response to white appropriation of black folklore and the black oral tradition.*]

Once Joel Chandler Harris invented Uncle Remus and adapted black folk storytelling to popular literary narrative, there was no going back. As framed by Harris and told by Uncle Remus, the tales seemed to confirm the nation's limited, false view of African-American history and personality. Harris's call, however distorted, cried out for an African-American response. Indeed, at the time Harris composed his static myth of the Negro and the old (and new) South, Charles Chesnutt was formulating literature's role in the process of historical change. "The Negro's part," Chesnutt wrote in his journal in 1880, "is to prepare himself for recognition and equality; and it is the province of literature to open the way for him to get it—to accustom the public mind to the idea; to lead people on, imperceptibly, unconsciously, step by step, to the desired state of feeling." Light enough to pass, Chesnutt affirmed his African-American identity, and in Cleveland, where he earned the highest score on the bar exam but worked for years as a legal stenographer, he wrote **"The Goophered Grapevine"** (1887), the first of his Uncle Julius tales.

Encouraged by white southern writers like George Washington Cable and the lawyer-novelist, Albion Tourgee, Chesnutt collected seven of these tales in *The Conjure Woman* (1899). After a brief success *The Conjure Woman* was neglected—perplexingly, because from the vantage points of form and voice (personality) it is an essential innovative contribution to African-American fiction. Chesnutt unfolds the tales in a complex double narrative frame. A white narrator frames in florid, legalistic prose stories told to him and his wife in dialect by a black oral storyteller, Uncle Julius McAdoo. These conjure tales counter Harris's uses of the animal tales and the often viciously sentimental plantation legends of Thomas Nelson Page and other literary proponents of the comic myth of slavery as a generally benevolent if somewhat peculiar institution.

Coming to *The Conjure Woman* from Harris's *Uncle Remus: His Songs and Sayings,* I am struck by the open and closed form of these respective narratives. In Harris, personality is static. Nothing happens to change Uncle Remus in character or outlook. He remains entirely consistent with Harris's initial ventriloquist's portrait. He is kind and grandfatherly. He knows how a boy should handle his mother and how he should avoid disreputable, trashy neighbors of a caste supposedly abhorrent to both slaves and masters. He also displays the whims of advancing age: petulance, silence, real and feigned lapses of memory. And the unquestioning, uncritical allegiance and adulation of his single audience dulls Remus's improvisatory reflexes. But this is emphatically not the case with Chesnutt's two narrators. In contrast to the formulaic, mechanical relationship between Uncle Remus and the little

Cover of the first edition of The Conjure Woman.

boy, the voices of Chesnutt's narrators, John and Uncle Julius, contend dynamically on the field of narrative. Chesnutt's frame keeps their personalities unfolding and not merely reiterative; subtly and, in the case of John, unwillingly, each becomes responsive in unanticipated ways because of his experience with the other. Unlike Remus and the little white boy, John and Uncle Julius are each performer and audience; they engage in a variation of call-and-response.

As collections, **The Conjure Woman** and *Uncle Remus: His Songs and Sayings* have in common several crucial elements of taletelling. Both retell stories from the past in a contemporary context, and both counterpoint dialect with a formal, sententious standard English. But Harris introduces and periodically interrupts Uncle Remus in a third-person voice, whereas Chesnutt hands responsibility for the narrative frame over to John, and within it Uncle Julius performs his acts of storytelling. Chesnutt respects fiction's artifice, and his form forces narrator and storyteller to battle for the audience's allegiance. In **The Conjure Woman** Uncle Julius uses tales and the occasion of storytelling to tell the truth about slavery and to overcome an apparent disadvantage of race and class, for his mastery of oral expression and tradition gives him certain advantages over John.

Most of all, Chesnutt enacts the fiction of a pluralistic American reading public by creating a double audience for Julius McAdoo's tales. John and his wife, Annie, represent different facets of human personality and of American social reality in the period after the Civil War. Their responses suggest a tension between contrary impulses of the individual human heart often repeated in the contest between head and heart, will and sympathy in the tales of Nathaniel Hawthorne. John is an eighteenth-century man who wants his truth—whether in fact, in history, or in fiction—measured and laid out according to exact specifications and premises. And his simple, superficial empiricism is more than a way of thought; it becomes a way of life, a way of response. But Annie is open to realities beyond her direct or indirect observation. She tests what she hears against her feelings and imagination. She understands that there is a mystery to things and that Julius possesses the storyteller's power to reveal what lies behind the surface of nature and human behavior. She is a responsive listener and through her responses to Julius's tales encourages readers to bring the commonplace and mysterious, known and unknown, into forthright relationship. Dramatically, Annie is the fulcrum, the swing vote, and the two men, John and Julius, contend for her allegiance, with Julius aware that she exercises indirect power over the household and that she has the exemplary power to change her husband's mind. Officially, according to background and position, she is of her husband's party. But as a woman, she keeps in touch with a range of sympathies and possibilities far wider than John's self-centered world of discrete, practical details.

Yet John is not simply a closed, rational mind. His skepticism is a function of how he thinks he should act, a paradoxically passive response to his society's norms of behavior. He migrates from Ohio to North Carolina for his wife's health and his business interests. Once there, he obeys the conventional male reflexes of power and southern custom in his dealings with Julius, a former slave who still lives on the quarters of the abandoned, rundown, old plantation. Julius is an African-American whose ingratiating manner paradoxically belies and enhances his craft as a storyteller and his identity as an individual. Gradually, his stories and the occasions they respond to exert a cumulative influence on John. John is swayed, often in submerged ways, by the mutual power of Julius's storytelling and his personality. At stake is the nature of craft. Julius's strategy allows his adversary maneuvering room. For instance, after John buys the old McAdoo place for its scuppernong vineyard despite Julius's tale of goophered grapevines, he hires Julius. His words express his need to save face, to rationalize. "I believe, however," John tells not Julius but his readers, "that the wages I paid for his services as a coachman, for I gave him employment in that capacity, were more than an equivalent for anything he lost by the sale of the vineyard." His words also reveal a Yankee shrewdness. After all, he discovered Julius savoring the grapes, so although Julius's tale of conjuration—of grapes and a slave bewitched—does not persuade John to take Julius's advice against buying the vineyard, the tale does move him to hire Julius as a coachman, an occupation that, during and after slavery, often put the African-American in the double role of spy and advisor. Here Chesnutt acknowledges the contradictions driving even the best relations between black and white Americans in his time. For John has things both ways. He scoffs at the mystery and metaphor of conjuring and dismisses Julius's biting indictment of slavery as biased, fanciful, and overdrawn. Yet though he condescends to Julius, at a deeper level he affirms the old man's usefulness and wisdom. For, as he writes, he knows that without Julius the restored vineyard would not be "often referred to by the local press as a striking illustration of the opportunities open to Northern capital in the development of Southern industries."

Despite John's doubts about the tales he hears, he recognizes Julius as a historian of this plantation and the Pateville locale. From Julius, he learns things about the people and the place essential to living there and doing business that he could not figure out on his own. His doubts about Julius's tales confirm his disregard for and perhaps fear of the insolubles in human experience. Nevertheless, he heaps praise on Julius as a storyteller. In **"The Marked Tree,"** John includes Julius in the class of world masters. "I suspected Julius at times of a large degree of poetic license—he took the crude legends and vague superstitions of the neighborhood and embodied them in stories as complete, in their way, as the Sagas of Iceland or the primitive tales of ancient Greece." Presently, John hedges, but the qualification is Chesnutt's way of calling readers to acknowledge Julius's achievement. "Had Julius lived in a happier age for men of his complexion the world might have had a black Aesop or Grimm or Hoffman—as it still may have, for who knows whether our civilization has yet more than cut its milk teeth, or humanity has even really begun to walk erect?" In the first place, between John's moralizing about the past and the future stands the actual achievement of Julius's storytelling. Second, according to Herodotus, Aesop was a slave, probably of African origin or descent. Finally, in his own time and place Julius is a citizen of good heart and will who adapts African and African-American techniques of call-and-response to his storytelling before an uninitiated white audience—as if declaring that after the Civil War all of his countrymen and women are necessarily members of the same tribe. As one who surrounds Julius's tales with a discourse close to legal writing, John should understand that the tales have more than an oral duration. For his part, Chesnutt, acting on his inner necessity to write fiction, places the spoken tale and its white audience's responses in a continuing, inclusive, pluralistic literary tradition.

Throughout *The Conjure Woman* Julius's individual tales pivot on the act and metaphor of conjuration. At the heart of the conjurer's art, like the storyteller's and the fiction writer's, is the power to turn one thing into another, to change the things of the earth and, as a consequence, alter relationships in the mind of the listener and reader. A conjurer possesses special powers. Using the juices, herbs, and powders of Nature, he steps outside ordinary ideas of cause and effect. But the conjurer's agency depends on craft as well as imagination; like the art of fiction, conjuring derives its power from thorough, indeed scholarly knowledge and the application of precise techniques and skills to the natural world.

Like the storyteller and the writer, the conjurer discloses reality's possibilities. Aunt Peggy and the others in *The Conjure Woman* bring an old African tribal art to bear on the environment of slavery. Through his tales and his participation in the work of interpretation Julius undermines

his white listeners' (and Chesnutt's white readers') static view of slavery. For one thing Aunt Peggy and the conjure man of the tales are free Negroes. They dare to cross conventional lines between slavery and freedom, black and white relationships. Both slaves and masters are rightly wary of antagonizing conjurers. People of each race, though more often slaves, consult conjurers, obey their rules, and pay for services rendered.

Here, Chesnutt intends a tie between the mobility and independence free Negroes enjoyed even in the midst of North Carolina plantations and the power to change the environment. Chesnutt's passion for history compels him to mix elements from the animal tales with those of more realistic folktales, the tales of John the slave, for instance. He uses tales not as an escape from history into myth but as one of history's unofficial sources—what Ellison calls that "stream of history which is still as tightly connected with folklore and the oral tradition as official history is connected with the tall tale" [Ralph Ellison, in "The Uses of History in Fiction," *Southern Literary Journal* 1, 1969]. And the debate among Julius, John, and Annie about the past raises questions about the prevailing social order in the dramatic narrative present of the 1880s. In **"The Dumb Witness,"** John displays a classic nineteenth-century view of racial hierarchy. Referring to the "low morality of inferior races," he claims that "our own race excels them all, when it wishes, because it lends to evil purposes a higher intelligence and a wider experience than inferior races can command." But the craft of Uncle Julius and the skills of his characters refute John's patronizing, backhanded claim for Caucasian "higher intelligence and wider experience." As a storyteller who both instructs and entertains, Julius revises the terms of discussion about race and personality. *The Conjure Woman* places the strongest *individual* levers of power in the hands of black conjurers and the strongest *institutional* levers in the hands of white masters. On this level, too, the battle is joined in the present between John and Julius, and won by Julius, often because he improvises an effective answer to John's negative response to the tale just told.

Julius never forces his tales on John or Annie. In every case one or both of them asks him for a story. Because of his venerable, lowkey, understated, unthreatening but always savvy voice, his tales persuasively indict slavery and affirm the principle of human equality Chesnutt sought to advance in his fiction. Julius's continuing presence around the plantation makes him centrally important to the narrator and his wife. At first, Julius obeys the conventional rules. He is respectful, speaks when spoken to. But his is the stance of a man who knows who he is and, though inquiring by nature, is less interested in these new northern white folks than they are in him. For them, he is a guide to an unfamiliar place and a people more legendary than actual to many northerners. He is inseparable from the natural, moral, historical landscape. And he possesses such a storehouse of tales that, whatever the present controversy, he can choose a story to advance his point of view and his specific objective. The connections between the tales Julius tells and his life in the present underline the complexity of his storyteller's craft and his progressive resolve to help create a community of both black and white citizens. Will he continue to have free access to the vineyard? Will he be able to use the lumber from a crumbling old kitchen for his new church? Will he persuade

John to rehire his grandson? Less self-interestedly, will he be able to ease Annie's melancholy, and can he stop time long enough for her young sister to work through her lover's quarrel with young Malcolm Murchison? These issues are small matters, and alongside the life and death action of the tales, they seem almost trivial. Julius knows this and makes the apparent disjunction serve a double purpose. The dialogic form of his return to the present both lessens the immediate tragic tension of the tale just told and intensifies what has been heard by allowing its after-effects to reverberate in the listeners' minds as if to prepare a space in which Julius can serve as interpreter of past and present.

As a collection, the tales express the diversity and complexity of African-American life during slavery. "The Conjurer's Revenge" and "The Gray Wolf's Ha'nt," for instance, turn wholly upon relations among blacks, with free Negroes avenging themselves upon slaves not by virtue of justice but through the power of conjuration exercised amorally. The other five tales are closely bound up with the influence of slavery on the basic conditions of human life. In them conjuring counters slavery's institutional power to fray or break the ties of human kinship. In this sense, Julius's tales locate the offical and unofficial forces at work during slavery.

At first, Chesnutt mutes his irony and appears simply to initiate an educated but provincial northerner in the ways of the South. In a rambling, satisfied voice John begins "The Goophered Grapevine" by tracing his and his wife's migration to North Carolina. A cousin sponsors him, and John feels so acutely the tourist's false familiarity that he regards Julius McAdoo as a curiosity, an old man sitting on a log with a hatful of grapes. Embarrassed, Julius grasps that these two strange Yankees jeopardize his poacher's privileged position. Introducing John and Annie to African-American storytelling, Julius, wearing a mask that evokes the minstrel manner along with folk speech and folk values, unfolds a tragic tale. He tries to persuade John not to buy the vineyard, knowing that even if he fails, he will have made a good impression for future dealings with an important new white man.

In Julius's tale of "The Goophered Grapevine" the natural and human orders are violated by the master's greed. To prevent his slaves from eating grapes and diminishing slightly his profits, Mars Dugal hires Aunt Peggy to charm the vineyard. Like Julius's role as storyteller, Aunt Peggy's position as conjure woman is complex, though unambiguous. (Although she conjures for whites as well as blacks, she insists on cash payment from whites, while the slaves' offerings are usually pilfered from the master's smokehouse or chicken yard.) After conjuring the vineyard and telling one of the slaves that "a nigger w'at eat dem grapes 'ud be sho ter die inside'n twel' mont's," Peggy, at the overseer's request, immunizes a new field-hand from the conjured grapes he has eaten by mistake. Henry, the new slave, is a good worker so Aunt Peggy does Mars Dugal a favor, too.

The tale turns on nuances of relationship. Once conjured, Henry's vitality, like the grapevine's, waxes and wanes according to changes in the seasons and also according to the vicissitudes of Mars Dugal's management. Unmindful of Henry's wishes, Mars Dugal hoodwinks other men who, like him, seek to profit from slavery's human traffic. For five years he sells Henry in the spring and buys him back for a pittance during the dead of winter. As long as Mars Dugal plays his grotesque tricks within the natural cycle to which Aunt Peggy has attached Henry's life, the natural order continues to function. But eventually Mars Dugal, outgambled and half-bewitched by a fast-talking Yankee, hires this confidence man to increase scientifically the yield on his scuppernongs. The charlatan's intervention disrupts the fragile balance between natural and moral forces restored by Aunt Peggy's conjuring.

"The Goophered Grapevine" is about the sources, uses, and consequences of power. Aunt Peggy's comes from a knowledge of living things, yet her individual power is subject to the larger institutional force of slavery. When the grapes wither and die, Henry dies, too, because his well-being depends on relationships in the world around him. Rounding out his tale, Julius testifies eloquently to the mysterious yet verifiable pattern of connection and causality in nature and consciousness.

> All dis time de goopher wuz a-wukkin'. When de vimes sta'ted ter wither, Henry 'mence' ter complain er his rheumatiz; en when de leaves begin ter dry up, his ha'r 'mence' ter drap out. When de vimes fresh' up a bit, Henry 'd git peart ag'in, en when de vimes wither' ag'in, Henry 'd git ole agi'in, en des kep' gittin' mo' en mo' fitten fer nuffin; he des pined away, en pined away, en fine'ly tuk ter his cabin; en when de big vime whar he got de sap ter 'n'int his head withered en turned yaller an died, Henry died too,—des went out sorter like a cannel.

Julius's account is also an exemplary tale for the present circumstance. After all, John, also a Yankee, eventually buys the vineyard and hires Julius to take advantage of his knowledge and lore, his presence as a genius of the place. He learns from Mars Dugal's experience that it is to his advantage to live tolerantly with "his mild suspicion that our colored assistants do not suffer for want of grapes during the season." He learns from Julius that this practice is part of the pact, the needful relationship between those who work the vineyard and the grapes, and that it is in the best interest of the owner to respect this relationship. Presumably, too, John learns about agriculture from Julius who, in the absence of an owner controlling the vineyard, was content to take only a "respectable revenue" from the grapes. So, because of the tale and Julius's sneaky, comic, understated manner of performance, the use of power undergoes a subtle change. As coachman and counselor, Julius now has an official and unofficial relationship with John and Annie. Contrary to John's view that Julius "seemed to lose sight of his auditors, and to be living over again in monologue his life on the old plantation," the old storyteller is shrewdly, deceptively, and constantly aware of his audience. His performer's guile and craft enable him to enlarge John's narrow scheme to include a simultaneously moral and historical frame of reference and rhetoric.

In response and as introduction to "Po' Sandy," the next story, John testifies to the diverse and wide range of tales in Julius's repertoire. "Some," he says, "are quaintly humorous, others wildly extravagant, revealing the Oriental cast of the Negro's imagination; while others poured freely into the sympathetic ear of a Northern-bred woman, disclose many a tragic incident of the darker side of slavery." John's comments are primarily self-revealing. The differences between him and Annie are differences of sensibility, and Chesnutt makes gender a figure for sensibility. "Northern-bred," both hear the same tales, but as a master storyteller and performer, Julius quickly senses that Annie's sympathy runs deeper than her husband's. Even *after* he has heard **"Po' Sandy"** and other tales and begun to write them down, John limits the full power of the tales to disclose "many a tragic incident of the darker side of slavery" to Annie. His response seems both a concession and a revelation of his lingering compulsion to view slavery in terms of a balanced moral equation. Yet his comments prepare the responsive reader to listen carefully to the forthcoming voices of Julius and Annie. Julius is finely sensitive to the sensibility called for by this story, for his essential purpose is to compel his audience to see and feel and understand the sinister values behind the institution of slavery. No doubt he knows about the coming split in the Sandy Run Colored Baptist Church, knows the old schoolhouse could provide his faction with a meeting place. But he is not about to play the minstrel with a story so expressive of his people's unalterable tragic past. Here and elsewhere, John misunderstands the complementary relationship between performance and entertainment; he tends to stereotype Julius and ignore the serious and profound uses to which Julius puts his comic gifts.

In this tale Sandy and Tenie (and also Sandy's first wife) are victims of the capricious ownership—the buying and selling and swapping—of human beings. That power knows no limits to its abuse. To keep her husband Sandy near her, Tenie turns him into a tree.

> "Shill I turn you ter a wolf?" sez Tenie.
>
> "No, eve'ybody's skeered er a wolf, en I doan want nobody ter be skeered er me."
>
> "Shill I turn you ter a mawkin'-bird?"
>
> "No, a hawk mought ketch me. I wanter be turnt inter sump'n w'et'll stay in one place."
>
> "I kin turn you ter a tree," sez Tenie. "You won't hab no mouf ner years, but I kin turn you back oncet in a w'ile, so you kin git sump'n ter eat, en hear w'at's a gwine on."

Within the prison of slavery, Tenie and Sandy sustain the essentials of their love and life. But Tenie is shipped off to nurse one of the master's relatives. While she is away, Sandy is cut down and, in another transformation, sawed into lumber for Mrs. Marrabo's new kitchen. Desirous "ter 'splain ter' im dat she had n'went off a-purpose, en lef' 'im ter be chop' down en sawed up," Tenie is tied up like a crazy woman by the mill hands, and excruciatingly watches Sandy die.

Julius ends the tale with a dying fall. Folks say, he tells John and Annie, that any remaining lumber from the tree that was Sandy "is gwine ter be ha'nted tel de las' piece er plank is rotted en crumble' inter dus'." Annie, the woman, understands instantly and completely. " 'What a system it was,' she exclaimed, under the sorrowful spell of the tale, 'under which such things were possible!'." True to form, John's narrow, literal mind misconstrues Annie's reference to such things. "Are you seriously considering the possibility of a man's being turned into a tree?" She demurs, seeming to yield to his intimidation, then murmurs with, as John describes her, "a dim look in her fine

eyes, 'Poor Tenie!'." Writing down the exchange, John undercuts his position during the time of Julius's actual storytelling, as if admitting that Julius's sense of tact and timing—his complex sense of performance—has nudged him toward a more compassionate historical awareness.

A week or two after Annie decides against using any of the old lumber for her new kitchen, Julius asks her if his Baptist faction "might not hold their meetings in the old schoolhouse for the present." John's irritation, he freely acknowledges, stems partly from the fact that he has just received a bill for the new lumber, and partly from Annie's admission that she has donated money toward the new church. Despite this, and perhaps in irrepressible admiration for Julius's consummate performing skill, John reveals how Julius disposed of even his last meanly literal question. " 'Oh,' replied Annie, 'Uncle Julius says that ghosts never disturb religious worship, but that if Sandy's spirit *should* happen to stray into meeting by mistake, no doubt the preaching would do it good'." Julius has been the articulate voice for Sandy and his ghost, and his message, intended for John through Annie, is that his storytelling has already put John through some beneficial changes. If that is the case, maybe the preacher's testifying will have similar salutary effects on the mind of a restless ghost. Julius's mischievous words, conveyed to John by Annie, reinforce his storyteller's whammy over John in their call-and-response combat. Their contention continues, but here Julius and John may begin to anticipate an eventual fraternal outcome to the contest.

In **"Mars Jeems's Nightmare"** the conjuring of Aunt Peggy *in* the tale and Uncle Julius *with* the tale leads to changes in values and to subsequent actions in the past and present. But John introduces the tale by affirming the view of the African-American held by the Plantation School. Julius, he tells us, "had attached himself to the old plantation, of which he seemed to consider himself an appurtenance." Writing *ex cathedra,* he concludes that "we found him useful in many ways and entertaining in others, and my wife and I, took quite a fancy to him." John's mask of genteel condescension veils the intensity of the conflict about to unfold. John hires Julius's grandson "mainly to please the old man." Irritated by his own spurious, sentimental generosity, he soon sours on the young man and calls him lazy, careless, and "trifling"—about the worst things he could say about a young Negro male. Julius responds by putting on his minstrel's mask. "I knows he ain' much account, en dey ain' much 'pen'ence ter be put on 'im. But I wuz hopin' dat you mought make some 'lowance fuh a' ign'ant young nigger, suh, en gib 'im one mo' chance." But John reasserts his identity as a practical northerner and rejects Julius's appeal to paternalistic southern ritual. According to his deserts a "fair trial" is sufficient. He fires the grandson, and Julius addresses the issue from behind his storyteller's veil.

Knowing that his most important listener is no longer John but Annie, Julius conjures with the tale as his goopher. He waits for a suitable occasion and finds it in a man furiously beating his horse. " 'A man w'at 'buses his hoss is gwine ter be ha'd on de folks w'at wuks fer 'em,' " remarks Julius, and he tantalizes John and Annie with dark hints about the offensive gentleman's grandfather and his bad dream "way back yander, long yeahs befo' de wah." John calls for more, and Julius responds with a tale. Mars Jeems McLean's "niggers wuz bleedzed ter slabe fum daylight ter da'k, w'iles yuther folks's did n' hafter wuk 'cep'n' fum sun ter sun."

To Julius, with his memories of slavery's abuses, differences of degree were bad enough. But in Jeems's case, some of the differences were in kind, as when, unsuccessful in love because his fiancee interprets his cruelty to slaves as a sign of his true character, he forbids love and courting among his slaves. Defied by one pair of lovers, he sells the woman and orders forty lashes for her man, Solomon. Solomon promptly enlists Aunt Peggy's aid. For two pecks of corn, she prepares a goopher, which sends away Mars Jeems and paradoxically leaves his slaves at the mercy of an overseer who is even harsher than Jeems. But soon Jeems returns in the form of a recalcitrant, amnesiac slave and for his insolence is mercilessly hounded but not broken. Transformed back into a white man by Aunt Peggy, Jeems turns his values and policies inside out. He pretends to enjoy his overseer's account of cruelty toward the unidentified slave, then, suddenly, capriciously fires him. The slaves love again and prosper, and Jeems's former sweetheart, hearing about his changed character, restores him to her affections. But Julius's concluding images of happy days on the plantation are received sarcastically by John. " 'And they all lived happy ever after,' I said, as the old man reached a full stop. 'Yes, suh,' he said, interpreting my remarks as a question, 'dey did'." Julius, always a master of timing, seizes the role of interpreter. " 'Dis yer tale goes ter show,' concluded Julius sententiously, 'dat w'te folks w'at is so ha'd en stric', en doan make no 'lowance fer po' ign'ant niggers w'at ain' had no chanst ter l'arn, is li'ble ter hab bad dreams, ter say de leas', en dat dem w'at is kin' en good ter po' people is sho' ter prosper en git 'long in de worl' '."

Julius revises the myth of the contented slave in favor of an attitude closer to that dream of American possibility proposed by the Declaration of Independence. Perhaps feeling pressured, John, too, retreats to first principles and accuses Julius of making up the tale. Julius's response bears witness to the complexity of the oral tradition: "My mammy tol' me dat tale w'en I wa'n't mo' d'n knee-high ter a *hopper-grass*" (my italics). By invoking his ancestor and by replacing grasshopper with hopper-grass, Julius affirms both the tale's longevity and his own improvisatory power. But John still does not grasp that tales as told, embellished, and retold have a function in daily life. In this case Julius embellishes a tale whose outcome upholds values central to the tradition held sacred by John and, particularly, his wife. Treat those less well off badly and you will have bad dreams and worse. Treat them better than you need to, and they and you will prosper.

Once again, Chesnutt advances his theme of change through small actions in the present. In John's absence, Annie hires back Julius's grandson. When John returns, he is quietly furious, yet the glimpse he now gives of the grandson is another persuasive reversal of stereotypes. "I saw a familiar figure carrying a bucket of water to the barn," he notes, and this image of the young man performing his duties replaces John's earlier portrait of shiftlessness and hopelessness. Julius, the storyteller and trickster, uses a tale to change both his grandson and his boss for the better.

In **"Sis' Becky's Pickaninny"** Julius's storytelling ad-

dresses Annie's psychological and spiritual depression and restores her to health. After two years in North Carolina, she becomes "the victim of a settled melancholy, attended with vague forebodings of impending misfortune." When Julius shows up and silently fingers his rabbit's foot as a sign of concern, John seizes eagerly on his presence. But he soon ridicules the old man, and his sententious little speech against superstition is Chesnutt's signal that the rabbit's foot will have metaphorical power both within the tale and its narrative frame.

> "Julius," I observed, half to him and half to my wife, "your people will never rise in the world until they throw off these childish superstitions and learn to live by the light of reason and common sense. How absurd to imagine that the fore-foot of a poor dead rabbit, with which he timorously felt his way along through a life surrounded by snares and pitfalls, beset by enemies on every hand, can promote happiness or success, or ward off failure or misfortune!"

Julius counters with a slapstick, almost minstrel response: "De fo'-foot ain't got no power. It has ter be de hin'-foot." Julius's outrageous, wonderful riff mocks John's refusal to admit mysterious, rationally unaccountable phenomena into his scheme of reality, and calls satiric attention to John's reference to the rabbit's hard, hapless life, apparently without the slightest awareness of the trickster's role performed by Br'er Rabbit in African-American folklore. Then, too, Julius's refutation of John's syllogistic logic, reminiscent of Jim's demolition of Huck's flawed argument about language in *Huck Finn,* establishes his power on John's ground. Julius's stubborn discrimination between effectual and ineffectual rabbit's feet also reinforces his power as storyteller, for his craft confers on everyday objects a form and meaning they have not had before for his audience. In the end, after he tells the tale and Annie responds sympathetically, he loans her his rabbit's foot because she has traveled outside her depression and entered imaginatively a historical world where grief and trouble more intense and terrible than hers are suffered and overcome.

Recall the profoundly historical simile of the old spiritual: "Sometimes I feel like a motherless child / A long ways from home." Everything about Julius's tale and its strategy of conjuring suggests that in the hands of slaves and for that matter in the hands of abolitionist forces in the North, ordinary weapons like "reason and common sense" were powerless to reverse the personal cruelty and tragedy that accompanied slavery. The tale's action examines the assumptions and institutional power of slavery. Sis Becky's master wants another master's horse. To get it he exchanges her but not her baby son. Colonel Pendleton's self-justifying, cowardly idea of kindness leads him to lie to Sis Becky about where she is going and for how long. Aunt Peggy's conjuring succeeds because through it the health of both woman and horse appears to decline, so that out of self-interest the two plantation owners disingenuously negotiate the return of each other's property. Here and in other Chesnutt tales a struggle goes on between property and the more fluid pursuit of happiness as primary human rights. **"Sis' Becky's Pickaninny"** projects an advance on the condition of happiness characterized in **"Mars Jeems's Nightmare."** Even when the spell of conjuring ends, the boy Mose retains the ability to sing like a mockingbird. He sings for white folks, improves his mother's life with the proceeds, and after becoming a successful blacksmith, buys her freedom, then his own. Freedom remains the objective and the last best expression of the pursuit of happiness. And conjuring, an example of transformation at a cost—Aunt Peggy always insists on payment—provides a catalyst for change.

Back in the present, as if demonstrating her worthiness of Julius's rabbit's foot, Annie responds to John's mockery of the tale's literal level. "Those are mere ornamental details and not at all essential," she tells him. "The story is true to nature, and might have happened half a hundred times, and no doubt did happen, in those horrid days before the war." She understands and succinctly expresses the form and meaning of the slave tales as told and performed by Julius in variations on what has been handed down to him. When John characteristically ignores Annie's case and asks Julius about the relevance of the rabbit's foot, Julius calls on Annie to be his interpreter. Her responses to the spell of the tale make her restoration to health and vitality a continuing condition. As a sign of friendship and appreciation, Julius loans her his rabbit's foot, a symbolic object he swears he "wouldn' sell, no indeed, suh, I wouldn'." His gesture, together with his tale and Annie's whole-souled response, affirms the pursuit of happiness as an inalienable right that ought to be available to every citizen, black and white, male and female, a right more essential than property.

Lest the act and metaphor of conjuring seem too easy, Chesnutt closes out ***The Conjure Woman*** with **"Hot-Foot Hannibal,"** a comic tale that turns tragic because the lovers who retain Aunt Peggy fail to learn the lesson of craft essential to their efforts to displace Hannibal from his position as the house slave favored by Chloe by the master and mistress. Chloe and Jeff concentrate so entirely on each other they forget Aunt Peggy's instruction to return " 'dis baby doll' " and her warning that "it's monst'us powerful goopher, en is liable ter make mo' trouble ef you leabe it layin' roun'." Perhaps the lovers assume that trouble can never be their lot. But they are wrong. Hannibal, banished from the big house to the fields, and still afflicted because of their negligence, guesses that Chloe and Jeff are responsible for his sudden change in estate. Guilefully and cruelly, he plays on Chloe's jealousy to set in motion another reversal of fortune. Conjuring, then, is a catalyst for possibility, but most attractive possibilities have a quotient of danger and may boomerang if discipline and craft are not observed.

Certainly, in the present, craft is a necessary condition for Julius if he is to help heal the lovers' quarrel between Annie's sister, Mabel, and young Malcolm Murchison. From John we learn that the "match thus rudely broken off " is in his self-interest as "another link binding [him] to the kindly Southern people among whom [he] had not long before taken up residence." But the potentiality for action belongs to Julius. He suggests the long way on a drive but draws back when Annie insists on the short way. To argue with her would violate good form. Besides, to fight and lose might close out his options. Instead, Julius keeps his distance and his discipline, though in his tale he recounts that Mars Dugal "would 'a' had old Aun' Peggy whip' long ago, on 'y *Aunt Peggy wuz a free 'oman, en he wuz 'feared she'd cunjuh him*" (my italics). Julius is con-

tent with this oblique reference to power's actual and potential checks and balances.

In cahoots with a recalcitrant mare, he tells an appropriate tale and so persuades Annie to take the lead and the long road. In the end the lovers seize the opportunity Julius has offered and work out a reconciliation. They marry and offer him a position. Skillfully, Chesnutt has Julius turn it down as a way of undermining John's smug, suspicious comment "that a most excellent understanding existed between [Julius] and Murchison after the reconciliation." But Chesnutt does something else, too. He allows John to record Julius's decision. "For some reason or other, however," he writes, "he preferred to remain with us." And why not? In life and in performance Julius finds his moveable frame, his foil, his opportunity to use form and convention to advance his interests, his values, and the well-being of the whole community of black and white citizens in generous progression. Yet John mutes his tone as if he, too, now knows these things, accepts them, and acknowledges that somehow he and Julius have become kin. And this kinship is palpably a consequence of craft, for in ***The Conjure Woman*** acts of voice lead to connections between contesting narrative personalities and points of view. Through storytelling Julius conjures the past, and by engagement with his audience he clarifies and in small ways changes the present situation. His performances may have changed John sufficiently that Julius need no longer resort to tricks in their relationship. To put it another way, John seems to have been conjured and to have accepted his transformation on a permanent basis. Because of John's grudging, gradual respect for Julius's craft, his attitude toward the former slave changes from arrogant paternalism to cooperation and perhaps even a preliminary acknowledgment of that democratic equality for which Chesnutt stands.

Recall the last words of ***The Conjure Woman:*** "The mare, I might add, was never known to balk again." John's voice now joins Julius's in affirming the continuing power of conjuring and storytelling. And the mare, in John's possession but Julius's care, is a figure for the potential effects of storytelling. In the last tale, Julius first caused the mare to balk, then released her from a momentarily useful, fixed position into one of motion and freedom from restraint, of fluidity and possibility. The mare's release corresponds to Chesnutt's liberation of African-American tales, their black storyteller, white audience and white narrator, too, from the literary stereotypes of Joel Chandler Harris and the southern Plantation School. On this point Chesnutt is specific. Two years after publication of ***The Conjure Woman,*** he declared his allegiance to a *"literature of necessity."* "The writings of Harris and Page and others of that ilk," he explained to Booker T. Washington, "have furnished my chief incentive to write something upon the other side of the very vital question." That question was, as Ralph Ellison wrote some sixty years later in "The World and the Jug," "the Negro struggle for freedom." Like Ellison, who told Irving Howe that "my reply to your essay is in itself a small though necessary action" in that struggle, and like Douglass before him, Chesnutt understood that literary freedom was bound up with the larger struggle. He understood, too, that the urgent relationship between storyteller and audience, between the word and the world needed imaginative expression in fiction.

Ellison once observed that *Huck Finn* was "a collaboration between a white American novelist of good heart, of democratic vision . . . and white readers, primarily." Chesnutt's form and Uncle Julius's storytelling voice allowed all Americans to become more truly "grounded" in the "reality of Negro American personality" than exposure to Twain's Jim made possible. Chesnutt wrote for all his countrymen. In its time *The Conjure Woman* invited white Americans also of "good heart, of democratic vision," to join the African-American audience. Confident he had mastered his craft, Chesnutt predicted his approach to fiction and folklore would "win out in the long run, so far as I am personally concerned, and will help the cause, which is vastly more important." As a writer Chesnutt helped the cause so much that *The Conjure Woman* continues to challenge writers to discover their own form and voices, to tell their own stories inspired by the tales of folklore and the oral tradition. And the cause remains the double craft of fiction and democracy. (pp. 39-57)

> *John F. Callahan, "The Spoken in the Written Word: African-American Tales and the Middle Passage from 'Uncle Remus: His Songs and Sayings' to 'The Conjure Woman',"* in his In the African-American Grain: The Pursuit of Voice in Twentieth-Century Black Fiction, *University of Illinois Press, 1988, pp. 25-61.*

FURTHER READING

Ames, Russell. "Social Realism in Charles W. Chesnutt." *Phylon* XIII, No. 2 (1953): 199-206.
> Commends Chesnutt as "the first distinguished American Negro author of short stories and novels" and considers his work "the forerunner of a substantial body of fiction written by Negroes which has maintained an unusual level of social realism."

Andrews, William L. "A Reconsideration of *Charles Waddell Chesnutt: Pioneer of the Color Line.*" *CLA Journal* XIX, No. 2 (December 1975): 136-51.
> Assessment of Chesnutt's life and career based on excerpted letters and journal entries reprinted in Helen M. Chesnutt's biography *Charles Waddell Chesnutt: Pioneer of the Color Line.*

———. "William Dean Howells and Charles W. Chesnutt: Criticism and Race Fiction in the Age of Booker T. Washington." *American Literature* XLVIII, No. 3 (November 1976): 327-39.
> Examines the influence of white literary critics such as Howells on Chesnutt's career and on the course of black literature predating the Harlem Renaissance.

Babb, Valerie. "Subversion and Repatriation in *The Conjure Woman.*" *The Southern Quarterly* XXV, No. 2 (Winter 1987): 66-75.
> Contrasts Chesnutt's use of black dialect in his conjure stories with that of Joel Chandler Harris in his Uncle Remus stories. Babb notes that dialect is used in the Uncle Remus stories to reinforce a white supremacist

order, while in Chesnutt's fiction the world view of the white northern landowner (who narrates the frame stories in standard English) is consistently subverted in the dialect narrative of former slave Julius McAdoo.

Bell, Bernard W. "The Early Afro-American Novel: Historical Romance, Social Realism, and Beyond." In his *The Afro-American Novel and Its Tradition,* pp. 37-75. Amherst: University of Massachusetts Press, 1987.
> Considers Chesnutt's novel *The Marrow of Tradition* a realistic depiction of social realities in the postbellum South and an important development in the trend toward realism in black literature.

Blake, Susan L. "A Better Mousetrap: Washington's Program and *The Colonel's Dream.*" *CLA Journal* XXIII, No. 1 (September 1979): 49-59.
> Considers Chesnutt's last novel a systematic and thorough refutation of Booker T. Washington's recommendations for black advancement through service to the white community, education, and "separate but equal" social policies.

Britt, David D. "Chesnutt's Conjure Tales: What You See Is What You Get." *CLA Journal* XV, No. 3 (March 1972): 269-83.
> Maintains that the stories in *The Conjure Woman* are characterized by tension between the different perspectives from which the framing stories and the conjure stories are narrated.

Brooks, Van Wyck. "Eugene O'Neill: Harlem." In his *The Confident Years: 1885-1915,* pp. 539-55. New York: E. P. Dutton & Co., 1952.
> Includes mention of Chesnutt in a discussion of black writers of the period. Brooks suggests that Chesnutt's early fiction suffered from stereotyped characterizations and outmoded literary conventions, but comments that "Chesnutt, as he went on writing, developed a stronger modern phase, dealing in three novels with the borderline of colour, and the problems of mixed blood and the Urban Negro."

Brown, Sterling. "A Century of Negro Portraiture in American Literature." *The Massachusetts Review* VII, No. 1 (Winter 1966): 73-96.
> Briefly mentions Chesnutt's novels of social realism and attributes an underlying social purpose to the *Conjure Woman* stories.

Burnette, R. V. "Charles W. Chesnutt's *The Conjure Woman* Revisited." *CLA Journal* XXX, No. 4 (June 1987): 438-53.
> Compares the texts of the conjure stories as they appeared in periodicals with revisions for book publication, focusing on changes in the character of Julius McAdoo.

Chametzky, Jules. "Regional Literature and Ethnic Realities." *The Antioch Review* XXXI, No. 3 (Fall 1971): 385-96.
> Maintains that Chesnutt's presentation, in his short fiction, of a black ethos, lifestyle, and values, was consistently misunderstood by the white literary establishment and his predominantly white readership, leading Chesnutt to write the more overtly didactic novels.

Chesnutt, Helen M. *Charles Waddell Chesnutt: Pioneer of the Color Line.* Chapel Hill: University of North Carolina Press, 1952, 324 p.

Affectionate biography that reprints numerous passages from Chesnutt's journals and correspondence quoting extensively from contemporary reviews of Chesnutt's published work.

Condit, John H. "Pulling a Chesnutt Out of the Fire: 'Hot-Foot Hannibal'." *CLA Journal* XXX, No. 4 (June 1987): 428-37.

Offers an analysis of the short story "Hot-Foot Hannibal."

Cooke, Michael G. "Self-Veiling: James Weldon Johnson, Charles Chesnutt, and Nella Larsen." In his *Afro-American Literature in the Twentieth Century: The Achievement of Intimacy,* pp. 43-70. New Haven: Yale University Press, 1984.

Includes discussion of "self-veiling": "pulling down a mask over [the] desire for independence and an unencumbered place" by the black narrator of the conjure tales, who both entertains and manipulates the white characters.

Delmar, P. Jay. "The Mask as Theme and Structure: Charles W. Chesnutt's 'The Sheriff's Children' and 'The Passing of Grandison'." *American Literature* LI, No. 3 (November 1979): 364-75.

Examines "the theme of the mask"—"how both whites and Blacks are constrained to hide their true personalities and, often, their true racial identities from themselves and each other"—in the two stories, and suggests that this theme unifies much of Chesnutt's fiction.

———. "Charles W. Chesnutt's 'The Web of Circumstance' and Richard Wright's 'Long Black Song': The Tragedy of Property." *Studies in Short Fiction* 17, No. 2 (Spring 1980): 178-79.

Examines the presentation in both stories of the view that blacks are denied full participation in the white economic system.

———. "Elements of Tragedy in Charles W. Chesnutt's *The Conjure Woman*." *CLA Journal* XXIII, No. 4 (June 1980): 451-59.

Discusses tragic elements in a number of the *Conjure Woman* stories and analyzes "The Gray Wolf's Ha'nt" as a fully developed tragedy that is dependent on characterization and not the background of slavery to bring about the tragic action.

———. "The Moral Dilemma in Charles W. Chesnutt's *The Marrow of Tradition*." *American Literary Realism, 1870-1910* XIV, No. 2 (Autumn 1981): 269-72.

Notes that Chesnutt does not offer solutions to the moral dilemmas presented in the novel, but rather, forces the reader to realize that none of the courses of action undertaken in the novel are likely to solve problems of racial enmity in American society.

———. "Coincidence in Charles W. Chesnutt's *The House behind the Cedars*." *American Literary Realism, 1870-1910* XV, No. 1 (Spring 1982): 97-103.

Considers the role of coincidental encounters and events in furthering the plot of *The House behind the Cedars*.

Dixon, Melvin. "The Teller as Folk Trickster in Chesnutt's *The Conjure Woman*." *CLA Journal* XVIII, No. 2 (December 1974): 186-97.

Considers ways that the black narrator of the conjure stories tricks the white northerners into meeting his own needs through recounting tales that similarly depict trickery through conjuring and witchcraft.

Elder, Arlene A. "Chesnutt on Washington: An Essential Ambivalence." *Phylon* XXXVIII, No. 1 (Spring 1977): 1-8.

Discusses reasons for Chesnutt's public support of Booker T. Washington despite their essential disagreement on the best means for black advancement.

Farnsworth, Robert. Introduction to *The Marrow of Tradition,* by Charles W. Chesnutt, pp. v-xvii. Ann Arbor: University of Michigan Press, 1969.

Discusses the place of *The Marrow of Tradition* in Chesnutt's career, commending Chesnutt's use of contemporary historical background and representation of different classes of black and white characters.

———. "Testing the Color Line—Dunbar and Chesnutt." In *The Black American Writer, Volume I: Fiction,* edited by C. W. E. Bigsby, pp. 111-24. Baltimore: Penguin Books, 1969.

Compares Chesnutt's and Paul Laurence Dunbar's approaches to racial issues. Farnsworth maintains that Chesnutt more successfully addressed "the immediate problems of southern disfranchisement, Jim Crow legislation, and racial intermarriage."

———. "Charles Chesnutt and the Color Line." In *Minor American Novelists,* edited by Charles Alva Hoyt, pp. 28-40. Carbondale: Southern Illinois University Press, 1970.

Discusses Chesnutt's treatment of race relations in a chronological sketch of his literary career.

Ferguson, SallyAnn H. "Chesnutt's 'The Conjurer's Revenge': The Economics of Direct Confrontation." *Obsidian: Black Literature in Review* 7, Nos. 2 and 3 (Summer and Winter 1981): 37-42.

Examines economic themes in several of the *Conjure Woman* stories, noting that the collection as a whole demonstrates obstacles to black economic success in the South.

———. "Rena Walden: Chesnutt's Failed 'Future American'." *The Southern Literary Journal* XV, No. 1 (Fall 1982): 74-82.

Considers the novel *The House behind the Cedars* as a fictional forum in which Chesnutt, through the mulatto characters Rena Walden and John Walden, demonstrated possible consequences of his proposals for racial amalgamation through intermarriage between blacks, whites, and native Americans. In a series of magazine essays Chesnutt had suggested that a large mixed-race population would help to eliminate race prejudice.

Fienberg, Lorne. "Charles W. Chesnutt and Uncle Julius: Black Storytellers at the Crossroads." *Studies in American Fiction* 15, No. 2 (Autumn 1987): 161-73.

Notes that Chesnutt paralleled the transitional, uncertain nature of race relations in the postbellum South in his depiction of dealings between the white northern landowners and the black former slave in the *Conjure Woman* stories.

Fraiman, Susan. "Mother-Daughter Romance in Charles W. Chesnutt's 'Her Virginia Mammy'." *Studies in Short Fiction* 22, No. 4 (Fall 1985): 443-48.

Suggests that racial themes are secondary to themes of

female identity and mother-daughter relationships in the short story "Her Virginia Mammy."

Gartner, Carol B. "Charles W. Chesnutt: Novelist of a Cause." *The Markham Review* 1, No. 3 (October 1968): 5-12.
    Notes the didactic and propagandistic nature of Chesnutt's fiction.

George, Marjorie, and Pressman, Richard S. "Confronting the Shadow: Psycho-Political Repression in Chesnutt's *The Marrow of Tradition*." *Phylon* XLVIII, No. 4 (Winter 1987): 287-98.
    Examines unresolved tensions between the rational message of cooperation and nonviolence, and the call for resistance to and violent overthrow of the racist social and political establishment, in *The Marrow of Tradition*.

Gibson, Donald B. "Charles W. Chesnutt: The Anatomy of a Dream." In his *The Politics of Literary Expression: A Study of Major Black Writers,* pp. 125-54. Westport, Conn.: Greenwood Press, 1981.
    Traces the development of Chesnutt's complex social and racial attitudes in his published fiction.

Gidden, Nancy Ann. " 'The Gray Wolf's Ha'nt': Charles W. Chesnutt's Instructive Failure." *CLA Journal* XXVII, No. 4 (June 1984): 406-10.
    Suggests that "The Gray Wolf's Ha'nt" fails to achieve the "delicate counterpoint of opposing views: the white narrator's, his convalescent wife's, Uncle Julius's" usually accomplished in the conjure tales, because of the incongruity between the comic function of the tale, which is related by Julius in order to obtain something of value from the northerners, and the tragic nature of the tale itself.

Giles, James R. "Chesnutt's Primus and Annie: A Contemporary View of *The Conjure Woman.*" *The Markham Review* 3, No. 3 (May 1972): 46-49.
    Suggests that Chesnutt introduced racial stereotypes—and in particular, demeaning characterizations of blacks—into the *Conjure Woman* stories to appease a racist white readership.

Giles, James R., and Lally, Thomas P. "Allegory in Chesnutt's *Marrow of Tradition*." *JGE: The Journal of General Education* XXXV, No. 4 (1984): 259-69.
    Considers Chesnutt's novel "an elaborate allegory of the American racial dilemma, with virtually all of its characters having an abstract symbolic function."

Gloster, Hugh M. "Negro Fiction to World War I." In his *Negro Voices in American Fiction,* pp. 23-100. Chapel Hill: University of North Carolina Press, 1948.
    Includes discussion of Chesnutt in a survey of black American writers of the period.

Gross, Seymour L. "Stereotype to Archetype: The Negro in American Literary Criticism." In *Images of the Negro in American Literature,* edited by Seymour L. Gross and John Edward Hardy, pp. 1-26. Chicago: University of Chicago Press, 1966.
    Considers Chesnutt's fiction a challenge to and refutation of limited and biased presentations of black characters in turn-of-the-century American literature.

Hackenberry, Charles. "Meaning and Models: The Uses of Characterization in Chesnutt's *The Marrow of Tradition* and

Mandy Oxendine." *American Literary Realism, 1870-1910* XVII, No. 2 (Autumn 1984): 193-202.
    Discusses the didactic purpose of characterization in two novels (one unpublished) by Chesnutt.

Harris, Trudier. "Chesnutt's Frank Fowler: A Failure of Purpose?" *CLA Journal* XXII, No. 3 (March 1979): 215-28.
    Examines the literary and didactic function of the black working-class suitor of the light-skinned heroine of *The House behind the Cedars.*

Haslam, Gerald W. " 'The Sheriff's Children': Chesnutt's Tragic Racial Parable." *Negro American Literature Forum* 2, No. 2 (Summer 1968): 21-6.
    Considers "The Sheriff's Children" as a parable for ongoing racial crisis in the United States perpetuated by white moral degeneration.

Hemenway, Robert. "Gothic Sociology: Charles Chesnutt and the Gothic Mode." *Studies in the Literary Imagination* VII, No. 1 (Spring 1974): 101-19.
    Considers ways that the *Conjure Woman* stories both conform to and diverge from the Gothic mode.

———. " 'Baxter's Procrustes': Irony and Protest." *CLA Journal* XVIII, No. 2 (December 1974): 172-85.
    Examines the subtle protest elements of "Baxter's Procrustes," which exposes certain ingrained prejudices to ridicule but removes the action from the arena of racial confrontation by presenting conflict between all white characters.

Hovet, Theodore R. "Chesnutt's 'The Goophered Grapevine' as Social Criticism." *Negro American Literature Forum* 7, No. 3 (Fall 1973): 86-8.
    Suggests that Chesnutt's first published story, "The Goophered Grapevine," is primarily a work of social criticism designed to cast doubts on the soundness of the white northerners' value system and their response to the South.

Ikonné, Chidi. "Symptoms of a Phenomenon: Charles Waddell Chesnutt." In his *From Du Bois to Van Vechten: The Early New Negro Literature, 1903-1926,* pp. 45-8. Westport, Conn.: Greenwood Press, 1981.
    Suggests that Chesnutt's depiction of the lives of black people in the *Conjure Woman* stories "anticipates . . . the realism of the more typical New Negro writers' treatment of such material."

Jackson, Wendell. "Charles W. Chesnutt's Outrageous Fortune." *CLA Journal* XX, No. 2 (December 1976): 195-204.
    Examines the reaction of the white literary establishment to Chesnutt's fiction, noting that the didacticism of his novels lost Chesnutt the small, conditional readership gained by the conjure stories.

Keller, Frances Richardson. *An American Crusade: The Life of Charles Waddell Chesnutt.* Provo, Utah: Brigham Young University Press, 1978, 304 p.
    Biography that includes discussion of the contemporary reception of Chesnutt's major fiction as well as commentary on his journalism and other nonfiction writing.

Lewis, Richard O. "Romanticism in the Fiction of Charles W. Chesnutt: The Influence of Dickens, Scott, Tourgée, and Douglass." *CLA Journal* XXVI, No. 2 (December 1982): 145-71.
    Suggests that Chesnutt's fiction is characteristic of Afro-

American response to the late nineteenth-century shift from literary romanticism to realism.

Mason, Julian D., Jr. "Charles W. Chesnutt as Southern Author." *The Mississippi Quarterly* XX, No. 2 (Spring 1967): 77-89.

Considers Chesnutt's place in American literature and within the southern literary tradition.

Ogunyemi, Chikwenye Okonjo. "The Africanness of *The Conjure Woman* and *Feather Woman of the Jungle*." *Ariel* 8, No. 2 (April 1977): 17-30.

Compares African themes in Chesnutt's *Conjure Woman* stories and Amos Tutuola's novel *Feather Woman of the Jungle*.

Reilly, John M. "The Dilemma in Chesnutt's *The Marrow of Tradition*." *Phylon* XXXII, No. 1 (Spring 1971): 31-8.

Notes that *The Marrow of Tradition* is informed by an ironic dilemma: though advocating the acceptance of blacks into the mainstream of white society, Chesnutt acknowledges that this is an almost unattainable goal.

Sedlack, Robert P. "The Evolution of Charles Chesnutt's *The House behind the Cedars*." *CLA Journal* XIX, No. 2 (December 1975): 125-35.

Examines manuscript versions written between 1889 and 1899 of the short story "Rena Walden" and the novel *The House behind the Cedars* (based on the short story), finding that each revision reveals "Chesnutt's growing militance as a polemicist and his increasing competence as an artist."

Selke, Hartmut K. "Charles Waddell Chesnutt: 'The Sheriff's Children' (1889)." In *The Black American Short Story in the 20th Century: A Collection of Critical Essays,* edited by Peter Bruck, pp. 21-38. Amsterdam: B. R. Grüner Publishing Co., 1977.

Summarizes the principal themes of Chesnutt's fiction and offers an extended analysis of "The Sheriff's Children," which Selke contends contains most of Chesnutt's characteristic literary themes.

Shulman, Robert. "*The Conjure Woman:* Double Consciousness and the Genteel Tradition." In his *Social Criticism & Nineteenth-Century American Fictions,* pp. 50-65. Columbia: University of Missouri Press, 1987.

Examines ways that Chesnutt offered commentary on both the genteel tradition in American letters and the racism of American society by contrasting the sensibilities of the white northerners and the former slave in *The Conjure Woman*.

Smith, Robert A. "A Note on the Folktales of Charles W. Chesnutt." *CLA Journal* V, No. 3 (March 1962): 229-32.

Considers traditional folkloric elements in Chesnutt's conjure stories.

Socken, June. "Charles Waddell Chesnutt and the Solution to the Race Problem." *Negro American Literature Forum* 3, No. 2 (Summer 1969): 52-6.

Examines Chesnutt's promotion in his nonfiction writings of black assimilation into the mainstream of American culture primarily through intermarriage with whites and light-skinned blacks.

Taxel, Joel. "Charles Waddell Chesnutt's Sambo: Myth and Reality." *Negro American Literature Forum* 9, No. 4 (Winter 1975): 105-08.

Examines Chesnutt's depiction of manipulation and trickery on the part of characters who outwardly conform to the archetype of the happy, docile slave.

Terry, Eugene. "The Shadow of Slavery in Charles Chesnutt's *The Conjure Woman*." *Ethnic Groups* 4 (May 1982): 103-25.

Maintains that Chesnutt's purpose in writing the *Conjure Woman* stories was to discredit the benign presentation of slavery by white Plantation School authors.

Walcott, Ronald. "Chesnutt's 'The Sheriff's Children' as Parable." *Negro American Literature Forum* 7, No. 3 (Fall 1973): 83-5.

Considers this story of a white sheriff with a legitimate white and an illegitimate mulatto child emblematic of southern unwillingness to acknowledge responsibility for the plight of free blacks.

Whitt, Lena M. "Chesnutt's Chinquapin County." *The Southern Literary Journal* XIII, No. 2 (Spring 1981): 41-58.

Identifies Chesnutt's fictional Chinquapin County with North Carolina's Cumberland County and considers the area a microcosm of the moral and sociological problems facing the South.

Wideman, John. "Charles W. Chesnutt's *The Marrow of Tradition*." *The American Scholar* 42, No. 1 (Winter 1972-73): 128-34.

Close examination of structure, narrative, and characterization in *The Marrow of Tradition*.

Winkleman, Donald M. "Three American Authors as Semi-Folk Artists." *Journal of American Folklore* 78, No. 308 (April-June 1965): 130-35.

Includes discussion of Chesnutt's use of folktale techniques in the conjure stories.

Wintz, Cary D. "Race and Realism in the Fiction of Charles W. Chesnutt." *Ohio History* 81, No. 2 (Spring 1972): 122-30.

Explores the dualism between Chesnutt's desire to accurately present black experience in his fiction and his desire to win acceptance by the white literary establishment.

Ford Madox Ford

1873-1939

(Born Ford Hermann Hueffer; also wrote under pseudonyms Fenil Haig, Daniel Chaucer, and Baron Ignatz von Aschendrof) English novelist, editor, poet, critic, biographer, historian, essayist, and autobiographer.

The following entry presents criticism of Ford's novel *The Good Soldier: A Tale of Passion* (1915). For discussion of Ford's complete career, see *TCLC,* Volumes 1 and 15.

The Good Soldier is generally regarded as Ford's greatest work. In this novel, Ford used a narrative technique called *progression d'effet,* whereby events are repeated or occur out of chronological sequence, thus multiplying perspectives on individual incidents and characters and giving them an ever changing, cumulative significance. In *The Good Soldier,* the *progression d'effet* lends the narrator, John Dowell, a complex psychology that supports a variety of interpretations. While critics continue to debate the ultimate meaning of *The Good Soldier,* they generally agree that it is a significant example of early twentieth-century modernist literature.

Although Ford had previously published several novels, critical works, and volumes of poetry, he was little known and in financial difficulty when he wrote the *The Good Soldier.* By Ford's account, he began the novel on his fortieth birthday, 17 December 1913, intending "to show what [he] could do" as a novelist and then to retire from literature. Ford, who had originally called the novel "The Saddest Story," facetiously suggested *The Good Soldier* when his publisher insisted on an alternative title. Ford later claimed he was horrified to find that his publisher had taken his suggestion seriously. *The Good Soldier* met with little critical or popular success when it appeared in 1915. Most reviewers found the novel's narrative unfocused and its subject sordid. Not until the 1950s did *The Good Soldier* begin to receive extensive critical attention.

Throughout *The Good Soldier,* plot is subordinated to narration. Using Dowell, an American living in Europe, as narrator, Ford transcends the melodrama of lies, petty vengeance, and adultery that constitute the events of the story, giving the novel artistic and psychological complexity. The impetus for the story is Dowell's discovery that his close friend of nine years, Edward Ashburnham, has cheated on his wife, Leonora, and has had an affair with Dowell's wife, Florence, among several other women. Dowell, the only person in his social circle unaware of Ashburnham's infidelities, had believed that his friend was the embodiment of the English gentleman. Whether he tells his story to find the truth, to banish the events from his memory, or to vindicate his part in what he calls "a long, sad affair" is a matter of critical debate, but most commentators concur that Dowell is an unreliable narrator, arguing that understanding his personality is the key to resolving the ambiguities of the novel. At times he appears sadly naive, missing completely the significance of events and punctuating his narrative with the words "I don't know." At other times he may impress the reader

as coldly calculating, purposely hiding the truth. While Dowell has been the focus of most commentary on this novel, Ashburnham, the "good soldier" of the title, is generally regarded as its main character. Ironically, Dowell portrays Ashburnham sympathetically, viewing him as a traditional English country gentleman whose two major weaknesses, passion and sentimentality, lead him into affairs in search of female approval. Critics have traced Ashburnham's values to those of the chivalric and courtly love traditions, and his eventual suicide over love for a woman is often seen to represent the conflict between outdated mores and those necessary to survive in twentieth-century society.

Critical commentary on *The Good Soldier* most often focuses on the artistry Ford displayed in structuring the novel. Using the *progression d'effet,* Ford emphasized Dowell's efforts to tell his story, depicting the forward and backward movement of the storyteller's consciousness as he remembers details that he temporarily forgot or gains new insights into his narrative. This technique enabled Ford to maintain a high level of narrative intensity throughout the novel, compelling the reader to take an active part in piecing together the events that Dowell relates in order to form a coherent story. Many critics find Ford's style in this novel reminiscent of that used by Joseph Conrad in *Heart of Darkness* (1902) and by Henry James in his later novels, particularly *The Golden Bowl* (1904). Consequently, critics assert that Ford's artistic success with *The Good Soldier* ranks him, with Conrad and James, among the great writers of the twentieth century.

(See also *Contemporary Authors,* Vol. 104 and *Dictionary of Literary Biography,* Vol. 34.)

The Athenaeum   (essay date 1915)

[*Although praising Ford's writing ability, this anonymous reviewer censures* The Good Soldier *for its "sordid theme."*]

Mr. Hueffer's book is unpleasant—about that there cannot be two opinions. For the two men he describes we can feel neither sympathy nor admiration. The one is that worst kind of hypocrite, a rake impregnated with lachrymose sensibility; the other would be the worst type of "complacent" husband, were it not for short-sightedness that even Georges Dandin would scorn to plead. His wife is even worse—dissolute with open eyes, yet assuming conscientious motives for her worst acts. The wife of the rake is, to a certain degree, tolerable; she is at least upright, led astray by a conception of her religion which persuades her to condone her husband's ill-doing with the idea, so far as one can make out, that his possible redemption to fidelity is better than the publicity and punishment he really merited. Of her the author says:—

> Perhaps Leonora was right; perhaps Roman Catholics, with their queer, shifty ways, are always right. They are dealing with that queer, shifty thing that is human nature.

At any rate, Mr. Hueffer exculpates no one; he presents his case impartially as a "real story," pleading, moreover, this reality as the reason for his discursive way of telling it. Here—from an academic point of view—he has some justification; he does achieve a certain sinister realism, at least in his characterization; the people and the scenes in which they move are thoroughly lifelike. But then Mr. Hueffer has the professional touch; he can express himself effectively, in description or epigram; also he can see certain things clearly. His book would have had distinct claims to great value had he only chosen a less sordid theme.

A review of "The Good Soldier," in The Athenaeum, *No. 4563, April 10, 1915, p. 334.*

Ford Madox Ford   (essay date 1927)

[*The 1927 edition of* The Good Soldier *marked the first appearance of Ford's letter dedicating the work to Stella Bowen, then his common-law wife. In the following excerpt from that letter, Ford comments on the writing of the novel and records some personal anecdotes about its reception.*]

My dear Stella: I have always regarded this as my best book—at any rate as the best book of mine of a pre-war period; and between its writing and the appearance of my next novel nearly ten years must have elapsed, so that whatever I may have since written may be regarded as the work of a different man—as the work of *your* man. (p. xvii)

What I am now I owe to you: what I was when I wrote the **Good Soldier** I owed to the concatenation of circumstances of a rather purposeless and wayward life. Until I sat down to write this book—on the 17th of December 1913—I had never attempted to extend myself, to use a phrase of race-horse training. Partly because I had always entertained very fixedly the idea that—whatever may be the case with other writers—I at least should not be able to write a novel by which I should care to stand before reaching the age of forty; partly because I very definitely did not want to come into competition with other writers whose claim or whose need for recognition and what recognitions bring were greater than my own. I had never really tried to put into any novel of mine *all* that I knew about writing. I had written rather desultorily a number of books—a great number—but they had all been in the nature of *pastiches,* of pieces of rather precious writing, or of *tours de force.* But I have always been mad about writing—about the way writing should be done, and partly alone, partly with the companionship of Conrad, I had even at that date made exhaustive studies into how words should be handled and novels constructed.

So on the day I was forty I sat down to show what I could do—and the **Good Soldier** resulted. I fully intended it to be my last book. I used to think—and I do not know that I do not think the same now—that one book was enough for any man to write, and at the date when the **Good Soldier** was finished London at least and possibly the world appeared to be passing under the dominion of writers newer and much more vivid. Those were the passionate days of the literary Cubists, Vorticists, Imagistes, and the rest of the tapageur and riotous Jeunes of that young decade. So I regarded myself as the Eel which, having reached the deep sea, brings forth its young and dies—or as the Great Auk I considered that, having reached my allotted, I had laid my one egg and might as well die. So I took a formal farewell of Literature in the columns of a magazine called the *Thrush*—which also, poor little auk that it was, died of the effort. Then I prepared to stand aside in favour of our good friends—yours and mine—Ezra, Eliot, Wyndham Lewis, H. D. and the rest of the clamourous young writers who were then knocking at the door.

But greater clamours beset London and the world which till then had seemed to lie at the proud feet of those conquerors; Cubism, Vorticism, Imagism, and the rest never had their fair chance amid the voices of the cannon and so I have come out of my hole again and beside your strong, delicate, and beautiful works have taken heart to lay some work of my own.

The Good Soldier, however, remains my great auk's egg for me as being something of a race that will have no successors, and as it was written so long ago I may not seem over-vain if I consider it for a moment or two. No author, I think, is deserving of much censure for vanity if, taking down one of his ten-year-old books, he exclaims: "Great heavens, did I write as well as that then?" for the implication always is that one does not any longer write so well and few are so envious as to censure the complacencies of an extinct volcano.

Be that as it may, I was lately forced into the rather close examination of this book, for I had to translate it into French, that forcing me to give it much closer attention than would be the case in any reading however minute. And I will permit myself to say that I was astounded at the work I must have put into the construction of the book, at the intricate tangle of references and cross-references. Nor is that to be wondered at, for though I wrote it with comparative rapidity, I had it hatching within myself for fully another decade. That was because the story is a true story and because I had it from Edward Ashburnham himself and I could not write it till all the others were dead. So I carried it about with me all those years, thinking about it from time to time.

I had in those days an ambition: that was to do for the English novel what in *Fort comme la mort* Maupassant had done for the French. One day I had my reward, for I happened to be in a company where a fervent young admirer exclaimed: "By Jove, the *Good Soldier* is the finest novel in the English Language!" whereupon my friend Mr. John Rodker, who has always had a properly tempered admiration for my work, remarked in his clear, slow drawl: "Ah yes. It is, but you have left out a word. It is the finest French novel in the English language!"

With that—which is my tribute to my masters and betters of France—I will leave the book to the reader. But I should like to say a word about the title. This book was originally called by me *The Saddest Story*, but since it did not appear till the darkest days of the war were upon us, Mr. Lane importuned me with letters and telegrams—I was by that time engaged in other pursuits!—to change the title, which he said would at that date render the book unsaleable. One day, when I was on parade, I received a final wire of appeal from Mr. Lane, and the telegraph being reply-paid I seized the reply-form and wrote in hasty irony: "Dear Lane, Why not *The Good Soldier*?" . . . To my horror six months later the book appeared under that title.

I have never ceased to regret it, but since the war I have received so much evidence that the book has been read under that name that I hesitate to make a change for fear of causing confusion. Had the chance occurred during the war I should not have hesitated to make the change, for I had only two evidences that anyone had ever heard of it. On one occasion I met the adjutant of my regiment just come off leave and looking extremely sick. I said: "Great heavens, man, what is the matter with you?" He replied: "Well, the day before yesterday I got engaged to be married and today I have been reading *The Good Soldier*."

On the other occasion I was on parade again, being examined in drill, on the Guards' Square at Chelsea. And, since I was petrified with nervousness, having to do it before a half dozen elderly gentlemen with red hatbands, I got my men about as hopelessly boxed as it is possible to do with the gentlemen privates of H. M. Coldstream Guards. Whilst I stood stiffly at attention one of the elderly red hatbands walked close behind my back and said distinctly in my ear: "Did you say *The Good Soldier*? " So no doubt Mr. Lane was avenged. At any rate I have learned that irony may be a two-edged sword. (pp. xvii-xxii)

Ford Madox Ford, in a dedicatory letter to Stella Ford on January 9, 1927, in his The Good Soldier: A Tale of Passion, *1951. Reprint by Vintage Books, 1983, pp. xvii-xxii.*

Walter Allen   (essay date 1954)

[*Allen is an English novelist of working-class life and a distinguished popular historian and critic of the novel. In the following excerpt, he extols* The Good Soldier.]

[*The Good Soldier*] springs out of [Ford's] own sufferings, so that in it the whole man is engaged. By religion, Ford was a Roman Catholic, but one cannot call him a Catholic novelist as Mauriac or Bernanos is. Human life, as Ford reveals it in his novels, is meaningless, and his values are purely stoic. Dowell, in *The Good Soldier,* asks:

> Are all men's lives like the lives of us good people— like the lives of the Ashburnhams, of the Dowells, of the Ruffords—broken, tumultuous, agonized, and unromantic lives, periods punctuated by screams, by imbecilities, by deaths, by agonies? Who the devil knows?

In the midst of tribulation Ford can only put forward a code of conduct: the façade of civilized life must be preserved at all costs; husband and wife, no matter how unhappy their marriage, do not make scenes before servants; and so on. As he remarks in *The Good Soldier:*

> Pride and reserve are not the only things in life; perhaps they are not even the best things. But if they happen to be your particular virtues you will go all to pieces if you let them go.

Judged as a technical feat alone *The Good Soldier* is dazzling, as near perfection as a novel can be. It is amazingly subtle, this account, by one of them, of the lives of four people who appear to have lived in harmony and friendship for more than ten years:

> Our intimacy was like a minuet, simply because on every possible occasion and in every available circumstance we knew where to go, where to sit, which table we should unanimously choose; and we could rise and go, all four together, without a signal from any one of us, always to the music of the Kur orchestra, always in the temperate sunshine, or, if it rained, in discreet shelters.

So Dowell, the narrator of the novel, saw the relationship while it existed; but Dowell is a deceived man, deceived at every turn of the action; his wife and the Ashburnhams have united to keep him in ignorance of the relationship between them. Yet, what is the truth? What is the truth about Ashburnham, the gallant, stupid Tory gentleman whose code is *noblesse oblige* and who cannot resist pretty women? What is the truth about Leonora Ashburnham, the narrow Irish Catholic who loves him, protects him, keeps up the appearance of a happy marriage in public and does not speak to him in private, who acts as procuress for him and in the last analysis is responsible, through defects in upbringing and perhaps in character, for his deterioration? What is the truth about Dowell himself, whose life is one long meaningless self-sacrifice? We do not know the answers, do not attain to full knowledge of the characters and the pattern they make between them, until the last pages of the book. Ford's technique resembles a kaleidoscope; with each chapter the kaleidoscope is shaken anew to reveal fresh and unexpected aspects of the Dowell-Ashburnham relationship.

But dazzling as it is, the technique is a means to an end, the exposure of the characters in all the poignancy of their intolerable situation; and at the end the pattern is restored, the partners have changed, but the figure is the same: they are still dancing their pathetic minuet. (pp. 394-96)

> *Walter Allen, "The Novel from 1881 to 1914,"
> in his* The English Novel: A Short Critical
> History, *1954. Reprint by E. P. Dutton & Co.,
> Inc., 1957, pp. 305-408.*

Elliott B. Gose, Jr.   (essay date 1957)

[*Gose is an American-born Canadian educator and critic. In the following essay, he analyzes Dowell as a passionless but essentially honest character whose perspective toward events and other people constantly changes as the novel progresses.*]

In his appreciative portrait of Theodore Dreiser, Ford Madox Ford recorded how in 1914, long before they ever met, he had read with emotion Dreiser's novel, *The Titan,* and then had written a laudatory review of it. Six months later in this country Dreiser read Ford's new novel, *The Good Soldier,* also with emotion and also to write a review [see *TCLC,* Vol. 15, pp. 70-1]. Here the similarity ends, however, for Dreiser was irritated by Ford's novel and especially by the portrayal of John Dowell, an expatriate from Philadelphia in "the United States of North America." This character, claimed Dreiser, "is no American. He is that literary packhorse or scapegoat," the "Englishman's conception of an American husband." In a sense this is quite true. No American would make the comment that Dowell does in analyzing his wife: "She did not want much physical passion in the affair. Americans, you know, can envisage such unions without blinking." Obviously such a conception, if taken as an attempt to state the literal truth about this country, must have sounded to a contemporary reader as though its author's acquaintance with America were limited to the novels of Henry James. Actually, of course, as an impressionist novel *The Good Soldier* does not intend to give a literal representation of the problem it explores. And since, as Ford emphasized in his portrait, he and Dreiser were temperamentally different, we should not be surprised at Dreiser's irritation or his final complaint that the novel as a whole is "cold narrative and never truly poignant" because the "formal British leanings" of the author "will not let him loosen up and sing."

Yet Dowell is not simply a Jamesian character in a novel influenced by the French impressionists, nor can we subordinate Ford's work to a study of his two masters, James and Conrad. For at his best he did more than combine in his work their subjects, attitudes, and techniques. Exactly how much we think he accomplished in *The Good Soldier,* however, depends on our reaction to the novel, and this in turn rests on our reaction to Dowell, the narrator of the story. Do we take him to be his author's mouthpiece, as Dreiser implied, or do we take him to be a weak and passionless self-deceiver, as Mark Schorer insists in his provocative introduction to the 1951 edition of the novel [see *TCLC,* Vol. 1, pp. 277-78]? In my opinion the real Dowell

lies somewhere in between these extreme views of him. Dreiser refused to suspend his disbelief. Schorer, because he is a responsible critic, accepts Ford's *donnée* as he sees it, but insists that Ford did not intend us to sympathize with Dowell or accept his interpretation of what happens in the novel. I would like to propose that we extend our sympathy to include not only Ford and the novel but also Dowell as narrator. As I see him, he is an essentially honest if not very passionate person whose attitude toward the characters and events with which he deals is in constant evolution as the novel progresses. Although we certainly cannot take all his prejudices as being Ford's, I believe we will find that the two make essentially the same evaluation of life.

We must begin, however, not with what we desire to prove but with what all readers of *The Good Soldier* would have to agree on: those "facts" in the novel which can be said to exist irrespective of any emotional coloring their narrator might wish to give them. Arranging the important events of the novel in chronological order, we find that in 1892 Captain Edward Ashburnham, the last of a line of well-bred Anglican, English landholders, married Leonora Powys, third eldest daughter of an impoverished Catholic army officer. In 1897 Edward was tried in a civil court for kissing a servant girl on a train; he was acquitted of any evil intention. Shortly thereafter, while the Ashburnhams were at Monte Carlo, Edward became involved with a courtesan and went badly into debt. After this incident Edward allowed his wife to take control of his estate and his finances, and got himself transferred to active duty in Burma, where he and Leonora stayed for seven years. When they returned in 1904, they brought with them a married woman with whom Edward had fallen in love. This woman died of heart failure at Nauheim, Germany, shortly after the narrator, John Dowell, and his wife, Florence, met the Ashburnhams there. Although the two couples were together only during the time they spent at the spa in Nauheim each summer, Florence soon became Edward's mistress. With Leonora's knowledge, but without Dowell's, this arrangement continued for nine years, until 1913. In that year, Florence committed suicide, partly because she had discovered that Edward was in love with his ward, a young girl named Nancy Rufford. Edward finally decided to send the girl to her father in India and asked the narrator to ride with them to the station from which she was to leave. Although neither Edward nor Nancy showed any emotion at parting, he later committed suicide and she went mad upon hearing of it.

The details of the last part of *The Good Soldier* (1915) have an interesting parallel in an anecdote from Ford's monograph on the English character, *The Spirit of the People.* There he told the story of two "good people," a man and wife, and "a young girl, the ward of the husband." Between the girl and the husband

> an attachment had grown up. P—— had not only never "spoken to" his ward; his ward, I fancy, had spoken to Mrs. P——. At any rate, the situation had grown impossible, and it was arranged that Miss W—— should take a trip round the world in company with some friends who were making that excursion. It was all done with with the nicest tranquillity. Miss W——'s luggage had been sent on in advance; P—— was to drive her to the station himself in the dog-cart. The only betrayal of any kind

of suspicion that things were not of their ordinary train was that the night before the parting P——had said to me: "I wish you'd drive to the station with us to-morrow morning." He was, in short, afraid of a "scene."

On the way to the station the two talked "in ordinary voices" of ordinary things, and finally parted without ever showing the emotion felt. Ford concluded that "in its particular way, this was a very fine achievement; it was playing the game to the bitter end. It was, indeed, very much the bitter end, since Miss W—— died at Brindisi on the voyage out, and P—— spent the next three years at various places on the Continent where nerve cures are attempted."

Although anyone familiar with *The Good Soldier* will notice many more similarities than I have space to point out, we may take it that the anecdote and the novel ("a true story," Ford claimed) have a common source. They are similar also in what their author thought they demonstrated about human beings. Of the conclusion to the anecdote in *The Spirit of the People,* Ford noted:

> It may have been desirable, in the face of the eternal verities—the verities that bind together all nations and all creeds—that the parting should have been complete and decently arranged. But a silence so utter: a so demonstrative lack of tenderness seems to me to be a manifestation of a national characteristic that is almost appalling. . . . [For, Ford felt] to the attaining of this standard the Englishman has sacrificed the arts—which are concerned with expression of emotions—and his knowledge of life, which cannot be attained to by a man who sees the world as all good.

In the six years between recording this analysis and beginning work on *The Good Soldier,* Ford was evidently strengthened in his belief. For in his critical study, *Henry James* (which appeared in London, 1913, the year that he started work on *The Good Soldier*), he recorded the following view of the state of society and its relation to art:

> The greatest service that any novelist can render the Republic, the greatest service that any man can render to the State, is to draw an unbiassed picture of the world we live in. . . . Regarding the matter historically, we may safely say that the feudal system in its perfection has died out of the world. . . . And, just at this moment when by the nature of things we know so many men and so little of the lives of men, we are faced . . . by a sort of beggardom of political theories. It remains therefore for the novelist—and particularly for the realist among novelists—to give us the very matter upon which we shall build the theories of the new body politic.

Ford believed, of course, that James was doing this in his novels. And in a sense he was, but his preoccupation was primarily with moral manners rather than with building "the theories of the new body politic." Applied to Conrad, however, the doctrine of this paragraph might have more relevance. In *The Heart of Darkness* and *The Secret Agent* he might be said to have been drawing "an unbiassed picture of the world we live in" with the hope of altering that world. But James was too much a product of the old order and Conrad by temperament too much removed from the contemporary scene, to deal as sympathetically as Ford did with the effect of society on individual passion. In ad-

dition, Ford's relation to the past, his concept of tradition, was different from James's or Conrad's. He had an anachronistic attitude which allowed him to say, as we have seen, that "the feudal system *in its perfection* has died out of the world." I have italicized three of these words because they so casually qualify a point which any twentieth-century man would say had been settled hundreds of years ago. Ford, however saw the English aristocracy of his time as the last in the long line of direct heirs to the feudal lords of the Middle Ages. And he made a member of that aristocracy one of the most important characters in *The Good Soldier.*

Probably the essence of Edward Ashburnham's character lies in his being a feudal gentleman. When, for instance, he wants to make the courtesan, La Dolciquita, his mistress, he cannot bear her practical suggestion that they put their relations on a financial basis. "You see, he believed in the virtue, tenderness, and moral support of women. He wanted more than anything to argue with La Dolciquita; to retire with her to an island and point out to her the damnation of her point of view and how salvation can only be found in true love and the feudal system. She had once been his mistress, he reflected, and, by all the moral laws, she ought to have gone on being his mistress or at the very least his sympathetic confidante." Unfortunately, like Edward's wife, La Dolciquita tends to put material and other interests ahead of emotional ideals. If it had not been for this quality in Leonora, Edward might never have wandered afield. In running his estate, he applied "the feudal theory of an overlord doing his best by his dependents, the dependents meanwhile doing their best for the landlord." But after marrying Leonora, he found that his generosity was making them "hard up." This situation brought out a "purposeful efficiency" in Leonora, who started giving him advice. Since, however, Edward believed that "no man can satisfactorily accomplish his life's work without loyal and whole-hearted co-operation of the woman he lives with," he took her argument and advice to indicate that she was "physically and mentally cold." This coldness was anathema to Edward, for "what really made him feel good in life was to comfort somebody who would be darkly and mysteriously mournful."

There are, then, two sides to Edward's character, and they provide a basis for the main conflict in the novel. On the one hand there is what we may call the internal Edward, driven "by the mad passion to find an ultimately satisfying woman." On the other hand there is the external Ashburnham, "the fine soldier, the excellent landlord, the extraordinarily kind, careful, and industrious magistrate, the upright, honest, fair-dealing, fair-thinking, public character." Edward is himself aware of this split. Shortly after his marriage he was "perfectly ready to become a Romanist" because Leonora was one, but he insisted that any male offspring "be educated in the [Anglican] religion of their immediate ancestors." As Dowell says, "This may appear illogical, but I dare say it is not so illogical as it looks. Edward, that is to say, regarded himself as having his own body and soul at his disposal. But his loyalty to the traditions of his family would not permit him to bind any future inheritors of his name or beneficiaries by the death of his ancestors."

Not only do we find a conflict within Edward between his own inextinguishable passion and his inherited sense of tradition; the two kinds of reality represented by these forces saturate the novel as a whole. We cannot understand the narrator's position, the tone and imagery, or the meaning of **The Good Soldier** unless we appreciate the importance of external and internal values. As Mark Schorer says, "We learn from what is perhaps the major theme of the book [that] appearances have their reality." Thus he calls Dowell's view of what happens "not so much the wrong view as merely *a* view." For according to Schorer, Dowell cannot see any of the characters objectively, but has to distort them to make his own shortcomings seem less. "If Florence is a harlot, she is so, in part, because of her husband's fantastic failure," which he tries to hide by accusing her of "calculated vice." Here as elsewhere in his analysis Schorer allows his dislike of Dowell to push him to an unwarranted extreme in interpreting the narrator's attitude. Although it is true that Dowell and the other characters are imperfect, I do not think that Ford intended us to judge them as harshly as Schorer does. He claims, for instance, that it is wrong to see "Florence's indiscretions [as] crimes, and Edward's, with Florence, follies at worst, and at best true goodness of heart." The problem is worth investigation.

As Dowell admits from the beginning of his tale, he has lived for forty-five years on the level of appearance. And, he says, until "six months ago . . . I had never sounded the depths of an English heart. I had known only the shallows." Dowell is in fact constantly reminding the reader of his shortcomings. After first meeting Florence in New York, he determined, he says, "with all the obstinacy of a possibly weak nature, if not to make her mine, at least to marry her." He finally prevailed upon her to elope with him—mainly because she wanted, not passion, but a "European establishment," which she coldly calculated that he alone could offer her. One night he appeared at her window with a rope ladder, and she greeted him with a warm embrace. Although it was the first such sign he had ever received from a woman, Dowell was in a hurry and quickly went back down with her luggage. "I fancy," he says, "that, if I had shown warmth then, she would have acted the proper wife to me, or would have put me back again. But, because I acted like a Philadelphia gentleman, she made me, I suppose, go through with the part of a male nurse." For soon after the ceremony Florence feigned heart trouble; the marriage was never consummated, and Dowell's only *raison d'être* became taking care of his wife.

From this evidence we should rightly conclude that Florence's later adultery is partly Dowell's fault. But we have to remember that she had not only as much say in deciding upon the marriage as Dowell but considerably more insight into their relation. She judged him as a man who lacked passion but who could give her what she wanted otherwise. She used deception, first to keep her husband in the role of nursemaid and second to become the lover of Jimmy, a dissolute character with whom she had had an affair before her marriage. She is, then, obviously more to blame than Dowell. But she is also more to blame than Edward Ashburnham. Whereas he acted from the pressures of a cold conventional marriage upon a warmly passionate temperament, Florence "was an American, a New Englander. She had not the hot passions of these Europeans." This is, of course, Dowell's view and certainly not Florence's. She in fact excused herself to Leonora "on the score of an overmastering passion." But Dowell punctures

this: "I always say that an overmastering passion is a good excuse for feelings. You cannot help them. And it is a good excuse for straight actions—she might have bolted with [Jimmy] before or after she married me." She might also have gone off with Ashburnham, except that in reality she really wanted his estate, Branshaw Teleragh.

But if Florence's self-advertised "overmastering passion" should have provided her with "a good excuse for straight action," why should Edward's passion not provide him with the same excuse? So far as their actions (or nonactions) are concerned, both are, of course, equally guilty. But the important question is how we are meant to take these actions; and this problem depends in turn on how the narrator takes them and how, accordingly, we judge him. The answer in this particular case, as in all others of importance, is that Dowell has valid reasons for condemning Florence and condoning Edward for their respective parts in the adultery. Actually he does not condemn either for the adultery itself: "I do not know where the public morality of the case comes in," he says, but "if I had known that they really and passionately loved each other . . . I truly believe that I would have united them, observing ways and means as decent as I could." The truth is, however, that they were not "really and passionately" in love with one another. Florence's selfish nature has been well enough established so that we can now turn to Edward.

To begin with, Dowell says that he is convinced that Edward "was sick of Florence within three years of even interrupted companionship and the life that she led him." Why, if this is so, did Edward not break off the awkward arrangement? Because Leonora had "assured him that, if the minutest fragment of the real situation ever got through to my senses, she would wreak upon him the most terrible vengeance that she could think of." Why on the other hand did he not run away with Florence? Because, as Dowell says, "he cared for his wife too much," not to mention his sense of responsibility for the estate, which she at that time controlled. Edward's motives are, in other words, based on considerations outside himself. Although unable to curb his physical passions, he has a code and feelings for others. Despite Edward's weakness, therefore, I believe that Ford intended us to view him sympathetically, just as I believe he intended us to view Dowell in the same way.

Dowell's early self is almost pathetically limited, but as usual, for all that he tries to enlist our sympathy for that self, Dowell paints an essentially honest picture. A lonely man, not even intimate with his wife, he spent his time waiting for her outside of spas. "But a day was to come when I was never to do it again alone. You can imagine, therefore, what the coming of the Ashburnhams meant for me." What he found with them, of course, was an external friendship, but one that was satisfactory for nine years. When it broke up, Dowell was again left by himself, with the realization that he knew "nothing—nothing in the world—of the hearts of men. I only know that I am alone—horribly alone." Not only does this statement indicate that Dowell is fully conscious of his position, it evidences once again the fullness of his honesty with the reader. This honesty appears constantly in his appraisal of the past. For instance, in apologizing for not having suspected at the time that Florence had committed suicide, Dowell says, "You may think that I had been singularly lacking in suspiciousness; you may consider me even to have been an imbecile. But consider exactly the position." This might be called a disarming prelude of falsified rationalization, but I do not think it is. Nor do I see how we can denigrate the following analysis of the shock that separated the man he was from the man he became. "I dare say that my week or ten days of affraissement—of what was practically catalepsy—was just the repose that my exhausted nature claimed after twelve years of the repression of my instincts, after twelve years of playing the trained poodle. For that was all that I had been. I suppose that it was the shock that did it—the several shocks."

The clue to the change in Dowell's character lies in the phrase "repression of instincts." Because he is an American (or at least Ford's version of one) Dowell had never given much thought to his instincts, but the complete repression of them during the twelve years of his marriage to Florence had been an extreme which finally caused an unconscious rebellion. The shock of Florence's death brought up from the depths of Dowell's mind a passion his conscious self had never suspected. As a result, two hours after his wife's death, he suddenly said, "Now I can marry the girl [Nancy]." His speaking this sentence is as much of a surprise to Dowell as it is to the unsuspecting reader. In fact Dowell finds it "a very amazing thing—amazing for the light of possibilities that it casts into the human heart. For I had never had the slightest conscious idea of marrying the girl; I never had the slightest idea even of caring for her. I must have talked in an odd way, as people do who are recovering from an anaesthetic. It is as if one had a dual personality, the one I being entirely unconscious of the other."

But Dowell had finally begun to put the two together, to try to reconcile the life of convention in which he had been passively happy for so long with the life of passion which demands active satisfaction if it is to be fulfilled. Like Edward Ashburnham, Dowell desires fulfillment, but unlike him he never achieves it, partly because of circumstance. This claim is, of course, Dowell's, but in making it he tries to generalize about all men: "I suppose I should really like to be a polygamist; with Nancy, and with Leonora, and with Maisie Maidan, and possibly even with Florence. I am no doubt like every other man; only, probably because of my American origin, I am fainter. At the same time I am able to assure you that I am a strictly respectable person . . . I have only followed, faintly, and in my unconscious desires, Edward Ashburnham." Here, as always, Dowell qualifies what he had to say to indicate that he does not really consider himself at all the kind of person Ashburnham was in his actions, that they are similar only in what they desire. With this view Mark Schorer is in vehement disagreement. Dowell, he says, is "incapable of passion, sexual and moral alike," and has "no heart at all, and hence no mind." Taking Dowell's picture of an earlier self as the true one, Schorer calls his later comparison of himself with Ashburnham the narrator's "weirdest absurdity." According to this view, Dowell has no right to say that, in his "fainter way," he also comes into "the category of the passionate, of the headstrong, and the too-truthful."

Yet, granted Dowell's purpose in the last part of the book, his statement is true. For he is trying to show that there are two types of persons in the world, those who can effi-

ciently repress their instincts and those who are betrayed in some way by their individual traits. He identifies himself with the second of these groups and finally comes to dislike the first:

> Conventions and traditions I suppose work blindly but surely for the preservation of the normal type; for the extinction of proud, resolute, and unusual individuals.

> Edward was the normal man, but there was too much of the sentimentalist about him and society does not need too many sentimentalists. Nancy was a splendid creature but she had about her a touch of madness. Society does not need individuals with touches of madness about them. So Edward and Nancy found themselves steam-rolled out.

But perhaps Dowell's sympathy for Edward is, as Schorer suggests, only a salve for his ego. Perhaps his love for Nancy is only a result of this "infatuation and self-infatuation." If so, like all of Dowell's other new attitudes, this one depends upon imitation. But we have concrete evidence that Dowell's love for Nancy is not the result of mere conscious emulation of Edward.

For the night that Edward sat with Nancy in the park and realized his love for her was also the night that Florence spied on them and realized the same thing. It was immediately afterward that she returned to the hotel and committed suicide. Two hours after this, in turn, Dowell's instincts were finally liberated when he voiced his theretofore unconscious desire for Nancy. This scene is, obviously, a crux, and I do not see how it can be read except to support Dowell's independent realization of love, a realization which liberates his ability to desire, causing in effect a revolution in his American personality. It is true that he does not act out his desires, but this fact, as we shall see presently, is important mainly for its irony.

Actually the contrast with Edward's consuming passion for Nancy is not intended to obliterate any similarity between Dowell and Edward, but precisely to emphasize the common instinct shared even by such dissimilar men. Seen in this perspective, their love for Nancy fits in with a theory which Dowell enunciates halfway through the novel. He finds it "impossible to believe in the permanence of any early passion," he tells us. "As I see it, at least with regard to man, a love affair, a love for any definite woman, is something in the nature of a widening of the experience. With each new woman that a man is attracted to there appears to come a broadening of the outlook, or, if you like, an acquiring of new territory." This section of *The Good Soldier* is central to an understanding of the problem raised by the novel, and I think we are intended to read it sympathetically, taking seriously both the presentation of Edward's problem and Dowell's analysis of it. We dare not, therefore, discount Dowell's opinion that "the sex instinct" is of little importance "in a really great passion." For he qualifies, "I don't mean to say that any great passion can exist without a desire for consummation. That seems to me to be a commonplace and to be therefore a matter needing no comment at all." What he feels does need comment is a man's "craving for identity with the woman he loves," something "long continued and withering up the soul of a man." Such a passion was Edward's for Nancy, but for once he was able to resolve the conflict it caused in favor of his external life. Refusing to touch her, he determined to stick "to what was demanded by convention and by the traditions of his house." And he sent her away, hoping only that she "would continue to love him . . . Well, he was a sentimentalist," concludes Dowell. Earlier he had generalized that "all good soldiers are sentimentalists—all good soldiers of [Edward's] type. Their profession, for one thing, is full of the big words— 'courage,' 'loyalty,' 'honor,' 'constancy'." Also "Edward was a great reader—he would pass hours lost in novels of a sentimental type—novels in which typewriter girls married marquises and governesses earls. And in his books, as a rule, the course of true love ran as smooth as buttered honey." This background and attitude accounted for "his intense, optimistic belief that the woman he was making love to at the moment was the one he was destined, at last, to be eternally constant to."

From Dowell's tone it is obvious that he considers Edward's sentimentality a weakness in his private life. Yet from Edward's attitude toward his tenants and his troops, we come to see that it is a virtue in his public life. Thus it is precisely this sentimentality which enables him to send off Nancy at the end of the novel as if he were a character in "a perfectly sad love story" enduring "a hopeless parting." And it is the same quality which determines his suicide after receiving Nancy's sardonic wire at the end of the novel.

> When he saw that I did not intend to interfere with him his eyes became soft and almost affectionate. He remarked:
>
> "So long, old man, I must have a bit of a rest, you know."
>
> I didn't know what to say. I wanted to say: "God bless you," for I am also a sentimentalist.

Ford could have handled Ashburnham's suicide (and indeed the novel as a whole) with the same objectivity which Conrad used to criticize society in *The Secret Agent*. Or he could have shaped the story with less social comment and made a kind of tragedy out of the ending. But he did neither of these things, partly because he was trying to strike a balance between them, holding his characters responsible for their actions on the one hand, and sympathizing with them because the fault is mainly in society, on the other. As Dowell says, "I call this the Saddest Story [the title Ford had originally intended to give the novel] rather than 'The Ashburnham Tragedy,' just because it is so sad, just because there was no current to draw things along to a swift and inevitable end. There is about it no nemesis, no destiny."

This observation, applied to the possibilities for tragic drama or fiction in general during the twentieth century, has become a commonplace in our culture. What we need to remark in particular about it is its similarity, in general attitude toward the relation between individuals and ultimate laws, to a statement Ford himself had made a year earlier in *Henry James.* Asserting the validity of his version of James's favorite theme, Ford had proclaimed that "life really is" a series of "meaningless episodes beneath the shadow of doom." This rather pessimistic summation answers very neatly the pessimistic question which Dowell asks near the end of *The Good Soldier:* "Are all men's lives like the lives of us good people—like the lives of the Ashburnhams, of the Dowells, of the Ruffords—broken, tumultuous, agonized, and unromantic lives, periods punctated by screams, by imbecilities, by deaths, by agonies? Who the devil knows?"

Actually, during the nine years that Dowell moved along happily on the surface of his relations with these people, he alone escaped completely the unromantic agonies of passion (or at least intrigue) in which the others were involved. Thus one of the important ironies in the novel is the twofold one of Dowell's life: while those about him were all in emotional turmoil, he wanted and was able to live calmly; but the moment before he discovered that turmoil it had stopped, and he was left without a chance to use his long-dormant faculty of passion. Dowell as narrator is conscious of this irony. Although he has moved through most of his life understanding only the external events, the appearance of things, as he tells his tale, he is also able to look back on the action with an appreciation of the internal reality of social situations. It is as though he were only understanding the affair himself as he tells his story.

The Good Soldier is, then, a novel presented to the reader from a continually developing point of view. Three fourths of the way through his story, for instance, Dowell says that he has "been writing away . . . now for six months and reflecting longer and longer," so that the reader should not be put out by any sharpened or altered judgments. Although Dowell gives the reader the benefit of a gradually deepening insight into his story, we have seen that he was from the first somewhat aware of the discrepancy between surface and interior reality. The irony which comes from this dual vision, as Schorer has noted, makes "no absolute commitments and can thus enjoy the advantage of many ambiguities of meaning and endless complexities of situation." As this analysis implies, Ford's irony not only influences our reaction to the subject matter, but shapes the tone of the novel as well. Speaking of the novel's stylistic irony, Schorer applauds Ford's "comic genius" in always putting such "rather simpleminded and, at the same time, grotesquely comic metaphors," into the narrator's mouth. It is true that the metaphors are often, if not grotesque, at least incongruous, but the reason is at once more complicated and more important than Schorer would lead us to expect.

In the first place Dowell, like Ford, is an impressionist. This means that he is usually trying to give the reader, not a coldly objective description of what happened, but the action as it appeared to him or as he imagines it appeared to one of the other characters. Schorer himself picks one example of this technique when he refers to Leonora's boxing the ears of Mrs. Maidan, one of her husband's mistresses, and Dowell's comment that she "was just striking the face of an intolerable universe." We may call this heroic exaggeration for comic effect, but unless we see that Dowell is trying to convey something of Leonora's feelings, we shall be unprepared for his second description of the same scene, a description which is exactly the opposite in emphasis. The fact, Dowell tells us, that "Leonora had almost attained to the attitude of a mother towards Mrs. Maidan . . . no doubt partly accounted for the smack in the face. She was hitting a naughty child who had been stealing chocolates at an inopportune moment." These two versions of the same incident are to some extent incompatible. But Dowell does not seem to be aiming at consistency. Rather he appears to be concerned with giving his reader as many possible insights into the affair as he can. Thus he tells us at one point that Leonora's depriving Edward of any possibility of "public service" caused his suicide, while at the end of the novel he makes the loss of Nancy responsible. Obviously both are true. For if Edward could have counted on either a life of public service or the love of Nancy he might have been able to live without the other. Unfortunately, circumstance cuts him off from both.

We may therefore account for Dowell's way of telling his story partly in terms of a conscious (almost philosophic) aim. But we must also consider an artistic necessity which had its influence upon Dowell's style. The actions of *The Good Soldier,* when seen in bare outline, may appear somewhat sensational. As Dowell says at one point, "It is melodrama; but I can't help it." He can help it, however, and does. For by virtue of his method of recounting them, Dowell raises the incidents of the novel from the melodramatic to the almost-classic. This feat is achieved by his continually twisting the reader's attention away from the incident (Edward's committing suicide or Leonora's slapping Mrs. Maidan) and focussing that attention on the implications of an action or the motive behind it.

For instance, when Nancy in her madness says "Shuttlecocks" to no one in particular, the incongruity of the remark short-circuits any real pathos of feeling in us. On the other hand, the word has meaning. For Dowell says he knows "what was passing in her mind"; Leonora had told him that Nancy once "said she felt like a shuttlecock being tossed backwards and forwards between the violent per-

Pastel of Ford by Stella Bowen.

sonalities of Edward and his wife." So actually Dowell's language reveals an attitude which is half comic (when Ford has him speak to keep the story under control) and half serious (when Dowell is allowed to speak in his own character).

Yet even when he is serious, Dowell often speaks for his author. He is not, therefore, simply being fatuous when he makes the Jamesian comment that "the death of a mouse from cancer is the whole sack of Rome by the Goths" and that for him "the breaking up of our little four-square coterie was just such another unthinkable event." Actually, as this quotation shows, Dowell is conscious not only of the drama of his story, but of himself as the narrator of it. And at another point, again speaking for himself and his author, he says,

> I have, I am aware, told this story in a very rambling way. . . . When one discusses an affair—a long, sad affair—one goes back, one goes forward. One remembers points that one has forgotten and one explains them all the more minutely since one recognizes that one has forgotten to mention them in their proper places and that one may have given, by omitting them, a false impression. I console myself with thinking that this is a real story and that, after all, real stories are probably told best in the way a person telling a story would tell them. They will then seem most real.

It was for this reason, Ford reported in *Joseph Conrad* (1924), that he and Conrad accepted the label of Impressionism when it was attached to them at the turn of the century. "We saw," Ford said, "that life did not narrate, but made impressions on our brains. We, in turn, if we wished to produce on you the effect of life must not narrate but render . . . impressions." In *The Good Soldier,* the straight chronology of narration is broken up by means of Dowell's digressions, which lead naturally and easily to shifts in time. The result is that he succeeds in "catching the very note and trick, the strange irregular rhythm of life," as Henry James defined the aim of the art of fiction.

Ford realized, however, that there was more to impressionism than the art which conceals art, the open naturalness at which he was so good. In his study of James he spoke admiringly of a quality which he termed "vibrating reality." In reading James's novels, the mind of the reader vibrates because it must pass "as it does in real life, perpetually backward and forwards between the apparent aspect of things and the essentials of life . . . between the great outlines and the petty details." Which is exactly what happens in *The Good Soldier.* As we have seen, Dowell is forever stepping in and fixing our attention not on the surface events, which are often melodramatic, but on the meaning of those events to their actors, on the several inner realities which he has since realized were present.

At the same time, Dowell is forced to judge the system of conventions under which he has lived. Such a system, he decides, keeps men from finding out much about each other:

> After forty-five years of mixing with one's kind, one ought to have acquired the habit of being able to know something about one's fellow beings. But one doesn't.

> I think the modern civilized habit—the modern English habit—of taking everyone for granted is a good deal to blame for this. . . .
>
> Mind, I am not saying that this is not the most desirable type of life in the world; that it is not an almost unreasonably high standard. . . .
>
> But the inconvenient—well, hang it all, I will say it—the damnable nuisance of the whole thing is, that with all the taking for granted, you never really get an inch deeper than the [external social facts].

Dowell realizes (as Ford had earlier) that the English code of living is admirable, but that it has too little room for man's individuality and instincts. The purpose both of author and narrator is, however, not so much to offer a solution to this problem as to present, as specifically as possible, the dilemma of individuals caught in a too-rigid society. It is understandable, therefore, that Violet Hunt's analysis of Ford's outlook on life at the time he was writing *The Good Soldier* should be so similar to Dowell's attitude in telling that story. Ford, she wrote in *I Have this to Say,* cultivated a "curious *laisser-aller* notion of shrugging off all to the last, so that, until a man lay on his deathbed, shriven and his peace made with God, he did not himself realize what had been his goal, his object in life, his heaviest sorrow, and eke which woman he loved best . . . Life, a series of affairs! And one is left with the last affair on one's hands." Similarly, only at the end of his tale does Dowell finally decide that Leonora should be blamed for losing control and sacrificing Edward and Nancy. On the other hand, Dowell realizes that the feudal code is dead, that Edward cannot live by it in the modern world. He does not, therefore, blame Leonora for remarrying an innocuous rabbit of a fellow and beginning to produce children in the best modern way.

In his book on James, Ford said that the novelist must "give us the very matter upon which we shall build the theories of the new body politic"; this statement not only defined a task which he attempted to carry out in *The Good Soldier,* it also came very close to formulating a relativistic theory of the rules that govern human behavior. On the other hand, we realize that Ford's was an old-fashioned kind of relativism when we remember his reasoning that the reconstruction of political theory is necessary because "the feudal system in its perfection has died out of the world." That is, Ford obviously wished for an ideal code like feudalism and, in his own way, worked to lay the groundwork for one. In 1913 he asserted as a positive goal his belief that "the greatest service any novelist can render the Republic . . . is to draw an unbiassed picture of the world we live in." He had come to believe this partly because his temperament and his experience had forced him to reject the Victorian concept that a man must measure up to his duty with no lapses and no excuses. In writing *The Good Soldier* in 1914, Ford developed his analysis and criticism by emphasizing the discrepancy between ideals and actions, between the values of external appearance and internal reality.

All this is not to say that Ford was writing a political tract in *The Good Soldier;* it deals with the affairs of people who interest us. But it is also a consciously artful novel, not a rousing, straightforward adventure tale. And we have seen that Ford's impressionism tends to shift the focus from the events to their importance to the characters involved. We are therefore naturally led to concentrate our attention on the theme and the abstract meanings which the novel offers covertly through its technique and overtly in Dowell's own analysis. His diffidence in trying to evaluate the events he has witnessed is not the sign so much of his stupidity as of a lack of ready-made solutions to the problems of our time. Because both narrator and author accept the human condition of change and uncertainty, neither will pass final judgment. Ford developed the theme inherent in that condition to create a novel characterized by admirably controlled artistry and compassion. (pp. 494-509)

> *Elliott B. Gose, Jr., "The Strange Irregular Rhythm: An Analysis of 'The Good Soldier',"* in PMLA, *Vol. LXXII, No. 3, June, 1957, pp. 494-509.*

James Hafley   (essay date 1959)

[*Hafley is an American educator and critic. In the following excerpt, he argues that* The Good Soldier *adheres to an essentially Catholic moral viewpoint.*]

No one denies that Ford Madox Ford's *The Good Soldier* is a fine novel: critics who have disagreed about everything else under the sun band together to describe it as one of the best novels of the century. But if it needs no advertising, no defense, *The Good Soldier* nonetheless might profit from the sort of re-examination that would, I think, correct a fairly serious misapprehension that has to do with its meaning, with the affirmation it makes about human experience. Walter Allen, for instance, calls this novel "dazzling, as near perfection as a novel can be," but believes that although "by religion, Ford was a Roman Catholic, . . . one cannot call him a Catholic novelist as Mauriac or Bernanos is. Human life, as Ford reveals it in his novels, is meaningless, and his values are purely stoic" [see excerpt dated 1954]. And Mark Schorer, in his extremely useful interpretation of the book, feels that "finally, *The Good Soldier* describes a world that is without moral point" [see *TCLC,* Vol. 1, pp. 277-78]. . . . Such readers seem to be perilously close to joining John Dowell, the narrator, in his incoherent vision of the significance of his story, by failing to take into account things like the carefully structured religious element in the novel—a novel actually as "Catholic" as any art-work can be said to be, and one in which the narrator's initial ignorance changes not to real awareness but to darker blindness in the light of the moral norm as that is established by Nancy Rufford and Edward Ashburnham. For *The Good Soldier* is a novel about faith, though a reader's faith in its narrator, at any stage, will obscure this fact.

The faith of the "insane" Nancy, who repeats over and over again *"Credo in unum Deum Omnipotentem,"* this simple sanity, appearing in a mad world to be madness, stands at the center of the novel's structure and builds to other acts of faith that reach out in various directions around it: that of "the Ashburnham who accompanied Charles I to the scaffold," of Maisie Maidan, and so forth. Nancy is mad only as Gregor Samsa is an insect in *The Metamorphosis.* Even Dowell, to whom Nancy's Credo "all means nothing . . . it is a picture without a meaning," finally goes by a faith, albeit the wrong one: his "I don't know" is the most important single refrain in the novel, but he himself never recognizes it as such, even though he manages the progression "I don't know; I don't know. . . . Who knows? . . . God knows" in the very first chapter. Verbs of knowing, which contrast with those of feeling and believing, dominate the novel, which is in a sense an epistemological treatise set to art. And Leonora, the villain of the piece, reminds one of another Leonore, called Fidelio, who in Beethoven's opera is an image of the faithful wife, freeing her husband, Florestan, a political victim, from prison; acting on hope rather than knowledge that it is he whom her efforts will liberate: the novel is on one level an ironic foil to *Fidelio,* for here Leonora emprisons her husband, a "victim" of belief in an old-fashioned, feudal way of life; and she acts upon grounds of a sadistic-masochistic hope, rather than any knowledge of her husband's infidelities.

It is vital to notice that Ashburnham can be convicted of only one act of adultery in the course of the novel: the one night he spends with La Dolciquita. He grieves over this mistake, and the other accusations made against him are clearly to be understood as false, false as most other data interpreted for us by Dowell; each such accusation results from either blind or deliberate misinterpretation of evidence. The first supposed sexual indiscretion of Ashburnham, the "Kilsyte case," is by its very name pointed out as innocent enough; it does kill the sight of Leonora and of the narrator, who complains of not having "the seeing eye" as Florence has. In the same way *Florence* is indeed *flourishing,* as are all the sufferers from the heart in this novel; and as a *Hurlbird* she is one of the birdies, the shuttlecocks, sent to and fro in the game of moral badminton played by Leonora and Dowell; Ashburnham, too, is such a bird: Leonora looks at him with the attention "a cat bestows upon a bird"; she watches him "as a fierce cat watches an unconscious pigeon in a roadway." But he has, after all, been guilty of only the one sin which serves both to make him human and to give the vicious world with its prowling lions the thirst for his blood which not all the virtue of his remaining life can satisfy. He has shown himself, however excusably, vulnerable; and the world is free after that to know what it wants about him.

Thus the whole problem of knowledge is linked to that of good-and-evil and innocence: in the photograph of the Powys girls, Leonora stands with her face obscured by the shadow cast from a bough of an apple tree; Edward looks at this picture of her standing beneath the tree of the knowledge of good and evil, and he chooses her for his wife because of what he doesn't know about her. Nancy, whose name means grace, is at first innocent, but finally becomes involved in the experiential arena of the conflict and emerges insanely virtuous, so to speak—she is freed from the struggle with the world and the self after her victory just as Edward is, and his death is a counterpart to her madness. These two examples of detachment are contrasted with the absurd snobbishness of the narrator, carrying about with him the wampum attesting to his ancestors' importance in "Pa.," and finally buying Ashburnham's estate from Leonora: the American millionaire buying out a way of life he never comprehends, a situation basically the same as that which obtains in Waugh's *Handful of Dust,* when Tony Last's estate becomes a kennel for foxes. In dealing with good-and-evil, Dowell—who of course never does do well—cannot find significance in manners because he fails to understand them as objective equivalents for states of moral sensibility, and regards them instead as ends in themselves.

> Permanence? Stability! I can't believe it's gone. I can't believe that that long, tranquil life, which was just stepping a minuet, vanished in four crashing days at the end of nine years and six weeks. . . . You can't kill a minuet de la cour. . . . The mob may sack Versailles; the Trianon may fall, but surely the minuet—the minuet itself is dancing itself away into the furthest stars, even as our minuet of the Hessian bathing places must be stepping itself still. Isn't there any heaven where old beautiful dances, old beautiful intimacies prolong themselves?

The novel form is the perfect one for exposing this man whose consciousness is totally divorced from conduct, whose conduct is never informed with consciousness, and who therefore feels himself betrayed by what are to him simply "appearances." Thus, verbs of acting are important in two senses in the novel: for Leonora and Dowell, to act is to pretend; for Ashburnham, Nancy, and even Florence, to act is to do; rich ironic plays are made on the resulting ambiguities; for instance, Dowell deplores what he calls "the endless acting," and whereas he is consciously deploring pretence he is subconsciously regretting the need for doing. Social ritual is for him at once reality and only illusion, all and nothing at all, whereas for Edward it has been—what it is as well for the conservative novelist like Jane Austen and Ford—an articulation of moral direction.

Now the specifically religious dimension enforces the good-and-evil theme ("What does one know and why is one here?" Dowell asks early in the action) with quite orthodox methods. Leonora, who finally leaves the Church altogether, is the bad Catholic on this level; as such she is poised against both Maisie Maidan, an innocent who dies in embryo, and Nancy Rufford, an innocent who lives and achieves virtue. These three are all Irish, and all, indeed, from the same convent. Florence, on the other hand, is the good Protestant; Dowell—who from time to time waxes sentimental about being "an old-fashioned Philadelphia Quaker," but who would like to marry the Catholic Nancy in an Anglican service because Anglicanism is the fashionable religion of his set—is the bad Protestant. Ashburnham, the good soldier himself, has his story told us by the bad Protestant, but is actually involved with the good Catholic (Nancy) and the bad one whom he has married. He had wished to become a Catholic, but Leonora paid no attention to his interest, and scoffed at his plan to build a chapel (at once indicative of his love for her and his respect for her religion) as wasteful of money. Leonora, like Dowell, loves money; her taking over of Edward's accounts is both impertinent and, as we discover later, unnecessary, since his duties—known to her as his extravagances—would not have caused them any financial difficulties.

The central scene in the novel, as far as this religious motif is concerned, is that in which Leonora secretly looks into Edward's room and sees him

> kneeling beside his bed with his head hidden in the counterpane. His arms, outstretched, held out before him a little image of the blessed virgin—a tawdry, scarlet and Prussian-blue affair that the girl had given him on her first return from the convent.

His shoulders heaved convulsively three times, and heavy sobs came from him before she could close the door. He was not a Catholic; but that was the way it took him.

Leonora slept for the first time that night with a sleep from which she never once started.

Leonora's initial reaction to this baptism by desire, which one gathers from that phrase "before she could close the door," is even more arresting than the callous "that was the way it took him" thrown off by Dowell, who truly believes what Leonora only wants to believe—that Edward's plight is merely a sexual frustration. Here, as in his total life, Ashburnham is trying desperately to live according to a set of values from which he has been tragically alienated: time and the modern world have made his efforts to operate in terms of his ancestors' traditions appear grotesque; the sympathetic, thoughtful landlord, the man careful enough with money to have told Dowell that he "could buy [his] special shade of blue ties cheaper from a firm in Burlington Arcade than from [his] own people in New York"; the man so generously concerned for unhappiness—so medieval in his attempts to protect women, especially, from suffering—this soldier is defined by contemporary standards as a sentimental spendthrift lecher, and he in turn defines those standards, the standards of Leonora and Dowell, as unthinkably vulgar. But just as he is alienated from his own past by the valueless present, so also he is alien to the Catholic tradition which Nancy's behavior dramatizes as a norm, and subject to the machinations of a wife who herself symbolizes all that is unthinkable in the modern world, not least its opportunistic hypocrisy; his attempts to understand Leonora, whom he has genuinely loved, are interpreted as successive acts of adultery.

If Leonora, whom one must ultimately call a murderess, is the center of evil, poor Dowell (who does his share of calling the others "poor") manages a neutral gray existence too insubstantial and debilitated for good or evil, similar to that of Conrad's "pilgrims" in *Heart of Darkness*. It is very difficult to agree with Mark Schorer that at the end of his experiences Dowell has a "new knowledge of an exposed reality." For though Dowell is a hypocrite, who tells us how bad his memory is, then shows us that it is bad only where Florence is involved, and that otherwise he can reproduce a detailed close-up easily enough; and though he is a liar, who in one breath despises and in another adores Ashburnham and Nancy, he is never consciously either liar or hypocrite, one gathers; Dowell's moral ugliness is simply another part of the vast ocean he sums up with "I don't know," cozily certain that he knows enough. But, like Leonora, he finally knows only enough to allow him to live comfortably, not enough to cause him heart trouble and suffering; he is not one of the blessed. His sad deficiencies are laid bare in his remark about Florence's Uncle John: "He wasn't obtrusive about his heart. You wouldn't have known he had one." Dowell has "drifted" before his marriage to Florence, yet he complains bitterly that her illness has been responsible for his drifting afterwards; "the laziest man in Philadelphia" is miserable at having to act as "a male sick nurse"; and the man who complains that Europe has been forced upon him keeps his wife a virtual prisoner there. "Heaven knows I was never an untidy man," he manages; then, just two pages later, "It occurs to me that some way back I

began a sentence that I have never finished." It is the sentence of his life, and it remains unfinished for want of a verb. His favorite word is "safe," and he is thus rather daunted by the "gambling" of both Edward and Leonora; he believes that "the whole world ought to be arranged so as to ensure the keeping alive of heart patients," but this is because he understands by the word "passion"—and his is "a tale of passion"—not suffering but only lust. Finally, and devastatingly, he asks for "the liberty of a free American citizen to think what I please" (it is the same liberty asked for by Leonora in freeing herself from the dogma of her Church), and one realizes that his inability even to consummate his marriage emphasizes the moral gap between him and Florence: she, with a heart, has descended from a family that had owned Branshaw Teleragh two centuries before the first Ashburnham's arrival there; heart trouble "runs in families," she says; Dowell, without a heart, can only pay cash for Branshaw Teleragh after the last Ashburnham's departure. "I cannot," he informs us but hardly needs to, "I cannot tell an etching from a photographic reproduction."

Yet if Leonora strikes us as intelligent in relation to Dowell, she is in turn to be measured by Nancy. Leonora demands of Dowell in Part One, "Don't you see what's going on?" In the same way Nancy asks Leonora towards the end, "Why are you all in the dark?" Dowell simply asks, talking of Edward, "Good God, what did they all see in him?" While Edward is inventing an army stirrup (when it is successful, Leonora is furious that he gives it to the War Office without being paid for it), and using Florence as a means of trying to return to amicable relations with Leonora, Leonora herself is inventing the fantastic stirrup that allows her to restrain Edward at the cost of her self-respect, her religion, and her soul. Yet Leonora is the epitome of modern sanity, and, after selling her husband's past, she "survives, the perfectly normal type, married to a man [Rodney Bayham] who is rather like a rabbit." This passage harks back to Leonora's "Edward has been dead only ten days and yet there are rabbits on the lawn," itself a neat image of the destruction of largesse by the inconsequential. And the narrator echoes it still later: "Yes, society must go on; it must breed, like rabbits."

One is at first, as a matter of fact, almost prepared to applaud Dowell's concluding remarks; but one recalls two things: first, that he is himself now "an American millionaire, who has bought one of the ancient haunts of English peace" though "even now I do not understand the technicalities of English life," so that his comprehension of Edward is still as unknowing as his sense of Nancy ("I am not, unfortunately, up in the Catholic hagiology"); second, that Ford has had Dowell remark at the turning point of the novel that "it is as if one had a dual personality, the one I being entirely unconscious of the other." If his "mysterious and unconscious self"—the self that might have a heart—attains to certain judgments at the end of the novel, Dowell's conscious self remains vulgar as ever in its failure to discover them. Leonora wears always at her wrist a tiny golden key to a dispatch box; "perhaps," says Dowell, "it was that in which she locked up her heart and her feelings"; but Dowell's consciousness carries no key; there is no such box for him. Leonora can see straight through Dowell, but it requires Nancy to see through Leonora.

Nancy's attitude is paradoxical; she manages a capacity for almost simultaneous seriousness and silliness, that gives her a great advantage in a shattered world: she can cross bridges that Ashburnham only dreams of and Leonora has burned, to reach worlds totally unattainable by the others. "At one moment she would be talking of the lives of the saints and at the next she would be tumbling all over the lawn with the St. Bernard puppy." She has the advantage, at first, of being a child and innocent. Dowell attributes her resiliency to her Catholicism, then admits that "it positively frightened me. I suppose that I was almost afraid to be in a world where there could be so fine a standard." A standard, that is to say, which allows for instant and complete dismissal of the world itself, "saturnalia that can end in a moment, like the crack of a whip." Loyalty to tradition, collectivism instead of individualism as the narrator elsewhere puts it, is what Nancy has in common with Ashburnham; but her tradition is still alive and functioning for her, whereas he stands at the very end of his, or better still beneath it and attempting to bear its great weight entirely on his shoulders. However they both— exactly like Christopher Tietjens of *Parade's End*— operate on the assumption that "salvation can only be found in true love and the feudal system," and consequently they both find, in their different ways, that paradoxical salvation from the world and the self. Appropriately, Edward is ultimately led by the child; for Nancy "felt as if Edward's love were a precious lamb that she was bearing away from a cruel and predatory beast." Each escapes the lion, Leonora, by losing himself in concern for the other's safety; and each achieves safety, the "foursquare" security for which Dowell has ludicrously longed throughout his life as he drifted in his prison of selfconscious heartlessness, searching for a "terrestrial paradise."

Perhaps one may fancy Dowell as gaining some satisfaction from the consolations of the "silent listener" to whom he addresses his tale; the careful reader can console him not at all. Even the fact that the events are not ordered chronologically should not, I suspect, lure one into facile acceptance of Dowell's own explanation that the order is associational; behind his order there is Ford's, and this again leads into the epistemological area explored by the novel. Upon a first reading, one responds to each of the novel's four parts by valuating the chief characters; the data in each part are selected to compose one possible response, until finally, in view of all the data, one's response is correctly enlarged and unified as the inevitable valuation. Thus, by the end of Part One there have been revealed facts which lead the reader to suppose that Edward and Florence are good, that Leonora is evil, and that Dowell is neither, incapable of either evil or good. This is generally correct; but by the end of Part Two, in view of the selection of facts there given him, the reader must decide that Florence is evil, that Leonora is good and possibly Edward, and that Dowell is good; Part Three composes a set of facts establishing Leonora and Dowell as evil, Edward as supremely good, and Florence as, at most, pitiable; finally, Edward becomes heroic, Leonora the villain, Florence irrelevant and Dowell ignorant. Part One ends with Mrs. Maidan's death; Part Two with Florence's; Part Three with one's sense of Leonora as Edward's murderess; and of course Part Four with Edward's death itself. In Part Three Nancy has begun to define the narrator as morally inert as well as stupid, and Leonora as the bad

Catholic. Dowell's own anti-Catholicism increases in this part to counterpoise the good Catholicism of Nancy, the moral norm, and the bad Catholicism and excommunication of Leonora. Thus, the hairpin curves that would have to be used to describe the reader's "knowledge" at any point in the novel parallel those descriptive of Dowell's: the reader's own experience of the novel dramatizes its theory of knowing-versus-believing in a manner not unsimilar to that used in Conrad's novel of the same year, *Victory*, also concerned with "fact" versus feeling, head versus heart, faith and charity versus knowledge and judgment.

Talking at one point about Edward, Dowell tells us that it was "as if the very words that he spoke, without knowing that he spoke them, created the passion as they went along. Before he spoke there was nothing; afterwards, it was the integral fact of his life." The narrator follows this with "Well, I must get back to my story"; but it is his own story that he has just then unknowingly described. In this rich story each sentence deserves to be savored; nothing less than a phrase-by-phrase analysis could do full justice to its delicate complexities—the wonderful series of puns on the key words *know, act, heart, passion,* for instance, and the ambiguities of the restraint-freedom tension, carefully controlled as those in the novels of Jane Austen or the poems of George Herbert. This brief account of the novel has succeeded if it has done no more than suggest that the world of *The Good Soldier,* far from being a moral vacuum or one in which only stoical confrontation of *nada* is possible, is instead a world as surprisingly traditional, as orthodox in its values and meanings, as any to be found in modern fiction. (pp. 121-28)

> *James Hafley, "The Moral Structure of 'The Good Soldier'," in* Modern Fiction Studies, *Vol. V, No. 2, Summer, 1959, pp. 121-28.*

Richard A. Cassell   (essay date 1961)

[*Cassell is an American educator and critic whose* Ford Madox Ford: A Study of Novels *is the first book-length critical examination of Ford's writings. In the following excerpt from this work, Cassell discusses a major theme of* The Good Soldier *and Ford's strategy in choosing Dowell to narrate the story.*]

More than any novel of Ford's written before it, *The Good Soldier* penetrates the social, moral, and psychological tensions working beneath the restraints of refinement imposed by the conventional behavior of the best people. This novel, in showing how social convention and communication allow for no public show of private emotion, is similar to *A Call,* but it penetrates more deeply and pessimistically the social dilemma of the leisured class. The protagonist and several characters in *A Call* are members of London society " 'going fanti,' running amuck through the laws of public opinion," as Ford had earlier described their life in *England and the English.* "In the body politic they do not 'count,' " Ford had also written in that lengthy essay, which serves for him almost as a writer's notebook:

> they are a shade more hopeless than the very poor, they will run their course towards ruin, physical decay, or towards that period of life when ginger

being no longer hot in a mouth that has lost all savours, they will become aged devotees and perhaps make for edification.

The Ashburnhams are not members of London society but of the landed gentry who, when not at their estates, spend their time on the Continent, in India, or traveling. They have diligently maintained in public the traditional controls over behavior, the pride, the reserve, "the saving touch of insolence that seems to be necessary." It might have been better if they had gone "fanti," for "the extraordinarily safe castle" they seem to be has crumbled from within, being destroyed by the release of the invading passions. "It was a most amazing business," Dowell says at one point, "and I think that it would have been better in the eyes of God if they had all attempted to gouge out each other's eyes with carving knives. But they were 'good people.' " The gentry compose a class who do "count" in the body politic, or, rather, they had "counted" before they had given over their sense of responsibility to a mere show of respectability to lead "normal, virtuous and slightly deceitful" lives.

The social restraints are paralyzing; eventually the tensions demand release. And when tensions are released, emotions go out of control and moral barriers collapse. The Ashburnhams and the Dowells are both victims and agents in a moral wasteland created by the release of sexual passions against the fortress of social manners, the calm respectable citadel. These people are forced to face the discovery that their lives lack any center of moral belief or action. Deceit, subterfuge, jealousy, and pimping are the chaotic devices to which they have to resort in order to keep up appearances. The consequences are loneliness, insanity, suicide.

Relentless in her pursuit of conformity, Leonora will do almost anything to possess her husband body and soul and to bring her marriage within the limits set by her narrow Irish Catholicism. Her view is that life is "a perpetual sex-battle between husbands who desire to be unfaithful to their wives, and wives who desire to recapture their husbands in the end." Willing to allow men their "rutting seasons," she expects that they eventually will settle down in the arms of their patient wives. Leonora is so instructed by the Mother Superior to whom she turns after Ashburnham's disastrous affair with the Spanish dancer. She is told: "Men are like that. By the blessing of God it will all come right in the end." She cannot wait; with a masculine determination she manages her husband's estate and love affairs, and hence destroys what she most wants to have and moves toward her own mental and moral collapse. In her final frustration and despair she forces Nancy on Ashburnham, an action which is a true measure of her misunderstanding of his sense of moral honor. She breaks away from the restraints of her religion, and, as Dowell writes, acts "along the lines of her instinctive desires." But these are not simple, for her ambivalent emotions have reached a crisis. Love, hate, pity, respect for Ashburnham tear her apart. While she desperately hopes this is his last affair, she knows it is a true passion, and though she is certain Ashburnham will not touch Nancy, she is aware that she has lost him for good. When the innocent, idealistic girl assures her that she and Ashburnham are soul mates, Leonora reveals Ashburnham's infidelities and extravagances, and both women, acting along the lines "of the sex instinct that makes women be intolerably cruel to the beloved person," force Ashburnham into a frightful moral crisis.

Florence had earlier done her part in destroying Ashburnham, but without even the excuse of Leonora's sincere passions, for Florence is an absolute materialist for whom emotions and sex are weapons needed to acquire the luxury and prestige of being the wife of a British landed gentleman. Essentially she is sexless, a condition Ford, oddly enough, saw all Americans as trying to attain. Dowell himself is the sexless American male, incapable of passion. Since his sudden realization that he is in love with Nancy is merely a partial release of frustrated emotion, he is actually more in love with love than with her. Blind to the feelings of others and lacking clear or useful moral yardsticks, he seeks recourse in self-pity and in emulation of the tortured Ashburnham.

Although foolish and sentimental through several adulterous affairs, Ashburnham is the only one able to meet a real moral test. He is the victim of the three women who surround him and of sheer bad luck. The Rodney Bayhams can keep a mistress quietly in Portsmouth and manage their estates economically, but Ashburnham must pick a prudish nursemaid, a mercenary courtesan, a woman with a blackmailing husband, a coldly ambitious woman, and finally his own ward, who has been brought up almost as a daughter. He is equally a victim of his own generous emotions and of his sentimental view of life, inspired by traditional schoolboy and military aphorisms of British honor and by sentimental fiction, where true love, once found, is eternal. Dowell, studying Ashburnham, comes to realize that the male passion is for tenderness, understanding, someone to talk to, and for identity with the woman loved, and that ultimately "for every man there comes at last a time of life when the woman who then sets her seal upon his imagination has set her seal for good." This Nancy does and without a word from Ashburnham. In one of those unconscious outbursts which occur frequently in the novel, he lets slip to Leonora that he will be satisfied if Nancy still loves him when she is five thousand miles away. When he is brought to doubt that she does, and when Leonora threatens to take over his bank account again after he has paid £200 to save a gardener's daughter from charges of killing her child, he has no resources or reasons left for living. His refusal of Nancy is a victory for the generous emotions over the selfish ones; his suicide is a victory for the moral anarchy of individual passions over the collective passions directed toward the order and well-being of the body politic. He is the last of a tradition. (pp. 153-57)

And yet the victory and the defeat are not so simple as I suggest. As Dowell reminds us, Ashburnham, by insisting that Nancy be sent away, acts conventionally: ". . . . it was in tune with the tradition of Edward's house. I dare say it worked out for the greatest good of the body politic." Leonora could have managed the girl's departure earlier and thus taken "the decent line," but since the return to Branshaw House "poor Leonora was incapable of taking any line whatever," acting irrationally as she shifted between pity and loathing for her husband. The decent line is the conventional one, but, ironically, convention will not allow for passion. Leonora ultimately sacrifices the conventional line to indulge the contrarieties of her passions; Ashburnham sacrifices his passion to the conventional line. The conventional line which determines social behavior, or appearance, is thus a reality, and as much a reality as the private passions that tend to destroy that line, unless those passions are controlled or sacrificed.

Ford exploits the ironies inherent in the psychological conflicts between the passions and the conventional line. *The Good Soldier* is literally his study of the heart of darkness encased within the calm surfaces of leisured upperclass manners. One of its principal themes is the "dark forest which is the heart of another." Florence, her uncle, Ashburnham, and Maisie Maidan supposedly suffer from bad hearts, but Maisie is the only one to die of a heart attack. Mr. Hurlbird goes through life thinking he has heart trouble, but he dies of bronchitis. Florence, using the ailment as a tactic in her campaign to achieve a European establishment, is essentially heartless. Ashburnham's heart is Leonora's deception, giving them a reason to stay in Nauheim several months a year, where living is relatively inexpensive. But he does suffer from an excess of heart, of too much sympathetic concern for others. The cold Leonora, once her heart shows itself, is torn between love and hatred. Ford fully explores the motivations of the heart. "I know nothing—nothing in the world—of the hearts of men," Dowell says early in the first chapter. And it is true; even after everything has been revealed to him and he has written the record of the affair, the secrets of the heart are still a darkness. Passion, generosity, deceit, disease, chivalry, innocence, sterility, craven sensuality— all are part of the undecipherable language of the heart.

Passion *versus* paralysis is the keynote of the struggle. The Ashburnhams are sexual innocents whose marriage had been arranged by their parents. Leonora, then only eighteen, "had been handed over to him, like some patient mediaeval virgin." Until a couple of years later, neither knew how babies are produced. Leonora was a Catholic born into a small, impoverished, land-owning family. Her convent had shielded her from thoughts of sex and had never bothered to explain the realities of adultery and sexual jealousies, and her family had shown her the necessity of maintaining a niggardly economy and respectability. Nancy comes out of the same convent and we are to see in the latter part of the book her suffering the shock of sexual discovery. Ashburnham, though equally innocent, is an Anglican of the feudal aristocracy with wealth, though not great wealth, and with an idealized conception of woman's character and function. He and Leonora are fatefully mismated. It is to be expected that Ashburnham, finding her cold, would turn to mysterious women with a past, or motherly women, or even to a flighty but dazzling woman like Florence; and it is to be expected that Leonora, finding him extravagant and sanguine, would seek to recoup his fortunes and direct his love affairs. But through it all, except for her rantings against his extravagance after the discovery of each new infidelity, they never talk of intimate matters and barely converse at all. Outside of expressions of remorse, Ashburnham remains silent, ignorant of how much she really knows. Their sexual life is paralyzed; their bedroom doors are always locked to each other, but Leonora blames their childlessness on the will of God. Actually, of the foursome, Florence is the only sexual initiate before marriage, but her union with Dowell is never consummated. She acquires her "heart" the first day of their honeymoon voyage to Europe, forcing Dowell to become the "sedulous nurse" from the very beginning. Although

Florence talks incessantly, she and Dowell also seldom speak to each other. Occasionally she throws him a coquettish glance to baffle him.

What should have happened to these people? In the depth of his bitterness against Florence, Dowell relates a recurrent dream of his, a "vision of judgment." Three figures stand, suspended in air, upon an immense plain, which is the "hand of God." Ashburnham and Nancy are embracing; Florence stands alone; Dowell feels the urge to help her, though he hates her "with the hatred of the adder." Leonora does not appear, but he imagines that she "will burn, clear and serene, a northern light and one of the archangels of God." He, himself, perhaps, will be given an elevator to run. This vision is not only a key to Dowell's self-deprecatory, almost masochistic temperament, but also the clearest clue to the ideal truth of the matter: Ashburnham should have been allowed Nancy, Florence should be alone, Dowell should seek to comfort her, and Leonora should be a devoted angelic manager. The vision belittles the human struggle for social, moral, and psychological equanimity by its denial of the realization of human hopes. Dowell laments near the finish of his memoirs that no one got what he wanted. "It is a queer and fantastic world. Why can't people have what they want? The things were all there to content everybody; yet everybody has the wrong thing. Perhaps you can make head or tail of it; it is beyond me." The reader is likely to feel at this point (Dowell has just declared himself in his unconscious desires as a faint follower of Ashburnham) that they are five ignorant fools hounded by bad luck but almost deserving what they get. But upon reflection one realizes there are still too many darknesses, a fact which Dowell constantly emphasizes by his questions. One illuminating fact does become evident, however. The world has been taken over by the emotionally and morally incompetent who relentlessly pursue respectability and conformity without the saving graces of honor and sympathy. Ford does not want to suggest a remedy but only to paint a picture, to leave a record. But it is clear that he is saying here what he has said often elsewhere: the best of England's past has been lost or, rather, has been driven out by a strident individualism governed by expediency rather than principle.

The Good Soldier is to Ford's fiction what *Madame Bovary* is to Flaubert's. It is Ford's record of wasted lives torn between dreams and what the world offers in their place. His upper class "good people" are as thoroughly dissected as Flaubert's middle class. Both novelists utilize limited centers of consciousness which must without faltering give us the intended impression of life or, at least, lead us to it. Both relentlessly pursue the horrors of their subjects; both retain a measure of affection for their protagonists. One significant difference is that while Flaubert's irony tends to dissipate into anger at life itself, as James perceived, Ford's leaves us in a mood of grim humor, bemused and suspended between pity, shock, and despair. Ford, unlike Flaubert, is writing comedy, although, like Flaubert, he sees the tragedy in the lives of the devoutly conventional. Ford's single reflector is not the main character, while Emma, Flaubert's primary reflector, is. Ford, as storyteller, places himself at one further remove from both his protagonist and his reader than Flaubert did and manages to achieve levels and shades of irony not open to Flaubert.

Considering the Ashburnham affair, with Dowell relegated to his proper minor role, the story is close to being a domestic tragedy relating the disintegration of two upper class families, one British, one American. To the extent that society is indicted, the story is a social tragedy, a catastrophe resulting from the inherent weaknesses and inhumanity of a debilitated society. Ultimately the domestic tragedy is illustrative of the social tragedy. The characters are not, however, merely types who serve to point up society's shortcomings; they are rather highly particularized individuals who because of environmental conditioning, certain strokes of bad luck, and the nature of their own temperaments are brought to their inevitable end.

Even though the Ashburnham affair evokes tragic implications, we are never allowed to react to the story with the emotions usually accompanying a tragedy of the classical type. Ford's technique of telling the story through the opaque eyes of a naive, bewildered, myopic, fatalistic American who slowly and painfully reveals the horrors to which until recently he had been an unseeing witness moves the story into the realm of the comic and ironic. The irony of allowing Dowell to tell the story he seems least qualified to tell must have suggested to Ford the value of such a narrator to make us see and feel the ironies inherent in the story. As Mark Schorer says: "Irony, which makes no absolute commitments and can thus enjoy the advantage of many ambiguities of meaning and endless complexities of situation, is at the same time an evaluative mood, and, in a master, a sharp one." [see *TCLC*, Vol. 1, pp. 277-78] The intricacies of the manner, the narrative point of view, the time-shifts, the language . . . , heighten the sense of the ridiculous and the grotesque and permit the fullest ironic exploitation of the situation. The reader is never to be satisfied with a simple interpretation or a single emotion. Ashburnham has several of the endearing qualities of Ford's gentleman of honor, but even his sacrifice of Nancy, which would ennoble him in a less distorted account, as James for instance might write, is largely vitiated by our view of him as a man who muddles through life, who seeks self-indulgent solace from several adulterous attachments, and whose sentimental innocence prevents him from telling his wife of his affairs for fear of sullying the virginity of her thoughts. And yet Ashburnham is the most worthwhile character in the whole novel. One wishes for him better luck than he has. Surprisingly enough, the reader's final view of him approaches Dowell's, although it is certainly difficult to see him as one of "the ancient Greek damned."

The novel eludes precise classification. In one sense it is a satire because it does, at least by implication, hold up to ridicule prevailing vices and follies, but unlike satire it does not have as its end the improvement of humanity or its institutions. There is literally at the end no hope of improvement, for Ashburnham and what he represents are dead. The emphasis is not so much upon depicting the amusing or ridiculous behavior of stereotyped characters, as in the comedy of manners, as it is upon seeking out the innermost emotions and motives of highly particularized people trying to live in a conventional world, which they ultimately illuminate and condemn by virtue of being the kind of people they are. So considered, the novel is closer in type to high comedy. It deals, first of all, with upper class life, but, more tellingly, it treats of its subject with a remarkable authorial detachment, evoking thoughtful if somewhat despairing laughter and a sense of tragic undertones, while constantly demanding the intellectual attention of the reader. "The world," Horace Walpole says in his famous adage, "is a comedy to those that think, a tragedy to those who feel." In this novel the characters feel more than they think; Ford thinks (primarily in his carefully worked out, intellectualized methods) as much as he feels. The result is an ironic view of life, of a world in which appearances hide a frightful reality and in which reality has too many faces.

Electing to tell the story through Dowell's eyes, Ford chose about the weakest of all possible vessels. . . . Ford's choice . . . was derived from his realization that using a morally complacent narrator with several shortcomings of insight was the best means of revealing the moral chaos of the affair he had in mind. Because Ford is not handling "middling experience," or attempting to give a simple view, he needs the advantages which his indirect, fragmentary, ironic method can give. (pp. 157-65)

Dowell is used to help clarify the action he narrates but in a special and indirect way. . . . [Ford] has Dowell force himself on us with all the irritating ways of an egotistic, sentimental, overtalkative gossip. Dowell startles us into attention, causing us to protest and to seek the balance of other interpretations. Our sense of superiority to him excites us to discover the truth. (p. 166)

Ford . . . achieves both humor and irony by such means as the time-shift, a careful ordering of the action for *progression d'effet,* and imagery. In addition, he makes his narrator disarmingly honest and capable of reporting action. Dowell records rather faithfully the physical details of places, speeches, and actions. By his being so thorough we get a truer picture than perhaps would be available from someone who felt he had things to hide, as, for example, Leonora would have. As a leisured American of good family living on the Continent, he is acutely sensitive to the customs and behavior of upper class society in the capitals and watering spots. Although no scene is fully reported or dramatized without the intervening comments or thoughts of Dowell, the novel none the less achieves the intensity of drama because the consciousness of the narrator is so limited, so full of self-justifications and distorted half-truths, and because the points of view of others are diligently reported. The implications of what it all means are left almost totally up to the reader.

It is in this way that *The Good Soldier* is dramatic in method. . . . In effect Dowell's consciousness is dramatized. He tells us everything we need to know; his reportings, his analyses are themselves dramatic events. His view, as Mark Schorer realizes, is not always the wrong one; it is "merely *a* view."

Elliott B. Gose, Jr. is right when he says that our evaluation of the excellence of *The Good Soldier* "depends on our reaction to the novel, and this in turn rests on our reaction to Dowell" [see excerpt dated 1957]. He sets Dreiser's view that Dowell is merely Ford's mouthpiece [see *TCLC*, Vol. 15, pp. 70-1] against Schorer's description of the narrator as a "weak and passionless self-deceiver." He himself takes a middle position, seeing Dowell "as an essentially honest if not very passionate person whose attitude toward the characters and events with which he deals is in constant evolution as the novel progresses." He adds that "we will find that the two [Dowell and Ford] make essentially the same evaluation of life." Dreiser's view is inadequate, Gose's seems to me to contain an error of emphasis, Schorer's to be more nearly the best reading. For Dowell is used both to make *and* render Ford's evaluation of the affair and, through it, of life. It is true that Dowell is not totally blind, for he is capable of insights, and some are Ford's, but he is at the same time (another certainly intentional irony) a living illustration of those insights. Given Dowell's innocence, his insights are hindsights, but hindsights are not always useless. With all of his pitiful self-glorification in identifying himself with Ashburnham as one of "the passionate, of the headstrong, and the too-truthful," with all of his self-indulgent bitterness, he none the less is competent to present Ford's analysis of society, of the anomalies of the good people in the present commercial age, although he cannot discover the reaches of the human heart or the secrets of human motivation. But neither can the others. Together, all their views point to Ford's conviction that humanity works at cross purposes with itself, that the heart is infinitely complex, and that it is not for one to know the heart of another, or even his own.

Such ignorance of the heart, as he says in **Women and Men,** leads a woman to say when a man irritates her: "What can you expect? He is a man." And when a woman irritates a man, he can only say, "What can you expect? She is a woman." The truth, Ford adds here, is that "actually since God made us all and the world is a trying place we are most of us poor people trying to make the best of a bad job." The muddle is caused by conflicts of the male and female point of view; the "abstract male" a woman chooses will be determined by the qualities ascribed to her father by her mother, and the male will have been brought up to believe in the inferiority of women. Quite literally, only unutterable confusion can result when such ideals face realities. All the characters in **The Good Soldier** are limited by the boundaries of their passions and insights— all differing, each shifting, but never coalescing. When these people are set against each other, the battle lines are drawn.

Using Dowell as the chronicler of the affair is one of the central ironies in **The Good Soldier.** To register his moral protest and yet to disappear, Ford needs a narrator who lacks strict moral preconceptions, who is, in fact, without narrow moral blinders which might prevent him from seeing or representing the view in contexts other than his own. During the act of reminiscence, collecting memories, making continuous, tentative, shifting judgments and analyses, Dowell comes to see that there was no excuse for what Florence did, that Leonora was wrong in what she did to reclaim Edward, and that Edward could not help what he did. Except possibly for Florence, he can see why they did what they did. But what should Leonora have done? At one point he says she should have let Ashburnham become a gentlemanly bum married to a drunken barmaid who would cause scenes in public. In another place he says Leonora should have shared Edward with Florence "until the time came for jerking that poor cuckoo out of the nest." He admits he would have pimped for Florence with Jimmy (as he probably later would have with Ashburnham) if he had known and had been convinced it was a true passion, for true passion transcends moral restrictions.

His fond *if's* and *should's* establish Dowell's moral confusions at the same time that they point to the only conditions for passion possible in contemporary life. For Dowell appears to be Ford's representative not only of the contemporary American but also of one predominant contemporary point of view, which can best be described as a moral relativism approaching inertia. He is a creature of fragments who lacks a view of life as a whole and who finds solace in both self-effacement and self-glorification and in a kind of self-indulgent loneliness. As an American from one of the first English Philadelphia families, he has ancestral longings for the feudal life, hence the appeal of Ashburnham, but as a leisured American who does nothing, not even manage his own affairs, he lacks the ballast of tradition and the duties it imposes, a ballast which Ashburnham possesses until even that is stolen from him. It seems that it is only out of Dowell's inertia and the detachment which it gives him, even in the midst of his pain and distorted self-analysis, that he is able to see as much and to paint as accurate a picture as he does. On the other hand, he cannot be the true representative of the Ashburnham tradition, nor is he, except in the most amorphous way, identifiable with Ashburnham; he is perhaps the last ironic heir of that tradition, a symbol of the directionless, sentimental, self-centered despair that has taken over.

Along with Leonora, Florence and Nancy, Dowell has lost the simplicity and clarity of moral purpose characteristic of the Ashburnham tradition. They are all representatives of the age of doubt about which Dionissia speaks in **Ladies Whose Bright Eyes** (1935 edition), and they have failed to reclaim the faith necessary to achieve an honorable contentment. In fact, among them, in destroying Ashburnham, they have destroyed the generous sentiments, the only basis of that renewal of faith. They suffer "broken, tumultuous, agonized, and unromantic lives, periods punctuated by screams, by imbecilities, by deaths, by agonies," a characteristic exaggeration by Dowell of the view of life Ford ascribed to James: "a series of [. . .] meaningless episodes beneath a shadow of doom." It is a declaration of the wasteland of the elders of Eliot's and Hemingway's lost generation.

There are three apparent breakdowns in the narrative point of view, but only one materially affects the total impression. Ford has the difficult problem of getting into Nancy's consciousness so that we can see her Catholic innocence faced with the shock of her first realization of the facts of divorce and of the unhappiness of the Ashburnhams, with her agonized discovery of love, and, finally, with her awareness that she is in love with Ashburnham and he with her. Almost every instance of a revelation of her consciousness breaks the narrative illusion. We are told that one night she drank a wine glass full of whisky and then "dragged her tall height up to her room and lay in the dark," where "she gave way to the thought that she was in Edward's arms, that he was kissing her on the face." It seems incredible that Nancy would ever tell this to Leonora in their long, agonized talks together. It does not seem likely either that she would tell Leonora that she saw her as becoming "pinched, shriveled, blue with cold, shivering, suppliant," or as a "hungry dog, trying to spring up at a lamb that she was carrying." It is equally difficult to conceive of these omniscient intrusions as coming only from Dowell's imaginative reconstruction of what must have happened, unless we consider them as his sentimental elaborations. [The critic adds in a footnote: "The other two apparent violations of the point of view must also be seen as Dowell's fanciful reconstruction of what might have happened. He tells us during the scene when Leonora boxes Maisie Maidan's ears that Maisie had gone to Ashburnham's room, after he had left, to return a case of scissors. 'She could not see why she should not, though she felt a certain remorse at the thought that she had kissed the pillows of his bed. That was the way it took her.' How does Dowell know this? Maisie writes in her last note to Leonora: 'You never talked to me about me and Edward, but I trusted you.' It is not the kind of thing Maisie would tell Leonora anyway. Later, . . . Dowell reports Ashburnham's thoughts on Nancy's telegram ('He thought she only pretended to hate him in order to save her face and he thought that her quite atrocious telegram from Brindisi was only another attempt to do that . . . '), but as he reports the arrival of the telegram and Ashburnham's quietly removing the penknife from his pocket, there is no time for any such statement from Ashburnham."] The intrusions are too important: Ford needs to explore Nancy's consciousness in order to give point and depth to the *progression d'effet* which will culminate in her offering herself to Ashburnham and in her eventual madness. But even though our credulity is threatened, Ford manages in almost every instance to sustain our suspension of disbelief by the skill with which he engages our attention and renders Nancy's involvement in the final crisis. (pp. 166-73)

> *Richard A. Cassell, in his* Ford Madox Ford: A Study of his Novels, *The Johns Hopkins Press, 1961, 307 p.*

John A. Meixner   (essay date 1962)

[*Meixner is an American educator and critic. In the following excerpt, he examines the narrative technique, imagery, and meaning of* The Good Soldier, *which he considers to express a complex, tragic vision of life in the twentieth century.*]

The culminating achievement of Ford's "cat's-cradle" vision, **The Good Soldier** is, at its core, a tragedy. It tells a lacerating tale of groping human beings, caught implacably by training, character, and circumstance, who cruelly and blindly inflict on each other terrible misery and pain: "poor wretches," as the narrator says, "creeping over this earth in the shadow of an eternal wrath." Yet around this awful core, and without diminishing its power, Ford in his complex and subtle art has placed a context of comic irony. This context—which Mr. Schorer has made the center of the book [see *TCLC,* Vol. 1, pp. 277-78]—Ford uses, as we shall see, to provide the novel's ultimate commentary on the nature of human life in the twentieth-century world. Indeed, in its juxtaposition of these two modes, **The Good Soldier** epitomizes in a classic way the altered tragic vision of our modern sensibility. (p. 153)

Rudyard Kipling once wrote that "There are nine and sixty ways of constructing tribal lays / And every single one of them is right!" Ford, who often referred to this jingle, granted that stories may be told by a multitude of means. But for each story, he insisted, there is one best method. And certainly this claim is true of **The Good Soldier,** for Ford could have transmitted his lacerating tale

of passion in no more effective way than through the eyes of Florence's deceived husband, John Dowell.

The artistic advantages of having Dowell narrate the story are enormous. Some are obvious and shared with almost all novels told by a first-person narrator. Characteristically the point of view heightens reality: the narrator personally witnessed and participated in these events—they must be so. The angle of vision is also an invaluable narrative convenience. A review of the action reminds us that the novel concerns itself with a steady, gradual alteration in character and relationship over a span of many years. It is the story of a long psychological struggle in which the individual incidents which crystallize a response and move a character another notch toward alienation and hatred or toward love and passion are in themselves not sharply dramatic, are like the life that most of us live from day to day. As the narrator once observes, in a key passage, the work is called "The Saddest Story" and not "The Ashburnham Tragedy"

> just because there was no current to draw things along to a swift and inevitable end. . . . Here were two noble people—for I am convinced that both Edward and Leonora had noble natures—here then, were two noble natures, drifting down life, like fireships afloat on a lagoon and causing miseries, heartaches, agony of the mind, and death.

To present this tale, a narrator is clearly necessary, enabling Ford to set side by side discontinuous incidents which have powerfully affected motivation. Even Dowell's name indicates his function in the story as a necessary center of composition—a "dowel" being, as the second definition in Webster's unabridged dictionary informs us, "a piece of wood driven into a wall, so that other pieces may be nailed to it." (Nor is such a meaning accidental, as can be seen by examining the names of the other characters, which also subtly imply special meanings. It surely is not chance that the two tender, sympathetic women of the novel, Mrs. Basil and Mrs. Maisie Maidan, have been given the name (1) of the basil herb, commonly called "sweet basil," and (2) of that feminine state which has been traditionally thought of as fresh, innocent, and gentle. Nor that the cold sensualist, Florence, bears the family name of "Hurlbird" with its emotional suggestion of ideality violated (the symbolic bird so violently used). Nor that Nancy, the character whom Ford ultimately feels and presents most intensely, bears the name of Rufford, significantly combining both the double "f" of Hueffer and Ford's first name. Nor, finally, that the tormented Edward has been given the name of Ashburnham.)

Dowell as narrator holds together, however, more than a chronologically diffuse action. He also enables Ford to shape the highly complex emotional and intellectual responses he wishes to arouse in his reader. Dowell is not after all a mere narrator, a clinical witness of the story he tells. He himself is engaged in its action.

Before examining Dowell's artistic function, however, we first must try to understand his character. For certainly, superficially considered, it is baffling. Although Ford provides various facts about him—his Philadelphia origin and wealth, for example—these are minimal and tell us little about his motivation. Where Edward, Leonora, and Nancy are "justified" with great detail and care, Dowell's background is scarcely explained at all. We learn nothing, for example, of his immediate family, nor are we given any cause, psychological or otherwise, for his lack of masculine vitality. He has no occupation: "I suppose I ought to have done something but I didn't see any call to do it. Why does one do things?" What he originally saw in Florence is unclear. "I just drifted in and wanted Florence," is the way he puts it: "And, from that moment, I determined with all the obstinacy of a possibly weak nature, if not to make her mine, at least to marry her." That he should never in twelve years of marriage have suspected either her unfaithfulness or her fraudulent invention of a bad heart, which had kept him from any conjugal claims, seems almost fantastic. In Dowell something of the common state of humanity is missing, a lack reflected in the responses of other characters. Edward, he tells us twice, thought of him as not so much a man as a woman or a solicitor. In behavior, he is often peevish, even fatuous. Ford's characterization of Dowell undeniably seems shaped under the comic spirit.

But that is only part of the story. For our sense of the objectively ludicrous in Dowell is very much qualified by the fact that we perceive his emotional life from within. He himself tells the story. And it is also qualified by our knowledge, which gradually becomes firmer and firmer, that this emotional life is that of an individual who is a psychic cripple.

In Dowell, Ford has created one of the most remarkable, certainly one of the most subtle, characterizations in modern literature. Almost completely from within he has caught and rendered the sensibility of a severely neurotic personality. Dowell is Prufrock before Prufrock, and not a mere sketch as in Eliot but a full-scale portrait. He is a man who, incapable of acting, is almost entirely feeling—a creature of pure pathos. Lonely and unrooted, Dowell is an alienated being, as he himself with fascinating indirection indicates in the opening chapters. With "no attachments, no accumulation," "a wanderer on the face of public resorts," always "too polished up," he felt "a sense almost of nakedness—the nakedness that one feels on the sea-shore or in any great open space." That was why the Ashburnhams had meant so much to him. They had, he implies, filled a frightening void. Dowell's absurdity does not induce laughter, but rather a grave sadness.

The narrator's spiritual invalidism is manifest in many ways—his atypical behavior, his almost painful self-deprecation, his peculiar images, and on occasion, certain incongruously repetitive and overly precise observations which Ford superbly uses to reassert this knowledge. (For example, his reference to the marriage rites of the Anglican Church and the use of the word "trotted" in the penultimate sentence of the book.) The plainest reference to his psychological state is brought out when he describes Leonora's reaction at their initial meeting. For at first, she was cautious and probing; but then into her eyes came a warm tenderness and friendly recognition. "It implied trust: it implied the want of any necessity for barriers." "By God, she looked at me as if I were an invalid—as any kind woman may look at a poor chap in a bath chair. And, yes, from that day forward she always treated me and not Florence as if I were the invalid." "I suppose, therefore," he continues wryly, "that her eyes had made a favourable answer. Or, perhaps, it wasn't a favourable answer." The

same motif of himself as the patient is reinforced a few pages later.

The clinical origin of Dowell's damaged spirit is not given, but its source does not really matter. Ford has rendered the inner life of that spirit, and that is sufficient. In fact, had more been presented of Dowell's background, the emphasis would have been taken away, as it should not be, from the central characters. "I don't know that analysis of my own psychology matters at all to this story," Ford pointedly has his narrator write at the opening of Part Three. "I should say that it didn't or, at any rate, that I had given enough of it."

The appropriateness of Dowell as the medium through which the careers of the Ashburnhams and their ward are told should by now be clear. Either in actual life—as students of mental disorders well know—or in *The Good Soldier,* the neurotic sensibility, turned in on itself, is apt to be heightened above the normal in its perception of emotional pain. It will be peculiarly receptive to the ache in the universe.

Dowell's sensitivity is further intensified by the recent shock of his sudden, appalled insight into the characters of his friends and their relationships. In quick succession he had been exposed to Edward's confidences, his calmly terrible self-destruction, and the discovery that his wife had been Edward's mistress. As he begins his account, his spirit is still reeling under the impact of his new knowledge.

Dowell's anguish is also rooted in his admiration and highly personal feeling for the Ashburnhams and their ward. In particular his emotion is grounded in his deep love for Edward and Nancy, a love which finds much of its source in their embodiment of what he values in life and in the pathetic identification he makes between himself and them. The depth of his love for the girl, with her rectitude and strange, half-tortured beauty, can be discerned in almost every description and response. They are further united in that each are innocents who for the first time have confronted the full evil of the world. Indeed in the last third of the book the reader all but ceases to see events through Dowell's eyes; although they are told by him, Nancy's seems the sensibility through which they pass.

As for his feeling for Edward, it naturally is more complicated. Dowell, like Nancy, admires Ashburnham for his collective responsibility and for his virtues as a good soldier, a considerate landlord, an upright magistrate. At first, being an American, he had taken these qualities for granted. "I guess I thought it was part of the character of any English gentleman," the duty of his rank and station. "Perhaps that was all that it was—but I pray God to make me discharge mine as well." If Edward had cuckolded him, Dowell could not hate him for it, for Florence did not mean that much to him really, as he comes to see, and Edward, the "luckless devil," had suffered too much torment. Dowell's love, finally, is based on the fact that Edward was what he himself longed to be and could not be. "I can't conceal from myself the fact that I loved Edward Ashburnham—and that I love him because he was just myself. . . . He seems to me like a large elder brother who took me out on several excursions and did many dashing things whilst I just watched him robbing the orchards, from a distance. And, you see, I am just as much of a sentimentalist as he was . . . "

Certainly, however, it is not sufficient for the narrator of such a passionate tale merely to be sensitive to the ache of its events. Otherwise, the effect would only seem distraught and excessive. To be communicated, the emotions must be contained within order. And this risk of sentimentality, particularly dangerous in a work as emotionally ambitious as *The Good Soldier,* Ford has masterfully guarded against.

The most obvious technical resource for the control of emotion is the prevailing ironic tone. The irony which Dowell feels is partly the product of his natural resentment against Florence, Leonora, and Edward, all of whom in varying degrees have misused him. And it is partly a personal defense, the summoning of the intellectual principle of irony to ward off painful feelings. "Forgive my writing of these monstrous things in this frivolous manner," he writes in one connection. "If I did not I should break down and cry." The irony thus provides for the novel a counterweight, a check on unbridled responses. Sensing this control, the reader can accept the passion as valid.

The greatest ironic resentment which Dowell feels is naturally directed toward Florence and Leonora. Of Florence spying on Edward and Nancy in the park by the Casino, he writes, "And that miserable woman must have got it in the face, good and strong. It must have been horrible for her. Horrible! Well, I suppose she deserved all that she got." Or, at another point, he comments on Florence's justification (given to Leonora) that she had deceived him because of a passion for Jimmy that was overmastering: "Well, I always say that an overmastering passion is a good excuse for feelings. You cannot help them. And it is a good excuse for straight actions—she might have bolted with the fellow, before or after she married me. And, if they had not enough money to get along with, they might have cut their throats, or sponged on her family. . . . No, I do not think that there is much excuse for Florence."

As for Leonora, his dislike, based on her unfeminine hardness, her selfish individualism, and her materialism, is tempered through most of the book by admiration and by his sympathy for her tortured position and deep, unsatisfied longings. Words written by Ford about James apply as well to *The Good Soldier:* "The normal novelist presents you with the oppressor and the oppressed. Mr. James presents you with the proposition, not so much that there are no such things as oppressors and oppressed, but that, even in the act of oppressing, the oppressor isn't having a very much better time than his victims." Dowell also carefully points out that Leonora's character deteriorated under the pressure of events. Florence, an unstoppable talker, broke down Leonora's pride and reserve. "Pride and reserve," Dowell writes, "are not the only things in life; perhaps they are not even the best things. But if they happen to be your particular virtues you will go all to pieces if you let them go. And Leonora let them go." In the end, however, when she is released by Edward's death and remarries, Dowell's dislike emerges plainly and brings at last to clear focus all the selfishness and craving for comfortable respectability at the basis of Leonora's personality. He even literally names her "the villain of the piece." Part of his response is personal. Several times she has sacrificed his happiness for her own, constricted, ends.

But his antipathy is also based on her destruction of the two persons he most loved—the "Beati Immaculati" (the "Blessed Immaculates") in the words affixed to the title page—and is expressed in the bitter irony of the following: "So Edward and Nancy found themselves steam-rolled out and Leonora survives, . . . married to a man who is rather like a rabbit. For Rodney Bayham is rather like a rabbit and I hear that Leonora is expected to have a baby in three months' time." The most terrible ironic thrust, however, is the *coup de canon* which ends the book. With the knowledge that Edward is going to kill himself, Dowell brings Nancy's telegram to Leonora. "She," the closing sentence reads, "was quite pleased with it."

Dowell's ironic view of Edward, as might be expected, is more prominent in the earlier stages of the novel, when he is still suffering from the knowledge of betrayal. Thus, his opening physical description of Edward: "When you looked [at his eyes] carefully you saw that they were perfectly honest, perfectly straightforward, perfectly, perfectly stupid." Or again of Edward after the Spanish dancer barred her door to him: "I dare say that nine-tenths of what he took to be his passion for La Dolciquita was really discomfort at the thought that he had been unfaithful to Leonora. He felt uncommonly bad, that is to say—oh, unbearably bad, and he took it all to be love. Poor devil, he was incredibly naive." Later, as Edward steadily increases in stature, Dowell's ironic tone toward him disappears only to emerge at key moments to serve as a subtle check to excess, and as relief. Thus after Nancy has been sent away and Leonora quietly exhibits her sense of triumph, Edward is heard to say beneath his breath, *"Thou has conquered, O pale Galilean,"* and Dowell comments: "It was like his sentimentality to quote Swinburne." Even Nancy, whom he presents with such tenderness, is not completely free from Dowell's irony, a check which only redoubles the sense of bitterness. Thus in describing the form of her insanity, he writes: "She hadn't made any fuss; her eyes were quite dry and glassy. Even when she was mad Nancy could behave herself."

Ford further guards against the dangers of a merely aching consciousness as his transmitting medium by adopting the methods of poetry. Imagery, allusion, juxtaposition, cadence—these characteristically poetic means—are all drawn upon by Dowell to formulate emotion. A man as feeling as he, if he is to be expressive, must be in fact a poet or nothing.

It is by images particularly that Dowell seeks to communicate his feeling of a personality or a situation. Thus, he writes of Florence:

> She became for me a rare and fragile object, something burdensome, but very frail. Why, it was as if I had been given a thin-shelled pullet's egg to carry on my palm from Equatorial Africa to Hoboken. Yes, she became for me, as it were, the subject of a bet—the trophy of an athlete's achievement, a parsley crown that is the symbol of his chastity, his soberness, his abstentions, and of his inflexible will.

And of Maisie Maidan, he observes:

> Why, even I, at this distance of time, am aware that I am a little in love with her memory. I can't help smiling when I think suddenly of her—as you might at the thought of something wrapped care-

fully away in lavender, in some drawer, in some old house that you have long left.

Of his feeling when Leonora for the first time, as he puts it, paid any attention to his existence, he writes: "She gave me, suddenly, yet deliberately, one long stare. . . . And it was a most remarkable, a most moving glance, as if for a moment a lighthouse had looked at me." The rightness of this extraordinary image for its purpose is stunning. That is precisely how the impact of a hard, coldly integrated personality like Leonora's would feel to a tremulous soul like Dowell's. At a more intense moment, as when the leagued Leonora and Nancy are daily censuring Edward, the images may literally become lacerating.

> Those two women pursued that poor devil and flayed the skin off him as if they had done it with whips. I tell you his mind bled almost visibly. I seem to see him stand, naked to the waist, his forearms shielding his eyes, and flesh hanging from him in rags. I tell you that is no exaggeration of what I feel.

At times Dowell's quest to image a feeling is baffled, and his struggle for a form is brought to our conscious attention. Of a crucial scene between the couples, when the relationship between Florence and Edward is faintly emerging, he writes: "I was aware of something treacherous, something frightful, something evil in the day. I can't define it and can't find a simile for it. It wasn't as if a snake had looked out of a hole. No, it was as if my heart had missed a beat. It was as if we were going to run and cry out; all four of us in separate directions, averting our heads." And on another occasion, when he is introducing Leonora, he attempts a peculiar image of the way Leonora looked in an evening dress. Not well, he thought, because it was always black, cleanly cut, and had no ruffling; her shoulders were too classical for it. "She seemed to stand out of her corsage as a white marble bust might out of a black Wedgwood vase." His own awareness of the strangeness of the image is indicated by the sentence that follows and closes the paragraph: "I don't know." As if to say, it is at least a try. His meaning is not so vague, however, and is reinforced by a more obvious image in the next paragraph when he observes that although he always loved Leonora, he had never had any sexual feeling toward her:

> As far as I am concerned I think it was those white shoulders that did it. I seemed to feel when I looked at them that, if ever I should press my lips upon them, they would be slightly cold—not icily, not without a touch of human heat, but, as they say of baths, with the chill off. I seemed to feel chilled at the end of my lips when I looked at her. . . .

In short, there was little of femininity about Edward's wife. In so many words, however, this is never said, not even in the expressive sentence which follows: "No, Leonora always appeared to be at her best in a blue tailor-made."

These examples are, by and large, bold and self-aware. Dowell is the conscious imagist trying to find forms for his experience. But the function of other images is subtler, more a part of the general emotional atmosphere. As an example we may take the second paragraph of Chapter Two, in which the dominant mood has still to be established. Perplexed as to how to tell his story, Dowell writes:

I shall just imagine myself for a fortnight or so at one side of the fireplace of a country cottage, with a sympathetic soul opposite me. And I shall go on talking, in a low voice while the sea sounds in the distance and overhead the great black flood of wind polishes the bright stars. From time to time we shall get up and go to the door and look out at the great moon and say: "Why, it is nearly as bright as in Provence!" And then we shall come back to the fireside, with just the touch of a sigh because we are not in the Provence where even the saddest stories are gay. Consider the lamentable history of Peire Vidal. Two years ago Florence and I motored from Biarritz to Las Tours, which is in the Black Mountains. In the middle of a tortuous valley there rises up an immense pinnacle and on the pinnacle are four castles—Las Tours, the Towers. And the immense mistral blew down that valley which was the way from France into Provence so that the silver-grey olive leaves appeared like hair flying in the wind, and the tufts of rosemary crept into the iron rocks that they might not be torn up by the roots.

In this paragraph Ford is both summing up in juxtaposed images the emotional dimensions of the novel and shaping the reader's responses and expectations. There is the warm, reassuring fireplace set, however, in the vast elemental context of the sea, the wind, and the stars; the moon which is not the soft, comforting moon of romance (this will not be that story); the sudden, by no means accidental, introduction of the "lamentable" story of Peire Vidal; and the shift to the motoring trip to Las Tours, with all its wracking emotive diction: *Black Mountains; tortuous valley; immense mistral* blowing down that valley (the earlier wind grown savage); *olive leaves like hair flying in the wind* (in the classic image of grief); and, finally, moving imagistically to the ultimate condition of the characters themselves, *the tufts of rosemary* (the name of no other flower, with its suggestion of love, purity, and tenderness, could have been more appropriately selected) *crept into the iron rocks that they might not be torn up by the roots.* A paragraph which has begun in comparative calm ends with great violence, and the reader's readiness for the cruel story before him is by so much more prepared. (pp. 156-66)

But if the poet Dowell draws heavily on the emotional resources of imagery, he does not neglect the power of allusion to shape and prepare feeling. Thus he frequently mentions the Protestant leader, Ludwig the Courageous, who "wanted to have three wives at once—in which he differed from Henry VIII, who wanted them one after the other, and this caused a good deal of trouble." The reference is significant both as preparation for the story of Edward and for the establishment of the religious conflict which shortly follows. Classical myth also is evoked by Dowell when he writes near the end: "I seem to see poor Edward, naked and reclining amidst darkness, upon cold rocks, like one of the ancient Greek damned, in Tartarus or wherever it was." Similarly, the Hebraic-Christian myth of the Garden of Eden is suggested, though never overtly, in the brilliant scene when Edward is falling in love with Nancy while Florence looks on. The powerful effect is that of a blessed Adam and Eve spied upon with passionate envy by the serpent.

One of the key emotive methods used by Ford in *The Good Soldier* is the device of setting side by side details which do not naturally connect, and thus compelling in the reader an imaginative, poetic leap and resolution between them. Such effective juxtaposition can be seen in Chapter Two, for example, in Dowell's apparently aimless but decidedly meaningful shift from discussing the character of Florence to telling the Provençal story of the troubador Peire Vidal and the crucial part played in it by La Louve, the heartless She-Wolf. Another example is Dowell's digression about his amusement, on a trip all four made, at seeing from the train window a brown cow hitch its horns under the stomach of a black and white one and pitch it into a stream. "I chuckled over it from time to time for the whole rest of the day. Because it does look very funny, you know, to see a black and white cow land on its back in the middle of a stream. It is so just exactly what one doesn't expect of a cow." In two more pages Leonora will be in the position of the overturned cow, as Florence begins her formal annexation of Edward. In a similar way the gray-faced head waiter of the hotel at Nauheim is juxtaposed with Edward. When Leonora wishes to appropriate a table reserved for others, the waiter objects. Although he knows that the Ashburnhams would give him much less trouble and tip him far more handsomely than the legitimate table holders, he is intent on doing his steadfast duty, which is the right and just thing. The notion of honor is thus subtly introduced, and the waiter's code is an analogue of Edward's.

In managing prose rhythm to help achieve his emotive ends, Ford demonstrates the utmost mastery. Economical and simple in diction, unpretentious in sentence structure, his language moves through an intricacy of cadences which richly but unobtrusively supports the complexity of thought and feeling. Conversational in tone, it is yet a prose which is as tightly drawn as can be imagined—a fact which becomes clearer on subsequent readings of the novel. Probably Ford's most striking rhythmic device is the effect of finality with which many paragraphs end. After moving appropriately through a series of sentences, the line of thought will suddenly be thrust into place in the concluding statement—like a bolt shooting home. Most often the thrust is ironic, like "Well, I suppose she deserved all that she got." At other times it will be a statement which has an impact because of revelation, surprise, or shock: "And, by God, she gave him hell." "Outside the winter rain fell and fell. And suddenly [Nancy] thought that Edward might marry someone else; and she nearly screamed." In the closing, most intense, section of the novel, no paragraph lacks its final jolt—in sensibility as though one's heart were being struck at again and again. Together with the tight control of the prose itself, the effect is an extraordinary feeling of constant pressure.

But in rendering emotion, Ford does not employ oblique means only. At the most intense moments he can be powerfully direct. Perhaps no word occurs more frequently in *The Good Soldier,* for example, than agony and its forms. It is, in fact, the emblem of the work. Or consider such direct statements of the situation as:

> are all men's lives like the lives of us good people—
> like the lives of the Ashburnhams, of the Dowells,
> of the Ruffords—broken, tumultuous, agonized,
> and unromantic lives, periods punctuated by
> screams, by imbecilities, by deaths, by agonies?

Or, again, Dowell's explanation of why a man must go to the woman he loves for renewal of his courage and solu-tion of his difficulties: "We are all so afraid, we are all so alone, we all so need from the outside the assurance of our own worthiness to exist."

The technical importance of Dowell in shaping the responses of the reader is not confined, however, to various poetic, ironic, and stylistic elements. He also enables Ford brilliantly to manage feelings by controlling the tempo and tension of the novel and the degree of its psychological penetration. The structure of *The Good Soldier,* as a result, is extraordinary in its gripping suspense, narrative drive, and emotional concentration.

The use of Dowell to bridge time, which we noted earlier, may now be examined more closely. Ford's problem was not unlike one James faced in writing a famous tale in which he wanted to present the spiritual changes in a young woman over a considerable period. To do this he selected a narrator who reports his encounters with her on four separate, revealing occasions, hence the story's title, "Four Meetings." In his book on James, published not long before *The Good Soldier,* Ford took special note of this tale by devoting three pages of discussion to it (including this sentence which seems particularly appropriate to Dowell: "Mr. James knows very well that he was giving just an extra turn to the tragedy of the story by making his narrator so abnormally unhelpful"). And in one important respect, the story would seem to have served as his technical model, for Ford focuses the action on three specific encounters among his characters. Thus, although the chronicle of *The Good Soldier* spans many years, it concentrates on the initial meeting of the two couples at Nauheim; the death of Florence and Edward's discovery of his love for Nancy in the same place nine years later; and the two-month period which follows at Branshaw after the Ashburnhams return to England. As a result the novel gains greatly in dramatic unity and immediacy. Unlike James, however, Ford is not limited to these major dramatic occasions. (It is partly the difference between the tale and the novel.) For, as we have seen, much of the book traces the careers, motivation, and actions of the characters in the periods before the couples meet and in the interval between the episodes. The reader becomes acquainted with them in full dimension, so that the crucial incidents take on considerable authority and depth. The important technical point, however, is that Dowell (or Ford) presents only the highlights of the "justifying" actions. One of the most unusual features of the novel in fact is that very few of its episodes last more than a page. A very important scene continues two pages, and only a few are longer. The novel has no lengthy exchanges of dialogue. In a scene of dramatic confrontation, the reader will be led up to the height of the incident; a character will speak an intense, key speech and may or may not be answered; and the episode is finished, its point burning like a brand into the reader's consciousness. Being extremely concentrated, the method wins for the book an emotional penetration rare in fiction.

This emotional penetration is, naturally, not attained only through concentrated impressions. It requires as well a plot development that will couple concentration with the highest degree of narrative tension, and this Ford achieves. The effect, as was said, is a series of surprises, brought about by new insights into facts and relationships—the constant turning of the screw.

Basically Ford uses the device of beginning in the midst of action. His tactic is to grip the reader's attention by presenting as forcefully as he can an emotional conflict at the peak of its intensity, and then, having aroused the desire to know more about it, to develop the background which led to the situation. His special skill is in so presenting the expository material that the tension is not quickly resolved, but keeps pulling the reader on and on. For these purposes Dowell is admirably contrived. His state of shock at what he has only recently discovered, together with his somewhat foolish, ineffectual character, goes far toward justifying the rambling method with which he tells the story. He himself is still in process; his personal attitudes toward the various other characters are not finally formed. As he begins to write, he does not even know the final outcome of the action: the closing two chapters, written on his return with Nancy from Ceylon, are completed months later. One probably need not add, however, that the ramblingness of the narrative is only seeming. "Not one single thread must ever escape your purpose," Ford always insisted, and none does in *The Good Soldier.* (pp. 167-71)

The greatest of Ford's narrative triumphs, however, is not so much that he prevents interest from slackening as that, consummately modulating the values of his novel, he has steadily intensified the force of its emotion. . . . Through a combination of literary devices, mostly involving his narrator, Ford in the opening chapters has skillfully kept his basic emotional materials at several steps removed. Because Dowell tends to fill the foreground during the early stages of the novel, the intense emotions of the other characters, of which he is reporter, come to the reader only in isolated bursts; and not deriving from integrated centers of personality which the reader can as yet be assured of and understand, these passionate outbursts remain "unplaced" and muted in penetrative force. Similarly, emotional power is moderated by Dowell's ironic tone. And finally, distance is achieved through the high degree of indirection with which the experience of the novel is transmitted—the peculiar juxtapositions which often require of the reader subtle, thoughtful yoking; and the abundant use of intellectual imagery. Later in the novel these screening elements begin to dissipate. The reader moves closer and closer to the characters, until their emotional responses are rendered with almost excruciating directness.

Among the most extraordinary of many extraordinary qualities about *The Good Soldier* is that although Ford has presented an account of drifting lives which, considered chronologically, fail to move toward any swift or inevitable end, he has nevertheless produced an artistic work which is singularly distinguished by its sense of swift inevitability. Ford's canons of economy and movement to produce the sense of relentless destiny in a novel are perfectly embodied in *The Good Soldier.* Every word is carefully chosen to advance the action; digressions relax tension, yet are only seeming digressions; the narrative moves faster and faster and with increasing intensity (*progression d'effet*). Finally the entire novel draws to one inevitable culmination, which, as Ford said, should reveal "once and for all, in the last sentence, or the penultimate; in the last phrase, or the one before it—the psychological significance of the whole." In *The Good Soldier* this culminating moment occurs one page from the end. All the facts of the story have been recorded, and the book seems to be trailing away without any final climax. Suddenly remembering, however, that he has not told how Edward met his death, Dowell depicts the scene at Branshaw when Nancy's telegram arrived. Until this point in the novel the telegram has been several times referred to indirectly, and vaguely described as "atrocious." Now Ford sets down the actual message, and its bright, hard words provide the final turn of the screw, the ultimate clinching cruelty. At one instant, and with a shock of perception, the reader understands both why Edward had to end his life and why Nancy, on learning of his suicide (and knowing its cause), had to go mad. In the face of such cruelty in the human heart, withdrawal from life is the only conceivable course for such sensitive beings. The reader has been magnificently prepared to feel the horror of it. All forces have contributed to the inevitable end.

Finally, one further point of Ford's art ought not to be overlooked—the size and depth given to the novel by its great number and variety of marvelously executed scenes, each of which is a model of artistry, with its own individual angle of attack, appropriate tone and mood, structural rhythm and prose cadence. There are episodes, for example, of social comedy: the two Hurlbird aunts in their Stamford home (with its picture of General Braddock), delicately trying to warn Dowell against their niece; the pathetic post-midnight elopement of Dowell and Florence in Waterbury, Connecticut, and its aftermath: the couple, "listening to a mocking-bird imitate an old tom-cat" while they dully wait in the woods for dawn; the photographing of Leonora and her six sisters at their impoverished manor house and the other hopeful expenditures made for the visit of the Ashburnhams and their marriageable son; Edward at Monte Carlo with the Spanish dancer; Leonora striking Maisie Maidan in a hotel corridor and her attempted recapture of poise on discovering that Florence had been a witness; or Dowell's fateful meeting with the odious Mr. Bagshawe, who knew of "Florrie" Hurlbird's affair with Jimmy. There are also the splendid scenes of graver import: Dowell's almost stream-of-conscious memory (a technique unusual in the book) of his catatonic state after Florence's death; Dowell and Leonora in the dead-world of Branshaw after Edward's suicide, with the rabbits already beginning to nibble the lawn; the narrator's magnificent, extremely moving disquisition on the growth and meaning of a man's love for a woman; the sequence, purely quivering in its feeling, when the simple Nancy discovers (through reading the newspapers) the existence of marital infidelity, perceives the bitter hate between the Ashburnhams, and, with a sense of age and wisdom and of superiority over Leonora, at once recognizes her own proud love for Edward; or the terrible scene at the end in which, with Dowell looking on, Edward and Nancy, those restrained "good people" of England, bid each other good-bye at the railroad station without any sign of emotion. ("The signal for the train's departure was a very bright red," Dowell writes; "that is about as passionate a statement as I can get into that scene.") Only a reader of the novel can understand the full variety and brilliance of such episodes, how admirably they have been selected to impel the action, or how masterfully they establish the breadth and solidity of the work.

The intense, complex experience of *The Good Soldier* and the means by which Ford successfully mounted it have by now been isolated. Still before us, however, is its larger significance. What, ultimately, is Ford saying in the novel? In his examination of character and of the agonies of human relationships the intention is apparent enough. But, like Flaubert, Ford does not express his full meaning obviously. Rather he subtly implies it, asking the reader to actively participate in understanding it. There are mysteries in *The Good Soldier,* and the mind cannot rest until it resolves them.

Earlier the novel was described as a classic rendering of the modern tragic outlook. What was meant, more specifically, was that in it Ford has presented a genuinely tragic experience but in circumstances, peculiar to the twentieth century, which condition that experience in a special, meaningful way.

Those elements which make for the tragedy of the action are classically Aristotelian: its sense of inevitability, its reversals of situation and meaning, its high poetry. Its protagonist, Edward Ashburnham, is a man much above the ordinary. He lives according to the high values of generosity, kindness, duty, and responsibility to those who depend upon him, and he can act for the right with will and determination. "The unfortunate Edward," Dowell writes. "Or, perhaps, he was not so unfortunate; because he had done what he knew to be the right thing, he may be deemed happy." If Edward at his introduction seems, like Dowell, essentially a creation of comedy—an indulgent libertine, athletically handsome but basically stupid and vacuous—his dignity and stature steadily grow during the book . . . until at its close he is an extremely impressive, noble figure. By no means a perfect man—the tragic protagonist never is—he is a good man who has never been guided by base motives. As Dowell makes clear, he was not a promiscuous libertine, but a sentimentalist. Sentimentality in fact is Edward's basic human weakness, his fatal flaw—even as, ironically, it is the source of much of his virtue. Most importantly, *The Good Soldier* arouses in the reader the cathartic emotions of pity and awe at the spectacle of its admirable, greatly suffering protagonist overwhelmed by hard cruelty in so terrible and unfeeling a way.

These are the classic attributes of tragedy, but this experience is significantly qualified by elements that are not tragic. The sense of destiny, for example, is merely formal. The lives of the characters actually trail away to no seeming conclusion. Nor does the tragic experience of Edward and Nancy move in the larger context of a universe which is purposeful, either in the classical Greek deterministic meaning or in that of the Hebraic-Christian Divine Plan. Instead Ford has placed the pair in a world in which, there being no purpose, there is hence no meaning to life on earth, only an ultimate knowledge of futility. At one place Dowell writes of himself and Leonora: "I cannot tell you the extraordinary sense of leisure that we two seemed to have at that moment. It wasn't as if we were waiting for a train, it wasn't as if we were waiting for a meal—it was just that there was nothing to wait for. Nothing." This motif of nothingness, which is actually announced in the opening chapter ("And there is nothing to guide us. . . . It is all a darkness"), is re-sounded almost at the very end of the novel when Dowell presents his final description of the insane Nancy: "It is very extraordinary to see the perfect flush of health on her cheeks, to see the lustre of her coiled black hair, the poise of the head upon the neck, the

grace of the white hands—and to think that it all means nothing—that it is a picture without a meaning."

The religious framework of the world, with its vision of harmony between God, man, and nature, has been shattered. This catastrophe and its consequences Ford crystallizes through brilliant juxtaposition in at least two key places in the novel. The first is the somewhat bathetic contrast (in the concluding chapter of Part One) between the powerful, compelling image of the palm of God and the comic, half-mocking (and half-weeping) image of the death and doll-like religious funeral of Maisie Maidan. More striking still, and more obvious in its meaning, is the conjunction of the only comments which are spoken by Nancy after she goes insane. "Credo in unum Deum Omnipotentem" is the first, and about it Dowell sadly, wearily comments: "Those are the only reasonable words she uttered; those are the only words, it appears, that she ever will utter. I suppose they are reasonable words; it must be extraordinarily reasonable for her, if she can say that she believes in an Omnipotent Deity." Almost at the end of the book Nancy speaks the other: a single word, repeated three times, "Shuttlecocks." That is how she felt between Leonora and Edward, and that was the way Edward had felt between the women. And that is the word, Ford is saying, for man's buffeted, purposeless existence in the world that has come into being.

We can now understand also the full ambiguity and subtlety of the scene in which, when Florence had disclosed a copy of Luther's Protest, Leonora cried out: "Don't you see that that's the cause of the whole miserable affair; of the whole sorrow of the world? And of the eternal damnation of you and me and them . . . " Her words, as we saw, are addressed essentially to the quietly meaningful touching by Florence of Edward's wrist. Although a staunch Roman Catholic, Leonora in reality is not a religious woman at all, operating rather according to the rigid code of the Church, to its letter rather than its spirit. Yet the reader does not yet know this fact and the words make their significant effect in his mind. By them Ford is saying that the rise of Protestantism, which symbolizes the entire modern, sceptical, fragmenting impulse, is the source of the destruction of the old consoling religious framework and the whole present sorrow of the world.

This sense of a nothingness at the heart of the universe can also be seen, of course, in the questionings of Hamlet and the rages of Lear. But the distance between Shakespeare's world, in which only chinks in the spiritual framework are spied, and our own period is great. As the modern era moves on into the time of the high prestige of science and Darwinism, the religious structure holds less and less power over the minds and actions of men. And with the change comes the disappearance of the heroic attitude. ("I am not Prince Hamlet," declares Prufrock; and Dowell says of himself in heaven: "Well, perhaps they will find me an elevator to run.") Gone also is the deep assurance that evil must, for all its ravages, be overcome. In *Lear* the disaster of the King and Cordelia is meliorated by the bitter deaths of Goneril and Regan. In *The Good Soldier* Edward and Nancy, who are the spiritual descendants of Lear and his youngest daughter, are destroyed, while Leonora, for whom the evil sisters are an essential prototype, triumphs without final punishment. In the rendering of man's spiritual plight in the twentieth century, *The*

James Joyce, Ezra Pound, John Quinn, and Ford in Paris, 1923.

Good Soldier is thus a major artistic document, an objective correlative of its age.

This twentieth-century world Ford represents specifically through various symbols. One is his selection of a pair of Americans as the peripheral characters to his tragedy. Ford conceived of his fictional Americans—as we observed in *The English Girl* and *A Call,* and as may be seen in his presentation of Millicent de Bray Pape in *The Last Post*—as unrooted creatures and, hence, as faint, ineffective personalities. Several times Dowell speaks of himself in these terms, and his wife he once calls a "paper personality" who at her death dropped completely out of recollection. Florence is also characterized by her American busybody but mindless desire to bring "a little light into the world." This meddling Dowell pointedly defines through a digressive anecdote about her uncle, who on his world tour took with him thousands of California oranges to give as "little presents" to strangers. The absurdity of the venture is epitomized brilliantly in the following passage:

> When they were at North Cape, even, he saw on the horizon, poor dear thin man that he was, a lighthouse. "Hello," says he to himself, "these fellows must be very lonely. Let's take them some oranges." So he had a boatload of his fruit out and had himself rowed to the lighthouse on the horizon.

"And so, guarded against his heart," Dowell adds (in a double sense), "and having his niece with him, he went round the world." This is the American in action, inno-

cent of what lies below the surface of life, and often, as in the case of Dowell's wife, cheerfully doing evil.

Another meaningful symbol may be seen in Ford's depiction of Florence dead on her bed: "looking with a puzzled expression at the electric-light bulb that hung from the ceiling, or perhaps through it, to the stars above." Strikingly paralleling this description is a movement of Edward's just before he takes his life: "He just looked up to the roof of the stable, as if he were looking to heaven . . ." We may note the contrast. For Edward, the agrarian stable (with its connotation even of the birth of Christ) and the searching appeal for heaven. For Florence, an electric light bulb, an almost by now classic symbol of the industrial substitution for Godhead, and the stars which coldly swing in the empty spaces above.

In dramatizing the nature of this dominant modern spirit, Ford did not rely, however, only on texture and subtly revealing incidents. He also built the point into the structure, so that the form itself defines and crystallizes its scope and large meaning; from beginning to end, the main action is transmitted through the sensibility of the narrator—an individual who brilliantly objectifies this lamed modern spirit. The ultimate importance (and final justification) of Dowell in the novel is as a concrete, functioning embodiment of the state of mind formed by the new conditions of the twentieth-century world: alienated and unrooted, helpless and "less than human," pathetic and absurd. As symbolic context, Dowell gives the tragedy a remarkably contemporary dimension. Ford has been praised for dramatizing in the Tietjens cycle the transition in England from one order of society to another, particularly in the composition of its governing classes; but in *The Good Soldier,* his *constatation* ["statement"] of change is still more penetrating. It is not limited to England, or its governing classes, or the public events of a decade. Rather it directly concerns itself, as we have noted, with a basic alteration that has steadily been going on in the attitudes and psychology of Western Man in general.

Having perceived the deeper significance of Ford's narrator, we must also consider the underlying meaning of his final fate. As owner of Branshaw Manor and nursemaid to the mad Nancy, neither of which roles gives him any satisfaction, Dowell's end suggests a grim, sad prophecy. Ford appears to be saying by it that the modern estranged spirit, symbolized by Dowell in particular and Americans in general, will supplant the older types and values (Edward, Nancy, and Branshaw; the seat of the stabler feudal attitudes based not on abstract capital but tangible land; even a Leonora). Yet this spirit, being sick, will not be the possessor of the dying, blighted remains, but, like Dowell, their joyless caretaker.

Ford's story, in the end, however, focuses not on the ascendancy of the future, not on the "new" man, but rather on the predicament and death of the old. Dowell (and Florence) are not, after all, at the center of the experience of *The Good Soldier.* That position is reserved for the three English characters who move in the spiritual environment the Americans represent. As personalities (and creations) they are in sharp contrast with the Dowells, are strengthened and deepened by their social, familial, and religious roots. They strive to put a face on life, to give it meaning and purpose, to shore value, even if only sentimental, against the ruins. None of them are personal ciphers, as modern writers frequently have made their entrapped characters. If in a sense they are victims, it is not in a simple reflex way; they are not mere products of society. In abundant measure they possess the will and passion to victimize themselves. Their personal strength gives them their grandeur and makes them worthy of such tragedy as Ford sees that the twentieth century enables.

But in the end, of course, futility is the context in which they move. Theirs is not the resolution finally of great tragedy, which in its heroism confirms the optimistic view of man's ability to transcend himself spiritually. Instead, for Edward and Nancy, it is the resolution of withdrawal, by suicide and insanity, from a world which is too horrible. Souls of a certain greatness have suffered greatly, but hopelessly and to no larger purpose—their values, lacking sanction, sentimental. This is the tragic absurdity (or absurd tragedy) of human life in a world bereft of meaning. The novel in every way earns its superlative claim. It does, indeed, tell "the saddest story." (pp. 181-89)

> *John A. Meixner, in his* Ford Madox Ford's Novels: A Critical Study, *University of Minnesota Press, 1962, 503 p.*

Joseph Wiesenfarth   (essay date 1963)

[*Wiesenfarth is an American educator and critic. In the following essay, he surveys criticism of* The Good Soldier, *discussing why the novel has been the subject of several conflicting interpretations and suggesting a method of finding more concrete meaning in it.*]

In the dozen years between the spring of 1949 and the winter of 1961, nine interpretations of Ford Madox Ford's *The Good Soldier* were published. This essay does not primarily offer a tenth. Rather its purpose is to show why such a variety of meanings has been tended for *The Good Soldier* and in so doing to suggest how the relative value of these and other interpretations may be adjudicated. To this end I shall briefly present the arguments of the most significant interpretations of *The Good Soldier,* suggest the difficulties attendant on ascribing meanings to even minimal units of the novel, point to the kinds of signs the novel offers and the resilient ambivalence they establish, and finally suggest an area of certainty in the meaning of the novel that seems invariably to underlay the probability of diverse opinions as to its proper interpretation.

Robie Macauley's "The Good Ford" is an attempt to discriminate value (the "good") in Ford's voluminous output [see *TCLC,* Vol. 15, pp. 79-81]. For Macauley Ford's monumental work is *Parade's End;* "his most perfect miniature performance" is *The Good Soldier,* "a splendid novel written just before the first World War." Macauley points to "Ford's strange powers of persuasion [which] make us sympathize with both [Edward and Leonora]; both seem equally right and equally wrong, equally good and evil. The final tragedy of Edward Ashburnham's suicide is no more terrible than the sudden slackening of his wife's mind."

Mark Schorer's "An Interpretation" is an implicit challenge to the point of view that Macauley's essay represents [see *TCLC,* Vol. 1, pp. 277-78]. By reference to what the novel is "about," Schorer questions the credibility of the narrator. In Schorer's view, *The Good Soldier* is a novel which "first of all . . . is about the difference between convention and fact." Because John Dowell is unable to distinguish between convention and fact and because self-interest—conscious or otherwise—colors his version of events in the story, he is an unreliable narrator. "His must be exactly the *wrong* view" of "a world that is without moral point."

Elliott Gose challenged Schorer's view of Dowell's credibility and distinguished a different point of focus to determine the novel's meaning. To Gose *The Good Soldier* primarily concerns the English society of Ford's day, a society in which individual freedom was limited by a social code that represented a decadent form of feudalism. Edward Ashburnham is the victim of the conflict between this society and his passionate nature. John Dowell is educated by his experience with this society and—though he is not thoroughly admirable—is a credible witness to the events which take place in it. Thus "Dowell often speaks for his author" and deserves the confidence of the reader.

Without recourse to Gose's essay, John A. Meixner presented views similar to his [for a revised version of Meixner's discussion, see excerpt dated 1962]. To Meixner *The Good Soldier* is a "lacerating tale of groping human beings, caught implacably by training, character, and circumstance, who cruelly and blindly inflict on each other terrible misery and pain." Thus Schorer's version of the novel as a "comedy" and Macauley's judgment of it as a " 'miniature' performance" are wrong. Since Meixner finds Schorer's impeachment of Dowell's credibility to be "inappropriate" and "uncongenial," his essay is devoted to penetrating to "the deeper significance of Ford's narrator," whom he sees as "a poet or nothing."

About the same time that Meixner's article was published, James Hafley's "The Moral Structure of *The Good Soldier*" appeared, and the credibility of Dowell was again called into question [see excerpt dated 1959]. Arguing that the novel is as " 'Catholic' as any art-work can be said to be" and marking Dowell's failure to understand the "carefully structured religious element," Hafley scores Dowell's "incoherent vision of the significance of his story"; he further points to a "theory of knowing-versus-believing" in the novel that makes it possible for one to distinguish facts from Dowell's interpretation of them. Hafley also challenged Schorer's view of *The Good Soldier* as a novel without "moral point"; Hafley describes "a world . . . surprisingly traditional . . . [and] orthodox in its values and meanings," and he acquits Ashburnham (as no previous critic had done) of all but "one act of adultery in the course of the novel: the one night he spent with La Dolciquita."

Hafley's and Schorer's challenging positions on the personal goodness and on the reliability of Dowell were questioned by Samuel Hynes in "The Epistemology of *The Good Soldier*" [see *TCLC*, Vol. 1, pp. 278-80]. Hynes examines the novel in relation to the limited possibility for knowledge in a novel in the tradition of a first-person narrator. Hynes maintains that "there is neither a "primary author' or 'knower' . . . in terms of which we get a true perspective of either Dowell or the events of the novel. There is only Dowell, sitting down 'to puzzle out what I know.' " Consequently, Hynes suggests that the "narrator's fallibility *is* the norm." The novel then becomes "a study of the difficulties which man's nature and the world put in the way of his will to know." Dowell does come to know something nevertheless; he understands what he "can't know" and that itself is a kind of knowledge "that Dowell did not have at the beginning of the affair." This knowledge of the narrator, then, in addition to Hynes's conviction that Dowell is both a selfless human being and *the* "Lover" in the novel, justifies Dowell in this interpretation of *The Good Soldier.*

A most recent and challenging interpretation of *The Good Soldier* has come from James Trammell Cox. In his "Ford's 'Passion for Provence' " Cox seeks to place Edward Ashburnham in a less than orthodox Catholic tradition—he seeks, in fact, to place him in the courtly love tradition. Cox theorizes that by this oblique approach to the novel Dowell's reliability can be examined. By tracing the action and imagery in *The Good Soldier,* Cox concludes that Edward represents the medieval knight-errant who is playing Lancelot to other men's Guineveres and that Dowell's report, which begins somewhat unreliably, finishes—after his return from India with Nancy—with reliability. Edward is consequently more the villain (although Ford did not quite allow him to be such) and Dowell more the serious man at the novel's end.

If *The Good Soldier* were an ordinary novel, it would be reasonable for readers to be exacerbated by this diversity in its interpretation. But the novel is not at all ordinary. One cannot even be certain of the meaning of its title page. If, after all, Edward Ashburnham is as guilty as Dowell

and Leonora suppose him to be, how can he be the eponymous Good Soldier? Shouldn't Ford be suspected of having intended an ironic meaning when he suggested the title to his publisher? Also, mustn't the subtitle, "A Tale of Passion," in consequence mean that the novel is about Edward and his mistresses—about the perversion of marital love? To these legitimate questions it is quite impossible to supply totally satisfactory answers. One cannot be quite sure about the "mistresses": Florence denies that she is Edward's mistress and the absence of real evidence to the contrary makes her denial as credible as Leonora's and Dowell's opposite assertions; Maisie's name is "Maidan," which suggests chastity; the encounter with the girl named Kilsyte ("kill sight") suggests misinterpretation on the part of Ashburnham's accusers. When Leonora attempts to make Nancy Edward's mistress, he orders the girl from his bedroom. There is in these instances a basis for the conjecture that Edward Ashburnham is not as guilty as the narrator suspects him to be.

Edward, then, might really be the Good Soldier. The "Passion" of the subtitle might not be lust. Rather, since everyone in the novel suffers, "Passion" might mean suffering (as it does when Christ's Passion is referred to). But who can postulate *with certainty* that Edward is either guilty or innocent? It is both *probable* that he is guilty and *probable* that he is innocent. Therefore it is probable that "Passion" means either lust or suffering—or, more complexly, both lust and suffering simultaneously.

The epigraph in no way helps to solve the problem. The first two verses of Psalm 118—from which the words of the epigraph are taken—are:

> Beati immaculati in via
> qui ambulant in lege Domini.
> (Happy are they whose way is blameless
> who walk in the law of the Lord.)

Who in *The Good Soldier* is blameless? Who in *The Good Soldier* walks undeviatingly in the law of the Lord? Who in *The Good Soldier,* above all, is happy? Is the epigraph the final irony of the novel? Is *The Good Soldier* Ford's gloss on the too human fracture between the ideal as enunciated by David and the real as lived by David? Is the Psalmist—himself a good soldier—the symbol of struggling humanity?

It is quite easy to propose these and further questions like them, but it is not easy to answer such questions. In fact, I do not think that the semiosis (the process in which a sign—a word—means) of *The Good Soldier* allows for such questions answers that have more than a degree of probability. It does not allow for answers that carry certitude. This is so because the elements of *The Good Soldier* are so complexly interrelated and, from different viewpoints, so contradictory that the problems already suggested by the nine words on the title page merely hint at the difficulty involved in interpreting the tens of thousands of words in the body of the novel itself.

These and similar difficulties are inevitable now that criticism has brought one to the impasse where it becomes impossible either to dismiss Dowell completely or wholeheartedly to accept him. This ambivalence complicates the task of exegesis. A case in point is Richard Cassell's suggestion that there are three breakdowns in point of view in *The Good Soldier:* Dowell reveals Nancy's reactions in situations in which he seems to have no access to information; he also notes that Maisie Maidan kissed the pillows on Edward's bed, but that information also seems outside his purview; likewise unavailable to Dowell are the thoughts of Edward (which Dowell reports) when he reads Nancy's telegram [see excerpt dated 1961]. These items and others like R. W. Lid's account of the inaccurate time scheme that Dowell provides for episodes in the novel mean one thing to those who favor Dowell's interpretation of events and something quite different to others who question the narrator's reliability [see Further Reading]. To Cassell, who accepts Dowell's testimony, these "apparent breakdowns" are assimilated into the novel's effect. A less sympathetic critic, however, could easily—and with as much probability—argue that these are merely a few instances of contradiction which highlight Dowell's distortion of facts and suggest that he cannot be trusted. Ford could be shown by this kind of critic to be the ultimate artist rather than the artist whose work shows, in Cassell's phrase, "apparent breakdowns." The critic who views Dowell's statements for the most part as interpolations could then suggest that other facts of an ambiguous character should also be used in favor of Ashburnham and against Dowell. As it happens, these "neutral" facts have been among those most interpreted by critics.

The reality of Edward's mistresses is such a neutral fact. *Were* there really mistresses, and if so *who* were these mistresses? Certainly La Dolciquita for one night and most probably for one week. Certainly not the Kilsyte girl and certainly not Maisie Maidan. Perhaps Mrs. Basil. Edward liked her, and her husband blackmailed him. But Edward denied that she was his mistress and had his solicitor threaten a public litigation to end the husband's demands for money. Perhaps Florence. Florence on one occasion before she married Dowell most probably slept with Jimmy; she might also have slept with Edward after her marriage. Leonora saw Edward leave Florence's room "at an advanced hour of the night"; but Florence maintained to Leonora that "she had merely been conversing with Edward in order to bring him to a better frame of mind" after Maisie's death. Leonora and Dowell affirm that Florence is Ashburnham's mistress, but Florence and Edward strongly deny the accusation. No matter how one presses the possibility of adultery, it cannot be proved as a certainty.

The problem here is obvious: an instance of adultery is not in evidence. The reader has only the assertion that the adultery not in evidence was in fact committed. That assertion, moreover, is made by one who was not a witness to the event he asserts to have taken place nor has he received his information from one who was a witness at the event in question. In the case of allegation by one party and denial by another, the reality of the disputed event remains questionable. The uncertainty of the event is its sole certainty.

There are other words and actions, however, of which the reader can be certain; but the problem of these events lies with their interpretation. Ultimately one cannot be certain of the meaning of some verifiable facts. Meixner, for instance, thinks that there is an equation of statements in Nancy's *"Credo in unum Deum Omnipotentem"* and her "shuttlecocks." To him the novel is one complete chaos in which "shuttlecocks" equals *"Deum."* Cox interprets these two statements in a different way; he sees Edward as Nancy's savior. "It is thus not too fanciful, perhaps, to assume that in her madness the two ideas she gives expression to in 'Shuttlecocks' and *'Credo in unum Deum Omnipotentem . . .* ' are not so disparate as they might seem: in both cases, she has Edward, who announces himself as 'master of this house,' the cloistral manor, on her mind." For Hafley the "faith of the 'insane' Nancy, who repeats over and over again *'Credo in unum Deum Omnipotentem,'* this simple sanity, appearing in a mad world to be madness, stands at the center of the novel's structure and builds to other acts of faith that reach out in various directions around it."

It is no wonder that critics who disagree on the way that Nancy's *"Credo"* is integrated into the novel's meaning also contest the meaning of the Protest scene (as Hafley and Meixner do), of Edward's bedside prayer (as Hafley and Cox do), of "sentimentalism" (as Hafley and Gose do); contest the meaning, in short, of any fact capable of different interpretations from different points of view.

In a novel like **The Good Soldier** such diversity of interpretation is inevitable. Facts like the *"Credo,"* the Protest scene, Edward at prayer, and so on exist amid so many non-facts (assertions) that meanings ascribed to facts are configured by the reading given to non-facts. The meaning that Hafley attaches to the Protest scene, the *"Credo,"* and Ashburnham's praying (all facts) is determined by the lack of credibility that he allows to Dowell's assertions (non-facts). The meaning that Meixner attaches to the *"Credo"* is conditioned by the credibility he ascribes to Dowell's assertions. The same is also true for other interpreters of **The Good Soldier.** Interpretation of facts is intricately connected with interpretation of assertions or non-facts, and these assertions are deemed valid or invalid in terms of John Dowell's credibility or lack of it. One, then, is pushed back to an ultimately insoluble problem—to know with certainty whether or not Dowell can be believed.

Dowell tells his story after Leonora has revealed to him her interpretation of actual and possible events in which he has ignorantly figured. Leonora, however, is a prejudiced interpreter; moreover she is not a thoroughly reliable one. She is wrong, for instance, about Maisie Maidan's coming from Edward's room; she is "baffled" by Ashburnham's dismissing Nancy from his bedroom. She may be wrong in her interpretation of Florence's coming from her husband's bedroom; she may be wrong about Mrs. Basil and about the Protest scene. In each of these cases the alternate meanings proposed are as probable as the ones offered by Leonora.

Dowell, too, is a prejudiced interpreter. Although the doctors had maintained that Florence had heart trouble, he now denies its possibility. Dowell is convinced of Florence and Edward's adultery even though there is no actual evidence of it. Also, Dowell is continuously fitting things together in patterns which suit his interpretation. After Leonora's remark that Florence was Edward's mistress, Dowell comes upon "a dozen unexplained things [which] would fit themselves in place." After Florence's death he decides on what led to it: "I pieced it together afterwards." His dead wife's life becomes to him "a problem in Algebra," something that "I have tried to figure out." Dowell "figured it out" that Mrs. Basil was Ashburnham's mistress." His explanation of the blackmail plot ends with the remark: "I fancy that was how it was." As he nears the end of his account of Edward's relations with Leonora, Miss Kilsyte, Maisie Maidan, Mrs. Basil, Florence, and himself, Dowell says, "You have the facts for the trouble of finding them; you have the points of view as far as I could ascertain or put them." This is not a very encouraging epistemological statement.

Nor is Dowell an encouraging interpreter and judge of events. In fact, at certain points in the novel he appears to be completely ridiculous. When he asks Edward the meaning of his D. S. O. decoration, Ashburnham replies: " 'It's the sort of a thing they give grocers who've honourably supplied the troops with adulterated coffee in wartime'—something of that sort. He did not quite carry conviction to me, so, in the end, I put it directly to Leonora." Dowell's "He did not quite carry conviction to me" is hardly perceptive. After Edward had expressed to Nancy his admiration for her, "he realized what he was doing, [and] curbed his tongue at once." Yet Ashburnham's spontaneous and self-reproved remark is to Dowell "the most monstrously wicked thing that Edward Ashburnham ever did in his life." This is certainly a naive judgment. Dowell's reaction to Nancy's refusal to enter the convent is ludicrous: "Well, I guess I was sort of a convent myself; it seemed fairly proper that she should make her vows to me." Dowell's (not Ford's) knowledge of Catholicism is clearly summarized in his " 'On Corpus Christi'— or it may have been some *other saint's* day . . . " (italics added). Dowell's interpretation of Ashburnham's relation to Mrs. Basil and the events subsequent to it is hardly profound: "Edward ought, I suppose, to have gone to the Transvaal. It would have done him a great deal of good to get killed." When Dowell learns that Leonora believed Florence to be Edward's mistress, he remarks that Leonora "so despised Florence that she would have preferred it to be a parlour-maid"; he then adds, in all seriousness, "There are very decent parlour-maids." After revealing that he feels himself following in Edward's footsteps and that he would "like to be a polygamist; with Nancy, and with Leonora, and with Maisie Maidan, and possibly even Florence," Dowell adds (for sake of edification?), "I am able to assure you that I am a strictly respectable person." All this naivete comes to a climax when Dowell decides— after having for page upon page related "the unimaginable hell" that Leonora has given her husband—that Edward and Nancy are the villains of the story.

These instances of naivete in approaching and properly judging rather simple happenings make a reader chary of Dowell's capacity to judge rightly the novel's more complex "neutral" facts. Not one nor all of these incidents, however, can *prove with certainty* that Dowell's story is the wrong one. Not at all. In spite of these arguments it is still probable that Dowell's version of the facts is true; but because of these arguments it is as equally probable that he is in error.

The reader is capable of making these judgments for himself because he is in no sense limited by the narrator's fallibility, as Hynes has suggested. Rather, it seems that by providing events similar to those already referred to, Ford allows the reader a sufficient number of incidents that are not cardinal to an interpretation of *The Good Soldier* and that permit the reader to judge the narrator's capabilities.

The narrator's fallibility thus becomes a primary fact for the reader to judge. That Dowell does not know what D. S. O. means, or that *Corpus Christi* is a saint's day to him, does not mean that the reader, when presented with D. S. O. and *Corpus Christi,* cannot know what they mean because of Dowell's ignorance. Rather, Dowell's judgments become primary facts that the reader, in his turn, *must* judge—and be especially careful to judge in light of contradictory evidence—when Dowell's remarks concern either assertions or facts that can be interpreted ambivalently.

Because of the complex semiosis in which signs operate in this novel, it seems that a critic interested in more than polemic must readily grant degrees of probability to other critics' views insofar as those views are reasonably argued. Thus it is unreasonable in a conflict of interpretations of *The Good Soldier* to maintain one's own view as the only correct one where the evidence—as in this novel—is not conclusive and tends to impress different critics in different ways. The simple truth of logic remains that the greater probability of one opinion does not and cannot destroy the probability of its contrary.

Consequently, it might be refreshing for the critic beset and jaded with many probabilities in one area to turn elsewhere in a work and examine a different dimension of it in an attempt to elucidate some facet of structure or meaning that is more likely to yield a more satisfying degree of probability or perhaps certainty itself. It seems that this is still possible for *The Good Soldier.*

One of the remarkable things about *The Good Soldier* is its manifest independence of systems of meaning that critics have found central to it. Ford has created something quite autonomous. Whether Dowell is correct or incorrect, whether Edward Ashburnham is guilty or guiltless, the novel survives as a tale of passion—as a tale of suffering. Ultimately the justice or injustice of the suffering that the characters endure is not nearly as important as the simple fact that they suffer and that the sufficient cause of their suffering is a lack of communication—especially between husband and wife. The simple inability of Edward and Leonora to sit down and talk with each other, the simple inability of husband and wife to blend their worlds of thought, action and emotion into a new and unified world of discourse, the simple inability of the Ashburnhams to be, in Edward's phrase, "better friends," is the cause of the bone-deep suffering in the novel. If Edward committed adultery again and again—according to natural justice— he *should* suffer; but his guilt or innocence is beyond proof; the novel's true certainty is that he *did* suffer. The same can be said for Leonora, Dowell, Florence, Maisie and Nancy: the degree of their innocence or guilt is unknowable, but that they suffered is the story's hard and resilient fact. And at the heart of the suffering of each is his inability to communicate in a timely and meaningful way with another who could understand him.

In its structure of ambiguous meanings and in the pervasive lack of communication that is *a* central meaning in the novel, *The Good Soldier* is like Henry James's *The Sacred Fount* and Ford's own *No More Parades.* Like the *Fount, The Good Soldier* presents few facts of which the reader can be certain. For the few facts that James offers in the *Fount,* he structures primarily two interpretations, the narrator's and Grace Brissenden's. Neither one is more certain than the other; each makes perfect sense. The true one is ultimately unknowable. In *The Good Soldier* there is only one interpretation given, Dowell's. But the reader stands to the certain facts in the story as the interpreters in the *Fount* stand to the certain facts in theirs. Each can produce a theory that has the consistency of a logical probability drawn from the signs given; none can arrive at certainty. In one sense, then (and not a pejorative one), the structure of *The Good Soldier* is a correlative of the certainty of one of its meanings—the lack of effective communication.

The Good Soldier also bears a relation to *No More Parades.* In that novel, by using a given set of facts and interpreting them from Christopher Tietjen's point of view and then by using the same facts and presenting their meaning from Sylvia's viewpoint, Ford dramatizes the heart-rendering gap in the world of discourse of husband and wife. The gap is never closed; on the contrary it is opened wider (as Christopher is assigned to the front) by Sylvia's failure to tell her husband the meaning of Perowne's interruption of what promised to be their reunion in consummated love. In this novel the reader knows the whole truth, but Christopher and Sylvia never do. They are like Edward and Leonora in *The Good Soldier;* they are the victims of their own silence. Perhaps Christopher and Sylvia's is not the saddest story, but it is a story that leads one to re-examine in retrospect how the one certainty of non-communication could and did effect all the suffering in that novel which did tell "the saddest story."

The value of isolating a certain and basic meaning in terms of non-communication seems evident: to each of the conflicting interpretations of *The Good Soldier* the divisive silence of Edward and Leonora in each other's company is something implicitly necessary. The manner in which this meaning is developed—in terms of facts and assertions, verifiable and non-verifiable meanings—cannot be reasonably questioned either. Also, the certainty of this meaning of non-communication and the certainty of how this non-communication means in the novel in no way destroy the probability of other and more elaborate meanings and structures in *The Good Soldier.* Rather, these certainties are basic to each of the existing probable interpretations of Ford's novel and, I conjecture, must remain so for other readings that the highly connotative and frequently ambiguous signs in *The Good Soldier* will subsequently suggest. (pp. 39-49)

> *Joseph Wiesenfarth, "Criticism and the Semiosis of 'The Good Soldier'," in* Modern Fiction Studies, *Vol. 9, No. 1, Spring, 1963, pp. 39-49.*

Charles G. Hoffmann   (essay date 1967)

[*Hoffmann is an American educator and critic. In the following excerpt, he regards the corrupt nature of humanity as the central theme in* The Good Soldier.]

The *donnée* for *The Good Soldier* is to be found in *The Spirit of the People* (1907), Ford's impressionistic study of England and the English. In it is the "true story" of a married man who fell in love with his young ward, until, when "the situation had grown impossible," the girl was sent on a trip around the world to save the marriage and prevent scandal. Ford was asked by the husband, who was

"afraid of a 'scene,' " to accompany them to the station; but the parting was so lacking in display of tenderness or any emotion, without so much as a goodby, that it seemed "to be a manifestation of a national characteristic that is almost appalling." The girl died en route at Brindisi, and Ford comments "that at the moment of separation a word or two might have saved the girl's life and the man's misery without infringing eternal verities." From this anecdote, like James's *donnée* for *The Spoils of Poynton,* Ford fashioned *The Good Soldier,* a masterpiece so closely interwoven in theme, character, structure, and technique that it reaches Flaubert's ideal of the perfect fusion of form and subject matter: "The Idea exists only by virtue of its form."

The Good Soldier is divided into four parts; while this structural division is not unusual in the conventional narrative, *The Good Soldier* does not progress chronologically. Rather, Ford relies upon *progression d'effet,* a theory of narrative progression developed by Ford and Conrad during their collaboration: "in writing a novel we agreed that every word set on paper . . . must carry the story forward and, that as the story progressed, the story must be carried forward faster and faster and with more and more intensity." Partly, this theory is the logical extension of Poe's theory of the short story; partly, it is based on Flaubert's concern with style in relation to subject and form. But what is unique is the idea that the story must be carried forward faster and more intensely as it progresses. *Progression d'effet* is best exemplified in Conrad's work by *Heart of Darkness,* in which Marlow (and his listeners, and, by extension, the reader) journeys more and more deeply into "the heart of darkness," penetrating at a faster and more intense pace into the psychological and moral darkness of man's evil self. It is best exemplified in Ford's work by *The Good Soldier* in which John Dowell (and his listener, and, by extension, the reader) unfolds, layer after layer, the surface manners of these "good people," penetrating at a faster and more intense pace to the psychological and moral core of rottenness.

Crucial to the control of the narrative is the role of the narrator, John Dowell. As his name suggests, Dowell holds the story together, linking the various parts and giving unity to the whole. Through his mind we "know" the others; through his *impressions* we "see" the events and relationships revealed in the novel. The choice of narrator is therefore essential to the rendering of impressions, and Ford chose a narrator who is centrally involved in the situation. Although Edward Ashburnham is the protagonist of the "story," Ford has created a novel with a double focus, just as Conrad utilized Kurtz and Marlow in *Heart of Darkness.* And indeed Dowell eventually identifies himself with Ashburnham. . . . The effect is quite similar to James's use of the governess as the narrator of *The Turn of the Screw,* for like Dowell's, it is her psychological and moral impressions of appearances and realities which are the central focus of the novel.

The "occasion" for the novel is Dowell's "telling" the story to an imaginary sympathetic listener some months after the suicide of Edward Ashburnham. As Dowell states at the beginning of Part Four, he is telling

> . . . the story as it comes. And, when one discusses an affair—a long, sad affair—one goes back, one goes forward. One remembers points that one has

forgotten and one explains them all the more minutely since one recognizes that one has forgotten to mention them in their proper places, and that one may have given, by omitting them, a false impression. I console myself with thinking that this is a real story and that, after all, real stories are probably told best in the way a person telling a story would tell them. They will then seem most real.

Thus the past is reconstructed not as a chronological report of what happened from beginning to end, but as a series of impressions as they are remembered and relived in the mind of the narrator. The intent of the narrator is to re-create for his listener the immediate experience of the event or scene, tempered, however, by the irony of present knowledge and re-examined in the light of later knowledge.

This going back and forward over the affair necessitates a manipulation of time sequences as though the story were being told "in a very rambling way so that it may be difficult for anyone to find his path through what may be a sort of maze." Yet *The Good Soldier* is anything but rambling; it has its own inner logic and order of time, as does Faulkner's *The Sound and the Fury*. The progression of the novel is, as Ford defined this "New Form" of the novel,

> . . . the rendering of an Affair: of one embroilment, one set of embarrassments, one human coil, one psychological progression. From this the Novel got its Unity. No doubt it might have its caesura—or even several; but these must be brought about by temperamental pauses, markings of time when the treatment called for them. But the whole novel was to be an exhaustion of aspects, was to proceed to one culmination, to reveal once and for all, in the last sentence, or the penultimate . . . the psychological significance of the whole. (Of course, you might have what is called in music your Coda.) (***Thus to Revisit***).

The narrative pattern of *The Good Soldier,* that path through the maze, is suggested by two controlling images—the first stated at the beginning of the novel, and the second at the end—"four-square coterie" and "shuttlecocks." The unity of the Affair, its oneness of embroilment and psychological progression, is suggested by the intimate cohesiveness of the group that excludes the outside world and by the group's appearance as a solid front of friendship that is permanent and stable. More importantly, the image of the four-square coterie suggests the various possible combinations of relationships among the four that are revealed as the novel progresses—Edward and Florence as lovers, Florence and Leonora as antagonists, Edward and John as rivals for Nancy yet in the end as alter egos, Leonora's love-hate of Edward that alternates between attraction and repulsion, paralleled by John's love-hate of Leonora—to say nothing of the fact that the Dowells and the Ashburnhams are on the surface seemingly happily married couples presenting to the public eye a solid front of friendship. The four-square coterie image alternates between suggesting a "stepping minuet," with all its implications of a graceful way of life that is dead, and "a prison full of screaming hysterics," just as the novel itself shuttles between keeping up appearances and giving way to hysteria.

Each of the four parts examines and re-examines different facets of the interrelationships of the two couples and the various individuals, like Maisie and Nancy, who are drawn into the center of the square by one or the other of the four. The focus of the novel shifts back and forth among the coterie like a shuttlecock as light is shed on an individual or on a relationship. The pattern is not haphazard: as a character or relationship is illuminated in a scene, light is thrown on all the other characters because of the interlocking unity of the group. It may be nothing more than Florence's laying her finger on Edward's wrist (Chapter Four, Part One), but it is sufficient to involve and reveal all four of them. Thus the novel progresses at a faster and more intense pace as each aspect contributes to the psychological significance of the whole, culminating in the final revelation. The listener-reader is drawn deeper and deeper into the labyrinthine way until the heart of darkness is reached and the heart of the matter is known: the core of rottenness in man.

The very rhythm of *The Good Soldier* with its alternations of mood and tempo (its progression and caesura) moves like parallel lines "more and more swiftly to the inevitable logic of the end." Time is not measured by the calendar or the clock as though events were categorically separated and unrelated in space and time. Ford's historical sense, his sense of the past, achieved in the historical novels, is here applied to his sense of the present: events, though they may *appear* to be so at the time they occur, are not isolated happenings unrelated to the past or the future. Thus the date, August 4th, is not merely a day on the calendar of the year 1874, 1899, 1900, 1901, 1904, or 1913; the dates, respectively, are those of Florence's birth, of her trip around the world, of her affair with Jimmy, of her marriage to Dowell, of the death of Maisie Maidan and the beginning of Florence's affair with Edward, and of Florence's suicide. The date is a living link with the past, a revelation of the present, and a portent for the future. It is an important and structural symbol in the novel.

At eleven o'clock on the night of August 4, 1914, as every English schoolboy knows, England declared war on Germany. At approximately the same hour on the night of August 4, 1913, as every reader of *The Good Soldier* knows, Florence Dowell committed suicide. It is principally by this device of the fateful date that Ford links the microcosm of his fictional characters with the macrocosm of a world at war, thereby enlarging the scope and significance of the novel. For what the novel explores are the causes of failure in human relationships, whether it be in love, marriage, friendship, national character, or international relations. The events leading up to Florence's suicide and Nancy Rufford's madness six months later are the causes of the breakdown of civilization, of a world gone suicidal and mad.

There are some discrepancies in references to dates in the novel, particularly in the sequence of events that occurred during the first four days of August, 1904. For example, the first meeting of the Ashburnhams and the Dowells at the watering spa of Nauheim, the trip to the castle at M— where Leonora learns that Florence is Edward's mistress, the boxing of Maisie's ears by Leonora which Florence witnesses, and the death of Maisie occur early in August and all but the first specifically on August 4th. But Dowell later states that Maisie's death occurred a month after the two couples had met, which would put the latter event early in July not August. In the manuscript version of *The*

Good Soldier Ford changed the date of the first meeting of the two couples from July, 1906 to August, 1904. Dowell's later statement would be consistent with the original July date, but apparently Ford did not catch the discrepancy in relation to Dowell's statement when he changed the date in the manuscript.

However, the larger pattern of narrative time in the novel is unaffected by the minor factual discrepancies, for the time sequences are consistent both with the theme and with the psychological progression of the novel. Narrative time in *The Good Soldier* is not merely a realistic, chronological account of events as they happened; for *The Good Soldier* is an impressionistic novel, not a naturalistic one. Time is rendered through the impressions and memories of the narrating consciousness of John Dowell, who is not an omniscient narrator. A Bergsonian account of "lived time," it is intensive, qualitative, intuitive, indivisible; it is a concept of time and memory in which the living past merges into the present.

Thus, the memory of the narrator does not "lapse"; the "truth" of his recollections is not sequential factualism but psychological impressionism leading to a comprehension of the past by the telescoping of events. Indeed, Ford *deliberately,* through his narrator, focuses attention on the "facts" of time so that the careful reader will realize that what is important is not calendar or clock time, but the psychological and symbolic interrelationships of events. The events reported as all having happened during the first four days of August, 1904, are one indivisible continuum of interlocking memory in the mind of Dowell, having, according to Bergson, an immanent existence in one's consciousness along with an awareness of the present moment.

Thus also, the Anglo-American world generally considers August 4, 1914, when England declared war on Germany, as the date for the beginning of World War I. But in actuality Austria declared war on Serbia on July 28th, thus beginning a series of interlocking events. A series of mobilization orders and ultimatums between Russia and Germany occurred from July 29th to August 1st, and Germany declared war on Russia on August 1st. France mobilized on that day; Germany on August 3rd declared war on France and invaded Belgium on the morning of August 4th, with England's declaration of war the result.

These fast-moving events, all interrelated and dependent on one another, were a continuum of crises in the historical sense; and in the psychological sense they could be telescoped into the action of one symbolic day. Similarly, Ford telescopes the events of August 4, 1904, and crowds the fateful day of August 4, 1913, with a similar series of crises—Ashburnham's romance with Nancy Rufford begins, Dowell learns his wife once had an affair with Jimmy, and Florence commits suicide. The macrocosm of a world at war is thus symbolically linked to the microcosm of the private world of the characters in crisis, and both are moving more and more rapidly toward catastrophe and the end of the world as they knew it.

The whole novel is structured, therefore, around the August 4th date. Although the exact date is first specifically mentioned at the beginning of Part Two, Part One narrates or refers directly or indirectly to all the important interrelated events connected with this date (the only exception being Florence's affair with Jimmy, which occurred on August 4, 1900). Part One ends with the death of Maisie on August 4, 1904. Part Two begins with a specific summary of the date as a portent in Florence's life and ends with the events of the night of August 4, 1913. Part Three begins with the revelation to Dowell of his wife's infidelity with Ashburnham (begun on or just before August 4, 1904; ended August 4, 1913) and of the reasons for her suicide, and it ends with a summary of Ashburnham's series of loves up to the death of Maisie and the taking on of Florence (which "caused" Maisie's death). Part Four reveals the consequences of Florence's suicide on that portentous date: it leads ultimately to Edward Ashburnham's suicide and to Nancy Rufford's madness. The interlocking events which are the cause of Florence's and Edward's suicide and Nancy's madness are like the events that led to World War I—each move caused a counter move because of the entangled embroilment of the nations and their alliances; each action of the characters caused a reaction in the others because of their entangled lives.

The Good Soldier, in spite of its title, is not a "war" novel in the sense that Hemingway's *A Farewell to Arms* and Remarque's *All Quiet on the Western Front* are, nor even in the sense that Ford's *Parade's End* is. Nor is *The Good Soldier* an allegory about the defects of society traced back to the defects of human nature as Golding's *Lord of the Flies* is. Yet *The Good Soldier* is a "war" novel in that it analyzes the seeds of destruction in human nature and, by extension, in human society on the verge of war; and it is an allegorical novel in that society is made up of types like the Ashburnhams and the Dowells, the "good people" who rule the nation and guide its destiny, and, with all the good (and bad) intentions in the world, bring it to ruin and disaster. The *rationale* of the novel is to reveal the process by which this happens.

This *rationale* is explicitly stated in the first chapter:

> You may well ask why I write. And yet my reasons are quite many. For it is not unusual in human beings who have witnessed the sack of a city or the falling to pieces of a people to desire to set down what they have witnessed for the benefit of unknown heirs or of generations infinitely remote; or, if you please, just to get the sight out of their heads.

> Someone has said the death of a mouse from cancer is the whole sack of Rome by the Goths, and I swear to you that the breaking up of our little four-square coterie was such another unthinkable event.

Thus, the break-up of the four-square coterie is the break-up of civilization itself, heading toward disaster. Though the dissolution of the intimate group seems to occur suddenly through a series of crises and catastrophes (suggesting the days of feverish diplomatic negotiations after the assassination of Archduke Ferdinand in the summer of 1914 and the crisis days of August 1st through 4th), the novel's main concern is with the causes of the break-up. Therefore, the emphasis in the novel is on the ironic discrepancy between the coterie's outward appearance of permanence and stability and the inner reality of its being cancerous from the start, just as cancer may fester for years and then break out with painful and mortal suddenness.

Yet the discrepancy between appearance and reality is a

double irony, for if the minuet image is false, then the whole of life, manners, and morality are false and the proper man is "a raging stallion forever neighing after his neighbour's womenkind." If man is nothing more than a beast, then war is his destiny; and all that man has achieved in civilized behavior is "a folly and a mockery." Dowell shrinks away from accepting such a conclusion: "For, if for me we were four people with the same tastes, with the same desires, acting—or, no not acting—sitting there and there unanimously, isn't that the truth? If for nine years I have possessed a goodly apple that is rotten at the core and discover its rottenness only in nine years and six months less four days, isn't it true to say that for nine years I possessed a goodly apple?"

However, by the end of the novel the reader can accept no other conclusion; for he comes to discover, as Dowell had discovered, that the very virtues of civilization are the cause of its downfall. Just as Swift strips away the appearance of man's pretense to Reason, so Ford penetrates deeper into the "dark forest" of the human heart to reveal the core of rottenness hidden from view. It is a small consolation to man to realize that his "goodly apple" was good only because he was ignorant of its rottenness. It is indeed "the saddest story" because the tragedy is that "it is all a darkness."

The rottenness at the core is a disease of the heart. This sickness of heart is similar to E. M. Forster's theme of the undeveloped heart in *Passage to India:* "For it is not that the Englishman can't feel—it is that he is afraid to feel. He has been taught at his public school that feeling is bad form. . . . He must bottle up his emotions, or let them out only on a very special occasion. However, Ford emphasizes much more than Forster the "cold" heart that is symbolized by Florence's locked bedroom door (and obversely by Leonora's door that is always open) and that is represented most obviously by Dowell's own lack of passion. Edward's passion is perverted into sentimentalism; Leonora's, into hate and martyrdom. All of them, however, keep up appearances of happiness; it is good form to do so.

The technique Ford employs in developing his theme of the heart is similar to Thomas Mann's use of physical disease or deformity as a symbol or symptom of spiritual sickness, except that in *The Good Soldier* even the physical disease itself is a sham and thus part of the moral rottenness. This literal deception of the heart, carried on by both Florence and Edward (with Leonora's tacit acceptance), is a corollary of the main theme: "this pitch of civilization to which we have attained, after all the preachings of all the moralists, and all the teachings of all the mothers to all the daughters *in saeculum saeculorum*" ["for ages and ages"] has amounted to nothing more than a mere morality of manners by which true immorality is hidden by appearances in order to avoid scandal. It is underlined by the fact that Maisie Maidan, the only truly innocent character in the novel, is the one who really suffers from serious heart trouble and who actually dies of heart failure; and yet the suggestion seems to be that she is able to preserve her innocence only because the disease is real.

At the beginning of the novel the reader learns that Florence "had, as the saying is, a 'heart.'" One is led to believe, as Dowell himself was, that she died of heart trouble. The irony here lies not in the fact that the reader is deceived by the narrator (the purpose obviously is that the listener-reader must be deceived in order to understand Dowell's shock of recognition that appearances are a deception), but that in a figurative sense Florence died of a "broken heart" when she learned Edward no longer loved her. Yet even the "broken heart" is not the final "truth"; what ultimately drove her to suicide was not the loss of Edward's love—she might have tried to win him back—but that the truth of her earlier infidelity with Jimmy was now known and she could no longer hope to retain her public image of a respectable married woman or to continue to deceive her husband. The true sickness of her heart was vanity.

Dowell also reveals at the beginning that "Captain Ashburnham also had a heart." Dowell (and the reader) learns that this is the story told to dispel any possible scandal involving Edward's leaving India to follow Maisie. Even Florence's father supposedly "had a heart," but he died of bronchitis at the ripe old age of eighty-four. Although there was nothing physically wrong with his heart, he spent his life guarding against his heart, suggesting that Florence's supposed heart trouble was hereditary. Significantly, Dowell inherits Mr. Hurlbird's fortune through Florence.

If Florence lacks heart, she does not lack passion. But Dowell does, at least until the end, when he falls hopelessly in love with Nancy. It is not that he did not "love" his wife (they even manage to elope romantically), but that Dowell, being a proper Philadelphia gentleman, did not respond to her one gesture of passion toward him the night of their elopement. Though Dowell is truly deceived by his wife's "heart," it nonetheless suits his passive personality to play the part of a male nurse. And Dowell's role as nurse, related as it is to the theme of the sick heart, is a key to the primary theme of the novel, for the dark forest of the heart, the core of the rottenness, is this disease of the heart which creates an evil not only out of basic human drives, but also out of the subtler morality of manners.

If Edward and Florence commit adultery, they do so, therefore, out of love and passion; if Leonora tortures Edward and drives him to suicide, she does it out of hate and jealousy; but Dowell's intellectual detachment and analytical observation are a subtler form of evil. In accepting his role as nurse to Florence, he must accept the responsibility for creating a "shock-proof world," for heading "off what the English call 'things'—off love, poverty, crime, religion, and the rest of it." In other words, Dowell must create a rarefied atmosphere that denies life itself. Dowell's tragedy, then, is his lack of commitment to life itself; in a moment of self-revelation near the end of Part One, he recognizes that he deserves neither heaven nor hell— "perhaps they will find me an elevator to run," an appropriately modern reward for one of the living dead.

The ultimate significance of Dowell's role as nurse is not revealed until near the end of the novel when, acting as nurse to Nancy, he says: "So here I am very much where I started thirteen years ago. I am the attendant, not the husband, of a beautiful girl, who pays no attention to me." Caretaker of a sick world gone mad, he is unable to minister to it because, as he reveals at the beginning, "I know nothing—nothing in the world—of the hearts of men. I only know that I am alone—horribly alone." He has experienced nothing; he has felt nothing; he "has nothing whatever to show for it." Ultimately, his is the greater evil; for he has denied life itself.

The Ashburnhams (and the Dowells) are "what in England it is the custom to call "quite good people.'" This categorization is a recurring statement throughout the novel and is essential to our understanding of the relationship of the microcosm of the novel's "affair" to the macrocosm of the world at large. With all its implications of governing class, of Anglo-Saxon tradition, of refinement of manners and morals, and of cultural heritage and the comfortable material life, these "good people" represent the best that civilization has to offer. Thus, the rottenness at the core of their lives is the rottenness of Anglo-American civilization, and the end of that four-square coterie is the end of that civilization itself.

Related to the concept of the "good people" is the idea of "the good soldier." Though Ford states in his dedicatory letter that he suggested the title "in hasty irony" and "never ceased to regret it" [see excerpt dated 1927], the title is suggestive of its theme. Edward Ashburnham is obviously the good soldier. In a literal sense, he is "a first-rate soldier," but also in a larger sense he is the good soldier of civilian life—he "was the cleanest-looking sort of chap; an excellent magistrate . . . one of the best landlords . . . a painstaking guardian" of the poor and of drunks. He was, in a word, a sentimentalist, "for all good soldiers are sentimentalists—all good soldiers of that type."

The irony of this appellation is revealed by Dowell immediately: "he was just exactly the sort of chap that you could have trusted your wife with. And I trusted mine—and it was madness." And, as though Ashburnham really believed it, "he would say that constancy was the finest of the virtues. He said it very stiffly, of course, but still as if the statement admitted of no doubt." In his sentimentality, he really did believe it. The emptiness of good form—of the appearance of courage, loyalty, honor, constancy—as opposed to the reality of being courageous, loyal, honorable, and constant, is the essence of his sentimentality and good soldiery. He believed intensely and optimistically "that the woman he was making love to at the moment was the one he was destined, at last, to be eternally constant to." The details of his self-deception are revealed in the rest of the novel, particularly in the last two parts. Yet even at the end when he faces up to himself, as any good soldier should, his honor is destructive of self and of others. In the best of good form, he quietly says goodby to Dowell, as though he were about to take a nap before tea; and he goes to cut his throat in the privacy of his room.

The climax of Part One (Chapter Four) illuminates the relationship between Florence and Leonora, but it also sheds indirect light on the relationship between Florence and Edward and that between Leonora and Edward. At Florence's insistence they all view the pencil draft of Luther's Protest. Looking into Edward's eyes, Florence says,

> "It's because of that piece of paper that you're honest, sober, industrious, provident, and clean-lived. If it weren't for that piece of paper you'd be like the Irish or the Italians or the Poles, but particularly the Irish. . . . "

And she laid one finger upon Captain Ashburnham's wrist.

Leonora, reacting violently to the scene, says to Dowell: "don't you see what's going on?" But when Dowell, though he instinctively suspects the truth, denies he knows, Leonora backs away from breaking up the coterie and instead refers to Luther's Protest: "Don't you see that's the cause of the whole miserable affair; of the whole sorrow of the world? And of the eternal damnation of you and me and them. . . . "

Ironically, Leonora's failure to inform Dowell of the true significance of Florence's laying of her finger on Edward's wrist illuminates one aspect of the macrocosm—man's inability to live in harmony and peace with his fellow man. Florence's militant Protestantism and Leonora's narrow Catholicism clash as abstract ideologies. Yet the reverberations of the clash illuminate the personalities involved in the reflected light of this scene. Dowell, passive and uncommitted to life, is relieved to understand it intellectually as a clash of ideas that is kept impersonal by Leonora because of Florence's "heart." Even Leonora withdraws from her vision of hell and becomes "just Mrs. Ashburnham again." Yet, as Dowell realizes later, Leonora's Catholicism is the key to her personality and particularly to her relationship with her husband as a philanderer. Florence's triumphant Protestantism is a reflection of her conquest of Edward; the finger on Edward's wrist is her victorious gesture that lets Leonora know that she has conquered Edward. Florence knows at the same time that Leonora, because of her Catholic sense of martyrdom and because Florence is supposedly a "heart" case, will do nothing overt.

Parts One, Two, and Four all end with a death scene; significantly, Part Three begins with a detailed description of Florence's death and ends implicitly with the theme of the death of the heart, Leonora's. The end of Edward's affair with Maisie was to be, according to Leonora's plan, the beginning of her again winning Edward's love. Though Leonora could not know that Maisie would die as she did, she took comfort in the fact that this affair had to be passionless because of Maisie's heart condition. But "Florence knocked all that on the head." Furthermore, one of the reasons Florence committed suicide was that Edward was already beginning his romance with Nancy Rufford; thus, all of Leonora's hopes, all of her reasons for waiting while Edward went through his "rutting season," were false to begin with. The minuet becomes a dance of death though all the formalities of that graceful dance are maintained: Leonora "had been drilled—in her tradition, in her upbringing—to keep her mouth shut." The death-wish is strong in all four of the coterie; but Leonora survives because of her Catholicism and because she enters into a normal marriage after the death of Edward. Dowell survives because he has been dead, emotionless and passionless, all along. As Dowell himself says, he must "get back into contact with life. I had been kept for twelve years in a rarefied atmosphere."

The death of Maisie is that of innocence; not only is she innocent (her attack is brought on by the shock of realization that Leonora has brought her to Nauheim so that Edward can make love to her), but her death is also the beginning of nine years of deception by the other three. It is only Dowell's ignorance that makes those years happy ones. The happiness itself was true; what was false was its basis. The suicide of Florence "knocked all that on the head" too. And, with the suicide of Edward about four months later, the whole edifice, the "safe castle" that seemed so permanent and stable, crumbles.

Color symbolism is an important corollary to the theme of heart. Whereas heart and passion are associated with red, pink is associated with the dilution, or, at least, suppression of emotions. When Dowell learns that Florence's death was a suicide, he remembers only the *pink* effulgence from the electric lights in the hotel lounge. When Edward receives Nancy's telegram, printed on *pink* paper, that she is having "a rattling good time" on her trip, he reads it without showing a trace of emotion and hands it to Dowell without a word. Then he goes quietly to his room and cuts his throat with a pen knife (one might imagine the *red* effluence of blood, but it is the only death in the novel that occurs "off-stage." Maisie, though she dies grotesquely with the lid of the portmanteau closing over her head, is quickly arranged by Leonora to look like "a bride in the sunlight of the mortuary candles." Florence's body is "quite respectably arranged" on the bed as though she had died peacefully).

Though Edward, pink-complexioned, displays no outward emotion on receiving the pink-paper telegram, his inner emotions are in turmoil; for the telegram is a double shock to him—in his sentimentality, he would have expected Nancy to suffer as he does; and in his heart he recognizes Leonora's triumph in separating Nancy from him. Only good form keeps him from showing his despair in front of Dowell, just as he brought Dowell along with him to the train station to see Nancy off in order to prevent "a scene": "There was upon those people's faces no expression of any kind whatever. The signal for the train's departure was a very bright *red;* that is about as passionate a statement as I can get into that scene" [italics added by the critic].

Ashburnham *does* act, even if his act is one of self-destruction. Dowell, however, on learning of his wife's death, "felt no sorrow, no desire for action, no inclination to go upstairs and fall upon the body of my wife." True, he too has received a shock: he has just learned that Florence had an affair with Jimmy before their marriage. But the truth is that his whole life has been a pinkish effulgence—not without feeling, in fact he is too much the man of sensibility, but without deep emotions or significant actions. He identifies himself with Edward at the end, which provides the novel with its double focus; but he himself admits he is the fainter image (revealingly, Edward talks to him as though he were "a woman or a solicitor"): "I loved Edward Ashburnham . . . because he was just myself. If I had had the courage and the virility and possibly also the physique of Edward Ashburnham I should . . . have done much what he did." Significantly, of course, Dowell does not do what Ashburnham did, for he lacks those very qualities of Ashburnham. It is the good form that makes Edward seem like Dowell; what is the appearance of respectability in Ashburnham is the actuality of Dowell's personality. As Dowell admits of himself, "I am able to assure you that I am a strictly respectable person. I have never done anything that the most anxious mother of a daughter or the most careful dean of a cathedral would object to. I have only followed, faintly, and in my unconscious desires, Edward Ashburnham."

Florence, Edward, and Leonora all have blue eyes, and both Florence and Leonora wear blue to heighten the blueness of the eyes. It is not objectivity but impenetrability that is symbolized by the blue eyes; the eyes alternate between expressing cold defiance and warm tenderness, yet neither coldness nor tenderness is the ultimate truth of these "windows of the soul"; but, like the waters of the blue sea, they only reflect the surface. Dowell's first sight of Ashburnham is that his face typified English unemotionalism: "There was in it neither joy nor despair; neither hope nor fear; neither boredom nor satisfaction." And Florence hides her face in her hands, Dowell's last sight of her alone.

Significantly, Edward's complexion (and Florence's and Leonora's) is smooth and clear, symbolizing the smooth, clear surface of their lives, apparently unmarked by any deep emotion. Leonora's one emotional outburst that results in overt action, the boxing of Maisie's ears, is smoothed over by the social lie that the small gold key suspended from her wrist had tangled in Maisie's hair. This is the key to her dispatch case which she keeps locked and in which, Dowell suggests, Leonora perhaps "locked up her heart and her feelings." Florence kept her bedroom door locked (the first time Dowell entered her bedroom was the night she died), and behind it she hid her heart and feelings. Leonora kept her door wide open, but only to hear "the approaching footsteps of ruin and disaster"; the first time in nine years she entered her husband's bedroom was to tell him she would divorce him so that he can marry Nancy, offering herself in a martyrdom that her church forbade. For nine years they hide from the rest of the world and from each other their true feelings until so intense is the hatred or jealousy being suppressed that it explodes in violent emotion and action.

"It would have been better in the eyes of God," Dowell comments, "if they had all attempted to gouge out each other's eyes with carving knives. But they were 'good people.' " It is significant that Dowell says "they" not "we," for if he had included himself it might have been his saving grace. It is Dowell who provides the "shock-proof world" for Florence. It is Dowell who displays no emotion on the death of his wife. It is Dowell who watches on the sidelines the game of shuttlecocks being played by the Ashburnhams and Nancy Rufford (Leonora's attempt to draw him into the "game" by suggesting he marry Nancy after Florence's death is unsuccessful). And it is Dowell who, knowing that Edward is about to commit suicide, does nothing to hinder it; he does not even comment, thinking that perhaps it would not be quite good form to say, "God bless you."

We are brought full circle to the anecdote that provided the *donnée* for **The Good Soldier.** For what is "appalling" ultimately—the final effect to which the novel has progressed in its last words—is that Dowell, Ashburnham's pale American image, is unable to say anything, even something sentimental, for fear of breaching "English good form." In the face of his friend's direct, challenging glare, he asks himself, "Why should I hinder him? I didn't think he was wanted in the world. . . . " A word, an action, might have saved the girl from madness and Edward from self-destruction, for "he was wanted in the world."

Thus, the novel ends on a double note of tragic irony. Dowell's failure to interfere, his neutrality in a world of violent, warring personalities, is as much if not more a cause of madness and self-destruction as Leonora's being pleased with the telegram which represents her triumph over Edward in the game of shuttlecocks. It is an appalling victory; Nancy and Edward were sacrificed to achieve Leonora's "happy ending with wedding bells and all"; for now she is free to marry Rodney Bayham and live a happy, normal life. Yet what is more appalling is Dowell's life as caretaker to Nancy, who to all appearances is a perfectly healthy and beautiful girl, whom Dowell is now "free" to marry but cannot because her reason will never be restored. The world will never be the same again though it will survive, as Leonora does, for "society must go on," but to Dowell who must nurse it—"it is a picture without a meaning." (pp. 75-91)

> *Charles G. Hoffmann, in his* Ford Madox Ford, *Twayne Publishers, Inc., 1967, 156 p.*

Patrick Swinden   (essay date 1973)

[*Swinden is an English critic and educator. In the following excerpt, he discusses Ford's use of the* progression d'effet *technique in* The Good Soldier.]

Ford's opinion, as expressed in a multitude of books on the art of fiction, was that the Victorians considered the novel an impure form, and that they had no use for a theory of the novel which allotted to it as an art-form limiting, though proper and exclusive, functions. Instead they had treated it as a mixed mode, in which the novelist could pontificate, describe, dramatise, self-dramatise, and generally taken upon himself the role of mediator and judge, both in respect of relations set up within his fiction and relations between aspects of his fiction and complementary aspects of the real world. (pp. 120-21)

Ford countered this accepted view of the novel with the Continental alternative. According to this, the novel was a pure form. It had functions and methods which were quite different from those of any other literary form, having nothing to do with the sermon, the tract, the essay, the moral treatise or the writing of history. These made up its first skin, as it were, which had been sloughed off in the course of the development of the form from Madame de Lafayette and Richardson to Jane Austen and Stendhal. With Flaubert the novel had once and for all come of age. It had developed a new and glossy skin which marked it out as an altogether different species of literature. Ford traced this development in **The English Novel** in a manner which is clearly positivist, the novel having now reached a level close to perfection in the work of the French realists, James and Conrad. (p. 121)

Ford substituted for the straightforward progress in time from one description of an event to another description of a later event, a chronologically erratic grouping of impressions of different aspects of a number of events. Now the point of view remains stable at the expense of the events it apprehends, rather than the other way about. The events adapt to the modes in which they are perceived, where before, the modes could chop and change as much as the author pleased so long as the 'story line' remained straight and went on its way diagrammatically from A to B to C and so on. Another consequence was that the events became more and more *mental* events since the plot became a pattern of impressions, subjective and relatively time-free, whereas before they had been objective events which minds operated on, and were seen to operate on, from the vantage-point of the impression-free narrator. Temperamental and emotional forces themselves became events. Where the old novel was mechanical, even if the mechanism included parts of organic tissue, the new novel would be organic, even if it had an artificial valve or two inside it. (p. 122)

With the closer approximation to real life and the developed impressionist technique consequent upon it must go a subjectivising of the plot and a deterioration of any definite structure of events. Events will become as fluid as the minds and interests operating upon, and indeed creating them. In substituting impressions of events for the events themselves, Ford should have found that the old 'well-made' novel was beyond recall. In fact he never lost faith in the usefulness of 'well-made' novels. Somewhere there had to be found a point midway between real events—of which, unlike Flaubert, Ford nowhere seriously questioned the status—and our shifting perceptions of them, and this 'somewhere' would be the point of vantage from which the novel was written. Hence point of view, time-shift and impressionist rendering of events would remain techniques. The novelist, no longer omniscient in the manner of Fielding, Scott or Thackeray, would remain in control by working his narrative techniques into a pattern as absorbing as the old plotted novel was absorbing. Impressionist point of view would be responsible for the development of whole sequences of action, and to that extent would be dominant; but the arrangement, whilst not defying impressionist principles, would be undertaken by a novelist who had reserved to himself the choice of whose point of view should open and close each sequence of scenes. The arrangement of sequences Ford called the *progression d'effet.*

The method, though not the phrase, was Flaubert's. Ford was fascinated by the way in which in *Madame Bovary* 'the most casual detail' was used to 'inevitably carry the story forward'. He noticed that the action of the *Education* is nothing but a succession of such casual details and that its plot is therefore little more than a 'constant succession of tiny unobservable surprises'. This was what all novelists should try to achieve: 'every word set on paper . . . must carry the story forward and, . . . as the story progressed, the story must be carried forward faster and faster and with more and more intensity'. In his own work Ford tried to replace this succession of details—fixed, definite and largely external—by mental agitations, plays of temperament and changes of attitude on the Jamesian and Turgenevian model. He never achieved their degree of subtlety and he often had recourse to a melodramatic or even farcical type of plotting which they had left far behind. But if Ford has a claim on posterity it is by virtue of his attempt to bring together the new preoccupation with subjective responses and impulses, and an acceptably thrusting narrative, fluctuating in its time-scheme and subject to arbitrary interruption, but able to call forth the same degree of interest and excitement that the novel composed on the old lines had done in its Victorian heyday.

He succeeded best in **The Good Soldier** (1915), a novel with a tight, dramatic form of a kind that might have been suggested by the study of French realist practice. In this case the study had been very particular. The Dedicatory

Letter to his wife Stella shows that Ford was trying to emulate Maupassant's treatment of a subject in *Fort comme la mort* [see excerpt dated 1927]. This is the story of a fashionable and successful Parisian painter, Olivier Bertin, his mistress, Any de Guilleroy, and her daughter Annette. Olivier and Any are becoming aware of their decline into middle age. Olivier is falling in love with Annette. Clearly, then, the way is open for comparisons between Maupassant's novel and Ford's in respect of the subject. . . . The action of the French novel is organised around Annette's return from the country, and the effect of her presence on the liaison between the two older characters. In Ford's novel, the arrival on the scene of Nancy Rufford is a late though crucial development, and although her importance throughout is testified to by the mysterious references in part I to 'the girl' and 'the poor girl', at least as much space is occupied by Ashburnham's affairs with Maisie Maidan and Florence Dowell. Comparisons between subjects do not turn out to be quite so telling as might have been expected. Perhaps Ford had other things in mind; perhaps he was as much interested in method as in subject. (pp. 122-24)

Fort comme la mort, a study of an ageing artist, has a subject as closely connected with Maupassant's own life in 1888-9 as *The Good Soldier* has with Ford's in 1913-15. The psychological method was therefore permissible. But it was not effective [in Maupassant's case]. In the event, Maupassant proved incapable of combining objective and psychological techniques satisfactorily. Passages like those incorporating Madame de Guilleroy's reflections on her age are unnecessary and crude; they merely summarise imprecisely what has been suggested earlier through the dialogue. The action of the novel is impeded by their presence rather than placed in a different light. By manipulating Any's conscious thoughts, Maupassant is making sure we have grasped the significance of the action proper; and we can see that that is what he is doing. . . . To grasp the importance of this mistake, in terms of what Ford learned from it, we must be aware of another very important thing that the two novels have in common. Both deal with a process of becoming aware. Maupassant's work is about the way two middle-aged people discover that they are indeed middle-aged and that this discovery involves difficult readjustments to each other and to the circles within which they move. It is, more precisely, about Olivier Bertin's gradual discovery that he is in love with Annette de Guilleroy. As a psychological novel it tries to make the reader understand these issues from the inside; to plot, perception by perception, incident by incident, the trajectory of an intermittent, almost imperceptible, process of understanding on the part of its two main characters, and in particular of Bertin. But at each stage of the process Maupassant seems to have felt the need for summing-up of the point already reached—not, since he is a realist, from the vantage-point of an omniscient narrator, but from the point of view of the character concerned. Because this point of view is a fully conscious one, and because it duplicates insights already achieved by objective methods of dialogue and description on previous pages, it is felt to be irrelevant. The work is already done. No amount of description of conscious reflection will take it any further.

Ford's novel is also about a process of becoming aware. But in his case the awareness of his character, Dowell, is not so improved at the end of the book as is that of the reader who has followed its development. Meditations in Dowell's first-person narrative contribute a great deal more than a summing-up of what we already know, whilst functioning in a manner less pat and less academically articulated than do Bertin's conclusions in Maupassant's novel. It begins to look as if, by studying *Fort comme la mort,* Ford hit upon a method of reproducing a character's developing awareness of his situation in such a way as to allow us, the readers, to understand more about that situation than the character himself does: not *as much* or *as little* as Bertin, but *more than* Dowell. To do this he disposed of the customary method of third-person narrative.

Outside of his collaboration with Conrad at the turn of the century, Ford had never used first-person narrative before. He was to do so only once again, in *The Marsden Case.* It can therefore be assumed that he had special reasons for using it here, especially as he had taken so much time meditating how to present his story. The way he uses it in *The Good Soldier* is strange, to say the least. Usually we rely on a fictional narrator to make the story he tells clearer as it proceeds. The more he tells us, the more we understand the nature and significance of the events he is describing. If he is handled ironically, then the discrepancy between what he tells us and what we are able to infer (from the dialogue, for example) brings us by an indirect route to an understanding of what really took place. In Ford's novel this does not happen. The situation of Edward Ashburnham, involving Leonora and Florence in the first part of the book and Leonora and Nancy in the last, becomes more and more difficult to get to grips with, as the character of Dowell, who is telling us about it, becomes clearer and clearer.

This is perplexing, since Dowell is in charge of the whole affair. We are told, by him, that all the points of view of the other characters are, finally, constituents of his own. We have to rely on him almost entirely. Many critics don't like to do this, because they think he is unintelligent. I think not, and that the key to *The Good Soldier* lies in our understanding of the way Dowell's intelligence works. Taken as a whole, his narrative is not that of an imperceptive or abnormally stupid man, however much his gullibility in the face of deceptions of the grossest kind in the past might lead us to believe he ought to be. The six months during which he has been sounding the depths of the English heart have not been wasted.

Much of the confusion over Dowell's character springs from his use of a polite language which fits what we judge to have been his previous conception of himself and his friends much better than it fits him now, in his effort to communicate what he has learned and what he is still learning. He habitually uses easy expressions like 'as close as a good glove's with your hand' and 'we were thrown very much into the society of the nicer English'. That is to say, he is in the habit of making assumptions about the world that are inconsistent with what we discover he has learned about it. The language he uses betrays the position he occupies between two outlooks on life. The course of his narrative jolts back and forth between interpretations based on old assumptions, and others based on the undeceived outlook he is still only partly in possession of when the novel opens, and which, throughout, he fights against as much as he accepts. The most difficult problem he is left with is how to judge Edward. Conventionally, he should be the villain; but it is Leonora, the wronged wife, whom Dowell dislikes. Edward is more often 'poor' Edward, 'poor' devil, than the hated seducer of his wife. Of course, this has something to do with Dowell's basic deficiency, his feebleness and lack of passion, But more than that it is a problem because:

> I guess that I myself, in my fainter way, come into the category of the passionate, of the headstrong, and the too-truthful. For I can't conceal from myself the fact that I loved Edward Ashburnham— and that I loved him because he was just myself . . . you see, I am just as much of a sentimentalist as he was. . . .

This seems to me to be thoroughly obtuse of Dowell. Nothing he has said or done up to this point would lead one to believe that his judgement here is correct. He is not passionate and he is not headstrong. But he does love Edward Ashburnham. He is honest about what he feels but he still cannot recognise why he feels it: namely, because Edward, like himself, and like Nancy, whom he also loves, is a victim; and he automatically identifies with victims, especially when they are more attractive to others than he is. His mind dwells obsessively on this aspect of character, sometimes distilling from it images of sadistic melodrama. The self-deception he practices (even at the very end of the novel) in supposing his sense of fellow-feeling with Edward has its origin in a common strength rather than a common weakness, is evidence of the incomplete awareness he has of the situation he describes.

In a way he knows this already. He frequently confesses to ignorance of life in general as distinct from ignorance of particular aspects of it: 'I am only an ageing American with very little knowledge of life.' Dowell's reflections have not yet brought him to a proper understanding of himself. In this respect it is Ashburnham's role that is like Bertin's in *Fort comme la mort.* They both commit suicide—Ashburnham certainly, Bertin probably—as a result of what they discover about themselves in the course of their relationship with a young girl. Dowell lives on, still only half aware of what has brought him to where he is. On the other hand, we remember Maupassant's attempt to integrate passages of psychological reflection in his novel. In this respect Bertin is certainly the model for Dowell, not for Ashburnham, since all the points of view, and meditations on them and on events, are Dowell's. Both Dowell and Bertin gradually become aware of their true feelings and their reasons for them, though in Dowell's case this is an incomplete process. The difference is that by substituting Ashburnham for Bertin as a type within the narrative, and by incorporating that narrative within the first-person framework of Dowell's recollections, Ford turned the 'coming-aware' psychological passages to greater advantage. These are no longer summaries but essential parts of the plot, since it is the course of Dowell's meditations and memories which dictates the form the plot takes.

The manipulation of Dowell as speaker of a first-person narrative has another advantage: it provides additional psychological justification for the use of the time-shift which becomes, for the first time in Ford's work, a basic structural principle and not, as elsewhere, a useful technique to be applied at selected points in the novel's devel-opment. Dowell explains what it is and why he has to use it at the beginning of part IV:

> . . . when one discusses an affair—a long, sad affair—one goes back, one goes forward. One remembers points that one has forgotten, and one explains them all the more minutely since one recognizes that one has forgotten to mention them in their proper places and that one may have given, by omitting them, a false impression. I console myself with thinking that this is a real story and that, after all, real stories are probably told best in the way a person telling a story would tell them. They will then seem most real.

The way Dowell tells the story is consistent with his character. True to his amateur status, he keeps reminding us of his difficulty. The fact remains, though, that Dowell's peculiar but apparently quite natural method of organising what he has to say tells us more about *him* than he is able to tell us about Edward, Leonora, Florence and Nancy. We are almost entirely dependent on his viewpoint for our knowledge, let alone interpretation, of events involving *them*. Independent evidence is in the nature of things difficult to come by.

Where it does exist, Dowell often understands its relevance to the affair as well as we might have done ourselves if it had been presented to us in the third person. For example, it is obviously important that Leonora is a Roman Catholic. The comedy of misunderstandings at the castle at M— (part I, chap. 4) would be a much cruder thing if we had no knowledge of this, and the reason for Leonora's putting up with Edward's earlier and pettier indiscretions with women would be less intelligible. At the time, at M—, Dowell allows himself to be easily taken in by Leonora. He takes her religious explanation of her conduct seriously, though without seeming to understand anything more about her character as a result of it; and he seems to be blind to the more obvious cause of her hysterical behaviour—namely, her realisation that Florence and her husband have been conducting an affair behind her back. His acceptance of Leonora's explanation tells us a lot about the kind of man Dowell's was then, and to some extent has remained up to the time of writing the story. For Leonora's words 'gave me the greatest relief that I have ever had in my life. They told me, I think, almost more than I had ever gathered at one moment—about myself.' What he understands about himself is his capacity to be self-deceived, not because of stupidity, but because of laziness: 'I verily believe . . . that if my suspicion that Leonora was jealous of Florence had been the reason she gave for her outburst I should have turned upon Florence with the maddest kind of rage.' Why? Because Florence would have made self-deception on his part impossible, by allowing another person to confirm suspicions he had hitherto carefully hidden from himself because he was 'too tired'. Once we grasp this characteristic of Dowell, present throughout the nine years during which he knew the Ashburnhams, it becomes less difficult to appreciate the complex, and not unintelligent, state of mind in which he tells the story. He is more of a coward than a fool, and his over-riding insistence on not being bothered, on not being put to the trouble of facing the consequences of what he knows is really the case, is not eradicated by the time he writes the story. The third paragraph of the first page of the novel should have alerted us to this fact. Clearly, one thing

Dowell must have learned earlier, and did not learn in the process of writing about the affair, was the spuriousness of Florence's heart condition. What he gradually becomes aware of in the course of putting down his thoughts, and in the six months before, is the extent to which his passive acceptance of a state of affairs he half knew to be dangerous has created the disastrous situation he finds himself in now. The seriousness of Dowell's behaviour and the tragedy of the situation it helps to bring about are both trivialised and misunderstood if Dowell is judged to be simply a fool. The tragedy lies in the fact that he knew well enough what he was doing, but neglected to admit to himself what the consequences might be when he and Florence fell in with the Ashburnhams at Nauheim. The superficially convenient aspects of the friendship—his identification with Edward as a victim of the sex war, his sympathy with Leonora as another heart-patient nurse—override his sense of the basic danger: Florence's promiscuity answering to Edward's. Dowell's fault is that of seeing always and only what he wants to see. His observations on English Catholics are shrewd, because his knowledge of them is fully consonant at this stage with his wish to avoid the issue of Florence's adultery: Catholicism provides an explanation for Leonora's behaviour without bringing in the other unpleasant matter, which can therefore be disregarded. He knows enough to want to be ignorant, and thinks he can convert the wish into a reality by pretending hard enough that it is already granted.

This makes Dowell an interesting and complex first-person narrator and excuses some of the uncertainty we sense in the portrayal of Edward, who is ostensibly the main character. After all, the plot itself, quite apart from Dowell's organisation of it, is very complicated. It deals with Edward's affairs with at least five women, the financial problems of the Ashburnham household (the ups and downs of Edward's financial affairs accompany and provide motives for much of the action of the novel), Dowell's courtship and marriage, Florence's affair with Jimmy, and the religious issue between Edward and Leonora. There is plenty of material for Dowell to work on; and the fact that that is what it is there for goes far to excuse the hints of intrigue and over-complication left over from Ford's earlier novels. The use of the time-shift throughout the narrative, justified by the mental habits of the particular narrator Ford has chosen, removes the feeling of artificiality which might otherwise have been present. The more often Dowell returns to an awkward conjunction of incidents—Bagshawe's arrival at Nauheim at a crucial time, for example, or Maisie Maidan's overhearing Edward and Florence, just as Florence, later, overhears Edward and Nancy—the less awkward, the less of a novelist's device we feel it to be: we get used to the fact that it happened and become absorbed in what Dowell spins out of it, in the connections he forms between it and other incidents.

The Good Soldier is a triumph of colloquial style properly adapted to the point-of-view method. It is also a triumph of *progression d'effet*. Ford was well aware of this, sufficiently so to draw our attention to his subtlety in handling it. Dowell calls his story 'the saddest story' rather than 'The Ashburnham Tragedy', 'just because it is so sad and just because there was no current to draw things along to a swift and inevitable end'. We must assume that Ford is showing himself confident of his method even when proposing to adapt it to a situation which we should expect

to resist it, since what is lacking, the 'current to draw things along to a swift and inevitable end' (associated with 'the elevation that accompanies tragedy' in the next sentence), is precisely what he meant by *progression d'effet*. His manipulation of the time-shift enabled him to make use of some of the strong points of both the classic drama and the novel. As in the case of the former, there is a restricted time-scale. The action revolves around two brief spaces in time: the final period at Nauheim during which Leonora struggles against Florence for possession of her husband, and Florence commits suicide; and the period at Branshaw Teleragh, during which the relationship between Edward and Nancy is broken by Leonora. There is a pendant to the latter, bringing Dowell back on to the scene and dealing with Edward's suicide. Everything else in the novel refers to one or other of these episodes; the frequent time-shifts, controlled by Dowell's changing interests, serving the same purpose as recapitulatory speeches by characters in classical tragedy. But this other material is treated novelistically, the dramatic material being incorporated in the pictorial proclivities of Dowell's temperament. Hence the compactness of the drama is accompanied by the diffuse excursions of the narrator into the past. All these excursions spring recognisably from Dowell's insistence on clarifying the meaning of what happened at Nauheim and Branshaw. The containment of the two dramatic centres of the novel within the pictorial structure of Dowell's meditation is therefore fully justified, since it is the piecing together of that structure which creates, and explains, the centres. It is the only way Dowell and ourselves (though with different conclusions) can understand their meaning. Hence the way the dramatic centres and the reflective movement backwards and forwards, from and into the past, are built up interdependently by means of the time-shift as the novel progresses, *is the progression d'effet*. The casual way in which Dowell says what he has to say makes the course of Edward Ashburnham's self-destruction, in spite of the imperfect rendering of his character, convincingly inevitable. The novelist's interference is not at all in evidence, and the objective record which Flaubert had achieved in the third person, and according to the conventional arrangement of the time-scheme, Ford achieved in first-person narrative, meandering according to the credible psychological impulsions of the narrator. Since the author succeeds in bringing this into line with his own requirements—those of providing readers with all the information needed to understand the affair—he remains invisible, as Flaubert did. The development of the plot of both *Madame Bovary* and *The Good Soldier* is inevitable. (pp. 125-33)

Patrick Swinden, "Time and Motion," in his Unofficial Selves: Character in the Novel from Dickens to the Present Day, *Barnes and Noble Books, 1973, pp. 120-57.*

David Eggenschwiler   (essay date 1979)

[*Eggenschwiler is an American educator and critic. In the following excerpt, he describes Ford's manner of manipulating the reader's responses to events in* The Good Soldier.]

For a quarter of a century *The Good Soldier* has caused dissention among the critical ranks. Ever since Mark

Schorer's famous essay [see *TCLC,* Vol. 1, pp. 277-78] divided readers as neatly as a debater's topic, we have argued whether John Dowell, the narrator, is a fool and a eunuch or a good fellow much like Ford himself, whether Edward Ashburnham, the central actor, is a hypocritical cad or a tragic (at least, melodramatic) hero, whether the author mocks or eulogizes the few, late vestiges of chivalry. And, indeed, we have not been perverse in our arguments, abusing a simple tale for the pleasure of critical dispute. For all its claims to a French pedigree ("the finest French novel in the English language"), **The Good Soldier** is an artful mongrel, a delightful and subtle mixture of genres that is bound to perplex those who are looking hard for consistency. Yet, if not perverse, we have still been at fault for handling the novel too roughly as we have required it to take sides in our disputes, to show its colors and stick by its guns. Ford has been so skillful in combining genres, managing transitions, and creating the illusion of coherence that the cooperative reader ought to float in suspended disbelief without the irritable striving after fact and certainty that comes when the story has been told, the illusions have been dispersed, and the novel is subjected to sensible tests for truth and order. In what I hope is a cooperative response I intend to describe rather than dispell Ford's literary illusions, to show how he transforms character, theme, plot, and (encompassing all these) genre so that we leave a very different novel than we entered, yet without feeling confused by a foolish narrator or duped by a sly author. If the novel as I describe it will not abide our questions on how, ultimately and comprehensively, to judge Dowell, Edward, and feudal values, I can only say that these questions have been often asked and variously answered, that they are concerned with a truth-in-art that is the subject of retrospect (when, in memory, we spread out the novel like a map and try to see it steadily and whole), and that I am more concerned with the manner in which Ford creates and recreates our immediate responses than with any summary judgments we should eventually reach.

To appreciate what Ford is doing in **The Good Soldier** we must first appreciate what is often slighted in interpretations: this is a very funny book, partly because the narrator is witty and quick to see incongruities, partly because the first half of the novel is essentially a comedy. As we read of the Dowells and Ashburnhams in Parts One and Two, we accept and enjoy a sexual farce with conventional character types and conventional relationships—all of which is heightened by the narrator, the cuckolded husband, who emphasizes the ludicrousness of all roles. Later we will understand that these relationships have some nasty consequences, but we should not therefore try to convince ourselves that this farce has really been a tragedy that an incompetent narrator has failed to understand. Whatever their consequences, the relationships in the foursquare coterie are basically funny.

Consider the cast of characters. Edward seems a perfect replica of a nineteenth-century fictional type: the attractive and not overly bright career officer (and cavalry, at that). He would have been quite at home in *Vanity Fair.* He is handsome in a conventionally manly way (fair hair, sunburnt complexion, blue eyes, bristling mustache); he dresses elegantly but not foppishly (the pigskin cases—for guns and collars and helmets and hats—strike the right balance); to men he talks of clothes, horses, and artillery;

to women he "gurgles" the ideals about love's redemption which he has picked up from popular novels; he is common-sensical about common-sensical things and sentimental about "all children, puppies, and the feeble generally"; above all, with his physique, his composure, his perfectly stupid blue eyes, he is decidedly attractive to women. And such a man is married to such a woman as Leonora; only the god of farce could have united this couple and only for ribald purposes. Leonora is cold and very proper: clean-run, splendid in the saddle, tall and fair, with chilly white shoulders and a little gold key with which to lock up her heart. Knowing the moral economy of farce, we know that proud, chilly Leonora is going to take her lumps.

And, if we consider only Parts One and Two, who could be better to attract this Edward and vex this Leonora than Florrie Hurlbird Dowell, the satiric version of the American innocent abroad. On the surface she is little and fair, as radiant as a track of sunlight as she dances over the floors of castles and over the seas, trying to leave the world a little brighter for her passage through it. Below that radiant surface she is a cruel little hypocrite, a silly social climber, and a cold sensualist. Acting the playful retriever to Leonora's lean greyhound, she seems perfect to arouse Edward's manhood, Leonora's scorn, and her own husband's perplexity. Dowell completes the foursquare group by playing the cuckolded husband to an extreme that makes him a triumph of the type. Twelve years a cuckold in an unconsummated marriage, and cuckolded by an expatriated painter in Paris and a British officer in Germany—this is remarkably absurd for both duration and symmetry. Yet Dowell, as narrator, is unsparingly amusing about his own past role, as he is about the roles that the other characters assume with such gusto and such taste for conventional parts. He presents himself, well-brushed and meticulous, as a Philadelphia gentleman, performing the most unromantically slapstick elopement, guarding his wife's bedroom with an axe while she dallies with her fat painter, trying in a frenzy to keep the little tart's mind off thoughts that might set it fatally aflutter while the other three characters treat him like an emotional invalid, preserving the illusion of the innocent minuet that he dances alone.

It is, indeed, the funniest, most conventional of stories, this adulterous farce, and the narrator has ornamented it with minor characters and incidents to sustain the charm and silliness of a comic world in which farce seems the norm. But as we recall the farcical plot, the witty narration, and the comic artificiality of Parts One and Two, we should also recall that Dowell begins the story by saying that it is the saddest he has ever heard. That is a problem; or, rather it should be a problem as we read the novel for the first time. After we have finished the book and seen Edward flayed alive and heard Nancy's mad *Credo,* we ought to consider it, all around, a very sad affair; but that is not the impression given by the first third of the book, and we ought to be a bit puzzled by Dowell's claim and by his occasional outbursts of passionate rhetoric that seem little suited to the predominate tone. And, indeed, we *ought* to be puzzled and even a trifle amused, because Ford has arranged things that way. He has used clever, ironic, melodramatic, and slightly befuddled Dowell for his complex narrative purposes and to the accidental confusion of sophisticated readers who, made too wary by un-

Stella Bowen.

reliable narrators, have mistaken Dowell, the narrative device, for a realistic neurotic. In short, when Dowell begins telling his tale he already knows almost all of the sad details of the Ashburnhams' lives; consequently, as he tells first of the foursquare coterie, of that part of the Ashburnhams' story that directly involves himself and Florence, he occasionally bursts out with grand themes and grand suffering that, since we know little of the whole context of the adulterous farce, seem perplexingly and amusingly extreme. Poor Dowell is made the victim of his own meandering narrative method and the triumph of Ford's precise one.

For a grand theme Dowell claims that society's decorums hide immoral passions. That is, and always has been, the natural theme of sexual comedy; and, if Dowell had not made such a to-do about it, no one would have written much about Ford's grappling in this novel with the modern loss of cultural values, the collapse of the Victorian compromise, and such like. But Dowell does make a to-do, likening the collapse of the coterie to the Goth's sack of Rome, suggesting that most men may be sexually raging stallions, and lamenting loudly that the human heart is unknowable. Now the human hearts that Dowell describes in Parts One and Two do not seem very bestial or mysterious; they seem naughty, as they have seemed for centuries

of conventional literature and life. He alone of the four characters has not known what hanky-panky has been going on; he has been duped in the most preposterous ways for twelve years; even at the last he must have others explain everything to him. Consequently, we seem to have an absurdly naive husband and admittedly befuddled narrator who exaggerates both the social importance and the emotional intensity of his cuckolding. What do we see in these early sections to justify references to Edward's "madness" or to a "prison full of screaming hysterics"? Leonora does have a few minutes of hysterics at the castle, but we are led to assume that she is merely the jealous wife who sees that her husband is at it again. We are told early that Edward and Florence are dead, but the deaths that we see in the first half of the novel—Maisie with her heels in the air, Florence arranged "decoratively" on her bed— are amusing; they do not suggest that, in this farcical world, death has much sting-aling-aling. We are even led to suppose that Edward died somehow for love of Florence, and, from what we are told of Florence, that hardly promises a good fatal passion. So, as long as we stay with the adulterous farce of the two couples and find out only as much about the Ashburnhams as fits that tale, we are apt to be a bit puzzled and amused at Dowell's melodramatic claims. It may be true that "the death of a mouse from cancer is the whole sack of Rome by the Goths," but only in the most abstract sense or only if it is your pet mouse. We are led to suspect the latter, to assume that Dowell is puffing up the significance of his private and objectively amusing little affair. That is not entirely true, but Ford has done a good job of making us think that it is.

At the end of Part Two the novel begins quietly to change, for Dowell has finished his introductory farce and is beginning to get on to other subjects. As long as he concentrates on himself and Florence and their relationships with others (the Ashburnhams, Jimmy, the Hurlbirds) the story will be essentially comic, for they are essentially a flat, comic couple. But by the middle of the novel Florence is packed away like poor little Maisie; she even gets a public dismissal ("You have no idea how quite extraordinarily for me that was the end of Florence"), and Dowell considers the Ashburnhams in the different contexts into which his own marital tale has flowed. Near the end of Part Two, Chapter One, the change is signalled with a pointed transition. Dowell has just described his marital history from his meeting Florence through the *menage à trois* with Jimmy, and he pauses for a moment to sum up that part of the novel as a way of having done with it and preparing to get on with other things:

> Well, there you have the position, as clear as I can make It—the husband an ignorant fool, the wife a cold sensualist with imbecile fears . . . and the blackmailing lover. And then the other lover came along. . . .

> Well, Edward Ashburnham was worth having. Have I conveyed to you the splendid fellow that he was—the fine soldier, the excellent landlord, the extraordinarily kind, careful and industrious magistrate, the upright, honest, fair-dealing, fair-thinking public character? I suppose I have not conveyed it to you. The truth is that I never knew it until the poor girl came along—the poor girl who was just as straight, as splendid, and as upright as he.

A fine change of direction—not particularly subtle, but precise, economical, and apparently straightforward. Dowell, Florence, and Jimmy get their brutal epithets as a way of fixing them and dismissing them from central importance in the novel. Then Edward re-enters as Florence's virile and gentlemanly lover, a contrast to pallid Dowell and vulgar Jimmy; but no sooner is he before us than he is metamorphosed from the stupid, sentimental ladies' man and cavalry officer into a paragon of public virtue. Of course Dowell has mentioned before that Edward was a fine magistrate and all, but those brief comments suggested a hypocritical split between apparent honor and secret adultery. Here is an Edward we have not seen before; and Ford, sly author, allows Dowell to accept the blame for not having represented Edward adequately. As he begins to turn his novel about, Ford does not try embarrassedly to hide his maneuvers. He is more devious than that: he has Dowell call our attention to the change, apologize frankly for past misunderstandings, and offer an apparently reasonable (but actually sophistic) cause for his misrepresentations. Here is the illusion of no illusions, the art of seeming artlessness, the benign trickery of the Tale-Teller.

Dowell is not changing his characterizations because he is coming, while he narrates, to understand more about those characters and their lives. This is not an epistemological novel about the narrator's gradual discoveries. As Dowell admits here, he has known for a long time about Edward's splendid character; he learned about it through the poor girl during various summers at Nauheim. If he did not convey that splendid character to us before, it was because that side of Edward had little to do with his relations with Florence and would have disrupted his role in the adulterous farce. Remember, too, that for nine years Edward helped to make his friend one of the silliest of cuckolds; now for ninety pages Dowell has been able to spit on Edward's grave, as he admits a desire to do; he has been able to condescend to Edward and make him an adjunct to the Dowells' minuets. Now the farce is ending, the comic ghosts are being laid to rest, and Edward is being resurrected through his relationship with the poor girl, who has flitted like the vaguest of shadows through the first chapters. From now on, the Dowells will be mere foils to the Ashburnhams, who will be given emotional, social, and even historical complexities that the sexual comedy would not have been able to bear.

But if Ford is disarmingly frank in reassessing Edward, he is not clumsy about it. By using Nancy Rufford to help supply the new point of view, Dowell can praise Edward yet ironically mock that praise as schoolgirl's gush: "She made him out like a cross between Lohengrin and the Chevalier Bayard. Perhaps he was. . . . But he was too silent a fellow to make that side of him really decorative." First comes the girl's sentimental excess, then Dowell's admission of its possible truth, qualified by "perhaps" and made mysterious by ellipses that hint of things we have not yet been told, and finally the urbane, understated compliment that locates this Lohengrin-Bayard in the manners and values of English gentlemen. For another one hundred and fifty pages Ford controls the narrative tone this precisely, adjusting our sympathy and detachment, making Edward seem admirable, ridiculous, or pathetic, and gradually transforming the comedy into a romantic tragedy without losing the frequent ironic tone that characterizes

the narrator and helps to make his final sympathies and tributes seem trustworthy. This control of tone is a triumph of rhetoric and vexation to readers who would decide whether Edward is a noble feudal hero or a sentimental fool. Although one ought to know how to respond to Edward in any specific passage (and Ford and Dowell are fair enough with us on this), one need not be able to pin him finally with the kind of pat judgment that Dowell makes of Jimmy or Florence or, indeed, of Edward in the first third of the novel. By the end Edward has eluded simple definition (although perhaps not simple, opposing definitions) and has been cast in various roles in various contexts.

As Ford transposes his novel he repeats themes, characterizations, incidents, and situations from the first two parts, but he transforms them to create different impressions. Dowell begins Part Three by telling that, immediately after his wife's death, he surprised himself by saying that now he could marry the girl. Because he had not previously thought of caring for her, this strange outburst makes him talk about dual personalities and the difficulties of knowing one's unconscious feelings. This theme reflects the main theme of Parts One and Two—the contrast between man's social appearance and his secret desires—but with such a difference: moral and social hypocrisy has become psychological mystery. The ambiguity of man's nature has deepened from its conventional form in sexual farce—proper gentleman and lustful stallion—to more general, more disturbing forms that include all of the main characters. So Edward, too, discovers suddenly, surprisingly, and tormentingly that he loves the girl; had he been conscious of it, he assures Dowell, "he would have fled from it as from a thing accursed." And we are no longer concerned with secret lust, the adulterous itch of farce, but with inexplicable love, with passion. Dowell makes the issue clear at this point: "Of the question of the sex instinct I know very little and I do not think that it counts for very much in a really great passion"; and he tells instead of feelings that would have had no place in the story of the Dowells and Ashburnhams: "We are all so afraid, we are all so alone, we all so need from the outside the assurance of our own worthiness to exist." Of course, Dowell still plays the cynic and describes the "great passion" as the last stop of a weary romantic traveler (Ford still qualifies romanticism with irony), but we have clearly changed our way of looking at man's buried life.

Later in the novel the theme reappears to underscore the sudden emergence of other intense passions. Commenting on Leonora's cruelty toward Edward at the last, on her hatred of his final virtue, Dowell says that "the human heart is a very mysterious thing." By now the theme, which had gotten us through a difficult transition in the middle of the book, has become merely rhetorical, a way of sighting over the horrible things people do and feel. The causes of Leonora's feelings are not mysterious, for Dowell has very precisely told us all of her past that we need to know to understand her hatred and he now describes precisely what she feels toward Nancy and Edward. Despite his frequent claims that people are unknowable and that he is befuddled, Dowell is an exact and extensive interpreter of what has happened, and *The Good Soldier* is extraordinarily clear and explicit about motives. If commentators have thought that the novel is about the impossibility of knowing truth, they have too readily believed Dowell's sad sighs and paid too little attention to the many truths—social, religious, and psychological—that Dowell tells us about the characters. Most of Dowell's claims of confusion and ignorance as narrator are means of creating a useful narrative tone and of allowing Ford to move convincingly through the various transformations of his tale. If Dowell pleads, and perhaps even feels, some confusion, I do not see why we should, for he guides us very well. He does cheat at times, though, only to apologize later for having given false or incomplete impressions, which he then corrects; but that deviousness is part of the teller's art in manipulating the reader and achieving his *progression d'effet*. It won't do as grounds for an epistemology.

Dowell most obviously changes the impressions of incidents when he gives new versions of Edward's romantic affairs from the Kilsyte case to Maisie Maidan. The first time around, the affairs—a servant girl, a courtesan, two fellow officers' wives—seem but the amusing stages of a sentimental adulterer's progress. But they seem different when Edward is no longer the flat farcical character, when we know more of his boyhood, his marriage, his difficulties with his estate, and especially his ideals of feudal responsibility and chivalric love, which dominate his character in the second half of the novel although they were of little concern in the first half. These are not changes of fact, but of emphasis, associations, and tone. Instead of hearing that Edward reads syrupy love stories, we hear that as a boy he read Scott and Froissart, which may be just as disastrous for an impressionable romantic but which are more culturally complex in their sentimentality. Instead of hearing briefly of a "perfectly commonplace affair at Monte Carlo" in which Edward smashes his fortune to enjoy the overpriced favors of a "cosmopolitan harpy" (an account in Part One that seems as well suited to Rawdon Crawley and his like), we are given a high comedy closer to *Don Quixote* in which Edward plays the courtly lover and fool, confusing sex and devotion, talking feudalism and eternal love while La Dolciquita talks cash and a month's rental. Mrs. Basil, scarcely more than the blackmailer's wife in Part One, is Edward's imagined "soulmate," who admires his ideals of landlordship and sympathizes with him as Leonora inhumanely reorganizes Branshaw along modern, efficient lines. Even Maisie is less the pretty little simpleton at Nauheim than she is the girl to whom Edward can carry cups of bouillon when he can no longer serve his tenants as the good landlord and the father of his people. In all these incidents Edward is still wonderfully comic—lovesick at the gambling tables in Monte Carlo or among the sheafs of severed vegetation in Burma—but he is comic in a lovable, touching way. His character, in the abstract, is not very different than it was in the first two parts, but it makes different impressions. Edward was not particularly touching before.

Furthermore, as Edward's role as chivalric lover develops, it becomes more romantic and less carnal. As Dowell says, the sex instinct does not count for much in a really great passion, and we are subtly preparing for Edward's passion for Nancy in which he renounces all sexual desire. So from La Dolciquita's bedroom he moves into the Burmese garden with Mrs. Basil, where "long passages of affection" overshadow occasional "falls," and then to the side of poor little Maisie, whose heart trouble insures the chastity of the relationship. The one exception to this development is the affair with Florence, which interrupts the sequence between Maisie and Nancy and which certainly is carnal. But the exception not only proves and justifies the pattern, it also demonstrates how artfully Ford manipulates his narrative to create the right illusions at the right times. The affair with Florence is the only one in Parts Three and Four that is not described from Edward's point of view. Dowell tells us openly that he cannot give us Edward's point of view on Florence because Edward, of course, never spoke to him about it, and this concern with narrative logistics, about which Ford is not always so scrupulous, is a reasonable excuse to keep the relationship between Edward and Florence out of the second half of the novel where it would have ruined the image of Edward that Dowell is creating. A colleague once asked me what Edward saw in Florence, and I was puzzled, not only because I did not know but also because it had not occurred to me to wonder. That was Ford's doing. The coarse, nasty, pedantic, coldly sensual Florence in Parts One and Two does not seem out of place as the mistress of the vapid Edward we see there; *that* Edward would likely be attracted to that "personality of paper." When we have come to appreciate Edward more, to have seen him fully and to have gotten the drift of his character and his fate, Ford has shuffled Florence out of the circle of Edward's passions and made Edward's relations with her the vaguest abstraction, something we have taken for granted so long that it does not perplex. In retrospect, if we rearrange the tale into chronological order and think objectively about motivations, we are bound to be puzzled; but if we stay with the tale in the order and manner of its telling, we shall ask only those questions that the form of the tale suggests to us at various times. The magician and artist make us look where they wish while the blind hand gropes in the secret place for the rabbit's ears.

When Florence is pulled back into the story for a dozen pages at the beginning of Part Four, she does not come to clarify her relations with Edward but to show how she "deteriorated" Leonora with her ill-timed adultery, her coarseness, and her cruel, vain talk about the Ashburnhams' estrangement. This role contributes well to the deepening of Leonora's character that occurs steadily throughout Parts Three and Four. From the chilly, proper wife of the farce she has become for us the financially insecure Irish girl, the unappreciated manager of her husband's estate, the proudly threadbare martyr, the fanatical Catholic wife, the patient and disappointed woman who waits for her husband's return. Although she does not gain much of our sympathy, she does gain our understanding, and we are prepared for her eventual deterioration into the wicked mad woman that Dowell claims her to be in her final assaults on Edward.

The last stages of the Ashburnhams' story is, indeed, as Dowell says, the saddest part. Although there are still ironic touches—Nancy's remembering that love withers the vitals, Edward's quoting Swinburne—they deepen the pathos by controlling it, by enriching the mixture. Now we have actions to justify the outburst of feeling that Dowell made in the first part of the novel. And if Ford has developed his novel from humor to pathos, from farce to tragedy, he also has transformed themes and situations from earlier sections, emphasizing the novel's unity and its development. The chivalric ideals of women and love that caused Edward ridiculously to kiss the servant girl and swear undying fidelity to La Dolciquita are now literally killing him in his relations with Nancy. The role of adulterous hypocrite that Edward played in Parts One and Two is passed on to Rodney Bayham, Leonora's leporine second husband with his separate establishment in Portsmouth and his trips to Paris and Buda-Pesth. And Leonora will be perfectly happy with this normal, virtuous, slightly deceitful husband, for the life of underdone roast beef and discreet adultery turns out to be the normal life of society and the proper setting for a woman who is splendid in the saddle. Edward, who once seemed to us the epitome of that life (to Leonora's vexation), turns out instead to be one of "the passionate, the headstrong, and the too-truthful [who] are condemned to suicide and to madness," to be one of the fatally splendid personalities that a romantic tragedy cannot allow to survive among the rabbits like Rodney. Could anyone, after having read the first ninety pages of the novel have predicted Dowell's final assessment of Edward or Dowell's claim that, because he can respond imaginatively to this ideal, he too is one of the passionate, the headstrong, and the too-truthful? Yet step by step, illusion by illusion, Ford has turned his novel about, and only those who refuse to yield to the illusions, who step back for a clear-headed appraisal, will call Dowell a liar or a fool at this point.

In Part Four Dowell also plays a tragic variation on this theme of social decorum versus private passion, the theme with which we began the farce at the other end of the tale. Now we have the Ashburnhams preserving the apparent charm of a pleasant country house-party at Branshaw while they are enduring agony and performing monstrous cruelties on each other. Now we have the secret "prison full of screaming hysterics" that Dowell had perplexingly referred to in connection with Nauheim. And now we find that the social decorum is not merely a cover for inadmissible feelings; it is also one of the causes of the tragedy, of the "monstrously, cruelly correct" actions of Leonora, Edward, and Nancy in their fated triangle. The horror of this "conventional line" is later imaged by Nancy after she has returned from Ceylon: well-dressed, quiet, beautiful, and "utterly well behaved as far as her knife and fork go," she sits at the luncheon table, utterly mad, a "picture without a meaning." As Dowell says in one of his most painful and precise witticisms, "even when she was mad Nancy could behave herself."

If we were to forget that this novel is read in time and that the order of its telling is not the order of the events it purports to describe, if we were to pick and sort and rearrange details from our notes in order to try for the "right" point of view toward the characters and incidents in order to find clues to the truth, why, we should be as confused as poor Dowell claims to be. Is Edward the normal hypocrite that he seems at first or the abnormal, too-truthful romantic that he seems at last? Is Dowell a eunuch or a headstrong, passionate man, both of which he suggests at different times? Are social conventions the form of a beautiful minuet, hiding horrible passions that threaten to destroy it, or is society the breeding ground of rabbits, the destroyer of splendid personalities? The answer to all of the questions is "yes," but that hardly satisfies a desire to know God's truth about these characters and issues. This is not to say that Ford irresponsibly obscures his moral position in the ways that Wayne Booth has ascribed to many authors who use impersonal narrative techniques. If we do not try too hard to outwit Dowell, we will know well

enough how to feel about things at any moment in the novel. We might not know exactly how to feel about society or Edward Ashburnham once we have separated them from the novel and made them abstract, but I don't know why we should want to. If we wanted to discover Ford's "views," we could get them more easily and reliably from his journalism than from his fiction.

I also do not see why, because we cannot produce decisive, comprehensive statements about themes or characters, we should conclude somewhat defensively that *The Good Soldier* is about the impossibility of knowing truth. As I have said, we learn many solid truths from our intelligent, interpretative narrator, and his frequent claims of ignorance and mystery seem less the subject of the book than a rhetorical device to help us suspend our disbelief as we accept his supposedly tentative, changing opinions. The relativity of knowledge was already a platitude when Ford wrote, and authors who have tried too conscientiously to demonstrate it have, like Pirandello at times, produced some quickly dated, theory-ridden works. Better, like Ford, to take the theory as a given and use it as a technique to manipulate the reader.

Finally, I do not see why we should conclude that, because Dowell's opinions change, the novel is about the teller's process of discovery, about Dowell's coming to deeper truths as he writes. This device has been used so well in modern fiction that we are too ready to let it explain problems that it will not quite solve. At the beginning of Part Four Dowell does tell us that he has been writing away for six months and "reflecting longer and longer upon these affairs"; so he explains his harshness toward Florence in his subsequent account. Again Ford is using a familiar theme to ease us over a transition, to gain consent by pointing to a narrative convention. If we tried to make this convention the essence of the novel, we would create more problems than we would solve. If we are to assume that the final view of Edward is the truest one, how are we going to imagine that "splendid personality" having a nine-year affair with Florence? And are we to imagine a passionate, headstrong Dowell counting his footsteps as he waits for poor Florence to finish her medicinal baths? And are we to reread Parts One and Two to find hidden clues to these passionate natures that are finally understood in Part Four? Surely not. We must let the novel itself show us how much we are to demand from its conventions. The impression that Dowell gives us of the four-square coterie are quite adequate to that subject; there is no reason to believe that they distort an objective truth to which we finally win through, either with or without the narrator's insight. It is enough that we *feel* an increasing penetration, for that is essential to the *progression d'effet*.

In sum, if we are not too eager to possess this novel through moral, psychological, or epistemological themes, we can more easily enjoy—and eventually understand—its changing illusions. In transforming *The Good Soldier* from a sexual farce to a romantic tragedy, Ford may well have written an impressionistic novel, using multiple points of view by a single narrator; but it seems best not to consider this book a demonstration of impressionism, any more than a study of sexual repression or social hypocrisy. It is better to stop looking for the key to a hidden coherence than to bruise the skillful illusions in our search. (pp. 401-14)

David Eggenschwiler, "Very Like a Whale: The Comical-Tragical Illusions of 'The Good Soldier'," in Genre, Vol. XII, No. 3, Fall, 1979, pp. 401-14.

Denis Donoghue   (essay date 1980)

[*Donoghue is an Irish educator and critic. In the following excerpt, he asserts that the meaning of* The Good Soldier *hinges on Dowell's role as storyteller—on the manner of his narrative rather than on the content of it.*]

In the first paragraph [of **The Good Soldier**], beginning with "This is the saddest story I have ever heard," the narrator presents himself as a storyteller, though he appears to take little pleasure in that role. He tells the story because he is the only one left to tell it or with an interest in telling it. Edward and Florence are dead, Nancy is mad, and Leonora is pursuing her new life by putting the old one behind her. The narrator, Dowell, is fated to tell the story, and he tells it with an air of fatality. But his genre is necessarily talk, garrulous enough to roam and digress, raise hares, engage in speculation and surmise. Ford is writing a book by pretending that Dowell is telling a story to a silent listener:

> So I shall just imagine myself for a fortnight or so
> at one side of the fireplace of a country cottage,
> with a sympathetic soul opposite me. And I shall
> go on talking. . . .

The pretense is insistently oral. "But I guess I have made it hard for you, O silent listener, to get that impression," he says at one point, one of many. The terminology of print and paper is voided. In part 3, Dowell describes his wife as "a personality of paper," in the sense that "she represented a real human being with a heart, with feelings, with sympathies, and with emotions only as a bank note represents a certain quantity of gold." The true element is air, breath: the story is given not as so many pages of print but as a mouthful of air. The pretense is maintained until twenty pages from the end. At the beginning of the fifth chapter of part 4, Dowell gives up all pretense of storytelling and insists upon the work as writing. "I am writing this, now, I should say, a full eighteen months after the words that end my last chapter. Since writing the words 'until my arrival,' which I see end that paragraph, I have seen again," and so on. The reason is that Nancy, who is with him ("sitting in the hall, forty paces from where I am now writing") is gone far beyond dialogue. No conceit, no romantic fancy, could allow Dowell to think of her any longer as his "dear listener"; she is "not there." So he gives up the pretense of speech and hands over the ending of his story to loneliness and print. And, worse still, he makes his written words turn upon Nancy, accusing her of cruelty comparable with Leonora's, a sinister conspiracy of the two women against Edward. Till that point, Dowell had taken the dear listener as a surrogate for the still dearer Nancy. Now that the pretense has to be dropped, Nancy is replaced by the severity of the written word, and punished for her absence; she is beyond speech, beyond hearing.

Going back to the first paragraph for a second, third, or fourth reading: Dowell's gestures are now familiar to us, especially his troupe of correction and his troupe of ignorance. For the first, we hear with now greater emphasis his revisions, when he says something and then backs away from its commitment. In the first paragraph, having said that the Dowells knew the Ashburnhams "with an extreme intimacy," he immediately qualifies the saying: "or, rather, with an acquaintanceship as loose and easy and yet as close as a good glove's with your hand." Intimacy seems to be vetoed by acquaintanceship, but the acquaintanceship is then warmed, like fingers in a good glove. A few pages later Dowell has a grandiloquent passage about the intimacy of the two couples as a minuet, and he leads the dance for half a page only to wave it away: "No, by God, it is false! It was not a minuet that we stepped; it was a prison. . . ." Much later he says, "And yet I do believe that for every man there comes at last a woman . . . ," and he changes the form of his belief even before the sentence is complete: "or, no, that is the wrong way of formulating it." When he says something, the saying makes it feel wrong, too much more often than not enough. A paragraph ends, "So, perhaps, it was with Edward Ashburnham," and the next paragraph begins, "Or, perhaps, it wasn't. No, I rather think it wasn't. It is difficult to figure out. . . ."

As for Dowell's trope of ignorance, I would not blame a reader who finds tedious his constant insistence that he knows nothing, that nothing can be known. "I know nothing—nothing in the world—of the hearts of men." "Who knows?" resounds through the book. Questions are posed, two alternative answers offered, but neither of them is an answer, and the whole episode is voided with an "I don't know" or "It is all a darkness" or "Perhaps you can make head or tail of it; it is beyond me." Facts are recited as if they were significant, but then the official significance attached to them is prised away, first with revisions and modifications, then with a gesture of ignorance. Why?

Think again of Dowell as narrator, or rather as storyteller. The question of reliable and unreliable narrators has often been raised in reference to him, but it is not the real question. Reliable or not, he is the only narrator we have, and we must make the best of him even when he makes the worst of himself. The real question is: What remains, now that nearly all the ostensible significance of the facts has been drained from them by Dowell's scepticism? And the answer is: Dowell himself remains. If you are listening to a storyteller, and he is telling the story subject to constant interruptions, his backward glances, revisions, corrections, and protestations of his own ignorance; these interrogations may damage the confidence with which you receive the story, but not the zest with which you attend upon the storyteller. The more he disputes the significance of the facts he recites, the more indisputable he becomes. We accept him precisely because he is evidently more scrupulous than we would be, in the same circumstances. Accepting him does not mean that we think him infallible but that we think him honest: he may still be obtuse, slow to sense the drift of things. No matter; we listen to his voice. Nothing in **The Good Soldier** is allowed to escape from Dowell's voice, until in the end he disowns voice itself and goes over to the cold fixity of print. It does not matter what he says, as distinct from the saying, which matters all the time. The force of the story, whether it is maintained, deflected, or subverted, returns intact to the teller. It is here that the story is performed; the unity of the tale is in the teller, not in the facts he recites. With

Dowell, the tropes of correction and ignorance which seem to warrant our discounting in advance nearly everything he reports, or at any rate our subtracting from its authority, have an entirely different effect; they keep him immune to his subject, or superior to it. The gestures by which he answers contingency make him immune to it. No wonder he survives its attack.

Dowell cannot defeat contingency in its own terms. He survives not only because, as the narrator, he must, but because he converts everything that happens into his own gestures, which are all the better for being his trademarks. Let me explain. Fredric Jameson argues in *Fables of Aggression* that Anglo-American modernism has been dominated by an impressionistic aesthetic rather than by Wyndham Lewis's externalizing and mechanical expressionism. The most influential formal impulses of modernism, he continues, "have been strategies of inwardness, which set out to reappropriate an alienated universe by transforming it into personal styles and private languages." Such wills to style now seem "to reconfirm the very privatization and fragmentation of social life against which they were meant to protest." Jameson does not discuss these strategies of inwardness in detail, but I assume he means, mostly, the impulses common to Joyce's early fiction and Eliot's early poems. Call those strategies Stephen Prufrock, for want of an official name. It is not clear that Dowell's way of dealing with crass contingency is by transforming it into a personal style and private language? His apparently obsessive themes (heart; Catholicism; good people; knowledge; service) should be construed, like Prufrock's fancies and Stephen's murmurs, as his poetic diction, a specialized vocabulary significant only in relation to him; his private language to which he resorts not only when he has nothing else to do but when a strategy of such inwardness is the only device he can practice. The chief attribute of such a diction is that it is self-propelling; that is (so far as the disinterested reader receives it), repetitive. A diction is that in our language which seeks to establish itself by repetition; it acts in a poem or a novel as a cell acts in politics, a clique, a party of like-minded people. In a poetic diction the words are not the same but similar in their origins, affiliations, let us say in the ideology they sponsor. What, besides the narrator, is John Dowell? He is an ideologist who deals with a flagrantly alienated universe by forcing it toward the inwardness of his diction. We say the diction is obsessive, but we really mean that it has established itself in advance of any contingency that might threaten to overwhelm it. Dowell, not a strong character in other terms, has the strength of the voice he is given, the strength to draw every event toward himself. If his voice remains unanswered, it also remains unanswerable; his style is answerable to contingency by virtue of being, in Jameson's sense, private.

Impressionism is as good a word as any to describe this device. Dowell is like Ford in this respect: the truth of an event is always the accuracy of his impression of it. He despaired of ever achieving an autonomous truth, independent of his sense of it; and he converted despair into scruple. The words he needs and uses are those which, with maximum resource and accuracy, convey his impression of a fact or situation, and they release themselves from further obligation. So the direction of force in *The Good Soldier* is always from the outer event to the inwardness which receives and transforms it. Tropes of correction and

ignorance arise from Dowell's sense that the event and his impression of it do not necessarily coincide; but this is misgiving congenital to idealists. Meanwhile his speech is an exercise of the only power he commands, the power to draw every event into himself and convert it into privacy and inwardness.

Why do we speak? The question is reasonable when asked of a Dowell, who has nothing but speech. We speak to exercise the faculty and power of speech. Again we speak from need, the need to recognize our need, including especially our sense of the inadequacy of speech. We speak to be completed and fulfilled; meanwhile to be appeased. In *The Good Soldier,* Dowell's speech is the only power he commands, and what speech commands is mostly the space of its presence, its resonance. Dowell's voice has every power in the world except the power to change anything or forestall it: it can do all things, provided that they are all the one thing, the conversion to inwardness by repetition. So there is no contradiction in referring to the power of Dowell's voice and recognizing that, for himself, he insists only upon helplessness. Up to the end and more especially at the end, Dowell insists that he is feeble, effete, a mere shadow of greater men: specifically, he insists, "I have only followed, faintly, and in my unconscious desires, Edward Ashburnham." As Prufrock says "No! I am not Prince Hamlet, nor was meant to be"; a Polonius, perhaps. But voice, in Dowell, is more powerful than anything he knows in himself: in his mere person he has nothing to match it.

That is to say: the power is in the role of the storyteller. It does not matter that he is obtuse, if he is obtuse; slow to grasp what Leonora knows when she rushes from the room at M— and speaks of "accepting the situation"; and naive generally about Ashburnham and Florence. No matter; the beauty of the book arises from the ironic relation between two factors—the primacy of Dowell's voice, if for no other reason than that it is the only voice we really hear; and his persistent effort to direct all our attention and nearly all our sympathy toward Edward, who has wronged him in every way that seems at first to matter but finally does not matter, since Florence was already bogus. The book draws every event or fact toward Dowell; while he insists that, by comparison with Ashburnham, he is nothing, a shadow at best of a greater self.

Much of our understanding of storytelling is due to two studies, Albert B. Lord's *The Singer of Tales* and Walter Benjamin's "The Storyteller," in *Illuminations,* a collection of his essays edited by Hannah Arendt. *The Singer of Tales* is a study of oral narrative, the epic construed as an oral art. Particularly we note the formulaic element in epic narrative, phrases which make a breathing space for the singer and establish the provenance of epic poetry as such: they correspond to Dowell's recurrent themes or motifs, which otherwise look like nervous tics and allow some readers to refer, too casually, to obsession. *The Singer of Tales* also supports, only less specifically, the notion of our attention, as listeners, being drawn always to the singer, the storyteller. The narrative always remains a mouthful of air, enacting not only ostensible events in a world at large but the proximity of the singer to his voice. Benjamin's essay mainly distinguishes between novel and tale; between fiction as a function of the printing press and fiction as story, oral narrative. The novel is meant to be read in solitude, and it features an elaborately detailed psychology. The tale is meant to be heard in common, it is a function of speech and, equally, of listening; its psychology is general rather than specific, more interested in the sort of thing people do than in any particular thing a particular person has done. In the tale, the explanation of the events is left loose, open-meshed; in the novel, the explanation is inscribed. We are discouraged from offering our own reasons to account for what people have done or failed to do. The events narrated in a novel generally proceed in accord with the linear, sequential form sponsored by pages and print: in the tale, the storyteller is free with the circuit of his story; he delivers things in the order in which he forms impressions of them, he remembers and forgets, he adverts to the slack of his narrative and stops to take it up. *The Good Soldier* has often been read as a precociously modern novel that anticipates many of the procedures of more recent French fiction in the fractures of its narrative. A simpler explanation is that it is what its subtitle says it is, a tale told by an amateur storyteller who does the best he can and takes every latitude offered by that genre.

Northrop Frye has pointed out in *Anatomy of Criticism* that a genre tends to be mixed rather than simple, and that fictions tend to result from mixtures of generic elements. Very few fictions are single-minded instances of their genres. So it is not an embarrassment to say that *The Good Soldier* is a mixture of novel and tale; though I would maintain that it is a tale incorporating, often with only a show of interest, some elements from the novel. The novel tends to place its events in society; its art is politics so far as its themes are evident; it concerns itself with the human relations provoked by a given society. These elements are active in *The Good Soldier,* but not as active as a list of its ostensible themes would suggest. We hear a good deal about property, travel, love-affairs, the season at Nauheim and other places, but the social atmosphere is notably thin: we are not encouraged to sense, beyond the four chief characters and the various women whom Edward loved, a social world densely wrought, going about its business. The social atmosphere is thin for a book that seems to present itself as an account of such things. But the explanation is that in its scheme of organization and judgment, *The Good Soldier* is only nominally a novel. The novel supplies only its decor, not its judgments. The judgments issue far more directly from the tale, in which characters are more types than individuals and psychological explanations are felt to be beside the point. Why does Edward do the things he does? Because he is the type to do them: that is Dowell's pervasive implication. His actions are not explained, as a novel would offer to explain them, by reference to his early circumstances, and so forth. Again: where blame must be laid, Dowell does not lay it upon society, but upon Fate. The ordinances of society are not invoked. The main conflict is not between self and society but between type and morality, and finally the blame is laid upon Fate, the force of nature that ordained the type in the first place. In Dowell's account of Edward and the Kilsyte girl, only Edward's nature is blamed, and thereafter the God of his nature. "There is no priest that has the right to tell me that I must not ask pity for him, from you, silent listener beyond the hearthstone, from the world, or from the God who created in him those desires, those madnesses. . . ." The same page has a rather Conradian passage about "that inscrutable and blind justice" which punishes you "for following your natural but ill-timed in-

clinations." A few pages later we hear of "the shadow of an eternal wrath"; later still, of "the ingenious torments that fate prepares for us" and our drifting down "the stream of destiny." Bad coincidences are attributed to "a merciless trick of the devil that pays attention to this sweltering hell of ours." And so forth. Dowell's accusations become more extreme as the story goes on, and in the end Fate becomes a neo-Darwinian mutation by which vivid organisms are suppressed so that ordinary, normal, prudent organisms may survive.

Since this development brings the major judgment of the book, I should round it out. The crucial passage comes at the beginning of part 4, chapter 5, where Dowell, thinking of Edward and Nancy and Leonora, says that events worked out "in the extinction of two very splendid personalities—for Edward and the girl *were* splendid personalities, in order that a third personality, more normal, should have, after a long period of trouble, a quiet, comfortable, good time." That last phrase, which refers to the married life of Leonora and Rodney Bayham, is enough to show what Dowell feels about the dispositions of Fate which have issued in a good time for such trivial people; and about the cost to other people. Dowell reverts to the point a few pages later:

> Conventions and traditions I suppose work blindly but surely for the preservation of the normal type; for the extinction of proud, resolute, and unusual individuals.

And again, later, mocking the happy disposition of blessings and punishments:

> Well, that is the end of the story. And, when I come to look at it, I see that it is a happy ending with wedding bells and all. The villains—for obviously Edward and the girl were villains—have been punished by suicide and madness. The heroine—the perfectly normal, virtuous, and slightly deceitful heroine—has become the happy wife of a perfectly normal, virtuous, and slightly deceitful husband. She will shortly become a mother of a perfectly normal, virtuous, slightly deceitful son or daughter. A happy ending, that is what it works out at.

Indeed, he cannot leave the point alone. On the next page he refers to the sinister conspiracy of Fate and Society:

> Mind, I am not preaching anything contrary to accepted morality. I am not advocating free love in this or any other case. Society must go on, I suppose, and society can only exist if the normal, if the virtuous, and the slightly deceitful flourish, and if the passionate, the headstrong, and the too-truthful are condemned to suicide and to madness. But I guess that I myself, in my fainter way, come into the category of the passionate, of the headstrong, and the too-truthful. For I can't conceal from myself the fact that I loved Edward Ashburnham— and that I love him because he was just myself.

The Byronism of these passages is of course odd, except that it is a Byronism of desire and not of deed. Society has nothing to fear from such desire, unless it forces itself into action and calls itself Edward Ashburnham. *The Good Soldier* is not "a novel without a hero," it is what it claims to be, a tale of passion in which passion is found in Edward and only its desire in Dowell. And since the ground of Edward's passion is his nature, the force that destroys it and destroys him can only be called Fate. If the force were contingent or conventional and not categorical, it could be called Society. But the book is a tale because its conflicts are social only betimes and by the way; the true conflict is aboriginal, it has to do with natures and principles. Fate is what we call Nature when its dealings with us are sinister not by chance but by design and malice. Society is a cultural term, and it arises in *The Good Soldier* only at the last moment and, even then, misleadingly; it is nothing more than the visible form of Fate, Fate's conspirator on the daily surface of life. The chief irony of the book is that these warring principles are narrated and invoked by a storyteller who knows them only in shadow and by the intermittent knowledge of his own desire. "I don't know why I should always be selected to be serviceable," he muses at one point. He seems born to be in attendance; diversely upon Florence, Edward, Leonora, and Nancy, but more fundamentally upon passions that he cannot feel in himself but only through others, especially through Edward. If he is superior to the events by being immune to them, he gains this immunity by being fated to know only indirectly and at several removes the passions that made the events. No wonder we recall him as rueful and sedentary, when his own feelings are present; and as rising only to the occasions provoked by others.

There is no contradiction in thinking of Dowell as Byronic in desire and again, in the way he thought of himself, as a nurse if not a poodle; because his Byronism is a value asserted in the modern world but known, and known well enough by him, to be archaic and belated there. It is precisely because the value is archaic that it has to be asserted, and may be. Dowell's Byronism remains nostalgic so long as it is doomed in practice and archaic in every form of itself short of practice. If it had the slightest chance of being embodied successfully and at large, it could be invoked and would not need to be asserted. So it stands for all those "lost values known to be lost" which R. P. Blackmur has ascribed to Ford's novels as the substance of their unmoored sensibility. "Each of these books," Blackmur remarks, "has something to do with the glory of an arbitrary prestige resting on values asserted but not found in the actual world: values which when felt critically deform rather than enlighten action in that world, so that the action ends in the destruction of the values themselves" [see *TCLC*, Vol. 15, pp. 77-79]. In Edward Ashburnham the destruction of Byronism is complete; it survives only as a pale shadow of itself, and only as a virtual value, in Dowell, where it never reaches further than mockery. Who are mocked? The "beati immaculati" who walk in perfectly normal, virtuous, and slightly deceitful ways which they appropriate as the way and the law of the Lord. But the mockery, valid enough in the usual anti-bourgeois tone of modern literature, is itself mocked by being ascribed to a man whose criticism of life is, in every limiting sense of the phrase, merely verbal. Dowell says of Edward and Nancy at the end:

> So those splendid and tumultuous creatures with their magnetism and their passions—those two that I really loved—have gone from this earth.

What does Dowell know, we may well ask, of tumult and magnetism, except as his own unconscious desire, carefully suppressed from the field of action and belatedly incited into words? For him, and not for him alone, the words become a substitute for the action that cannot otherwise be taken. If we forgive him, it is because he has not quite forgiven himself.

We return to our starting point: Dowell as narrator, reciting the deeds of others and the suffering which in part he shares with them. His reliability is not the problem. He is central to the story because he is the storyteller. The pathos of the book is that the passion to which Dowell appeals has no continuing place in the world. In many senses, we have approved its loss; in a residual sense, our approval is itself compromised. We do not want Byronism back, but we cannot be sanguine about the ease with which we have repudiated all such desires. (pp. 46-54)

> *Denis Donoghue, "Listening to the Saddest Story," in* The Presence of Ford Madox Ford: A Memorial Volume of Essays, Poems, and Memoirs, *edited by Sondra J. Stang, University of Pennsylvania Press, 1981, pp. 44-54.*

Lawrence Thornton (essay date 1984)

[*In the following excerpt, Thornton asserts that Edward's downfall in* The Good Soldier *primarily stems from his inability to differentiate between the idealized realm of history and Romantic literature and the contingent elements of reality.*]

In *The Good Soldier* Ford shows us two worlds simultaneously coming apart at the seams: the "four-square coterie" of the Dowells and Ashburnhams and the society of Edwardian England on the eve of the First World War. The disintegration of these worlds is manifested in the conflict between the bourgeois, dogma-ridden Irish Catholic, Leonora, and her aristocratic Anglican husband, Edward. But the theme of disintegration is also present in the materials of Romance associated with Edward's background and his habitual reading of sentimental literature. Ford's achievement rests not only on the "intricate tangle of references and cross-references" that constitutes the remarkable impressionistic structure of the novel, but also on his ironic deployment of historical motifs that inform Edward's imagination and define the central vision of *The Good Soldier.*

A medieval ideology guides Edward's attitudes towards himself and everyone with whom he comes in contact. In his study of the English novel Arnold Kettle discusses those elements of feudalism and its literature that exert an irresistible influence on Edward's imagination. "Feudalism," argues Kettle, "the society of the Middle Ages, had as its principal characteristic a peculiar rigidity of human relationships and ideas which sprang inevitably from the social structure. . . . Their whole interest, their very existence as the kind of people they were, demanded the preservation . . . of the *status quo.*" Rigidity within this context means stasis, attitudes frozen in time, unamendable to other persuasions. *The Good Soldier* consistently dramatizes the consequences of stasis or rigidity as it is reflected in Edward's imagination. But even more important to the argument of this [discussion] is the fact that Ford's novel develops a dialectic between Edward's fantasies and the irretrievability of the past, reflecting the deadweight of gone worlds. (pp. 98-9)

Edward's passions cannot be separated from his aristocratic, feudal view of the nature of relationships between men and women. . . . [He] dehumanizes his women . . . by making them projections of his reading so that we are always conscious of a distance between a woman and the person Edward imagines her to be. Such imaginative projection could succeed during the flowering of courtly love because those associated with the courts believed in the same fictions—the ladies and knights were rigidly typecast, seeing themselves mirrored in their roles, seeing only the roles of those surrounding them. But a society of personae can survive only so long as everyone believes in personification—when only Edward takes seriously the tenets of courtly love and the feudal concept of social order, then we have . . . a conflict between a personal fiction and social reality, which can only result in the destruction of the individual because the perpetuation of his fictions is inimical to the welfare of society. The social order of the Middle Ages and Edwardian England was complex and multilayered, but the Romantic personal fiction is simple and denies by definition any and all ties beyond the "community of the elect." What we have here finally is a dialectical opposition between stasis and kinesis, past and present, history and the contemporary, evolving social moment. A large part of Edward's attraction to the static world of feudalism lies in the fact that it does not change, that it presents a world in which all variables are known. . . . (pp. 99-100)

The conflict engendered by this dialectic occupies much of the third chapter of Part III of *The Good Soldier,* where John Dowell explains the basic difference between Edward and Leonora:

> You see, Edward was really a very simple soul—very simple. He imagined that no man can satisfactorily accomplish his life's work without loyal and whole-hearted co-operation of the woman he lives with. And he was beginning to perceive dimly that, whereas his own traditions were entirely collective, his wife was a sheer individualist. His own theory—the feudal theory of an overlord doing his best for his dependents, the dependents meanwhile doing their best for the overlord—this theory was entirely foreign to Leonora's nature. She came of a family of small Irish landlords—that hostile garrison in a plundered country. And she was thinking unceasingly of the children she wished to have.

The first of their many differences occurs when Edward speaks of his "desire to build a Roman Catholic chapel at Branshaw" for Leonora. "Real trouble between them" began at this point, for Edward was "truly grieved at his wife's want of sentiment—at her refusal to receive that amount of public homage from him. She appeared to him to be wanting in imagination—to be cold and hard." From that moment Edward reacts against what he considers to be the mundane economic responsibility Leonora increasingly insists on, dimly perceiving in each of her objections a threat to his imagined world. At the same time, Leonora's original passion for Edward becomes confused by frustration, for in Edward's extravagance she sees her own security, and that of any children she might have, threatened by impecunious tenants and Edward's troops.

These differences in class ideologies are not confined to Edward's relationship with Leonora. While his sentimental "heart" leads Edward into his various affairs, his conduct in those affairs generally reflects the traditional attitudes and privileges of his class. For example, Edward can "console" the Kilsyte girl *because* she is a member of the working class, and, while it seems only natural for him to offer her the benefits of his comforts, the girl does not feel the same way: "All of her life, by her mother, by other girls, by school-teachers, by the whole tradition of her class she had been warned against gentlemen. She was being kissed by a gentleman. She screamed. . . . " Similar class attitudes can be traced in Edward's relationships with La Dolciquita, Maisie Maidan, and even in the platonic entanglement with Nancy (Mrs. Basil and Florence are ladies of the court) where we see distorted, but perceptible, signs of the feudal doctrine of *droit de seigneur.*

In what follows I hope to show that Edward's passions are undeniably authentic and moving, but that his search for an ideal woman can only lead to disaster because of his heritage, whose simplified paradigm of life is further skewed by his Romantic imagination. Edward is incapable of distinguishing between the ideal, closed, static world of history and Romantic literature and the problematic, open, unpredictable elements of reality. This naiveté leads to devastating consequences for Ford's "Beati Immaculati."

The first three chapters unfold against this complex social background, and by the time we reach the end of the third chapter we have encountered the major elements that define the strange *ménage* that centers on a man who is being flayed alive by his own emotions and his wife's jealousy. Chapters 1 and 2 introduce the themes of romance and social disintegration in allusions to the troubadour Peire Vidal and to the French revolution. In the third chapter we are taken back nine years to the German spa Bad Nauheim, where "the whole round table [was] begun." This time shift introduces a second, more ironic, evaluation of what Dowell characterizes as the "minuet of the Hessian bathing places." There are striking images contrasting the platonic minuet with the "mad house" of human emotions, as well as seemingly incongruous anecdotes dealing with Leonora's failed attempt at sex with Rodney Bayham in the dark recesses of a carriage and with the indefatigable energy of Vidal who sought the favors of a chatelaine in the Provençal countryside. These stories of arrested and frustrated passion are given in the memoirs of John Dowell, who has recorded his impressions of a life spent "wander[ing] upon the face of public resorts," a life which led him, years later, to the country house where Edward Ashburnham was suffering from the final passion of his life: "That poor devil beside me was in an agony. Absolute, hopeless, dumb agony such as surpasses the mind of man to imagine."

The imagery of these initial chapters is remarkably rich and varied; it is also characteristically violent. Ford proceeds, by way of abrupt juxtapositions, from ordered but superficial forms to the chaotic reality underlying them. Nowhere in the novel is this method more apparent than in Dowell's opening evaluations of his experiences at Bad Nauheim. After sketching in the social background of the Ashburnhams and of himself and his wife, Dowell's attention shifts to images of disintegration—"the sack of a city or the falling to pieces of a people," decay—"Someone has said that the death of a mouse from cancer is the whole sack of Rome by the Goths, and I swear to you that the breaking up of our little four-square coterie was such another unthinkable event," and disbelief—"Permanence?

Stability! I can't believe it's gone." His incredulity over the fate of their coterie continues in a speech organized around an image of a highly sophisticated society that reflects the typical elements of the closed world of Romance:

> I can't believe that that long, tranquil life, which was just stepping a minuet, vanished in four crashing days at the end of nine years and six weeks. Upon my word, yes, our intimacy was like a minuet, simply because on every possible occasion and in every possible circumstance we knew where to go, where to sit, which table we unanimously should choose; and we could rise and go, all four together, without a signal from any one of us, always to the music of the Kur orchestra, always in the temperate sunshine, or, if it rained, in discreet shelters. No, indeed, it can't be gone. You can't kill a minuet de la cour. You may shut up the music-book, close the harpsichord; in the cupboard and presses the rats may destroy the white satin favours. The mob may sack Versailles; the Trianon may fall, but surely the minuet—the minuet itself is dancing itself away into the furthest stars, even as our minuet of the Hessian bathing places must be stepping itself still. Isn't there any Nirvana pervaded by the faint thrilling of instruments that have fallen into the dust of wormwood but that yet had frail, tremulous, and everlasting souls?

But in the time it takes for the rhythm of that last sentence to settle into his consciousness, Dowell sees the contradiction of his experience:

> No, by God, it is false! It wasn't a minuet that we stepped; it was a prison—a prison full of screaming hysterics, tied down so that they might not out-sound the rolling of our carriage wheels as we went along the shaded avenues of the Taunus Wald.

Despite the intensity of their desires, Ford's characters discover, each in his own way, that it is not in the measured form of the minuet, but rather in the violent prison "full of screaming hysterics" that the meaning of their lives is reflected.

In his evocation of the minuet, Dowell wistfully hopes for an order that transcends the mutability of time, a kind of romantic synchronicity capable of surviving social anarchy and guaranteeing permanence. By taking the minuet as a symbol of social perfection, Dowell's attitude merges with Edward's, for the highly structured musical form mirrors the "peculiar rigidity of human relationships" within Edward's historical vision of society. One could also argue that the music of the "Hessian bathing places," as well as the songs of the troubadours with which we associate Edward through Peire Vidal, are both meant to evoke a shock-proof world. Unlike Edward, however, Dowell comes to understand that there is a discrepancy between his desire and reality, admitting in his conclusion that the harmony of the minuet only masks the dissonance of human experience. While Edward never discriminates between the dancer and the dance, Dowell learns that the elegant but static form must inevitably be left behind in the diachronic world of change, disorder, and nihilism. (pp. 100-03)

The violence that lies beyond the "shaded avenues of the Taunus Wald" is transposed to another setting when Dowell introduces the "lamentable history of Peire Vidal" during his recollection of a trip into Provence:

> Two years ago Florence and I motored from Biarritz to Las Tours, which is in the Black Mountains. In the middle of a tortuous valley there rises up an immense pinnacle and on the pinnacle are four castles—Las Tours, the Towers. And the immense mistral blew down that valley which was the way from France into Provence so that the silver-grey olive leaves appeared like hair flying in the wind, and the tufts of rosemary crept into the iron rocks that they might not be torn up by the roots.

The essence of *The Good Soldier* is symbolized in these images of discord and stress, and, by reminding us that "hair flying in the wind" is the "classical image of grief," John Meixner emphasizes the central emotion of the novel [see excerpt dated 1962]. There is no question that the violence of the mistral is in perfect accord with the violent passions that drive Vidal in his attempts to win the favours of La Louve, and the two paragraphs Ford gives over to Vidal's antics a few pages later describe, in comic terms, the same kind of agonies as Edward suffers in each of his affairs, but especially in his unrequited passion for Nancy Rufford.

Vidal is the fool of love, a direct link to the Provençal courts and feudalism, but we miss his significance if we see him merely as a symbol of the ethics of passion that once flourished in Provence. There is a disjunction between Vidal's antics which, comic as they are, were an acceptable part of the courtly social world and Edward's, which are socially out of place because they are out of time. Ezra Pound's poem about Vidal—"O Age gone lax! O stunted followers, / That mask at passions and desire desires"—chastises modern man for sublimating his emotions, but it also registers a difference between Vidal's age and Edward's. Vidal's love is heroic because it expresses a very limited, but nevertheless real, social attitude toward love; Edward's represents the degenerated ideal of love that has come down to him through Romantic literature. The source of Edward's fantasies can be found in the self-consciousness of his narcissism; the source of Vidal's in the will of a stratum of medieval society. Thus the juxtaposition of Edward and Vidal reveals a tension between Vidal's twelfth century Provence and Edward's modern India and Europe. But the main point to emphasize here is that their ideals of love cannot be separated from Romantic egocentrism that forces roles to displace personality. So the irony often mentioned in Edward's resemblance to Vidal is really more deeply rooted in the novel's thematic texture than has been noticed, particularly in the disturbing questions Dowell raises at the end of his narrative about the conflict between passion and society and the fantasies men entertain about themselves. (pp. 104-05)

Edward's adolescent fantasies were confirmed by the sentimental literature he read even when he was a military cadet:

> At Sandhurst . . . he was keen on soldiering, keen on mathematics, on land-surveying, on politics, and, by a queer warp of his mind, on literature. Even when he was twenty-two he would pass hours reading one of Scott's novels or the Chronicles of Froissart.

And he was especially attracted to

> novels in which typewriter girls married marquises and governesses earls. And in his books, as a rule,

the course of true love ran as smooth as buttered honey. And he was fond of poetry, of a certain type—and he could even read a perfectly sad love story. I have seen his eyes filled with tears at reading of a hopeless parting.

Edward's sentimental vulnerability is balanced by his wife's decidedly unromantic views of love and marriage. Within a few years Leonora's attitudes become antithetical to all that is assumed in her husband's "sentimental view of the cosmos." She has come to see "life as a perpetual sex-battle" between unfaithful husbands and faithful suffering wives, a position Dowell attributes to the absence of a literary sensibility:

> Man, for her, was a sort of brute who must have his divagations, his moments of excess, his night out, his, let us say, rutting seasons. She had read few novels, so that the idea of a pure and constant love succeeding the sound of wedding bells had never been very much presented to her.

The comic irony of Edward's reading, of course, is that it has produced a dedication to those "divagations" which offend the ethics of popular romantic fiction while confirming those of adulterous courtly-love liaisons.

It is sentimental literature, along with radically different class ideologies, that separates Leonora and her husband. Edward tries for a while to draw Leonora into his fictive world, but she cannot enter because she does not have the requisite imaginative sensibility, and Edward begins to look for others who can satisfy his literary desires—as well as his physical ones. Opposed to Edward's optimistic belief that his divagations reflect a superreality is Leonora's religious tradition, which counsels resignation in the face of such indulgences. This is comically but painfully apparent when Leonora seeks advice about Edward's adventure with the Spanish dancer from the Mother Superior of her old convent. "Men are like that," the nun says. "By the blessing of God it will all come right in the end." What we have here is a difference between optimistic, passionate expectation and pessimistic, resigned acceptance of fate; and the dramatic consequences of these differences are obvious in *The Good Soldier.* Leonora cannot be drawn into Edward's imaginative world because it denies all that she has learned about reality. For her, Edward is not ennobled by his sentimental views; he is only made to appear more irresponsible, more prone to "moments of excess."

But what drives Leonora away attracts Mrs. Basil, Maisie Maidan, and Nancy (La Dolciquita and Florence are special cases—the first responds to Edward only as a business liaison, the second as a sexual object). "What did they all see in him?" Dowell wonders. "Suddenly, as if by a flash of inspiration," he knew: "All good soldiers are sentimentalists—all good soldiers of that type. Their profession, for one thing, is full of the big words—'courage,' 'loyalty,' 'honor,' 'constancy.' " Dowell then sketches in what Edward at times "blurted out" concerning "the sentimental view of the cosmos that was his," at the center of which were received ideas about the redemptive effects of a woman on a man and the virtues of fidelity. "So you see," Dowell concludes, "he would have plenty to gurgle about to a woman—with that and his sound common sense about martingales and his—still sentimental—experiences as a county magistrate; and with his intense, optimistic belief that the woman he was making love to at the moment

was the one he was destined, at last, to be eternally constant to. . . . " As I suggested earlier, Edward's sentimentality is never far away from narcissism, and the women he finds irresistible are largely attractive because they see him as he sees himself. Maisie Maidan was star-struck, "perpetually asking her boy husband why he could not dress, ride, shoot, play polo, or even recite sentimental poems, like their Major." For Nancy Rufford, Edward was the "Cid; he was Lohengrin, he was the Chevalier Bayard." Such affirmations of his ego-ideal beguile Edward with the force of magic one associates with fairy tales, and it is unquestionably a fantasy world Edward hopes to enter with all of his women (even with Leonora when they are first married)—a fantasy world characterized by the absence of pain that issues from moments of insight, accidents of character, or social demands that complicate reality—a world frozen in time where feelings respond to the dictates of a medieval code.

The violent, tragic effects of Edward's beliefs are dramatized in the last half of *The Good Soldier* where Ford develops the bizarre triangle formed by Leonora, Edward, and Nancy. Nancy has grown up with Edward and, as we have seen, worshipped him: "He was for her, in everything that she said . . . the model of humanity, the hero, the athlete, the father of his country, the lawgiver." While she was a child, Edward accepted these accolades as a grateful and happy guardian, but, when he suddenly senses that she has become a woman, he develops a passion for her that exceeds anything he experienced with his former mistresses or his wife. The effects of Edward's newly discovered passion are devastating for both Nancy and Leonora. His unspoken but clearly felt demands literally push Leonora over the edge, causing her mind to "waver," and the instability we sense in Nancy from the moment she is introduced is tragically heightened by the confusion of feelings she develops towards this man. By attempting to force Leonora and Nancy into the field of his imagination, Edward deprives both of them of their own ground, for his solipsistic concerns serve to cut them off from all connections with the security of their private worlds and traditions. While the result of this appropriation is muted until they all return to Branshaw Teleragh, Leonora's suffering begins at Nauheim.

The ground is cut from under Leonora on the night Edward discovers his passion for Nancy and speaks to her of the great sentimental verities. Leonora "had guessed what had happened under the trees near the Casino," and, from that moment of intuition until Edward's death, is consumed by jealousy and frightening visions of chaos encroaching on what she believed was an ordered world. But Leonora does not know that Edward never intended to tell Nancy more than he did that night, nor to do anything more than worship her in his sentimental way. "He was very careful to assure me that at that time there was no physical motive about his declaration," Dowell writes. "It did not appear to him to be a matter of a dark night and a propinquity and so on. No, it was simply of her effect on the moral side of his life that he appears to have talked." Leonora's ignorance of this indulgence in innocent admiration leads her to keep a strict vigil, never allowing Edward and Nancy to be alone together except in crowded places in broad daylight. Her suspicions are justified because during this time Edward had begun to show the tell-tale signs of unrequited love—that is, a disjunction between his imagination and reality—with which Leonora was familiar from his previous infatuations. It is only a matter of time before her suspicions are confirmed that it is Nancy, and not memories of the now dead Florence, who is the source of the latest, and what proves to be the last, of Edward's passionate afflictions.

The events of the last three weeks at Nauheim are extraordinarily dramatic; time seems to have been suspended in this elegant spa where we are aware only of profound emotions slowly intersecting each other in a dream-like world. Leonora watches Edward "as a fierce cat watches an unconscious pigeon in the road way," Edward remains silent and drinks late into the night, and Nancy is sent to bed at ten and performs a "nightly orison" with Leonora for Florence. While Nancy remains ignorant of the conflict between her guardians, Leonora is consumed by the agony of jealousy, and beneath his somnambulistic torpor Edward is being torn to "rags and tatters" by his feelings for the girl. All of this emotion is masked by superficial conversation that can best be illustrated by a comment Ford once made about Henry James: "His characters will talk about the rain, about the opera, about the moral aspects of the selling of Old Masters to the New Republic, and those conversations will convey to your mind that the quiet talkers are living in an atmosphere of horror, of bankruptcy, of passion as hopeless as the Dies Irae!" The unvoiced suffering Ford points to dominates the Ashburnhams at Nauheim, and one scene in particular conveys these Jamesian qualities. On the last night of their stay, Leonora relents in her vigilance and allows Edward to take Nancy on a final visit to the Casino. Later that night,

> Leonora could hear Edward going about his room, but, owing to the girl's chatter, she could not tell whether he went out again or not. And then, much later, because she thought that if he were drinking again something must be done to stop it, she opened for the first time, and very softly, the never-opened door between their rooms. She wanted to see if he had gone out again. Edward was kneeling beside his bed with his head hidden in the counterpane. His arms, outstretched, held out before him a little image of the blessed virgin—a tawdry, scarlet and Prussian-blue affair that the girl had given him on her first return from the convent. His shoulders heaved convulsively three times, and heavy sobs came from him before she could close the door. He was not a Catholic; but that was the way it took him.

Edward's pain prefigures the emotional disaster that lies in wait for all of them at Branshaw Teleragh, for from this moment the "Beati Immaculati" will move under the "shadow of an eternal wrath . . . drifting down life, like fireships afloat on a lagoon and causing miseries, heartaches, agony of the mind, and death."

Readers are inclined to see Leonora as the source of these miseries and Edward as a heroic figure who gives all for love, but Ford's treatment of Leonora is considerably more sympathetic than it may first appear to be. Up to this point Leonora has been presented as a woman who is cold and unresponsive and whose vision has been delimited by the rigorous Catholicism inherited from her Irish background. Once the *ménage* arrives at Branshaw, Leonora's distress forces her into acts that she would very likely have avoided had she the strength and insight of normal health.

Dowell tells us that "with the slackening of her vigilance, came the slackening of her entire mind. This is perhaps the most miserable part of the entire story, for it is miserable to see a clear intelligence waver; and Leonora wavered." With the relaxation of tension following her conviction that Edward will not seduce Nancy comes a vulnerability to all the emotions she has repressed over the years. The destructive, violent acts that follow upon this vulnerability are the result of an intense concentration of contradictory and unresolvable emotions of maternal love for Nancy, jealousy of her as the final passion of Edward's life, disgust for Edward's weakness in giving in to this passion, and pity and respect for his decision to leave Nancy alone. The crisis Leonora helps to precipitate at Branshaw is largely the result of neurosis and hysteria in a woman who for years has been driven closer and closer to the breaking point by her husband's extraordinarily insensitive and irresponsible behavior.

An uneasy silence pervades Branshaw for a while as the days are filled with Leonora's absorption in her migraines and Edward's in his silences and drink. But this hiatus in what Dowell characterizes as a "duel with invisible weapons" ends when Nancy's innocence is shaken by her recognition of a "profound difference" between her guardians because of Edward's gift of a horse to a young man whose family has long been in the service of the Ashburnhams. In this act Nancy sees a further example of Edward's heroic generosity, but in response to her praise of Edward Leonora bursts out: "I wish to God that he was your husband and not mine. We shall be ruined, we shall be ruined. Am I *never* to have a chance?" Nancy's enthusiasm could not have come at a worse moment since that day Leonora had been occupied with feelings of hatred and jealousy for both Nancy and Edward. Just before Nancy had spoken to her, Leonora had heard them return to the house:

> At that moment Leonora hated Edward with a hatred that was like hell, and she would have liked to bring her riding-whip down across the girl's face. . . . Yes, Leonora wished to bring her riding-whip down in Nancy's young face. She imagined the pleasure she would feel when the lash fell across those queer features, the pleasure she would feel at drawing the handle at the same moment toward her, so as to cut deep into the flesh and to leave a lasting wheal.

Leonora's jealousy of Edward is redirected to Nancy who has innocently brought before Leonora one more time her husband's financial irresponsibility. In the gift of the horse is concentrated all of Leonora's frustrations, and the sexual jealousy that lies at the center of her feelings simply blots out all perspective and leads to a series of actions that are among the most painful and most psychologically accurate graphs of human emotions in modern literature. Ford presents a double challenge to his reader here: to understand why Leonora feels as she does, and to understand that the rational world has been left forever in the past for all three of these sufferers. It is partly this explosion of feeling and its consequences that Dowell had in mind earlier when he described the underlying reality of the "four-square coterie" as a place filled with "screaming hysterics."

And this is when Dowell arrives to find Edward in "hopeless, dumb agony such as surpasses the mind of man to imagine." What he finds continues the tension between appearance and reality, the superficial talk in perfect accord with the Ashburnhams's British decorum that masks the sense of the Dies Irae. But it is only a mask and Dowell learns that "what had happened was just hell":

> Leonora had spoken to Nancy; Nancy had spoken to Edward; Edward had spoken to Leonora—and they had talked and talked. And talked. You have to imagine horrible pictures of gloom and half lights, and emotions running through silent nights—through whole nights. You have to imagine my beautiful Nancy appearing suddenly to Edward, rising up at the foot of his bed, with her long hair falling, like a split cone of shadow, in the glimmer of a night-light that burned beside him. You have to imagine her, a silent, no doubt agonized figure, like a spectre, suddenly offering herself to him—to save his reason! And you have to imagine his frantic refusal—and talk. And talk! My God!

Their words "flayed the skin off him." In Leonora's accusations and Nancy's offering of herself to save his life, "they were like a couple of Sioux who had got hold of an Apache and had him well tied to a stake. I tell you there was no end to the tortures they inflicted upon him."

The type of this confrontation is Dowell's story of Vidal, with Leonora acting the role of La Louve's husband who "remonstrated seriously with her" when she rejected the troubadour's love. But in the passion of his life Edward is steadfastly virtuous, suffering "like one of the ancient Greek damned." "Drunk or sober," Dowell writes, Edward "stuck to what was demanded by convention and by the traditions of his house," avoiding one of the oldest taboos of mankind, for what is often glossed over is the blatantly incestuous nature of his passion for Nancy. In resisting her innocent offer of herself to save his reason, Edward upholds the feudal-romantic tradition that Leonora's hysterical reaction almost succeeded in destroying. At the same time, we need to remember that it was Edward's view of himself as a composite lord of the manor and courtly lover that precipitated the situation with Nancy, while Leonora's years of suffering are responsible for her hysteria and the revenge she attempts. There are no easy answers here, no measuring out of unmitigated guilt or virtue. As Hugh Kenner has said, Ford is "in an impasse of sympathy for all sides" [see *TCLC*, Vol. 1, p. 278].

It is inevitable that Edward commits suicide because the absence of any acknowledged suffering in Nancy's telegram violates his imagined world. It is also inevitable that Nancy is driven into incurable madness when she learns of Edward's death—despite what she had learned about him from Leonora, he was still the symbol of order in a world that had come crashing down around her. In light of these tragic events, as well as Leonora's having found peace with Rodney Bayham and Dowell's new role as Nancy's nurse whom he enshrines in the silent rooms of Branshaw, Dowell's final evaluation of their communal experience is especially disturbing. "It is," he says, "a queer and fantastic world":

> Is there then any terrestrial paradise where, amidst the whispering of the olive-leaves, people can be with whom they like and have what they like and take their ease in shadows and in coolness? Or are all men's lives like the lives of us good people—like the lives of the Ashburnhams, of the Dowells, of

Ford, 1939.

the Ruffords—broken, tumultuous, agonized, and unromantic lives, periods punctuated by screams, by imbecilities, by deaths, by agonies. Who the devil knows?

Dowell has learned much since he first sat down to order his impressions of the "coterie," and these questions reverberate ironically against his earlier naive evocation of the inviolable minuet. That naiveté is faintly perceptible in his answers to these questions, particularly in the bitterness we sense against the parameters society imposes on idiosyncratic desires and behavior. "Yes," he muses, "society must go on." "Edward was the normal man, but there was too much of the sentimentalist about him and society does not need too many sentimentalists. Nancy was a splendid creature but she had about her a touch of madness. Society does not need individuals with touches of madness about them." And these speculations conclude with his notion that "Edward and Nancy found themselves steam-rolled out and Leonora survives, the perfectly normal type, married to a man who is rather like a rabbit." Edward's Romantic imagination posited "a community of the elect, a circle of solidarity . . . set apart from the common herd," but Dowell has learned that the romantic's inability to see himself and others as individuals enmeshed in the common life of humanity threatens the integrity of both the individual and the social order.

There is much of Ford himself in Edward Ashburnham,

and perhaps the most telling observation about this congruence is Ezra Pound's: "That Ford was almost an *halluciné* few of his intimates can doubt. He felt until it paralyzed his efficient action, he saw distinctly the Venus immortal crossing the tram tracks." But, while Ford may have personally mourned the loss of "courtesie" and the plot that Romance gave to one's passional life, he was deeply aware of the destructive qualities inherent in Edward's view of history. Edward's attempt to actualize his idiosyncratic vision fails, Ford argues, because the love it manifests only masks solipsism and devalues the loved one since it forces each of Edward's women into his imaginative world where they become fictional projections of his fantasies. The direct result of this tension between desire and reality is that values in *The Good Soldier* remained mired in the realm of possibility, because Edward's romanticism lacks any consciously apprehended principles. . . . Edward reductively interpolates Romanticism, for his sentimental, unexamined feelings are imposed on the complex ideals of this movement, distorting it in his narcissistic expropriation of its tenets to his own ends. Such distortion suggests a nihilistic view of human experience only if we do not see that the values of the novel are not negated, only suspended, and that the alienation of the "Beati Immaculati" carries with it the condition necessary for escape. That condition involves movement away from solipsism to integration, from the "rigidity of human relationships" as Edward conceived of them to a new perspective where individuals can be seen as themselves as well as members of the social order. The division we sense in *The Good Soldier* between Edward's fantasies about social purpose and what he helplessly *does* to those nearest him is resolved in *Parade's End,* where Ford reimagines an English country gentleman whose idealism and medieval code of conduct spring from compassion rather than from a sense of inherited duty, where Christopher Tietjen's love for Valentine Wannop and his often repeated motto—"I stand for monogamy and chastity"—graph the distance between a man of honor and an engaging but sentimental and corrupting *puer eternus.* Having regressed to the ideals of feudalism and the courts of love, Edward is stranded in a static world out of time. (pp. 105-14)

Lawrence Thornton, " 'A Queer and Fantastic World': Romance and Society in 'The Good Soldier'," in his Unbodied Hope: Narcissism and the Modern Novel, *Bucknell University Press, 1984, pp. 98-114.*

Vincent J. Cheng   (essay date 1985)

[*In the following excerpt, Cheng considers the significance of religious controversy in interpreting* The Good Soldier.]

Ford Madox Ford's *The Good Soldier* is a celebrated novel whose intricacies have been vigorously explored by critics in the last thirty years. This essay makes a small foray towards investigating a larger topic which has, however, remained relatively unexplored: the importance of religion in this novel, especially of the Roman Catholic and Anglican religions. By investigating the ways in which the Catholic and Protestant religions are presented, we can perhaps make out the shadowy outlines of Ford's own

moral sentiments and religious sympathies within this enigmatic "tale of passion."

This complex tale, concerning events spanning a period of twenty-three years, is told to us by a rambling first-person narrator, John Dowell. He relates the stories of Leonora and Edward Ashburnham; Leonora is a sheltered Roman Catholic convent girl from Ireland who marries Edward Ashburnham, a sentimental Anglican and a member of the English landed gentry. Edward is an unfaithful husband who, for many years, conducts an adulterous affair with Florence, the narrator's wife. Leonora is quite aware of the situation, but Dowell learns of the adultery only after the principals have died.

While most of the details of these events are revealed to us in dialogue, there *are* a few scenes or incidents that are fully and novelistically portrayed. One such scene is the well-known "Protest" scene in the Schloss at Marburg in Part One of the novel; it serves as an illuminating case study of the role of religion in this novel.

After Florence has led the foursome to the town of M— and has dramatically unveiled Luther's protest, Leonora hysterically questions Dowell: "Don't you know that I'm an Irish Catholic?" Mark Schorer interprets this scene as one of "the wonderfully comic events . . . the frequent moments when the author leads his characters to the most absurd anticlimaxes, as when, at the end of the fourth chapter, Leonora, in a frenzy of self-important drama, demands: 'Don't you know that I'm an Irish Catholic?' " I have long been bothered by this statement of Schorer's, for it has always struck me that Leonora's question and outburst are not a bit anticlimactic, but precisely and devastatingly to the point. Schorer also poses the key (but since neglected) issue which this essay tries to address: "What, again, is the meaning of the narrator's nearly phobic concern with Catholicism, or of the way in which his slurs at Leonora are justified by her attachment to that persuasion?" Another popular version of the anticlimactic interpretation is that it is Leonora who consciously deflates the tension of the situation, in an effort to protect Dowell from reality. Jo-Ann Baernstein, for example, speaks of "the 'protest scene' in which Leonora shielded Dowell from the incipient adultery by talking of Protestants and Catholics" [see Further Reading].

Such readings seem to me to miss the pointed thrust of the scene. What is the importance, one might ask (but commentators seem loath to ask), of religion—of Roman Catholics and Protestants—in this novel? Surely it is not a minor concern. Ford once described himself as "a sentimental Tory and a Roman Catholic" (*Memories*), which seems to be a facile conflation of Edward and Leonora. Yet this book is hardly kind to its Roman Catholics, but rather tender towards sentimental Tories. Nor is the religious element limited to this one scene. Reading carefully for detail, we see that the religious issue is ubiquitous, and that religion must play an important role in this novel. A few salient facts suffice to illustrate: Leonora is a staunch Roman Catholic, going on periodic retreats, seeking guidance from her "spiritual advisers" for her marital problems. Florence and Edward are Anglican. Dowell is a Quaker, which leaves him, characteristically, an outsider, and a non-aggressive one by both temperament and religious conviction. While Edward is an Anglican and an heir to the feudal tradition of the British landed gentry, he is willing to convert to Catholicism should Leonora wish it, but insists, to her mortification, that any sons they may have be raised Anglican. Leonora, being Roman Catholic, cannot divorce Edward, and must make the best of her marriage in spite of Edward's infidelities. Dowell seems to qualify everyone and everything as either Roman Catholic or Protestant, and clearly dislikes Roman Catholics: "I must confess I felt a little angry with Leonora . . . I took it as one of the queer, not very straight methods that Roman Catholics seem to adopt in dealing with matters of this world. . . . Perhaps Leonora was right; perhaps Roman Catholics, with their queer, shifty ways, are always right." It is the sight of Edward sitting in his room silently reading the Anglican prayer book which leads Leonora to risk relaxing her vigilance over Edward and Nancy Rufford. Note that both Nancy, and Maisie Maidan before her, are just what Leonora once was: innocent Roman Catholic girls right out of the convent, the kind of girls who retire to a chapel in the midst of a field hockey game to pray for victory. In fact, Maisie and Leonora are from the same convent; no wonder that Leonora watches over Maisie and Nancy. After Nancy leaves Branshaw, Edward quotes, beneath his breath, from Swinburne's "Hymn to Proserpine," with its resounding religious implications: "Thou hast conquered, O pale Galilean." Nancy, after she goes mad, merely sits and chants the opening of the Nicene Creed: *"Credo in unum Deum Omnipotentem."* And finally, the main narrative of Part Four and of the book itself—excluding Dowell's dramatic afterthought, his two-page finale recounting of Edward's suicide—ends with Dowell's spiteful comment about Leonora's marriage to Rodney Bayham: "The child is to be brought up as a Romanist."

In light, then, of all these religious details underlying the novel, perhaps the "Protest" scene, and other scenes dealing with religion, deserve a careful re-reading. Let us begin [where] the two couples ride a train to the ancient city of M—. We are subtly prepared for the religious conflict (centering on the issue of adultery) that will ensue, when Florence tells of "how Ludwig the Courageous wanted to have three wives at once—in which he differed from Henry VIII, who wanted them one after the other, and this caused a good deal of trouble." Henry VIII, of course, founded the Anglican sect as a result of his adulteries; Edward himself later conceives the idea of becoming a polygamist. The conversation on the train is only slightly sublimated in its sexual implications: Florence wishes to "educate" Edward Ashburnham, and asks Leonora why she refuses to do so, to which Leonora replies that "it might injure his hand—the hand, you know, used in connection with horses' mouths." Dowell is quite oblivious to this secondary level of discourse, and watches one cow toss another into a stream; he continues to muse about Ludwig the Courageous and Luther. They then enter "the great painted hall where the Reformer and his friends met for the first time under the protection of the gentleman that had three wives at once and formed an alliance with the gentleman that had six wives, one after another (I'm not really interested in these facts but they have a bearing on my story)."

These facts have a much greater bearing than Dowell imagines, for it is in this atmosphere of adultery, bigamy, and divorce, that Florence exhilaratingly points out: "There it is—the Protest. . . . Don't you know that is why we are all called Protestants?" Dowell stupidly feels

relieved because "she was better and she was out of mischief "; he is dead wrong, for Florence's tactic is nothing if not searingly offensive and startlingly belligerent:

> She continued, looking up into Captain Ashburnham's eyes: 'It's because of that piece of paper that you're honest, sober, industrious, provident, and clean-lived. If it weren't for that piece of paper you'd be like the Irish or the Italians or the Poles, but particularly the Irish. . . . ' And she laid one finger upon Captain Ashburnham's wrist.

This moment, this laying of a finger on a wrist, is electric and frightening. Florence is ritually laying claim to her adulterous prize, threatening to shatter the traditional social order symbolized by marriage and by "playing the game." The moment is insidious, and prophesies anarchy and the disintegration of order. Even Dowell becomes aware of the sudden tension in the air, something betokening the break-up of the "minuet" and "four-square coterie": "I was aware of something treacherous, something evil in the day. I can't define it. I can't find a simile for it. . . . It was as if we were going to run and cry out; all four of us in separate directions, averting our heads."

Florence's finger on the wrist of her prize is balanced now by Leonora desperately clutching Dowell's left wrist. Leonora, always so admirable and controlled as the proper English lady, suddenly stops playing the game, and becomes hysterical:

> "I can't stand this," she said with a most extraordinary passion; "I must get out of this." . . . And it was a panic in which we [Dowell and Leonora] fled! We went right down the winding stairs . . . "Don't you see," she said, with a really horrible bitterness, with a really horrible lamentation in her voice, "Don't you see that that's the cause of the whole miserable affair; of the whole sorrow of the world? And of the eternal damnation of you and me and them. . . . Oh, where are all the bright, happy, innocent beings in the world? Where's happiness? One reads of it in books!"

Surely this is no conscious or calculated attempt to shield Dowell from the grown-up reality of adultery; this is real hysteria.

Dowell, of course, does not "see." He does not understand the significance of that little piece of paper which to a Roman Catholic betokens Anglicanism and adultery, nor of the stinging lash of Florence's words. But Leonora is reeling under Florence's direct slap at her and her Irish Catholicism. I paraphrase Florence's (previously quoted) words to Edward: "Edward, if not for that piece of paper you wouldn't today be honest, sober, industrious, provident, and clean-lived. You'd be a Catholic—that is, dishonest, drunken, lazy, irresponsible, and immoral. You'd be like the Catholics are, but particularly like your wife. . . . I, of course, am clean and Anglican like you, and with my hand I now lay claim to you, rescuing you from the fangs of that Roman serpent standing beside you."

Dowell does not see, has no inkling of the incipient adultery. But Leonora feels the sting fully; I paraphrase her quoted remarks to Dowell: "Don't you see what's going down? My religion has been assaulted and, as a result, your wife is about to commit adultery with my husband (the two are the same, since my faith is the True Defender of the sacred sacrament of Holy Matrimony). Don't you see that that piece of paper, that paper which gave rise to Protestantism and thus to evil, to rampant divorce and adultery—that *that's* the cause of this whole miserable affair, as well as of the sorrow in the world, that piece of sacrilegious paper which dooms us all to the raging fires of everlasting Hell?"

Leonora becomes hysterical because the central pillars of her life, of Roman Catholicism, under the shadows of which she went to school and grew up, and on whose firm foundation she built a marriage that might not be dissolved, these pillars are being toppled by Florence. Leonora is hysterical because this collapse signifies the breakdown of a social convention—marriage—whereas she believes Catholicism would have preserved the sanctity of marriage. If not for the Protest, Florence's sort of adultery would never have existed, for Leonora realizes that Florence is making an unequivocally adulterous overture by hinting that Edward would be better off with Florence's Connecticut Protestantism than with Leonora's Irish Catholicism.

Dowell, of course, does not see, and it is in this context that Leonora asks him, in her "clear hard voice, 'Don't you know that I'm an Irish Catholic?' " Her question is explosive and thoroughly to the point; it is hardly anticlimactic. Dowell advises, "Do accept the situation. I confess that I do not like your religion. But I like you so intensely. . . ." But for Dowell "the situation" consists only of a difference in religious affiliation, whereas Leonora knows it includes adultery. The final proof that Leonora *is not* consciously shielding Dowell comes, here, as we realize that Leonora, in fact, assumes that Dowell *already* sees, that he does know—so that shielding him would be out of the question—for she replies: " 'Oh, I accept the situation,' she said at last, 'if you can.' " There is a terrific irony here, and the scene ends.

After this, Dowell tells us about the history of Edward and Leonora's marriage and of Edward's adulteries—all of which, one could argue, has much to do with religion. However, what is interesting in our reading of the "Protest" scene is how Dowell's subsequent and conflicting treatment of this same reveals, and is typical of, his attitude towards Catholics, Anglicans, and especially Catholic Leonora. Dowell tells the tale in such a way as to give the impression that Leonora consciously manipulated Edward and Florence so as to shield him (Dowell) and keep him in the dark about his wife's adultery—when in fact Dowell, narrating the tale, knows perfectly well that Leonora had simply assumed he knew. As Dowell himself admits . . . , after Edward's death Leonora had "to talk (to Dowell) about a much wider range of things than she had before thought necessary." After all, we have just had the events of the "Protest" scene narrated to us in great retrospective detail; surely it is a version of events which Dowell can hardly repudiate, since it is *his* version and narration.

Yet—in Part Four of the novel, when we have a brief reprise of the "Protest" scene in Dowell's recollection—this later impression by Dowell is significantly different from, and inconsistent with, the earlier treatment: Here, Dowell says that, immediately after seeing the "Protest," "suddenly there came into [Leonora's] mind the conviction that Maisie Maidan had a real passion for Edward; and

this would break her heart. . . . She went, for the moment, mad." The previous treatment in Part One gave no hint that Maisie might have been on Leonora's mind at the time. Secondly, at this point in Part Four, Dowell the narrator seems now consciously aware that the issue during the "Protest" scene was not merely a matter of religious leaning, but also had to do with adultery. And, most striking here is Dowell's unfairness to Leonora. He says that at the time she

> ought to have said: "Your wife is a harlot who is going to be my husband's mistress. . . . " That might have done the trick. But even in her madness she was afraid to go as far as that. She was afraid that, if she did, Edward and Florence would make a bolt of it and that, if they did that, she would lose forever all chance of getting him back in the end. She acted very badly to me. Well, she was a tortured soul who put her church before the interests of a Philadelphia Quaker.

Dowell is condemning Leonora for putting self-interest ahead of telling him the truth; as the early version of this conversation makes quite clear, however, and as Dowell is well aware, Leonora did not tell him about the adultery because she assumed that he *knew,* that he had understood the significance of that piece of paper and had chosen to "accept the situation." It was Leonora, after all, who was reluctant to accept the situation, and who was thus thinking in the better interest of both Dowell and herself. In Part Four, we see Dowell undertake a concerted campaign to attack and denigrate Leonora's character.

Leonora, as far as Dowell is concerned, is at fault either way. In his narrative at this point, either she did not enlighten Dowell because she assumed he knew—which seems to be the case—and therefore she can only be guilty of underestimating Dowell's obtuseness, or she was aware that he didn't know and tried consciously to protect him, as Dowell now implies: "She had to give [Edward] . . . to understand that if I ever came to know of his intrigue she would ruin him beyond repair. . . . I rather imagine that she would have preferred damnation to breaking my heart." If the latter were true, then Leonora is only trying to be kind to the one innocent in the foursome. Yet, even so, Dowell spitefully condemns her: "That is what it works out at. She need not have troubled." She simply can't win.

At this point Dowell's dislike of Leonora becomes fully apparent. He depicts her as a manipulating tigress ("She was not a Roman Catholic for nothing"), managing both Edward's adulteries and his estate. And Dowell is deliberately misleading in order to blacken Leonora: for example, he conjectures that it was primarily Leonora's tight rein over him that made Edward cut his throat ("He might have stuck it out otherwise"), while at the end of the novel Dowell makes the loss of Nancy the cause of death. Dowell's aim here is not to be consistent, but to make Leonora seem a cruel murderess.

We know that many of Dowell's spiteful comments about Leonora's own actions and thoughts are mere speculations because, rather than say "Leonora told me" as he often does, he prefaces all these remarks with "I think" or "I imagine" (and yet how can we believe the speculations of a man who, on the previous page, "imagined that it would be up to me to propose to Nancy that evening"?): *"It is impossible to say* that Leonora, in acting as she then did, was not filled with a sort of hatred of Edward's final virtue. She wanted, *I think,* to despise him" (italics added). Or: "*I think* that she must have taken Nancy through many terrors of the night and many bad places of the day." Dowell conjectures much evil about Leonora—but what does he really *know*? How could he possibly know that "At the moment Leonora hated Edward with a hatred that was like hell, and she would have liked to bring her riding-whip down across the girl's face. What right had Nancy to be young and slender and dark . . . ?" Is it very likely that Leonora would tell him such things? "And at the same time, Leonora was lashing, like a cold fiend, into the unfortunate Edward." But this biased view is all conjecture, for Dowell himself goes on to admit that "God knows what was in Leonora's mind exactly," or, later, "God knows what Leonora said." Nevertheless, he does not hesitate to damn her by speculating about what she *might* have thought or said.

If we read these pages carefully, we see that it is quite possible that Leonora, a mother-figure to the innocent young convent girl Nancy Rufford, with whom Leonora must have identified, may not have been motivated, as Dowell implies, by gratuitous cruelty toward Edward when she lashed out against his insistence that Nancy return to India, but out of concern for her young ward. She is even willing to divorce Edward so as to save Nancy: "If you want me to divorce you I will. You can marry her then. She's in love with you." Leonora goes as far as to suggest to Nancy that "you must belong to Edward. I will divorce him"; Nancy responds properly that "The church does not allow of divorce. I cannot belong to your husband." Dowell would like to believe that Leonora was relaxing her religious scruples and was now being motivated by baser passions—perhaps because "the religious [her spiritual advisers] she now avoided"; he speculates: "You may put it that, having been cut off from the restraints of her religion, for the first time in her life, she acted along the lines of her instinctive desires." But Dowell's reports of the *actual* conversations in which Leonora offers to divorce Edward and to bring him and Nancy together all suggest a selfless attempt to save Nancy (from her father) and Edward (from himself), even at the risk of her own loss and damnation. She tells Nancy: "Edward's dying—because of you. . . . You must stay here . . . to save Edward. He's dying for love of you"; "You must stay here; you must belong to Edward. I will divorce him. . . . You see that it is your duty to belong to him. He must not be allowed to go on drinking." But, in his conjectures, Dowell dismisses this possibility:

> God knows what was in Leonora's mind exactly. I like to think that uppermost in it was concern and horror at the thought of the poor girl's going back to a father whose voice made her shriek in the night. And, indeed, that motive was very strong with Leonora. But *I think* there was also present the thought that she wanted to go on torturing Edward with the girl's presence. She was, at that time, capable of that. . . . She *probably* said a good deal more to Edward than I have been able to report.

So that when . . . Dowell does give a number of verifiable, visual details, he says, "Leonora *told* me these things"; the implied contrast is clear: the other details were merely speculations. Dowell has certainly misunderstood her mo-

tives before. And all of Leonora's actions at Branshaw are perfectly understandable from the much simpler perspective of motherly concern. After all, as the description of Nancy . . . reminds us (she sat "perfectly still . . . as she had been taught to sit at the convent. She appeared to be as calm as a church"), Nancy Rufford, like Maisie Maidan, is also a Roman Catholic convent girl under Leonora's protection—and Leonora does not want to have the blood of a correligionist on her hands a second time.

As Dowell grows in his hatred of Catholic Leonora, he conversely grows in his admiration and sympathy for Anglican Edward by the end of the novel. He comments bitterly:

> Society does not need too many sentimentalists. . . . Society does not need individuals with touches of madness about them. So Edward and Nancy found themselves steam-rolled out and Leonora survives, the perfectly normal type, married to a man who is rather like a rabbit. For Rodney Bayham is rather like a rabbit and I hear that Leonora is expected to have a baby in three months' time.

Or, "Society must go on, I suppose, and society can only exist if the normal, if the virtuous, and the slightly deceitful flourish, and if the passionate, the headstrong, and the too-truthful are condemned to suicide and madness. . . . Yes, society must go on; it must breed, like rabbits." It is clear that Dowell here stands behind the atavistic Edward, doomed to extinction in the modern, rabbit world of the Leonoras and Rodneys.

In the last two chapters of the novel, Dowell openly admits that he "cannot conceal . . . the fact that I now dislike Leonora." He describes her as partaking in "a fantastic display of cruelty" towards Edward. But, we might wonder, who was cruel and who was selfish? For, as Dowell admits, "Leonora says that, in desiring that the girl should go five thousand miles away and yet continue to love him, Edward was a monster of selfishness. He was desiring the ruin of a young life." Even Dowell admits that, in fact, the love between Leonora and Nancy may have been as important as, or more important than, Edward's and Nancy's love. Typically, Dowell says, "I don't know. I know nothing."

At the end of the book, we return overtly to the religious issue. After seeing Nancy off at the train station, Edward returns to acknowledge Leonora's victory with a line from Swinburne's "Hymn to Proserpine"—"Thou hast conquered, O pale Galilean"—referring to Christ's victory over the pagan deities. Did Edward or Ford see the tale as a religious victory for Leonora? Dowell envisions a pagan Edward: "I seem to see poor Edward, naked and reclining amidst darkness, upon cold rocks, like one of the ancient Greek damned, in Tartarus or whatever it was." He sees Leonora as alive and pregnant. "The child is to be brought up as a Romanist."

There are two alternative ways to end this "saddest story." One is to have a happy ending:

> Well, that is the end of the story. And, when I come to look at it, I see that it is a happy ending with wedding bells after all. The villains . . . have been punished by suicide and madness. The heroine—the perfectly normal, virtuous, and slightly deceit-

ful heroine [with the queer, shifty ways of Roman Catholics]—has become the happy wife of a perfectly normal, virtuous, and slightly deceitful husband. She will become a mother of a perfectly normal, virtuous, slightly deceitful son or daughter. A happy ending, that is what it works out at.

Such an ending Dowell obviously dislikes.

At this point, the story seems over. But Dowell suddenly remembers that he has forgotten to say how Edward met his death. An oversight by Dowell? Hardly. This is the alternate ending to the story that Dowell wants, and he has saved it for a final, dramatic climax. He wants to end not merely by denigrating Leonora, but by celebrating Edward as the noble sentimentalist, the last of his race, looking "up to the roof of the stable, as if he were looking to heaven," bidding Dowell a "soft and almost affectionate" farewell, and then, in the high Roman fashion, killing himself. But Dowell cannot resist aiming one last, barbed shaft at Leonora in the final lines of the book: "I trotted off with [Nancy's] telegram to Leonora. She was quite pleased with it." But the final devastating irony is at Dowell's expense; Nancy's *credo* is entrusted to his care. Perhaps in depicting such a biased and anti-Catholic narrator, Ford in fact wrote a moral tale much more sympathetic towards the Catholic faith than has usually been assumed by focussing on the moral relativism and emptiness of a beleaguered, faithless world exemplified by the tale and its teller. (pp. 238-47)

Vincent J. Cheng, "Religious Differences in 'The Good Soldier'; The 'Protest' Scene," in Renascence, *Vol. XXXVII, No. 4, Summer, 1985, pp. 238-47.*

FURTHER READING

Andreach, Robert J. "Ford's *The Good Soldier:* The Quest for Permanence and Stability." *Tennessee Studies in Literature* X (1965): 81-92.
    Argues that Dowell attempts to find permanence and stability in his life through telling the story.

Armstrong, Paul B. "The Epistemology of *The Good Soldier:* A Phenomenological Reconsideration." *Criticism* XXII, No. 3 (Summer 1980): 230-51.
    Examines "the epistemology of reading and representation in *The Good Soldier.*"

Aswell, Duncan. "The Saddest Storyteller in Ford's *The Good Soldier.*" *College Language Association Journal* XIV, No. 2 (December 1970): 187-96.
    Contends that Ford originally called *The Good Soldier* "The Saddest Story" as both an assessment of Dowell's narrative ability and as a judgment upon a society that makes it difficult for people to learn from their experience.

Baernstein, Jo-Ann. "Image, Identity, and Insight in *The Good Soldier.*" *Critique: Studies in Modern Literature* IX, No. 1 (1966): 19-42.
    Analyzes the use of animal imagery in *The Good Soldier,*

arguing that it adds new insight into Dowell's statement of identity with Edward at the end of the novel.

Bailin, Miriam. " 'An Extraordinarily Safe Castle': Aesthetics as Refuge in *The Good Soldier.*" *Modern Fiction Studies* 30, No. 4 (Winter 1984): 621-36.
    Studies "the ways in which Dowell employs aesthetic principles in order to control and to evade the disruptive nature of the experience he recounts."

Barnes, Daniel R. "Ford and the 'Slaughtered Saints': A New Reading of *The Good Soldier.*" *Modern Fiction Studies* XIV, No. 2 (Summer 1968): 157-70.
    Attempts to reconcile the different opinions held by James Hafley (excerpted above) and James Trammell Cox (below).

Bender, Todd K. "The Sad Tale of Dowell: Ford Madox Ford's *The Good Soldier.*" *Criticism* IV, No. 1 (Winter 1962): 353-68.
    Argues that Dowell represents "modern man whose character has been steamrolled by society" while Edward represents to Dowell what he might have been. Bender considers Dowell's sadness at Edward's eventual downfall to color the narrative, giving the novel tragic power.

Bonds, Diane Stockman. "The Seeing Eye and the Slothful Heart: The Narrator of Ford's *The Good Soldier.*" *English Literature in Transition* 25, No. 1 (1982): 21-7.
    Contends Dowell attempts to escape from awareness of his problems by telling his story but "some of his narrative techniques force upon him the very understanding that he seeks to avoid."

Bort, Barry D. "*The Good Soldier*: Comedy or Tragedy?" *Twentieth Century Literature* 12, No. 4 (January 1967): 194-202.
    Concludes that *The Good Soldier* is "a savage comedy of manners . . . in which people are unable to cope with the world because they have never learned to understand it."

Cheng, Vincent J. "A Chronology of *The Good Soldier.*" *English Language Notes* XXIV, No. 1 (September 1986): 91-7.
    Orders the plot chronologically to clarify some details of the story.

Cohen, Mary. "*The Good Soldier*: Outworn Codes." *Studies in the Novel* 5, No. 3 (Fall 1973): 284-97.
    Considers *The Good Soldier* an attack on the weakness of English society for maintaining the outdated codes of the chivalric and courtly love traditions.

Cox, James Trammell. "Ford's 'Passion for Provenance'." *ELH* 28, No. 4 (December 1961): 383-98.
    Argues that the courtly love tradition helps to illuminate the meaning of *The Good Soldier.*

Creed, Walter G. "*The Good Soldier*: Knowing and Judging." *English Literature in Transition: 1880-1920* 23, No. 4 (1980): 215-30.
    Offers a provisional interpretation of the novel's characters to show that they can be understood through internal evidence rather than through biographical information about Ford.

Ganzel, Dewey. "What the Letter Said: Fact and Inference

in *The Good Soldier.*" *Journal of Modern Literature* 11, No. 2 (July 1984): 277-90.

> Views *The Good Soldier* as an "elaborate puzzle in which significant facts are left to the reader's deductive imagination" by Dowell, a narrator incapable of understanding the events of his own tale.

Green, Robert. "*The Good Soldier*: Ford's Cubist Novel." *Modernist Studies* 3, No. 1 (1979): 49-59.

> Discusses the relationship between Ford's techniques and aesthetic goals and those of Modernist artists, especially Cubist painters.

Hanzo, T. A. "Downward to Darkness." *The Sewanee Review* LXXIV, No. 4 (Autumn 1966): 832-55.

> Studies archetypal patterns in *The Good Soldier.* As Hanzo writes: "The events of the story reverberate with a knowledge given in man's primordial encounter with the mystery of existence."

Hartford, Gordon. "Ford and *The Good Soldier*: A Bid for Tragedy." *English Studies in Africa* 23, No. 2 (1980): 93-102.

> Compares events in Ford's life with those in the novel.

Henighan, T. J. "*The Desirable Alien*: A Source for Ford Madox Ford's *The Good Soldier.*" *Twentieth Century Literature* 11, No. 1 (April 1965): 25-9.

> Marks the influence on *The Good Soldier* of Violet Hunt's sections of the travel book, *The Desirable Alien at Home in Germany* (1913), which included two chapters and a preface by Ford.

Hessler, John G. "Dowell and *The Good Soldier*: The Narrator Re-Examined." *The Journal of Narrative Technique* 9, No. 1 (Winter 1979): 53-60.

> Asserts that Dowell's "narrative stance as helpless questioner is, ultimately, an emotional strategy of evasion."

Hoffmann, Charles G. "Ford's Manuscript Revisions of *The Good Soldier.*" *English Literature in Transition: 1880-1920* 9, No. 3 (1966): 145-52.

> Analyzes Ford's revisions of three manuscripts of the novel, concluding that "*The Good Soldier* is so nearly a perfect masterpiece because of careful stylistic and thematic revisions."

Hood, Richard A. " 'Constant Reduction': Modernism and the Narrative Structure of *The Good Soldier.*" *Journal of Modern Literature* 14, No. 4 (Spring 1988): 445-64.

> Examines the narrative structure of *The Good Soldier* and its relationship to Modern literature and art.

Hurt, James. "The Primal Scene as Narrative Model in Ford's *The Good Soldier.*" *The Journal of Narrative Technique* 8, No. 3 (Fall 1978): 200-10.

> Considers the psychological and narrative implications of Dowell's infantile view of sex inspired by a primal scene fantasy, in which a child imagines seeing his or her parents copulating, misinterprets their act as violent, and continues as an adult to unconsciously link sex with violence.

Jacobs, Carol. "*The* (too) *Good Soldier*: 'A Real Story'." *Glyph: Johns Hopkins Textual Studies* 3 (1978): 32-51.

> Describes the ambiguity of *The Good Soldier,* showing that the reader "is tossed back and forth between possibilities."

Johnson, Ann S. "Narrative Form in *The Good Soldier.*" *Critique: Studies in Modern Fiction* XI, No. 2 (1969): 70-80.

> Examines the narrative structure of the novel in order to provide insights into Dowell's personality.

Jones, Lawrence William. "The Quality of Sadness in Ford's *The Good Soldier.*" *English Literature in Transition* 13, No. 4 (1970): 296-302.

> Attempts to demonstrate that the tragic qualities of *The Good Soldier* are typical of those in later absurdist plays that comment on "the situation of human beings in an essentially meaningless universe."

Lentz, Vern B. "Ford's Good Narrator." *Studies in the Novel* 5, No. 4 (Winter 1973): 483-90.

> Compares Ford's theory of fiction with Dowell's comments on his narration, arguing "that Ford regarded Dowell as a totally reliable narrator of a very complex fiction."

Levenson, Michael. "Character in *The Good Soldier.*" *Twentieth Century Literature* 30, No. 4 (Winter 1984): 373-87.

> Investigates techniques of characterization that Ford employs in *The Good Soldier.*

Lid, R. W. "On the Time-Scheme of *The Good Soldier.*" *English Fiction in Transition* 4, No. 2 (1961): 9-10.

> Finds some discrepancies in Ford's use of time in the novel.

Loeb, Harold. "Ford Madox Ford's *The Good Soldier*: A Critical Reminiscence." *The Carleton Miscellany* VI, No. 2 (Spring 1965): 27-41.

> Biographical interpretation by an acquaintance of Ford.

Lynn, David H. "Watching the Orchards Robbed: Dowell and *The Good Soldier.*" *Studies in the Novel* 16, No. 4 (Winter 1984): 410-23.

> Argues that "albeit lame and isolated," Dowell is a hero "who undergoes a moral education, tells his tale as a means of imposing order on chaos, and makes a final heroic gesture of human responsibility and love."

McCaughey, G. S. "The Mocking Bird and the Tomcat: An Examination of Ford Madox Ford's *The Good Soldier.*" *The Humanities Association Bulletin* XVI, No. 1 (Spring 1965): 49-58.

> Appreciative overview of plot and characterization in the novel.

McDougal, Stuart Y. " 'Where Even the Saddest Stories Are Gay': Provence and *The Good Soldier.*" *Journal of Modern Literature* 7, No. 3 (September 1979): 552-54.

> Discusses the significance of Ford's frequent references to Provence, suggesting that that region's melancholic legends represent contentedness in Ford's novel.

McLaughlin, Marilou B. "Adjusting the Lens for *The Good Soldier.*" *The English Record* XXII, No. 3 (Spring 1972): 41-8.

> Argues that understanding Leonora is central to interpreting *The Good Soldier.*

Micklus, Robert. "Dowell's Passion in *The Good Soldier.*" *English Literature in Transition: 1880-1920* 22, No. 4 (1979): 281-92.

> Maintains that Dowell's narrative reveals his "passion for vengeance."

Moser, Thomas. "Towards *The Good Soldier:* Discovery of a Sexual Theme." *Daedalus* 92, No. 2 (Spring 1963): 312-25.

Traces the development of attitudes towards sexuality in Ford's novels, concluding that the successful portrayal of passion in *The Good Soldier* indicates Ford's "triumph not merely of literary skill but of knowledge, self-acceptance and, even, courage."

———. "Impressionism, Agoraphobia, and *The Good Soldier,* 1913-1914." In his *The Life in the Fiction of Ford Madox Ford,* pp. 122-95. Princeton: Princeton University Press, 1980.

Provides historical background and biographical material relating to Ford's writing of the novel.

Mosher, Harold F., Jr. "Wayne Booth and the Failure of Rhetoric in *The Good Soldier*." *Caliban* VI (January 1969): 49-52.

Argues that *The Good Soldier* is not "a successful poetic construct," but rather "an unsuccessful didactic one."

Pierce, William P. "The Epistemological Style of Ford's *The Good Soldier*." *Language and Style* VIII, No. 1 (Winter 1975): 34-46.

Offers a close analysis of grammar, sentence structure, and the function of style in the novel.

Reichert, John. "Poor Florence Indeed! or: *The Good Soldier* Retold." *Studies in the Novel* 14, No. 2 (Summer 1982): 161-79.

Reinterprets narrative evidence in *The Good Soldier* that is usually accepted as proof that Florence Dowell was Edward Ashburnham's mistress, and questions common critical assumptions about reasons for Florence Dowell's actions, including her suicide.

Rentz, Kathryn C. "The Question of James's Influence on Ford's *The Good Soldier*." *English Literature in Transition: 1880-1920* 25, No. 2 (1982): 104-14.

Acknowledges the influence of Henry James on *The Good Soldier,* but contends that Ford successfully shaped his novel "according to his particular vision and temperament," resulting in "a chaotic, violent novel quite different from the comparatively tidy and restrained Jamesian works."

Schow, H. Wayne. "Ironic Structure in *The Good Soldier*." *English Literature in Transition: 1880-1920* 18, No. 3 (1975): 203-11.

Attempts to arrive at an understanding of the novel's moral structure through an examination of the irony inherent in the relationships between characters, and between form and meaning in this novel.

Siemens, Reynold. "The Juxtaposition of Composed Renderings in Ford's *The Good Soldier*." *The Humanities Association Bulletin* XXIII, No. 3 (Summer 1972): 44-9.

Examines ways that Ford rendered characterization and advanced plot in *The Good Soldier* by means of juxtaposing situations and actions and "a range of items within them which includes colors, dates and numbers, objects, and images."

Snitow, Ann Barr. "From Comic Irony to Romance." In her *Ford Madox Ford and the Voice of Uncertainty,* pp. 159-90. Baton Rouge: Louisiana State University Press, 1984.

Evaluates *The Good Soldier* as "Ford's masterpiece of comic irony," the culmination of his years of experimentation with narrative and with exploration of the tension between contradictory aspects of existence.

Thornton, Lawrence. "Escaping the Impasse: Criticism and the Mitosis of *The Good Soldier*," *Modern Fiction Studies* 21, No. 2 (Summer 1975): 237-41.

Attributes the lack of critical consensus regarding interpretations of *The Good Soldier* to Mark Schorer's 1951 essay focusing attention on the narrator, John Dowell [see *TCLC,* Vol. 1, pp. 277-78], and subsequent criticism that accepted Schorer's interpretation. Thornton suggests that the focus of the novel is actually the futility of Edward Ashburnham's love for a girl young enough to be his daughter.

Tracy, Laura. "Ford Madox Ford's *The Good Soldier* and the Tietjens Tetralogy: Knowledge is Power." In her *"Catching the Drift": Authority, Gender, and Narrative Strategy in Fiction,* pp. 64-102. New Brunswick, N. J. : Rutgers University Press, 1988.

Maintains that the effect of the literary techniques Ford developed, such as nonchronological narration and the incomplete or gradual revelation of key information, is to engender confusion in the reader and to empower the author by establishing him as the sole possessor of full knowledge of the situation.

Ricardo Güiraldes

1886-1927

(Full name Ricardo Guillermo Güiraldes) Argentine novelist, poet, essayist, and short story writer.

An important figure in Argentine literature of the early twentieth century, Güiraldes is best known for his novel *Don Segundo Sombra,* which is widely considered the classic novel about the gaucho, or South American cowboy. Esteemed for its evocative imagery, lyrical prose, and accurate portrayal of rural customs, *Don Segundo Sombra* captured the imagination of the Argentine public at a time when interest in the gaucho culture was at its peak and has been hailed as a masterpiece of Spanish-American literature. Although Güiraldes also participated in the founding of a progressive literary journal and wrote several other novels and volumes of experimental poetry, his other achievements have been overshadowed by the renown of *Don Segundo Sombra.*

Güiraldes was the second son of a prosperous Argentine cattle rancher. His parents, like many wealthy Argentines, maintained a residence in France in order to be close to the cultural centers of Europe, and it was there that Güiraldes spent most of his first four years. However, a downturn in the economy brought the family back to Argentina in 1890, and shortly thereafter they settled at La Porteña, their cattle ranch in the pampas, or grasslands, outside Buenos Aires. Güiraldes's parents hired private tutors to continue his education in French and German; at the same time, his father also encouraged him to take part in the operation of the ranch, where he heard songs and stories about the feats of legendary gauchos. One of the ranch hands, an old gaucho named Don Segundo Ramírez, later served as the model for the character Don Segundo Sombra. Though Güiraldes frequently neglected his studies to develop his skills as a rancher, he nevertheless developed a wide-ranging interest in literature, focusing in particular on French authors, and began writing poetry and prose. He later attended the University of Buenos Aires, studying both architecture and law, but withdrew from his classes, preferring to read independently.

Güiraldes left Argentina in 1910 to travel throughout Europe and Asia; during this period he began writing short stories and prose poems based on his memories of the Argentine pampas and on the dramatic gaucho stories he had heard as a child. Upon his return to Argentina in 1912, he published a number of his gaucho stories in *Caras y Caretas,* a popular Argentine magazine that featured regional literature. In 1915, Güiraldes published *Cuentos de muerte y de sangre,* a collection of short stories, and *El cencerro de cristal,* a volume of prose poetry influenced by the work of the French Symbolist writers Stéphane Mallarmé and Jules Laforgue. Both volumes were virtually ignored by the public, and the few critics who commented on them generally ridiculed Güiraldes's efforts as the products of an inferior and imitative talent. Güiraldes withdrew most of the unsold copies of the two works from sale and threw them down a well on his ranch. When his semiautobiographical novel *Raucho: Momentos de una ju-*

ventud contemporánea, published in 1917, received a similar response, Güiraldes went to Paris hoping to find a more receptive audience for his work.

In Paris, Güiraldes was welcomed and encouraged by a number of French writers, including Valéry Larbaud, a prominent poet and critic who wrote an article praising Güiraldes's works. While there, Güiraldes had several of his poems published in French and finished writing a draft of the novel *Xaimaca,* based on an earlier trip to Jamaica, but he realized that the rapidly vanishing culture of the gauchos was his most compelling interest, and in 1920 he returned to Argentina to gather material for *Don Segundo Sombra,* which he envisioned as the definitive gaucho novel. In 1924, Güiraldes, Jorge Luis Borges, and several other writers founded *Proa,* a literary journal devoted to publishing the work of unknown poets and educating the public about the latest trends in French and Spanish literature. Although *Proa* attracted some attention abroad, it was unpopular in the conservative literary atmosphere of Buenos Aires, and it failed after a year. At this time, Güiraldes began to suffer from an illness later diagnosed as Hodgkin's disease, but he finished *Don Segundo Sombra* before seeking help from doctors in Paris. Not long after *Don Segundo Sombra* appeared in Buenos Aires in 1926, the prominent author and critic Leopoldo Lugones wrote a lengthy review praising Güiraldes's novel as a masterpiece of Argentine literature. Other critics in Argentina, France, and Spain also praised the novel, ranking it with two other classic works portraying the gaucho: Domingo Faustino Sarmiento's biography/essay *Facundo: Civilización y barbarie* (1845) and José Hernández's epic poem *Martín Fierro* (1872-79). *Don Segundo Sombra* was awarded the Argentine National Prize for Literature shortly before Güiraldes died in Paris in 1927.

Often described as a *Bildungsroman,* a novel which traces the development of a young protagonist from adolescence to maturity, *Don Segundo Sombra* is written as the recollections of an unnamed orphan (sometimes referred to by critics as "Fabio," or "the son of Fabio Cáceres"). At the beginning of the novel, the narrator is an adolescent living with his two maiden aunts in a small, rural town. Bored with his life there, he runs away with Don Segundo Sombra, an almost mystical old gaucho known for his courage and strength. The boy travels with Don Segundo for five years, learning the skills of a gaucho and achieving emotional and intellectual maturity. The story concludes with the narrator, having discovered his parentage, inheriting his father's estate and accepting the responsibilities of a ranch owner, while Don Segundo returns to the wilderness of the pampas. Although Güiraldes made use of the same subject matter treated by numerous other writers, critics remark that his skillful rendering of Argentine folklore in a style that combines gaucho colloquialisms with the symbolic and linguistic richness of French lyric poetry distinguishes *Don Segundo Sombra* from the melodramatic gaucho tales that formed the basis of Argentine popular entertainment in the early twentieth century. Critics further note that this lyrical quality contributes to the elegiac tone of the novel, evoking a lament for the rapidly disappearing gaucho way of life.

PRINCIPAL WORKS

El cencerro de cristal (poetry) 1915
Cuentos de muerte y de sangre (short stories) 1915
Raucho: Momentos de una juventud contemporánea (novel) 1917
Rosaura (novella) 1922
    [*Rosaura* published in *Tales from the Argentine,* 1930]
Xaimaca (novel) 1923
Don Segundo Sombra (novel) 1926
    [*Don Segundo Sombra: Shadows on the Pampas,* 1935]
Poemas místicos (poetry) 1928
Poemas solitarios (poetry) 1928
Seis relatos porteños (short stories) 1929
Obras completas (essays, novels, novella, poetry, short stories, and letters) 1962

Ricardo Güiraldes (essay date 1910)

[*In the following excerpt, Güiraldes explains his objectives as a writer.*]

Literature does not have to have loud shouting, graftings and complicated theories. Quite the contrary, it must be as pure as possible—get rid of all artifices that are foreign to it and let it stand on its own merits.

Nowadays people confuse writers, or better said scribblers, with men of letters. They don't draw a line between the former, who use language merely as a medium of communication, and the latter, who make language a creation of art. My mission is to look at life from a healthy and intelligent point of view and to translate it into an artistic expression; and by artistic I also mean simple. I shall not seek public approval; I shall be honest with myself. I will polish and continue polishing my language until I will have achieved that simplicity which makes greatness. This is why I have sought out the gaucho and the pampas as my subject matter from among all other themes.

The gaucho is by nature the son of the pampa; both are inseparable from each other; each possesses the simplicity that I have been trying to achieve. In fact, my inclination toward unadorned plainness may well have come from the influence of the gaucho upon me. The gaucho casts out all that is pusillanimous and infirm from his great soul, which is simple and sound, and above pettiness.

. . . . .

The beauty of the vast, uniform plain, the great spectacle of those days and nights in the pampa that follow upon each other with equal splendor, but which are never the same, have instilled in me a love for that which is simple and great . . .

I have to carry out this work of mine without worrying about the opinions of others . . .

My writing can have a literary style without having to use only words approved by the Royal Spanish Academy. Our pampa has its own vocabulary which has come from the need to create new terms. The use of these expressions are as proper—indeed as necessary—as the best.

. . . . .

I can write literature with what we may call "gaucho" vocabulary in as pure a style as the most Castilian . . . (pp. 30-2)

> *Ricardo Güiraldes, in an extract in* Ricardo Güiraldes and "Don Segundo Sombra": Life and Works *by Giovanni Previtali, Hispanic Institute, 1963, pp. 30-32.*

Harriet V. Wishnieff (essay date 1929)

[*In the following review, Wishnieff discusses Güiraldes's technique in* Don Segundo Sombra.]

Not since the epoch-making innovations of Rubén Darío's *Azul* and *Prosas Profanas,* more than thirty years ago, has a more interesting work, from the technical standpoint, been produced in Spanish America than Ricardo Güiraldes's novel, **Don Segundo Sombra.** It meets every requirement of the new "dehumanized" art; the action is slight, diffuse, devoid of climax, creating at times the sensation of a motion picture *al rallenti* ["in slow motion"]. The subconscious psychological impressions and motives are sought after and insisted upon. The language is difficult, deliberately, and the syntax elliptical and arbitrary. The plot is so frankly romantic that it becomes the satire of a plot, the old cliche of the long-lost son and missing heir reduced ad absurdum, to show how unnecessary a plot is—a modern contention. And yet, remarkable though it might seem in a book of this type, it is not interesting alone as an example of the newest literary art; it possesses a vital and eternal significance for the Argentine nation. In what may often seem aimless pages Güiraldes has fixed for all time the enduring charactristics of the gaucho. The nameless hero of the book—Don Segundo Sombra is his mentor—exists by virtue of his one ambition: to become the embodiment of those qualities considered essential in a good gaucho, and the story is the account of this *werden* ["becoming"].

The gaucho has disappeared from the reality of the Argentine, engulfed in the flood of immigration and the economic development of the past sixty years. But he lives as a legend, an ideal, haloed by all his virtues and with most of his vices transmuted, cherished by every son of the Argentine. His songs, his dances, the history he has made, the very defects of his language have permeated the fiber of his country's civilization, and he has been and is being immortalized in every phase of its culture.

> Harriet V. Wishnieff, "The Vanished Gaucho," in The Nation, New York, Vol. 129, No. 3345, August 14, 1929, p. 176.

Anita Brenner   (essay date 1935)

[*Brenner was a Mexican-born American author, journalist, and critic who translated Güiraldes's novella Rosaura. In the following excerpt, she offers a favorable assessment of Don Segundo Sombra.*]

Waldo Frank says in his introduction to [**Don Segundo Sombra;** see Further Reading] that it "occupies a place in Argentinian letters not unrelated to that of *Huckleberry Finn* in ours." It is the story of an orphan boy, he points out, on his own in a frontier day. Other critics remark that it is more like a Western thriller, since it is a story about cowboy life, and they compare Güiraldes to Jack London. To me it suggests irresistibly *Moby Dick* because of its underlying theme—the pursuit of some enormous mystery, and against that the shaping of human lives in a noble pattern, on a grand, exciting scale.

These different aspects of the book have a common denominator, the thing sensed in it by everybody who reads it. It is unmistakably an American book. It has the feel of space, endless and generous and dangerous; the vigor and nobility of youth; the casual ruthlessness, the horseplay, and the enormous hopefulness of the primitive. Its thread of mysticism—the inarticulate emotions of a man riding alone at the head of thousands of cattle, across hundreds of miles—is also the sense, the excited awe, of explorers, prospectors, whalers, migrants, and pioneers.

Don Segundo Sombra, the hero of the book, rides into the life of the boy who tells the story when that boy is a small-town tough, escaping from two pious and petty "aunts" to go fishing and to hang around saloons. He has become a shrewd little guttersnipe and spends his time clowning maliciously, picking up spare pennies however he can, or brooding uncomfortably by the river. Sly subtleties in public places have made him well aware that there is a shadow on his birth. His aunts are not exactly fond of him. Yet an "uncle" whose ranch he once visited gave him two ponies and a poncho, so that when Don Segundo Sombra,

the almost legendary *gaucho,* rides into his town at dusk one day, a complete vision of escape flashes into his head. He departs, with his ponies and his poncho, to lead a brave man's life, the *gaucho* life of Don Segundo Sombra.

What he pursues when he rides out to find Don Segundo Sombra is this: "I stood still and watched the silhouette of horse and rider strangely magnified against the glowing sky. It was as if I had seen a vision, a shade, a something which passes and is more a thought than a living thing; a something that drew me as a deep pool draws down within it the current of a river." So he attaches himself to the *gaucho,* watches him, listens, obeys. And together with him rides from ranch to ranch, from round-up to fair, to make a marvelously colorful and dramatic tale.

Güiraldes says Don Segundo Sombra was a real person. Frank says he met him when he was in the Argentine. But in the story Don Segundo Sombra is also a complete ideal, like our own frontier heroes. He is courageous, silent, modest, witty, and completely sure of himself. Of course he can rope, saddle, ride, break horses, dance and sing, and tell stories better than anybody else. But he was something more than these things. He was *gaucho* inside as well as out, and therefore, says the boy who took him as a model, "only Don Segundo seemed to escape the fatal law that events play with us and make us dance to every vagrant tune." As he broke green horses, as he dominated broncos, so he dominated life itself. He had "the strength of the pampas." The silent land gave him "something of its greatness and its unconcern." And because he had somehow eliminated fear, "the result was that while the rest of us were heading toward death, he seemed to be on the way back."

Don Segundo Sombra as a complete personification of young Argentine, young America, and manhood making its own fate is probably the triple reason that the book has long since become a classic in the Spanish language, one of those literary mountain peaks at once a widely popular story and a book to be studied in school. (pp. 133-34)

> Anita Brenner, "Man's Fate on the Pampas," in The Nation, New York, Vol. 140, No. 3630, January 30, 1935, pp. 133-34.

M. J. Benardete   (essay date 1935)

[*In the following review of Don Segundo Sombra, Benardete comments on Güiraldes's idealized portrayal of the gaucho way of life.*]

To Hispanic literature, Argentina has contributed three outstanding works around the life of the *gaucho:* Sarmiento's *Facundo,* Hernández' *Martín Fierro,* and Güiraldes' **Don Segundo Sombra.** Only the student of Spanish culture would be interested in their subtle differences. To the American reader desirous of a good story, **Don Segundo Sombra** offers an optimistic outlook, unburdened by any intellectualism. This episodic novel will hold his interest as he reads of the herders always moving on, hiring themselves out now at one ranch, now at another, till the herd is driven to its destination or the ponies and mares are taught to accept the saddle without arching their backs or playing tricks on their riders. There is no love story, and sex is a negligible element. Don Segundo, the mentor of the boy in the story, is the surviving representative of the

Pampas. The heroes of Sarmiento and Hernández were fierce fighters against the authorities and the Indians, but the hero of Güiraldes, though he moves within organized society, exemplifies only the admirable virtues of the *gaucho* outlaw. Through his disarmingly simple story, Güiraldes has built up a poetic atmosphere that illumines and justifies the ways of the Pampas.

Don Segundo Sombra is like *Don Quixote* on a different level. Both tell of the closing chapter in a people's history and the most secret yearnings of their authors. Ricardo Güiraldes, the son of a rich rancher, imaginatively projects himself into the life of his *guacho* (orphan waif) who willed to become a *gaucho*. The boy, through his contact with the uneventful daily tasks of herders and horse-tamers, succeeds in hardening himself to the demands of the Pampas, and when he is a master in his trade discovers he is the son of a rich ranch owner. This is not like our success stories, for the hero then feels most disconsolate, and blindly wishes to escape his fate. In spite of the three more years of life with Don Segundo, his "godfather," the young man is defeated in his will to be the poor *gaucho* of the Pampas. We are made to understand that Argentina's past, her tradition and her masculine mode of life received a deadly blow from the sudden wealth thrust upon her. ". . . . I grieved at the poverty I was losing. Why? Because in poverty lived all my days as a wandering herder; and deeper still, that vague need to be forever on the move, which is like a thirst for the road and a lust, each day increasing, to possess the round earth."

Like all truly Hispanic literary work, *Don Segundo Sombra* is more than the creation of one man. It illustrates with precision Menéndez Pidal's theory about the production of a popular Spanish book. A highly sensitive man of letters picks up a theme very dear to the hearts of his fellows. By remaining faithful to the tradition of the people he utilizes their folkways and their values. Güiraldes has written a folktale with the flavor and naïveté of the best traditions of the Pampas. Stories, customs and the tasks of the folk are described with the art of a genius. Since his purpose in writing this novel was to underscore the positive virtues of the *gaucho,* when the *gaucho* has ceased to be a social class, and the lyrical qualities of the Pampas, no image passes his censorship that does not fit the story and its environment. He wields the simile with an adroitness learned in the most exacting of literary schools. And through his style we come to have a feeling for the intuitive realities of the Pampas.

> M. J. Benardete, "Spirit of the Pampas," in The New Republic, *Vol. LXXXII, No. 1059, March 20, 1935, p. 166.*

Arturo Torres-Ríoseco   (essay date 1942)

[*Torres-Ríoseco was a Chilean-born American scholar of Spanish-American literature. In the following excerpt, he discusses Güiraldes's works, noting that the primary importance of his early writings lies in their relation to his masterpiece,* Don Segundo Sombra.]

[Ricardo Güiraldes's] brief life is chiefly significant as a background for the composition of his one great book, with its frankly autobiographical elements. Güiraldes' own existence—his many years passed in the ranch of La

Porteña coupled with his wide culture and his travels abroad, his change from a gaucho's boyhood to the manhood of a cultivated gentleman—this simple pattern underlies the action (it can hardly be called plot) of *Don Segundo Sombra.* In this same connection, his earlier books are interesting largely because they contain elements—though only elements—of the traits which were to distinguish his gaucho masterpiece. Thus, **Raucho** (1915) studies the character of a youth removed from his early rural environment; **Tales of Death and Blood** (1915) and the posthumous **Six Stories** (1929) exhibit a strange penetration of native Argentine themes; **Xaimaca** (1923) reveals elements of nostalgia; and **Rosaura** (1922) is written in that advanced technique which is such a feature of Güiraldes' work.

But none of these books exhibits any of that dazzling originality which was to make the appearance of **Don Segundo Sombra** in 1926 an event in the history of Spanish American letters. This unique book has won a permanent place as an Argentine classic, both for its merits as a work of art and for its perfect interpretation of the gaucho. Don Segundo, as Güiraldes has created him, is not so much a human being of flesh and blood, as a myth—the ideal gaucho, the symbol of the pampas. The author himself informs the reader that this character, by his very name, is a *sombra*, a shadow; and he writes thus in his very first picture of Don Segundo:

> Motionless, I watched him move away, the silhouette of man and horse strangely enlarged against the luminous horizon. It seemed to me that I had a phantom, a shadow, something that passes and is more of an idea than a real being; something which drew me with the force of a hidden pool sucking the current of a river into its depths.

Above everything else, this Don Segundo is a complete man, master of himself in every situation, possessor of his soul. His nobility derives from his concept of liberty, which compels him to lead a life of solitude and anarchic individualism, and to wander ceaselessly across the plains. (pp. 164-65)

As a novel, **Don Segundo Sombra** can perhaps best be compared to *Don Quixote.* Like Cervantes' immortal work, it belongs to that purely Spanish type of novel in which the chief interest lies in the character portrayed, and the action is hardly more than a series of episodes. Nor does the resemblance end here. For Don Segundo, like Don Quixote, is a knight of the ideal; an ideal of simple manliness and freedom. Here perhaps lies the secret of Güiraldes' work: he has sought to ennoble a historic national character so often caricatured in circus pantomimes and bandit novels—and he has amply succeeded. For the shadowy figure of Don Segundo will forever stretch across the pampas, not as a picture drawn from life, but as a legendary symbol of a heroic type that was. (p. 166)

> Arturo Torres-Ríoseco, "Gaucho Literature" *in his* The Epic of Latin American Literature, *Oxford University Press, Inc., 1942, pp. 133-67.*

Jefferson Rea Spell   (essay date 1944)

[*In the following excerpt, Spell surveys Güiraldes's*

major works. Although he praises the author's tech-
nique, Spell argues that Güiraldes lacks the essential
qualities of a great novelist.]

[Ricardo] Güiraldes reveals himself both as man and writer in his very first work. Although a cosmopolite, his creative impulse springs entirely from the Argentine. Of the first nineteen prose sketches in *Cuentos de muerte y de sangre,* four relate incidents in the life of its military chieftains; three recount happenings in the wars of independence; and some twelve narrate occurrences in connection with Argentine ranch life. Of particular interest among these are **"Al rescoldo" ("Embers")**, in which Güiraldes's celebrated character, Don Segundo Sombra, appears for the first time and narrates one of the tall tales for which he is famous; and **"La estancia vieja" ("The Old Ranch")**, based on an old theme—the punishing of the image of a saint for refusing a request. In this case an old rancher brought a downpour by punishing an image of Our Lady after she had steadfastly failed to bring rain during a long drought. A group of four stories, entitled "Aventuras grotescas" ("Grotesque Adventures"), deals with Argentine urban life. Three of them—**"Máscaras" ("Masks")**, **"Ferroviaria" ("A Train Trip")**, and **"Sexto" ("The Sixth")**—are notable for their salaciousness, not a striking element in Güiraldes's works but one that particularly appeals to the Argentinean, as Manuel Gálvez comments in his *Hombres en Soledad.* The last three stories in the collection, "Trilogía cristiana" ("Christian Trilogy"), deal, as the title suggests, with the Christian religion and are noteworthy for their rhythmic flow of language. Quite sincere in tone, **"Güele,"** one of the stories, tells of the miraculous conversion of an Indian chieftain of the Argentine; the two remaining stories, one caricaturing a scene in Heaven (**"El juicio de Dios") ("Divine Judgment")** and the other portraying the struggles of Saint Anthony against the flesh (**"San Antonio"),** are quite in the spirit and manner of Anatole France and thematically quite at variance with the general tone of the collection.

Two stories from *Cuentos de muerte y de sangre,* **"Al rescoldo"** and **"Trenzador" ("A Leather Worker")**, are reprinted in *Seis relatos.* The remaining four, thoroughly Argentine in background, are: **"Diálogo y palabras" ("A Dialogue and Words")**, which exemplifies in a dialogue between two ranch workers Güiraldes's mastery over dialectical peculiarities of the River Plate region; **"Esta noche, noche buena" ("This Christmas Eve")**, an amusing tale that portrays certain Christmas customs among the lowly folk of the Argentine; **"La politiquería" ("The Knack of Politics")**, an account of a peon that had a charmed life; and **"Telesforo Altamira,"** a story of a down-and-out individual in Buenos Aires that had once been somebody.

In general, however, in these early *cuentos* Güiraldes does not appear in the light of a teller of stories, but rather as an artificer in words. Tropes abound, many of which strike the reader for their surprising air of freshness. A winding road is compared to a lasso that has been carelessly cast aside; the travel of gossip is likened to the spread of grease in a hot frying pan; and the nimbleness of a pig's snout is compared with the quickness of an eye. Some of the figures are very poetic, for instance the metaphor in **"Al rescoldo"** in which embers are described as velveting themselves in ash. But his poetic fancy takes at times a Gon-

goresque turn, as the conceit in the description of a young girl in **"Arrabalera" ("Suburban")**:

> On her neck she wore a ribbon of black velvet, and, harmonizing in color with it, down near her mouth, was a mole of surpassing beauty, which was black—perhaps from striving to be the pupil of an eye, in order to contemplate in ecstasy the coquettish passing of her little moist tongue over her lips.

Quite different from the *Cuentos* is *Rosaura,* which comes nearer to meeting the standards of the short story of Poe or Maupassant than anything else that Güiraldes wrote. The setting is a small town in the Argentine pampas, Lobos, in the early years of the present century. When the story begins, the railroad, which had recently connected Lobos with Buenos Aires, had already jarred the town from its long, peaceful slumber. Infected with idle curiosity, if not absolute restlessness, many of the townspeople had acquired the habit of gathering at the station each day at train time in order to catch a glimpse of the outside world.

Among such was the young and pretty Rosaura Torres, who, one day, in company with two girl companions, attracted the attention of a very handsome young man on the train. When they stared at him, he was irritated by their rudeness and attempted to shame them by fixing his gaze intently upon Rosaura, who remained completely unperturbed. Recovering his good humor as the train was leaving, he bowed pleasantly to the girls, evidently dismissing them from his mind. Rosaura, however, unmistakably affected by the stranger, returned home somewhat in a daze. In the weeks that followed she saw again and again the same young man on the train, and her love increased, for although he made no advances, he showed clearly an interest in her. If he came near her, as he sometimes did when he got out of the train and walked up and down the platform, poor Rosaura almost swooned, so great was her emotion.

Still greater was her concern when she discovered that he was far above her socially. She was in very comfortable circumstances—her father was the owner of the best livery-stable in Lobos—but Carlos Ramallo was the son of an extremely wealthy landowner and had been educated in Europe. Self-conscious, by nature quiet and unassuming, Rosaura bore her anguish silently. Finally, at a dance given in the town to honor Carlos, Rosaura met him formally; and he showed clearly that he preferred her to all the other girls in Lobos. Their acquaintance improved, for when he stopped in Lobos, as he frequently did, the two saw each other and talked. Although poor Rosaura was now considerably occupied with dress patterns and the fashioning of new clothes, her mind was in a constant swirl, so possessed was she by her infatuation for Carlos. A fatal day it was for her when he told her he was going to spend six months in England, where his father was sending him to study certain methods in farming.

How slowly those months dragged by for Rosaura! Then one day when she and her dearest friend, Carmen, were at the station, they saw Carlos again. A woman, evidently his wife, was with him on the train. He saw Rosaura, but bowed very coolly to her. In deep despair, she returned home. A few days later, accompanied by Carmen, she went again to the station. She was wearing the dress she wore on the night she met Carlos at the dance, and in her bosom she had tucked a brief note that he had written to her at one time; Carlos was on the train and with him was the same woman. Visibly moved, Rosaura walked away along the track; but when the locomotive neared her, she uttered a scream and threw herself under its wheels.

In *Rosaura* the various narrative elements are exceedingly well developed and unified. One tone, that of tragedy, dominates the plot, which moves swiftly and without interruption, incident by incident, to its tragic culmination. But by far the outstanding quality of the story is its portrayal of the modest, sensitive village girl Rosaura under the spell of a great love, which she repressed and yet inwardly nourished until the realization of the utter futility of her dreams broke the barriers of her will and led her to destroy herself. Güiraldes proceeds impressionistically in sketching in the background against which the tragedy is enacted. Without actually saying much about Lobos, with only a remark here and there about any of its inhabitants—such as Doña Petrona, who sometimes spoke to Rosaura as she was on her way to or from the station—he succeeds in leaving a very definite impression of the town and its people. A very important element of the setting is the train itself; the locomotive appears as a sinister force from the beginning of the story to the end. It is to be regretted that Güiraldes, with the inimitable style that characterizes everything he wrote and the mastery of the technique of the modern short story that he exhibits in *Rosaura,* did not write other stories like it.

The main characters in Güiraldes's longer works are, as in his *Cuentos,* distinctively Argentine. Represented as well-to-do ranch owners, the Galváns, who might very well be Güiraldes's own family, appear in all of his longer works. In *Xaimaca* the central figure is Marcos Galván; and in *Don Segundo Sombra* Leandro Galván and his son Raucho appear as minor characters. These last two characters figure largely in *Raucho.* The story itself begins with the sorrow of Don Leandro over the death of his wife, but it soon centers about Raucho, whose life might be regarded as typical of a wealthy young Argentine. In a magically poetic style, Güiraldes recreates the scene of Raucho's childhood, the headquarters of the Galván ranch, with its family residence, its stables, other outhouses, and corrals; and he animates that scene with descriptions of the activities of the workers on the ranch, of the pastimes of Raucho and his brothers, and of such incidents as the arrival from time to time of peddlers with wares to sell. Then follows an account of Raucho's schooldays in Buenos Aires, attended with love affairs and his first acquaintance with prostitutes. Those days over, Raucho returned to the ranch, with whose activities he had long been familiar; there, for some months, freer than ever in his life from the authority of his father, he was very active, helping with the management of the property. Particularly impressive, in this part of the book, are poetic passages descriptive of the four seasons of the year, and the realistic touches that color the rounding up and branding of the cattle, the shearing of the sheep, and the invasion one year of the entire countryside by great swarms of locusts.

Then, little by little, Raucho grew weary of the country. He began to read, especially the French writers—Lorrain, Maupassant, Verlaine. He went frequently to Buenos Aires to talk to French women about Paris; finally he went to live there permanently, joined the Jockey Club, and took a mistress. Not until the eve of his departure for Europe did he return to the ranch, where for a few days he amused himself with a buxom girl of the countryside, and with shooting birds out on the edge of a lake, a spot that fascinated him peculiarly, for there—with only wild birds of all sorts about—he felt quite removed from the rest of the world.

Then came at last the long anticipated journey to Europe; and with it his impressions of the sea, of Río, of Lisbon, of Paris, which he already knew thoroughly from his reading. There, he abandoned himself to all the sensual pleasures the city afforded; and when his father commanded him to return home, he refused, his mind being deranged by drugs and drink. When Raucho finally fell sick, his brother made the trip and brought him home. Whatever love Raucho had had for Paris, faded gradually away as he neared America. His joy on the way from Buenos Aires to the ranch was unrestrained; but he was not entirely at peace until he went out and sat down under a willow near the river bank, where "the whistling duck pierced the night with his shrill cry," and then on his own native soil he "fell asleep, flat on his back, his arms outstretched—crucified thus by the calmness that had pervaded and possessed his soul."

Even more convincing than *Raucho* that the experiences it records are absolutely genuine is *Xaimaca,* Güiraldes's second novel and his most poetic work. This sense of reality arises from the fact that *Xaimaca* is a travel book—one of the most delightful in Spanish-American literature—in which, even to the names of boats and hotels, there is a scrupulous regard for fact. Entirely in keeping with the exaltation of the central figure, Marcos Galván, who jots down his impressions while on a journey, is the highly imaginative treatment of the material.

Scarcely had Marcos begun his journey by train from Buenos Aires to Peru when he became interested in a young woman, Clara Ordóñez, who was accompanied by her brother, Peñalba. The places through which the travelers, who soon become friends, passed are poetically described: the Argentine plains, the city of Mendoza, the Andes, and the city of Santiago with its lofty, picturesque mound of Santa Lucia on which the three travelers took tea. Journeying by automobile from Santiago to the port of Valparaiso, they were forced by an accident to spend a part of the night in a Chilean village, where they witnessed native dances and other quaint rural customs.

The bond that united the three travelers grew stronger. Clara responded to the interest Marcos had taken in her, and his love for Kipling endeared him to Peñalba. Consequently, shortly after they had embarked for the voyage northward along the west coast of South America, Marcos decided to abandon his plan of stopping in Peru and to continue with his friends to Jamaica. He was delighted with all that he saw from the boat—a shoal of fish, a shark, a whale, and the interesting birds of the region; the Pacific itself awakened in him all that he had read, probably in Loti, of the distant Orient, which is repeatedly brought to mind. Wherever the boat stopped, Marcos and his friends went ashore: in Iquique they ate crabs; from Arica they went by train to Tacna, where they ate river-shrimp; and at Paita, Peru, Marcos was charmed by the Indian venders, descendants of the indigenous race, who swarmed with their wares into the boat.

For Marcos all of these sights and experiences were highly colored by his intense emotional state—by his love for Clara, for between the two there already existed a very intimate, personal relationship. Of a very rich Argentine family, she had married according to dictates of her parents for money and position, and the marriage had turned out badly. Genuine and without restraint, however, was her love for Marcos, whose account of the ecstasy into which he was transported by his passion is truly a glorification of carnal love.

In time the travelers came to Panama, with its lighthouse and beautiful bay; they suffered from the heat as they passed through the Canal; in Colón, whose negroes and Oriental shops fascinated Marcos, they spent several days at the Washington Hotel; and then in a few days reached their destination, Jamaica. The beauty of the tropical region struck them all, especially Marcos, who, "his mind carbureting perfectly," likened the island to an immense avocado on a great blue tray, the botanical garden to a piece of the forest that the English had disciplined and shaved, and the sound of the impact of the rubber tires of the automobile against the wct pavement as "a sticky, whistling" noise.

All went gloriously for Marcos and Clara until Peñalba discovered the relation that existed between them and forced him to leave Jamaica. Dejected, truly lovesick, Marcos set out for Buenos Aires by the same route he had come. His melancholy was apparent to the passengers, particularly to a North American girl who became enamoured of him and would have given herself to him; but, romantically true to Clara, he declined her love.

Episodic, and in this respect like *Raucho* and *Xaimaca,* Güiraldes's masterpiece, *Don Segundo Sombra,* consists of a series of incidents that trace the development of an Argentine boy to early manhood. His name is never mentioned, but the reader suspects from the very outset that he is the illegitimate son of Fabio Cáceres, a rich ranch owner, who had sent him to a small country town to be educated. Already weary of school when we see him for the first time, and weary, too, of Cáceres's two maiden sisters with whom he lived, the boy had become a loafer about the public places in the town. He came to admire intensely an individual he saw from time to time—a roaming ranch worker, an expert breaker of horses, Don Segundo Sombra by name, a man of great courage, physical strength, and probity. One evening in a tavern the boy rendered Don Segundo a service that probably saved his life, and the two became friends. It was then that the boy decided to run away from home, to attach himself in some way to the man he admired; and the next morning he set out on his pony for a ranch to which he knew Don Segundo was going.

When the latter arrived at the ranch, he took the boy, who had already found employment there, definitely under his protection. For five years he was directly under the tutelage of Don Segundo; at the end of that time he was an expert cowboy and horse-breaker; he was proficient in leather work and in the treatment of the diseases of livestock; he knew how to play the guitar and to dance the popular dances; and, from the standpoint of moral conduct, he had learned to show "endurance and fortitude in the struggles of life; to accept fatalistically and without grumbling whatever happened; to have moral force in sen-

timental affairs; to distrust women and drink; to be prudent among strangers; and to be true to his friends."

Even after his probationary period the boy continued with his mentor. The two went to work on a ranch on the seacoast, the owner of which was half-crazed; here the boy saw strange sights, among them an enormous colony of crabs that filled him with awe. In the same neighborhood, in a great round-up in which the two took part, the boy's horse was gored and he himself suffered a broken collar bone. After attending to his protégé's injury, and placing him in the home of a rancher in the district, Don Segundo left to follow his work elsewhere. But a fight with a jealous suitor over a girl, both of whom lived at the ranch where he was recuperating, soon terminated the boy's stay there. He joined Don Segundo again, but ill fortune continued to pursue him, for at a horse race he lost both his money and several of his horses. Other experiences as a cowboy followed. At a ranch where he took a job of breaking horses, the owner took a fancy to him and invited him to remain; at a country tavern he witnessed a brawl in which a man was killed; and on the pampas at night he was faced with a stampede of the herd of cattle he was helping drive to market.

Then one day while he was reflecting on the adverse fortune that had lately attended him, he received a letter from a lawyer in the town where he had lived a as young boy informing him that his erstwhile protector, Fabio Cáceres, recently dead, had acknowledged the boy in his will as his legitimate son and left him a large estate. Irritated by the deference all his friends began to show him, he would have refused the property, but for the advice of Don Segundo. After he assumed his new rôle as proprietor, he acquired through the influence of Raucho Galván, the son of his guardian, a taste for literature, and frequent visits to Buenos Aires transformed him in a measure into a cultured person; but he did not lose his democratic attitude toward those of lower social rank. Don Segundo remained with him for more than three years; then, feeling that his work of moulding a man had been completed, restless again for his old life, he took leave of his protégé and returned once more to the pampas.

The two main characters, like the tale itself, are a bit romantic. Somewhat shadowy, as befits his name, Don Segundo Sombra, who possesses so many virtues—courage, endurance, moral and physical strength, leadership, the art of entertaining in various ways, and unusual skill in the work in which he made his living—and none of the vices which afflict humanity, is an idealized rather than a real character. We know him only through a source that is prejudiced in his favor, his protégé, who tells us what he is and what he does. The boy is also idealized, but he is less of one cloth than Don Segundo. Skilled, first of all, in everything that pertains to life on the plains, finally a cultivated man with a love for reading, he stands as an exemplar of Güiraldes's own ideal of a man. Of him there is, too, a side that we never see of Don Segundo, and that is his inner world, his thoughts and reflections on life, which in his rôle of autobiographer he constantly reveals.

The very effective portrayal of the background for these Argentine characters has contributed probably more than any other feature to winning for the book the high praise that has generally been accorded it. When Don Segundo's ward takes stock of himself at the end of five years, he enumerates a long list of towns and ranches, all of the province of Buenos Aires, which had seen them pass many times, "covered with dirt and mud, behind a herd of cattle." Of the appearance of this region, with the exception of the dunes and crab-infested bogs of the seacoast, there is in the book practically no description. Certain phenomena of nature, on the other hand, particularly in reference to their effect on the teller of the tale, are frequently commented upon: the cold; the heat of the summer's sun; the rain, as he is driving a herd of cattle; or the night, as he is sitting with others by the campfire.

The part of the setting, however, that is really striking is the varied panorama of rural and small-town life in the province of Buenos Aires. While there is some detailed description of places, the salient characteristic in nearly all of the various scenes is the human element, which imparts, through its lively, natural vernacular, a decidedly animated tone—whether it be the coarse joking in the tavern where we first see the hero of the tale; or the bantering of the cowboy at the ranch where he obtained his first job; or the raillery of the "tape" Burgos when he tried to pick a quarrel with Don Segundo; or the love-making between Paula and our hero, when he was recuperating at the ranch. In this connection, too, mention must be made of two tales that Don Segundo tells in quaint, dialectical language: one, a supposed incident in the life of our Lord when He was on this earth; the other, a veritable fairy tale of demons, witches, enchantments, and disenchantments.

In addition to vernacular speech the author attains local color through the description of certain manners and customs with which Don Segundo and his pupil come in contact in their wanderings. Some of these portrayals are veritable essays in themselves: the account, for instance, of a country dance, which among a diversity of details includes certain popular songs as an accompaniment to the dances; the description of a cock-fight, at which our hero had the good fortune to bet on the winner; and, later, of a horse race, at which he lost almost everything he had; the account of a Sunday spent at a country saloon, where a friend was forced in self-defense to kill a man; and the portrayal, probably the most masterful in the book, of a great round-up, which is made so vivid that one almost smells the dust, hears the lowing and bellowing of the cattle, and sees the cowboys, in mad pursuit, racing after and lassoing them. Many passages in the book, such as the following, reveal the keenness of Güiraldes's observation in regard to cattle:

> Without moving, I let the herd of cattle pass. Some, as they looked toward the ranch houses, bellowed. Weary, the yearlings went by slowly. From time to time, when one would hook another, a hollow space for some meters about would form; but it would soon fill up again, and then the march would go on, slowly, relentlessly.

In a measure this passage reveals how the chief aesthetic value of the book is attained—by rendering into poetry, through the use of rhythmical and figurative language, experience which is generally regarded as common, prosaic, or even sordid.

Güiraldes, however, with all of his excellent qualities as a writer—now that we have come to a final evaluation of him—is not the truly great novelist that some enthusiastic critics would have us believe. His novels, after all, are limited in scope, rather one-sided. For, while his style is poetic, while his sharp-toned pictures of certain strata of Argentine society remain with one long after his books are read, he is sadly lacking in two essentials of a great novelist: he gives no evidence of ability to develop character or to weave a plot that is much beyond that of the picaresque novel.

In spite of these shortcomings, **Don Segundo Sombra** has entered the ranks of international literature in both German and English translations and has received high praise from other than Argentine and Spanish critics. (pp. 192-204)

> *Jefferson Rea Spell, "Ricardo Güiraldes, Stylistic Depicter of the Gaucho," in his* Contemporary Spanish-American Fiction, *The University of North Carolina Press, 1944, pp. 191-204.*

Arturo Torres-Ríoseco   (essay date 1951)

[*In the following essay, Torres-Ríoseco praises* Don Segundo Sombra *as an outstanding example of the* gauchesco *genre and as a classic novel of universal appeal.*]

In 1926, just twenty-five years ago, **Don Segundo Sombra** was published in Argentina. The critics unanimously praised this work, and since then the reputation of **Don Segundo Sombra** has become more and more solid. Today the novel is considered a classic.

Don Segundo Sombra belongs to the *gauchesco* genre, inasmuch as it deals with the life of the pampa, its men, its work, and its atmosphere. The style of the book is that of the inhabitants of the province of Buenos Aires; it has the regional idiom which its author, Ricardo Güiraldes, knew as well as Spanish. Nevertheless, **Don Segundo Sombra,** although it is a gauchesco work, has nothing in common with the truculent novels of Eduardo Gutiérrez, the initiator of this genre, nor with the most important poems of the popular epic, *Martín Fierro* and *Santos Vega.*

Don Segundo Sombra is narrated in the first person by a young gaucho, who learns the various tasks of the pampa under the guidance of Don Segundo Sombra, whom he calls his godfather. The essential purpose of the novel is to show the affection and admiration that the boy feels for his mentor. From the first time he sees him, "huge under his light colored poncho," until he takes leave of him and remains "like one who is bleeding to death," the young gaucho reveals the deep loyalty that he feels for his master and makes us realize its quality.

Under the direction of Don Segundo he learns "the manliest of occupations," that is, all the knowledge of the man of the pampa: the cattle driver's skill, the tricks of the horse breaker, the expert use of the lasso and the boleadoras [a lariat with balls at both ends], the technique of developing a good horse, the making of halters, reins, cinches.

When at the end of the novel the young man inherits a large ranch, Don Segundo remains with him for three years; then he leaves and disappears into the pampa, thus fulfilling the destiny of one who cannot take root anywhere but must always move on.

Don Segundo Sombra is more an idea than a man; hence, the word "sombra," shadow, something which is beyond concrete reality. Don Segundo is the symbol of manliness, he embodies the feeling of liberty, perfection in one's work, dignity in simple or great acts, patience, stoicism, and the kindness and humor of all the gauchos of the past; he is the ideal gaucho whom Güiraldes carried within himself, but who was also a man of flesh and blood whose name was Segundo Ramírez.

That which the little gaucho admires in his master is this: coolness in danger, honesty, absolute courage, modesty, the perfect knowledge of the cowboy's profession, and disdain for wealth. Don Segundo is a gaucho, that is to say, he is the "son of God, of the countryside, and of himself." Don Segundo defines himself when he exclaims on addressing the boy: "If you are a gaucho, a real gaucho, you will not change, because wherever you go your spirit will go before you leading you like a bell mare."

The young boy is the intelligent, admiring, and faithful disciple. Don Segundo might have done with him whatever he wanted; he could have made him a caudillo, an outlaw, a bad gaucho, a slave to his will, but he preferred to shape him in his own image, a perfect gaucho in his simplicity and greatness. The little gaucho possesses besides that which Don Segundo seems to have lost with age: the youthful emotion of the first experiences of beauty, the intense joy of the pampa at dawn, the feeling of rain on dry pastures and the horses' bodies, the pleasure of seeing clear light on the fields and water. The great joy of living in liberty, which in Don Segundo is always latent but tempered by his mature philosophy, belongs to youth in its fullness. The little gaucho lives Don Segundo's early youth, that youth which Don Segundo must have lived in order to become the hero that he was. When the boy becomes the owner of a farm he will search in books and in culture for the profound joy of new discoveries and revelations with the same intensity as he did in the pampa.

The structure of the novel is based on these two characters. The interest of the story is maintained by the continuous succession of inner and outer experiences. The background is the pampa, which gives the characters their emotional life, their idealism, and their experiences. The novel is movement and space—movement in so far as constant traveling is concerned and the vital succession of sensations and emotions; space in a real sense of places and numberless mirages.

" 'Riding, riding, riding,' exclaims the little gaucho," and Don Segundo's existence is just this: "a constant desire to travel, which is like a network of roads, and an eagerness to possess everything, which increases every day." That is why when the young gaucho has to remain on the farm he feels that his life is ended; and in order not to die completely, he tries to find a new life in books. If the pampa is full of roads, the souls of the two characters are full of horizons which invite them to their fullest expression.

As narrator the young man has written the novel after he has become a wealthy farm owner and a man of culture, that is, after he has acquired a literary style. Let us remember that from childhood the little gaucho has had a fine sensibility and a deep rooted pride ("I had learned already to swallow my tears and not to believe in flattering words"), that he has become a philosophic and stoic man

under the watchful eyes of Don Segundo, that continuous travels have kindled his imagination and a thousand experiences have enriched his inner world. Thus we shall understand better Güiraldes' manner of expression when he writes:

> Way up yonder the starry sky seemed to be a huge
> eye, full of shining sands of sleep. Sleep fell upon
> me like a pile of straw on a sparrow.

Güiraldes fuses the poetic faculty of the young man and the realism of his vision. "Way up yonder" keeps the rustic flavor of the gauchesque idiom; "full of shining sands" is a poetic expression which denotes a literary standard, the mark of a good writer. "Sleep," an abstraction, becomes a concrete image to the gaucho who has often seen a pile of straw fall upon a sparrow. Given these examples we may understand better Güiraldes' style. He uses constantly and accurately the language of the country folk, but without wishing to be always picturesque and exotic, as is the case of José Hernández in his poem *Martín Fierro*.

The most frequent resources of this style are: description of little things pertaining to country tasks, things that are so insignificant that it seems they shouldn't have a name; use of verbs already forgotten by the people of the cities but dear to the gauchos; nouns used exclusively by the cattle driver; adjectives and adverbs which have become worn through continuous regional usage; half finished interjections and sentences, and emphatic repetitions. But all these are genuine forms, not invented by the author; and with them he can give us accurate and faithful descriptions of real scenes of gaucho life, such as the following of a country store:

> Meantime, while my self-trust swelled like the day,
> we had come to a country store. It was a single
> building, rectangular-shaped; the taproom was on
> the right of an open hall with benches where we sat
> down side by side like swallows on a wire. The
> storekeeper handed out the drinks through a coarse
> iron grating that caged him from the great room
> with its tiers of gay-labeled bottles, flasks and jugs.
> Skin sacks of maté leaf, demijohns of liquor, many-
> shaped barrels, saddles, blankets, horse pads, lassos
> littered the floor. And through this welter of stock
> the owner had made a narrow trail as cows made
> a path, and he came and went along it bearing
> drinks, smokes, maté, saddle fittings. Across from
> the taproom were a couple of columns of cement,
> joining the roof of the house into an arbor for the
> patio of gnarled paradise trees. And farther off was
> a taba field. The trail in front of the store bellied out
> wide enough to hold the herd.

Other linguistic phenomena—archaisms, Indian words, phonetic variations, ultracorrectness, analogies—have less importance for us, since their use may be found in other regions, whether it be in Spanish America, in Spain, or in New Mexico. In reading *Don Segundo Sombra* one does not find those phrases of erudite pedantry which disfigure the style of so many gauchesque writers, phrases that may impress the foreign reader but never the inhabitant of Argentina.

Don Segundo Sombra is more than just a gauchesque novel; it has the proportions of a work of universal appeal. Its hero is conditioned to regional life by what is perishable—language, clothing, occupation, a way of life—but by his deepest vital processes Don Segundo may aspire to the status of a universal man. The dignity of his person imposes respect anywhere, and we can imagine that Don Segundo might enter a drawing room in Paris or New York, wearing boots, spurs, and *chiripá* [a long fringed shawl], without anyone daring to laugh at him. On horseback Don Segundo might have accompanied in his rides through Hyde Park that English *gaucho* whose name was R. Cunningham Graham ("Don Roberto" to the Argentineans), or W. H. Hudson, the famous author of *Far Away and Long Ago*.

His dignity, the preciseness of his words and actions, would make him stand out in any social gathering. As a novel, **Don Segundo Sombra** fulfills the strictest Spanish concept of the genre: pure realism, a fine sense of humor, concentration of interest on two characters, rapid succession of a gallery of interesting types, internal and external movement. In this way **Don Segundo Sombra** follows, at a respectable distance, in the footsteps of the *Lazarillo de Tormes* and the *Quijote*.

Don Segundo Sombra puts an end to the bizarre forms of the works of its class, to the stupid repetition of melodramatic and violent episodes, to the grandiose plots devoid of psychology, to mediocre sentimentalism and eroticism. Nevertheless, the novel does not lack feeling, but on the contrary possesses that deep emotion that one finds in human actions which are the result of a genuine realism. **Don Segundo Sombra** is rich in human experience. With the ideas of this novel one could write an essay entitled "Gauchismo and Philosophy" which would deal with self-reliance and the harmony between human limitations and ambitions. Another essay, which might study the formation and development of character, could be called "Gauchismo and Pedagogy"; such an essay might revolutionize contemporary methods of education, which insist on cluttering the mind of the student with pseudoscience, pedantic information, and half-truths, forgetting that harmony of knowledge, morals, and character which humanistic culture has left to us.

After a quarter of a century the novel of Ricardo Güiraldes is alive and no longer requires favorable criticism or the help of patriotism for its success. It is useless both to defend it or attack it. As in the case of *Don Quijote*, sequels have been written to **Don Segundo,** but none of these even remotely compares with the original.

I have often been asked if **Don Segundo Sombra** is the best Spanish-American novel. Knowing that I undertake a great responsibility, I have answered "yes." **Don Segundo** is an exemplary novel, and as such it should be placed beside the classic novels of our language. (pp. 274-80)

> *Arturo Torres-Ríoseco, "The Twenty-Five Year Anniversary of Don Segundo Sombra," in* New Mexico Quarterly, *Vol. XXI, No. 3, Autumn, 1951, pp. 274-80.*

G. H. Weiss (essay date 1958)

[*In the following excerpt, Weiss interprets the works of Güiraldes in relation to political and cultural change in Argentina during the twentieth century.*]

Ricardo Güiraldes stands between the past and the future of his nation, and contrary to what has hitherto been as-

serted, he looks not only to the past for the purpose of recalling it with poetic nostalgia, but also towards the future. The problem of making past and future blend rather than repel each other fills his mind. Argentina's past is his inheritance, her future his ideal.

Güiraldes realizes that the Argentine character and the national way of life cannot be considered solely in terms of the national territory or of the Pampa. He is convinced that obstinate clinging to the ways of old is undesirable if progress towards a richer culture is to be made, but he also sees that if the culture of Europe is absorbed indiscriminately, there may result, not the desired improvement, but a decadence of old virtues and strengths. All of Güiraldes' writings, his novels, short stories, narratives, poems, notes, commentaries, give expression to this problem and envisage the Argentina of the future.

The novels and short stories of Güiraldes constitute a panorama of the evolution of the Pampa, heart of Argentina, an evolution slowed by the political strife that followed the Wars of Independence and by a dictatorship of some twenty years, an evolution that was the great concern of Domingo Faustino Sarmiento as writer, educator, and President. With his typical impetuousness Sarmiento was ready to sacrifice tradition for a new, and what he considered better way of life. He was eager to transform the Pampa

Güiraldes in traditional gaucho dress, 1922.

as rapidly as possible, if necessary, by force. Sarmiento saw only defects at home and virtues abroad. Güiraldes is more careful. He sees both defects and virtues at home, and danger in the absorption of culture in the manner of an intoxicating drink, to escape from one's poverty into a realm of unreliable delight.

The equipment which the gaucho of old brought when he came face to face with an enemy were his attributes of the Pampa: strength of muscle and of will, a need to dominate and a fear of being destroyed. He was ready for hand to hand combat to subdue his opponent and impose his own will, but in his early encounters with European culture he perceived that the struggle was not to take place on familiar ground. To his satisfaction, however, he soon saw that the onrush of foreign ways became dissipated as it spread over his land. The will of the Pampa appeared triumphant and her man retained his pride of conqueror. The gaucho's descendant, the man of the Pampa depicted by Güiraldes, on the other hand, finds European culture advancing upon him in ever expanding waves, dislodging tradition and demanding that he become the agent of his own transformation. Although this man still prides himself on an integral gaucho personality, such a personality is now more and more a mental reality.

The *estanciero* ["rancher"] class is first in the Pampa of Güiraldes to face the cultural forces of the outside world in their commercial-financial, scientific, and artistic manifestations. Some of the members of this class, like young Raucho, the protagonist of the novel ***Raucho,*** return to the Pampa after brief and uneven schooling in the city, while others, like Raucho's brother Alberto, enter more definitely upon the paths of city life and European culture: ". . . entraba en la Facultad para mediados de marzo." The roots and the trunk remain in the Pampa, while some of the branches move outwards, but even the branches that remain in the Pampa turn eventually towards the lights of the city and of Europe. In a moment of tedium the uncouth son of the rich *estanciero,* who in adolescence was more assiduous in his attendance at brothels than at school, also longs for culture. Ill prepared to understand the true values of culture, he gulps down some French novels and poems for their sensous appeal, and after exhausting the night-life "culture" of Buenos Aires, he embarks to seek the wider horizons of Paris. He visualizes culture in the form of the Parisian model, or conceives of it as an affair with the actress of the day. He identifies culture with dissipation, and in the pursuit of such culture, he squanders his energies and wealth. Through Raucho's adventure in culture, which ends in a total collapse, Güiraldes points to the fact that a national danger is implicit in an erroneous concept of culture, that unless the man of the Pampa learns (perhaps in the school which Raucho so neglected) to follow less the bent of his will and to comport himself with greater moral and social awareness, his person and his patrimony will be wasted in the modern world.

The novelette ***Rosaura*** also serves as a warning of the danger contained in a fascination with glitter for which the man of the Pampa is not ready. The town of Lobos, in the Province of Buenos Aires, typical of provincial towns in Argentina during the late nineteenth and early twentieth centuries (and not entirely unlike the capital city itself), is still materially and spiritually Pampa in the throes of becoming Europeanized. As the *loberitas* and the *loberos*

gaze into the train which every evening at six thirty-five breaks the darkness of their small station, they behold a picture of light, comfort, luxury—the modern outside world. The express train soon departs, however, leaving behind it a trail of poisonous smoke. This vision of the outside world is a dangerous phenomenon for the *loberos* to accept as part of their lives, for its only reality in Lobos is in the tracks, the small station, and the rapid passage of the locomotive with its cars. The younger *loberos* like to dwell in this illusion for brief moments, but they invariably return to the facts of their daily existence as the train departs. One among them, the sensitive Rosaura, is possessed by a strong will for the perfect life and forgets that the tracks, the station, and the train are but meagre points of contact with the wonder-filled outside world, that the passage from her own into the world symbolized by the train is not an easy one, that her glimpses of that world may not reveal its true character. Rosaura's illness is symptomatic for Güiraldes. . . . (pp. 149-50)

Some of Güiraldes' stories reflect the period of the Wars of Independence, some the following period of internal political struggles, others the period of Rosas, still others the later frontier wars against the Indians, and others, conditions in the last years of the nineteenth and first fifteen or twenty years of the twentieth century. The latter period is also portrayed in the novels ***Raucho, Rosaura, Don Segundo Sombra,*** and ***Xaimaca,*** which, in spite of its variety of exotic locales and platonic spirituality, reveals concern with the social scene in Argentina.

Don Segundo Sombra is a synthesis of the panorama of Argentine evolution developed by Güiraldes throughout his other works. It represents the entire process of historical change even though it speaks but of the present moment, the moment that Güiraldes lived. Don Segundo is the symbol of the personality formed by the Pampa of the past. Young Fabio Cáceres, who, anonymous like the man of the Pampa throughout his history until the final moments of the novel, when he receives a name and a social status, his due inheritance, moves alongside don Segundo as the embodiment of the present in its evolution towards the future. Fabio's mother belonged to the lower classes of the Pampa; his father was of the *estanciero* class. There is in Fabio's person, therefore, a social and cultural *mestizaje* ["half-caste"], which it will become his duty to expand and refine into a new personality, for with his name and his wealth, his father bestows upon him a mission. According to the letter of don Leandro Galván accompanying the notification of inheritance, it will be Fabio's function to carry forward the ideas and ideals of his late father into the world of the future. Fabio Jr. is the product of a socially condemned union. He begins life as a social *mestizo* and a *guacho,* or illegitimate child. Circumstances or his own choice will determine which is to be his social plane. A child still, he has the choice of accepting his father's protection (not his recognition) and thus live in a social no-man's land, or freeing himself by reverting to the class of his mother. The second becomes his choice when he attaches his fate to that of don Segundo, but with the approach of majority circumstances compel him to make another choice, and assume the burden of his country's future. Bernardo Gicovate [see Further Reading] states:

> If Don Segundo is the symbol and the nostalgia of the past, Fabio, his adopted son, is a representation of the present, the new twentieth-century Argenti-

na burdened with a history. . . . Towards the end of the book, the young man thinks he has already learned all the lessons and his education is at an end. Fabio Cáceres thinks he has found his America in the way of life he has chosen and which he wants to lead forever. His pride and assuredness are yet to be tested. He must learn to accept and not to choose his place in the world. At this point the author introduces the climatic lesson of life: Fabio must learn now a twofold sacrifice. He must sacrifice the way of life he loves and he must sacrifice also his own certainty of his completeness as a man. He learns that a new cycle of life and experience is open to this illegitimate child of an old culture. His education will never be complete, but he must try endlessly to assimilate the tradition of the Western World presented him through Raucho and his books and yet he must preserve sacramentally his pristine gaucho self, although the freedom and joy will be his no more.

If Fabio were merely forced to *accept and not to choose* a place in the world of the future, the preservation of his *pristine* gaucho self would become problematic, if not impossible. Güiraldes' search for the new does not imply an eradication of the past by submission, but rather its fertilization, so that a personality combining the strengths of national tradition with the moral and intellectual qualities evolved by the culture of Europe might emerge. This personality will be a re-creation of the self, a rebirth achieved by the will of the man of the Pampa. Fabio must therefore become judge over himself, and once more, the creator of his own destiny. This process of recreation of the national self and penetration into the currents of universal culture has no little resemblance to the process advocated by some of the intellectuals of the Spanish Generation of '98.

The task that Fabio faces is difficult and one for which he is half prepared. His immediate reaction is to turn away. First to recognize the need of an adaptation to new conditions is don Segundo, who, strikingly, belongs more definitely to the past than Fabio. Don Segundo does not appreciate the true value of change, but long experience in life makes it evident to him that change is inevitable, but, though inevitable, it may turn out to be a surface occurrence. He inspires Fabio with his confidence in survival at a critical juncture by impressing upon him that *once a gaucho always a gaucho,* but Fabio will have to rely upon himself to evaluate his past and his future—to live towards the realization of Güiraldes' ideal Argentina.

The separation between Fabio and don Segundo marks the beginning of Fabio's new life as *gaucho-estanciero* in the face of a new world. Fabio's friend Raucho is the symbol of the new personality that Fabio must make his own, but which he must also transcend. [The critic adds in a footnote that "Raucho is a combination of the word *gaucho* with the initial of Güiraldes' first name, Ricardo. . . . According to Güiraldes' own statement, the novel **Raucho** was begun as autobiography. . . ."] There are two Rauchos in the works of Güiraldes, representing two aspects of the same problem. The Raucho of **Don Segundo Sombra** is a modern, enlightened man of the Pampa who has incorporated into his personality some of the best elements of European culture. The other Raucho, the protagonist of the earlier novel, represents a stage akin to that of Fabio. His early years were spent closer to the Pampa than to the city with its cultural influences. When the time

for change arrives his character is fully formed, and the attempted change, based on an erroneous concept of culture, on last minute, makeshift preparation, bears evil rather than good.

As has already been suggested, Güiraldes' novels and short stories constitute a panorama of Argentina in evolution. Güiraldes' interest lies not in the portrayal and characterization of individuals, but in the selection of those traits which are the common denominator of all men in a broad region, core of the Argentine nationality, the Pampa. He gathers those ways and traits which have revealed the greatest power to withstand change and views them in the light of new influences, of a possible future evolution. Man, in Güiraldes' panorama of the Pampa, is bound to his surroundings in a wedlock that cannot be suddenly broken without fatal consequences. The man of the Pampa must not give up his vigorous way of life, for it is in this life, not in commercial activity (for which Güiraldes expresses contempt on more than one occasion), that the health of the individual and of the nation lies, but a new atmosphere of morality and reason must pervade the Pampa. The code of honor prevailing in the Pampa is to be modified by the eradication of bloody deeds. Güiraldes' attitude towards such deeds, even though he cannot help admiring the *gaucho's* lively sense of honor and his dexterity with the knife, is always one of shock and condemnation. It is to an individual attuned to nature, endowed with her powers, but freed from her extreme domination, that Güiraldes looks forward in the *argentino* of the future.

During his first stay at Galván's *estancia* ["ranch"], when he was about to set out on his quest of a personality congruent with the traditional way of life, Fabio did not meet Raucho, of whom no mention was made at the time, perhaps because Fabio's footsteps did not as yet lead him in the direction of cosmopolitan culture. On his return to the same *estancia,* however, to receive title to his inheritance, now an *estanciero* himself, Fabio does come into contact with Raucho, an *estanciero's* son acquainted with literature in several languages, a young man of the world whose mind and spirit have been refined in the outside world, a young man who returns to the Pampa to dedicate himself joyously to its way of life on his own social plane. The Raucho of **Don Segundo Sombra** does not carry his strengths of the Pampa to Europe to corrupt them there, but rather, brings to the Pampa the seeds of Europe's higher culture. While Raucho represents the *argentino* who is moving out to meet his destiny in a wider world, his fellow-*estanciero* Fabio is the incarnation of the conservativism which must accept Raucho's lesson and transform itself into a flexible, open-minded, progressive patriotism. During the process of evolution these two forces, conservativism and progress, will keep each other in balance.

The gaucho knew that his occasional victories over nature did not imply superiority, but he did not feel that his freedom or his integrity were impaired by submission to the will of nature. He believed, rather, that wisdom and strength were to be gained from such a submission, which could be utilized later to advantage in his dealings with his fellow men. It is precisely this type of reasoning that induces don Segundo to bow to the force of historical progress—to accept arrest when he and Fabio are apprehended for disrespectfully galloping by the police station in the town of Navarro; to advise Fabio that he accept the *estancia* left him by his father and assume the responsibilities of his new station. In both instances don Segundo recognizes a power greater than his own, and instead of resisting, he favors an acceptance with the mental reservation that there is in his acceptance an act of choice. He is convinced that by opposing this inner freedom to the new ways that are forced upon him, he will be able to slow and modify their advance sufficiently to preserve his Pampa personality. Don Segundo is, in fact, creating the equilibrium of the old and the new which Güiraldes considers necessary for the proper evolution of Argentina. Thus, through compulsion, resistance, and compromise, the man of the Pampa will gradually move in the direction of an inner mental and spiritual life and will attain a higher plane of civilization.

The Argentina of the future that Güiraldes envisions will still be agrarian, centering about the *estancia,* depending for leadership upon the *estanciero* class, but a nation mellowed by intelligence and moral refinement. Its men will have outgrown ignorance and violence, their God will transcend sectarian boundaries, their politics will have rid itself of *caciquismos* ["bosses"] with their disregard for constitutional processes and perversions of justice. The new *argentino* will abhor war and imperialism (caused, in Güiraldes' opinion, by greed and the notion of racial superiority), he will live in a society where wealth is equitably distributed. The Argentine woman will have been delivered from the degrading domination of *machismo* and *don juanismo* and from an upbringing that condemned her to isolation and thwarted her normal mental and psychological development.

A free, democratic, enlightened nation, whose rule of life will be generosity and self-imposed morality—such will the Argentina of the future be—Argentina, the ideal of Ricardo Güiraldes. (pp. 150-53)

> *G. H. Weiss, "Argentina, the Ideal of Ricardo Güiraldes," in* Hispania, *Vol. XLI, No. 2, May, 1958, pp. 149-53.*

G. H. Weiss (essay date 1960)

[*In the following excerpt, Weiss examines the influence of Güiraldes's philosophy on his literary technique.*]

Ricardo Güiraldes rejected the role of philosopher, but life was the theme of his meditations and of his literary art. What he could not and would not express in philosophic systems or in the language of philosophy, he attempted to make visual in the symbol of his art, and for this task, although lacking the basis of a formal higher education, his thinking was supported by an assorted reading in philosophy that included Hegel, Schopenhauer, Nietzsche as well as many Hindu spiritualists.

From his first published book of poems, *El cencerro de cristal* (1915)—the various sections of which, "Camperas," "Viaje," "Ciudadanas," "Plegarias astrales," "Realidades de ultramundo," give evidence of a dual orientation, earthly and supra-terrestrial—all of Güiraldes' works, including his masterpiece, *Don Segundo Sombra* (1926), endeavor to capture the material and spiritual nature of the universe. *Don Segundo Sombra* reflects the cos-

mic duality in its title, in which the concreteness implied by a proper name mingles with the mystery of the suprahistorical emanating from the word *Sombra* ["shadow"]; but it also, more clearly perhaps than any of the other works, encompasses in its very style and structure the unity and multiplicity of life.

Even before he had completed his extensive travels through the Orient and Europe, Güiraldes had begun depicting in short stories and poems the scene of his native Pampa, the way of life and the way of being of its people. Observation of different scenery and customs, of different psychologies and religious practices led him to the belief that he could best intuit and express the universal brotherhood of man, the cosmic unity of all things, by intensifying his search not only for the similarities between the alien peoples and his own, but also by seeking out the differing and seemingly unique features of his race, his land, and his people—by expressing his own personality and his own heritage in his art. Although it may appear paradoxical, by thus consciously placing himself at the center of his art, Güiraldes endowed it with balance and perspective, for in order to penetrate into his art the panorama of life had to pass through a focus established by the contrary forces of a Pampa psychology and a cosmopolitanism of mind. So Güiraldes found the true subject of his art and established himself in a point of view. It now remained for the artist to develop a technique and a style sufficiently elastic both to encompass his subject and to coincide with his point of view. In one of his professions of aesthetics, Güiraldes declared that he felt free to use any and all forms and devices that would aid him in expressing his subject, because his subject, life, could not be forced into a single mold, nor, for that matter, into any combination of molds. The best he could hope for, even with complete liberty in the choice of artistic means, was a partial but suggestive representation.

It would appear that such an artistic principle might lead to a chaotic agglomeration of devices, and Güiraldes' compositions do at first give the impression of being made up of disconnected visions animated by impulses of kinesthetic and psychic experience. Yet close observation discloses the elusive pattern into which the individual glimpses of life are gathered to constitute a large symbol, which in turn combines with the other symbols of Güiraldes' works, to unfold the panorama of national historical progression within the dynamism of nature and the mystery of the cosmos. A form is, after all, inevitable, but should derive from the subject, rather than be imposed upon it. This cumulative structure, on the basis of single images blending into a panorama of the living universe, resulted from Güiraldes' theory that beauty and truth are expressions of each other, and that the state most to be desired by man is that of never ceasing expansion in consciousness, even though full knowledge can never be attained.

Although they are cumulative in structure, Güiraldes' compositions generally, and his novels in particular, are by no means rambling or disjointed. They possess unity of idea and of plan. The episodes of Güiraldes' novels are strung like beads on a tenuous filament, the plot. Introduced at the beginning of the novel, the plot almost disappears in the subsequent chapters, reappears and is brought to its climax towards the end of the work. Thus, dominating at the beginning and at the end, plot is subordinated in the intervening chapters to descriptions of nature (with their cosmic implication), and to *cuadros de costumbres* ["sketches of manners"] (with their national, historical implication). Güiraldes' plots are rudimentary, made up of conventional ingredients. Within the texture of Güiraldes' compositions, however, these are transformed into the protoplasm of a living artistic creation, of a symbol of Argentina's social and cultural evolution, of man's movement in the mystery and beauty of the cosmos.

Güiraldes' works are essentially descriptive and narrative. Their true dramatic quality arises not from form, nor from plot, but from the subject matter itself—from the explosions of cosmic power in nature and man. Thus, storms in the Pampa, invasions of the locust, man's passions provide the vital, dramatic element, and are presented descriptively.

Not only does Güiraldes relegate plot action and dialogue to a subordinate position, but he also foregoes the development of individual character. Indicative of the fact that individuality was not Güiraldes' primary concern is the lack of a name for some of his characters—for example, the protagonist in **"El remanso,"** the murderer of **"Nocturno,"** the hunchback in **"Compasión,"** the heroine of **"Máscaras,"** and even Fabio himself, in *Don Segundo Sombra,* until he acquires a name upon being legally recognized as the son and heir of the deceased don Fabio Cáceres. Güiraldes' main interest lay in the depiction of Pampa atmosphere and way of life, as well as in the selection of those personal traits which are usually considered to constitute the national character—a primitive sense of honor and the need to impose one's will, whether it be found in the *patilludo jefe* Facundo Quiroga, the blue-eyed don Juan Manuel, the vengeful Captain Zamora, the unyielding Zurdo, the highly temperamental don Venancio Gómez, the reckless protagonist of **"El remanso,"** Atanasio Sosa, Encarnación Romero, Camilo Cano, *el negro* Britos, or Fabián Tolosa.

In his ever increasing inclination towards a cosmic perspective, Güiraldes found in the subconscious an avenue of approach to true knowledge, and his fascination with this level of experience is frequently revealed in his works. Some of the clearest examples of the use of the subconscious may be found in *Don Segundo Sombra:* don Sixto Gaitán's nightmare (ch. XV) concerning the death of his small son, an occurence corroborated on the following morning; and especially Fabio's delirium—ch. XVIII, which becomes reality in ch. XXVI. The second example is directly related to plot development, for in his delirium Fabio sees himself in the act of receiving title to a name and a social position from the hands of don Leandro Galván. The event, as it occurs in ch. XXVI is almost a verbatim repetition of the delirium in ch. XVIII.

His interest in Hindu spiritualism, his theosophic readings and experiences, mixed with the abundant remnants of his Catholic heritage, increasingly affected Güiraldes' thinking and left a definite stamp, as has already been suggested, not only upon the content of his writings, but also upon their form. The mystic number 3, for example, plays an impressive role in both these aspects. Not only is it abundantly present by direct reference, but is also to be found in the repetition of ideas, the division of sentences into three parts, in the accumulation of adjectives and verbs in series of three, in the grouping of incidents and chapters—particularly in *Don Segundo Sombra.*

The novel *Don Segundo Sombra* consists of twenty-seven chapters that fall into three general divisions, the chapters of each division falling into series of three (with the exception of six chapters which form series of two's), and each chapter, in turn, divisible into three aspects or series of three aspects. The long transition between chs. IX and X of the novel, five years, creates the impression of a division into two parts, or books. If the biography of Fabio Cáceres Jr., which serves as a unifying thread, is considered, however, it will be observed that a more logical division is obtained by viewing the work as divided into three parts: departure, quest, and return. The first section covers the childhood of Fabio, his meeting with don Segundo, his escape and first adventures in Pampa life: the second is dedicated mainly to folkloric elements and descriptions of nature, although it includes some events in Fabio's life of roaming under the tutelage of don Segundo (chs. X-XXIV): while the third part corresponds to a return and a movement towards a way of life which Fabio did not expect to follow (chs. XXV-XXVII). There also occur three instances of reminiscence at the edge of a body of water, and these flashbacks contain a large portion of Fabio's life. Thus, time in *Don Segundo Sombra,* can also be viewed as a threefold past: the past recalled by the young protagonist, the present at which it is recalled, and both viewed as past in the total reminiscence that is the novel. (pp. 353-55)

There is also evident in *Don Segundo Sombra* a marked tendency to base each chapter upon three main situations or events, which, in turn, are dependent upon three (or series of three) subsidiary events or situations. This triadic feature in the construction of *Don Segundo Sombra* is a persistent one—to be found in the recurrence of key events and situations: three reminiscences at water's edge; three meetings with Pedro Barrales; . . . three instances of struggle with a bull on the part of Fabio; three instances of danger for don Segundo . . . three crucial moments in the course of Fabio's attempt to attach his existence to that of don Segundo (his lack of certainty as to whether don Segundo will go to Galván's *estancia* in search of work; the English foreman's refusal to accept Fabio upon his first petition for work; Fabio's uncertainty as to whether he will be permitted to join the arreo with which don Segundo is leaving Galván's *estancia*). The last-named three situations, are, in fact, crucial to the progress of the plot, for without their favorable resolution the destinies of Fabio and don Segundo could not have been joined. (p. 356)

In the consideration of the structural features of *Don Segundo Sombra,* reference must be made to the function of Pedro Barrales. Since, in typical gaucho fashion don Segundo and Fabio move through life and the Pampa without a predetermined direction, it is Pedro's function to maintain a connection between the young hero on his quest and his point of departure. Pedro serves as a kind of guide post indicating the way back. From the point of view of geography or ground covered, Fabio's return begins rather early, but it takes on its profounder meaning of *return* as late as ch. XXV, upon the third meeting with Pedro. Thus the early beginning of the return movement is suggestive of an operation of Destiny.

The novel *Don Segundo Sombra* is a circle, symbolic of the unending cycle of life. On the circumference of this circle there appear three points, three moments of Argentina's history, represented by three characters: don Segundo, Fabio, and Raucho—the past, the present, and the ideal future into which the present is already changing. Like don Segundo, who comes out of the night in the first chapter of the novel, to disappear into approaching night in the last chapter, the generation symbolized by Fabio moves between two shadows, that of the past, from which it draws the strength of an identity, and that of the future, which it must accept in an act of understanding (not of surrender). Thus, in willing collaboration with the new forces emerging therefrom, this generation transforms the national personality of Argentina, and lifts the individual to a higher plane in the realm of spirit.

In conclusion, it may be said that in spite of his refusal at the age of nineteen to occupy his mind with problems which were not related to the concrete world and which defied a rational solution, from the very outset of his literary career Güiraldes' compositions disclosed a spiritual inclination—a tendency to surpass the limits set by the earth and the mind. In spite of his subsequent rejection of scholarly procedures, of philosophic systems and vocabulary, his major works (as well as his directly autobiographical compositions contained in *Poemas solitarios, Poemas místicos,* and the personal notes of *El sendero*) reveal a Güiraldes concerned not only with Argentina's social and cultural evolution, but with his own, and man's position in the cosmic totality. Thus is realized the author's dictum that beauty and truth are manifestations of each other, for all the ideas and spiritual strivings, expressed in the panorama of his works, find their synthesis in the balance of content and form of his masterpiece, *Don Segundo Sombra.* (pp. 356-57)

> *G. H. Weiss, "Technique in the Works of Ricardo Güiraldes," in* Hispania, *Vol. XLIII, No. 3, September, 1960, pp. 353-58.*

Enrique Anderson-Imbert   (essay date 1969)

[Anderson-Imbert is an Argentine-born literary historian, critic, novelist, and short story writer. He has published more than twenty books of essays and criticism, including his study Historia de la literatura hispanoamericana (Spanish-American Literature: A History). *In the following excerpt from that work, he offers a structural analysis of* Don Segundo Sombra.]

With the appearance of the verses in *The Crystal Bell (El cencerro de cristal)* in 1915, Ricardo Güiraldes (1886-1927) presented his credentials as a reader of French poetry and daring poet: as a reader, he preferred the symbolists and, above all, Jules Laforgue; as a poet he tried a good deal, succeeded at times, and managed some advances which later were to be called "creationism" and "ultraism." *Stories of Death and Blood (Cuentos de meurte y de sangre)*, also of 1915, were in reality "anecdotes heard and written because of our affection for the things of our land." These *Stories* were neither well constructed nor well written. But the "affection for things of our land," for the Argentinian countryside and its folk, was to inspire better works. There were already two interesting novelettes: *Raucho* (1917), in whose protagonist we see the

same educational upbringing as in the author who, wearied of Buenos Aires, wearied of Paris, was attracted to the country, and *Rosaura* (1922), a simple, sentimental, and melancholy story of small-town loves. The second is of especial interest because the constructive and emotional unity are much more obvious than in all his other works. Quite apparent, also, is the influence of Laforgue on his poetic, metaphoric, impressionistic language, ironic in its expression of tenderness. Güiraldes appreciated the prose poem—in Baudelaire, Flaubert, Villiers de l'Isle-Adam, Aloysius Bertrand—and in poetic prose he published in 1923 his most characteristic book: *Xaimaca,* which is typical of his double and harmonic aptitude as a lyricist and narrator. The novel *Xaimaca*—a voyage from Buenos Aires to Jamaica, with a love adventure—was forgotten because of the success of *Don Segundo Sombra* (1926). There were factors foreign to purely literary merits that entered into this success, such as the nationalist feelings of the reader, the surprise of finding, in gaucho clothes, a metaphoric language fashionable in postwar literature, and a conception of the novel, also fashionable in those years, according to which the poetic tone was more important than the action and the characterization. The action is contemplated through a curious esthetic lens that retires objects to a distance, yet enlarges them. The cattleman Don Segundo, for example, is a "phantom, a shadow, an idea" that appears to be emerging from tradition. He is not the gaucho of the Facundo nor of the Martín Fierro epoch, but he does come from those backgrounds and the narrator is overcome with admiration for his aura of historic legend: "What a leader of the bushwhackers (*montonera*) he would have been!" Although we see him as a laboring and civilized cattleman, he is not a contemporary man, but "something that is passing." The novel, in this regard, is in the form of a farewell. It evokes an Argentina that is passing and the narrator takes leave of it with the tenderness of a poet. One by one the scenes of country life make up a poetic of regional customs: the small town, the general store, the saddle-breaking, natural love, the slaughtering of cattle, the square dance, folkloric tales, cockfights, scenes of Creole politicking, fairs, encounters of old friends in the nomadic life of the Argentine plains, horse herding, the round-up, knife duels, horse racing for money, stampedes. Within this body of lyrical evocations of customs, there is the skeleton and musculature of a novel. That is, these lyrical evocations of customs move at a novel's pace, but with a simple, minimal action. In the form of memoirs Fabio Cáceres relates details of his life.

There are twenty-seven chapters that might be divided into three parts, though not all the readers will agree on the location of the divisions of this tripartition. Those who like symmetry might propose three parts of nine chapters each. First: an orphan boy of fourteen, who does not know who his father was and who, up to now, has roamed the streets of a country town like a rogue, is suddenly fascinated by the appearance of the gaucho, Don Segundo Sombra, and decides to hang on to him like a burr. He runs away from home and is initiated into "the most manly of occupations": steer-herding on the pampas. This exposition, into which a family secret is inserted, comes to a close with an interruption in the narrative sequence. Second part: five years have passed, and our protagonist-narrator tells us that Don Segundo Sombra has made a gaucho out of him. From this point, the following nine chapters are nine sketches of rural customs. This part, descriptive not only of customs but also of landscapes, culminates in chapter XVIII, when the protagonist-narrator, on coming to from a fainting spell, has the rare experience of seeing into the future: he hears, or believes he hears, what he will indeed hear in chapter XXVI, that from a cowhand he has become a rich cattleman. Third part: his labors as a cowboy continue, with a few adventurous sketches included. The protagonist returns to his home town and there finds out who his father was. He inherits his name and property, becomes a cultured man, and has the urge to become a writer. The book ends with Don Segundo Sombra's farewell. This symmetrical division, although defensible, suggests a rigorous structure that the novel is far from having. An asymmetrical division composed of three retrospective moments is one that the protagonist-narrator himself proposes: first chapter, in which, at the edge of a brook, the fourteen-year-old youth evokes his childhood; tenth chapter, in which, at the shores of a river, he evokes his five years of living with Don Segundo Sombra; chapter XXVI, in which, on the banks of a lagoon, he evokes his three years as the owner of a ranch. There are other structural elements in the novel: the appearance and disappearance of Don Segundo Sombra (chapters II and XXVII), both actions occurring at dusk and described almost with the same words ("I thought I had seen a phantom, a shadow, something that passes by and is more an idea than a person"; "What went off into the distance was more an idea than a man"); the narrator's premonition of the future on coming to after fainting—encased in another supernatural episode, that of Don Sixto, the invisible devil, and the death of his son—and the repetition of the scene, nine chapters later; the narrator's family mystery that opens the novel, and its final clarification. But let us not exaggerate: **Don Segundo Sombra** is not a novel of a complex and harmonic architectural structure. The order is rather that of a collector of scenes and landscapes who wants to complete an album of pages linearly juxtaposed. The action changes pace, it moves slowly, it hurries along, and it even leaps over time, only to return later to complete itself in a flashback (the separation of the two lovers in chapter VI, which closes the love scene begun in chapter V); but it never reaches the fluidity of the psychic life of the narrator. "Gradually my recollections had brought me up to the present," Fabio says in his first retrospection (chapter I). How coincidental that recollections should be organized in such a logical sequence! These are memories written like a clear and coherent soliloquy that arranges the episodes with the object of moving the urban reader by presenting him with a stylization of country life. There are no interior monologs to reveal directly the profound life of the narrator. "Brief words fell like ashes of inner thoughts," Fabio tells us; but either we do not hear them or, if we do, they have already lost their fleeting intimacy. Nevertheless, the greatest achievement of the novel is the oneness of its point of view. "Enclosed within a character that did not allow me to pour myself out in him except with great prudence," Güiraldes explained to Valery Larbaud, "I have been obliged to restrain my desires to achieve perfection of expression." And, in fact, what elegant temperance this is, to resist the temptation of displaying his powers as a cultured writer! "I don't wish to speak about that," says the narrator referring to his education and travels to the world's capitals, "in these lines that describe a simple soul." He avoided dissonances between the style and the theme, and his efforts were dissimulated and always subtle. And so, as he fashioned the usual gaucho similes, transforming them into new metaphors, he also thinned down the sulky, malicious speech until it took on literary subtlety, as in "I have lost a ring in the cornfield," spoken by the girl, chapter IV, in which "ring"—as in Chaucer—means virginity.

But the protagonist's change in social position, with his subsequent literary education, capably solves the problem that intrigues the reader from the very first pages: What will happen farther on, he may ask, to make the little gaucho who is telling us his memoirs acquire a perspective on his own life that is so literary, so wise in metaphoric procedures? Because the perspective with which the protagonist is contemplating the countryside, its men, and his own adventures is always idealizingly poetic. At times he looks down upon himself from the sun: "the first look from the sun found me sweeping"; more normally he looks at himself from a moon, high and distant, illuminated by cosmopolitan literature. It has already been noted that among the many refinements that Güiraldes puts into the soul of his protagonist—metaphors, rare sensations, synesthesia—there is evidence of that literature that offers cases of parapsychological states, telepathy, and paramnesias. It is true that the little gaucho Fabián always had a delicate nervous constitution (with esthetic delights, superstitious shudderings, a propensity to tears, and the imagination of one who enjoys hearing the stories that Don Segundo elaborated in his campfire chats), but without that jump from cowhand to ranch owner—and, consequently, without the time distance between the adventures he experienced and the memories he evoked—the book would not be convincing. In his evocative flights the protagonist considers as feats what to Don Segundo were everyday events: to lasso, to break horses, to wrangle steers were feats for one who, through later education, learns that the cultured public of the city, having read about them in many books, would also consider them as such. A stylistic analysis would show the complicated inventive operations with which **Don Segundo Sombra** was created. Operations that were very subtle, very lyrical, very cultured; but one of these was intended to objectify the collective soul of the traditional Creole Argentina, and this achievement in descriptive transparency is what gained international recognition for the novel. It was thought to be a realist novel, almost a telluric novel. Not at all. Güiraldes, a rich ranch owner, educated in the latest currents of French literature, did not express the real viewpoint of the cattlemen: as he let Fabio Cáceres speak, he put symbols of distance in his mouth ("for those old timers"), extemporaneous judgments, philosophical reflections foreign to the world of the gaucho and, especially in chapter XXVII, scorn for the wealth and comfort that falsified the social reality of the Argentine countryside. But, in spite of this social falsification, the novel has an admirable stylistic truthfulness. Fabio Cáceres, now a mature man and writer, relives his cowboy years and describes them in a language of refined expressive dignity, yet true to the actual vision of country life. The vision is that of a lyrical poet, but the things he sees are only those that are there before him. No matter how original his metaphors may be, they never go beyond the horizons of the pampa: they fuse and transmute things familiar to cowboys and cattlemen. Even the most realistic details are doubly artistic: because they are chosen for their starkness and because of their evocative effect. Güiraldes combined the language spoken from birth by the

Creoles with the language of the Creolist educated in European impressionism, expressionism, and ultraism. In spite of his realist dialogs, his folklore, his rural comparisons, his pampa dialect of cowhands and cattlemen, **Don Segundo Sombra** is an artistic novel. Cáceres, without leaving his pampa, strives for a style rich in rare and brilliant images. (pp. 546-51)

> Enrique Anderson-Imbert, "1910-1925," in his Spanish-American Literature: A History, Vol. Two, *edited by Elaine Malley, translated by John Falconieri and Elaine Malley, revised edition, Wayne State University Press, 1969, pp. 453-564.*

Peter R. Beardsell   (essay date 1981)

[*In the following excerpt, Beardsell examines the treatment of violence in Güiraldes's works.*]

While he was working on **Don Segundo Sombra,** during the Radical government of Alvear, Ricardo Güiraldes witnessed a national prosperity which, without reaching all classes of society, seemed to augur well for Argentina. Though disenchanted with the materialism and coarseness of Buenos Aires itself . . . , he had reason to believe that the material influence of the Pampa—which in the 1920s dominated the country's economy far more than it does today—could produce a healthy nation with an independent identity. Fifty years after his death it is striking to notice how far those expectations have been disappointed. **Don Segundo Sombra**'s message that the country should not forget its gaucho heritage does not seem at first sight to have had much relevance as Argentina coped with economic depressions, mass movements, labour disputes, industrial expansion, foreign commercial domination, and military dictatorships. Güiraldes could therefore be seen as the champion of a lost cause: the vague, nostalgic wish that the nation's rural past should in some way be used in the construction of the future.

Before we dismiss **Don Segundo Sombra** to the archives, however, we would do well to remember that (apart from representing the highest stylistic attainment in Argentina at that time) it stands as an historical record of the attitude of a social and intellectual class whose influence on the nation's mentality has been considerable. In the novel, therefore, we may discover reasons for the sometimes pernicious effect of this influence. At the heart of the problem is the ambivalence that Güiraldes betrays in his attitude towards the gaucho heritage. He undoubtedly admired and idealised the gaucho, but with implicit reservations of a kind not widely recognised by the critics. My contention here is that **Don Segundo Sombra** suggests a close relationship between, on the one hand, the virtues of dignity, courage, fortitude, virility, daring and physical prowess, and on the other hand, the vices of violence, revenge, anarchy and homicide.

The issue might well be overlooked were it not for the enigmatic chapter in which Antenor Barragán kills a man who has challenged him to a knife fight (XXIII). It is, in fact, a unique chapter in that the true protagonist of the episode is neither Fabio nor Don Segundo. Since it does nothing to advance the plot, we expect its relevance to be explicable in terms of the illustration of local customs or a new lesson learned by the narrator, as is the case with a great many of the chapters between X and XXV. Without denying the element of *costumbrismo* here, we would find the deeper meaning of the chapter in the psychological effect exerted on Fabio by the way a young man he has befriended is compelled to kill another man, and by the bloody outcome of what at first seemed a harmless situation.

After completing the job of breaking in some horses, Fabio and Don Segundo are ready to resume their gradual journey north. They make a last visit to a local bar, where they pause for a drink with acquaintances, one of whom is Antenor Barragán. This young man, we are told, is an expert in the prestigious mock knife-fights known as *visteos*, in which the two contestants go through the motions of a real bout, but mark their opponent's cheek with a sooty finger instead of slashing it with a knife. In the scene that follows, his skill is put to the test not merely in a game but in a genuine duel. When a stranger provokes Antenor with the taunt that the young man would be terrified at the sight of a real knife, the onlookers notice that he has indeed turned pale and seems afraid. Antenor's reply that he is a peaceful man who practices the art of the *visteo* for fun, not because he is looking for a quarrel, serves only to cause discomfort among his watching friends and to draw increasing taunts from the stranger. At this point Don Segundo intervenes, urging Antenor to accept the challenge and to amuse himself. We notice that although Fabio and the other onlookers are at first surprised by Don Segundo's unexpected intervention, nobody makes any objection or shows any notable reaction once he has said his piece. It is clear that everyone accepts the common sense of his words, recognising in them a code of behaviour to which they adhere. Antenor is in danger of losing his considerable prestige. Don Segundo, respecting him, wishes him to protect his honour, prove himself a man, and teach the intruder a lesson. (Besides, he is aware of Antenor's skill and could be confident of his ability to win.) The gaucho's role is therefore to act as a conscience, to voice a common respect for the code according to which a man is bound to defend his honour and prove his courage. It is important to notice that no protest is raised against the use of knives and the object of slashing a man's face.

When Antenor, with consummate ease, produces a cut from the stranger's moustache to his ear, everyone takes the duel as finished. Up to this point events have followed an expected and presumably acceptable convention. Now, however, the violence inherent in the situation suddenly breaks out of control, for the stranger is determined that the fight must be to the death. Güiraldes gives no indication of any reaction among the onlookers to this new development, and Don Segundo is significantly silent. We are left to infer that the passion of the stranger can not be contained, and that events must be allowed to take their inevitable course. We imagine the onlookers to recognise a death-wish in the stranger, or a sense of offended honour so great that only the adversary's death can atone. It is not long before Antenor has dealt the final blow and fled from the scene. Güiraldes summarises the course of the duel with the utmost brevity. When describing the cock-fight in chapter XIII he traced the various manoeuvres of the two contestants in some detail. What interests him now, however, is not the fight itself but the bloodiness of the outcome. Clearly, he wishes to suggest that Fabio is struck by the spectacle: the flow of blood, the dying breath, the stiffening of the corpse. . . . Then follow the reactions of the spectators. The first to speak expresses revulsion: "Porquería . . . nos alabamos de ser cristianos . . . y a lo último somos como perros . . . ; sí, como perros" ["Disgusting. . . we brag about being Christians. . . and in the end we are like dogs . . . ; yes, like dogs"]. His word "somos" includes not only the two combatants but all those present; all who have allowed the barbarous act are guilty of animal-like behaviour. In a more controlled, though equally damning reaction, a second speaker regrets the effect of excessive pride. It is of great significance that this man's comments, which advocate the suppression of one's pride rather than the avenging of offended dignity, run counter to the code that the onlookers appeared to accept previously. More important still, they seem contrary to the role played by Don Segundo two pages earlier. The sense that these two speakers have voiced the general sentiment of those present is confirmed by the comment of a third man. All seem to recognise the lack of any guarantee that once a degree of violence is endorsed it may be held in check.

Although nobody—not even Fabio—comments on Don Segundo's previous intervention, Güiraldes is certainly aware of the gaucho's difficult position now that he had advocated a course of action that has produced unacceptable results. Unlike the other onlookers, he shows little reaction, and certainly no regret or revulsion. But Güiraldes has him defending his own role on the grounds that he himself has always managed to handle such situations without killing anyone (implying perhaps that Antenor should have done the same), and that in any case, according to the rules the duel should have ended as soon as blood was drawn. It is quite possible that Güiraldes hoped to exonerate his gaucho in this way, and perhaps a willing listener would accept the excuse. But we may well find the attempt unconvincing; we may well await (in vain) some further clarification of the author's own view, some reconciliation of the concensus opinion with that of Don Segundo. Instead, Güiraldes proceeds to bring the episode to a cool, clinical end. The doctor, far from being horrified, is merely impressed by the strength and precision of Antenor's knife-thrust, leaving Fabio deeply influenced by the way a human being has become an inanimate object.

At the beginning of the following chapter, when Fabio meditates on the events he has witnessed, the theme is that of the power of fate over a man's life. Rather than betray any doubt concerning the perfection of Don Segundo as a model, the narrator interprets the episode as an illustration of the irresistible force of destiny. If there are any reflections on Don Segundo's role, they concern only the remarkable way in which he alone can avoid such blows of fate. While thoughts of this kind are quite legitimate for the impressionable Fabio, they are surely not the only ones he ought to have at this juncture. For a good part of the nineteenth century the gaucho's lawless or violent behaviour was considered part of the barbarity that opposed civilisation. Güiraldes was among those who thought that the time had come to bury Sarmiento's thesis that the city must overcome the country. However, in failing to give Fabio an awareness of the dubious aspects of Don Segundo's role, he is side-stepping this vital issue. If he disapproves of the outcome of Antenor's duel he must have his

own reservations about Don Segundo's intervention; he must also recognise a flaw in the gaucho code to which this was a response. We can only assume that, since his overall intent is to idealise the gaucho heritage, he wishes to avoid any emphasis on features that detract from the favourable picture. His views on the matter, though never openly expressed in the novel, are implicit in the sequence of events from chapter XXII onwards.

In XXII, Fabio reveals sufficient independent skill in breaking horses for the *patrón* to offer him permanent employment. Güiraldes therefore implies that he has acquired all the technical accomplishments of the herdsman's repertoire and that, since the offer of a job does not include Don Segundo, he now has the opportunity of terminating his apprenticeship and ceasing to follow the gaucho. Fabio declines, not on the grounds of friendship but because he believes Don Segundo still has things to teach him. . . . In the following chapters Fabio learns nothing from Don Segundo. It is true that he needs his friend's steadying influence and moral support during the difficult transition from herdsman to landowner in the last three chapters of the novel, but these are more the services of a friend than a teacher. In effect, the only major lesson that Fabio ought to learn from Don Segundo after his chance to leave him in chapter XXII is that the traditional gaucho values are not always fully acceptable in the society that Argentina is to develop. Although the narrator himself does not appear to be conscious of this lesson, the reader can be in no doubt that Güiraldes recognised it, for this is one reason why Don Segundo must ride away.

It is worth noticing at this stage that the code observed during the Antenor Barragán duel is connected with the more general gaucho cult of virile behaviour. In its most refined form the gaucho's *hombría* ["manliness"] is proved by his inner fortitude and resistance, as we shall see below; in its crudest form, however, no distinction is made between these inner qualities and more physical things such as the display of strength, skill, and daring, the participation in combat, and the physical domination of another person. This is why the term *machismo* is appropriate. As in the Antenor episode, the male's relationship with the female is occasionally at issue. When Fabio makes his sexual conquest of Aurora, this is part of his development into a true *macho;* when Don Segundo dominates the scene at a dance, he is displaying his *machismo.* But Güiraldes virtually excludes women from ***Don Segundo Sombra*** (in sharp contrast with ***Xaimaca***), with the result that *machismo* is normally revealed in the men's struggle with the land, with climatic conditions, with animals, and with each other. What most concerns us here is the extent to which the cult of *machismo* leads to situations where violence exceeds tolerable proportions, and human life is placed needlessly in jeopardy.

In his **"Notas sobre 'Martín Fierro' y el gaucho,"** Güiraldes begins by insisting on the distinction between "gaucho" and "matrero." He takes the latter to be the specific term for a type of gaucho given to lawless behaviour. Martín Fierro, he argues, was compelled by adverse circumstances (except in his fight with the negro) to act like a "matrero"; it is not his fights that should determine the impression of a gaucho conveyed by the poem, but rather "el libro mismo en su índole íntima. La filosofía que constituye el fondo de sus razones así como su modo de hablar . . . " ["the very record of his intimate nature. The philosophy that constitutes the basis of his reasoning as well as his way of speaking . . . "]. If we apply the same reasoning to Güiraldes' novel we may conclude that the general impression rather than a specific moment should form our view of the gaucho as he is represented by Don Segundo. Güiraldes' argument seems to suggest that the characteristic of a "matrero" is not essentially and inherently a gaucho trait.

This line of argument is not supported, however, by the general presentation of Don Segundo. When the gaucho is first introduced, in chapter II, it is precisely those elements that Güiraldes would seem to associate with a "matrero" that predominate. The man is preceded by a reputation for being "fiero" ["fierce"], for having had "una mala partida con la policía" ["a run-in with the police"], and for having killed someone with a knife. No sooner has he appeared on the scene than we see him in action, demonstrating his supreme prowess as a fighter. In chapter XIV, when a policeman seeks to display his own *machismo* while arresting Don Segundo, the latter reduces the policeman to a ridiculous spectacle and at the same time shows that he is above sheer obedience to the law *per se*. This is all part of the process of magnifying the gaucho's image; it proves that the author expected Fabio to be filled with awe and admiration, and it suggests very strongly that Güiraldes himself admired those features in Don Segundo.

There is abundant evidence, moreover, that Güiraldes could not resist portraying certain types of violence in his books. A number of the short stories in *Cuentos de muerte y de sangre* already depict challenges and contests between two men: **"Facundo", "Don Juan Manuel", "Justo José", "El capitán Funes", "Venganza", "Nocturno", "La deuda mutua",** and **"La donna è mobile".** Although not all lead to the shedding of blood, it is evident that Güiraldes enjoyed situations where courage is put to the test, where either words or deeds create tension, or where the menace of a violent outcome is felt. Often a brutal death does indeed occur. In **"Nocturno",** for example, the narrative begins at the point where an offended man promises revenge; after seven introductory lines, without pausing to intimate the cause of the offence (which is not what interests him here), Güiraldes moves directly to the description of an assault in the darkness, a vain attempt by the young *estanciero* to defend himself, the deep knife-thrust that kills him, and the departure of the anonymous assailant. There is no moral comment by the author, nor any indications of repulsion; only the occasional word like "tragedia" to betray an attitude. Occasionally Güiraldes narrates an episode in which the violence is not the outcome of a contest between two men. In **"El Zurdo"** a gaucho reveals his bravado by flinging insults at his executioners; in **"De mala bebida"** a drunken *estanciero* needlessly murders a peasant; and in **"El remanso",** impatience, bad temper, and the failure to recognise danger are all punished by death. Brutal episodes of this kind seem to have held a fascination for Güiraldes at the same time as they disturbed him. He clearly recognised them as part of the traditional rural scene. One story, **"Compasión",** suggests an ironical view of the attempt to apply "civilised" codes of behaviour in "barbarous" settings. A man who stops a fight and saves the loser from worse punishment is not thanked; the loser waylays him and beats him up. Offend-

ed pride and the need to inflict revenge prove stronger than gratitude.

Between these short stories (written 1911-1915) and *Don Segundo Sombra* Güiraldes wrote three books (*Raucho, Rosaura,* and *Xaimaca*) that are poetic and sentimental rather than heroic and brutal. Indeed, when we consider *Don Segundo Sombra* as a whole, we are probably most conscious of the meditative, folkloric and static elements. This disguises the fact that Güiraldes had not lost his fascination with the tough, wild character of the pampa. There is plenty of violence in the novel quite apart from the Antenor Barragán episode: a cock-fight (chapter XIII), a perilous journey through crab-beds and swamps (XV), dangers and injuries during a round-up (XVI and XVII), a stampede and a storm (XXIV). There are, moreover, other contests and confrontations between men: Don Segundo and the *tape* Burgos (II), Don Segundo and the officious corporal (XIV), Fabio and Numa (XIX), Fabio and Pedro (XXV).

We must recognise that one of the prime functions of these episodes is as tests and trials for the characters. An admirer of the qualities of manliness and stoicism, Güiraldes constantly set his national heroes (Don Segundo, Fabio, and their herdsmen friends) in situations where they were required to learn and develop those virtues. Even Sarmiento, we should remember, had admitted the positive contribution of the gaucho's life-style in creating a national character. . . . Almost every chapter of *Don Segundo Sombra* contains at least one situation in which men display their skill or valour, resist boldly in the face of danger or hardship, or dominate some kind of adversary. (pp. 302-08)

In the last years of his life Güiraldes became increasingly interested in theosophy, spiritualism, Yoga, and Eastern religions generally. While he was undergoing physical suffering this reading assisted him in learning to exert the power of mind over body. He noticed that pain could have a constructive role, for the victory of resisting it brought pleasure. . . . To shun pain and to yield to it were, Güiraldes believed, both forms of cowardice. In the light of these views, we may readily understand why it was necessary for his heroes to undergo sufferings in order that they should develop their nobler, spiritual capacity. It is clear that the innate sense of *machismo* attributed to gauchos overlaps with these essentially intellectual and mystical concepts. This means that Güiraldes' early instinctive admiration for the influence of the Pampa found its vindication in the philosophical views that he gradually evolved, and suggests that his exaltation of the gaucho in *Don Segundo Sombra* was based on firm personal beliefs rather than a national vogue.

It is quite evident, nevertheless, that the rugged action and the violence (besides the local customs) satisfied a taste among the urban readers of the novel in 1926. . . . When we compare *Don Segundo Sombra* with other Argentine books about gauchos we find that violent action and bloodshed are among the ingredients that it shares with them. The fights of Martín Fierro (in Hernández's poem) with the negro, the gaucho, the police force, and the Indians spring readily to mind, as do the deaths of don Francisco and his son at the end of Benito Lynch's *Los caranchos de La Florida.* Needless to say, this was not an exclusively gauchesque phenomenon. Horacio Quiroga's stories were often exciting their readers with their wild, grotesque, or horrific events, while further afield, Rómulo Gallegos was exploring the problem of barbarity in the Venezuelan plains in *Doña Bárvara,* José Eustasio Rivera was illustrating the atrocities committed on the Amazon rubber plantations in *La vorágine,* Mariano Azuela was narrating the bloody course of the Mexican Revolution in *Los de abajo,* and Alcides Arguedas was probing the conflicts between white men and Indians in *Raza de bronce.*

Apart from the inference that a taste for melodrama was common among readers, and allowing for the integrity of each author's purpose, we must acknowledge that one of their aims was to portray a reality—the reality of violent behaviour in Latin America's untamed environment. A note of censure is not always immediately perceptible. Quiroga, for example, approaches Güiraldes in his view that a man ennobles his character by exposing himself to danger and physical trials. Gallegos's hero reaches a compromise with barbarity in his efforts to overcome its excesses. On the other hand, Azuela is not alone in showing revulsion for mankind's brutality. Above all, these other authors were not intent on *idealising* a national heritage (one in which *machismo* and violence formed an integral part), with the result that they appear less approving than Güiraldes of the violence that they portray.

Among Spanish American writers as a whole there seems to be a growing awareness of the ridiculous, if not the dangerous, aspects of *machismo*. . . . It is significant that Jorge Luis Borges—an Argentine author of a later generation who illustrates the code of *machismo* in gaucho legend—gives a far more equivocal treatment than Güiraldes. As L. A. Gyurko has shown, Borges "presents a paradoxical vision. He combines romantic idealisation and ironic undercutting, adulation of the vibrant display of courage and élan . . . and burlesque of the cult." The Antenor episode suggests very strongly that Güiraldes recognised problems with the code. But his failure to present any clear link of the lessons of chapter XXIII with those of the rest of the novel (particularly with an episode like that in chapter XIV where Don Segundo handles the law in a manly yet almost anarchic fashion) betrays an excessively simplistic and insufficiently critical approach to the national heritage. (pp. 308-10)

> *Peter R. Beardsell, "Don Segundo Sombra and Machismo," in* Forum for Modern Language Studies, *Vol. XVII, No. 4, October, 1981, pp. 302-11.*

Jorge Luis Borges   (essay date 1982?)

[An Argentine short story writer, poet, and essayist, Borges was one of the leading figures in contemporary literature. His writing is often used by critics to illustrate the modern view of literature as a highly sophisticated game. Justifying this interpretation of Borges's works are his admitted respect for stories that are inventions of art rather than realistic representations of life, his use of philosophical conceptions as a means of achieving literary effects, and his frequent variations on the writings of other authors. In his literary criticism, Borges is noted for his insight into the manner in which an author both represents and creates a reality with words, and the way in which those words are variously interpreted by read-

ers. With his fiction and poetry, Borges's critical writing shares the perspective that literary creation of imaginary worlds and philosophical speculation on the world itself are parallel or identical activities. In the following interview with Roberto Alifano, Borges explains Güiraldes's involvement with the journal Proa *and discusses* Don Segundo Sombra.*]*

Alifano: *How did you happen to meet Ricardo Güiraldes?*

Borges: I met him in a hotel that was on Maipú Street between Córdoba and Viamonte Streets. Brandan Caraffa introduced me to him. Brandan wanted to found a literary journal, *Proa,* and he came to tell me he had talked with Pablo Rojas Paz and with Ricardo Güiraldes and that they had decided to create a magazine, from which I could not be left out. That publication was to meet the needs of the new literary generation. I, of course, was very flattered with their attitude toward me. And I said to my mother: "By God, this is wonderful! They've told me that I couldn't be missing from a magazine for young writers that some of my friends are creating with Güiraldes. This is really gratifying." My mother agreed completely with my opinion, and Brandan Caraffa and I went the next day to the hotel where Güiraldes was staying.

What year did that take place?

My dates are vague, but it must have been around 1924 or 1925. Ricardo Güiraldes was older than I by ten or twelve years; of course, to a young man, ten years are a lot, although later it is the same to be sixty or seventy, seventy or eighty. Güiraldes was, indeed, what people called back then *"un escritor de fuste"* (a writer of consequence). I remember that at the meeting he said to us: "I am older than you are, young men, and I am really moved that you have met with Brandan Caraffa" (with Caraffita, as he used to call him affectionately), "and that you have decided that a magazine for young writers cannot be published without my collaboration." I understood then that behind all that was Brandan Caraffa's scheme to bring out the magazine. At that point, Pablo Rojas Paz arrived and my suspicions were confirmed. "I am very flattered," said Rojas Paz, "by this honor that you do me. . . ." And I interrupted him: "Yes, a few days ago Ricardo Güiraldes, Brandan Caraffa and I met and agreed that a magazine for young writers could not manage without someone like you." Güiraldes, who understood the scheme, winked at me, Brandan Caraffa laughed, and a short time later *Proa* appeared.

Where did the funds for Proa come from?

Well, each of us gave fifty pesos. But I suspect that the magazine cost much more than the amount we gave. I think Güiraldes added the necessary funds to cover the cost of production. Güiraldes was a very generous man, and he was always willing to donate money for all cultural enterprises, especially if those projects were supported by young people.

Güiraldes was a man in love with the Argentine pampa, despite the fact that he came from Buenos Aires, indeed, was born right in the downtown area of Buenos Aires.

Yes, he was born in his parents' home (people used to be born in their own homes in the old days), and this house was in the very center of downtown, between Florida and

Paraguay Streets. He spent his childhood and adolescence there, but he used to travel frequently to San Antonio de Areco, where his family had a ranch. Later, Güiraldes bought an apartment in Solís Street, close to Congreso Plaza, where we used to visit him. One of the things I remember about that apartment was the large library Güiraldes had there. That library had two sections: One of its wings had books by French and Belgian Symbolists and a smattering of Argentine authors; the works of Leopoldo Lugones were there; also works by Poe translated into French. The other wing had books on theosophy. Güiraldes was interested in those ideas, and, like the rest of us at that time, he was also a devoted reader of Lugones.

His writing was influenced by Lugones. We used to speak ill of Lugones, but deep down we felt that to write well was to write like Lugones. I think that influence is noticeable in Güiraldes's novel **Don Segundo Sombra.** The range of his essay *El payador* (The Itinerant Singer) encompasses a more complex milieu, one that goes back to that time in Argentine history known as "The Conquest of the Desert." In the work of Lugones many events take place; in **Don Segundo,** on the other hand, few events take place other than the theme of friendship. I remember that I gave a copy of **Don Segundo** to my friend, the boss of the Palermo district, Nicolás Paredes, who had been the protector of Evaristo Carriego. A few days later, I asked him what he though of Güiraldes's book, and he, perhaps because of his loyalty to the novels of Eduardo Gutiérrez or to *Martín Fierro,* denied that he liked it. He said to me: "Tell me, Borges, when does that *criollo* fight? I kept on turning the pages expecting a bloody fight, but it never happened." There is a complete literary definition in that, don't you think? Paredes wanted a book full of action, with knife duels, which is why **Don Segundo** disappointed him so much.

Don Segundo *is a sort of elegy that gives the impression that everything is happening for the last time, don't you think so?*

Yes, I do. And perhaps Güiraldes felt that more than anybody else. It's true; everything happens in that book as though it were happening for the last time. There is a breaking in of horses, and one feels that it is the last breaking in of horses; there is a cattle drive, and one feels that it is the last cattle drive. Everything happens for the last time. Güiraldes is a *criollo* gentleman who seems to be bidding farewell to everything with an habitual courtesy. He says goodbye, with evident nostalgia, to that world which was disappearing, to that world which was slowly dying out. I have attempted to classify **Don Segundo** by suggesting that it is not a novel, but an elegy, an admirable elegy.

I am sure that one social circumstance that influenced Güiraldes was that, in the area where he had his ranch, Italian and Spanish immigrants had begun to establish farms that were progressively displacing the gaucho.

Ah, yes, around that time agricultural farms began to flourish, which meant that the *criollo* world, the world of the gaucho, was disappearing from the countryside. Now, of course, many people say that at no point in that book are farms mentioned. Well, one could answer that **Don Segundo** is not an historical novel, nor does it intend to be realistic. Güiraldes's book is conceived as an elegy about that old world of cattlemen. That is why there are

no references to new things. Like all elegies, **Don Segundo** ends by bidding farewell, and that brings to mind an analogous passage in *El payador,* where Lugones speaks of the gaucho who leaves with his poncho fluttering in the wind and with a flag at half mast. I think that Güiraldes echoed that passage intentionally to remind us of Lugones, since he was a devoted admirer of Lugones.

It has been said that you personally knew the gaucho who inspired Güiraldes. What was don Segundo Sombra like?

Yes, I met that gaucho, who was called Segundo Ramírez Sombra. He was a heavy-set and relatively short man, and was quite introverted. An employee of the National Library—the son of a cattle driver whom Güiraldes mentions in the prologue to his book—told me that the hoodlums of San Antonio de Areco, jealous because the book was dedicated to don Segundo, disliked him intensely. The Toro Negro and his son the Torito, who were famous local hoodlums and who had been bodyguards to Güiraldes's father, were the ones who hated the poor man most. When those bullies would come into a tavern, don Segundo would flee through the back door—he was afraid of them. Don Segundo was, moreover, a foreigner in that region, since he was born in the province of Santa Fé. Don Segundo was not a hoodlum but a working man who did not bother anyone. The famous hoodlums could not understand why Güiraldes had based his book on that "wretch."

Güiraldes was a man who had a profound knowledge of all aspects of rural life.

Yes, Güiraldes knew all the secrets of the countryside. He was also a guitar player and singer. Güiraldes spent hours singing and talking. I'll tell you something I have not told anyone before: Güiraldes often came to my house for lunch. He would arrive around ten in the morning, and after lunch, he would delight us with his guitar playing and his *milongas.* One day as he was bidding farewell, my mother pointed out that he was leaving his guitar behind. And Güiraldes answered her, "I did it on purpose, doña Leonor. As I told you, I am leaving for France next Saturday, and I wanted something of mine to remain with you." So that for six or seven months we kept in our house the guitar of Ricardo Güiraldes. (pp. 99-102)

> *Jorge Luis Borges, in an interview with Roberto Alifano, in* Twenty-Four Conversations with Borges: Including a Selection of Poems; Interviews 1981-1983, *by Roberto Alifano, translated by Nicomedes Suárez Araúz, Willis Barnstone and Noemí Escandell, Lascaux Publishers, 1984, pp. 99-102.*

John Donahue   (essay date 1987)

[*In the following excerpt, Donahue examines the role of nature in* Don Segundo Sombra *and Owen Wister's novel* The Virginian *(1902), attributing likenesses between the two works to the similar geographic features of North America and Argentina and explaining the dissimilarities as the result of differing cultural myths.*]

Environment and culture shape human beings, both as individuals and as societies. In all the vast plains of the Americas where a cattle industry developed, a human type evolved a distinct way of life: the *gaucho* in Argentina, the *charro* in México, the *llanero* in Venezuela, the *guaso* in Chile, and the *cowboy* in the United States and Canada. Domingo Faustino Sarmiento, an Argentine intellectual who was an avid reader of James Fenimore Cooper, was perhaps the first to state clearly in regard to the Americas that wherever a similar combination of geographical features occurs, parallel customs and occupations have evolved among otherwise unrelated peoples, but the observation has since become almost a commonplace. Naturally, people with parallel customs have produced similar bodies of literature, but the mythic underpinnings of that literature are not necessarily the same, as a comparison of two outstanding novels shows.

Don Segundo Sombra, by Ricardo Güiraldes, is generally considered the masterpiece of literature dealing with the Argentine gaucho. Published in 1926, it represents the culmination of the gaucho theme. As Owen Wister's *The Virginian* (1902) stands out in the tradition of the Western in North America, ***Don Segundo Sombra*** likewise towers above other creations in the genre. As Wister attempts to synthesize historical changes in the West, Güiraldes likewise attempts to reconcile the factions in Argentine culture that shaped the perspective on the gaucho. Thus the two novels are appropriate for comparison. In both novels geography exerts its influence on the characters. Both the gaucho and the cowboy owe their existence to a coincidence of historical and environmental factors, but although both novels highlight the physical environment, the interplay between man and environment is markedly different in the two novels. *The Virginian* is the heir of the romanticism of Wordsworth and Rousseau, touched by the Protestant work ethic and Jeffersonian democracy, and is finally the product of two central myths of identity in the United States, that of the frontier and that of the garden, both myths that celebrate nature. ***Don Segundo Sombra,*** on the other hand, is the product of a culture that glorified urban virtues and distrusted nature. The differences in culture and cultural myth account for the differences in the role the environment, or nature itself, plays in the two novels.

When Frederick Jackson Turner elaborated his theory of the significance of the frontier in molding the institutions and character of democracy in the United States, he changed the focus of historical analysis. For Turner, the frontier was the edge between savagery and civilization, the force that stripped the pioneer of the baggage of European civilization and forced him to create a new civilization, transformed and distinctive. The development of American society, Turner argued, could be studied in terms of European ideologies. (pp. 166-67)

Many similarities could be enumerated between the settlement of Anglo North America and the settlement of Latin America, but similarities and differences depend on the standard of comparison used and the method of analysis applied. In *The Frontier in Latin American History,* Alistar Hennessy explores the possibility of applying Turner's frontier hypothesis to the study of Latin American history. The approach produces questions rather than answers but highlights a difference of paramount importance for the history of the two frontiers: the original settlement patterns of Latin America did not produce a clearly identifiable frontier line between savagery and civilization. In some areas the Spaniards found sedentary peoples onto whose cultures, institutions, and social structures they grafted their own. In other areas Spanish settlers did displace nomadic or seminomadic tribes. Furthermore, the colonial policies and the political and social structures of the Spanish and English colonizers were markedly different. Most Latin American nations are still in the frontier state of development, but unlike the United States, Hennessy writes, they are "frontier societies lacking a frontier myth." He explains that the persistence of cultural traits on the Latin American frontier means that we cannot really talk of the environment shaping a new man. "It is not easy to jettison cultural baggage in the Latin American environment. Monuments, whether pre-Columbian or colonial are ubiquitous, and the greater degree of racial intermixing has bequeathed a complex pattern of varied cultural traditions and contrasting ways of looking at the past." Latin Americans did not attribute to the frontier the significance that Anglo-Americans did because they had neither had the same experiences nor did they have the cultural necessity for constructing a frontier myth. For the United States, the frontier provided "a legitimizing and fructifying nationalist ideology." But for the people of Latin American countries, "without democracy, there was no compulsion to elaborate a supportive ideology based on frontier experiences and their putative influence on national character and institutions."

Interpretations of the European settlement frontier in Latin America must start from a set of suppositions different from Turner's. As John A. Crow points out [in *The Epic of Latin America*], the civilization of Spain was urban rather than rural, and building cities was perhaps one of the greatest achievements of the Spanish colonizers. Interpreters of Latin American history and culture over the past 150 years, men such as Domingo Faustino Sarmiento (Argentina), José Enrique Rodó (Perú), Ezequiel Martinez Estrada (Argentina), Octavio Paz (México), and Hernán Arciniegas (Colombia), reflect in their thinking a preference for the urban and the intellectual over the rural and the materialistic. (pp. 167-68)

The mid-nineteenth century in Argentina saw the emergence of two political and cultural factions, those who championed the native, Argentinian ways and those who favored the Europeanization of Argentina through industrialization and the wholesale importation of European styles and manners. Sarmiento belonged to the latter faction. His *Facundo: Civilization and Barbarism* (1845), the biography of the gaucho lieutenant to the dictator Rosas, was intended as a study of the barbarous influence of the Pampa on its inhabitants. Sarmiento grudgingly admires many qualities of the gaucho in his natural state, but he nevertheless indicates that the gaucho and the Pampa embody all that was backward and uncivilized in an Argentina determined to modernize itself. In his understanding of the role of the physical environment in the evolution of cultural personality, Sarmiento resembles Frederick Jackson Turner, but unlike Turner, who saw the frontier and the successive phases of barbarism and civilization as positive forces in the evolution of a uniquely American character, Sarmiento condemned the process as leading to the antithesis of the European character he desired for his homeland. Successive Argentine governments broke up the gaucho culture by conscripting the gauchos into military service and encouraging immigrant farmers to settle the Pampa.

As Hennessy points out, the frontier myth and the garden myth go hand in hand, sustaining each other, and the lack of a garden myth in Latin America helps explain the lack of a frontier myth. Frontier communities in Latin America may have had democratic traits, but they were not strong enough to offset the image of the interior as dark and menacing in contrast to the civilization of the cities as that image was forcefully articulated by Sarmiento. Whatever democratic values existed on the frontier, it is unlikely that they "would have flowed back and influenced thinking in the cities, given the state of communications, lack of information, and absence of any agrarian myth comparable to Jeffersonianism which predisposed many in the U. S. to conjure up a 'garden image' of the newly opening West." In the United States, however, the frontier myth and garden image are linked in the earliest colonial writings. The Puritans, Richard Slotkin argues, developed an elaborate concept of their mission in the New World as a new Exodus of Israel from Egypt, a temporary exile for fugitives from an "idolatrous land, a period of trial which would make them worthy of entering into a new Promised Land, a New Jerusalem." The age of independence continued the marriage of frontier and garden myths. According to Norman Foerster, the distinguishing feature of the age in which the colonies were forged into the United States was a "new gospel of nature." The Transcendentalists, such as Emerson and Thoreau, praised the effects of nature on the spirit and stressed its role in the formation of the American character and its role as a healthy balance to the dead tameness of civilized life. Today Wallace Stegner speaks of the American wilderness as a "geography of hope." "We need wilderness preserved," he writes, "as much of it as is still left, and as many kinds—because it was the challenge against which our character as a people was formed."

A survey of the relationship between man and nature in Latin American literature and history offers a very different picture. . . . In *La Vorágine,* José Eustasio Rivera, a contemporary of Ricardo Güiraldes, writes of the Venezuelan plains, "It's a man-eating abyss . . . , a huge mouth that devours men whom hunger and despair have placed between its jaws." Carlos Fuentes, a Mexican novelist, calls nature "the enemy that devours men, destroys their will, strips them of their dignity, and leads them to annihilation." As Edward Larocque Tinker comments, this negative attitude toward nature colors Latin American thinking. In Latin American literature and culture, then, nature and the frontier are simply two factors among many that form human existence and affect the development of culture. They carry no mythic attributions of regeneration or purification. Hence, the Latin American attitude toward the physical environment is dispassionate or realistic rather than emotional and mythic.

The process through which the cowboy and the gaucho entered the literature of their respective homelands reflects the relative importance given them. Wister's cowboy took his place in a growing tradition. He is an extension of Cooper's Leatherstocking or of the heroes of the nineteenth century dime novel. Güiraldes's gaucho, on the other hand, entered literature as a result of nationalistic political and literary factors associated with the rise of the Argentinian Republic. Argentine poets used gaucho folklore as a source of inspiration for their works—José Hernandez's two part *Martín Fierro* (1872 and 1879) was the most successful literary treatment of the gaucho before *Don Segundo Sombra.* Popular literature took up the theme of the persecuted gaucho who resorted to banditry to survive, thereby creating a plethora of folk heroes similar to those found in the dime novels. Yet by the time of *Don Segundo Sombra* the historic gaucho culture had perished, leaving behind no myth to grant the gaucho a continuing life in the imagination, and Güiraldes's novel is the last important work on the theme. Wister wrote in a tradition with a future as well as a past; Güiraldes had only a past. This circumstance, too, adds to the difference in tone between the two books.

The physical setting of *The Virginian* is Wyoming in the 1880s, the Wyoming Owen Wister visited when he first headed west. The scenery varies from the rolling plains surrounding Medicine Bow to the wooded mountains separating Sunk Creek from Balaam's ranch to the majestic Tetons. The area is in transition; the Plains are being invaded by the railroad, although it is still 263 miles from Judge Henry's ranch. There are two towns in the area, Medicine Bow and the nameless town where the wedding and showdown take place. Most important, the entire area is changing from wilderness and free range to fences and civilization. The Virginian's friend James Westfall has married and committed the unforgivable sin of fencing off a patch of ground to grow potatoes. Even Judge Henry is experimenting with new methods of cattle raising, fenced pastures, an irrigation system, and the cultivation of crops such as alfalfa. The Virginian has purchased land with coal deposits for future development when the railroad expands.

As Enrique Williams Alzaga points out [in *La pampa en la novela argentina*], the Pampa described in *Don Segundo Sombra* is not the Pampa of 1926 but that of an earlier generation, the Pampa Güiraldes knew as a child, before the final division of the open range into estancias devoted to the cultivation of crops as well as to ranching. The Pampa in this novel lacks the variety of orographic relief found in *The Virginian,* extending for miles without a tree to break the horizon. Don Segundo and Fabio visit many small towns, some named, others nameless. The relatively large towns have a church, a *comisaría* (police station), and, of course, a *pulpería* (saloon), but many are smaller. The two wanderers drift from mountain foothills through semidesert to swamplands and seacoast. The many references to fences and wire dividing off properties show that the division of the Pampa into estancias has begun and that this area, like Wister's Wyoming, is in a period of economic transition.

Both settings are cultural hinterlands. Wyoming's ties are to the east, to Vermont and New Hampshire, the home states of Molly's people, and to the hero's home state, Virginia. The eastern norms are duly modified to suit Wyoming taste. Argentina's hinterland, the Pampa, is culturally linked not only to Buenos Aires but to Paris and London as well. Molly may read Shakespeare, but she has never been to Stratford. Raucho, Fabio's companion and teacher at the end of the novel, has traveled and studied abroad, particularly in Paris and London, and we may assume that this will be the destiny of Fabio as well. Argentinian landowners are Europe-oriented in their cultural preferences, and the concept that European norms should be modified to suit native taste is tantamount to heresy.

The most striking similarities in the treatment of nature in the two books stem from the similarities in the physical environment, similarities that produced the similar figures of gaucho and cowboy. In both novels the dominant perception of the natural environment is of overwhelming size and grandeur. The narrator of *The Virginian* speaks of the unending gulf of space that swallows up the east-bound train and that later swallows up Medicine Bow as he makes his way to Judge Henry's ranch. Concepts of distance need adjustment to a larger scale—the Virginian has "dropped over" to pick him up, a journey of some 263 miles; the Judge casually speaks of the neighborhood, referring to a circle of some eighty miles. Fabio Cáceres, the narrator of **Don Segundo Sombra,** makes similar comments, comparing the Pampa to an ocean that swallows up a ship; a herd of several thousand cattle leaves no mark on an indifferent Pampa. The individual, face to face with the unending prairie, feels lonely and solitary, dwarfed by the immensity of the environment. For Fabio the loneliness is a palpable reality, a stream of water running down his spine. The Virginian observes that loneliness can drive some men mad or frighten others away from the Plains, but he, himself, cannot live without it. Being a gaucho or a cowboy means learning to be alone.

The majesty of nature inspires admiration and elation. The sense of grandeur elevates the individual whom the immensity dwarfs. This grandeur brings with it a distaste for civilization and for the environment created by man. Fabio and Don Segundo refer to settlements as *"pueblitos mezquinos,"* wretched villages. According to the narrator of *The Virginian,* towns like Medicine Bow "lay stark, dotted over a planet of treeless dust, like soiled packs of cards . . . They seemed to have been strewn there by the wind and to be waiting till the wind should come again and blow them away." Both the cowboy and the gaucho are led to contemplate the finite nature of man and his works and to glimpse, through the grandeur of nature, the reality of the infinite and the eternal.

In his ability to arrive at the transcendent, the Virginian fits nicely into the Cooper mold, but he lacks Leatherstocking's almost pantheistic outlook. Leatherstocking sees God in nature, whence he acquires his moral sense. The frontiersman seems to accept Emerson's dictum that nature is a moral teacher. The Virginian points to nature and says it is proof that God exists, but he himself doesn't worry about God, other worlds, or religion. As David B. Davis writes [in *The Western: A Collection of Critical Essays,* edited by James K. Folsom] "The cowboy is the enunciation of the goodness of man and the glory he can achieve by himself . . . , a faith that man needs no formal religion once he finds a pure and natural environment."

The Virginian resembles the gaucho in his unconcerned, if not indifferent, attitude toward the transcendent. Nature inspires in Fabio and in Don Segundo a sense of grandeur, an awe of something greater than man and his works, but this does not carry over into identification with a godhead or into reflections on morality. The Pampa is a force beyond finite man, but it does not reflect the generous spirit of a transcendent god nor does it produce a man who is morally upright, good, glorious, or imbued with a high sense of morality and justice. The Pampa produces a man who can take care of himself and survive on its terms, nothing more.

Love of solitude and self-reliance are the first changes produced by nature in the men of the plains, but specific skills emerge as well. A man develops a keen sense of sight, and acuteness of vision, and an unerring sense of direction, what Fabio refers to as his "valor de baquiano." The gaucho is like a sea captain who navigates over unmarked open sea, using his own instincts, and the stars, and a keen vision that surely and easily identifies distant objects. The image of the navigator also occurs several times in *The Virginian.* . . . Such knowledge and ability cannot be acquired in schools but only through experience, and only those who can acquire those abilities survive. The horsemen of the plains learn to read nature as others would a map.

While both the cowboy and the gaucho traditions stress the influence of nature in the formation of their heroes, **Don Segundo Sombra** traces the development of a neophyte gaucho through the full process, while *The Virginian* focuses on the adventures of an Easterner guided by a mature cowboy. *The Virginian* is notoriously lacking in details of the cowboy's life, and this has led Davis to comment that *The Virginian* is the story of a cowboy without cows. The romantic frontier tradition inherited from Cooper discouraged emphasis on realistic detail; cattle drives, hard work, boredom, monotony, loneliness, and dull tasks must be subordinated to more exciting pastimes. Consequently, we see the Virginian only in those moments when the work is done, such as on the return trip from Chicago, for example, when he must manipulate his rebellious crew into coming back to the ranch. The Virginian's cowboy skills are second to his amorous and managerial skills. Davis points out that the "Western environment . . . sorts men into their true places, it does not determine men. It brings out the best in heroes and the worst in villains, but it does not add qualities to the man who has none." Wister's discussion of aristocracy and democracy in *The Virginian* illustrates his faith in the Western environment as a social separator that brings the cream to the top while the commonplace milk settles to the bottom. The physical environment is one force that, according to the frontier myth, allows true merit and natural nobility to prosper and eventually to lead society.

While Wister traces the large scale effects of nature on the cowboy, Güiraldes, in contrast, provides copious details of the practical role of nature in forming the working gaucho. The first stage is to *hacerse duro,* to toughen up. On his first cattle drive, Fabio learns what misery really is: the thick white dust rising from thousands of hooves, the throbbing head, the aching muscles and legs, the swollen feet, the unbreatheable air, the rainstorms without shelter, the sleepless nights on duty. He becomes indifferent to suffering, to harsh weather, and to the strain of life in the open. He acquires the gaucho's characteristic stoical attitude, but his stoicism is not based on passivity and resignation so much as on the will to succeed, to survive. The physical environment provides the gaucho with the challenge to prove himself and to develop the stamina, the skills, and the self-reliance needed for life in such intimate contact with a harsh, demanding environment.

The Pampa is not romantic background; it is a force in the daily lives of Fabio and Don Segundo. The slightest changes of mood in nature leave their mark. The Pampa lives and breathes along with Fabio; even his moments of thoughtful, quiet reflection are born of the Pampa. This humanization of nature, however, lacks a symbolic dimension. According to Giovanni Previtali, the features of the Pampa parallel the attributes of its inhabitants. Güiraldes ascribes an impassive exterior and stoicism to both the gaucho and to his environment. This intimate relationship between man and nature contrasts with the role of nature in the American Western novel, where it serves as a social separator or as a backdrop to action, not as an equal partner in human drama.

Nature may be harsh, but the open plains furnish both gaucho and cowboy a freedom unknown in organized, civilized society. The struggle to survive pares away unnecessary preoccupations and worries; accountable to no one but themselves, the gaucho and cowboy are free to wander as the wind, boasting of their freedom. Don Segundo cannot abide the fixed ways and rigid codes of life in a settlement; Fabio says that the continual presence of other people produces in him a great weariness and uneasiness. The Virginian and his saddle pals in the pride of their freedom look upon all signs of civilization with suspicion and dread. The new school house, fenced-off land, and farm houses symbolize the dawn of a new era and the death of their world.

Both the gaucho and the cowboy see organized society as inimical to personal freedom. To the gaucho, the Pampa means freedom from the persecution of government and army, from the restraints of organized society. The gaucho rejects the city-oriented civilization that is spreading to the Pampa from the urban centers. Martín Fierro escapes from the army to the freedom and independence of the Pampa and the Indians, who, in spite of the risks and dangers they present, are more welcoming than the civilization the army seeks to foster and spread. Don Segundo, we are told, has had difficulties with the army and with the police; only the Pampa can satisfy his lust for freedom and independence. To the cowboy, the Western Plains means freedom to roam, to seek adventure, to live as one pleases. According to the Virginian, "If there was a headstone for every man that once pleasured in his freedom here, you'd see one most every time yu' turned your head."

Romanticism gave rise to both the gaucho and the Western novels; the Western, however, remains true to its romantic heritage while the gaucho novel more accurately fits into the later traditions of realism and naturalism. For Wordsworth, perhaps the most characteristic spokesman for the romantic idea of nature, nature offered man physical and mental health as well as a refuge from the industrialized urban world. Civilized urban man had cut himself off from the vital springs of existence, leading to his spiritual poverty and alienation. The solution was a return to nature, that kind, generous, healing mother. (pp. 168-73)

The Western gives us not only Wordsworth's nature but also Rousseau's natural man. Cooper's description of Natty as a "man of native goodness," possessed of little of civilization but its highest principles, established the pattern for subsequent Westerns. The natural man preserves the best of civilized life without the accompanying evils of organized society. Emerson reiterates this view in his essay "Nature" declaring that "every natural process is a version of a moral sentence. The moral law lies at the center of nature and radiates to the circumference. It is the

pith and marrow of every substance, every relation and every process." Wordsworth's "One echo from a vernal wood / may teach you more of man / of moral evil and of good / than all the sages can" echoes clearly.

The Virginian is a later manifestation of the natural man. The external markings have changed from the time of Natty Bumppo but the essence remains unaltered as we see in Wister's first description of the cowboys:

> Youth untamed sat here for an idle moment, spending easily its hard-earned wages. City saloons rose into my vision, and I instantly preferred this Rocky Mountain place. More of death it undoubtedly saw, but less of vice, than did its New York equivalents. And death is a thing much cleaner than vice. Moreover, it was by no means vice that was written upon these wild and manly faces. Even where baseness was visible, baseness was not uppermost. Daring, laughter, endurance—these were what I saw upon the countenances of the cowboys. . . . In their flesh, our natural passions ran tumultuous; but in their spirit sat hidden a true nobility, and often beneath its unexpected shining, their figures took a heroic stature.

Wilson Clough [in *The Necessary Earth: Nature and Solitude in American Literature*] attributes the success of the cowboy theme to a nostalgic view of the past, an idealized view of man in nature, preserved from the corruptions of the big city centers of population. The cowboy is still "capable of living by a private code, free to move from job to job largely a law unto himself. He is the last symbol of a passing era, a combination of the knight in armour, Natty Bumppo and the West's own grandeur."

Latin American romanticism necessitates a different treatment of nature in the gaucho tradition. Romanticism in Spain and Latin America turned to nature for its pictorial value, for its distinctive regional qualities, for its local color. Nature remains primarily a pictorial element, as well as a necessary element to explain human character. The gaucho would not exist if nature were not constantly at work shaping and molding him. Nature was not seen as a transcendental power, although moments of harmony between man and nature, such as those in Güiraldes, are to be found. We do not find for nature the love and tender feelings of the Virginian. Güiraldes does not project onto nature a symbolic value but remains faithful to his realistic bias, never losing sight either of the hostile environment in which the gaucho lives or of the thin layer of varnish that separates the civilized man from the savage. Escaping organized society is not a rush into the warm embrace of a wise and protective mother but into an environment that is ferocious, unforgiving, and implacable.

The vision of nature in the gaucho novel resembles that of Hobbes, Darwin, and the naturalists rather than that of Wordsworth and Rousseau. Nature is not a generous mother who cares for man but rather a conjunction of blind forces in which only the strongest survive. Fabio frequently feels the hostility of nature; there are traps to catch the unwitting and the unwary. Recalling an episode when he nearly lost his life in quicksand, Fabio concludes that the Pampa quickly eliminates the weak. In one of the most striking scenes of the novel, Fabio watches crabs eat one another. The beach is full of half-devoured carcasses and of survivors in various stages of mutilation. This savage scene, an example of Güiraldes's naturalistic perspective, makes Fabio think about his need for human companionship. The Pampa does not shelter or restore man— consolation is to be found within oneself or with other humans. Nature is, at best, indifferent. This view contrasts sharply with the perspective of the Western novel, where nature rather than society provides solace.

Nature engenders stoicism in the gaucho. In ***Don Segundo Sombra,*** in contrast to the sanguine *Virginian,* there is no expression of an outlook that could be labelled optimistic. I do not mean to suggest that the Western does not reveal examples of a naturalistic view; on the contrary. The Virginian thrives while the inept Shorty is destroyed. Trampas, unlike the Virginian, absorbs the worst influences of the environment and of society, and he is killed. The fittest survive and the weak perish. The fundamental distinction between the gaucho novel and the Western is that in the latter the individual is able to contribute to his destiny, to forge a future for himself and his country. The gaucho prefers to lament his situation and to dream of the past while he despairs of the future. Argentina's frontier myth lay in Sarmiento's assertion that the superior urban civilization would eventually wipe out the gaucho as evolution had eliminated the dinosaur. The gaucho sees no future for himself in a world that views his way of life as the epitome of backwardness and savagery and his continued existence as a blight on the attractive modern image of the country.

In the Western, the land is given symbolic value and geography loses its realistic dimension. The first American colonists came to the new world seeking a new start for humanity. The theme of the Promised Land, of Zion, runs throughout the Western tradition. In Medicine Bow, the narrator of *The Virginian* catches a glimpse of this Paradise:

> serene above the foulness swam a pure and quiet light, such as the East never sees; they might be bathing in the air of creation's first morning. . . . Beneath sun and stars their days and nights were immaculate and wonderful. . . . at the door began a world of crystal light, a land without end, a space across which Noah and Adam might come straight out of Genesis.

The West is the Promised Land which can become Paradise Regained through human effort, including the Biblical command to subdue nature. Echoes of the Protestant work ethic abound. The possession and exploitation of the land is almost a religious duty.

The Spaniards came to the New World seeking wealth, not Paradise, nor did they ever see the settlement and exploitation of the land in terms of a garden myth or a new Zion. The Conquistadores sought gold, El Dorado, cities whose streets were reportedly paved with gold and silver, but the true wealth of Latin America, as was recognized later, lay in its agriculture. The early Spanish settlers did not share the Protestant work ethic. The gaucho loved work, Angeles Cardona de Gibert tells us, not because it could produce wealth but because it was necessary and enjoyable. Working to amass property and wealth was quite foreign to him. Fabio's father takes him to see his ranch, fields, and herds of cattle, but Fabio shows little interest in property and wealth. When Fabio inherits the estate, he laments his fate because becoming a property owner means ceasing to be a gaucho. For the Virginian, on the other hand, the acquisition of property and the rise to a position of prominence amply compensate for the loss of freedom of cowboy life. The two can be complementary rather than antithetical.

In both the cowboy novel and the gaucho novel, nature is the force that determines the specific type of the characters. The struggle to survive in a lonely, harsh environment develops man's stamina and special skills. The environment allows man the opportunity to glimpse the eternal and to recognize his own, finite nature, to put civilization and human accomplishments into perspective. In the gaucho novel, realistic interaction with nature focuses the gaucho's life. Bad weather, parching sun, and loneliness affect him directly. Nature can reduce him to the level of a brute, drive him mad, or even kill him, although it can also inspire in him a sense of the spiritual and the eternal. The land, however, never becomes the mythic landscape of the cowboy story. The similarities between the treatment of nature in the two regional literatures are environmental: humans do adapt to similar environments in similar ways. The differences are cultural.

The cowboy novel reveals a double romantic inheritance from Wordsworth and Rousseau. Nature is loved as a generous, kind mother, the consolation and refuge of man. Characters and writers have faith in the goodness of man and nature and consequently mistrust organized society and its institutions. From this inheritance spring the frontier and garden myths that value nature at the same time that they glorify the conquest of nature for the service of man as part of the settlement of the Promised Land. Nature is the source of wealth and prosperity as it is transformed by the Protestant work ethic operating in a capitalistic free enterprise system. Western geography symbolizes the challenge to conquer, to subdue, and to build a better future. Realism in this tradition is stylistic, not the undergirding of a basic point of view. The gaucho novel treats nature differently partly because Latin American romanticism attributed to nature a passive, pictorial role and partly because the cultural bias, especially in Argentina, valued the urban and intellectual life. Nature and rural life were barbarous and backward, not healthy and sane. Despite the fact that some moments of splendid harmony develop between man and nature, for the most part a Hobbesian or Darwinian attitude takes the place of a Wordsworthian one. Nature is not a nurturing mother to the gaucho; at best it is indifferent and often is the setting for a brutal struggle. This lack of a central symbolic role for nature, a myth pointing to a brighter future, may explain why Güiraldes's ***Don Segundo Sombra*** marks the end of the gaucho tradition in literature while Wister's *Virginian* marks the midpoint of a tradition that has continued to evolve through popular literature and film into a distinctive body of art. (pp. 173-76)

John Donahue, "Nature in 'Don Segundo Sombra' and 'The Virginian,'" in Great Plains Quarterly, *Vol. 7, No. 3, Summer, 1987, pp. 166-177.*

FURTHER READING

Beardsell, P. R. "French Influences on Güiraldes: Early Experiments." *Bulletin of Hispanic Studies* XLVI (1969): 331-44.

Examines the influence of French writers on the content, style, and technique of Güiraldes's early poetry. Beardsell praises Güiraldes's ingenuity but comments that "the poems in prose of *El cencerro de cristal* . . . seem today to be of uneven value. Often they are too obviously exercises and experiments; only when Güiraldes succeeds in creating something personal and original with the material of his idols is the result more satisfying."

———. "The Dichotomy in Güiraldes's Aesthetic Principles." *Modern Language Review* 66, No. 2 (April 1971): 322-27.

Analyzes the conflict between Güiraldes's views of art as a reflection of national and regional traditions and as a highly personal means of expression.

Chapman, Arnold. "Pampas and Big Woods: Heroic Initiation in Güiraldes and Faulkner." *Comparative Literature* XI, No. 1 (Winter 1959): 61-77.

Explores the similarities between *Don Segundo Sombra* and William Faulkner's story "The Bear" (1942). Chapman claims that "Güiraldes and Faulkner are linked by a common comprehension of the phenomenon America." The protagonists of the two novels both face "an American problem, that of spanning the gap between a primitive world in equilibrium, apparently perfect in the harmony of its parts, and a clearly imperfect, changing, unhappy, hybrid society."

Frank, Waldo. Introduction to *Don Segundo Sombra: Shadows on the Pampas,* by Ricardo Güiraldes, translated by Harriet de Onis, pp. vii-xi. New York: Farrar & Rinehart, 1935.

Compares *Don Segundo Sombra* with Mark Twain's *Huckleberry Finn* (1884), discussing differences between the cultural heritages of North America and Argentina.

Gates, Eunice Joiner. "A Note on the Resemblances between *Don Segundo Sombra* and *Don Quijote.*" *Hispanic Review* XIV, No. 4 (October 1946): 342-43.

A brief note pointing out similarities between characters and episodes in the two works.

———. "The Imagery of *Don Segundo Sombra.*" *Hispanic Review* XVI, No. 1 (January 1948): 33-49.

A detailed description of the imagery in *Don Segundo Sombra.*

Gicovate, Bernardo. "Notes on *Don Segundo Sombra:* The Education of Fabio Cáceres." *Hispania* XXXIV, No. 4 (November 1951): 366-68.

Interprets the development of Fabio as a metaphorical lesson for twentieth-century Argentina: "If Don Segundo is the symbol and the nostalgia of the past, Fabio, his adopted son, is a representative of the present, the new twentieth-century Argentina burdened with a history."

Irving, T. B. "Myth and Reality in *Don Segundo Sombra.*" *Hispania* XL, No. 1 (March 1957): 44-8.

Refutes the common view of Don Segundo as a symbol of the ideal man, suggesting Fabio Cáceres as an alternative.

Predmore, Michael P. "The Function and Symbolism of Water Imagery in *Don Segundo Sombra.*" *Hispania* XLIV, No. 3 (September 1961): 428-30.

Argues that "the image of moving water gives symbolic expression to the gaucho's pattern of existence and to his spiritual needs."

Sisto, David T. "A Possible Fictional Source for Don Segundo Sombra." *Hispania* XLII, No. 1 (March 1959): 75-8.

Compares Don Segundo with Segundo Rodríguez, the protagonist of Javier de Viana's short story "La yunta de Uroboli" (1899).

Weiss, G. H. "The Spirituality of Ricardo Güiraldes." *Symposium* 10, No. 2 (Fall 1956): 231-42.

Discusses the development of Güiraldes's personal philosophy, noting that "he attempted, by the sheer power of his own will, to effect his spiritual rebirth—and he failed."

Sinclair Lewis

1885-1951

(Born Harry Sinclair Lewis; also wrote under the pseudonym Tom Graham) American novelist, short story writer, essayist, journalist, critic, dramatist, and poet.

The following entry presents criticism of Lewis's novel *Babbitt* (1922). For a discussion of Lewis's complete career, see *TCLC,* Volumes 4 and 13; for a discussion of the novel *Main Street,* see *TCLC,* Volume 23.

A classic example of early twentieth-century American social satire, *Babbitt* is usually considered Lewis's most significant novel. At once a hilarious tour through the starched provincial milieu of a typical midwestern booster and a serious commentary on American values, *Babbitt*'s lampoon of insular middle-class society and its naive preoccupation with business immediately resulted in a critical uproar, with liberal commentators largely approving of Lewis's point of view and conservative critics articulating a defensive hostility. Lewis's portrait of Babbitt, however, is complex enough to transcend the limitations of pure satire, and the novel continues to be of interest to critics and scholars today.

Babbitt was begun in the late summer of 1920, shortly after the publication of *Main Street.* The latter novel, a damning indictment of the mediocrity and pettiness of the rural American small town, was an extraordinary critical and popular success, establishing Lewis's reputation as a novelist of international importance. His conception of *Babbitt* was unequivocally ambitious. In a letter to his publisher Alfred Harcourt, Lewis explained, "I want the novel to be the G. A. N. [Great American Novel] in so far as it crystallizes and makes real the Average Capable American. No one has done it, I think—no one has even *touched* it, except Booth Tarkington in *Turmoil* and *Magnificent Ambersons.*" As for the novel's protagonist, George F. Babbitt, Lewis described him in equally universal terms: "He is all of us Americans at 46, prosperous but worried, wanting—passionately—to seize something more than motor cars and a house *before it's too late.*"

The verisimilitude of *Babbitt*'s fictional tableau of the American middle class derives in large part from the authority of its characterizations. Lewis was adept at mimicry, and friends were frequently amused by his ability to appropriate the speech, gestures, attitudes, and mannerisms of passing strangers. Preliminary research on *Babbitt* began with Lewis's frequent travels across the country in the nineteen-teens, during which he carefully studied the spectrum of American character "types," such as the traveling salesman. After finalizing the subject of *Babbitt*—the medium-sized American city—Lewis spent several months during 1921 observing and recording the social patterns of middle-class businessmen in Cincinnati, Ohio, which became the model city for Zenith in *Babbitt.*

Lewis completed the first draft of the novel in Europe, where in 1921-22 he spent about a year traveling with his wife, Grace Hegger Lewis. *Babbitt* was published a few months after their return to the United States, on Septem-

ber 14, 1922. With a prepublication printing of 80,500 copies, its commercial success was assured, and, in general, initial critical reaction was just as favorable. The vast majority of periodical reviewers in America—including Ludwig Lewisohn, H. L. Mencken, and Rebecca West—enthusiastically praised the acuity of Lewis's satire, while in England, where the novel also sold well, commentators applauded Lewis's vivid portrayal of a philistine, materialistic society, which they considered a reasonably accurate representation of America. Critical perception of the severity of Lewis's satire notwithstanding, even in medium-sized American cities, the principal victims of Lewis's satire, intensely hostile or negative reactions to the novel were comparatively rare. In fact, newspapers in five of these cities—Cincinnati, Duluth, Kansas City, Milwaukee, and Minneapolis—claimed that their town had provided the model for Zenith, while the celebration of a "Babbitt Week" in Minneapolis resulted in a bitter civic feud with neighboring St. Paul.

Lewis conceived the setting of *Babbitt* as a mythical realm based on recurring patterns of everyday life he observed in small towns throughout America. Consequently, he invented a typical midwestern state, "Winnemac" (a synthesis of Wisconsin, Minnesota, and Michigan), and a prototypical middle-class citizen, George F. Babbitt: forty-six years old, a successful real estate speculator with an income of around ten thousand dollars a year, resident of a fashionable suburb, married with two young children. The first quarter of the novel consists of a resume of a day in Babbitt's life, and includes extremely detailed descriptions of Babbitt's household, business routine, and social life. Beyond the obvious satirical intent of these descriptions, the novel also explores the internal crisis of Babbitt's psyche, the result of the protagonist's ultimate dissatisfaction in his conformable life. After a trip to Maine where he complains about the tedium of his existence to his liberal friend Paul Riesling, Babbitt's confidence in the system suddenly fades, and he embarks on a rebellious course against Zenith's conformist values. He initiates a series of extramarital affairs, offers support to such liberal causes as workers' rights, and pointedly refuses to join the Good Citizens' League, an organization devoted to upholding Zenith's middle-class value-system. The pressure on Babbitt to conform increases, however, when his friends begin to desert him and the volume of his business declines. The final crisis occurs with his wife Myra's illness. After seeing her through a serious operation, Babbitt decides that his former secure, comfortable life is preferable to his current state of precarious freedom. The ties to his liberal friends are rapidly undone and he joins the Good Citizens' League, promising to zealously uphold its values. At the novel's end, Babbitt is depicted as a passive victim of social forces, and he can only project his ideals onto his son, who he hopes will follow a more independent path in the future.

Although critical commentary on *Babbitt* in the twenties and thirties focused on the novel's social relevance—that is, on the question of whether it accurately represented American middle-class society or merely expressed Lewis's biased judgment against it—since 1945 critics have been almost exclusively concerned with the tension between satire and realism that animates the novel's narrative. The majority of commentators view the novel as a successful parody lacking in artistic depth, citing Lewis's obsession with capturing patterns of vernacular speech, stereotyped behavior, and other surface details, and his relative indifference to nuances of plot, style, and characterization typical of more sophisticated fiction. Many critics also suggest that Lewis's interest in Babbitt's "revolt" injects an element of realism in the novel that severely dilutes its parodic effect. On the one hand, critics point out that Lewis seems to be condemning Babbitt as a cultural archetype while, on the other, sympathizing with him as an individual. As a result, modern critics generally agree that the work lacks thematic coherence, and must be seen as a complex synthesis of several, sometimes conflicting, narrative functions.

(See also *Contemporary Authors*, Vol. 104; *Dictionary of Literary Biography*, Vol. 9; *Dictionary of Literary Biography Documentary Series*, Vol. 1; and *Concise Dictionary of American Literary Biography*, 1917-1929.)

Sinclair Lewis   (essay date 1921?)

[*The following essay, originally intended to serve as an introduction to the first edition of* Babbitt *(1922), first appeared in a collection of Lewis essays entitled* The

Man from Main Street *in 1953. Here, Lewis describes the unvarying socio-economic characteristics of the medium-sized American city, which became the model for the fictional city of Zenith in* Babbitt.]

This Is the Story of the Ruler of America

The story of the Tired Business Man, the man with toothbrush mustache and harsh voice who talks about motors and prohibition in the smoking compartment of the Pullman car, the man who plays third-rate golf and first-rate poker at a second-rate country club near an energetic American city.

Our conqueror, dictator over our commerce, education, labor, art, politics, morals, and lack of conversation.

There are thirty millions of him, male and female, and his autocracy is unparalleled. No czar controlled the neckware and dice-throwing of his serfs; no general in the most perilous climax of war has codified his soldiers' humor or demanded that while they engaged the enemy they admire narratives about cowpunchers and optimistic little girls. But this completeness our ruler has attained.

Though English morals and French politics and German industry have been determined by the Sound Middle-Class, the Bourgeoisie, the Pumphreysie, have never dared also to announce standards in sculpture and table-manners. For in those lands there are outcasts and aristocrats who smile at the impertinence of the unimaginative. But in America we have created the superman complete, and the mellifluous name of the archangelic monster is Pumphrey, good old G. T. Pumphrey, the plain citizen and omnipotent power.

> *Note: Above too much hints of another Main St. Most of this and all of "pos. part of Intro." cd be used, say, as Chapter [word indistinct] in Part III or IV.*

Though this is the individual romance of one G. T. Pumphrey and not the breviary of his community, that community enters his every moment, for it is himself, created in his varnished image. Monarch City is every "progressive, go-ahead, forward-looking, live, up-to-date" city of more than eighty thousand in the United States and Western Canada, with 8 or 10 venerable exceptions.

These exceptional cities Pumphrey visits with frequency, and stirs their theaters, hotels, books, and wholesalers to emulate the perfection of Monarch City, that even we who faint may win at the last to purity, efficiency, and ice water.

Distinctly, however, Pumphrey is not a satiric figure, nor a Type.

He is too tragic a tyrant for the puerilities of deliberate satire. And he is an individual, very eager and well-intentioned, credulous of pioneering myths, doubtful in his secret hours, affectionate toward his rebellious daughter and those lunch-mates who pass for friends—a god self-slain on his modern improved altar—the most grievous victim of his own militant dullness—crying in restless dreams for the arms of Phryne, the shirt of Jurgen and the twilight sea that knows not purity nor efficiency nor 34 × 4 casings.

As a Part Of Introduction, or in the story, or just implied in the story, or in an appendix on Main Street vs. the Boulevard vs. Fifth Ave.

They are complex phenomena, these American cities of from 80,000 to 1,000,000. They are industrially magnificent. They supply half the world with motor cars, machine tools, flour, locomotives, rails, electric equipment—with necessities miraculous and admirable. They are provided with houses more elaborate than any palaces, with hotels and office buildings as vast as and more usable than any cathedral. Their citizens are not unaccustomed to Fifth Avenue, to Piccadilly, to the Champs Élysées. Hither comes Galsworthy to lecture, Caruso to sing, Kreisler to play (even though they do beg him always to play the Humoresque), and here, in a Little Theater, a Schnitzler play may have a hearing as soon as Vienna, long before London. Yet they are villages, these titanic huddles. They import Kreisler as they import silks—not because they passionately love music or silks, but because those obvious symbols of prosperity give social prestige. To attend a concert is almost as valuable a certificate of wealth as to be seen riding in a Pierce-Arrow car. It is not an elegant and decorous listening to a great violinist which attests musical understanding; it is a passionate playing of one's own music—though the playing may be very bad indeed; may be nothing but the agitated scratching of four old cellists in a beery cellar. Since there is—as yet—no instrument which measures ergs of spiritual energy, the matter cannot be neatly and statistically proven, but one suspects that there is not one of these cities with a million, or half a million, people which has one tenth of the joyous mental activity of little Weimar, with its 35,000—among whom once moved no Crackajack Salesmen, perhaps, but only Goethe and Schiller.

And those glorious Little Theaters—those radiant and eager Little Theaters—indeed they do revel in Glaspell and Eugene O'Neill and Ervine—for one season or two; and then the players who have gone into this new sport for social prestige grow weary; the professional producer grows yet wearier of begging for funds, and of seeing newspapers which give a column to a road-company in a musical comedy, and two columns to a wedding between patent medicines and steel, present a brilliant performance of Shaw in two paragraphs with four solecisms; he goes his ways, and the Little Theater is not.

Villages—overgrown towns—three-quarters of a million people still dressing, eating, building houses, attending church, to make an impression on their neighbors, quite as they did back on Main Street, in villages of two thousand. And yet not villages at all, the observer uneasily sees, as he beholds factories with ten thousand workmen, with machines more miraculous than the loaves and fishes, with twice the power and ten times the skill of a romantic grand duchy. They are transitional metropolises—but that transition will take a few hundred years, if the custom persists of making it a heresy punishable by hanging or even by ostracism to venture to say that Cleveland or Minneapolis or Baltimore or Buffalo is not the wisest, gayest, kindliest, usefullest city in all the world. So long as every teacher and journalist and workman admits that John J. Jones, the hustling sales-manager for the pickle factory is the standard in beauty and courtesy and justice—well, so long will they be sore stricken with a pest of J. J. Joneses.

It is not quite a new thought to submit that though admittedly Mr. Jones somewhat lacks in the luxuries of artistic taste and agreeable manners, yet he is so solid a worker, so true a friend, and so near to genius in the development of this astounding and adventurously new industrial system, that he is worthier, he is really more beautiful, than any Anatole France or [word omitted]. Are his pickle machines with their power and ingenuity a new art, comparable to vers libre, and is there not in his noisiest advertising, his billboards smeared across tranquil fields, a passion for achievement which is, to the unprejudiced discernment, a religious fervor, an esthetic passion, a genius such as inspired the crusader and explorer and poet? Is not his assailant a blind and reactionary fellow who demands in this rough glorious pioneer outworn standards and beauties dead and dry?

Only it happens that these generous inquirers who seek to make themselves comfortable by justifying their inescapable neighbor, Mr. Jones, give him somewhat too much credit. Mr. Jones, the salesmanager, Mr. Brown, the general manager, Mr. Robinson, the president—all the persons in the pickle hierarchy most to be accredited with passion and daring and new beauties—are nothing in the world but salesmen, commercial demagogues, industrial charlatans, creators of a demand which they wistfully desire to supply. Those miraculous, those admittedly noble machines—they were planned and built and improved and run by very common workmen, who get no credit whatever for pioneering. Those astounding pickle formulae, they were made by chemists, unknown and unglorified. Even those far-flung billboards, the banners of Mr. Jones's gallant crusade—their text was written by forty-a-week copywriters, their pictures—their very terrible pictures—painted by patient hacks, and the basic idea, of having billboards, came not from the passionate brain of Mr. Jones but was cautiously worked out, on quite routine and unromantic lines, by hesitating persons in an advertising agency.

And it is these workmen, chemists, hacks, who are likely to be eager about beauty, courageous in politics—Moon-Calves—children of the new world. Mr. Jones himself—ah, that rare and daring and shining-new creator of industrial poetry, he votes the Republican ticket straight, he hates all labor unionism, he belongs to the Masons and the Presbyterian Church, his favorite author is Zane Grey, and in other particulars noted in this story, his private life seems scarce to mark him as the rough, ready, aspiring, iconoclastic, creative, courageous innovator his admirers paint him. He is a bagman. He is a pedlar. He is a shopkeeper. He is a camp-follower. He is a bag of aggressive wind.

America has taken to itself the credit of being the one pioneering nation of the world; it has thereby (these three hundred years now) excused all flabbiness of culture and harshness of manner and frantic oppression of critics. And, strangely, Europe has granted that assertion. Never an English author descends upon these palpitating and grateful shores without informing us that from our literature one expects only the burly power and clumsiness of ditch-diggers. We listen to him, and are made proud of the clumsiness and burliness—without quite going so far as to add also the power.

It is a national myth.

England has, in India, Africa, Canada, Australia, had quite as many new frontiers, done quite as much pioneering—and done it as bravely and as cruelly and as unscrupulously—as have we in pushing the western border from the Alleghenies to Honolulu. Thus France in Africa, Holland in the West Indies, Germany all over the world. And England has quite as many Rough Fellows as America. Lord Fisher criticizing the British navy in the tones of a tobacco-chewing trapper—is he so much less of a Rough Fellow and Pioneer and Innovator than the Harvard instructor reading Austin Dobson by candle-light? The silk salesman, crossing the Arizona desert—in a Pullman—is he so much bolder a ditch-digger than Ole Bill, the English Tommy?

A myth! America is no longer an isolated race of gallant Indian-slayers. It is a part of the world. Like every other nation, it is made up of both daring innovators and crusted crabs. Its literature and its J. J. Joneses are subject to the same rules as the literature and the bustling innumerous J. J. Joneses of England or Spain or Norway. Mr. Henry van Dyke is no newer or more pioneering than Mr. H. G. Wells—and subject to no more lenient rules or more provincial judgments.

Of this contradiction between pioneering myth and actual slackness, these Monarchs, these cities of 300,000 or so, are the best examples. Unfortunately American literature has discerned as types of communities only the larger or older cities—as New York, San Francisco, Richmond—and the villages, with nothing between. Yet there is a sort of community in between, an enormously important type—the city of a few hundred thousand, the metropolis that yet is a village, the world-center that yet is ruled by cautious villagers. Only Booth Tarkington, with his novels flavored by Indianapolis, and a few local celebrities eager to present the opulence of their several Monarchs, have dealt with these cities which, more than any New York, produce our wares and elect our presidents—and buy our books. Yet they are important enough to quarrel over—they are great enough to deserve the compliment of being told one's perception of the truth about them.

Just use "city man & country girl" How dif from N. Y.

To say that they are subject to the same rules as Munich or Florence does not at all mean that they are like Munich or Florence. They have grown so rapidly, they have been so innocent and so Republican and so Presbyterian and so altogether boosting and innocent, that they have produced a type of existence a little different from any other in the world. It may not continue to be so different—it some time may be subject also to fine tradition and the vision of quiet and honest work as against noisy selling of needless things—but this fineness it will not attain without self-study, and an admission that twenty-story buildings are not necessarily nobler than Notre Dame, and that the production of 19,000 motor cars a day does not of itself prove those cars to be better built than cars produced at one a day.

This foreshadowing of a future adoption of richer tradi-

tions does not, of course, mean at all that in the future these Monarchs are to be spiritually or physically like Munich or Florence. It is a paradox of psychology that it is precisely the richest philosophies, with the largest common fund of wisdom from all ages, which produce the most diverse and lovely products, while it is the thinner and hastier philosophies which produce the most standardized and boresomely similar products.

German Munich and Italian Florence are vastly and entertainingly different in all that counts—in passions, wines, aspirations, and furniture—for the reason that they have both digested and held and brilliantly changed a common wisdom of Plato and Shakespeare and Karl Marx. But German Milwaukee and Italian Hartford are uncomfortably alike because they have cast off all the hard-earned longings of mankind and joined in a common aspiration to be rich, notorious, and One Hundred Per Cent American.

It is this fact which is the second great feature of the American cities of 300,000—and as important as their other feature of unconquerable villageness. It is this fact which makes a novel that chanced to be local and concrete and true in regard to Omaha equally local and concrete and true regarding twenty other cities. Naturally, they are not all precisely alike. There is a difference resulting from situation—from a background of hills or plain, of river or seacoast; a difference from the products of the back-country—iron, wheat, cotton; a distinct difference from the various ages—the difference between Seattle and Charleston.

But these differences have for a long time now tended to decrease, so powerful is our faith in standardization. When a new hotel, factory, house, garage, motion-picture theater, row of shops, church, or synagogue is erected in gray Charleston, rambling New Orleans, or San Francisco of the '49ers, that structure is precisely, to the last column of reinforced concrete and the last decorative tile, the same as a parallel structure in the new cities of Portland or Kansas City. And the souls of those structures—the hospitality of the hotels, the mechanical methods in the garages, the minutest wording of the sermons in the churches—are increasingly as standardized as the shells.

It would not be possible to write a novel which would in every line be equally true to Munich and Florence. Despite the fundamental hungers equally true to all human beings, despite the similarity of manners and conversation in the layer of society which contentedly travels all over the world, despite the like interest of kissing at Fiesole and at Gansedorf, so vastly and subtly are the differences in every outward aspect, every detail of artistic aspiration and national pride and hope, that the two cities seem to belong to two different planets.

But Hartford and Milwaukee—the citizens of those two distant cities go to the same offices, speak the same patois on the same telephones, go to the same lunch and the same athletic clubs, etc., etc., etc.

Novel unlike M. St. cf Carol [Kennicott] on standardized life in U. S.

The test of the sameness is in the people. If you were by magic taken instantly to any city of over 80,000 in the United States and set down in the business center, in a block, say, with a new hotel, a new motion-picture theater, and a line of newish shops, not three hours of the intensest study of the passing people—men on business errands, messenger boys, women shopping, pool-room idlers—would indicate in what city, indeed in what part of the country, you were. Only by traveling to the outskirts and discovering mountains or ocean or wheat fields, and perhaps Negro shanties, Mexican adobes, or German breweries, would you begin to get a clue—and these diverse clues lessen each year. They know it not but all these bright women and pompous men are in uniforms, under the discipline of a belligerent service, as firmly as any soldier in khaki. For those that like it—that is what they like; but there are those of us who hesitated about being drafted into the army of complacency. (pp. 6-13)

> *Sinclair Lewis, "Unpublished Introduction to 'Babbitt',"* in The Merrill Studies in Babbitt, *edited by Martin Light, Charles E. Merrill Publishing Company, 1971, pp. 6-13.*

Ludwig Lewisohn   (essay date 1922)

[*A German-born American novelist and critic, Lewisohn was considered an authority on German literature, and his translations of Gerhart Hauptmann, Rainer Maria Rilke, and Jakob Wassermann are widely respected. In the following essay, Lewisohn evaluates the principal thematic and stylistic features of* Babbitt.]

With one accord both the simple and the sophisticated will ask at once: Is *Babbitt* as good as *Main Street*? There need be no hesitation in answering: it is better. There is a higher concentration of substance, a more scrupulous testing of style, the rhythm of life and of the form used as symbol are felt to be identical. Unwary readers will think a good deal of *Babbitt* raw material and use the limp word "photographic." Nothing, on the contrary, is more remarkable than the way in which Mr. Lewis has produced a perfect illusion of reality by letting the creative imagination select and mold and guide and lift the vast mass of observation which must be his. A central and controlling intention, partly artistic, partly intellectual, has worked from within outward to create the picture and the symbol, the thing shown and the thing to be shown forth as one. A precious example of Mr. Lewis's method is the annual address delivered by George F. Babbitt before the Real Estate Board of the city of Zenith. No booster or Rotarian ever made such a speech. But it is the speech that every booster and Rotarian has made in his dreams. It is the essence of Rotarianism thrice purified by the ironic vision of a creative mind. It is Rotarianism made eternal and perfect for our delectation and the terror and laughter of posterity.

From the small town Mr. Lewis has proceeded to the typical American city, from quietness, rudeness, and bickering to the granite arched and nickel-plated splendors of sound business, great hotels, cottage-colonies, boulevard systems, and up-to-date offices. He gives us the visible image of Zenith; he gives us the noise, the hustle, the glare; beneath it—buried deep and voluntarily—he shows us the helpless hush, the spiritual stagnancy, the dimness and confusion. Babbitt is himself and a symbol and also a symbol of his city. His life is speed without aim, matter without form, activity without desire. Activity without desire! It was Lee Randon's trouble in Hergesheimer's story. It

is the deep trouble of poor George Babbitt. With a forlorn cheerfulness he says, at the end of things, to his son: "Practically I've never done a single thing I've wanted to in my whole life!" A mechanical civilization and a system of morals with which the will can no longer identify itself—these forces move on of their own impetus. They are implicated with this economic structure and threaten the dissenter with exile and hunger. Thus life is lived by a fundamental fear. Babbitt, for all his joviality and bluster, is a creature of fear. He fears his business associates, his friends, his political representatives, his wife. He fears for his business which gives him prosperity without wealth, for his home that gives him order without comfort, for domestic affections that keep out forlornness but do not warm his soul. He has never done what he wanted to do; he possesses nothing that he truly wants. His friend, Paul Riesling, a more sensitive spirit, is destroyed by the conflict. Fear drives Babbitt back from his timid wanderings to the celebration of things as, for him, they are.

This somber ground-work of the story is implicit in every line of the book. It is implicit only. The surface is all movement and ironic gayety, marvelously authentic talk and vivid people. Interpretation is limited to a phrase or an adjective. But from the few scenes and phrases that illustrate the relations of George Babbitt and his wife, a history of the inner truth of a typical American marriage could be developed. And from that one may derive the story of poor, ruffled Tanis and of the girl in the manicure shop; and from the fate of Paul and Zilla a good deal is to be inferred concerning the story of strange religious movements in America, and from the political scenes and the strike the character of our governmental methods and forces.

This account of *Babbitt* has purposely omitted those elements in the book that will not lack public appreciation. There is an exactness and ironic felicity in the rendering of the surface of American life that is astounding. The various meetings and banquets, especially the gathering of the alumni of the State University, the business conferences, the dispiriting social experiments, the advertisements of Frick, the scenes at the Athletic Club, the ecclesiastical activities of Dr. Drew—all these are in no need of praise. Nor is Mr. Lewis's command of the American idiom which, granting a necessary symbolic concentration and hence exaggeration, is simply consummate. But all these things could be found in a brilliant *feuilleton* or sketch. What gives *Babbitt* its artistic value is Mr. Lewis's profound recognition that these noisy lives are lived by fear and without desire. Under his virtuosity is his sense of the tragic in life, his steady closeness to those permanent values by which he condemns the bright and busy scene he delineates. It would be futile to attempt to inquire into the absolute aesthetic value of such a book as *Babbitt,* nor would the inquiry be important. What is certain is that to us the book represents a deed of high cultural significance and that the future historian of American civilization will turn to it with infinite profit, with mingled amusement, astonishment, and pity. (pp. 284-85)

> *Ludwig Lewisohn, in a review of "Babbitt," in* The Nation, *New York, Vol. CXV, No. 2985, September 20, 1922, pp. 284-85.*

Upton Sinclair   (essay date 1922)

[*An American novelist, dramatist, journalist, and essayist, Sinclair was a prolific writer who is most famous for* The Jungle *(1906), a novel that portrays the unjust labor practices, filth, and horrifying conditions of Chicago's meat-processing industry, and which prompted passage of the Pure Food and Drug Act of 1906. A lifelong, outspoken socialist, Sinclair addressed the excesses of capitalist society in most of his works and demanded, in his critical theory, the subservience of art to social change. In the following essay, Sinclair affirms the effectiveness of* Babbitt's *damning social satire of America's commercial classes.*]

Fifteen years ago I ran a Socialist colony for six months, and there turned up at the place two runaway students from Yale, who applied for the job of furnacemen, and general utility men. I don't know whether they came to us because they were Socialists, or whether we made them Socialists. One of them was a lanky redheaded youth by the name of Sinclair Lewis, conveniently shortened to Hal. He turned into a popular novelist of the *Saturday Evening Post* variety, and for a long time I wondered where the Socialism had gone to. Apparently it was fermenting inside, because Lewis kicked over the traces and wrote a novel to suit himself, and it proved the biggest success of our time. I reviewed it in these columns a couple of years ago—*Main Street.*

The book brought its author a fortune, and I wondered if this was going to spoil him. Now I am ready to get out in the middle of the street and shout hurrah, for America's most popular novelist has just sent me his new book, and it is a scream. I am here to enter my prediction that it will be the most talked about and the most read novel which has been published in this country in my life-time. Incidentally it is the most effective piece of social satire that America has yet produced, and you understand this is something hard for me to say, because I have been trying as hard as I know how for the past twenty years to do the same thing myself. The trouble with me is I hate the commercial classes so heartily that I can't bring myself to get inside their skins, but I suppose that Lewis is a little gayer by nature than I am, and he has done it. I am just as glad as if I had written the book myself, because I have been waiting a long time for somebody else to come along and do a part of the job, and here he is!

This time the scene of the story is a medium-sized American city; the title of the book is *Babbitt,* and that is the name of a prominent and successful real estate operator, who combines in himself all the deliciously absurd and unspeakably loathsome qualities of the "booster" and the "go-getter." Never has there been such a mass of ridicule. I found myself thinking, as I read the book, what a ghastly job it must have been to associate with those people long enough to gather all the minute details about their lives, their homes, their conversations and their ideas about life. I spent six or seven weeks in the Chicago stock-yards for *The Jungle,* but I believe I would rather spend six or seven years there than spend six or seven days in the environment of *Babbitt.*

Everything is here; Babbitt's home, and his wife and children, his automobiles and his dinner parties, his "booster" clubs and his civic reform societies and his churches. Some of it is so funny that it begins to seem like caricature; but then you stop and ask yourself, is it possible to caricature commercial America?

Anyhow, Babbitt is very fond of talking, and he delivers his ideas on every subject to everybody who can be got to listen. For example, he has ideas on the subject of labor unions; he thinks they should be crushed, and he thinks that in order to crush them business men ought to join the Chamber of Commerce, and if they don't join, they should be compelled to join! The book is a series of amusing contrasts such as that. We see Babbitt going in with the street-car crowd, to put through a series of crooked deals where they make a lot of money by selling real estate secretly to their own company. Babbitt "gets his," of course, and he is perfectly satisfied and happy, only just about that time a terrible thing happens; he discovers that one of his real estate salesmen has been doing something dishonest! Babbitt is terribly excited, and we attend the scene while he gives this salesman a lecture on morality.

Babbitt's wife is tremendously anxious to "rise in society," and Babbitt goes to his old college reunion in order to meet a rich banker, who was a college chum. He insists and urges until the rich banker consents to bring his wife to a dinner party at Babbitt's home; then the family labors for a week in tremendous excitement to prepare a great feast, and the banker and his wife come, and are bored to death, and they don't invite the Babbitts to dinner in return, and poor Mrs. Babbitt cries herself to sleep. Babbitt decides that these college reunions don't pay, because as a result of going to this one he got in touch with a former classmate who has made a failure of life, a poor wretch who fastens on to him, and insists that Babbitt and his wife shall come to a dinner party at this poor wretch's home. Babbitt and his wife try to get out of it, but the wretch insists, and so they go and are bored to death, and they don't invite the poor wretch and his wife in return. And we see Babbitt and his wife reproducing in every detail the actions and conversations of the banker and his wife, who were bored to death by the Babbitts.

I am sorry to have to praise this book so much, because, as it happens, it comes out one day ahead of my own novel, *They Call Me Carpenter,* and I am hoping that some of you will save a part of your money to buy a copy of that! (pp. 28-30)

Upton Sinclair, "Standardized America," in The Merrill Studies in Babbitt, *edited by Martin Light, Charles E. Merrill Publishing Company, 1971, pp. 28-30.*

Robert Littell   (essay date 1922)

[*Littell was an American critic, journalist, and author. During the 1920s he worked as an associate editor of the* New Republic *and as a drama critic and columnist for the* New York Evening Post *and the* New York World. *In 1927 Littell began a long association with* Reader's Digest, *becoming senior editor of that publication in 1942. In the following essay, he argues that the severity of Lewis's satire in* Babbitt *trivializes the novel's characterizations.*]

It was not as a novel that *Main Street* was interesting, because a novel is a picture of life and of people, and life is a whole and people have three dimensions, plus an inscrutable core of individuality about which their recreator in fiction must not seem to have too complete a knowledge if he wishes them to appear real. Sinclair Lewis was almost always in visible and tyrannical possession of his characters' souls: they spoke, but how obviously at his prompting; they moved, but how plainly because he pulled the strings. Only occasionally—with Dr. Kennicott—did he achieve the difficult art of not seeming to be inside a character's head, of seeming to let him go his own way. Something mattered to him more than people: the trivial and repressive mind of a small town, the fungus of dullness, venom and misunderstanding which grows over ideals and aspirations and stifles them.

But Mr. Lewis did not give us a rounded picture of this, because he was more bent on destroying than describing. All through *Main Street*—the same is true of *Babbitt*—his dislike for his subject outstripped his interest in it, and gave the book its predominating flavor, which was acid.

Why then does *Main Street* remain a significant book, and one that Americans will probably remember for some time? Isn't it mostly because so many people bought it that we realized for the first time that as a nation we were beginning to become self-conscious? If *Main Street* lives, it will probably be not as a novel but as an incident in American life.

Main Street was a complaint, *Babbitt* is an indictment. The scene is shifted from a small town to a city. And in a city the dragon which rules over a small town vaguely, if really enough, becomes an army of dragons with a lot of heads, and the dragons all have names and live in identifiable caves, and Mr. Lewis explores these caves and calls the dragons by their real names. The Boosters' Club, the Rotary Club, the Y. M. C. A., the Church, the newspaper, the bank, the street railway, the Realtors' Association, these are the dragons who conspire to make and keep George F. Babbitt, an ordinary, decent-hearted, soft, average, mediocre American business man, a slave to their own vulgar, noisy, cheap, insincere, illiterate standards of life, by offering him their usual rewards of specious good-fellowship, an ugly but comfortable home, an automobile, and a perishable popularity.

While Mr. Lewis undoubtedly has an eye—and in several places a very warm heart—for Babbitt's emotional travails, his gnawing doubts, his booms of confidence, the shabby emotional back-alleys in which he seeks release from an intolerable struggle, Mr. Lewis's chief effort is going after the scalps of the dragons. This he achieves with enormous success. I don't believe anyone has his particular talent for describing the relentless gladhandedness of the lunchers at the Athletic Club of Zenith, nor the grotesque, silly emptiness and self-conceit of the Realtors' delegations as they assemble at the railway station. Mr. Lewis does this sort of thing extraordinarily well, though one wonders why one so seldom laughs at these caricatures, until one notices that he himself is not so much laughing at these ridiculous people as trying with all his might to kick the life out of them. He enjoys mimicking them so hugely that he does it a great deal too much, and the people whose speech he mimics seem all to draw their talk from the same source. It is an inexhaustible source: page after page of the book is spread thick with the same composite of slang, repetition, triviality and crude generalization.

In *Main Street* there was the same font of slangy, trivial, repetitious speech used indiscriminately by most of the characters. In *Babbitt* a great deal more of the talk is about general ideas. The boosting business man's ideas about labor, freedom, politics are in the lime-light, and Mr. Lewis is concerned in showing us over and over again how undigested, dogmatic but above all how illiberal they are. A defence of a liberal point of view by ridicule and savage attack on its opposite can almost be said to be the undercurrent of *Babbitt.* This shows us again how much more specific is Mr. Lewis's second tirade against our society.

The moral pointed out in *Main Street* was fairly vague: You cannot live in a small town and not be emotionally squashed. *Babbitt's* moral is more precise; Mr. Lewis has passed from emotional ground to somewhere nearer politics. If you are a business man in a large town you cannot try to be liberal and survive. Such and such dragons, who exist in actual life, will certainly step on you.

The dragons are the household gods of the big city, which is the home of people who have arrived. The ambition of the small town citizen is to leave its restraint. It is much easier to appeal to his dissatisfaction than it is to try to tell the large city's booster that his gods are devils, especially if you indict his gods as specifically as Mr. Lewis has done. Will the readers he is aiming at in Babbitt resent the attack more than the Main Streeters did? It will be interesting to see.

Babbitt is hideously true to the worst things in America. The fact that it is not the whole truth makes it not so much a novel as a terribly damaging attack on nearly all of our worst faults, and a brilliant piece of propaganda for some future America which will be rid of them. To destroy evil it isolates evil: that is not fiction. It is rather a contribution to the prevailing mood, among intellectuals. There's a lot more to America, even that part of her next door to the Boosters' Club, than the crude and frantic gospel of the Boosters. There's a rich, easy-going humor, a genuine if not always effective kindliness, intimately mixed with the Booster streak. Isn't Mr. Lewis, by contrast with a writer interested in giving us characters of such a genuine American admixture, mentally almost an exile from America?

Does he not reject us? Is he not unwilling to be as interested in us, all of us and every part of us, as if we were children from whom no moral responsibility for the state of the society they live in can be expected? I wonder if he would be interested in writing about a community whose members he felt to be irresponsible, though they were human beings none the less. I suspect that he is more interested in motives than in people. I feel, in both *Main Street* and *Babbitt,* that what most prevents his characters from becoming real is his ineradicable tendency to entertain moral judgments about them—though I usually agree with those moral judgments. The mood of a novelist, if not one of love alone, should at least be odi et amo. I feel that Mr. Lewis is saying odi nearly all the time.

Robert Littell, in a review of "Babbitt," in The New Republic, *Vol. XXXII, No. 409, October 4, 1922, p. 152.*

Rebecca West (essay date 1922)

[*West is considered one of the foremost English novelists and critics to write during the twentieth century. Her early criticism was noted for its militantly feminist stance and its reflection of her Fabian socialist concerns. Her first novel,* The Return of the Soldier *(1918), evidences a concern that entered into much of her later work—the psychology of the individual. West's greatest works include* The Meaning of Treason *(1947), which analyzes the motives of Britain's wartime traitors—notably, William Joyce ("Lord Haw-Haw")—and* Black Lamb and Grey Falcon *(1942), a record of the author's 1937 journey through Yugoslavia. West's literary criticism is noted for its wit, aversion to cant, and perceptiveness. In the following essay, West affirms the brilliance of* Babbitt's *social satire.*]

Main Street was a good book. One was as glad that it attained the incredibly tremendous triumph of being an American bestseller as one might be when a thoroughly nice girl wins the Calcutta Sweepstake. But on reading *Main Street* one did not in the least feel as if one were dancing round a bonfire. Heat and light and exhilaration were foreign to the hour. It was a sincere, competent, informative, even occasionally passionate piece of writing, but it had not that something extra and above the logical treatment of its subject—that "peacock's feather in the cap," as Yeats has called it—which makes the work of art. Moreover, it had not much in it of its author's own quality, and that was felt as a serious deprivation by those who were acquainted with Mr. Lewis and his literary past, by those who knew, for example, of the entertaining investigation into spiritualism he conducted on behalf of one of the American magazines. (During the course of this, swathing with seriousness a remarkable personal appearance which bears a strong resemblance to that of Mr. George Grossmith, but made more glorious with red hair, he sat down beside many mediums and asked chokingly for a message from his "dear friend, Mr. H. G. Wells, the English novelist, who recently passed over"; and usually got one.) But these deficiencies are rectified in *Babbitt.* It has that something extra, over and above, which makes the work of art, and it is signed in every line with the unique personality of the writer. It is saturated with America's vitality which makes one obey the rhythms of its dance music, which gives unlimited power over audiences to their actresses whether they be artistically dog-lazy like Ethel Levey, or negligible like Peggy O'Neill. And combined with this, Mr. Lewis has an individual gift of humour, a curiously sage devotion to craftsmanship, and a poetic passion for his own, new country.

To write satire is to perform a miracle. One must hate the world so much that one's hatred strikes sparks, but one must hate it only because it disappoints one's invincible love of it; one must write in denunciation of ugliness and put the thing down in unmistakable black and white, yet keep this, as all written things, within the sphere of beauty. But Mr. Lewis has been equal to these things. He writes of vulgar Zenith City and its vulgar children, yet never writes a vulgar line. He is merciless to George F. Babbitt, that standardised child of that standardised city, with his pad-cheeks and his puffy hands, his hypocrisy and his ignorance, his dishonesty and his timid sensualities; and he reveals him lovable and pitiable, a strayed soul disconso-

late through frustrated desires for honour and beauty. He can flame into transports of exasperation with the religion of business and its paunchy priesthood—marvellous transports these are, for what we have here is the Celt getting angry with the Englishman. For Zenith City and Babbitt are amazingly English. They represent that section of America which seems the least affected by the Latin and Jewish and Celtic leavens; the resemblance of kinship is patent, even blatant. Oh, never star was lost here but it rose afar! Look West where whole new thousands are! In Zenith City what Leverhulme! And the Celt in the person of Mr. Lewis cannot bear it. Vindictively he reports their flat, endlessly repetitive, excessively and simultaneously ignorant and sophisticated conversation at dinner parties and in smoking-cars. He snatches out of the paper enraged parodies of the *Poemulations* they read instead of poetry—by T. Cholmondeley Frink, who was not only the author of *Poemulations,* which, syndicated daily in sixty-seven leading newspapers, gave him one of the largest audiences of any poet in the world, but also an optimistic lecturer and the creator of "Ads. that Add." *"I sat alone and groused and thunk, and scratched my head and sighed and wunk and groaned. There still are boobs, alack, who'd like the old time gin-mill back; that den, that makes a sage a loon, the vile and smelly old saloon! I'll never miss their poison booze, whilst I the bubbling spring can use, that leaves my head at merry morn as clear as any babe new-born!"* He describes with deadly malice the proceedings at the lunch of the Zenith Boosters' Club. "The International Organisation of Boosters' Clubs has become a world-force for optimism, manly pleasantry, and good business." Its members all wore a button marked "Boosters—Pep!" At each place at the lunch-table, on the famous day when George F. Babbitt was elected Vice-President, was laid a present, a card printed in artistic red and black:

SERVICE AND BOOSTERISM.

Service finds its finest opportunity and development only in its broadest and deepest application and the consideration of its perpetual action upon reaction. I believe the highest type of Service, like the most progressive tenets of ethics, senses unceasingly and is motived by active adherence and loyalty to that which is the essential principle of Boosterism—Good Citizenship in all its factors and aspects.

DAD PETERSEN.

Compliments of Dadbury Petersen Advertising Corp.

"Ads not Fads at Dads."

"The Boosters all read Mr. Petersen's aphorism and said they understood it perfectly."

Yet behind all this is a truth. There is something happening in among these hustling congregations of fat and absurd men. The present condition of George F. Babbitt may be discomfortable. Loathing at the smooth surface of his standardised life, destitute of interstices that might admit romance, may move him to vain and painful flights towards the promise of light; to his comical attempts to find spiritual comfort in the Chatham Street Presbyterian Church; to his efforts to make a synthetic substitute for love out of the kittenish contacts of Mrs. Janis Judique. ("And shall I call you George? Don't you think it's awfully nice when two people have so much—what shall I say?—analysis that they can discard all these conventions and understand each other and become acquainted right away, like ships that pass in the night?") Little as he has, he yet possesses a promise. The value of that possession can be estimated by comparing Babbitt with his English analogue, Sir Gerald Doak, whom Mr. Lewis shows, touring the States in a state of panic because a title bought by the accumulations of industry in Nottingham brings on him the attentions of earnest hostesses who (misled by their conception of the British aristocracy) talk to him about polo and the galleries of Florence. Paunch for paunch these two sound business men seem much the same. But there is for Babbitt a certain advantage; or perhaps, in the transitional and blundering state of affairs revealed in this book, it should be called a certain opportunity. He moves in a setting so vast and so magnificent that surely it must ultimately dictate vastness and magnificence to the action it contains. There are in this volume a few pages, which must be counted among the masterpieces of satire; they profess to give a verbatim report of the speech delivered by Mr. George F. Babbitt at the Annual Dinner of The Zenith Real Estate Board. In it Mr. Lewis' exasperation rises to the pitch of genius. It dances on the chest of Babbitt's silly standardised self and his silly standardised world. There is one absurd passage, when Babbitt cries:

> "With all modesty, I want to stand up here as a representative business-man and gently whisper, 'Here's our kind of folks! Here's the specifications of the standardised American Citizen! Here's the new generation of Americans: fellows with hair on their chests and smiles in their eyes and adding machines in their offices. . . . So! In my clumsy way I have tried to sketch the Real He-man, the fellow with Zip and Bang! And it's because Zenith has so large a proportion of such men, that it's the most stable, the greatest of our cities. New York also has its thousands of Real Folks, but New York is cursed with unnumbered foreigners. So are Chicago and San Francisco. Oh, we have a golden roster of cities—Detroit and Cleveland with their renowned factories. Cincinnati with its great machine-tool and soap products, Pittsburgh and Birmingham with their steel, Kansas City and Minneapolis and Omaha that open their bountiful gates on the bosom of the oceanlike wheatlands, and countless other magnificent sister-cities, for by the last census, there were no less than sixty-eight glorious American burgs with a population of over one hundred thousand! And all these cities stand together for power and purity, and against foreign ideas and communism. Atlanta with Hartford, Rochester with Denver, Milwaukee with Indianapolis, Los Angeles with Scranton, Portland, Maine, with Portland, Oregon. A good live-wire from Baltimore or Seattle or Duluth is the twin brother of every like fellow booster from Buffalo or Akron, Forth Worth or Oskaloosa!"

It is a bonehead Walt Whitman speaking. Stuffed like a Christmas goose as Babbitt is, with silly films, silly newspapers, silly talk, silly oratory, there has yet struck him the majestic creativeness of his own country, its miraculous power to bear and nourish without end countless multitudes of men and women. He is so silly, so ill-educated (though as he says, "the State University is my own Alma Mater, and I am proud to be known as an alumni") that

he prefers to think of it bearing and nourishing countless multitudes of featureless standardised Regular Guys. But there is in these people a vitality so intense that it must eventually bolt with them and land them willy-nilly into the sphere of intelligence; and this immense commercial machine will become the instrument of their aspiration.

> Before he followed his wife, Babbitt stood at the westernmost window of their room. This residential settlement, Floral Heights, was on a rise; and though the centre of the city was three miles away—Zenith had between three and four hundred thousand inhabitants now—he could see the top of the Second National Tower, an Indiana limestone building of thirty-five storeys.
>
> Its shining wall rose against April sky to a simple cornice like a streak of white fire. Integrity was in the tower, and decision. It bore its strength lightly as a tall soldier. As Babbitt stared, the nervousness was soothed from his face, his slack chin lifted in reverence. All he articulated was, "That's one lovely sight!" but he was inspired by the rhythm of the city; his love of it renewed. He beheld the tower as a temple-spire of the religion of business, a faith passionate, exalted, surpassing common men; and as he clumped down to breakfast he whistled the ballad, "Oh, by gee, by gosh, by jingo," as though it were a hymn melancholy and noble.

(pp. 78, 80)

Rebecca West, "Notes on Novels," in New Statesman, *Vol. XX, No. 497, October 21, 1922, pp. 78, 80.*

Americanus   (essay date 1922)

[*In the following excerpt, Americanus praises the acuity of Lewis's observations of the middle-class American milieu.*]

To consider first the sociological aspect of *Babbitt,* it looks as though Mr. Lewis had sent this book to be a corroboratory illustration of much that Mr. Waldo Frank said in *The New America.* With perfect realism, which is a thing quite distinct from verisimilitude, Mr. Lewis has told the story "of a man, his family, and his one great friendship." In so doing, he has limned the spiritual state of the bulk of America. George F. Babbitt is typical of the nationally adolescent state of mind which appears between the complete extraversion of the pioneer and the articulate consciousness of an established culture. Babbitt has material prosperity and the external interest of his business, but he is not happy. He is restless with a vague sense of the futility of his existence and all the things he is expected to believe are worth while. The reason for his restlessness he does not see. The mantle of the pioneer has fallen upon him and covered his eyes. The traditions of repression are still too strong to be broken, for they have the reinforcement of the herd's approbation. And the penalty exacted by the herd for transgression is, as this book clearly shows, destruction. Although the herd is composed of restless beings like Babbitt himself, there is among them still too much work to be done, too much muscular activity to be gone through with, to admit of any real experience, for experience is an intensely personal thing and demands time and meditation.

This restlessness, this sense of the unsatisfactoriness of

life, is not evenly spread over the population, nor is it always unrecognized. We catch glimpses in Mr. Lewis's book of an extremely complacent, nay, self-satisfied group of wealthy and atrophied tyrants who brood heavily over the rest of the population. And at the other extreme, Mr. Lewis gives us a peep at the small group of the younger generation which is actively revolting against the pioneer spirit. But hear the restlessness of the great body of the middle class expressed in the words of Babbitt's friend:—

> "I bet if you could cut into their heads [the men he and Babbitt know] you'd find that one-third of 'em are sure-enough satisfied with their wives and kids and friends and their offices; and one-third feel kind of restless but won't admit it; and one-third are miserable and know it. They hate the whole peppy, boosting, go-ahead game, and they're bored by their wives and think their families are fools—at least, when they come to forty or forty-five they're bored—and they hate business, and they'd go——. Why do you suppose there's so many 'mysterious' suicides? Why do you suppose so many Substantial Citizens jumped right into the war? Think it was all patriotism? . . . Good Lord, I don't know what 'rights' a man has! And I don't know the solution of boredom. If I did, I'd be the one philosopher that had a cure for living. But I do know that about ten times as many people find their lives dull, and unnecessarily dull, as ever admit it; and I do believe that if we busted out and admitted it sometimes, instead of being nice and patient and loyal for sixty years, and then nice and patient and dead for the rest of eternity, why, maybe, possibly we might make life more fun."

Babbitt himself is not so articulate. "Wish I'd been a pioneer, same as my Grand-dad," he says to himself, rather wistfully. "But then I wouldn't have a house like this. I——. Oh, gosh, *I don't* know!" Finally he admits to his son, "I've never done a single thing I've wanted to in my whole life! I don't know's I've accomplished anything except just get along. I figure out I've made about a quarter of an inch out of a possible hundred rods." In those words, Babbitt takes on the proportions of a tragic figure.

Main Street was rather the raw material for a novel; *Babbitt* is the finished product. The advance of the latter over the former is amazing. Only a few hardy souls ever reached the end of *Main Street* by legitimate means. But there is no such trouble with *Babbitt*. While it is by no means "light reading," the interest does not flag. And this is rather a triumph, for *Babbitt* is wholly made up of the dull and inept events in the everyday life of a mediocrity.

Main Street was too much a mere collection of material, a cataloguing of facts. There was almost nothing there beyond those things which made us acquainted with the *milieu,* which let us see, hear, smell and feel it. But a work of art, to be one, to hold us and to satisfy our aesthetic emotions, must make us take up an attitude toward what it portrays. We must be pleased or displeased with it; afraid of it or curious about it. But we must also desire to possess it, or strive to alter it in some way. The artist in making his synthesis must balance these three elements with the utmost care. He may emphasize one element to produce the effect he desires to make upon the beholder, but he must maintain his balance with the other two. This Mr. Lewis did not do in *Main Street,* but in *Babbitt* he has managed it. Possibly this is because he is surer in his

own mind now what his attitude is toward American life in general and toward the *milieu* he portrays in particular. At any rate, none of the details in *Babbitt* is insignificant. Moreover, his powers of observation and analysis have developed wonderfully, and he has learned the art of satire. He has learned it to perfection. We feel now that his hate is the flame which springs up out of the fire of a deep and understanding affection. This is further vouched for by the fact that he has found his sense of humour again. The Messianic delusion has passed, and he can view the scene with equanimity. He has grown out of vituperation into real criticism. Moreover, he is now dealing more with human problems than with the difficulties of environment. Consequently, although he is still quintessentially American, his work begins to take on a more universal significance. Mr. Lewis is one of the best of the younger generation of American writers who are proving so ably the growing articulateness of their country. (p. 929)

> Americanus, *"Georgie from Main Street," in* The Spectator, *Vol. 129, No. 4929, December 16, 1922, pp. 928-29.*

Stuart P. Sherman   (essay date 1922)

[*In the following excerpt from a pamphlet commissioned by Lewis's publishers to enhance his critical reputation, Sherman presents* Babbitt *as a pure extension of* Main Street's *negative appraisal of American life, faulting* Babbitt *in comparison to its predecessor, however, for its exclusion of any redeeming values.*]

Babbitt is not a sequel to *Main Street* but a parallel and coordinate extension. It is a picture of contemporary American society not in the small towns and villages but in the cities of some numerical pretentions. Zenith, the prosperous middle-western city of 350,000, in which George F. Babbitt, the prosperous "realtor" establishes himself on Floral Heights, is inhabited largely by people who had in their youth ambition enough to get up and get out of the "hick burgs". They flatter themselves that, leaving behind them all the elements that constituted the dinginess and dreariness of Gopher Prairie, they have pressed forward to the mark of the high calling of hustling, right-thinking, forward-looking boosters, good-fellows, and 100% Americans. For Iron they have substituted copper sinks in the kitchen; for the Saturday night tubbing, the daily bath; for golden-oak, near-mahogany; for the Ford the limousine; for the dirty, ramshackle, huddle of shops and visibly suspended tobacco-chewing shopkeepers blocks of aspiring office buildings and hotels with manicure girls attending in the Pompeian Barber Shop; for the somnolent barn-like church an up-to-date competitive "community centre" with press-agents, military organization, and pep-masters; for cigars and poker in the parlor with Sam Clark and "the boys" monogrammed cigarettes and mixed auction bridge at the country club; for "open meetings" of the Thanatopsis society week-end parties with prohibition anecdotes and cocktails.

With comprehensive and mordant notation of detail coupled with a formidable power of generalization, Mr. Lewis shows how the city attempts to solve the problem of the small town. Between Gopher Prairie and Zenith, there is the material progress of a generation—a long march in America. But between Gopher Prairie and Zenith, civilization, according to this record,—civilization, judged by the decisive tests—has not advanced an inch. The quantity of human happiness has not increased, nor has its quality improved. The people are not more open-minded, nor more upright, nor more beautiful, nor more interesting. This is not "the story of Carol", and the unrest among young women, which she so vividly illustrated, finds here no adequate representative. The "leading lady" does not lead. Myra Babbitt, Mrs. George F., is a woman, "definitely mature", who has, in a dull fashion, accepted her universe: "She was a good woman, a kind woman, a diligent woman, but no one, save perhaps Tinka her ten-year old, was at all interested in her or entirely aware that she was alive"—a tragical sentence, applicable enough to the average middle-class American woman of forty. But this is primarily a story of a man's unrest. This is the story of Babbitt; the graduate of a state university, the "swaddled American husband", the prosperous American broker, the Rotarian, the leading citizen, the consequence and cause of civilization as it exists in Zenith, and the embodiment of nearly all its vices and its virtues.

Babbitt is a more important character than Dr. Kennicott in that he is more nearly ubiquitous. Less trustworthy as a man, he will perhaps be found more interesting as a "hero" because he has less of character and more of temperament. Unlike the Doctor, he is highly self-conscious, he has a "soft" streak, he is an egotist, and he is eager for the applause and admiration of men and women, not excluding his wife, for whom he feels an habitual tolerance, and including his stenographer, whom he wishes to impress as a "great man", and his manicurist, to whom he is willing, in relaxed and erratic moods, to appear as a person with possibilities of romance. In the morning Mr. Babbitt wears a well-made, well-pressed grey suit with white piping on the V of the vest. In the evening he wears, when there is important company, a "Tuxedo" which Mrs. Babbitt vainly insists that he should call a "dinner-jacket"— that is the precise "note" of their social status. He is diligent in business and not more crooked than William Washington Eathorne, President of the First State Bank, a chilly old gentleman who lives in an old brick house of the Civil War period, and who impresses Babbitt as "the real thing" by quietly ringing for a whiskey toddy, instead of mooing and baying around the subject, as in his own circle is the custom when the host produces something illicit from the ice-box.

This is one of the many incidents by which Mr. Lewis illustrates the peculiar pathos of his hero's situation. With all that the civilization of Zenith can offer at his disposal, Babbitt is restless and unsatisfied. He has money enough, things enough, physical comforts enough. He has, like great numbers of our prosperous middle-class, reached the point where the multiplication of things gives no addition of content. There is a gnawing hunger in him but he can think of nothing that he wants to eat. In a vague way he desires "the right thing" for himself, for his family, for his community; but there is no authoritative standard, there is no one to tell him, there is nothing in the society of Zenith to show him by example, what the "real right thing" is. Consequently, in the restlessness of satiety and inner boredom, Babbitt unintelligently and unimaginatively gropes for his missing felicity in unfruitful directions: in imitating Mr. Eathorne, in speechmaking and prominence at business men's conventions, in running off to the Maine woods where one can wear old clothes and chew tobacco and "cuss" in freedom, and finally in various experiments in marital infidelity. But from all these ventures he returns with the taste of sand and ashes in his mouth. And the only gleam that lights the final pages of the book is his indulgent humor towards his children, one of whom is studying the drama and labor statistics, while the other, his son, has just revealed his secret off-hand marriage. To the boy he says:

> "Practically I've never done a single thing I've wanted to in my whole life. I don't know's I've accomplished anything except just get along. . . . Well, maybe you'll carry things on further. I don't know. But I do get a kind of sneaking pleasure out of the fact that you knew what you wanted to do and did it. Well, those folks in there will try to bully you, and tame you down. Tell 'em to go to the devil! I'll back you. Take your factory job, if you want to. Don't be scared of the family. No, nor all of Zenith. Nor of yourself, the way I've been. Go ahead, old man! The world is yours!"

I have no high expectation regarding Babbitt's son. He gives as little promise as his father of capacity for finding delight in the things of the mind. The daughter may conceivably become an interesting individual, perhaps only an intense and difficult one.

Babbitt is not a representation of the highest American standards of morals and manners. But neither is *The Rise of Silas Lapham* nor *Huckleberry Finn* nor Henry James's *The American.* Neither is *Vanity Fair* a representation of the highest standards of morals and manners in England, nor is *David Copperfield,* nor *Pride and Prejudice.* It is not the business of the realistic novelist nor dramatist, to confine his studies to those small and isolated spots in which the society of his contemporaries approaches perfection. To propose such an aim is absurd. A jury of award which accepted it would at once be obliged to exclude from its consideration practically everything that is worth considering. In the age of Elizabeth the acceptance of such an aim would have excluded from consideration the chief tragedies of Shakespeare and all the comedies of Ben Jonson. The most important business of the capable painter of contemporary society from Balzac to the present day has been the portrayal of the great representative types. In an immense and motley democracy booming furiously through the stages of material progress, few of the great representative types know anything about the "highest standard of manners and morals in America".

All that we may fairly demand of our novelists—and it is a large demand—is that they themselves, as observers of the human spectacle, should be aware of this "highest standard", should paint their great representative types at a point of view at which the best society is at least within their vision. It is a large demand but it is a fair demand to make of a class of men who undertake to govern us through our imaginations. It is a fair demand to make of men whose profession involves a connoisseurship of truth and beauty. It is a necessary demand, if their criticism of life is to have any social value. *Vanity Fair,* for example, though it is for the most part a picture of a selfish and disagreeable world, is obviously written by a man who understands what an unselfish and agreeable world might be, while Mr. Dreiser's *Genius,* for another example, is a picture of a selfish and disagreeable world, written by a man incapable of conceiving anything else.

Now Mr. Lewis, with increasing clearness of apprehension and vitality of presentment has devoted himself to the portrayal of the representative. There is no denying the vigor or the representativeness of the types presented in *The Job, Main Street,* and *Babbitt.* Nor is there doubt in anyone's mind that Mr. Lewis's contemporary scene is drenched in irony and raked with satire. The one rather serious objection which one hears raised against his work is that the standards, the existence of which are implied in any consistently satiric picture of society,—the standards by which Mr. Lewis judges, for instance, Gopher Prairie and Zenith are not sufficiently in evidence. The publication of *Babbitt* is likely to increase the frequency of that objection; for while in *Main Street,* there are at least four persons, including Carol, with quite definite conceptions of what ought to be done to increase beauty and interest in Gopher Prairie, in *Babbitt* these quite definite improvements have been made, without essential increase of beauty or interest in the lives of the citizens; and no one in the book seems to understand what to do next. We are on the brink of a Tolstoian problem. The artistic charm and vivacity of this novel, to say nothing of its social stimulation, would have been heightened by somewhat freer employment of those devices of dramatic contrast of which Mr. Lewis is a master—by the introduction of some character or group capable of reflecting upon the Babbitts oblique rays from a social and personal felicity, more genuine, more inward than any of the summoned witnesses possesses. Eventually, if Mr. Lewis does not wish to pass for a hardened pessimist, he will have to produce a hero qualified to register in some fashion the results of his own quest for the desirable; he will have to give us his Portrait of a Lady, his Pendennis, his Warrington and his Colonel Newcome. Meanwhile I am very well content to applaud the valor of his progress through Vanity Fair. (pp. 15-20)

> Stuart P. Sherman, in his The Significance of Sinclair Lewis, *Harcourt Brace Jovanovich, 1922, 20 p.*

Charles A. Beard   (essay date 1928)

[*Beard was one of the most influential American historians of the early twentieth century. Through his numerous works he directed the course of historiography from the scientific formalism of his predecessors, who believed that natural law governs the course of history, toward the liberal reformism of the progressives, who viewed history as a record of social, economic, and intellectual choices made by individuals and groups, advocated political and social change based on their studies of the past, and thus sought to improve the future. Beard applied his reformist ideology to several areas of study, becoming widely recognized for his expertise in municipal government, educational development, and domestic and foreign policy. In his most famous and controversial work,* An Economic Interpretation of the Constitution of the United States, *he proposed the thesis that underlies most of his works: that America's past can be best interpreted through an examination of its economic forces. Although Beard's studies have been severely criticized for*

their economic bias, they have nevertheless exerted a profound influence on modern historical thought. In the following essay, Beard refutes the standard interpretation of Babbitt as the inevitable product of bourgeois materialism, arguing that cultural aspirations and mercantile interests are not necessarily antipodes.]

George F. Babbitt is certainly all dressed up. He has an automobile, a town house, a country house, a charming wife, and two promising children. His business is growing, his factory is expanding, the pile of green and yellow papers in his strong-box is swelling. He belongs to five clubs, twelve lodges, and twenty-three associations for the improvement of mankind at home and abroad. A thousand editors tell him every day about his greatness, his prowess, and his imperial destiny. As he rolls down to his office in his limousine wearing his natty clothes, radiating assurance, and feeling himself an heir to the mantle of the greatest Roman negotiator, he basks in the worshipful glances of the commonalty. College presidents wait in his outer chambers until he finds time to consider their prayers. Clergymen pay court to him in the interest of cathedrals, missions, and good works. Advertising agents tell him that Christ was created in his image and intimate that the angels are a little bit lower in the firmament than his most excellent self. He has more food, clothes, and shelter than any of his trading colleagues on the face of the earth. Even the quantity of his wines and liquors is not diminished as the result of the prohibitory labors of the benevolent government at Washington. He has more goods and better. His stomach wants not; neither does he shiver in the blasts of winter. He is never in prison, but when he is sick he is visited by the most competent of servants with tools of every device imaginable and chemicals of every known substance. Business goes on before him by day as a cloud and gaudy entertainment at night as a pillar of fire. He gives more generously to the poor and to good works than his brethren of commerce in any land; his modesty blushes when the headlines tell his left hand what the right has done.

All this is undeniable, and yet Mr. Babbitt is not entirely happy. True, no gloomy shadows darken his rotund and florid countenance. He wears none of Dante's lean and hungry look. He does not put away his earthly things like Buddha and seek refuge in places of sorrow and sufferings. He handles his charity cases through an expert in efficiency and propriety. But withal he is visibly disturbed and discontented. If a thousand editors praise him, they also print articles, books, reviews, and literary opinions that betray doubts with respect to his immaculate and invincible majesty. Novelists hawk at him. *The American Mercury* slams his toys about as if they deserved none of the ceremonial tribute paid to them by the professors of adulation and collection. He is flatly notified that he is an intellectual child furnished with an eighty-ton locomotive and a sixteen-inch gun by a fate which owes nothing to his ingenuity. He is told that he cannot appreciate art, literature, science, poetry, statecraft, warcraft, music, and the glories of saints' dreams. His noblest words, such as "uplift," "service," and "community good," are assailed as mere cloaks concealing a shallow mind, a cheap sentimentality, and a hard determination "to get his," legally, if possible, with the assistance of shrewd counsel; in any event to get it. No sooner do his publicity men coin a new phrase for a lofty emotion than reporters and critics openly and covertly begin to make it appear as sounding brass, concealing some new adventure into the realm of the higher hokum.

Even his favorite magazines and newspapers contain advertisements that hourly insult him by suggesting that he is ignorant, untutored, and uncultured. He is informed that he is stupid because he cannot order ham and eggs in intelligible French and is offered a home course which will enable him to master that noble tongue in fifteen minutes a day for ten days. He is laughed at because he does not know who wrote *The Ring and the Book* or whether Confucius lived before or after the opening of the Ming dynasty, and he is promised a key to the mystery of all things in the form of a scrap-heap prepared, predigested, indexed, and hand-tooled by one of the master minds of the twentieth century. He stumbles at a dinner party trying to discuss Einstein's theory of relativity with the wife of his broker who has taken a parlor course in physics under the celebrated Professor Doomuch at the University of Weissnichtwo, engaged in eking out academic wages. On the way home in his motor car, Mr. Babbitt is taken to task by his wife for attempting to talk real estate to the lawful spouse of a glorified bond salesman and is told to his face that he should improve his style by reading Elbert Hubbard's *Perfect Guide for American Gentility*. If he aspires to climb into the more ethereal college atmosphere disconsolate Babbitt is advised in a flaming advertisement to buy culture on the wholesale principle by the cubic foot and to take it in little gulps at his own pleasure without submitting to the irksome grind of daily stints. To make a long story short, George F. is treated with scorn by the self-constituted guardians of the higher sophistication and then baldly instructed to save his reputation, with his hair, by using standardized specifics. Beyond question, his stock is below par among the dabblers in dainties.

By all this uproar, Babbitt is visibly disturbed. He patronizes learning. He founds scholarships, gives funds to music and art schools, attends conferences of the learned societies on public affairs, helps along the Little Theatre Movement, endures readings by poets, holds salons for lions in town and country house, displays college presidents, archeologists, historians, novelists, connoisseurs, gentlemen of beautiful letters to his kind at capacious dinners, issues through his publicity boys oracular statements on the progress of the arts in America, and even hires space in the *Mercury* to take a shot at the Editor and assure him that *homo boobiens* is not a bad fellow after all. He buys art objects by the ton, trainload, and cargo; acquires the patois of the art sales agent; and in the presence of a Titian or Corot can pull a face as long and wise as a prohibition clergyman in the presence of a joyful drinking party. He even takes part in the meetings of professors, reads papers on recondite subjects, writes books on local history or public questions, and warms up to the poignant intellectuals as if to say that he knows a thing or two about Freud, Proust, Croce, Spengler, Whitehead, Agrippa, Lewis Mumford, and Van Wyck Brooks.

All this is true to historical form. When primitive man got his belly full, he began to decorate the walls of his cave—perhaps his wife did it while he was bringing home the bacon. In every civilization of the past, riches have produced patronage; patronage has afforded emancipation from rough work; and leisure has brought forth art in varied forms. And culture, it seems, takes on the color of its

Dust jacket of Babbitt.

host. There is a culture appropriate to an age of fighting feudal lords, merchant servitors, and clerical dignitaries. There is a culture appropriate to the age of the grand bourgeois. There is a culture of the proletarian glorification. No doubt by spending enough money, long enough, Babbitt could refashion the arts in his own image and behold himself mirrored in the blandishment of his defenders.

But there is another side to patronage. It is well illustrated in the eleventh chapter of Buckle's first volume, dealing with the demoralizing influence of Louis XIV's lavish patronage on science, letters and the arts of France. There it is shown with a bewildering wealth of evidence that the open-handed bounty of the Grand Monarch, far from stimulating the genius which is supposed to have decorated his long reign, stunted and stifled it. Nearly all the great artists and men of letters who gave glory to the period flourished before the effects of his largess got in their deadly work; while during the last twenty-five years of Louis's reign, "when his patronage had been longest in operation, it was almost entirely barren of results." Painting was favored with cash, but at length the creative power of painters "fell so low that, long before the death of Louis XIV, France ceased to possess one of any merit; and when his successor came to the throne, this beautiful art was in that great country almost extinct." And what of historical and imaginative writing? Speaking of this department of culture Buckle laments that "the men of letters, pensioned and decorated by the court, had degenerated into a fawning and hypocritical race who, to meet the wishes of their master, opposed all improvements and exerted themselves in support of every old abuse." Buckle may be extreme, but, if there is nourishment for the arts in patronage, there also lurks in the wine cup of luxury a deadly potion— deadly to the spirit of freedom, sacrifice, faith, and love, which is the everlasting source of inspiration to those who imagine, worship, and labor in the realm of the creative arts. So if Mr. Babbitt thinks that he can follow in the footsteps of Mæcenas, the results are likely to be laughable rather than heroic.

But all such criticisms refer to externals. The only doom pronounced on George F. Babbitt that really matters, that runs to the roots of his conduct and aspiration, is to the effect that he is destined to cultural sterility and vulgarity by the very nature of his money-making trade. It is said by the more severe critics that mercantile operations and their inexorably shadowing psychology are forever at war with the creative arts, no matter how large and colorful may be the borrowed plumage bought to decorate the fruits of financial speculation. Can a man who devotes his best energies, not to drawing, designing, carving, dreaming, and making, but to shuffling papers, scheming, trying to force people to buy things, getting as much as he can for as little as possible, taking advantage of social conjunctures to enlarge his treasure, seeing nature only from the window of a Pullman car, the deck of a steamer, the seat of a limousine, or the well-groomed turf of a golf course— can such a man summon from the deeps of his being rich, wayward, divine emotions which are the source of cultural flowering, heroic daring, and sacrificial ardor?

In short, is not a race of bankers, bond salesmen, and advertising agents condemned by the very nature of its work, its hopes, its hard passions, its artificial environment and its petty routine, to a life of cultural futility, no matter what gauds it buys, what ornaments it chooses for decoration, what diversions it selects for leisure hours? Is there any cultural hope in a race dedicated to money-making?

Numerous and impressive are the negative answers. For more than two thousand years great thinkers have regarded the mercantile craft as demoralizing to the human spirit and the foe of all grand art in life, manners, conduct, letters, sculpture, and painting. Aristotle believed that there was "no room for moral excellence" in any of the employments of merchants, that the life of tradesmen was "ignoble and inimical to virtue," and that they ought to be excluded from citizenship in any state desirous of stability and dedicated to the good life. The Senators of Rome, according to Dill, the historian of Roman culture, were forbidden "by ancient law as well as sentiment . . . to soil themselves by trade or usury," and this rule was theoretically in force "down to the last age of the Empire." Did not Juvenal reserve his sharpest satire for the new rich, the money-trafficker, master of fine houses and many slaves, patron of pimps, bawds, and beggars, enemy of toil and simplicity? And long after Juvenal did not Matthew Arnold disclose the money-making bourgeois as the true Philistine, foe of the arts, lover of the eternal commonplace, demoralizer of taste? Was not the Southern gentleman's phrase "damned Yankee" a linguistic sign of his contempt for the merchant and capitalist? Many a planting Senator of the United States in the golden age before the Second American Revolution must have rolled under his tongue with gusto that immortal line: "C. Pompeius Trimalchio Mæcenatianus was pious, stout, and trusty; he rose from nothing, left HS. 30,000,000, and never heard of a philoso-

pher." If citations from great authorities are to be admitted to court, the case of George F. Babbitt is hopeless; he cannot go anywhere; he is condemned to tramp his treadmill until the end, while his girth grows larger and his strong-box swells with green and yellow paper.

Considered in the mass, this solemn chatter about the cultural sterility of the money-maker looks impressive—until its source is considered. The brutal fact is that contempt for the trader has been and is now the emotion of the landed gentleman and is nothing but an expression of the social psychology of this class. It is not the fruit of ethics, observation, or abstract speculation, but the offspring of group pride and social pique, fortified by a clerical heritage handed down from the Middle Ages when priests were also landed proprietors, not the possessors of stocks and bonds. To suppose that the criticism of the trading class has universal validity akin to the compelling power of a mathematical formula is like imagining that the scorn which the white-collar clerk feels for the country yokel is of divine origin. Once understood, it dissolves in laughter as the mist dissolves in sunshine. The zeal with which vociferous defenders of the proletariat unite with landed proprietors in damning the man of commerce—after the fashion of Spengler—deceives no one, except sophomores in the school of life. Hence George F. Babbitt need not conclude from reading Aristotle, Cicero, Dr. Johnson, Jefferson, Matthew Arnold, and Sinclair Lewis, that his case is intrinsically hopeless, that he suffers from an economic disease fatal to culture.

Neither need he despair of his strain. It is true that those now prostrate before the gods of heredity and eugenics offer him little hope. According to historical records, Americans are nearly all descendants of peasants, artisans, and petty merchants. Even the lordly Cavalier of Virginia disappears in the ranks of the small folk when viewed in the devastating light of T. J. Wertenbaker's analysis of Old-Dominion genealogical tables. If there is something in the germplasm of Superior Persons that produces artists, poets, imaginative writers, and great thinkers, then the outlook is not favorable for G. F. Babbitt.

But in truth, he should not worry. Science has not yet broken the whirling circle of cause and effect and determined the respective values of heredity and environment. All pretenses to the contrary are solemn shams. No doubt Galton and his school have shown that genius often appears in families of high talent, but even in making this disclosure they cannot pretend to say how much of the power displayed by the second and third generation is due to blood inheritance and how much to the economic opportunity and intellectual environment, provided by fortunate ancestors. Moreover, the honor roll of powerful minds originating in undistinguished families is so long and so impressive that Babbitt need not be disturbed about the lowly origins of his class or its potentialities as a source of culture under right conditions of aspiration and inspiration. No comparative study has yet measured the cultural fruitage of aristocratic classes against that of the humbler orders, but there is enough evidence in hand to puncture all the claims of exalted stock to special proliferation in this sphere, to say nothing of a monopoly. Speaking of the governing aristocracy of Rome in the age of Cicero, Mr. W. Warde Fowler says: "It is in the main a society of gentlemen, dignified in manner and kindly towards each other, and it is also a society of high culture and literary ability, though poor in creative genius and unimaginative. On the other hand, it is a class which has lost its interest in the State and is energetic only when pursuing its own interests; pleasure-loving, luxurious, gossiping, trifling with serious matters, shortsighted in politics because anxious only for personal advance. '*Rari nantes in gurgite vasto*' are the men who are really in earnest."

It is a lesson in caution to discover how little genius, apart from state, war, and churchcraft, has appeared in the aristocracies of Europe from the age of Pericles to the era of Hindenburg, Mussolini, and Winston Churchill. Socrates was a stonecutter, by courtesy a sculptor—one of Aristotle's despised tradesmen. Demosthenes was the son of a rich business man, whose estate was destroyed by princely grafters in the great age of Greek culture. Cicero's origin is obscure. Certainly he was a provincial and a *novus homo,* perhaps from the artisan class. "The men who are the glory of Roman letters in epic and lyric poetry," says Dill, "were born in quiet country towns in Italy or in the remoter provinces." Sir Isaac Newton's father was a yeoman farmer. Diderot was the son of a cutler—but why enlarge upon the obvious. From the nameless and the obscure, from whom Babbitt took his rise, have also sprung makers of culture. Even the mercantile class despised by the landed warrior and the revolutionary proletarian has made its contribution to art, letters, and philosophy.

So there is no reason for believing that Babbitt's cultural strain is incurably diseased. The source of his vexation must be elsewhere. Wise indeed is the seer who can discover it, but in this hour of visceral fullness perhaps a few minutes may be devoted to inquiring into it and guessing about it. Perhaps after much hammering on the subject a few sparks may fly upward and glow for a moment on the horizon.

To the present inquirer it seems that the fatal weakness in criticisms launched against Babbitt by the sophisticates lies in the assumption that culture is like a garment that can be put on and taken off; that it is a kind of decoration, not a mode of life; that it is a ritual made evident by sounds and genuflections, not the spirit in which a man does the work that falls to his lot in the destiny of things; that understanding comes from borrowing, not from the contemplation of that which is fair and of good repute; that a man who never made or did a beautiful thing or never desired to do or make it can be civilized by any process whatever; that culture is a leisure class acquirement, unrelated to work, to responsibility, to material things, to the creation and transfer of goods, to the basic purposes of those who live it.

All these suppositions are wrong. No doubt the great cultures of the world have been in various respects derivative—the extent of the diffusion of the arts even in the most primitive ages almost passes belief; but every commanding culture that the world has witnessed has been in some mysterious manner assimilated to the life and spirit of the people who have developed it. Japan, for example, borrowed heavily from China in every department, but Japanese art is not Chinese, as everyone knows who has studied at first hand the amazing revelations of Japanese spirit in architecture, gardening, painting, and sculpture. No, culture springs from life and work; sincerity and sustained effort are among its sources.

Hence it is absurd for Babbitt to run from himself. By acquiring a fortune at the age of forty as a mortician and then acquiring a country estate, a town house, a library, and a gallery, he cannot make himself a Pliny or transform the administration of Calvin Coolidge into an Augustan Age. Neither can he call into life the great arts and a great civilization by sowing money among the multitude of white-collar beggars clamoring at his gates—for such arts as he produces by that process will inevitably smell of embalming fluid. Neither can he rise above the role of Trimalchio by giving heed to the poignant youngsters who insist on telling him that the key to the Eleusinian mystery of civilization is to be found in London, Berlin, Paris, Rome, Tokio, or Peking. Let him consider the fate of Ticknor, Irving, and Motley who rushed off to Europe and took on "polish," as compared with Emerson, Whitman, and Mark Twain who stood fast in America—on the soil that nourished them and their ancestors—and who still rule us from the tombs.

Babbitt's historic mission is here or nowhere. He is an organizer and an administrator in a machine age, not a warrior or priest in a feudal age. The clans Emilii, Cornelii, and Julii are not his clans and nothing under the starry and shining canopy of heaven can make him over in their image.

Hope for him, if there is any, lies in introducing sincerity, thought, beauty, and greatness of spirit into his own work, here and now—the business of building, making, and distributing. Could he imagine a banking house refusing to float a loan merely because it was not destined to some high constructive purpose? Could he imagine the swelling superpower corporations of his country engaged in discovering not how little electric current they can sell for a penny but how much? Could he imagine advertising without claptrap? Could he conceive of his tribe undertaking the reconstruction of an industrial wilderness, wiping out slums and jungles, and making a city over with a view to beauty and the good life—instead of unearned increment and a full stomach? Could he imagine the editor of his favorite paper admitting that his news columns are full of colored lies? Could he imagine public dinners without speeches, philanthropy without publicity, noble work as unobserved as the delicate traceries hidden from popular gaze in the vaulted roof of a medieval cathedral, prayers realized but unsaid, faith justified by works unpraised in the daily *Blather,* truth nourished in a secret chamber of the heart instead of service blazing on the front of a profiteering establishment, great collective effort for any purpose other than war or exploitation, hours of covert labor unrewarded by money, cheers, editorial soft-soap, or clerical smear?

If so, Babbitt may become civilized. When he is full enough of husks and wind he may, like the prodigal son, consider his Maker. *Surtout, Monsieur Babbitt, pas de zèle.* (pp. 21-8)

Charles A. Beard, "Is Babbitt's Case Hopeless?" in The Menorah Journal, *Vol. XIV, No. 1, January, 1928, pp. 21-8.*

Frederick J. Hoffman   (essay date 1949)

[*In the following excerpt, Hoffman analyzes Lewis's cri-*

tique of bourgeois ideology in Babbitt, *arguing that the author's recognition of Babbitt's essential humaneness late in the novel conflicts with the story's parodic intentions.*]

In his novels of the 1920s, Sinclair Lewis offered every available perspective upon the middle class. He was its critic and Judge, its satirist and parodist, minister to its victims, Balzacian commentator upon its many-sided life, and "liberal" guardian of its political activities. **Main Street** (1920) treated the Midwestern metaphor of the small town, trying to discover, as Lewis said, how "much of Gopher Prairie's eleven miles of cement walks" was "made out of the tombstones of John Keatses." With **Babbitt** (1922) he began a full-scale investigation of the small Midwestern city, the "Zenith" city with 250,000 to 300,000 inhabitants, and growing steadily. He searched indefatigably for every kind of venality, corruption, stupidity, and demagoguery, every tendency toward fascism in middle-class society, every pressure upon the "man of good will" to abandon his rights as a democratic citizen. He was so successful in accumulating evidence, so fond of echoing and parodying the grandiose absurdities of his subject, that his novels became (or threatened to become) fantasies woven from the kinds of fact that Mencken reported in his "Americana."

Lewis's portrait is at once a skillful organization of middle-class detail, a series of caricatures of middle-class types, a parody of middle-class habits, forms of speech, gestures, and a fantasy world, derived from the real but unreal in its actual effect. His interest is primarily anthropological; he is the student of a strange tribe that exists in a world (Winnemac) that includes all states of the Midwest but is none of them, behaves in a way that resembles the behavior of the actual middle-class world, but in vigor and extreme of gesture transcends it. As an analyst of this half-real, half-fantasy world, Lewis gives it all forms of attitude, belief, faith, gesture: a "piety of things"; a full complement of rituals (together with totem signs and magic slogans); a metaphysic ("Service and Boosterism"); an ethic ("Gotta hustle"); a religion (Dr. John Jennison Drew's "Salvation and Five Per Cent" church, where "everything zips"); an aesthetic (red-blooded, efficient, sentimental "Poemulations" by Chum Frink); and a fully articulated political philosophy (Republicanism and the wisdom of Harding and Coolidge).

The Zenith setting is itself an architectural and religious symbol of the faith, a temple dedicated to the religion of business. Its Athletic Club is a masterpiece of eclectic display: the entrance lobby "Gothic, the washroom Roman Imperial, the lounge Spanish Mission, and the reading-room in Chinese Chippendale." In this world, in the Floral Heights residential region, lives Babbitt, the symbolic hero, scapegoat, and prodigal son. His religious faith is associated almost entirely with "things"—gadgets, automatic and mechanical and efficient instruments of a busy man's life. To maintain his morale he has to buy more things, whether he needs them or not: their "thinginess," quite apart from need or practicality, sustains him. His outward expression of "the faith" is "hustle," which gives the appearance of absorption and direction and quiets the suspicions of the tribe; any attempt to remain isolated from it is a form of backsliding. In a noisy confraternity lies the best resort of orthodoxy.

Babbitt wears the uniform of the solid citizen, as his mind wears uniform opinions. The "standard suit" is a gray business suit, and in its pockets he carries certain badges of his loyalty: a fountain pen and silver pencil, a gold pen-knife, a silver cigar-cutter, "a large yellowish elk's-tooth," a looseleaf pocket notebook (containing, among other things, verses of C. Cholmondely Frink and newspaper editorials), and the Boosters' Club button ("his V.C., his Legion of Honor ribbon, his Phi Beta Kappa key").

The Babbitt "program" involves a dedication to Unselfish Public Service ("a thing called Ethics . . . if you had it you were a High-Class Realtor"), a proper reverence for the "spiritual value of things," and intellectual stimulus from "rubbing up against high-class hustlers every day and getting jam full of ginger." It demands the right kind of political activity; campaigning for the "right kind" of loyal Americans, warning against the "Red professors" in the university, guarding the local political scene against its enemies. Most of all, it requires a tribal solidarity with "the boys": Vergil Gunch, Professor Joseph K. Pumphrey (of the Riteway Business College, instructor in Business English, Scenario Writing, and Commercial Law), Orville Jones (owner of the Lily White Laundry, the "biggest, busiest, bulliest cleanerie shoppe in Zenith"), Chum Frink, Dr. Howard Littlefield, Ph.D., and the rest.

At the peak of his success as a tribal Booster, Babbitt delivers the annual address before the Zenith Real-Estate Board. This is a summing up of the "parody Babbitt" and of his stock-in-trade of tribal opinions and evaluations. It is a literary ordering of Mencken's accumulations of what "the booboisie" thinks. Its substance is contained in Babbitt's description of "Our Ideal Citizen": he is "first and foremost" busy ("busier than a bird-dog"), and he has no time for daydreaming "or going to sassiety teas or kicking about things that are none of his business," but spends all his time "putting the zip into some store or profession or art." The slang puts the daydreamers in their place; the warning that no one should "kick about things that are none of his business" identifies the solidarity of the group, jealously guarded. Our citizen is also a "he-man," an extrovert, a conscientious family man; for entertainment he plays "a few fists of bridge, or reads the evening newspaper, and a chapter or two of some good lively Western novel if he has a taste for literature." He is a good, sound, efficient man in his taste for the arts; nothing of the bohemian about him—"in America the successful writer or picture-painter is indistinguishable from any other decent businessman"—and he should be properly rewarded, have his chance "to drag down his fifty thousand bucks a year."

The middle-class stereotype is a hundred-per-cent standardized American, a full-blooded, he-man, native American citizen:

> Here's the specifications of the Standardized American Citizen! Here's the new generation of Americans: fellows with hair on their chests and smiles in their eyes and adding machines in their offices. We're not doing any boasting, but we like ourselves first-rate, and if you don't like us, look out—better get under cover before the cyclone hits town!

There are those who "don't like us"; but one advantage of Zenith over big cities like New York is that there are very few "foreign-born" people in it, with their "foreign ideas and communism."

The "Regular Guys" are creating a new civilization of vital, standardized living, which is the great hope of the future and must be protected from "the long-haired gentry who call themselves 'liberals' and 'radicals' and 'non-partisan' and 'intelligentsia' and God only knows how many other trick names!" There are certain instructors "over at the U" (of which "I am proud to be known as an alumni") who "seem to think we ought to turn the conduct of the nation over to hoboes and roustabouts." These are the men to watch; if we're going to pay them our good money, "they've got to help us by selling efficiency and whooping it up for national prosperity!" Only when they are set right, and the communist-socialist foreigners are locked up, can this he-man tribe of Moose, Elks, Lions, and other right thinkers proceed on the road to a glorious standardized civilization, a paradise of gadgets and standardized proprieties.

This is, of course, as far as the parody Babbitt can go. But *Babbitt* is a novel as well, and its hero is a personality; Lewis had the choice of making him simply a mouthpiece of middle-class views (as is Lowell Schmaltz of *The Man Who Knew Coolidge*) or of breaking into the pattern of his gestures and appearance to give him a sensitivity, make him a doubter of his own loud confidence. Lewis was careful to plant suspicion of a "complex" Babbitt from the start: the businessman Babbitt does not seem the same person when the very latest alarm clock with its cathedral chime and its phosphorescent dial rouses him from dreams of the "fairy child." Further, he has a friend, Paul Riesling, who is not a mixer, who sits apart from "the boys," and encourages Babbitt to doubt the whole tribal structure. Riesling is obviously the "criminal type," and his friendship is a great risk to Babbitt; when Riesling tries to kill his wife and is given a three-year sentence, Babbitt loses confidence and morale. This is the beginning of his treachery, his flirtation with "alien" ideas. It is the novel, as distinguished from the parody.

It is interesting that Lewis should have made the two Babbitts so very distinct from each other. The doubting Babbitt, upon yielding to his temptations, becomes an anti-Babbitt, a rebel and scapegrace, violating the social, political, and sexual taboos, and for a while taking pleasure in his defiance. He associates with the bohemian "Bunch" instead of with the Athletic Club boys or regular guys; he refuses to join any more Booster organizations; he is unfaithful to his wife, neglects his family, sneers at the architectural harmony and social stability of Floral Heights, openly flouts Prohibition. Worst of all, Babbitt begins to defend his friend, Seneca Doane, who remembers him from the university as "an unusually sensitive chap." He begins to play the role of the liberal, argues against those who condemn Doane's middle-of-the-road liberalism, defends the strikers and admires men who march with them in a protest parade. Lewis has saved Babbitt from himself, has given him this "fling" of sanity and intelligence, and has thus revealed his own private confidence in the soundness and the fundamental decency of the extracurricular Babbitt.

Lewis's own position was that of a liberal humanist; in a **"Self-Portrait"** (1927) he admitted that the parody-artist was not his real self:

> All his respect for learning, for integrity, for accuracy, and for the possibilities of human achieve-

ment are to be found not in the rather hectic and exaggerative man as his intimates see him, but in his portrait of Professor Max Gottlieb, in *Arrowsmith.* Most of the fellow's capacity for loyalty and friendship has gone into Leora in that same novel and into the account of George F. Babbitt's affection for his son and for his friend Paul.

Lewis saves his greatest respect and affection for the man and woman of integrity, of an instinctive sense of decency. The double view of Babbitt is thus a consequence of Lewis's mixed emotion concerning the middle class. Its most hideous extremes of boasting, vulgarity, and cheapness of mind are fully given in the parody figure of Babbitt in the "gotta-hustle" public world; but Babbitt is himself saved from the parody. In the end one discovers he is only weak—not malicious, illiberal, ungenerous, and fascistic, but sentimental and basically decent. In so revising the portrait of Babbitt, Lewis has to shift the center of his characterizations. Babbitt, who is in the beginning the epitome of all the violations of decorum that Lewis hates, must—because of his revolt—move downstage. The really villainous incarnation of the middle-class evil is not Babbitt but Vergil Gunch. His hostile eyes follow Babbitt as he moves from one petty defiance of the tribe to another; he proposes that Babbitt join the Good Citizens League as a testament of renewal of the faith; he leads the move toward extradition, which strikes fear in Babbitt's heart.

Vergil Gunch succeeds finally in convincing Babbitt that his extra-tribal spree is sinful. "The independence seeped out of him, and he walked the streets alone, afraid of men's cynical eyes and the incessant hiss of whispering." A minor family crisis helps to solve the major tribal crisis. Myra Babbitt is stricken, and at once he reacts with all tribal and family correctness; he drops all his "inner dramas" and asks his wife's forgiveness for them. "The boys" return, with fulsome gestures of regular-guy affection; and Babbitt, almost in tears because he can now stop fighting them, is restored to full membership. He moves quickly to resume his status; as a newly accepted member of the Good Citizens League, he is "fired up" over "the wickedness of Seneca Doane, the crimes of labor unions, the perils of immigration, the delights of golf, morality, and bank-accounts." He goes to the efficient Reverend Doctor Drew, who efficiently prays with him (watch in hand) for five minutes, after which he must rush off to a meeting of the Don't-Make-Prohibition-a-Joke-Association. And now Babbitt knows he is safe from the terror of being alone, outside the tribe, isolated "from the Clan of Good Fellows."

The crucial fact about *Babbitt* is that it is two novels—or two types of literary exposition poorly combined in one work. The Babbitt of the address before the Real-Estate Board is one character, a perfect representation of its limited kind; but Lewis creates another, a sensitive, humane Babbitt, who in his person and in his behavior cancels the validity and nullifies the success of the other. The parody Babbitt is so indisputably the imaginative product of the Lewis-Mencken view of the middle class that he cannot also be an anti-Babbitt, a Babbitt conspiring against himself. In order to humanize a parody figure, Lewis must make him over into a person with at least some of the sensitivity of a Seneca Doane. Babbitt must become a complex man in order that "something happen." What happens to the parody Babbitt is within its own context merely a succession of "Americana" incidents; the novel demands more of crisis, a stronger narrative line. Besides, Lewis does not want to leave us with a pure caricature; he likes the middle class and would only point up its absurdities and follies. So, midway in the novel, Babbitt changes from a raucous, naïve Booster to a vaguely resentful doubter; and the center of the criticism shifts from Babbitt to "the boys" and especially to Vergil Gunch. The middle class is saved from its worst sins, and its worst sins have at the same time provided high comedy.

Lewis touched upon every critical image applied to the middle class in the 1920s. The chief of these is, of course, Mencken's image of an inverted business mythology; but there is also—and perhaps underlying it—the liberal humanistic position of Seneca Doane, which, in Babbitt's brief flirtation with his ideas, is drawn into the range of a possible middle-class self-criticism. Babbitt briefly recognizes the heroism of strikes and the selflessness of sympathizers who put their "alien, red notions" on public display. But all of this is dominated throughout by the great middle-class tribal fantasy, to which the extremes of standardization of thought, ownership, and belief contribute. This, the dominating motif of middle-class criticism in the 1920s, is by all odds the most memorable quality of the novel. Because of it, **Babbitt** is especially representative of one phase of thinking and writing in the decade. (pp. 408-15)

> *Frederick J. Hoffman, "The Text: Sinclair Lewis's 'Babbitt',"* in his The Twenties: American Writing in the Postwar Decade, *revised edition, The Free Press, 1962, pp. 408-15.*

Sheldon Norman Grebstein   (essay date 1962)

[*In the following excerpt, Grebstein discusses the artistic conception, thematic background, and contemporary social and economic issues of* Babbitt, *asserting that in his portrait of Babbitt, Lewis successfully conflated the symbolic with the subjective.*]

By late summer, 1920, just several weeks after completing **Main Street,** Lewis was already planning his next novel. It was to be "the story of the Tired Business Man, of the man in the Pullman smoker, of our American ruler." The book's title, Lewis decided, would be the name of its central character. "Babbitt" was the name he chose.

From its inception Lewis intended the book to be a serious treatment. Both the composition and reception of **Main Street** had wrought a profound, although not a total, change in Lewis and in his attitude toward writing. He saw that he had become a novelist of international importance and that his work would thenceforth be given the most careful attention. Consequently, he found himself unable to return to the potboiling fiction he had earlier found easy and profitable, and he wrote to Alfred Harcourt, "I don't believe I shall ever again be the facile *Post* trickster I by God was." In the same letter and in a prospectus for the new novel, he declared his intention to depict its protagonist as an individual, for he hoped to correct one of the faults which critics had found in **Main Street,** that of "exterior vision," its superficial and typed characters. But this hero and his environment would also be representative of America, Lewis believed, because

only in the United States was life so standardized that a writer could treat one city as if it were like all others of its size, regardless of its location.

The ambitiousness and seriousness of his conception is best revealed, perhaps, in this letter to Harcourt, December 28, 1920:

> I want the novel to be the G. A. N. [Great American Novel] in so far as it crystallizes and makes real the Average Capable American. No one has done it, I think; no one has even *touched* it except Booth Tarkington in *Turmoil* and *Magnificent Ambersons;* and he romanticizes away all bigness. Babbitt is a little like Will Kennicott but bigger, with a bigger field to work on, more sensations, more perceptions. . . . He is all of us Americans at 46, prosperous but worried, wanting—passionately—to seize something more than motor cars and a house *before it's too late.* Yet, utterly unlike Carol, it never even occurs to him that he might live in Europe, might like poetry, might be a senator; he is content to live and work in the city of Zenith, which is, as everybody knows, the best little ole city in the world. But he would like for once the flare of romantic love, the satisfaction of having left a mark on the city and a let-up in his constant warring on competitors, and when his beloved friend Riesling commits suicide he suddenly says, "Oh hell, what's the use of the cautious labor to which I've given everything"—only for a little while is he discontented, though. . . . I want to make Babbitt big in his real-ness, in his relation to all of us, not in the least exceptional, yet dramatic, passionate, struggling.

Much of **Main Street** had been drawn directly from Lewis's experience, for he knew from direct observation the patterns of small town speech and behavior. Although **Babbitt** depended far less upon what Lewis had lived, it also contained something of his personality. A number of Lewis's friends have remarked about the similarity between the character of Babbitt and that of his creator. One has written: "At the bottom, Lewis is solidly bourgeois. He loves real estate and mortgages and bank accounts. Fundamentally, he is a Rotarian." Another has pointed out that in his informality, cordiality, impulsiveness, candor, riotessness, and in his hatred of affected and arty people, as well as in other personal qualities, Lewis resembled Babbitt. An incident related by William Rose Benét concerning what he called the "essential Lewis" further illustrates this matter. Benét and Lewis were dining together when a stranger, a traveling salesman, came to their table and engaged them in conversation. Lewis soon got him talking about himself so that he revealed more than he knew—to the fascination of Lewis but to the boredom of Benét. After the man had gone, Benét asked Lewis if he truly liked that sort of person, and Lewis replied, "That's the trouble with you, Bill. You regard him as *hoi polloi,* he doesn't even represent the cause of labor or anything dramatic—but I understand that man—by God, I love him."

As regards Lewis the artist, **Babbitt** displays his ability to project himself into virtually any environment and capture its essence. His gift for impersonation and mimicry enabled him at any given time to be almost anyone he wanted. He could strike up an acquaintanceship with a stranger on a train or in a hotel or restaurant and, by pretending to be of the same background, completely win the man's confidence. His remarkable memory enabled him to record American speech on a mental soundtrack, to be replayed at will—a talent crucial to the astounding fidelity of detail and idiom both typical of his work and necessary to its satiric effectiveness. In this manner Lewis had been gathering material for *Babbitt* in the years of his travels over the American continent. Moreover, his own experience in the various publishing jobs he had held from 1910 to 1915, including his work as advertising manager for the Doran Company, had given him some insight into the principles of salesmanship. Finally, the student of Lewis's career perceives that in the character of Eddie Schwirtz in *The Job,* and in a number of short stories, Lewis had anticipated some of the characters and situations of *Babbitt.*

Thematically, *Babbitt* is an extension and expansion of *Main Street.* Having described the forces of conformity at work in a typical small town, it was foreseeable that Lewis would now enlarge his canvas. Accordingly, he created an average mid-western state called Winnemac (Wisconsin, Minnesota, Michigan), placed in it the imaginary but familiar city of Zenith, and depicted two years in the life of one of its representative citizens, George F. Babbitt: middle class ($9,000 a year), forty-six years of age, somewhat overweight, resident in a fashionable suburb, father of two children, dealer in real estate, good fellow. Again in *Babbitt,* as he had in *Main Street,* Lewis combined and solidified ideas and attitudes already in existence but awaiting a local habitation and a name. Indeed, we may discern in Lewis's novel certain perceptions about American life which had been advanced by such keen observers of our civilizaton as Thorstein Veblen, Randolph Bourne, and H. L. Mencken.

While much of Veblen's thought is today in disrepute, especially those concepts based on Sumnerian sociology, Veblen's theories of pecuniary emulation, conspicuous consumption, the pecuniary standard of living and canons of taste (these are developed in *The Theory of the Leisure Class,* 1899), all have great pertinence to the mode of Babbitt's daily life. Furthermore, Veblen's analysis of business enterprise and business principles (*The Theory of Business Enterprise,* 1904) goes far toward explaining the larger structure of Babbitt's society.

As Veblen saw it, wealth symbolizes honor and prestige in modern society; it is necessary for acceptance by our fellows. For status we need money, and without that status there can be no self-respect. Yet once we accumulate a certain sum, it is not enough. We are driven ever to increase what we own, to rise as far above the average as we can. Moreover, money brings power, or the sense of power; and, since man's striving for money also springs from his sense of purposeful activity—what Veblen calls "the instinct of workmanship"—we have come to see success as money and to measure success by money. But the possession of money is not alone sufficient to satisfy man; he must demonstrate his wealth, either by his own freedom from labor and/or by the amount of goods and services he and his family consume. Since money becomes the *summum bonum* and the surest way in a business society to success and power, the aim of business is to gain money; all is subordinated to profit, even if the profit is gained at the community's loss. Nor are profit and wages necessarily related to true value.

Finally, the members of an industrial and business society, such as that of the modern Western world, are inevitably affected in their modes of thinking by the machine process upon which industry depends. Because the machine process inculcates standardization, exact quantitative knowledge, and a sense of material causality, it inevitably collides with and weakens tradition, traditional morality, and all conduct based on sentimental and metaphysical precepts. Only the tradition of ownership prospers under such conditions; property rights become the highest rights. However, despite the deterioration and change ultimately produced by the machine process, the standardization it enforces tends to prevail in the lives of the industrial population and to repress any disturbance which might upset the delicate balance and adjustment between the various parts of the society. The balance must be maintained.

The ideas of Randolph Bourne apply to *Babbitt* in a different sense but with no less pertinence. Bourne pointed out that America's older generation had grown conservative and stodgy. It had stopped thinking about and trying to answer life's more difficult questions; in fact, it pretended there were no questions. While it was no longer so strict in its religion and its belief in religious dogmas, it persisted in maintaining the forms and rituals. The elders disengaged themselves from such vital matters as death, which frightened them; sex, which brought them panic; and psychology, which mystified them. Having fallen into the comfortable routines of business, church, and family life, they recognized no change and failed to meet the age's new needs and demands. The young, Bourne concluded, must transform all this and must not become victim to their parents' complacency. Bourne admitted to the friendliness of the American, especially the midwesterner, but warned against its consequences. "An excessive amiability . . . will, in the end, put a premium on conformity." "Folksiness," he wrote, "evidently has its dark underlining in a tendency to be stampeded by herd-emotion." And, "Social conscience may become the duty to follow what the mob demands, and democracy may come to mean that the individual feels himself somehow expressed—his private tastes and intelligence—in whatever the crowd chooses to do."

Likewise, H. L. Mencken in *The American Credo* (written in collaboration with George Jean Nathan) offered an analysis of the American character which is perfectly applicable to *Babbitt:*

> The thing which sets off the American from all other men, and gives a peculiar colour not only to the pattern of his daily life but also to the play of his inner ideas, is what, for want of a more exact term, may be called social aspiration. That is to say, his dominant passion is a passion to lift himself by at least a step or two in the society that he is a part of—a passion to improve his position, to break down some shadowy barrier of caste, to achieve the countenance of what, for all his talk of equality, he recognizes and accepts as his betters.

This desire to rise socially, Mencken asserted, was at the root of American restlessness. However, Americans fear one another. Since the majority determines the individual's status, the individual fears the majority. His only way to success is to assume protective coloration, to lose himself in the crowd, and then to be approved by it as one of its members. Failure consists of being unmasked, of standing out as an individual; consequently, the American fears to question ideas and institutions. Ultimately, he fears simply to question.

Thus, Babbitt lies within a context of economic and social analyses which suggest some of the novel's intellectual affiliations, whether or not they were actually influences upon it. But when we analyze the novel itself, we discover that it has its own entity.

Babbitt begins with the description of a modern city—a city "for giants." The remainder of the novel provides an extended ironic commentary on this statement, as it demonstrates how Babbitt and the others of his kind who live in this city are pygmies, not giants. Our initial glance at Babbitt is likewise focused through Lewis's ironic lens, for the only beauty and magic left in his life are the visitations of an elusive dream girl, reminiscent somewhat of Melville's Yillah, who beckons to Babbitt in his slumbers. As Lewis continues to concentrate on the hero for the narrative's first one hundred pages, the irony deepens.

We are given closely detailed descriptions of Babbitt's house, yard, bathroom; the routine of his morning shave; Mrs. Babbitt's contours; his method of dressing, his eyeglasses, his tie, the contents of his pockets; his minor aches and pains and the state of his digestion; his opinions on dress suits and on his children. We are told of his pride in his automobile, his attitude toward his neighbors, his route to his office. We watch him as he dictates letters, prepares a sales campaign, and composes advertisements for cemetery plots. We follow him to lunch at the Zenith Athletic Club and listen to his badinage and his conversation. We see him, in short, in all the significant activities of his life, at home, at work, with his friends; and in the last five of the one hundred and two pages which have depicted twenty-four hours in the history of George F. Babbitt, Lewis recounts to us the sinful or meaningful or interesting things others are doing and saying in Zenith as Babbitt goes to sleep on his sleeping-porch, gallant and intrepid at last in the pursuit of his dream girl.

The total effect of this first section of the novel is, just as Lewis intended, overwhelming in its emphasis upon the smallness, the pettiness, the triviality, and the lack of joy and freedom in the existence of a typical member of a money society. His house, conspicuous in its material comforts and illustrative of its owner's success, is a shelter but not a home. His stolid wife and his children who insult one another and argue at the breakfast table about who will get the car (less a vehicle than a symbol of status) are, if anything, even more trivial and shallow. Although Babbitt performs no truly useful function in his work as a "realtor," he is successful enough at it financially. His field is real estate but he adds nothing to its value nor is informed about it. He knows nothing about architecture, landscaping, economics. He does not really know such essential facts about his community as how good the police and fire departments are, or the quality of the schools. Although engaged in land development, he is ignorant of the fundamentals of sanitation. Nor does he need to possess any of this information. As Veblen had written, the business system is large enough to absorb those who take profit without rendering service or creating anything of worth.

Furthermore, Babbitt's business ethics are elastic. They can be stretched to condone bribery, lying, bullying, and conspiracy, although Babbitt discharges one of his employees for employing the same methods. The point (Veblen's) is that right and wrong, the traditional morality, are now determined by what is expedient and profitable, by what brings in a financial return yet is not flagrant enough to disturb the system's equilibrium. Where Babbitt might be troubled by moral qualms, the remnants of the old morality and religion, he can justify his practices under the name of good, smart business, which is what everyone is doing. In this way Babbitt also has his efforts rewarded by his peers, for in following them he shares in the recognition which the group provides for the obedient (Mencken and Bourne).

Everywhere Babbitt is surrounded by pals who slap him on the back, call him by affectionate nicknames, joke with him. His entrance at the Athletic Club brings a volley of greetings. He is elected vice-president of the Boosters Club. He is chosen to make a speech before the Zenith Real Estate Board. He attracts attention and praise by his speech-making during an election campaign and by his participation in a drive to raise Sunday School attendance at his church. But Babbitt's conformity and forced geniality have their price because all the while there is only one person, Paul Riesling, to whom he can admit that he is somehow not fully satisfied, not really happy; and his only means of breaking out and still maintaining the appearance of respectability is to take a Maine vacation without his wife and, once there, to sit up late, drink, and play poker.

Only in the hotel barbershop can Babbitt unleash his senses and glory in the sybaritic abandonment of a haircut, a shampoo, and a manicure; the group demands that at least the pretense of propriety prevail. Thus, Babbitt is disturbed by Paul's open hatred of his wife Zilla, shocked at Paul's flagrant violation of the code by carrying on an affair, and horrified when Paul turns on Zilla and physically assaults her. Yet it is acceptable to Babbitt that as "one of the boys" he should get drunk and visit a house of prostitution during the course of an out-of-town convention. He avows dedication to law and order, but with ill-concealed pride at this proof of his status and power, he procures and serves bootleg whiskey at a party.

He declares himself a democrat, yet he is thrilled to meet one of the town's richest men, proud to have another to his home for dinner (a dismal failure), and contemptuous when one of his less successful college classmates in turn invites him to dinner (a dismal failure). When he does get a glimmer of the realities of class and caste structure, it is forgotten in the frenzied activities of the innumerable clubs and organizations which the system provides to keep its citizens from too much thinking. One of the highest moments of his life is his meeting with Sir Gerald Doak, an Englishman, who likes the same pastimes as Babbitt, has the same disdain for the intellectual, the same lust for success symbols, and the same smug sense of the power of his kind. Lewis's point? Babbittry is not only a native disease; it is pandemic.

But somehow Babbitt does grow restless and thoughtful

in his constricted existence. Paul Riesling's frustration arouses muted response in Babbitt. At the same party whose success is reassurance of his popularity, he gets another impulse toward revolt; for a moment he realizes how dull it all is, how stupid his friends are, how hollow their congeniality. He comes to see that he neither understands nor approves of his children, nor they of him. When he falls ill for a day or two, he realizes the emptiness of his life, his work. It is "all mechanical." He begins to take the hard look, characteristic of the individualist, the sensitive man, at himself. In a word, he begins to move away from the mass and to search out true value—an act which inevitably threatens the delicate balance of the system and which, consequently, it cannot permit.

Babbitt's rebellion starts harmlessly and predictably enough with some mild and furtive attempts at romance: a weak pass at his secretary, a slightly stronger one at a neighbor's wife, a date with a manicurist, and finally an affair with a pretty widow. The group frowns on such philandering, but it does not absolutely forbid it if in moderation and in secrecy. However, when his affair becomes dissipation and when Babbitt openly declares his independence by publicly defending the cause of labor during a strike—thus challenging both the social and economic bases of his world—it is time for the maverick to be driven back to the herd. Accordingly, representatives of the newly formed "Good Citizen's League," a kind of rotarian Ku Klux Klan, call on Babbitt and ask him to join. He refuses; the pressure builds; he loses business and his friends avoid him. Then his wife falls ill and her illness causes him to realize how much she and the safe, comfortable existence she represents mean to him. He renounces his liberty, becomes a member of the Good Citizen's League, and with its members pledges himself to uphold the ideal of equality in everything but wealth—and for everyone except the working class. As the novel concludes, only one avenue of hope and freedom is left to Babbitt (and this is, of course, reminiscent of *Main Street*), that his son will not make the same mistakes.

In *Babbitt* we can distinguish the two elements, the two layers of meaning comprising Lewis's method. As a novel it is the story of one man's struggle against the forces besetting him, a man who is closer to the Wellsian than the Sophoclean. On this level *Babbitt* might be read as the story of a man approaching old age—the male menopause—and having a last fling. Typically, he becomes dissatisfied with his daily routine, his work, his friends, his home and family. He almost inevitably seeks an illicit relationship which will restore the sense of life's danger and adventure he had as a youth and reassure him that he is still sexually attractive. He rejects the values he has accepted as an adult, whatever those values, and tries to return to the values and ideals of his youth. In some cases the rebellion goes so far that the man overturns his whole life, takes the firm's money and his secretary, and runs off to Brazil. Babbitt travels a little distance along just such a road.

On the second level, Babbitt is not a realistic character but a parody, a type, a symbol. By means of this Babbitt, Lewis uses the book as a vehicle for satire and social history, the portrayal of a whole way of life in a representative American city. In this context Lewis gives us a superficially authentic but distorted account of the conditions of life in an industrial and commercial society, which is dominated by the profit motive and acquiescent to the pressure toward sameness and standardization.

The success of *Babbitt* as a novel results from the merger of the two elements, for the story of the brief rebellion of one middle-aged man cannot be separated from the account of that man's role in a society which he has made and which has made him. We perceive that the doubts Babbitt suffers are shared by his friends and associates. Paul Riesling revolts even more drastically by trying to destroy his wife, the symbol of his imprisonment in a desolate world. Chum Frink the poet, who is one of the voices of the society, confesses drunkenly, like a character in an E. A. Robinson poem, that he has betrayed his talent; he could indeed have become a poet, not the hack versifier he is. The camaraderie, the noise, the activity of the Athletic Club and the Booster's Club, the Fascistic program of the Good Citizens League—all indicate a basic malaise, an unhappiness with life as it is. As Maxwell Geismar and Ludwig Lewisohn have noted, this sense of fear and dread underlying the novel is a high artistic achievement by Lewis. Like Babbitt, the other inhabitants of this purgatory try to resolve or forget their inner torment by arranging a busy and gimmick-filled outer world, by their frenetic pursuit of money and what it buys, by the chase to acquire class and caste symbols—a chase so exhausting that no energy remains to enjoy what has been achieved. Their symbols become ends in themselves. In such a world individuality and self-knowledge are difficult, perhaps impossible. Thus, individual revolt comes too late for Babbitt; he cannot see himself clearly for the first time at forty-eight and make changes. The children must determine the future, and they must do it by heeding their own desires, by defying the world and doing what they want.

Among the most tragic things which have happened to Babbitt is his loss of capacity for pleasure. He who seeks so ardently for recreation, for entertainment in a culture which has never been more materially conducive to pleasure, cannot really be entertained. Not only is he fearful of what people would say if he followed his dream-girl in actuality, he is so stifled by routine that he has lost most of his capacity to feel. Herein Babbitt demonstrates what Thomas Henry Huxley had said was the penalty of civilization—weariness, ennui. Where there should be standards of taste, value, and beauty adequate to the height of the material existence, where, in other words, there should be a soul, we find a vacuum. Too comfortable, well fed, long-lived, and rational to believe in heaven and hell, not talented or dedicated enough to believe in himself or his work, he can only believe in what his friends and the mass media tell him. Once he learns that they lie, that his gods are brazen idols, he becomes stripped of his capacity for faith.

But Lewis's conclusions about Babbitt's future are not entirely negative. He shares with Lewis's other heroes a yearning for self-realization and fulfillment. If it is too late for him to find fulfillment, at least he may achieve realization. This realization, once established, will never again allow Babbitt contentment or peace of mind, will never again permit him to warm himself against the bodies of the herd, but it is worth more than any of these. Babbitt is not of heroic dimensions—nor could he ever be so in the conditions of his world; but he is an adult or promises to become one at the novel's end. He walks out to face the world and live in it, although it is no longer Eden.

In this portrait of Babbitt there appears once more the question of Lewis's ambivalence toward his heroes. Whereas he had clearly *approved* of his earlier heroes, despite their faults, he obviously does not approve of Babbitt. Babbitt is a coward, a braggart, a hypocrite, a liar, a cheat, a poor husband and father, a worker whose work contributes nothing toward human betterment. Yet we *like* Babbitt and are indulgent to him, just as Lewis is and intends, for Babbitt is also kind, loyal to his friends, basically simple and decent. He is a combination of strength and weakness, vice and virtue. His family and friends sense his decency and lean on him a little for it. He is so perfectly representative that the Good Citizens League feels his membership is important. Why, then, does Lewis portray a way of life so explicitly evil and destructive, and yet convey affection for the man who is its chief type and symbol? Perhaps because Lewis himself, as I have indicated, experienced kinship with Babbitt. Perhaps because at the same time Lewis realized and attacked the power of *things* in American life, he admired the ingenuity of those things, the technology which made them, and the operation and power of the system which markets them. Utterly to damn Babbitt would have meant to damn America.

Although this ambivalence is undeniably present in ***Babbitt,*** it is much less obvious than in ***Main Street*** and it is consequently less damaging to the novel and less perplexing to the reader. In fact, Lewis's affection acts as a catalyst in the novel, thickening it and providing a complexity too often missing in his work. Where ***Babbitt*** falls short of the highest art, it does so from Lewis's inability to leave room for the reader's imagination. Almost nothing is implicit in ***Babbitt;*** we are told everything. When we share Babbitt's thoughts and fears, we share them all; there are no greater depths to be plumbed. Only two matters are left unclear: how Babbitt came to be the way he is, and what he should do about it. Although he is given a vague family background and a mother and half-brother who appear in the novel briefly, we learn nothing about Babbitt as a child or adolescent. We are told that in college he was a liberal, with lofty ambitions and ideals but we do not know what changed him. Surely it is hard for us to believe he could ever have been a wild and dangerous dreamer. In this sense Babbitt as a character is weaker than Carol and inferior to Hawk Ericson.

As for the possible methods of change in ***Babbitt,*** we have already seen that Lewis believes little is possible for Babbitt himself. However, the reader remains confused about what Lewis is *for.* Beyond an obvious sympathy for union labor, a hatred of the kind of Harding-Coolidge policies Babbitt admires, and a contempt for the cultural and aesthetic sterility of middle-class life, we do not know specifically what Lewis wants us to do. If he wants socialism, he does not say so. He simply wants people to be better. The novel's social program here reminds me of the scene in *All My Sons,* when Joe Keller, a more recent Babbitt, turns to his son Chris, and asks him what his son wants from him, and Chris shouts, "You can be better!"

While the book lacks proposals upon which to build the foundations of a new society, its impact upon its own time was very great. Appearing in the same year as Harding's declaration "If I could plant a Rotary Club in every city and hamlet in this country I would then rest assured that our ideals of freedom would be safe and civilization would progress," *Babbitt* reminded Americans that there were higher aspirations than "normalcy." It summarized every criticism advanced against the middle class in the 1920's, and it rendered a superb account of the devastating effects of a material culture. Others have since written of the average American businessman, but only Lewis's name for him survives in our vocabulary—as Lewis predicted it would, as a synonym for both a state of mind and a way of life. It is the outstanding social satire of its generation, if not of American literature, and it continues to engage us by the quantity of its truth and the vigor of its execution. Sinclair Lewis invented Babbitt; his creation endures. (pp. 73-85)

Sheldon Norman Grebstein, in his Sinclair Lewis, *Twayne Publishers, 1962, 192 p.*

Charles Child Walcutt (essay date 1966)

[*Walcutt is an American educator and critic who has written extensively on American literature. In the following excerpt, Walcutt explains his conception of* Babbitt *as programmatic parody of America's cultural insecurities.*]

Babbitt has been incredibly popular all over Europe as the ultimate exploration of the go-getting American businessman of the twenties. It is still on more reading lists for American Studies in Continental universities than one likes to count. Its horrible popularity is Phoenix-like: we may reduce it to ashes, but it will rise to peck at us, renewed, indestructible.

Babbitt burst like the apocalypse on the early twenties. Its hero's name became a byword that is still with us. The book supports my contention that, in the long run, ideas are more important to the success of a novel than character or plot, even though they do not necessarily assure distinction. Proof of the fascination of ideas lies in the fact that the plot of ***Babbitt*** is quite infantile, the characterization is incredibly poor, and yet the book was and still is read with delight. The influence of ***Babbitt*** abroad is incalculable. Western Europe has had two images of the United States. One is of a soulless commercial monster controlled by uneducated fools who in turn are frightened by mobsters. It is a land of folly and disorder, a land of incredibly bad taste, bad manners, half-baked ideas, hare-brained get-rich-quick schemes, political corruption, lynchings, hillbillies, poor education, and social chaos. The second image is of a nation with the most stable government in the whole world (a government that has kept its form through uncounted revolutions in the other "civilized" nations), with the most advanced technology, with the readiest imagination to generate new ideas and make use of them, with the highest and most practically active idealism and generosity that any nation has ever evinced, and—*mirabile dictu*—with the best poets, novelists, dramatists, composers, and architects in the world. This latter image is reflected in the influence of American styles and gadgets, the enthusiasm for American movies and American popular music, the spread of American painting, and the extraordinary currency of American books in Europe. But most of all it is by the written word that the mind is made up or changed, and ***Babbitt*** is the American written word that seems to have been most widely read and to have spread the "bad" image of the United States.

Babbitt is powerful satire. It holds the American Way up to bitter castigation, representing its follies in a sequence of concrete incidents that jump nimbly from item to item of the presumed American scene. In the early 1920's it answered a strange and special American need, which must be traced and explained. This country went into World War I with total dedication and idealism. For centuries our backs had been turned on Europe while we developed the West and wondered about the Great American Novel. The war brought a massive reversal, for unaccustomed as we are to half-measures, we determined not merely to help the Allies against the Hun but to revise the whole calendar of European injustice, oppression, and bigotry. We would free her from the dead hand of the past; we would mark her map anew with reasonable borders; we would, in fine, make the world safe for democracy. It was not a war but a crusade, and America has never been more passionately committed to any cause. Then came the Treaty of Versailles, where American idealism was betrayed by Old World evil and guile, leaving us nothing but empty hands and disenchantment, demonstrated on the political front by our refusal to join the League of Nations. Once more we washed our hands of Europe.

But hand washing was not enough. Our stains, like those of Lady Macbeth, became obsessions that would not give us peace. Anger and frustration changed to guilt—a national guilt that made us turn upon ourselves and abuse everything American. The reaction is psychologically common enough, and in the 1920's it found a warehouse full of emotional fireworks ready to be touched off. The attack on the small town was launched by Anderson's *Winesburg, Ohio* (1919). H. L. Mencken writing in the *American Mercury* made us rejoice to think ourselves a nation of boobs. Lewis joined the pack in full cry with *Main Street* (1920), which spelled out in detail the stifling social bigotry of the small town. F. Scott Fitzgerald in *The Great Gatsby* (1925) anatomized the corruption of the American Dream between the irresponsibility of the well-bred Buchanans and the phony illusions of Gatsby whose dream was tinsel. Hemingway hit the scene very soon to trace the scars on the body of hope, and in 1926 *The Sun Also Rises* began with an epigraph about the Lost Generation of shattered, disillusioned, expatriated heroes.

Babbitt makes a climax of self-abuse. It sets out to ridicule one aspect of American life after another, and we must look at it item by item in order to see how totally impossible it would be for any character to be all the characters that George Babbitt is said to be. He is, in fact, a moving image of American insecurity; the reader's guilts, fears, and shames are exploited, one after another, to make him react to one shameful, sentimental, nostalgic, or exasperated situation after another. He identifies with Babbitt as he experiences these emotions, and so he may be conned at first reading into thinking that Babbitt is a possible person, but the illusion vanishes with a second reading. The numerous Babbitts subsumed under the single name may be itemized by episodes.

Our hero, forty-six, pink, pudgy, balding, wakes to the rasping sounds of suburban morning, which he resists by snuggling down into a few moments of reverie about his "fairy girl" of romance. He is made ridiculous by details;

his alarm clock "was the best of nationally advertised and quantitatively produced alarm-clocks, with all modern attachments, including cathedral chime, intermittent alarm, and a phosphorescent dial"; he creeps out from under a blanket that was "forever a suggestion to him of freedom and heroism. He had bought it for a camping trip which had never come off. It symbolized gorgeous loafing, gorgeous cursing, virile flannel shirts." Gritty, petulant, repetitious, he struggles up to consciousness till his "sleep-swollen face was set in harder lines," then bumbles through washing and shaving and assumes the aggressive role of dynamic businessman. (Chapter 1.) The presentation continues to ridicule him by associating him with such objects as B.V.D. underwear, silver cigar-cutter, elk's tooth, and Boosters' Club button; these banal objects match the flow of banalities from his lips: his opinions are canned, superficial, shallow, and ludicrously self-contradicting. Let the following passage of Babbitt's opinion stand for fifty others like it that are scattered through the book. Reading the headlines at breakfast, he proclaims:

> "But this, say, this is corking! Beginning of the end for those fellows! New York Assembly has passed some bills that ought to completely outlaw the socialists! And there's an elevator-runners' strike in New York and a lot of college boys are taking their places. That's the stuff! And a mass-meeting in Birmingham's demanded that this Mick agitator, this fellow De Valera, be deported. Dead right, by golly! All these agitators paid with German gold anyway. And we got no business interfering with the Irish or any other foreign government. Keep our hands strictly off. And there's another well-authenticated rumor from Russia that Lenin is dead. That's fine. It's beyond me why we don't just step in there and kick those Bolshevik cusses out." [Chapter 2.]

The catalogue of banalities pronounced by Babbitt is a sparkling tribute to Sinclair Lewis's documentary zeal; if there was a stupid opinion on anything uttered during the period, there it is coming again from the mouth of the hero. One cannot help being delighted by the rich authenticity of what Lewis's ear has caught and his pen recorded:

> "How do those front tires look to you?"
>
> "Fine! Fine! Wouldn't be much work for garages if everybody looked after their car the way you do."
>
> "Well, I do try and have some sense about it." [Chapter 3.]

Everybody who dreams of escaping to the north woods, who catches himself uttering obvious remarks about the weather, who wishes from time to time that his life were more significant, or who makes a fool of himself giving up smoking every other week will know lively twinges of guilt as he laughs at the barren but pretentious soul of George F. Babbitt of Zenith in the American Middle West. This guilt is periodically relieved by renewed doses of the hero's socioeconomic opinions, for to these the reader can feel immeasurably superior:

> "A good labor union is of value because it keeps out radical unions, which would destroy property. No one ought to be forced to belong to a union, however. All labor agitators who try to force men to join a union should be hanged. In fact, just between ourselves, there oughtn't to be any unions allowed at

all; and as it's the best way of fighting the unions, every business man ought to belong to an employers'-association and to the Chamber of Commerce. In union there is strength. So any selfish hog who doesn't join the Chamber of Commerce ought to be forced to." [Chapter 4.]

Babbitt is a hardheaded, enterprising real-estate broker, which means that he knows how to bribe a politician, how to fix up a false front to hide the fact that he is also developing and building, and how to turn the screws down hard when he has a client or renter at his mercy. He is sharp, knowledgeable, energetic, hypocritical, and as crooked as he ever needs to be to get anything he wants. As the evidence of his success mounts along with the evidence of his colossal ignorance of anything but the data of his business, the image of American commerce goes down, down, down. It goes down so fast and so far and so fantastically that one is led to generalize on the fact that satire causes distortions which make chameleons of people.

And not many pages pass before Lewis, making a virtue of necessity, acknowledges that his hero is a quick-change chimera: "He was, just then, neither the sulky child of the sleeping-porch, the domestic tyrant of the breakfast table, the crafty money-changer of the Lyte-Purdy conference, nor the blaring Good Fellow, the Josher and Regular Guy, of the Athletic Club. He was an older brother to Paul Riesling, swift to defend him, admiring him with a proud and credulous love passing the love of women." (Chapter 5.) Acknowledges, yes, but he continues to multiply Babbitt's roles at a dizzy pace. As Babbitt jumps from a position to its opposite, he plays the gamut of pride and guilt, of stupid arrogance and secret shame, of loud-mouthed Josher and the man with a hundred gnawing insecurities.

It seems just possible that this pattern is a symptom of the neurotic self—and thus a reflection of the nation stretched in agony between indignation and guilt, between abusing ungrateful Europe and abusing its own booboisie-dominated self. As an individual or a nation agonizes in such continual incongruity, its sense of self dissolves. It finds itself adopting a series of poses, among which it moves with weakening confidence. It thrashes about in bewilderment, abusing itself and assailing the "others" before whom it fancies itself to be cutting a sorry figure, and it continually reveals that it is harried by uncertainty. The amorphous character of the hero and the acidulous venom of the style in *Babbitt* reveal these frightening doubts which are relieved by explosive laughter rather than by insight.

The episodic ridicule of American life continues. Correspondence courses suffer next, and Babbitt as usual contradicts himself in every sentence. A flashback shows how he was tricked into a loveless marriage, which is not without affection now, and which has brought three typical children into the household.

Babbitt and his wife give a painful dinner party, with too much food and drink, boisterous talk, and table-tapping. After it, Babbitt is bored and disgusted with his life. He plans a trip—wifeless!—to the Maine woods with Paul Riesling, finds the experience boring, then good when it is almost over; returns to more frantic work; participates ridiculously in golfing and movie-going. Then he makes a great, utterly fatuous speech to the State Association of Real Estate Boards and discovers Talent. Local fame

comes with a flood of Booster speeches that he delivers. The Babbitts prevail upon a social leader to come to dinner. The party is a fiasco and the invitation is not returned. In the following chapter the situation is reversed: The Babbitts go to dinner at the home of an old friend who is down on his luck. The dinner is a fiasco and the invitation is not returned. Next the church-as-Rotary-Club is lampooned. Getting involved in fund-raising brings Babbitt close to a very rich and pious old man named Eathorne, with whom he is able to work up some shady and profitable deals, the best of which is privately buying options on land that he is acting as broker to buy for the Traction Company's new line. Thus he is able to sell the land to himself and then to the Traction Company at a fat profit.

When Paul Riesling, who is Babbitt's sentimental escape-valve, shoots his nagging wife and is sentenced to three years in prison, Babbitt goes into a prolonged depression and yearns for Adventure and Escape. These come when he takes a manicurist to dinner, talks to a "radical" lawyer named Seneca Doane, whose flattery and name-dropping he gobbles up so avidly that he begins to wonder whether his Boosters aren't too hard on the workingman. Now labor trouble breaks out with several major strikes and demonstrations. The Boosters naturally are 5000 per cent for a firm hand: " 'I don't believe in standing back and wet-nursing these fellows and letting the disturbances drag on,' " says one Clarence Drum. " 'I tell you these strikers are nothing in God's world but a lot of bomb-throwing socialists and thugs, and the only way to handle 'em is with a club!' " (Chapter 27.)

That morning Babbitt had seen Seneca Doane in a tiny workers' parade that was broken up by the militia. For the worst reasons of vanity, discontent, and confusion (and not even really on the strikers' side) he nevertheless takes the liberal view: "Babbitt heard himself saying 'Oh, rats, Clarence, they look just about like you and me, and I certainly didn't notice any bombs.' " (Chapter 27.) The "fellows" begin to look at him as if he is "nutty," and he begins to draw the reader's sympathy because the businessmen are so stupid and brutal against him. They eye him suspiciously, and he feels "vaguely frightened."

Sharing this crumb of right feeling, Babbitt is drawn to a sultry widow named Tanis Judique, who so flatters his damaged ego that he defies his Booster pals at the daily lunch, slips into heavy drinking and wild parties—and balks at joining the Good Citizens' League, recently organized to combat "red ruin and those lazy dogs plotting for free beer." Now, Babbitt's leftish swerve has been motivated by pique plus Seneca Doane's name-dropping; his affair with Tanis Judique is entirely selfish and sensual; his drinking is wildly excessive; yet he becomes sympathetic because the Boosters are such boobs and because Lewis plays on the reader's insecurities. "Anybody" could be caught in the toils of his lower nature if the unlucky circumstances conspired. And poor bewildered stubborn childish Babbitt becomes the prey of a small-scale witch hunt. He shakes Tanis off, then yearns for her, quarrels with his wife, and is going in frantic circles—when Lewis pulls the weeping fortissimo stop on his sentimental organ. Babbitt's wife has acute appendicitis; in the emergency all the old homey loyalties rush back in, friends rally round, and Babbitt is so overwhelmed by their forgiveness that he vows never to stray again. He instantly becomes the leading red-baiter of Zenith. It is quite nauseating.

The fact that Lewis can make the reader feel some sympathy for Babbitt, in his final rosy glow of togetherness, shows again how cleverly Lewis has worked on him. The novel's plot is held together like autumn leaves in a gust, which is to say that the incidents are held together by the covers of the book and little else. The hero has no character; he is a complex of banalities, uncertainties, and huffiness. Only such a meandering and inconclusive action could produce so cipherous a man, and only the clever concreteness of Lewis's appeals to the reader's fears could delude him into *feeling* that he had indeed identified with him.

Most significant for our inquiry is the fact that the flimsiness of the action, the superficiality of the characterization, and the meanness of the controlling idea are organically balanced and unified. The organism, however, is a kind of stunted cactus, raised in an agronomy of venom and guilt. (pp. 241-47)

> *Charles Child Walcutt, "The Idea Men," in his* Man's Changing Mask: Modes and Methods of Characterization in Fiction, *University of Minnesota Press, 1966, pp. 240-300.*

Philip Allan Friedman (essay date 1966)

[*In the following essay, Friedman explains his conception of* Babbitt *as a synthesis of satirical devices and traditional realism.*]

In her revised memoir of their marriage Sinclair Lewis' first wife writes, "**Main Street** was not a satire until the critics began calling him [Lewis] a satirist, and then seeing himself cast in that role, it is possible that **Babbitt** thus became a true satire." I have found that, on the contrary, almost all the major reviews of his first best-seller stress its photographic realism rather than its satire.

Lewis himself said that **Babbitt** would have been written no matter how poorly **Main Street** had sold: "I was making notes," he tells us, "for **Babbitt** at the time I was putting the finishing touches on **Main Street**." At first he denied that Babbitt would be "a satiric figure" or "a Type." "He is too tragic . . . for the puerilities of deliberate satire." [See excerpt dated 1921?] No doubt he feared that, since satire involves distortion by the use of rhetorical devices, his book would not be read as a close image of American society. But when he got further into the composition, he wrote to his publishers on November 5, 1921, that he saw the developing novel as "satiric, rather more than **Main Street**." In another letter, dated December 13, 1921, he reiterated this idea: "I see that, being inherently more satiric than **Main Street, Babbitt** must not be anything like so long, or it will be tedious." Thus, perhaps under provocation from H. L. Mencken, whose idea it was years before, perhaps feeling at last free to do so, he deliberately created a consummate satiric type.

We can analyze how Lewis—sometimes grossly, more often with the great naturalness of a born mimic and a stabbing perception of incongruities in life—integrated certain discoverable properties of satire with realistic methods, making his novel something more than a mere fulfillment of the categorical imperatives laid down for the genre. He had produced a mixed breed, satiric realism. To this day no published examination of **Babbitt** has attempted an extensive formal analysis of this mixture of ingredients, some obvious, others not so apparent.

Often, to make us identify with the principal character, Lewis begins sentences with so-called objective phraseology such as: "It is true," "Statistics show," and the like. Thus he introduces us to Zenith (in the state of Winnemac), a seemingly appropriate name for a city that at first sight is highly developed in the arts of living. But if we are taken in by the author's veracity of external detail throughout the early sections, we are alienated to an extent, dependent upon our own conditioned attitudes, by the views of prominent citizens.

Lewis immediately pins down his type by means of a satiric epigram: George Follansbee Babbitt "made nothing in particular . . . but he was nimble in the calling of selling houses for more than people could afford to pay." As an instrument of satiric invective, the epigram compels us to see Babbitt in his real societal position. He is like his name sounds, we learn as we continue to read; and he is almost like what his name means: frictionless metal. He and his kind are a sort of neutral buffer between the top and the bottom rungs of the social ladder, held in place by the "prizes" at the top and by fear of being cast to the bottom.

That he put Babbitt in the real-estate business shows Lewis' awareness of its symbolic relationship to American civilization. Babbitt is a dealer in land that was once freely given.

Enlarging the picture of industrialized society, Babbitt's dream-fairy scene, a device of the Comic Spirit used by Mark Twain and others, creates the initial atmosphere of irony. With all the material enjoyments that are his, Babbitt yet finds his pleasure only in the imaginative reality of his dreams. The higher irony occurs when mechanical civilization, symbolized by the Ford car, invades his dream and takes precedence over the chase. Yet throughout the novel Babbitt is subject to one of Gulliver's errors: attributing an incorrect cause for an effect, seeing "the spiritual" as dominating mechanical progress, movements of Efficiency, Rotarianism, *et alia.*

Everything conducive to showing us how trivial and functionless a person can become in a city of steel, ostensibly erected for giants, is amassed satirically. Thus Lewis provides "props" that are sufficient to "prop up" the characterization. When Babbitt puts on his spectacles, he looks deceptively like a solon of business instead of a flabby-faced, pink, fat man who is trying only to follow rules he never made and dares not question. When he changes the contents of one suit to another, it is a "sensational event." An item such as the Boosters' Club lapel button proclaiming "Boosters—Pep!" was to him like a Legion of Honor ribbon or a Phi Beta Kappa key: it was "of eternal importance, like baseball or the Republican Party." Of course this arrangement of items provides an intentional anticlimax, indicating, by humorous descent from the eternal to the mediocre and commonplace, Babbitt's false sense of values.

Because the depiction of Babbitt's family life is satire within the much larger compass of the novel's structure, Babbitt's relationship with his wife Myra cannot be revealed in all its nuances. Its middle-class typicality must demonstrate the submerging of romantic aspirations and must earn our sympathy for Babbitt as he looks upon his wife with mild disgust. Even in the early part of the novel, brief references to the idealist Babbitt once was and the "clinging vine" Myra was, show that Lewis is never wholly the satirist consigning his "hero" to the devil.

Lewis describes Myra, in a doubly-significant phrase, as "definitely mature" after several years of marriage. When her maturity is defined as composed of a creased face, a baggy carcass, and a mind that is no longer aware of feminine niceties of appearance before her husband, we are affected by the biting contrast with real maturity. By middle-class standards Myra is "what is known as a Good Wife . . . " Juxtaposing words from two differently connotative spheres, Lewis draws a masculinely graphic picture of what habituation to married life has made her—"sexless as an anemic nun." Married love in a middle-class existence becomes for Babbitt a mere habit engendered by associations, circumstances, and conveniences, a habit circumscribed by the possibilities of prosperity or adversity in business.

In fact, to paraphrase Lewis, Babbitt's house is not a home. His children are cause only for his groaning, as in the famous breakfast scene; and they in turn consider him dull. He is as loyal to his family as to a legal contract; that is, he is often, but not always, loyal. He wants to live in that atmosphere of applause which is a paradise of fools, and his society sustains his desire. "But Babbitt was virtuous," smiles Lewis with Comic Spirit, continuing in an antithetical vein that has Babbitt cheating "only as it was sanctified by precedent."

Keeping his main character in interaction with other characters, Lewis catalogues most of the middle class's hypocrisies and rationalizations through Babbitt's spoutings with his friend Paul Riesling and with others. The more Babbitt deceives others in business, the more he deceives himself. Babbitt constantly puts himself on display as he would one of his realty selections. Just how ludicrous his thinking can be we learn from the inconsistency of his statements concerning labor-management relations—statements made during a decade when unions were steadily losing strength because of the Red Scare: a good labor union, Babbitt insists, is one that keeps out radical unions; in fact, no union at all is the best union. But the best way to fight labor is by the union of businessmen. When his salesman threatens "to squeal all I know," Babbitt is temporarily discomforted: "I wonder—No, I've never done anything that wasn't necessary to keep the Wheels of Progress moving." He does not admit even to himself having fallen from middle-class grace because as a double irony the reality of middle-class morality has nothing to do with the conventional ideals it professes. Life in middle-class America, and elsewhere today as industrialization spreads the growth of the middle class, is a sordid calculation of moments.

Many critics have remarked that Lewis lacked depth as a novelist because he probed the generic, not the individual, qualities of his central character. But the force of their argument is self-contained only if one agrees to their initial definitions of the so-called pure novel, at one time perhaps a valid area of conceptualization. True, Lewis' satire is often gross in leaving almost nothing to inference. But in the overall view of *Babbitt* as satiric realism, considering the intentional breadth of Lewis' satiric scope, this work is powerful.

The satire is the more powerful in the very fact that for a long time Babbitt does not realize the cause of his restlessness and covers it with self-assured bluster. Had Lewis given Babbitt immediate understanding of his own dilemma and an early opportunity to resolve it, the strength of the social indictment would have been diminished. Lewis views a whole class and a whole city through the eyes of a man first prejudiced for their progress and then ironically tripped up by his class-imposed vision.

Like Dickens, Lewis could transfix the variations of the middle-class type, all of whom merge into this institution in their social relationships. With tags or auditory labels which, when often repeated, become catch phrases, Lewis sets and strengthens his minor characterizations. He also uses tag names to great effect. For instance, the "Great Scholar," Howard Littlefield, indelibly confirms his name in being a little man in his field. The social snobs are the McKelveys, representing the upper class, and the Babbitts themselves, the middle-class social climbers. Perhaps with too obvious dramatic irony Lewis exhibits the Babbitts turning up their noses at the Overbrooks at the same time that the Babbitts themselves are suffering from having been snubbed by the McKelveys. The intellectual snob of this menage, T. Cholmondeley ("Chum") Frink, Lewis describes with mock encomium as not only a syndicated poet but also "an optimistic lecturer and creator of 'Ads that Add'." Frink obviously connotes a fraud.

Before William A. ("Billy") Sunday, the ranting baseball player turned raving preacher, found himself impaled by Lewis' barbs in *Elmer Gantry,* he could have discovered himself thinly disguised in *Babbitt* as Mike Monday. This time Lewis flays the type of religious hypocrite with satiric invective: "As a prize-fighter he [Monday] gained nothing but his crooked nose, his celebrated vocabulary, and his stage presence. The service of the Lord had been more profitable. He was about to retire with a fortune."

A more significant figure in the novel is the demoniac Vergil Gunch. Lewis does not satirize him in the same way that he does the other characters, because Gunch is too sinister a force—a type become all evil. He represents the nemesis which makes every apostate-Babbitt eventually recant. It is no coincidence that his occupation is that of a coal dealer with its associative reference to blackness and the fires of Hell. His tag names reinforce the complete duality of his nature, his devilish two-facedness. Half of his personality fits in a humorous way the poet's name he bears. He can be jolly and oratorical, though his accusing silences also persuade; and he is chummy with the members of the theater's lesser arts, vaudeville and burlesque. The name "Gunch" has the quality of the word "goon," which would appropriately suggest his serving as the chief instrument of the bigger business elements in Zenith. When he first appears in a scene, his hair *"en brosse,"* his name is mentioned in close context with the word "hunch." It may not be too hypothetical to suggest that "hunch," somewhat inappropriately used by Lewis except for its proximity to "Gunch," was intended to indicate the contraction of "gods' hunch" in the name. This view strengthens the conception of Vergil Gunch as the thought controller for the gods of American business.

In the famous dinner-party scene of Chapters VIII through IX, in the best Dickensian tradition, Lewis makes Gunch a malevolent antagonist of those who expose small-town provincialism. What he speaks is not so much ludicrous as deadly: "You don't want to just look at what these small towns are, you want to look at what they're aiming to become . . . they all want to be just like Zenith!" Developing the mood that will result in Babbitt's later abortive rebellion, Lewis permits him to see his life in Zenith as constricting and Gunch as the watchdog of conformism, almost an impersonal and depersonalizing instrument of an industrialism rampant.

As we see, Lewis has both contempt and empathy for most of these complacent egoists. They have accepted as inevitable the fact that their friends are really boring to them for the same reasons of banal behavior they cannot perceive in themselves. Lewis satirizes the whole gamut of opinions and institutions in Gunch-ridden, Babbitt-conforming middle-class society, except for what in a later decade Arthur Koestler called the mouthings of the Babbitts of the Left. Lewis knew them, too, but preferred not to complicate his novel with such modulations of types, perhaps because he did not wish to hurt the infant labor movement. Rather he has Clarence Drum (whose tag names suggest the bullying martial spirit attempting to conceal the coward's heart) view striking laborers as "a lot of bomb-throwing socialists and thugs." The Fascist-minded "Minute Man" advocates violent measures against unions in anticipation of violence.

To the businessmen riding the rails, the old "coons," who were always called "George," were good servants because they knew their place. Babbitt decries the disrespectful yearnings of the young "niggers" who do not want to be porters and cotton pickers into eternity. One obviously Jewish chameleon, taking on the standardized colors of Babbitt, inveighs against the increase of foreigners in the country. We also discover the Jewish anti-Semite in Sidney Finkelstein, one of the "Regular Guys."

Lewis would find the middle-class rush to obtain the ornaments of "culture" laughable if it were not so pitiful. Lewis understands that culture is never a businesslike pursuit. It is an evocation of a people's high spirits and noble aims. But Chum Frink asks for funds to establish a symphony orchestra on the ground that "The thing to do . . . is to *capitalize Culture*." The italicizing, of course, derives from the older forms of exaggeration, by which Lewis directs our attention not only to the spelling directions contained in the expression itself but also to the commercial emphasis of any middle-class venture into these higher spheres of activity. Babbitt's own cultural entertainments are the movies, where usually he gushes sentimentality. Lewis would have agreed with George Herbert Mead that the movie houses offered escape to those emotionally frustrated and bottled up. His observation is also in consonance with that of Morris R. Cohen and other thinkers of the twenties and later: watching a baseball game "gave outlet for the homicidal and sides-taking instincts which Babbitt called 'patriotism' and 'love of sport'."

What Babbitt does not understand, if acceptable to his group, he praises; if unacceptable, he condemns. Higher education, typified by the State University, he praises for the reason that it is good business to say you are a B.A. Lewis has previously prepared us for the paradox of Babbitt's dictating to teachers, although knowing nothing about their average salary and caring less. Lewis is saying that American education is forced to impart efficiency but not humanity and appreciation of true culture. The Babbitt-warren among the academic fraternity, under the influence of their business brethren, vulgarize pragmatic philosophy in identifying truth with material success, beauty with utility.

Lewis pictures religion in the middle-class world either as a repressive puritanism which easily converts people like Zilla Riesling from potential to full-fledged fanatics or as another form of "boosting" like that illustrated by the Reverend Dr. Drew who writes about "The Dollars and Sense Value of Christianity." If Babbitt gives to the church his greatest treasure, his money, he insures himself heavenly reward. Even Babbitt, when in revolt against his class, becomes figuratively asphyxiated by the pastor's gaseous harangue on "How the Saviour Would End Strikes." Lewis gives us credit for the intelligence to extend the pastor's drivel to mean that though the workers starve on their wages, they should live on the boss's smiles. Lewis implies that most American churches subserve the demands of the real religion—the "religion of business."

"Boosting" provides Babbitt, as religion does not, with various avenues of escape from domestic boredom, with an arena for the expression of his self-conceit, and with places where he can meet the "right" businessmen. In a vein of high burlesque, Lewis takes off the report of the Resolutions Committee at the State Real Estate Board convention. The exalted language magnifies the trivial intent of the report, which thinks nothing of debasing the view of God for its purpose. And Lewis parodies the circular bombast of the Boosters' Club's aims in Dadbury Petersen's announcement, but he has already topped this effort at refining high burlesque into its verbal form, parody, when he mimics the one-hundred-percent American in Babbitt's speech on the Ideal Citizen. The novel drives home the point that such organizations as Rotary International do not really give Babbitt a chance to express his individuality. They make him stay rooted in confusion of values.

The ironic climax, Paul's tragedy, injects the cosmic irony of universal boredom into the novel, for it makes Babbitt see the futility of his existence. "What was it all about? What did he want?" As a satirist Lewis need not present the dramatic contrast of people following a better way of life which Babbitt could emulate. Like the radical lawyer Seneca Doane, Lewis approves of material standardization but abhors the fact that with all their material success too many Americans in their complacent arrogance are unaware that they concentrate on being like one another. He condemns through Doane "the traditions of competition" in a society which makes the type of slave for whom there is least hope of freedom, the slave of other men's ideas.

Lewis' implied alternative is no well-knit philosophy of living; he leaves it to the revolutionist theoreticians and other ideological activists to provide absolute faith in causes and programs. Romantically inclined, he believes that man is full of undiscovered possibilities for creating a better life, but that these possibilities are suppressed at an early age. For Babbitt subordinates himself to the group, to the disciplined conformity of psychological socialism. Lewis perceives nothing inherently evil in human nature to cause the surface boils of society which he loves to prick. The basis of his satire is society's committing the *reductio ad absurdum* of preventing individualism in the name of individualism.

Lewis conceived the later sections of the novel as "much more straight narrative, much less satiric, than the earlier part, so it could run longer than could all satire." The satire prevails, however, although Lewis applies fewer rhetorical devices, because it takes on the larger proportions of cosmic irony. For it is a universal boredom, the same *weltschmerz* Paul felt, that now Babbitt cannot escape, in addition to the dullness generated by his environment. His clandestine affair with Tanis Judique and his binges with the "Bunch," whom Lewis mercilessly satirizes for their pretended bohemianism, are all merely excesses of middle-class behavior and do not relieve his great loneliness. As has often been noted, Lewis' kindred affection for the very type he is satirizing comes to the surface in the novel, sometimes to the confusion of his purposes. Where he could have been scathing, he is indulgent. He gives us the painful social consequences of Babbitt's groping for self-realization among a herd of "nice" people who are bold for causes when they are afraid for themselves. But in making Babbitt more human Lewis also reinforces his contention that, in a too-standardized industrial society, being an individual, not merely individualistic, is a luxury which only a man blessed with a permanently high income can afford. With terrifying ironic realism, he dramatizes the truism that when a vice wishes to disguise itself, it assumes the appearance of its opposite virtue. However, Lewis did not intend that Babbitt should become as intellectually cognizant as Seneca Doane of the reactionary elements composing the Good Citizens' League. Actually Babbitt is not so much opposed to such an organization's goals as he is interested in voicing a vestigial individualism in American society. His one really un-Babbittlike act has been his previous willingness to perjure himself to help his friend Paul. Except for this, his behavior remains that expected of a middle-class egoist. Even so, we sympathize and empathize with him when the businessmen conduct a crusade to make him once more a "decent" citizen. We foresee that his submission to the GCL is inevitable. As the tyranny of the Gunches increases, we watch in ironic suspense how Babbitt's nerve proportionately fails. And we even feel some compassion for him at this juncture because Lewis' satiric realism borders on tragedy.

It is a good psychological touch for Babbitt to embrace his wife in her need; Lewis saves the situation from bathos by revealing the shallowness of Babbitt's reaction. But it would have been more satiric and less unrealistic had the little fat man been caught longer in the "big squeeze" of the business community before an opportune pretext to recant arose. Even so, there is some satire in Babbitt's rationalization of his return to the fold and in his becoming more the conformist than ever.

In the first half of the last chapter, Lewis again resorts to the classical convention of contrasting the profession of honesty, integrity, and virtue with the practice of dishonesty, compromise of integrity, and vice. And he demonstrates with greater irony that vice parading as virtue, evil as good, and folly as wisdom have earned the most reward and highest esteem on earth. The irony is refined into Bab-

bitt's realization that "he had been trapped into the very net from which he had with such fury escaped and, supremest jest of all, been made to rejoice in the trapping." Lewis knows that Babbitt wants to think that he had really escaped.

After such irony, we are not fully prepared for what Lewis intended in the remaining pages of the novel. In later years, he declared that he had not changed his opinion of Babbitt and that he had not been unkind in his portrait of the middle-class businessman, adding: "If you read the last chapter of the book you'll find I treated Babbitt well." But the only "kindness" Lewis performed was what the reality of the novel demanded, that Babbitt be permitted to live. The contrived ending is both satirically realistic and a projection of Lewis' romantic hope for the future. This hope is tenuous, however, because he gives meager evidence, except in the last few pages, when we are not prepared for it, that Ted's behavior is anything more than adolescent bravado. The romanticism weakens the natural logic of the novel qua novel, and only the predominant satiric realism concerning Babbitt's final and futile gesture makes us overlook Lewis' artistic failure with respect to Ted. Or did Lewis realize, and intend us to see, that Ted would become no more mature than his father? Sometimes his *post facto* statements must be discounted.

Is not this whole final incident of Ted's elopement and Babbitt's blessing to his son in effect an ultra return to babbittry—an incident richer in satire than is the opening scene of the novel? Now again Babbitt feeds the fairy child to the giant of conformity, and this is the wide-awake dreamer—this is the Death of a Salesman who must go on living. The reader who imagines that Lewis has given us another Babbitt at this point, does so because he identifies (Lewis relentlessly makes him identify) with Babbitt. In the final analysis, the reader shudders to see himself so realistically presented, and therefore cries out in protest to the mirror, "This is a new Babbitt. I knew he would become objective and realistic enough to see the right path." Lewis thus achieves the ultimate in satire—to let Babbitt see himself clearly for a while, then permit him to live with that bitter view, accepting his inevitable "What is, is," which Babbitt will ever "boost," making even himself believe that he wants it that way. The mote is not in Babbitt's nor Lewis' eye.

Lewis' satiric realism will survive so long as Babbitts survive in their *essentia*, their outward behavior doing violence to the moral sentiments they profess. However, Babbitts are no longer merely funny or faintly pathetic (were they ever just this?). As Lewis implies, the Babbitts are dangerous to the future of civilization. The truth about them is not simply their inertia but, unfortunately, their active behavior—conformism and philistinism in action. Imperishable types? (pp. 64-75)

> *Philip Allan Friedman, " 'Babbitt': Satiric Realism in Form and Content," in* The Merrill Studies in Babbitt, *edited by Martin Light, Charles E. Merrill Publishing Company, 1971, pp. 64-75.*

D. J. Dooley   (essay date 1967)

[*In the following excerpt from his biographical and criti-*

cal study of Lewis, The Art of Sinclair Lewis, *Dooley argues that Lewis was incapable of sustaining his conception of Babbitt as pure caricature given the protagonist's protracted struggle to exert a measure of control over his moral destiny.*]

The first hundred pages of ***Babbitt*** describe, almost in mock-heroic fashion, a day in the life of the Average Business Man. The Substantial Citizen is taken at his own valuation; each event of his day is of world-shaking importance, and must be captured in photographic detail: Business Man shaving, Business Man changing suits, Business Man starting car, Business Man completing deal, and so on. The effect would be highly ironic if the author maintained his detachment. But instead of allowing us to infer the limitations of his hero, Lewis himself points them out: he stresses that in a city which seems built for giants George F. Babbitt is really a pygmy.

Babbitt is portrayed as the archetype of the Booster, loud-mouthed, unthinking, and insensitive. His speech, compounded of the clichés and prejudices of his group, is not the expression of a sentient, rational human being. His symbols of truth and beauty are the mechanical devices which surround him, even though he understands nothing of their workings. Success for him means conformity to the pattern of living delineated by the one true American art, advertising:

> Just as he was an Elk, a Booster, and a member of the Chamber of Commerce, just as the priests of the Presbyterian Church determined his every religious belief, and the senators who controlled the Republican Party decided in little smoky rooms in Washington what he should think about disarmament, tariff, and Germany, so did the large national advertisers fix the surface of his life, fix what he believed to be his individuality. These standard advertised wares—toothpastes, socks, tires, cameras, instantaneous hot-water heaters—were his symbols of excellence; at first the signs, then the substitutes, for joy and passion and wisdom.

Though he loves "to speak sonorously of Unselfish Public Service, the Broker's Obligation to Keep Inviolate the Trust of His Clients, and a thing called Ethics, whose nature was confusing," the value of his work to society is exactly nothing. Beyond this, Seneca Doane, the middle-of-the-road liberal who seems to represent Lewis's point of view, maintains that he exercises a fearful despotism:

> "What I fight in Zenith is standardization of thought, and, of course, the traditions of competition. The real villains of the piece are the clean, kind, industrious Family Men who use every known brand of trickery and cruelty to insure the prosperity of their cubs. The worst thing about these fellows is that they're so good and, in their work at least, so intelligent. You can't hate them properly, and yet their standardized minds are the enemy."

Doane's assessment is in keeping with the unpublished introduction—written when Lewis had not yet made his final decision concerning his hero's name and was calling him Pumphrey—which begins, "THIS IS THE STORY OF THE RULER OF AMERICA" and ironically refers to "Our conqueror, dictator over our commerce, education, labor, art, politics, morals, and lack of conversation." Lewis declares that the thirty million men of this type have an un-

paralleled autocratic control, for no rulers in past history have ever interfered so completely in their subject's activities:

> Though English morals and French politics and German industry have been determined by the Sound Middle-Class, the Bourgeoisie, the Pumphreysie, have never dared also to announce standards in sculpture and table-manners. For in those lands there are outcasts and aristocrats who smile at the impertinence of the unimaginative. But in America we have created the superman complete, and the mellifluous name of the archangelic monster is Pumphrey, good old G. T. Pumphrey, the plain citizen and omnipotent power.

But Lewis does not sustain this view of his central character. He often shows Babbitt as a caricature of a real person, ironically prevented from becoming fully human by the restrictions which all the people of his class impose upon their society. However, Babbitt does possess an inner life, a yearning for the exotic and a native decency which separate him from his back-slapping associates—the Vergil Gunches and Chum Frinks—and link him with a misfit, Paul Riesling. Babbitt can be regarded as a buffoon: his name has entered the dictionaries as a synonym for blatancy; but that is not the whole of him.

Nor is he an "archangelic monster," a "superman complete." The more subtle conception of a character who, though sympathetic, is still the villain of the piece gives way to the more melodramatic conception of an *homme moyen sensuel* struggling helplessly against powerful ogres. Babbitt's moral failure is partly excusable: he tries to revolt against conformity, but finds that it is impossible to do so and still survive. The Babbitts are only pawns in the hands of the real villains, the racketeers like Colonel Snow, Jake Offutt, and Henry Thompson. Lewis has fallen back upon a commonly held opinion concerning the

Lewis, 1923.

source of evil in the American Garden of Eden; Henry F. May writes,

> When the muckrakers brought them to light, cruelty and misery seemed a disgrace to America and the twentieth century. They were the product, not of any innate evil either in human nature or modern society, but of the corrupt power of a few. . . . Powerful and corrupt individuals had perverted the country's institutions and dammed for their own benefit the rivers of progress.

Lewis accepts the middle-class myth that the Babbitts are not to blame. Though we can convict Babbitt of hypocrisy and affectation—and one main thread of the book is the comic exposure of these—he is the victim of a tragic irony: he acts as though he had some control over his own affairs, becoming almost heroic in a struggle which he has no chance of winning.

Curiously, however, Lewis allows him to sink back from defiant hero to Average Business Man again. Eventually he swears allegiance to the Good Citizen's League:

> Within two weeks no one in the League was more violent regarding the wickedness of Seneca Doane, the crimes of labor unions, the perils of immigration, and the delights of gold, morality, and bank-accounts than was George F. Babbitt.

Although he has seen how ugly is the behavior of the Booster's Club and how empty are its oracles, he is happy to be welcomed back into it. And with an incredible disregard of his own bitter experiences, he tells his son, "Go ahead, old man! The world is yours!"

Just as there are two Babbitts, there are two themes. Lewis is partly concerned with sociological analysis, with an anatomy of the businessman's world. He employs the satirist's techniques of selection and distortion; the day in Babbitt's life which takes up the first quarter of the book shows us a caricature of a businessman engaged in a parody of business activity. After that, there is a series of satirical episodes connected only by the fact that Babbitt has something to do with them. The Real Estate Boards convention shows us hysterical local patriotism and males in a happy state of nature. Lunches at the "Roughnecks' Table" at the Athletic Club, a college reunion, a civic election, and various other events round out the picture of group behavior and exhibit the full range of group opinion and prejudice. The universality of Babbittry is made apparent when Babbitt discovers that his sales techniques are just the thing which religion needs. Lewis's method thus permits a general satiric attack, beginning with a single point, the main character, and tracing around him the whole circle of society.

In his desire to be as comprehensive as possible, Lewis connects some of the satire only very loosely with Babbitt. When young Ted receives some correspondence-school circulars, Lewis is given an opportunity to ridicule them. Since Babbitt knows a real, live, A-one poet, Chum Frink, Lewis can parody the verse and satirize the outlook of an Edgar Guest. When Mrs. Babbitt conducts a revolt of her own in the direction of Higher Thought—presumably suggested by New Thought—Lewis forces his hero to sit through a lecture by Mrs. Opal Emerson Mudge on "Cultivating the Sun Spirit." In a survey of what is going on in Zenith when Babbitt goes to bed, Lewis brings in Mike Monday (Billy Sunday) and lets him evangelize for the length of a page. The loose form of the novel allows Lewis plenty of scope for take-offs on people familiar to the citizens of all the Zeniths.

"Form letters, advertisements, six-page conversations about prohibition, evangelical sermons by Mike Monday, all are put in, head first. And out of this, about two-thirds way through the book, Mr. Lewis gets down to the business of writing a novel with created characters and very nearly pulls it off "—So wrote the *Dial* reviewer. But in the melodramatic story of how Babbitt, now a hero, battles his former friends, now villains, the characters are simple and unreal, the plot is full of improbabilities, and Lewis does not come close to pulling it off. A possible criticism is that, whereas Lewis can amuse us with his Boosters' Club, he cannot frighten us with his Good Citizens' League. The qualities of the characters are as heightened and exaggerated as they were before; previously the exaggeration led to laughter, and it is very difficult for the reader to change his response just because Lewis tells him to do so: these fairy-tale giants and ogres cannot hurt us. But perhaps there is something particularly monstrous about these hearty, laughing, mechanical men beginning to torture someone; at any rate, their Vigilante Committee is horrifying, and the growth of Babbitt's fear after their ostracism of him is made very real. Yet it is hard to accept the turns of the plot, especially the new awareness with which Babbitt is endowed and then his loss of it and relapse into his former state.

Edward Wagenknecht contends that the change in Babbitt is prepared for or nonexistent, since Lewis skillfully prevents his hero from ever declining into a mere stalking-horse—in college, for example, he was "an unusually liberal, sensitive chap" who wanted to be a lawyer and take the cases of the poor for nothing. Virginia Woolf, however, seems nearer the mark when she describes Lewis's attempts to convey Babbitt's sensitivity as awkward and unconvincing. Commenting on the dream of a fairy child—"Her dear and tranquil hand caressed his cheek. He was gallant and wise and well-beloved; warm ivory were her arms; and beyond perilous moors the brave sea glittered"—she observes that this is not a dream at all but "the protest of a man who has never dreamed in his life, but is determined to prove that dreaming is as easy as shelling peas." Babbitt's inwardness, of course, is just what Lewis did not want to show if he were to hold to his original conception of a man who lived by externals, by things which could be bought and sold and advertised. He could have shown the uncertainty which mocked the confident exterior, the fear in a handful of dust; instead, he tried to convince his readers that Babbitt's naive questionings and affirmations represented something deep and true and unperverted.

What Frederick J. Hoffman calls the parody Babbitt [see excerpt dated 1949], therefore, is the vivid and memorable one. The most frequent tributes to the book were that Babbitt was characterized with gusto and that Lewis had succeeded in presenting the commonplace in lively terms; he had caught the American businessman in all his vulgarity and "vile gregariousness," as H. G. Wells put it in a letter of congratulation. He had, in fact, created a whole herd of Babbitts, all of them voicing the same crude prejudices and platitudes, all of them employing the same slangy, repetitious, bombastic utterance, all of them full of hearty boyish humor based on elaborate exaggeration and deliberate misrepresentation. They live in virtue of their talk; if some critics have disputed the opinion that Lewis had a marvelous ear for American speech, he undoubtedly had a knack for making speech sound authentic. In conversation or in satiric monologues delivered in a racy, convincing idiom, the Babbitts give themselves away; Babbitt's speech to the Zenith Real Estate Board provides what Hoffman terms a whole summary of tribal opinions and evaluations, a literary ordering of Mencken's accumulations, in the "Americana" section of his *Mercury,* of what the booboisie thought.

Mencken delightedly wrote that for the first time the type had been captured in fiction: "For the first time a wholly genuine American has got into a book—not the lowly, aspiring, half-pathetic American of the hinterland, but the cocky, bustling, enormously successful American of the big towns—the Booster, the Master of Salesmanship, the Optimist, the 100 per cent Patriot and Right-Thinker." Was this a large enough subject for a novel? Virginia Woolf did not think so. Rather patronizingly, she wrote that if Lewis had been born in England he might have proved himself the equal of Wells and Bennett, but, denied the riches of an old civilization, he had been forced to criticize rather than explore, and the object of his criticism—the life of Zenith—was unfortunately too meager to sustain him. But the complaint of Cooper and Hawthorne and many another American novelist that the American scene offered a paucity of literary material was not and could not be Lewis's complaint. When Babbitt delineates his concept of the Ideal, Standardized Citizen and contrasts the new civilization of vital standardized living with the decadence of Europe, Lewis is implying that the whole nation has got into a blind alley of Babbittry. Surely this is a major subject for satire; Lewis found it and exploited it, but unfortunately he was not satisfied with it—he gave rein to his naive romanticism and brought in some entirely alien fairy children, giants, and ogres.

With *Babbitt* Lewis began what was to be his characteristic method of composition, based on an intensive study of a subject. First came a preliminary stage of investigation, often requiring research trips and the services of an expert adviser, and always involving the taking of copious notes. Then came a stage of amazingly detailed planning. "He wrote his novels from precise and copious outlines of the characters, their professions or trades, and their haunts," wrote Dorothy Thompson, "building the structure of the book as an architect designs a house." He had always drawn detailed maps of the more important fictional towns in his books. Charles Breasted, who was shown those for the novels from *Our Mr. Wrenn* on, noted, however, that between Gopher Prairie and Zenith "the detail increased until it was almost like an annotated commercial map. . . ." In his arguments with George Soule over the importance of scene, Lewis had maintained that the remembered background, the "scene which one knows by the ten thousand unconscious experiences of living in it," was the only one which a writer could express adequately. When he had to deal with an environment not lived in and remembered in this way, he apparently felt that he would have to familiarize himself with it to the greatest possible extent. He knew the streets in the business section of Zenith and the residential area of Floral Heights because he

had examined their real-life prototypes with the greatest care; he tried to construct them with all the fullness of cities he knew. "By this folder full of maps," Breasted wrote, "Lewis had translated the world of his imagination and experience into something so close to reality that in listening to him one promptly became wholly convinced of their actuality." When to his maps, charts, and notes recording examples of the various types of folly which he was investigating he added full biographies of all the important characters in his projected novel and an outline of the action, he had a formidable mass of material; his complete plan might be as long as an average novel.

From the first, *Babbitt* made its mark; it was quickly acclaimed as a classic burlesque of the businessman and his world. From expected quarters, especially in the Midwest, there came growls of resentment and protest, but Anne O'Hare McCormick reported in the New York *Times* just a month after the book's publication that even the Rotarians were reading it. Some people thought that Lewis filled his books with spleen; many thought that he hated his native land; but very many thought that he had made a brilliant attack on a vulnerable segment of American society. The reception of *Babbitt* abroad was equally favorable. "After *Babbitt* was published in London," writes Harrison Smith, "there was an immense curiosity about the man who had revitalized American literature, so that he was welcomed everywhere." The curiosity was not entirely attributable to the view that Lewis's fearless criticism had revitalized American literature; his novels seemed to justify the stereotype of the typical American as uncouth, materialistic, and ignorant of the finer things of life. Therefore Europeans generally viewed Babbitt as Mencken did, as a portrait of the wholly genuine American [see *TCLC*, Vol. 4, pp. 246-47]. They took seriously, of course, only the parody Babbitt, not the hesitant and soul-searching one. "To be labeled a 'Babbitt,' " says the article on the novel in the *Encyclopaedia Americana,* "carries with it the packaged stigma of obtuseness, philistinism, blatant optimism, want of humor, and a smug, uncritical acceptance of one's own standards, however narrow, benighted, and unlovely they may seem to others." Whether or not Lewis wanted to attach other connotations to the name, this is what it has come to convey, both in America and in Europe. Sherard Vines wrote, "it was *Babbitt* which so impressed its portraiture on this island as almost to create a myth of America as one vast Babbitt warren; and at least replaced the old popular image of the thin American with a goatee beard, by that of a fat American with spectacles." Similarly George Bernard Shaw declared that "Mr. Sinclair Lewis has knocked Washington off his pedestal and substituted *Babbitt,* who is now a European byword." (pp. 83-93)

D. J. Dooley, in his The Art of Sinclair Lewis,
University of Nebraska Press, 1967, 286 p.

Helen B. Petrullo   (essay date 1969)

[*In the following essay, Petrullo discusses Lewis's controlled disposition of satirical devices within* Babbitt's *narrative structure.*]

Man Ray's famous camera portrait of Sinclair Lewis, which shows poised above a heavy overcoat collar a face that looks both bewildered and introspective, has become emblematic of the man. Few critics of his works, from the twenties to the present, have been able to forget the "divided" man behind that face. At this juncture in the criticism of Lewis's novel-satires of the twenties, an approach more fruitful than the biographical, I believe, is to study them analytically and to judge them by the criteria of prose satire, rather than of the novel. In applying these criteria to **Babbitt,** I find that Lewis, in effect, has done what Jack Burden daydreams of doing for himself in Warren's *All the King's Men:* he has brought Babbitt's various "you's" together at "barbecues" and exposed what they say to each other.

Lewis's practice in **Babbitt** closely approximates Ricardo Quintana's brilliant description of Swift's characteristic method—the creation of a "situational satire." The ways in which Swift develops an argument and establishes a moral focus is an elucidating frame of reference for studying Lewis's structuring, which must necessarily yield an inferable standard against which the heterogeneous contextual society is measured.

In creating a situation generative of satire Quintana finds that all of Swift's normal satiric devices are used to produce "an exhibition" where "everything is one degree removed from reality." Behind the created situation there is "an imaginative point of view, making possible and controlling a kind of translation into terms peculiar to a certain angle of perception." In *An Argument Against Abolishing Christianity,* there is, Quintana says, "a disputation that is more than a colloquy between A (who views abolition with concern) and B (all who, for various reasons, would abolish). A is likewise a multiplicity of voices, each point of view that is pressed into service carrying with it a somewhat different personality. It is a dialogue between the speaker's various selves, each of whom has a myth wherewith to confound his adversary; the full pattern of the 'argument' emerges solely from eccentric points of reference."

A moral standard is educed from the full pattern of the argument. To make explicit that which is implicit in Quintana, I would add that the "normal" may at times represent one of the "eccentric points of reference" and that within the created situation, one absurdity, or voice, confronts other absurdities, including *what is.* In the resulting competition of voices, the reader is coerced into making his own "translation," from which the moral focus emerges.

Approaching **Babbitt** as situational satire permits a concentration on the structuring—the selection of the various elements, their positioning, functions, and interrelationships. The contemporary milieu remains as the viable context of the satire even though the impressive verisimilitude that Lewis has fabricated out of genuinely realistic details is admitted at the outset to be "one degree removed from reality," because of the selection and emphasis of the fictional elements. We can objectively examine the methods Lewis used to entice a complacent and self-righteous America to lower its barriers to self-awareness enough to peruse the mirrored ugliness that constricts the lives of its individuals and stunts the development of its society.

Babbitt is of course the central figure in the overall "situation" that encompasses the total action, and in that action he offers enough selves to engage the sympathetic identification of most readers at some point. From his wardrobe of masks, Babbitt plucks faces to meet the exigencies—head of family, entrepreneur, shady dealer, crony, host, politician, alumnus, rebel, outdoorsman, pious moralist, romantic, church layman, orator, loyal friend, husband out-on-the-town. During the course of the narrative, Lewis creates a montage image of Babbitt that rivals the Athletic Club's eclectic architectural collage. While the Club is imposing and misnamed, its clashing styles chosen for pretension's sake, out of necessity Babbitt is an unprepossessing alloy, properly named. As mouthpiece for Zenith's glories, unifying center for its described activities, and temporary defector from its conventions, Babbitt is also the main satiric vehicle. For the whole action, his speech before the Real Estate Board is the artistic center. The speech of praise by the loyal, credulous Babbitt, in its passionate boosting of the city and its long-winded all-inclusiveness, would become through simple inversion an equally inclusive indictment. Lewis's technique is more subtle than an irony that involves only simply inversion, however, for the object of his satire—the city itself, and beyond it the culture which Zenith epitomizes—is too complex to be attacked effectively by an instrument that only requires the taking of a meaning directly opposite to the one presented. The indictment of the city is tempered and clarified, even as it is extended, by the concatenation of the many voices that figure in the action.

Character, setting, and events are plotted to provide a full background against which Babbitt's glowing account of the city is measured. While the setting cannot be treated in detail here, we can observe that the beginning paragraphs develop a basic incongruity between the new city and the lingering remnants of the old town, between the emerging city seemingly built for giants and the little, insignificant people dwarfed by its shining towers. The deceptiveness of appearances is immediately impressed upon the reader. From the initial telescopic view, Lewis proceeds to a microscopic examination: the bright, new "home" which should have been a retreat for laughter and tranquility is shown to be no more of a sanctuary than a "good hotel room", and Babbitt's office in one of the glistening skyscrapers is "a vault, a steel chapel," where business was worshipped and "loafing and laughter were raw sin."

The various satiric voices that present points of view different from Babbitt's including the anonymous narrator's are strategically deployed through the developing narrative, making possible the introduction both before and after Babbitt's speech of other evaluations of the city. No voice equals Babbitt's, before his defection, in sheer, apparently unselfish if indiscriminate, loyalty to Zenith, although the narrator says that a stranger suddenly dropped in Zenith could not have told it from "a city of Oregon or Georgia, Ohio or Maine, Oklahoma or Manitoba." Drunk or sober, the early Babbitt brags about the superiority of his burgeoning metropolis and sometimes puts his foot, unawares, into his mouth as in the exchange with another "realtor" while they are being taxied "toward the red lights and violent automatic pianos and stocky women" of Monarch's sirloin district: "A broker from Minnemagantic said, 'Monarch is a lot sportier than Zenith. You Zenith tightwads haven't got any joints like these here.' Babbitt raged, 'That's a dirty lie! Snothin' you can't find in Zenith. Believe me, we got more houses and hootch-parlors an' all kinds o' dives than any burg in the state'."

When introducing characters, Lewis sometimes uses contrastive techniques, as in the descriptions of Babbitt's next-door neighbors, between whom Babbitt occupies a middle social position. On one side is the Bohemian, whiskey-drinking, music-playing Dopplebrau who, young at forty-eight, is the secretary to a plumbing firm; on the other, the "archidiaconal" Howard Littlefield who, old at forty-two, is a Phi Beta Kappa in economics from Yale and the employment manager and publicity counsel to the Zenith Street Traction Company—a commercial pedant who pontificates about the sanctity of business.

Occasionally Lewis uses seriation as a technique for presenting characters, as on the first day while Babbitt goes about his normal activities. Although the roles of these characters in the action are insignificant, the descriptions of them and their activities are part of the gross piling up of data that contributes to the feeling that Zenith is a city of teeming vulgarity and nefarious life. In his encounters with the characters, Babbitt reveals other aspects of his life, other masks that he assumes.

Jake Offutt, a gang-politician who "fixes" inspectors, never appears directly, but he had played briber for Babbitt in the Glen Oriole housing development, which has stinking sewers. Conrad Lyte, an entrepreneur with hollows below his eyes that resemble silver dollars, appears in person at the closing of a shady deal engineered by Babbitt which forced a small grocer to pay double what a piece of property was worth. At the Athletic Club, Babbitt runs into pals from other businesses: Joseph H. Pumphrey, owner of Riteway Business College; Sidney Finkelstein, a department store owner, always anxious to deny his Jewishness; Chum Frink, syndicated author of *Poemulations* and composer of "Ads. that Add"; Paul Riesling, a roofing dealer; and Virgil Gunch, a coal dealer and president of the Boosters' Club.

Lewis frequently uses the "encyclopaedic" method to amass data. He uses the device very effectively to create the feeling of a nether Zenith alive with people engaged in multifarious activities when he catalogues nine events that take place while Babbitt prepares for bed at the end of the first day: Horace Updike, the city's professional bachelor, makes love to plutocratic Lucile McKelvey; a cocaine-runner shoots a prostitute who is drinking cocktails with him at Healey Hanson's speakeasy; two men work on a report of their experiments with synthetic rubber; four labor leaders debate whether to call a strike of coal miners; a G. A. R. veteran dies on a farm outside Zenith, unaware of the transformations that have taken place around him; a factory operates a night shift to produce tractors for the Polish Army; Mike Monday, a muscular evangelist, who averts strikes by turning workmen's minds "from wages and hours to higher things," winds up a "Christ-boosting" harangue; Seneca Doane argues with an intellectual revolutionist; Lloyd Hallam finishes a rondeau at his bookshop; and, most incisive of all the little events, Babbitt's father-in-law, the old-fashioned and frugal Yankee type, Henry T. Thompson, listens to Jake Offutt plan how to "milk the cattle" by getting Babbitt to grab land for the gang, because Babbitt can make it look as though they are "dyin' of love for the dear peepul."

A party is one of Lewis's favorite ways of bringing together a group of people and letting them expose themselves through talk. The five couples who have dinner at Babbitt's house, while unveiling their prejudices, especially against the working classes, reveal a number of things about their society: the thinness and shallowness of individuals when seen outside their occupations, the way in which the business ethic saturates their lives and dominates their conversation, and the pathetic role of the women in this world. Toward the end of the party when the men grow lethargic with booze, food, smoke, and talk, the women emerge from the shadows with the best entertainment they can offer: card-table spiritualism.

Equally revealing is the conception of the city which evolves from the men's shallow pontifications. Chum Frink, just returned from a lecture tour among the small towns, rejoices to be back in "civilization." Together the men exultingly construct their vision of "civilization." It is a dozen movie houses, an opportunity for those with initiative to achieve success, the possibility of wearing a "Tux," culture and an appreciation of the Beautiful—that is, magazine poetry instead of newspaper ditties, and a recognition of "artistic things and business punch equally." This sad picture is climactically projected with deadening magnification into the future with Virgil Gunch's observation that all the little towns "want to be just like Zenith."

Lewis often exploits the basic similarity of the voices to show up the unrelieved sameness of the common dough, while at other times he uses a personality who speaks from a position almost diametrically opposite that of the status quo. Such attitudes qualify the dominant disposition generated within a particular situation. With the central characters—George and Myra Babbitt, Paul and Zilla Riesling, and Gunch—the tactic is to expose the variations within the voice of each. Babbitt can be sarcastic, especially with his cronies and with himself when he has been desperately trying to recapture his youth with the "Bunch," but he is most effective in the unwitting satire that streams out of his praise of Zenith. The voice of the anonymous narrator participates in every scene.

The sarcastic comments of the narrator generally have relevance beyond the event or character immediately in view. When he says that Zilla Riesling "was a crusader, and like every crusader, she exulted in the opportunity to be vicious in the name of virtue," the thrust goes beyond Zilla to Babbitt crusading in his speech against university professors and to the Good Citizens' League, introduced in the latter half of the book, which sends little delegations around to let a person know when he is deviating from the accepted standards. Again, when Babbitt has been praising himself for his fine management of the Glen Oriole housing development, the narrator observes that in these transactions Babbitt was not "too unreasonably honest" and cooly indicts Zenith's virtue, which is cheating "sanctified by precedent."

The cult of individualism, often a favorite scapegoat for many of the ills of our society, plays along the surface of the narrative, while below Lewis adroitly manipulates its contradictory meanings. Babbitt's ego-centrism is not quite the individuality of an Emersonian unique individual for the narrator tells us that in actuality "the large national advertisers fix the surface of [Babbitt's] life, fix what he believed to be his individuality." In a parody of the metaphysical concept of oneness, Lewis drives home the incongruity of ego-centrism posing as individuality *qua* personality in a repressive conformist society. The Boosters' Club, the argument runs, permitted only two members from any segment of business because it was believed that on encountering "the ideals of other occupations" a person would realize "the metaphysical oneness of all occupations." The satiric thrust is double-pronged: Lewis ridicules the pompous debasing of the idea itself, and he uses the idea as an ironic counterpoint to the fact that the American community has only one occupation: making money.

Myra Babbitt, epitome of all the cow-like, silently suffering wives, provides an explicit contrast to Zilla Riesling; on the other hand, she comes through at times, surprisingly, as the voice of common sense and common human experience as when she protests against the false claims of advertisements for mail-order education. Pitiable as Myra is in her ignorance, hangdog loyalty, and dead level conventionality, she too longs for something to fill the empty spaces in her life. Spiritualism and gossip are spices that substitute for food. Following Paul's shooting of Zilla, Myra was "radiant with" horrified interest in the tragedy of a friend. Despite Zilla's shrill haranguing of Paul, before the shooting and afterward in her evangelical phase, she could pin a creature to the wall with truth, as when she told Babbitt that he was "about as broad-minded and liberal as a razor-blade."

Paul Riesling, the only genuinely introspective and sensitive character in the book, openly criticizes Zenith's monotonous uniformity. The force of habit which he offers as the reason for not leaving Zenith, though he despises the city, is the same reason Guy Pollock of **Main Street** gives for enduring the virus of Gopher Prairie. Flatly condemning the idea that it is one's moral duty to work hard at business, Paul opens up another view of George and his fellow boosters when he suggests that all their morality is merely phony posturing. Paul takes George's earnestness as an index to how "essentially immoral" he is underneath. In a conversation that followed Babbitt's catching Paul in a Chicago restaurant with Mrs. Arnold, Paul unintentionally draws an ironic parallel between George and Zilla. He warns George that Zilla is "perfectly capable" of having him "shadowed" and of going to Chicago and "busting into a hotel dining-room and bawling" him out in public.

Up to the time of his famous speech, Babbitt expresses his discontent in musings, or more vividly, in fantasies. His daydreams take the place of Riesling's "bats" and Chum Frink's drunken, solitary talking to himself. In exposing Babbitt's need to find a vicarious emotional life in fantasy to compensate for the lack of one in his everyday existence, the daydream becomes a "satiric voice" in a dramatic, if only mentally imaged situation. The puerility of the imagined escape with the fairy child in no way affects the authenticity of the daydreams. Significantly, the daydreams disappear when Babbitt finds a live fairy child—Tanis Judique.

Two voices speak from outside the "community." Dr. Kurt Yavitch, a revolutionist and a famous histologist of unspecified origins, acts as foil to the native Seneca Doane, a labor lawyer. Doane is a middle-of-the-road liberal who defends standardization and bigness in material things; he

resists, however, "standardization of thought." Dismissing Doane's liberalism as vague, Yavitch caustically condemns Zenith as a hateful city that "has standardized all the beauty out of life. It is," he says, "one big railroad station—with all the people taking tickets for the best cemeteries. . . . "

Against a carefully constructed background of scenes, characters, events, and varied points of view, Babbitt, catapulted to oratorical eminence and a "fame enduring for weeks," delivers his rapturous account of the city of Zenith as "the finest example of American life and prosperity to be found anywhere." The man with a family, an automobile, and a bungalow on the edge of town is "the ideal type to which the entire world must tend, if there's to be a decent, well-balanced, Christian-go-ahead future for this little old planet." Babbitt is a perfect *miles gloriosus* as he piles sentimental clichés on go-getting business clichés until he announces, finally, that he has given "the specifications of the Standardized American Citizen." Even then he cannot stop talking. He must make his city the exemplar of all American cities.

The major threat to "idealism" and to "sound government" is not the outright socialist but the undercover cowards, particularly the university professors whom the crusading Babbitt declares "are the snakes to be scotched." Babbitt pleads with his fellow realtors that it is as much their duty "to bring influence to have those cusses fired"— the blab-mouth, fault-finding, cynical university professors—"as it is to sell all the real estate and gather in all the shekels we can." The injection of the slang word "shekel" establishes unequivocally the tonal value of the speech.

Few literary examples express attitudes toward education and basic human freedom as sinister as the one voiced by Babbitt. James Thurber and Elliott Nugent later treat the subject of academic freedom in *The Male Animal,* but their portrayal of the ignorant, fascistic bullies on a university's board of trustees does not match this speech as a general threat to freedom, partly because Babbitt's is so larded with flattering, euphemistic, cliché-ridden bunk.

Lewis, accused of having no values, surely expresses some in this instance. Rarely have university professors been as complimented and applauded as when Babbitt lambastes them for being the principal opposers to Zenith's kind of "idealism." Seneca Doane's enlightened liberalism, strategically introduced into the narrative but never pressed as an alternative—to the dismay of the critics who demand a substitute for the pictured blight—is the kind of liberalism that Lewis later defends in **It Can't Happen Here.** Within the situational satire, Doane's voice suggests potentials alien to the perspectives of orating Babbitts and bullying Good Citizens Leaguers. When Babbitt's speech is "translated" in terms of the full fictional situation, it has few peers in modern American literature as indirect, but vitriolic, denunciation—and it denounces not only Zenith but the whole society for which that city stands as model.

In the concluding assurance to the audience that the Standardized Citizen will give the dissenter "a square-toed boot" that will teach him to respect "the He-man" and to "root for Uncle Samuel, U.S.A.!," Babbitt adumbrates the actual method that will be used against the Zenith workers on strike, against the city's lone conscientious objector, and against himself during his brief defection. Babbitt, in effect, tells his listeners that the latent violence beneath the public masks of unsatisfactory lives can be easily mobilized for licensed brutality—in the name of public good.

Following Babbitt's speech the narrative develops a steadily increasing sense of unpleasantness, of constricting forces at work in the city, and of the pervasiveness and impregnability of the commercial ethic. Other aspects of characters are revealed and additional areas of life in Zenith are depicted, but essentially nothing changes.

Lewis has been criticized for creating only type-characters and for giving these only surface treatment. The technique used in **Babbitt** might be described as a breaking up of the old compact "Character" of the seventeenth century into several typifying aspects which are then deployed along the line of the narrative, each aspect emerging within a dramatic situation. The character of the "summer friend" Virgil Gunch is developed in this way. His jovial backslapping side predominates in the first half of the narrative, although we see glimpses of his adamant prejudices against labor when he insists, cocktail in hand, that prohibition is a good thing for workers. In the events following Babbitt's speech, Gunch's sinister side is deployed as a complement to the good fellow. During the Zenith strike, Gunch shadows Babbitt because he has expressed a mild sympathy for the workers; later Gunch openly spies on the rebellious realtor at lunch with Tanis Judique at the best hotel. As the voice of public morality, he invites Babbitt to join the Good Citizens' League. After the vigilance committee has failed in its threatening follow-up visit, Gunch practices on Babbitt the fine art of snubbing. Obviously Gunch is not the representative of an enlightened public conscience. His type belongs instead to the secret police who use blackballing, spying, threats, and force to persuade waverers and dissenters to conform. With other members of the police, as with Babbitt after his scared-rabbit capitulation, Gunch can be a jovial friend.

Lewis explores religion and old established wealth conjoined in the publicity-hungry Reverend John Jennison Drew's competitive struggle to make his Sunday School, ranked fourth in the city, first in weekly attendance. Babbitt's proposal that the Sunday School be converted into quasiarmy units to attract youngsters is accepted by the committee without a demur. William Eathorne, a banker who serves on the committee, the narrator tells us, belongs to the "tiny hierarchy"—one of "the dozen contradictory Zeniths"—for which "the other Zeniths unwittingly labor and insignificantly die." Babbitt endears himself to the reader when in a moment of seditious honesty he sees Eathorne as a little fuzzy-faced "quarter-sized squirt."

At the end, Babbitt thinks that he has changed, but after two years he is still where he began. He has learned two things, however: he cannot escape Zenith even if he goes away forever, just as none of us can escape our past; he learns too that the coercive forces of his society will not tolerate any deviations from its narrow, rigid standards. In this situation the satirist presents a grim picture of the unchanging conditions even as he expresses a submerged wish for change, or for some disruption of the solidifying tendencies.

The fear engendered by threats and the genuine feeling of being isolated from his community drive Babbitt back into conformity. Of his accommodation, it can be said that a person needs to think sufficiently well of himself to have enough starch in his system to get through the day. The attack in this novel-satire goes beyond a Babbitt who can never leave his city to the deprivations the environment forces him to suffer and to the very restricted means it allows for obtaining the sufficient starch. Within the community Babbitt can only survive by being a strutting cock who supersells Zenith's kind of "idealism." In his unpublic life the starch is derived from fantasies and from furtive and episodic "adventures." Unlike Othello, who "takes in" himself after his irrational murder of Desdemona, Babbitt must constantly deceive himself for survival.

So Babbitt, at the end of the story, like Voltaire's Candide and like Karel Capek's nations in *War With the Newts,* has not changed in any fundamental way. He declares after his reinstatement into the community that he will do better in the future, that is, when he retires and can run things for himself. He deceives himself once more with the philosophy of materialistic acquisitiveness which requires that one put off "life" until retirement. Babbitt, however, is never able to delude himself so thoroughly as Melville's Bildad, who applauds his own sagacious recognition that a man's religion is one thing, the practical world another.

The final action, the elopement of Ted Babbitt and Eunice Littlefield, daughter of the archdeacon of business, is of the same quality as Babbitt's daydreams, and it might, therefore, be called a "fantasied" denouement. As a foreshadowing of the younger generation's jettisoning of their elders' stuffy restrictive mode of life, it has the character of a wish-fulfilling prediction. As a defiant revolt against an oppressive world, Babbitt derives vicarious pleasure from seeing his surrogate Ted flout decorum. The new situation, however, is never tested against the forces controlling Zenith. Actually, the author departs from the probable when he portrays two children of the vengeful "American gothics" as having the simple honesty, courage, and aplomb to return after an elopement to spend their first night in the boy's own bed. This sally is the book's brightest slap at hypocrisy and stultifying decorum.

Lewis's Zenith is barely a city and yet it is already a dystopia, but as Lewis Mumford has shown in his "Utopia, The City and the Machine," utopias have always been marked by evils, compulsions, and regimentations. These perennial characteristics, Mumford believes, come about because the "abstract intelligence" is "actually a coercive instrument: an arrogant fragment of the full human personality, determined to make the world over in its own over-simplified terms."

Material self-advancement is the "intellectual" abstraction on which Zenith is founded. It is not self-advancement in any intangible way, but self-aggrandizement. The horror of **Babbitt,** ultimately, is the recognition that the denial of all pleasure and all affective life is a sublimation that reaches no higher than money-grubbing.

Juvenal complained of an imperial Rome decaying because of corruption, degeneration, and neglect. Zenith is a "coming" city, still in the process of construction; yet it has been rightly described as a city of the dead, a city of "human simulacra," and "a native *Inferno* of the mechanized hinterland." Just as this city does not recall decaying Rome, neither do its citizens resemble decadent, luxury-loving, corrupt Romans. They are closer to the fallen angels of Milton's *Paradise Lost* who madly ransack hell to build a Pandemonium. (pp. 89-96)

Helen B. Petrullo, " 'Babbitt' as Situational Satire," in Kansas Quarterly, *Vol. 1, No. 3, Summer, 1969, pp. 89-97.*

Robert W. Lewis   (essay date 1972)

[*In the following essay, Lewis argues that the search for romantic love is the predominant theme of* Babbitt.]

Reflecting on the serious novels of the Twenties, one is struck by the recurrence of heroes whose quests end in defeat because their goals entail, in whole or in part, a dream of romantic love. Heroes as different as Dreiser's Clyde Griffiths (*An American Tragedy,* 1925), Fitzgerald's Gatsby (*The Great Gatsby,* 1925), and Hemingway's Lieutenant Henry (*A Farewell to Arms,* 1929) share a common fate: they are all trapped and defeated because they believe in an abstract kind of love that somehow doesn't accommodate itself to reality. At the end of the Twenties, Joseph Wood Krutch wrote "Love—or the Life and Death of a Value" (in *The Modern Temper,* 1929), and although his essay is not literary criticism, he describes the cultural demise of a love that is related to the lure that these questing (and representative) heroes of the Twenties follow. (Dreiser, as a matter of fact, uses the word *lure* in several chapter titles in the earlier *Sister Carrie.* Fitzgerald has Nick Carraway think of Gatsby as pursuing a *grail.*) The lure or the dream is of romantic love—it is a love which is essentially illicit rather than domestic and marital; it is not essentially erotic but rather etherealized; it is happy only in suffering; it requires and luxuriates in obstacles such as husbands, differences in social class, wars, separations, etc.; and it evaporates instantly if it is realized—it is always a striving, a longing; and marriage spells the end of it.

Another novelist of this important decade who was more popular but less "serious" than Dreiser, Fitzgerald, and Hemingway was Sinclair Lewis. His best novels were written in the Twenties, and they too reveal a continuing, obvious concern for the idea of passion or romance, the reaching beyond. In commenting on *Babbitt* (1922), Lewis said that he attacked sentimentality and "romance" because he was a sentimentalist and romantic at heart. And he wanted to create Babbitt as a passionate *wanter.* It is certainly easy enough to see many of his protagonists like Babbitt, Carol Kennicott, Arrowsmith, and even Elmer Gantry as akin to Flaubert's Emma Bovary. At 19, Lewis had written a poem "Launcelot" in the tradition of courtly love and under the influence of Tennyson. It was perhaps his first publication, and he later referred to it and to himself as a "romantic." He had read and admired Walter Scott in his youth, and he never overcame his romantic proclivities. In 1935, on re-reading his short stories, some of which were first published nearly twenty years before, he was surprised at his earlier optimism, and he discovered that, rather than being a satirist or realist, he was "actually a romantic medievalist of the most incurable sort." In jest he referred to his own life and the era 1885-1935 as a half century of romance, of knights, of castles, and "maidens

in silver and flowered silks [who] danced to strange music, freed from the pious caution of duller days."

In his early fiction he had written about broken friendships that led to yearning, frustration, and grief for loveless men (*Our Mr. Wrenn,* 1914, and *The Trail of the Hawk,* 1915). *The Job,* 1917, was also about escape, the loneliness of misfits, and the failure of an ideal. In his first big success, *Main Street* (1920), he depicted his heroine Carol Kennicott as a romantic, full of desire and longing for that which she could not have. Even the recent heroic pioneering past of her Midwest, as alluded to in the opening section, was as remote as Camelot. While writing *Babbitt,* Lewis noted his conscious intent to write of the average man who wants passionately to fill a void in his life unfilled by automobiles, real estate, and bootleg gin. And "he would like for once the flare of romantic love."

Cathartic literature will naturally have its paradoxes and ambiguities, and not all of them will be meaningful. Lewis persisted with the theme of romantic love without resolving his early attraction to it. In *Elmer Gantry* (1927), "true love" is associated with divine or Christian love and is corrupted by "mere" lust that, cleverly and ironically, opens the doors to Gantry's success as a preacher. In *Arrowsmith* (1925) and *Dodsworth* (1929), Lewis again depicted heroes like Babbitt who were essentially romantics, but their fates were better than Babbitt's. The pendulum seemed to be swinging back; Lewis was never again as negative about romance. Regarding *Cass Timberlane* (1945), Lewis' own fictionalized love story, Schorer asks if he was "an unwitting victim of America's matriarchal complex, or did he really believe that passionate love of woman involves male abandonment of dignity, integrity, emotional balance, and honor?"

Diana Trilling saw *Cass Timberlane* as being full of clichés about love and marriage, and other critics as different as Constance Rourke, Maxwell Geismar, and Gerald W. Johnson have detected the romantic proclivity and the *Child's-Garden-of-Verses* philosophy. How wonderful that our first Nobel Prize author was a *realist* (*pace* Henry James), a *satirist* (*pace* Voltaire and Swift), and a *hard worker* (*pace* Benjamin Franklin), and yet a fabulist, properly "indignant because he was unhappy" and "His indignation betray[ing] his essential romanticism." As a "100-percent American," Lewis *expected* happiness and was committed to its "pursuit." He thought Americans were unhappy and because of stupidity, cowardice, or greed. Lewis might denounce Americans, but he defended American ideals.

A victim of this dream whose romantic agony is at first glance absurd and seems at best tangentially relevant to his story is George Follansbee Babbitt. Babbitt seems to be an unlikely companion to the thwarted Horatio-Alger hero, Clyde Griffiths, the bootlegging Jay Gatsby, and the stoic soldier Frederic Henry. But his very *commonness* (attested by the generic meaning of his name today) makes him a particularly good victim to examine if one wants to see the endemic and epidemic nature of the corruption of love in the America of the Twenties. Babbitt is the bourgeois complement to the other more traditionally "romantic" heroes I have mentioned who have all lived on the fringe of respectable society.

In addition to this thematic and historical idea, a second

purpose for examining the novel *Babbitt* is to refute a common opinion that it not only is episodic but is without form or structure. In his 1922 review of the novel, H. L. Mencken wrote that *Babbitt* "is better designed than *Main Street*," [see *TCLC,* Vol. 4, pp. 246-47] but "There is no plot whatever, and "Every customary device of the novelist is absent." Gilbert Seldes writing in *The Dial* also praised the book but "failed to find any satisfactory aesthetic organization." In 1927 Rebecca West—a novelist herself and thus, one would think, attuned to such matters as organization—wrote, "*Babbitt* as a book was planless; its end arrived apparently because its author had come to the end of the writing pad . . . " Also in 1927 Joseph Wood Krutch wrote that in both *Babbitt* and *Main Street* "there was no continuous, steady march of incident." More recently Mark Schorer in his critical biography quotes Lewis as writing that he had originally " 'planned to make the whole novel 24 hours in his [Babbitt's] life, from alarm clock to alarm clock.' " And the first seven chapters follow that plan. The next 27 chapters, however, came (again in Lewis' words), " 'more or less unconsciously.' " Schorer doesn't accept Lewis' statement of unconscious composition at its face value, but he too regards the organization as defective: the last "twenty-seven chapters are systematically planned if rather aimlessly assembled set pieces that, taken together, give us the sociology of middle-class life. . . . There is no plot to effectively contain and unite these interests, but their fragmentariness is in part overcome by the fact that Babbitt moves through all of them in the course of his rising discontent, his rebellion, his retreat and resignation. Each of these three moods, in turn, centers in a more or less separate narrative: the first in the imprisonment of Paul Riesling after he shoots his wife; the second in Babbitt's attempt to find sympathy in Tanis Judique and 'the Bunch'; the third in the pressures brought on him by the Good Citizens' League and his wife's happily coincidental emergency operation. It is not surprising that the general thematic and narrative movement, like the central figure himself, is sometimes lost to sight in the forest of marshaled mores." Later Schorer adds, "Perhaps it is futile to approach any Lewis novel as a work of art."

But, by definition, every novel is a work of art, and one approach to it, and the central approach, is as art. If ordinary methods or analyses don't reward the critic, then perhaps he has to search further. In his study, *Sinclair Lewis,* Sheldon Grebstein notes that on one level of understanding, Babbitt's dream of romance is a key to understanding Lewis' method [see excerpt dated 1962]. While the novel is obviously read and has been appreciatively read as a broad satire on the mid-continent, middle-class American way of life, the corruption of love is rather more important than the other corruptions of business, politics, religion, and education that Lewis takes swipes at. Romantic love does not play as dominant a role here as it does in novels like *The Great Gatsby* and *A Farewell to Arms,* but it nevertheless plays a crucial role, and observing its development one also sees the structural unity it provides.

Babbitt affords a good view of the failure of romantic love unaccompanied by any understanding of causes. Considered as a story about love, it has unity and a certain neatness of structure that a reader who regards it as a general scatter-gun satire fails to see. Babbitt's crucial and peculiar delusion is a belief in romantic love. The crass success worship, the hollow materialism, and the personal and community corruption in *Babbitt* are more or less common to all the Zeniths in America and all the characters in the novel. "Chum" Frink is more of a booby than Babbitt, Howard Littlefield, Ph.D., more of a sham, William Washington Eathorne more corrupt, and the Reverend John Jennison Drew, M.A., more of a hypocrite. As the protagonist, Babbitt focuses these traits, but he adds another which none of the other characters seems to have—the dreaming of romantic love. The central conflict is between this dream and reality; all other action derives from it.

Nothing is wrong with being a real estate salesman—or as Babbitt would have it, a realtor—nor is anything wrong with living in a suburban Floral Heights and, in general, being middle class. But how ironical that a stalwart pillar of this materialistic society should nourish himself on the wildest dream, the dream of the fairy girl or child. There is no question in Babbitt's subconscious that it is not real estate nor bootleg gin but love that makes the world go round. When we first meet him on his "unromantic" sleeping porch, he *seems* "prosperous, extremely married and unromantic. . . . Yet Babbitt was *again* dreaming of the fairy child, a dream more romantic than scarlet pagodas by a silver sea.

"For years the fairy child had come to him. Where others saw but Georgie Babbitt, she discerned gallant youth. She waited for him, in the darkness beyond mysterious groves. When at last he could slip away from the crowded house he darted to her. His wife, his clamoring friends, sought to follow, but he escaped, the girl fleet beside him, and they crouched together on a shadowy hillside. She was so slim, so white, so eager! She cried that he was gay and valiant, that she would wait for him, that they would sail—

"Rumble and bang of the milk truck."

When the slim fairy girl flees—that is, during Babbitt's waking hours—"doubts regarding life and families and business" claw at him. The novel describes Babbitt's growing malaise that is basically a romantic longing in which he becomes increasingly and painfully aware of the difference between the subconscious dream and the vulgar reality. The malaise is too powerful to be allayed by the antidote of the dream. Because his sexual urges are sublimated to a dream existence, he suffers from their inhibitions and frustrations during his waking hours. The first block of seven chapters covering one day in Babbitt's life symbolically begins and ends with his dream of the fairy child. This dream metaphorically embraces Babbitt's day in which he seems happy and prosperous.

We meet this important fairy child at intervals until Chapter XXIII (there are altogether 34 chapters) where she is directly referred to for the last time. At that point about two-thirds of the way through the narrative, Babbitt's malaise has become insufferable, and this Chapter XXIII is the turning point in the novel where the sublimation breaks forth. The only friend Babbitt has, Paul Riesling, has shot his wife who, like Babbitt's Myra, has fallen far short of her husband's expectations. Zilla Riesling is a bitch, but what is more instructive is the American male's tendency to marry the Zilla type (or to create her) and his turning to male companionship when the honeymoon is over. Paul and Zilla Riesling are counterparts of the Babbitts, and the tragedy that strikes them brings Babbitt's malaise to a head:

"He was restless. He vaguely wanted something more diverting than the newspaper comic strips to read. . . .

"There it was again: discontent with the good common ways. . . .

"If she were here Myra would be hinting, "Isn't it late, Georgie?" He tramped in forlorn and unwanted freedom. . . . The world was uncreated, a chaos without turmoil or desire."

Up to this point Babbitt has been satisfied with ogling and merely dreaming about the fairy child, but now he has had enough of that. Presumably his Athletic Club friends ogle also, but as far as we know they do not dream; they are not deluded by the vision of romantic love embodied—or rather disembodied—in a fairy girl. It is the embodiment or fulfillment that destroys the dream, from Tristan and Iseult sleeping with a sword between them to the Harold-Bell-Wright sort of lovers whose love story must be ended with marriage, preferably before its consummation. The formerly domestic and faithful Babbitt destroys his fairy girl when he thinks he finds her.

His dream changes to conscious quest with a thought. For the first time in the novel, "He was thinking. . . .

"What did he want? Wealth? Social position? Travel? Servants? Yes, but only incidentally.

". . . he stumbled into the admission that he wanted the fairy girl—in the flesh. If there had been a woman whom he loved, he would have fled to her, humbled his forehead on her knees."

But Babbitt loves only in the romantic sense of the word, neither the *agape* of disinterested and selfless brotherly love nor the lost-in-Eden *eros* of "simple" sexual love. At this juncture the fairy girl disappears as Babbitt attempts to banish his malaise by embodying her in a succession of fleshly charmers. First, he experimentally contemplates his secretary, Miss McGoun. He goes a little further with his friend's wife, Louetta Swanson; he kisses a lock of her hair as they dance and later squeezes her hand. Though she is just a neighborhood coquette, he identifies Louetta with the fairy girl and thus destroys her. His dream is hardly mentioned again, for too much reality destroys romance.

The next chapter, XXIV, introduces Tanis Judique, who later becomes Babbitt's mistress, and Ida Putiak (what wonderful names!), the manicurist whom he awkwardly tries to seduce. He kisses Ida in a taxi. Her hat falls off.

" 'Oh, let it be,' he implored.

" 'Huh? My hat? Not a chance!' " Ida Putiak replies, and the third embodiment of the fairy girl begins to fade, fade away.

With Tanis Judique, Babbitt is most successful, and consequently the image of her as a romantic lover endures longest. She is coy and for a time keeps our Tristan Babbitt guessing, though the reader has no doubt what her game is. Her apartment *seems* to the rejected and dejected Babbitt a warm love nest of understanding. Tanis Judique must surely be the fairy girl. She has an "appealing" voice,

"lustrous eyes," rosy cheeks, a "delicate nose, gentle chin," and (joy!) "a slender body." She *seems* "immensely sophisticated," but for all that she sings "My Creole Queen" with "intolerable sweetness," transporting Babbitt to ecstasy.

"He thought of Tanis always. With a stir he remembered her every aspect. His arms yearned for her. 'I've found her! I've dreamed of her all these years and now I've found her!' he exulted."

But instead of living in a leafy bower as did Tristan and Iseult or Deirdre and Naoise, Babbitt romances Tanis in a movie theater during the day and in her steam-heated flat at night. True to the traditions of courtly love, however, Babbitt's greatest happiness is in anticipation. The last third of the novel is the unhappy fulfillment of his dream which turns out to be sordid as well as banal and even less attractive than his dull, unromantic life with his wife Myra. The romantic tradition dictates that one cannot find love within marriage, but it also demands a constant seeking, a perpetual courtship. Love is somewhere over the rainbow. If there are no legal or social barriers such as marriage to separate the true lovers, they must create them or lose their romance.

At the climax of the novel, Babbitt breaks away from Tanis, for no barrier has arisen to give them an excuse for separation, sweet sorrow, or unrequited love. Besides being of the wrong sex, Myra is a far cry from Tristan's King Mark or Naoise's King Conchubar, the third sides of those famous and archetypal triangles. If she had tried to disrupt or thwart Babbitt's romance, it could have lived longer, being properly nourished by trials and sorrows. If no resistance exists, neither can romantic love, and Tanis and Myra both are almost too cooperative. Who wants both his wife *and* his mistress to be permissive!

"In a barren freedom of icy Northern wind he sighed. "Thank God that's over! Poor Tanis, poor darling decent Tanis! But it is over. Absolute! I'm free!' "

Free of what? Symbolically, of his self-delusions that include more than the dream of the fairy girl. Babbitt begins to take stands. He is, for once, truthful with his wife and friends; he refuses to buy the shams of middle-class virtue in marriage and business. He tells Myra he has been calling on a woman, he tells the Boosters that immigrants are

Lewis and his wife in 1917.

not necessarily undesirable, and he refuses more positively than ever to be pushed into joining the reactionary Good Citizens' League. The loss of his dreams and his resistance are not finally triumphant, however, for Babbitt feels lost and "the independence seeped out of him." He may envision a life of truth and freedom, but he is not strong enough to realize it himself.

He is only saved by a near tragedy, Myra's acute appendicitis, which shocks Babbitt into a rudimentary understanding of his pitiful position and his former delusions. He does not verbalize the latter, and he does happily seize the first opportunity to rejoin his friends in the Good Citizens' League, but he acts as though he has destroyed the fairy girl forever, even if his understanding of her and the delusion she represents is incomplete and he has no positive hope that Myra or he will change greatly.

At least, "he did not compare her with Tanis; she was not merely A Woman, to be contrasted with other women, but his own self, and though he might criticize her and nag her, it was only as he might criticize and nag himself, interestedly, unpatronizingly, without the expectation of changing—or any real desire to change—the eternal essence."

The point seems clear enough: Babbitt will still be a realtor, though perhaps a less hypocritical one, and he will still lead a rather dull existence in Floral Heights, only experiencing freedom of spirit vicariously through his more independent son Ted. But at least he has discovered the Antilles of a continent of love that is at once newer and yet more mature than the misty hot-and-cold world of romantic love that he has paradoxically destroyed by discovery.

At the beginning of the novel, Lewis describes Babbitt as a man who finds it difficult to love anybody but himself. He is fond of Paul Riesling and in his dull, unimaginative way he is also in love with love. At the end of the novel he has learned the futility of romantic love and the difficult necessity of loving in another way those dull people around him—including, of all people, his wife: "He . . . began to see her as a human being, to like and dislike her instead of accepting her as a comparatively movable part of the furniture, and he compassionated that husband-and-wife relation which, in twenty-five years of married life, had become a separate and real entity." The second love that Babbitt discovers is, ideally, a combination of care, responsibility, respect, and knowledge (to borrow Erich Fromm's four-part description of love). This lesson in love that traces his growing malaise and then disenchantment is the central story of the novel. It is true that at the end of the novel Babbitt has surrendered to the forces of mediocrity and hypocrisy, but he is not back where he started on his unromantic sleeping porch dreaming of the fairy child. He has dramatized Jay Gatsby's, Clyde Griffiths', and Frederic Henry's fatal quests and lived to tell about it. (pp. 7-14)

Robert W. Lewis, " 'Babbitt' and the Dream of Romance," in North Dakota Quarterly, *Vol. 40, No. 1, Winter, 1972, pp. 7-14.*

George H. Douglas   (essay date 1972)

[*In the following excerpt, Douglas argues that the artis-tic significance of* Babbitt *hinges on Lewis's vivid rendering of the struggle between freedom and social convention in the protagonist.*]

Some will say that **Babbitt** is the kind of novel that would no longer be widely read if it were not a historical monument, part of the American pageant. Indeed it is widely held today that Sinclair Lewis himself is not a writer of very considerable importance. Mark Schorer concluded his massive biography of Lewis by remarking that "he was one of the worst writers in modern American literature." But in spite of this sort of judgment there is something of compelling interest about Lewis and his work—indeed, if this were not so, it would be hard to imagine why Schorer would devote 800 pages to him. There is something about Lewis that we can't quite purge from our national psyche, something we can't easily put aside. But what is it?

It's not a matter of art—at least in one very important meaning of that word. If there is a single thing that all the critics agree upon today, it is that Lewis was a poor master of the art of the novel—his plots were foolish and unbelievable, his characters wooden and superficial (anything resembling character development was unknown to Lewis), his human understanding and tragic insight feeble and undisciplined.

In the early years Lewis was much praised by the critics because he had a well-tuned ear and an uncanny ability to record the speech of his fellow countrymen, because he seemed to have absorbed every idiosyncrasy of the national species and was possessed of a certain malicious genius that enabled him to transfer it all to paper. He was our great national photographer, said E. M. Forster—"neither a poet or preacher, but a fellow with a camera a few yards away." When he chose to snap the lens, he came away with an exact likeness of his subject.

Of course we know that even this is not precisely true. And **Babbitt** is a good case in point. Reading the novel today, one thing is clear. The realistic details—the photographs if you like—are usually of poor quality. The details of Lewis' portraits are almost always askew, and the things he was supposed to be able to do best, like render the atmosphere of a local Rotary luncheon or a salesman's inane conversation, always seem off the mark. Zenith, Ohio, the setting of **Babbitt,** never comes into focus as a real American city—sometimes its description suggests a city of 25,000 people, sometimes a city of 250,000. One gets the feeling that Lewis didn't really know what kind of city he was writing about, and what's more didn't really care. (Theodore Dreiser, in *Jennie Gerhardt,* did a better job of realistically capturing the flavor of Columbus, Ohio, a city he had never seen, than Lewis did with any of his oft-visited representative American towns.)

Most of Lewis' minor details are equally out of focus. Babbitt's real estate business is described with a curious lack of precision. Sometimes we are given to understand that Babbitt is a small businessman dealing in inexpensive suburban property; in other places he appears to be a fairly large-scale operator involved in big projects. Oddities of this sort abound in the novel, and always one has the impression that Lewis wasn't really interested in getting things right, that he was sloppy and careless when it came to putting down a picture of the American scene—even those aspects of it that interested him the most.

Well, then, if we can no longer take Lewis seriously as a master of the art of the novel, if we can't even take him seriously as a precise and indefatigable realist or journalist, are there any laurels left for him? Yes, there are, and we are obliged to admit that Lewis commands a place of some kind in the American pantheon, and that he still speaks to us with force and authority. For while he may no longer be an important "novelist," although the specific objects of his satire may now be little more than indistinct historical relics, Lewis is a significant writer because he grappled doggedly with some elemental qualities of our experience, including a number that he was the first to identify. What is more important, they are qualities that are as persistent today as they were in the 1920s.

No novel of Lewis' illustrates this better than *Babbitt.* It has often been observed that one of the great contributions of this work was that it succeeded in naming an American phenomenon, and the act of naming, of course, has always been one of the primary functions of the poet or artist conceived in the widest sense. By this I do not mean that all Lewis did was to catch the essence of the smug, complacent booster or joiner, the self-satisfied and unimaginative small-town businessman. This he did, of course, but if that were the limit of his achievement, *Babbitt* would be to us today a faded novel, its chief character a mere curiosity of second-rate American literature. The truth is that Lewis had hit upon, and long struggled to understand, a deeply rooted disease of the American spirit. There is no single name for this disease but its symptoms are familiar enough.

Lewis was tormented, as other American writers were before him—writers as diverse as Cooper and Thoreau—by the contrast between the promise of America and the often unhealthy results of American life. Lewis always thought Americans to be a good people, a promising people, and he looked for great things from them, but American social life had about it a suffocating quality that wouldn't allow this goodness to breathe.

Lewis never really enjoyed his great talent for ticking off the symptoms of this disease. It has often been remarked that he could never work up a fair and complete portrait of his fellow Americans because he despised them so heartily that he had not detached perspective on them. But he was no Jonathan Swift. Indeed, he was an imperfect satirist precisely because he could never really hate the Babbitts and Elmer Gantrys he went after, but was always searching for something good to come from them, a search which, nevertheless, continually proved futile.

Babbitt is a perfect manifestation of the national malady that fascinated Lewis throughout his career. In spite of the utter complacency and conformity in which Babbitt later became enmeshed, we are told that in college he was "an unusually liberal, sensitive chap," who wanted to be a lawyer and dreamed of taking cases of the poor without fee. Even in later life, after Babbitt has given up, and slipped into complete spiritual inertia, we find him struggling to get out of his stereotyped life, the supposed virtues of which he is always publicly trumpeting. Not that Babbitt himself is a great tragic figure—he is too puny a soul for that—but he isn't exactly a cipher or empty vessel either. Like so many Americans, he had begun life under favorable skies, with the whole world open to him, but somehow he got stuck, allowed himself to fall into rigid pat-

terns of behavior from which he could never extricate himself.

But he knew he was stuck. He knew he had started out with a vast possibility for personal action in a free land, and that he had sold himself out. At the end of the book we find him trying to convince his even more foolish and vacuous son, Theodore Roosevelt Babbitt, to do something individual, something worth while. "Practically I've never done a single thing I've wanted to do in my whole life," he admits dolefully. Still, he had spent his life making abortive attempts to extricate himself from the social conditions in which he had become entangled—he reached out for a friendship with Paul Riesling, a tender and sensitive poet. No use. He tried a brief love affair, but gave it up rather than face ostracism on the part of the community. Always he knew, in the depths of his soul, that he was entitled to break loose—such is the American right and destiny—always he knew that he wanted to do so, but in the end he gave up the battle and accepted the immolation of self and soul.

The tale thus speaks eloquently of one of the saddest and most enduring American verities. I say most enduring since it is obvious that *Babbitt* is no outdated story of small-town business society, vintage 1920. The great issue that tormented Lewis is still with us, even though we no longer think of the small-town Rotarian as being a spiritual center of gravity in our society, even though Babbitt's manners and morals are no longer important enough to get under our skin. Prestige and respectability have moved to big government, to the technostructure of the large corporations, to the research universities—away from Zenith or Gopher Prairie. But there is no reason to think that Babbitt has not shifted with the times, no reason to doubt that he appears in new clothing in these newer institutions, and continues his struggle to find some fresh air and freedom in them.

And there is no reason to believe that the stultification of desire, the standardization of manners, morals and ideas is a product of the small town alone. Or that "businessmen" have a monopoly on it. Our society, our major institutions, because of their very largeness and complexity, always involve a certain rigidity of action, require a certain amount of uniformity and conformity of behavior (the social scientists began discovering this after World War II, thirty years after Lewis had identified the phenomenon with precision). Of course, we can all freely choose, in theory at least, to make our noble individual contributions. We can take up the law, or medicine, or social work, or we can become college teachers. But it is part of the tragedy of our modern life that even the lofty professions have about them in our society a certain inflexibility that we cannot easily escape. We become locked into these pursuits, we adopt the respectable habits of thought that go with them, and we break out of them only at our peril. The professor just as easily as a small-town real estate dealer binds himself into a set of conventions from which there is no easy release.

The conditions under which this kind of thing happens fascinated Lewis, and, if he could never completely explain it, he was the first to give it an artistic rendering. Lewis' Midwestern youth obviously had impressed upon him the sharp contrast between the great destiny of America—its openness and flexibility—and the painful limits that were finally forced upon its social life. This was his major theme. Perhaps there always lingered in him a feeling of desperate contrast between the wide open spaces of northern Minnesota with its brisk fresh air, and the constricting space of the stale settlements nearby. Like James Fenimore Cooper he wished for an America that was open, one where a man could always go out beyond the established communities, away from the church, away from lawyers, away from the sellers of land. But like Cooper, too, Lewis came to see that this was all an impossible dream. In a vestigial way it was the dream dreamed by all Americans, even the lowest Babbitt in the land, and Lewis always hoped that Babbitt would continue to dream it and that some day the dreaming would do some good. Meanwhile, it was Lewis' genius to have perceived how and why in the complex social world of the 20th century, this great American dream was often nothing but a faint and powerless shadow, consigned to the dark recesses of the mind. (pp. 661-62)

> *George H. Douglas, " 'Babbitt' at Fifty—The Truth Still Hurts," in* The Nation, *New York, Vol. 214, No. 21, May 22, 1972, pp. 661-62.*

Martin Light   (essay date 1975)

[*In the following essay from his book-length study of Lewis,* The Quixotic Vision of Sinclair Lewis *(1975), Light examines Lewis's treatment of Babbitt as middle-class archetype, stressing the undercurrent of romantic rebellion that lies beneath his bourgeois conformity.*]

Babbitt, not as much a tale of a quixote as is **Main Street,** nonetheless contains undercurrents of romance, and a reading of the book from [this] point of view . . . will reveal some interesting aspects of it.

The book opens with a fantasy. George F. Babbitt, asleep, dreams of a fairy child, an idealized younger sister, imaginary and chaste, "a dream more romantic than scarlet pagodas by a silver sea." Babbitt is not a great reader, as Don Quixote is, but Babbitt's mind is shaped by poetry, by editorials, and by films. For example, in his wallet he kept "clippings of verses by T. Cholmondeley Frink and of the newspaper editorials from which Babbitt got his opinions." Frink can sing songs of vagabondia: "When I am out upon the road, a poet with a peddler's load, I mostly sing a hearty song, and take a chew and hike along, a-handing out my samples fine of Cheero Brand of sweet sunshine. . . ." From his newspapers Babbitt gathers information that he garbles: "New York Assembly has passed some bills that ought to completely outlaw the socialists!. . . A mass-meeting in Birmingham's demanded that this Mick agitator, this fellow De Valera, be deported. Dead right, by golly!"

Quixotic romance surrounds Babbitt. The architecture of his Athletic Club, for instance, is pseudo-gothic. "The lobby, with its thick pillars of porous Caen stone, its pointed vaulting, and a brown glazed-tile floor like well-baked bread-crust, is a combination of cathedral-crypt and rathskellar." Further:

> The entrance lobby of the Athletic Club was Gothic, the washroom Roman Imperial, the lounge Spanish Mission, and the reading-room in Chinese Chippendale, but the gem of the club was the dining-room, the masterpiece of Ferdinand Reitman, Zenith's busiest architect. It was lofty and half-timbered, with Tudor leaded casements, an oriel, a somewhat musicianless musician's-gallery, and tapestries believed to illustrate the granting of Magna Charta. . . . At one end of the room was a heraldic and hooded stone fireplace which the club's advertising-pamphlet asserted to be not only larger than any of the fireplaces in European castles but of a draught incomparably more scientific.

Babbitt's movie theater is the Château, and there he enjoys three kinds of films: "pretty bathing girls with bare legs; policemen or cowboys and an industrious shooting of revolvers; and funny fat men who ate spaghetti." From all these sources, Babbitt derives his romanticism.

Babbitt has his quixotic adventures, too. He wishes he had been a pioneer. His motor car, says Lewis, was "poetry and tragedy, love and heroism." And further: "His office was his pirate ship but the car his perilous excursion ashore." His trips to Maine are his greatest adventures. There he intends to shake loose the family and his wife; there he intends to fish in the male companionship of his friend Paul Riesling and the fishing guides. But such adventures fail him, and shortly after he returns to Zenith you would hardly know he had been away. Another of Babbitt's adventures is to a convention, where he goes out on the town with the boys, and presumably to a prostitute, though nothing very specific is stated.

Babbitt has the power of enchantment, also. As he bathes, he is "lulled to dreaming by the caressing warmth." He is "enchanted" by the dripping water. When he gets into bed, "instantly he [is] in the magic dream," and his fairy child comes to him. In the exhilarations of drinking a cocktail, he feels the urge "to rush places in fast motor cars, to kiss girls, to sing, to be witty." In fancy, he sees himself as a romantic hero, for "the Romantic Hero was no longer the knight, the wandering poet, the cowpuncher, the aviator, nor the brave young district attorney, but the great sales-manager." At the Booster Club, the members designate special titles for the officers and imagine themselves transformed thereby. "It gave to Americans unable to become Geheimräte or Commendatori such unctuous honorifics as High Worthy Recording Scribe and Grand Hoogow."

On his second trip to Maine, "all the way north he pictured the Maine guides: simple and strong and daring, jolly as they played stud-poker in their unceiled shack, wise in woodcraft as they tramped the forest and shot the rapids"—"like a trapper in a Northern Canada movie." But this fancy is dispelled by a truer picture: "In their boarded and rather littered cabin the guides sat about the greasy table playing stud-poker with greasy cards."

But his greatest adventure is his affair with Tanis Judique—and here he exercises his fancy also, transforming her and her friends into persons they are not. His language becomes that of magazine fiction: thinking about what Tanis will wear, Babbitt says, "I can't decide whether you're to put on your swellest evening gown, or let your hair down and put on short skirts and make-believe you're a little girl." He transforms Tanis with these words: "Child, you're the brainiest and the loveliest and finest woman I've ever met! Come now, Lady Wycombe, if you'll take the Duke of Zenith's arm, we will proambulate in to the magnolious feed!" He thinks, "I've dreamed of her all these years and now I've found her!"

Their most memorable excursion "was a tramp on a ringing December afternoon, through snow-drifted meadows down to the icy Chaloosa River. She was exotic in an astrachan cap and a short beaver coat." At the end of the book Babbitt returns to the reality of his wife's appendectomy in order to break these illusions.

Because Babbitt was intended to represent a type, the standardized American citizen to whom he pays homage in his speech before the real estate board, Lewis found himself, while working on the book, puzzling over the problems of typicality and individualization in character-making. Having tried out the babbitt-type, the hustler, the booster, and the charlatan as targets for satire in short stories and several novels, Lewis was by 1921 sensitive to criticism that he was repeating himself. With so many similarities among character, differentiation became a matter of subtle manipulation of details. Lewis's task was to note the differences if he was to individualize effectively. He was aware of the difficulties: "It is true that the Babbitt of Boston, the Babbitt of Charleston and the Babbitt of Seattle are confusingly alike. . . . It is the job of the writer of fiction to discover the differences beneath the similarities." At once, however, Lewis voiced his bitter feeling that in this matter he had been mistreated by unsympathetic critics: "No matter how you differentiate, unless you portray such obviously exceptional, such meretriciously 'quaint' characters as Yankee philosophers or bootleggers, if ever you deal accurately with real contemporaries in Hart, Schaffner & Marx clothes, the critics will accuse you of 'creating nothing but types.' It's a way critics have."

This petulance was as characteristic of Lewis as was his uncertainty about whether he created caricatures of "real" figures. But when his sense of humor overcame his touchiness, Lewis was able to laugh at his struggle in differentiation. To our amusement, in *The Man Who Knew Coolidge* Lowell Schmaltz talks about the differences among the babbitts of America. The joke comes full circle as Schmaltz directs his scorn toward Lewis himself: "There's a lot of sorehead critics of America that claim we're standardized," but there are, he notes, significant differences. Schmaltz undertakes to show the differences between himself and another Zenith citizen of his acquaintance, a George F. Babbitt by name. Although they both belong to the Athletic Club and to the service clubs, although they have their places of business in the same block and live within a quarter of a mile of each other, although they both like golf and good lively jazz on the radio, yet—

> Well, like this, for instance: I drive a Chrysler, and Babbitt doesn't. I'm a Congregationalist, and Babbitt has no use whatsomever for anything but his old Presbyterian church. He wears these big round spectacles, and you couldn't hire me to wear anything but eyeglasses—much more dignified, *I* think. He's got so he likes golf for its own sake, and I'd rather go fishing, any day. And—and so on. Yes sir, it's a wonderful thing how American civilization, as represented, you might say, by modern advertising, has encouraged the, as a speaker at the Kiwanis recently called it, free play of individualism.

Like George F. Babbitt, Lowell Schmaltz evaluates people by tabulating their possessions, and measures individuality by such unimportant and minute distinctions as only such experts in what David Riesman called "marginal differentiation" can perceive. Besides, standardization, in the last analysis, was what Schmaltz and Babbitt most valued, and attention to marginal differences was their empty homage to an older American value of individualism which lingered in their consciences. Yet Lewis made Schmaltz different from Babbitt in ways that Schmaltz cannot see—in Babbitt's discontentment and in his momentary response to the humanitarianism of his friends Paul Riesling and Seneca Doane. Later, in the characterization of Dodsworth, moreover, Lewis moved farther from Schmaltz and from Babbitt. Lewis states that Dodsworth, though he shares some of their attributes, is neither a Schmaltz nor a Babbitt. It is interesting to see how Lewis, serious in *Dodsworth,* as he was not in the passage from *The Man Who Knew Coolidge,* indicates the differences:

> To define what Sam Dodsworth was, at fifty, it is easiest to state what he was not. He was none of the things which most Europeans and many Americans expect in a leader of American industry. He was not a Babbitt, not a Rotarian, not an Elk, not a deacon. He rarely shouted, never slapped people on the back, and he had attended only six baseball games since 1900. He knew, and thoroughly, the Babbitts and baseball fans, but only in business.
>
> While he was bored by free verse and cubism, he thought rather well of Dreiser, Cabell, and so much of Proust as he had rather laboriously mastered. He played golf reasonably well, and did not often talk of his scores. He liked fishing-camps in Ontario, but never made himself believe that he preferred hemlock boughs to a mattress. He was common sense apotheosized.

While shouting, back-slapping, and self-conscious masculinity are the primary characteristics of the babbitt-type, Sam Dodsworth has better manners and more sensitivity (though he probably has "mastered" very little art and literature).

Lewis's attention to the matter of types and individuals resulted, I believe, from his desire to be thought of as something more than a satirist. He expressed his feelings in a letter to his editor, in which he said *"all* my keenest eagerest thought tends to sneak off into my plans, thoughts, notes about *Fitch* [an early title for *Babbitt*]—which will, I believe, correct any faults of 'exterior vision,' of sacrifice of personality to types and environment, which in his New Republic review Francis Hackett finds in *Main Street*." In another letter he spoke of George Babbitt as being bigger than Will Kennicott, with "more sensations, more perceptions. . . . He is . . . prosperous but worried, wanting—passionately—to seize something more than motor cars and a house *before it's too late.*" Lewis continued, "I want to make Babbitt big in his real-ness, in his relation to all of us, not in the least exceptional, yet dramatic, passionate, struggling." It was carefully planned that Babbitt would have unexpected inner complexities: "where the surprise is going to come in is that, being so standardized, Babbitt yet breaks away from standards, a little, when the time comes." Lewis, hoping to overcome the limitations of caricature, tried consciously to make Babbitt real, yet before the novel was finished, Lewis had conceded something to its inevitable tone and was looking toward his next book where he would try again: "It [*Babbitt*] is satiric, rather more than *Main Street;* and for that reason I think—I hope—that the novel after *Babbitt* will be definitely non-satiric—except, of course, for occasional passages." That Babbitt remains a type, a caricature, in spite of Lewis's efforts to make him complex, is what some critics find deficient in what they otherwise recognize as Lewis's most brilliant novel.

Much of the differentiation among the various babbitts depended upon Lewis's handling of the tone of voice of his characters. Lewis was haunted by the voices of salesmen, managers, businessmen, and boosters. Self-exposure—the method of his satire—is accomplished by speeches in which his characters give their ignorance away. We know from William Rose Benét's reminiscence (quoted earlier) that Lewis practiced his mimicry in California as early as 1909. About that time, Lewis was working on his first novel, *Our Mr. Wrenn.* When it appeared in 1914, *Wrenn* contained some early and crude versions of the babbitt-voice, with the ineffectual hesitancies and the clichés which were to characterize it.

The handling of the tone, opinions, and character of Eddie Schwirtz, the paint salesman in *The Job,* was a significant development in Lewis's portraiture. Before his voice takes over (for, after the first pages of his initial appearance, we do not see Eddie; we hear him—and at great length), he is described as forty and red-faced, with a clipped mustache, a derby hat, and an uneven tie. When he and Una Golden are hiking and he feels the stirrings of love, he says, "I'm a poor old rough-neck, . . . but to-day, up here with you, I feel so darn good that I almost think I'm a decent citizen. Honest, little sister, I haven't felt so bully for a blue moon." In such a speech one finds the elements of all the babbitt-voices yet to come—that rather unreal overloading of clichés, the "manly" diction ("rough-neck," "so darn good") which is ultimately weak and mindless. I believe that Lewis is suggesting that clichés are the only words a babbitt-type dare use to express emotions, which the Schwirtzes and Babbitts fear. Their misunderstanding of emotion is what makes them comic, grotesque, or dangerous. Yet there is a curious little passage that comes a few pages later in *The Job,* where Schwirtz speaks in a strangely natural and affecting way; it contains much potential for a humanizing of Babbitt and Paul Riesling and Dodsworth, though Lewis used it only occasionally. Eddie tells Una about the death of his wife: "My wife died a year later. I couldn't get over it; seemed like I could have killed myself when I thought of any mean thing I might have said to her—not meaning anything, but hasty-like, as a man will. Couldn't seem to get over it. Evenings were just hell; they were so—empty. Even when I was out on the road, there wasn't anybody to write to, anybody that *cared* . . . " It is as if for a moment Lewis has heard the cadences of Jim or Huck. But there is nothing like it again in *The Job* and not enough of it elsewhere in Lewis.

The voice of George F. Babbitt introduces an important new tone that results from fatigue and is expressed in whining and self-pity. The fatigue has been caused by deep discontent. Babbitt, who thinks of himself as the very backbone of America, is given to weak hesitations and ineffectual curses and commands. At the opening of the novel our Ideal Citizen is talking to himself, as he strug-

gles with the toothpaste in the bathroom: "Verona been at it again! 'Stead of sticking to Lilidol, like I've re-peat-ed-ly asked her, she's gone and gotten some confounded stickum stuff that makes you sick!" Her "stickum stuff" is too feminine for a regular guy like Babbitt, but the triviality of the matter and his inability to make his daughter do as he wishes belie his picture of himself. Then self-pity overcomes him: "He was raging, 'By golly, here they go and use up all the towels, every doggone one of 'em, and they use 'em and get 'em all wet and sopping, and never put out a dry one for me—of course, . . . I'm the only person in the doggone house that's got the slightest doggone bit of consideration for other people and thoughtfulness and consider there may be others that may want to use the doggone bathroom after me and consider—'." His ineffectuality is shown not only in the weak profanity, but more importantly in the wasted words of his redundancies.

Babbitt sees himself as friendly, affable, and masculine, yet the he-man is soon fretting about the effect of banana fritters upon his digestion. He sees himself as imposed upon, for he works hard and ought to be rewarded with peace of mind. "I may not be any Rockefeller or James J. Shakespeare, but I certainly do know my own mind, and I do keep right on plugging along in the office and—." This man who knows his own mind relies upon the editorials of his newspaper, upon the sermons at his church, and upon the speeches he hears at his Boosters Club meetings in order to know what to think. To his daughter's expression of a desire to do social work, Babbitt gropes for words, stumbling and sputtering out clichés:

> "Now you look here! The first thing you got to understand is that all this uplift and flipflop and settlement-work and recreation is nothing in God's world but the entering wedge for socialism. The sooner a man learns he isn't going to be coddled, and he needn't expect a lot of free grub and, uh, all these free classes and flipflop and doodads for his kids unless he earns 'em, why, the sooner he'll get on the job and produce—produce—produce! That's what the country needs, and not all this fancy stuff that just enfeebles the will-power of the working man and gives his kids a lot of notions above their class."

Midway in his speech he fizzles, so he resorts to repetition of "flipflop and doodads." Suddenly he remembers an editorial: "get on the job and produce—produce—produce! He has moved a long way from a simple response to his daughter's remark. In such ineffectual language does he challenge the world of business and politics.

Although Lewis's plans for the characterization of Babbitt resulted from his desire to create a rounded figure, displaying interior as well as exterior vision, Babbitt's character was to begin, Lewis wrote his publisher in December 1920, in the man's typicality; he is to be "the typical T. B. M. [tired business man], the man you hear drooling in the Pullman smoker." But, Lewis went on, "having once so seen him, I want utterly to develop him so that he will seem not just typical but an individual." Discontentment was to be the principal device for suggesting Babbitt's inner self. Tired of the work routine, Babbitt "would like for once the flare of romantic love, the satisfaction of having left a mark on the city, and a let-up in his constant warring on competitors." But "only for a little while is he discontented, though." Babbitt is to surprise the reader by breaking away from the standards—a little.

How did Lewis plan to make Babbitt come alive? First, Babbitt's typicality, as Lewis saw it, must be extracted from hundreds of observations of induviduals. Lewis's work through 1920 had prepared him to know what the man in the smoking car sounded like when he spoke. Nevertheless, Lewis did considerable research for this book, visiting Cincinnati and other cities of two, three, and four hundred thousand people. From his notes, he was able to put into the book a mass of accurate detail about clothes, houses, furnishings, cars, clubs, real estate enterprises, and conventions. Therefore, we have great confidence in Babbitt's typicality in respect to things and opinions: his toothpaste and bath-towels, his gray suit and his spectacles, the contents of his pockets, his Booster's Club button; and his indecisive and inconclusive discussion with his wife Myra about the choice of suits, his concern for his stomach, the opinions he gleans from his newspaper's editorials, his scorn for socialist agitators, and his faith in the strength of the towers of Zenith—all these observations we are delighted to recognize as true. The contradictions in his opinions ring true also: "We got no business interfering with the Irish or any other foreign government"; still, "it's beyond me why we don't just step in there [Russia] and kick those Bolshevik cusses out."

But during the account of the first two hours of Babbitt's day, Lewis plants evidence of the discontentment which is intended to reveal the interior Babbitt. It begins with irritability about the wet towels in the bathroom and the little chunks of toast and the socialist threat and his rebellious and bickering children. Soon, so early in the day, we hear the great burst of fatigue: "Oh, Lord, sometimes I'd like to quit the whole game. And the office worry and detail just as bad. And I act cranky and—I don't mean to, but I get—So darn tired!"

He says much the same thing before lunch, during lunch, after lunch, and in the evening. As the day ends, "his feet were loud on the steps as he clumped upstairs at the end of this great and treacherous day of veiled rebellions." To his friend Paul Riesling he had complained,

> "I don't know what's the matter with me today. . . . Kind of comes over me: here I've pretty much done all the things I ought to; supported my family, and got a good house and a six-cylinder car, and built up a nice little business, and I haven't any vices 'specially, except smoking. . . . I belong to the church, and play enough golf to keep in trim, and I only associate with good decent fellows. And yet, even so, I don't know that I'm entirely satisfied!"

In this little speech, we have what I think is the essential insight of the book. Lewis gives us the babbitt-vision of the American Dream. Babbitt has lived according to its inspiration, but it is a dream which leaves the dreamer restless and betrayed.

Paul Riesling believes that there is a widespread undercurrent of dissatisfaction among businessmen; they seem content, yet one-third of them feel restless and won't admit it, while another third are simply miserable and know it. "They hate the whole peppy, boosting, go-ahead game,

and they're bored by their wives and think their families are fools."

Lewis has discovered that a babbitt can suffer the tensions of conformity, though conformity was not supposed to bring tension. A part of Babbitt's early-morning fatigue comes from indecisions and contradictions. So sensitive is he to marginal differences that deciding what suit to wear is an exhausting problem with many subtleties. Then he engages in a discussion with his wife which (though I shall abbreviate it) takes him through confusions like these:

> "I feel kind of punk this morning. . . . You oughtn't to serve those heavy banana fritters."
>
> "But you asked me to have some."
>
> "I know, but— . . . it would be a good thing for both of us if we took lighter lunches."
>
> "But Georgie, here at home I always do have a light lunch."
>
> "Mean to imply I make a hog of myself, eating down-town? . . . Why don't you serve more prunes at breakfast? . . . "
>
> "The last time I had prunes you didn't eat them."

Such an exchange would indeed be wearing. Babbitt's fatigue engages both our sense of humor and our pity. It is both sound psychological insight and effective social criticism.

There is the additional tension of social-climbing: the Babbitts would like to enter the higher social level of the rich. At Babbitt's party, he and his friends congratulate themselves, however, on having reached the metropolitan middle-class ("those Main Street burgs are slow"). Beyond the satire of the party itself, which is excellent ("these small towns . . . all got an ambition that in the long run is going to make 'em the finest spots on earth—they all want to be just like Zenith"), Lewis reveals Babbitt's sense of guilt in having left the home village. And there is tension caused by contradictions in business practices. "The whole of the Glen Oriole project was a suggestion that Babbitt, though he really did hate men recognized as swindlers, was not too unreasonably honest." But, Lewis continues, "Babbitt was virtuous. He advocated, though he did not practise, the prohibition of alcohol; he praised, though he did not obey, the laws against motor-speeding; he paid his debts; he contributed to the church, the Red Cross, and the Y.M.C.A.; he followed the custom of his clan and cheated only as it was sanctified by precedent." In the next scene, Lewis shows us Babbitt swindling a helpless storekeeper. The Puritan business ethic encourages pragmatic decisions which then fatigue the conscience.

Babbitt also frets over the problem of faithfulness to the wife he takes no interest in. "In twenty-three years of married life he had peered uneasily at every graceful ankle, every soft shoulder; in thought he had treasured them; but not once had he hazarded respectability by adventuring." Now he is restless and discontented. He dreams of a fairy-girl, a divine playmate. He is worried, too, about his relationships with his employees: "He liked to like the people about him; he was dismayed when they did not like him. . . . He was afraid of his still-faced clerks."

If these tensions disturb the private Babbitt, what of the

public image of the Solid American Citizen? Babbitt's speech before the Real Estate Board describes his vision of himself. Lewis's parody is his means of attacking attitudes he detests:

> "Our Ideal Citizen—I picture him first and foremost as being busier than a bird-dog, not wasting a lot of good time in day-dreaming or going to sassiety teas or kicking about things that are none of his business, but putting the zip into some store or profession or art. At night he lights up a good cigar, and climbs into the little old 'bus, and maybe cusses the carburetor, and shoots out home. He mows the lawn, or sneaks in some practice putting, and then he's ready for dinner. After dinner he tells the kiddies a story, or takes the family to the movies, or plays a few fists of bridge, or reads the evening paper, and a chapter or two of some good lively Western novel if he has a taste for literature, and maybe the folks next-door drop in. . . . Then he goes happily to bed, his conscience clear, having contributed his mite to the prosperity of the city and to his own bank-account."

Yet in reality Babbitt sleeps fitfully and dreams of escape and rebellion.

On page 303 (with one-fourth of the novel remaining) Babbitt meets the socialist Seneca Doane, who recalls that in college Babbitt was "a liberal, sensitive chap," who had dreamed that he would become a lawyer, assume the causes of the poor, and fight the rich. With Doane's encouragement, Babbitt's overt rebellion begins. His quixotism stirs. He will draw strength from Nature; he will seek a princess outside of marriage; he will defend honesty in business and support social reform; he will right wrongs. But powerful forces are at work to call the quixotic adventurer and reformer back home:

> Vast is the power of cities to reclaim the wanderer. More than mountains or the shore-devouring sea, a city retains its character, imperturbable, cynical, holding behind apparent changes its essential purpose. Though Babbitt had deserted his family and dwelt with Joe Paradise in the wilderness, though he had become a liberal, though he had been quite sure, on the night before he reached Zenith, that neither he nor the city would be the same again, ten days after his return he could not believe that he had ever been away. Nor was it at all evident to his acquaintances that there was a new George F. Babbitt.

His friends note only a mild liberalism and a flicker of conscience. Both, however, worry them. They think him merely a crank at first. Then they decide to drive him out of their society or make him return. He becomes afraid of the terrorism of Vergil Gunch and the Good Citizens' League. When he comes back to the fold, however, a different terror remains with him—the terror of defeat: "They've licked me."

Lewis had planned from the beginning that Babbitt would break away from the standard "only for a little while." For all his careful planting of discontentments and tensions, Lewis had decided not to give Babbitt much sensitivity or intelligence. He was conceived of as a generic figure; Lewis had early pledged to have everyone soon talking of babbittry. It is impossible, however, to read Babbitt's last speech—his advice to his son to do what he

wants to do—without realizing that Lewis had allowed Babbitt to know to a small extent what his experience of rebellion has meant. But George is still very much a babbitt, frightened, guilty, and conformist, and both his way of addressing his son and that son's character itself leaves little confidence of growth. "Yet we *like* Babbitt," writes Professor Sheldon Grebstein [see essay dated 1962], "and are indulgent of him, just as Lewis is and intends." The book, he goes on, "is the outstanding social satire of its generation, if not of American literature." Howell Daniels believes that the novel is admirable because Lewis has brought Babbitt fully before us by means of the rendering of his past and his "capacity for wonder," conveyed "in a prose which moves easily between Babbitt's world of fact and the world of fantasy."

So much babbitt-talk derived from such popular media as editorials, westerns, films, and romantic fiction; Babbitt's desire to escape into a mock-Thoreauvian wilderness; and the importance of the glorious princess of his dreams as embodied in Tanis Judique—these give to Lewis's novel a pattern by which he can challenge middle-class society in America. ***Babbitt*** is a remarkable book, in large part because of Lewis's parodies of conversation, oratory, and print, which open to us, through exposures of the corruptions of language, the parallel faults of society. (pp. 73-84).

> *Martin Light, in his* The Quixotic Vision of Sinclair Lewis, *Purdue University Press, 1975, 162 p.*

Walter H. Clark, Jr. (essay date 1976)

[*In the following excerpt, Clark argues that* Babbitt's *scenographic narrative is given a formal unity by the presence of the tragic themes of Babbitt's friendship with Paul Riesling and his dream of the fairy child.*]

Here is a description of George Babbitt's alarm-clock:

> It was the best of nationally advertised and quantitatively produced alarm-clocks, with all modern attachments, including cathedral chime, intermittent alarm, and a phosphorescent dial. Babbitt was proud of being awakened by such a rich device. Socially it was almost as creditable as buying expensive cord tires.

The questions planted in the reader's mind about the society that could produce such an object are telling, as are the insinuations about the purchaser. We can see at once that George F. Babbitt is in for a hard time from his narrator. A closer examination shows something of how the irony is released, and reveals a narrative strategy that is characteristic of the novel in its entirety. The strategy I have in mind might be described as undercutting, or cutting back. Consider the alarm-clock. What we are told first is that it is the *best*. This is the highest possible praise, and gives the passage an initial positive thrust. The details appear in the guise of supporting evidence, but when we hear them described as "attachments" we begin to realize that their real function is to provide a frame for what has been left out, the clock's time-keeping properties. The passage is almost surrealistic as description in that the clock's essential function has been subtracted. What we have from the narrator is a strong *give* followed by an oblique *retraction*. The treatment of Babbitt is similar. "Babbitt was proud . . . " This is a given. In consideration of the best, one has reason to be proud. The retraction follows. "Socially . . . " This changes the thrust of the entire passage from valuation of an object to valuation of self. Babbitt is not proud of the alarm-clock for what it is or can do. He is proud of himself for owning it. The pairing of *best* at the start with *expensive* at the end frames the undercutting in the passage. The reader is encouraged to attribute a positive dynamic to the description, only to discover that its real business is to dispraise both the clock and Babbitt. This pattern occurs over and over through the novel, and is manifest, not only in such set pieces as Babbitt's speech to the Booster's Club, but also in the basic design of the novel itself.

My arguments for the coherence of the novel run counter to the views of most critics. Mark Schorer, for instance, whose biography is the definitive work on Lewis, remarks in an afterword to the New American Library edition of **Babbitt** that the novel's structure is episodic and "quite fantastic," and suggests that the book be treated as a piece of documentation rather than a novel. Nevertheless, I shall devote the rest of this paper to an attempt to show that a concealed tragic plot informs the novel up to the very final pages. Parenthetically, I feel the novel is too surrealistic to be read as more than notation for documentary.

The view of the novel as episodic rests on an analysis that takes the confusion of the world of Zenith at face value. The first seven chapters of the novel deal with a typical day in Babbitt's life. After that a number of disparate threads are followed: Babbitt's social ambitions, business deals, two pastoral interludes, philandering, experiments with social rebellion, and ultimate acquiescence to the status quo, realized at the altar of Myra Babbitt's appendicitis. If this surface were all there were to the novel it would be difficult to make a case for greater structural coherence, but I believe that two aspects of the novel deserve closer attention. One is Babbitt's friendship with Paul Riesling. The other is the dream of the fairy child, and the remembrance of the dream which recurs throughout the novel.

Babbitt is "fonder of Paul Riesling than of anyone on earth except himself and his daughter Tinka." "He was an older brother to Paul Riesling, swift to defend him, admiring him with a proud and credulous love passing the love of women." At the center of his day's activities, which comprise the opening of the novel, is a luncheon with Paul. Babbitt learns that Paul is having trouble with Zilla, his wife. Paul suggests that the two of them take a camping trip alone in Maine. Later on, when the trip takes place, Babbitt faces his own dissatisfaction with life in Zenith, but upon his return devotes himself once again to the struggle to rise in business and society. At the moment which marks his success, just as he is elected vice president of the Boosters, he learns that Paul has shot his wife. Though Zilla recovers, Paul is sent to prison. Babbitt tries to recapture the spirit of his relationship with Paul, first by returning to Maine, then, seemingly, by imitating Paul's unfaithfulness. His efforts become less comical as they become more self-destructive, and he is on the way to ruin when Myra Babbitt gets appendicitis. Babbitt rallies to his wife in her time of need. He repudiates his philandering, brings his dalliance with liberal political causes to an end, returns to the fold of Zenith, and is "saved."

I hold that the buried plot implicit in this series of events is basically tragic. Babbitt projects on Paul, and values in Paul, those characteristics which Zenith scorns, but which make a man admirable in our eyes. He and Paul together make a man larger than life in the world of Zenith. When Paul is sent to prison, Babbitt gradually ceases to cope. Events are trending toward a realization of tragic potential when Mrs. Babbitt's illness intervenes. The same sort of give and retraction that we noticed in the passage on the alarm-clock seems to be operating at the level of plot.

The dream of the fairy child has the significance of a communication from an oracle. It is Babbitt's subconscious telling him of the crucial lack in the world of Zenith: love and human contact. The fairy child is associated with Tinka, and Paul Riesling, the two people he is said to love other than himself. It may be that the fairy child is a manifestation of his *anima*. Whatever the case, he is like Oedipus in misconstruing the oracle. The crucial passage linking the loss of Paul with the dream of the fairy child, and illustrating Babbitt's misinterpretation of the dream, occurs about two thirds of the way through the novel:

> What did he want? Wealth? Social Position? Travel? Servants?
>
> Yes, but only incidentally.
>
> "I give it up," he sighed.
>
> But he did know that he wanted the presence of Paul Riesling; and from that he stumbled into the admission that he wanted the fairy girl—in the flesh. If there had been a woman whom he loved, he would have fled to her, humbled his forehead on her knees.

I would like to examine the themes of Babbitt's relation to Paul Riesling, and the dream of the fairy child in slightly greater detail in the hope that the tragic aspects of plot may be made to stand forward a bit more clearly. Take Babbitt's world as a kind of hell. Though it has the superficial, if detailed, appearance of the America of the Twenties, the spiritual properties ascribed to it could as easily be ascribed to many other times and places. The novel's representational technique is subtractive. It achieves surrealism through leaving out. There is, for example, no individuation of character. As Babbitt makes explicit in his address to the Zenith Real Estate Board, everyone in this world is like everyone else. Even the frustrated idealism of Babbitt and Paul Riesling is grotesquely mirrored in the drunken ecstasy of a Chum Frink: "Know who I am? I'm traitor to poetry . . . I could've been a Gene Field or a James Whitcomb Riley." And the social pyramid from its top, Sir Gerald Doak, to its bottom, the guide Joe Paradise, is motivated by the same mercantile and rapacious aim. Only Seneca Doane falls outside these strictures, and of course the narrator. The most significant subtraction is that of love and human contact—which is why this world must be described as a hell. In part the effect is accomplished by poisoning the female figures, who are portrayed as either washed out, like Myra Babbitt, or ravening, like Zilla and Tanis Judique. But in most general terms the narrator simply does not discover any human warmth in the society he is describing.

The effect is to place Babbitt's feelings for Paul in relief. In this world of clones no man displays such love and loyalty as Babbitt's for Paul, not even Paul himself. He is irritated by Babbitt's interference in Chicago, turns from him in prison, and as early as the lunch scene shows that his view of Babbitt is unclouded by such feelings as Babbitt's for him. ("You've been the rock of ages to me, all right, but you're essentially a simp.") Babbitt's love and loyalty are insufficient to qualify him as a tragic hero because he lacks strength of character and understanding. Still, if we think of Babbitt and Paul as combining, then we can see that person as more admirable than the other people in Zenith. But Babbitt's affection for, and loyalty to, Paul lead to his downfall. And the account of this downfall is capable of arousing a strong response in the reader.

Babbitt's virtue is also his weakness in that he uses his affection for Paul as an unconscious way of buffering himself from the unpleasant facts of his world. In loving Paul he avoids recognizing the absence of love all around him. In fending for Paul he works at maintaining the precarious balance of his own family relationships. And the qualities which he projects on Paul are those which it would be awkward to recognize in himself. Like a talisman, his affection for Paul enables him to survive Zenith. Loss of the talisman must lead either to destruction or to understanding and growth. Without it Babbitt can no longer remain static.

The dream of the fairy child is still another threat to stasis. It calls for interpretation, like any oracular revelation, but Babbitt is reluctant and unhandy in dealing with it. He never questions it explicitly. It is we who must infer the loveless enslavement of Zenith from which he escapes in the dream (hence the curative powers of the visit to Maine with Paul), and it is my suggestion, not his, that the meeting with the fairy child stands simply for human touch with another human spirit. (It will be remembered that Tinka, of whom Babbitt is so fond, is the child of the family). There are clear indications that Babbitt mishandles the dream by responding to it on too literal a level. The child of the narrator's first description is immediately transposed (by Babbitt?) into a girl. When Babbitt thinks of her during the day she is a girl, but when he falls asleep at the end of this first day he dreams again of a child. A similar mishandling is implicit in the series of ineffectual escapades with women, which are played out in the latter portions of the novel, and which are explicitly tied to the dream of the fairy child. These are escapes *within* the world of Zenith, but not *from* it. They mime escape, but in their pitiable lovelessness only illustrate Babbitt's inability to rise above the mode of life in which he is engrossed and entrapped.

The lunch with Paul, then, concentrated as it is upon the aridity of Paul's relationship with Zilla, his desire to escape from her, and his willingness to solace himself with other women, cannot but add to the disturbance already created by the dream of the fairy child. There is a potential tragic irony in Babbitt's concern for Paul. The acceptance of Paul's suggestion that they go to Maine together is at once an indication of Babbitt's affection and concern for Paul, an example of his determination to hold on to the talisman of his friendship, and a first soundless, invisible tearing of his own accommodation to the world of Zenith.

The conclusion of the Maine idyll creates the impression that Babbitt's stability has been restored. It is appropriate, I think, that for a long time after (nearly a quarter of the book) we follow the cut and slash of Babbitt's social and business forays. The friendship with Paul serves as a palliative. It enables Babbitt to function amid the brutality of Zenith, but it bears the seeds of destruction.

Babbitt's reaction to his discovery of Paul's dalliance is extreme. Leaving aside the conventional aspects of his response (". . . I don't propose to see a fellow that's been as chummy with me as you have getting started on the downward path . . . "), there are a number of conscious or unconscious motives to be associated with his actions and reactions. Most obvious is his genuine concern for Paul's well-being, which conflicts with his respect for Paul's right to do what he wants. At the same time his identification with Paul means that Paul's actions threaten the stability of his own marriage, which we know is already under a cloud. What if Babbitt were to act as Paul is acting? One way to prevent this is to keep Paul on the rails. Nor need one imagine what Leslie Fiedler would make of the trip to Maine in order to read the workings of jealousy into the following account:

> The woman was tapping [Paul's] hand, mooning at him and giggling. Babbitt felt that he had encountered something involved and harmful. Paul was talking with rapt eagerness of a man who is telling his troubles. He was concentrating on the woman's faded eyes. Babbitt had so strong an impulse to go to Paul that he could feel his body uncoiling, his shoulders moving. . . .

Surely we are entitled to look for deepseated reasons in attempting to account for Babbitt's remarkable reluctance to leave things alone between Paul and Zilla at this particular stage of their trouble.

Something of what I have described above seems implied by the phrase, "the obscenity of fate," employed by the narrator to describe the situation after Babbitt learns that Paul has shot Zilla. It points to the operation of fate as a kind of machine, in the workings of which Paul is caught. Babbitt is struck by the fact that something valued as human is about to be absorbed by a process. If that is a fair way to account for what is repulsive in obscenity, we can describe the world of Zenith as itself obscene, and distinguish a conflict in the novel between what little is warm and human and the juggernaut of process. At all events Babbitt is as much in the toils of fate as Paul.

Whether or not he is conscious of this fact, we can trace a struggle in Babbitt from the time of Paul's attack on Zilla. It takes a double form; on the one hand he tries to recapture Paul, and on the other to replace him. We see the first in his visits to Paul in jail and his return to Maine, and the second in his escapades with women, and his friendliness toward Seneca Doane. The attempt to *recapture* Paul's spirit fails, but the attempts to *replace* Paul do not merely fail. They activate the efficient causes of a destruction that has been building since the opening of the novel. Though Babbitt's affair with Tanis Judique ultimately comes to nothing, it is clear that there is material for a major scandal—scandal of the sort that might cause Mrs. Babbitt to divorce him and Henry Thompson to force him out of the real estate business. The consequences of the friendship with Seneca Doane, which are spelled out so explicitly in the sequence of events leading up to Mrs. Babbitt's attack of appendicitis, are perhaps more germane to a tragic interpretation of the novel. For Seneca Doane is in many ways a parallel to Paul Riesling. Each personifies qualities which Babbitt values. To a considerable degree, the qualities that Babbitt values must define his character since so much of his claim to tragic dignity rests on his potential. Paul looks to art. Babbitt's respect for Paul gives testimony to his own capacity for aesthetic feeling. This is further evidenced by some few of his perceptions. At the same time Paul serves a magical purpose in that Babbitt projects his own dormant aesthetic sensibilities on Paul, and thus disencumbered is able to abide the darkling plain which is Zenith. The attachment to Paul is unattended by any dangers since Zenith is totally blind to aesthetic values, and has no concern for their presence or absence. Paul's downfall, and thus Babbitt's downfall, insofar as he is dependent on Paul, comes about through matters totally beyond Babbitt's control. Babbitt's relationship with Seneca Doane is necessarily more sketchy than that with Paul Riesling. Babbitt looks up to Seneca in the same way that he looked up to Paul. However, the ideals for which Seneca stands, and which give him value in Babbitt's eye (concern for others, both as individuals and in the body social), are in direct opposition to the values of the marketplace. Zenith cares about Seneca Doane. It fears him, and it hates the ideals for which he stands. And so Babbitt's admiration for, and identification with, Seneca Doane prove self-destructive in a much more rapid and immediate way than his identification with Paul, and in a manner much more directly tied to the core of the novel. For it is not possible that Babbitt keep his friendship with Seneca Doane a secret talisman as he had that with Paul, since the values which must make the pledge good require him to take a public stand. As with the affair of Tanis Judique it is plain to the reader in what direction events are heading. The way appears clear, and has long been prepared, for a tragic catastrophe and illumination.

But this is not to be. We are surprised to find that it is Tanis who rejects Babbitt and not the other way around. The possibilities of revenge on her part are thus done away with. But it is Mrs. Babbitt's illness, and Babbitt's reaction to it, that constitutes the most powerful cut-back against the tragic inertia that has been steadily building up to this point. We can look back at Paul's failure to kill Zilla and assimilate it to the main plot as an intimation of Babbitt's own failure to win through to catastrophe and understanding. The reader who has been aware of the deeper significance of the plot finds himself non-plussed at this point. It is only upon still further reflection that he realizes the impossibility of the protagonist's measuring up to the requirements of the tragic plot. Plot and character have been at odds with one another. The novel is not itself a tragedy, but it makes use of tragic plot and perspective for its own purposes. More specifically, it sets out to be a tragedy, then makes a great point of being a not-tragedy. If this be granted we can go on to ask what it means for Babbitt and Zenith that the author should so deliberately develop tragic inertia around them, only to undercut it at the end.

I would try to answer this question not so much in terms of Babbitt as in terms of Zenith. Babbitt, all are agreed, is no tragic hero. The most poignant thing we can say about him is that he has traces of tragic potential, traces of heroic virtue. The narrator speaks at one point of " . . . the dozen contradictory Zeniths which together make up the true and complete Zenith . . . . " Tragedy and com-

edy require the assumption of a certain stability of the world in which they take their form. The thesis of this novel, I think, is that these conditions do not exist in such a place as Zenith. Zenith is a world of social uniformity, spiritually fragmented. Beneath its show of uniformity there is no human contact, no religious or humane belief. There may be fate (mechanism) in Zenith, but there are no Fates, no Gods. The world of Zenith, in short, is not a world where tragedy can exist. The logical contradictions which comprise the warp of Babbitt's Address to the Zenith Real Estate Board are representative of the mental confusion of the inhabitants of this world, the most ordinary objects of which reflect a confusion of values. Babbitt is awakened by a modern alarm-clock with cathedral chimes. The house he lives in has only one thing wrong with it. It is not a home. The very name "Zenith" contradicts actuality. Morally speaking, there is simply too much noise in Zenith for the harmony that tragedy and comedy require. The people in this world do not know what they are doing and cannot control their own actions. Nor is there any higher power to set them on the right path or to guarantee the action of the novel as a whole. The contradictions apparent in the plot, therefore, can be seen as emblematic of contradictions inherent in the world that is being represented. *Babbitt* employs contradiction as a fundamental and persuasive strategy in depicting a world of contradiction, a chaotic hell. The suggestions of tragic form simply invite the reader to see this world against the background of one where tragedy is truly possible. (pp. 277-85)

> *Walter H. Clark, Jr., "Aspects of Tragedy in 'Babbitt'," in* The Michigan Academician, *Vol. VIII, No. 3, Winter, 1976, pp. 277-85.*

T. Motylyova   (essay date 1976)

[*In the following excerpt, Motylyova observes, from a Marxist perspective, Lewis's critique of bourgeois society in his early fiction, focusing on his portrait of the typical American businessman in* Babbitt.]

Lewis' creative work . . . consists of more than just satire. Positive, even heroic characters often make their appearance in his novels. But the satiric element is always present—such is the nature of this great writer's talent; he was exceptionally keen in observing the base and comical aspects of life. The element of satire—in *Arrowsmith,* for example—heightens the drama of conflict between the honorable, thinking man and the proprietors, careerists, and the shallow and petty men with whom life inevitably brings him into contact.

The four novels which Sinclair Lewis published in fairly rapid succession after the First World War are thematically completely unrelated: *Main Street* (1920) is the story of an intelligent, cultured woman trying to resist the onslaughts of provincial philistinism; *Babbitt* (1922) portrays a typical, "average" businessman; *Arrowsmith* (1925) is a novel about the fate of a scholar; *Elmer Gantry* (1927) describes the career of a roguish preacher. Nonetheless they could be viewed as a sort of cycle united by a common overall theme. They show in an uncompromisingly critical light what is commonly called "the American way of life"; Sinclair Lewis' criticism is not directed against Americans as a nation, nor against the nature of man as such, but rather against a social system built on the private ownership of property and the pursuit of profit. Social and psychological analyses are here fused together. And it is no coincidence that these novels in particular marked the beginning of his meteoric rise to international fame and brought him the Nobel Prize in 1930, making him the first American author to be so honored. (pp. 263-64)

The central characters of Lewis' works are always taken from those social strata with which the author was well acquainted from his youth, with whom he had had personal contact or which fell under the range of his extensive literary and journalistic impressions. They are representatives of the working intelligentsia—doctors, jurists, those involved in commerce and even middle-class businessmen and politicians. But the working and exploited masses are in some form or other represented on the pages of his novels: the farmers and craftsmen treated by the provincial "Doc" Kennicott (*Main Street*) or by the young doctor Arrowsmith in the novel of the same name; the steel founders and construction workers of the city of Zenith, whom the respectable George F. Babbitt fears, and whom he tries to flatter in his demagogic speeches; the prisoners whose fate Ann Vickers tries to make more tolerable through her naive reformist activities; or, finally, the oppressed Blacks with whom Neil Kingsblood, hero of **Kingsblood Royal** draws close and with whom owing to unexpected circumstances and the dictates of conscience he expresses his solidarity. The very nature of the milieu depicted by Lewis creates an essential distinction between his work and that of those American novelists whose heroes and plots are completely closed within the exclusive world of wealth and property (including the great and bitter novels about the life of the rich that were composed by F. Scott Fitzgerald). The life of the working class which constituted a majority of the population never became a primary theme in Lewis' novels. But in almost all his best works it was an open question, keen, vital, disturbing both the author and his heroes.

Lewis' novels most often have the same name as that of the central figure in the novel. And this was not simply a whim. The plots of these novels unfold as the history of an individual in his relations with society. Here the author is in part paying tribute to traditional American individualism: he was inclined to approach many problems and their resolution precisely from the point of view of a single individual with his spiritual needs, his fate and his views. At the same time this structural principle made it possible for Lewis to reveal more fully the inner world of his heroes.

A man comes face to face with life (or comes to some turning point in life). How does he bring his natural potential to realization? In what form will he interact—or has he interacted—with the surrounding world? Will he submit completely to the evil laws of the world of property or will he dare to hold his ground, to defend his searching, rebelling self ? Or in the end will he find some sort of intermediate ground, some kind of compromise? Almost all of Sinclair Lewis' fundamental works, though varying in plot and occasionally completely dissimilar in their conceptual frame, are constructed as variations on the theme of the individual's conflict with his environment. Often the conclusion is vague or conciliatory in nature, which reflects both the contradictory position of the writer himself, and at the same time the fact that the problems which his heroes face are not resolved by life itself.

The relationship between the individual and his environment has not only a social and moral aspect for Sinclair Lewis but also something more concrete and professional. The writer is convinced that each man must have his own occupation in life. (The drama of Carol Kennicott, the heroine of **Main Street,** is motivated not only by the fact that Carol cannot get along with the petty bourgeois of Gopher Prairie, but primarily because she has not found an occupation for herself which satisfies her soul and corresponds to her abilities.) It goes without saying that Lewis sees clearly the difference between sensible, creative work and empty, meaningless activity: the preacher Elmer Gantry and the political careerist Gideon Planish are plainly involved with the latter, not with real work. But be that as it may, Lewis portrays each of his heroes in that environment, that sphere of activity, which is connected with his type of work. And many of Lewis' novels, as critics have often noted, are a sort of sociological investigation from which one can learn much about the world of provincial "operators" (**Babbitt**), the state of science and health services in the United States (**Arrowsmith**), the women's movement and the penitentiary system (**Ann Vickers**), religious organizations and sects (**Elmer Gantry**) and so on.

No matter how unstable Lewis' world view or how susceptible to fluctuations, there was a definite complex of ideas which took shape in his mind while he was still young and to which he remained true through the various turning points in his life. His attitude toward capitalism was and remained critical (even though he did try occasionally to find sympathetic and reasonable representatives of the bourgeois). He was irreconcilably opposed to the greed and narrow-mindedness of men of property. He sharply condemned militarism and aggressive wars and racial oppression in its various forms. He was quick to identify the class nature of fascism and was uncompromisingly opposed to it. He made a sober assessment of the darker aspects of the American political system, though he could not completely abandon his illusions regarding bourgeois democracy.

Sinclair Lewis was a fierce opponent of everything that might inhibit the individual. This in part explains why he did not accept organized forms of revolutionary struggle. At the same time, however, Lewis, championing the freedom of the individual took a passionate stand against the hypocrisy and falsity, against reducing a man to a common level, and he opposed standardization everywhere he found it.

Hence the birth of **Babbitt,** a novel about a "standardized" American.

The literature of critical realism, from Balzac to Dreiser, has often provided colorful portrayals of bourgeois figures—energetic, businesslike entrepreneurs capable of acting independently with style and initiative, but at the same time acting unscrupulously and without conscience. Mr. Babbitt is not altogether scrupulous himself. But in essence he is neither free nor *independent* in his actions. His businesslike mien is largely illusory.

Such a depiction of the bourgeois was new, not just for American, but for world literature. It is not surprising that progressive literary circles in the United States welcomed *Babbitt.* The novel was perceived as a literary discovery of sorts. The outstanding critic H. L. Mencken [see *TCLC,* Vol. 4, pp. 246-47], who assumed a sharply anti-bourgeois position in the twenties, ended his review of the novel in the following manner: "In all these scenes there is more than mere humor; there is searching truth. . . . I know of no American novel that more accurately presents the real America. It is a social document of a high order."

Sinclair Lewis speaks forthrightly and clearly about his hero: ". . . he made nothing in particular, neither butter nor shoes nor poetry, but he was nimble in the calling of selling houses for more than people could afford to pay." Thus from the very start Babbitt stands out as a social superfluity. We see Babbitt at various moments in his working day—dictating letters, pondering a report, closing a deal—and we become more and more convinced of the truth of the author's initial characterization. In truth Babbitt does not create, and is incapable of creating values of any sort, whether material or spiritual. He is the representative of a class which, in the well-known words of the *Communist Manifesto,* at one time played a revolutionary role in history, but in the 20th century has abandoned its role as an organizer of production and in the main has been transformed into a parasitic and consuming class.

Babbitt, too, is depicted close-up as just this sort of person: a consumer, a man who possesses an enormous number of things which actually he does not need. The books in the house which nobody reads, the latest super custom-made cigarette lighter, and even the car—for Babbitt and his family these objects are significant above all in that they lend social prestige to their owners. And in fact "in the city of Zenith, in the barbarous twentieth century, a family's motor indicated its social rank as precisely as the grades of the peerage determined the rank of an English family".

At a leisurely pace, with characteristically reserved and ironic intonations, the novelist describes the external appearance and behavior of his hero. Even in the laudatory epithets there lurks an element of censure which from time to time breaks out into the open. "The gray suit was well cut, well made, and completely undistinguished. It was a standard suit. White piping on the V of the vest added a flavor of law and learning. His shoes were black laced boots, good boots, honest boots, standard boots, extraordinarily uninteresting boots. . . . A sensational event was changing from the brown suit to the gray the contents of his pockets. He was earnest about these objects. They were of eternal importance, like baseball or the Republican Party. They included a fountain pen and a silver pencil (always lacking a supply of new leads) which belonged in the righthand upper vest pocket. Without them he would have felt naked." The reader sees more and more clearly that it is not Babbitt who owns things, but things that own Babbitt. He leads a contented life in wealth and comfort. But he has neither happiness nor freedom.

Babbitt, it would appear, is an extremely uncomplicated individual. But his psychological portrait is marked by flexibility and mobility. However poor in spirit he may be, however lacking in mental facility, Babbitt is vaguely dissatisfied with himself and with his life, and is trying somehow to change his mode of living. The first seven chapters of the novel devoted to one day in Babbitt's life are in essence an exposition, a prologue. The real action of the novel unfolds in the succeeding chapters, where we witness Babbitt's clumsy attempts to break the inertia of his standard existence—and the inevitable failure of these attempts.

Critics of various countries interested in Lewis' novels have traditionally devoted attention to the internal dynamics of the image of Babbitt. The well-known Italian writer and anti-fascist Cesare Pavese, a translator and extremely perceptive critic of American literature, wrote the following as far back as 1930:

> Babbitt affects us precisely because he shows us how being an average man, a common man, a normal man, is like being a puppet. What reader of the novel, while reading it, has not every so often squirmed, asking himself how many times he himself has been a Babbitt?
>
> And, I repeat, the book's greatness lies in the fact that Babbitt is restless, that Babbitt—in this respect more than ever Babbitt—does not want to be a Babbitt, and that all his efforts fail, leaving him terribly resigned, terribly good-natured, and ready to begin again. At a certain point, every cliché, every glad-handing phrase, every gesture, every ridiculous scene—and the reader knows how full of them the book is—becomes a barb which we see stuck in Babbitt, and he doesn't notice, but from it his character emerges, tortured, quite stoic, and still without heroism, the most common—and thus the most extraordinary—martyr the world has ever seen.

The word martyr, of course, is applied to Babbitt with a touch of irony, for his dreams of happiness, his pretentions to independence and freedom of thought, are in essence as destitute as he himself is: there is no real, profound dramatic tension in his experiences, nor can there possibly be. Nonetheless it is significant that Lewis does not make his hero a complete obscurantist and dimwit, but endows him with a measure of real human feelings: a genuinely friendly attachment to Paul Riesling, love for his son, and timid—oh, so timid!—gleams of critical consciousness. All this does not mean that Sinclair Lewis entertained secret feelings of tenderness toward Babbitt and Babbittry. Rather it signifies that the accusation inferred in the novel is directed primarily at the entire bourgeois class, and not at a single individual.

The most perspicacious readers of the novel, both in America and abroad, were quick to recognize the typicality of Babbitt. We ought to add to Cesare Pavese's judgement yet one more testimony, that of a prominent West-European writer. Kurt Tucholsky, a well-known satirist and publicist writing in pre-Nazi Germany greeted the publication of *Babbitt* in German translation (1925) with an ecstatic review. "This is the most topical novel to come to my attention recently—it is totally a product of our times," he exclaimed. Tucholsky noted the innovative literary devices employed by the novelist—the inclusion of expertly stylized business documents, notices, newspaper articles, an originally applied montage of short cinematic clips extending the frames of action. But what was most contemporary and most valuable in the novel, he affirmed, was the image of Babbitt himself. He saw in it something very much like the German philistine Wendriner, the personage he created for his own satirical feuilletons. "The Germans will laugh at this American. But Mr. Wendriner will never realize that he is also a Babbitt; that if one reproduced his notions, thoughts and current ideas benevolently and without commentary people would also laugh; that values which he finds irrefutable and indestructible are just as absurd; that his Dresden Bank, his ball at the opera, his literature, symphony concerts, the electric apparatus in his apartment and his bargains are just as senseless and foolhardy as those of Babbitt."

Sinclair Lewis was the first to create a typical image, embodied in relief, of a life process which now, a half century later, is being pondered by many writers and sociologists in Western Europe and the United States: the depersonalization of the individual, the standardization of the tastes, opinions and behavior of people living in the capitalist world. And this process as delineated on the pattern of Babbitt becomes all the more convincing because the hero of the novel is not a marionette, not a conventional, hyperbolized figure, but a real, live man, drawn, as it were, from within, with concreteness and psychological authenticity.

In the course of the action the reader sees more and more clearly the mechanism whereby bourgeois society affects the individual. When Babbitt tries to break through the barriers surrounding him, and especially when he tries to avoid joining the so-called Good Citizens' League, his fellow townsmen, relatives, neighbors, business partners and church officials make a concerted effort to compel him, literally *compel* him, to "think things over". His father-in-law and companion Henry Thompson unambiguously hints that if Babbitt does not join the Good Citizens' League the firm will be faced with failure and the family with ruin. Former friends avoid him.

Lewis' keenness of vision with respect to social matters is manifested with particular strength in the episodes devoted to the Good Citizens' League. He was among the first in world literature to discern, already in the twenties, the signs of fascism in the capitalist world, though he was thousands of miles removed from its birthplace in Mussolini's Italy. He revealed those specific national methods of activity and forms of ideological camouflage which served as a refuge for those organizations and groups of fascist cast in his own country. "All of them [members of the league] agreed that the working classes must be kept in their place; and all of them perceived that American Democracy did not imply any equality of wealth, but did demand a wholesome sameness of thought, dress, painting, morals, and vocabulary. . . . The longest struggle of the Good Citizens' League was for the Open Shop—which was secretly a struggle against all union labor." It is only a small step from this sort of struggle to acts of political terrorism. "One evening a number of young men raided the Zenith Socialist Headquarters, burned its records, beat the office staff, and agreeably dumped desks out of the window."

This was the beginning of the anti-fascist theme in Sinclair Lewis' work, one to which he returned ten years later, after Hitler's coup in Germany, developing it in his satirical novel *It Can't Happen Here,* and later, during the Second World War, in *Gideon Planish.* (pp. 268-76)

T. Motylyova, "Sinclair Lewis and His Best Novels," in 20th Century American Literature: A Soviet View, *translated by Ronald Vroon, Progress Publishers, 1976, pp. 261-84.*

Joel Fisher (essay date 1986)

[*In the following excerpt, Fisher explains the significance of Lewis's analysis of the relationship between individual and national identity in* Main Street *and* Babbitt, *arguing that the eclipse of individual liberties in the latter work is adumbrated by the "marriage contract" theme of* Main Street.]

Sinclair Lewis's critical reputation could not easily be lower than it is at present. In the discussion that follows I want to suggest that a radical re-evaluation of this reputation, and of Lewis's achievement as a novelist, is necessary; not just because he ought to be read and studied seriously in his own right, but also because in his best fiction he addresses very important issues of narrative technique and of historical and structural analysis. And I believe that without a proper understanding of Lewis's engagement with his material in these areas, most notably in *Main Street* (1920) and *Babbitt* (1922), the two texts I want to concentrate on here, any account of the re-shaping of American fiction in the years after the First World War must be seriously incomplete.

Lewis has proved to be an extremely easy writer to dismiss from any literary or intellectual canon, and not without good reason. His fictions are direct, accessible, and for the most part actively simple. Like Wells and Bennett in England he is a provincial writer of materialist romances, apparently left behind by Modernism; like Upton Sinclair he is a clumsy and over-productive fictionaliser of obvious social problems; in the 1920s he is a man of middle age writing stories about middle-aged characters for a middle-aged readership in a literary and intellectual climate obsessed and characterized by youth; he is a wildly inconsistent writer, who in his weakest work unquestionably justifies Schorer's description of him as "one of the worst writers in modern American Literature." And probably more than any other twentieth-century writer of comparable stature, Lewis has been a victim of literary history-writing. With only the very weak platform of spectacular popular success to support him, he stands as the clearest (and unfortunately also the most vociferous) representative of the American fiction that Hemingway and Fitzgerald and their apologists were careful to be seen to be superseding in the 1920s and 1930s.

If Lewis is read and studied at all now, it is as a marginal figure. He is not a free-standing object thinking for himself, but an example of extreme contingency, who is on the one hand a symptom and on the other an artifact. As a symptom he is a Popular Novelist, blatantly deriving his writing technique and his conspectus from sources that are already outmoded: Dreiser for the documentary realism; Sinclair and Norris for the naively imposed analytical problem plot; Dickens watered-down through Bennett for the idea of the empathic comic monster; Mencken for the crude and heavy satire which is rigorous in its application but often apparently groundless. As an artifact he becomes, because of his third-hand techniques and his undemanding intellectual level, of merely sociological interest: if you want a fictional correlative of *Middletown* you go to Lewis's Zenith, and vice versa. So in this sense, making few demands of Lewis's text and accepting received opinion, you can very easily categorize him as a briefly successful charlatan whose corpus is made up of attempts to make the Popular Novel look intellectually viable by putting a

Lewis with Dorothy Thompson.

mask of verisimilitude and profound analysis on to a base of cheap stock romance plots, sentimental conservation of the idlest sort, and easy polemic employed almost entirely for its comic value.

Lewis's fictions are plainly synthetic, and it would be impertinent to argue that they are not. His central stories about characters are implausible and artificial, and his writing is a derivative collage that acknowledges its antecedents clearly. If the fictions were synthetic to no end other than the selling of books and the making of money, then it would seem reasonable to applaud Lewis for his short-term accomplishment and let the sort of negative reading I have outlined stand as a final judgment. But I want now to try and demonstrate virtually the exact opposite.

I want to show that Lewis's ways of making fictions (with the caveat that my arguments are based on Lewis at what has generally been agreed to be his best; I can think of no arguments that would defend him at his worst) are calculatedly synthetic, and that what have been read as limitations are in fact part of a comprehensive and radical intellectual exercise. The nature of this exercise is reasonably easy to identify and describe, but difficult to define in accepted critical terms. This is partly because of Lewis's scale, and partly because of his eclecticism. He does not appear to recognize barriers of taste and discipline and mode. On the surface of a Lewis novel there is no differentiation between social realism and implausible satire and

equally implausible romance, and no sense that they might be in any way incompatible; and in the analysis that informs and constructs the fiction there is no differentiation between history, politics, sociology, psychology, law and simple rhetoric. If something can be used to make a point it is used to make a point, and no other consideration is necessary.

This means that you can read Lewis in two very distinct ways. You can either say that, like Twain before him and Mailer after, he is a very acute intellectual hooligan who decides not to notice that there might be any necessary disparity between accessible popular fiction and fiction which makes a useful and profound analysis of society and individuals, or you can say that he is a crass and literal-minded writer who at his best unwittingly trespasses into areas that are usually the prerogative of more disciplined and sophisticated minds. Given the quantity of poor fiction in the Lewis corpus, the latter reading is obviously safer and in little danger of falsification. But I want to try and argue the former case.

It is both straightforward and productive to start with Lewis's own clearest attempt to define his work: "I am the diagnostician." This suggests the weaknesses as well as the strengths. In the later and weaker fiction, the diagnosis is very often the finite diagnosis of a discrete area, like the issue of race in *Kingsblood Royal.* But in the earlier and stronger fiction, Lewis is attempting a great deal more. A diagnostician finds out what is wrong, and in order to do this he needs to have a model of the precise nature and structure of the object under examination. In *Main Street* and *Babbitt* Lewis is establishing this model. He is slicing into America and into the ways in which the individual American constructs his identity at a historical moment which he rightly identifies as a crucial turning-point; and in doing so he is describing and defining structure, history and society both as determinants and objects of discourse. As a working diagnostician Lewis is entirely a pragmatist. He wants to use his fictions to find out things he believes can be found out and need to be found out. The way he gets the results is of little or no importance, and this, in its most direct formulation, is the reason for the sense of eclecticism and derivative collage. Lewis is not borrowing and shifting around for artistic effect or intellectual credibility; in any case he achieves neither; he is furiously analysing, using any technique that comes to hand, and then discarding it as soon as it has served its purpose. All other considerations are subordinate to the main function of making the diagnosis.

Lewis's opening claim for *Main Street,* the notorious statement that "This is America," is grandiloquent, but it does not by any means misrepresent the book. Read consecutively, *Main Street* and *Babbitt* make up an extraordinarily ambitious attempt to define America and the individual American at the start of the 1920s. The remarkable fact about this attempt, and the fact that has unfortunately rendered it virtually invisible to critics, is that Lewis is making an analysis of America in the vernacular. By ignoring and thus transcending mode and manner and by writing what is unashamedly popular fiction, he is defining America *on its own terms;* not working through any imposed or contrived analytical system, but working in the peculiarly American idiom of the contractual creation of nation and individual identity, and of the necessary structural links between the two.

Before actually engaging with **Main Street** and **Babbitt,** I want briefly to rehearse the bases of the contractual framework Lewis uses in making his diagnosis. Since Lewis works into his larger analyses by examining the individual American, it seems most realistic to work into the contractual framework in the same way.

If you say that the relationship between individual and nation is dependent on the existence of an *a priori* written contract, establishing a nation built to represent individual moral and ethical values, then the contractual result is that the individual is made subject to a uniquely total form of control. The paradox of this control is that it is the result of a liberation. In a nation that refuses publicly to admit that any individual member might possibly be in a condition of alienation from the main structure, because the structure is ostensibly built of and for and by the individual American, control moves to a significant extent away from the superficial area of politics. The control is instead articulated and exercised through the less accessible area of the individual American's identity construction, and it is probably best described as a system of contractual determinism. Because the American nation contains by definition the individual American's "inalienable Rights" to "Life, Liberty and the pursuit of Happiness," the individual American, providing he believes life, liberty and happiness to be desirable qualities and qualities that define his identity as an individual, cannot conceive of his existence except as a member of the nation. He therefore has no option but to construct his identity on the terms the nation prescribes.

Until the closing of the frontier, all this is hypothetical. The individual American is protected by a nominal States' Rights argument, because as long as the paradigm is of the individual making the nation, power remains with the individual. And even if this is only a matter of popular mythology, it cannot be tested objectively until the nation exists physically, and the nation cannot be said to exist physically rather than hypothetically until settlement is complete. This is compounded by the fact that while settlement is still happening, political and economic control systems are largely nominal. They are not established systems of control, but blueprints for a nation that can only become a nation when it has assimilated its own land. (The Frederick Jackson Turner frontier thesis, with its emphasis on land and abundance and character, is effectively a euphemistic statement of this point; and the way in which the Turner conception of the frontier uses the very potent border between contractual determinism and popular mythology accounts to a great extent for its centrality in historical thought.)

The frontier does not close at a specific point, and it does not close in isolation. The contractual position of individual and nation cannot be divorced from the social and economic context that dictates nation and national definition. The period between, say, 1870 and 1920 sees two movements: on the one hand the closing of the frontier, and on the other the development of an urbanized, industrial society. Neither movement is neat or categorical, but both represent decisive and incontrovertible shifts in the perception of America and the American. The combination of the two movements categorically signals the end of the period of luxury in which, whatever the actual state of affairs, the individual American might reasonably believe that his existence and identity were not heavily determined by nation and structure.

This becomes a critical matter of intellectual debate immediately after the First World War. As the first mobilisation of the American nation in a foreign conflict, the War marks the point at which the nation first functions as an entity which is invented and complete rather than in process of invention; it is, if you like, the definite statement by America to the individual American that the frontier is now closed, and the literary examinations that follow detail the meanings and their consequences. Hemingway's and Fitzgerald's have generally been read as the most direct fictional responses, but their re-shapings and evaluations are limited by an implausible romanticism. Both use the War, rightly, as a schismatic event that makes a definition and demands analysis, but they use the schism to impose an artificial division between materialist reality and the individual utopianism of an American Dream. The annoying point is that Hemingway and Fitzgerald both correctly engage with the main issue of identity construction, but they do it by making a Romantic approach which is logically impossible if you acknowledge the implications of the nation's contractual control of its individual member.

In *The Great Gatsby* Fitzgerald dramatizes the impossibility of the co-existence of utopianism and materialism in the same identity or the same nation, and in *Tender is the Night* he documents the consequent shattering of identity and national utopianism in their European footings, America having been abandoned to the materialist forces that must necessarily destroy individual utopianism. This is essentially Hemingway's thesis also: but having identified the schism, he insistently details the impossibility of continuing a utopian Americanism that depends on elemental contact with the American land, for once the whole of the American land has been usurped by materialism, the one place in which utopian Americanism can certainly never exist is America. In this context Lewis's status is magisterial. In his diagnostic fictions he identifies, lays out and analyses the factors that stimulate Hemingway's and Fitzgerald's Romantic secessions; and because Lewis does not secede and allow the individual American to run away to Europe or dissolve in obsessive fantasy, he is in a position to describe and technically analyse the way in which the individual American is both used and re-defined by corporate materialist America.

The analytical device most consistently at the center of Lewis's diagnosis in **Main Street** is his use of the marriage contract as the focus of the contract between individual and nation in America. This is a particularly strong example of Lewis's technique of giving an account of America on its own terms, because what he actually does is to articulate and invoke a connection automatically present in the contractual structuring of nation and identity in America. In European bourgeois society the marriage contract represents the larger contract between individual and state because it represents the accessible point at which a naturalized contract of identity and subscription to state is articulated and publicly legitimized. In America and in American fiction it is more than this and can more reasonably be put forward as a matter of general rule. Because of the inextricable bonding of the individual American to America it both articulates the individual's subscription to the structure, thus stating public legitimacy, and at the same time *naturalizes* the state's legal control of the individual, by engaging a hypothetical, discursive idea of identity and nation with the naturalizing ideas of fertility, reproduction, pair-bonding and home-making. In this sense every American marriage points not merely to the contract itself, but to the way the contract is used as the mandate for occupying America, assuming legal control and then settling the nation in order to naturalise the legal control. (pp. 421-26)

Lewis adds to the idea of the marriage contract as the focus of the contract between individual and nation its obvious corollary, that if marriage in America implicitly states the naturalization of legal control, it also automatically gives a matrix of meaning on the same terms to the range of individual definitions and statuses that take their meaning from their relationship to the marriage contract. H. L. Mencken begins to identify the way Lewis uses this in *Main Street*:

> Superficially the story of a man and his wife in a small Minnesota town, it is actually the typical story of the American family—that is, of the family in its first stage, before husband and wife have become lost in father and mother. [H. L. Mencken, "Consolation," *Smart Set*, January 1921.]

This superficial story is the narrative vehicle that Lewis uses to frame and carry *Main Street*'s most obvious function of social and sociological survey, so that Carol Kennicott's marriage into Gopher Prairie is used to introduce an ironic representation of the paradigm unit of agrarian America, the Mid-Western small town. The small town is small-minded, narrow, hypocritical and philistine. It does not in any sense represent a Jeffersonian yeoman democracy; on the contrary, its function is almost wholly parasitic, and it seems to exist only in order to take money away from the land and its small farmers. The exploiters are WASPs, and the exploited farmers Swedes and Germans. The most distinguished and authoritative citizen is the banker Stowbody, and the most imposing building the bank. *Main Street*'s basic narrative follows Gopher Prairie from this decadent and contradictory state in the years leading up to the First World War to the beginning of post-war Boosterism (Honest Jim Blausser and the White Way) and plainly hopeless attempts at growth, competition and industrialization. All this is presented in the manner of verisimilitudinous report; but to accept this on its surface level and look no further, as E. M. Forster seems to do in limiting his comments to praising Lewis's photographic technique, is to risk missing much of the point.

The surface of *Main Street* is the presentation of the problem. The function of the novel is to move from the presentation of symptoms to actually making the diagnosis, and the analytical use of the Kennicott marriage is at the centre of the process. At the start of the novel, as Carol Milford, Carol is unambiguously set up as an archetype, "the spirit of that bewildered empire called the American Middlewest." This is not only (because it must be admitted that it *is* in part) a flamboyantly vulgar opening statement: it is also Lewis's first diagnostic move in setting up his model of America, and Carol's personal history is carefully structured to support it. She is the orphan daughter of

a Massachusetts judge who came West to Mankato ("white and green New England reborn") and died there; so if Lewis's literal statement that Carol is the spirit of the Mid-West is to be taken literally, she has been created by law in the East, kept briefly and artificially in a re-creation of the East in the Mid-West, and left an orphan in the geographical centre of the continent to make her contract with both husband and land. As the outstanding girl at Blodgett she is made the obvious product of an institutionalised liberal humanism, and at Blodgett it is her ambition to engage with a prairie town, and the place she eventually does engage with, Gopher Prairie, is immediately and literally set up as an archetype: Carol sees in it "not only the heart of a place called Gopher Prairie, but ten thousand towns from Albany to San Diego."

If Carol Milford is the abstract and disengaged utopianism produced by the legal birth of America in the East, Will Kennicott is her necessary complement, the elemental contact with land and human life that must fuse with the invented nation in order to close the frontier and complete America. (Hemingway's use of a sporting doctor in "Indian Camp" to make a similar statement closely echoes this characterization.) Will Kennicott is notably inarticulate, though by no means insensitive; the point is not that he is a hick and a boor, but that he lacks abstraction and the capacity to explain his feelings. In this sense he is as much a victim as Carol, and the question of whether Carol or Will is Lewis's main focus character is ambiguous for much of the length of *Main Street*.

Gopher Prairie is the ironic setting for this epic contract-making: taking Lewis at his most direct, Carol's and Will's marriage is the theoretical idea of America and Gopher Prairie is its practical product. When Carol arrives in Gopher Prairie she finds a European peasantry already installed, and the ideal she represents being used as a facile apologia for commercial parasitism. Her introduction to the community makes it clear that she is not structurally necessary; that she is of interest only to the extent to which she has purchasing power (hence the emphasis on shops and shop-keepers) and commodity value (hence the emphasis on "society" and the newspaper reports of her arrival). This setting is *Main Street*'s materialist base. While, through the Kennicott marriage, legal and natural America are making their final contractual connection, the agrarian ideal that the nation was created to serve has become a travesty.

The meaning of the Kennicott marriage as a description of "the family in its first stage" now becomes fully clear. Lewis is using the marriage to adumbrate the move from the *de jure* closure of the frontier to its *de facto* closure, first detailing the marriage itself, the definite engagement of ideal and land against the commercial base that neither ideal nor land can accommodate, then moving through to the outbreak of war in Europe, the changes in Gopher Prairie, the birth of the two Kennicott children, and hence the actual results of the contract-making and its necessary subordination to the commercial base. In the course of this the central characters move into middle age, and this is also a clear analytical point in the making of the diagnosis. Twain's protagonists in *Tom Sawyer* and *Huckleberry Finn* are adolescents. They can still light out for the Territories, and cannot make a formal contractual engagement because the frontier is still open. Fitzgerald's impossible secessionists in *Tender is the Night* form and break identities of spurious youth, because Fitzgerald's impossible division of utopian America and materialist America depends on identifying youth with a utopianism that can carry on an independent existence. Only Lewis states the necessity of aging and makes a model of the construction of the mature, post-frontier American identity.

The model is by no means pleasant. In **Main Street** Will Kennicott is from the start tainted and compromised by commercialism, and this has a plain analytical meaning because the taint comes through Will's land-dealing activities. If America has a commercial base, naturalized contact with the American land must necessarily become commercialized also. For Lewis this is an accepted and established fact in approaching **Main Street**'s central question, of whether it is possible for the force of ideal America that Carol represents either to alter this situation or to exist away from it. The answer, and on this point Lewis's answer differs little from Hemingway's and Fitzgerald's, is that neither is possible. The ideal, based on the necessity of making the contract, can exist only with reference to naturalized contact with America, which in turn can now exist only with reference to the commercial base. The conclusion of **Main Street** makes this statement. After the birth of her son, and during America's involvement in the First World War, Carol goes to Washington; so during the event that defines the *de facto* closure of the frontier, and hence also of the nation's contractual control of individual identity construction, she goes back East to the home both of the contract and of the machinery of government.

Will comes to fetch Carol from Washington, they return to Gopher Prairie, and Carol has a daughter. The son, taking literally Lewis's use of gender in his analytical model, is a continuation of Will and all that he represents; and the daughter is a continuation of Carol. The fact that the marriage is resumed, and resumed in Gopher Prairie, makes clear Lewis's conclusion that the force of ideal America cannot escape from the necessity of bonding with natural America, whatever the state of natural America, and the birth of the daughter re-emphasizes the fact that this is Lewis's image of the future of America.

Babbitt details the practical and analytical consequences of this tainted contract-making. Babbitt himself is the new archetype of middle-aged, post-frontier America, and he is a figure of Behaviourist nightmare. Because as an individual he is governed by the forces of uncontrolled materialism that have been mandated by the completion of the contract, his identity is made out of the marketing devices and jargons of the Zenith business community, and out of the commodity fetish objects that indicate style and status in Zenith. He is in this sense a victim (as, for Lewis, every individual American must always be primarily a victim) of the contract; but at the same time he is a monster character who represents inordinate power. There are two basic reasons for this. First, as a realtor Babbitt controls the crucial interface of land and property-dealing. This analytical continuation of the betrayal of land-holding, taking up the points made about Will Kennicott's deals in **Main Street,** becomes Babbitt's most cherished image of himself; he believes that the realtor stands at the base of society because community and civilization cannot exist without someone having first sold the land. This is a bizarre and apparently rather facile joke, but as a diagnostic

statement it has considerable moment and needs to be taken entirely seriously. There is no force in Zenith to suggest that Babbitt's reading of America is not correct; because Zenith is Lewis's diagnostic model of the America that must necessarily result from the mismade contract, Babbitt must be right.

Second, Babbitt is, as Rebecca West puts it, "a bonehead Walt Whitman" [see essay dated 1922]. He is the paradigm product of a contractual system in which the spirit of utopian invention has become, and must remain, the major motive force of a commercial machine that is its logical antithesis. Just as Lewis's contemporary Dale Carnegie can prescribe systems of identity construction and ethical behaviour (most notoriously in *How to Win Friends and Influence People*) based on the central idea of utopian America and borrowed from Emerson and William James and then present the product as a prescription for commercial success, because his own sense of identity has in it no sense of the necessary contradiction between utopianism and exploitative commerce, so Babbitt's energized and spirited American vision becomes an integral and essential part of the grotesque circle depriving him of the individuality that should be at the heart of the vision.

As an account of the stage of America consequent on the contract made in **Main Street, Babbitt** points also to the dissipation of the pre-industrial ideals of natural contact with American land. The cults of masculinity that Lewis uses to characterize Will Kennicott, and which are so central to Hemingway's attempts to secede into elemental Americanism, have become on one hand the emasculated tourist attractions of Babbitt's trips to Maine, and on the other the rhetorical devices (he-men, go-getters, regular guys) of the Zenith marketing culture.

Having put forward his diagnosis, Lewis subjects it to the crucial test of Babbitt's attempted escape from Zenith's Watsonian determinism. To do this he uses the same technique as in Carol's separation from Will in **Main Street;** while Myra Babbitt is away, the marriage contract is suspended in order to allow George Babbitt to experiment with different bases of social contract. The results of this period of experiment are entirely self-defeating. While politically Babbitt makes his brief identification with Seneca Doane and Liberalism, his parallel social attempts at redefinition with Tanis Judique and the Bunch represent subscription to a rootless hedonism, characterized by a commitment to materialist consumerism that differs from Floral Heights commodity fetishism only in its lack of pretence to solidity and permanence. Babbitt cannot escape from the system and the structure; he can only lose status within them.

And just as Carol's return to Gopher Prairie after the interregnum in her marriage is used to reinforce and restate **Main Street**'s diagnosis, so is Babbitt's return to his marriage and to the world of Gunch and Frink and the Athletic Club.

The return operates analytically on two levels. The first is an apparently crude moment of epiphany, when the surgeon Dilling operates on Myra Babbitt's appendicitis. On the surface this is domestic melodrama of the cheapest sort, but its meaning is far more profound. The marriage, and hence the contract, is saved because Myra Babbitt's life is saved. And the life is saved in a way that shows very clearly the convergence of the forces that keep Babbitt under strict control, because the hospital and the operation provide the focal point at which technology and materialism engage with basic humanity and matters of life and death. Myra Babbitt's operation is Lewis's demonstration that Will Kennicott's elemental contact with humanity and land is still, and will always remain, the first and most important building-block of America and American community. While this remains the case, neither utopian idealism nor individual identity can ever be separated from it. Zenith unquestionably maintains its right to be America and to construct Babbitt as its archetypal representative.

This conclusion leads to another, because its implications are dramatized in the way Babbitt is returned to his normal existence by the Good Citizens' League. Lewis points up the connection by making Dilling a prominent member of the GCL. The GCL is, as Lundquist neatly puts it [see Further Reading], a representation of "the fascistic tendencies that are constantly on the verge of destroying freedom in the United States," and it stands as *Babbitt* 's valedictory statement. Latent hysteria and its horrifying implications (examined in part in *Elmer Gantry*) are the only logical product of the progress of America that Lewis describes and analyses in *Main Street* and *Babbitt.*

And after these two brutal conclusions *Babbitt* ends, like *Main Street,* with marital resolution and an image of the future. Ted Babbitt marries Eunice Littlefield, so that another generation of Babbitts will presumably follow in due course. But for the new generation of Babbitts (babbitt metal being notable only for its extreme malleability), there is a crucial change of occupation and mode. Lewis's characters' departure from the law, and hence their original invention as individual Americans, is now complete. Carol Milford's father was a lawyer, and so were two of her prospective lovers; George Babbitt trained as a lawyer, although he ended up as a realtor, and his main ambition for Ted was that he become a lawyer; but at the end of *Babbitt,* Ted Babbitt has married, and thus made his contract of subscription to nation and structure, as a mechanical engineer. This is the basis of the new model of America that Lewis goes on to examine in *Dodsworth.* If the law stands for the utopian legal creation of America, then *Babbitt* 's ending signals the point at which, because the contract is made and the nation completed, the individual American finally and definitely ceases to be in direct contact with the founding determinants of America. The period of interregnum is over, and the individual has contact instead with the new paradigm of the machine. This is Lewis's image of mature, post-frontier America.

It has not been my intention in the discussion to try and establish Lewis as a particularly felicitous or accomplished writer, because he is neither. To an almost unique extent, he disregards any conception of the fiction as a finished or intrinsically valuable object; it is no more or less than a collection of piecemeal devices that happen to have come in useful in making the diagnosis. And reading Lewis, as with reading Twain, whose attempts to make a vernacular analysis of America through vernacular fiction echo Lewis's in many ways, is an exercise that almost continuously begs the question of whether you are dealing with something extremely simple and direct, or something so large and ambitious that it can only ever be achieved partially and intermittently. For the reasons I outlined at the start, it has generally seemed easier to regard Lewis as being extremely simple. There are certainly very many points in the Lewis corpus at which he achieves nothing at all; and putting forward any theories about the extent to which *Main Street* and *Babbitt* are calculated and to which they communicate well beyond the level of their writer's skill by some lucky instinct is very difficult, mainly because of the unconstructive nature of most of Lewis's own comments about his work and the paradox of an intensely fastidious and disciplined writer whose private existence and utterances were celebrated for their complete lack of control.

But as soon as you do Lewis the courtesy of reading him as if he might be doing something more than writing semicompetent stories about characters, it rapidly becomes clear that, in spite of his limitations, his best work is the work of a major American writer. *Main Street* and *Babbitt* are not texts that happen to give a good surface account of a transitional period, and Lewis is not a writer who happens to be a good transitional writer. Even though his fictions ultimately imply a good deal of contempt for the novel as an aesthetic object, Lewis makes a remarkable and highly flexible use of the novel as a diagnostic and communicative device. He is also a writer who makes a uniquely comprehensive and structurally profound analysis of a crucial period of American history, and in doing so makes an extremely important analysis of the construction of the individual American's identity. (pp. 427-33)

> *Joel Fisher, "Sinclair Lewis and the Diagnostic Novel: 'Main Street' and 'Babbitt',"* in Journal of American Studies, *Vol. 20, No. 3, December, 1986, pp. 421-33.*

Caren J. Town   (essay date 1987)

[*In the following essay, Town distinguishes between the types of narrative voices that appear in* Babbitt, *arguing that the novel ultimately reads as an unresolved synthesis of disparate genres.*]

There is a scene, two thirds of the way through Sinclair Lewis's *Babbitt,* in which the main character, George F. Babbitt, picks up a book, hoping to read himself to sleep. The section, from *The Three Black Pennies* by Joseph Hergesheimer, reads like this:

> A twilight like blue dust sifted into the shallow fold of the thickly wooded hills. It was early October, but a crisping frost had already stamped the maple trees with gold, the Spanish oaks were hung with patches of wine red, the sumach was brilliant in the darkening underbrush. A pattern of wild geese, flying low and unconcerned above the hills, wavered against the serene ashen evening. Howat Penny, standing in the comparative clearing of a road, decided that the shifting regular flight would not come close enough for a shot. . . . He had no intention of hunting the geese. With the drooping of day his keenness had evaporated; an habitual indifference strengthened, permeating him. . . .

Babbitt puts the book down, disappointed that it was not the adventure story he thought it would be, and disconcerted, the narrator says, by the "discontent with the good common ways" the passage suggests to him. But shortly after, when Babbitt drives off to an adventure of his own with Tanis Judique, a widowed client of his real estate firm, the narrator's description of his trip to see her begins to sound like the passage from *The Three Black Pennies.* It reads:

> He drove happily off toward the Bellevue district, conscious of the presence of Mrs. Judique as of a brilliant light on the horizon. The maple leaves had fallen and they lined the gutters of the asphalted streets. It was a day of pale gold and faded green, tranquil and lingering. Babbitt was aware of the meditative day, and of the barrenness of Bellevue— blocks of wooden houses, garages, little shops, weedy lots.

At this point it is difficult to tell which book this is—*The Three Black Pennies* or **Babbitt.** Lewis's narrator has assumed the voice of Hergesheimer's narrator, or more precisely, Lewis's narrator has assumed Babbitt's voice, as filtered through his recent reading of *The Three Black Pennies.* In this passage, as in many others in the novel, what Babbitt reads—from novels to advertising copy— influences the narrator's descriptions of him: the narrative becomes increasingly influenced by the surrounding culture, voices, and ideologies. The end result is that the narrator of **Babbitt,** who often comments satirically on the main character, increasingly assumes his character's outlook and consequently his values, with a resulting loss of satirical distance. As these incidents multiply it becomes harder and harder for the reader to read the novel as purely a satire of Babbitt's business boosterism and to consider Babbitt as merely a fool. The narrator is finally not the only one who sympathizes with Babbitt; the reader is also seduced by the desires of narrator and character.

The most common critical response to this anti-satirical strain in a novel which appears to treat its main character satirically is, first, to declare the novel hopelessly divided and probably artistically flawed and, secondly, to use Lewis's biography as proof of the author's divided psyche and as explanation for the novel's multiple perspectives. Sheldon Grebstein so argues when he says Lewis was a writer constantly at war with himself [see excerpt dated 1962], as does Martin Light, who sees **Babbitt** (and also Lewis's life) as the struggle between the Quixotic character (or author) and his community [see excerpt dated 1975]. Perhaps the best articulation of this position is made by Howell Daniels, who says that Lewis's characters tend to be individuals "continuously in a state of self-creation, seeking a humanity which their creator is perhaps incapable of providing [because, one would assume, Lewis could not provide it for himself]."

Yet I think it is possible to account for the many voices in **Babbitt** without resorting to biography, or without declaring that a multiplicity of perspectives necessarily means an artistic failure. Mikhail Bakhtin has pointed out in *The Dialogic Imagination* that this multi-vocal quality is exactly what defines a novel. Any utterance, he says, is a "contradiction-ridden, tension-filled unity of two embattled tendencies in the life of language." The novel form in particular, he says, borrows from all sorts of literally genres and into these genres it "inserts an indeterminacy, a certain semantic openendedness, a living contact with undefined, still-evolving contemporary reality (the open-ended present)."

Babbitt is full of such movements between genres, between satire and sympathy, realism and romance, and yet the novel continues to attract and intrigue readers. It is the narrator's empathy for the main character, who is in many ways a fool, that encourages the reader to keep reading. On the one hand the novel presents the reader with a satirical portrait of the American businessman, while at the same time it sympathizes with the frustrations and longings of that character. Therefore, a simple critical distinction between either a satirical or a sympathetic approach to this world and this character can have little value, for the novel is both a critique and a celebration of the society and character it describes: Babbitt is simultaneously condemned and admired, and the reader is simultaneously appalled and amused.

Babbitt is not obsessed with a tension between these oppositions but instead manages to absorb inconsistency into the main character's world view. This fact seems to be a recognition of what Jacques Lacan says about language, memory, and personality, that "all discourse aligns itself along the several staves of a score." That is, the relationship between the various signifiers and the signified is always simultaneous (not linear, as Saussure thought). The following example shows how Babbitt himself embraces inconsistency, regardless of how exasperated it makes the other characters in the novel feel. Shortly before he visits Tanis Judique, Babbitt, who has until now been a staunch supporter of Calvin Coolidge and the Republican Party, tries to convince his long-suffering wife Myra that he has become a liberal. When she reminds him, in her all-too-literal way, that he once condemned liberals, he says "Rats! Women never can understand the different definitions of a word. Depends on how you mean it." Myra responds, characteristically, "Of course I *know* you. . . . I know you don't mean a word you say . . . " The trap awaiting critics here is that they tend to believe Myra and ignore what Babbitt is trying to tell her about himself, that for Babbitt (both the character and the novel) the interpretation of words and of characters should vary with the situation. Babbitt is a liberal at that moment because he *says* he is; the word is defined by the context of his experiences, of his associations, and finally of his conversations.

But Babbitt's next response to Myra shows that both the immediate audience and the wider social context must be considered when interpreting the novel. Immediately after he defends his position as a liberal, Babbitt begins to worry about what the neighbors will think. Although he rages, "I want you to distinctly understand . . . when I say a thing, I mean it, and I stand by it," he replies, "and— Honest, do you think people would think I was too liberal if I just said the strikers were decent?" Almost immediately the reader is returned to and trapped by Babbitt's middle-class mind and middle-class fears, which nevertheless the reader has been taught to appreciate and to worry about as well.

Babbitt assumes many different guises, and the narrator many different voices, as the narrative progresses. It is in these vacillations that the novel becomes more than just satire. Babbitt is treated both sympathetically *and* satirically. The reader, too, begins worrying about what the neighbors will think about Babbitt's newfound liberalism, while at the same time wondering how he can be so small-minded. In fact, it is never easy to form an opinion about Babbitt. He can be a loyal friend to his college chum Paul

Riesling when Paul shoots his wife in a quarrel, and he can be a dishonest businessman when dishonesty is necessary to make money; he is a loving husband and a philanderer; he is both a romantic hero and a fat, middle-aged Booster. Although Babbitt, as the narrator says, can "never run away from Zenith and family and office, because in his own brain he bore the office and the family and every street and disquiet and illusion of Zenith", he embodies the unrest of his seemingly self-satisfied class, and he also embodies the desires of his readers. Babbitt exists as a lack which must be supplemented, with the narrator ever adding to a center which does not exist. Babbitt's characterization is supplemented by the narrator, by the language of advertising, by the desires of his readers and most importantly by the desires of his narrator which seep into the description. A well-known passage summarizes Babbitt's relationship to the language of advertising and the world around him:

> Just as he was an Elk, a Booster, and a member of the Chamber of Commerce, just as the priests of the Presbyterian Church determined his every religious belief and the senators who controlled the Republican Party decided in little smoky rooms in Washington what he should think about disarmament, tariff, and Germany so did the large national advertisers fix the surface of his life, fix what he believed to be his individuality. These standard advertised wares—toothpastes, socks, tires, cameras, instantaneous hot-water heaters—were his symbols and proofs of excellence; at first the signs, then the substitutes, for joy and passion and wisdom.

First the signs and then the substitutes. Babbitt's possessions in the beginning of the novel show to the world—and to the readers—what kind of man he is, but eventually these outward manifestations begin to take the place of character description. The same thing happens in the language of the text, and the characters, Babbitt especially, begin to speak like magazine ads, or magazine stories. During Babbitt's trip to the wilderness, his conversation with the men he meets in the train's smoking compartment sounds very much like, and is probably based on, the dialogue from a story in *American Magazine,* and the language of all the main characters resembles nothing so much as the ad copy in that same magazine. Babbitt's speech to the real estate board is a masterpiece of cliché and invective, with its "Real He-man, the fellow with Zip and Bang" and "rational prosperity" and its indictments against "blab-mouth, fault-finding, pessimistic, cynical University teachers" and European writers and painters who are "shabby bums living in attics and feeding on booze and spaghetti." The limitations of both his morality and his language are parodied here, and what Babbitt really is, or really desires, is lost in an avalanche of hackneyed language and overworked advertising slogans.

The fairy child comes to represent what is lacking in this novel, and it is significant that her appearance is relegated to the nighttime world of Babbitt's dreams. She symbolizes the vacillation between the real and unreal, between the achieved and the desired, that Babbitt experiences throughout the novel. Although Babbitt is, superficially, a contented man, he dreams nightly of a fairy child who is alternatively a childhood friend, a perfect partner, and a mysterious seductress, and as he tosses and turns on his sleeping porch, the novel tosses and turns between romance and realism. Although in the first half of the novel the sound of a car engine can bring him back to reality and us back to the satire, Babbitt's dreams of the fairy child eventually begin to spill over into his daytime life: he begins to see the child in his son's girlfriend, in his secretary and his manicurist, in his neighbor's wife, and ultimately in Tanis Judique.

In much the same way the language of romance begins to spill into the language of the novel. Babbitt's automobile becomes "poetry and tragedy, love and heroism," and his office his "pirate ship", his writing of ad copy "artistic creation", his lunch hour exit almost like "plans for a general European war." He often sees himself as a pirate, a general, a lost child, and especially, a romantic hero. For example, during a post-party seance, when his guests call up the spirit of Dante, the narrator says of Babbitt: "He had, without explanation, the impression of a slaggy cliff and on it, in silhouette against menacing clouds, a lone and austere figure." No explanation is necessary for the reader who is aware of the potential for language to mimic desire: he and his friends have just been thinking about Dante, and now Babbitt has become him, just for a moment. He has also become the perfect companion to the fairy child. Babbitt has made himself, through his language, into a lover.

Yet these dreams of "perilous moors" and the "brave sea" where the fairy child waits are always followed by deflations and unfavorable images of containment. Babbitt's attempts to find a real-life counterpart to the fairy child are quickly contained. Each of his forays into the world of romance ends in disaster. His secretary is too practical to be interested in him, the manicurist is just out for a good meal, and even Tanis eventually becomes a clinging vine who is, after all, much older than his fairy child ought to be.

The containment continues throughout the novel. For example, Babbitt's home town, Zenith, is described as a city "built for giants", and immediately afterward Babbitt is described as having "nothing of the giant in [his] aspect." His grey suit, while well-cut, well-made, and capable of turning him into a Solid Citizen, is however "completely undistinguished." Babbitt is a virtuous businessman who speaks often of "Vision and Ethics" but cheats his customers "only as it was sanctified by precedent." Although midway through the novel Babbitt is "converted to serenity" after his vacation to the woods, the conversion is called into question shortly after when Babbitt is asked to help increase the membership and bank account of his church. The place where the committee meets to discuss his ideas (the house of the wealthiest church member) is described as having a porch "like an open tomb."

The second half of the novel, which is dominated by a labor strike, is full of images of the containment of individual liberty, of radicals, of unconventional thought. At one point they come together in a passage which both discusses and demonstrates how the language of the characters limits them. At a dinner party, Babbitt's male guests discuss the provinciality of small-town life:

> "You bet!" exulted Orville Jones. "They're the best folks on earth, those small-town folks, but oh, mama! what conversation! Why, say, they can't talk about anything but the weather and the ne-oo Ford, by heckalorum!"

"That's right. They all talk about just the same things," said Eddie Swanson.

"Don't they, though! They just say the same things over and over," said Vergil Gunch.

The conversation continues on in this vein for quite some time. While Lewis obviously intends satire here, the impoverishment of the language is more than just satirical. The reader is made to feel the mental impoverishment that this language suggests. These are characters who not only do not realize that they are saying nothing but who also would have no ability to correct the problem *if* they knew. In the same way that the reader indentified with Babbitt's fears, he now feels the desire to escape from such a prison of language.

Even his trips to the wilderness are spoiled by his inability to escape convention and by the utter and complete tameness of this "wild" world which contains backwoods guides who secretly dream of opening shoe stores. Although Babbitt attempts to escape this conventionality through political action, envisioning himself late in the novel as "the veteran liberal strengthened by the loyalty of the young generation," he eventually succumbs willingly to the pressures of the Good Citizens' League (whose sole purpose is to subdue minorities and radicals) and has to sublimate his desires through his son. Babbitt and the fairy child cannot hold up under the combined pressures of the pathos of his wife's illness and the harassment of the Good Citizens' League, and the novel ends, like all good sentimental fiction, with Babbitt's returning to the fold. Babbitt comments on his entrapment: "He felt that he had been trapped into the very net from which he had with such fury escaped, and supremest jest of all, been made to rejoice in the trapping." If such is the case for Babbitt, the same thing could be said about the reader, and the narrator here is the jester. The reader has begun, by the end of the novel, to fear the consequences of Babbitt's revolt and to welcome his return to the fold.

Although the novel capitulates to containment, the language and the character cannot ever be completely contained. Babbitt is never clearly a dream lover but he is also never completely a wide-awake realtor. He is a "neither/both," as Warwick Wadlington calls it, a character who is neither romantic hero nor bumbling businessman but both at once. He assumes a new identity with every person he meets, with everything he reads, with every material thing he buys; and in each situation, the narrator assumes a new voice to describe him.

Babbitt exists in a central position between his friend Paul, who is all "self," and willing to destroy anything that gets in the way of his vision, and Myra, who is all "world," and is incapable of existing without the other characters. Paul is the stereotypical romantic hero, alienated from his environment, thwarted in love, and doomed to a tragic fate. Myra is the self-sacrificing, self-effacing, realistic heroine who has become part of the furniture of her household. Babbitt is somewhere in between. He is defined by Myra's and Paul's desires, by the world of advertisements and materialism which surrounds all the characters in the novel, and finally by the narrator and by the readers. He is a character embodying both comedy and tragedy, and demanding both a satirical smile and a sympathetic sigh.

Lewis demonstrates in this novel what I call the art of sus-

pended compromise. That is, in **Babbitt** he has created a character who moves between worlds, who invokes both our pity and our rage, who is both hero and clown. The reader is not forced, in fact is not allowed, to choose between responses, or even to reach a compromise between them. This refusal of the novel to admit to being either a romance or a satire in no small measure explains its problematic critical reception, while it also explains its enduring appeal for readers. In a criticism devoted to oppositions and tensions, between the machine and the garden, between the novel and the romance, between the light and the dark, there is no place for a realtor who might dream of being Rhett Butler, but most readers, who both sympathize with and smile at Babbitt, have no difficulty imagining just such a combination of reality and romance. (pp. 41-7)

> *Caren J. Town, "A Dream More Romantic: 'Babbitt' and Narrative Discontinuity," in West Virginia University Philological Papers, Vol. 33, 1987, pp. 41-9.*

FURTHER READING

Bucco, Martin. *Critical Essays on Sinclair Lewis.* Boston: G. K. Hall & Co., 1986, 242 p.

    Collection of notable essays covering Lewis's entire oeuvre, including *Babbitt.*

Coard, Robert L. "Mark Twain's *The Gilded Age* and Sinclair Lewis's *Babbitt.*" *The Midwest Quarterly* XIII, No. 3 (April 1972): 319-33.

    Compares Mark Twain's *The Gilded Age* and *Babbitt* in order to "illuminate the satirical techniques of two celebrated practitioners and . . . say something about the continuity of American satirical tradition."

Hines, Thomas S., Jr. "Echoes from 'Zenith': Reactions of American Businessmen to Babbitt." *Business History Review* XLI, No. 2 (Summer 1967): 123-40.

    Assesses the diversity of critical reactions toward *Babbitt* voiced by the American business community in the 1920s.

Lundquist, James. "Moralities for a New Time" and "The Question of Art." In his *Sinclair Lewis,* pp. 33-86. New York: Frederick Ungar, 1973.

    Concise critical discussions in each chapter focus on the conflict between Babbitt's private, rebellious self and public, conforming self.

Mencken, H. L. "Hints for Novelists." In *The Bathtub Hoax and Other Blasts & Bravos from the "Chicago Tribune,"* edited by Robert McHugh, pp. 67-71. New York: Alfred A. Knopf, 1958.

    Argues that the novel formula perfected in *Babbitt*—"a character sketch of a single individual, and yet a vivid and penetrating portrait of a whole civilization"—should be applied to a series of similar American social types.

Norris, Hoke. "Babbitt Revisited." *The Yale Review* LXVIII, No. 1 (Autumn 1978): 53-70.
> Historical synopsis of the material conditions and consumer commodities described in *Babbitt*.

O'Conner, Richard. "Meet Mr. Babbitt." In his *Sinclair Lewis,* pp. 71-81. New York: McGraw-Hill, 1971.
> Thematic and biographical overview of *Babbitt*.

Parrington, Vernon Louis. *Sinclair Lewis: Our Own Diogenes.* Seattle: University of Washington Book Store, 1930.
> Argues that in his portrayal of Babbitt, "Mr. Lewis completely fails to understand the fine ethical values that underlie and animate the common American life at which he aims."

Quivey, James R. "Release Motif and Its Impact in Babbitt." *Sinclair Lewis Newsletter* I, No. 1 (Spring 1969): 4-5.
> Asserts "the near total futility of each attempt [by *Babbitt*'s characters] to gain release from both the external influences of Zenith and from the inner tensions of consciousness."

Rothwell, Kenneth S. "From Society to Babbittry: Lewis' Debt to Edith Wharton." *Journal of the Central Mississippi Valley Association Studies Association* I, No. 1 (Spring 1960): 32-7.
> Argues that Edith Wharton's *The Age of Innocence* "was actually the master blue print for *Babbitt*."

Schorer, Mark, ed. *Sinclair Lewis: A Collection of Critical Essays.* Englewood Cliffs, N.J.: Prentice-Hall, 1962, 174 p.
> Compendium of critical essays edited by Lewis's biographer; includes significant early reactions to *Babbitt*.

Schriber, Mary Sue. "You've Come a Long Way, Babbitt! From Zenith to Ilium." *Twentieth Century Literature* 17, No. 2 (April 1971): 101-06.
> Compares *Babbitt* with Kurt Vonnegut's novel *Piano Player,* focusing on the depiction of the fictional cities of Zenith and Ilium.

Wilson, Christopher P. "Sinclair Lewis and the Passing of Capitalism." *American Studies* XXIV, No. 2 (Fall 1983): 95-108.
> Argues that in his formative period that ended with the publication of *Babbitt,* "Lewis played a seminal role in puncturing and reformulating the literary understanding of American capitalism."

Jack London

1876-1916

(Born John Griffith London) American novelist, short story writer, essayist, journalist, autobiographer, and dramatist.

The following entry presents criticism of London's novel *The Call of the Wild* (1903). For a discussion of London's complete career, see *TCLC*, Volumes 9 and 15.

The Call of the Wild is considered London's greatest literary achievement and a classic of American literature. The story of Buck, a dog who becomes the leader of a wolf pack during a physically and psychologically challenging journey in the Yukon wilderness, *The Call of the Wild* exemplifies the adept use of animal protagonists for which many of London's works have been praised. Popular as an adventure story, the novel also endures as an object of critical study due to its philosophical and literary depth.

A popular and prolific short story writer during the late 1890s, London achieved international fame with *The Call of the Wild,* one of a series of works based on his observations while prospecting for gold in the Klondike in 1897 and 1898. Intending to produce a work that would redeem the species of sled dog that his short story "Bâtard" had vilified, London remarked that *The Call of the Wild* "got away from me, and instead of 4000 words, it ran 32000 before I could call a halt." London completed this novel in one month, and, in January 1903, he sold a shortened version of it to the *Saturday Evening Post.* In accepting an offer of $2,000 for the book from Macmillan the next month, London unfortunately agreed to waive his right to royalties. Macmillan's promotion of the novel was extensive, and *The Call of the Wild* became an instant success.

Commentators have explicated *The Call of the Wild* in three principal ways: as an allegory of human nature, as well-written escapist literature, and as London's symbolic autobiography. Critics advancing an allegorical interpretation of the novel maintain that London used the popular genre of the animal story to convey his philosophical principles. Strongly influenced by the writings of Charles Darwin and Friedrich Nietzsche, London viewed life as a struggle for survival in which scientific laws govern all events and religious faith and moral standards are meaningless. London referred to himself as a "materialist monist," one who, disavowing the possibility of spiritual reward, acts wholly on instinct, achieving pleasure from the struggle for life and power. Thus Buck, the canine protagonist in *The Call of the Wild,* represents London's conception of the physically and socially ideal being; removed from his lazy and aimless position as a household pet, Buck becomes a strong, agile, and skillful sled dog, earning admiration and respect from the animals and people that he encounters. In responding to his environment and instincts, Buck learns "the law of club and fang," gaining an understanding of his physical disadvantage in fighting a man who wields a club as a weapon and strengthening his own will to survive. Many critics suggest that this lesson, along with the emphasis on Buck's intelligence and

physical stature as genetically determined, exhibit London's belief that ideal human beings are shrewd, self-aware, individualistic, and able to capitalize on inherited strengths, a characterization reflecting Nietzsche's conception of the amoral *Übermensch* ("superman"). While Buck is generally seen, in one critic's words, as a "product of biological, environmental, and hereditary forces," a hero in the tradition of naturalistic fiction, some critics find the interpretation of *The Call of the Wild* as an allegory of Darwinian or Nietzschean principles to be contradictory and incomplete. During Buck's transformation from innocuous pet into "dominant primordial beast," for example, London attributes to Buck strange, atavistic memories of his wolf-ancestors. These memories, as Earle Labor notes, suggest a "deeper music than that of the ordinary phenomenal world," a spiritualism that contradicts the naturalistic philosophy that most critics find in the novel.

While the allegorical interpretation of *The Call of the Wild* is the most widely accepted, critics also note the value of the novel as escapist fiction that offers adventure, vivid descriptions of the northern wilderness, and a simple and elegant style that led Maxwell Geismar to describe the work as a "prose-poem, a novella of a single mood, admirably sustained." London has also received praise for his skillful narration of the novel from the point of view of an animal. James Lundquist, in commenting on the credibility with which London portrayed the thoughts of animals, notes: "It is London's 'dog psychology' that contributes the most to the unique effect of the novel and what also makes a lot of critical terminology essentially useless in dealing with it."

The third reading commonly subscribed to by critics emphasizes autobiographical elements in *The Call of the Wild*. Determined to overcome the impoverished conditions into which he was born, London became, at a very young age, the type of "rugged individualist" often featured in his short stories and novels. Working at a series of occupations, including that of sailor on a sealing ship and trail-breaker on a gold mining expedition in the Klondike, London developed physical strength and a sense of adventure, qualities celebrated in his works. Andrew Flink points out that London identified himself with Buck in several passages of the novel. For example, a one-month internment for vagrancy that London served in a Pennsylvanian penitentiary, Flink contends, is reflected in Buck's experience as a captive of dog traders. Both London and Buck emerged from captivity wiser, stronger, and more independent.

Some critics have faulted *The Call of the Wild* as inconsistent with London's philosophy of pragmatic individualism, especially in the sentimental description of the relationship between Buck and his master Mr. Thornton and the romantic conclusion in which Buck's apotheosis is complete, and he is mythologized by the Yeehat Indians as a fierce and cunning "Ghost Dog." Generally, however, commentators agree with Fred Lewis Pattee that *"The Call of the Wild*, which is the crowning work of [London's] career, perfectly illustrates his methods when at his best. His zest of life is in it and the undiminished enthusiasm of youth."

(See also *Short Story Criticism*, Vol. 4; *Concise Dictionary of American Literary Biography*, 1865-1917; *Contemporary Authors*, Vols. 110 and 119; *Dictionary of Literary Biography*, Vols. 8, 12, and 78; and *Something about the Author*, Vol. 18.)

J. Stewart Doubleday   (essay date 1903)

[*In the following excerpt, Doubleday praises* The Call of the Wild *for its graphic realism.*]

The power of Jack London lies not alone in his clear-sighted depiction of life, but in his suggestion of the eternal principles that underlie it. The writer who can suggest these principles forcibly and well, though he may not be actually great, has something in him closely allied to greatness. Mr. London is one of the most original and impressive authors this country has known. His voice is large and vibrant, his manner straightforward and free. . . . (p. 408)

The Call of the Wild is the story of a dog, reared in comfort in Southern California, but afterwards broken to the sled on the desolate Alaskan trail, where his experiences are related with a candor and ring of genuineness, exciting yet ofttimes heartrending in the extreme. The philosophy of the survival of the fittest runs through every page of Mr. London's book; the call of the wild evidently signifies the appeal (and in Buck's case, the triumph) of barbarian life over civilized life; in fact, this dog becomes, after a series of bloodcurdling incidents ending at the murder of a beloved master, the eventual leader of a pack of timber wolves, in whom, following a fang fight for individual supremacy, he recognizes the "wild brother," and joins the savage horde. The book, very brief, is filled from cover to cover with thrilling scenes; the Northern Territory is brought home to us with convincing vividness; every sentence is pregnant with original life; probably no such sympathetic, yet wholly unsentimental, story of a dog has ever found print before; the achievement may, without exaggeration, be termed "wonderful."

Yet it is cruel reading—often relentless reading; we feel at times the blood lashing in our faces at what seems the continual maltreatment of a dumb animal; we can scarce endure the naked brutality of the thing; our sense of the creature's perplexity in suffering is almost absolutely unrelieved; we sicken of the analysis of the separate tortures of this dog's Arctic Inferno. Not seldom we incline to remonstrate, "Hang it, Jack London, what the deuce do you mean by 'drawing' on us so?" But we forgive the writer at last because he is true! He is not sentimental, tricky; he is at harmony with himself and nature. He gives an irresistible groan sometimes—like Gorky; but this is only because he does, after all, feel for humanity—yes, down to the bottom of his big California heart.

It must be patent to all, we think, that the man who can, through the simple story of a dog set us thought-wandering over illimitable ways, is a man of language to be respectfully classed and reckoned with. There is nothing local or narrow about Jack London. Sectionalism is smaller than he. His voice is the voice of a man in the presence of the multitude, and he utters the word that is as bread to him. He has not, to say truly, much humor; the theme of necessary toil and suffering overburdens and drowns the casual note of laughter—he is buoyant rather than bright. Sometimes we are wearied by his too ecstatic hymning of the primitive, the rude, the elemental in spirit and nature—we begin to desire a little more mildness and beauty, a possible mercy and femininity, a hope; but these we must look for in other writers than the stalwart youthful leader of the promising Far West. In his own field he is master; and more than this we ought not to exact of any man. (pp. 408-09)

> *J. Stewart Doubleday, in a review of "The Call of the Wild" in* The Reader, *Vol. II, No. 4, September, 1903, pp. 408-09.*

The Atlantic Monthly   (essay date 1903)

[*In the following excerpt, the reviewer, denying that* The Call of the Wild *is an allegory, offers a favorable estimate of the novel as an illumination of the nature of animals.*]

The Call of the Wild is a story altogether untouched by bookishness. A bookish writer might, beginning with the title, have called it An Instance of Atavism, or A Reversion to Type. A bookish reader might conceivably read it as a sort of allegory with a broad human application; but its face value as a singleminded study of animal nature really seems to be sufficiently considerable. The author, too, must be allowed to stand upon his own feet, though one understands why he should have been called the American Kipling. His work has dealt hitherto with primitive human nature; this is a study of primitive dog nature. No modern writer of fiction, unless it be Kipling, has preserved so clearly the distinction between animal virtue and human virtue. The farther Buck reverts from the artificial status of a man-bounded domestic creature to the natural condition of the "dominant primordial beast," the more strongly (if unwillingly) we admire him. There is something magnificent in the spectacle of his gradual detachment from the tame, beaten-in virtues of uncounted forefathers, his increasing ability to hold his own among unwonted conditions, and his final triumph over the most dreaded powers of the wilderness:

> He was a Killer, a thing that preyed, living on the things that lived, unaided, alone, by virtue of his own strength and prowess, surviving triumphantly in a hostile environment where only the strong survived. Because of all this he became possessed of a great pride in himself, which communicated itself like a contagion to his physical being. . . . To sights and sounds and events which required action, he responded with lightning-like rapidity. He saw the movement, or heard the sound, and responded in less time than another dog required to compass the mere seeing or hearing. He perceived and determined and responded in the same instant. His muscles were surcharged with vitality, and snapped into play sharply, like steel springs. Life streamed through him in splendid flood, glad and rampant, until it seemed that it would burst him asunder in sheer ecstasy, and pour forth generously over the world.

The making and the achievement of such a hero constitute, not a pretty story at all, but a very powerful one. (pp. 695-96)

A review of "The Call of the Wild," in The Atlantic Monthly, *Vol. XCII, No. DLIII, November, 1903, pp. 695-96.*

Maxwell Geismar   (essay date 1953)

[*Geismar is one of America's most prominent historical and social critics. Although he has often acknowledged that literature is more than historical documentation, Geismar's own critical method suggests that social patterns and history, more than any other phenomena, affect the shape and content of all art. Geismar's major enterprise—a multi-volume history of the American novel from 1860 to 1940—clearly demonstrates his fascination with the impact of external forces on literature. His praise of such writers as Ernest Hemingway, John Dos Passos, and John Steinbeck, and his criticism of others, such as Henry James and the post-World War II writers, depends almost exclusively on how these artists were affected by and responded to the conditions in their particular societies. Many of Geismar's contemporaries, and many scholars today, have criticized his inability to see art as anything beyond social documentation. In the following excerpt, he assesses the narrative strengths and* weaknesses of The Call of the Wild, *which he describes as a celebration of animal instincts.*]

We are told by London's daughter that **The Call of the Wild,** in 1903, was begun and finished in one month as a companion piece to another dog story, and it was in fact a sort of prose-poem, a novella of a single mood, admirably sustained. The sketch of the great Chilkoot Divide, which stood between the salt water and the fresh, "and guards forbiddingly the sad and lonely North," set the tone; just as the early episode in which Buck was 'broken' into the "reign of primitive law," the first step in his education as a pack dog, starts his reversion to the wild. One notices how delicately London kept his story within the limits of credible animal behavior. The human beings are good or bad, efficient or useless, only to the degree that they affect the well-being of the dogs—and here indeed the brutes often rose to a stoic dignity not granted to the humans. There was the death of Curly as the huskies rush her and she is lost beneath the bristling mass of bodies ("So that was the way. . . . Once down, that was the end of you.") or the description of Sol-leks, a one-eyed battler, very Hemingwayish, who "asked nothing, gave nothing, expected nothing." There was Dave, the dog who fell sick but refused to relinquish his place in the team until he was driven away and shot; and the brief, sparkling scene when Buck first learns how to sleep, completely buried in a warm, snug ball under the Alaska snow.

An excellent passage described Buck's first act of theft, "the decay . . . of his moral nature . . . in the ruthless struggle for existence,"—a favorite theme, as we know, in the naturalism of the 1900's, and more convincing at times in a canine hero than in a dentist or financier. From Stephen Crane and Frank Norris, too, the novels of the time were filled with the howls, oaths, imprecations of heroes who harkened back to primitive epics—this was a noisy literature—just as here the song of the huskies, "with the aurora borealis flaming coldly overhead, or the stars leaping in the frost dance, and the land numb and frozen under its pall of snow," was "one of the first songs of the younger world in a day when songs were sad." Thus Buck learned to kill and to defend himself:

> It was no task for him to learn to fight with cut and slash and the quick wolf snap. In this manner had fought forgotten ancestors. They quickened the old life within him, and the old tricks which they stamped into the heredity of the breed were his tricks. They came to him without effort of discovery, as though they had been his always. And when, on the still cold nights, he pointed his nose at a star and howled long and wolf-like, it was his ancestors, dead and dust, pointing nose at a star and howling down through the centuries and through him.

And so London carried us back—with an ease and sureness of perception that appeared also to be "without effort of discovery"—through the ages of fire and roof to the raw beginnings of animal creation. . . . The theory of racial instinct, of memory as inherited habit, that was at the start, through long aeons, a very conscious and alert process of behavior indeed—this theory, as developed by such figures as Samuel Butler, Bergson or Jung, was very clear here, of course. Similarly, the scene in which Buck finally deposed Spitz as the leader of the team, surrounded by the ring of huskies waiting to kill and eat the vanquished king, was a perfect instance of the 'son-horde' theory which

Frazer traced in *The Golden Bough,* and of that primitive ritual to which Freud himself attributed both a sense of original sin and the fundamental ceremony of religious exorcism. But what is fascinating in *The Call of the Wild* is the brilliance of London's own intuitions (quite apart from any system of psychology) in this study of animal instincts which are the first, as they are the final biological response to the blind savagery of existence.

If London's portraits of twentieth century supermen almost always sound fabricated and false, this legend of the super-brute—the dominant primordial beast—was completely natural, delicate and even tragic in the purlieu of a dog world and in its flickering reflections of the buried night-life of the race. And there was another theme that became a favorite in the 1920's. The shifting, tortuous relationship of the hunter and the hunted had its roots also in this instinctive Darwinian cosmos. Indeed, when the memories of his heredity that gave, in Buck's eyes, a seeming familiarity to things he had never seen before are fully quickened and alive again, he experienced in the joy of the kill itself "an ecstasy that marks the summit of life, and beyond which life cannot rise." The moment of impending death was the moment of life at its most intense pitch, when London's hero, too, was sounding the deeps of his nature, and those strains, deeper than he, which went back to the womb of life. "He was older than the days he had seen and the breaths he had drawn. He linked the past with the present and eternity throbbed through him in a mighty rhythm to which he swayed as the tides and seasons swayed." And the underlying structure of dream and myth in *The Call of the Wild* was summarized, of course, in the final episode where all the premonitions of 'the trap' in this primordial world—and of those "wayfarers to death" in an earlier episode of the story—were more than justified.

Could anything be better than the long trip into the wilds in search of a hidden valley of treasure, from which no man had ever returned: this "great journey into the East," past the tall peaks which marked the backbone of a continent, into a land of gold and death? "They went across divides in summer blizzards, shivered under the midnight sun on naked mountains, between the timber line and the eternal snows, dropped into summer valleys amid swarming gnats and flies, and in the shadows of glaciers picked strawberries and flowers as ripe and fair as any the Southland could boast." In the fall of the year, the little expedition had penetrated the weird lake country where wild fowl had been; and through another winter they wander "on the obliterated trails of men who had gone before," and then reach the deserted lodge with its long-barreled flint-lock that had been worth its weight in beaver skins in the younger days of the Territory. And the resemblance of London's northern scene to some opium-haunted paradise of De Quincey or an Arctic Xanadu is even more marked here. "Like giants they toiled, days flashing on the heels of days like dreams as they heaped the treasure up." The surprise attack of Swiftian savages, the Yeehats: the final scene in which the bodies of men and dogs alike are found feathered by arrows like porcupines, while the trail of Buck's master leads to the muddy pool, "discolored from the sluice boxes," from which no trace led away: this climax was inevitable in the logic of the fable.

So, too, with Buck's irrevocable return to the wild; his

grim pursuit of the dancing savages, for now he had killed man, "the noblest game of all"; and his later reputation as a phantom dog who ran at the head of a wolf pack. "Night came on, and a full moon rose high over the trees into the sky, lighting the land till it lay bathed in ghostly day." Probably the episodes that take place in 'civilization' are weakest in *The Call of the Wild,* and there was a sentimental relationship between Buck and John Thornton; but even there London showed a warmth and delicacy of affection that was not often displayed in the world of men's affairs. The success of this admirable little tone-poem, which sang a song of the younger world, throws a sharper light on the works of London which had preceded it and on the two books [*The Sea-Wolf* and *The Kempton-Wace Letters*] which brought to a close the first glittering burst of his talent. (pp. 149-153)

Maxwell Geismar, "Jack London: The Short Cut," in his Rebels and Ancestors: The American Novel, 1890-1915, *Houghton Mifflin, 1953, pp. 139-218.*

Charles Child Walcutt   (essay date 1956)

[*Walcutt is an American critic who has written extensively on American literature. In the following excerpt, he discusses the conflict between animal instinct and ethics in* The Call of the Wild.]

[The Call of the Wild] is episodic. Buck, a splendid California ranch dog, is stolen and sold into Alaska, to become a sled-dog in the gold rush. Going thus "into the primitive" he quickly learns "the law of club and fang." "Jerked from the heart of civilization and flung into the heart of things primordial," his first experience on the Alaskan coast brings home the nature of the eternal struggle. A friendly dog is knocked down in a fight, and instantly "she was buried screaming with agony beneath the bristling mass" of huskies who had been watching the unequal fight. "So that was the way," Buck learned. "No fairplay. Once down, that was the end of you."

Buck's fitness is measured by his primordialism, by the way "he was harking back through his own life to the lives of his forbears." He learns fast and is soon clever enough to steal some bacon to supplement his meager rations of dried fish. The author's comment upon this action is illuminating:

> This first theft marked Buck as fit to survive in the hostile Northland environment. It marked his adaptability, his capacity to adjust himself to changing conditions, the lack of which would have meant swift and terrible death. It marked, further, the decay or going to pieces of his moral nature, a vain thing and a handicap in the ruthless struggle for existence. It was all well enough in the Southland, under the law of love and fellowship, to respect private property and personal feelings; but in the Northland, under the law of club and fang, whoso took such things into account was a fool, and in so far as he observed them he would fail to prosper. . . .

[Here] the "moral nature" can be thrust aside without the reader's losing respect for Buck, because Buck is a dog. . . . Buck's forgotten ancestors "quickened the old life within him, and the old tricks which they had stamped into the heredity of the breed were his tricks. They came to him without effort or discovery, as though they had been his always"; and the reader seeks no higher ethical virtues in Buck.

By Chapter III, Buck is "The Dominant Primordial Beast"; and the story proceeds as the conflict for mastery between Buck and Spitz, the treacherous and hated lead-dog of the team. "It was inevitable that the clash for mastery should come. Buck wanted it. He wanted it because it was his nature, because he had been gripped tight by that nameless, incomprehensible pride of the trail and trace—that pride which holds dogs in the toil to the last gasp, which lures them to die joyfully in the harness, and breaks their hearts if they are cut out of the harness." Spitz is experienced. Buck is intelligent and big; he has imagination, and his prowess increases. Always it is the life-impulse in him expressing itself. London pauses in a muscle-flexing digression to explain the nature of this impulse:

> There is an ecstasy that marks the summit of life, and beyond which life cannot rise. And such is the paradox of living, this ecstasy comes when one is most alive, and it comes as a complete forgetfulness that one is alive. This ecstasy, this forgetfulness of living, comes to the artist, caught up and out of himself in a sheet of flame; it comes to the soldier, war-mad on a stricken field and refusing quarter; and it came to Buck, leading the pack, sounding the old wolf-cry, straining after the food that was alive and that fled swiftly before him through the moonlight. He was sounding the deeps of his nature, and of the parts of his nature that were deeper than he, going back to the womb of Time. He was mastered by the sheer surging joy of life, the tidal wave of being, the perfect joy of each separate muscle, joint, and sinew in that it was everything that was not death, that it was aglow and rampant, expressing itself in movement, flying exultantly under the stars and over the face of dead matter that did not move.

This is the materialistic philosophy transformed by the celebration of the single vital and inescapable fact which even materialism recognizes as valuable—life. Seen from within, the struggle represents the surge of life, and the struggle is dominated by will. It is will in the sense of impulse, life-urge, ecstasy of power, rather than ethical choice. It is presented as an animal trait, inherited and consequently not really "free." If Buck were a man there would have to be some kind of ethical responsibility. With Buck there need be only this animal expression of the life-instinct that is derived from his "racial memory" of his ancestors.

Although the story is seen substantially from Buck's point of view, there is always inevitably present (and carefully controlled by London) the reader's moral judgment of men and their actions. Thus one admires the dogs' noble courage, hates the tenderfeet, and loves the kind John Thornton who saves Buck. Much of the aesthetic effect of the novel attaches to these feelings. Chapter VI is devoted to the love of dog and man, and here the reader's feelings are entirely human and civilized as he responds to the presentation of Buck's devotion to Thornton while in all other respects he is becoming increasingly wild. He twice saves Thornton's life and wins a $1600 wager for him by pulling a tremendous load.

Finally, on a trip into the wilderness, Buck's atavism surges up within him. He has racial dreams of remote times, when fear dominated his primitive master:

> When he watched the hairy man sleeping by the fire, head between his knees and hands clasped above, Buck saw that he slept restlessly, with many starts and awakenings, at which times he would peer fearfully into the darkness and fling more wood upon the fire. . . . Through the forest they crept noiselessly, Buck at the hairy man's heels; and they were alert and vigilant, the pair of them, ears twitching and moving nostrils quivering, for the man heard and smelled as keenly as Buck . . . and Buck had memories of nights of vigil spent beneath trees wherein the hairy man roosted, holding on tightly as he slept.

The same primordialism that makes him "remember" the hairy man draws him toward the wolves whom he hears howling at night. He makes friends with the pack and, when John Thornton is killed, he joins the pack and lives thereafter as a magnificent wolf—more cunning and fierce than all the others and the relentless foe of the Indians who had killed his master. In this story the conflict of animal impulse and ethical nature is successfully evaded because the hero is a dog of whom ethical action is not expected—though the most moving passages in the book are those that deal with Buck's love for Thornton and which, consequently, appeal strongly to the reader's sense of moral rightness and goodness.

The Call of the Wild is a masterpiece of thrilling and colorful narrative, but it does not—indeed it cannot—tell anything about the nature of "atavism" or the operation of determinism.

The discrepancy between London's philosophical ideas and the "naturalistic" use he is able to make of them in his novels appears in his explanation of *White Fang,* companion volume to *The Call of the Wild.* Published in 1906, *White Fang* deals with a wolf who is domesticated through circumstances and, particularly, the love of a man. London wrote of it:

> Life is full of disgusting realism. I know men and women as they are—millions of them yet in the slime state. But I am an evolutionist, therefore a broad optimist, hence my love for the human (in the slime though he be) comes from my knowing him as he is and seeing the divine possibilities ahead of him. That's the whole motive of my *White Fang.* Every atom of organic life is plastic. The finest specimens now in existence were once all pulpy infants capable of being molded this way or that. Let the pressure be one way and we have atavism—the reversion to the wild; the other the domestication, civilization.

As a theory this is all very well, but in the novels there is no explanation of the atavism and the domestication; their only justification is that they *happen.* No "pressures" are depicted which tell why Buck goes wild and White Fang becomes tame. The facts speak for themselves; as facts they are convincing; but the science or philosophy behind them receives no serious attention. (pp. 104-07)

Charles Child Walcutt, "Jack London: Blond Beasts and Supermen," in his American Literary Naturalism, A Divided Stream, *University of Minnesota Press, 1956, pp. 87-113.*

Abraham Rothberg (essay date 1963)

[*Rothberg is an American novelist and critic. In the following excerpt, he offers a comparison of the allegorical qualities of* The Call of the Wild *and* White Fang.]

With his second novel, London became an important writer; *The Call of the Wild* is the most perfectly realized novel he ever wrote. Out of his fearful plunge into the London abyss and his consequent retreat in fiction to the primitive world of dogs and Alaska came an allegory of human life. A study of atavism, or reversion to type, it was also an allegory of man's conditions in the society of London's time as well as a revelation of the deepest emotions London felt about himself and that society.

The novel has three levels, the first and narrative one the story of a dog, Buck, who reverts to type, learns to survive in a wolf-like life, and eventually becomes a wolf. The second, or biographical level, reveals what London himself lived and felt in climbing out of the abyss of poverty and deprivation to prestige as a writer and wealth. Buck was symbolically Jack London struggling for success and domination, learning the law of club and fang, "put into harness," and finally becoming the shaggy wolf rampant. The third level is political and philosophical, exemplifying the doctrines of social Darwinism in fictional form. The fittest survive by adaptation to the man with the club (the stronger individual) and the strength of the herd (the power of the masses). By this adaptation man or dog may be temporarily defeated but ultimately will triumph. Man or dog becomes hardened to nature physically and also hardened spiritually to greed, thievery, cunning, violence, and individualism in society and nature. Finally, when man or dog has gained sufficient strength and craft, he may prey on those weaker than himself, knowing that, as London saw it, "Mercy did not exist in the primordial life. It was misunderstood for fear, and such misunderstanding made for death. Kill or be killed, eat or be eaten, was the law."

London was not only treating animals like human beings, but treating human beings like animals, recognizing no essential difference between man and animal. In *The Call of the Wild* he equated men with dogs and wolves, and equated the harshness of the trail with the harshness of society, implying that force, savagery and cunning were equally the ways to success in both areas. London's vocabulary also carried and reinforced his meaning. Buck is "put into harness," the human phrase for working. He becomes "lead-dog," or in man's parlance, "top-dog." He is forced to meet and bow to "the man with the club," an almost cliché expression for power and authority. Buck leads the "wolf pack," to which he finally reverts, a predatory term still in use in our own day. The very fact that London deals with a "dog's life"—Humankind's frequent comment on its own condition is that "It's a dog's life."—indicates how thoroughgoing was his view.

Beneath man's veneer of civilization, London saw a prehistoric beast who fought and conquered through might and deceit, whose nature was fierce and cruel in the extreme. Scratch the veneer, and the prehistoric beast shone through, atavism took place, and man reverted to the "wolf." Buck, the civilized dog, devolves to where he not only kills but enjoys killing. London's love of violence and bloodshed is here, and elsewhere, rendered as a "wine-of-life," "strength-through-joy," emotion, and to Buck he gives it as a lust "to kill with his own teeth and wash his muzzle to the eyes in warm blood."

The only thing that keeps Buck from the wild is his love of man, just as love had held London, and just as love as well as fear holds most of mankind from the war of all against all, in spite of Hobbes' dictum that "Man is as a wolf to man." In life, however, love eventually dies or is killed, as John Thornton is killed by the Yeehats, and then Buck (and therefore man) reverts to the savagery of the wolf-pack, following the primordial call of the wild.

With *White Fang,* his fifth novel, London returned to the dog-eat-dog life. Though once more in fictional retreat from human life, London was still writing about human problems. As *The Call of the Wild* had been a study in regress, so London intended to make *White Fang* a study in progress, a case history of evolution not devolution, of civilization rather than of atavism. This book, too, is three-tiered. On the surface or narrative level it is the story of the wolf-dog, White Fang, who comes up from savagery to civilization. On a biographical level, the novel reiterates Jack London's childhood struggles and fight for life in a hostile environment. Like London's childhood, White Fang's puppyhood is miserable. Different from the other dogs in camp because he is three-quarters wolf, he becomes an outcast. The other dogs sense that he is "different" and "instinctively felt for him the enmity the domestic dog feels for the wolf." They all join in persecuting him and because "the tooth of every dog was against him, the hand of every man," White Fang becomes a fighting dog. London's illegitimacy, his quasi-paranoia, and his own hostility and aggression against people and society are, in this fiction, subjected to his myth-making and converted from unpleasant compulsions to necessary virtues. Even White Fang's love for his mother, Kiche, and her subsequent rejection of him are described in emotional terms similar to those London used to describe his relationship to Flora London.

The final philosophical level was meant to convey mankind's ascent from bestiality to civilization. Love regenerates the wolf by making him a domesticated dog, and the logical inference is that if a dog can listen to the "call of the tame" because of love, then why not man? White Fang is transformed by his love for Weedon Scott; in short, London has the wolf-dog change his whole mode of life by an act of will and for *nonmaterial* motives. Such a revolutionary change, according to London, gives the lie to the "very law of life," which London maintains is self-assertion not self-sacrifice, material motives—money, meat, power, not idealist ones like love. In addition, the materialist-determinist London introduces idealism and will as the means not only of regenerating a wolf-dog, but by extension, of remodeling society.

Unfortunately for London's express intention, the novel's most forceful sections are devoted to the war of all against all, which London portrays with fidelity and power. Individual assertion and adaptation remain the best methods of survival. Not only is the law of the wilderness depicted as eat or be eaten, but London explicitly makes it the law of society as well: "Had the cub [White Fang] thought in man-fashion, he might have epitomized life as a voracious appetite, and the world as a place wherein ranged a multitude of appetites, pursuing and being pursued, hunting and being hunted, eating and being eaten, all in blindness and confusion, with violence and disorder, a chaos of gluttony and slaughter, ruled over by chance, merciless, planless, endless." Once White Fang has gone to live with the Indians and so begun his evolution, he soon discovers that the law of civilization—even primitive Indian civilization—is as cruel and remorseless as that of the wild. In fact, White Fang's contact with Indian's and white man's society makes him *devolve,* not evolve, grow more savage than less, and become a professional killer. And London's depiction of the laws of civilization and savagery are identical, except for the "Love Master," Weedon Scott—and the term *master* is here, as vocabulary is elsewhere in London, revealing.

Although London proposed to show the plasticity of life and the reverse of primordialism, he was still revealing the same violence, romanticism, killing, and "wine-of-life" intensity in savagery. The exaltation of fighting and killing is never really eliminated in the "evolutionary" process. As Buck ended his call to the wild by achieving the "heights" of killing a man, so White Fang ends his call to the tame in the same way, by killing the convict Jim Hall. Although both acts of violence are performed out of loyalty and affection for "love masters," and against murderers and a would-be murderer, they remain brutal killings. White Fang's reward is his acceptance by Weedon Scott's family, and the novel ends in the unbelievable bathos of White Fang becoming the "Blessed Wolf."

Buck had listened to the call of the wild and White Fang presumably to the call of the tame, but White Fang's acceptance of civilization is only partial, at best contingent and unconvincing, while Buck's rejection is total and quite convincing. On both biographical and allegorical levels, London's retreat from the cities and from socialism was in full force, while in fiction he clung with a desperation born of despair to the vain hope that the wolves might come in to sit at the fires and be dogs, a belief he had already actually abandoned both in his behavior and in his heart. (pp. 8-12)

> *Abraham Rothberg, in an introduction to* The Call of the Wild and White Fang *by Jack London, Bantam Books, 1963, pp. 1-17.*

Raymond Benoit　(essay date 1968)

[*In the following excerpt, Benoit discusses* The Call of the Wild *as an example of the pastoral tradition in American literature.*]

Enough is known of London's Darwinism, Nietzscheism and Socialism. Not so current, perhaps, is the extent to which his works reflect the pastoral protest that Mr. John Sisk finds so pervasive in our literature. In his article, "American Pastoral," Mr. Sisk finds the gist of the pastoralism to be "a critical view of simplicity . . . in context with the non-simple (therefore the less innocent, less wise, less integrated) which it measures. . . . There is always the awareness of an older, debilitated, hopelessly artificial and complex civilization, at once watching with awe and being dramatically criticized and found wanting." London used just this pastoral mode in *The Call of the Wild:* the myth of Buck, the great dog, is an embodiment of the American dream of escaping from the entangling com-

plexity of modern living back to a state as unencumbered as the sled that Buck pulls. Buck, from this angle, is as much an American hero as Rip Van Winkle—he shakes superfluities from himself. From the moment he learns to dig a hole in the snow to sleep in, all his southern heritage, the nurture of Santa Clara Valley, begins to fall away:

> The snow walls pressed him on every side, and a great surge of fear swept through him—the fear of the wild thing for the trap. It was a token that he was harking back through his own life to the lives of his forbears; for he was a civilized dog, an unduly civilized dog and of his own experience knew no trap and so could not of himself fear it.

The significant word is "unduly." London's point in this novel and in all his novels is that agrarian America in becoming industrialized had traded the undulations of celestial music, as Thoreau stated, for factory bells, and had as a consequence lost contact with that saving nature which ultimately mattered. "Much of the old brutal ignorance that had in it also a kind of beautiful childlike innocence is gone forever," Sherwood Anderson lamented in *Winesburg, Ohio;* and in 1920, "Couldn't she somehow, some yet unimagined how," Sinclair Lewis asked of Carol Kennicott, "turn it back to simplicity?" The question reverberates with the force of an archetype through our literature, through Faulkner (*Sartoris*), through Hemingway (*In Our Time,* especially "Big Two-Hearted River"), and into contemporary American poetry (Robert Bly, James Wright, Gary Snyder). Part of a context, then, the value of *The Call of the Wild* is just that this motif of pastoralism is so very clear in it. Good in its own right, it is a cartoon, in a way, of more major accomplishments. Readily understood, it is an excellent and useful introduction because it hones the point so cleanly that Hemingway and Faulkner, among others, do much more fancy whittling to attain. Not just about a dog, the book is a ritual enactment of the American wish to turn back to simplicity. Buck goes to Alaska and there London reduces life to its lowest terms, discovers under so much complexity what life is essentially all about. Buck in Alaska takes his rightful place among those heroes in American literature who counteract in our imagination, by living more fully, those others we revere for getting ahead, like Spitz the lead-dog, "cold and calculating," whom Buck ritually defeats. For from the beginning our worship has been schismatic, Franklins on the one side and Thoreaus on the other, of our twin ideal that the Puritan John Cotton characterized as "diligence in earthly affairs and deadness to the world." There is no doubt where Buck belongs:

> each day mankind and the claims of mankind slipped farther from him. Deep in the forest a call was sounding, and as often as he heard this call, mysteriously thrilling and luring, he felt compelled to turn his back upon the fire and the beaten earth around it, and to plunge into the forest, and on and on, he knew not where or why; nor did he wonder where or why, the call sounding imperiously, deep in the forest.

The claims of mankind are represented in the novel by Charles, Hal and Mercedes, nurture's interlopers in the North to whom Buck is sold by Perrault and Francois. Buck had been uneasy during the transaction and his fear is later justified when he first sees the camp of his new owners, "a slipshod and slovenly affair, tent half stretched, dishes unwashed, everything in disorder. . . . " It is the opposite of the clean well-lighted place that Buck's later master and Nature's Nobleman, John Thornton, keeps. Thornton's two partners, Hans and Pete, "were of the same large type as Thornton, living close to the earth, thinking simply and seeing clearly. . . . " Such a pastoral trinity is in meaningful contrast to the wrangling threesome of Charles, Hal and Mercedes "slack in all things, without order or discipline." They are products of artificial and complex civilization and as such are measured by the established norm of simplicity and found hopelessly wanting:

> Starting from a dispute as to which should chop a few sticks for the fire (a dispute which concerned only Charles and Hal), presently would be lugged in the rest of the family, fathers, mothers, uncles, cousins, people thousands of miles away, and some of them dead. That Hal's views on art, or the sort of society plays his mother's brother wrote, should have anything to do with the chopping of a few sticks of firewood, passes comprehension; nevertheless the quarrel was as likely to tend in that direction as in the direction of Charles's political prejudices. And that Charles's sister's tale-bearing tongue should be relevant to the building of a Yukon fire, was apparent only to Mercedes, who disburdened herself of copious opinions upon that topic, and incidentally upon a few other traits unpleasantly peculiar to her husband's family. In the meantime the fire remained unbuilt, the camp half pitched, and the dogs unfed.

The language itself ("disburdened herself of copious opinions") takes on the messy headiness of abstraction that is the syntactic equivalent of the effete, over-complicated society the book criticizes. The phrases, "sort of society plays his mother's brother wrote" and "Charles's sister's tale-bearing tongue," are a verbal exhibit of civilization's bedeviling complexity; they are onomatopoetic of the sputtering exasperation with which the pastoral writer by definition views such entanglement. When Buck is the subject, however, the prose moves with his rhythmic gait to the tune of "no ideas but in things": "Fish, in open pools, were not too quick for him; nor were beaver, mending their dams, too wary."

Characteristically, Charles, Hal and Mercedes overload the sled just as they overload the syntax. The dogs are overworked and clubbed when they become too weak from lack of food to pull the load that civilization demands. Charles, Hal and Mercedes (civilization) fail to pull down their vanity and learn of the green (in this case, white) world; they are judged and condemned by London to a death caused by the weight of their own baggage which cracks the river ice.

By so criticizing society, *The Call of the Wild* is akin to yet another very archetypally American book— *Huckleberry Finn*. It also involves a flight for freedom from the debilitating influences of civilization. Like Huck, Buck's been there before and he will never go back. "Simplify, simplify" Thoreau urged; London's prose style communicates this content as much as the content itself. "At home it was all too complicated" says Krebs, one of the first in a long line of Hemingway's pastoral heroes. And like Hemingway's uncomplicated style, clean and well-lighted to both match and be his theme, London's prose opens out to be in structure what it is in theme: like Buck,

"free in the open, the unpacked earth underfoot, the wide sky overhead." (pp. 246-48)

> *Raymond Benoit, "Jack London's 'The Call of the Wild'," in* American Quarterly, *Vol. XX, No. 2, Summer, 1968, pp. 246-48.*

Earl J. Wilcox   (essay date 1969)

[*In the following excerpt, Wilcox finds* The Call of the Wild *to be a "Darwinian epic."*]

Both Jack London's intentions and his accomplishments in *The Call of the Wild* account for the artistic success of the book. For the story which London intended to write— about a dog who merely reverts to the wild—developed into a full, 32,000 word novel. And the simplicity intended in the implicit atavism in the dog's reversion also became a more complex discussion than London apparently bargained for. But a fortuitous combination of events led London to produce the most popular and the best piece of fiction he ever wrote. Thus while he gauged his audience accurately in writing a popular account of Darwinian literature, at the same time the novel gave him an opportunity to explore the philosophical ideas which had been fermenting in his mind but which he had not found opportunity to express in full in his fiction.

Joan London reports her father as saying that he did not recognize "the human allegory in the dog's life-and-death struggle to adapt himself to a hostile environment." And even after he had reread his story several times, he allegedly said, "I plead guilty, but I was unconscious of it at the time. I did not mean to do it." London's disclaimer has been eagerly accepted by critics who point to the discrepancies in both his plot and his philosophy. . . . But London *was* aware of his intentions in the novel, at least in some of the "allegorical" aspects. For sometime later, in defending himself against charges of President Theodore Roosevelt and John Burroughs, who had accused him of being a "nature-faker," London states his artistic purpose in *The Call of the Wild* and *White Fang:*

> I have been guilty of writing two animal stories— two books about dogs. The writing of these two stories, on my part, was in truth a protest against the "humanizing" of animals, of which it seemed to me several "animal writers" had been profoundly guilty. Time and again, and many times, in my narratives, I wrote, speaking of my dog-heroes: "He did not think these things; he merely did them," etc. And I did this repeatedly to the clogging of my narrative and in violation of my artistic canons; and I did it in order to hammer into the average human understanding that these dog-heroes of mine were not directed by abstract reasoning, but by instinct, sensation, and emotion, and by simple reasoning. Also, I endeavored to make my stories in line with the facts of evolution; I hewed them to the mark set by scientific research, and awoke, one day, to find myself bundled neck and crop into the camp of the nature-faker.

Throughout the discussion in the essay, London relies on his rather thorough knowledge of Darwinian thought to defend his assertions. If London were not drawing inferences about man in his "dog-heroes," his entire literary career, particularly in relationship to the naturalistic movement, is called into question. For to leave the implications of his struggle-for-survival thesis in the realm of "lower" animals is to relegate the stories to mere animal adventures. Indeed, there would seem to be no London achievement worth quibbling about. But, in fact, both the first short stories and the first novel—in which human beings are clearly the protagonists—these precise themes and motifs are basic philosophy. The extent to which London makes the Darwinian or Spencerian allegory directly applicable to human existence is surely left for the reader to decide. For while there is confusion in London's understanding between the explicit relationships of the evolutionary and atavistic concepts developed by Darwin and the views advanced by Spencer, London seems little concerned about delineating either with a nice distinction. Nevertheless, precise qualification which focuses on naturalistic implications of the novel accounts for the meaning of the work.

The plot of *The Call of the Wild* is so familiar, because of its wide-spread popularity, that to review it would appear unnecessary, particularly in view of the haste with which London wrote it. Since he is ostensibly concerned with dogs in the naturalism here, however, a brief statement of the plot may be helpful. In simplest terms, Buck, a magnificent dog, lives on Judge Miller's ranch in California. He is kidnapped and taken to Alaska where through numerous hardships and encounters with the "wild" he recognizes his affinity to it and reverts to his primordial state.

It is clear that Buck is not precisely one of the pure breed for whom London held greatest respect, because Buck is a cross between a St. Bernard and a Scotch shepherd. Still, Buck's pre-eminence, as London later explains, results from the lucky combination of his parents, a familiar philosophical idea emanating from London's views on natural selection. While the Judge is away at a meeting of the Raisin Growers' Association, Buck is stolen by Manuel, a ranch laborer, and sold for fifty dollars to a man who wants to use Buck in the Northern country.

In the suggestive initial chapter, "Into the Primitive," Buck first learns the difference between the "cold" world to which he is being taken and the "warm" world from which he comes. He has not been accustomed to harsh treatment, but being an exceptionally wise dog, he quickly adjusts. In fact, his adjustment and his adaptability become his salvation. Buck's first reaction to rough treatment is in a spirit of rebelliousness. But, London tells his reader before he has gone a dozen pages into the narrative, Buck recognizes a new "law" when he sees it:

> He saw, once for all, that he stood no chance against a man with a club. He had learned the lesson, and in all his after life he never forgot it. That club was a revelation. It was his introduction to the reign of primitive law, and he met the introduction halfway. The facts of life took on a fiercer aspect; and while he faced that aspect uncowed, he faced it with all the latent cunning of his nature aroused.

And each dog who is brought receives the same treatment:

> As the days went by, other dogs came, in crates and at the end of ropes, some docilely, and some raging and roaring as he had come; and, one and all, he watched them pass under the dominion of the man in the red sweater. Again and again, as he looked at each brutal performance, the lesson was driven

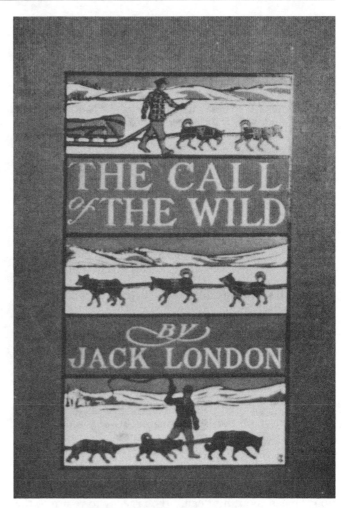

Front cover for The Call of the Wild.

home to Buck: a man with a club was a law-giver, a master to be obeyed, though not necessarily conciliated. Of this last Buck was never guilty, though he did see beaten dogs that fawned upon the man, and wagged their tails, and licked his hand. Also he saw one dog, that would neither conciliate nor obey, finally killed in the struggle for mastery.

How easily London has transferred his concept of law from the early stories to this intriguing adventure of man's best friend is readily observable through the eyes of Buck, for Buck directs the reader's sympathies to the "good" and the "bad" as they pass through his life. The story is, of course, not an objective account of the struggle, not in any way an "experiment" in Zola's frame of reference. Nevertheless, it is a forceful and powerful adventure through which London explores the latent possibilities of his Darwinian and Spencerian views.

Buck is finally sold to two Frenchmen who take him into the Klondike. There Buck learns a corollary law of the club, the law of fang. It is by these laws that Buck's "primitive" ancestors lived. And Buck's own translation is succinctly noted: "He had been suddenly jerked from the heart of civilization and flung into the heart of things primordial." Contrasted with the soft world from which Buck has come, in the primordial "all was confusion and action,. . . . There was imperative need to be constantly alert; for these dogs and men were not town dogs and men. They were savages, all of them, who knew no law but the law of club and fang."

Buck's first experience with the law of fang is in observing another dog, Curly, make friendly overtures to a husky. Curly is quickly struck, and as soon as she is down, ". . . [the pack] closed in upon her, snarling and yelping, and she was buried, screaming with agony, beneath the bristling mass of bodies." And Buck's mind quickly reaches its first significant conclusion:

> So that was the way. No fair play. Once down, that was the end of you. Well, he would see to it that he never went down. Spitz ran out his tongue and laughed again, and from that moment Buck hated him with a bitter and deathless hatred.

From this moment Buck's most dangerous enemy is Spitz, a dog who has arrived with Buck for the new adventures. The allegory in their action is too obvious, the melodramatic tone is unmistakably clear: even as Scruff MacKenzie (an early London protagonist in a short story) fought for his life, Buck early discovers both the "rules" of the "game" and the "laws" which govern the environment into which he has come.

London's implicit suggestion that the law of club and fang is supreme in the wild is weakened somewhat by his insistence that Buck learns unusually fast. And part of Buck's education grows out of his rebelliousness as much as his need for survival. For Buck apparently needs only one lesson to know whom to approach, when to act, and how to act. Always, London says, "he was learning fact," and, later Buck is described as an "apt scholar." Nevertheless, his schooling becomes important, for his mobility in adjusting to the environment precipitates the early sensations he has about his "call," the urgency to return to the primordial world from which he has evolved. Using a familiar naturalistic image, the "trap," London describes the prescience which surrounds Buck as he dreams of being caught and devoured by the pack. Even when he experiences his first snowfall and wakes to find himself buried,

> . . . a great surge of fear swept through him—the fear of the wild thing for the trap. It was a token that he was harking back through his own life to the lives of his forebears, for he was a civilized dog, an unduly civilized dog and of his own experience knew no trap and so could not of himself fear it.

Watching and learning, Buck discovers that self-preservation means more than defensive action. Offensive maneuvers are also a part of the "law," particularly in regard to the procurement of food. Like Theodore Dreiser's Carrie, who "adjusts" to Chicago to live, Buck steals food to live. But London cannot resist propagandizing, and he comments in non-Dreiserian terms.

> This first theft marked Buck as fit to survive in the hostile Northland environment. It marked his adaptability, his capacity to adjust himself to changing conditions, the lack of which would have meant swift and terrible death. It marked, further, the decay or going to pieces of his moral nature, a vain thing and a handicap in the ruthless struggle for existence. It was all well enough in the Southland, under the law of love and fellowship, to re-

spect private property and personal feelings; but in the Northland, under the law of club and fang, whoso took such things into account was a fool, and in so far as he observed them he would fail to prosper.

. . . For once Buck learns to adjust, "his development (or retrogression) was rapid." Experience is his teacher, even as it had been Sister Carrie's or Stephen Crane's Maggie. But his morality is not questioned by the reader because Buck is a dog—or because London chooses to ignore the moral implications of Buck's thievery. For Buck's "new" way of life is new to him only momentarily. As London closes out his discourse on the law of club and fang, he comments on Buck's strange awareness of memories of a previous life in which his ancestors had lived precisely as he is now having to live in his struggle for survival. As the culture of generations of civilizations fell from Scruff MacKenzie, the same process occurs through Buck's atavism.

> The domesticated generations fell from him. In vague ways he remembered back to the youth of the breed, to the time the wild dogs ranged in packs through the primeval forest, and killed their meat as they ran it down. It was no task for him to learn to fight with cut and slash and the quick wolf snap. In this manner had fought forgotten ancestors.

Buck's evolutionary process is a combination of natural selection and of other Darwinian "accidents" through which he has evolved. The probability of his existence, a product of no clearly definable pattern, had characterized, for example, the view of Fortune La Perle (in an earlier London short story), who also knew life as chance. About Buck, too, London again asserts,

> Thus, as token of what a puppet thing life is the ancient song surged through him and he came into his own again; and he came because men had found a yellow metal in the North, and because Manuel was a gardener's helper whose wages did not lap over the needs of his wife and divers small copies of himself.

It is London the pessimist who speaks for Buck in this cryptic manner.

The highest achievement of the novel is clearly Chapter III, "The Dominant Primordial Beast." Following themes, images, and tonal qualities upon which Frank Norris had dwelt in his descriptions of McTeague and Trina, and with which Stephen Crane described his central figures in *Maggie,* London is emphatic and convincing: "The dominant primordial beast was strong in Buck, and under the fierce conditions of trail life it grew and grew." By now Buck has had many hours of schooling which have prepared him for the supreme test. The lead dog, whose job it is to keep the others in line, even if killing is necessary, is Spitz. From the first, Spitz and Buck have been deadly enemies. When Spitz tries to steal Buck's bed, Buck reacts, and "The beast in him roared." Even when Francois or Perrault, the masters, try to separate the dogs, Buck is eager to continue the fracas. Once in the grip of the new morality, " . . . fairplay was a forgotten code" and Buck springs on Spitz. While these minor clashes characterize the long trips which Buck and his friends are making, Buck discovers also that he is soft from years in civilization. Buck's feet tell the tale: ". . . [they] were not so compact and hard as the feet of the huskies. His had softened during the many generations since the day his last wild ancestor was tamed by a cave-dweller or river man."

The inevitable, bloody showdown between Buck and Spitz is soon to come. And "Buck wanted it. He wanted it because it was his nature. . . ." For Buck had endured thus far because he was different from the Southland dogs: "He alone endured and prospered, matching the husky in strength, savagery, and cunning."

London leads his reader along at a rapid pace as he points toward the supreme effort of Buck's life, his fight with Spitz. In the precision of moving toward the battle, London again shows the explicit parallel between the lives of the dogs whom he is describing and the lives of humanity whom he also has in mind. In perhaps the most poetic passage London ever wrote, he says:

> With the aurora borealis flaming coldly overhead, or the stars leaping in the frost dance, and the land numb and frozen under its pall of snow, this song of the huskies might have been the defiance of life, only it was pitched in minor key, with long-drawn wailings and half-sobs, and was more the pleading of life, the articulate travail of existence. It was an old song, old as the breed itself—one of the first songs of the younger world in a day when songs were sad. It was invested with the woe of unnumbered generations, this plaint by which Buck was so strangely stirred. When he moaned and sobbed, it was with the pain of living that was of old, the pain of his wild fathers, and the fear and mystery of the cold and dark that was to them fear and mystery. And that he should be stirred by it marked the completeness with which he harked back through the ages of fire and roof to the raw beginnings of life in the howling ages.

Finally, Buck is given the pre-eminent position as leader of the pack because the others respect his strength and his skill. Even Spitz resists open fighting, though grumbling has set in among some of the pack before the final stretch of a long journey between Dawson and Salt Water.

The call which has been haunting Buck returns one evening as he and the others relax after a day in the traces. A snowshoe rabbit is treed, and the pack is off after it. While leading the pack in the chase, Buck remembers his primordial past:

> All that stirring of old instincts which at stated periods drives men out from the sounding cities to forest and plain to kill things by chemically propelled leaden pellets, the blood lust, the joy to kill—all this was Buck's, only it was infinitely more intimate. He was ranging at the head of the pack, running the wild thing down, the living meat, to kill with his own teeth and wash his muzzle to the eyes in warm blood.

And in the description of this thrill of the chase, the joy, the ecstasy of living, London evinces a significant materialistic attitude that links him profoundly with the naturalists. Buck becomes, perhaps, the epitome of London's own materialistic impulses, in his exulting in the joy of living, the joy of life for its own sake. For Buck is also "mastered by the verb 'to live'," in precisely the same manner of Jan, the Unrepentant, and Sturgis Owens, and Scruff Mackenzie—all human protagonists in London's first short stories. Later, London depicted Wolf Larsen, a man, in similar terms; here it is Buck, the dog, who finds the life-urge, the sense of impulse, the will to live, dominating all else.

> There is an ecstasy that marks the summit of life, and beyond which life cannot rise. And such is the paradox of living, this ecstasy comes when one is most alive, and it comes as a complete forgetfulness that one is alive. This ecstasy, this forgetfulness of living, comes to the artist, caught up and out of himself in a sheet of flame; it comes to the soldier, war-mad on a stricken field and refusing quarter; and it came to Buck, leading the pack, sounding the old wolf-cry, straining after the food that was alive and that fled swiftly before him through the moonlight. He was sounding the deeps of his nature, and of the parts of his nature that were deeper than he, going back into the womb of Time. He was mastered by the sheer surging of life, the tidal wave of being, the perfect joy of each separate muscle, joint, and sinew and that it was everything that was not death, that it was aglow and rampant, expressing itself in movement, flying exultingly under the stars and over the face of dead matter that did not move.

This formula is characterized by impulse emerging from self-forgetfulness, and the individual who partakes does so without reason. In the comment, it is obvious that man and animal become one in this materialistic view.

Following immediately in the narrative is the passage which tells of Spitz's intention to prevent Buck's remaining the leader. The fight to death ensues. When Spitz attacks, Buck knows the meaning instantly:

> In a flash Buck knew it. The time had come. It was to the death. As they circled about, snarling, ears laid back, keenly watching for the advantage, the scene came to Buck with a sense of familiarity. He seemed to remember it all,—the white woods, and earth, and moonlight, and the thrill of battle. . . . To Buck it was nothing new or strange, this scene of old time. It was as though it had always been, the wonted way of things.

The resulting battle is a bloody, ugly affair. It is won by Buck because he has imagination. The quality of mind which produces Buck's victory is indeed a strange and perplexing psychological feat for a mere animal, but as odd as it appears, it does not leave room for mercy. That was "a thing reserved for gentler climes." Buck reigns supreme, "the successful champion, the dominant primordial beast who had made his kill and found it good." London is not explicit in arguing for survival as the motivation for Buck's fight, though it is certainly implicit in all that Buck does from the first encounter with Spitz. The capture of the rabbit is likewise not necessary for survival, but it is artistically relevant since it precipitates Spitz's desire to attack Buck.

After this chapter, which itself is episodic, the remainder of the novel seems almost anti-climactic, though in reality it is not. For London still manages in the scenes following to carry out his central thesis, Buck's return to a former, primitive state. So Buck becomes the leader of the pack, and the team successfully makes its trips between Dawson and other cities. In the leisure between trips, while lying by the fire, Buck's mind wanders back to Judge Miller's home, and London makes the dream of the call nearer:

> The Sunland was very dim and distant, and such memories had no power over him. Far more potent

were the memories of his heredity that gave things he had never seen before a seeming familiarity; the instincts (which were but the memories of his ancestors become habit) which had lapsed in later days, and still later, in him, quickened and became alive again.

And in Buck's dreams of the ancestral world of the primitive, described in a manner very similar to the setting in London's earlier **"The First Poet"** and the later book, *Before Adam,* Buck sees another man:

> This other man was shorter of leg and longer of arm, with muscles that were stringy and knotty rather than rounded and swelling. The hair of this man was long and matted, and his head slanted back under it from the eyes. He uttered strange sounds, and seemed very much afraid of the darkness, into which he peered continually, clutching in his hand, which hung midway between knee and foot, a stick with a heavy stone made fast to the end. He was all but naked, a ragged and fire-scorched skin hanging part way down his back, but on his body there was much hair. In some places, across the chest and shoulders and down the outside of the arms and thighs, it was matted into almost a thick fur. He did not stand erect, but with trunk inclined forward from the hips, on legs that bent at the knees. About his body there was a peculiar springiness, or resiliency, almost catlike, and quick alertness as of one who lived in perpetual fear of things seen and unseen.

With each passing day Buck and his mates are given sleds too heavy to pull, until finally their masters overwork them, and the entire pack crawls, half-dead into Dawson. There Buck is sold to a group of tenderfeet who try also to pack too much on a sled for the tired dogs to pull. In this dull little episode, Buck learns that not all people have a knowledge of even the rudiments of survival, for "Hal," "Charles," and "Mercedes" first quarrel, then fight, and finally resort to beating the dogs into moving the heavy sleds. John Thornton, an informed and interested trapper, warns the tenderfeet to stop beating the dogs and to go no further on the frozen river. After seeing their particularly harsh treatment of Buck, he rescues Buck from the group, and the naive trappers dash on, only to fall through the ice and drown.

In the penultimate chapter, the one most often remembered but far less characteristic of the book's themes, London sentimentalizes his story to make effective the contrast of the last chapter where Buck answers the call of the wild. Thornton becomes Buck's savior, and the life with Thornton revives memories of the soft days before Buck came north. Still the episode only quickens Buck's dilemma: Buck cannot decide between the call of Thornton's love and the lure of the wild. In the structural *tour de force* of the novel, London parallels Buck's journey back to the wild with the literal journey the sled teams take to the wild country of Alaska:

> He was older than the days he had seen and the breaths he had drawn. He linked the past with the present, and the eternity behind him throbbed through him in a mighty rhythm to which he swayed as the tides and seasons swayed. He sat by John Thornton's fire, a broad-breasted dog, white-fanged, and long-furred; but behind him were the

shades of all manner of dogs, half-wolves, and wild wolves. . . .

> So peremptorily did these shades beckon him, that each day mankind and the claims of mankind slipped farther from him. Deep in the forest a call was sounding, and as often as he heard this call, mysteriously thrilling and luring, he felt compelled to turn his back upon the fire and the beaten earth around it, and to plunge into the forest. . . .

London says that "Buck earned sixteen hundred dollars in five minutes for John Thornton," in summarizing the events that characterize Buck's "love of man." But the love and the fame of his feats in civilization cannot forever restrain Buck. The more he is on the trail with the man he loves, the more also the vision; and in all his visions, the "trap" is prominent. Except for his love for Thornton, Buck's return to his "first" love becomes complete. In daydreams, while his masters work their claims, Buck wanders through the wilds until at last he cannot resist the call: "And he knew it, in the old familiar way, as a sound heard before." In answering the call, Buck finds a friend in the wolf he has heard. But the two ways of life persist in his mind, even with increased perplexity as he returns to be with Thornton briefly. At last Buck's killing a bull moose assures him that it is with the wild he belongs:

> There is a patience of the wild—dogged, tireless, persistent as life itself—that holds motionless for endless hours the spider in its web, the snake in its coils, the panther in its ambuscade; this patience belongs peculiarly to life when it hunts its living food; and it belonged to Buck as he clung to the flank of the herd. . . .

Trying to break completely with civilization, Buck discovers that it is not easy to leave the man he loves, but returning to find his master dead, Buck knows that "the last tie was broken. Man and the claims of man no longer bound him." Thornton's death, Buck discovers, is at the hands of a tribe of Yeehats. In his revenge, Buck achieves his highest aim, his action pointing to the implicit allegory of the novel: "He had killed man, the noblest game of all, and he had killed in the face of the law of club and fang." Symbolically, the law of survival has become explicit; the law of tooth and fang both pays and extracts its fee in the merging of the killing of the Indian-man by the dog-man.

Once in the wild permanently, Buck soon successfully defends his life against a pack of wolves; then he knows that he was right to answer the call.

London's Darwinian epic is neatly concluded:

> And here may well end the story of Buck. The years were not many when the Yeehats noted a change in the breed of timber wolves; for some were seen with splashes of brown on head and muzzle, with a rift of white centering down the chest.

It is the Ghost dog, as elusive in its forays into the Indians' camp as the Evil Spirit into which the dog eventually evolves in the Indian mythology. London apostrophizes the call, noting that Buck still exists in the folklore of the Yeehats, the primitive forerunner of man. And Buck and his "pack" still permeate the world:

> But he is not always alone. When the long winter nights come on and the wolves follow their meat into the lower valleys, he may be seen running at

the head of the pack through the pale moonlight, or glimmering borealis, leaping gigantic above his fellows, his great throat a-bellow as he sings a song of the younger world, which is the song of the pack.

The naturalism that characterizes this novel is not consistently developed. But neither is the naturalism always of a rigid, definable pattern in, for example, Norris's romantic ending of *McTeague,* or Dreiser's or Crane's notable lack of reform (to choose random motifs historically associated with naturalism). In *The Call of the Wild* one does not learn how atavism is biologically or scientifically plausible, nor does one learn how the implicit determinism at work behind Buck's existence comes about. In London's mind, it is merely an assertion, an accepted, "irrefragable fact," not a scientifically controlled experiment. The book gives no help to either the sociologist or the biologist who turns here expecting to find Taine's, Darwin's, or Spencer's theories put into practice in fiction. Indeed the ideas of Spencer and Darwin are certainly confused in the philosophy which does come through. For Spencer felt that whatever evolutionary processes should work out in creating a complex society, the individual would never notice the changes. In Buck, however, the dominant operating pressure is clearly an evolutionary process, though not rationally defended by London, which the individual not only senses but ultimately knows. While Jung's and Freud's psychology later supported London's legend of the purlieu of a dog world, Darwinism was generally not intent on showing that in the descent of man the intuitive memories of a former state were a prerequisite to man's having been there. Nevertheless, while some technical difficulties preclude one's making rigid and categorical assertions about London's understanding and use of naturalistic theory, he was clearly writing for a popular audience that had no doubt about either his intentions or his accomplishments. (pp. 91-101)

> *Earl J. Wilcox, "Jack London's Naturalism: The Example of 'The Call of the Wild'," in* Jack London Newsletter, *Vol. 2, No. 3, September-December, 1969, pp. 91-101.*

Mary Kay Dodson (essay date 1971)

[*In the following excerpt, Dodson discusses* The Call of the Wild *as it reflects the Naturalist doctrine of biological determinism.*]

In the naturalistic sense, man is considered an animal. Hereditary, environmental, and biological forces determine what he is; he has little or no control over what he is and what he does. In 1900 London wrote that "the different families of man must yield to law, which has no knowledge of good or ill, right or wrong." As London grew older, his materialistic view of life grew stronger. Fifteen years later he wrote: "I am a hopeless materialist. I see the soul as nothing else than the sum of the activities of the organism plus personal habits, memories, and experiences, plus inherited habits, memories, experiences of the organism." He also wrote that "man is not a free agent, and free will [as the power of ethical choice] is a fallacy exploded by science long ago." London was also a believer in Darwin's ideas about the struggle for existence. Since this survival depends on superior force or guile, London formulated the idea that man's will (as vital impulse or force) was the one

positive fact upon which an individual could base his actions. In glorifying strength, he glorified the will (as vital force) which seems always to exist in a character who has superior cunning or power. London's writings reflect his naturalistic philosophy. The primary symbol he uses for the purpose of showing the relationship between strength and the struggle for survival expressed in terms of Darwin's scientific determinism is the beast. His beasts are depicted both explicitly and implicitly. Buck, the protagonist in *The Call of the Wild,* is the most forceful example of the former, whereas Wolf Larsen, in *The Sea-Wolf,* is the best example of the latter. (p. 130)

One of London's greatest successes in his writing about the vast northern wilderness is *The Call of the Wild.* The universe determined scientifically by heredity and environment is wrought very masterfully in the novel. . . . The use of Buck is London's most explicit portrayal of the "beast." Buck's transformation from a domesticated, gentle dog into the dominant primordial beast is inevitable because of the naturalistic universe; his heredity and environment force him to kill or to be killed. The amiable Buck was kidnapped from Judge Miller's California ranch by Manuel, a ranch-hand, and sold. Then he was transported to the Yukon to be used in a dog team which was run by Perrault, a French Canadian. Buck learned quickly that he would have to adapt in order to survive. He was cruelly treated in the beginning of the book; after Perrault sold him, he was almost killed by his new master. John Thornton, his final owner, saved him from this cruel master.

In *The Call of the Wild,* the portrayal of men as beasts is shown as well as the portrayal of dog as beast. When Buck is caged after he has been stolen, he is tormented by his captors. He has been put in a baggage car and has had nothing to eat or drink for two days. As can be expected, Buck is very angry. "In his anger he had met the first advances of the express messengers with growls, and they had retaliated by teasing him. When he flung himself against the bars, quivering and frothing, they laughed at him and taunted him. They growled and barked like detestable dogs. . . ."

Buck's first introduction to primitive law—the law of the club and fang—came at the hands of Perrault who beat him into submission with a club. Buck learned quickly that he must avoid the club; he was an intelligent dog who fought not only by instinct, but also by his head. He "possessed a quality that made for greatness—imagination." His imagination helped him not only to survive, but also to adapt.

Buck's father was a huge St. Bernard and his mother a Scotch shepherd dog. During the four years he lived at Judge Miller's, he became accustomed to the genteel life. "But he had saved himself by not becoming a mere pampered house dog. Hunting and kindred outdoor delights had kept down the fat and hardened his muscles; and to him, as to the cold-tubbing races, the love of water had been a tonic and a health preserver." Because Buck was in good physical condition, one aspect of his adaptation to the Yukon territory was made easier; he was capable of doing the work for which he had been stolen.

The powerful influence of Buck's heredity is carefully presented. He was not homesick because his memories of

California were very dim and distant, and therefore not very powerful. "For more potent were the memories of his heredity that gave things he had never seen before a seeming familiarity; the instincts (which were but the memories of his ancestors become habits) which had lapsed in later days, and still later, in him, quickened and became alive again." Even though Buck's father too had been a companion of Judge Miller's, Buck quickly recognized his hereditary instincts. He responded to them because he was placed in an environment in which these hereditary factors were essential to survival. Had he remained in his comfortable surroundings at the ranch, he never would have felt this influence of his heredity.

Buck realized that his new environment was his natural habitat especially when he made friends with the wolf. The two of them

> came down into a level country where were great stretches of forest and many streams, and through these great stretches they ran steadily, hour after hour, the sun rising higher and the day growing warmer. Buck was wildly glad. He knew he was at last answering the call, running by the side of his wood brother toward the place from where the call surely came. Old memories were coming upon him fast, and he was stirring to them as of old he stirred to the realities of which they were the shadows. He had done this thing before, somewhere in that other and dimly remembered world, and he was doing it again, now, running free in the open, the unpacked earth underfoot, the wide sky overhead.

Buck, in responding to the call of the wild, was responding to the call of his ancestors—his heredity. As his hereditary forces came into the fore, he began to depend less and less upon the only decent human being he had encountered since leaving Judge Miller's. He learned to kill, but not just for the sake of killing; he killed to feed himself. "The blood longing became stronger than ever before. He was a killer, a thing that preyed, living on the things that lived, unaided, alone, by virtue of his own strength and prowess, surviving triumphantly in a hostile environment when only the strong survived. Because of all this he became possessed of a great pride in himself, which communicated itself like a contagion to his physical being." His appearance was almost that of a gigantic wolf. The physical characteristics of his father and mother were blended in him:

> From his St. Bernard father he had inherited size and weight, but it was his shepherd mother who had given shape to that size and weight. His muzzle was the long wolf muzzle, save that it was larger than the muzzle of any wolf; and his head, somewhat broader, was the wolf head on a massive scale. His cunning was wolf cunning, and wild cunning; his intelligence, shepherd intelligence and St. Bernard intelligence; and all this, plus an experience gained in the fiercest of schools, made him as formidable a creature as any that roamed the wild.

Thus Buck explicitly embodies the theory of naturalism. He is a product of biological, environmental, and hereditary forces. (pp. 132-34)

Mary Kay Dodson, "Naturalism in the Works of Jack London," in Jack London Newsletter, *Vol. 4, No. 3, September-December, 1971, pp. 130-39.*

Jonathan H. Spinner (essay date 1974)

[*In the following excerpt, Spinner illustrates the ways in which violence serves a redemptive purpose in* The Call of the Wild.]

The Call of the Wild has usually been placed in the limbo of the "boys book," a designation that conjures up a cheap, though exciting "action-packed adventure story." To be sure, it is a story filled with action and adventure. However, there is something deeper in this novella, something beyond the usual frontier "Shoot-em-up." For London describes an education, spiritually as well as physically, of a being suffering through the dilemma of existence of the modern world. What is presented by London is a syllabus for the twentieth century, a syllabus that states that the way to solve the dilemma of existence in a harsh world is to accept and glory in the cleansing fire of violence.

A syllabus usually states what the lesson to be learned consists of, what the problem to be solved is. The lesson that Buck must learn is how to cope with his loss of identity, his feeling of alienation, and his loss of faith in a world he neither created nor knew existed. In other words, Buck's problem is how to survive in a hostile world; not surprisingly, it is the same problem faced by modern man.

I may seem to be overextending the concept of a "dilemma of existence" for a dog, even one as larger-than-life as Buck. But London makes it clear that Buck certainly does suffer from a loss of identity and a feeling of alienation when he is first "dognapped" and thrown into a crate prior to being sent to the Klondike, for Buck

> could not understand what it all meant. What did they want with him, these strange men? Why were they keeping him pent up in this narrow crate? He did not know why, but he felt oppressed by the vague sense of impending calamity.

These reactions are compounded by a loss of faith in both man and dog, first stated when he is finally freed on the Dyea beach, as his first day there is

> like a nightmare. Every hour was filled with shock and surprise. He had been suddenly jerked from the heart of civilization and flung into the heart of things primordial. . . . Here was neither peace,nor rest, nor a moment's safety. All was confusion and action, and every moment life and limb were in peril. There was imperative need to be constantly alert; for these dogs and men were not town dogs and men. They were savages, all of them, who knew no law but the law of club and fang.

These chaotic feelings are the central focus of the first two chapters of the novella. Gradually, Buck is able to cope with such inner confusion as he learns of his new outer world. He quickly discovers certain natural laws in this universe far away from his Southland home. Buck sees "once for all, that he stood no chance against a man with a club." As far as how a dog in the Klondike is expected to fight, he learns that there was "no fair play. Once down, that was the end of you." And Buck learns another natural law of the North, that of the true relationship between man and dog, when he discovers that when Francois has fastened upon him was "an arrangement of straps and buckles. It was a harness, such as he had seen the grooms put on the horses at home."

These, Buck learns, are the Northland dog's three great laws: fear of man; no quarter among themselves; and the true constant in the equation, hard work. What permits Buck to absorb these lessons without being destroyed as other dogs are destroyed is the "latent cunning of his nature aroused," his "adaptability." Having once gained the knowledge of these three laws, Buck quickly learns all the other necessary tricks of survival in a hostile world. As he learns them with great speed, London states, the greater the

> decay or going to pieces of his moral nature, a vain thing and a handicap in the ruthless struggle for existence. It was all well enough in the Southland, under the law of love and fellowship, to respect private property and personal feelings; but in the Northland, under the law of club and fang, whoso took such things into account was a fool, and in so far as he observed them he would fail to prosper.

It is this "decay" that is at the heart of Buck's learning process, and is the core of London's lesson. In a harsh and brutal world, it is imperative that Buck give up civilized ways for "instincts long dead." In order for Buck to solve the dilemma of his existence, a dilemma created by modern Fates, uncaring as their ancient sisters, it is necessary for Buck to shed his "domesticated generations" and become a "dominant primordial beast." Like modern men, Buck is thrown out of paradise somewhere much further than east of Eden, by forces unknown to him, beyond his control, and rooted in the industrial world, forces somehow tied into men finding "a yellow metal in the North, and because Manuel was a gardener's helper whose wages did not lap over the needs of his wife and divers small copies of himself."

By the third chapter, Buck has learned, in an unconscious way, all the tricks of survival. But London, being a wise teacher, does not end the story here, with a quick and successful fight against Spitz, and Buck's assumption of the mantle of lead sled dog. London does not wish to present a story of how a dog learns to survive in the wilderness. That is the nature of the usual adventure story. Rather, London wants to create a moral tale, a fable, and it is necessary that Buck become conscious of the changes in himself, even as the reader is informed. Further, London also wants to go beyond the lessons Buck has already gained; his true aim is the exploration and exploitation of his own Northland gold—the instinctual nature of blood and violence, the call of the wild.

London must, however, set the stage in the reader's heart by showing how treacherous and frightened Spitz is, by having him attack Buck in dangerous situations. It is not enough to win the adventure-story-buff's head by giving the story a pseudo-Darwinistic "survival of the fittest" patina, since the "fair play" credo is the accepted one in this genre. Thus, when the maddened huskies attack the camp, it is Spitz who slashes at Buck during the fighting. After being pursued by the rabid Dolly, it is Spitz who attacks Buck as he is trying to catch his breath. By setting up this situation, London is able to exploit it by having Buck then act in like spirit and attack Spitz at inopportune times, while saying that for Buck, "fair play was a forgotten code."

One other element is added by London to this equation, an element that acts as a catalyst for the final showdown between Buck and Spitz, even as it promises to be one of the active ingredients in the rest of the story. It is the vital element of wildness, first expressed by Buck when he joins the wolf huskies in their "nocturnal song." For Buck

> this song of the huskies might have been the defiance of life, only it was pitched in minor key, with long-drawn wailings and half-sobs, and was more the pleading of life, the articulate travail of existence. It was an old song, old as the breed itself— one of the first songs of the younger world in a day when songs were sad. It was invested with the woe of unnumbered generations, this plaint by which Buck was so strangely stirred. When he moaned and sobbed, it was with the pain of living that was of old the pain of his wild fathers, and the fear and mystery of the cold and dark that was to them fear and mystery. And that he should be stirred by it marked the completeness with which he harked back through the ages of fire and roof to the raw beginnings of life in the howling ages.

Thus, when Dub scares out a snowshoe rabbit, the stage has been set not only for Buck to become the "dominant, primordial beast" by killing Spitz, but has been prepared as well for the succeeding acts leading to Buck's complete acceptance of the "call of the wild."

By ascending to the head of pack, Buck has merely crossed over from being a good Southland dog to being a good Northland dog. Only half of London's syllabus has been expounded and absorbed by Buck and the reader. It is time for Buck to begin to break two of the three natural laws he has learned so far as a Northland trace dog, as he learns new rules about violence as a way out of the modern dilemma of the "monotonous life" in which he worked with "machinelike regularity."

Like the situation surrounding Spitz' death, London sets up this further change in Buck's outer way of life by giving him tantalyzing glimpses of this paradise of instinctual violence that lies within Buck's reach. By having Buck dream of happier possibilities, London has shown the reader Buck's future potential. And by having Buck dream of the "far more potent . . . memories of his heredity," London is able to contrast these "memories of his ancestors" against "the Sunland" of Judge Miller's ranch, for which Buck is "not homesick," and thus use the weight of the pre-historic past to defeat the more recent, upstart civilized garden of eden in the "sun-kissed Santa Clara valley." Of course, since London is attempting to educate his human audience more than he is the dog Buck, it is not surprising that the first of Buck's dreams features a man "shorter of leg and longer of arm" sitting by a fire surrounded by "the eyes of great beasts of prey."

Having hooked the reader by a vision of his own possible ancestral paradise, London now proceeds to have Buck violate two of the three natural laws he has learned about the Northland, with the reader, if not applauding, at least understanding Buck's reasons for his actions. Buck is first shown what hard work does to every dog who survives the continual fights with the other sled-dogs, when Dave, one of the hardest working and most compulsive of the dogs, becomes ill yet refuses to stop pulling in his place in the sled-harness. A choice is given to Buck between the "natural" way of the wild, dying an honorable death in combat, and the "unnatural" way of the world of man by dying a death filled with "convulsive efforts" in the sled-harness.

Thus, a dog like Buck, filled with pride and dignity, must choose to break the Northland law of hard work.

London clarifies Buck's choice when the team is sold to Hal, Charles, and Mercedes. Already beaten by the thirty-day drive from Dawson to Skagway, Buck and the rest of the team are sold to Southland people totally unequipped to handle a sled in the Klondike. Buck quickly realizes their lack of expertise as he "watched them apprehensively as they proceeded to take down the tent and load the sled. There was a great deal of effort about their manner, but no businesslike method." Buck's apprehension is proven to be more than a suspicion in the succeeding weeks, as the greenhorns' lack of expertise, combined with their cruelty destroys the sled-team's already exhausted abilities. However, something else besides physical strength is destroyed as well; Buck learns that hard work done for people who neither understand nor appreciate it leaves one, as modern man has already learned, "jaded and tired . . . (and) bitter. His heart was not in the work."

So much for one of the laws of the Northland, hard work. Yet another law is to be broken on this trip with the greenhorn Southerners, the law of the man with the club. This condition of the Klondike was the first that Buck was exposed to, and the most fearsome of the three. To overcome it then, is to free Buck from man. Buck does not defeat it by killing Hal, who torments Buck and the rest of the team; rather, like oppressed beings in the modern world, the dogs become "insensible to the bite of the lash or the bruise of the club. The pain of the beating was dull and distant." And compared to these beatings administered by a man, so much like death, is the natural world that is filled with the "bursting, rending, throbbing of awakening life."

At this point, John Thornton is brought into the story. Buck has reached the nadir of his existence in the Northland, a situation of life beyond the dilemma of existence, brought on by physical exhaustion and human cruelty beyond that first experience had by him on the Dyea Beach. If two laws of Klondike life are swept aside by Buck, it is because of the actions taken by beings outside Buck's control that force him to choose life over the death-giving aspects of these laws. John Thornton is necessary partially to release Buck from death, spiritually as well as physically.

The physical death facing Buck is clear enough, for as Hal beats him Buck feels that

> the blows did not hurt much. And as they continued to fall upon him, the spark of life within flickered and went down. It was nearly out. He felt strangely numb. As though from a great distance, he was aware that he was being beaten. The last sensation of pain left him. He no longer felt anything, though very faintly he could hear the impact of the club upon his body. But it was no longer his body, it seemed so far away.

As John Thornton springs to Buck's defense with a "cry that was inarticulate and more like the cry of an animal," he forces Buck into a new position, a position at once free of the Northland laws of hard work and respect for the man with a club while still tied to mankind and his civilization through the love for one man. And Thornton understands, perhaps unconsciously, what kind of animal he

has helped, as he refers to Buck as " 'You poor devil.' " For Thornton, Buck will be an angel; to others, he will seem to be a devil, and a rather powerful one at that.

As Buck regains his strength under Thornton's ministrations, he senses two changes in himself. First, "love, genuine passionate love, was his for the first time"; secondly, "the strain of the primitive, which the Northland had aroused in him, reamined alive and active." These changes are the last of the lessons of the Klondike, and they are the last of the choices Buck will have to make to determine his pattern of existence. That both love and violence are equally powerful lures is indicated by the actions Buck is willing to take in either case. For Thornton, Buck is willing to jump a chasm, to attack a man, to brave rapids, to pull a sled weighing a thousand pounds.

But there is the "stuff of his dreams." There is,

> deep in the forest a call . . . sounding, and as often as he heard this call, mysteriously thrilling and luring, he felt compelled to turn his back upon the fire and the beaten earth around it, and to plunge into the forest, on and on, he knew not where or why; nor did he wonder where or why, the call sounding imperiously, deep in the forest.

So there it is, the call of the heart against the call of the wild.

It is the Northland's, and London's, final lesson to Buck and to people of the twentieth century, that there is no choice involved. There is only one syllabus to be followed, only one passion that will cleanse the soul, and that is violence, not love. Love of this world is transient, because it depends on loving flesh-and-blood, which may wander away or in Thornton's case, be too weak to survive physi-

Scene from a film adaptation of The Call of the Wild.

cally, and so disappear. Since neither London nor twentieth century man truly believes in God's love, only one passion can truly be called enduring, that of violence. Buck, like mankind in our time, chooses that which seems strongest, which will help him best survive in a cruel world.

Even with Thornton still alive, Buck is almost completely overwhelmed by the call of violence. Perhaps it is London's bit of irony that as Thornton is drawn to gold, to undreamed-of wealth, the perennial El Dorado of civilized man, Buck is drawn to his own El Dorado, the merciless ways of the wild. And as Thornton and his companions discover their sought-after mother-lode, so Buck discovers his own gold mine, his own treasure in the wild. Buck also discovers, through his dreams, what is at the root of his relationship to men other than Thornton, the basis for the relationship between all men and all dogs: man's fear of the unknown, of other beasts, of the wild itself. Buck realizes that man needs the dog to protect him from that which, every day and night, called to him and "filled him with a great unrest and strange desires."

When Buck discovers the wolf, he discovers a substitute for his love for John Thornton: the companionship of the wild pack. Buck knows that his choice is coming soon, and he guiltily "never left camp, never let Thornton out of his sight" for two days and nights, for he is "haunted by recollections of the wild brother." This substitute for his love for John Thornton, like the bond between teenagers in a gang, is strengthened by his "blood longing." London's lesson, like the lessons of the worst of the twentieth century, is that one must be "a killer, a thing that preyed, living on the things that lived," in order to survive "triumphantly in a hostile environment where only the strong survived."

Buck's long hunt of the bull moose is part of that blood longing, just as his detection of a "new stir in the land . . . different from the life which had been there throughout the summer." What he discovers on his return to camp is death, the death of John Thornton, not life. But there is something new in the land, as both the Yeehats who killed Thornton, and the wolves who come to devour Thornton's remains discover; it is Buck who is new, a Buck who is to become the incarnation of the Evil Spirit. For Buck, there is "a great void . . . somewhat akin to hunger, but a void, which ached and ached, and which food could not fill." There is also, however, the breaking of all ties with mankind and the loss of all fear of him. As Buck proves himself to the wolves and joins them to run "side by side with the wild brother," London's last lesson is driven home, his syllabus completed, and violence is shown to be the only way to overcome the dilemma of existence in the twentieth century.

London writes "and here may well end the story"; Buck leads the wolf pack, throws fear into the Yeehats, and generally becomes the embodiment of so much of twentieth century man has come to applaud, the cleansing force of violence. But Buck, having fulfilled his dreams of his ancestors' genetic call, remembers another vision, a vision not too distant in his own past, that of his love for a man, John Thornton. By the "yellow stream (that) flows from rotted moose-hide sacks and sinks into the ground," Buck "muses for a time, howling once, long and mournfully, ere he departs." Perhaps Buck's memorial visit is of greater

sincerity than our present-day nostalgic remembrances of things past; but readers of today still may better understand Buck than did London's first readers of some seventy years ago. For Buck remembers and yearns, for a moment, for that time in his life that was filled with love, like mankind when it speaks of belief in God nowadays, and how human beings in the past once believed fully, and God loved us completely. Like Buck, however, we soon return to our fellows and to our violence singing "a song of the younger world, which is the song of the pack." (pp. 73-8)

> *Jonathan H. Spinner, "A Syllabus for the 20th Century: Jack London's 'The Call of the Wild'," in* Jack London Newsletter, *Vol. 7, No. 2, May-August, 1974, pp. 73-8.*

Earle Labor   (essay date 1974)

[*In the following excerpt, Labor discusses the structure and themes of* The Call of the Wild.]

Neither of London's two most successful works of long fiction is a conventional novel: **The Call of the Wild** is a mythic romance; **White Fang,** a sociological fable. Both works are, of course, beast fables in that they provoke our interest—unconsciously if not consciously—in the human situation, not in the plight of the lower animals. By using canine rather than human protagonists, London was able to say more about this situation than he might have been otherwise permitted by the editors of magazines like *The Saturday Evening Post* and *Cosmopolitan* who were extremely careful not to offend the genteel sensibilities of their Victorian readership. Just as two generations earlier Poe had muffled sexual aberrations under the dark mantle of Gothicism, so London hid sex under a heavy cloak of fur as in the vivid scene of "love-making in the Wild, the sex-tragedy of the natural world" in the early pages of **White Fang** when old One Eye and the ambitious young wolf fight to the death while "the she-wolf, the cause of it all," sits and watches with sadistic pleasure. And we also have the example of Buck's ethical retrogression in **The Call of the Wild:** his learning to steal and rob without scruple and to kill without pity does not morally offend us because he is just a dog, not a human. (p. 69)

Joan London tells us that so far as her father was concerned, this masterpiece was "a purely fortuitous piece of work, a lucky shot in the dark that had unexpectedly found its mark," and that, when reviewers enthusiastically interpreted **The Call of the Wild** as a brilliant human allegory, he was astonished: " 'I plead guilty,' he admitted, 'but I was unconscious of it at the time. I did not mean to do it.' " However, he was not entirely oblivious to the story's unusual merit; in a letter to his publisher George Brett, he wrote: "It is an animal story, utterly different in subject and treatment from the rest of the animal stories which have been so successful; and yet it seems popular enough for the *Saturday Evening Post,* for they snapped it up right away."

Though London may not have understood the full import of this statement, his story was in fact "utterly different" from the humanized beasts in Kipling's "Mowgli" stories and from the sentimental projections of Margaret Marshall Saunders's *Beautiful Joe* and Ernest Seton's *Biogra-*

phy of a Grizzly, which were enormously popular in London's day and which can still be found in the children's sections of public libraries. Charles G. D. Roberts, writing about the appeal of such literature at the turn of the century, explained that "the animal story, as we now have it, is a potent emancipator. It frees us for a little while from the world of shop-worn utilities, and from the mean tenement of self of which we do well to grow weary. . . . It has ever the more significance, it has ever the richer gift of refreshment and renewal, the more humane the heart and spiritual the understanding which we bring to the intimacy of it." This explanation holds true for *The Call of the Wild* as well as for the other wild animal stories: London's work offers the "gift of refreshment and renewal," as well as a certain escapism. The difference is its radical departure from the conventional animal story in style and substance—the manner in which it is, to use the psychoanalytic term, "overdetermined" in its multilayered meaning.

Maxwell Geismar [see excerpt dated 1953] gives a clue to the deeper layer of meaning when he classifies the work as "a beautiful prose poem, or *nouvelle,* of gold and death on the instinctual level" and as a "handsome parable of the buried impulses." We need only interpolate that these "buried impulses" are essentially human, not canine, and that the reader identifies more closely than he realizes with the protagonist of that *nouvelle.* The plot is animated by one of the most basic of archetypal motifs: the Myth of the Hero. The call to adventure, departure, initiation, the perilous journey to the "world navel" or mysterious life-center, transformation, and apotheosis—these are the phases of the Myth; and all are present in Buck's progress from the civilized world through the natural and beyond to the supernatural world. His journey carries him not only through space but also through time and, ultimately, into the still center of a world that is timeless.

Richard Chase [in his *The American Novel and Its Tradition*] points out that in the type of long fiction most properly designated as the *romance,* character becomes "somewhat abstract and ideal," and plot is "highly colored": "Astonishing events may occur, and these are likely to have a symbolic or ideological, rather than a realistic, plausibility. Being less committed to the immediate rendition of reality than the novel, the romance will more freely veer toward mythic, allegorical, and symbolistic forms." All of these remarks are directly applicable to *The Call of the Wild,* in which the richly symbolistic form ultimately becomes the content of the fiction. The seven chapters of the work fall into four major parts or movements. Each of these movements is distinguished by its own theme, rhythm, and tone; each is climaxed by an event of dramatic intensity; and each marks a stage in the hero's transformation from a phenomenal into an ideal figure.

Part I, consisting of three chapters, is, with its emphasis on physical violence and amoral survival, the most Naturalistic—and the most literal—of the book. Its rhythms are quick, fierce, muscular. Images of intense struggle, pain, and blood predominate. Chapter I, "Into the Primitive," describes the great dog's kidnapping from Judge Miller's pastoral ranch and his subsequent endurance of the first rites of his initiation—the beginning of the transformation that ultimately carries him deep into Nature's heart of darkness: "For two days and nights he neither ate nor drank, and during those two days and nights of torment, he accumulated a fund of wrath that boded ill for whoever first fell foul of him. His eyes turned blood-shot, and he was metamorphosed into a raging fiend. So changed was he that the Judge himself would not have recognized him; and the express messengers breathed with relief when they bundled him off the train at Seattle."

The high priest of Buck's first initiatory rites is the symbolic figure in the red sweater, the man with the club who relentlessly pounds the hero into a disciplined submission to the code of violence and toil. "Well, Buck, my boy," the man calmly observes after the merciless beating, "we've had our little ruction, and the best thing we can do is to let it go at that. You've learned your place, and I know mine." Like all of London's heroes who survive the rigors of the White Silence, Buck has passed the first test: that of adaptability.

Chapter II, "The Law of Club and Fang," takes the hero to the Northland. On the Dyea beach he encounters the dogs and men who are to become his traveling companions in the long hard months ahead. He also continues to absorb the lessons of survival. Curly, the most amiable of the newly arrived pack, is knocked down by a veteran husky, the ripped apart by the horde of canine spectators. The scene remains vividly etched in Buck's memory: "So that was the way. No fairplay. Once down, that was the end of you." Later, as he is broken into his traces for the trail, he awakens to the great driving motivation of the veteran sled-dogs: the extraordinary love of toil. But more significant is the metamorphosis of his moral values. He learns, for example, that stealing, an unthinkable misdeed in his former state, can be the difference between survival and death:

> [His] first theft marked Buck as fit to survive in the hostile Northland environment. It marked his adaptability, his capacity to adjust himself to changing conditions, the lack of which would have meant swift and terrible death. It marked, further, the decay or going to pieces of his moral nature, a vain thing and a handicap in the ruthless struggle for existence. It was all well enough in the Southland, under the law of love and fellowship, to respect private property and personal feelings; but in the Northland, under the law of club and fang, whoso took such things into account was a fool, and in so far as he observed them he would fail to prosper.

Chapter III, "The Dominant Primordial Beast," marks the conclusion of the first major phase of Buck's initiation; for it reveals that he is not merely qualified as a member of the pack but that he is worthy of leadership. In this chapter, there is a pronounced modulation of style to signal the glimmerings of Buck's mythic destiny; instead of sharply detailed physical description, we begin to encounter passages of tone-poetry:

> With the aurora borealis flaming coldly overhead, or the stars leaping in the frost dance, and the land numb and frozen under its pall of snow, this song of the huskies might have been the defiance of life, only it was pitched in minor key, with long-drawn wailings and half-sobs, and was more the pleading of life, the articulate travail of existence. . . . When he moaned and sobbed, it was with the pain of living that was of old the pain of his wild fathers,

and the fear and mystery of the cold and dark that was to them fear and mystery.

London's style becomes increasingly lyrical as the narrative rises from literal to symbolic level, and it reaches such intensity near the end of Chapter III that we now realize that Buck's is no common animal story:

> There is an ecstasy that marks the summit of life, and beyond which life cannot rise. And such is the paradox of living, this ecstasy comes when one is most alive, and it comes as a complete forgetfulness that one is alive. This ecstasy, this forgetfulness of living, comes to the artist, caught up and out of himself in a sheet of flame; it comes to the soldier, war-mad on a stricken field and refusing quarter; and it came to Buck, leading the pack, sounding the old wolf-cry, straining after the food that was alive and that fled swiftly before him through the moonlight. He was sounding the deeps of his nature, and of the parts of his nature that were deeper than he, going back into the womb of Time. He was mastered by the sheer surging of life, the tidal wave of being, the perfect joy of each separate muscle, joint, and sinew in that it was everything that was not death, that it was aglow and rampant, expressing itself in movement, flying exultantly under the stars and over the face of dead matter that did not move.

This paragraph is a thematic epitome of the whole work, and it functions as a prologue to the weird moonlit scene in which Buck challenges Spitz for leadership of the team, a scene noted by Geismar as "a perfect instance of the 'son-horde' theory which Frazer traced in *The Golden Bough,* and of that primitive ritual to which Freud himself attributed both a sense of original sin and the fundamental ceremony of religious exorcism."

Even though Buck has now "Won to Mastership" (Chapter IV) he is not ready for apotheosis; he is a leader and a hero—but he is not yet a god. His divinity must be confirmed, as prescribed by ritual, through death and rebirth. After the climactic pulsations of Chapter III, there is a slowing of beat in the second movement. Death occurs symbolically, almost literally, in Chapter V ("The Toil of Trace and Trail"). Clustering darkly, the dominant images are those of pain and fatigue as Buck and his teammates suffer under the ownership of the three *chechaquos:* Charles, his wife Mercedes, and her brother Hal—"a nice family party." Like the two Incapables of "In a Far Country," they display all the fatal symptoms of incompetence and unfitness: "Buck felt vaguely that there was no depending upon these two men and the woman. They did not know how to do anything, and as days went by it became apparent that they could not learn. They were slack in all things, without order or discipline." Without a sense of economy or the will to work and endure hardship themselves, they overwork, starve, and beat their dogs—then they turn on one another: "Their irritability arose out of their misery, increased with it, doubled upon it, outdistanced it. The wonderful patience of the trail which comes to all men who toil hard and suffer sore, and remain sweet of speech and kindly, did not come to these two men and the woman. They had no inkling of such a patience. They were stiff and in pain; their muscles ached, their bones ached, their very hearts ached; and because of this they became sharp of speech, and hard words were first on their lips in the morning and last at night." This ordeal is the second long and difficult phase of Buck's initiation. The "long journey" is described in increasingly morbid imagery as the "perambulating skeletons" and "wayfarers of death" approach closer to their fatal end in the thawing ice of Yukon River; the journey ends with Buck's symbolic crucifixion as he is beaten nearly to death by Hal shortly before the ghostly caravan moves on without him and disappears into the lethal river.

Buck's rebirth comes in Chapter VI, "For the Love of a Man," which also functions as the third and transitional movement of the narrative. Having been rescued by John Thornton, the benign helper who traditionally appears in the Myth to lead the hero toward his goal, Buck is now being readied for the final phase of his odyssey. Appropriately, the season is spring; and the mood is idyllic as he wins back his strength, "lying by the river bank through the long spring days, watching the running water, listening lazily to the songs of the birds and the hum of nature. . . ." And, during this same convalescent period, the hints of his destiny grow more insistent: "He was older than the days he had seen and the breaths he had drawn. He linked the past with the present, and the eternity behind him throbbed through him in a mighty rhythm to which he swayed as the tides and seasons swayed. . . . Deep in the forest a call was sounding. . . . But as often as he gained the soft unbroken earth and the green shade, the love for John Thornton drew him back. . . ." The passionate devotion to Thornton climaxes in the final scene of Chapter VI when Buck wins a thousand-dollar wager for his master by moving a half-ton sled a hundred yards; this legendary feat, which concludes the third movement of the narrative, foreshadows the hero's supernatural appointment in the fourth and final movement.

Chapter VII, "The Sounding of the Call," consummates Buck's transformation. In keeping with this change, London shifts both the setting and the tone. Thornton, taking the money earned by Buck in the wager, begins his last quest "into the East after a fabled lost mine, the history of which was as old as the history of the country . . . steeped in tragedy and shrouded in mystery." As the small party moves into the wilderness, the scene assumes a mythic atmosphere and the caravan is enveloped in a strange aura of timelessness:

> The months came and went, and back and forth they twisted through the uncharted vastness, where no men were and yet where men had been if the Lost Cabin were true. They went across divides in summer blizzards, shivered under the midnight sun on naked mountains between the timber line and the eternal snows, dropped into summer valleys amid swarming gnats and flies, and in the shadows of glaciers picked strawberries and flowers as ripe and fair as any the Southland could boast. In the fall of the year they penetrated a weird lake country, sad and silent, where wild-fowl had been, but where then there was no life nor sign of life—only the blowing of chill winds, the forming of ice in sheltered places, and the melancholy rippling of waves on lonely beaches.

The weirdness of the atmosphere is part of the "call to adventure" described by Joseph Campbell in *The Hero with a Thousand Faces,* which "signifies that destiny has summoned the hero and transferred his spiritual center of gravity from within the pale of society to a zone unknown. This fateful region of both treasure and danger may be variously represented: as a distant land, a forest, . . . or profound dream state; but it is always a place of strangely fluid and polymorphous beings, unimaginable torments, superhuman deeds and impossible delight." This "fateful region of both treasure and danger" is a far cry from Judge Miller's pastoral ranch and from the raw frontier of the Klondike gold rush: it is the landscape of myth. The party finally arrives at its destination, a mysterious and incredibly rich placer-valley where "Like giants they toiled, days flashing on the heels of days like dreams as they heaped the treasure up."

His role fulfilled as guide into the unknown zone to the "World Navel," Thornton and his party are killed by the savage Yeehats; and Buck is released from the bond of love to fulfill the last phase of his apotheosis as he is transformed into the immortal Ghost Dog of Northland legend; he incarnates the eternal mystery of creation and life: "[And when] the long winter nights come on and the wolves follow their meat into the lower valleys . . . a great, gloriously coated wolf, like, and yet unlike, all other wolves . . . may be seen running at the head of the pack through the pale moonlight or glimmering borealis, leaping gigantic above his fellows, his great throat abellow as he sings a song of the younger world, which is the song of the pack."

Though *The Call of the Wild* was perhaps no luckier than any other great artistic achievement, it was "a shot in the dark" in an unintended sense—into the dark wilderness of the unconscious. And as with other great literary works, its ultimate meaning eludes us. But at least a significant part of that meaning relates to the area of human experience which cannot be translated into discursive terms and which must therefore be approached tentatively and obliquely. After granting this much, we may infer that the animating force of London's wild romance is the vital energy Jung called *libido* and that London's hero is a projection of the reader's own *self* which is eternally striving for psychic integration in the process called *individuation*. Such an inference accounts for the appropriateness of London's division of his narrative into seven chapters which fall naturally into four movements: quaternity symbolizing, in Jung's words, "the ideal of completeness" and "the totality of the personality"—seven, the archetypal number of perfect order and the consummation of a cycle. But, of course, we do not need such a technical explanation to know that the call to which we respond as the great Ghost Dog flashes through the glimmering borealis singing his song of the younger world is the faint but clear echo of a music deep within ourselves. (pp. 71-8)

> *Earle Labor, in his* Jack London, *Twayne Publishers, 1974, 179 p.*

Andrew Flink (essay date 1978)

[*In the following excerpt, Flink suggests that London's experience in the Erie County penitentiary is reflected in* The Call of the Wild.]

> I plead guilty, but I was unconscious of it at the time. I did not mean to do it.

So spoke Jack London about his most enduring novel, *Call of the Wild.* He was, of course, referring to the underlying story-behind-the-story that some saw as human allegory.

Along these lines, James Glennon Cooper [in his "The Womb of Time: Archetypal Patterns in the Novels of Jack London," *Jack London Newsletter* 8 (1975)] made the observation that:

> London put many things into his stories he did not mean to include. Conscious intention and unconscious accomplishment were often [so] far apart . . .

and

> The breaching of the barrier between the consciousness and the unconscious once accomplished, allows more and more images to emerge from the depths of the unconscious.

In Jack London's life his sensitivity was assailed by two major events, the rejection of fatherhood by Chaney, a subject I touched on in "*Call of the Wild*—Parental Metaphor" [see Further Reading], and the experience of the Erie County Penitentiary both of which seemed to be highly traumatic for him. The Erie County experience, shock that it was, became the turning point of his life . . . steering him to education and ultimately to writing.

It's interesting to note, however, that while John Thornton seemed to be a parental metaphor, the story of Buck, before meeting John Thornton, might well be considered a "writing out" of the Erie County experience. With this in mind I'd like to take you on an excursion that might prove interesting by pointing up some parallels that exist between London's experiences in Erie County and Buck's experiences after being taken from the ranch in Santa Clara. In view of London's statement that he was "unaware of what he'd done" and in keeping with James Glennon Cooper's viewpoint about the unconscious, I'm going to proceed on the idea that London wasn't aware, cite some examples of why I think so and let you decide.

First, London's description of Buck is very much a description of London himself. From *War of the Classes* we read London's own words:

> . . . I was healthy and strong, bothered with neither aches or weaknesses.

and:

> . . . a stomach that could digest scrap iron and a body which flourished on hardships . . .

He describes Buck as:

> [his] muscles [became] hard as iron and he grew callous to all ordinary pain . . .

or:

> He could eat anything no matter how loathsome or indigestible.

London's description of Buck coincides clearly with what he'd written of himself.

Add to this the following reference to Buck's age on page 18 of *Call of the Wild:*

> During four years since his puppyhood

One year in the life of a human is 7 for a dog. This would make Buck twenty-eight human years old, London was twenty-seven when he finished Buck's story.

From the beginning of *Call of the Wild,* London touched on a common denominator between his brilliant novel and the Erie County experience. Manuel's treachery was the turning point in Buck's easy going life of a ranch dog. Taken from the ranch he's suddenly thrown into a situation completely foreign and strange to him. His freedom is curtailed, and he's exposed to cruelty and barbaric treatment. In **"Pinched"**, London finds himself in much the same situation, freedom suddenly curtailed leading to the inhumanity he witnessed as a convict.

Buck was sold to pay a gambling debt with which he had no connection. London was arrested to pay a debt he felt he never incurred. Both were victims of money, Buck sold to pay a gambling debt, London " . . .was nabbed by a fee hunting constable."

> Buck accepted the rope . . . [placed around his neck by Manuel] . . . with quiet dignity

and with faith in the way of things to go fair and just. London, by the same token, allowed himself to be taken to jail with the idea in mind that he could present his case and justice would prevail. In *The Road* London states:

> He'd have never run after me, [the arresting officer], for two hoboes in the hand are worth more than one on the getaway. But like a dummy I stood still when he halted me.

Later, London's eyes were opened wider by the facts. He was sentenced to thiry days by a biased and unfeeling court—only thirty days, but a month that would force a decision out of him that was to affect the rest of his life.

In **"Pinched"** London faces the reality of jail—he was behind bars! He describes the holding cell.

> "The hobo" is that part of a prison where the minor offenders were confined [together] in a large iron cage.

Buck, after leaving Manuel, is placed in a crate and there he stayed until such time as the dog taming sequence by the man in the red sweater. The visions of bars were common between the two situations. London states it as: "[he] [Buck] . . . raged at them through the bars."

While in the "hobo" London said that: "Here we met several hoboes who had already been pinched this morning, and every little while the door was unlocked and two more were thrust in on us."

Buck witnesses a situation that was similar: "As the days went by other dogs came in crates and at the ends of ropes, some docilely and some raging and roaring as he [Buck] had done."

To this point there would seem to be a close parallel between the experiences suffered by Buck and by London. The visions of bars in the crate where Buck was imprisoned and the implication of bars described by London in **"Pinched"** as " . . . a large iron cage", follow closely with each other. A relationship would certainly seem to exist. Here are some more examples:

London was transferred with other convicts to Buffalo by train from Niagara Falls. Buck also was transferred among other ways, by train.

States London: "Down the streets of Niagara Falls we were marched to the railroad station, stared at by curious passers-by . . . "

London and the others were, like Buck, placed on the train. London writes that " . . . he [Buck] was trucked off the steamer into a great railway depot, and finally he was deposited in an express car."

Like London, who was subjected to the shame by the people of Niagara Falls and who felt: "Afire with indignation was I at the outrage . . . "

Buck also felt: " . . . [the] more outrage to his dignity [and] his anger waxed and waxed."

Later when his indignation cooled and London began to settle down to the task of survival in Erie County, Buck likewise had the same change of heart. London says: "My indignation ebbed away and into my being rushed the tides of fear. I saw at last clear-eyed, what I was up against."

Buck echoes: "He was beaten (he knew that); but he was not broken. He saw once and for all that he had no chance against a man with a club. He had learned the lesson, and in all his after life he never forgot it."

Could this last sentence be the key to this entire idea? London left Erie County with the avowed intention of getting an education, to "open the books", and later to become a writer. He never forgot the Erie County experience, speaking of it later in years as "unprintable and unthinkable", describing it in **"Pinched"** as "unbelievable and monstrous" and writing it years later into *Call of the Wild* with the following: "The facts of life took on a fiercer aspect; and while he faced that aspect uncowed, he faced it with all the latent cunning of his nature aroused."

While in Erie County London certainly did face it with "all the latent cunning of his nature aroused." He became a trustee and gained some degree of autonomy, however small. But the gnawing spectre of hunger seemed to be a major problem and food was hard to come by.

> We were a hungry lot in the Erie County Pen . . . .
>
> I used to steal their grub while serving them. Man cannot live on bread alone and not enough of it.

Buck's problem was similar: "So greatly did hunger compel him, he was not above taking what did not belong to him."

From London's assessment that what he encountered was "unprintable and unthinkable" and that he, according to [his wife] Charmian, had understated the case in what she refers to as " . . . a hint of what he calls the 'unprintable' details . . . " either consciously or unconsciously, London must have been reliving the Erie County experience as he wrote *Call of the Wild.* What he experienced must have been a great shock. Imagine the effect of the kind of brutality described in **"Pinched"** and the **"Pen"** on someone as sensitive as London and who had the compassion for people that he had—one can only imagine what horrors he saw that he didn't write about. This along with the fact that he was only eighteen when he lived this experience it must have made an indelibly deep impression and who, like Buck: " . . . in all his after life he never forgot it."

The depth of the impression might be measured with the following from **"The Pen"**:

> There was a young Dutch boy, about eighteen years of age, who had fits most frequently . . .

> He prefaced his fits with howling. He howled like a wolf.

Compare that with what Buck witnessed: "Dolly, who had never been conspicuous for anything, went suddenly mad. She announced her condition by a long, heartbreaking wolf howl that sent every dog bristling with fear."

Immediately after being taken into custody, London's confusion as to why he was there became very evident as seen from this example from *The Road:*

> I was forced to toil hard on a diet of bread and water and to march the shameful lock-step with armed guards over me—and all for what? What had I done? What crime had I committed against the good citizens of Niagara Falls that all this vengeance should be wreaked upon me? I had not even violated their "sleeping-out" ordinance. I had slept outside their jurisdiction in the county that night. I had not even begged for a meal, or bartered for a "light piece" on their streets. All I had done was to walk along their sidewalk and gaze at their picayune waterfall and what crime was there in that?

> . . . I wanted to send for a lawyer. The guard laughed at me. So did the other guards. I really was incommunicado.

Buck was equally confused:

> There he lay for the remainder of the weary night, nursing his wrath and wounded pride. He could not understand what it all meant. What did they want with him, these strange men? Why were they keeping him pent up in this narrow crate? He did not know why, but he felt oppressed by a vague sense of impending calamity. Several times during the night he sprang to his feet when the shed door opened expecting to see the judge, or the boys at least. But each time it was the bulging face of the saloon keeper that peered in at him by the sickly light of a tallow candle.

London's statement about being incommunicado would seem to match up with the implied incommunicado experienced by Buck.

Buck's overwater voyage from Seattle to Dyea reads like a symbolic birth from London's tramp existence and its restless uncertainty of what his future held, to a definite plan with accompanying goals.

> When the heroes of *Call of the Wild, Nostromo,* and *Moby-Dick* must each cross a body of water in a small conveyance, the event represents a common "unconscious core" in the minds of the authors. The body of water reflected from this core represents the point of separation between life and death, but the "cask and water of the exposure myth become the womb and the amniotic fluid in which the fetus grows to birth.

The release from Erie County brought a new awareness to Jack London. It not only gave him a clearer picture of the brutalities of life, but it also made him want to do something about it. The difficulties ahead (to become a writer) were formidable. In "Dominant Primordial Beast" London wrote a paragraph that almost seems to be the essence of London himself at the point in time when he wrote *Call of the Wild.* He'd found his niche, he was moderately successful and maybe even elated:

> There is an ecstasy that marks the summit of life and beyond which life cannot rise. And such is the paradox of living, this ecstacy comes when one is most alive, and it comes as a complete forgetfullness that one is alive. This ecstasy, this forgetfullness of living comes to the artist, caught up and out of himself in a sheet of flame; . . .

To say in one of the strongest passages of the story that " . . . the artist is caught up and out of himself . . . " might well be leading into the very heart of the *Call of the Wild* in which London "wrote out" his feelings about himself. This occurs early in the novel when Buck is learning to survive after the experience of the sellout by Manuel and the subsequent events. To this point London's psyche had been something very elusive to him and he said of himself; "I had been reborn but not renamed and I was running around to find out what manner of thing I was."

Buck's case was worded differently but the content is the same: "He was sounding the depths of his nature, and of the parts of his nature that were deeper than he, going back to the Womb of Time."

It seems that each one, Buck and London, was searching for his own personal identification—London's search began upon his release from Erie County and culminating in his goal as a writer. Buck's rebirth began in the north and with the struggle to survive eventually becoming a " . . . great gloriously coated wolf, like, and yet unlike all other wolves." London's struggle to become a writer must certainly have included self-evaluation as one means to an end. Again we have a significant phrase: "He was sounding the depths of his nature, . . . "

The significance for both Buck and London is carried farther and the idea reappears later as the chapter titled "Sounding of the Call". A repeated use of "sounding" and "depths" brings to mind not audible sound but rather sound as a means of measuring depth, in the same manner as river pilots used soundings as navigational aids.

Buck pursued:

> . . . the call . . . sounding in the depths of the forest. It filled him with a great unrest and strange desires. It caused him to feel a vague, sweet gladness for he knew not what. Sometimes he pursued the call into the forest, looking for it as though it were a tangible thing . . . .

There's an interesting phrase, pursuing the call as though it were tangible. Relate this phrase to one I mentioned earlier written by and about London from *War of the Classes:* "I was running around trying to find out what manner of thing I was."

Buck followed the call into the forest in an attempt to take a "sounding of the call" in order to learn "what manner of thing I [London] was . . . "

What does all this mean? Maybe nothing! Then again it might mean that the *Call of the Wild* became the success it did because of the factors of: first, the trauma of Erie County, the nebulous parentage, and the fact that *Call of the Wild* was an autobiographical purging of the two strongest elements of his life up to the point of writing this haunting story, London's cartharsis, as it were. This too could be one reason why the story just about wrote itself.

> . . . [it] [*Call of the Wild*] got away from me and instead of 4,000 words it ran 32,000 before I could call a half.

This might imply a kind of compulsion or a "pursuit of the call into the forest, looking for it as though it were a tangible thing . . . ", London's "conscious intention and unconscious accomplishment."

What can we conclude from all this? Maybe these examples I've outlined might serve to pick out some pattern regarding London's creative powers. It would certainly tend to point up his sensitivity to his life's experiences and how they influenced his writing, either consciously or unconsciously. London's sensitivity was acute, his total recall a thing of wonder and the Erie County experience along with his parental problem became something for him to acknowledge and cope with—perhaps *Call of the Wild* is how he did it. His writings are laced with a restlessness and maybe this too is significant in some way, as though he never felt secure in spite of his successes and the following his name attracted (and still attracts). I feel that London was "sounding the deeps of his nature" all through his life but especially during his life as a writer. Maybe there's some personal significance for him in this respect when he has Buck return to the site of John Thornton's death where:

> . . . he muses for a time, howling once, long and mournfully, ere he departs.

Or that London felt the " . . . sheer surging of life . . . " by putting Buck's story on paper.

Jack London's " . . . superb meteor, every atom in magnificent glow . . . " was formed from the Erie County experience to the completion of *Call of the Wild,* the completion of which found him:

> . . . leaping gigantic above his [London's] fellows, [a leading writer among writers] his great throat a-bellow [expressing himself as a writer in a strong voice and being heard] as he sings the song of the younger world, which is the song of the pack.

(pp. 12-18)

Andrew Flink, " 'Call of the Wild'—Jack London's Catharsis," in Jack London News-letter, *Vol. 11, No. 1, January-April, 1978, pp. 12-19.*

John S. Mann   (essay date 1978)

[*In the following excerpt, Mann suggests that various "doubles," or pairings of antithetical characters and plot elements, contribute to the enduring popularity of* The Call of the Wild *and to the value of the novel as an object of critical study.*]

Dogs and men are fundamentally alike in the Klondike world of Jack London's *The Call of the Wild:* "There was imperative need to be constantly alert; for these dogs and men were not town dogs and men. They were savages, all of them, who knew no law but the law of club and fang." Dogs and men answer the call of their savage natures and their terrifying environment in a violent, bloody, and continual struggle for survival. The primitive fears and desires which surface in Buck—the splendid animal on whom the story centers—also control his human masters. London describes the dog's "development"—his regression to instinct—in terms of *human* personality and action, so that by the end of the tale Buck emerges as a fully-realized "character" whose motivation can be thoroughly understood. *The Call of the Wild* remains, curiously, a dog story made humanly understandable: it is a story of the "transformations" that a dog undergoes in the development of a new identity.

London patterns the relationships between dogs and humans with special care, and they strike the reader with clarity and richness. In part this justifies one's discovery in the story of a controlling metaphor, a theme, usually applied to a peculiar facet of human character. The theme of the "double" in fact illuminates *The Call of the Wild* in several important ways, offering focus for revelations about Buck and his human masters alike. The double as theme, as idea, as complex symbology provides a radiant metaphorical center for the whole landscape of Buck's tale. It encompasses character—the presentations of Buck, men and other dogs, and their necessary relations—but it also touches the action, the points of view involved in the telling of the story, and its atmosphere and setting in significant ways. Doubles and "doubling" themselves become controlling, almost obsessive preoccupations in London's narrative. Accordingly, a consideration of the double can help to account for the fascination the book has had for readers in the seventy-odd years since its publication in July, 1903. It can also suggest ways in which the book, surely one of London's best, is worthy of continued serious critical attention. (p. 1)

If the theme of the double usually depicts men as deeply divided within themselves, at war with their own natures and with their surroundings, then its first manifestation [in *The Call Of the Wild*] is in the opposing values, the polar attractions, of civilized and uncivilized worlds at work on the consciousness of a dog. The story develops through the impact of Buck's new Klondike environment upon his habits and expectations, conditioned as they are by his four-year sojourn in the civilized Santa Clara Valley of California. The logic of Buck's experience is to drive him increasingly, dramatically into the wild, so that even the interruption of this process by the civilizing love of John Thornton is not enough to return him to men and civilization.

London called the process "the devolution or decivilization of a dog." Buck's first theft of food from the government courier Perrault early in the book marks "the decay or going to pieces of his moral nature, a vain thing and a handicap in the ruthless struggle for existence." Stealing food helps Buck stay alive, and the narrator remarks that "the completeness of his decivilization was now evidenced by his ability to flee from the defence of a moral consideration and so save his hide." The remainder of the story parallels the outer conflict between Buck and his new Klondike environment with the inner conflict between the savage character of his buried nature and the patterns of conduct imposed on that nature by civilized society. Like the chief character in O'Neill's *Emperor Jones,* Buck faces experiences that force "instincts long dead [to become] alive again. The domesticated generations fell from him."

London dramatizes this split between civilization and savagery in several interesting ways, each involving a kind of double in turn. Though he once commented that "God abhors a mongrel," he carefully states that Buck is of mixed breed—half St. Bernard and half Scotch shepherd. This racial split in Buck's physical nature shrewdly underscores the inner conflict between civilized values and their opposites.

More important in defining the antithetical parts of Buck's nature is London's constant use of images of war throughout the book. Civilization and savagery fight a "war" inside Buck; much of Chapter Three chronicles the "secret growth" of the "dominant primordial beast" within him. Marks of war are everywhere in the plot of *The Call of the Wild:* in the huskies' savage killing of the Newfoundland, Curly; in the fight of Buck's team with a pack of starving huskies; in the constant fighting among the dogs on the team; in the murder of John Thornton and his partner by marauding Yeehat Indians; in Buck's battle with the wolf pack at the end of the book. Buck fights a literal war with his rival Spitz, first as a rebellious underling deposing the leader of the dog team, and later in a significant affirmation of his savage inheritance:

> In a flash Buck knew it. The time had come. It was to the death. As they circled about, snarling, ears laid back, keenly watchful for the advantage, the scene came to Buck with a sense of familiarity. He seemed to remember it all,—the white woods, and earth, and moonlight, and the thrill of battle. Over the whiteness and silence brooded a ghostly calm. . . . To Buck it was nothing new or strange, this scene of old time. It was as though it had always been, the wonted way of things.

The war between Buck and Spitz provides London with one of his clearest metaphors for Darwinian struggle and survival. The taste of Spitz's blood remains with Buck, drawn back and waiting for the other dogs to finish off the wounded rival: "Buck stood and looked on, the successful champion, the dominant primordial beast who had made his kill and found it good."

Francois, the team driver, notices the change in Buck the next day in a significant phrase: " 'Eh? Wot I say? I spik true w'en I say dat Buck two devils!' " As if in confirmation of that statement, London further dramatizes the theme of the double in an explicit set of controlling oppositions. Each of these projects Buck's inner and outer conflicts in things of opposite value. The original opposition between civilization and the wild encompasses all the others. The civilized world of the Southland, described continually in the book as warm, soft and easy, is opposed to the wild Northland, a terrifying arena of cold, hard brutality and sudden, violent death which yet—in London's most intriguing paradox—is finally seen as life-giving for the transformed Buck. The human world of ethical impulse and civilizing sanctions against violence is placed against the savage world of animals and savage men. More civilized dogs like Newfoundlands and even huskies find primitive counterparts in the wolves whose howl at the end of the story is the very sound of the wild.

Less obviously, London "doubles" the story into opposing worlds. Buck begins in the waking world of reality and ends in a silent, white wasteland which is also the world of dream, shadow, and racial memory. Buck survives to embrace life at the end of a book informed by death as the horrifying, rhythmic reflex of an entire order of things. Life in *The Call of the Wild* is a survival built on the death of other living creatures.

Between these opposing worlds and these opposing values Buck hovers continually in the action of the tale. Even the call of the wild itself, to which Buck responds with growing intensity throughout, receives double focus, twin definition: it is both lure and trap. In the second chapter, when Buck learns "The Law of Club and Fang," he builds his first warm sleeping nest in the snow, to discover the next morning:

> It had snowed during the night and he was completely buried. The snow walls pressed him on every side, and a great surge of fear swept through him—the fear of the wild thing for the trap. It was a token that he was harking back through his own life to the lives of his forbears; for he was a civilized dog, an unduly civilized dog, and of his own experience knew no trap and so could not of himself fear it. The muscles of his whole body contracted spasmodically and instinctively, the hair on his neck and shoulders stood on end, and with a ferocious snarl he bounded straight up into the blinding day, the snow flying about him in a flashing cloud.

The alluring world of snow and silence remains no less a tomb at the end of the book; though Buck is able to respond to it and still survive, John Thornton cannot.

It is impossible to view such doubled worlds and values, such connected oppositions, for very long without returning to London's pairing of dogs and humans with a renewed sense of its interest and complexity. Both Maxwell Geismar and Charles Child Walcutt [see excerpts dated 1953 and 1956] have pointed to London's skill in keeping the story within an animal point of view while retaining for balance and proportion a wise degree of human perspective. In fact, *The Call of the Wild* does retain a double point of view throughout, and London's cunning alternation of dog and human perspectives becomes the essential mark of his craft in the story. London often maintains the two points of view simultaneously; the impact of the double perspective on the reader makes it worthwhile to follow its development more closely in the action of the book.

The relations between Buck and the humans he encounters are marked, not surprisingly, by opposing forces, actions, roles, or values: love and hate, master and slave, uneasy truce and open war, hunter and victim. Buck enters the story in his sustaining California environment as ruler of all he surveys: he is "king,—king over all creeping, crawling, flying things of Judge Miller's place, humans included." Taken out of that happy valley, he is starved and mistreated by his captors and then subdued by the brutal club of a shrewd, red-sweatered man. The man conquers Buck and Buck hates him; yet the beating brings with it the curiously ambiguous relation between master and slave: "When the man brought him water he drank eagerly, and later bolted a generous meal of raw meat, chunk by chunk, from the man's hand." Buck's understanding of human beings will henceforth be defined by power and the politic dispensing of the necessities of life.

The next three chapters bring Buck under the benevolent tutelage of Perrault and Francois, masters still, but fair and, above all, schooled in the ways of the North. Buck's own competence increases apace. Though life on the trail is hard, Buck finds increasing joy in work. Humans and dogs grow markedly together: the trail demands teamwork from both. As humans and dogs form a cohesive unit, however, Buck begins fighting the other animals. His struggle for mastery in fact replays his own battle with the red-sweatered man; at the end of Chapter Three he mortally wounds Spitz and, though slave of humans, becomes master of the team. He retains this mastery though most of Chapter Four ("Who Has Won To Mastership") and leads a record run to Dawson and back; he continues to lead through Chapter Five, in spite of new owners and the increasing fatigue of endless trips from the coast to the interior.

This curious sharing of human and animal points of view and roles receives added point in Chapter Five in the interpolated fable of Charles, Hal, and Mercedes. Theirs is the fate of incompetence, weakness, and the failure to rid themselves fast enough of Southland, civilized values; the reader hates them because they mistreat the dogs through ignorance and kill off all but a few. London's manipulation of his readers' sympathy here suggests the way human and canine perspectives begin to fuse in the Klondike and foreshadows the end of the story. Buck can make it; the humans cannot: "By this time all the amenities and gentlenesses of the Southland had fallen away from the three people. Shorn of its glamour and romance, Arctic travel became to them a reality too harsh for their manhood and womanhood."

The appearance of John Thornton in Buck's life seems the signal for more human values—chiefly love—to mitigate the severity of Buck's previous experience. Yet once again the double remains a controlling presence. John Thornton's initial response in saving Buck is that of an animal: "And then suddenly, without warning, uttering a cry that was inarticulate and more like the cry of an animal, John Thornton sprang upon the man who wielded the club." Buck responds in turn with a human emotion in Chapter Six: "Love, genuine passionate love, was his for the first time." Though London uses words like "adoration" and "madness," he makes it clear that Thornton is "the ideal master." Buck has become a love-slave, the reverse of his relationship to the red-sweatered man. Remarkably, Buck and Thornton grow alike, almost exchange roles. For example, Thornton begins to talk to Buck; and a "miners' meeting" absolves Buck of guilt, as though he were a human on trial, in an incident at Circle City in which he defends Thornton from " 'Black Burton'." Buck gains increasing "fame" in the Klondike, adopts traditional dog roles in saving Thornton's life and in winning a $1600 bet for his master with an amazing feat of strength. Thornton is murdered, and Buck avenges his death. At the end of the story, however, he has become least civilized, most open to the wolf's howl which gains his final allegiance. Love for a human master co-exists with primal savagery, each paradoxically intensifying the other.

Thus London develops his intricate system of relations between humans and dogs through a series of double im-

pulses and actions: fusions and separations, loves and hates, adoptions and rejections. The tale's action meanwhile drives Buck more deeply into the wild. This double perspective becomes the craft of the book. In process, it gives us the action of *The Call of the Wild* while it symbolically restates its major themes.

In the latter part of the book, atmosphere, setting, landscape become all-important; and they, too, reflect the theme of the double. Writing to his young friend Cloudesley Johns in 1900, London had commented on the importance of atmosphere in terms curiously reminiscent of Poe's "Philosophy of Composition": "Atmosphere stands always for the elimination of the artist, that is to say, the atmosphere is the artist; and when there is no atmosphere and the artist is yet there, it simply means that the machinery is creaking and that the reader hears it." Practically, London did not "eliminate" himself from *The Call of the Wild*—indeed he could not—though he solves the problem of atmosphere wonderfully in the story.

As Buck's journey to the Klondike separates him from the civilized life of the Southland, so the sled-runs from the seacoast to the interior cross a "divide" that separates men from the wild. In Chapter Two, London introduces this divide as a major feature of the Klondike landscape: "It was a hard day's run, up the Cañon, through Sheep Camp,

London during his goldmining expedition in Alaska.

283

past the Scales and the timber line, across glaciers and snowdrifts hundreds of feet deep, and over the great Chilcoot Divide, which stands between the salt water and the fresh and guards forbiddingly the sad and lonely North." Divides like this recur throughout the book, and each time Buck crosses one, he enters a world whose constituent parts are silence, wildness, an increasingly nonhuman void—whatever is opposite to the world he has left. In the last chapter, Buck, Thornton, and two other men enter more deeply the "uncharted vastness":

> They went across divides in summer blizzards, shivered under the midnight sun on naked mountains between the timber line and the eternal snows, dropped into summer valleys amid swarming gnats and flies, and in the shadows of glaciers picked strawberries and flowers as ripe and fair as any the Southland could boast. In the fall of the year they penetrated a weird lake country, sad and silent, where wild fowl had been, but where then there was no life nor sign of life—only the blowing of chill winds, the forming of ice in sheltered places, and the melancholy rippling of waves on lonely beaches.

Here, London emphasizes the "divide" with striking clarity in paradoxes like "summer blizzards" and "midnight suns," in the rapid crossings into new seasons and landscapes, and in the sense that the interior of the North is a closed country which must be "penetrated."

Earle Labor has described this interior wilderness of the North in one of London's own metaphors and, following one of his own story titles as the **"White Silence,"** emphasizes its inviolability and austere force in opposition to man's puny insignificance. The landscape, the setting of the tale, its atmosphere—all become increasingly charged with symbolic and psychological meaning, so that the "divide" crossed in Buck's journey is one of interior character and world as well as outer reality. Buck journeys from the waking world into its double, the world of dream. As early as Chapter Four, Buck begins dreaming by the campfire of a "hairy man" in an older world, a human companion and double evoked by instinct and heredity from the depths of his consciousness. Buck dreams increasingly as the story continues: he dream of "shades" of older dogs and wolves and even becomes the hairy man's shadow-companion and *equal* in dream-visions of hunt and escape in a primitive time. Even the humans seem affected at the end of the book. Thornton and the others journey "into the East after a fabled lost mine"; their discovery of gold seems to bring them into another world than the waking one: "Like giants they toiled, days flashing on the heels of days like dreams as they heaped the treasure up."

Buck has been moving toward this dream-world double of the waking world throughout the book. He "enters" it in consciousness as well as in unconsciousness several times and then suddenly, literally, at the end. What Buck journeys toward is the instinctual life, the buried life within.

All of these things are recapitulated and intensified in the stunning last chapter of *The Call of the Wild,* where the theme of the double develops with special clarity. The logic of "The Sounding of the Call" is dream-logic, even though the action remains entirely compelling in its effort to move Buck completely, finally from the world of men to the world of natural creatures. Buck's experience has already made him "older," drawn him closer to natural, not human, rhythms: "He linked the past with the present, and the eternity behind him throbbed through him in amighty rhythm to which he swayed as the tides and seasons swayed." He meets his dream-companion, the hairy man who "heard and smelled as cleanly as Buck," as an equal in a world behind and within the present waking world. His meetings with this human double closely parallel the "call" he hears with greater and greater frequency from "the depths of the forest." He begins to respond to "irresistible impulses." Suddenly, one night, he slips out of camp to encounter a timber wolf, a literal double. They run together, cross a "bleak divide," a "watershed," into a new country: "Buck was wildly glad. He knew at last he was answering the call, running by the side of his wood brother toward the place from where the call surely came. Old memories were coming upon him fast, and he was stirring to them as of old he stirred to the realities of which they were the shadows."

This encounter with Buck's literal double destroys the precarious balance between the civilized and primitive qualities of Buck's nature. He becomes a skilled hunter and kills a large black bear. As the "blood longing" grows he begins to look more and more like a wolf. He remains "haunted by recollections of the wild brother, and of the smiling land beyond the divide and the run side by side through the wide forest stretches." He leaves camp, humans, and fire each night to undergo an "instant and terrible transformation" like some woodland Jekyll-Hyde. In an epic chase and battle taking him miles and days away from Thornton, he kills a moose, highest and strongest of Klondike animals. After each hunt, however, he returns, so that the action of the chapter displays a doubling, a shifting back and forth between the world of John Thornton's human love for Buck and the world of the forest and his wild wolf-brother.

He returns from the moose hunt to find John Thornton dead. Thornton's admirable simplicity and competence contain one flaw, which London states early in the final chapter: "He was unafraid of the wild." His fate remains, in James I. McClintock's rewarding suggestion, "the tragedy of youthful, energetic protagonists testing their vitality against the brutal forces of nature only to be drawn catastrophically toward the demonic, the irrational and death-dealing." Buck does not make the same mistake; because he apprehends the wild, he can turn it to his advantage in slaughtering Thornton's Yeehat murderers. The Yeehat bodies lie as nothing more than animal "carcasses," the remains of "the noblest game of all." With Thornton's death and in killing his first men, Buck moves irrevocably into the wild: "John Thornton was dead. The last tie was broken. Man and the claims of man no longer bound him."

The tone of the last chapter has meanwhile been shifting subtly. London's prose begins to sound more lyric, evocative, dream-like, idyllic. As Buck pursues the "call," he "would thrust his nose into the cool wood moss, or into the black soil where long grasses grew, and snort with joy at the fat earth smells. . . . " His senses are more and more tuned to nature itself, so that he can feel that "a change was coming over the face of things":

> He could feel a new stir in the land. As the moose were coming into the land, other kinds of life were

coming in. Forest and stream and air seemed palpitant with their presence. The news of it was borne in upon him, not by sight, or sound, or smell, but by some other and subtler sense.

When he encounters and subdues the wolf pack, it is with all the natural, non-human sanction that London's prose can command.

Then, suddenly, the dog Buck enters the realm of myth and the story ends. He leads the pack and becomes a kind of Ur-dog: he changes the timber wolf breed by siring a whole race of dogs mixed like him. He persists, in the legends of the Yeehats, as a "Ghost Dog" who haunts their camps and hunting grounds. In the last four paragraphs London fuses Buck totally with the natural world, so worlds and seasons sing through his final wolf howl. The song has now become "a song of the younger world, which is the song of the pack." Running along the snow under the pale moonlight and flaming aurora borealis, Buck becomes a vision, an incarnation.

Perhaps London's evocation of the natural world of the North lends the special, feral grace to the prose of *The Call of the Wild.* In any case, it aids his development of the theme of the double in the consciousness of a dog—the working out of individual action amidst the conflict and final transformation of the divided self. Joan London may be right in suggesting that her father's trip to the East End London slums so horrified him that he fled in Buck's story "to a world of his own devising, a clean, beautiful, primitive world in which . . . the fit, be they man or beast, could and would survive." Yet attempts to make Buck solely a human character in a social allegory remain curiously unproductive. The identity which Buck affirms is the product of the doubled values, landscapes, actions, and psychological impulses in the story, not of abstract notions about existing social reality. The "choice" Buck makes has, moreover, a peculiar attraction for London himself:

> There is an ecstasy that marks the summit of life, and beyond which life cannot rise. And such is the paradox of living, this ecstasy comes when one is most alive, and it comes as a complete forgetfulness that one is alive. This ecstasy, this forgetfulness of living, comes to the artist, caught up and out of himself in a chain of flame; it comes to the soldier, war-mad on a stricken field and refusing quarter; and it came to Buck, leading the pack, sounding the old wolf-cry, straining after the food that was alive and that fled swiftly before him in the moonlight. He was sounding the deeps of his nature, and of the parts of his nature that were deeper than he, going back into the womb of Time. He was mastered by the sheer surging joy of each separate muscle, joint, and sinew in that it was everything that was not death, that it was aglow and rampant, expressing itself in movement, flying exultantly under the stars and over the face of dead matter that did not move.

The metaphors of this passage (from Chapter Three) summarize the doubling impulses of the story in their paradoxical connections of life and dead matter, old and young worlds, the human reality of things and the timeless world of nature and race memory. The *energy* of the passage suggests London's primary achievement in *The Call of the Wild:* he discovered an action and a character that would elevate the savage world of Darwin to the pure and terrible world of myth. (pp. 1-5)

John S. Mann, "The Theme of the Double in 'The Call of the Wild'," in The Markham Review, *Vol. 8, Fall, 1978, pp. 1-5.*

Charles N. Watson, Jr.   (essay date 1983)

[*In the following excerpt, Watson discusses the rites of passage that lead to the mythologizing of Buck as the "Ghost Dog."*]

The Call of the Wild can no more be dismissed as a dog story than *Moby-Dick* can be dismissed as a whale story. Indeed, Alfred Kazin's fine insight [in his introduction to *Moby-Dick*]—that Melville's Ishmael "sees the whale's view of things," that he speaks for the primordial, transhuman world of nature—can equally well be applied to London. Both Melville and London attain a kind of double vision, sensing the alien character of the natural world while at the same time feeling a deep kinship with it. This is not a matter of observing, as some critics have done, that the dog story involves a human "allegory," a term implying that Buck is merely a human being disguised as a dog. Rather, the intuition at the heart of the novel is that the processes of individuation in a dog, a wolf, or a human child are not fundamentally different. Somehow, out of the dim memories of his own childhood, London recaptures the groping steps by which the very young deal with the mystifying sensations of their world, learning that snow is cold and fluffy, that fire burns, that some people are kind and others cruel. This is the "primordial vision" that Earle Labor [see excerpt dated 1974] has rightly insisted is a distinctive facet of London's imagination.

But *The Call of the Wild* is about society as well as about the wilderness—or rather, like *A Daughter of the Snows,* it is about the conflict between the two, a conflict that reaches its height in the final chapter, when Buck finds himself unable to choose between the civilizing influence of John Thornton and the increasingly insistent call of his primitive brothers. The conflict is resolved when Thornton dies and Buck leaves civilized life for good, but that departure is only the culmination of a movement toward the wild that has been taking place throughout the book. The movement is not steady; sometimes Buck will advance one step toward the wild only to be cast back again toward civilization. Still, the fundamental movement is clear, and it can be regarded from two seemingly opposite perspectives. Approached from the assumptions of Zola-esque naturalism it will seem atavistic—a reversion to savagery, a process of degeneration. On the other hand, from the standpoint of romantic primitivism, it will appear to embody the forward movement of an initiation rite, through which Buck attains maturity and even apotheosis as a mythic hero.

Both of these views accurately describe the action of the novel. Indeed, London himself reveals the same ambivalence when he says of Buck: "His development (or retrogression) was rapid." This "divided stream" of American naturalism was first recognized by Charles Child Walcutt [see excerpt dated 1956], who saw the materialistic thrust of the new naturalism at odds with the strains of transcendental idealism and romantic individualism that continued to exert a strong influence on American fiction. Frank Norris and Jack London offer particularly good examples of this uneasy combination. Norris, in fact, devoted several of his critical essays to promoting the idea that Zola and other naturalists, including himself, were actually romanticists. The result for all of these novelists is a fruitful tension between the naturalistic impulse, with its emphasis on society and environment, and the romantic impulse, which emphasizes the power of the exceptional individual to act on his own. Such a tension, as so many critics have observed, is one of the most fundamental themes of American fiction.

This indigenous American quality can be seen more clearly if one observes the structural parallels between *The Call of the Wild* and *Adventures of Huckleberry Finn.* As the two novels begin, each young protagonist lives in society under the protection of a benevolent foster parent. Each undertakes a journey away from that sheltered world, encountering in his travels several varieties of civilized virtue and folly. Intermittently, however, he feels the counterinfluence of the natural world and the anarchic impulse toward escape; and when each at the end is nearly adopted by another benevolent foster parent, he instead heeds the call of the wild and lights out for the Territory.

Despite manifest differences of tone and narrative method—*The Call,* for example, lacks the satirical, picaresque qualities of Twain's novel—these structural and thematic parallels suggests that both *Huckleberry Finn* and *The Call* are sustained at least in part by a common vision. What they share is the perennial American dream of escape and freedom associated with the natural world. As critics of *Huckleberry Finn* have repeatedly recognized, it is the river itself, and the life Huck and Jim lead there, that holds the strongest fascination for the reader. In this idyllic world, the stirrings of primitive life reassert themselves when the two fugitives, rejecting the dessicated piety of civilization, reinvent a natural mythology as they speculate about the origin of the stars, wondering "whether they was made, or only just happened." Jim suggests that "the moon could a *laid* them," and Huck allows that "that looked kind of reasonable . . . because I've seen a frog lay most as many, so of course it could be done." Just as Huck begins to reexperience the world mythopoetically, from the ground up and from the sky down, London's Buck must discover, in himself and in the wilderness, the primordial sensations that lead him to reject the conventions of civilized life. Hence it is no disparagement to say that both of these are "escape novels," for the impulse toward escape—toward the world of wish and dream—exists in all of us, and one of the functions of fiction is to fulfill it. There is, no doubt, a higher function that fiction can serve: to take us not merely away from our daily realities but into a reality we have not yet experienced or have experienced only imperfectly. The best "escape fiction"—including *Huckleberry Finn* and *The Call of the Wild*—serves that purpose, too.

During the long middle section of the novel, Buck is at the mercy of his owners, and the structure of episodes is governed chiefly by the contrast between two Klondike types, the hardened sourdough and the ignorant *chechaquo.* Francois and Perrault, with their rough but humane discipline and their hardy devotion to work, contrast sharply with the hapless incapables: the mindlessly vicious Hal and Charles, who club the dogs for failing to perform impossible tasks, and the self-indulgent, sentimental Mercedes, who protests the whipping of the "poor dears" even

while insisting that the bone-weary dogs pull her own weight on the already overloaded sled. This trio, in turn, contrasts sharply with Buck's final master, the kindly John Thornton.

But these episodes offer more than a gallery of Klondike types. They also serve to establish the civilized values against which the wilderness must compete, for human society in this novel is not an irredeemable disaster. Indeed, its most attractive virtues serve as a necessary counterweight to the ever more insistent call of the wild. Of central though qualified value is the pride of work, and even more deeply attractive is the value of love. For Buck, both love and work fulfill a profound need, though neither can finally compete with the deepest need of all—the one ecstatically fulfilled in the blood ritual of the hunt.

In his early years on Judge Miller's estate, though no "mere pampered house-dog," Buck resembles Vance Corliss of *A Daughter of the Snows,* living the easy life of a "sated aristocrat," developing his muscles not through work but through play. The abrupt transition to the Northland introduces him to the world of labor. "No lazy, sunkissed life was this," he finds, "with nothing to do but loaf and be bored." Instead he must perform the tasks that in the Southland were assigned to draft-horses. Yet once he has absorbed this blow to his dignity, he discovers that "though the work was hard . . . he did not particularly despise it." Gradually accommodating himself to the harness, he experiences the "nameless, incomprehensible pride of the trail and trace—that pride which holds dogs in the toil to the last gasp." As it does for Conrad's Marlow in "Heart of Darkness," work constitutes a source of order in the midst of primitive chaos.

Nevertheless, Buck's attitude toward work grows increasingly ambivalent. Part of the reason lies in the nature of the work itself, especially in the cautionary example of two other dogs of the team, Dave and Sol-leks, who seem the very incarnation of passionate devotion to toil. Otherwise uninspired and phlegmatic, they are "utterly transformed by the harness." The labor of the trail seemed "the supreme expression of their being." Under the inspiriting mastership of Francois and Perrault, such devotion seems admirable, almost heroic; but after the team passes into the hands of the "Scotch half-breed," the work gets harder, more routine, and less rewarding. Though Buck continues to take pride in it "after the manner of Dave and Sol-leks," he no longer enjoys it, for it is "a monotonous life, operating with machine-like regularity." The "pride of trail and trace" has become the drudgery of the work-beast—a fate dramatized when Dave wears down in the traces and must be shot. Thereafter the ineptitude of Hal, Charles, and Mercedes reduces what is left of the nobility of labor to meaningless, grinding, and ultimately fatal toil.

The decreasing attractions of the work itself are accentuated by the ever more alluring alternative of the wild. The conflict heightens when the team first reaches Dawson, where in the civilized daylight world it seems "the ordained order of things that dogs should work." But though by day these dogs haul cabin logs and firewood and freight, most of them are of the "wild wolf husky breed" in whose "nocturnal song, a weird and eerie chant," it is "Buck's delight to join." On the trail, as well, though the work is "a delight to him," it becomes "a greater delight slyly to precipitate a fight amongst his mates and tangle the traces." This act is more than a momentary imp of the perverse; there is method in it. What Buck seeks as an alternative to order and work is the deeper satisfaction of the irrational, the anarchic, and the demonic, symbolized by the hunt and the kill. Challenging the leadership of Spitz by plunging the team into disorder, he hopes to precipitate the climactic fight that will confirm his devotion to the primordial life.

The trail and the mining camp thus provide halfway stations between the extremes of civilization and savagery, calling forth the values of hardihood, discipline, and devotion. The other civilized value—the value of love—is also associated with contrasting landscapes. The loving-kindness that Buck experiences with Judge Miller and John Thornton is associated with the Southland, and with its central images: fire, sun, daylight, summer, and warmth. The antithesis of this world of love is, of course, the Northland wilderness, whose images are darkness, frost, moonlight, winter, and cold. London weaves these images into the texture of the novel, subtly establishing the natural rhythms of Buck's divided life.

Like work, love is a source of order—not the order of disciplined movement but that of the stability and security of an enclosed space. Its locale is not the trail but the fireside or the sunlit clearing. In the beginning, Buck basks securely on Judge Miller's estate in the "sun-kissed" Santa Clara Valley, and "on wintry nights he lay at the Judge's feet before the roaring library fire." The secluded domesticity of the house, "back from the road, half hidden among the trees," as well as the "rows of vine-clad servants' cottages, an endless and orderly array of outhouses, long grape arbors, green pastures, orchards, and berry patches," make the estate an oasis of pastoral serenity, just as the fire in the library suggests an island of civilization in the midst of a wintry darkness.

But though temporarily under the protection of a benevolent owner and the maternal warmth of the Southland, Buck will soon be abducted into a life of wandering orphanhood in the North. A measure of his loss, of his need for an enfolding maternal presence, arises during his first night on the trail when he searches for a warm place to sleep. Seeing the light and warm glow in the tent of Francois and Perrault, he seeks refuge there but is driven back violently into the cold, where, "miserable and disconsolate, he wandered about among the many tents, only to find that one place was as cold as another." At last he learns the trick of burrowing under the snow, discovering paradoxically that the only warmth lies there.

Afterwards, under the firm discipline of the two Frenchmen, his movement toward self-sufficiency is rapid. But the extraordinary kindness of John Thornton soon causes him to regress to the dependency and idealistic devotion of childhood and consequently to experience the foster-child's fear of abandonment: "For a long time after his rescue, Buck did not like Thornton to get out of his sight. From the moment he left the tent to when he entered it again, Buck would follow at his heels. His transient masters since he had come into the Northland had bred in him a fear that no master could be permanent. He was afraid that Thornton would pass out of his life as Perrault and Francois and the Scotch half-breed had passed out. Even in the night, in his dreams, he was haunted by this fear."

Yet this regression is temporary. By the time Thornton is killed, Buck has completed his rite of passage into adulthood, and his grief, though deep and genuine, is but the last of his civilized emotions, his farewell to his life as a son. Not even this deeply affectionate relationship can entirely heal the division in Buck's nature, for in spite of its "soft civilizing influence" on him, "the strain of the primitive . . . remained alive and active. Faithfulness and devotion, things born of fire and roof, were his; yet he retained his wildness and wiliness. He was a thing of the wild, come in from the wild to sit by John Thornton's fire, rather than a dog of the soft Southland stamped with the marks of generations of civilization."

Earlier, in camp on the long trail, Buck's ambivalence had been expressed in two fireside dreams. One is of the "Sunland" of his youth, but the other is of a different fire, beside which a hairy man squatted in fear and beyond which, "in the circling darkness, Buck could see many gleaming coals, two by two, always two by two, which he knew to be the eyes of great beasts of prey." The demonic fascination of those glowing eyes will at last become irresistible. Appealing to the inchoate emotions of the nocturnal world, they call forth a response like that evoked by the haunting, glittering landscape of the Northland wilderness:

> With the aurora borealis flaming coldly overhead, or the stars leaping in the frost dance, and the land numb and frozen under its pall of snow, this song of the huskies might have been the defiance of life. . . . When he moaned and sobbed, it was with the pain of living that was of old the pain of his wild fathers, and the fear and mystery of the cold and dark that was to them fear and mystery. And that he should be stirred by it marked the completeness with which he harked back through the ages of fire and roof to the raw beginnings of life in the howling ages.

At the center lies the fire of warmth and safety; beyond its perimeter are the cold fire of the northern lights, the white glitter of the stars, and the pall of snow. When Buck finally leaves John Thornton, feeling "compelled to turn his back upon the fire and the beaten earth around it," he will conclude a movement that has been underway from the beginning—a movement into the world of his "wild fathers."

Psychologically, this countermovement is a rejection of maternal security, which restricts even while it protects. Increasingly Buck seeks out those "wild fathers," who can be cast as opponents and whose potency is signaled by the brandished club, the flashing white fang, and the many-pronged antler. Against them Buck will test his strength and finally, in deadly combat, make their power and independence his own. In two clearly ritualistic acts—the defeat of Spitz and the killing of the old bull moose—Buck establishes first his supremacy over the half-civilized world of the dogteam, and second his right to lead the wolfpack in the wild as the fabled "Ghost Dog."

Into these rituals London weaves one further strand: the evocative Melvillean symbol of whiteness. This symbol, in fact, is a recurrent one in London's writing. It appears in the early story **"The White Silence,"** where the title signals "the ghostly wastes of a dead world," convincing man of his insignificance. It recurs in the eerie terror of the "white death" that Smoke Bellew and Labiskwee encounter during their flight through the mountains in **"Wonder of Woman"**—a "weird mist" with the "stinging thickness of cold fire." And finally, as the White Logic, it becomes the central image of *John Barleycorn,* where it implies the ultimate reality, the coldly terrifying truth to be found beyond all comforting illusions. In *The Call of the Wild,* it is not only the menace of the frozen landscape; it is also the personification of that landscape in a white beast, whom Buck must hunt, defeat, and displace—whom he must, in a sense, become.

Buck's first crucial rite of passage occurs in the stirring conflict with Spitz. As the lead dog doomed to be deposed by a younger, stronger rival, Spitz is the symbolic father, the incarnation of the demonic white wilderness of Buck's ancestors. Their climactic encounter, with its atmosphere of ghostly whiteness and its impression of ritualistic compulsions, seems an instinctive reenactment of an episode that has taken place since the beginnings of animal life. The fight is preceded and foreshadowed by a ritualistic hunt for a white rabbit, during which Buck and Spitz compete for the honor of the kill. In the "wan white moonlight" the rabbit flashes across the snow "like some pale frost wraith," while Buck, leading the pack and scenting the kill, anticipates the baptismal moment when he will "wash his muzzle to the eyes in warm blood." In this moment of anticipation comes the exaltation of mystical experience:

> There is an ecstasy that marks the summit of life, and beyond which life cannot rise. And such is the paradox of living, this ecstasy comes when one is most alive, and it comes as a complete forgetfulness that one is alive. This ecstasy, this forgetfulness of living, comes to the artist, caught up and out of himself in a sheet of flame; it comes to the soldier, war-mad on a stricken field and refusing quarter; and it came to Buck, leading the pack, sounding the old wolf-cry, straining after the food that was alive and that fled swiftly before him through the moonlight. He was sounding the deeps of his nature, and of the parts of his nature that were deeper than he, going back into the womb of Time. He was mastered by the sheer surging of life, the tidal wave of being, the perfect joy of each separate muscle, joint, and sinew in that it was everything that was not death, that it was aglow and rampant, expressing itself in movement, flying exultantly under the stars and over the face of dead matter that did not move.

Employing a familiar romantic conception of inspiration, London here brilliantly evokes those rare instants when the self is dissolved into a transcendent moment of union with the currents of life.

But at this moment of triumphant anticipation, with the "frost wraith of a rabbit still flitting before him, [Buck] saw another and larger frost wraith leap from the overhanging bank into the immediate path of the rabbit. It was Spitz." As Spitz's "white teeth broke its back in mid air," the dogs raised "a hell's chorus of delight" and the inevitable death-struggle was on. Buck "seemed to remember it all,—the white woods, and earth, and moonlight, and the thrill of battle. Over the whiteness and silence brooded a ghostly calm." As the dogs circle around the combatants, waiting for the kill, the aura of ritual intensifies. Near defeat, Spitz sees "the silent circle, with gleaming eyes, lolling tongues, and silvery breaths drifting upward, closing

in upon him as he had seen similar circles close in upon beaten antagonists in the past," until finally "the dark circle became a dot on the moon-flooded snow as Spitz disappeared from view."

As Maxwell Geismar has noted [see excerpt dated 1953], this whole scene resembles the rites of sacrifice and succession that J. G. Frazer found among primitive tribes and described in *The Golden Bough.* Even more important is Freud's argument, in *Totem and Taboo,* for a link between such social rituals and the Oedipal conflict. According to such theories, the ritual sacrifice reenacts the primal patricide, in which a son, cast out of the horde by his father, returns at the head of a band of brothers to kill the father and usurp his leadership. Though London may not have known about such theories from Frazer, and certainly not yet from Freud, his knowledge of Melville's *Moby-Dick* (1851) could have suggested to him a similar cluster of images and rituals centering on the demonic associations of whiteness.

Melville's narrative of the hunt for the fabled white whale must have been on London's mind during the writing of *The Call of the Wild,* as it certainly was a few months later when he wrote *The Sea-Wolf.* He may have recalled, for example, the scene in "The Quarter-Deck" when Captain Ahab and his harpooners swear a diabolic oath to hunt Moby Dick to his death. As the rest of the crew "formed a circle round the group," their "wild eyes met his, as the bloodshot eyes of the prairie wolves meet the eye of their leader, ere he rushes on at their head in the trail of the bison." Just as Melville based his romance in part on a legendary sperm whale, London may have known of a "ghost dog" story then current in Alaskan folklore. Without question, he knew Melville's chapter "The Whiteness of the Whale," in which several images of demonic whiteness are drawn from landscapes of snow. Conjuring up the "eternal frosted desolateness" of snowcapped mountains, Ishmael imagines "what a fearfulness it would be to lose oneself in such inhuman solitudes." Later, he associates the "dumb blankness, full of meaning, in a wide landscape of snows" with the "colorless, all-color of atheism from which we shrink." These images, which Earle Labor has compared to London's description of the ominous landscape in **"The White Silence,"** are equally pertinent to *The Call of the Wild,* in which the hunt for the white rabbit is climaxed by the death-struggle with the white dog.

London would have been especially alert to Melville's instances of fabulous white beasts of the American wilderness, whose qualities anticipate those of Spitz and, later, of Buck himself. Most notable is Melville's observation that "to the noble Iroquois, the midwinter sacrifice of the sacred White Dog was by far the holiest festival of their theology, that spotless, faithful creature being held the purest envoy they could send to the Great Spirit with the annual tidings of their own fidelity." It is precisely such a ritual sacrifice of the totem animal that Freud saw as a symbolic reenactment of the primal crime of patricide, which is so strongly implied in Buck's killing of Spitz.

The final phase of the initiation into the white wilderness occurs when Buck accompanies Thornton in the search for the "fabled lost mine" of the East. The journey is explicitly a "quest," the mine "steeped in tragedy and shrouded in mystery." As they penetrate the "uncharted vastness" of the wilderness, they come to a land that London evokes with a haunting lyricism:

> They went across divides in summer blizzards, shivered under the midnight sun on naked mountains between the timber line and the eternal snows, dropped into summer valleys amid swarming gnats and flies, and in the shadow of glaciers picked strawberries and flowers as ripe and fair as any the Southland could boast. In the fall of the year they penetrated a weird lake country, sad and silent, where wild-fowl had been, but where then there was no life nor sign of life—only the blowing of chill winds, the forming of ice in sheltered places, and the melancholy rippling of waves on lonely beaches.

In such a land, the gold hunt itself takes on an aura of the fabulous. The questors find themselves on a path that "began nowhere and ended nowhere, and it remained mystery." When at last they find gold-diggings of unimagined richness, they toil "like giants" and their days are "like dreams." Yet the men's quest for riches ends, after all, like any merely mundane quest—in death. Just as in *Moby-Dick* the great shroud of the sea covers over the defeated questors, the gold is reclaimed by the wilderness, where, as the years pass, "a yellow stream flows from rotted moose-hide sacks and sinks into the ground, with long grasses growing through it and vegetable mould overrunning it and hiding its yellow from the sun."

But while the men are defeated, Buck succeeds, for he is summoned by a call not to wealth but to mature selfhood and triumphant life. Despite his love for Thornton, he is filled with a "great unrest and strange desires" as a preternatural sixth sense responds to the ever more insistent call of the "mysterious something" lurking beyond the circle of the fire. Discovering his brotherhood with the wolf and drawn increasingly into wild company, he engages in a final initiation ordeal, the stalking and killing of the old bull moose, whose gigantic fourteen-prong antlers advertise his sexual dominance over his herd of cows and his readiness to resist all challenges to his authority. With the coming of winter, "the young bulls retraced their steps more and more reluctantly to the aid of their beset leader." Finally, at twilight "the old bull stood with lowered head, watching his mates—the cows he had known, the calves he had fathered, the bulls he had mastered. . . . He could not follow, for before his nose leaped the merciless fanged terror that would not let him go." Here the challenge to the horde, and its basis in sexual rivalry, is even clearer than in Buck's fight with Spitz. Buck is the figurative son, whose defeat of the bull moose prepares him to assume his place not in the mooseherd but in the wolfpack. His assumption of that place, in the dead of winter, completes his initiation into the demonic white wilderness of his ancestors.

The word "demonic" deserves stress, for Buck's selfless exploits with John Thornton may serve to obscure some infernal undercurrents. Almost from the beginning, Buck has been something of a demon. His imprisonment in the crate transforms him into a "raging fiend." As he clashes with the man in the red sweater, he is "truly a red-eyed devil," while to Francois his demonism is multiplied to that of "two devils." In the final chapter, as he leaves the civilizing influence of the camp, he undergoes a "terrible transformation," becoming a "thing of the wild" who can steal along softly, "cat-footed," or "crawl on his belly like a snake." Avenging the murder of Thornton, Buck ravages the Yeehats with such ferocity that he seems to them the "Fiend incarnate," and as he prepares to lead the wolf-pack, the atmosphere of ghostly, demonic whiteness resembles the haunting landscape in which he first triumphed over Spitz. With the coming of night, "a full moon rose high over the trees into the sky, lighting the land till it lay bathed in ghostly day." Soon into the moonlit clearing the wolves "poured in a silvery flood," challenging Buck, one by one, until each is defeated. At length they draw back, their "white fangs showing cruelly white in the moonlight," until an "old wolf, gaunt and battle-scarred," comes forward to howl the pack's admission of defeat.

There remains only for Buck to pass into Indian legend as the "Ghost Dog that runs at the head of the pack." If London remembered a Northland legend of a ghost dog, he may also have recalled Melville's description of the White Steed of the Prairies, "with the dignity of a thousand monarchs in his lofty, overscorning carriage":

> He was the elected Xerxes of vast herds of wild horses, whose pastures in those days were only fenced by the Rocky Mountains and the Alleghenies. . . . A most imperial and archangelical apparition of that unfallen, western world, which to the eyes of the old trappers and hunters revived the glories of those primeval times when Adam walked majestic as a god, bluff-bowed and fearless as this mighty steed. . . . always to the bravest Indians he was the object of trembling reverence and awe. Nor can it be questioned from what stands on legendary record of this noble horse, that it was his spiritual whiteness chiefly, which so clothed him with divineness; and that this divineness had that in it which, though commanding worship, at the same time enforced a certain nameless terror.

In his combination of divinity and demonism, his "spiritual whiteness" evoking both "reverence" and "terror," the White Steed becomes the incarnation of the primeval wilderness precisely as Buck becomes to the Indians both a sign of the "Evil Spirit" and yet, as the Ghost Dog, the object of a kind of spiritual awe. His ascendancy as father and leader is signaled by the "change in the breed of timber wolves," some now being seen with a "rift of white centring down the chest." As the great white whale triumphantly swims away from the sinking *Pequod,* so does Buck elude the desperate Yeehats, "running at the head of the pack through the pale moonlight or glimmering borealis, leaping gigantic above his fellows." His apotheosis as the Ghost Dog of the North is complete. (pp. 38-52)

> *Charles N. Watson, Jr., "Ghost Dog: 'The Call of the Wild'," in his* The Novels of Jack London: A Reappraisal, *The University of Wisconsin Press, 1983, pp. 33-52.*

Richard Fusco   (essay date 1987)

[*In the following excerpt, Fusco contends that Buck's acceptance into the wolf pack is a social advancement rather than a regression into the primitive.*]

Jack London's *The Call of the Wild* traces one animal's

gradual reversion to its primordial instincts. During the course of the novel the dog Buck experiences a gamut of life styles from civilization to apparent primitiveness. If a reader analyzes the story only superficially, he could erroneously conclude that London's protagonist does indeed surrender totally to ancient urges, which the author identifies as "the call of the wild." Buck's metamorphosis is not as complete as a cursory reading might lead one to believe, however. Buck still retains vestiges of social advancement in his eventual leadership of the wolf pack. In preparing for the wild, the dog undergoes a socialization process of three stages, each represented by Buck's dealings with a differing sort of family. His fourth and final, ideal family resembles the compromise between civilization and primitive man Rousseau described for the idealized political state. Thus, London's concept of a propitious universe is not nature operating in chaos, but instinct tempered somewhat by learning.

Curiously, this misinterpretation of *The Call of the Wild* resembles in form a misconception critics often harbor about Rousseau's ideal society. Arthur O. Lovejoy identifies this problem as "[t]he notion that Rousseau's *Discourse on Inequality* was essentially a glorification of the state of nature, and that its influence tended wholly or chiefly to promote 'primitivism,' is one of the most persistent of historical errors." Lovejoy describes Rousseau's four phases of man's development as (1) a primitive, animalistic stage, (2) a transitory stage, (3) a family-scale social unit stage, and (4) modern civilization. Rousseau did reject the artificiality of contemporary society, but he did not suggest that men revert to the first stage of their development. Lovejoy points out:

> Rousseau could not bring himself to accept either extreme as his ideal; the obvious way out, therefore, was to regard the mean between these extremes as the best state possible. In the third stage, men were less good-natured and less placid than in the state of nature, but also were less stupid and less unsocial; they were less intelligent and had less power over nature than civilized man, but were also less malicious and less unhappy. In thus regarding the state of savagery, which some have called the "state of nature," not as a kind of natural perfection, an absolute norm, but as a mixed condition, intermediate between two extremes equally undesirable, Rousseau once more differed profoundly from his primitivistic predecessors.

Consequently, Rousseau saw small clans as the best of all possible political and social structures, permitting the healthiest compromise between reason and instinct.

Although no biographical evidence exists that Rousseau's writings directly influenced *The Call of the Wild,* London apparently employed a similar philosophic system in constructing his novel. *The Call of the Wild* does trace one character's eventual rejection of the artificialities of modern society in favor of a clan-type existence. Buck's associations with four families symbolize the phases of his regression to the wild. First, for four years Buck lived on Judge Miller's "sun-kissed Santa Clara Valley" ranch. London presents Buck as a fully integrated member of Miller's family and, hence, of civilization. Despite Buck's avoidance of "becoming a mere pampered house-dog," his life is carefree—especially when compared to the harsher fate that awaits him. His relations with other "family members"—both men and animals—arouse Buck's impulse to dominate those around him, but his power has no foundation. His chief flaw lies in his innocence: he knows nothing of mankind's treachery. Consequently, a gardener's helper easily steals and sells the dog because of the latter's naive trust of all men. Buck's early life in California contains another, more glaring superficiality, though—the absence of love:

> This [love] he had never experienced at Judge Miller's down in the sun-kissed Santa Clara Valley. With the Judge's sons, hunting and tramping, it had been a working partnership; with the Judge's grandsons, a sort of pompous guardianship; and with the Judge himself a stately and dignified friendship.

In sum, the civilization that Miller's ranch represents has underdeveloped Buck's potential—both emotional and otherwise.

On one hand, Buck's second family, the dog sled team, places the dog in a world apparently stripped of civilization's veneer. After weathering the shock of his transition to a bleak and brutal existence, Buck attempts to dominate his new world and does succeed in establishing his authority over the team. On the other hand, the order and purpose of his new family bear the artificial imprint of civilization, represented by the men who drive the sled. The team exists not for its own benefit but to transport men and mail. Consequently, the team must suffer the whims of its human masters. When a backlog of Yukon mail must be delivered, Buck's tired family must transport it. Later, three greenhorn miners buy the team and set out upon a foolhardy journey. The family must follow its owners through exhaustion and to death. Only providence and John Thornton save Buck. Although Buck's primordial instincts begin to awaken while with the team, he also learns much on a conscious level, particularly about the dynamics within family relationships. He uses this knowledge to assert authority not only over the dog team but also later over the wolf pack, his final family.

Buck's third family consists of John Thornton, his partners, and his dogs, which represent a further phase of Buck's advancement toward the wild. In many ways Buck's life with Thornton resembles his life with Miller. It differs, though, in that love rather than "stately and dignified friendship" bonds the dog and the miner. Thornton's family is still not ideal, however, because Buck remains subject to man's caprices. For example, to see how far Buck will go in obeying him, Thornton orders the dog to leap over a steep cliff. Only by tackling Buck does the miner prevent the dog from doing so. Later, Buck must pull a sled loaded with a thousand pounds of flour because a rival miner had maneuvered Thornton into a foolish bet. For the most part, though, the good-natured Thornton forbears asking Buck to do anything with a superficial motive behind it. In fact, except for two life-threatening events, the miner requires little of Buck's services. He allows the dog the freedom to roam the wilderness alone, during which time Buck perfects his survival skills. Through these solitary hunting trips Buck realizes that he can live without man. His only remaining link with civilization lies in his love for Thornton. Consequently, Thornton's death at the hands of the Yeehats releases the dog from all obligations.

Buck does not remain alone: he joins a fourth family—a wolf pack, signifying his rejection of the total primitiveness of an anarchic wilderness. Eventually, based upon the principles of love and survival he learned as a member of his three former families, he assumes the leadership of the pack. Under Buck's direction the pack exhibits behavioral characteristics beyond those governed by instinct. For example, in killing the Indians who murdered Thornton, Buck conquers his fear of man:

> He had killed man, the noblest game of all, and he had killed in the face of the law of club and fang. He sniffed the bodies curiously. They had died so easily. It was harder to kill a husky dog than them. They were no match at all, were it not for their arrows and spears and clubs. Thenceforward he would be unafraid of them except when they bore in their hands their arrows, spears, and clubs.

The dog brings this knowledge to his new family, and, in consequence, the pack becomes more prone to attack stray Yeehat hunters than ever before. The wolf pack becomes so fierce that the Indians ascribe supernatural traits to it. Every autumn during moose season hunters refuse to enter the "certain valley" where Buck, the "Ghost Dog," rules.

In sum, Buck's ideal family permits his instincts freer bent, but, as Rousseau recommends, the dog does not surrender totally to primordial urges. Considered within the framework of London's socialistic beliefs, communal ties do enrich the individual if they are not carried to the extremes of modern civilization. Thus, the dog's new-found world seems primitive to the reader only in that it is stripped of all civilized pretense. (pp. 76-9)

> *Richard Fusco, "On Primitivism in 'The Call of the Wild'," in* American Literary Realism 1870-1910, *Vol. 20, No. 1, Fall, 1987, pp. 76-80.*

FURTHER READING

Allen, Mary. "The Wisdom of the Dogs: Jack London." In her *Animals in American Literature,* pp. 77-96. Urbana: University of Illinois Press, 1983.

Discusses *The Call of the Wild* in the context of London's Klondike stories, examining the Darwinist and naturalistic theories therein.

Clayton, Lawrence. "The Ghost Dog, A Motif in *The Call of the Wild." Jack London Newsletter* 5, No. 3 (September-December 1972): 158.

Uncovers a relation between an obscure Eskimo folk myth and the motif of the "Ghost Dog" in the conclusion of *The Call of the Wild.*

Flink, Andrew. "*Call of the Wild*—Parental Metaphor." *Jack London Newsletter* 7, No. 2 (May-August 1974): 58-61.

Examines the similarities between London's father and the character John Thornton in *The Call of the Wild.*

Frey, Charles. "Contradiction in *The Call of the Wild." Jack London Newsletter* 12, Nos. 1-3 (1979): 35-7.

Calls attention to "the contradiction in Buck (and, perhaps, in Jack London as well) between life as a woeful 'puppet thing' and life as 'ecstasy.'"

Hedrick, Joan D. *"The Call of the Wild."* In her *Solitary Comrade: Jack London and his Work,* pp. 94-111. Chapel Hill: The University of North Carolina Press, 1982.

Critical plot summary.

Lundquist, James. "Meditations on Man and Beast." In his *Jack London: Adventures, Ideas, and Fiction,* pp. 77-113. New York: Ungar, 1987.

Praises the realism in London's characterization of Buck.

Perry, John. "The Dominant Primordial Beast." In his *Jack London: An American Myth,* pp. 127-46. Chicago: Nelson-Hall, 1981.

Surveys the critical history of *The Call of the Wild* and offers a comparative study of London's use of dogs and wolves in his fiction.

Reed, A. Paul. "Running with the Pack: Jack London's *The Call of the Wild* and Jesse Stuart's *Mongrel Mettle." Jack London Newsletter* 18, No. 3 (September-December 1985): 96-8.

Compares characterization and technique in *The Call of the Wild* with Jesse Stuart's novel *Mongrel Mettle,* concluding that in both stories "the irony and symbolism of a dog's point of view sheds a truly original and interesting light upon the human drama."

Solensten, John. "Richard Harding Davis' Rejection of *The Call of the Wild." Jack London Newsletter* 4, No. 2 (May-August 1971): 122-23.

Suggests that Davis's novel *The Nature Faker* is a humorous attack on London's espousal of Darwinism in *The Call of the Wild.*

Upton, Ann. "The Wolf in London's Mirror." *Jack London Newsletter* 6, No. 3 (September-December 1973): 111-18.

Examines London's identification with and liberal use of wolves as characters in his fiction.

Katherine Mansfield

1888-1923

(Born Kathleen Mansfield Beauchamp; also wrote under the pseudonym Boris Petrovsky) New Zealand short story writer, critic, and poet. For further discussion of Mansfield's career, see *TCLC*, Volumes 2 and 8.

Mansfield is a central figure in the development of the modern short story. An early practitioner of stream-of-consciousness narration, she applied this technique to create stories based on the illumination of character rather than the contrivances of plot. Her works treat such universal concerns as family and love relationships and the everyday experiences of childhood, and are noted for their distinctive wit, psychological acuity, and perceptive characterizations.

Mansfield was born into a prosperous family in Wellington, New Zealand, and attended school in England in her early teens. She returned home after completing her education, but was thereafter dissatisfied with colonial life, and at nineteen she persuaded her parents to allow her to return to England. Biographers believe that Mansfield either arrived in London pregnant as the result of a shipboard romance, or that she became pregnant after her arrival as the result of an affair with a man she had known in New Zealand. She entered into a hasty marriage with George Bowden, a young musician, and left him the next day after which her mother arranged for her removal to a German spa, where she miscarried. Mansfield returned to England after a period of recuperation, during which she wrote the short stories comprising her first collection, *In a German Pension*. Offering satiric commentary on the attitudes and behavior of the German people, these stories focus on themes relating to sexual relationships, female subjugation, and childbearing. Critics have found that these stories, although less technically accomplished than Mansfield's later fiction, evince her characteristic wit and perception—in particular her incisive grasp of female psychology—as well as her early experimentation with interior monologue. Determined to pursue a literary career, between 1911 and 1915 Mansfield published short stories and book reviews in such magazines as the *Athenaeum*, the *Blue Review*, the *New Age*, the *Open Window*, and *Rhythm*. In 1912 she met editor and critic John Middleton Murry and was soon sharing the editorship of the *Blue Review* and *Rhythm* with him. The two began living together, and married in 1918, when Bowden finally consented to a divorce.

In 1915 Mansfield was reunited in London with her only brother, Leslie Heron Beauchamp, shortly before he was killed in a military training accident, and Beauchamp's visit is believed to have reinforced Mansfield's resolve to incorporate material drawn from her New Zealand background into her fiction. The collections *Bliss, and Other Stories,* and *The Garden Party, and Other Stories*—the last that Mansfield edited and oversaw in production—contain many of the New Zealand stories, including "Prelude," "At the Bay," "The Garden Party," "The Voyage," and "A Doll's House," as well as other examples of her mature

fiction. The success of these volumes established Mansfield as a major talent comparable to such contemporaries as Virginia Woolf and James Joyce. Never in vigorous health, Mansfield was severely weakened by tuberculosis in the early 1920s. Nonetheless, she worked almost continuously, writing until the last few months of her life, when she undertook a faith cure at a "psychical institute" in France. She died in 1923 at the age of thirty-four.

Early assessments of Mansfield were based largely on the romanticized image presented by Murry in extensively edited volumes of her private papers, as well as in reminiscences and critical commentary that he published after her death. His disposition of her literary estate is considered by some commentators to have been exploitative: he profited from the publication of stories that Mansfield had rejected for publication, as well as notebook jottings, intermittent diaries, and letters. The idealized representation of Mansfield promulgated by Murry, termed the "cult of Katherine," is undergoing revision by modern biographers aided by new editions of her letters and journals.

Mansfield's best and most characteristic work is generally considered to be contained in *Bliss, and Other Stories* and *The Garden Party, and Other Stories*. These volumes collect many of Mansfield's highly regarded New Zealand stories as well as the widely reprinted and often discussed "Bliss," "The Daughters of the Late Colonel," "Je Ne Parle Pas Français," and "Miss Brill," which are considered among the finest short stories in the English language. These stories display some of Mansfield's most successful innovations with narrative technique, including interior monologue, stream of consciousness, and shifting narrative perspectives. They are commended for the facility with which Mansfield represented intricate balances within family relationships, her depictions of love relationships from both female and male points of view, and her portrayals of children, which are considered especially insightful. Mansfield is one of the few authors to attain prominence exclusively for short stories, and her works remain among the most widely read in world literature.

(See also *Contemporary Authors*, Vol. 104.)

PRINCIPAL WORKS

In a German Pension (short stories) 1911
Prelude (short story) 1918
Bliss, and Other Stories (short stories) 1920
The Garden Party, and Other Stories (short stories) 1922
The Doves' Nest, and Other Stories (short stories) 1923
Poems (poetry) 1923
The Little Girl, and Other Stories (short stories) 1924;
    also published as *Something Childish, and Other Stories*, 1924
Journal of Katherine Mansfield (journal) 1927
The Letters of Katherine Mansfield. 2 vols. (letters) 1928
The Aloe (short story) 1930
Novels and Novelists (criticism) 1930
The Short Stories of Katherine Mansfield (short stories) 1937
The Scrapbook of Katherine Mansfield (journal) 1939
Katherine Mansfield's Letters to John Middleton Murry: 1913-1922 (letters) 1951
The Urewera Notebook (journal) 1978
The Collected Letters of Katherine Mansfield. 2 vols. (letters) 1984-87
The Critical Writings of Katherine Mansfield (criticism) 1987
Letters between Katherine Mansfield and John Middleton Murry (letters) 1988
Poems of Katherine Mansfield (poetry) 1988

Andrew Gurr and Clare Hanson   (essay date 1981)

[*In the following excerpt, the critics consider the diversity demonstrated in Mansfield's fiction and comment on some principal characteristics, including Mansfield's status as a New Zealand expatriate, her use of the modern, plotless short story form, and the influence of Symbolism on her work.*]

As a writer Katherine Mansfield produced no single magnum opus. Consequently there is no obvious focus for assessing her achievement or even for identifying her distinctive qualities. Readers who follow Leonard Woolf's

preferences will take *In a German Pension* as her most characteristic achievement, and rank the other stories accordingly ['Her gifts were those of an intense realist, with a superb sense of ironic humour and fundamental cynicism. She got enmeshed in the sticky sentimentality of Murry and wrote against the grain of her own nature,' Leonard Woolf, in his *Beginning Again: An Autobiography of the Years 1911-18*, 1964]. The childhood stories will seem stickily sentimental, products of a maudlin escapism. Readers who find her social analysis, particularly of the oppressed position of women, to be her most conspicuously acute and illuminating feature will similarly range the stories according to a preference for which there is a good deal of supporting evidence but which still provides only a limited perspective on the whole achievement. And the view which takes the New Zealand stories, especially '**Prelude**' and the other stories written for the *Karori* collection, as most characteristic will also be limited in so far as it draws attention away from the distinctive qualities of the stories set in Bavaria or London or France. It is difficult to find a central organising principle for assessing her achievement that does not lead to neglect of some aspect of her work. She shines out through too many lantern-faces for any single perspective to give an adequate view. The best we can do is identify the different perspectives, and which face they lead up to. Of them all, probably the broadest is the one relating her exile to the powerful evocation of New Zealand in the major stories of her last years.

The last seven years of her life, the years of her mature achievements from '**Prelude**' onwards, were years of retreat into art isolation made perfect only inside the private circle of the childhood world that she constructed with such meticulous precision. She continued to use Murry and Ida Baker for physical protection, but in her stories she went where neither could hope to follow. She had written work based on her relationship with Murry—'**Je Ne Parle Pas Français**', '**The Man without a Temperament**', '**Psychology**'—but all of them were in some degree part of the dialogue which they maintained throughout their lives together. As such they perhaps lack the complete detachment and freedom, which writing out of more distant recollections provided.

Rather more than half the stories in her total *oeuvre* are based on or set in New Zealand. Murry's version of her outlook—that she hated the closed-off complacency of bourgeois suburban New Zealand until Leslie's death, when, as she put it, 'quite suddenly her hatred turned to love'—is a thorough oversimplification. She was trying out a narrative by 'Kass' about two little 'Beetham' girls early in 1910 ('**Mary**', published in the *Idler*, March 1910. 'Kass' also appears in '**The Little Girl**' of 1912). '**A Birthday**', set amongst the Bavarian stories of *In a German Pension*, has a New Zealand setting. The story which first drew Murry's attention, '**The Woman at the Store**', written towards the end of 1911, was based on her memory of the camping holiday she underwent (over 240 miles on horseback) in the Ureweras shortly before she finally left New Zealand in 1908. And two stories written in 1915 before she began '**The Aloe**' have distinct affinities with the later New Zealand material. '**The Apple Tree**', first published in the *Signature* in October 1915 under the title '**Autumn I**', is a gently derisive anecdote about her father, told from the viewpoint of his children, girl and boy. '**The**

Wind Blows', published as 'Autumn II' in the *Signature,* is a more oblique piece about brother and sister, poignant, discontinuous, foreshadowing the symbolist technique which evolved as 'The Aloe' changed in the following years to 'Prelude'. Both stories were presumably triggered by the reminiscences of their childhood that she was sharing with Leslie at the time. His death, which took place just before the two stories appeared, changed the tentative, exploratory impulse into a powerful compulsion. From then on she drove towards the ultimate goal of a complete evocation of Karori in a series of minutely detailed epiphanies.

'Prelude' showed her that her New Zealand background was the best quarry for her artistic materials. It contained so much of the experience which, up to that time, she had most deeply lived. Only such experience could be the proper food for her art. This realisation is recorded in a famous journal entry of 1916:

> I feel no longer concerned with the same appearance of things. The people who lived or whom I wished to bring into my stories don't interest me any more. The plots of my stories leave me perfectly cold. Granted that these people exist and all the differences, complexities and resolutions are true to them—why should *I* write about them? They are not near me. All the false threats that bound me to them are cut away quite.
>
> Now—now I want to write recollections of my own country. Yes, I want to write about my own country till I simply exhaust my store . . .
>
> Ah, the people—the people we loved there—of them, too, I want to write. Another 'debt of love'. Oh, I want for one moment to make our undiscovered country leap into the eyes of the Old World. It must be mysterious, as though floating. It must take the breath. It must be 'one of those islands . . .'

From this point on, when she began to see her New Zealand background as an artistic positive, something which would both nourish her as an artist and enable her to express something wholly individual, she gained enormously in confidence as a writer.

There is no doubt that she worked at her highest creative level on material that was removed from her in space and time. This is because she was a Symbolist writer, interested not in social contexts and realities, but in the imaginative discovery or recreation of the ideal hidden within the real. With the aid of distance in time and space it is the idealising imagination, or perhaps more precisely what Pater [in 'The Child in the House,' in his *Miscellaneous Studies,* 1910] would call 'the finer sort of memory', which can best discover the ideal essence of experience, which is obscured in the confusion of immediate impressions and perceptions.

Katherine Mansfield and Rudyard Kipling are among the very few writers in English to establish a reputation entirely on the basis of the short story form. It is no accident that they were writing at approximately the same time. The development of the short story in England lagged behind that in America and Russia chiefly because of differences in opportunities for magazine publication. By the 1890s, however, a huge expansion in the numbers of quarterlies and weeklies created the situation described by

H. G. Wells [in his introduction to his *The Country of the Blind, and Other Stories,* 1911]:

> The 'nineties was a good and stimulating period for a short story writer . . . No short story of the slightest distinction went for long unrecognised . . . Short stories broke out everywhere.

Two entirely different types of story flourished together at the close of the nineteenth century. First, there was the story with a definite plot, which was the lineal descendant of the Gothic tale; and second, there was the new, 'plotless' story, concentrating on inner mood and impression rather than on external event. The latter was associated especially with the *Yellow Book,* the famous 'little magazine' of the nineties, and with the circle of writers gathered round its publisher John Lane—George Egerton, Ella D'Arcy, Evelyn Sharp and others. The innovatory quality of many of the stories published by these writers, and the contribution that they made to the development of the short story, is now becoming increasingly evident.

The plotless story seems to arise naturally from the intellectual climate of its time. In a world where, as the German philosopher Nietzsche declared, God was dead, and evolutionary theory had produced a sharp sense of man's insignificance in a changing universe, the only alternative seemed to be the retreat within, to the compensating powers of the imagination. With such a retreat came the stress on the significant moment, which would be called 'vision' or 'epiphany' by later writers such as James Joyce—the moment of insight which is outside space and time, vouchsafed only fleetingly to the imagination, but redeeming man's existence in time.

In fiction a shift in time-scale seems to accompany this emphasis on the moment. Throughout the nineteenth century the unit of fiction had been the year—from *Emma* to *The Ambassadors* we can say that this was so. In the late nineteenth and early twentieth century, the unit of fiction became the day. Elizabeth Bowen has written of this, saying that Katherine Mansfield was the first writer to see in the short story 'the ideal reflector of the day'. It is perhaps significant, however, that many other writers began their careers with short story writing in this period—Forster, for example, with the aptly named *The Eternal Moment,* and also D. H. Lawrence, James Joyce, and Virginia Woolf. It can even be suggested that the novels of these writers—Lawrence excepted—are in a sense simply extended short stories. Virginia Woolf's *Mrs Dalloway* is an obvious example, but there is also Joyce's *Ulysses,* originally projected as a story for his collection of stories called *Dubliners,* to be titled 'Mr Hunter's Day'. It is as though the short story is the paradigmatic form of the early twentieth century, best able to express its fragmented and fragmentary sensibility.

Katherine Mansfield certainly saw her kind of story as a quintessentially modern form, a point she makes more than once in her reviews of fiction for the *Athenaeum.* She was also very conscious in her use of epiphany as the focal point of her stories. In one of her reviews she discusses the way in which internal crisis has replaced external crisis of plot in modern fiction, at the same time warning against the loss of all sense of crisis or significance which she detected in the work of some modern novelists:

Without [the sense of crisis] how are we to appreciate the importance of one 'spiritual event' rather than another? What is to prevent each being unrelated—complete in itself—if the gradual unfolding in growing, gaining light is not to be followed by one blazing moment?

It is usual in discussing Katherine Mansfield as a story writer to emphasise the influence of Chekhov on her technique. The relationship between her fiction and the plotless story of the nineties, however, is probably more important. She modelled her early stories on those of the *Yellow Book* writers, and it is from them, not Chekhov, that she would have learnt the techniques of stylised interior monologue, flashback and daydream which became so important in her work. By 1909, which was when she probably first read Chekhov, his techniques must have seemed distinctly old-fashioned by comparison with much English fiction.

Chekhov was probably more interesting to her as a type of the artist, especially after she contracted the tuberculosis from which he also suffered, rather than being a specific influence on her work. The two writers differ fundamentally in that Chekhov is a far more realistic writer than Katherine Mansfield. His characters are always rooted firmly in a social context, and social forces are shown to have a decisive influence on the course of their lives and feelings. The difference is best shown by a comparison of his story 'Sleepy' with Katherine Mansfield's version of it, **'The-Child-Who-Was-Tired'** (1909). Chekhov's story is a restrained, pathological study, in which action is convincingly related to a specific social and psychological context. Katherine Mansfield's story is a symbolic fable, in which certain elements of the original plot are exaggerated and key images repeated in order to express a general, rather than a specific truth: the harshness of woman's lot in life. Although she read and admired Chekhov's stories throughout her career, a limit must be set on any comparison between the two writers. Any easy identification of the two is misleading.

Katherine Mansfield's talents were peculiarly suited to the short story form, as, in a different way, were those of Kipling. She did, however, try on at least three occasions to write a novel. There is the early attempt, *Juliet* (1906); then a novel to be based on the life and experiences of a schoolfriend she had known both in London and New Zealand, *Maata* (written intermittently between 1908 and 1915); finally the novel, *Karori,* which was to be built around the **'Prelude'** and **'At the Bay'** material, and to be based on the Burnell family. She was planning this last novel as late as 1921-22. Speculation about what she might or might not have written is futile, but clearly she continually wanted to experiment with new forms and to widen the boundaries of her talent. Another way of getting out of the critical rut of seeing her solely as a master of the concentrated short story is to recognise the clear development in her later work towards the use of the story cycle form. Two distinct cycles emerge: that centering on the Burnell family (**'Prelude'**—**'At the Bay'**—**'The Doll's House'**) and that centering on the Sheridans (**'The Garden Party'**—**'Her First Ball'**—**'By Moonlight'**—**'The Sheridans'**). Although they are all New Zealand stories, the two cycles are quite separate, and are clearly associated in Katherine Mansfield's mind with different themes. Broadly speaking, the Burnell sequence is concerned with the difficulties of the child or young adult coming to terms with the brutal realities of life (the egotism and cruelty of other people, the pressures of sexuality and so on), whereas in the Sheridan sequence there is a much more elegiac note: the theme is, as Katherine once wrote of Hardy's poems,

that love and regret touched so lightly—that autumn tone, that feeling that 'Beauty passes though rare, rare it be . . . '

The fact that the two sequences were quite distinct is clear from a journal note written as Katherine Mansfield was planning **'The Sheridans'**:

I must begin writing for Clement Shorter today [this refers to a contract she had with the *Sphere*] 12 'spasms' of 2,000 words each. I thought of the Burnells, but no, I don't think so. Much better, the Sheridans, the three girls and the brother and the Father and Mother and so on . . .

And in that playing chapter what I want to stress chiefly is: Which is the real life—that or this?—late afternoon—these thoughts—the garden—the beauty—how all things pass—and how the end seems to come so soon.

The stories in the Sheridan and Burnell cycles are linked together by character, setting and theme, and by repeated images and motifs. A 'dynamic pattern of recurrent development' is established, so that the reader's experience of an individual story is enriched by and enriches his experience of the others in that sequence.

Katherine Mansfield did not herself separate the short story and novel form as absolutely as genre-conscious modern critics have done, and the cycle of related stories may be seen as a kind of bridge for her between the two forms—rather as in William Faulkner's *Go Down Moses,* or, more relevantly, in Joyce's *Dubliners,* a sequence of stories linked together loosely but firmly by a common setting, related characters and related themes. Joyce similarly employs the symbolist technique of imagery repeated throughout the stories.

The relationship between Symbolism and Katherine Mansfield's short story art has been insufficiently recognised. It is accepted that her contemporary, Joyce, was influenced decisively by his early contact with Symbolist literature, but Katherine Mansfield's critics and biographers have failed to register the similar influences at work in her case. They have dismissed her early writing in the Symbolist mode as immature and, by implication, irrelevant, not seeing the intimate connection between this early work and the particular nature and scope of her achievement.

The main influence on her in the period up to 1908 when she left New Zealand for the last time was that of Arthur Symons, who also influenced so many other early twentieth-century writers, notably Yeats and Eliot. Symons's role was as a communicator and purveyor of ideas. It was through his critical books that Katherine Mansfield was introduced to French Symbolist poetry and to other diverse, broadly Symbolist writers like the Belgian Maurice Maeterlinck and the Italian Gabriele D'Annunzio. She also absorbed very thoroughly the condensed version of Symbolist aesthetic theory which Symons presented in his books. Indeed, her early attempts to piece together an aesthetic rely almost entirely on the writings of Symons, and to a lesser extent Wilde. From these two, she took ideas which continually influenced her art. One was the Symbolist belief that in literature an abstract state of mind or feeling should be conveyed not through descriptive analysis but through concrete images or symbols. Such a theme must be evoked, not described, if it is to be successfully conveyed in art. If we read her stories in the light of this ideal—one which she refers to repeatedly in letters and notebooks—it becomes apparent that in a Mansfield story almost every detail has a symbolic as well as a narrative function. The details, or images, are intended to work in concert to create a mood or evoke a theme which is never directly stated. These oblique and indirect stories must thus be read with the same close responsiveness as a Symbolist or Modernist poem, if the full effect is to be realised.

She was also influenced by the Symbolist belief in the organic unity of the perfect work of art. Even in her earliest stories she strove to achieve the 'unity of impression' advocated by Poe, and she wrote many years later that 'If a thing has really come off it seems to me there mustn't be one single word out of place, or one word that could be taken out.' This particular quotation might tend to suggest that she was concerned only with a superficial perfection of style, but her other references to the 'essential form' of the true work of art make it clear that for her such form was truly organic, uniting form and content indissolubly.

Though the work of art could be considered as analogous to natural organic life, it was also, paradoxically, outside organic life, outside reality. She certainly inherited the Symbolist belief in art as an autotelic activity, a fact which should be stressed as a corrective to the impression, frequently given by critics, that she was a writer with a 'mission' or purpose. In fact she was clear in her belief that, though art must be nourished by life, it had its own laws and nature, which were quite distinct from those of reality. The artist must be completely aware of the distinction, and must not confuse the two spheres, nor attempt to impose his vision on life:

> That is to say, reality cannot become the ideal, the dream; and it is not the business of the artist to grind an axe, to try to impose his vision of life upon the existing world. Art is not an attempt of the artist to reconcile existence with his vision; it is an attempt to create his own world *in* this world.

From Symbolist theory and practice came her interest in extending the boundaries of prose expression. Baudelaire and Mallarmé in their prose poem experiments were interested in steering prose away from its innate structural tendency towards abstraction and analysis, towards a more concrete expressiveness. They and other Symbolist writers—including Pater—attempted to convey meaning in prose not only through the use of words as conceptual counters, but also by exploiting the 'physical properties' of language, and 'sound sense'. They repeatedly used the musical analogy for prose, to signify an ideal of non-discursive expressiveness, and this is an image which is also used by Katherine Mansfield, for the same reasons, in her frequent discussions of what she was trying to do with her prose medium. For example, she wrote of **'Miss Brill'**:

> After I'd written it I read it aloud—numbers of times—just as one would *play over* a musical com-

position—trying to get it nearer and nearer to the expression of Miss Brill—until it fitted her.

(pp. 14-23)

Katherine Mansfield's reputation is of a writer with an exquisite and delicate sensibility. Her writing is most often described as though it were a kind of verbal equivalent of an Impressionist painting, and stress is laid on the physical 'surface' of her work—its tone, colour and texture. She is commonly praised for her acuteness of ear, her visual memory, her exquisite rendering of impressions of the natural world. There is a string of verbal nouns—flash, colour, sparkle, glow—by means of which her critics have tried to convey the effect that her work has had on them. But it can more usefully and accurately be compared to Post-Impressionist rather than to Impressionist painting, for we need more emphasis on the solidity of the structure of her stories and on their weight of implication. (p. 24)

> *Andrew Gurr and Clare Hanson, in their* Katherine Mansfield, *St. Martin's Press, 1981, 146 p.*

C. A. Hankin   (essay date 1983)

[*In the following excerpt from her* Katherine Mansfield and Her Confessional Stories, *Hankin assesses the autobiographical, confessional nature of the stories in Mansfield's first published collection,* In a German Pension.]

Katherine Mansfield's journey to Bavaria in 1909 was the first of many attempts to escape personal unhappiness through changing her environment. No matter where she lived, it seems, some other place was always preferable. After coming home to New Zealand from school, she could only think of England; within a year of having her wish to return to London fulfilled, she was crying out, 'To escape England—it is my great desire. I loathe England.' [A story fragment, dated 1914 and never published], so frank in other ways, suggests that for Katherine travel was a kind of drug, providing an escape from reality not dissimilar to that afforded by fantasy. Elena, as her journey by train comes to an end, thinks about

> these strange pangs of excitement that set upon her at the end of a journey. Any journey—it was always the same. . . . The unknown place to which she travelled had in her head a fanciful image. . . . And although these things never came to pass it did not matter. Faced with reality she did not even regret them. They faded out of her mind until they were forgotten, then on the torn web of the old dream the new dream began silently to spin. . . . Yes, yes, I am coming.

Here, the relationship between travel and fantasy (or the imagination) is admitted openly. In real life there appears to have been a close association between Katherine Mansfield's bursts of creative activity and her journeys of escape. Indeed, from the time of this first removal from England to Bavaria a pattern for writing was established: first there would be an emotional crisis; then the search for release, for a new life as it were, through the change to a more desirable location. Once in that location, the mind of the author would begin reworking with a new objectivity the details of the situation from which she had broken away. But Katherine Mansfield's act in putting her personal unhappiness to artistic use was not merely one of transcendence; it was one of defiant self-affirmation. Whatever else went wrong in her life, she could assert herself as a writer, even as she controlled and refashioned the troubling events in a more satisfactory manner. Although her stories far surpass mere autobiography, at their best they always have their origins in, and in some way reflect, the particular emotional crisis she was endeavouring to overcome.

Katherine's experiences in Bavaria provided her with the material for her first collection of short stories, *In A German Pension.* Published in December 1911, the book made an immediate impact, and it gave its author a firm foothold in the London literary scene. Curiously, in later years she repudiated this first work as a 'succès scandale'. Critical commentators followed her lead. The *German Pension* stories, they said, were uncharacteristic of Katherine Mansfield's writing, not only in their technical awkwardness and strident tone, but also in their thematic concern with sexual relationships and childbearing. The early appeal of the collection, most said, was to the anti-German sentiments felt by Britons in the years preceding the First World War.

Towards the end of her life, Katherine Mansfield had private reasons for not wanting the book republished. Yet, from the time of its first reissue in 1920, *In a German Pension* has remained continuously in print. The failure of some commentators and anthologists to see this work as an integral part of the Mansfield corpus would appear unrealistic, then. In fact, neglect of these stories has distorted the picture of Katherine Mansfield's artistic development. In spite of their ostensible focus on the manners and attitudes of German men and women, the stories reiterate in their themes Katherine's youthful uneasiness about relationships between the sexes; and they are clear forerunners of some of the great stories in which sexual ambivalence remains thematically central. But the enduring interest of the collection lies in the intuitive grasp of female psychology which informs the stories.

Into her caustic portraits of German people, whether at work or at play, Katherine Mansfield poured her own emotional reactions to the sad affair with Garnett Trowell, to her hasty marriage, and to the trauma of pregnancy and miscarriage. Her response to pregnancy was primarily physical. 'My *body* is so self-conscious', she commented in her journal before leaving London. 'Je pense of all the frightful things possible—"all this filthiness".' In Bavaria she described 'a terrible confusion in your body which affects you mentally, suddenly pictures for you detestable incidents, revolting personalities'. A preoccupation with the physical aspects of the relations between men and women is to the fore in the *German Pension* stories. Especially striking is the way in which a portrayal of the Germans' gross eating habits barely disguises a persistent correlation between the devouring of food and the sexual devouring, as it were, of a woman's body. In such stories as **'Germans at Meat', 'Frau Brechenmacher Attends a Wedding', 'At Lehmann's'** and **'Bains Turcs',** Katherine Mansfield reveals an overwhelming fear of physically dominant men and of male sexual appetite, often through the symbolism of food.

Some commentators, seeking to dismiss as an aberration what they considered the 'distasteful' aspects of the *German Pension* stories, have argued that Katherine Mans-

field was writing under the alien influence of Beatrice Hastings, the ardent woman's liberationist from the *New Age.* But the appearance of closely related themes in both her mature works and her youthful writing suggests otherwise. Anxieties about physical relations—anxieties which she came increasingly to express in terms of eating—are evident in the juvenilia. Even as a girl there seems to have been a link in her mind between food and physical dominance. Resenting her father's dominating presence in 1906 and precociously aware of his sexual appetite, she had written disgustedly of his behaviour at meal times: 'A physically revolted feeling seizes me. . . . He watches the dishes go round, anxious to see that he shall have a good share.'

In the *German Pension* stories, Katherine Mansfield made little attempt to disguise her private obsessions. **'Germans at Meat'** focuses upon the links between sexuality and eating. The narrative, a rather contrived conversation around a pension dinner-table between the German guests and the prim young English narrator, has the ostensible purpose of exposing the gustatory greediness of the Germans. It is not the satirical asides of the narrator, however, which give the piece its interest: it is the tension which develops between her and the physically dominant 'Herr Rat' as the two engage in ambiguous small talk. Herr Rat, anxious like Harold Beauchamp to 'have a good share' of the food, is unpleasantly aggressive as he boasts: 'As for me, I have had all I wanted from women without marriage.' What he wanted from women is never spelled out, but he relentlessly details the quantities of food needed to satisfy his appetite. The narrator's revulsion against Herr Rat and his physical appetites is conveyed indirectly as a German widow elicits from her the information that she is a slight eater and a vegetarian. 'Who ever heard of having children upon vegetables?' exclaims the widow. The correlation between food and sexuality becomes explicit when the widow says that while she herself has had nine children, her own achievement cannot be compared with the feat of a friend who 'had four at the same time. Her husband was so pleased he gave a supper-party and had them placed on the table.'

'Frau Brechenmacher Attends a Wedding' is an undisguised attack upon the sexually dominant male. In portraying the indignities and the suffering heaped upon women in marriage, Katherine Mansfield might almost be dramatising her own expressed belief that 'it is the hopelessly insipid doctrine that love is the only thing in the world, taught, hammered into women, from generation to generation, which hampers us so cruelly'. If the polemic which informs the work is sometimes too direct for comfort, the very sharpness of the narration makes this an unforgettable story. The author illustrates her theme in terms of two women, one who has endured marriage for years and one who is about to be married. In the opening section of the story, Frau Brechenmacher is shown rushing to and fro at the command of her bullying husband. Her husband's name suggestive of one who 'breaks', Frau Brechenmacher must attend the wedding to witness the ritual preparation for the breaking of yet another woman's spirit.

It is through the symbolism of food that Katherine Mansfield again drives home her meaning. The bride, who has been deserted by the father of her illegitimate child and who is now being forced into an arranged marriage, has 'the appearance of an iced cake all ready to be cut and served in neat little pieces to the bridegroom beside her'. She might almost be the victim of some primitive sacrifice, such is the effect of the explicit linking of male sexuality and cannibalism. When Herr Brechenmacher presents the newly-weds with a silver coffee pot containing 'a baby's bottle and two little cradles holding china dolls', the latent cruelty of the wedding-feast reaches a climax. Lifting the lid, the bride seems to understand the meaning of the gift; she 'shut it down with a little scream and sat biting her lips'.

Frau Brechenmacher, instinctively empathising with the girl in her humiliation, imagines that 'all these people were laughing at her . . . all laughing at her because they were so much stronger than she was'. The operative word is 'stronger', and the story ends with the focus on the older woman and her fear of physical abuse. Her husband, eating greedily on their return home, reminds his wife of the trouble she gave him on their wedding-night: 'You were an innocent one, you were. . . . But I soon taught you.' Just what the woman, now mother of five children, has been taught is conveyed by the closing sentence: 'She lay down on the bed and put her arm across her face like a child who expected to be hurt as Herr Brechenmacher lurched in.'

Frau Brechenmacher's fear of her physically dominant husband (and her refusal to eat with him) shows in primitive form attitudes which Linda Burnell displays towards her husband in the later story **'Prelude'**.

Another *German Pension* story, **'At Lehmann's'**, shows Katherine Mansfield exploring with a similar unsubtle emphasis on physicality the theme of initiation (a theme which in altered form is central to such later stories as **'The Little Governess', 'Her First Ball'** and **'The Garden Party'**). Sabina, the servant girl at Lehmann's café, is innocent about the facts of life: 'She knew practically nothing except that the Frau had a baby inside her, which had to come out—very painful indeed. One could not have one without a husband—that she also realised. But what had the man got to do with it?' The climax of the story is of course Sabina's sudden understanding of what the man *had* got to do with it, and the shattering of her childish naïveté and illusion. There is a degree of dramatic irony in the girl's failure to see any link at first between her excitement at the attentions of a visiting young man, whose 'restless gaze wandering over her face and figure gave her a curious thrill deep in her body, half pleasure, half pain', and Frau Lehmann's ugly body in the final stage of pregnancy. But making quite sure that she—and the reader—make the connection is Katherine Mansfield's juxtaposition of the girl's first kiss with the 'frightful, tearing shriek' that heralds the birth of the baby. Shrieking too, Sabina pulls away from her would-be lover and rushes out of the room.

Again and again in the *German Pension* stories Katherine Mansfield underlines her sense that sexual love for women is fraught with physical danger. Victims of the stronger sex, women face the ultimate exploitation: the burden of constant childbearing. Her attempts to find a solution to the problem in fictional terms are various. In **'The-Child-Who-Was-Tired'**, the servant girl (who performs the duties of mother) finally smothers the baby which will not stop crying. But the answer which appears most frequently in these stories is an avoidance of normal heterosexual relations. Widows are singularly blessed. In **'Frau Fischer'** the character of that name is a widow, and the 'fortunate possessor of a candle factory'; equally fortunate is Frau Hartmann, the owner of a pension. 'We are such a happy family since my dear man died', she tells her guests. Pretending to be married—to a sea captain who is conveniently away on long voyages—the English narrator of the story announces that, for her part, she considers 'childbearing the most ignominious of all professions'.

Women's revenge on men, in one form or another, is a thematic element in many of the *German Pension* stories. And lesbianism, or something very close to it, is the alternative to domination by men which Katherine Mansfield explores in **'The Modern Soul'** and **'Bains Turcs'**.

In dealing with bisexuality, Katherine Mansfield was entering difficult territory. She was not only exposing in fiction the motivations of women whose psychology resembled her own; she was writing about a subject which in the aftermath of the Wilde trial was considered morally wrong, if not 'forbidden'. As a result, there is no urgent presentation of a message in **'The Modern Soul'** and **'Bains Turcs'**. Rather the author is concerned so to disguise and encode her theme that the stories can be read on two levels: at a superficial level which appears to present satiric caricatures of German men and women, and at a deeper level where psychological dramas of some complexity can be seen unfolding. There is an ambiguity, then, in the texture of these two stories which reveals itself in devious plot structures, confusing shifts of point of view, innuendo and a heavy reliance upon symbols—especially symbols connected with eating.

'The Modern Soul' is about the ambivalent relationship of a narcissistic young actress, Fräulein Sonia Godowska, with her mother on the one hand and with a conceited middle-aged professor on the other. Observing and commenting on the behaviour of this group is the English narrator. As the story opens, the focus is on 'Herr Professor'. Exhausted from trombone-playing in the woods, he is depicted greedily devouring a bag of cherries. From the outset his conversation is spiced with innuendo that leaves us in little doubt about the correlation between his prowess as an eater of fruit (so obviously symbolic of a woman's body) and his sexual prowess. 'There is nothing like cherries for producing free saliva after trombone playing, especially after Grieg's *Ich Liebe Dich*', he announces happily. At a concert that evening it becomes clear that the Professor (who has bragged about the quantity and variety of fruit he has eaten in the present location) intends Fräulein Godowska as his next conquest. 'To-night you shall be the soul of my trombone', he tells her. His reappearance with the trombone symbolically underlines his desires: he 'blew into it, held it up to one eye . . . and wallowed in the soul of Sonia Godowska'.

Amusing though the ridiculous portrayal of this character is, the impact of the story hinges on the reader's perception of the trap which is prepared for him. After the concert it is not the Professor but the narrator whom Fräulein Sonia singles out for a walk in the woods. To her the actress confides that she is 'furiously sapphic.' The focus now shifts from the Professor's expectations to the confused psychology of the woman whose sexual inversion is bound to thwart him. 'Not only am I sapphic,' she continues, 'I find in all the works of all the greatest writers . . . some sign of myself—some resemblence.' If a combination of sapphism and narcissism nourishes her creative 'genius', so, apparently, do Sonia's intensely ambivalent feelings for her mother. Terming Frau Godowska her 'tragedy', the daughter insists, 'I love my mother as I love nobody else in the world—nobody and nothing! Do you think it is impossible to love one's tragedy? "Out of my great sorrows I make my little songs", that is Heine or myself.'

The ending of this story whose secret subject is the frustration of a conceited man's sexual desires is fittingly ironic. Sonia reveals that the attachment to her mother precludes any normal relationship with a man; besides, 'genius cannot hope to mate'. What she would like is to marry 'a simple, peaceful man . . . who would be for me a pillow'. By casting the unwitting Professor in this role, Sonia effectively turns the tables on him. The exploiter is about to become the exploited.

Out of her own inner knowledge, Katherine Mansfield portrays in **'The Modern Soul'** not only the battle of the sexes. She probes, in her characterisation of Fräulein Sonia, the longings of an immature woman who, like a little girl, wishes to marry her father and retain sole possession of her mother. And whether she knew it or not, she illustrates the link between a neurotic fixation on childhood, bisexuality and creative endeavour.

'Bains Turcs', although published some time after the *German Pension* collection, belongs with the group of stories that Katherine Mansfield wrote out of her experiences in Bavaria. Like the earlier works, it has a German cast of characters seen through the eyes of a self-conscious English narrator; and it conveys a disparaging attitude towards men. More directly than in **'The Modern Soul'**, Katherine Mansfield contemplates in **'Bains Turcs'** the alternative to marriage offered by lesbian relationships. But here too the author approaches her dangerous theme with some evasion, relying heavily on the concealing devices of word associations and picture-language, or symbols. The overall effect of the story is dreamlike, so that it is difficult to determine the deliberateness with which we are being allowed a glimpse into the characters' unconscious minds. What we do gain from a close reading of **'Bains Turcs'** is a strong sense of Katherine Mansfield's ability to tap, for the purposes of fiction, the workings of the unconscious mind.

Reminiscent of Cerberus, the many-headed dog guarding the entrance to Hades, the cashier at the entrance to the Turkish baths gives an immediate impression of dominance with her 'masses of gleaming orange hair—like an over-ripe fungus bursting from a thick, black stem'. Such luxuriant fecundity suggests that this is a place ruled by women; and indeed, the only man in the establishment, an elevator attendant, is likened to a 'dead bird'. In contrast to the cashier, by whom he is scolded, the man seems impotent. A 'tiny figure disguised in a peaked cap and dirty white cotton gloves', he is referred to derisively by the narrator as 'the figure', 'the midget' and 'the creature'.

The train of thought which depersonalises the man before reducing him to the level of an animal takes another direction when the narrator, who has come to enjoy the baths,

settles into the comfort of the 'Warm Room'. 'Yes, it might have been very fascinating to have married an explorer', she thinks, 'and lived in a jungle, as long as he didn't shoot anything or take anything captive. I detest performing beasts.' The implication is that, while man in the shape of a sexless elevator attendant can be an object of mockery, man in the shape of a sexually virile predator (who might take the narrator captive) is a definite threat. Mentally attempting to render this imaginary male impotent too, the narrator reduces him to the level of a 'performing beast'.

Having thus dismissed the opposite sex, the narrator turns her attention to two women in the baths whose looks and behaviour suggest an attractive substitute for marriage. With their 'gay, bold faces, and quantities of exquisite whipped fair hair', they seem to exist in an exclusively happy world of their own. Their shared act of handling and eating mandarins, as they scrutinise and discuss laughingly the bodies of the other bathers, accentuates their apparent intimacy. The other women in the room, as if signalling a veiled recognition of the lesbianism implicit in this scene, vented 'the only little energy they had . . . in shocked prudery at the behaviour of the two blondes'.

But, as if the theme were coming too close for comfort, the focus shifts from the perceiving mind of the narrator to a new character, 'a short stout little woman with flat, white feet, and a black mackintosh cap over her hair'. Mackintosh Cap demonstrates an obsessive concern with the two blondes: 'They're not respectable women—you can tell at a glance. At least I can, any married woman can.' Then she launches into an account of her own marriage and the five children who have been born to her in six years. Yet

Mansfield and John Middleton Murry, 1918.

her championing of the married state is belied by a physical interest in her own sex she is unable to suppress. 'Are you going to take your chemise off in the vapour room?' she asks the narrator. ' "Don't mind me, you know. Woman is woman, and besides, if you'd rather, I won't look at you. . . . I wouldn't mind betting", she went on savagely, "those filthy women had a good look at each other." ' The narrator's comment, 'I could not get out of my mind the ugly, wretched figure of the little German with a good husband and four children, railing against the two fresh beauties who had never peeled potatoes nor chosen the right meat', conveys her recognition of the jealousy which underlies the discrepancy between the woman's words and the feelings she exposes. It is the narrator, too, who at the end of the story suggests the psychological interpretation of what we have observed through her eyes: 'And as the two [blondes] walked out of the ante-room, Mackintosh Cap stared after them, her sallow face all mouth and eyes, like the face of a hungry child before a forbidden table.'

Katherine Mansfield has been illustrating in this second section of the story the process whereby a wish that has been repressed by the conscious mind can make its way back to consciousness—in the form of a denial of that wish. Overtly denying her own deepest feelings as she rails at the two lesbians, Mackintosh Cap's longing for a similar intimacy is revealed through the very intensity of her fixation. In the striking final sentence, Katherine Mansfield rounds off the exposure of the woman's character. Appearing momentarily to have regressed to the condition of a baby whose sole interest is in possession of its mother's breast, Mackintosh Cap exhibits the despair of a rejected female child; a despair which can survive in adult life as the repressed longing for a physical relationship with another woman.

The understanding of female psychology which emerges in **'Bains Turcs'** is remarkable. But, because the author is herself ambiguously involved in the mental processes of her characters, the story is aesthetically unsatisfying. There is no manifestly logical connection between the narrator's thoughts in the opening scene, her observation of the two blonde women, and the conclusion to the story. Only an interpretation of the symbolism and word pictures can make it clear that all the female characters who appear in the narrative are logically linked by their rejection of men and their accompanying attraction to their own sex. (pp. 61-70)

> C. A. Hankin, in her Katherine Mansfield and Her Confessional Stories, *St. Martin's Press, 1983, 271 p.*

Joanne Trautmann Banks   (essay date 1985)

[*In the following excerpt, Banks traces Mansfield's development as a short story writer through a chronological examination of her fiction.*]

Katherine Mansfield lived precociously. In 1908, at twenty, the young New Zealander had already committed herself to freedom in London, daily writing, and serious publishing—which is just as well, for Mansfield was destined to live only half a lifetime.

When she died at thirty-four of tuberculosis, she left a substantial body of writing. Poems, diaries, and letters there were, but chiefly short stories, of which she is arguably her generation's best practitioner in English. (p. 64)

[Within] her short lifetime Mansfield grew markedly in intellectual discernment, aesthetic accomplishment, and emotional maturity. Ultimately, she became a creator of worlds that are, at their best, as honest, compassionate, and formally exquisite as those of her spiritual mentor, Anton Chekhov. To be sure, at the end of her life, she was still occasionally turning out a merely clever story, polished and not thoroughly felt. But on the whole, the previous judgment stands. It is helpful, therefore, to an overall understanding of Mansfield to follow the phases of her development.

One of the earliest of these seems to have grown out of her ability to amuse her family and friends with impersonations—quick, vivid, enacted presences. That skill, added to a relatively contrived turn of plot or control by the author, is the basis for several of the so-called "German stories" collected as *In a German Pension* (1911). The hilarious **"Germans at Meat"** is representative. Just a few gestures vividly capture the characters around the table at a health spa. The Widow plucks a hairpin from her head and, before returning it, casually uses it to pick her teeth, all the while intoning axioms on the relation of vegetarianism, the English suffragettes, and fecundity. Herr Rat, blowing on his soup, alludes just as casually to his sexual experience, en masse, as it were. The Germans' enormous appetites are matched by rotund self-satisfaction. The mood darkens when the Germans suggest to the narrator, a young Englishwoman of refinement, that England ought to fear an invasion, but her stance of mild sarcasm and complete self-possession keeps the gluttons merely funny and in their place.

There are deliciously wicked delights here and there in the German stories. The opening of **"A Modern Soul,"** for instance, has some of the qualities of Restoration comedy. But on the whole, **"Germans at Meat"** is probably the best of an unsatisfactory lot. They are the work of a bright, young writer with a strictly limited vision. Mansfield's Germans are indeed arrogantly vulgar, but they are set up too easily as targets. Moreover, the uneasiness that some readers are certain to feel in the presence of ethnic humor is reinforced in these stories, particularly in **"Germans at Meat,"** where the title and the reference to potential political hostilities oil the way to inflexible conclusions. Amusing stereotyping—a constant danger for comic short fiction—is what is really going on. More important, in terms of what Mansfield will do with her narrative voice later, the narrator of these German stories manipulates her fellow boarders in order to bring out the worst in them for us to laugh at. Responding to Herr Rat, for instance, she reports to her reading conspirators: " 'How interesting,' I said, attempting to infuse just the right amount of enthusiasm into my voice." This narrator is smug. She is telling us about herself rather than dramatizing herself so that we can thoroughly believe in her. She is also protecting herself, of course. No one can deny that this young woman is the most superior person in the group, however difficult she may be to know well, or perhaps because of that difficulty. There is a certain cruelty and cynicism here that will not be purged for several years.

In addition to the rigidly satiric voice in these early stories, there is one other striking tone. The young Mansfield is angry about woman's lot. She has a self-devouring anger that runs to bitterness, a quality that makes stories such as **"Frau Brechenmacher Attends a Wedding," "A Birthday,"** and **"At Lehmann's"** less artistically appealing than some of her later treatments of women's roles, such as **"Mr. Reginald Peacock's Day"** and the masterful **"Prelude"** and **"At the Bay."**

"Frau Brechenmacher" and **"A Birthday"** are essentially the same story narrated from the points of view first of the wife, then of the husband. The village wedding in the first story is the occasion for the men to humiliate the bride, who has borne an illegitimate child (a daughter and no happier than her mother). The groom, it is said, literally stinks, but, as the village women put it, "Every woman has a cross to bear." The story's sexual innuendos become blatant after Frau Brechenmacher, the overworked mother of five young children, the eldest another burdened female, goes home to remember her wedding night, for which she had been completely unprepared. Not that she is much better prepared now for sexual abuse: "She lay down on the bed and put her arm across her face like a child who expected to be hurt as Herr Brechenmacher lurched in."

Mansfield carries the universal condemnation perceived by the Frau—"all over the world the same . . . how *stupid*"—into the middle-class household of **"A Birthday,"** where the abuse is more subtle, but equally violent. Andreas Binzer condemns himself: "I'm too sensitive for a man," he wails, but everywhere is evidence of his insensitivity to his wife's situation. She is in painful labor with her third child in four years, but she worries about her husband. He pities himself because he does not have more support. It is surely disloyal of him to find his wife's photograph unattractive and to imagine her as dead as he awaits the results of her confinement. The servant girl, here and elsewhere in Mansfield a choric commentator on the main action, returns to her kitchen, loathing men and vowing sterility. Her real problem—hers, Frau Binzer's, Frau Brechenmacher's—is that she is "bursting for want of sympathy."

Mansfield came to dislike her German stories. They represented in her mind clever but trivial juvenilia. As for the themes in her stories—particularly the relationship between men and women and the isolation of the young woman—these she would continue to write about, refining them as her sensibility matured. But first she would write another sort of story altogether. In turning toward her homeland, she treated ethnicity with a completely different emphasis from that of her early stories. Her stories set in New Zealand were comparable, in fact, to some of the first of the American local-color stories, with the addition of a certain amount of psychological subtlety.

The change of locale and tone is remarkable. **"The Woman at the Store"** (1911) opens with a description of the New Zealand wilderness that would have struck English readers as exotic: "there was nothing to be seen but wave after wave of tussock grass, patched with purple orchids and manuka bushes covered with thick spider webs." Then, equally surprising from an author who had been presenting herself as a sophisticate, comes her attempt at rough dialect: "It's six years since I was married, and four miscarriages. I says to 'im, I says, what do you think I'm doin' up 'here? If you was back at the coast, I'd 'have you

lynched for child murder. Over and over I tells 'im—you've broken my spirit and spoiled my looks, and wot for—that's wot I'm driving at." The plot is also startling. Two men and a woman, who is the narrator and may be the men's sister, have been riding in the wilderness for a month. They come upon an isolated store, where a woman is alone with her nasty, pathetic six-year-old daughter. Claiming that her husband has been gone as usual for weeks, she welcomes the trio to the extent of sleeping with one of the men. During the night the child, to spite her mother, draws a picture for the visitors. It shows her mother shooting her father and burying him.

Upon reflection, this and the other New Zealand stories of this phase do not seem so far removed from Mansfield's early artistic choices. The first-person narrator, for instance, while socially and psychologically more attuned to the main participants in these stories, is still superior to the action in the old way. From the German stories, Mansfield likewise carries over her skill in accurately hearing the voices of her characters. And her adeptness at portraying social classes other than her own had been demonstrated not only in the German stories such as **"Frau Brechenmacher Attends a Wedding"** and **"The Child-Who-Was-Tired,"** but as early as her first story published in England, **"The Tiredness of Rosabel."** As in these stories and others, in **"The Woman at the Store"** we have an exhausted female at the mercy of a brutal man and childbearing. "Wot for?" is the question Mansfield has been asking from the beginning.

Now the violence in the male-female relationship explodes outward. Somewhat controlled in the European settings, it becomes murder in New Zealand. The woman in the store kills the husband who has all but destroyed her. She is half-mad as a result of her psychological and physical isolation. **"Ole Underwood"** presents another "cracked" New Zealander; he has murdered his wife. In **"Millie"** we see a third isolated person, torn between what Mansfield regards as feminine aspects of character—chiefly maternal feelings—and masculine—the primitive, eye-for-an-eye justice of the men, who are out to punish a murderer. Millie is so far from civilization, as represented rather mawkishly by the print of a garden party at Windsor Castle, that she easily gives in to the hot, mad joy of killing.

As dramatic as these New Zealand stories are, the plotting is not so very different from, say, **"The Sister of the Baroness,"** which turns on contrivances only slightly less subtle. Furthermore, Mansfield is still resorting to clever versions of the nineteenth-century surprise ending. Linked to the emphasis on action is the de-emphasis on character. In all these New Zealand stories, Mansfield puts a wide distance between herself and the characters, comparable to the distance achieved by the satire in some of the German stories. The distance is as much moral as aesthetic. Simple explanations for the murders are made, but no interpretations are drawn. Finally, we do not care very much about any of these people. A coldness thus is cast over the exciting plots, whose action is, in any case, off-stage. At this point in her work, Mansfield is far more interested in art than in humanity.

She was not yet ready to return, heart and soul, to her homeland. She had first to prepare the way by mining her childhood. Suddenly, in the middle of the wilderness New Zealand stories, she writes **"The Little Girl,"** a story so fine as to set her on the way to becoming—with, say, Isaac Babel and Frank O'Connor—one of our greatest portrayers of children in short fiction.

Mansfield depicts children sympathetically; at the same time, in her best stories she achieves the right distance on childish emotions. In **"The Little Girl"** the sensations of little Kezia, who is perhaps five years old, are always expressed in terms of her size: her father is huge, his voice loud, the far jollier father next door perceived through a hole in the fence. Father beats her unjustly. He intimidates her and is a hard giant compared to her soft, comforting grandmother. Then, one night when mother and grandmother are out of the house, the little girl awakens from a nightmare to find her father by the bedside. He scoops her up and takes her to his bedroom, an eminently masculine place, with newspaper and half-smoked cigar, which he now casts out to make room to warm his little daughter in his bed. Then tired out from working so hard, he falls asleep. Kezia reflects: "He was harder than the grandmother, but it was a nice hardness. . . . 'Oh,' said the little girl, 'my head's on your heart; I can hear it going. What a big heart you've got, father dear' ": an insight which, if she can retain it, may one day allow Kezia to trust men and to marry satisfactorily.

There were five years between these early New Zealand stories and the magnificent **"Prelude"** (1917). During that time Mansfield wrote, apparently, very few stories, and only one completely good one, the famous **"The Little Governess."** But clearly she was changing enormously in those years. So, of course, was the European world. The war was as stimulating and devastating an event for Mansfield as it was for every other young person with a mind open to experience. For Mansfield there was, in addition, the personal grief over the loss of her younger brother, Leslie, with whom she had grown increasingly intimate before his death. The English writer Vita Sackville-West, who was also one of her country's finest gardeners, used to say that her garden at Sissinghurst—its beauty, she supposedly meant, its wild suggestiveness within a strictly controlled form—was an answer to war. Mansfield could have meant **"Prelude"** to counter the international and personal horror in something of the same manner. She is never directly political in her stories, rarely even makes reference to matters in the so-called larger world, but the domestic **"Prelude"** is such a complete, beautiful, and fully human world as to make international battle seem a very passing phenomenon indeed.

The method of **"Prelude"** is in many ways its content. Its title the name of a musical form, the story reflects Mansfield's early training—she played the cello, sang, and for a time thought of a career in music. The prelude as developed by Bach is a very free form, and with Chopin becomes highly suggestive and imaginative, almost appearing improvised. In Mansfield's hands, the form is plotless. People move; there are clearly identified "scenes," each with completed action; but there is no strictly linear cause and effect. (What a distance she has come from **"The Woman at the Store."**) Connecting the scenes is a larger movement consisting of exactly pointed rhythms and balances. For instance, the story moves gracefully toward the mother, Linda Burnell, giving detailed attention to the other characters, but preparing us subtly for the penultimate scene, section 11, with its pivotal weight on Linda

and her vision. The final section settles into a more objective tone through the device of a letter from Beryl to someone in the outside world. Thus are some details firmly rooted, and yet the story ends airily. The whole is much like the aloe plant, which provides the central symbol for the story: "High above them, as though becalmed in the air, and yet holding so fast to the earth it grew from, it might have had claws instead of roots." The lyrical composition is attached to a mimetic base and never allowed to become wispy impressionism.

And where is the narrator in this composition? Far from the self-conscious teller of the German satires and the reporter of action in the early New Zealand adventures, Mansfield's narrator has here magically hidden herself. She conceals herself first in one character, then another—a child, a woman, a servant, a man . . . a duck. She switches so fast from perspective to perspective that we do not see any movement at all. Nor have we the usual sense of the omniscient narrator, a voice distinct from all the others and somehow above the action, even when she describes a phenomenon like the dawn in section 5. The narrator conceals herself in the rising day as skillfully as in the other characters, though without in any way personifying the natural experience. So completely in control is this author that she can afford to give up more obvious methods of control. It is as if Mansfield were not the composer of this prelude so much as its performer.

Yet the method never overpowers the people. Each is vividly drawn. None is judged. The flirtatious, yearning, self-loathing Beryl is accepted just as she is. Mrs. Fairfield is the ideal comforter, but she is no more important a thread of this richly human tapestry than are any of the children—themselves affectingly distinct from one another—or the compelling, mysterious Linda Burnell herself. **"Prelude"** is the story of a family understood so compassionately that what might otherwise be seen as faults are simply taken as aspects of living. We are as inclined as Mrs. Fairfield is, for instance, to accept Linda's inability to mother her children intimately. Partly that is owing to our sympathy for her lot—the old one, too many children too fast—but it is due even more to the sharply delineated tenderness of her characterization.

The husband, Stanley, also profits from the method. To be sure, the household is overwhelmingly female. So is the element that holds it together: "she spoke to her mother with the special voice that women use at night to each other as though they spoke in their sleep or from some hollow cave." In addition, Stanley Burnell comes in for his share of criticism, here and in the sequel story, **"At the Bay."** Here, for instance, Linda knows him to be a big, loyal dog of a man, but too dominating, too easily hurt. She loves him, she says, and admires him, but simultaneously she hates the hooks by which he anchors her. On attaining her Lawrencian vision, she is freed to laugh. Lest the reader come to feel condescending toward Stanley, we also see him in the light of devoted husband. We see the joy with which, when his wife asks him at night to light a candle, "he leapt out of bed as though he were going to leap at the moon for her."

The portraits of husband, wife, and the child Kezia firmly mark Mansfield's new maturity. The Burnells' is a satisfactory marriage in spite of woman's lot. All the ingredients of the relationships—the sweet dailyness, on the one hand, and the painful loss of independence, on the other— are suspended in a gel of family strength. The husband is no longer an ogre. More admirable still, Linda Burnell, based on Mansfield's mother, whom she felt had not loved her enough, is here given the right to her own values. Through the charming Kezia and her entirely realistic adventure, Mansfield recaptures the little girl she was, the one she was chasing in the story called **"The Little Girl."** In **"Prelude,"** Mansfield demonstrates her newly honed ability to use her art to focus life both within, and above, the fray.

In the same year, 1917, Mansfield's experimental stories began to appear with greater frequency. Technically, these stories are of two distinct types. One is dialogue, an example of which she apparently wrote as early as 1911. Of course, the ancients used this "experimental" form; and her stories were based, we are told [by Antony Alpers in his *Life of Katherine Mansfield* (see Further Reading)], on Theocritus. **"Late at Night," "Two Tuppenny Ones, Please," "The Lady's Maid,"** and **"The Black Cap"** belong to this type. The first three are actually monologues and startlingly like the "dialogues for one voice" by Colette, a writer whose life-style Mansfield admired, and whose work was currently being published in *Le matin*. The second type is a more truly experimental form—a very short tone poem doubtless intended to be as colorful and luminous as a postimpressionist painting. Examples are **"See-Saw," "Spring Pictures,"** and **"Bank Holiday."** None of these short experimental stories is of the least moral or aesthetic interest to the general reader. But they provide important sources for speculation about Mansfield's continued development as an artist.

Both types of experiments are attempts at objectivity. In the visual ones Mansfield describes something that exists out there, as it were, and that can be simply taken down as data. And the dialogues are bits of drama, commonly understood to be the most objective of literary genres. They are all in some way related to the freedom she was achieving in 1917 as she created and revised the grand experimental design of **"Prelude."** The earlier New Zealand stories—**"The Woman at the Store"** and the others—are falsely, coldly, objective by comparison. She may have been trying to refine her self and her narrative voice out of existence, as Joyce's Stephen Dedalus advised the artist. There would then be psychological payoffs too. Her self, frequently elusive, unlovable, and now subclinically tubercular, might thus be avoided.

The experimental stories disappointed Mansfield, and the public gave them scant attention. Even **"Prelude"** was received in silence; so she had no encouragement to continue in this vein. She may also have learned that objectivity of the sort she sought was a temporary illusion on both the aesthetic and psychological levels. Whatever the case, after the experimental stories of 1917, various strong narrative voices reenter her fiction. Subtle stances are taken that nonetheless leave characters and ideas their freedom. Still, Mansfield did learn something positive from the experiments. Just as scientists often labor long with negative or little results and suddenly come via that very route to meaningful discoveries, so did Mansfield create her best work after the experimental stories. In other words, the experimental stories were in some way like artist's sketches for the larger works. This is very clear in the case of

"The Lady's Maid," which directly precedes **"The Daughters of the Late Colonel"** in Murry's chronology, and which we know from biographical sources is to a degree based on Mansfield's intimate woman friend, "Leslie Moore" (Ida Constance Baker), just as is Constantia in **"The Daughters."** It is likewise clear in the case of another more or less experimental story, the exciting **"The Wind Blows,"** which in method and content helps to set up **"Prelude."** In some mysterious way, when good writers are writing badly, they are often on the eve of writing better. (Curiously, in her last story, **"The Canary,"** she returns to an experimental form.)

A cluster of justly admired stories followed the experimental work: **"Bliss"** (1918), **"Je Ne Parle Pas Français"** (1918), **"The Man without a Temperament"** (1920), **"The Stranger"** (1920). Mansfield's creative power had been released. Beginning with **"The Daughters of the Late Colonel"** (also 1920), she completed nineteen successful stories in as many months. That a few of these are trivial does not matter in the midst of the almost unbroken string of gems: **"Life of Ma Parker," "The Voyage," "Miss Brill," "Marriage à la Mode," "The Doll's House," "The Fly."** Her second long masterpiece, **"At the Bay,"** also belongs to this period. Its recapturing of the thematic and technical perfection of four years before demonstrates Mansfield's agility. She had hit her stride: she had slipped her methods on like a dress and with them focused her themes.

In maturity, Mansfield learned to write sotto voce, as the narrator in **"A Married Man's Story"** puts it. He continues: "No fine effects—no bravura. But just the plain truth, as only a liar can tell it." The narrative voice became a quiet undertone—its function to reveal simple, preferably concrete, reality, not in some slice-of-life mode, but polished by the tricks of the crafty fictionalist in order to focus upon the kernel of meaning. It delicately furthered broadly moral ends.

This means that the narrator takes extremely subtle stands, intimately close to the action. For instance, even in her comedy the mature Mansfield never mocks as she did in her German stories. Her naive girls and women (**"The Daughters of the Late Colonel," "The Singing Lesson," "Her First Ball," "Taking the Veil,"** and the superbly Austenian **"The Doves' Nest"**) are protected from their own silliness by the author's intimacy with them. Even when Mansfield chooses some ironic distance, as in the unusually skillful handling of the corrupt but naive narrator in **"Je Ne Parle Pas Français,"** she hovers nearby, never too superior. But she gently directs the reader's reactions, making the stories of this period different from **"Prelude"** and **"At the Bay,"** where she successfully attempts to withhold almost all judgment. Comparatively, the last stories show a return to plot—nothing like the adventurous New Zealand stories, but a line that moves softly to an end. Sometimes those endings are neat, entirely too clever no doubt, and even "thematic," but normally they underline the ambiguity and tolerate it: "Rot!" whispers the Man Without a Temperament; *Isn't* it, darling?" concludes Laurie in **"The Garden Party"** about life itself.

In these last stories, Mansfield further refined her special skill for narrative description. For instance, in **"The Voyage"** the descriptions monitor the little girl's mood, and underscore in a lovely, indirect manner, the theme of the story: "It was dark on the Old Wharf, very dark. . . .

Here and there on a rounded woodpile, that was like the stalk of a huge black mushroom, there hung a lantern, but it seemed afraid to unfurl its timid, quivering light in all that blackness; it burned softly, as if for itself." The method here consciously comes from music. It is rhythm and timbre as much as content. Occasionally Mansfield will modulate the description into something that carries the heavier weight of symbolism: the pear tree in **"Bliss,"** the fur neckpiece in **"Miss Brill."** She plays no games about this sort of thing. Either the symbols are a natural part of the setting, or she makes the point straightforwardly. Tidily married couples are doves (**"Mr. and Mrs. Dove"**). Our lives may be snuffed out like flies' (**"The Fly"**). A canary's lyrical sweetness and sad fragility is as close to an analogue of life as we shall get (**"The Canary"**).

In the best Mansfield stories both description and dialogue brilliantly bring the characters to life. Although they do not evoke the reader's deepest affections, there is a certain very moving quality about her people. William in **"Marriage à la Mode"** is a good example. So, of course, are all the children—those in **"The Doll's House"** and **"The Voyage"**—and the childlike adults like Miss Brill and the speaker in **"The Canary."**

The range of characters and social settings is broad. Mansfield can convincingly create women, men, children, and, sometimes, animals. In addition to the very young—even an infant in **"At the Bay"**—she depicts older people like Mr. Neave in **"An Ideal Family"** and Miss Brill. She presents people in isolation, in romantic or marital couples (not necessarily the same thing for her), and in families. If there are rarely large groups, that is due to the nature of the short story genre as much as to Mansfield's abilities. In terms of social class, she is most thorough about the middle class, but from the beginning she was able to portray working-class girls, particularly servants. Because she was one of life's alert wanderers, Mansfield observed enough cultural and natural detail to be able to set her stories in several countries: Germany, France, New Zealand, and England.

Her themes, however, are not as varied, but that fact scarcely distinguishes her from many other first-rate writers. She wrote most often about innocence challenged. She brilliantly portrayed characters looking back on that innocence like the remains of a dream, as in **"Sun and Moon."** Often her girls and women suffer unfairly; they have too many children; they have too little money (**"The Child-Who-Was-Tired," "The Doll's House," "Pictures,"** and **"Miss Brill"**); men are insensitive to them (**"The Little Governess"** and **"This Flower"**). She wrote about narcissism in both women and men, and how it causes people, particularly couples, to drift apart (**"Prelude," "Marriage à la Mode," "The Man without a Temperament," "Bliss," "Mr. Reginald Peacock's Day," "Revelations," "The Stranger," "Honeymoon,"** and **"A Cup of Tea"**). Innocence lost, unfairness to women and children, the penalties of isolation and narcissism: these few themes, with one important exception to be discussed later, are the bases for most of Mansfield's work.

If there is a quintessential Mansfield story, it is **"The Garden Party."** When a man says to the heroine in Jean Stafford's "The Interior Castle," "My dear, you look like something out of Katherine Mansfield," it is this story that he has equated with its author's sensibility. Its typical elements and treatments include: a New Zealand domestic setting; a family consisting of a down-to-earth father, a frivolous mother, three daughters, and one son; pretty feminine clothes and gestures; a fashionable party; flowers (lilies) described as to seem gently symbolic of both the gaiety of the party and the approaching death; empathy with a working-class widow, who has five little children; offstage violence; self-involvement leading unwittingly to cruelty; and an innocent young heroine, who walks the line between sentimentality and real experience.

The story opens onto a setting reminiscent of the romantic comedy of an Austen or a James. The mood is upbeat: "ideal," "perfect," "delicious." Even the rose bushes have been blessed. The comic figure of the mother is introduced, saying something superbly egotistical: "Treat me as a honoured guest." Laura has a charm as lacey as a garden-party dress. She flies, she skims, over the lawn. Childlike, she adores her bread-and-butter, her cream puff. She blushes. She and her brother Laurie are as close as Shakespeare's Violet and Sebastian. In addition, the leader of the party of workers has the deepest blue eyes and a nose for lavender. Life is sweet and amusing. It moves gaily, full of potential.

Without spoiling that scene in the least, Mansfield begins to present the oppositions to the "ideal" that will create story. One of the workmen is pale and haggard. The splendid yellow-fruited Karaka-trees must be hidden by the marquee. The canna lilies are "wide open, radiant, almost frighteningly alive on bright crimson stems." Jose begins singing a lyric about the death of hope, the waking from a dream—while wearing a smile that undercuts the song's warning. Still, the mother keeps the laughter fueled. Her handwriting as reckless as she is, she thinks she has ordered "egg and mice" sandwiches for the party.

In the exact middle, the story turns. "Something had happened," writes Mansfield bluntly. A young workman from one of the cottages at the foot of the hill has been killed, leaving a wife and five children.

As we have been slyly led to expect, Jose has not the imagination to empathize. She substitutes prejudice for understanding, assuming that the man must have been drunk. Laura, who has already been identified as "the artistic one," has the beginnings, at least, of true imagination. Realizing that the sounds of the forthcoming party will be offensive to the widow, she insists upon canceling it. But soon the picture in her mind's eye becomes "blurred, unreal," and she can no longer sustain the reality of other people's pain (especially since at the moment she looks absolutely smashing in a new hat). The story is once more at a romantic pitch, and the reader is almost as willing to postpone confrontation with the incident as Laura is. The stream of life overwhelms us: "The band struck up; the hired waiters ran from the house to the marquee. Wherever you looked there were couples strolling, bending to the flowers, greeting, moving on over the lawn. They were like bright birds that had alighted in the Sheridans' garden for this one afternoon, on their way to—where?"

That is the question, of course, and its answer has already been implied: They are on their way to the universal stopping place. After the party when the father is "tactless" enough to reintroduce the subject of the "horrible affair," it is inevitable that Laura, who has a "different" view of matters, should be the one to call on the widow. Her bright frock and her pretty hat are grotesquely out of place as she enters the world of poverty and death, now far more real than garden parties. For one awful moment she looks into the face of grief—the young widow's "face, puffed up, red, with swollen eyes"—and then upon the face of death itself.

What can Mansfield say about a young person's first look at death? How can she honestly render this nearly indescribable event? Wisely, she forgoes her own insights to let Laura's nature shape the experience. The denouement may be taken as superficial if this division of author from subject is not kept constantly in mind.

We know Laura to be artistic, a little sentimental (Jose is correct on that point), and, with the possible exception of her brother and father, with whom she shares certain family characteristics, more imaginative than the rest of the Sheridans. She bears the marks of youthful narcissism, but she has flashes of real empathy for people around her. In fact, for her there is something mildly erotic about working men, so unlike the "silly boys" who come to supper on Sundays. Delicately rebellious, she flaunts social conventions by eating bread in public. Most important, she has refused to shut her eyes to anything. When she thinks of the poverty-stricken scene at the bottom of the hill, it is "disgusting and sordid" to her. "But still one must go everywhere; one must see everything." In short, at this stage of her life, Laura is in search of undifferentiated experience.

When this charming child-woman looks at the dead man, she sees, therefore, what her nature dictates. The young man is dreaming. "He was wonderful, beautiful. . . . All is well, said that sleeping face." "This marvel," Laura thinks: "While they were laughing, and while the band was playing, this marvel had come to the lane." Death has come in the back door to the garden party as the most important guest. Laura knows that something ritualistic is required by way of acknowledging that the dead young man has reached a place beyond frivolous arrangements. Sobbing childishly, she offers the nervous, poignant, "Forgive my hat"—which, as a response to death, may be as useful as anything else.

Waking then from the dream, running from everything, from the beautiful face of death as well as the swollen face of grief, from party frocks and those poor dark people with their oily voices, she experiences an emotional high. Like many such feelings, its component parts are fused so tightly that it cannot be analyzed. "What life was she couldn't explain." But that does not matter. She is in the loving arms of her brother, who understands that Laura has been reborn into her own world.

So to the short list of Mansfield's major themes, we must add a final one. In **"The Garden Party," "At the Bay"** (section 7), **"The Daughters of the Late Colonel," "Life of Ma Parker," "Six Years After,"** and in her last two stories, **"The Fly"** and **"The Canary,"** she looks at death in its living aspect, grief. Wedged between her brother's death and her own, these stories represent an interesting compromise between being awash with grief in life and coming to terms with it, however briefly, in art. Only the unfinished **"Six Years After"** fails to provide a satisfactory artistic stasis. Written with some of the finest insights

of her career, this shipboard story of a mother's grief for her adored young son remained unfinished because the grief as expressed was unendurable and the story drifts off threateningly: "And the little steamer, growing determined, throbbed on, pressed on, as if at the end of the journey there waited . . . "

The grief in the completed stories is usually handled by being forgotten, or, as in the pathetic case of Ma Parker, being unutterable because there is no one to hear. In other words, grief is not really *handled* at all.

Life is so full that grief gets displaced. Grandmother and Kezia, thinking of two deaths in **"At the Bay"**—one past, one (the Grandmother's) to come—are diverted back into life by tickling each other. Soon both have "forgotten" what they were talking about. Similarly, the colonel's daughters are caught up in the conventions of postfuneral courtesy. In any case, grief is not the operant emotion in response to the death of their comically brutal father. That event simply resurrects the old grief for their mother, thirty-five years dead—not that the sisters realize this fact. Looking at a photograph of their mother, the middle-aged, unmarried Josephine wonders how their lives would have been different had their mother lived. Then, hearing some sparrows peeping on the window-ledge, she feels their "crying, so weak and forlorn" inside her. By the end of the story, both sisters have "forgotten" what it was they needed to say to each other.

In Mansfield's sharpest depiction of grief, **"The Fly,"** the main character, called "the boss," finds that after six years of mourning for his son, he can no longer "arrange to weep." Instead, he experiments sadistically with a fly—as do the gods with us mortals. When the poor creature finally dies, the boss is seized with "a grinding feeling of wretchedness," but he too has forgotten the grief he had been trying to experience: "For the life of him he could not remember."

In Mansfield's last story, **"The Canary,"** someone is finally able to express grief in the customary manner. Speaking directly, through a monologue, the narrator recalls the small details of the dead bird's life and acknowledges what he meant to hers. She also attempts to interpret the bird's life and death in larger terms: "I must confess that there does seem to me something sad in life. It is hard to say what it is. I don't mean the sorrow that we all know, like illness and poverty and death. . . . But isn't it extraordinary that under his sweet, joyful little singing it was just this sadness—ah, what is it?—that I heard?" Transmuted into a floating feeling of diffuse sadness, wretchedness, or simply unreality, grief in the Mansfield stories falls residually like ash. (pp. 64-76)

Joanne Trautmann Banks, "Virginia Woolf and Katherine Mansfield," in The English Short Story, 1880-1945: A Critical History, *edited by Joseph M. Flora, Twayne Publishers, 1985, pp. 57-82.*

Kate Fullbrook   (essay date 1986)

[*Fullbrook is an English educator and critic whose* Katherine Mansfield *analyzes Mansfield as an important English Modernist. In the following excerpt from that work, Fullbrook closely examines several of Mans-*

field's most accomplished short stories from 1921, finding that they recapitulate characteristic concerns of Mansfield's fiction while displaying advances in literary technique.]

The early 1920s were the culminating years for literary modernism in English. Pound's *Mauberley* came out in 1920; Lawrence's *Women in Love* and Richardson's *Deadlock* in 1921; Eliot's *Waste Land,* Joyce's *Ulysses,* Yeats's *Later Poems* and Woolf's *Jacob's Room* in 1922. 1921 was the *annus mirabilis* for Katherine Mansfield's later work, during which she produced a crop of brilliant stories that themselves provide a review of all the concerns which had shaped her fiction and which extend her treatment of them through the application of her late technical subtlety.

The overriding interest in the stories of 1921 remains the unpredictability of the self and the impossibility of direct communication between individuals. Katherine Mansfield stressed this point again in 1922, when, in a letter to Murry, she insists on her familiar preoccupation: 'We are all hidden, looking out at each other; I mean even those of us who want not to hide.'

Moments of connection, much less communication, are rare in Katherine Mansfield's work, but in **'At the Bay'** (1921), one of the Burnell stories, she provides accounts of several moments when the barriers between her characters break down. Like **'Prelude'**, **'At the Bay'** is an impressionistic story held together by running motifs of animal images and of varieties of symbolic response to the sea.

'At the Bay' has a pastoral opening, patterned by images that embody the characters, their actions, their deficiencies and the mysterious influences that work upon them. The scene set is primal, an alternative Genesis: the sea is divided from the safety of the land, a flock of sheep and a wise old shepherd with his dog appears, a rebellious cat surveys the controlled, domestic animals with disdain, a huge gum-tree spreads its arms over the whole of the scene. Against the background of these 'timeless' images, the Burnells go into action, locked in roles that are fixed by their historical moment. Stanley plays his usual role of macho buffoon, beginning his day with an officious encounter with his brother-in-law, Jonathan, during his morning dip. It is all that Stanley can do with the possibilities of the unconscious which the sea, in the story, represents. The prose moves from the lyricism of the opening images to the self-important bluster of Stanley's mind, and it stays in this register until the women of the family bundle him into the coach for work. As he leaves, the whole house relaxes, with the narrative catching the change from the women's tension to their harmony in relief at his departure. Even Beryl, still driven by her lack of success in ensnaring a husband, and still engaged in a nervous flirtation with Stanley, is glad to see him go:

> 'Good-bye, Stanley', called Beryl, sweetly and gaily. It was easy enough to say good-bye! And there she stood, idle, shading her eyes with her hand. The worst of it was Stanley had to shout good-bye too, for the sake of appearances. Then he saw her turn, give a little skip and run back to the house. She was glad to be rid of him!

> Yes, she was thankful. Into the living-room she ran and called 'He's gone!' Linda cried from her room:

> 'Beryl! Has Stanley gone?' Old Mrs. Fairfield appeared, carrying the boy in his little flannel coatee.

> 'Gone?'

> 'Gone!'

> Oh, the relief, the difference it made to have the man out of the house. Their very voices changed as they called to one another; they sounded warm and loving and as if they shared a secret. Beryl went over to the table. 'Have another cup of tea, mother. It's still hot.' She wanted, somehow, to celebrate the fact that they could do what they liked now. There was no man to disturb them; the whole perfect day was theirs.

> 'No, thank you, child,' said old Mrs. Fairfield, but the way at that moment she tossed the boy up and said 'a-goos-a-goos-a-ga!' to him meant that she felt the same. The little girls ran into the paddock like chickens let out of a coop.

> Even Alice, the servant girl, washing up the dishes in the kitchen, caught the infection and used the precious tank water in a perfectly reckless fashion.

> 'Oh, these men!' said she, and she plunged the teapot into the bowl and held it under the water even after it had stopped bubbling, as if it too was a man and drowning was too good for them.

Katherine Mansfield deftly dramatises the relaxation of the women into mutual kindness as they make their various gestures of relief with the departure of Stanley. The women of all ages and social conditions respond more strongly to their moment of liberation than their external behaviour can indicate, but for an instant they are united in the communal expression of freedom grasped with pleasure.

Another writer concerned with portraying the condition of women might have left it at that: with symbolic Alice symbolically drowning all men in her symbolic sink in her symbolic kitchen while the women move in a harmony of rapture through the house. But Katherine Mansfield's moment of shared release is over in an instant. Alice stays at her sink; Beryl's frustration is not eased. The unity is, after all, only temporary; nothing essential has changed. Once the emotional reflex of relief has passed the characters go their separate ways, their female condition of restraint blending with other facets of their personalities to shape them in the series of duet-like encounters that follow. The little girls run off to play with their cousins; Alice visits a jolly widow happy with her independence (' "freedom's best" ', she tells Alice); Kezia confronts the idea of death in a moving conversation with her grandmother; Linda feels a stab of love for her new son, who, up to this point, has left her only hostile or indifferent, and has a moment of connection with Jonathan.

There are only a few instances in all of Katherine Mansfield's fiction where she suggests what a true meeting between the sexes might entail. The most powerful of these occurs in **'At the Bay'** during Linda's conversation with Jonathan. It is important to notice that the fellow feeling in this encounter is only possible because Jonathan falls hopelessly short when measured against standards of orthodox masculine behaviour and success which are typified by Stanley. Linda, as in **'Prelude'**, is unhappy, still enmeshed in the expectations of her class and era. Jonathan, however, interests her.

> Linda thought again how attractive he was. It was strange to think that he was only an ordinary clerk, that Stanley earned twice as much money as he. What was the matter with Jonathan? He had no ambition; she supposed that was it. And yet one felt he was gifted, exceptional. He was passionately fond of music; every spare penny he had went on books. He was always full of new ideas, schemes, plans. But nothing came of it all. The new fire blazed in Jonathan . . . but a moment later it had fallen in and there was nothing but ashes, and Jonathan went around with a look like hunger in his eyes.

Jonathan himself understands what is wrong; he loathes the half of the sexist equation that defines the worth of a man largely by the money he can make, and yet he realises that his own life has been set in its pattern of unease by the very values he rejects.

> 'It seems to me just as imbecile, just as infernal, to have to go to the office on Monday,' said Jonathan, 'as it always has done and always will do. To spend all the best years of one's life sitting on a stool from nine to five, scratching on someone's ledger! It's a queer use to make of one's . . . one and only life, isn't it?'

Jonathan is kept 'in jail' by his marriage and family. ' "I've two boys to provide for," ' he says, but he is wistfully pulled toward a larger life, a world that he sees as a ' "vast dangerous garden, waiting out there, undiscovered, unexplored" '. And it is too late to change. He says, in response to Linda's empathy and sympathy: ' "I'm old—I'm old." ' He bends his head and to Linda's sad surprise shows the grey speckling his hair. Like Kezia with her grandmother in the same story, the characters bow together before knowledge of mortality; age and sexual differences are brushed aside in recognition of the inevitability of death and in wonder at the fixity of personal history.

This single, moving instance of unmasked connection between a woman and a man emphasises the similarities rather than the divergences in the human condition. The moment depends on the fact that Jonathan is capable of wonder and is intellectually alive, and that Linda is in sympathy with these qualities despite her own choice of bourgeois safety. Even if Jonathan is a failed rebel, it is crucial that his disgust with masculine roles is one of the most significant aspects of his character. Sensitivity and rejection of a totally materialist view of the world point to the ways in which the existential bad faith, which Katherine Mansfield sees as generally poisoning life, might be overcome. It is, of course, a traditional spiritual and intellectual solution that is offered, but it is a tradition that Katherine Mansfield herself embraces. Yet even in this rare moment of meeting in her fiction, the direct occasion for abandoning roles is the intimate realisation of mortality. The joy in the characters' easiness together is touched by the corruption of death. Katherine Mansfield sees love and death, pity and fellow feeling, and the realisation of human boundaries and possibilities meeting in a solemn and stoic frame.

If sexual *rapprochment* such as that which takes place between Linda and Jonathan is portrayed as possible to characters able to abandon, even momentarily, the divisive effects of social convention (and one must point out that *both* Linda and Jonathan are failures if judged by the standards of social orthodoxy), and see instead the commonality in the human condition, the experiences of Beryl, in her dealings with the Kembers, illustrate the power that the failure to fulfil conventional sexual expectations has to warp all other relationships. In **'Prelude'** as well as in **'At the Bay'**, Beryl is shown in the process of being driven literally mad by her lack of a husband—a case that balances against Linda's equal distress in her marriage. In Beryl, Katherine Mansfield delineates the process that creates the embittered spinster by providing no option in life but marriage for the respectable woman. Attractive, lively Beryl, able to measure her success as a human being only by the acquisition of a man, enraged by her lack of success as an unmarried aunt, emotionally unfulfilled, financially dependent, is caught in the period between hope of changing and despair at the permanency of her condition. She lives chiefly in her divided imagination; the prose that depicts her consciousness is alternately swooning, romantic and fanciful, and angry, violent and tyrannical. Beryl consistently lashes out at the world which, as far as she can see, allows her only one avenue to happiness which she, by herself, can do nothing to secure. Because she lives so much in her own mind, and is absorbed by its contradictions, she does not even see the disastrous nature of her sister's marriage. Marriage to Beryl seems the answer to every problem, including that of the torment of the internal divisions which assail her. Her hysteria (and she is another of Katherine Mansfield's characters likely to lose herself in moments of panicky breakdown) is rooted in her definition as a woman, and her blind need is punctuated by moments of illumination. In **'Prelude'**, at night, she regards herself in the mirror:

> Oh God, there she was, back again, playing the same old game. False—false as ever . . . False even when she was alone with herself, now. . . .
>
> 'Oh,' she cried, 'I am so miserable—so frightfully miserable. I know that I'm silly and spiteful and vain; I'm always acting a part. I'm never my real self for a moment.'

Beryl's sense of herself as masked presupposes a different self beneath the mask, waiting for liberation. The narrative, however, does not verify this belief. The mask *is* Beryl, as much as the doubtful and self-critical response to that mask is also a secret part of her identity. But the whole of her discontinuous character has only one function—to save herself from what she sees as her social isolation, her cultural placelessness. In **'At the Bay'**, since no acceptable attachment presents itself, Beryl turns to the unacceptable Kembers.

Escaping from her mother on the beach, Beryl plunges into the sea with 'fast' Mrs Kember, whose disregard for the proprieties goes further than her cigarettes, her 'lack of vanity, her slang, and the way she treated men as though she was one of them, and the fact that she didn't care twopence about her house'. Katherine Mansfield draws a hard line around the relationship between the two women—the external marks of Mrs Kember's 'liberation' say nothing about her moral quality. In fact, she is a sexual predator as much as the men she so closely imitates. Her lesbian predation of Beryl is emphasised in her parody of male seduction, her leering compliments to Beryl about her body, her 'stolen' caressing touches. Like a 'rat', Mrs Kember leaves Beryl, who plays up to her, feeling as if 'she was being poisoned by this cold woman . . . how strange, how horrible!' But Beryl needs to hear the kind of crude seductive comments Mrs Kember makes, and will listen to her in the absence of any man to make them instead. At the end of the story, she does have her chance at a man. Harry Kember, the equally predatory husband of the rat-woman, calls her into the garden at night. Beryl joins him but ends in running away, leaving the silence and 'the sound of the sea . . . a vague murmur, as though it waked out of a dark dream'. What Katherine Mansfield shows Beryl drawing back from is not Mrs Kember's lesbianism nor Harry Kember's extramarital embrace, but something *both* characters represent. It is the Kember's predation, their being seducers, *victimisers* rather than lovers, that is Katherine Mansfield's concern.

'At the Bay', despite its moments of connection, ends with danger in Beryl's escape from further psychological corrosion. What she flees from is simultaneously her own desire and its fulfilment, and a victimisation that would distortedly enact the marriage she needs for personal validation. The sound of the sea, image of these confusions and possibilities, takes the narrative back to timelessness, and to the chaotic mumblings of dream and desire.

Kezia probably has a less important role in **'At the Bay'** than in any of the Burnell stories, but she is once again at the centre of **'The Doll's House'** (1921). The little girls in this story, like Nora in the play by Ibsen after which it is named, and like the little girl in **'Pearl Button'**, are female rebels in revolt against the sexual and social rules that are meant to divide them into hostile and permanently alienated camps. Kezia is the heroine, and the story concerns her breaking her family's injunction against allowing the 'impossible' Kelvey girls to see the Burnells' new doll's house.

Lil and Else Kelvey are the pariahs of the playground. They are poor children who are used by the school and the parents of the other girls as negative object-lessons of what, for females, is beyond the pale. The Kelveys are 'shunned by everybody'.

> They were the daughters of a spry, hard-working little washerwoman, who went about from house to house by the day. This was awful enough. But where was Mr. Kelvey? Nobody knew for certain. But everybody said he was in prison. So they were the daughters of a washerwoman and a gaolbird. Very nice company for other people's children! And they looked it. Why Mrs. Kelvey made them so conspicuous was hard to understand. The truth was they were dressed in 'bits' given to her by the people for whom she worked.

The narrative mimics the tone of the self-righteous, disapproving, genteel community (and these are women's tones, women's voices defending their class territory). Aside from the fundamental class snobbery in operation here, there is an explicit outline of what conformity to female stereotype must mean. Women must not work, they can only be fully validated on the production of a suitable male from whom they ought to derive their status, their being is closely bound up in their clothes. Self-sufficiency, hard work, and cheerful courage (supposedly valued by the

same culture) are unacceptable: Mrs Kelvey and her daughters fail on every sexist point.

On a day that the outcasts have been particularly tormented in the schoolyard, Kezia violates her mother's ban on the girls. Seeing them coming down the road she is torn, in a moment reminiscent of Huck Finn's espousal of the 'nigger' Jim, between the social conscience her culture has been developing and an individual stroke of consciousness.

> Nobody was about; she began to swing on the big white gates of the courtyard. Presently, looking along the road, she saw two little dots. They grew bigger, they were coming towards her. Now she could see that one was in front and one close behind. Now she could see that they were the Kelveys. Kezia stopped swinging. She slipped off the gate as if she was going to run away. Then she hesitated. The Kelveys came nearer, and beside them walked their shadows, very long, stretching right across the road with their heads in the buttercups. Kezia clambered back on the gate; she had made up her mind; she swung out.

As in **'Pearl Button'** the gate is a sign of vacillation between being shut into or moving out of convention. And again, the central character swings free. Kezia asks the Kelveys in and they have a chance to see the doll's house before Aunt Beryl shoos them off. The shadows of the girls, 'stretching right across the road with their heads in the buttercups', is what decides Kezia to make her move. The delicacy and beauty of the highly original image contrasts strongly with the clipped, factual language of crude perception that records Kezia's sighting of the girls, and the text reflects the shift from the crudity of dispassionate observation to Kezia's sympathetic recognition of the outlaw children. The shadows that merge the little girls with the beauty of the flowers simply ignore the confining man-made road and its straight lines. Kezia does the same as she obliterates the class lines of her acculturation and recognises the Kelveys as in some sense equals. And in doing so, Kezia denies the values their rejection represents.

The doll's house itself is a complex symbol that precisely suits the story. Given to the Burnell girls by Mrs Hay ('Sweet old Mrs Hay', a woman whose bland, rustic, vegetable name connotes her conformity), the doll's house has to be left outside. As Beryl thinks:

> No harm could come to it; it was summer. And perhaps the smell of paint would have gone by the time it had to be taken in. For, really, the smell of paint coming from that doll's house . . . the smell of paint was quite enough to make anyone seriously ill. . . .

The doll's house is completely furnished, down to 'the father and mother dolls, who . . . were really too big for the doll's house', just as real people are 'too big' for the kind of married life that the doll's house metonymically represents. Even when new, the doll's house smells revolting, like the institution it imitates. And just as the Kelveys are used as a negative lesson for the Burnell girls, the doll's house is meant for positive female instruction. It is an invitation to sweet domesticity, to boast about possessions; it provides an opportunity for a complete childish parody of the approved method for women to locate their identities in their houses and in the things and people they manage to stuff into them. But the doll's house is also a fabulous toy, a playground for the wayward imagination, and it contains one item that particularly catches Kezia's fancy: a tiny lamp that almost looks as if it could be lit. Katherine Mansfield once more uses the classic association of lamps and knowledge to indicate the rebelliousness of Kezia's reaction to the house. Although the lamp is false, as is the system of values embodied by the house and summed up in the persecution of the Kelveys, it is the *idea* of the lamp that catches Kezia's attention. The linkage of Kezia and the Kelveys earlier in the story is repeated via the mediation of this image. Else nudges Lil at the very end of the story: 'she smiled her rare smile. "I seen the little lamp," she said softly. Then both were silent once more.' The image unites the girl-children, the outcast and the privileged, in their imaginations which refuse the patterns dictated by their culture and create alternative patterns of their own. (pp. 106-17)

['The Garden Party', 'The Daughters of the Late Colonel', and 'Life of Ma Parker'] are stories about mortality, particularly women's consciousness of mortality, and I can think of no other woman writer, with the exception of Emily Dickinson, who gives the subject such close attention. For all that has been made of the connection between Katherine Mansfield's own awareness of impending death at this time, it is necessary to note that her interest in the subject in her writing of 1921 was concentrated on the effect of death on the living, and it adds another dimension to her consistent portraiture of women's isolation and exclusion.

'The Garden Party' is a case in point. As in 'Bliss', Katherine Mansfield sets up a situation in which a woman is suddenly displaced from a frenetic social whirl that supposedly defines the totality of her being. The Sheridans in the story are a variant of the Burnells; the setting is New Zealand and the characters prototypical colonials.

The Sheridan children, all young adults, are giving a party. The excited, happy narrative sees what they see in the terms that they see it—their fine house on a hill, bustling in preparation for the party, full of good things to eat, lovely things to wear, wonderful, expensive flowers to enjoy. The background is crammed with people to order about; the servants 'loved obeying'; friendly workmen swarm in the garden putting up a marquee; deliveries are made from shops; a band has been hired to put the finishing touches on the pleasures of the afternoon. The confident description is soaked in the values of middle-class authority as the genteel bourgeoisie prepares to play and enjoys every minute of the preparation. The pleasures at hand are both material and aesthetic, and even the perfect weather seems to endorse everything the Sheridans stand for. But the narration, insidiously, also undercuts its own exuberance with irony. Here, for example, is one of the daughters, Jose, practising for the display of her musical talents at the party:

> *Pom!* Ta-ta-ta *Tee*-ta! The piano burst out so passionately that Jose's face changed. She clasped her hands. She looked mournfully and enigmatically at her mother and Laura as they came in.
> This Life is *Wee*-ary,
> A Tear-a Sigh.
> A Love that *Chan*-ges,
>   This Life is *Wee*-ary,
> A Tear-a Sigh.
> A Love that *Chan*-ges,

> And then . . . Good-bye!

> But at the word 'Good-bye,' and although the piano sounded more desperate than ever, her face broke into a brilliant, dreadfully unsympathetic smile.

> 'Aren't I in good voice, mummy?' she beamed.

Katherine Mansfield mocks Jose's 'female accomplishments' in the same ironic manner and for the same reasons as Jane Austen does in *Pride and Prejudice*. Just as Mary bored the company in 1813, displaying her vanity rather than her love for music, so Jose produces the same eminently false effect in 'The Garden Party' of 1921. It is something of a shock to recognise the same device working so effectively in this twentieth-century story. Katherine Mansfield's attack on the inadequacy of the education of 'the daughters of educated men' is deepened by the story's account of the suffering taking place in the workmen's cottages just below the Sheridans' privileged hill. The false sentiment of Jose's song echoes the emotional disaster near at hand. The worker's world, which 'mummy' does not fully recognise (though the story emphasises the fact that she and her children live by and through their control of that world), is the scene of a casual tragedy. A workman has been killed in an accident; the news arrives during the preparations for the party. And the question of what is to be done in response to the news arises for only one character.

The character is Laura, a vaguely mutinous Sheridan daughter who, in the course of the story, acts as an intermediary between the two worlds—that of privilege and gaiety, and that of hardship, death and sorrow—and in the process is forced, if only momentarily, into the role of outsider.

We see Laura first in that most typical of middle-class occupations—romantic identification with an idealised working class. Laura, 'who loved having to arrange things', is assigned to direct the workmen who erect the marquee. Actually she directs nothing; the workmen know their job and choose the best site for the marquee in spite of her alternative suggestions. Laura's class loyalties vie with her sense of adventure; as she deals with the men their ease finally overcomes her slightly wounded dignity when they do not treat her with the deference afforded to a middle-class matron. Looking over the plan the foreman has hastily drawn, Laura dips her toe into rebellion:

> Oh, how extraordinarily nice workmen were, she thought. Why couldn't she have workmen for friends rather than the silly boys she danced with and who came to Sunday night supper . . . It's all the fault, she decided . . . of these absurd class distinctions. Well, for her part, she didn't feel them. Not a bit, not an atom . . . Just to prove how happy she was, just to show the tall fellow how at home she felt, and how she despised stupid conventions, Laura took a big bite out of her bread-and-butter as she stared at the little drawing. She felt just like a work-girl.

This is, of course, transparent affectation, but it is also a potentially significant masquerade, small as the gesture of taking a bite of bread-and-butter might be. What the significance might be is suggested when the news of the death reaches the Sheridans. Laura, still influenced by her thoughts about the workmen, wants to stop the party, but her mother simply cuts her off:

> 'You are being very absurd, Laura,' she said coldly. 'People like that don't expect sacrifices from us. And it's not very sympathetic to spoil everyone's enjoyment as you're doing now.'
>
> 'I don't understand,' said Laura, and she walked quickly out of the room into her own bedroom.

Several truths of unequal significance operate in this passage. Death *cannot* be conquered by stopping a party. Pleasure *is* rare enough to deserve protection. The workers do *not* have any expectations. And Laura really does have no idea what she is doing. (That her mother damns herself and her class goes without saying, but at the same time *any* life that paused with every death would soon be unliveable).

Laura's knowledge of the workmen is almost nonexistent. Their lane was forbidden territory in her childhood and since she has 'grown up' she has only walked through it once with her brother (and *alter ego*), Laurie. On the walk she sees the lane as 'disgusting and sordid. They came out with a shudder. But still one must go everywhere; one must see everything.' Laura in no way connects herself with the lane. But this distanced social voyeurism turns into something very immediate with the news of the death, and just for a moment, at the centre of the story, Laura steps outside her class and circumstances into a confrontation with the equality of all humanity in the face of mortality. What Laura 'sees' at this point is far more important than what she has 'seen' during her educational tour of a working-class habitat. For a moment, the social vocabulary of her tribe fills Laura with disgust.

But only for a moment. What draws Laura back from the isolation of her response to death is another confrontation, this time with her own face framed by a lovely hat that itself is the image of the pleasures of life that only youth and privilege provide. What she sees in a mirror, walking away from her mother, is her identity:

> the first thing she saw was this charming girl in the mirror, in her black hat trimmed with gold daisies and a long black velvet ribbon. Never had she imagined she could look like that. Is mother right? she thought. And now she hoped that her mother was right.

It is an extraordinary moment of conscience callousing over, with the lovely black hat repeating the colour of death. Katherine Mansfield's characteristic attention to detail allows her to conflate conscience and consciousness, beauty and vanity, bodily and mental satisfaction as Laura's politics turn on a glimpse of herself in the mirror. Giving up her chance for a public display of her beauty would be sacrificial; Laura slips easily back into the frivolity of the garden-party. On the next page she is afraid of being 'teased' about even thinking of making her egalitarian gesture.

Since Laura's class complacency is safe and the party is over, Mrs Sheridan gives her daughter a lesson in 'proper' charity. She sends her to the dead man's cottage with scraps from the party. In her stunning hat, her mind filled with the delights of the party, Laura self-consciously walks into the cottage with her basket and into the ceremonies of death. The two social rituals—the celebrations of the rich family, and the solemnity of death for the poor one—stress the discontinuity of experience. The man's wife, huddled like some primitive wounded thing by the fire, looks up at Laura, 'Her face, puffed up, red, with swollen eyes and swollen lips, looked terrible'. Laura, ashamed and embarrassed, blunders into the room with the dead man, and as the corpse is exhibited to her with tender, ritualistic pride, her response remains in the aesthetic mode of the party: 'he was wonderful, beautiful', a 'marvel', much better, in fact, in terms of beauty than her hat for which she now blurts out an excuse. The reader must recall the earlier significance of the hat and all that it has meant for Laura's conscience to understand the meaning of that apology. The story ends with Laura's confusion as she tries to express her feelings to Laurie and the meaning she has drawn from this encounter with death.

'The Garden Party' is radically inconclusive. It is especially interesting in its portrayal of simultaneous but opposing goods, and in its treatment of the confusion of motivations and principles in life as opposed to the clarity of abstract ideas. Katherine Mansfield stressed this aspect of the story in a letter [dated 13 March 1922] to William Gerhardi:

> And yes, that is what I tried to convey in **'The Garden Party.'** The diversity of life and how we try to fit in everything, Death included. That is bewildering for a person of Laura's age. She feels things ought to happen differently. First one and then another. But life isn't like that. We haven't the ordering of it.

Katherine Mansfield's writing does, however, impose an order. It rejects the one that Laura accepts when she allows her aesthetic and class assumptions to dominate her at the moment when another kind of response was available to her. Laura only tastes the solitude that is the main diet of the women in many other stories, but the easiness with which a character can be thrust from full membership of a community to absolute exile in an instant, and the way in which such exile depends upon individual consciousness, underscores Katherine Mansfield's insistence on the fragility of identity.

While Katherine Mansfield's portrayal of the relationship between the self and others is always bleak, her late stories, as well as her early ones, are often comic. As Claire Tomalin points out about **'The Daughters of the Late Colonel'** [in her introduction to **Katherine Mansfield: Short Stories,** 1983], this very funny story 'offers an almost flawless description of two sisters who have been rendered unfit for life: not entirely a laughing matter.' In turning themselves into perfect objects for their father's will, the two old ladies have denuded themselves of their own. As Tomalin goes on to say of the story, 'it is quite possible to enjoy its jokes about early twentieth-century womanhood and miss the devastating nature of what it is saying.' The querulous, timid narration itself expresses the central experience of the daughters as they try to grope their way out from under their masks after the death of their father.

The title of **'The Daughters of the Late Colonel'** gives the circumstances of the story away. The two women, Constantia and Josephine, have indeed been 'constant' to their rumbling old father. These two pathetic creatures have existed only in relation to him, have lived only as 'daughters' and never in their own right. When the Colonel is dead, the world slips its moorings for the women who have been so stripped of the capacity for independent action by their life-long deference that they are scarcely sane.

> 'Oh,' groaned poor Josephine aloud, 'we shouldn't have done it, Con!'
>
> And Constantia, pale as a lemon in all that blackness, said in a frightened whisper, 'Done what, Jug?'
>
> 'Let them bu-bury father like that,' said Josephine, breaking down and crying into her new, queer-smelling mourning handkerchief.
>
> 'But what else could we have done?' asked Constantia wonderingly. 'We couldn't have kept him, Jug—we couldn't have kept him unburied. At any rate, not in a flat that size.'
>
> Josephine blew her nose; the cab was dreadfully stuffy.
>
> 'I don't know,' she said forlornly, 'It is all so dreadful. I feel we ought to have tried to, just for a time at least. To make perfectly sure. One thing's certain'—and her tears sprang out again—'father will never forgive us for this—never!'

Like frightened birds kept too long in captivity the two sisters cannot even think of flying. At the conclusion of the story, as they try to speak to one another of the future and to tell truths unrelated to their father's rule, they falter.

> A pause. Then Constantia said faintly, 'I can't say what I was going to say, Jug, because I've forgotten what it was . . . that I was going to say.'
>
> Josephine was silent for a moment. She stared at a big cloud where the sun had been. The she replied shortly, 'I've forgotten too.'

Like the lives they might have had but which are no longer even memories of possibilities lost, the very words that might mean freedom have lapsed; the two sisters fall into the sun-darkening silence that has been their women's portion all along. Inured in their father's house they will rot with his furniture. Freedom has atrophied with lack of use. The two old women will continue as victims of a father who denied them the right to live.

Katherine Mansfield was angered by accusations of 'cruelty' and 'sneering' in the story. As she explained, again to William Gerhardi, the story was meant 'to lead up to that last paragraph, when my two flowerless ones turned with that timid gesture, to the sun. "Perhaps *now* . . . " And after that, it seemed to me, they died as surely as Father was dead.'

It is finally, this theme, the 'sunlessness' of women's lives, and perhaps all lives, that is the dominant impression left by Katherine Mansfield's late fiction. It is the fiction of catastrophe, with varieties of deprivation, unhappiness and despair in control of human consciousness which Katherine Mansfield is constantly pushing to the breaking-point. The most important impulses behind the writing are emotions of anger and pity, and in her late work Katherine Mansfield at times abandoned the emotional cynicism of modernism to compose stories which are pure outcry.

'Life of Ma Parker' is the best of these sketches of despair.

As always, Katherine Mansfield provides a social base for her tale in the form of a 'literary gentleman' who is shown priding himself on his 'handling' of Ma Parker, his aged, cheap, exhausted char, whom he overworks and underpays, and then undermines with accusations of petty theft. As the story switches to Ma Parker's consciousness, the way the world looks changes completely. She has a kind heart and merely pities the man for his messes as her mind fingers the memories of her disastrous life. Her husband died young of his baker's trade leaving her with the six of their thirteen children who survived. Her daughters 'went wrong', her boys 'emigrimated', and her last remaining girl was thrown back on her hands after the death of her husband, bringing with her a frail grandson who has been the light of Ma Parker's life and whom she has just buried. The contrast of the extraordinary stoicism of the woman and the tenderness of her love for the fragile child is painfully moving:

> 'Gran! Gran!' Her little grandson stood on her lap in his button boots. He'd just come in from playing in the street.
>
> 'Look what a state you've made your gran's skirt into—you wicked boy!'
>
> But he put his arms round her neck and rubbed his cheek against hers.
>
> 'Gran, gi' us a penny!' he coaxed.
>
> 'Be off with you; Gran ain't got no pennies.'
>
> 'Yes you 'ave. Gi' us one!'
>
> Already she was feeling for the old, squashed black leather purse.
>
> 'Well, what'll you give your gran?'
>
> He gave a shy little laugh and pressed closer.
>
> She felt his eyelid quiver against her cheek. 'I ain't got nothing,' he murmured. . . .

This battered old woman, as 'squashed' as the purse that has held so little, has in fact possessed riches, and has lost them all. Katherine Mansfield refuses to mitigate the pathos of memories, and the story turns on the last of the little boy's remembered words. The theme, 'I ain't got nothing', is picked up forcefully when Ma Parker, finally overcome by her grief at her loss, somnambulantly walks out of the flat into the cold street.

> There was a wind like ice. People went flitting by, very fast; the men walked like scissors, the women trod like cats. And nobody knew—nobody cared. Even if she broke down, if at last, after all these years, she were to cry, she'd find herself in the lock-up as like as not.

Images of hostility and threat—wind and ice and scissors and cats and prisons—provide the final exclusion, generated by a consciousness that is left with only its own incredible stoicism. There is nowhere even for Ma Parker to cry. The narrative swoops in and out of her vocabulary to a general outcry of desolation and deprivation.

Katherine Mansfield's reputation for most of this century—that of a delicate female stylist with a reassuring line in colonial nostalgia—is rightly being revised. Her stories instead demand to be read as unremittingly critical accounts of social injustice grounded in the pretence of a 'natural' psychological and biological order that is disproved by the experience of consciousness. Image and plot, symbol and idea—all the elements of her fiction function as protests against any ideology of fixture and certainty. Katherine Mansfield's general commentary on her age is couched in her exposition of, her imaging of, contemporary women's consciousness, and in a prose attuned to catch the form of that experience. She implicitly demands the right to see women and their lives as the particulars from which the general historical situation can be deduced. But her fiction goes beyond an attempt to 'reflect' the age in which she lived; it is a body of work that incites to revolt through its critical appraisal of the circumstances Katherine Mansfield sees and records. (pp. 117-28)

Kate Fullbrook, in her Katherine Mansfield, *The Harvester Press, Sussex, 1986, pp. 106-29.*

Clare Hanson   (essay date 1987)

[*In the following excerpt, Hanson examines some characteristics of Mansfield's literary criticism and considers its role in her life and literary career.*]

'Not being an intellectual', Katherine Mansfield wrote to John Middleton Murry in 1920, 'I always seem to have to learn things at the risk of my life.' The remark suggests some of the dangers inherent in the enterprise of attempting to establish KM's reputation as a critic. She is alluding here, with some hostility, to Murry's book of critical essays *The Evolution of an Intellectual* (1920), and distancing herself from the kind of professional criticism produced by Murry, which did not often represent something learnt 'at the risk of [one's] life'. In an earlier letter she expressed her distaste for Murry's intellectual approach: a note of conviction is sustained rather than undermined by her admission of feelings of vulnerability in writing as a (relatively) uneducated woman and as a colonial—the 'little Colonial' from Karori.

> But this intellectual reasoning is never *the whole truth*. It's not *the artist's truth*—not *creative*. If man were an intellect it would do, but man ISN'T. Now I must be fair, I must be fair. Who am I to be certain that I understand? There's always Karori to shout after me. *Shout* it.

From such a perspective KM's formal critical writings might be seen as anomalous: it could be argued that the reviews she wrote in 1919 and 1920 for the *Athenaeum*, in particular, were written against the grain, from a desire to placate Murry. Yet KM put 'her all' into these reviews, and devoted nearly two years of her short writing life to them, at the expense of her fiction. While we must acknowledge the reservations she felt about formal literary criticism and the English upper-middle-class male values embodied in it, we must recognise too that her critical writings represent a genuine attempt to take on the literary establishment on its own terms. KM wanted to 'preach', to convert, and could and would take up the opposition's weapons in order to do this. The extent to which she at the same time subverted and undercut contemporary literary-critical forms must by the same token be recognised.

KM's critical writings are not well known (unlike those of Virginia Woolf, for example), and it has been suggested that her finest critical insights came in an impromptu fashion, and were dashed off in moments of inspiration in letters and journals. This rather romantic view both fosters and depends on an over-emphasis on the immediately accessible 'personality' of the author, which, it is supposed, is reflected in all her writings. . . . I would like to shift attention away from the attractive personality of 'Katherine Mansfield', back to the writing, in this case that body of critical work which lies so solidly across the path of the would-be KM reader or critic. What meaning, and what status, should we assign to it?

The difficulties of decision in this particular case are compounded by the presence of J. M. Murry in KM's life as in her work. Murry acted as KM's agent and took responsibility for the publication of her life and writings in a process of re-presentation which began years before her death. Antony Alpers has suggested [in an August 1983 conversation with the critic] that Murry introduced a kind of 'fuzziness' into the public picture of KM. Certainly there is an unmistakable preference for the softer focus and rosier hue in Murry's view, as is suggested in Lytton Strachey's acid summing up of the discrepancy between the portrait of a lady produced for the public in Murry's 1927 *Journal,* and the woman he thought he had known: 'But why that foul-mouthed, virulent, brazen-faced broomstick of a creature should have got herself up as a pad of rose-scented cotton wool is beyond me' [quoted in *Lytton Strachey: A Critical Biography,* by Michael Holroyd, 1968].

For a variety of perfectly understandable reasons it would seem that Murry frequently miscast and misread KM both as a person and as a writer. At the very beginning of their relationship KM *wrote* to him (significantly) about her loathing of the role of 'wife':

> Yes, I hate hate *hate* doing these things that you accept just as all men accept of their women. I can only play the servant with a very bad grace indeed. It's all very well for females who have nothing else to do. . . .

Eight years later, still in the same vein, she wrote of Murry's refusal to accept the fact that for her, as for Virginia Woolf, the roles of 'wife' and 'writer' were—not just because of illness—incompatible:

> My only trouble is John. He ought to divorce me, marry a really young healthy creature, have children and ask me to be godmother. I shall never be a wife and I feel such a fraud when he believes that one day I shall turn into one.

Murry's failures of vision affected important areas of professional life: it was while he was acting as KM's literary agent, for example, that he released what Anthony Alpers calls the 'detested 1913 photograph' for publicity purposes. The photograph was rejected by KM not just because it gave a false picture of her as brimming with rude health, but because it gave a misleading picture of her *as a woman* and/or as a writer. KM complained too, when ***Bliss, and Other Stories*** was published, about what she perceived as a conflict inherent in the presentation of 'Katherine Mansfield' both as a woman and a writer. She felt threatened with silence specifically because of this conflict [and wrote in a letter to Murry]:

Just while I'm on the subject I suppose you will think I am an egocentric to mind the way Constable has advertised my book and the paragraph that is on the paper cover. I'd like to say that I mind so terribly that there are no words for me. No—I'm DUMB!! I think it so insulting and disgusting and undignified that—well—there you are! It's no good suffering all over again. But the bit about 'Women will learn by heart and not repeat'. Gods! why didn't they have a photograph of me looking through a garter. But I was helpless here—too late to stop it—so now I *must* prove—no, convince people ce n'est pas moi. At least, if I'd known they were going to say that, no power on earth would have made me cut a word. I wish I hadn't. I was wrong—very wrong.

To come down to more tangible textual matters, it is clear that Murry had a hand in the bowdlerisation of KM's fiction as well as of her letters and journals. In the quotation above, KM is referring to the fact that **'Je Ne Parle Pas Français'** (one of the only two stories, she said in 1922, that satisfied her to any extent) had been adulterated for its publication by Constable. The original text, as published by the Heron Press in 1919, is far bolder—the story ends, for example, with two additional paragraphs:

I must go. I must go. I reach down my coat and hat. Madame knows me. 'You haven't dined yet?' she smiles.

'No, not yet, Madame.' [Constable text ends here.]

I'd rather like to dine with her. Even to sleep with her afterwards. Would she be pale like that all over?

But no. She'd have large moles. They go with that kind of skin. And I can't bear them. They remind me somehow, disgustingly, of mushrooms.

Many references to sexuality (important for the particular kind of 'corruption' KM was evoking here) have been cut for the Constable edition: KM felt she had 'picked the eyes out of [her] story', at Murry's and Michael Sadleir's instigation, to ensure its publication. Of course, she was responding to social pressures, not only to Murry, in doing this, and it would be wrong to suggest that Murry should take sole responsibility for the ways in which his wife's work and personality were presented to the public. It is unfair, I think, to take the line taken by Leonard Woolf, who [in his *Beginning Again: An Autobiography of the Years 1911-18*, 1964] claimed that Murry had a malevolent influence on KM which was in some way outside her control:

I think that in some abstruse way Murry corrupted and perverted and destroyed Katherine both as a person and a writer. . . . She got enmeshed in the sticky sentimentality of Murry and wrote against the grain of her own nature.

But Murry did certainly suggest, during KM's lifetime, that she should hide some of her cutting edge from the public, and after her death he ensured that her sharpness did not often appear. He was far more concerned than KM with the question of what it was decorous for a woman writer to say, and the effect of his editing of KM's life and works has undoubtedly been to obscure the clarity, the harshness and, I would suggest, the more 'masculine' qualities of her mind.

In KM's critical writings Murry's influence is directly detectable in certain turns of phrase and in a kind of portentousness which appears particularly in the earlier reviews. KM and Murry wrote enthusiastic manifesto articles together for *Rhythm* in 1912, and something of the Murry tone still lingers in the first reviews KM wrote for the *Athenaeum*—in the closing lines of a review of Maugham's *The Moon and Sixpence,* for example:

But great artists are not drunken men; they are men who are divinely sober. They know that the moon can never be bought for sixpence, and that liberty is only a profound realisation of the greatness of the dangers in their midst.

But KM quickly pulled herself up: she commented crisply when she pasted this review into her notebook, 'Shows traces of hurry & at the end, is pompous!'

Her achievement was precisely to create her own voice—the least portentous of voices—while working within many constraints, both in the *Athenaeum* reviews and in her critical writing in letters and journals. Seen in this context, of an achieved critical point of view, Murry's influence (apart from specific questions of style or tone) is perhaps best seen as symbolic—he acts as a convenient scapegoat, a representative of many of the values of the contemporary literary establishment which KM wished to resist.

What KM really wanted to do in her criticism is explained in a letter of 1920 in which she admonished Murry regarding the *Athenaeum:*

In my reckless way I would suggest all reviews were signed and all were put into the first person. I think that would give the whole paper an amazing lift-up. A paper that length must be *definite, personal* or die. It can't afford the 'we'—'in our opinion'. To sign reviews, to put them in the 1st person stimulates curiosity, *makes for correspondence,* gives it (to be 19-eleventyish) GUTS. You see it's a case of leaning out of a window with a board and a nail, *or* a bouquet, *or* a flag— administering whichever it is and retiring *sharp.* This seems to me essential.

It is tempting to suggest that KM's dislike of the impersonal third-person style of contemporary reviewing is distinctively 'feminine', and on these grounds to align her with a writer such as Dorothy Richardson, who was a conscious campaigner against the rigid, impersonal, rulebound qualities of 'male prose'. Yet this would be misleading and the adoption of such convenient distinctions might obscure the real complexity of KM's position as a woman writer at a particular point in time, writing for a particular audience. It does not take much reflection to see, for example, that KM's writing, both creative and critical, has qualities which, in such terms, would have to be considered 'masculine', though it is also true that it is very difficult to determine when she is consciously cultivating a 'masculine' tone for defensive purposes.

In broad terms, KM wanted her criticism to be more personal, and more concrete, very much as she wished her fiction to be 'personal' and concretely affective, and she adopted rather similar strategies to achieve this. She sought the freedom of a tone in which she could be, as far as that was possible, 'most herself, and least personal', a tone achieved through placing of the self in a dramatic context and through the use of symbolism and indirect allusion rather than direct statement. She adopted a persona in her criticism just as she did in her fiction: a persona which is androgynous—tough, 'masculine' and fearless on the one hand, yet capable of the finest (feminine) judgements and discriminations on the other. A prevailing note of irony dissolves tensions between male and female, writer and work: we can see such irony in operation, defusing potentially disabling oppositions, in this extract from a review of M. Austen-Leigh's *Personal Aspects of Jane Austen:*

> It seems almost unkind to criticise a little book which has thrown on bonnet and shawl and tripped across the fields of criticism at so round a pace to defend its dear Jane Austen. . . . Can we picture Jane Austen caring—except in a delightfully wicked way which we are sure the author of this book would not allow—that people said she was no lady, was not fond of children, hated animals, did not care a pin for the poor, could not have written about foreign parts if she had tried, had no idea how a fox was killed, but rather thought it ran up a tree and hissed at the hound at the last—was, in short, cold, coarse, practically illiterate and without morality? Mightn't her reply have been, 'Ah, but what about my novels?'

KM's criticism is also marked, like that of her modernist contemporaries Woolf and Eliot, by a striking and vivid use of metaphor. Such criticism is often called 'impressionistic'—the term has been applied particularly often to the sometimes flamboyant criticism of Virginia Woolf. Yet KM's literary criticism is the reverse of impressionistic in the derogatory sense of diffuse or vague. Through the use of metaphor she achieves two major objectives.

First, she enforces an extension of our critical capacity—we are led into an acknowledgement of relationships and suggestive analogies of whose existence we had previously been unaware. And it is important to note that in this context, of a discourse of persuasion, metaphor works very much as it does in some metaphysical poetry, to evoke and create very precise images and qualities.

Secondly, however, KM is able to exploit the 'luminous halo' surrounding the lighted core of any given metaphor: she is able to utilise the wider, less well defined attributes or associations of a particular image in order to suggest indirectly a point of view which she was unable openly to state. This kind of 'secondary' indirection is particularly important when we are considering the formal, and, in some respects, restrictive context in which the *Athenaeum* reviews were written. To take an example, in her review of Virginia Woolf's *Night and Day,* KM is able through her use of the metaphor of the ship for this novel to bring to our notice not only its solid, craftsman-like qualities and its seriousness (it is or it has been launched on the sea, which serves KM again and again as a metaphor for knowledge, consciousness and discovery), but also its heaviness and its rather unyielding aspects. These qualities of the ship are actually foregrounded by KM as she develops the metaphor:

> To us who love to linger down at the harbour, as it were, watching the new ships being builded, the old ones returning, and the many putting out to sea, comes the strange sight of *Night and Day* sailing into port serene and resolute on a deliberate wind. The strangeness lies in her aloofness, her air of

quiet perfection, her lack of any sign that she has made a perilous voyage—the absence of any scars. There she lies among the strange shipping—a tribute to civilisation for our admiration and wonder.

KM similarly uses an extended metaphor in order briskly to dispose of Mrs Wharton:

> But what about us? What about her readers? Does Mrs Wharton expect us to grow warm in a gallery where the temperature is so sparklingly cool? We are looking at portraits—are we not? These are human beings, arranged for exhibition purposes, framed, glazed, and hung in the perfect light. They pale, they grow paler, they flush, they raise their 'clearest eyes', they hold out their arms to each other 'extended, but not rigid', and the voice is the voice of the portrait.

KM's use of metaphor in her critical writings is thus not only a matter of personal preference in the sense that she was (or, rather, had become) a symbolist writer, delighting in obliquity and 'fine shades': it also served a very definite tactical purpose, enabling her to be 'definite and personal' in her criticism despite the constraints and conventions of her medium.

Other strategies employed by KM to subvert critical forms from within include the impassive retelling of a story simply in order to make it ridiculous. The tone of many of the novel reviews reminds us of Leonard Woolf's memorable picture of KM [in *Beginning Again*]:

> I don't think anyone has ever made me laugh more than she did in those days. She would sit very upright on the edge of a chair or sofa and tell at immense length a kind of saga of her experiences as an actress or of how and why Koteliansky howled like a dog in the room at the top of the building in Southampton Row. There was not the shadow of a gleam of a smile on her mask of a face, and the extraordinary funniness of the story was increased by the flashes of her astringent wit.

Another tactic KM often adopts is the use of a rhetorical question to open a review, and then of a suspended conclusion—the effect is that of disclaiming responsibility for the criticism which has just been produced. An example is **'Anodyne'**, a withering account of a 'pastime novel', which opens with the bland question, 'What is a "sweetly pretty" novel?' and ends, 'though you would not doubt the issue of the fight, you cannot be absolutely certain how the victory will be obtained, and so—you read on'. At the end of the review KM is, as it were, like the cat which has neatly regained its balance after performing a superb trick—and then, like Kezia in **'Prelude'**, tiptoes away.

So KM, working flexibly within cultural and social restrictions and conventions, manages to a considerable extent to fit her own prescription and to be 'definite and personal' in her criticism. In looking more closely at this criticism it is useful, if rather artificial, to make a distinction between its general interest and value and its particular relevance for a consideration of KM's own fiction. In making high claims for her literary criticism, one is by implication inviting a reassessment of her creative work. I suggest that this is especially important in the case of KM, for in her work, as in that of many modernist writers, there is a particularly close connection between critical and creative writing. Modernist literature is by its nature oblique, allusive, formally experimental, and may exhibit a certain logical discontinuity. Most modernist writers have in consequence found it necessary to prepare and create the audience for their work, explaining their aims and techniques in critical manifestos which have acted as glosses on their work. Examples are T. S. Eliot's essays in the *Criterion,* or Virginia Woolf's early essays. I would suggest that the fiction of KM, too, would benefit from being read in the light of her expressed aesthetic aims, and that such a reading would lead to a fuller understanding and appreciation of her allusive and elusive art.

In order to understand KM's 'personal' aesthetic in this sense—her *particular* aims as a writer—we must focus predominantly on her technical and practical remarks on writing, more evident in the letters and journals, as we would expect, than in the formal reviews. The most important aspect of KM's aesthetic to emerge from such scrutiny is its symbolist bias. KM was a symbolist writer in the sense that her work belongs to the post-Symbolist tradition in European literature. KM's earliest literary mentors were Arthur Symons and Oscar Wilde, the two most important representatives or 'translators' of the French Symbolist movement. KM's familiarity with the work of Symons, in particular, becomes clear from a study of her early . . . notes on his work . . . ; Wilde too appears frequently in the early notebooks as a tutelary figure. The central idea which she took from these writers was the belief that in literature abstract states of mind or feeling should be conveyed through concrete images rather than described analytically. This view is expressed with remarkable clarity in an early notebook entry which appears among her annotations of Symon's *Studies in Prose and Verse* (1904):

> The partisans of analysis describe minutely the state of the soul; the secret motive of every action as being of far greater importance than the action itself. The partisans of objectivity—give us the result of this evolution sans describing the secret processes. They describe the state of the soul through the slightest gesture—i.e. realise flesh covered bones—which is the artist's method for me—in as much as art seems to me *pure vision*—I am indeed a partisan of objectivity—

It is a view to which KM held throughout her career. Compare, for example, this 1919 letter to Murry on her own indirect method in fiction (she is writing about the effect of the war on her contemporaries):

> I can't imagine how after the war these men can pick up the old threads as though it had never been. Speaking to *you* I'd say we have died and live again. How can that be the same life? It doesn't mean that life is the less precious or that the 'common things of light and day' are gone. They are not gone, they are intensified, they are illumined. Now we know ourselves for what we are. In a way it's a tragic knowledge. . . .
>
> But, of course, you don't imagine I mean by this knowledge let-us-eat-and-drinkism. No, I mean 'deserts of vast eternity'. But the difference between you and me is (perhaps I'm wrong) I couldn't tell anybody *bang out* about those deserts; they are my secret. I might write about a boy eating strawberries or a woman combing her hair on a windy morning, and that is the only way I can ever men-

tion them. But they *must* be there. Nothing less will do.

An abstract theme must be suggested through concrete images and symbols, and thus returned to its origin in concrete experience. Thus, in a Mansfield story, we might expect to find that most of the 'narrative' details work in this way, having a symbolic as well as a narrative function: in this respect her work may be closely linked with that of Joyce (of whom, incidentally, she could not conceivably have been aware in 1908, the date of the notebook entry on the revelation of the soul 'through the slightest gesture'). Both writers—independently—effected a revolution in the short-story form by introducing into it techniques of systematic allusion derived ultimately from French Symbolist poetry.

There is a limit, however, to the extent to which the all-purpose label 'symbolist' will fit KM. In one important respect her aesthetic differs from that of the symbolists: it is a difference that by its nature becomes clearer if we look beyond KM's letters and journal to her formal critical writing. A belief strongly expressed in the reviews is that art has an ethical *dimension,* if not an ethical function: KM did not in this respect assent to the symbolist belief in art as an entirely autotelic activity. While she did not suggest that the artist should in any crude sense set out to preach or prove a point, she did believe that the 'true' artist's work would make an ethical 'impression', and that it was the duty of the critic to register this impression and measure its depth and quality. This is a role which she plays, in the least abrasive manner, in much of her critical writing—for example, in a 1920 review of Galsworthy's *In Chancery,* in which she laments his inability to regard his characters 'from an eminence' both moral and intellectual:

> It is a very great gift for an author to be able to project himself into the hearts and minds of his characters—but more is needed to make a great creative artist: he must be able, with equal power, to withdraw, to survey what is happening—and from an eminence.

While noting this 'ethical' aspect of KM's aesthetic, however, it is important too to observe the almost Jamesian distinctions which she herself made about the scope and function of the ethical element in art. She explains her position most clearly in a journal note on the philosophy of Vaihinger. Here she asserts the intrinsic identity of ethical and aesthetic ends ('the ideal') but suggests that this ideality can, paradoxically, only be achieved *within* the work of art itself, removed from *practical* use and function:

> Reality cannot become the ideal, the dream; and it is not the business of the artist to grind an axe, to try to impose his vision of life upon the existing world. Art is not an attempt of the artist to reconcile existence with his vision; it is an attempt to create his own world *in* this world.

The second major aspect of KM's 'personal' aesthetic is her emphasis on memory, which she places at the centre of the artistic process. Memory is both selective, isolating the salient features of a particular event or experience, and synthetic, superimposing and juxtaposing remembered scenes and images so that in time (in the fullest sense) experience is literally reconstituted. This process is not mechanical but organic, and it too has an ethical dimension which is rooted in the individual artist's temperament and disposition. These beliefs are expressed most forcefully in the review of Dorothy Richardson's *The Tunnel* which opened KM's series of reviews for the *Athenaeum*. Here, the moral and idealising aspects of memory are evoked through apocalyptic imagery:

> There is one who could not live in so tempestuous an environment as her mind—and he is Memory. She has no memory. It is true that Life is sometimes very swift and breathless, but not always. If we are to be truly alive there are large pauses in which we creep away into our caves of contemplation. And then it is, in the silence, that Memory mounts his throne and judges all that is in our minds—appointing each his separate place, high or low, rejecting this, selecting that—putting this one to shine in the light and throwing that one into the darkness.
>
> We do not mean to say that those large, round biscuits might not be in the light, or the night in Spring be in the darkness. Only we feel that until these things are judged and given each its appointed place in the whole scheme, they have no meaning in the world of art.

Memory idealises, in the fullest sense, and makes (ethical) judgements and discriminations; it is important to recognise this element in KM's richly worked and polished fiction, which is 'slight' or 'episodic' only in the most nominal technical sense.

Besides shedding light on KM's own aims and achievement in fiction, her criticism has an interest and value which extends far beyond particular insights into contemporary writers. The formal reviews written for the *Athenaeum* (as opposed to the working-notes found in letters and journals) constitute a formidable body of criticism, a framework of (sometimes veiled) polemic and advocacy. It has already been indicated that one of the important themes of KM's criticism is that of the effects of the First World War: this is partly a simple function of the timing of the reviewing-stint, but also stems from KM's clear belief that the war had, or should have, entirely changed man's perception of himself. She wrote to Murry that 'we have to face our war', the implication being that artists could not dismiss the war as the responsibility of other people, as many, she felt, wished to do. While illness made KM particularly susceptible to intimations of frailty and mortality associated with the war, one cannot deny the justice of her charge that for many artists the war simply had not been 'felt'. For most, direct personal suffering had been avoided, and the war had not brought a greater consciousness of man's inhumanity to man. When KM wrote that as a result of the war 'now we know ourselves for what we are', she was speaking, she felt, for a tiny minority—a minority which included most notably D. H. Lawrence. . . . (pp. 1-13)

The major thrust of KM's polemic in the *Athenaeum* reviews is in an area related to her feelings about the war: she was concerned above all with 'seriousness in art', concerned that the literature of her day should, using whatever techniques were necessary, address the deeper issues of life—'nothing less will do'. She felt that much of the fiction she encountered was trivial, and consequently her attempts at definition of what is worthwhile in art occur as frequently in a context of denunciation (for instance, of the third-rate novels of Gilbert Cannan, or of the 'pastime

novel') as in one of admiration and congratulation. Like all reviewers, KM was deluged with inferior novels: what makes her outstanding as a critic is the deft and deadly way in which she analyses the failures she so often encounters and, more rarely, illuminates the successful, achieved work of art.

It is important in this context to point out that KM was writing for the *Athenaeum* in a period which appeared a desert in terms of fiction: as Antony Alpers has remarked [see Further Reading], reading the *Athenaeum* reviews one comes fully to appreciate the climate of mingled dearth and expectation in which '**The Garden Party**', *Jacob's Room* and *Ulysses* were so rapturously received. It was a desert more apparent than real, as Lawrence, Joyce, KM and Woolf were all writing in the years before 1922—but were not, for a variety of reasons, being published. Compared to the dramatic developments taking place in visual art at the same time, literature seemed to be lagging dully behind.

It is fortunate that KM was able with such frequency to turn reviews of novels which disappointed her into occasions for the exploration and celebration of those qualities which make for distinction. In a review of Joseph Hergesheimer's *Linda Condon,* for example, she uses the Yeatsian image of the tree to suggest the organic wholeness of the successful work of art—*not* achieved in this particular instance:

> If a novel is to have a central idea we imagine that central idea is a lusty growing stem from which the branches spring clothed with leaves, and the buds become flowers and fruits. We imagine that the author chooses with infinite deliberation the very air in which that tree shall be nourished, and that he is profoundly aware that its coming to perfection depends upon the strength with which the central idea supports its beautiful accumulations.

The extended metaphor is one of the most often used tools through which she places, though often in negative terms, moral and aesthetic qualities. So, to register just a few, she uses metaphors for familiarity and change (the shallow and the deeper seas, the known and the unknown hotel); employs consumer metaphors for fictions which are no more than conventional confections or 'digestible snacks', uses 'artful' metaphors for artful novels where the characters resemble portraits hanging in a gallery; or evokes in detail the atmosphere of the 'Garden City novel' with homes 'which seem to breathe white enamel and cork linoleum and the works of Freud and Jung'.

As these allusions should make sufficiently clear, it is extremely difficult to disentangle ethical and aesthetic motives and beliefs in KM's literary criticism. It may be useful here to make a distinction between the 'ethical' and the 'moral': 'moral' might be used to refer to the practical sphere, to matters of action and conduct, while 'ethical' would denote a more disinterested ethical sense, rather like the 'undestroyed freshness' of Maisie in James's *What Maisie Knew,* which is, as it were, as much a matter of taste as of judgement. It is in this light—in relation to the 'ethical' in this sense—that we can perhaps best see KM's insistence on the relation between the ethical and the aesthetic, and on the relation between 'life' and 'art'. It is by no means a naïve insistence. In, for example, a review of *Mary Olivier: A Life* by May Sinclair, KM uses Blake's

Murry and Mansfield, 1922.

image of the 'bounding line' to suggest that widest possible ethical and aesthetic perspective which, she felt, should distinguish the great novel (and which was of course lacking in Sinclair's work):

> But if the Flood, the sky, the rainbow, or what Blake beautifully calls the bounding outline, be removed and if, further, no one thing is to be related to another thing, we do not see what is to prevent the whole of mankind turning author.

She goes on:

> Is it not the great abiding satisfaction of a work of art that the writer was master of the situation when he wrote it and at the mercy of nothing less mysterious than a greater work of art?

The suggestion that the world of art and the world of 'fact' are analogous and conterminous (it is the world itself which is of course the greater work of art) reflects KM's very modernist feeling for the unreality and insubstantiality of any external world conceived of as existing outside the (involuntarily) creative mind of man. (pp. 13-15)

> *Clare Hanson, in an introduction to* The Critical Writings of Katherine Mansfield, *edited by*

Clare Hanson, Macmillan Press, 1987, pp. 1-20.

Gillian Boddy   (essay date 1988)

[*Boddy is a New Zealand educator and critic. In the following excerpt from her* Katherine Mansfield: The Woman and the Writer, *she considers Mansfield's development as a short story writer, discussing influences, styles, themes, characterization, and literary techniques.*]

A brief look at K. M.'s letters and journals shows that she was a compulsive writer. Her international reputation as one of the world's best-known short story writers, based on only eighty-eight collected stories, remains secure today. Nevertheless K. M. believed:

> You know . . . I shall not be 'fashionable' long. They will find me out. . . . I like such awfully unfashionable things—and people. I like sitting on doorsteps, and talking to the old woman who brings quinces, and going for picnics in a jolting little wagon, and listening to the kind of music they play in public gardens on warm evenings, and talking to captains of shabby little steamers, and in fact, to all kinds of people in all kinds of places. But

what a fatal sentence to begin. It goes on for ever. In fact, one could spend a whole life finishing it. But you see I am not a highbrow. Sunday lunches and very intricate conversations on Sex and that 'fatigue' which is so essential and that awful 'brightness' which is even more essential—these things I flee from.

This was how she saw her work and her place in literature. It was, she knew, from life's 'tremendous trifles' that she created her stories. She chose ordinary people, everyday events: a charwoman, a child's dolls house. In this, the creation of something timeless from simple things, she was an innovator. (p. 153)

Her work has been constantly debated, analysed, criticised. For some critics she was a writer's writer, to others a teller of tales. Others saw her work not as stories but as fragments or recollections. A more recent attempt to define the exact nature of her writing is Professor C. K. Stead's analysis of them as 'fictions' as opposed to narratives. At several stages in her life K. M. hoped to write a novel—these attempts included *Juliet, Young Country*, **'The Aloe'**, *Maata, Karori*. Even **'The Aloe'**, since published as a separate volume, was never truly completed. It seems very possible that her particular creative gift was for the short story alone; that her unique flashes of creativity could not be sustained. Perhaps she was right in saying that she could never write, 'a whole novel about anything'.

Three of her greatest stories, **'Prelude', 'The Daughters of the Late Colonel'** and **'At the Bay'** are similar to novels in that they are divided into twelve sections or episodes, an unusual device. Each episode has a different focus. They are also longer than the average short story. Many of her New Zealand stories also fall into two cycles: one, the larger, about the Burnell family, the second about the Sheridans. K. M. seems to have felt able to sustain her interest, and the reader's, in these characters. Indeed the stories most critics regard as her finest are from these two groups. Professor Ian Gordon's *Undiscovered Country* fits these together with other stories and journal entries in such a way as to suggest what a novel based on these might have been like. Did K. M. therefore do herself an injustice in saying she would not succeed in writing a novel? If not a novel, perhaps the novella, a piece of prose the length of Ernest Hemingway's *The Old Man and the Sea*, might have been a possible form?

Some of her comments about reviewing do suggest that she regarded contemporary novels 'as simply rubbish on the whole'. For her the short story was apparently the superior genre and the one at which she would have been content to excel.

K. M.'s earliest vignettes published in the *Native Companion,* and her 1908 story **'The Education of Audrey'** show the unmistakable influence of Oscar Wilde in their subject matter, exotic mood and ornate style. From this she moved towards a more naturalistic type of story. Many of the early stories published in **In a German Pension** and **Something Childish but Very Natural** are immature, superficial, and technically often weak. She herself commented in February 1920:

> I cannot have the **German Pension** republished under any circumstances. It's far too *immature . . .* it's not good enough. . . . It's posi-

tively juvenile and besides that it's not what I mean: it's a lie.

Though they were often bitter, cynical and disillusioned satires, those early stories foreshadowed her later ones in style, theme and characterisation. There is wit, perception and some early, if uneven attempts at the interior monologue technique which she later developed so successfully. Often overlooked, they contain the prototypes of characters who would later fully develop 'in the round'—Frau Brechenmacher's husband was to evolve into the 'Boss' in **'The Fly'** and the Binzer family became the Burnells.

Many of the **German Pension** stories focus on the situation of a young woman, often alone and vulnerable to avaricious, prying strangers. Her ambivalence about her own sexuality and women's traditional child-bearing role was also explored in them. The young bride in **'Frau Brechenmacher Attends a Wedding'** had 'the appearance of an iced cake all ready to be cut and served in neat little pieces to the bridegroom.' Little Frau Brechenmacher lay waiting for her drunken chauvinistic husband, 'her arm across her face like a child expecting to be hurt'. Often the central rather ingenuous female figure was frequently forced to face reality when predatory, physically stronger men made unexpected crude advances.

Frequently the characters in these early stories are caricatured through exaggeration and oversimplification, even labelled as such—Herr Rat, the Young Man, the Coral Necklace. Others are more fully and skillfully developed. The skill with realistic dialogue is already evident, the setting and atmosphere are often clearly evoked. The sharp, sometimes cruel observation of human frailties and stupidities revealed through selected telling details is already fundamental to her stories. The later subtlety is not yet a feature but certain techniques that mark her later writings are already part of her style. These include the compounding of words for effect as in 'a "fancy-not-recognising-that-at-her-first-glance" expression'; the skilful variation of sentence length, including the 'ungrammatical' minor sentence; the quick flash of colour; and the frequent use of simile and metaphor. The central character, often the same woman narrator, is already sometimes revealed through implication and symbolism rather than external description.

These early stories contain the embryonic treatment of the themes she would continue to explore—the essential aloneness and isolation of the human predicament; the conflict between love and disillusionment, between wistful childlike idealism and life's harsh reality, between beauty and ugliness, joy and suffering. For K. M., the juxtaposition of these themes seemed to illustrate life's inevitable paradoxes.

After the destruction of the war she wrote:

> Now we know ourselves for what we are. In a way its a tragic knowledge. Its as though, even while we live again we face death. But *through Life:* thats the point. We see death in life as we see death in a flower that is fresh unfolded. Our hymn is to the flower's beauty—we would make that beauty immortal because we *know.* . . .

Eventually she was to see beauty in the inevitability of life's paradoxes but in those early stories it only repelled and frightened her.

Two of her first adult stories set in New Zealand, **'The Education of Audrey'** written in 1908, and **'Old Tar'** have received little critical attention. Each is interesting for different reasons. Not only does **'The Education of Audrey'** show the strong influence of Oscar Wilde, its atmosphere redolent with candles and gardenias, it is also the only one of her stories to combine New Zealand and London in setting. Like its predecessor, the unfinished *Juliet,* it is not great writing but rather quaintly contrived and pretentious, particularly in its philosophising about 'Art' and 'Life'. The heroine's capitulation in the last line is also uncharacteristic. Nevertheless it contains some vivid moments and, more importantly, the use of a phrase that was to become almost a talisman—'Do you remember?' One passage in which Audrey reflects on her inappropriately childlike feelings of happiness is strikingly similar to the opening paragraphs of **'Bliss'**, written some ten years later. A comparison of the two suggests something of her development over those years.

'Old Tar', printed in the *Westminister Gazette* and the *New Zealand Times* in 1913, also offers some intriguing comparisons. The theme of disillusionment, of reality shattering a dream, was one she would rework more successfully many times. Nevertheless this is a stronger story, the touches of colour are painted with a surer brush: 'There was no wind; just a breeze rippled over the grass and shook the manuka flowers like tiny white stars down the yellow clay banks of the new road.' This surely is the world of **'The Aloe'**, **'Prelude'** and **'The Doll's House'**. In her description of Tar, 'a little pale freckled boy with a flop of black hair', K. M. gives us one of her first pictures of a 'real' child. Mrs. Tar who:

> turned into a fine lady and talked of nothing but the inconvenience she'd suffered living in the shop for the sake of her 'usband's father and his sentimentalness.

is one of many characters who would be epitomised through the humour of their speech. This and the phonetic spelling of Tar's speech were two devices she continued to use in order to create realistic dialogue. What is more significant is the strong presence in this early New Zealand story of the sea, and of the wind 'snuffling' around the big white house as it was to do later in **'The Aloe'** and **'Prelude'**.

A study of these stories and other early stories such as **'How Pearl Button Was Kidnapped'**, **'A Birthday'**, the haunting **'The Woman at the Store'**, **'Ole Underwood'** and **'Millie'** show that the New Zealand setting and memories which K. M. was to explore so effectively had already been recognised, valued and drawn upon. Thus her 'New Zealand' short stories were not, as was so often thought, the sudden, direct result of her brother Leslie's death in 1915. She returned to this storehouse of memories yet again, early in 1915. This time the results were to be far more significant.

In February 1915 K. M. met her brother briefly and accidentally in London. In Paris in March she began 'my first novel', now identified as **'The Aloe'**. She had in fact begun several 'novels' before: the adolescent *Juliet,* and *Maata* in August 1913, for which she had written a draft outline of thirty-two chapters but had finished only two by mid-November that year. A third had been begun in December

that year, *Young Country,* set in Wellington, but only two chapters were again completed. Her ambitious calculations for '24 pages per day i.e. 5000 words—for 15 days 75,000 words' were not carried out.

'The Aloe' would be different. K. M. was still working on it during May 1915. During Leslie's visit to London that summer they revisited the past together. **'The Wind Blows'** was written out of those memories and published in October, the month he died.

Ignoring the war and her own chaotic existence and deep unhappiness she turned again, in her grief, to New Zealand and tried to recreate those early days of their shared childhood:

> I want to write about my own country until I simply exhaust my store—not only because it is 'a sacred debt' that I pay to my country because my brother & I were born there—but also because in my thoughts I range with him over all the remembered places. I am never far away from them. I long to renew them in writing.
>
> Ah the people, the people we loved there—of them too I want to write—another 'debt of love'. Oh, I want for one moment to make our undiscovered country leap into the eyes of the old world. It must be mysterious, as though floating—it must take the breath. It must be 'one of those islands'. . . . I shall tell everything—even of how the laundry basket squeaked at '75'—but all must be told with a sense of mystery—a radiance—an after glow because you my little sun of it, are set. You have dropped over the dazzling brim of the world. Now I must play my part. . . .

It was not easy however to fulfil that sacred debt, to give shape to those memories until, on rediscovering **'The Aloe'** among her papers, she knew it was right and began work on it again.

In **'The Aloe'** and in later stories such as **'At The Bay'** and **'The Doll's House'** she showed her particular skill in creating the world of children, a world of light and shade, overshadowed by the problems of the adult world. She captured the very sound of their voices, their moments of loneliness, fear and happiness. She was one of the first short story writers to evoke this childhood world so clearly, and to regard it as important enough to write about. We share their games of make believe, fantasies, important projects and adventures, their delights and guilt. Few knew better than K. M. the reality and value of the past within us:

> I think the only way to live as a writer is to draw upon one's real, familiar life—to find the treasure. . . . And the curious thing is that if we describe this which seems to us so intensely personal, other people take it to themselves and understand it as if it were their own.

There have been few writers whose life and work seem so inseparable, but there seems little point in debating whether it was her experiences in New Zealand or in England which had the greater influence on her work—she could not have written as she did without the particular combination of both those very different worlds, her own peculiar form of 'geographical schizophrenia'. Rebelling in her youth against the narrow, conventional bourgeois life of colonial New Zealand she had fled to London, Europe and

'Life'. Her experiences there provided her with the basis for many of her stories, including the German ones preferred by Leonard Woolf. Satirical, increasingly sophisticated, they had a quality of toughness in their clear-sighted depiction of society and its values. Increasingly disillusioned by that world, by her contemporaries and by the frequently unsatisfactory nature of her relationship with Murry; by her illness and increasing isolation; by the growing awareness that she had no certain future, she turned back increasingly to the past. Eventually she used those last pictures of childhood in what she acknowledged to be a 'dream' New Zealand, to reconcile the discordant elements in her European stories and many earlier New Zealand ones; and to attempt to resolve the conflicts in herself and in the world as she had known it. D. H. Lawrence remarked of his *Sons and Lovers* that, 'one sheds one's sicknesses in books'. For K. M., too, writing was a kind of therapy.

In her best stories K. M. created something beyond the limitations of time and place. They were the spontaneous but carefully crafted product of her experience of life:

> Even if one does not acquire any fresh meat—one's vision of what one possesses is constantly changing into something rich and strange, isn't it? I feel mine is. 47 Fitzherbert Terrace, p. e., is colouring beautifully with the years and I polish it and examine it and only now is it ready to come out of the store room and into the uncommon light of day.

Frequently K. M. recognised the strong autobiographical element in her work even when she had not consciously intended it. She described it later to Murry, 'Funny thing is I think you'll always come walking into my stories. . . . "The man she was in love with".' And, she warned him, 'You will recognise some of the people.' All too often, particularly in New Zealand, people were recognised and quite naturally did not always welcome that recognition. Even the names of many of her characters show the link between fact and fiction, as in Fairfield, the anglicised version of Beauchamp. To her father she wrote in 1922:

> I meant to draw your attention, if I may, to one little sketch, **'The Voyage'**, which I wrote with dear little Grandma Beauchamp in mind. It is not in any way a likeness of her, but there are, it seems to me, traces of a resemblance.

To L. M., whose full name was Ida Constance Baker, she wrote from Cornwall about her story **'Carnation'**, 'I've even put you in as Connie Baker!' Later **'The Lady's Maid'** was perhaps a kind of recognition of L. M.'s selflessness. Certainly she was the model for the sympathetic, gently humorous portrayal of Constantia in **'The Daughters of the Late Colonel'**. At times too K. M. felt she had actually brought 'the dead to life again'.

Interestingly, the first page of the manuscript of **'The Doll's House'** begins, 'When dear old Mrs Hay went back to Wellington . . . ' K. M. then crossed the name out, replacing it with the more anonymous town. Similarly, the early story **'A Birthday'** is clearly set in Tinakori Road, despite the family's German names. At other times K. M. could not herself trace the origin of a particular story. It just evolved. After all,

> When does one *really begin* a journey—or a friendship—or a love affair? It is those beginnings which

are so fascinating and so misunderstood. There comes a moment when we realise we are already well on our way—déjà.

Certainly it is difficult to disentangle fact from fiction. K. M. deliberately chose at times to write about her own experiences, her own emotions and fantasies, but often she seems not to have fully understood them herself. They reveal far more of her, her attitudes and her complex personality than she intended. This adds to their fascination—and their relevance. In her intriguing, detailed study of the 'psychological basis' of K. M.'s stories, C. A. Hankin remarks: 'Regardless of what she might say in her letters, however, Katherine Mansfield's truest expression of what she felt for the people close to her appears in her stories' [*Katherine Mansfield and Her Confessional Stories,* 1983].

One fascinating example of the way in which K. M. used her own experiences deliberately as the basis for a story seems to have been overlooked. Readers and critics have all agreed that the story **'An Indiscreet Journey'**, is based on K. M.'s own journey to visit Carco in Gray in 1915, the four-day escapade Murry dismissed as a 'fiasco'. In the story the narrator has a letter written to 'My dear niece' asking her to visit her aunt in 'X'. Written by her soldier lover it was, in fact, a ruse intended to convince the Commissaire Militaire that her journey through wartime France was legitimate.

Among Murry's letters to K. M. is one small sheet in another handwriting. Dated 26 March 1915, this letter in French from Aix-les-Gray to 'Ma Chère amie' is signed 'Marguerite Bombard'. It thanks K. M. for her last letter from Paris, speaks of their meeting there again after the war as they had promised, but suggests that in the meantime she should visit Gray as 'Maman' has put a room at her disposal. The letter continues very affectionately then instructs K. M. to obtain a pass. Marguerite Bombard's letter is, like the lover's in the story, an 'unfamiliar letter in the familiar handwriting'. It is, in fact, the only known letter still in existence from Carco to K. M. K. M. had returned to Paris to stay in Carco's flat on 18 March. It would appear she had written to him and he felt sufficiently confident to reply in this way, suggesting another visit. Perhaps they had parted on better terms than Murry had imagined? Her reply, if there was one, is unknown. She returned to England on 31 March, revisiting Paris for twelve days in May. Like the original escapade, the idea of transforming Marguerite Bombard (alias Carco) into Julie Boiffard, Aix-les-Gray into 'X' and the inclusion of the letter in the story was the kind of game that K. M. would have enjoyed.

Her own experiences provided her with the raw material, but she did not seek merely to give a photographic reproduction. Perhaps too much emphasis has been placed on analysing precise autobiographical details; on discussing whether portraits of certain people were either fair or accurate or whether a certain place was really as she described. Like an impressionist painter she worked to convey the light and shade, the overall impression or mood; details were altered, outlines blurred and places, people or occasions merged into a composite picture. Art always transcended reality and real events or people were shaped and manipulated to fit the impression she wished to create.

K. M. was a dedicated artist with 'a passion for technique', determined to find clarity, to 'write simply, fully, freely. . . .' Truth, above all, came to be the aim of her writing:

> You see for me—life and work are two things indivisible. It's only by being true to life that I can be true to art. And to be true to life is to be *good, sincere, simple, honest.*

She hoped in this way to enable others to see clearly. She felt eventually that neither her life nor her earlier work had been 'true'.

Throughout her life K. M. was constantly evaluating her style ('horrible expression!') and her craft, looking for greater discipline and clarity, altering and perfecting her method of narration, working to find that 'special prose' that was neither poetry nor prose. A comparison of **'The Aloe'** and the final version **'Prelude'** shows how stringent she was in her criticism of her own work.

Vincent O'Sullivan's elegant edition of **'The Aloe'** with its parallel printing of **'Prelude'** on the facing pages assists such a comparison and gives an accessible insight into K. M.'s creative process. She reworked the original story to tighten it in both structure and style in order to gain the particular effects she desired and, as a result, there is greater precision and coherence. A succession of adjectives is replaced by one precise word; extraneous details stripped away; interesting but superfluous characters, incidents and narrative passages are eliminated. Other incidents or details are added, particularly those which reveal more of the central characters.

A comparison of **'The Common Round'** and **'Pictures'** shows the same ruthless discipline. Some manuscripts show considerable alteration, revision affecting single words or whole passages. Others seem to have flowed spontaneously, requiring little change despite occasional marginal notes such as 'too much description!' Even **'The Daughters of the Late Colonel'**, written as it was at such a furious pace, was not greatly altered on a later reading, although the title was changed from 'Non-Compounders'—a reference to school days at Queen's College.

There is careful craftsmanship in her varied style, at times curt, terse, brittle, at others flowing, almost poetry, depending on the mood or situation she was describing. Her sentence construction reflected this care. She was well aware of the effect of a minor or simple sentence, in contrast to longer complex ones. To achieve the specific overall effect she desired she worked consciously at her technique. Even her use of dashes and dots was deliberate—it was not simply a matter of 'a feminine dash'. Of **'Miss Brill'**, her 'Insect Magnificat' she wrote:

> I choose not only the length of every sentence, but even the sound of every sentence. I choose the rise and fall of every paragraph to fit her, and to fit her on that day at that very moment. After I'd written it I read it aloud . . . until it fitted her. . . . If a thing has really come off it seems to me there mustn't be one single word out of place, or one word that could be taken out. That's how I AIM at writing. It will take some time to get anywhere near there.

K. M. developed the ability to enter the very minds and souls of her characters. The process of writing was 'a kind of *possession'*. Describing her story **'The Voyage'** she wrote:

> I might have remained the grandma for ever after if the wind had changed that moment. And that would have been a little bit embarrassing for Middleton Murry.

As a result of this remarkable empathy, some of her finest characters are revealed through their own thoughts, memories and feelings and not by external analysis or dissection so that the reader too is able to identify with them as they meet her own requirement that:

> New people have appeared in that other world of ours, which sometimes seems so much more real and satisfying than this one. That they have a life and a being of their own we do not question; even that they 'go on' long after the book is finished.

The reader slips without noticing from one character's mind to another; there is no break or narrative comment necessary. We do not need to be told at the beginning of **'The Doll's House'** that 'perhaps the smell of paint would have gone off' is said in disapproving tones by an adult. We simply know.

One word can reveal the point of view through which an incident or character is seen, and simultaneously more about the character whose vision we share. Through K. M.'s skill with dialogue the characters become living, speaking people. The choice of words, the catching of subtleties of contrasting pronunciation, intonation and inflection convey so much. The children usually speak in short sentences, simply, in 'children's language'. The adolescents and adults speak quite differently depending on their mood. From this we infer a great deal about the speakers. A skilled actress and impersonator, she had a remarkable facility with dialogue, especially children's, which allows her stories to be successfully dramatised, not only for television and radio but in the classroom and on stage. Her own dramatic pieces show how she herself experimented in the area of drama. A sense of rhythm and timing, an awareness of the nuances of speech characterise much of the dialogue, in these and other stories. These dramatic experiments also showed her how a story could progress without a narrator. She was to continue to work towards this elimination of the narrator in her writing, so having a profound influence on short story writing.

Moments of lethargy at times led to an almost physical inability to put pen to paper and consequent deep depression:

> I do still lack application. . . . There's so much to do and I do so little. Life would be almost perfect here if only when I was *pretending* to work I always was working. . . . Look at all the stories that wait and wait just at the threshold. Why don't I let them in? . . . *Next day* Yet take this morning for instance. I don't want to write anything. Its grey, its heavy and dull and these stories seem unreal & not worth doing. I don't want to write; I want to *Live.*

Nevertheless she was determined always to become 'a better writer'. Writing to Murry, she condemned Virginia Woolf for ignoring the war in her novel *Night and Day* which seemed to her 'a lie in the soul. . . . I feel in the *profoundest* sense that nothing can ever be the same—that as artists we are traitors if we feel otherwise; we have to take it into account and find new expressions new moulds for our new thoughts & feelings.' In her published review of the book she was more tactful, but Virginia Woolf was not deceived. K. M. felt the need to develop her own techniques, 'how are we going to convey these over tones, half tones, quarter tones, these hesitations, doubts, beginnings, if we go at them *directly?* . . . I do believe that there is a way . . . Its the truth we are after, no less (which, by the way, makes it so exciting)'.

Characteristically, she often felt she had failed. In the middle of the manuscript of **'Her First Ball'** she wrote:

> All that I write—all that I am—is on the border of the sea. It's a kind of playing. I want to put *all* my force behind it, but somehow, I *cannot!*

It was always the next story which would contain everything. In her search for 'the new word' she rejected the style and content of her early stories as well as many of the conventions of short story writing. Even at Fontainebleau, when her work was widely recognised, her idea of the short story was changing. Tired of her 'little stories like birds bred in cages', she hoped some new kind of writing would be the natural result of the spiritual rebirth she envisaged. She had always realised that carefully selected details were incredibly important, 'one can get only so *much* into a story; there is always a sacrifice.'

Inevitably it was her own attitudes which determined that selection. There was 'an infinite delight & value in detail' but it was not for detail's sake alone. Through the careful selection of detail she could *suggest,* and that should be enough. She could not tell anybody 'bang out' about the

> 'deserts of vast eternity'. . . . They are my secret. I might write about a boy eating strawberries or a woman combing her hair on a windy morning & that is the only way I can ever mention them. But they *must* be there. Nothing less will do.

Therefore, instead of telling 'directly' she frequently worked obliquely through implication, suggestion and symbolism. The little lamp in **'The Doll's House'** must surely be one of the most readily understood symbols in prose. A reader may know nothing of terms such as 'symbolism' but the little lamp will inevitably take on a deeper significance. Ordinary inanimate objects seem almost to take on a life of their own.

One of the most important techniques K. M. used in order to 'convey those over tones, half tones' was the use of contrast. At times the carefully developed contrasts provide the framework or structure for the story's events and also suggest the themes.

Frequently too the use of colour, light and shade are important in creating the atmosphere vital to the stories. In **'At the Bay',** the morning sun streamed through the open window 'on to the yellow varnished walls and bare floor. Everything on the table flashed and glittered. In the middle there was an old salad bowl filled with yellow and red nasturtiums.' The beginning of **'The Woman at the Store',** however, is very different: 'The white pumice dust swirled in our faces, settled and sifted over us . . . the sky was slate colour. . . . There was nothing to be seen but wave after wave of tussock grass.' Another contrast is the setting of **'The Wind Blows'** which is mainly an uncharacteristic monochrome.

Another of the characteristics of K. M.'s writing to which critics have paid much attention is her use of imagery. She seems to have been a writer who thought naturally in metaphor. Particularly apt images remain in the reader's mind. Our Else is 'a tiny wishbone of a child . . . a little white owl.' She and her sister are chased away from the doll's house 'like two little stray cats'. Sleek, insinuating, Mrs Harry Kember in **'At the Bay'** swims away 'like a rat'. In **'The Woman at the Store'** the narrator remarks:

> there is no twilight in our New Zealand days, but a curious half-hour when everything appears grotesque—it frightens—as though the savage spirit of the country walked abroad and sneered at what it saw.

When writing about children the imagery is peculiar to their world and strikingly apt, so the doll's house, for example, is 'spinach green', its door like 'a little slab of toffee'. Frequently she used animal imagery and symbolism as a device for hinting at hidden layers of meaning. A striking example of this occurs in **'Bliss'** when Bertha Young stands looking at the tall pear tree 'perfect . . . against the jade-green sky'. Below 'a grey cat, dragging its belly, crept across the lawn, and a black one, its shadow, trailed after. The sight of them, so intent and so quick, gave Bertha a curious shiver.'

The use of symbolism linking the concrete and the abstract, one of the most remarkable features of her work, was at times contrived, as she herself felt in **'Mr and Mrs Dove'.** In other stories a single action or detail skilfully conveys an emotion, image and mood, the external and the internal become one. Certain images recur from her earliest sketches at Queen's College. Others like the wind, flowers and insects and particularly the metaphor of the fly occur constantly, both in her notes and letters as well as in her stories. Like the sun, sea and darkness, mist and trees, they were all an integral part of her vision of life and the fabric of her stories.

Impatient with those who specialised in 'cheap psychoanalysis' she herself was a perceptive writer of unusual psychological insight, so it is not surprising that much has been written about her symbolism and her imagery. (pp. 154-68)

Generally her symbols and images are skilfully woven into the vivid texture of the story; at other times one is selected as the centre of the total pattern, such as the lamp in **'The Doll's House',** the pear tree in **'Bliss'.** The use of natural elements in particular provides a central symbolism, a recurrent underlying motif linking many of her stories. These then were some of the methods that typified K. M.'s writing, enabling her to convey evanescent moods, to capture the essence of a fleeting moment. But what of the total pattern, the form of her stories?

Describing the form of **'Prelude'** to Dorothy Brett she remarked, 'It's more or less my own invention', and that form was to be gradually perfected and refined. Other important features of that form were the stream of consciousness technique, her use of flashbacks and her skill in conveying the multipersonal viewpoint. These are clearly illustrated in **'The Daughters of the Late Colonel'**—'a huge long story of a rather new kind. It's the outcome of the **'Prelude'** method—it just unfolds and opens . . . It's a queer tale though.' Past and present become fused as the story evolves through the characters' minds. The external narrator is almost eliminated. As so often in her work, the reader is dropped into the story and simply confronted by a particular situation. There is no preliminary establishing and identification of time and place. The reader is immediately involved; it is assumed that he or she has any necessary prerequisite knowledge and is, in a sense, part of the story too.

Some stories make use of interior monologue throughout, others combine some interior monologue or stream of consciousness with more conventional techniques. It is the multi-personal viewpoint, in particular, which has marked her writing. Often, although the story is told through a variety of viewpoints, the focus is most frequently on the central protagonist so that we share that character's experience in particular. At other times, characters or events are viewed through the eyes of different characters, being described in the language and syntax peculiar to that character. As a result of the multi-personal viewpoint we often see the characters from several angles, providing us with a constantly changing perspective.

Today K. M.'s 'episodic' or 'slice of life' technique is perhaps taken for granted but her stories were really the first of significance in English to be written without the conventional plot. The expected sequence of events: exposition, rising action, climax and conclusion have often been replaced by concentration on a moment or episode or loosely linked series of moments. The interest lies not so much in what *happens* but in *why* it happens.

The famous American short story writer, Edgar Allan Poe, had laid down clearly the principles of short story writing. English writers such as Kipling and H. G. Wells had continued to write stories with a carefully structured plot. Other writers, little known today had, however, been experimenting in a magazine, the *Yellow Book*, famous in the 1890s. There does not, however, appear any clear reference in her letters and journals to the *Yellow Book*, and she herself believed that what she was attempting was innovatory.

Sylvia Berkman, who like Marvin Magalaner and T. O. Beachcroft sees many similarities in her work to that of James Joyce, describes her stories as 'the swift, illuminated glimpse into a character or situation at a given moment' [see Further Reading]. By showing us a character at a particular moment so much more is disclosed. At times, it is as if by giving the reader that glimpse of a specific character at a specific moment, as if through an open doorway, she shows them making a gesture or speaking in a way that is typical of that character. That moment allows the reader's imagination to do the rest.

The conventions of time and tense become irrelevant. This flexible manipulation of time was something K. M. was still consciously trying to perfect in the last years of her life. 'What I feel it needs so peculiarly is a very subtle variation of "tense" from the present to the past & back again—and softness, lightness. . . . '

There is no step-by-step development of plot but this does not mean, as one critic has suggested, that we are not moved by her stories because 'nothing happens' to her characters, or that they are merely 'incidents' not short stories. For her people, as for the rest of us, there are the moments of 'the soul's desperate choice'; the moment of

crisis, external or internal, the discovery of 'the big snail under the leaf—the spot in the child's lung'. Her stories may appear formless but there is, in fact, a careful pattern of parts. They were tightly constructed, around that moment of crisis or turning point which in a way determined the pattern of the story. She explained this apparent lack of ordered events:

> The diversity of life and how we try to fit in every-
> thing. Death included. That is bewildering . . .
> things ought to happen differently. First one and
> then another. But life isn't like that. We haven't the
> ordering of it . . .

Not surprisingly, she once showed great indignation about:

> a stupid man . . . bringing out an anthology of
> short stories and he said the more 'plotty' a story
> I could give him the better. What about that for a
> word! It made my hair stand up in prongs. A nice
> 'plotty' story, please. People *are* funny.

This view did not lessen her admiration for Jane Austen's skill with plot. 'She makes modern episodic people like me, as far as I go, look very incompetent ninnies.' She and Jane Austen were, however, alike in their rather deliberately limited range of subject matter and their ironic pictures of sophisticated society's pretensions and conventions, for K. M. had gradually abandoned her early malicious, sometimes clumsily obvious satire for a more subtle and delicate irony.

Occasionally, too, like earlier writers such as Jane Austen, she addressed the reader in an intimate tone, inviting participation in the story and collusion with the narrator. K. M.'s last story, **'The Canary'**—a monologue—involves the reader in such a way, 'there does seem to me something sad in life. . . . I don't mean the sorrow that we all know. . . . '

Often that sadness was juxtaposed with humour, an aspect that has been too often overlooked. She was a writer with an acute wit, a gift for mimicry and a true sense of the ridiculous. At times the humour was obvious and satirical, as in the German stories, with the caricature of the Norman Knights in **'Bliss'**; at others it is more subtle, a delicate irony. **'The Daughters of the Late Colonel'** illustrates a gentle compassionate humour in the portrayal of two spinster sisters who had dared to bury their bullying father 'without asking his permission'. **'At the Bay'** is not only a superb evocation of mood and feeling, it is also a story with considerable humour.

The humour in her work was often gained from a single word, sometimes deliberately misspelled, mimicking the speaker's voice, even when it is a silent voice heard only in the character's mind. It is derived from exaggeration and caricature, from a careful contrasting of characters, the placing of a character in a particular situation; from the use of cleverly selected details, unconscious self revelation, word association.

H. E. Bates, while recognising a vivid clarity and a strangely personal quality, found her writing frequently immature and monotonous; the stories told in 'a kind of mental soliloquy, fluttering, gossipy, breathless' by her characters, 'all chattering overgrown schoolgirls busy asking and answering breathless facile questions about love and life and happiness' [*The Modern Short Story,* 1941]. This surely is a very narrow view which ignores many of her characters. Certainly some are weakly drawn types— particularly in the early stories—but others are truly alive, not drawn on a grand scale, but real people in a real world.

It is true that the majority of the characters in K. M.'s stories are female. She was frequently concerned with the particular relationships in which women were involved— with their children, with each other and with men. The role of women in society is central to much of her work, and most obviously so in the German stories.

It is therefore, as H. E. Bates and others have suggested, at times a 'female' world we are shown. In **'The Luftbad'**, which is set in a women's sunbathing enclosure in Wörishofen where the women are 'in their nakeds' there are, not surprisingly, no men. The point of view from which we view incidents, characters and relationships is frequently female and it is more often the female characters who win our sympathy. Some, like Beryl in **'At the Bay'**, are disillusioned by unexpected and coarse male advances. In others, the male characters' potential for seduction or physical violence is only hinted at.

Often too the worlds of male and female seem quite separate, only tenuously linked. The men seem quite alien at times to that world in which women are comfortable. One of K. M.'s most unattractive characters, Harry Young in **'Bliss'**, epitomises this. He 'loved doing things at high pressure', was an ambitious greedy poseur who dismissed his baby daughter with the words, 'My dear Mrs Knight, don't ask me about my baby. I never see her. I shan't feel the slightest interest in her until she has a lover'. In **'At the Bay'** Stanley leaves home feeling 'The heartlessness of women! The way they took it for granted it was your job to slave away for them while they didn't even take the trouble to see that your walking stick wasn't lost.' Meanwhile, without the irritant of his presence, even the women's voices changed, 'they sounded warm and loving as if they shared a secret.'

In the same story, however, Jonathan Trout is shown as an atypical male. He is more articulate than Stanley, willing to talk about 'cranky' ideas and dreams; happier talking in the garden than sitting in his 'jail' of an office. Through him K. M. gives a picture of what men might be if only they were allowed to be, and had the courage to break free from the role society has traditionally allotted them. Linda, who finds Jonathan attractive, is aware that even beneath Stanley's everyday exterior there is a more sensitive man.

The traditional role of women in society is also closely examined. Linda spends her time calming Stanley down, 'and what was left of her time was spent in the dread of having children'. The woman 'at the store' was once a barmaid 'pretty as a waxdoll' who 'knew one hundred and twenty-five different ways of kissing'. After six years of marriage and four miscarriages she has become a pathetic figure. 'Her front teeth were knocked out, she had red pulpy hands', she is driven to murder by loneliness and despair. Elsewhere, as in **'Pictures'** and **'Miss Brill'**, K. M. explores the dilemma of older women, lonely, without family or support.

At times the male and female characters do achieve a kind of closeness and understanding, though it is rarely sexual but more akin to the kind of sympathetic bonding that often links the women in her stories. More often though the men are shown to be too inarticulate, uncommunicative and emotionally unevolved for this intimacy to take place. The boss in **'The Fly'** who 'had arranged to weep' but 'no tears came' is perhaps the most frightening example of such men, and at the same time a plea for them to change. Clearly then her characters are not 'all chattering overgrown schoolgirls' as H. E. Bates would have us believe. (pp. 168-72)

In moving away from the concept of the short story as a narrative and in suggesting through her work the immense possibilities of what could be done once the artificialities of conventional plot were eliminated, K. M. had a profound influence on the development of the modern short story—an influence freely acknowledged by Elizabeth Bowen and others. As T. O. Beachcroft states, she belongs with 'Eliot, Joyce and Virginia Woolf' as 'part of a new dawn' [see Further Reading]. Once K. M. and others had claimed the right to experiment, others followed, frequently achieving a combination of the two methods.

It is particularly interesting to look at the views of her contemporaries. Thomas Hardy, John Galsworthy and H. G. Wells all regarded her very highly, whereas D. H. Lawrence had answered Catherine Carswell's enthusiasm for **'Prelude'** with the impatient reply, 'Yes, yes, but prelude to what?' She would, he felt, reject the stories that contained her unique combination of sentiment and charm and stop writing until she could find a different kind of story. It was a strangely accurate prediction. Although he saw similarities to Dickens in her vivid use of specific details and colour and her touches of humour, Lawrence felt that Murry was wrong about her, and wrong to try to promote her work so assiduously after her death:

> She was *not* a great genius. She had a charming gift, and a finely cultivated one. But *not more*. And to try, as you do, to make it more is to do her no true service . . . she is delicate and touching—but not great! Why say great.

While dryly admitting her jealousy, Virginia Woolf felt that K. M. was one of the best women writers. **'Prelude'** was one of the first volumes published by the Hogarth Press because Virginia felt it to be, 'a good deal better than most stories'. In her diary she went further, recognising in it 'the living power, the detached existence of a work of art'.

Their relationship was a difficult one, however, and Virginia found little to admire in K. M.'s later stories. Shortly after her friend's death which, she said, had moved her greatly, she wrote to Jacques Raverat:

> My theory is that while she possessed the most amazing *senses* of her generation so that she could actually reproduce this room for instance, with its fly, clock, dog, tortoise if need be, to the life, she was as weak as water, as insipid, and a great deal more commonplace, when she had to use her mind. That is, she can't put thoughts, or feelings, or subtleties of any kind into her characters, without at once becoming, where she's serious, hard, and where she's sympathetic, sentimental.

It is also possible to criticise the very restricted circumscribed range of her work, but like Jane Austen she chose to write only of what she had known and seen. 'The artist takes a *long look* at life. He says softly, "So this is what life is, is it?" And he proceeds to express that. All the rest he leaves.' Nevertheless she was well aware of the limitations imposed upon her by her illness and her isolation: 'I'm so *stale*—oh for a "weekend" or even a ciné or a theatre or the sound of music'.

Naturally K. M. was considerably disturbed when it was suggested to her that had she not been ill, she might never have been able to write as she had.

Her illness certainly led to a feeling of urgency, 'It's always a race to get in as much as one can before it disappears'. She seemed often to write in bursts, sudden moments of crystallisation. A particularly interesting example of this occurs in the manuscript of **'The Doll's House'.** One page begins with the story's last few lines. Beneath an erratically drawn line is the preceding section about Willie Brent, 'he'd come to the front door. . . . ' Beneath that is a much earlier section, part of the scene at the school, 'Lil Kelvey's going to be a servant when she grows up. . . . ' An arrow indicates how these fragments were to be finally fitted together, like pieces in a jigsaw.

In spite of illness, unhappiness and bleak frustration K. M. retained a tremendous spontaneous enthusiasm for life. 'God! I'm *rooted* in Life. Even if I hate Life, I can't deny it. I spring from it and feed on it.' Often this enthusiasm had been for her vision of life, rather than for life's reality. Yet she knew she must learn to accept that reality: 'I don't believe a writer can ever do anything *worth* doing until he has—in the profoundest sense of the word— ACCEPTED Life.' Gradually she came to know herself; to gain the courage to accept life for what it really was:

> But do you really feel all beauty is marred by ugliness and the lovely woman has bad teeth? I don't feel quite that, . . . Beauty triumphs over ugliness in Life. That's what I feel. And that marvelous triumph is what I long to express. . . . Life is, all at one and the same time, far more mysterious and far simpler than we know. It's like religion in that. If we want to have faith, and without faith we die, we must *learn* to accept.

Some of her finest stories are about that triumph, and that acceptance, and with her ability to capture fleeting moods and vibrant warm colours they have enduring relevance.

Some stories do not work, but at her best, K. M. succeeded in writing something between 'a poem and a reflection, a novel and an anecdote'. All readers will have those stories which for him or her epitomise the particular quality of her writing and which lead them to glimpse a moment of truth; the realisation of the inevitability of life and the 'beauty in that inevitability'.

Despite John Middleton Murry's efforts, the amount of work on which her worldwide reputation rests is comparatively slight. Her technical innovations and skill alone would have had an important influence on modern writing. Her finest stories are, however, far more than technical masterpieces. In speaking to that 'secret self we all have', they establish her place in literature. Through her we see the world we have always known—but we see it more clearly. (pp. 180-82)

Gillian Boddy, in her Katherine Mansfield: The Woman and the Writer, *Penguin Books, 1988, 325 p.*

J. F. Kobler   (essay date 1990)

[*Kobler is an American educator and critic. In the following excerpt, he examines the development of new forms and narrative techniques in Mansfield's New Zealand stories.*]

Mansfield described what happened on 24 March 1915 as the Muses descending upon her, causing her to fall "into the open arms of my first novel," **"The Aloe."** The circumstances of her life may also have had something to do with her having "a great day" of writing. Her short affair with Francis Carco, a dedicated Bohemian writer and also a friend of Murry's, was over; her relationship with Murry had improved; and although her physical health was still poor, she had moved back to Paris alone with firm intentions of writing. Surely the greatest influence, however, on this sudden flowing of creative juices was the presence in England of her twenty-one-year-old brother, Leslie Beauchamp, who had arrived in February for military training, opening the doors of memory to their childhoods in New Zealand. If Chummie's coming back into Mansfield's life was instrumental in her beginning to produce some fifty pages of manuscript in Paris, his death in a hand-grenade accident in France on 7 October 1915 effectively ended her work until she could recover from the shocking loss. The significance of Chummie, his death, and Mansfield's recognition of what she had to do with her material is caught in this passage from her *Journal:* "But all must be told with a sense of mystery, a radiance, an afterglow because you, my little sun of it, are set. You have dropped over the dazzling brim of the world. Now I must play my part." The playing of her part in turning the manuscript of **"The Aloe"** into the published **'Prelude'** began in February 1916 and took until 10 July 1918, the day Virginia and Leonard Woolf sent out the first copies of the hand-set book.

Although Mansfield knew, as she said in a letter to the Honorable Dorothy Brett, artist and close friend, that she had something here "more or less my own invention," her statement about this new form says more about what she "tried to catch" from her people and her homeland than how she actually caught it. Mansfield's feeling of inadequacy in describing exactly how her prose works in **'Prelude'** and later stories has been duplicated down through the years by most critics, who see very well the word-magic occurring in front of their eyes but can catch in their own words only glimmerings of how that magic works. Most obviously and simply it involves the removal of a narrator as an active and direct agent in the telling of the story. The narrator, whether Katherine Mansfield or an alter ego of the author, is present in most of the stories written from the German experiences, clearly visible and audible in the first-person pronoun. The events in these stories do not just happen; they are shaped by the narrator's view of how they happened.

Of course, in reality Mansfield's consciousness cannot possibly be missing from **'Prelude'** or any other story. Some human consciousness has to be at work in all stories, unless we are going to move beyond magic and start fantasizing about muses and stories that write themselves. The magic lies in Mansfield's being able to move prose fiction closer to the dramatic form, in which characters can speak for themselves. One of the enduring fictions of the theater was transformed before our very eyes by Mansfield and many other twentieth-century writers into a now-enduring technique of literature.

Despite these general "truths" about the new prose fiction, there is still the magical truth that the "nonvoice" of Katherine Mansfield in her stories has a different sound from that of other authors—say, James Joyce, to name one of her near-contemporaries. The reader of well-tuned ear and even a modicum of experience will never confuse the sounds of a Joyce and a Mansfield story. Murry's notion, quoted earlier, that Mansfield was able to write as she did because she looked at life through a "crystal-clear" set of lenses is just not possible. Neither could she have retained a child's vision despite her adult experiences; whatever her stories may lack in tedious, cold, philosophical positions, they are not expressions of a child's mind. If Mansfield lacks a dogmatic view of life and, with Laura in **"The Garden Party,"** finds the meaning of life inexpressible in a mere phrase, so much the better. If Mansfield did not blindly accept the old-fashioned idea of a central self that needed discovering but did lean toward belief in the possibility of multiple selves, so much the better—at least for a fiction that tries to let every character present herself or himself directly through word and action but without turning those characters loose on the stage.

'Prelude' begins, "There was not an inch of room for Lottie and Kezia in the buggy." This is no storyteller's opening line but a magician's interception of a reader's eye in midpassage.

Compare that Mansfield sentence with the opening sentences of the first two stories in Joyce's *Dubliners:* "There was no hope for him this time: it was the third stroke" ("The Sisters") and "It was Joe Dillon who introduced the Wild West to us" ("An Encounter"). Although each sentence begins in the middle of an action, describing the action without any comment on it, the reader soon discovers in "The Sisters" and the line from "An Encounter" makes explicit that the Joyce stories both have first-person narrators. Mansfield's does not. So who in the story knows there is "not an inch of room" for what most readers will surely assume to be two children? Every character involved in the action can see the lack of room, but the reader does not yet know who those persons are.

Only as the paragraph develops does the reader learn who is taking part in the scene. The reader who thinks of this as a staged scene happening before his very eyes can better grasp how the magic works. The characters on the stage would be discovering the lack of room by looking at the buggy, simultaneously with the audience's learning the same thing through the same act of looking. In effect, the characters in the story are learning things about their scene at the same moment the reader is; there is no privileged viewpoint of some omniscient narrator, telling about events that have already occurred. The action has not previously taken place; it is taking place.

Not everyone involved in this simple action, however, knows the same things for the same reasons. For example, the statement that "Linda Burnell could not possibly have held a lump of a child on [her lap] for any distance" is loaded with precise implications and with an exposure of Linda's mental processes that a theater audience could not possibly "know" from what it physically sees. But a theater audience would know something that the reading audience can only assume: that Linda Burnell is pregnant. Physically, then, it would be dangerous for her to try to hold any child on her lap for very long. Are these her children? A theater audience might know from the list of characters in the playbill; from the scene itself and from the relative ages of the two adult females, our hypothetical theater audience might guess that the two little girls (the reading audience must assume their femaleness from their names) are the children of the pregnant woman. A character named Pat appears. The name may be either male or female, but maleness is assumed by the reader because Pat is physically strong enough to swing two persons up "on top of the luggage." But what about that phrase *a lump of a child* in the sentence quoted above? To whom are these darling little girls (the theater audience can see them; the reading audience assumes they are darlings from this paragraph and verifies it in the next one) mere "lumps"? To their mother, Linda, of course, as the story will continue to demonstrate but which fact may be assumed here at the beginning. Linda implies that the girls cannot make this trip because the "bags and boxes" on the floor of the carriage "are absolute necessities that I will not let out of my sight for one instant"—meaning that having Lottie and Kezia out of sight may also be happily out of mind, for Linda.

This extended analysis of one paragraph is meant to demonstrate several things about Mansfield's prose in **'Prelude'** and many subsequent stories: It is finely crafted; the reader must be constantly alert as to what the text is doing to perception; the point of view is multiple and shifting; and the nonexistent narrator must be watched closely, lest she sneak in and do a little sleight of hand. If the form of the story is complex and tantalizing, it only fits with the content and with the author's ambivalence toward her homeland and her own family members, who without a doubt are represented by the Burnells of the story.

Mansfield's mother's name was Annie Burnell Dyer Beauchamp. The story itself is entitled **'Prelude'** because the life depicted here for Kezia (Katherine) and the members of her family is but the prelude to later life and fiction. In the story Mansfield not only begins to develop her new style but creates events that will be instrumental in the development of her thematic interests in later stories. One of those themes involves the apparently inherent difficulties with love between men and women . . . , as it occurs in several stories. In **'Prelude'** Linda and Stanley Burnell convincingly represent the masculine and feminine principles that Mansfield so often depicts in her stories. Despite the absence of any direct authorial judgment in the story, every reader knows that Stanley Burnell is depicted unfavorably as he goes about being the kind of man his New Zealand (and English and American) society of the late nineteenth century expected him to be. He does nothing around the house except carve the duck at dinner, because women "never seemed to care what the meat looked like afterwards." He demands that his mother-in-law get him his slippers. He is implicitly compared by his wife to her dog, of whom she is very fond, but she wishes the dog "wouldn't jump at her so, and bark so loudly and watch her with such eager, loving eyes." Stanley hates servility in men but requires it of his women. In short, he is portrayed as the typical and societally admired male chauvinist of the time. No matter how typical he may be, the power of his portrait and the fundamental fact that he paints his own picture keep the typical from shading into the stereo-typical. Mansfield's method causes Stanley to condemn himself through word and deed, while at the same time Linda's attitude toward him (again without externally imposed narrative directives) softens his chauvinistic personality.

What Linda does to and for her own portrait while helping to color Stanley's is more complex and probably more interesting to most readers than anything Stanley does. Although Mansfield guides her story into Stanley's mind on occasion, it is clear from both the quantity and the quality of Linda's inner life that Mansfield takes Linda's interior world far more seriously than she takes Stanley's. While it is true that his great and surely superficial happiness in his present life stands in contrast to Linda's deep unhappiness, that simple distinction is not the only dividing factor that Mansfield crafts between the two.

Any analysis of what Mansfield's skillful maneuvering of Linda's and Stanley's outer words and actions means in relation to their inner lives is made additionally tricky by the problem of determining causes and effects. Narrators often do such work for the reader (as Mansfield's surrogate does in many of the *German Pension* stories), but here there is no guiding voice. When the Burnells wake up to a beautiful morning after their first night in their new house, Stanley is "enormously pleased" and his obviously superficial, smug thought process goes like this: "Weather like this set a final seal on his bargain. He felt, somehow, that he had bought the lovely day, too—got it chucked in dirt cheap with the house and ground." Mansfield and the reader both know that Stanley has his rational causes and effects badly confused, as undoubtedly Stanley would also know if he stopped to [think of] things in another way. Although he thinks an obviously silly thing here, it can speak well for his personality in a reader's mind, because his natural feeling stands in violent conflict with his pursuit of the practical. In a later incident, the effect that societal training has on Stanley in causing him to do something contrary to a natural and, by implication, good impulse is demonstrated when he thinks "he wouldn't mind giving" his driver Pat "a handful" of cherries but counters this feeling with the safe rationalization that he had better wait until Pat "had been with him a bit longer." In Stanley's defense and in further explanation of Mansfield's success as creator of him, it should be recognized that Stanley is too happy in his actual living at this point to worry (or think) much about the nature of life. Does he not demonstrate life daily in the very doing of it? Why ruminate when one can dominate?

Almost naturally, it seems, Linda and her sister Beryl Fairfield do a great deal of thinking, mostly about how unhappy they are in their present conditions. Yet Mansfield depicts their two minds as being quite different. Linda is clearly the more sympathetic of the two, perhaps largely because she is more honest with herself but also because Mansfield plays on the female-male situation to show that Linda is unhappy in a condition (marriage) that Beryl yearns for. Nothing in the characterization of the sisters even implies they are so different that Beryl would be happy if they changed places. Rather, Beryl is established as the romantic unmarried woman who believes marriage cannot help but bring happiness, even though she lives daily with evidence to the contrary. Beryl seems to blame Linda for Linda's unhappiness, but overall the story shows that Mansfield blames the kind of marriage that most women like these had to make as being the cause of Linda's current unhappiness and implicitly predicts that in marriage Beryl would encounter the same life and thoughts. Although some readers think badly of Linda because she does not love her children, surely in so casting her, Mansfield becomes an early questioner of another assumption of that society: that all women have a maternal instinct.

Linda's marriage has produced those emotions in her and her honesty about them; the absence of such feelings in Beryl and the presence in her of romantic notions about how marriage, as such, will bring her happiness contribute to the reader's feeling that this kind of marriage is the culprit, not either of the partners personally. The fault lies, the story says, not with the women and not with this husband but with all traditional marriages between unequal partners. Almost no other kind occurs in Mansfield's stories; their success rate is exceedingly low. Although Mansfield regularly goes into Linda's mind, the following quotation well demonstrates the nature of Linda's feelings and Mansfield's portrayal of them as completely honest and natural. The passage follows Linda's recognition that despite "all her love and respect and admiration" for Stanley, she hates him; the action that brings all these thoughts to the surface is his responding with far too much joy and enthusiasm to her simple request that he light a candle:

> It had never been so plain to her as it was at this moment. There were all her feelings for him, sharp and defined, one as true as the other. And there was this other, this hatred, just as real as the rest. She could have done her feelings up in little packets and given them to Stanley. She longed to hand him that last one, for a surprise. She could see his eyes as he opened that.

Linda will not and cannot tell Stanley she hates him. As she recognizes with silent laughter, life (the life that their society forced on such women) is absurd. This kind of life is, indeed, absurd for a woman. Too many women in too many Mansfield stories suffer these indignities for Linda to be seen as strange and unusual, as a misfit in this world.

Linda's unmarried sister Beryl yearns after exactly this sort of life. The great irony is that she already has it, but the man who works to supply her food and shelter is not her own man. Things would be different if Beryl had a husband of her own, she thinks; but the story says that they would not be. Mansfield establishes through the thoughts of these two sisters a basic difference in attitudes. Linda, suffering to learn it but learning it just the same, knows that she is a complex being who can both love and hate her husband; she knows, as the passage quoted above demonstrates, that she has no true self to be discovered. Beryl has not yet learned that the concept of a true self is a Platonistic ideal that has no bearing on real human beings. She thinks of herself as "always acting a part." She tells herself that she is not ever her real self. She upbraids herself for putting on a show "for Stanley's benefit" just the previous evening; "when he was reading the paper her false self had stood beside him and leaned against his shoulder on purpose."

In this societal structure, the current "rules" about marriage mean that despite her misery Linda will "go on having children and Stanley will go on making money and the children and the gardens will grow bigger and bigger"; likewise, Beryl will go on believing that her real self does not want to steal her sister's husband, that only her false self would dare to "put her hand over his, pointing out something so that he should see how white her hand was beside his brown one." The Beryl that she believes she really is and has achieved at "tiny moments" is "rich and mysterious and good," and life is also all of those things.

Life for the mother of these two women—the grandmother of Kezia—is, in contrast, wanting her pantry shelves well supplied with her homemade jam. Totally practical and the hardest-working member of the family, Mrs. Fairfield immediately tackles the kitchen of the new house and soon everything in the kitchen has been arranged in patterns. She surveys her work, smiles, and thinks how satisfactory it is.

Why is Mrs. Fairfield so calm, self-contained, practical, and hardworking? Since this story goes no more often into her consciousness than it does into Stanley's, a superficial reading might be that Mansfield no more knew what

makes stoical grandmothers tick than she knew what makes men like Stanley tick. Realizing the possible danger to her credibility of employing this method of writing to go into the minds of characters she could not "know" internally, Mansfield simply avoided trying to do so. Such an interpretation has to be tempting to any reader who is trying to avoid the issue of Mansfield's possibly inconsistent philosophy about human nature: Do we have true selves or do we not? The question should never be asked of Mansfield, even though she may depict some characters who think one way and some who feel another. Mansfield does not know the answer either. The grandmother is what she is, and never mind how she got that way.

A few of Mrs. Fairfield's actions, however, do seem to require some interpretation, especially as they relate to her grandchild Kezia, who loves her and depends on her in much the same way young Kass Beauchamp loved her Granny Dyer. The first night in the new house, Kezia is waiting for her grandmother to come to bed, the last to do so in the household. As the grandmother gets into bed, she sighs. Kezia sticks her head under the old woman's arms and gives "a little squeak." Mansfield's description of the grandmother's response is noteworthy because two very minor words (*but* and *only*) are important keys to the grandmother's state of mind: "But the old woman only pressed her faintly, and sighed again, took out her teeth,

Mansfield, 1913.

and put them in a glass of water beside her on the floor." These are sighs of resignation to her fate as a woman and to the need to do the things that must be done, such as taking good care of false teeth.

In the story **"At the Bay,"** probably originally intended to serve as a second chapter in the novel that was never finished, Grandmother Fairfield again is forced by Kezia to sigh about things. Kezia asks her why she is "stopping and sort of staring at the wall?" Following a paragraph that describes their setting and reads almost like stage directions, Kezia again asks why her grandmother seems so preoccupied. In response, "the old woman sighed, whipped the wool twice round her thumb, and drew the bone needle through." Mansfield follows with a gem of a sentence that reflects the old woman's stoicism and serves as both a reflection of her attitude and an attitude toward her reflecting: "She was casting on," doing what she is here to do.

The grandmother, however, does tell Kezia what she has been thinking about: Kezia's dead Uncle William. Following a short discussion of Uncle William, Kezia asks her grandmother if thinking about him makes her sad, at which point Mansfield's story enters the grandmother's thought processes: "Did it make her sad? To look back, back. To stare down the years, as Kezia had seen her doing. To look after *them* as a woman does, long after *they* were out of sight. Did it make her sad? No, life was like that."

How does a reader interpret Mrs. Fairfield's view of life— as wisdom gained with age? as resignation forced on her by conditions she accepted? In truth, the interpretation must not be made at this point in the story, because the "act" involving Kezia and her grandmother is not yet finished. Kezia has yet to ask if everyone has to die. She responds vigorously to Mrs. Fairfield's statement that even Kezia will die someday: "What if I just won't?" Mrs. Fairfield's response is to "sigh again" (with Mansfield calling direct attention to the act as occurring again) and to draw "a long thread from the ball." Work must go on in this life, despite our need to sigh over it occasionally. This scene in **"At the Bay"** ends with Kezia tickling and kissing her grandmother in an effort to love her into promising never to die and leave Kezia alone. The old woman is finally forced to drop her knitting (put the practical work aside), to swing "back in the rocker" and begin "to tickle Kezia." They are "laughing in each other's arms" when Mrs. Fairfield proclaims, "Come, that's enough, my squirrel! That's enough, my wild pony!" She sets "her cap straight" and commands Kezia to "pick up my knitting." The section of the story ends with the sentence "Both of them had forgotten what the 'never' was about."

Life is like that. The young do not expect to die; the old have a resigned wisdom. The young are as natural as squirrels or wild ponies; the old can be tickled and loved into dropping their work for a few moments. And when we are in the act of truly loving each other, young and old, we are very likely to forget our demands to say *never, forever, always,* or any of the other words that cause individuals to box themselves into one condition that they then label life.

Mansfield most often uses her fictional techniques to go into the consciousness of a young woman struggling with her feelings of love and hate, with her emotions as a woman in a world clearly dominated by men, as we might well expect from a romantic, autobiographical writer who lived in such a world; however, the methods of objective characterization (both internal and external) that Mansfield began to develop in these two stories of the Burnell family helped her also to create other characters with equal verisimilitude. Understandable is Murry's appreciation of the words of one of his wife's printers: "But these kids are *'real'!* "

Other stories that grew out of Mansfield's childhood in New Zealand include the very early story **"New Dresses,"** the minor stories **"The Little Girl"** and **"The Voyage,"** and the more significant **"The Doll's House."** . . . **"The Little Girl"** is another Kezia story, one in which Kezia sees her father as "a figure to be feared and avoided." The sense of relief she feels every morning when he goes off to work foreshadows the freedom that comes on all the Burnell women when Stanley leaves for work in **"At the Bay"**: "Oh, the relief, the difference it made to have the man out of the house. Their very voices were changed as they called to one another; they sounded warm and loving and as if they shared a secret."

But if the characters and most of the emotions are the same in **"The Little Girl"** (first published in 1912) and **"At the Bay"** (published ten years later), the narrative technique is not. In **"At the Bay"** Mansfield has eliminated the first-person narrator of the earlier story but has not yet found her way into Kezia's mind in the manner she will later. The first sentence of **"The Little Girl"** reads, "To the little girl he was a figure to be feared and avoided." That statement is clearly an external generalization about Kezia's attitudes and actions rather than an immediate opening leap into an ongoing action, as is the previously quoted beginning of **'Prelude'**: "There was not an inch of room for Lottie and Kezia."

The plot of **"The Little Girl"** concerns Kezia's innocently tearing up her father's "great speech for the Port Authority" to use for stuffing in the pincushion she is making for his birthday. Her hands are slapped with a ruler, causing her to sob, "What did Jesus make fathers for?" Kezia's superficial observation of the five Macdonald children playing in the yard next door with their father causes her to decide that not all fathers are like hers, a conclusion that readers of Mansfield's stories may have trouble endorsing. This story, however, ends on what feminist critic Kate Fullbrook [in her *Katherine Mansfield,* 1986] takes as a positive note, when Kezia, after a nightmare, is taken into her father's bed, because both her mother and her grandmother are out of the house, and discovers that, for cuddling, his body is harder than her grandmother's but is "a nice hardness." She begins to feel sorry for his having to go to work every day and being "too tired to be a Mr. Macdonald." The story ends with Kezia, her head resting on her father's chest, proclaiming, "What a big heart you've got, father dear." Although Fullbrook finds the end sentimental, she approves of what Mansfield "is trying to do here," that is, to posit tentatively "a female sexuality whose basis is reflective, based on similarity rather than difference."

Frankly, I have great difficulty being hopeful not about the actual existence of greater female-male rapprochment than has been thought possible in Western culture (largely by males and male psychologists such as Freud and Jung, as Fullbrook accurately charges) but about Mansfield's forecasting in her own time the possibility of such a coming together. Even more difficult to see is Mansfield's having opened "a new account of the links between male and female." Rather, I read the sentimental conclusion of the story at face value, which is that the "funny feeling" that comes over Kezia because her father tells her to rub her feet against his legs for warmth is a deluded feeling rather than a revelatory one. The man is still gaining ascendancy through his ability to deliver physical comforts to the female. Hearing his heart beating is ironically a purely physical thing. Although little Kezia may equate "a big heart" with the ability to love another person, there is no evidence in this story or in later stories about Kezia's father that the action of the heart is transformed into actions of self—giving love. Mansfield's stories taken as a whole say that big and little girls who think well of men or who try to be their equals are in for rude awakenings—which is what Kezia may get in the morning from her father.

Probably the most interesting fact about **"The Voyage"** is that Mansfield apparently stopped working on **"At the Bay"** on 11 August 1921 in order to write the story in recognition of the third anniversary of her mother's death. The story merely recounts the boat trip of Grandmother Mary Crane and her granddaughter Fenella to Mrs. Crane's home, following the death of Fenella's mother. At home they find Grandfather Walter Crane in a huge bed, with just his silver-bearded face showing outside the covers. This element of the story may recapture (surely not from Mansfield's own memory) a boat trip in the writer's first year to visit her paternal grandparents. The father in this story, by the way, appears only briefly to see the travelers off. He sounds stern to Fenella but looks tired. He hugs his mother and says, "God bless you." When she returns that blessing and adds "my own brave son!" Fenella thinks, "This was so awful," and turns her back on them. Is this response to be read as a child's normal reaction to gushing adults or as a recognition of some falseness in the display of emotion? When Fenella asks her father how long she is going to stay at her grandmother's, he will not look at her. She is holding on to his lapels, but he shakes her off "gently." This depiction certainly seems to be another of those mixed views of a father, written by a daughter who had a confusing love/hate relationship with her own father.

In **"The Doll's House,"** finished at the end of October 1922, Mansfield returns to the Burnells at a time that seems a few years later than that of the other stories about Kezia and her family. The story implies that they have been living in their house in the country for some time now, and Kezia, Lottie, and Isabel are all in school. There is no mention of a son; Father Stanley does not appear; Mother Linda utters but two sentences. **"The Doll's House"** is about the children—especially Kezia, who violates the family rules by inviting the outcast Kelvey girls to look at the wonderful dollhouse sent to the Burnell children by "dear old Mrs. Hay," after a stay with the family. The fabulous dollhouse is the talk of the school, and the children are allowed to invite their school friends to come see it, though under terribly strict rules for children: no more than two at a time, just to look, not to stay to tea, not "to come traipsing through the house," but to stand quietly in the courtyard admiring the little house as, the

story implies, everyone should admire the Burnells and their big house.

Much scapegoating occurs in this story. The Burnells do not approve of the school to which the girls go, but there is no choice. They must go and be mixed all together, the children of a judge, a doctor, a storekeeper, even a milkman; however, "the line" is drawn at the Kelveys, whose mother is a "hardworking little washer-woman" and whose father is thought to be in jail. The children at school learn from their parents, taunting and teasing the Kelvey girls—Lil and our Else (she is always called that) Kelvey—in sport. One of the girls hisses at the Kelveys, "Yah, yer father's in prison!" These scapegoating words "deeply, deeply" excite all the other girls, who are so released from their own fears and limitations by heaping them on the Kelveys that they skip rope faster and harder, doing more "daring things" than they have ever done before.

One day Kezia, who is said only to have "made up her mind," speaks to the Kelvey girls and invites them to look at the dollhouse. Although Mansfield writes of Kezia's hesitation in inviting them, she offers neither internal nor external reasons for Kezia's going against her mother's explicit orders. Lil, who is even more a victim of socialization than is Kezia, is afraid to accept the invitation, but our Else, who never speaks, implores with her eyes; thus, they go to look at the dollhouse. Descriptions of the Kelvey girls include their looking like "two little stray cats" and standing "still as a stone." When Aunt Beryl discovers the invasion of her courtyard, she shoos the Kelveys out "as if they were chickens." Later she thinks of them as rats. These images add up to the point that the adult Burnells do not even consider these little girls human. That Mansfield is depicting the psychology of scapegoating becomes even more obvious with an otherwise pointless paragraph about Aunt Beryl's feelings after she has chased the Kelveys away and shouted "bitterly" at Kezia, "Wicked, disobedient little girl." Aunt Beryl's "afternoon had been awful" because of a letter "from Willie Brent, a terrifying, threatening letter" that demands she meet him or expect a visit from him at her front door. Now, having "frightened those little rats of Kelveys and given Kezia a good scolding," Beryl's pain is lifted, the "ghastly pressure" is gone, and she can return to "the house humming."

But our Else has the last word. The furnishing in the doll's house that Kezia loves most "frightfully" is a tiny lamp "in the middle of the dining-room table." Well out of sight of the Burnells, the Kelvey girls sit down to rest and our Else speaks her only words in the story: "I seen the little lamp." Only Kezia in the Burnell family is capable of seeing and demonstrating the light of love—or human understanding, compassion, or whatever a reader wants to call it.

That Mansfield found her new form by going back to the emotional days of her childhood attests to the great influence of that early time on her life; her feelings of love and hate for her parents were so mixed that only by giving them different shapes and names could she come to grips with them. (pp. 14-27)

J. F. Kobler, in his Katherine Mansfield: A

Study of the Short Fiction, *Twayne Publishers, 1990, 172 p.*

FURTHER READING

Aiken, Conrad. "Mansfield, Katherine (1921)," "Mansfield, Katherine (1922)," and "Mansfield, Katherine (1927)." In his *Collected Criticism,* pp. 291-93, 293-97, 297-99. London: Oxford University Press, 1958.
    Favorable reviews of *Bliss, and Other Stories, The Garden Party, and Other Stories,* and the *Journal of Katherine Mansfield,* assessing Mansfield as an important literary talent.

Alpers, Antony. *The Life of Katherine Mansfield.* Rev. ed. London: Viking Penguin, 1980, 466 p.
    Extensively researched biography that includes critical commentary.

Baldeshwiler, Eileen. "Katherine Mansfield's Theory of Fiction." *Studies in Short Fiction* VII, No. 3 (Summer 1970): 421-32.
    Examines statements about narrative form and technique drawn from Mansfield's published letters, journals, and book reviews.

Bateson, F. W., and Shahevitch, B. "Katherine Mansfield's 'The Fly': A Critical Exercise." *Essays in Criticism* XII, No. 1 (January 1962): 39-53.
    Reprints Mansfield's "The Fly" and offers a close textual analysis. R. A. Jolly, R. A. Copland, and E. B. Greenwood responded to this essay (cited below).

Beachcroft, T. O. "Katherine Mansfield." In his *The Modest Art: A Survey of the Short Story in English,* pp. 162-75. London: Oxford University Press, 1968.
    Addresses the question of Chekhovian influence in a discussion of Mansfield's innovations in the short story form.

Berkman, Sylvia. *Katherine Mansfield: A Critical Study.* New Haven: Yale University Press, 1951, 246 p.
    Important biographical and critical survey.

Blanchard, Lydia. "The Savage Pilgrimage of D. H. Lawrence and Katherine Mansfield: A Study in Literary Influence, Anxiety, and Subversion." *Modern Language Quarterly* 47, No. 1 (March 1986): 48-65.
    Contends that in the novels *The Lost Girl* and *Women in Love* by Lawrence and "Je ne parle pas français," "Bliss," and "Marriage à la Mode" by Mansfield, each writer was responding to messages conveyed in the work of the other.

Bowen, Elizabeth. Introduction to *Stories by Katherine Mansfield,* by Katherine Mansfield, edited by Elizabeth Bowen, pp. v-xxiv. New York: Vintage Books, 1956.
    Biographical and critical sketch discussing salient characteristics of Mansfield's fiction and the difficulties of selection faced by an editor of her work.

Boyle, Ted E. "The Death of the Boss: Another Look at Katherine Mansfield's 'The Fly'." *Modern Fiction Studies* XI, No. 2 (Summer 1965): 183-85.
    Disputes the interpretation by John V. Hagopian (cited below) of the boss as a largely sympathetic figure with an imperfect understanding of death, suggesting that the story deals with the spiritual death of the boss.

Brewster, Dorothy, and Burrell, Angus. "Soundings: Fiction of Anton Chekhov and Katherine Mansfield" and "Salvaging the Short-Story: Chekhov and Mansfield—Continued." In their *Dead Reckonings in Fiction,* pp. 42-70, 71-100. New York: Longmans, Green and Co., 1925.
    Assesses shared characteristics of the fiction of Chekhov and Mansfield, noting in particular that both avoided the traditional short story form emphasizing plot and climax.

Brophy, Brigid. "Katherine Mansfield." In her *Don't Never Forget: Collected Views and Reviews,* pp. 255-63. New York: Holt, Rinehart and Winston, 1966.
    Biographical and psychological sketch of Mansfield that has been interpreted as hostile despite Brophy's professed admiration for Mansfield.

Corin, Fernand. "Creation of Atmosphere in Katherine Mansfield's Stories." *Revue des langues vivantes* 22, No. 1 (1956): 65-78.
    Examines ways in which Mansfield created atmosphere—defined as the general emotional effect, mood, and tone of a piece of fiction—and considers the function of atmosphere in her fiction.

Cox, Sidney. "The Fastidiousness of Katherine Mansfield." *The Sewanee Review* XXXIX, No. 2 (April-June 1931): 158-69.
    Contends that Mansfield's life and works alike are characterized by her fastidious nature, which lent a quality of precision to her fiction.

Daiches, David. "Katherine Mansfield and the Search for Truth." In his *The Novel and the Modern World,* pp. 65-79. Chicago: University of Chicago Press, 1939.
    Discusses Mansfield's application of a highly individual, nontraditional set of values in her works, resulting in her illumination of an intensely personal, nonobjective truth.

Gordon, Ian A. Introduction to *Undiscovered Country: The New Zealand Stories of Katherine Mansfield,* by Katherine Mansfield, edited by Ian A. Gordon, pp. ix-xxi. London: Longman Group, 1974.
    Surveys the principal themes of Mansfield's fiction with a New Zealand setting and presents the stories in a sequence intended to "reinforce and illuminate the themes and preoccupations that sustain the underlying unity of her work."

Gottwald, Maria. "New Approaches and Techniques in the Short Story of James Joyce and Katherine Mansfield." In *Literary Interrelations: Ireland, England and the World, Vol. 2—Comparison and Impact,* edited by Wolfgang Zach and Heinz Kosok, pp. 41-7. Tübingen: Gunter Narr Verlag, 1987.
    Examines affinities between the literary techniques of Joyce and Mansfield.

Gregory, Alyse. "Artist or Nun." *The Dial* LXXV (November 1923): 484-86.

Negative review of the posthumous collection *The Doves' Nest,* published by John Middleton Murry.

Gubar, Susan. "The Birth of the Artist as Heroine: (Re)production, the *Künstlerroman* Tradition, and the Fiction of Katherine Mansfield." In *The Representation of Women in Fiction: Selected Papers from the English Institute, 1981,* edited by Carolyn G. Heilbrun and Margaret R. Higonnet, pp. 19-59. Baltimore: Johns Hopkins University Press, 1983.
   Includes discussion of Mansfield's fiction in an assessment of ways in which "the changing reality and image of childbearing" is reflected in women writers' views of themselves.

Hagopian, John V. "Capturing Mansfield's 'Fly'." *Modern Fiction Studies* IX, No. 4 (Winter 1963-64): 385-90.
   Summarizes some critical interpretations of "The Fly" and offers a reading that rejects extra-textual, biographical interpretations in favor of the conclusion that the story "is an embodiment in language of an emotionally-charged, powerfully poignant human experience" not peculiar to Mansfield.

Hanson, Clare. "Moments of Being: Modernist Short Fiction." In her *Short Stories and Short Fictions, 1880-1980,* pp. 55-81. London: Macmillan, 1985.
   Includes discussion of Mansfield's innovative narrative techniques and comparison of Mansfield with James Joyce, Virginia Woolf, and Samuel Beckett.

Hynes, Sam. "Katherine Mansfield: The Defeat of the Personal." *The South Atlantic Quarterly* LII, No. 4 (October 1953): 555-60.
   Contrasts Mansfield's stylistic clarity with what Hynes terms the chaotic moral structure of her fiction. Defining moral structure as "the view of the world which emerges from [the] work," Hynes pronounces a coherent structure necessary to artistic maturity and asserts that Mansfield never successfully achieved such a structure in her fiction.

Jolly, R. A.; Copland, R. A.; Greenwood, E. B.; and Bateson, F. W. "The Critical Forum: Katherine Mansfield's 'The Fly'." *Essays in Criticism* XII, No. 3 (July 1962): 335-51.
   Responses by Jolly, Copland, and Greenwood to F. W. Bateson and B. Shahevitch's "Katherine Mansfield's 'The Fly': A Critical Exercise" (cited above) addressing perceived inadequacies of that analysis. Bateson's response to the criticisms is also included.

Kaplan, Sydney Janet. " 'A Gigantic Mother': Katherine Mansfield's London." In *Women Writers and the City: Essays in Feminist Literary Criticism,* edited by Susan Merrill Squier, pp. 161-75. Knoxville: University of Tennessee Press, 1984.
   Examines Mansfield's portrayal in her fiction of the urban landscape, noting her ironic, energetic response to the liberating effect of city life.

King, Russell S. "Katherine Mansfield as an Expatriate Writer." *The Journal of Commonwealth Literature* VIII, No. 1 (June 1973): 97-109.
   Examines how Mansfield's expatriate status influenced her view of art, the characters she portrayed, "and, perhaps, even the manner in which she [shaped] her stories around a moment of conscious or unconscious revelation."

Kirkpatrick, B. J. *A Bibliography of Katherine Mansfield.* Oxford: Clarendon Press, 1989, 396 p.
   Extensive bibliography listing books and pamphlets; contributions to books, periodicals, and newspapers; books translated by Mansfield; translations of Mansfield's works into foreign languages; large print editions; Braille, embossed, and talking books; extracts from unpublished letters, journals, and other material; stage and film scripts; radio and television productions; ballet, musical, and stage productions; films; and manuscripts.

Kleine, Don W. " 'The Garden Party': A Portrait of the Artist." *Criticism* V, No. 1 (Winter 1963): 360-71.
   Considers the dual nature of the conclusion of "The Garden Party," in which the protagonist's acquisition of adult perceptions about life and death also illuminates for the reader "the ardent, entranced sensibility" of a young girl.

Littell, Robert. "Katherine Mansfield." *The New Republic* XXXIV, No. 430 (28 February 1923): 22.
   Obituary tribute commending Mansfield's ability to portray "moods, and small joys, and small griefs."

Magalaner, Marvin. *The Fiction of Katherine Mansfield.* Carbondale and Edwardsville: Southern Illinois University Press, 1971, 148 p.
   Critical survey of Mansfield's work, focusing on technique, psychology, language, and theme. Magalaner includes a chapter discussing Mansfield's literary criticism.

Mantz, Ruth. *The Life of Katherine Mansfield.* London: Constable & Co., 1933, 349 p.
   Biography sanctioned and overseen by John Middleton Murry.

——. "K. M.—Fifty Years After." *ADAM International Review,* Nos. 370-75 (1972-73): 117-27.
   Reminisces about the process of editing Mansfield's posthumous papers with John Middleton Murry.

Maugham, W. Somerset. "The Short Story." In his *Points of View,* pp. 142-88. London: Heinemann, 1958.
   Includes discussion of Mansfield's life and works in a chapter devoted to study of the short story.

Maxwell-Mahon, W. D. "The Art of Katherine Mansfield." *Unisa English Studies* XVII, No. 1 (April 1979): 45-52.
   Examines Mansfield's published journals and letters for explicit statements of the artistic principles underlying her fiction. Maxwell-Mahon is critical of John Middleton Murry for publishing an edited synthesis of diaries, informally kept notebooks, and other loose personal papers as Mansfield's *Journal.*

Meyers, Jeffrey. "Katherine Mansfield and John Middleton Murry: Nausicaa and Polypheme." In his *Married to Genius,* pp. 113-44. London: London Magazine Editions, 1977.
   Account of the relationship between Mansfield and Murry.

——. *Katherine Mansfield: A Biography.* London: Hamish Hamilton, 1978, 306 p.
   Revises the idealized portrait of Mansfield created by Murry.

Modern Fiction Studies, Special Issue: Katherine Mansfield 24, No. 3 (Autumn 1978): 337-479.

Includes biographical and critical essays by T. O. Beach-croft, Geraldine L. Conroy, Richard F. Peterson, Mary Burgan, Marvin Magalaner, Don W. Kleine, and Adam J. Sorkin, and a secondary bibliography by Jeffrey Meyers. Essays by Ann L. McLaughlin, Toby Silverman Zinman, and Cherry Hankin from this issue are excerpted in *TCLC,* Vol. 2.

Moore, James. *Gurdjieff and Mansfield.* London: Routledge & Kegan Paul, 1980, 261 p.
Dual biographical accounts of Mansfield and psychic healer George Ivanovitch Gurdjieff intended to correct longstanding myths about their lives and their association just before Mansfield's death.

Moore, Leslie [pseudonym of Ida Baker]. *Katherine Mansfield: The Memories of L. M.* London: Joseph, 1971, 240 p.
Reminiscences by a longtime friend and companion of Mansfield.

Murry, John Middleton. *The Autobiography of John Middleton Murry: Between Two Worlds.* New York: Julian Messner, 1936, 500 p.
Autobiography by Mansfield's second husband.

Nathan, Rhoda B. *Katherine Mansfield.* New York: Continuum, 1988, 168 p.
Examines Mansfield's principal themes, techniques, and influences.

Neaman, Judith S. "Allusion, Image, and Associative Pattern: The Answers in Mansfield's 'Bliss'." *Twentieth Century Literature* 32, No. 2 (Summer 1986): 242-54.
Traces allusion, imagery, and associations in the short story "Bliss" to the Bible and to William Shakespeare's *Twelfth Night.*

Nebeker, Helen E. "The Pear Tree: Sexual Implications in Katherine Mansfield's 'Bliss'." *Modern Fiction Studies* 18, No. 4 (Winter 1972-73): 545-51.
Analyzes the sexual symbolism of the pear tree in the short story "Bliss."

O'Connor, Frank. "An Author in Search of a Subject." In his *The Lonely Voice: A Study of the Short Story,* pp. 128-42. Cleveland: World Publishing Co., 1963.
Assesses Mansfield's personality and fiction.

O'Sullivan, Vincent. "The Magnetic Chain: Notes and Approaches to K. M." *Landfall 114* 29, No. 2 (June 1975): 95-131.
Discusses literary influences, imagery, and the biographical content of Mansfield's fiction.

Palmer, Vance. "Katherine Mansfield." *Meanjin* XIV, No. 2 (Winter 1955): 177-85.
Discusses the genesis of the "cult of Katherine" in the editions of Mansfield's journals and letters published by John Middleton Murry, and commends the attempt of biographer Antony Alpers to present a more balanced account of Mansfield's life.

Rohrberger, Mary. "The Modern Short Story—Analyses of Representative Works: Katherine Mansfield, 'The Fly'." In her *Hawthorne and the Modern Short Story: A Study in Genre,* pp. 68-74. The Hague: Mouton & Co., 1966.
Examines aspects of the symbolic role of the boss in Mansfield's short story "The Fly."

Satterfield, Ben. "Irony in 'The Garden-Party'." *Ball State University Forum* XXIII, No. 1 (Winter 1982): 68-70.
Contends that Mansfield's portrayal of Laura Sheridan, the protagonist of "The Garden Party," was intended ironically to underscore the character's lack of comprehension when faced with the reality of death and intimations of her own mortality.

Schneider, Elisabeth. "Katherine Mansfield and Chekhov." *Modern Language Notes* L, No. 6 (June 1935): 394-97.
Considers similarities between Chekhov's short story "Spat khochetsia," which appeared in English translation in 1903, and Mansfield's "The-Child-Who-Was-Tired" from *In a German Pension* (1911), suggesting that Mansfield's story was an "unconscious imitation" rather than a work of plagiarism.

Stead, C. K. "Katherine Mansfield and the Art of Fiction." *The New Review* 4, No. 42 (September 1977): 27-36.
Examines biographical sources of Mansfield's fiction.

————. Introduction to *The Letters and Journals of Katherine Mansfield: A Selection,* by Katherine Mansfield, edited by C. K. Stead, pp. 9-22. London: Allen Lane, 1977.
Discusses "Murry's promotion of his wife's literary remains" and Stead's own methods of selection in printing an assortment of Mansfield's letters and journal entries.

Sutherland, Ronald. "Katherine Mansfield: Plagiarist, Disciple, or Ardent Admirer?" *Critique: Studies in Modern Fiction* V, No. 2 (Fall 1962): 58-76.
Contends that similarities between short stories by Mansfield and Chekhov can be attributed to Mansfield's admiration for the Russian author and not to plagiarism.

Taylor, Donald S. "Crashing the Garden Party, I: A Dream—A Wakening." *Modern Fiction Studies* IV, No. 4 (Winter 1958-59): 361-62.
Response to Warren S. Walker's "The Unresolved Conflict in 'The Garden Party' " (cited below) suggesting that contrary to Walker's contention, the clash between the social attitudes of the protagonist, Laura Sheridan, and those of her mother, is not dropped, but rather, is subordinated in Laura's larger struggle to comprehend death.

Thomas, J. D. "Symbol and Parallelism in 'The Fly'." *College English* 22, No. 4 (January 1961): 256, 261-62.
Examines the symbolic value of the fly in Mansfield's story and draws parallels between the characters of the boss and Woodifield.

Tomalin, Claire. *Katherine Mansfield: A Secret Life.* London: Viking, 1987, 292 p.
Extensively researched biography that addresses several events in Mansfield's life that have been neglected by previous biographers.

Waldron, Philip. "Katherine Mansfield's *Journal.*" *Twentieth Century Literature* 20, No. 1 (January 1974): 11-18.
Addresses errors of dating and transcription, as well as vagaries of editing, in the volumes of Mansfield's journal edited by John Middleton Murry.

Walker, Warren S. "The Unresolved Conflict in 'The Garden Party'." *Modern Fiction Studies* III, No. 4 (Winter 1957-58): 354-58.
Suggests that of two chief conflicts addressed in "The Garden Party"—the struggle between the fear and ac-

ceptance of death and the clash of social attitudes between Laura and her mother—the second is left unresolved. Donald S. Taylor (cited above) and Daniel A. Weiss (cited below) responded to this essay.

Weiss, Daniel A. "Crashing the Garden Party, II: The Garden Party of Proserpina." *Modern Fiction Studies* IV, No. 4 (Winter 1958-59): 363-64.

> Response to Warren S. Walker's "The Unresolved Conflict in 'The Garden Party' " (above), suggesting that the resolution of class conflict in the story is "a subordinate component of the primary theme—Laura's discovery of death, and its coextensiveness with life."

Wright, Celeste Turner. "Darkness as a Symbol in Katherine Mansfield." *Modern Philology* LI, No. 3 (February 1954): 204-07.

> Addresses the symbolic nature of darkness in Mansfield's fiction, where it often signifies loneliness and isolation.

Melville Davisson Post

1869-1930

American short story writer, novelist, and essayist.

A popular and prolific American author of the early twentieth century, Post is best known for his short stories of mystery and detection. Distinguished by their economical prose style and innovative plots, these works feature several memorable detective heroes, including Post's most famous character, Uncle Abner.

Born and raised in the mountainous West Virginia countryside, Post traced his ancestry to early settlers of the state. This setting and family background figure prominently in a number of his later short stories, especially the Uncle Abner series. Post completed his primary education at a local grammar school and took college preparatory courses at Buckhannon Academy before enrolling at West Virginia University, where he studied law. After graduating in 1892, Post practiced law for the next eleven years. In 1896 he published his first collection of short stories, *The Strange Schemes of Randolph Mason,* which focuses on the machinations of a dishonest lawyer whose devious use of fine points of law enables his guilty clients to escape justice. The Mason stories were an immediate sensation, provoking strong public reaction both for and against their highly original protagonist and prompting Post to augment his success with a second volume about Mason, *The Man of Last Resort.* Several changes in the criminal law codes of the time have been attributed to the publication of these works. In 1901 Post published a nondetective novel, *Dwellers in the Hills,* as well as numerous stories in which Mason reforms and uses his considerable legal prowess for more worthy causes. Written initially for periodicals, these stories were collected in *The Corrector of Destinies* in 1908. In 1911 Post began writing the Uncle Abner stories, and a few years later reached the height of his popularity with the publication of "The Doomdorf Mystery," an Uncle Abner case that met with wide acclaim when it appeared in the *Saturday Evening Post.* These stories were collected as *Uncle Abner, Master of Mysteries.* During his last years, Post wrote several novels as well as detective stories featuring such sleuths as Monsieur Jonquelle, Sir Henry Marquis of Scotland Yard, and Walker of the Secret Service. Post died in 1930 after a fall from a horse.

In several essays Post articulated his precepts for the construction of detective and mystery fiction, basing his ideas largely on Aristotle's literary theory, which stressed the central importance of plot and the unity of time, place, and action. In addition, Post emphasized the necessity of an element of surprise in detective and mystery stories. Post's chief contribution to the development of the form, however, was his reworking of the traditional approach to the solution of the mystery. Rather than unfolding the problem to be solved and then retrospectively presenting the steps to its solution as had been done by Edgar Allan Poe, Sir Arthur Conan Doyle, and others, Post evolved a plot structure in which these two stages of the narrative could take place simultaneously, and his economical use of language allowed the story to move at a faster, more exciting pace. While Post's earlier stories do not exhibit this approach consistently, his later works, particularly the Uncle Abner series, reflect his innovations, and commentators have concentrated their attention on these. "The Doomdorf Mystery" is Post's most widely read Uncle Abner tale and its spare but lyrical prose style and swiftly moving plot aptly illustrate Post's theories. The story opens following the death of Doomdorf, a hated and feared operator of a moonshine still. Present at the scene with Uncle Abner and a law officer are the two prime suspects: an old woman who has killed Doomdorf in effigy and a man who has prayed for his death. In the course of a few hours, Uncle Abner examines evidence involving the bullet-riddled corpse, a shack that has been neither entered nor exited, and the time of day the murder occured, advancing a surprising explanation of death by accidental causes. Other Uncle Abner stories display a similar narrative economy, often ending with a surprise for impact. The Uncle Abner series is also noted for its pervading theme of the inevitability of justice in human affairs and for the character of Uncle Abner, who with his trust in Providence and in his own intuition, is, according to Tom and Enid Schantz, "a figure so heroic in stature that he seems more a product of American folklore than the creation of a single intellect." Critics of Post's work often discuss his relationship to established masters of mystery and detective fiction, calling him the best in his field since Poe and applauding his ingenious plots and surprise endings. While some have faulted Post's method of story construction because it occasionally withholds necessary information from the reader, he is more often praised for his characterization and prose style as exemplified in the Uncle Abner stories.

(See also *Contemporary Authors,* Vol. 110.)

PRINCIPAL WORKS

The Strange Schemes of Randolph Mason   (short stories) 1896
The Man of Last Resort; or, The Clients of Randolph Mason   (short stories)   1897
Dwellers in the Hills   (novel)   1901
The Corrector of Destinies: Being Tales of Randolph Mason as Related by His Private Secretary, Courtlandt Parks   (short stories)   1908
The Gilded Chair   (short stories)   1910
The Nameless Thing   (short stories)   1912
Uncle Abner, Master of Mysteries   (short stories)   1918
The Mystery at the Blue Villa   (short stories)   1919
The Sleuth of St. James's Square   (short stories)   1920
The Mountain School-Teacher   (novel)   1922
Monsieur Jonquelle, Prefect of Police of Paris   (short stories)   1923
Walker of the Secret Service   (short stories)   1924
The Man Hunters   (nonfiction)   1927
The Revolt of the Birds   (novel)   1927
The Bradmoor Murder: Including the Remarkable Deductions of Sir Henry Marquis of Scotland Yard   (short stories)   1929
The Silent Witness   (short stories)   1930
The Methods of Uncle Abner   (short stories)   1974
The Complete Uncle Abner   (short stories and essay) 1977

The New York Times Book Review   (essay date 1920)

[*In the following review of* The Sleuth of St. James's Square, *the critic praises the skill and originality of Post's detective fiction.*]

Ever since the days of Edgar Allan Poe and "The Murders in the Rue Morgue," those tales of crime classed together under the general title of detective stories, have followed more or less along the same lines. A crime is committed, various innocent persons are suspected, and then at last some particularly ingenious individual appears who solves the riddle, reconstructing the case, and explaining it to an admiring audience. Mr. Post's stories [in *The Sleuth of St. James's Square*], however, depart somewhat from this usually accepted convention; the tale of the crime and its detection proceed together, at one and the same time. And this alone would, of course, give them a claim on one's attention. But they are not only unusual in construction; they are very well written, and, with but few exceptions,

close with a twist which will surprise even the skilled and habitual reader.

Sir Henry Marquis, chief of the Criminal Investigation Department of Scotland Yard, who is, of course, "The Sleuth of St. James's Square," appears in all of the tales, though in several of them only as the introducer of the person who relates the story. For three of them—**"The Wrong Sign," "The Fortune Teller"** and **"The Hole in the Mahogany Panel"**—go far back to the days when Virginia was a crown colony, and are ostensibly taken from an ancient diary. The majority of the tales, however, have to do with the present day and with adventures ranging all the way from India and the Gobi Desert to London and the United States. They are, with scarcely an exception, stories which completely absorb the reader's attention, and, of course, his individual tastes will influence that same reader's preference. But, to our thinking, the best of the stories, taken in the order in which they are printed in the book, are **"The Reward," "The Lost Lady," "The Cambered Foot," "The End of the Road"** and **"A Satire of the Sea."**

Mr. Post is one of those natural story-tellers who are not made, but born with the narrative gift. His is a fecund imagination, and if he makes use of the wonderful jewels, secret codes, spies and counterfeiters familiar to detective fiction, there is always, or very nearly always, something novel in his way of manipulating his material, some new turn or twist which gives freshness to the narrative. All those who like to be first puzzled and then surprised will heartily enjoy reading of the experiences and exploits of *The Sleuth of St. James's Square.* (pp. 21, 23)

> "A New Sleuth," in The New York Times Book Review, *December 12, 1920, pp. 21, 23.*

Blanche Colton Williams   (essay date 1920)

[*Williams was an American educator, biographer, and literary critic who specialized in the study of the short story. In the following excerpt, she provides a survey of Post's fiction.*]

Of all American writers who have converted to fictive purposes the science of logic, two are preëminent. They grew up, some fifty years apart, in the same section of the United States, and by a pun the surname of one is the superlative of the other. They are Edgar Allan Poe and Melville Davisson Post.

The first of these formulated the laws of the short story. He originated the detective story, his model for which served writers half a century. That model is well known: a crime has been committed, or is about to be committed, and the agent of the law bends his efforts to apprehending the criminal or to preventing the crime. It was left for the second to invent a new type of detective tale.

As Mr. Post has himself remarked, the flood of detective stories succeeding Poe's poured forth "until the stomach of the reader failed." He, a lawyer of parts, who has pleaded before the bar of the Supreme Court of West Virginia, the United Circuit of Appeals, and the Supreme Court of the United States, recognized that, notwithstanding stories of crime, "the high ground of the field of crime has not been explored; it has not even been entered. The book stalls have been filled to weariness with tales based upon plans whereby the *detective* or *ferreting* power of the State might be baffled. But, prodigious marvel! no writer has attempted to construct tales based upon plans whereby the *punishing* power of the State might be baffled."

Deducible from the preceding paragraph is the originality of Mr. Post's inventions. And by inference emerges the truth that only a lawyer or student of criminology has the precise knowledge adequate to the task. To write a series of detective stories wherein the criminal must go unpunished presupposes ability to differentiate between crime in the sense of social wrong and crime punishable by law. For law is not reason: not all wrongs, great though they may be, are crimes.

Here, at once, enters a new need. Poe had required an acute and subtile intellect, a highly trained ratiocinative mind, for his detective. These he incorporated in Monsieur Dupin. Mr. Post required, first of all, an unmoral intelligence, preferably that of a skilled unscrupulous lawyer who would instruct men how to evade the law. Hence, arose the figure of Randolph Mason.

Of the stories in **The Strange Schemes of Randolph Mason,** "The Corpus Delicti," reprinted by *The Review of Reviews* as a masterpiece of mystery fiction, is the most gruesome and the most powerful. But if it brings a shock to the layman, it conveys only a striking instance of legal lore to the lawyer. Samuel Walcott, in danger from Nina St. Croix, goes in his distress to Mason. Mason gives directions that must be faithfully followed. The reader is then treated openly to the performance of a diabolically contrived crime. In the guise of a sailor, Walcott enters Nina's home, stabs her to death, dismembers her body, destroys it by means of decomposing agents and through the bath tub drain removes all traces of his ghastly work. He is arrested, however, as he leaves the house and is brought to trial. To the astonishment of the Court, the defendant Mason moves that the Judge direct the jury to find the prisoner not guilty. In the bout that follows between himself and the prosecuting attorney, Mason observes: "This is a matter of law, plain, clear, and so well settled in the State of New York that even the counsel for the people should know it. . . . If the *corpus delicti,* the body of the crime, has been proven, as required by the laws of the commonwealth, then this case should go to the jury. If not, then it is the duty of the Court to direct the jury to find the prisoner not guilty." The Judge so directs, and the undeniably criminal Walcott walks out, a free man.

Now, had Poe or Conan Doyle told this story, he would have bent the energies of the detective to discovering what had become of the body (the reader would have learned only when Dupin or Sherlock Holmes saw fit to spring his discovery), and would have haled the criminal before a bar at which he would be convicted. Mr. Post frankly gives away the murder, and shifts his emphasis to showing how the State was baffled.

Of other stories in the same volume, **"The Sheriff of Gullmore"** and **"Woodford's Partner"** are, perhaps, the most satisfactory. In the latter Mason finds a criminal way, not, however, a crime before the law, to protect an honest young man from whom has been stolen twenty thousand dollars entrusted to him. An extreme application of the sophism that the means justifies the end, it draws to some extent upon the reader's sympathy. In the former, a sheriff who has defaulted, and whose bondsmen may be called to cover his defalcation, shifts the responsibility to his successor as he goes out of office. If here, as in succeeding stories, Mr. Post has seemed to show the villain how to circumvent the consequences of his villainy, he has also, as he maintains, warned the friends of law and order.

Mr. George Randolph Chester, whose *Get-Rich-Quick Wallingford* stories resemble in certain respects those of Mr. Post, was once asked whether sharpers had not received pointers from Blackie and Wallingford. "They have," he replied with something like enthusiasm, "but they are now behind prison bars!" One does not like to read with the feeling that some criminal may profit by the plan unfolded; it is more pleasant to harbor the thought that the law will take note, as well as the lawless . . . In any event, Randolph Mason has the fascination, and the repulsion, of the serpent.

The succeeding volume, **The Man of Last Resort,** informing by its sub-title that the stories deal with the clients of Mason, has been praised as a strong plea for moral responsibility made in vivid and earnest style. The author observes in the Preface that a few critics contended the first volume was dangerous because it explained with detail how one could murder or steal and escape punishment. He answers them by the fact that law-making ultimately lies with the citizens, and changes in the law must come about through public sentiment. "If men about their affairs were passing to and from across a great bridge and one should discover that certain planks in its flooring were defective, would he do ill if he pointed them out to his fellows?" Perhaps the close of the volume further enforces the cause of righteousness: Mason is in a bad case of acute mania, raving like a drunken sailor: "The man of last resort was probably gone. There was now no resort but to the steel thing on the table."

One more volume, however, appeared with this trickster for central character: **The Corrector of Destinies.** An element of novelty enters in the fact that Randolph Mason's secretary, Courtlandt Parks, heretofore spoken of in the third person, becomes the narrator.

A strong appeal Mason has for the reader is the eagerness with which he welcomes a struggle against Fate or Destiny. It appears as a determinant of his acts throughout. With Chance, or Fate, or Destiny, Robert W. Chambers evolves a light or pleasing love story; with the same forces Melville Post effects a revision of the Greek concept. "Fate is supreme," says Sophocles through the Œdipus trilogy. "Perhaps," says Post through the triptych of Mason volumes, "but probably not. Fate may be averted." He admits, through his dramas, that sometimes there is the inevitable "come-back," as in **"Mrs. Van Bartan"** (in **The Man of Last Resort**).

Mr. Post recognizes that in a story, the story's the thing, that no degree of literary excellence can atone for lack of plot. He addresses himself at once to the popular and the critical reader. If there lives a writer of stories who is the "critic's writer," he is the man. He expressed himself unmistakably in **"The Blight"** [see Further Reading]: "The primary object of all fiction is to entertain the reader. If, while it entertains, it also ennobles him this fiction becomes a work of art; but its primary business must be to entertain and not to educate or to instruct him." In answering the question, "What sort of fiction has the most nearly universal appeal?" he holds that the human mind is engaged almost exclusively with problems, and that "the writer who presents a problem to be solved or a mystery to be untangled will be offering those qualities in his fiction which are of the most nearly universal appeal." Men of education and culture—but never critics of stories!—have taken the position that literature of this character is not of the highest order. He cites Aristotle's *Poetics:* Tragedy is an imitation, not of men, but of an action of life . . . the incidents and the plot are the end of a tragedy." The plot is first; character is second. The Greeks would have been astounded at the idea common to our age that "the highest form of literary structure may omit the framework of the plot." The short story is to our age what the drama was to the Greeks. Poe knew this. And he is the one literary genius America has produced.

Yet Mr. Post's ideal of plot is no mere mechanical contrivance. He once expressed his pleasure to the present writer that "there are people who see that a story should be clean cut and with a single dominating germinal incident upon which it turns as a door upon a hinge, and not built up on a scaffolding of criss-cross stuff." In all these underlying principles of his work, principles stated with the frankness of Poe, Melville Post strikes an answering chord in the critic who finds in his stories the perfect application of the theories he champions.

Mr. Post also holds a brief for his large employment of tragic incident: "Under the scheme of the universe it is the tragic things that seem the most real." He pleases the popular audience because he writes of crime. He knows, as Anna Katharine Green knows, its universal appeal. Mrs. Green once wrote: "Crime must touch our imagination by showing people, *like ourselves,* but incredibly transformed by some overwhelming motive." Further, we are interested because what most interests us in human beings is their hidden emotions; crime in normal people must be the result of tremendous emotion. We like to read detective stories of crime because we like to figure on the solution of the mystery. Motive and mystery, in short, are the sources of entertainment, rather than the crime itself. But murder is interesting because of its finality: it is the supreme crime, because it is irreparable.

Mrs. Green thinks that nine times out of ten the crime is selfishness, which has many forms. If one form of selfishness is the desire to be freed from some obligation or duty, Mr. Post uses it as a motive in **"The Corpus Delicti."** Walcott murdered Nina because he desired liberty and because she was about to disclose the secret that would have disgraced him and cost him his life. But he also employs unselfishness as a motive. In **"Woodford's Partner,"** William Harris commits crime to save his younger brother from disgrace. Camden Gerard, of **"The Error of William Van Broom,"** becomes a thief unpunishable by law, that he may pay the school bills of his sister.

Uncle Abner is proof that Mr. Post had by no means exhausted his fecundity in creating the unmoral Mason. His sense of justice and his sense of balance have produced a hero the antithesis of his hero-villain. Whereas Mason delighted in struggling against pagan Fate, Uncle Abner finds joy in furthering the beneficent operations of Providence. These two men express, respectively, the heathen and the Christian ideal; and they are as complementary as Jekyll and Hyde. This is the significant accomplishment of Mr. Post. He has demonstrated that wrong may triumph over man-made laws, which are imperfect after all the centuries; but that right must win under the timeless Providence of God. Uncle Abner as described by his nephew, Martin, who recounts most of the exploits, is an austere, deeply religious man, with a big iron frame, a grizzled beard and features forged by a smith. His gift for ferreting out crime, which is as great as that of Sherlock Holmes and, in accordance with the author's purpose, requires not nearly so long to arrive at conclusions, works to throw down the last barrier behind which the criminal is entrenched. Small space is required to mete out justice. Take **"The Concealed Path,"** for example: after four thousand words or so ending in the revelation of the murderer, Abner's pronouncement of doom is swift. . . .

> He raised his great arm, the clenched bronze fingers big like the coupling pins of a cart.
>
> 'I would have stopped it with my own hand,' he said; 'but I wanted the men of the hills to hang you. . . . And they are here.'
>
> There was a great sound of tramping feet in the hall outside.
>
> And while the men entered, big, grim, determined men, Abner called out their names:
>
> 'Arnold, Randolph, Stuart, Elnathan Stone, and my brother, Rufus!'

The death of a criminal may be the subject of investigation, as in **"The Doomdorf Mystery."** The flawlessness of this story was appreciated by every critic who read it on its appearance in *The Saturday Evening Post,* July 18, 1914. For unity, strength, and integration of detail no better story has been written. Abner and Randolph arrive at the house of Doomdorf meaning to remonstrate with him over his illicit brewing. They find the circuit rider Bronson on his big roan horse in the paved courtyard. They knock and are admitted by a little, faded woman. They continue to Doomdorf's door, which, finding bolted, they burst open. Doomdorf is lying on his couch, shot through the heart. The mystery lies in the manner of the murder: the locked door and the barred windows seem to preclude human agency; suicide is eliminated inasmuch as the gun rests on its rack. The mystery is not lessened when the circuit rider declares he is responsible and when, later, the woman declares, "I killed him!" In the dramatic revelation, the reader is held breathless. The bottle of distillate on the table catches the sunbeam and focusing it upon the lock of the gun on the wall ignites the percussion cap. The symmetry of the story is perfected through the preacher's prayer that the Lord would destroy Doomdorf with fire from heaven, and through the woman's practice of magic which urged her to create a wax image and to thrust a needle through its heart. Doomdorf had died by immutable and natural laws working through his own hell-brew to poetic justice; or in answer to prayer, as the circuit rider believed; or through her sorcery, as the woman believed; or by the mysterious justice of God, as Abner saw it.

As in **"The Concealed Path,"** murder is used for chief interest in **"The Wrong Hand,"** **"The Angel of the Lord,"** **"An Act of God,"** **"The Age of Miracles,"** **"The Straw**

Man," "The Adopted Daughter," and "Naboth's Vineyard."

A difficult task lay, one might think, in convincing the reader of the murder in **"The Adopted Daughter."** Suppose you are told that a crack shot has put a bullet through a man's eyeball so as to leave no mark of death. Impossible, you say; the bullet must come out somewhere. But the author allows his murderer to use a light charge of powder that lodges the bullet in the brain. Well, you counter, why wouldn't the shrunken eyelid betray the death-wound? That is the center about which the author has woven the web of his story. You may also reflect that expert marksmanship is required. Mr. Post treats you to a dramatic instance or so of impromptu efficiency that requires *more* skill than is needed to shoot a man through the eyeball. He knows the value of the *a fortiori* argument.

To the critical eye the weakness of most of these tales is apparent; but they are not obtrusive to a reader who seeks entertainment. For example, in **"The Adopted Daughter,"** Sheppard Flornoy's eye has been shot out by his brother Vespasian. The latter saws off the head of an ivory pawn and forces it into the bullet hole to round out the damaged eyeball. No criminal would be likely to keep the pawn after sawing off the head. Yet it is this tell-tale object which, joined to suspected motivation for the fratricide, excites Abner's suspicion.

The scenes of these adventures are in Virginia in the days before the carving out of West Virginia. Although the stories more nearly approach the Poe type than do the Mason group, yet novelty is secured through shift of emphasis and through the setting. Dupin recalls to us the crime of the city; Sherlock Holmes lives in London. Abner is a man of the hills, whose detective work leads him among the hill people.

In *The Mystery of the Blue Villa* the author reveals knowledge of settings into which, in real life, his travels have led him. Port Said figures in the titular story—a story which lacks the freshness of Mr. Post's plots in that it is a variant of an old one. It has found subsequent treatment by Albert Payson Terhune in *A Catch in It Somewhere.* But it is only fair to note that the fine hand of coincidence may have directed both Mr. Post and Mr. Terhune. Paris, Nice, Cairo, Ostend, and London, with Washington and New York thrown in for home flavor, make up the settings of these tales. In this volume, as in the first, the reader thrills to a series of climaxes in plots so logically built as to seem a natural growth of events leading to or away from the dominant incident. They add nothing, perhaps, to the writer's fame, save in their indication of his broadening interests and in their suggestion of the Great War as an occasional background. **"The Miller of Ostend,"** indeed, is a superb example of war horror. **"The Witch of Lecca"** points to study of witchcraft and the Black Art, and develops with amazing resourcefulness a single incident. The author's manner is everywhere derived from the American plus the French: he combines the ratiocinative processes of Poe with the dramatic presentation of Daudet and Maupassant.

Among Mr. Post's most absorbing interests and pastimes, if one may judge by his articles in current magazines, are codes and ciphers. Readers of *Everybody's* will recall a cover picturing a code letter such as was discovered in the days of the War, and illustrating a factual story by Mr. Post. He has used a similar code letter in **"The Pacifist"** (in *The Mystery of the Blue Villa*). His constant curiosity about the ways men seek to outwit their fellow creatures promises further entertainment to his large class of readers. But it is to be remembered that before the age of fifty he had established himself in narrative one of the immortals.

Mr. Post has written not only the type of story with which he has scored so successfully again and again. Besides *The Gilded Chair,* a novel of love and adventure, he published in 1901—between the second and third Randolph Mason books—*Dwellers in the Hills.* It is impossible to read this work, which as to plot is a short story, and in deliberate use of irrelevant but enriching detail a novel, without the certainty that it is from Mr. Post's own experiences, and that he is limned in the narrator, Quiller. For the alien to read it is to acquaint himself with life in the hills of West Virginia some two score years ago. For the rural Southerner of Mr. Post's generation to read it is to ride in memory a gallant steed—like Quiller's El Mahdi—along a country road bordered by sedge and ragweed; to note the hickories trembling in their yellow leaves; to hear the partridge's "bob white" call, the woodpecker's tap, and the "golden belted bee booming past"; to cross the stream fringed with bullrushes; to hear men's voices "reaching half a mile to the grazing steers on the sodded knobs"; to meet a neighbor's boy astride a bag of corn, on his way to the grist-mill; to stop at the blacksmith's, there to watch the forging of a horse-shoe; or at the wagoner's, to assist in the making of a wheel; to taste the sweet corn pone and the striped bacon, and to roast potatoes in the ashes—to re-live a sort of natural "mission furniture" period of existence.

To read the book is also to construct the boy that was Melville Davisson Post, a process the more compelling because of the half-hidden, half-expressed relationships. If you know, for instance, from *Who's Who* or other sources, that his father was Ira Carper Post, you will notice that "Carper" creeps out in this book (as it does in the "Randolph Mason" books [*The Strange Schemes of Randolph Mason, The Man of Last Resort,* and *The Corrector of Destinies*] for other characters), and you find yourself wondering just [what is] the kinship between fictive heroine and actual human being. His use of family and State names is constant throughout his volumes: Randolph, Davisson, Blennerhassett and Evelyn Byrd are a few that set ringing the bells of history, conveying a mood that holds long after the peals have died away. . . .

Mr. Post was born April 19, 1871, and grew up, you are sure, to appreciate the art of riding (which consists in becoming part of your horse) no less than his lessons in the classics. From his fiction you are so sure of these truths that you hardly need for confirmation his factual articles testifying to the value of Aristotle, nor a published photograph that portrays him in riding togs with a noble dog at his side. Through the dramas he presents, you somehow have borne in upon you that he is a community man and a statesman, one ready to take his part in all that affects the good of neighborhood or nation. You turn to the record and find your deductions or vaporous guessings established facts. He has not all these years devoted himself wholly to writing nor yet to the law. He has been interested in railroads and coal, in education and in politics. His art of story-telling has been strengthened by his legal training and—what does not always follow from mere recognition of critical canons—by application of scientific standards to his own fiction. He learned before he was thirty that the mastery of an art depends only upon the comprehension of its basic law; that the short story, "like any work of art, is produced only by painstaking labor and according to certain structural rules." He is convinced that "the laws that apply to mechanics and architecture are no more certain or established than those that apply to the construction of the short-story" [see Further Reading, *Saturday Evening Post,* 27 February 1915]. In his enthusiasm for economy he would brand into the hand of everybody the rule of Walter Pater: "All art does but consist in the removal of surplusage." (pp. 293-308)

> Blanche Colton Williams, "Melville Davisson Post," in her Our Short Story Writers, 1920. Reprint by Dodd, Mead and Company, 1941, pp. 293-308.

The New York Times Book Review (essay date 1923)

[*In the following review, the critic praises* The Corrector of Destinies.]

Though the "Randolph Mason" stories may, strictly speaking, be called mystery stories, nevertheless one derives from them exactly the same type of esthetic satisfaction that one derives from very good detective stories. Randolph Mason, the Corrector of Destinies, as the author has christened him, is one kind of a detective—the kind who, in the character of an attorney, detects flaws and loopholes in the law and makes use of them.

This third collection of stories [*The Corrector of Destinies*] centering about the same character is a fitting climax for the series. It deserves all the success of *The Strange Schemes* and *The Clients of Randolph Mason.* If any gentle reader has entertained a fond hope that in this last series the great hero-lawyer might become humanized, then that same gentle reader merely placed himself in the ranks of those others whom Mason hoodwinked. As in the preceding stories, he is represented as cold, emotionless, a kind of disembodied intellect manipulating human affairs, a New York attorney specializing in the art of knowing and observing the letter of the law and violating its spirit.

He feels no compunction in instructing one of his clients to pass Confederate money in payment for the return of her ancestral jewels, because, technically, the passing of Confederate bills for the money of the United States is no crime against its laws. To be sure, the client is a beautiful woman, and her jewels had been unlawfully taken from her and unlawfully held, but one cannot help feeling that neither beauty nor justice had a great deal to do with Mason's feeling for his case—if feeling it may be called. His love of his profession is not, as in the case of Arthur Train's famous Mr. Tutt, an interest in human nature and in the administering of poetic justice; it is rather a desire to prove his own invincibility.

The atmosphere of awe and wondering admiration in which Mason is enveloped would scarcely seem to be warranted by his knowledge of the law, which is obscure rather than profound. He is neither a scholarly lawyer nor a student of human nature. He is an intellectual trickster.

The general tone of all these stories is as unemotional as the character of their hero. They are brisk, clear-cut and they move with rapidity. Set in a New York background, they are charged with the spirit of American commerce. Their romance is the romance of Wall Street. There is little or no love element in the entire collection, and that little is subordinated to the legal theme. Mr. Post has turned out a group of mystery stories that are "most uncommon good."

> A review of "Randolph Mason, Corrector of Destinies," in The New York Times Book Review, August 26, 1923, p. 24.

Grant Overton (essay date 1924)

[*Overton was an American novelist and literary critic. In the following excerpt, he examines the role of plot in several of Post's short stories.*]

Who that read in the *Saturday Evening Post* of 18 July 1914 a short story called **"The Doomdorf Mystery"** forgets it now? No one, I think; and it was a very short story, and it appeared over ten years ago. The magazine which published it—if one had read no others—has published 2,500 short stories since. **"The Doomdorf Mystery"** is one in a thousand, literally.

The creature, Doomdorf, in his stone house on the rock brewed a hell-brew. "The idle and the vicious came with their stone jugs, and violence and riot flowed out." On a certain day two men of the country rode "through the broken spine of the mountains" to have the thing out with Doomdorf. "Randolph was vain and pompous and given over to extravagance of words, but he was a gentleman beneath it, and fear was an alien and a stranger to him. And Abner was the right hand of the land."

About the place were two persons, a circuit rider who had been rousing the countryside against Doomdorf and who had called down fire from heaven for the creature's destruction. A little faded woman was the other.

In his chamber, the door bolted from the inside according to custom, Doomdorf lay shot to death.

The circuit rider asseverated that heaven had answered his prayer. The little, frightened, foreign woman showed a crude wax image with a needle thrust through its heart. She had killed Doomdorf by sorcery.

Randolph exclaimed with incredulity. Murder had been done; he was an officer of justice. But Abner pointed out that when the shot was fired, by evidence of Doomdorf's watch, the circuit rider was on his way to the place, the woman on the mountain among the peach trees. The door was bolted from the inside, the dust on the casings of the two windows was undisturbed and the windows gave on an hundred-foot precipice as smooth as a sheet of glass. Had Doomdorf killed himself? And then got up and put the gun back carefully into the two dogwood forks that held it to the wall? Says Abner: "The murderer of Doomdorf not only climbed the face of that precipice and got in through the closed window, but he shot Doomdorf to death and got out again through the closed window without leaving a single track or trace behind, and without disturbing a grain of dust or a thread of cobweb. . . . Randolph, let us go and lay an ambush for this assassin. He is on the way here."

This masterly tale, so far as the explanation is concerned, could doubtless have been chanced upon by Melville Davisson Post in those old records which he, a lawyer, would need to consult. Its kernel or nubbin could spring from the simplest scientific knowledge, the acquisition of any boy in high school. Its marvellous art is another affair. One might have the explanatory fact and make no more of it than a curious coroner's case. One could narrate it without any use of imagination and the result would be a coincidence without meaning.

The manner of Doomdorf's assassination depends very greatly upon coincidence. But given the series of coincidences, it was due to the operation of a natural law. Mr. Post had, initially, two difficulties to overcome. The first was fiction's rule of plausibility. The second was art's demand for emotional significance, a more-than-meets-the-eye, a meaning.

Truth is stranger than fiction dares to be. Truth compels belief, fiction must court it. To overcome the handicap imposed by the manner of Doomdorf's killing with its conspiracy of chances, Mr. Post plunges his reader at once into coincidences far more improbable—the presence on the scene of the circuit rider, the double confession of circuit rider and the woman to having killed Doomdorf. He storms the reader's stronghold of unbelief, the wall is breached, and no Trojan Horse is necessary later to bring his secret into the city. In fiction, there is no plausibility of cause and effect outside human behavior. The implausible (because unmeaning) manner of Doomdorf's death is superbly supported by two flanks, the behavior of the evangelist and the behavior of a terrified, superstitious and altogether childlike woman.

Art's demand for meaning requires much more than a certain plausibility of occurence. The manner of Doomdorf's death need not have been dependent on his evildoing; it must be made to seem so. The glass water bottle standing on the great oak table in the chamber where he slumbered and died could as easily have held water as his own raw and fiery liquor. There are two kinds of chance or coincidence in the world. One kind is meaningless; our minds perceive no cause and effect. The other kind is that in which we see a desired cause and effect. The writer of fiction must avoid or overcome the first kind if he is to write plausibly and acceptably; but upon his ability or inability to discern and employ the second kind depends his fortune as an artist.

In other particulars **"The Doomdorf Mystery"** exemplifies the artistry of the author. If I have not emphasized them, it is because they are cunning of hand and brain, craftsmanship, things to be learned, technical excellences which embellish but do not disclose the secret of inspiring art. The story is compactly told; tension is established at once and is drawn more tightly with every sentence; and the element of drama is much enhanced by the forward movement. Doomdorf is dead, but "Randolph," says Abner, "let us go and lay an ambush for this assassin. *He is on the way here.*" Not what has happened but what is to happen constitutes the true suspense. The prose style,

by its brevity and by a somewhat Biblical diction, does its part to induce in the reader a sense of impending justice, of a divine retribution upon the evildoer. But it is also a prose that lends itself to little pictures, as of the circuit rider, sitting his big red-roan horse, bareheaded, in the court before the stone house; or of the woman, half a child, who thought that with Doomdorf's death evil must have passed out of the world; or of Doomdorf in his coffin with the red firelight from the fireplace "shining on the dead man's narrow, everlasting house." The comparative loneliness, the wildness, and the smiling beauty of these mountains of western Virginia are used subtly in the creation of that thing in a story which we call "atmosphere" and the effect of which is to fix our mood. The tale is most economically told; the simplest and fewest means are made to produce an overwhelming effect. I have dwelt on it at length because it so perfectly illustrates the art of Melville Davisson Post, so arrestingly different from that of any of his contemporaries—different, perhaps, from anyone's who has ever written.

Mr. Post is one of the few who believe the plot's the thing. He has said [see William's excerpt dated 1920]:

> The primary object of all fiction is to entertain the reader. If, while it entertains, it also ennobles him this fiction becomes a work of art; but its primary business must be to entertain and not to educate or instruct him. The writer who presents a problem to be solved or a mystery to be untangled will be offering those qualities in his fiction which are of the most nearly universal appeal. A story should be clean-cut and with a single dominating germinal incident upon which it turns as a door upon a hinge, and not built up on a scaffolding of criss-cross stuff. Under the scheme of the universe it is the tragic things that seem the most real. "Tragedy is an imitation, not of men, but of an action of life . . . the incidents and the plot are the end of a tragedy [Aristotle in his *Poetics*]." The short story, like any work of art, is produced only by painstaking labor and according to certain structural rules. The laws that apply to mechanics and architecture are no more certain or established than those that apply to the construction of the short story. "All art does but consist in the removal of surplusage [Walter Pater]." And the short story is to our age what the drama was to the Greeks. The Greeks would have been astounded at the idea common to our age that the highest form of literary structure may omit the framework of the plot. Plot is first, character is second.

Mr. Post takes his stand thus definitely against what is probably the prevailing literary opinion. For there is a creed, cardinal with many if not most of the best living writers, which says that the best art springs from characterization and not from a series of organized incidents, the plot;—which says, further, that if the characters of a story be chosen with care and presented with conviction, they will make all the plot that is necessary or desirable by their interaction on each other. An excellent example of this is such a novel as Frank Swinnerton's *Nocturne* or Willa Cather's *A Lost Lady.* Yet it is not possible to refute Mr. Post by citing such books for he could easily point to other novels and stories if modesty forbade him to name his own work. Though there cannot and should not be any decision in this matter, for both the novel of character and the novel of incident are proper vehicles, it is interesting to consider plot as a means to an end.

The Greeks used plot in a manner very different from our use today. At a certain stage toward the close of a Greek tragedy the heavens theoretically opened and a god or goddess intervened, to rescue some, to doom others of the human actors. The purpose was to show man's impotence before heaven, but also to show his courage, rashness, dignity and other qualities in the face and under the spell of overwhelming odds. The effect aimed at by the spectacle of Greek tragedy was one of emotional purification, a purging away in the minds of the beholders of all petty and little things, the celebrated *katharsis* as it was called. To the extent that modern fiction aims to show man's impotence in the hands of destiny or fate, his valiance or his weak cowering or his pitiful but ineffectual struggle, the use of plot in our day is identical with that of the Greeks. One may easily think of examples in the work of Thomas Hardy, Joseph Conrad, and others. The trend has been toward pessimism as an inscrutable destiny has replaced a set of scrutable, jealous, all-too-human deities in the Olympian pantheon.

With Edgar Allan Poe the attempt was begun—indeed, was successfully made, for the time being, at least—to replace the divine with a human agency. Although the Greek drama had perished, all through the Middle Ages and afterward the effort had kept up to preserve the essence of miracle as an invaluable element in human drama. There were both miracles and miracle plays. In place of the Greek *deus ex machina,* "the god from the machine" with his interventions in human affairs, the world had its Francis of Assisi and its Joan of France. But for whatever reason the divine agency was gradually discredited, the force called Providence or destiny came increasingly to be ignored, and even so great a dramatist-poet as Shakespeare, unable or unwilling to open the heavens to defeat Shylock, could only open a lawbook instead.

What men do not feel as a force in their lives cannot safely be invoked in an appeal to their feelings, and Poe, a genius, knew it. In some of his stories he used in place of the Greek *deus ex machina* the vaguely supernatural, impressive because vague. In other stories he took the human intelligence, sharpened it, and in the person of Monsieur Dupin made it serve his purpose. M. Dupin, not being a god, could not be omniscient; as the next best thing, Poe made his detective omniscient after the event. If the emotional effect of a Dupin remorselessly exposing the criminal is not as ennobling as retributive justice administered by a god from Olympus, or wrought by Christian miracle, the fault is not Poe's. It is we who limit the terms of an appeal.

Mr. Post has himself commented on the flood of detective stories that followed Poe's "until the stomach of the reader failed." Disregarding merely imitative work, let us have a look at such substitutes as have been managed for divinity and fate. We commonly call one type of story a detective story simply because the solution of the mystery is assigned to some one person. He may be amateur or professional; from the standpoint of fictional plausibility he had, in most cases, better be a professional. Poe had his M. Dupin, Gaboriau, his M. Lecoq; Conan Doyle, his Sherlock Holmes. Mr. Post has Abner, his M. Jonquelle, prefect of police of Paris; his Sir Henry Marquis of Scotland Yard; his Captain Walker, chief of the United States Secret Service. If we are looking for Mr. Post's difference from Poe and others we shall not find it here. The use of a detective is not inevitable; when there is none we call the tale a mystery story. The method of telling is not fixed; and it is doubtful if anyone will surpass the extreme ingenuity and plausibility of Wilkie Collins in a book like *The Moonstone,* where successive contributed accounts by the actors unfold the mystery at last. One of the few American writers whose economy of words suggests a comparison with Mr. Post was O. Henry. And O. Henry was also a believer in plots, even if the plot consisted, as sometimes it did, in little more than a few minutes of mystification.

Poe had replaced the god from the machine with the man from the detective bureau, but further progress seemed for some time to be blocked. All that anyone was able to do was to produce a crime and then solve it, to build up a mystery and then explain it. This inevitably caused repetition. The weakness was so marked that many writers tried to withhold the solution or explanation until the very end, even at the cost of making it confused, hurried, improbable. Even so, no real quality of drama characterized the period between the crime at the commencement and the disclosure at the finish of the tale. I do not know who was the first to discover that the way to achieve drama was to have the crime going on, to make the tale a race between the detective and the criminal. The method can, however, be very well observed in Mary Roberts Rinehart's first novel, *The Circular Staircase* (1908); and of course it is somewhat implied in the operations of Count Fosco in Wilkie Collins's *The Woman in White,* many years earlier. But this discovery constituted the only technical advance of any importance since Poe. As a noticeable refinement upon this discovery Melville Davisson Post has invented the type of mystery or detective-mystery tale in which the mysteriousness and the solution are developed together. Not suitable for the novel, which must have action, this formula of Mr. Post's is admirable for the short story, in which there is no room for a race with crime but only for a few moments of breathlessness before a denouement.

This refinement of Mr. Post's whereby repetition is avoided, the development of the mystery and its solution side by side, is usually hailed as his greatest achievement. I happen to think that he has in certain of his tales achieved something very much greater. It seems to me that in some of his work Mr. Post has put the *deus ex machina* back in place, has by a little lifted the mere detective story to the dignity of something like the old Greek tragedy, and in so doing has at least partially restored to the people the purge of pity and the cleansing of a reverent terror.

For whatever tribute one may pay him on the technical side, and every book of his increases the tribute that is his due, the thing that has remained unsaid is his use of plot for ennobling the heart and mind of the reader. He is right, of course, when he says that the primary business of the writer must be to entertain; but more rightly right when he adds that it is possible to do the something more in a work which may aspire to be called a work of art. Anna Katharine Green once wrote: "Crime must touch our imagination by showing people like ourselves but incredibly transformed by some overwhelming motive." The author of *The Leavenworth Case* and all those other novels which have entertained their hundreds of thousands, despite appalling technical shortcomings which she never ceased to struggle with but was never able to overcome, was one of the terribly few to command our respect and our admiration in this crucial affair. She was one of the few with whom plot was never anything but a means to an end, and that end, the highest. Of others, it is easy to think at once of O. Henry; it is in this that I would compare him with Mr. Post, and not in any lesser detail such as the power to tell a story with the fewest possible words. All the emphasis that has been put on short story construction in America, all the trumpeting that has proclaimed American writers as the masters of the short story on the technical side will ultimately go for nothing if the fact is lost sight of that a short story is a cup to be brimmed with feeling. And as to the feelings poured into these slender chalices, by their effects shall ye know them.

There is a curious parallel between Mr. Post and another contemporary American writer, Arthur Train. Both began as lawyers, and both showed unusual ability in the practice of the law. Both are the authors of books in which the underlying attitude toward the law is one of that peculiar disdain which, perhaps, only an experienced lawyer can feel. Mr. Train's stories of Ephraim Tutt display an indignation that is hot enough under their surface of weathered philosophy and levity and spirit of farce. But as long ago as 1896 Mr. Post had published *The Strange Schemes of Randolph Mason,* his first book of all and one that must detain us a moment. (pp. 41-51)

A young man not yet twenty-five, [Mr. Post] conceived that "the high ground of the field of crime has not been explored; it has not even been entered. The book stalls have been filled to weariness with tales based upon plans whereby the detective or ferreting power of the State might be baffled. But, prodigious marvel! No writer has attempted to construct tales based upon plans whereby the punishing power of the State might be baffled." And he reflected that the true drama would lie in a duel with the law. He thereupon created the figure of Randolph Mason, a skilled, unscrupulous lawyer who uses the law to defeat the ends of justice. Of these stories the masterpiece is probably **"The Corpus Delicti."** Well-constructed, powerful, immensely entertaining, surely these dramas are of the essence of tragedy, surely they replace Poe's detective with somebody far more nearly approaching the Greek god from the machine. In considering the effects of these remarkable tales we can hardly lose sight of their moral purge of pity and terror, their sense of the law man makes as a web which man may slip through or break or brush aside. Why, a true god from the machine, Mr. Post implies, is not necessary to us; we can destroy ourselves; heaven has only to leave us alone. This, in its turn, produces the much stronger secondary effect: the cry for a true god to order and reward and punish us.

Uncle Abner has been well contrasted with *The Strange Schemes of Randolph Mason.* "He has demonstrated that wrong may triumph over man-made laws, which are imperfect after all the centuries; but that right must win under the timeless Providence of God" [see Williams excerpt dated 1920]. In *Uncle Abner* the *deus ex machina* is fully restored. When it was known how Doomdorf had died, "Randolph made a great gesture, with his arm extended. 'It is a world,' he said, 'filled with the mysterious

joinder of accident!' 'It is a world,' replied Abner, 'filled with the mysterious justice of God!" ' (pp. 51-3)

[Mr. Post] is the author of other books besides *Uncle Abner* which reveal his love for the West Virginia countryside and his power to make his stories take root and grow in that setting. Of his *Dwellers in the Hills* Blanche Colton Williams says, in *Our Short Story Writers:*

> To read it is to ride in memory along a country road bordered by sedge and ragweed; to note the hickories trembling in their yellow leaves; to hear the partridges' call, the woodpecker's tap, and the "golden belted bee booming past"; to cross the stream fringed with bulrushes; to hear men's voices "reaching half a mile to the grazing steers on the sodded knobs"; to meet a neighbor's boy astride a bag of corn, on his way to the grist mill; to stop at the blacksmith's, there to watch the forging of a horseshoe; or at the wagoner's to assist in the making of a wheel; to taste sweet corn pone and the striped bacon, and to roast potatoes in the ashes. . . .

With the exchange of West Virginia for Kentucky, this is also the background and the mood of *The Mountain School-Teacher,* but this short novel is an allegory of the life of Christ. A young schoolteacher appears in a mountain village. We first see him striding up a trail on the mountain, helping a little boy who is having trouble with an ox laden with a bag of corn. In the village the schoolteacher finds men and women of varied character. Some welcome him, and they are for the most part the poor and lowly; some regard him with suspicion and hate. The action parallels the life of Christ and is lived among people who are, despite nineteen centuries, singularly like the people of Christ's time. In the end comes the trial of the schoolteacher on trumped-up charges. "If He came again," the author seems to say, "it would happen as before."

Such fiction does not come from a man who is primarily interested in railroads and coal, education and politics, nor from one whose final interest is to provide entertaining fiction.

In recent books Mr. Post has allowed his fiction to follow him on his travels about the earth. *The Mystery at the Blue Villa* has settings in Paris, Nice, Cairo, Ostend, London, New York and Washington; the war of 1914-18 is used with discretion as an occasional background. Mr. Poe's mysticism can be quickly perceived in certain stories; the tragic quality is ascendant in such tales as **"The Stolen Life"** and **"The Baron Starkheim"**; and humor is not absent from **"Lord Winton's Adventure"** and **"The Witch of Lecca."** A story of retributive justice will be found in **"The New Administration."** The scenes of most of the episodes in *The Sleuth of St. James's Square* are in America; the central figure about whom all the cases turn is Sir Henry Marquis, chief of the investigation department of Scotland Yard. The material is extremely colorful—from all over the world, in fact. *Monsieur Jonquelle, Prefect of Police of Paris* has the same characteristics with the difference of the central figure and with various settings. The reader will observe in these books that the narrative standpoint is altered from story to story; to take *Monsieur Jonquelle,* some of the tales are related by the chief character, some by a third person, some by the author. The reason for the selection inheres in each affair and is worth some contemplation as you go on. *Walker of the Secret Service* is pivoted upon a character who appears in **"The Reward"** in *The Sleuth of St. James's Square.*

This new book of Mr. Post's is a brilliant example of his technical skill throughout; it has also a special interest in the fact that the first six chapters are really a compressed novel. Walker, of the U. S. Secret Service, is introduced as a mere boy of vigorous physique who falls under the influence of two expert train robbers. The several exploits he had a share in are related with a steady crescendo of interest. At the end of the sixth chapter we have a clear picture of the fate of the two chiefs he served. The peculiar circumstances in which young Walker was taken into the Secret Service are shown; and the rest of the book records some of the famous cases he figured in. The motivation is that of **Uncle Abner.**

> Crime always fails. There never was any man able to get away with it. . . . Sooner or later something turns up against which he is wholly unable to protect himself . . . as though there were a power in the universe determined on the maintenance of justice.

Two of the most striking stories, **"The Expert Detective"** and **"The 'Mysterious Stranger' Defense,"** are developed from courtroom scenes—indeed, **"The Expert Detective"** is a single cross-examination of a witness. Probably this tale and one called **"The Inspiration"** must be added to the shorter roll of Mr. Post's finest work, along with **"The Corpus Delicti"** and **"The Doomdorf Mystery."**

The general method has been said, correctly, to combine the ratiocination of Poe's stories with the dramatic method of the best French tellers of tales. The details of technique will bear and repay the closest scrutiny. But in certain stories Melville Davisson Post has put his high skill to a larger use than skill can accomplish; for those of his accomplishments an endowment and not an acquisition was requisite. When one says that of the relatively few American writers with that endowment in mind and heart he was able to bring to the enterprise in hand a skill greater than any of the others, one has indeed said all. (pp. 53-6)

> *Grant Overton, "The Art of Melville Davisson Post," in his* Cargoes for Crusoes, *D. Appleton & Company, George H. Doran Company, and Little, Brown, and Company, 1924, pp. 41-59.*

Melville Davisson Post (essay date 1924)

[In the following excerpt, Post describes his method for writing mystery and detective stories.]

The modern plan for the mystery or detective story can no longer follow the old formula invented by Poe and adopted by Gaboriau, Conan Doyle, etc. All life has grown quicker, the mind of the reader acts more quickly, our civilization is impatient at delays. In literature, and especially literature of this type, the reader will not wait for explanations. All explanations must be given to him in advance of the solution of the mystery.

It became apparent upon a very careful study of the mystery story that something must be done to eliminate the obvious and to get rid of the delay in action and the de-

tailed and tiresome explanation in the closing part. It occurred to me that these defects could be eliminated by folding together the arms of the Poe formula. Instead of giving the reader the mystery and then going over the same ground with the solution, the mystery and its solution might be given together. The developing of the mystery and the development toward the solution would go forward side by side; and when all the details of the mystery were uncovered the solution also would be uncovered and the end of the story arrived at. This is the plan which I followed in my later mystery-detective stories —the **Uncle Abner** series, **Monsieur Jonquelle,** and **Walker of the Secret Service.** This new formula, as will at once be seen, very markedly increases the rapidity of action in a story, holds the reader's interest throughout, and eliminates any impression of moving at any time over ground previously covered.

It requires a greater care and more careful technique, for *every explanation which the reader must receive in order to understand either the mystery or the solution must be slipped into the story as it proceeds without any delay in its action.* There can be no pause for explanation. Each explanation must be a natural sequence and a part of the action and movement. The reader must never be conscious that he is being delayed for an explanation, and the elements of explanation must be so subtly suggested that one receives them as he receives the details of a landscape in an adventure scene, without being conscious of it.

In undertaking to build up a story on this modern formula, one must first have a germinal or inciting incident upon which the whole story may turn as upon a hinge. Out of this controlling incident, the writer must develop both the mystery and its solution and must present them side by side to the reader in the direct movement of the story to the end. When the mystery is finally explained, the story is ended. There can be no further word or paragraph; there can be no added explanation. If a sufficient explanation has not preceded this point, the story has failed. If the reader has been compelled to pause at any point in the story long enough to realize that he is receiving an explanation, the story has failed.

But it will not be enough if the writer of the mystery-detective story is able cleverly to work out his story according to this formula. He must be able to give this type of story the same literary distinction that can be given to any type of story. To do this he has only to realize a few of the primary rules of all literary structure. He must remember that everything, every form of character, has a certain dignity. This dignity the writer must realize and respect. Flaubert told Maupassant that in order to be original he had only to look at the thing which he wished to describe long enough and with such care that he saw in it something which no one had seen in it before. That rule ought to be amended to require the writer to look at every character and every situation long enough and with sufficient care to realize the dignity in it—that element of distinction which it invariably possesses in some direction—and when he has grasped that, to respect and convey it in his story.

It may as well be said that no one form of literary structure is superior to another. The story dealing with the life and action of our highest types does not in itself result in any better literature than the story dealing with the lowest or most abandoned types; nor are physical adventures to be graded below metaphysical adventures. The mystery-detective story may be structurally so excellent and its workmanship so good that it is the equal of any form of literature.

The obvious is at the base of all boredom. The thing that provides our perpetual interest in life is that the events lying just ahead of us cannot be determined. It is the mystery in the next moment, the next hour, the next day that we live to solve. If by any mental process we could ascertain the arrival of events ahead, no human being could endure the boredom of life. Something of this mystery, this uncertainty, must be caught up for the reader in the short story if his interest is to abide to the end. The skill of the author in preserving this uncertainty and mystery in events—in this imitation of life—will indicate the place to be assigned to him in the art he has undertaken. (pp. 57-9)

> *Melville Davisson Post, in an excerpt in* Cargoes for Crusoes *by Grant Overton, D. Appleton & Company, George H. Doran Company, and Little, Brown, and Company, 1924, pp. 57-9.*

Howard Haycraft   (essay date 1941)

[*Haycraft is an American editor and critic who has written extensively on mystery and detective fiction. In the following excerpt, he discusses the strengths and limitations of Post's Uncle Abner stories.*]

Several years spent in the practice of criminal and corporation law in his native state gave [Post] the background for **The Strange Schemes of Randolph Mason,** a volume of short stories dealing with an unscrupulous lawyer who used his knowledge of legal loopholes to defeat justice. (p. 94)

The MASON stories qualify as detection only in an oblique sense, if at all. But there is no doubt that they helped to pave the way in Post's mind for UNCLE ABNER, whose sleuthing is of the purest ray. A rockhewn Virginia squire of the Jeffersonian era, whose position as protector of the innocent and righter of wrongs in his mountain community compelled him to turn detective with some of the most convincing results known to the short story form, UNCLE ABNER (who never appeared in a novel) had a long career in the popular magazines, beginning in 1911. The book collection of the tales, *Uncle Abner: Master of Mysteries,* did not appear until 1918, but has been in print continuously ever since.

Post, who received record prices for his magazine work, considered himself the champion of plot-technique in the short story. Indeed, he is probably the most creditable exponent of the formularized short story that America has developed; and his skill in this direction, however detrimental it may have been to his "artistic" reputation, brought to the detective story a new technical excellence that was to have far-reaching effects. His clipped, economical style was admirably suited to the form, and his deft, selective plot manipulation was a strong and healthy contrast to the rambling diffuseness of most of his countrymen who were active in the field at the time.

Nevertheless, in his preoccupation with plot formulas,

Post underestimated some of his own greatest talents. The ABNER stories are still read and re-read after more than a quarter-century less for the intensive plots of which their author was so proud—strikingly original in their time but mostly hackneyed by imitation to-day—than for the difficult-to-define quality that separates the sheep from the goats in any form of literature: in Post's case, as nearly as can be expressed, his richly sentient realization of character, place, and mood. Had he been willing to emphasize this side of his talent more, his stature as a true literary artist might have been greater than now seems likely. As it was, his never quite expressed serious abilities were sufficient to set him, in the less pretentious form of the detective story, head and shoulders above his contemporaries and to make him the peer of almost any practioner of the genre who has written since. (pp. 95-6)

Superlatively fine as they are, the UNCLE ABNER stories have not altogether escaped criticism. Their most serious fault, in the opinion of certain critics, is the author's failure in a few of the tales to make all the evidence explicit. In at least one instance this criticism is justified beyond any doubt. [In a footnote, Haycraft explains: "In the ABNER story, "An Act of God," Post proves by a phonetic misspelling the forgery of a document purportedly written by a deafmute. The brilliant solution is spoiled by the fact that he does *not* allow the reader to scan the document. Had he done so, the tale might well be ranked as one of the most nearly perfect in all the literature."] But in other cases, one wonders if a basic misunderstanding on the part of the critics themselves may not be at fault? Certainly, we must insist on fair play. But the detective story, whether long or short, does not exist in which there is not *some* "off-stage" work—if only in the detective's mind. To have matters otherwise would be to deprive us of our puzzle in mid-career. In nearly every case, Post's offense is merely the logical extension of this principle; and one feels, somehow, that the writer of the *short* detective story (handicapped and restricted in ways that the author of a novel never knows) should be allowed the widest possible discretion and latitude in this respect. Had Post met the demands of the quibblers to catalogue and label every clue, there would in many instances have been no mystery and no story. . . . It is not without relation that, for all Post's genius in physical device, ABNER's detection in the final analysis nearly always hinges on *character*. It is his judgment of men's souls that leads him to expect and therefore to find and interpret the evidence, where lesser minds (including, perhaps, the literal ones of his decriers) see naught.

In all, Melville Davisson Post created the surprising total of six detective characters: UNCLE ABNER, RANDOLPH MASON (to some degree); SIR HENRY MARQUIS of *The Sleuth of St. James's Square* and *The Bradmoor Murder;* MONSIEUR JONQUELLE of *Monsieur Jonquelle: Prefect of Police of Paris;* WALKER of *Walker of the Secret Service;* and COLONEL BRAXTON of *The Silent Witness.* All are good in their kind, but none of the others seriously challenges the immortal Virginia squire.

No reader can call himself connoisseur who does not know UNCLE ABNER forward and backward. His four-square pioneer ruggedness looms as a veritable monument in the literature. Posterity may well name him, after

DUPIN, the greatest American contribution to the form. (pp. 96-7)

Howard Haycraft, "America: 1890-1914 (The Romantic Era)," in his Murder for Pleasure: The Life and Times of the Detective Story, *D. Appleton-Century Company, Incorporated, 1941, pp. 83-102.*

Charles A. Norton   (essay date 1973)

[*In the following excerpt, Norton evaluates Post's literary career.*]

Judging the lifetime literary accomplishments of Melville Davisson Post is not a simple task. His present fortune is to belong to that group of authors, due to some seemingly unwritten law, who are subjected to near-total neglect. This is partly traceable to the phenomena that mediocre work and sometimes inferior work, which meets a public fancy, will draw all attention away from those items which do have a significant value causing what is worthy of critical attention to be ignored. Thus, only with a thorough application of research and item by item review can we conclude that Post has not received proper recognition for his several contributions to the literature of America. While there are no reasons to judge his contributions either as unmatchable or indispensable (terms which can be used only rarely), what he did accomplish may still be considered of importance, even if only of minor importance because of the depreciated rating of short fiction at this time. Also, we must allow that his contributions are not in any great quantity—much of what he wrote has been fairly judged and assigned to the limbo it deserves.

The most obvious injustice to his neglected accomplishments has resulted, ironically, from the recognition granted Post as an author of mystery and detective stories. Undoubtedly, this restricted praise is the product of an erroneous view, one which once established is mirrored by those who avoid doing original investigations. . . . The necessity for a reordered recognition of Melville Davisson Post is plain—however, viewed realistically, this does not guarantee the possibility of its success. Too often, history reports, such efforts tend to fall victim to the same obstacle they strive to overcome.

It appears that Post was attracted to enigmas; in fact he created them when they did not exist. Therefore, he undoubtedly brought upon himself, to a large extent, the very enigma that has been the legacy of his career as a writer. Post wrote to make money, and having such a goal, he proceeded on the basis that an author's principal aim should be primarily to write material that would entertain the reader. Post assumed that such work would attract the most readers, be most saleable, and earn the greatest sums of money. These points he developed with great success and remarkable skill. The result was that he became in the years between 1910 and 1930 one of the more frequently read writers of magazine fiction, and he received the top prices for his work. As his fame as a writer of mystery and detective tales grew, he accepted the role and even promoted it. Seeing perhaps the profit in being himself a mystery, he limited published knowledge of his personal life to a few guarded facts and ambiguous statements. Thus, by revealing to the public only his shadow and by ignoring

Melville Davisson Post.

his real talents, Melville Davisson Post aided his own demise.

The history of the mystery and detective story as a type of literature is lengthy and complex if one seeks to trace every one of its features back to their earliest source. The mystery and detective story, as we are most familiar with it, had its principal modern advent in the work of Edgar Allan Poe. Almost all of today's mystery and detective fiction can be said to have evolved from Poe's efforts in this category. There were a number of near-imitators of Poe's work who contributed memorable tales over the next several decades, plus some works less imitative. Following Poe, the modern mystery and detective story flourished as readers, writers, and books grew steadily in number. When A. Conan Doyle came upon the scene after 1887 with his cleverly-drawn detective, Sherlock Holmes, whose name is almost synonymous with the term "detective," he added impetus to the form. As Post noted in the "Introduction" to his first collection of stories in 1896, the reader was caught in a near "flood" of such stories. It was for this reason, being already enigmatic and unique in his approach, Post sought to invert the commonplace plot. In his attempt he created Randolph Mason, not as a detective, but as an attorney, waging a personal vendetta against Fate and lacking any moral standard but his own. Mason abetted various criminal acts, including murder, by casting his extraordinary powers and intelligence against the laws of the state. This was Post's first contribution, one which, while it never predominated, nevertheless is found in varied modes with great regularity in the modern tale of this field.

Despite success and fame as a result of two books of Randolph Mason stories (unique offerings, but mostly mediocre in construction), Post's next contribution was another complete change of style. *Dwellers in the Hills* is not only a minor masterpiece, but is completely removed from the mystery and detective category. This short novel is an ode to childhood, to nature, to adventure, and to life. The relationship of a remarkable boy and a magnificent horse recorded here has been seldom matched by any other writer. *Dwellers in the Hills* is a worthy contribution to American literature, but it is almost totally unknown to the general reader, even those who have read Post's more popular materials. More persons need an opportunity to read this short, but beautifully written and exciting book.

In Post's next three books there is again much mediocre and some inferior work. Although the third Randolph Mason book, *The Corrector of Destinies,* the novel, *The Gilded Chair,* and the unusual, disguised collection, *The Nameless Thing,* all have instances of brilliance, for the most part they deserve a measure of the neglect they have been accorded. Again in these three books little appears to assign Post to the mystery and detective tale classification exclusively. Only in *The Nameless Thing* do we find some such material. This last is a little understood collection, never properly criticized, put together in an interesting if not original fashion. It also contains one of the best and most neglected of Post's mystery and detective tales, first published serially under the title **"A Critique of Monsieur Poe."**

Post had been writing and publishing tales about his finest character, Uncle Abner, for seven years before they were collected into the deservedly famous *Uncle Abner, Master of Mysteries.* It is not only the best of Post's work, but one of the truly great collections of mystery and detective stories of all time. The chief contributions made here by Post are through his character, Abner. Here is the first great "non-detective" who solves crimes. Also with Abner, we find a character who does not wait upon the law, but administers justice as he sees it in accordance with the powers of Providence—although he often cooperates with and always sides with the law in a manner justified in the frontier setting of the tales. Perhaps Abner's method of solving crimes is one of the most important contributions, for he operates not only on shrewd intelligence in sorting out significant clues, but he has the added ability to read human nature. In these Abner stories, in nearly every instance, Post has devised plots that have various aspects of the tragic drama. Many good things have been said about these stories and many more remain to be said—they are a supreme accomplishment.

Profiting from his fame, Post was able during the remaining years of his life to publish nine more books, but none a challenge to his *Uncle Abner* stories. Six of these books have many elements in them that give credence to the classification of Post as an author of mystery and detective tales. In them are found some of the more commonplace detective characters he developed, the Britisher, Sir Henry Marquis; the Frenchman, Monsieur Jonquelle; and the bungling American Chief of the Secret Service, Walker. Also in these six books there are other elements which permit the further opinion that although it is partially correct to classify them as mystery and detective works, they are only borderline cases. Many of their stories and features are not closely related to the typical mystery and detective tale, but are significant in having a wider appeal. The last of these books again features a lawyer hero, Colonel Braxton, who operates much in the manner of Abner—but unfortunately these stories were not written with an equal skill. Discounting Post's one nonfiction book as inferior, there remain two other works, both novelettes and neither having any resemblance to a mystery-detective work. Both of these are unique books, but only mediocre in execution. *The Mountain School-Teacher,* a reconstruction of the life of Christ, appeals to a limited audience and perhaps says more than most readers realize. *The Revolt of the Birds,* a hazy tale, almost a fable, enlightens momentarily, then struggles to a dreamy conclusion.

Through all his work, the good and much of the bad, Post also added other worthy contributions that deserve more notice than they have been given. In Randolph Mason, Post helped lay the ground for acceptance of the anti-hero. He introduced often into his stories criminals as leading characters and, in a minor, primitive way, gave a start to the hard-boiled facet of the field. More generally, but also more importantly, he helped develop the sharpened technique that improved the form of the plotted short story. This he coupled with an economical use of language that helped to give short fiction some of the fast-paced action that is a distinctive feature of the modern variety. Although no single author deserves any special credit for this development of style, Post deserves as much credit as any should have earned.

Melville Davisson Post, in addition to being an author of many mysteries, was a man of many mysteries. He was an enigma in life and remains an enigma—a man who received some fame and praise, but not enough—and that he received for the wrong reasons. (pp. 229-33)

> *Charles A. Norton, in his* Melville Davisson Post: Man of Many Mysteries, *Bowling Green University Popular Press, 1974, 261 p.*

Allen J. Hubin   (essay date 1977)

[*In the following excerpt, Hubin characterizes Post's Uncle Abner stories as uniquely American in theme and characterization.*]

It is widely agreed that the uniquely American form of the mystery-detective story is that involving the hard-boiled sleuth. This variant was born in the early 1920s in the pages of *Black Mask* magazine, and was carried to notable literary heights by Dashiell Hammett in that same decade.

The hard-boiled detective story has proved immensely durable, not only sustaining such excellent writers of later decades as Raymond Chandler and Ross Macdonald, but also giving rise to a horde of imitations plumbing all manner of extremes within this subgenre, and running up through the present day. By 1940 such fiction had leaped United States boundaries; indigenous imitations were beginning to turn up in England, and later on the continent. But however international in authorship and publication and setting the hard-boiled story has become, it seems steadfastly to remain peculiarly American in essentials. The reasons for this can probably be found in features of

American culture and retained elements of the frontier and the Wild West.

I would like to suggest that Melville Davisson Post's Uncle Abner tales represent another peculiarly American form of the detective story; but here the analogy with hard-boiled fiction breaks down.

The stature of the Abner narratives was recognized early; by 1941 (in his *Murder for Pleasure*) Howard Haycraft was observing that "posterity may well name [Uncle Abner], after Dupin, the greatest American contribution to the form" [see excerpt above], and in 1942 (in his *The Detective Short Story*) Ellery Queen was stating firmly that **Uncle Abner** was "the finest book of detective short stories written by an American author since Poe" [see Further Reading]. There has long been a critical consensus, at least in the United States, that the Abner tales constitute a magnificent achievement—and one that was seemingly born fully developed rather than—like the hard-boiled story—evolving over several years.

Is this the reason why Uncle Abner appears to be *sui generis,* why no subsequent American writers—with the possible exception of William Faulkner in *Knight's Gambit*—attempted to build upon, imitate, or develop further the Abner model? Has there been a general recognition that the Uncle Abner stories, and Abner himself, were and are complete in themselves?

The various fictional cleric-detectives (such as Father Brown) that have dotted the ratiocinative landscape might be cited in rebuttal. But Uncle Abner was not a clergyman, and in the intensity of his religious beliefs, in his passion for justice, in his identification with the people and the land, I believe he stands uniquely apart.

Uncle Abner is also more distinctly American in acceptance than the hard-boiled story, which in the hands of Hammett as well as less able American practitioners was quickly recognized as a salable commodity in England and elsewhere. It is a matter of record that, although Post reportedly enjoyed a literary reputation in England through the appearance of his first novel (**Dwellers in the Hills**), **Uncle Abner** was not brought out in Britain until a small publisher, now defunct, issued the book in 1972.

Further, England's Julian Symons says in his highly regarded *Mortal Consequences* (1972; *Bloody Murder* in England) that "the attraction the stories have for Americans simply does not exist for others. To English readers, Uncle Abner is likely to seem a distant and implausible figure" [see Further Reading]. I find this curious, for the ties of Abner and his people to England are clearly evident in the stories, and Abner is twice described as "a man who might have followed Cromwell." Abner is profoundly a man of his Virginia country and mid-nineteenth-century period; but can it be true that no such character, strong and devout and wise, could have tramped the farther hills of England during the last century?

Yet the fact of Abner's low appeal to the English remains, and he stands to this day as peculiarly American. (pp. vii-ix)

[There are] three strong elements in the Abner stories: the land, God and His sovereignty, and the law and justice (which are not always, as we shall see, the same thing).

The land, the Virginia country shortly before the Civil War, is evoked so vividly it seems to breathe, "a country of little hills and narrow well-sodded valleys, lying westward from the great slope of the Alleghenies, toward the Ohio. It was old cattle country."

It was also the symbol of substance. "Land was the evidence and insignia of distinction in Virginia. . . . One's importance was measured by his acres."

Such high significance begets greed and covetousness, which in turn beget murder, and so it is in several Abner stories. "Dilworth had a pagan worship of his land. He would have gone to crucifixion to extend his acres."

Abner's views of God and law and justice are closely related. Abner himself represents justice, though he sees "justice in the larger and human aspect" and stands "for the spirit, above the letter, of the truth."

"I have read St. Paul's epistle on charity," says Uncle Abner, "and, after long reflection, I am persuaded that there exists a greater thing than charity—a thing of more value to the human family. Like charity, it rejoiceth not in iniquity, but it does not bear all things or believe all things, or endure all things; and, unlike charity, it seeketh its own. . . . Do you know what I mean, Smallwood? I will tell you. It is Justice."

Some hold that chance, random chance, governs the affairs of men. Abner insists that we are ruled by the Providence of God, and argues that "it favors the just." Elsewhere he calls chance "a fool's word like many others in our tongue. There was a purpose in every moving of events. Because the understanding of that purpose was denied us, we disclaimed the purpose. It was a way writ large in the affairs of men."

"It is a world," someone else suggests to Abner, "filled with the mysterious joinder of accident." Abner will have none of this: "It is a world filled with the mysterious justice of God." And Abner fears that "the justice of the law might contravene the justice of God."

But this does not mean that Abner would substitute his perception of divine justice—or any individual's own perception of justice—for human law: "The law and the orderly procedure of the law must be strengthened. The land was running into violence. The direct action of angered persons would presently supersede the law. Men would be judged and punished in hot blood and all orderly procedure of government would go to pieces. It was better for the guilty to go free than to put the land in chaos."

So Abner is profoundly conscious of God's providence, His justice, of the rightness of things, and the wrongness of other things. When he comes upon the starkest evil, the handservants of Satan, the power of the telling grows. I think of a passage recounted by Martin, Abner's nephew and the narrator of the stories:

> Before this fire stood Dix. He was holding out his hands and turning himself about as though he were cold to the marrow; but with all that chill upon him, when the man's face came into the light I saw it covered with a sprinkling of sweat.
>
> I shall carry the memory of that face. The grin was there at the mouth, but it was pulled about; the eyelids were drawn in; the teeth were clamped togeth-

er. I have seen a dog poisoned with strychnine look like that.

I lay there and watched the thing. It was as though something potent and evil dwelling within the man were in travail to re-form his face upon its image. You cannot realize how that devilish labor held me—the face worked as though it were some plastic stuff, and the sweat oozed through. And all the time the man was cold; and he was crowding into the fire and turning himself about and putting out his hands. . . .

I could smell the singe of the fire on him, but it had not power against this diabolic chill. . . .

The man had taken off his boots and he twisted before the fire without a sound. . . . I thought the man would burn himself to death. His clothes smoked. How could he be so cold? . . .

Then, finally, the thing was over! . . . He grew composed and stepped back into the room. . . .

It was Dix; but not the Dix that any of us knew. . . . Something that had been servile in him, that had skulked behind disguises, that had worn the habiliments of subterfuge, had now come forth; and it had molded the features of the man to its abominable courage.

Abner soon appears on the scene, and when he sees Dix's new face and the new boldness upon him, he says, "While one is the servant of neither, one has the courage of neither; but when he finally makes his choice he gets what his master has to give him."

Thus the existence and power of Satan were real and evident to Abner, and Satan's horrible corrupting sovereignty emerges again elsewhere in the stories. Of a man called Dale, Martin says: "There was everything fine and distinguished in his face, but his face was a ruin. It was a loathsome and hideous ruin. Made for the occupancy of a god, the man's body was the dwelling of a devil . . . one low and bestial, that wallowed and gorged itself with sins."

And again: "He was a man one would have traveled far to see—yesterday or the day ahead of it. He had a figure out of Athens, a face cast in some forgotten foundry by the Arno, thick-curled mahogany-colored hair, and eyes like the velvet hull of an Italian chestnut. These excellences the heavenly workman had turned out, and now by some sorcery of the pit they were changed into abomination. Hell-charms, one thought of, when one looked the creature in the face."

But what of Abner himself? He is a bachelor, a landowner, and a cattle raiser. He is introduced in the first story as "one of those austere, deeply religious men who were the product of the Reformation." Later we are told that he is "a big, broad-shouldered, deep-chested Saxon, with all those marked characteristics of a race living out of doors and hardened by wind and sun." His jaw is great, his chin massive, "his voice slow and deep."

Abner is a stern and solemn man; he does not seem to laugh, and indeed in all the stories there is little sense or expression of joy. But the atmosphere is by no means one of unrelieved gloom; rather Abner is a man engaged in serious business, and the stories are full of purpose—and, as we have seen, of Purpose.

Riding through the hills and among the people, Abner encounters the weak and the victimized and the evil. When he senses wrongness, he usually invokes his God; the men—and they are all men in this masculine world—jeer, and one says, "I would shoestrap such a God!" Then, arguments based on justice being unavailing, Abner must produce evidence of malefaction—and so he does.

The evidence comes from Abner's knowledge of man and his lusts, of the land and the animals and the seasons; it comes from Abner's deductions, his reading of signs and marks and tracks, his interpretation of events. Many of his interventions take place out-of-doors, and one is reminded of Hesketh Prichard's November Joe, "detective of the woods"—but Abner is the infinitely superior creation.

Abner might be expected to exalt reason and intelligence, as these are his tools and indeed the foremost weapons of the fictional detective. But he doesn't. In one of the stories, someone says of reason: "We have that, and God has nothing better!" Abner replies, "I cannot think of God depending on a thing so crude as reason. If one reflects upon it, I think one will immediately see that reason is a quality exclusively peculiar to the human mind. It is a thing that God could never, by any chance, require. Reason is the method by which those who do not know the truth, step by step, finally discover it."

Another character argues for the strength of human intelligence: "Is there any place in this scheme of nature for His intervention? Why, sir, the intelligence of man that your Scriptures so despises can easily put His little plans of rewards and punishments out of joint. Not the good, Abner, but the intelligent, possess the earth. The man who sees on all sides of his plan, and hedges it about with wise precautions, brings it to success. Every day the foresight of man outwits your God." Abner does not answer immediately, but in the end he thunders, his voice "echoing like a trumpet" above a storm: "Outwit God! Why, Mr. Evlyn Bird, you cannot outwit me, who am the feeblest of his creatures!" (pp. xi-xv)

Allen J. Hubin, in an introduction to The Complete Uncle Abner *by Melville Davisson Post, University of California, 1977, pp. vii-xvi.*

FURTHER READING

Anderson, Jack Sandy. "Melville Davisson Post." *West Virginia History* XXVIII, No. 4 (July 1967): 271-81.
    Biographical and critical introduction to Post's fiction.

Barzun, Jacques, and Taylor, Wendell Hertig. *Catalogue of Crime,* pp. 455ff. New York: Harper & Row, Publishers, 1971.
    Reviews a number of Post's short story collections.

Boucher, Anthony. Introduction to *Uncle Abner, Master of Mysteries,* by Melville Davisson Post, pp. 7-8. New York: Collier Books, 1962.
    Brief introductory remarks. Boucher concludes that the Uncle Abner stories' "foremost importance is in their

non-detective aspects: their penetration into human nature, their ventures in moral theology, above all, their rich warm evocation of life in western Virginia in the early part of the last century—as detailedly real as Sherlock Holmes's end-of-century London and possibly, to an American, even more nostalgic."

Marble, Annie Russell. "Melville Davisson Post." In her *A Study of the Modern Novel: British and American Since 1900,* pp. 292-95. New York: D. Appleton and Co., 1928.
General discussion of Post's fiction and nonfiction.

Penzler, Otto. "Collecting Mystery Fiction: Melville Davisson Post." *The Armchair Detective* 18, No. 2 (Spring 1985): 167-72.
A listing of collectible editions of Post's fiction that contains critical commentary on his works and reputation.

Post, Melville Davisson. "The Blight." *The Saturday Evening Post* 187, No. 26 (26 December 1914): 21, 25-6.
Outlines Post's formula, based on Aristotle's dramatic theories, for developing well-written and popular short stories.

———."The Mystery Story." *The Saturday Evening Post* 187, No. 35 (27 February 1915): 21-5.
Further elaboration of Post's theories on writing short stories with particular emphasis on the mystery story.

Queen, Ellery. *"The Strange Schemes of Randolph Mason"* and *"Uncle Abner."* In *Queen's Quorum,* pp. 36-9. Boston: Little, Brown and Co., 1951.
Praise for several collections of Post's short stories. Queen states: "In the same way that Chesterton's *The Innocence of Father Brown,* among all the books of detective short stories written by English authors, ranks second only to Doyle's *The Adventures of Sherlock Holmes,* so . . . Melville Davisson Post's *Uncle Abner* . . . is second only to Poe's *Tales* among all the books of detective short stories written by American authors. This statement is made dogmatically and without reservation: a cold-blooded and calculated critical opinion which we believe will be as true in the year 2000 as we wholeheartedly believe it to be true today. These four

books, two American and two British, are the finest in their field—the *crème du crime.* They are an out-of-this-world target for future detective-story writers to take shots at—but it will be like throwing pebbles at the Pyramids."

Schantz, Tom, and Schantz, Enid. "Introduction: The Book of Abner." In *The Methods of Uncle Abner,* by Melville Davisson Post, pp. vi-x. Boulder, Colo.: Aspen Press, 1974.
A discussion of plot, style, and characterization in Post's Uncle Abner stories.

Symons, Julian. "The Short Story: The First Golden Age." In his *Mortal Consequences: A History—From the Detective Story to the Crime Novel,* pp. 76-90. New York: Harper & Row, Publishers, 1972.
Includes a brief evaluation of Post's Uncle Abner stories. Symons, a noted English mystery writer, concludes: "To English readers, Uncle Abner is likely to seem a distant and implausible figure, and if one judges in terms of plot the stories have surely been overpraised."

Van Dine, S. S. [pseudonym of Willard Huntington Wright]. Introduction to *The Great Detective Stories,* pp. 3-37. New York: Charles Scribner's Sons, 1927.
Critical introduction to a collection of detective stories which includes Post's "The Straw Man." Van Dine concludes that Uncle Abner "is one of the very few detectives deserving to be ranked with that immortal triumvirate, Dupin, Lecoq, and Holmes. . . . In conception, execution, device and general literary quality these stories of early Virginia, written by a man who thoroughly knows his *métier* and is also an expert in law and criminology, are among the very best we possess."

Wood, Warren. "A Master Story-Teller." In his *Representative Authors of West Virginia,* pp. 172-90. Ravenswood, W. Va.: Worth-While Book Co., 1926.
Provides an overview of Post's short stories and novels.

William Sharp

1855-1905

(Also wrote under the pseudonyms Fiona Macleod and H. P. Siwaärmill) Scottish poet, novelist, short story writer, biographer, essayist, and dramatist.

Acknowledged as the foremost Scottish writer of the Celtic Renaissance, a predominantly Irish literary movement of the late nineteenth and early twentieth centuries, Sharp helped revive the dormant mythology of his homeland's past in his poems, novels, dramas, and short stories. He is best known for the mystical, romantic works he published as "Fiona Macleod," whose identity he concealed from his contemporaries. Speculation regarding Sharp's relationship to "Fiona Macleod" began immediately upon his use of the pseudonym and continued until the secret was revealed following his death. Denounced by some as a calculated hoax intended to increase his readership and analyzed by others as a case of dual identity, Sharp's feminine persona created what Richard Le Gallienne described as "one of the most picturesque sensations" of the 1890s and continues to overshadow criticism of his literary output.

Born in Paisley, Sharp was educated at the Glasgow Academy and at Glasgow University. In the summer of 1873 he joined a troupe of Gypsies as they roamed throughout the western Highlands of Scotland, and his fascination with this region later became a hallmark of the "Fiona Macleod" material. In 1878 he moved to London where, through his friendship with the painter and poet Dante Gabriel Rossetti, he became associated with the Pre-Raphaelite movement, an influential circle of artists and writers who sought to imitate in their works such qualities of pre-Renaissance art as religious symbolism, lavish pictorialism, and natural sensuousness. The influence of Rossetti and other Pre-Raphaelites is evident in Sharp's early poetry, particularly his first collection, *The Human Inheritance,* which appeared in 1882, the same year that he published a biography of Rossetti.

In 1891 he published what critics consider his most important early work, *Sospiri di Roma,* the poetry collection in which he first employed a feminine persona. *Vistas,* a collection of verse dramas published in 1894, displays a concern with mystical themes and subjects that reflects Sharp's growing interest in Celtic lore. While his output until this point in his career seemed to mark him as a minor talent, his circumstances changed when a psychic impulse—or a deliberate bid for readership—led to the invention of "Fiona Macleod," the alter ego Sharp publicly claimed was his uneducated cousin, a dweller of the Scottish Highlands and a romantic visionary. Beginning in 1894 with *Pharais: A Romance of the Isles,* "Fiona Macleod" attained the popularity and critical acclaim that had eluded Sharp, and interest in the works of "Fiona Macleod" led many who were familiar with Sharp's work to suspect him as the author. Other commentators rejected that suggestion, claiming Sharp incapable of the imagination required to create the works. Critics theorize that the sensation over the identity of "Fiona Macleod" contribut-

ed to the success of the works published under that name, and Sharp went to great lengths to perpetuate the mystery, writing pseudonymous letters and even submitting an entry for "Fiona Macleod" to *Who's Who.* In his private correspondence, Sharp occasionally referred to an anxiety regarding his identity, admitting, "Sometimes I am tempted to believe I am half a woman." He continued to write poetry and essays under his own name with moderate success, while the works of "Fiona Macleod"—notably the poetry collection *From the Hills of Dream* and the verse drama *The House of Usna*—earned enthusiastic reviews from such admirers as W. B. Yeats, who at the time was a leading figure of the Celtic Renaissance. For all but a few close friends, the mystery of "Fiona Macleod" remained unsolved until Sharp's death in 1905.

Katharine Tynan wrote in 1906, "One is obliged always to think of William Sharp and Fiona Macleod as two instead of one, although the two may have lodged under one mortal roof," and until recently critics have tended to proceed as if there existed two independent bodies of work. Of the two, "Fiona Macleod" has clearly attracted more critical attention, and few of those who have examined Sharp's non-Celtic writings have considered him more than, in Cornelius Weygandt's appraisal, "a skillful literary practitioner, a higher sort of hack." Most critics agree that his poetry is transparently imitative of Rossetti and John Keats, his prose of Rossetti and Walter Pater. His biographies of English authors earned the respect of his contemporaries, but are generally considered to have had no lasting effect on the reputations of their subjects. For the most part, commentary on Sharp has focused on discovering antecedents to the development of "Fiona Macleod." For instance, *A Fellowe and His Wife,* an epistolary novel coauthored with Blanche Willis Howard, is noted not for its literary attributes but because Howard assumed the male role and Sharp the female.

Filled with fantasy, lyrical descriptions of landscape, and a spirituality not generally found in Sharp's work, the novels, short stories, poetry, and dramas of "Fiona Macleod" are considered representative of the Celtic Renaissance, a movement that sought to reconstruct early Celtic history and literature, and to create a new literature out of that heritage. For retelling ancient Celtic legends, for setting new tales in the historic Highlands, and for making abundant use of Gaelic vocabulary, "Fiona Macleod" was hailed as a valuable agent of cultural awareness, and sometimes as a visionary in "her" own right. So convincing was Sharp's female persona that Ernest Rhys wrote in 1900 that the poems of "Fiona Macleod" were "filled and quickened to life by the imagination of Woman's earthly and Spiritual Beauty, her Divine and natural Mystery." Dissenting from the general praise for these works, the American critic Paul Elmer More complained in 1913 of an inclination towards vagueness and an "inability to distinguish between an idea or even a genuine emotion and the fluttering of tired nerves" throughout the works of "Fiona Macleod." More maintained that Sharp "fell again and again into meaningless rhetoric that makes the loosest vapourings of 'A. E.' or Mr. W. B. Yeats seem solid and compact of reason." Later examinations of Sharp's career have viewed the two previously distinct bodies of work as a unified entity, perceiving a consistency in the philosophical themes of all of Sharp's works, as well as a logical pattern of stylistic development. From this perspective the use of a feminine pseudonym, with its attendant controversy, is only one aspect of the career of a significant figure of the Celtic Renaissance.

PRINCIPAL WORKS

Dante Gabriel Rossetti: A Record and a Study (biography) 1882

The Human Inheritance. The New Hope. Motherhood (poetry) 1882

Earth's Voices. Transcripts from Nature. Sospitra, and Other Poems (poetry) 1884

Life of Percy Bysshe Shelley (biography) 1887

Life of Heinrich Heine (biography) 1888

Romantic Ballads and Poems of Phantasy (poetry) 1888

The Children of To-morrow (novel) 1889

Life of Robert Browning (biography) 1890

Sospiri di Roma (poetry) 1891

A Fellowe and His Wife [with Blanche Willis Howard] (novel) 1892

The Life and Letters of Joseph Severn (biography) 1892

*The Pagan Review (essays, dramas, poetry, and short stories) 1892

Pharais: A Romance of the Isles [as Fiona Macleod] (novel) 1894

Vistas (dramas) [first publication] 1894

The Mountain Lovers [as Fiona Macleod] (novel) 1895

The Sin-Eater, and Other Tales [as Fiona Macleod] (short stories) 1895

From the Hills of Dream: Mountain Songs and Island Runes [as Fiona Macleod] (poetry) 1896

Green Fire: A Romance [as Fiona Macleod] (novel) 1896

The Washer of the Ford, and Other Legendary Moralities [as Fiona Macleod] (short stories) 1896

The Laughter of Peterkin [as Fiona Macleod] (short stories) 1897

The Dominion of Dreams [as Fiona Macleod] (short stories) 1899

Silence Farm (novel) 1899

The Divine Adventure. Iona. By Sundown Shores: Studies in Spiritual History [as Fiona Macleod] (allegory and essays) 1900

Progress of Art in the XIX Century (history) 1902

The House of Usna [as Fiona Macleod] (drama) [first publication] 1903

Literary Geography (essays) 1904

The Winged Destiny: Studies in the Spiritual History of the Gael [as Fiona Macleod] (essays, short stories, and prose poetry) 1904

Where the Forest Murmurs [as Fiona Macleod] (essays) 1906

The Writings of Fiona Macleod. 7 vols. [as Fiona Macleod] (poetry, short stories, novels, prose poetry, allegory, essays, and dramas) 1909-10

Selected Writings of William Sharp. 5 vols. (poetry, short stories, essays, and dramas) 1912

*Sharp wrote these works under various pseudonyms and published the volume as a magazine.

Oscar Wilde (essay date 1888)

[*Wilde was one of the most prominent Irish literary figures of the late nineteenth century. Perhaps more than any author of his time, he is identified with the nineteenth-century "art for art's sake" movement, which defied the contemporary trend that subordinated art to ethical instruction. For Wilde, originality of form was the only enduring quality of a work of art. In the following excerpt, Wilde reviews* Romantic Ballads and Poems of Phantasy, *attacking the theoretical approach to poetry outlined in Sharp's preface to the volume.*]

Mr. William Sharp takes himself very seriously, and has written a preface to his **Romantic Ballads and Poems of Phantasy,** which is, on the whole, the most interesting part of his volume. We are all, it seems, far too cultured and lack robustness. There are those amongst us, says Mr. Sharp, who would prefer a dexterously turned triolet to such apparently uncouth measures as "Thomas the Rhymer," or the ballad of "Clerk Saunders," and who "would rather listen to the drawing-room music of the Villanelle than to the wild harp-playing by the mill-dams o' Binnorie, or the sough of the night wind o'er drumly Allan water." Such an expression as "the drawing-room music of the Villanelle" is not very happy, and I cannot imagine anyone with the smallest pretensions to culture preferring a dexterously turned triolet to a fine imaginative ballad, as it is only the Philistine who ever dreams of comparing works of art that are absolutely different in motive, in treatment, and in form. If English Poetry is in danger— and, according to Mr. Sharp, the poor nymph is in a very critical state—what she has to fear is not the fascination of dainty metre or delicate form, but the predominance of the intellectual spirit over the spirit of beauty. Lord Tennyson dethroned Wordsworth as a literary influence, and later on Mr. Swinburne filled all the mountain valleys with echoes of his own song. The influence to-day is that of Mr. Browning. And as for the triolets, and the rondels, and the careful study of metrical subtleties, these things are merely the signs of a desire for perfection in small things, and of the recognition of poetry as an art. They have had certainly one good result—they have made our minor poets readable, and have not left us entirely at the mercy of geniuses.

But, says Mr. Sharp, everyone is far too literary; even Rossetti is too literary. What we want is simplicity and directness of utterance; these should be the dominant characteristics of poetry. Well, is that quite so certain? Are simplicity and directness of utterance absolute essentials for poetry? I think not. They may be admirable for the drama, admirable for all those imitative forms of literature that claim to mirror life in its externals and its accidents, admirable for quiet narrative, admirable in their place; but their place is not everywhere. Poetry has many modes of music; she does not blow through one pipe alone. Directness of utterance is good, but so is the subtle recasting of thought into a new and delightful form. Simplicity is good, but complexity, mystery, strangeness, symbolism, obscurity even, these have their value. Indeed, properly speaking, there is no such thing as Style; there are merely styles, that is all.

One cannot help feeling also that everything that Mr. Sharp says in his preface was said at the beginning of the century by Wordsworth, only where Wordsworth called us back to nature, Mr. Sharp invites us to woo romance. Romance, he tells us, is "in the air." A new romantic movement is imminent. "I anticipate," he says, "that many of our poets, especially those of the youngest generation, will shortly turn towards the ballad as a poetic vehicle, and that the next year or two will see much romantic poetry."

The ballad! Well, Mr. Andrew Lang, some months ago, signed the death-warrant of the ballade, and—though I hope that in this respect Mr. Lang resembles the Queen in *Alice in Wonderland,* whose bloodthirsty orders were by general consent never carried into execution—it must be admitted that the number of ballades given to us by some of our poets was, perhaps, a little excessive. But the ballad? "Sir Patrick Spens," "Clerk Saunders," "Thomas the Rhymer"—are these to be our archetypes, our models, the sources of our inspiration? They are certainly great imaginative poems. In Chatterton's "Ballad of Charity," Coleridge's "Rhyme of the Ancient Mariner," the "La Belle Dame sans Merci" of Keats, the "Sister Helen" of Rossetti, we can see what marvellous works of art the spir-

it of old romance may fashion. But to preach a spirit is one thing, to propose a form is another. It is true that Mr. Sharp warns the rising generation against imitation. A ballad, he reminds them, does not necessarily denote a poem in quatrains and in antique language. But his own poems, as I think will be seen later on, are, in their way, warnings and show the danger of suggesting any definite "poetic vehicle." And further, are simplicity and directness of utterance really the dominant characteristics of these old imaginative ballads that Mr. Sharp so enthusiastically, and, in some particulars, so wisely praises? It does not seem to me to be so. We are always apt to think that the voices which sang at the dawn of poetry were simpler, fresher, and more natural than ours, and that the world which the early poets looked at, and through which they walked, had a kind of poetical quality of its own, and could pass, almost without changing, into song. The snow lies thick now upon Olympus, and its scarped sides are bleak and barren, but once, we fancy, the white feet of the Muses brushed the dew from the anemones in the morning, and at evening came Apollo to sing to the shepherds in the vale. But in this we are merely lending to other ages what we desire, or think we desire, for our own. Our historical sense is at fault. Every century that produces poetry is, so far, an artificial century, and the work that seems to us the most natural and simple product of its time is probably the result of the most deliberate and self-conscious effort. For Nature is always behind the age. It takes a great artist to be thoroughly modern.

Let us turn to the poems, which have really only the preface to blame for their somewhat late appearance. The best is undoubtedly **"The Weird of Michael Scott,"** and these stanzas are a fair example of its power:—

> Then Michael Scott laughed long and loud:
> "Whan shone the mune ahint yon cloud
> I speered the towers that saw my birth—
> Lang, lang, sall wait my cauld grey shroud,
> Lang cauld and weet my bed o' earth!"
>
> But as by Stair he rode full speed
> His horse began to pant and bleed;
> "Win hame, win hame, my bonnie mare,
> Win hame if thou wouldst rest and feed,
> Win hame, we're nigh the House of Stair!"
>
> But, with a shrill heart-bursten yell,
> The white horse stumbled, plunged, and fell,
> And loud a summoning voice arose,
> "Is't White-Horse Death that rides frae Hell,
> Or Michael Scott that hereby goes?"
>
> "Ah, Lord of Stair, I ken ye weel!
> Avaunt, or I your saul sall steal,
> An' send ye howling through the wood
> A wild man-wolf—aye, ye maun reel
> An' cry upon your Holy Rood!"

There is a good deal of vigour, no doubt, in these lines; but one cannot help asking whether this is to be the common tongue of the future Renaissance of Romance. Are we all to talk Scotch and to speak of the moon as the "mune," and the soul as the "saul"? I hope not. And yet if this Renaissance is to be a vital, living thing, it must have its linguistic side. Just as the spiritual development of music, and the artistic development of painting, have always been accompanied, if not occasioned, by the discovery of some new instrument or some fresh medium, so, in the case of any important literary movement, half of its strength resides in its language. If it does not bring with it a rich and novel mode of expression, it is doomed either to sterility or to imitation. Dialect, archaisms, and the like, will not do. Take, for instance, another poem of Mr. Sharp's, a poem which he calls **"The Deith-Tide"**:—

> The weet saut wind is blawing
> Upon the misty shore;
> As, like a stormy snawing,
> The deid go streaming o'er:—
> The wan drown'd deid sail wildly
> Frae out each drumly wave:
> It's O and O for the weary sea
> And O for a quiet grave.

This is simply a very clever *pastiche,* nothing more, and our language is not likely to be permanently enriched by such words as "weet," "saut," "blawing," and "snawing." Even "drumly," an adjective of which Mr. Sharp is so fond that he uses it both in prose and verse, seems to me to be hardly an adequate basis for a new romantic movement.

However, Mr. Sharp does not always write in dialect. **"The Song of Allan"** can be read without any difficulty, and **"Phantasy"** can be read with pleasure. They are both very charming poems in their way, and none the less charming because the cadences of the one recall "Sister Helen," and the motive of the other reminds us of "La Belle Dame sans Merci." But those who wish to thoroughly enjoy Mr. Sharp's poems should not read his preface; just as those who approve of the preface should avoid reading the poems. I cannot help saying that I think the preface a great mistake. The work that follows it is quite inadequate and there seems little use in heralding a dawn that rose long ago, and proclaiming a Renaissance whose first-fruits, if we are to judge them by any high standard of perfection, are of so ordinary a character. (pp. 33-41)

> *Oscar Wilde, "A Note on Some Modern Poets," in his* The Writings of Oscar Wilde, *1907. Reprint by Doubleday, Page & Company, 1923, pp. 23-50.*

W. B. Yeats   (essay date 1896)

[*The leading figure of the Irish Literary Renaissance and a major poet in twentieth-century literature, Yeats was also an active critic of his contemporaries' works. As a critic he judged the works of others according to his own poetic values of sincerity, passion, and vital imagination. In the following essay, Yeats favorably reviews* From the Hills of Dream, *praising its intensity and its mastery of Gaelic legend.*]

In France, where every change of literary feeling brings with it a change of literary philosophy, the great change of our time is believed to be a return to the subjective. We no longer wish to describe nature like the "nature poets," or to describe society like the "realists," but to make our work a mirror, where the passions and desires and ideals of our own minds can cast terrible or beautiful images. If the French are right—and every new book which seems at all of our time is, I think, a proof that they are—we are at the beginning of a franker trust in passion and in beauty than was possible to the poets who put their trust in the external world and its laws. Some of the poems in *From the Hills of Dream* would have been almost impossible ten years ago. For ten years ago Miss Macleod would have asked herself, "Is this a valuable and a sober criticism upon life?" and we should probably have lost one of the most inspired, one of the most startling, one of the most intense poems of our time, her incomparable **"Prayer of Women."**

> O spirit that broods upon the hills,
> And moves upon the face of the deep,
> And is heard in the wind,
> Save us from the desire of men's eyes.
>
> . . . . .
>
> Ah, hour of the hours,
> When he looks at our hair and sees it is grey;
> And at our eyes and sees they are dim;
> And at our lips, straightened out with long pain;
> And at our breasts, fallen and seared like a barren hill;
> And at our hands, worn with toil!
> Ah, hour of the hours,
> When, seeing, he seeth all the bitter ruin and wreck of
>   us—
> All save the violated womb that curses him—
> All save the heart that forbeareth . . . for pity—
> All save the living brain that condemneth him.
>
> . . . . .
>
> O spirit and the nine angels who watch us,
> And Thy Son and Mary Virgin,
> Heal us of the wrong of man:
> We whose breasts are weary with milk
> Cry, cry to Thee, O Compassionate.

This poem was, I understand, first written in Gaelic, and Miss Macleod is always best when she writes under a Gaelic and legendary and mythological influence. Emotions which seem vague or extravagant when expressed under the influence of modern literature, cease to be vague and extravagant when associated with ancient legend and mythology, for legend and mythology were born out of man's longing for the mysterious and the infinite. When Miss Macleod writes of "the white Peace" which "lies not on the sunlit hill," nor "on the sunlit plain," nor "on any running stream," but comes sometimes into the soul of man as "the moonlight of a perfect Peace," I find her thought too vague greatly to move or impress me; but when she writes of "the four white winds of the world, whose father the golden sun is, whose mother the wheeling moon is, the north and the south and the east and the west," and of "the three dark winds of the world; the chill breath of the grave, the breath from the depth of the sea," and "the breath of to-morrow," I am altogether moved and impressed. I feel, indeed, throughout this book two influences—a Gaelic influence, which Miss Macleod has mastered and remoulded, and an influence from modern literature which she has not yet been able to master and mould; and this is, perhaps, why *From the Hills of Dream* seems to me so much more unequal, so much more experimental, than *The Sin-Eater* or *The Washer of the Ford.* Many of the poems which have the strongest Gaelic influence, and therefore the most authentic inspiration, are in wild and irregular measures; and this is a pity, because the best critics are not convinced that wild and irregular measures are perfectly legitimate. The poems in rhyme and in regular measures which seem to be latest in date are, however, a great advance upon their fellows, and have occasional passages of a charming phantasy, like the second, third, fourth, and fifth stanzas in **"The Moon Child,"** or of a beautiful intensity, like this passage, which expresses something almost beyond the range of expression.

> She had two men within the palm, the hollow of her hand;
> She takes their souls and blows them forth as idle drifted sand;
> And one falls back upon her breast that is his quiet home,
> And one goes out into the night and is as wind-blown foam;
> And when she sees the sleep of one, ofttimes she riseth there,
> And looks into the outer dusk and calleth soft and fair.
>
> (pp. 92-3)

W. B. Yeats, "Miss Fiona Macleod as a Poet," in The Bookman, *London, Vol. XI, No. 63, December, 1896, p. 92-3.*

Ernest Rhys   (essay date 1900)

[*Rhys was an English poet, novelist, editor, and critic. He is perhaps best known for his work as the editor of* Everyman's Library, *a series of more than 1,000 volumes that offered inexpensive reprints of world literary classics as well as some original works of critical commentary. Although his editorial achievements tend to overshadow his writings, Rhys was also a poet and novelist whose works reflect the influence of the writers of the Celtic Revival. Along with W. B. Yeats and T. W. Rolleston, Rhys was a founding member of the Rhymers' Club, a group of Irish, Welsh, and English poets whose works were influenced by the French Symbolist movement and who opposed the increasing preoccupation in Victorian poetry with science, history, and religion. In the following essay, Rhys discusses the mystic and Celtic qualities of the works of "Fiona Macleod."*]

It is not eight years since **Pharais** appeared, and it is too soon to attempt a map of the illusive region into which it first led us, the continually changing region of Miss Fiona Macleod's fantasy. A romance written by a mystic, so **Pharais** might be considered. Its human people lived in a conditional Paradise, hung a little nearer the sky than common earth; a people subject to beings more vital and powerful than themselves: sea and wind, the elements and the spirits of the elements. **The Mountain Lovers** followed; a pastoral, exquisite in colour, but too unusual, too much haunted with a mountain wildness for the crowd. Later books, stories like **The Sin-Eater** and **The Dan-nan-Ron,** showed, with no want of originality, more of what may be called the dramatic probabilities, and of certain qualities, vivid and poignant, which were taken to promise a new Gaelic saga—perhaps a new kind of tale-telling altogether. Was the tale-teller then, dear to so many who care nothing for high fantasy, to grow in this writer, and the mystic to decline? When the reply to this came, it was in **The Dominion of Dreams,** whose very title is a challenge to the ordinary intelligence, and the realist, in us. Last of all, we have **The Divine Adventure,** a tale, an intense fable of the spirit, set among the same scenes, in which all the vanities of the fabulist are left out. After which, while drawn to go on speculating, the reader would be bold who would set bounds to the writings of so incalculable a writer.

The poet and tale-writer who is at heart a mystic is, at any time, a rare comer, and the writer who, writing in English, attempts like Miss Fiona Macleod and Mr. W. B. Yeats to bend the archaic Celtic stock, which is both stubborn and subtle, to the modern usage, is come on an errand of miracle. There is a superb tradition for the new English poet who is content to follow in the lyric line of the great masters before him, and to add his grain or more of originality to the forms they used and the kind of subjects they chose; and there is an inspiring tradition for the mystic to-day who will turn to Germany or the south, to forerunners like Novalis and Jacob Boehme, or to St. Francis and St. Martin, or the Catholic Mystics late and early, for his masters. But for the writer on Celtic themes, who, not using their natural tongue, has to employ names that are unfamiliar, allusions blunted in translation, and legends confused between the Pagan and Christian colours they bear, the road is much harder. How Mr. Yeats has succeeded in triumphing over its difficulties, as a visionary, and a poet in art, we have seen: but even now he has scarcely had his full tribute. Miss Macleod has come later upon the scene; but it is only by her latest work that she, in turn, can hope—or so one fears—to have her recognition, and be known even by outsiders as more than the "obscure chronicler of obscure things" that she termed herself in her dedication of **Pharais** to an English friend.

It is only through her latest writings, **"The Divine Adventure,"** the essay toward the writing of what she terms a "spiritual history" of Iona, and some shorter pieces, that one can hope to know what the writer thinks of her region of thought and its possibilities. In the Iona essay and in the shorter pieces there are many significant things which count among those intended to let readers into the secrets of a writer's writing craft, philosophy, sense of art, and what not besides. In these pages she offers many luminous little asides, suggestions for the better understanding that delays perhaps to arrive between author and reader, or considerations of the Celtic habit in literature; and affords in this way a tentative *apologia* for her life, and its imaginative expression.

"For myself," she writes, in the essay which she has entitled, all short, **"Celtic"**—"I would say that I do not seek to reproduce ancient Celtic presentments of tragic beauty and tragic fate, but do seek in nature and in life, and in the swimming thought of timeless imagination, for the kind of beauty that the old Celtic poets discovered and uttered." And she continues: "There were poets and myth-makers in those days; and to-day we may be sure that a new mythus is being woven, though we may no longer humanise and euhemerise the forces of Nature and her silent and secret processes, for the mythopoeic faculty is not only a primitive instinct, but a spiritual need." To find a sensitive instrument for this need grows harder to-day at every turn of the imagination. With the currents of thought setting altogether in other directions, how is the imagination in this kind to get stimulus, and gather its associations, and fashion its other-world; how is it to build its region about it? The author of **Pharais** has solved this matter by going to the western isles and the sea-confines of the Hebrides, where the smoke of cities, and the dust of the mob, have not yet destroyed the lingering vestiges, beautiful and alack! perishable, of the Ionic Gael.

What inestimable good-fortune for any poet or mystic today to be native to a region, full of the sea's mystery and mountain charm and the memory of the old Gaelic world, whose natural wildness is not yet lost, whose wonder has not been pricked by the pens of the disillusionist. Not everyone cares, it is true, for the wild scenic effect of Iona. Montalembert, who visited it when he was writing his *Monks of the West,* thought it only desolate. "The gloom and shine of the mountains that throw their shadow on the sea," which Miss Fiona Macleod never tires of describing . . . "the haunted shore which none loves save with passion . . . the land of hills and glens and heroes, as one of the ancient poets called it, *Tir nam Beann s'nan gleann' s'nan ghaisgach*": these did not appeal to him. But many of us will remember the reproach of the late Duke of Argyll and overlord of Iona, as he recalled the stigma which Montalembert—a master of the Celtic picturesque—had put upon its seascape. And even Montalembert must have given way before Miss Macleod's fervour of delight in the illimitable pale wave, the dusk of the underwater, the spell-bound silences of these island places, and the unfathomable gulfs of sky over unfathomable gulfs of sea. Nor is this all. For her it is not a mere rapture of the picturesque. If she hails the delicate pomp of summer skies, when that comes to a region often austere, and vexed by wet winds and cold mists, she loves the place, apart from its golden moods and purple splendours. She loves this island world for itself, as one of its strange children, Alison Achanna, "the anointed man," loved it, with a kind of obsession, which made the mournful, stony places, and the bleak sodden pastures of Eilanmore, even in the autumn rains, into holy ground.

And so it comes that Miss Macleod, in her essay on **"Iona,"** making pause for a confession, tells us that there is another Iona than the chroniclers have known or the gazetteers have put into their Scotland. It is the place of heart's desire, the white isle of the Gaelic dreamer, which none can understand who does not see it as played upon by the cross lights of Pagan and Christian tradition, as coloured by the blended and changing colours of Paganism, and romance, and spiritual beauty. And even this is not all. For there is yet an Iona that is more than a Gaelic Mecca, more than a place illumined by the desires of the world; the Iona that is the little home of the heart, "that, if we will it so, is a mirror of your heart and mine."

This is, one may think, to make a transcendent claim for any spot of earth. But this is the feeling, tender, human, uncontrolled and hardly controllable, which, called up by other less famously alluring spots of earth in the western islands and highlands, has lent warmth to her fable, warm life to her dreams. This intense feeling for place is the common heritage, you may say, of her race, and not enough in itself to account for a new imagination of life, wider than that of any particular people, and as essential as any vision, æsthetic or spiritual, must be, to appeal powerfully to the universal human spirit. To be a neo-Celt merely, with a passion for one's inherited corner of the world and its old association, and with a power to express it, is not enough. It is, in fact, to another intensive element in Miss Fiona Macleod's writing that one must turn to account for the last impulse of her work, which helps to give it the effect of being more than a highly original literary entertainment. In all her work one seems to trace it; in her later work alone it becomes quite clear, and is consciously presented. It is, in brief, a new emotion of the woman's ancient predicament, and of her love and its revolt against fate, added to a strange conviction of a mysterious predestined part to be played by her hereafter in the moving drama of spirit and sense. It would be impossible, obviously, to declare in passing the final virtue of such a message, veiled as it is in every device of allegory and romance. But of the emotion with which it is presented, and returned to, and of its quickening power upon the writer's imagination, none that reads can doubt. It is the secret, no doubt, of much that in Miss Fiona Macleod's work is, at a first glance, inchoate, over-wrought, too impassioned for pure art; and it explains, too, the presence in her writings of the ideal St. Bridget, whose neo-Celtic recall may prove to be the first word of a New Mysticism.

As for the form of her writings, and the Gaelic colour which she uses so profusely—too profusely, it may seem to the critical Saxon, at times—these add very much to the difficulty of estimating them. There would seem to be a very deliberate theory on the writer's part of her whole craft as a writer; but, in spite of her account of it, it is not easy to say at once how it acquired its particular bias. One traces in it foreign influences—the sensation and impressionism of the later French school, the phrase of M. Maeterlinck, the cadence of a Rossetti, the rhythm even of Mr. Yeats—along with those things that can be termed Gaelic and native. But the result is there, vital and individual and, allowing for the earlier violence of style and for mannerisms which in the later writings tend to disappear, harmonious and natural, one feels, to the writer's habit of thought, and to a temperament restless, emotional, intense.

To understand her method as a writer of tales and parables, it is necessary to turn to the archaic folk she has summoned out of the old Gaelic world. Long ago, Eugenius Philalethes (the brother of Henry Vaughan the Silurist) and other mystics talked of the alchemy by which a flower might be re-created from its ash and made to bloom again. In art it is possible to "quick the dead," as an old writer termed it: into their ancient memory blow imagination and the new emotion of a living heart, and the thing is done. But so passionate are the actors of the old Gaelic theme in Miss Fiona Macleod's pages—Scathach the Sad Queen, and Connla the Harper—that it seems possible to urge too much flame under the ribs of death. Like Heine, like Hugo at his best, their imaginer and new creator is in her historical recall only an historian of the heart. Do not be misled by her archaic colours, and her splendid fantasy of an heroic Queen of the Isles; of a harper with a demon in his harp, like Cravetheen, or of a Skald like Ulric, into thinking you have there the real presence of a barbaric prime. That life, that presence, are never to be recaptured. An adumbration of their going and coming, the shadow of a shadow, may be thrown upon one's canvas and painted there; but the picture must be warmed again with a different colour, the umber have a modern crimson added, if it is to reach your current vision. And this Miss Fiona Macleod has done.

Here is the portrait in full fantasy of Scathach, an Amazon of the Hebrides in the barbaric days. And first her face: "Pale as wax, and of a strange and terrible beauty. They could not look long in her eyes, which were black as darkness, with a red flame wandering in it. Her lips were curled delicately, and were like thin sudden lines of blood in the still whiteness of her face." And for her form:

> She was tall, and of great strength, taller than Connla, stronger than Ulric. Long black hair fell upon her shoulders, which, with her breast and thighs, were covered with pale bronze. A red and green cloak was over the right shoulder, and was held by a great brooch of gold. A yellow torque of gold was round her neck. A three-pointed torque of gold was on her head. Her legs were swathed with deerskin thongs and her feet were in coverings of cowskins stained red.

There is all the particularity of the old romancer in this latter description—the romancer who has his eye on the colour and the romantic circumstance. But in the "strange and terrible beauty" one detected a tell-tale generic touch. And now listen:—

"You die to-night," she says to Connla and Ulric, her captives. Later they appeal to her, through one of her women, in vain.

"It is because she loved Cuchullin," the woman said; "and he was a poet, and sang songs, and made music as you do; . . . and you have put memories into the mind of Scathach. But she will listen to you harping and singing before you die."

In all this intense conception of the Sad Queen, confronting her own tragedy with that of another, seeking solace for her inconsolable heart, one cannot help feeling that the true emotion is a modern one, not only allied to the revolt of woman against the tyranny of fate and time, and the order devised by man, but felt by the writer herself so profoundly, so passionately, that in Scathach she is compelled to work out her own problem, only giving it in the end, as poets do, an allegorical solution.

Scathach slays Connla because she loves Cuchullin, and Connla is but Cuchullin in another taking, to whom death is as nothing, since love is everything and its loss is death and its gain life.

"Take Connla the Harper," she says, "because he has known all things, knowing that little infinite thing, and has no more to know, and is beyond us, and lay him upon the sands with his face to the stars, and put red brands upon his naked breast, till his heart bursts and he dies."

With that the emotion called up by the fable is suddenly eased and satisfied; for Connla—not for Scathach, who will never be satisfied. Scathach, indeed, recalls the lines from Miss Macleod's extraordinary poetic cycle of the passion and sorrow of women, in which we are told of the fate of those who are doomed—

> To see the fairness of the body passing,
> To see the beauty wither, the sweet colour
> Fade, the coming of the wintry lines
> Upon pale faces chilled with idle longing,
> The slow subsidence of the tides of living.
> To feel all this, and know the desolate sorrow,
> Of the pale place of all defeated dreams,
> And to cry out with aching lips, and vainly,
> And to cry out with aching heart, and vainly,
> And to cry out with aching brain, and vainly,
> And to cry out with aching soul, and vainly,
> To cry, cry, cry, with passionate heartbreak, sobbing
> To the dim wondrous shape of Love Retreating.

In Scathach, we have but this voice, given a different inflection of barbaric pride. But if she were all barbaric she would not move us as she does. Such as she is, she lets us see the working of the favourite fable in Miss Macleod's fantasy, whose conception is always at bottom the same; two people, man and woman, Alasdair and Lora, Alan and Sorcha, Ula and Ulad, Scathach and Cuchullin—in the one predicament: striving and crying to deliver their love from obstacles of Nature and time, and seeing in their fellow mortals and the elements alike but the demons and angels that can destroy or save. In this way the people become passions, the elements become personified: the seals become men: the ninth wave becomes a demon: the trees imprison the spirits of lost creatures. Auguries and omens hang on every cloud. The sand is the piteous dust of dead beauties; the ocean is the blood of slain princes.

As with her archaic Gael, so with her Gaels of to-day. With some vivid exceptions, they are personifications rather than actual persons. Take the extraordinary story, one of the Achanna series, **"The Dan-nan-Ron."** Its heroine is a girl of Eilanmore—Anne Gillespie. Her lover, Manus MacCodrum, comes of a small clan in North Uist—dark skinned, brown, among a race of fair islanders, and known as the Sliochd nan Ron—the Clan of the Seals. Anne lives with the Achannas, her three cousins, and one of them bearing the name (which it costs one a shiver to accept) of Gloom, plays on the *feadan,* a primitive flute, the strange tune of the Dan-nan-Ron, the Song of the Seal; which becomes a kind of leit-motiv in the tale. The three Achannas bitterly resent Anne's going from their house; and here is tragedy's excuse. They protest, but it is of no avail. And though Marcus Achanna meets his doom at her lover's hands within an hour, and Gloom Achanna attempts revenge with the aid of his sinister *feadan,* she sails away that night, knowing nothing of the murder, and is married to Manus. But evil fate follows them—a fate of which Gloom Achanna with his pipe is the personification. Within the year she dies in childbed; and a melancholy akin to madness descends on Manus MacCodrum. Then the *feadan* of Gloom Achanna begins to haunt him again with the Dan-nan-Ron; and under its spell, he is drawn to the sea and to the Great Reef of the Seals. The last scene is extraordinary. Like one possessed—laughing, screaming, gesticulating—he is seen running towards the rocks and the reef, where, with clenched fists, naked, mad, dehumanised, he advances on a bull-seal, who pins him to the rock. The other seals join in with fury and all but tear him to pieces; and when at last his torn body is dragged from the reef and disappears in the sea, it is amid a crowd of leaping, struggling seals, "their fangs red with human gore." Last touch of all, Gloom Achanna is seen turning away from the reef, his revenge accomplished, playing on his *feadan* as he leaves the sea.

In this pale transcript from a bold original, much is overlooked and much tempered. There is a barbaric note in the account of Manus's death not often found in literature. The word "gore" in the phrase quoted is indicative. We are spared no red stroke of the butcher in the transcendent fantasy of the romancer. It would be hard to find any recent literary creation where imaginative beauty and sheer physical sensation are so mingled.

Gloom Achanna comes and goes continuously in Miss Macleod's pages, and in all he is the dramatic shadow of that evil destiny, which lies in wait in the Hebrides as it does everywhere else. He is the Satan, the Mephistopheles of this sea-play, whose rôle it is to wile the virtue and life-principle out of others. He uses his magic pipe and its fatal tunes as if he had misread Cornelius Agrippa, when that subtle master wrote: "Birds are allured with Pipes. Music hath caused friendship between men and Dolphins. The sound of the harp doth lead up and down the Hyperborean Swans."

Another personification that might be set beside this Gaelic Mephistopheles, and one freer from sensation and hot colours, is that of the wild child-spirit, Oona, in *The Mountain Lovers.* As Gloom Achanna pipes, so she dances and sings, and at her music the mountain and forest of Ben Iolair sigh in satisfaction and lend their ears; and Nial, the dwarf, the soulless man, begins to long for a soul:

> Wild fawn, wild fawn
> Hast seen the Green Lady?
> The merles are singing,
> The ferns are springing,
> The little leaves whisper from dusk to dawn—
> "Green Lady, Green Lady!"
> The little leaves whisper from dusk to dawn—
> "Wild fawn, wild fawn!"

The Mountain Lovers is another romance of that ecstasy of nature which in Miss Fiona Macleod's writings supplies the intervals which other tale-writers might fill with conversation and commoner reports of men. To take it up after some carpet comedy, or cloak-and-rapier romance, or after the hearty humours and realities of the other Scotland of Mr. Barrie or "Ian Maclaren," is to be startled by the mixed passion and innocence of its pages. Dawn, sunrise, moonrise, the wind, the storm: these are its events. Sunset opens the book with a scene in which the dancing child Oona is but the incarnation of the forest life and its changing hours:

> She was like the spirit of woodland loneliness: a lovely thing of fantasy that might recreate its beauty the next moment in a medley of sunrays, or as a floating golden light about the green boles, or as a wind-flower swaying among the tree-roots with its own exquisite vibration of life. So elemental was she, then and there, that if she herself had passed into the rhythm of her rapt dance, and so merged into the cadence of the wind among leaves and branches, or into the remoter murmuring of the mountain burns and of the white cataracts, nothing of it would have seemed unnatural. She was as absolutely one with nature as though she were a dancing sunbeam, or the brief embodiment of the joy of the wind. . . .

> As the child danced, a human mote in that vast area of sun-splashed woodland, the light flooded in upon her scanty and ragged dress of brown homespun, from which her arms and legs emerged as the white chestnut-buds from their sheafs of amber. Her skin was of the hue and smoothness of crudded cream, where not sunburnt to the brown of the wallflower. Dark as were her heavily-lashed eyes, her hair—a mass of short curls, creeping and twisting and leaping throughout a wild and tangled waviness—was of a wonderful white-like yellow, as of the sheen of wheat on a windy August noon, or the strange amber-gold of the harvest-moon when rising through a sigh of mist. . . . To and fro, flicker-

ingly as a leaf-shadow, the small body tripped and leapt. Sometimes she raised her arms when, with tossed-back head, she sprang to one side or forward; sometimes she clapped her hands, and a smile for a moment dreamed—rather than lay—upon her face. But none seeing her could have thought she danced out of mere glee. . . . Either the child was going through this fantastic by-play for some ulterior reason, or she was wrought by an ecstasy that could be expressed only in this way. Perhaps no one who had met a glance of those wild-wood eyes could have doubted that she was rapt by an unconscious fantasy of rhythm.

It requires some courage to write like that in the day of the document novel and M. Zola; and it would be difficult to justify to any halting critic the "ulterior reason" suddenly recalled to overweight the conclusion of this exquisite scene. Purely idyllic here, later in the story the child Oona takes part in a dramatic idyl, which is one of the most imaginative things in all the range of Miss Macleod's romance, but which is no more likely to conciliate the unbeliever. It is where the blind man Torcall, overtaken by drowsiness, is led by Oona through the forest to the side of the sleeping woman Anabal, whom he had once loved, and learnt bitterly to hate. There, as he too sinks to sleep, Oona joins the hands of the two sleepers, and the woman thinks it the hand of her dead husband. But the scene must be read, to be felt. A Greek dramatist might have conceived it; only a neo-Celtic romancer could have written it. Its conclusion is as sensational and as remorseless as anything in Hugo. In all this, however, it is the passions and emotions that seem most to live, and seize like dæmonic things on men and women; the men and women are but the instruments and symbols of fate, love and hate, spent desire, unavailing sorrow, and tragic death. But death is not the end. Death is but an episode in the region of Ula and Ulad.

In succeeding stories, if the method, as was said, became more real, more humanly devised, the allegorist and the fabulist were still there. It was in *The Dominion of Dreams* that the two tendencies at last took an unmistakable form, and were definitely set in order, and put into a kind of artistic apposition by the writer's own conscious device. In one section were stories, **"By the Yellow Moonrock"** and **"Children of the Dark Star,"** for example, where Hebridean earth still dusted the stage, and where Gloom Achanna was tied to reality by an unreal man of letters. In the next section, the Dreamer and Mystic ruled absolute, and led one on in the steps of a visionary like Ivor M'Iain, to the "low line where the moors crept into the sky," and so to the haunted region of the Wells of Peace and Ulad the Lonely.

> There is a land of Dream,
> I have trodden its golden ways,
> I have seen its amber light. . . .

But there is an Isle of Emain beyond the sea, and there is a "Distant Country of Splendour and Terror" beyond even the region of dreams; the country of which we read in one of these piteous episodes of Love's "untold story." Here is a fragment of it, broken off to show how (as if in a difficult recall of things too bitter for remembrance) the teller of the story has conceived the picture of the two lovers, fateful "bodily images of a flame that was not mortal, and of desires that were not finite." It is the most intimate chapter in all this book of the heart:—

> Year by year their love deepened. I know of no love like theirs; it was, in truth, a flame. . . . How could she tell what she was to him? He could not tell her what words fail to tell. But she knew her own heart; she heard it in those silences where women listen. . . . They turned the same way, not knowing it. How could they know, being blind? Blind children they were. He feared the flame would consume them. She feared it would consume itself. Therein lay the bitterness. But for her, being a woman, the depths were deeper. He had his dreams. . . . When, at last, the end came—a strange, a tragic, an almost incredible end, perhaps, for love did not veer, and passion was not slain, but translated to a starry dream, and every sweet and lovely intercourse was theirs still—the suffering was too great to be borne. . . . She loved to the edge of death by will. Will can control the mortal things of love. She put her frail strength into the balance, then her memories, then her dreams. At the last she had already put all in the balance, all but her soul. That, too, she had now put there. . . . They lived long after this great change; but that came to her no more which had gone. For him, he grew slowly to understand a love more great than his. His had not known the innermost flame—that is pure fire.

The spectator of this extraordinary soul's tragedy loses much by having it reduced to its elements. It is a mystery, of which some inkling is given in those subtle lines of a metaphysical poem that used to be attributed to Shakespeare:—

> So they lov'd, as love in twain
> Had the essence but in one:
> Two distincts, division none:
> Number there in love was slain.

But Love's Martyr, in this different way of love, and as a result of the breaking by one of its two actors of some occult, but imperious spiritual law—brings us this mysterious sequel—that while for her, who was most the Martyr, there was a Death-in-life, for him there was a new deliverance of the second self which has soul, will, and imagination apart from the ordinary self of body, mind, and sense.

Having brought us thus far on the road, it is easy for the fashioner of these things to carry us on to the top and crest of her mount of vision. It is but a step in fact from the **"Distant Country"** to the **"Divine Adventure."** The last words of the passage quoted above become the refrain of the extended parable also, which leaves the mystery of love—love, that is, between man and woman—and turns to the mystery of life and death. It is written with a solemn tenderness, an eloquence of the heart, such as could only come to a writer who had known the burden of the heart's desire and bitter loss, and the rest. There is little or nothing in it of the early manner of the writer. The old glut of images has been eased; the early excess of fantasy, that fury of the pen, which hurled words like stones at every image, everything described, that too urgent originality, have given way to the reticence and the calm of other planes of thought.

It is to **The Divine Adventure,** then, as was suggested at the opening of these pages, that one has to turn for the fru-

ition of the Gaelic tree of mystery, which was first set in **Pharais.** It is the grave dispassionate sequel to those legends of love's passion and fury, and consolation in the natural world. It would never have been written, had they not been written first; had they not been filled in particular with the emotion, which has been pointed out in them, of the woman's love, and life-in-death, and restless seeking for symbols to express herself, her earthly sorrows, her spiritual aspiration. Its accent is like little in the familiar voice of literature, though once and again it might recall to Cymric ears that of an old mystic, Morgan Llwyd, where he says, discoursing of Paradise with the voice of Lazarus: "My natural life was put out like a candle or as if one did fall asleep into sensible visions of the night. I found myself full of thoughts, but very quiet, having no lust, or will, or motion of my own."

But poor Morgan Llwyd, a poet born out of time to a harsh birthright, set the edge of his imagination against the beauty of the visible and revealed world. It is a truer mysticism which holds with the writer of **The Divine Adventure** that the soul has to learn to become "one with the wind and the grass and with all that lives and moves, to take its life from the root of the body, and its green life from the mind, and its flower and fragrance from what it may of itself obtain, not only from this world, but from its own dews, its own rainbows, dawn stars and evening stars." In this way the Body becomes the friend, and not as with the ascetics, the clog and foul garment, of the Soul.

The old mysticism, Catholic or Puritan, was often shadowed by the old asceticism; and the last word of the old asceticism went to the decrying and misconceiving of the beauty and wonder of the Woman, a word whose echo we have heard, indeed, in the corridors of a different philosophy as lately as Schopenhauer and Nietzsche. The new mysticism, as it lurks in these fables and parables of a neo-Celtic dreamer, is more human. It is filled and quickened to life by the imagination of Woman's earthly and Spiritual Beauty, her Divine and natural Mystery—whether it be a St. Bride of the Isles, or a Sorcha dying in the bitterest way of Motherhood. It is in a more tender sense of Nature, as seen through the eyes of a Woman's longing, and in the vision of Motherhood, that it gains its emotion, and finds its spiritual key to the interpretation of the revealed world. Whether it is to serve as the vision of the older mystics has served—whether it, in its turn, is to gain or to suffer from its attempt to expand the natural imagery into the supernatural—it is yet far too early to say. In the writings of Miss Fiona Macleod, if it has urged at times a too strenuous impulse toward figurative thought, it has tended both to vivify to marvellous new life, and to distort a little, at last, the beautiful mythology of the ancient Gaelic world; and this alike in the romantic memory and in the spiritual recall of its heroes and saints, and its fateful, beautiful women.

But this is to do an injustice, in the end, to a rare imagination, whose working it is more easy to wonder at than altogether to understand. It is well to remember that the writer of **Pharais** and **The Mountain Lovers, The Laughter of Peterkin,** and the **Barbaric Tales,** and the writer of many of the rhymes and so-called runes which fill the pages of **From the Hills of Dream,** would count as a poet and talewriter of great originality if there were no other claim to make. Lately too, the Stage Society made an interesting attempt, without, perhaps, quite understanding all the difficulties of it, to put on the stage of the Globe Theatre Miss Macleod's play and refrain of the *House of Usna;* which suggests again that her aims are not to end only in allegory and in subtle Essays of the Soul. But Love and Death, Destiny and the Fear of Death, were the burden too of this stage-fantasy of Concobar and the loss of Deirdre the Beautiful. Great emotions were its men; passions and cries on the wind were its women. And when Duach spoke to Concobar, "O King, there is no evil done upon the world that the wind does not bring back to the feet of him who made it," the hearer could not fail to hear in it the accent, full of fate and disaster, that he had heard in *Darthool and the Sons of Usna,* and to feel that the search for a dramatic form was not likely to alter much the imagination of the writer.

And as for attempting to penetrate the other mystery, which seems at intervals to have troubled the polite detectives of literature, the secret of the writer's personality, that would be as out of place here, as it is, after all, unnecessary. Enough if we know that these dreams and fables of Iona and the western isles were not concocted in Kensington, but are authentic in the sense that they have the salt airs that the Achannas tasted genuinely blowing through their keen pages.

"I have no liking," wrote their author in a letter once,

> for personal publicity. My writings are for the unknown public, not myself. . . . My life is mainly spent in the Western Highlands and Isles, and save for a week or so now and again in Edinburgh, I am never in towns which depress me beyond words, and which I care for only for the music that I can hear there. For the rest, I was born more than a thousand years ago, in the remote region of Gaeldom known as the Hills of Dream. There I have lived the better part of my life; my father's name was Romance, and that of my mother was Dream.

How the isles of this heritor of the old Gaelic spirit have furnished her region in art, we have seen. It would be harder to discover the process by which that region, undergoing a sea change, became like the other Pharais in the vision of St. Martin, where he "saw flowers that sounded," and "heard notes that shone." One ends, as one began, in paying tribute to the charm and natural magic, the beauty, the genius indeed, of her writings, and in trying to point to what may come to be accepted as their last errand and effect. This done, their account may best make its pause at this strange passage in the essay on **"Iona,"** which it is hardly fair to take from its context, but which appears to be the natural ending, figuratively presented, of the essayist's quest of those things, importunate and profound, whose symbol in older romance was the High Mystery of the Holy Grail:—

> It is commonly said that, if he would be heard, none should write in advance of his times. That, I do not believe. Only, it does not matter how few listen. I believe that we are close upon a great and deep spiritual change; I believe a new redemption is even now conceived of the Divine Spirit in the human heart, that is itself as a woman, broken in dreams and yet sustained in faith, patient long-suffering, looking towards home. I believe that though the Reign of Peace may be yet a long way off, it is drawing near; and that Who shall save us anew shall

come divinely as a Woman . . . but whether through mortal birth, or as an immortal breathing upon our souls, none can yet know.

> Sometimes I dream of the old prophecy that Christ shall come again upon Iona; and of that later prophecy which foretells, now as the Bride of Christ, now as the Daughter of God, now as the Divine Spirit embodied through mortal birth in a Man—the coming of a new Presence and Power; and dream that this may be upon Iona, so that the little Gaelic island may become as the little Syrian Bethlehem. But more wise it is to dream, *not of hallowed ground, but of the hallowed gardens of the soul,* wherein She shall appear white and radiant. Or that, upon the hills, where we are wandered, the Shepherdess shall call us home.

(pp. 1045-56)

Ernest Rhys, "The New Mysticism," in The Fortnightly Review, *Vol. LXVII, No. CCC-CII, June 1, 1900, pp. 1045-56.*

Katharine Tynan   (essay date 1906)

[*Tynan was an Irish poet, novelist, and critic. Although she was the author of more than a hundred novels, Tynan is remembered principally as an early member of the Celtic Revival and as a minor poet of nature and devotional lyrics. Tynan was associated with such prominent Irish literary figures as W. B. Yeats and A. E., but her work does not significantly share the characteristics of Celtic spirituality and pagan myth so prominent in the works of her contemporaries. Her literary themes more often derive from Christian legend, and she maintained an orthodox Catholicism throughout her life. In the following excerpt, Tynan reconciles the artistic identities of William Sharp and "Fiona Macleod."*]

I remember very well the arrival in April, 1894, of **Pharais,** by Fiona Macleod, which came to me with a letter, bespeaking my interest in the book, from William Sharp. I found the little book profoundly depressing; and the same, in a deeper sense, was the experience of a friend of mine whose state of health at the time made her more susceptible to the gloomy influence of the book with its dwelling upon and harking back to the subject of childbirth. **"The Chant of Women"** she found, as any impressionable woman would in the circumstances, well-nigh intolerable.

In Mr. Sharp's acknowledged **Vistas,** published about the same time by the same publisher, Frank Murray, of Derby, a series of cheerless Maeterlinckian dramatic episodes, there is also a childbirth scene.

> THE SISTER OF MERCY. Hush! for the Love of God! The woman is in labour. (*There is a sound as of someone drowning in a morass: a horrible struggling and choking.*)
>
> THE PRIEST. O God, have pity on us!
>
> THE SISTER OF MERCY. O Christ, have pity on us!
>
> THE MAN. O Thou, have pity on us!
>
> THE PRIEST. (*Chanting*) O Death, where is thy sting?

THE OTHER. (*In the shadow*) In thy birth, O Life.

THE PRIEST. (*Chanting*) O Grave, where is thy Victory?

THE OTHER. (*In the shadow*) I am come. (*There is a sudden cessation of sound. The Sister of Mercy lifts something from the bed. There is a low, thin wail. . . .*)

THE SISTER OF MERCY. She is dead.

There, in some dozen lines, the whole process of birth, one of the most patient processes of nature, is supposed to be done with and over. It is as artless as the old stage device of writing on a blank background: "This is a wood"; but it is not so intentionally artless. And there is the new-born infant with "a low, thin wail"; whereas the first sound from the lungs, newly expanding and filling, is a strange flat sound more like the strangled quack of a duck than anything else one can think of. "The low, thin wail" is a convention which many writers besides William Sharp have accepted cheerfully; and that is odd enough, since any doctor, any nurse, any mother, could have turned the convention out-of-doors.

Over that scene, with its grotesque accompaniments of chanting priests and the like, I must have murmured something like what my friend said over the opening sentence of *Pharais;* but I never thought to compare the two, although I read them within a short time of each other.

Vistas must have marked the passing over of William Sharp into Fiona Macleod. It is easy enough now to see the bridge in it, with one's later knowledge.

Of course it was a day when there was a little bad fashion of dragging questions of sex into everything literary, and one was not surprised at the predominance of the sexual interest in *Vistas.* In fact, the commonness of it must have put one off the scent, for when one found the work of Fiona Macleod sharing the same quality it was nothing unusual. I suppose it was due to the multiplicity of Mr. Sharp's doings that he failed to verify facts so easily verified.

So far as I know, William Sharp's work, before *Vistas,* had few qualities to impress themselves on the mind. There were some twelve years between *The Human Inheritance* and *The Flower o' the Vine,* years which had held all manner of work, books on art, biographies, boys' stories, novels, a deal of editing: yet in *Flower o' the Vine* he had come no nearer to the achievement he reached as Fiona Macleod than he had done twelve years before. I take up *Earth's Voices,* which followed two years after *The Human Inheritance.* It is not at all a distinguished book. It is quite creditable flowing verse, the verse of a man loving beauty and literature, but rather as a *dilettante* than as an artist. I take a passage at random which seems quite representative:—

All day she lay there like a flower
Rent from its place by the wind's power
And broken: nor as time waned fast
And the fierce tempest wheeled and passed,
Saw she the peaceful afternoon
Bring transient rest till once again
The changing wind and driving rain
Swept the sea-spray o'er each lagoon.

At last even of this second pain
Of silence she grew tired, and so
She rose and wandered to and fro,
Where the cold grey insistent waves
Swung heavily upon the shore,
And murmuring to herself, she said,
"O happy they that in their graves
Lie still and quiet; who feel no more
Life's bitterness: O happy dead!
Would God I in my narrow bed
Slept the long sleep."

Just a little reminiscent of *Mariana in the Moated Grange* and of a mood of Rossetti. In *Flower o' the Vine,* ten years later, we find a far greater pretension, and at times a far more marked imitativeness; for indeed one is not sure that the earlier books are imitative at all. But in *Flower o' the Vine* the imitativeness is at times quite remarkable. **"The Son of Allen"** so imitates "Sister Helen" that one almost suspects a jest.

And I saw you ride one sweet May morn,
When the missel-thrush sang on the flowering thorn,
O better if you had ne'er been born, Son of Allen.
I would that God had strangled my soul,
But living, to-night I seek one goal.

And again there occurs—

Her song it seemed far away
But oh, her kiss was sweet;
She led me to some green retreat,
And there within her arms I lay
The livelong day,—

which is certainly not an improvement on "La Belle Dame sans Merci."

At this period the real personality, the real art, which were to reveal themselves in Fiona Macleod had not come into sight in William Sharp's work. He was, so to speak, floundering in search of expression, and was speaking now in one man's manner, now in another's. For instance, in *Ecce Puella,* a gathering-up of magazine work, which appeared in 1896, the contents nearly all belonging to an earlier date, there are some things which are palpably derived from Walter Pater, and from the prose of Dante Rossetti. *The Journals of Piero Di Cosimo* might be an early Pater, an uninspired Rossetti. It is an extraordinary piece of precious writing. But in this volume also occur **"The Hill Wind,"** and **"The Sister of Compassion,"** which to some discerning minds identified William Sharp with Fiona Macleod. If I had happened to read them while yet the matter was a mystery I should have believed them to be imitative, like the other work which I have referred to. Here is a passage from **"The Hill Wind"** in the Fiona manner:—

Holding the branch downward she smiled as she saw the whiteness of her limbs beneath the tremulous arrowy leaves and the thick cluster of scarlet and vermilion berries. Whenever the gnats, whirling in aerial maze came too near, she raised the rowan branch and slowly waved them back. Suddenly . . . her arm stiffened, and she stood motionless, rigid, intent. It was the Voice of the Sea, the dull, obscure, summoning voice that whispered to the ancient Gods, and called and calls to all Powers and Dominions that have been and are; the same that is in the ears of Man as an echo; and in the House of the Soul as a rumour of a coming hour.

In this prose in the Fiona manner one gets the long, detailed word-painting which even in Fiona was apt to weary. But at the time **"The Hill Wind"** and **"The Sister of Compassion"** were written Fiona had already attained her greatest height, for in the same year was published *The Washer of the Ford,* which contains, in my opinion, in **"The Last Supper"** and **"The Fisher of Men,"** the most beautiful things Fiona ever did.

In Fiona there is the curious mixture of the Pagan and the Catholic which is very common in certain artistic temperaments, especially among the Celts. Very often to the real Catholic it is an unpleasing mixture, especially when it comes to the discussion of sacred things, and Fiona's verse, about the miracle of the Incarnation, for instance, often offends, as did the more Pagan, less Catholic, **"Passion of Brother Hilarion,"** in Mr. Sharp's *Vistas.* It is a common subject with both—for one must continue to think of them as two personalities—the subject of the man or woman who casts away God and everything for an unholy love; and the choice was significant of a certain unhealthiness which is in Fiona as well as in William Sharp. But there is no unhealth, only exquisite, lingering tenderness in **"The Last Supper"** and **"The Fisher of Men."** It is the child that begins the tale in **"The Last Supper,"** or rather the old man who had been a child when this happened:—

> I had the sorrow that day. Strange hostilities lurked in the familiar bracken. The soughing of the wind among the trees, the wash of the brown water by my side, that had been companionable, were voices of awe. The quiet light upon the grass flamed.
>
> The fierce people that lurked in shadow had eyes for my helplessness. When the dark came I thought I should be dead, devoured by I knew not what wild creature. Would Mother never come, never come, with saving arms, with eyes like soft candles of home?
>
> Then my sobs grew still for I heard a step. With dread upon me, poor wee lad that I was, I looked to see who came out of the wilderness. It was a man, tall and thin and worn, with long hair hanging a-down his face! Pale he was as a moonlit cot on the dark moor, and his voice was low and sweet. When I saw his eyes I had no fear upon me at all. I saw the mother-look in the grey shadow of them.
>
> "And is that you, Art lennavan-mo?" he said, as he stooped and lifted me.
>
> I had no fear. The wet was out of my eyes.
>
> "What is it you will be listening to now, my little lad?" he whispered, as he saw me lean, intent, to catch I knew not what.
>
> "Sure," I said, "I am not for knowing: but I thought I heard a music away there in the wood."
>
> I heard it for sure. It was a wondrous sweet air as of a playing the *feadan* in a dream. Callum Dall the piper could give no rarer music than that was; and Callum was a seventh son and born in the moonshine.
>
> "Will you come with me this night of nights, little

> Art?" the man asked me, with his lips touching my brow and giving me rest.
>
> "That I will, indeed and indeed," I said. And then I fell asleep.
>
> When I awoke we were in the huntsman's booth— that is, at the far end of the Shadowy Glen.
>
> There was a long, rough-hewn table in it, and I stared when I saw bowls and a great jug of milk, and a plate heaped with oat-cakes, and beside it a brown loaf of rye-bread.
>
> "Little Art," said he who carried me. "Are you for knowing now who I am?"
>
> "You are a prince, I'm thinking," was the shy word that came to my mouth.
>
> "Sure, lennav-aghrày, that is so. It is called The Prince of Peace I am."
>
> "And who is to be eating all this?" I asked.
>
> "This is the last supper," the Prince said, so low that I could scarce hear: and it seemed to me that he whispered: "For I die daily, and ever ere I die the Twelve break bread with me."

In my opinion Fiona Macleod never afterwards reached the height of achievement of these two stories. It is the height of the spiritual in the Celt which has its dark counterpart in him. For with strong religious faith comes superstition, the one the shadow of the other, and where the one lights up the other darkens. There is much that is darkening and dreadful in Fiona Macleod's work even when it is most remarkable from a literary point of view. **"The Dan-nan-Ron," "The Ninth Wave," "The Sin-Eater,"** have all to my mind a dreadful power of depressing the reader. These are the superstitions of Paganism side by side with the light of religion.

That they should have the power to depress is a tribute to their literary quality. I may say that my first experience with *Pharais* left me with a sense of dislike and fear for the work of Fiona Macleod. I felt that it was not good reading for the sensitive and imaginative. I had had the same sense in reading *Vistas,* but there mingled with a certain irritation as against one who chooses a bad literary convention, the result of which can be nothing else than to depress and darken.

Neither William Sharp nor Fiona Macleod brought into their work any hint of the saving sense of humour. To be sure Fiona was always writing at the top of her voice, in a passion which had no room for the ludicrous. I believe William Sharp did write one or two novels which had an intention of humour, but I do not think they amused anybody. That the sense was there, however, was proved in some of Fiona's correspondence, and doubtless the two personalities in one body must have been often grimly amused as the deception thickened and the whole world was at fault.

Personally I find no quality at all admirable in the poetry of Fiona, any more than in the poetry of William Sharp. What Fiona will live by is her poetic prose: and if one has the three paper-bound volumes published by Patrick Geddes and Colleagues, *Tragic Romances, Spiritual Tales,*

Barbaric Tales, one has pretty well all that is really worth preserving of Fiona's work. (pp. 570-75)

One is obliged always to think of William Sharp and Fiona Macleod as two instead of one, although the two may have lodged under one mortal roof. The more one thinks upon it all, the more is one convinced that this was no foolish and vulgar mystification. It may have manifested itself indeed at first in "the desire to escape from a name," which one of Mr. Sharp's friends speaks of. Afterwards—well, there were two complete and different personalities working. It would be very interesting to know how much William Sharp himself believed in Fiona Macleod. That he or she had the power of inspiring, in her case at least, vehement love of the work and vehement dislike, as well as vehement belief, is proved by the many who were in the secret and kept it—not one or two, not persons bound by ties of consanguinity or otherwise to Mr. Sharp, but grave, responsible persons, the last in the world to lend themselves to a fraud on the public, or that section of it best worth considering.

How far did William Sharp himself believe in Fiona Macleod? Perhaps Mrs. Sharp's forthcoming biography of her husband may enlighten us. Perhaps not. It is not always easy for those nearest to a man to be frank, at least while the clay is new over him, with themselves or others. Did he believe in her? Was it a difficult and obscure mental case, or something belonging to mysteries to which we have as yet no key? It reminds one of the old days of possession, when a wandering spirit entered into and took possession of a man, spoke with a voice not his, uttered words of which he had no knowledge, spoke words of wisdom out of a simple habitation. If one could accept some such theory as this much would be explained.

That finally the mystery will be relegated to the region of mental phenomena seems likely enough.

A friend of Mr. Sharp's, who was in the secret from the beginning, writes to me, with permission to publish his letter:—

> There was no *deception,* however: for the popular way of putting it that he simply masqueraded as Fiona Macleod lacks all real understanding, I don't believe either our physiology or psychology, or even the incipient re-union of both, can yet fully explain any such strange combination of normal and abnormal elements, but that there was a strong tendency to a dissolution of personality into distinct components, and that F. M. represented the highest product of this recurrent process, I have little doubt. You know more or less doubtless of the stories of dual and even triple personality which medical psychologists, especially, have established; of varieties of religious experience and so on. Well, here was the process at work upon a higher type than those as yet observed and recorded, and associated with a definite variety of poetic experience. Dr. —, of —, whose acquaintance I have just made, but who appears to have known W. S. and F. M. alike more fully and deeply if not also longer than I, holds substantially the same view: and I have no doubt that his forthcoming biography, for which I understand he prepared considerable material, and which doubtless Mrs. Sharp will soon finish, will confirm it. I do not take upon me to say beforehand, of course, that all his own interpretation is to be trusted—no one's probably is free from error

or imperfection or vanity—but I expect it to be substantially honest and veracious, and so of great interest alike to literary critic and to psychologist; while even the medical man may find in this some element or explanation of the many diseases which have too early broken down that magnificent frame.

I can vouch for the fact that if I were free to give the name of the writer of this letter it would carry considerable weight.

Who it was that wrote Fiona Macleod's letters is yet a mystery. That the dual personality did not write in different hands seems proved by the fact that when Mr. Sharp was abroad Miss Macleod's letters came from Edinburgh as steadily as ever. The same lady, perhaps, impersonated Fiona Macleod when Mr. Sharp took her to see the greatest of our novelists, a thing which would be altogether reprehensible if there were not some such explanation as my correspondent suggests.

My own experience is that for years I had a friendly, dropping correspondence with Fiona Macleod. No one could have been more generous and apparently more frank than my correspondent; and there was a warmth of appreciation of the work of other people which betokened a very rich and sweet nature. That big forgiveness, too, of my first hostile criticism has always seemed to me more masculine than feminine, and doubtless it was the masculine part that forgave so fully and freely.

Most of Fiona's books came to me in those years from herself, and one of her letters is, I think, of sufficient general interest, as bearing on the mystification, for me to reproduce it. I had apparently been writing to her for some materials for an article about her. It will be observed with interest that Fiona, the letter-writer, had the sense of humour which Fiona, the literary woman, never allowed to look into her pages.

c/o Miss Rea,
The Outlook Tower,
Castlehill,
Edinburgh.

24: 3: 97.,

Dear Mrs. Hinkson,

The re-issue of my shorter tales has brought me so many letters: then my present visit to Edinburgh is a brief one: and once more my uncertain health has been like a foe knocking at my gates: for all which triple reason I beg you to forgive me for not having sooner acknowledged your kind little note. . . .

I did not wish to trouble you with all the 3 vols. of the re-issue set. . . . but as you say you intend an article about me and my work in the *English Illustrated Magazine* I have directed the publisher to send you the volumes.

The third, ***Tragic Romances,*** contains my strongest contemporary short story by common consent (viz., **"Morag of the Glen"**); and what I myself think to be the best, the shorter story called **"The Archer."**

Oh, yes, dear Mrs. Hinkson, I am now well aware of much of the mystery that has grown up about my unfortunate self. I have even heard that Fleet Street journalist rumour to which you allude—with the addition that the said unhappy scribe was bald and old and addicted to drink.

Heaven knows who and what I am according to some wiseacres! A recent cutting said I was Irish, a Mr. Chas. O'Connor, whom I know not.

A friend of a friend told that friend that I was Miss Nora Hopper and Mr. Yeats in unison—at which I felt flattered, but amused. For some time, a year or two ago, there was a rumour that "Fiona Macleod" was my good friend and relative, William Sharp. Then when this was disproved I was said to be Mrs. Sharp. Latterly I became the daughter of the late Dr. Norman Macleod. The latest is that I am Miss Maud Gonne—which the paragraphist "knows as a fact." Do you know her? She is Irish and lives in Paris; and is, I hear, very beautiful—so I prefer to be Miss Gonne rather than that Fleet Street journalist!

Seriously, I am often annoyed by these rumours. But what can I do? There are private reasons, as well as my own particular wishes, why I must preserve my privacy.

I do most urgently wish not to have my privacy made public, partly because I am so "built," and partly for other reasons: but I would not perhaps let this stand in the way of the urgent wishes of friends were it not that there are other reasons also. But this much I will confide in you and gladly: I am *not* an unmarried girl, as commonly supposed, but am married.

The name I write under is my maiden name. Perhaps I have suffered as well as known much joy in my brief mature life: but what then? All women whose heart is in their brains must inevitably suffer. . . . Two friends in London have my photograph, and perhaps you may see it some day: but now I do not even let friends have a photograph, since one allowed someone to take a sketch of it for an American paper. I can't well explain why I'm so exigent. I must leave you to divine from what I have told you. . . . Of course I don't object to its being known that I come of an old Catholic family, that I am a Macleod, that I was born in the Southern Hebrides, and that my heart still lies where the cradle rocked.

If perchance I should be in London this Autumn or early Winter, on my way to the Riviera (for I am not strong) I hope to be able to make your acquaintance in person. I have heard of you from several friends and particularly from Mr. William Sharp, who is a great admirer of your writings, both in prose and verse.

> Believe me, dear Mrs. Hinkson,
> Cordially yours,
> Fiona Macleod.

Needless to say that meeting never came off, but some time in the same winter, 1896-97, Miss Lilian Rae, to whose care Fiona Macleod's letters were always addressed, in those days, did come to see me, and spent an afternoon with me. She seemed a pleasant, shrewd, frank little Scottish lady, and her way about the mystery was a bit of perfect acting. She simply did not acknowledge that one existed, treated the discussion of the subject as mere folly. But then William Sharp himself, one would have said, was the frankest and simplest of men.

How then, supposing he really believed in Fiona, did he persuade so many people to believe in her or act as though they did? Perhaps the forthcoming biography may enlighten us.

I may say that of late years, as William Sharp's health waned towards the close, Fiona's work lost its note of passionate personality. If she had not written **The Washer of the Ford** and **The Sin-Eater,** the **Divine Adventure** and the **Dominion of Dreams** would have been not much more than interesting. They were beautiful in parts, but they had the old fault of Fiona's work, diffuseness, and they had only at times the old fire that was genius. (pp. 576-79)

> *Katharine Tynan, "William Sharp and Fiona Macleod," in* The Fortnightly Review, *Vol. LXXIX, No. CCCCLXXI, March 1, 1906, pp. 570-79.*

Elizabeth A. Sharp   (memoir date 1912)

[*In the following excerpt, Sharp chronicles her husband's motivation for writing as "Fiona Macleod" and provides excerpts from his correspondence defending his actions.*]

The *Sospiri di Roma* was the turning point. Those unrhymed poems of irregular metre are filled not only with the passionate delight in life, with the sheer joy of existence, but also with the ecstatic worship of beauty that possessed him during those spring months we spent in Rome [1891], when he had cut himself adrift for the time from the usual routine of our life, and touched a high point of health and exuberant spirits. There, at last, he had found the desired incentive towards a true expression of himself, in the stimulus and sympathetic understanding of the friend to whom he dedicated the first of the books published under his pseudonym. This friendship began in Rome and lasted throughout the remainder of his life.

And though this newer phase of his work was at no time the result of collaboration, as certain of his critics have suggested, he was deeply conscious of his indebtedness to this friend, for—as he stated to me in a letter of instructions, written before he went to America in 1896, concerning his wishes in the event of his death—he realised that it was "to her I owe my development as 'Fiona Macleod' though, in a sense of course, that began long before I knew her, and indeed while I was still a child," and that, as he believed, "without her there would have been no 'Fiona Macleod.' "

Because of her beauty, her strong sense of life and of the joy of life; because of her keen intuitions and mental alertness, her personality stood for him as a symbol of the heroic women of Greek and Celtic days, a symbol that, as he expressed it, unlocked new doors in his mind and put him "in touch with ancestral memories" of his race. So, for a time, he stilled the critical, intellectual mood of William Sharp to give play to the development of this new found expression of subtler emotions, towards which he had been moving with all the ardour of his nature.

From then till the end of his life there was a continual play of the two forces in him, or of the two sides of his nature: of the intellectually observant, reasoning mind—the actor, and of the intuitively observant, spiritual mind—the dreamer, which differentiated more and more one from the other, and required different conditions, different environment, different stimuli, until he seemed to be two personalities in one. It was a development which, as it proceeded, produced a tremendous strain on his physical and mental resources; and at one time between 1897-8 threatened him with a complete nervous collapse.

And there was for a time distinct opposition between these two natures which made it extremely difficult for him to adjust his life, for the two conditions were equally imperative in their demands upon him. His preference, naturally, was for the intimate creative work which he knew grew out of his inner self; though the exigencies of life, his dependence on his pen for his livelihood—and, moreover the keen active interest "William Sharp" took in all the movements of the day, literary and political, at home and abroad—required of him a great amount of applied study and work. (pp. 4-7)

Pharais was the first of the books written and published under the pseudonym of "Fiona Macleod." The first reference to it is in [his] diary: "Have also done the first part of a Celtic romance called *Pharais*." The next is in a letter written to Mrs. Janvier from St. Andrews, on 12th August, 1893, before the author had decided on the use of a pseudonym:

> The white flowers you speak of are the moon-daisies, are they not?—what we call moonflowers in the west of Scotland and ox-eye daisies in England, and marguerites in France? . . . It is very strange that you should write about them to me just as I was working out a scene in a strange Celtic tale I am writing, called *Pharais,* wherein the weird charm and terror of a night of tragic significance is brought home to the reader (or I hope so) by a stretch of dew-wet moonflowers glimmering white through the mirk of a dusk laden with sea mists. Though this actual scene was written a year or two ago—and one or two others of the first part of *Pharais*—I am going to re-write it, your letter having brought some subtle inspiration with it. *Pharais* is a foil to the other long story I am working at. While *it* is full of Celtic romance and dream and the glamour of the mysterious, the other is a comedy of errors—somewhat in the nature, so far, of *A Fellowe and His Wife* (I mean as to style). In both, at least the plot, the central action, the germinal *motif,* is original: though I for one lay little stress on extraneous originality in comparison with that inner originality of individual life. . . . I have other work on the many occupied easels in the studio of my mind: but of nothing of this need I speak at present. Of minor things, the only one of any importance is a long article on a subject wherein I am (I suppose) the only specialist among English men of letters—the Belgian literary Renaissance since 1880. It is entitled **"La Jeune Belgique,"** and will appear in (I understand) the September number of *The Nineteenth Century* . . .

> . . . We must each "gang our ain gait." I'm singularly indifferent to what other people think in any matter where I feel strongly myself. Perhaps it is for this reason that I am rarely "put out" by adverse criticism or opinion—except on technical shortcomings. I do a lot of my own work here lying out on the sand-dunes by the sea. Yesterday I had a strange experience. I was writing in pencil in *Pharais* of death by the sea—and almost at my feet

a drowned corpse was washed in by the tide and the slackening urgency of the previous night's gale. The body proves to be that of a man from the opposite Forfar coast. It had been five days in the water, and death had played havoc with his dignity of lifeless manhood. I learned later that his companion had been found three days ago, tide-drifted in the estuary of the Tay. It was only a bit of flotsam, in a sense, but that poor derelict so sullenly surrendered of the sea changed for me, for a time, the aspect of those blithe waters I love so well. In the evening I walked along the same sands. The sea purred like a gigantic tigress, with a whisper of peace and rest and an infinite sweet melancholy. What a sepulchral fraud. . . .

> Life seems to move, now high and serene and incredibly swift as an albatross cleaving the upper air, now as a flood hurled across rocks and chasms and quicksands. But it is all life—even the strangely still and quiet backwaters, even, indeed, the same healthful commonplace lagoons where one havens so gladly often. . . .

>   (pp. 7-10)

When in the following year the book was published the author, forgetting that he had ever written Mrs. Janvier about it, sent a copy of it to her, and said merely that it was a book in which he was interested. Whereupon she wrote and asked if the book were not his own, and he replied:

> . . . Yes, *Pharais is mine.* It is a book out of my heart, out of the core of my heart. I wrote it with the pen dipped in the very ichor of my life. It has reached people more than I dreamt of as likely. In Scotland especially it has stirred and created a new movement. Here, men like George Meredith, Grant Allen, H. D. Traill, and Theodore Watts hailed it as a "work of genius." Ignored in some quarters, abused in others, and unheeded by the "general reader," it has yet had a reception that has made me deeply glad. It is the beginning of my true work. Only one or two know I am "Fiona Macleod." Let you and my dear T. A. J. preserve my secret. I trust you.

> You will find more of me in *Pharais* than in anything I have written. Let me add that you will find *The Mountain Lovers,* at which I am now writing when I can, more elemental still, while simpler. . . . By blood I am part Celt, and partly so by upbringing, by Spirit wholly so. . . . One day I will tell you of some of the strange old mysteries of earlier days I have part learned, and part divined, and other things of the spirit. You can understand how I cannot do my true work, in this accursed London.

A little later he wrote:

> . . . I resent too close indentification with the so-called Celtic renaissance. If my work is to depend solely on its Gaelic connection, then let it go, as go it must. My work must be beautiful in itself—Beauty is a Queen and must be served as a Queen.

> . . . You have asked me once or twice about F. M., why I took her name: and how and when she came to write *Pharais.* It is too complex to tell you just now. . . . The name was born naturally: (of course I had associations with the name Macleod). It, Fiona, is very rare now. Most Highlanders would

tell you it was extinct—even as the diminutive of Fionaghal (Flora). But it is not. It is an old Celtic name (meaning "a fair maid") still occasionally to be found. I know a little girl, the daughter of a Highland clergyman, who is called Fiona. *All* my work is so intimately wrought with my own experiences that I cannot tell you about *Pharais,* etc., without telling you my whole life.

As a matter of fact *Pharais* was not the first written expression of the new work. It was preceded by a short story entitled **"The Last Fantasy of James Achanna"** that in the autumn of 1893 was sent to *The Scots Observer.* It was declined by Mr. Henley who, however, wrote a word of genuine encouragement. He accepted Mr. Henley's decision, and the story was never reprinted in its first form. It was re-written several times; it was included in **The Dominion of Dreams** as **"The Archer."** During the writing of **Pharais** the author began to realise how much the feminine element dominated in the book, that it grew out of the subjective, or feminine side of his nature. He, therefore, decided to issue the book under the name of *Fiona Macleod,* that "flashed ready made" into his mind. Mrs. Janvier wrote later and asked why he, a man, chose to send forth good work under the signature of a woman. He answered:

> . . . I can write out of my heart in a way I could not do as William Sharp, and indeed I could not do so if I were the woman Fiona Macleod is supposed to be, unless veiled in scrupulous anonymity. . . .
>
> This rapt sense of oneness with nature, this *cosmic ecstasy* and elation, this wayfaring along the extreme verges of the common world, all this is so wrought up with the romance of life that I could not bring myself to expression by my outer self, insistent and tyrannical as that need is. . . . My truest self, the self who is below all other selves, and my most intimate life and joys and sufferings, thoughts, emotions and dreams, *must* find expression, yet I cannot save in this hidden way.

He was wont to say "Should the secret be found out, Fiona dies." Later in the year he wrote: "Sometimes I am tempted to believe I am half a woman, and so far saved as I am by the hazard of chance from what a woman can be made to suffer if one let the light of the common day illuminate the avenues and vistas of her heart. . . . " (pp. 11-14)

> *Elizabeth A. Sharp, in her* William Sharp (Fiona Macleod): A Memoir, 2 Vols., *Duffield & Company, 1912.*

Paul Elmer More   (essay date 1913)

[*More was an American critic who, along with Irving Babbitt, formulated the doctrines of New Humanism in early twentieth-century American thought. The New Humanists were strict moralists who adhered to traditional conservative values in reaction to an age of scientific innovation and artistic experimentalism. In regard to literature, they believed a work's support for the classic ethical norms to be of as much importance as its aesthetic qualities. More was particularly opposed to Naturalism, which he believed accentuated the animal nature of humans, and to any literary movement, such as Romanticism, that broke with established classical tradi-*

tion. His importance as a critic derives from the rigid coherence of his ideology, which polarized American critics into hostile opponents (Van Wyck Brooks, Edmund Wilson, H. L. Mencken) or devoted supporters (Norman Foerster, Stuart Sherman, and, to a lesser degree, T. S. Eliot). He is especially esteemed for the philosophical and literary erudition of his multivolume Shelburne Essays *(1904-21). In the following excerpt from that work, More traces Sharp's development as a writer, discussing the strengths and weaknesses of his writing style.*]

The writer who concealed himself under the name of Fiona Macleod has just been brought into prominence by the publication of a complete edition of his works and by an admirable biography from the hand of his wife [see excerpt dated 1912]. He may seem out of place among the greater forces of romanticism, yet his position as one of the leaders of revolt against certain aspects of our civilization gives him some significance, and there is, or at least was, a mystery about his double and epicene personality which piques attention and renders him curiously symbolical of the movement he represented. For twelve years, until his death in 1905 permitted the revelation, his identity with the woman of the Highlands was kept secret by the small circle to whom it was known. The situation had a comical element when William Sharp, as chairman of the Stage Society, brought out one of the plays of his supposed friend, Fiona Macleod, at the Globe Theatre, and during the rehearsals chatted with his Celtic fellows about play and author. When the secret of Fiona's existence was ended there rose in its place the question of Mr. Sharp's double activity—for all through the twelve years he had purposely continued his critical writing under his own name—and certain amateur psychologists began to spread the rumour of a mysterious dual personality in the man, as if he had really possessed two souls, one masculine and Saxon, the other feminine and Gaelic. Mrs. Sharp, in her biography, rather fosters this impression, and it is evident that Sharp liked to puzzle himself and his friends by the presumption of an extraordinary inspiration. As a matter of fact there is nothing at all supernatural or even very strange in the matter. The wistful, ghostly vein that runs through the works of Fiona Macleod was marked in William Sharp from a child, and if most of his writing before he assumed the Gaelic name shows the ordinary qualities of Anglo-Saxon London, that was simply because he wrote for the market what the market demanded. (pp. 119-20)

In 1878 [Sharp] came to London and took a place in a bank; but literature . . . lured him, and after a while he threw himself on his pen for support and gradually, through many hardships and moments of despair, won for himself a profitable hold on the publishers. Naturally, as a servant of the press he wrote what the readers of magazines and popular biographies desired, hiding close in his heart the wayward mysticism and grandiose philosophy he had learned from nature. Yet those hidden springs of inspiration were never forgotten, and in his intimate letters we hear continually of great projected epics and other poems that were to solve the riddles of life. From the specimens of these suppressed masterpieces given by Mrs. Sharp in the biography, we conjecture that their loss to the world is not deplorable. For example:

> There is in everything an undertone . . .
> Those clear in soul are also clear in sight,
> And recognise in a white cascade's flash,

The roar of mountain torrents, and the wail
Of multitudinous waves on barren sands,
The song of skylark at the flush of dawn,
A mayfield all ablaze with king-cups gold,
The clamour musical of culver wings
Beating the soft air of a dewy dusk,
The crescent moon far voyaging thro' dark skies,
And Sirius throbbing in the distant south,
A something deeper than mere audible
And visible sensations; for they see
Not only pulsings of the Master's breath,
The workings of inevitable Law,
But also the influences subordinate
And spirit actors in life's unseen side.
One glint of nature may unlock a soul.

No doubt the youthful bard and his confidante thought he was uttering some startling spiritual truth and, as is the way with youthful bards and their accomplices, cursed the world for its obstinate deafness. As a matter of fact that sort of pantheistic revery was exasperatingly easy then, and now; Wordsworth and Shelley and a little contempt for reason are the formula responsible for a stream of that kind of thing that trickles clammily through the nineteenth century. For whatever solid basis there is in the work of Fiona Macleod we must thank the hard prosaic experience of William Sharp, which gave him some discipline in common sense and kept his aspirations in long abeyance.

Two friendships in these early years should not be forgotten. As a boy he had fallen in love with his cousin Elizabeth, and, after years of waiting and despite some family opposition, they were married. If she was not precisely the muse of Fiona Macleod, for that honour belongs to an unnamed woman with whom he became acquainted later in life, she cherished his ambitions and responded sympathetically to his dreams of a Celtic revival. Another friend, who influenced him profoundly, was the figure that looms so large in all the literary history of the day, Dante Gabriel Rossetti, then a broken man secluding himself in the stealthy, heavy-aired retreat he had made for himself at 16 Cheyne Walk, but still the *deus præsens* in the imaginative world in which Swinburne and Watts-Dunton and Walter Pater and Philip Bourke Marston and other scented souls were breathing dim or gorgeous hopes. The first book that brought general recognition to Sharp was his study of Rossetti, and years afterwards, in a dedication to Walter Pater of a projected new edition, which, however, he never finished, he expressed what Rossetti meant to them:

> We are all seeking a lost Eden. This ideal Beauty that we catch glimpses of, now in morning loveliness, now in glooms of tragic horror, haunts us by day and night, in dreams of waking and sleeping—nay, whether or not we will, among the littlenesses and exigences of our diurnal affairs. It may be that, driven from the Eden of direct experience, we are being more and more forced into taking refuge within the haven guarded by our dreams. To a few only is it given to translate, with rare distinction and excellence, something of this manifold message of Beauty—though all of us would fain be, with your Marius, "of the number of those who must be made perfect by the love of visible beauty." Among these few, in latter years in this country, no one has wrought more exquisitely for us than Rossetti.

The dominance of Rossetti's vision of artificial beauty must not be forgotten when we read the works of Fiona Macleod.

By the year 1892, when Sharp was thirty-seven, he was in a position to command his own time to a certain extent, and with his wife he settled down for a while in a little cottage at Rudgwick, Sussex. His first ambition was to edit a magazine which should be unhampered by any policy save his own whims and ambitions, and he actually wrote and printed one issue of the *Pagan Review.* Fortunately he carried that fantastic project no further. Then came the inspiration of Fiona Macleod. He himself in a letter to Mrs. Thomas Janvier, who was one of the few in the secret, explained why he assumed this disguised personality:

> I can write out of my heart in a way I could not do as William Sharp, and indeed I could not do so if I were the woman Fiona Macleod is supposed to be, unless veiled in scrupulous anonymity. . . .
>
> This rapt sense of oneness with nature, this *cosmic ecstasy* and elation, this wayfaring along the extreme verges of the common world, all this is so wrought up with the romance of life that I could not bring myself to expression by my outer self, insistent and tyrannical as that need is. . . . My truest self, the self who is below all other selves, and my most intimate life and joys and sufferings, thoughts, emotions and dreams, *must* find expression, yet I cannot save in this hidden way.

There is, as I have said before, not quite so much mystery in this whole proceeding as Mr. Sharp and some of his friends would have us believe—the mystery in fact is mainly of that sort of mystification which has pleased so many other romantic writers, and which has its roots in the rather naïve desire to pose as the prophetic instrument of some vast renovation of ideas, when really the prophet's mind, instead of labouring with ideas, is floating in a shoreless sea of revery and tossing with indistinguishable emotions. Nor is it at all strange that Sharp should have taken a woman's name. He had for one thing the inspiration of his lately found friend in Rome, of whom we get only tantalizing glimpses in the biography and in his dedications—the woman who stood to him as the personification of the *Anima Celtica,* the Celtic Soul still brooding, as he describes it, in the "Land of Promise whose borders shine with the loveliness of all forfeited, or lost, or banished dreams and realities of Beauty." Moreover, the feminine element, the *Ewig-Weibliche,* has always been prominent in the ideals of romantic *Schwärmerei,* and it was natural that this latest incarnation of the old hopes and visions should have appeared in the guise of a feminine form. . . . The earliest book to appear under the new signature was *Pharais,* published in 1894; *The Mountain Lovers,* which with *Pharais* forms the first volume of the collected works, came out in 1895, and thereafter, for the ten remaining years of Sharp's life, there was a succession of stories, sketches, essays, poems, and dramas, making in the complete edition seven fair-sized volumes. *Pharais* caught the attention of the discerning at once, and the interest in the unknown writer never flagged. She became a cult with some, and with others a recurring escape from the world and from thought.

With advancing years the restlessness that from childhood had been characteristic of Sharp's temperament grew to what can only be described as feverish excess. The first glimpse we have of him as a baby is in the form of a runaway storming a make-believe castle in fairy-land, and at the end, until held in the leash by ill-health, we see him still drifting, or rather running, from place to place, seeking febrile exhilaration from the sea or unearthly peace from the hills, always in a wild haste to overtake some vanishing impalpable goal of the heart's desire. He who boasted valiantly that his soul knew its home in nature was, like so many of his tribe, a victim in fact of an incurable nostalgia. He died in Sicily in 1905, beloved and regretted. Over his grave an Iona cross was raised, and on it were cut the inscriptions chosen by himself:

> Farewell to the known and exhausted,
> Welcome the unknown and illimitable—

and

> Love is more great than we conceive, and Death is
> the keeper of unknown redemptions.

I cannot at all agree with Mr. Sharp's estimates of the works of Fiona Macleod. He apparently valued most the later writings in which the human motives disappear in a haze of disorganized symbolism, whereas the normal reader is likely to find his interest centering, with some minor exceptions, in the tales of *Pharais* and *The Mountain Lovers.* In these the discipline Sharp had acquired from long apprenticeship to the press kept him within the bounds of reason, while the new freedom and the Celtic imagery added a note of strange and fascinating beauty. There is more of passion in *The Mountain Lovers;* the scenes about the lonely haunted pool, the terrible unrelenting love and madness of the blind old man, the elfish fear and wisdom of the dwarf, the yearning of the girl Oona that a soul may be born in her wild worshipper—the whole tissue of emotions in this solitude where the influences of forgotten gods are more numerous than the human beings, has the sombreness and awe of real tragedy. But on the whole *Pharais,* with its quieter beauty and subtler pathos, seems to me the more memorable work; Fiona Macleod never equalled that first lovely creation. The story of *Pharais,* briefly stated, is of a fair young woman on one of the lonely outer isles; of her husband upon whom the mind-dark, that is to say the clouding forgetfulness of melancholy, has fallen; and of their child who is born to them blind. The elements of the tale may sound depressingly gloomy, but in fact they are so lost in brave human sympathies, so mingled with the symbolic sadness of the winds and especially of the infinite voices of the encompassing sea, that the effect is not depression but the elevation of the finer romantic art. When the little child is buried, and the mourners return home, the voices are filled with tragic lamentation:

> . . . The island lay in a white shroud. At the extreme margin, a black, pulsating line seemed to move sinuously from left to right.
>
> Suddenly a deeper sound boomed from the sea, though no wind ruffled the drifts which already lay thick in the hollows. Till midnight, and for an hour beyond, this voice of the sea was as the baying of a monstrous hound.
>
> None in the homestead slept. The silence, broken only by that strange, menacing baying of the waves as they roamed through the solitudes environing the isle, was so intense that sometimes the ears echoed as with the noise of a rush of wings, or as with

the sonorous suspensions between the striking of bell and bell in monotonously swung chimes.

> Then again, suddenly, and still without the coming of wind, the sea ceased its hoarse, angry baying, and, after lapse within lapse till its chime was almost inaudible, gave forth in a solemn dirge the majestic music of its inmost heart.

And at the last, when the husband carries the lifeless burden of his wife out into the white shroud of the new-fallen snow, and, for a moment recovering his reason, knows his loss and the mystery of life, the human emotions are again involved in the vision and sound of the sea:

> Idly he watched a small, grey snow-cloud passing low above the island.
>
> A warm breath reached the heart of it, and set the myriad wings astir. Down, straight down above the isle and for a few fathoms beyond it, they fluttered waveringly.
>
> The fall was like a veil suspended over Ithona: a veil so thin, so transparent, that the sky was visible through it as an azure dusk; and beneath it, the sea as a blue-flowing lawn wherever its skirts trailed; while behind it, the rising sunfire was a shimmer of amber-yellow that made every falling flake glisten like burnished gold. . . .
>
> The sea lay breathing in a deep calm all around the isle. But, from its heart that never slumbers, rose as of yore, and for ever, a rumour as of muffled prophesyings, a Voice of Awe, a Voice of Dread.

Having found his public in these two tales, Mr. Sharp, I think, a little abused its good-nature. A few of the shorter stories have a weird beauty not without some relation to human experience, and some of the nature-essays, written at the very end of his life and brought together under the title of *Where the Forest Murmurs,* display an intimate union of symbolism and real observation such as many in these latter days have attempted but few have achieved. He never, for instance, did anything better in its way than **"The Hill Tarn,"** which tells how an old gillie climbed one mid-winter day to a solitary pool in the mountains, and what strange sight there met his eyes:

> . . . He started before dawn, but did not reach the lochan till a red fire of sunset flared along the crests. The tarn was frozen deep, and for all the pale light that dwelled upon it was black as basalt, for a noon-tempest had swept its surface clear of snow. At first he thought small motionless icebergs lay in it, but wondered at their symmetrical circle. He descended as far as he dared, and saw that seven wild-swans were frozen on the tarn's face. They had alit there to rest, no doubt: but a fierce cold had numbed them, and an intense frost of death had suddenly transfixed each as they swam slowly circlewise as is their wont. They may have been there for days, perhaps for weeks. A month later the gillie repeated his arduous and dangerous feat. They were still there, motionless, ready for flight as it seemed.
>
> How often in thought I have seen that coronal of white swans above the dark face of that far, solitary tarn: in how many dreams I have listened to the rustle of unloosening wings, and seen seven white phantoms rise cloud-like, and like clouds at night drift swiftly into the dark; and heard, as mournful bells through the solitudes of sleep, the *honk-honk*

of the wild-swans traversing the obscure forgotten ways to the secret country beyond sleep and dreams and silence.

Take away the conventional inanity of that last phrase and you have here a passage which contains an image at once rare and actual and in itself suggestive of the most romantic interpretation. If Mr. Sharp had written always, or even often, in that vein, he would have accomplished something memorable and large in English letters; but too frequently the symbolism runs quite away with him and leaves one vaguely wondering whether he really had anything in his mind to symbolize. Many of the old Gaelic traditions and legends which he has attempted to revivify strike one in his rendering as mere empty vapouring. Though he never united himself unreservedly with the so-called Celtic movement and deprecated its too common hostility to prosaic sense and to everything Saxon, even bringing upon himself the obsecrations of some of the fiercer enthusiasts, yet in his inability to distinguish between an idea or even a genuine emotion and the fluttering of tired nerves he fell again and again into meaningless rhetoric that makes the loosest vapourings of "A. E." or Mr. W. B. Yeats seem solid and compact of reason. His two plays based on old Irish legends are frankly in the school of the so-called Psychic Drama, which is the ambition of many young writers for the stage in other countries as well as in Ireland. The ultimate aim of this *théâtre de l'âme,* he says in the introduction to one of these plays, is "to express the passion of remorse under the signal of a Voice lamenting, or the passion of tears under the signal of a Cry, and be content to give no name to these protagonists." He has not, indeed, gone quite to this extreme of inanity in his actual production, but he has gone far enough to empty his characters of all individuality, and in making them the mere mouthpieces of the vaguest bubbles of revery has left them passionless nonentities. Compare his work in this kind with that of Mr. Synge, who died just recently. Mr. Synge had too much feeling for his audience and too strong a grasp on personal emotion to lose himself utterly in this shadow-world, and his characters, for all his Celtic twilight, have some of the blood of real life in them. The simple fact is that Mr. Sharp, having got the trick of this sort of symbolic writing, found it delightfully easy and indulged in it without restraint. Possibly he deceived himself into believing that to write without thought is to write with inspiration; in reality he was abusing an outworn convention. Take a stanza of his poems—almost any stanza will do:

> Oh, fair immaculate rose of the world, rose of my dream, my Rose!
> Beyond the ultimate gates of dream I have heard thy mystical call:
> It is where the rainbow of hope suspends and the river of rapture flows—
> And the cool sweet dews from the wells of peace for ever fall.

Now it is quite possible that these phrases—"rose of my dream," "ultimate gates of dream," "rainbow of hope," "river of rapture," "wells of peace"—it is quite possible that these phrases when first struck out corresponded to some yearning for an ideal clearly conceived and strongly imaged, but as they are used and endlessly reiterated by Mr. Sharp, and by others of his school, they become a pure poetic convention emptier of specific content than the

much-abused *clichés* of the pseudo-classical poets. They require no effort on the part of the poet, and convey no shock of meaning to the reader. You remember the Grand Academy of Lagado which was once visited by a certain Mr. Gulliver, and the pleasant device of the academicians to produce literature without waste of brain. Well, something like that might seem to be the method employed in turning out a good deal of this late romantic prose and verse. All you need do is to have a frame of shifting blocks on which are inscribed severally the conventional phrases, and then by the turn of a crank to throw them into new combinations, and, presto, the thing is done. Dr. Johnson said the last word on this sort of composition when he demolished Ossian: "Sir, a man might write such stuff for ever, if he would *abandon* his mind to it."

In fact there is in all this literature a double misunderstanding, as must be pretty clear from what has been already said about it. Sharp and those who were working with him believed that they were faithfully renewing the old Celtic idealism, and they believed also that in this revival there was the prophecy of a great spiritual and imaginative renovation for the world; whereas in simple truth their inspiration came essentially from a source that had nothing to do with any special character of the Celts, and so far from being heralds of youth they are the fag end of a movement that shows every sign of expiring. Now it is well not to exaggerate on either side. Something of the ancient Celtic imagination has undoubtedly been caught up by these young enthusiasts. There is to begin with in the writings of Fiona Macleod a good deal of the actual legendary matter, taken in part from written records and in part from the fragmentary and fast-disappearing tradition among the Gaelic-speaking people of the Highlands and the Western Islands. The mere use of the names and myths of a time is likely to carry with it something of the emotional content that has become associated with them. The new and the old schools of the Celt have thus certain traits in common—the sense of fateful brooding, the feeling of dark and bright powers concealed in nature and working mysteriously upon human destiny, the conception of passions as forces that have a strange life in themselves and come into the breasts of men as if they were ghostly visitants, the craving for unearthly but very real beauty, the haunting belief in a supernatural world that lies now far away in the unattainable West, and now buried beneath our feet or just trembling into vision, the mixture of fear and yearning towards that world as a source of incalculable joys or dark forgetful madness to those who break in upon its secret reserve. All these things, more or less explicit, you will find in the saga literature of Ireland as it has been paraphrased by Lady Gregory in her *Cuchulain of Muirthemne* or translated more literally by Miss Hull and other scholars; and you will find them in the books of Fiona Macleod and Mr. Yeats. But withal the essential spirit of the sagas is quite different from that of these imitators—as different as tremendous action is from sickly brooding. The light in the old tales is hard and sharp and brilliant, whereas our modern writers rather like to merge the outlines of nature in an all-obliterating grey. The heroes in the sagas are men and women that throb with insatiable life, and their emotions, whatever mysticism may lie in the background, are the stark, mortal passions of love and greed and hatred and revenge and lamentable grief; whereas it is the creed of the newer school, fortunately not always followed, to create a literature, which, instead of dealing with the clashing wills of men, shall, in the words of Fiona Macleod, offer "the subtlest and most searching means for the imagination to compel reality to dreams, to compel actuality to vision, to compel to the symbolic congregation of words the bewildering throng of wandering and illusive thoughts and ideas." What Fiona Macleod meant by this "theatre of the soul" can be made clear by a single comparison. There is in the book of Lady Gregory a version of the *Fate of the Sons of Usnach,* being an account of the marvellous loveliness of Deirdre and of the ruin it wrought, which, in spite of some incoherence, is one of the unforgettable stories of the world. When Deirdre is born a Druid comes to the house, and sees the child, and utters this vision of the future:

> O Deirdre, on whose account many shall weep, on whose account many women shall be envious, there will be trouble on Ulster for your sake, O fair daughter of Fedlimid.
>
> Many will be jealous of your face, O flame of beauty; for your sake heroes shall go to exile. For your sake deeds of anger shall be done in Emain; there is harm in your face, for it will bring banishment and death on the sons of kings. . . .
>
> You will have a little grave apart to yourself; you will be a tale of wonder for ever, Deirdre.

Now Mr. Sharp has adopted the story of *The House of Usna* for his theatre of the soul, and this is what he has to say in a song of Deirdre:

> Dim face of Beauty haunting all the world,
> Fair face of Beauty all too fair to see,
> Where the lost stars adown the heavens are hurled
> There, there alone for thee
> May white peace be.
>
> For here, where all the dreams of men are whirled
> Like sere, torn leaves of autumn to and fro,
> There is no place for thee in all the world,
> Who drifted as a star,
> Beyond, afar.

Between the very woman Deirdre of the saga and this "dim face of Beauty" a whole civilization has passed; the force that is moving Fiona Macleod is in its essential quality not from the Celt or Gael, but, as the phrase adopted by her implies, from the *théâtre de l'âme* of Maeterlinck, and far behind him from the whole romantic movement of Europe. We have seen the earlier grandiose schemes of William Sharp melted down in practice to a commonplace imitation of Wordsworth and Shelley and Keats; these later productions of Fiona Macleod, though they show more literary skill and take much of their glamour from reminiscences of Celtic legend, are essentially drawn from the same failing well from which in its abundance those poets drew their sturdier dreams of pantheism. Here is the twilight and not the dawn of a great movement. (pp. 124-41)

> *Paul Elmer More, "Fiona Macleod," in his* The Drift of Romanticism: Shelburne Essays, *eighth series, Houghton Mifflin Company, 1913, pp. 117-43.*

Cornelius Weygandt (essay date 1913)

[*A historian and critic, Weygandt was one of the first American scholars to examine contemporary Irish drama, introducing its major practitioners to American readers in his* Irish Plays and Playwrights. *In the following excerpt from that work, Weygandt praises Sharp's achievement in revitalizing the Celtic heritage of Scotland in his writings.*]

There were relations other than that of a common purpose between William Sharp and the Irish writers of the Celtic Renaissance. He was a friend of Mr. Yeats, a correspondent of Mr. Russell, and the chief commentator in the English reviews on the work of the Irish group of its writers. At one time, after 1897, the relationship promised to be very close, indeed. William Sharp, experimenting in psychics with Mr. Yeats, found occasion to interest him in "Fiona Macleod," and as a result of that interest Mr. Yeats came to think the new writer might write Celtic plays for performances he intended to arrange for Irish literary organizations. Thus it is that Mrs. Sharp has to include in her memoir of her husband a long letter to "Fiona Macleod" from Mr. Yeats, in which he suggests: "The plays might be almost in some cases modern mystery plays. Your **'Last Supper,'** for instance, would make such a play." Mr. Sharp, apparently, did not follow up this suggestion, but shortly after the first performances of "The Irish Literary Theatre" in 1899 he wrote the two plays that, together with *Vistas,* comprise all the dramatic writing that he has to his name. That *The Immortal Hour* and *The House of Usna* were intended for "The Irish Literary Theatre," I think there is little doubt, and it was only, I take it, when circumstances dictated that only plays by Irish writers should be put on by that theatre that Mr. Sharp looked elsewhere for their presentation. Only *The House of Usna* was, however, placed,—in the spring performances in London of The Stage Society, on April 29, 1900. Two months later *The House of Usna* was published in the July number of the *National Review*. It pleased more, if we are to judge by the reviews, in the pages of the magazine than on the stage, but I hardly know why. *The House of Usna* is profoundly moving read in the study, surely, and if acted in such simplicity and enthusiasm as is that of the Abbey Theatre Players, I should think it would appeal as do the verse plays of Mr. Yeats. No play I have read carries me further into antiquity than this, none preserves more of what imagination tells us must have been the wilder beauty of what still are places of wild beauty, of the savagery of that old life of the hero tales of Ireland. Mr. Yeats's plays do not so recapture the past, they take us rather to places out of time, where all things are possible, because the world we know is put aside and all but forgot. Even on the stage, however, the new beauty of *The House of Usna* was recognized, a beauty as distinctive as that of the two plays of M. Maeterlinck that were produced with it, *Interior* and *The Death of Tintagiles,* but it was adjudged not to be drama in the accepted sense of the word. *The House of Usna* is written in a prose that has many of the effects of verse, but that is less luxuriant than the prose of *Vistas. The Immortal Hour,* published shortly afterwards in the *Fortnightly Review* (1900), is written in blank verse that shows its author has been carefully attentive to the free rhythms of the blank verse of Mr. Yeats, but it is neither so poetic nor so dramatic as *The House of Usna.* Both plays are written out of the old legends that are the common property of Irish and Scottish Gael, and in both Sharp has treated his material with his wonted freedom of adaptation, a freedom that is generally justified by his results, his instinctive surety of reconstruction of myths being such as to make one wonder, with Mr. Russell, if Sharp is not, in some fashion, a reincarnation of a shanachie that sang as contemporary in the wars of Gael and Gall.

A common preoccupation with the plays of M. Maeterlinck is another bond between the founder of the Abbey Theatre and Sharp, a preoccupation passing rather quickly from Mr. Yeats, but long retaining its hold on the changing selves of Sharp. For all his early interest in "spiritual things," an interest very definitely expressed in ***Romantic Ballads*** (1888), Sharp would not have come to ***Vistas*** (1894) without the guidance of M. Maeterlinck, and he admits as much in his preface to these "psychic episodes." ***Vistas*** he often referred to as heralding a "great dramatic epoch," and he evidently regarded them as, in a way, drama, but it is hardly likely that he dreamed of their enactment on the stage. Many of them are essentially dramatic, but their method of presentation is almost always lyric or narrative rather than dramatic, even in the Maeterlinckian sense of the word.

It is possible, however, that Sharp might have written other of his projected plays, "The Enchanted Valleys," "The King of Ys," "Drosdan and Yssul," and their many fellows he had projected by title, and others, too, had not developments in Dublin, as I have said, carried Mr. Yeats away from him during 1899 and 1900, and had Sharp himself not during this drifting written that article **"Celtic"** which so aroused many in Ireland on its appearance in *The Contemporary Review*. In this essay, basically a literary protest, "Fiona Macleod" declared "herself" against Separatist politics and affirmed "her" belief, as "she" had in ***The House of Usna,*** that the future greatness of Ireland was to come, not through independence, but through the rebirth of her ancient spirituality in other nations to whom she had given her children.

> The Celtic element in our national life [wrote "Fiona Macleod"] has a vital and great part to play. We have a most noble ideal if we will but accept it. And that is, not to perpetuate feuds, not to try to win back what is gone away upon the wind, not to repay ignorance with scorn, or dullness with contempt, or past wrongs with present hatred, but so to live, so to pray, so to hope, so to work, so to achieve, that we, what is left of the Celtic races, of the Celtic genius, may permeate the greater race of which we are a vital part, so that, with this Celtic emotion, Celtic love of beauty, and Celtic spirituality, a nation greater than any the world has seen may issue, a nation refined and strengthened by the wise relinquishings and steadfast ideals of Celt and Saxon, united in a common fatherland, and in singleness of pride and faith.

There was, however, if less intimacy with the Irish writers in these later years, no less admiration of their art, an admiration that led not only to praise of them in critical articles, but to a greater praise of imitation of their art. So possessed, indeed, was Sharp by the verse of the younger Irish poets as he read them to write of them, that when he turned to verse as "Fiona Macleod," he fell into their rhythms and reproduced the colors of their styles. Writing in prose as a critic of Mr. Yeats, Sharp came to write in verse as Mr. Yeats wrote, as in **"The Dirge of the Four Cities"**: writing of "A. E." in prose as critic, Sharp came to write in verse as "A. E." wrote, as in **"Flame on the Wind"**: writing of "Moira O'Neill," in prose as critic, Sharp came to write in verse as "Moira O'Neill" wrote, as in **"I—Brasil"**: writing in prose as critic, of "Ethna Carberry," Sharp came to write in verse as "Ethna Carberry" wrote, as in **"The Exile."** So it was, also, that, coming to write of Celtic literature after study of Renan and Arnold, Sharp attained to something of their large utterance.

Sharp sees the Celtic Renaissance, however, always in relation to English literature, and always, it should be added, with French literature and Greek literature in the background. In this wide outlook, in his freedom from political prejudice, in his sympathy with Celtic literature and his knowledge of it, is his greatest strength as a critic of the Celtic Renaissance. His greatest weakness is his willingness in this writing, as elsewhere in his writing, to abide by first impressions, to abide also by the first-come phrase or epithet, banes of the ready writer. But read his essay **"Celtic"** after you have read the great essays of Renan and Arnold, and read it alongside of what Mr. Yeats has to say of that literature, and you will find it, as I said, of the stature of these. You will at the same time find in this writing the answer to the contention that there were really two personalities in William Sharp. Even Mrs. Sharp, who writes so restrainedly about this question of dual personality, believes the analytical faculty belonged to William Sharp, the imaginative to "Fiona Macleod." But in this criticism of the Celtic Renaissance which is signed "Fiona Macleod," there is as much analysis as is to be found anywhere in his work as William Sharp. So obviously was he identifying "F. M." with "W. S." in this critical writing that Mrs. Janvier, of those in the secret, wrote to him to take warning lest he betray himself. She pointed out to him that such a display of learning as he was making in the later "Fiona Macleod" work would surely lead to discovery. But he did not heed. The truth probably was that he wrote about Celtic things as "Fiona Macleod" because he perhaps felt about them, as "Fiona Macleod," as one who is bilingual thinks about work he is doing, say in German, in German, and about work he is doing in English, in English; but just as surely I believe, because what "Fiona Macleod" wrote commanded more respect than what William Sharp wrote, a readier entrance into the magazines, and better pay. If there are those to whom such an explanation seems belittling to William Sharp, I can only say that they cannot have realized that he was a driven man earning his living by his pen. I am not, I confess, a sentimentalist in such matters, and while I do not wholly like his procedure in maintaining the fiction of "Fiona Macleod," it does not seem to me a very heinous sin.

He who would write of the work of William Sharp, indeed, must be resolute to remember that it is to be considered as an essay in the art of letters. There are so many temptations toward writing of it as a scientific problem,—for who is not interested in "dual personality"?—or as a "psychic revelation," if one is bitten—and who is not?—by curiosity about hidden "things"; or as an irritating hoax, if one has been befooled—and who, for one moment or another has not been?—into believing that this writing under the pseudonym of "Fiona Macleod" was the confession of a woman. The romance of it remains, no matter from what point of view you consider it, and, despite your preoccupation with this or that phase of it, the beauty of literary art of parts of it. Parts of it, I say, for to me no writer of our time was more uneven in his work. My point of view, indicated perhaps brutally, and with a firstly and secondly is:—

Firstly, that until he was nearly forty, William Sharp was no more than a skillful literary practitioner, a higher sort of hack, who had done some better writing of a tenuous kind of beauty but imitative in substance and art, in *Sospiri di Roma* and *Vistas,* and that after forty, when he was developing one undeveloped side of himself as "Fiona Macleod," he developed another undeveloped side of himself in *Silence Farm.* That he attained in a sort of writing, and greatly, that he had not attained in before, in *Silence Farm,* has not been acknowledged, so easy has it been to those interested in his work to lose sight of all else in their pursuit of the "Fiona Macleod" side of his nature. It is true of *Silence Farm,* as of almost all his other work done under the name of William Sharp, that it is imitative; but it is equally true that a large part of the "Fiona Macleod" work is imitative, too. *Silence Farm* is done under the influence of the later work of Mr. Hardy, but the material of *Silence Farm* is its author's own, and the color of the writing is as distinctly of the Lowlands as the color of *Tess* is of Wessex. That *Silence Farm* is better work in its kind, though that kind is less original than some of his writing as "Fiona Macleod," I have been forced against my prejudices to believe. If I did not so believe I would not have spoken of it side by side with *Tess.*

Secondly, that as "Fiona Macleod," William Sharp did much good writing in almost everything published under the pseudonym, achieving wholeness of good tissue in certain sketches and tales and verses on rather varying kinds of subjects, but that his work as "Fiona Macleod" that is really distinguished is in stories of prehistoric Scotland and Ireland, and of Scotland and Ireland in the earliest historic time. In these tales of the Gaels of old time he for the first time breaks ground for others. Before he wrote **"Silk o' the Kine,"** and **"The Harping of Cravetheen,"** **"The Annir Choile,"** and **"Enya of the Dark Eyes,"** there were no short tales of like temper and content and style in literature.

To me little is significant in the early verse of "Fiona Macleod," as little was significant in all the verse of William Sharp until the time of *Sospiri di Roma.* And for all the beauty of these pictures in words of the Campagna it is but a transient beauty. It was not until he was mastered by the new beauty that Mr. Yeats brought into English poetry that the verse of William Sharp won to itself abiding beauty and glamour and inevitable phrase. *The House of Usna* (1900) brought to me "Dim face of beauty haunting all the world," and the 1901 edition of *From the Hills of Dream, The Enchanted Valleys;* but it was not until after his death that I came upon his best verse of all, the verse of his last five years, which was gathered together posthumously in the 1907 edition of *From the Hills of Dream,* and included as **"The House of Beauty"** in *The Poems and Dramas* of 1911. Who does not know these sets of verses and **"The Dirge of the Four Cities,"** does not know the ultimate accomplishment of William Sharp in poetry.

That the "'Fiona Macleod' mystery" ended with the death of William Sharp is, then, my belief, as it is that it began before he conceived of exploiting a feminine subself he had long been aware of in himself. The beginnings of that sort of writing that made "Fiona Macleod" a reputation are to be found very early in his writing, in **"The Son of Allan"** of 1881, in the **"Record"** of 1884, in the preface to the *Romantic Ballads* of 1888, in the *Vistas* of 1894. That these earlier expressions of "spiritual" states and guesses at mysteries are not, except for certain parts of *Vistas,* so well written as the best writing of similar kind by "Fiona Macleod," is true, and perhaps, at first glance, a matter of wonder. It is, however, I think, not difficult to find an explanation of the better quality of the later work, and that explanation is afforded, firstly and most largely, by the Celtic Renaissance. A man of thirty-five, to all who know him a very vital force, a very original personality, who has all his life wanted to make beautiful things in words out of his dream of life, has disappointed himself and his friends. He is suddenly afforded the opportunity, by the interest in Gaelic subjects that the Celtic Renaissance has awakened, to gain a hearing for work of a kind he has long wanted to do. He had not done such work previously, because he had to live by his pen and could work consistently only at the sort of thing that would sell. He was well known as a journeyman of letters, so well known for bookmaking, and the ways of getting commissions from London editors and publishers, that his knowledge of Highland life would be questioned. All in London knew him as a Londoner. It would be useless for him to say that the Celtic Renaissance had brought back his childhood to him, a childhood as definitely dominated by a Highland nurse as Stevenson's was by the Lowland Alison Cunningham. It would be useless to tell of his summers in Argyllshire and among the inner isles, his intimacy with fishermen who were as elemental as his own dreams of old time. It would have been cast up to him that the editor of *The Canterbury Poets* could not be an original writer, and the very nine days' wonder of *Vistas* would have been pointed to to prove that he might now do well enough, as an imitator, perhaps of Mr. Yeats, as he was in *Vistas* successful as an imitator of M. Maeterlinck, but that an original Highland writer could not come out of Hampstead. There is no doubt in my mind that it was the part of wisdom for Sharp to put out the new work under a pseudonym, worldly wise if you will, but wise, too, with a higher wisdom. If he could keep the side of him he had never yet exhausted through hackwork apart from his other work, it would grow as it could not if it were a part of his daily stint.

Why Sharp chose a woman's name for his pseudonym has troubled many, but this choice was, I think, as was the assumption of a pseudonym, the part of wisdom. I do not believe, as he at times liked to believe, that he attained a woman's standpoint. He had been complimented on all sides for his composition of the wife's letters in *A Fellowe and His Wife* (1892), in which Mrs. von Teuffel wrote the husband's. Sharp enjoyed their writing as a *tour de force* and he probably believed they were very womanly. I should say that they showed insight into womanly ways of looking at things rather than a dramatic identification of himself with woman such as is George Meredith's. Sharp had already been experimenting with pseudonyms, that of "H. P. Siwaärmill," an anagram on his own name, being that he recurred to most often. He had written the whole of *The Pagan Review* in 1892 under eight different pseudonyms, and though, in the estimation of those to whom "Fiona Macleod" is all but a sacred name, it be sacrilegious to say it, William Sharp loved all sorts of fantastic tricks, hoaxes, mystifications, though in almost all his writing save in *Wives in Exile* he was seriousness itself. But the chiefest reason of all, in my estimation, for his assumption of a woman's name as his pseudonym was that it afforded greater protection against discovery. There are those who believe that he chose it because he wanted a chance to express that womanly element of human nature there is in all men, and there are others who believe that he was the possessor of a real dual personality in which the "Fiona Macleod's self" was a woman's consciousness; but he very infrequently, after *The Mountain Lovers* (1895), kept in mind in the writings he published as "Fiona Macleod's" that their author was supposed to be a woman, and it is wonderful, indeed, that he was able to preserve the secret until the end. In the earlier "Fiona Macleod" writing there is no revelation of the wide acquaintance with literature that was Sharp's, but despite his harassment by the constant identification of himself with "Fiona Macleod," he gradually allowed to creep into that writing more and more of what was known to be the knowledge of William Sharp, a knowledge unlikely to be also that of a Highland lady who lived apart from the world. His friends pointed out to him the danger he was running in writing from what was obviously a man's standpoint, as in his tales of the wars of Gael and Gall, and of revealing several sorts of interest that were known to be his, but their warnings were in vain. He was apparently unable to limit himself to the restrictions of the part of himself he had essayed to restrict himself to.

For my own part I was now sure the writing must be Sharp's and now sure it could not be his. I did not know of his intimate concern with questions of feminism until I read Mrs. Sharp's *Memoir,* so that outspoken chant, the **"Prayer of Women"** in *Pharais,* "Fiona Macleod's" first book, colored my outlook on all the writing that followed. I had no doubt at all but that *Pharais* was written by a woman, but **"The Dan-nan-Ron"** and **"Silk o' the Kine"** in *The Sin-Eater* (1895) seemed to me hardly a woman's. *The Washer of the Ford* (1896) was written from the man's point of view, too, but *Green Fire* (1896) seemed feminine again. So I wobbled in my opinion until *The Divine Adventure* (1900) and the critical writings of the volume that story gives title to, and the critical writing in *The Winged Destiny* (1905), made me believe again that "Fiona Macleod" was surely Sharp. I did not come upon the articles that now make up *Where the Forest Murmurs* (1907) until after the death of Sharp and the disclosure of the secret. Had his death not divulged the secret of the identity of "Fiona Macleod," it seems to me that collection must have disclosed it. Had Sharp lived after this there would not have been possible for him much further work from the seclusion his pseudonym gave him, and I doubt, once the secret was out, it would have been possible for him to write of things Celtic with the old gusto.

After all has been said it must be confessed, I think, that Sharp did not know the Highlander, either of the mainland or of the islands, very intimately. He wrote much better of his dream of life on the west coast in prehistoric times—out of his imagination of what that life must have been, an imagination founded on the reading of the old legends and modern collections of folk-lore, such as the

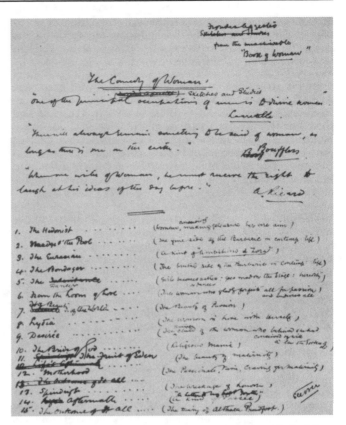

Manuscript page with projections for stories by "Fiona Macleod."

Carmina Gadelica of Mr. Carmichael—than he did out of his knowledge of Highland life of today. The Achannas are in many of his tales of modern times, and wherever they are there is unreality, if not melodrama. Unreality, too, there is, in many phases, in the modern tales, and "highfalutinness" everywhere in them. And both unreality and "highfalutinness" offend in these modern tales as they would not in the tales of far times, though in these, as a matter of fact, they are not so much in evidence.

It would almost seem that the approach to reality drove Highland atmosphere from the stories. In **"The Sin-Eater,"** one of the best of his writings that might be classed as a short story, the sin-eater and his confidant are Highlanders, but the description of the scene of his misfortune, the steading of the Blairs, might well have been that nearest to *Silence Farm.* It is faithfully described, the scenes about the little home, whose owner lies dead, having the very smack of realism. In the latter part of the story the scene shifts to the coast and the tang of the story turns Gaelic and unreal. Was it thus, I wonder, always to the imagination of William Sharp, Lowland life real, Highland life mystical?

Sharp was handicapped, of course, in coming to the subject material he could best handle late in life, *Pharais* (1894) and *The Mountain Lovers* (1895), the first books published as by "F. M.," being just as definitely 'prentice-work in their kind as was *Children of To-morrow* (1890) in its kind. Of the long stories other than *Children of To-morrow* published in his own name, *A Fellowe and His Wife* (1892) and *Wives in Exile* (1896) have no very serious intention, though both are well done after their kind, records of imaginings, respectively, of experiences of art life in Rome, and of yachting experiences in the Irish Sea. It was not until *Silence Farm* (1899), as I have said, that, as William Sharp, he found himself.

"The Gypsy Christ" (1896), which might well have been developed into a full-fledged romance, is less original than any of his longer writings. It is, like "The Weird of Michael Scott" and *A Northern Night,* closely allied to essays of his other rôle, that of "F. M.," to catch and express "the tempestuous loveliness of terror," such as the catastrophe of *The Mountain Lovers, The Barbaric Tales,* and those short stories in which Gloom Achanna is hero-villain. (pp. 251-65)

Of the long stories published as by "F. M.," Sharp repudiated *Flora MacDonald* because it was too much in the way of "ordinary romance," and *Green Fire* for the same reason and because it was largely about Brittany, a country with which, by some strange chance, he did not make himself familiar, though he had visited and learned to know well at least parts of all the other Celtic countries. It is to my mind, however, if not so definitely of a wholeness of texture as *Pharais* or *The Mountain Lovers,* or so singular, less monotonous than either. All three of these stories disappoint my memory of them when I again read them. This is, I believe, because all three of them—and for that matter many of the short stories as well—are incompletely realized, or because—in the case of two of them, *The Mountain Lovers* and *Green Fire*—they are unevenly written. Their high intention and atmosphere remain with you after you have put the books aside, and in the course of time you forget their hurried writing, their inconsistencies, and their qualities of the "Shilling Shocker," the result of their author's failure to attain "the tempestuous loveliness of terror" that are in so many of them, long or short. As aids to this effacement of the cheapening elements are the very materials of the tales, their characters, now elemental, now other-worldly, and their background of mountains that uplift the spirit, and of menacing sea. (pp. 266-67)

It is their aloofness from the everyday story, their unusual use of the supernatural that has given the longer stories written out of the "Fiona mood," as Mr. Sharp once spoke of his possession, their appeal to most readers, but there is here in America a class who put the highest valuation on the shorter stories Mr. Sharp called "spiritual tales." To those who hold this view *The Divine Adventure* is of the nature of revelation. To me it is hardly this, but very interesting, not so much for its putting of the relations of Body, Will, and Spirit to one another in life and at death, as for its beautiful writing, and for its definite betrayal, when its author is writing most intimately, of a man's attitude, though he published the story as the work of "Fiona Macleod." These "spiritual tales" do not belong, all of them, to his "Fiona Macleod" period, for *Vistas* (1894) contains many of them, though they are cast here in dialogue form, and there are others among the work published under his own name. In fact, the writing under the two names never becomes liker in quality and intention than when it is "spiritual." The sketch from Part II of *The Dominion of Dreams* (1899), entitled "The Book of the Opal," for instance, is written on the very key of *Fragments of the Lost Journals of Piero di Cosimo* (1896), far apart as is their subject material, and "The Hill-Wind" by

"W. S.," dedicated as it is to "F. M.," might well be a rejected passage from *The Mountain Lovers.* There is the color of the Highlands and Islands about many of these mystical stories, about "The Hill-Wind," by "W. S." and "The Wind, the Shadow, and the Soul," the epilogue "F. M." wrote to the *Dominion of Dreams;* but most of these shorter mystical tales have not the tang and savor of farm-home on lonely moors, or fisher's hut on the lonelier machar, that is characteristic of most of the tales, long and short, that deal with modern days.

Nor are the meanings of these "spiritual tales" consistently indicated in symbols taken from Scottish life, nor is their supernaturalism native to it. Mrs. Spoer (Ada Goodrich-Freer), in her "Outer Isles" (1902), tells us "The Celtic Gloom" amuses the Hebridean. If so, what effect would such discussion as that of "The Lynn of Dreams" and "Maya" have upon him? But if such essays are not written out of Highland life, they are none the less interesting, and in the case of "Maya," with its consideration of waking dream, beautiful as art, and valuable, too, as a contribution to science.

So far does Sharp go in his belief as to the apprehension of thought through powers other than those of the senses, that in *The Winged Destiny* he can look forward to a time "when the imagination shall lay aside words and pigments and clay, as raiment needless during the festivals of the spirit, and express itself in the thoughts which inhabit words—as light inhabits water or as greenness inhabits grass." Not only does he foresee such a time, but he foreshadows it, heralds it in some of his sketches, "Aileen" for one, by attempting it. Perhaps he has succeeded, perhaps not. To me the attempt is a failure, not, I think, because he is writing for to-morrow, for that age when the spiritual awakening he so often prophesied shall have come, but because he is attempting what cannot be done in any age. If he were seeking only suggestion, well and good. But he seeks more, and fails, I think, to attain more. It seems to me impossible that the suggestions he creates can ever be more than suggestions. They cannot become definite concepts that will mean the same thing to all men. Suggestion, the opening-up of vistas, is a high attribute of the art he follows; but he is not content with suggestion, he would seek more definite expression of what, after all, is not thought but mood. So it is that he is most successful when conveying mood and less successful when conveying esoteric thought. As a critic, of course, on a plane easier for the conveyance of thought, Sharp is definite enough, completely successful in conveying the ideas that he intends to convey.

Often, I fear, when Sharp intends "spiritual history," either in a tale wholly devoted to this purpose, as *The Divine Adventure,* or as explanatory to the incidents of some more tangible tale, he is really only playing with words, beautiful words, words sometimes so beautiful that we are apt to forget that words are to be used not alone for beauty's sake. Often, again, I fear, he will introduce beautiful symbols simply for their beauty and not because they have a real purpose, not because they will more intimately convey, even to the initiated, the intent of his writing. That these practices are the result of carelessness, sometimes, as well as of his subservience to beauty, the fascination that words merely as words or visions merely as visions exert upon him, is, I think, true. It is but seldom, I believe, that the underlying thought is incoherent. In almost all of his earlier writing, however, even in the earlier "Fiona" writing, he is very careless. He contradicts himself in his short stories as to facts, he gets his family relationships tangled in a way that cannot be explained by any process of nature, and so, too, I think, he gets his symbols mixed, or deludes himself into the belief that something that was hastily written "came to him" that way and so should be preserved in that exact expression, even though to him at the second reading it meant nothing definite. He jumps to conclusions again and again in what he writes about birds, where I can follow him on a certain footing of knowledge. If he is so careless about facts, if he can, even though it is a slip, confuse Mary Magdalene and the Virgin Mary, if he can mention birds in a description of Highland landscape that is characteristic of a certain time of year when birds of that species would be in the Highlands only by accident at that time of year, it is more than likely, slips though these may be, that there will be similar slips in all he writes, no fewer, it is likely, in his writings of psychic things than elsewhere.

There is possible, of course, no hard-and-fast classification of his writings. Class shades into class almost imperceptibly. It is particularly difficult to draw the line between the several kinds of stories and sketches he writes that involve supernaturalism of one kind and another. There is possible, however, a rough-and-ready distinction between those stories of his which are esoterically mystical and those which, while concerned with the supernatural, are concerned with it in the way familiar in old romance. Of this "usual supernatural" are those in which "second sight" is the motive, second sight which is always to be looked for as the commonest supernatural motive in the writing of all Gaels, either Alban or Irish. Sharp introduced "second sight" into **"The Son of Allan"** (1881); it is in *Pharais* (1894), the first of his "F. M." work; it is developed at some length in **"Iona"** (1900), which is a microcosm of all his writing. In **"Iona,"** Sharp puts himself on record as holding stoutly belief in the reality of the power:—

> The faculty itself is so apt to the spiritual law that one wonders why it is so set apart in doubt. It would, I think, be far stranger if there were no such faculties. That I believe, it were needless to say, were it not that these words may be read by many to whom this quickened inward vision is a superstition, or a fantastic glorification of insight.

The Achannas, in the uncanny stories in which they are heroes and villains, are all possessed by the power of the second sight, but second sight is not the most remarkable of their supernatural powers. Hypnotic suggestion Gloom uses as an everyday agent in his affairs. It is through hypnotic suggestion that he puts madness upon Alasdair M'Ian, playing to him the Pibroch of the Mad, Alasdair M'Ian, in telling whose story "Fiona Macleod" revealed—I suppose, by chance—something of the struggle of William Sharp to succeed in letters. Much more frequently, however, he uses a supernatural power that is further removed from those in which modern science is interested, such as the machination of fairies that made Allison Achanna the **"Anointed Man"**—that, in plain speech, had driven him fey; or such as the lure of the serpent goddess that drove to his death the piper hero of **"By the Yellow Moon Rock,"** or the exchanging of human child for fairy child that is the burden of **"Faraghaol."**

It is much more likely that William Sharp would have made more of this changeling motive had it not come so near to the question of dual personality, which it would be dangerous to him to discuss, as would that question so closely akin, the question of people who are "away,"—that is, with the fairies,—a kindly explanation of insanity, chronic or recurrent. As William Sharp he has touched on the question of dual personality several times in his verses, and very definitely in *A Fellowe and His Wife.* In this last-named book he says, in a letter that the Countess Ilse writes to her husband in Rügen: "This duality is so bewildering. I to be myself, whom you know, and whom I know—and then that other I, whom you do not know at all and whom I only catch glimpses of as in a mirror, or hear whispering for a moment in the twilight." That he could not take up the topic so definitely in his later writings must have, indeed, been a cross to him, for there was hardly any other question, unless perhaps that of "ancestral memory," which interested him more deeply. It might be argued, I suppose, that he did discuss it in *The Divine Adventure,* in considering the relations of Spirit, Will, and Body. Mrs. Sharp, I take it, so holds when she says in her *Memoir* that the William Sharp work was that of the Will and the "Fiona Macleod" work beyond the control of the Will. And it is true that these three, the Spirit, Will, and Body, though each is given a distinctive personality, each a memory distinct from the memory of the others, are all but the component parts of one man. Mrs. Sharp does not, however, anywhere avow directly a belief in the possession of a real dual personality by her husband, and she definitely contradicts Mr. Yeats for his expression of belief that "William Sharp could not remember what as 'Fiona Macleod' he had said to you in conversation."

Very different from these short stories I have been discussing are three of the four contained in the volume entitled *Madge o' the Pool* (1896), published as by William Sharp. Of the one that is somewhat in the manner of certain of the "F. M." stories, the **"Gypsy Christ,"** I have spoken. Two, **"The Coward"** and **"The Lady in Hosea,"** are but "the usual thing." **"Madge o' the Pool"** is the one really worth while. In this story, with such river pirates as we have met, sentimentalized, in "Our Mutual Friend," as material, Sharp writes as realistically as he does in *Silence Farm,* and with a sympathy and pathos that his objective method cannot exclude.

There are episodes or sketches, some of them what Sharp calls "prose imaginings," throughout his many books, that one may hardly call short stories, or myths, or studies in folk-lore, or criticism, or any of the other many kinds of writing that he essayed. Perhaps "memories" would be the proper general term for writing of this kind. In almost every one of these episodes or sketches there is a germ of a story, and some, I suppose, regard them as but unrealized art. But I for one am glad Mr. Sharp did not "work them up." In them are some of his best writing and some of that most personal and intimate. . . . [**"Aileen,"** **"Barabal,"** and **"Sheumas, a Memory"** are] memorable, and memorable, too, are **"The Sea Madness"** and **"The Triad."** **"The Triad"** is almost his *credo,* certainly a statement of the things he holds "most excellent"—"primitive genius, primitive love, primitive memory." Here Sharp recurs, as so often in his writing, to "ancestral memory," that possession of men by which they are aware of what was in the world before they were, through oneness with the universal memory into which they are absorbed in dream or vision or of which they become aware by what we call intuition. If such a power be restricted so that its possessor recalls only certain parts of antiquity, he is virtually in the state of him who believes he remembers what he remembers because of previous incarnations. I have no personal opinion to express on the subject, but if such memories exist in us because of our participation in a universal memory or because of reincarnation, it is easy to explain why Sharp is best in his writing of myths, his pictures of the wild beauties of love and war and dream in barbaric Erin and Alba. It is because he is the reincarnation of the shanachie of the Dark Ages. When he thought of reincarnation, however, in relation to himself, he thought, I have no doubt, of himself as the reincarnation of a druid, one who had been aware of mysteries; but what he really was, in life, with his magnificent enthusiasm and brávado,—picturesque raiment after all and no more for the high-hearted and inherently ailing body of him,—was this reincarnation of the shanachie, such as one as his own Oran the Monk turned tale-teller. If you doubt that he was shanachie, not druid, compare the two legends in **"Beyond the Blue Septentrions."** The ordered beauty of the legend that tells of the derivation of the name of Arthur from Arcturus falls familiarly on our ears. It is evidently made under a lamp by one who has read many old legends. It is no druidic revelation. The other, that which ends with the three great hero-leaps of Fionn from the Arctic Floes to the Pole, from the Pole up to Arcturus, from Arcturus to the Hill of Heaven itself, is fantastic, bizarre, extravagant to grotesqueness, with the very flamboyance of old Irish legend and modern Irish folktale. In other words, it is in the very manner of the shanachie of the Dark Ages, whether his work was recorded then as court poem or has been handed down by word of mouth among the folk. (pp. 273-81)

The range of the shanachie is wide, and wide, too, the range of Sharp in the rôle of shanachie of barbaric life on both sides of the Moyle. Among such writings there are few tellings of the order of the folk-tale, more of the order of the hero saga, many—perhaps the best of them—of an order all his own that has developed, it is likely, from the old "Saints' Lives," but to which he has given a ring of authenticity that makes them seem descended from an antiquity as remote as that of folk-tale or hero-tale. **"The Flight of the Culdees"** brings before you with vividness what must have been the life of the Celtic missionaries in the days when the men out of Lochlin began to seek the Summer Isles; and **"The Annir Choile"** and **"The Woman with the Net,"** what was the fate they meted out to those among themselves who slipped back into the pleasant old ways of paganism. These are written out of his own revisualization of the past. More immediately sprung of the old legends are **"The Three Marvels of Hy,"** which tells of the inner life of Columba and his brethren on Iona, and **"Muime Chriosd,"** which utilizes folk-lore as old or older than the legends collected by Mr. Alexander Carmichael in his pursuit of the stories of St. Bride among the peasantry of the Outer Isles. **"The Song of the Sword"** and **"Mircath"** have in them the battle-madness of the Viking, whetted to its keenest intensity as he meets the hard resistance of the Hebrideans; and **"The Laughter of Scathach"** and **"The Sad Queen,"** that more terrible fury of the Amazon who ruled in Skye. Than this last-named story Sharp has done no starker writing, but it is so evidently from a man's point of view that it confirmed many in the belief that "Fiona Macleod" could not be a woman.

"The Washer of the Ford" has its roots in folk-lore, but it is so remoulded in the mind of the writer that it is rather a re-creation of the old belief than a restoration of it. There are those who would rather have had Sharp follow the tales as they are told by Campbell of Islay, Cameron of Brodick, and Carmichael of South Uist, but to me, unless the tale is one familiar to many readers, such a remoulding, if done with power, is surely a prerogative of the artist. But when he takes a well-known legendary character, as well known among the Gaels as Achilles among English school-boys, and changes his hair from black to golden and his stature from short to tall, utterly transforming not only our picture of him, but the significance of his deeds, then I object, as I would object if he had made the fair-haired and great-statured Achilles into such "a little dark man" as the Red Branch legends record Cuchullin to have been. Nor would I quarrel even with his changing of the spirit of the old tales if he had always, as he has almost always, substituted a new beauty for the old beauty of the legend in its bardic or folk form. It is in the few instances in which his dream of the old tale does not lift to so great a power in its way as the old tale possessed in its way that I protest. Of such a nature are some of the changes Sharp made in his retelling of the "Three Sorrows of Story-Telling" in **"The Laughter of Peterkin,"** which, it must be remembered, however, was hurried work, almost hack-work.

Sharp was particularly successful, I think, in his handling, in the three tales—he calls them "legendary moralities"—in which he brings Christ to the straths of Argyll. These three are **"The Last Supper," "The Fisher of Men,"** and **"The Wayfarer."** The last is the least successful of the three, but significant in its attack on certain forms of Presbyterianism for their attempts to kill out, as un-Christian, the old ways of life among the Highlanders. This charge was made fifty years ago by Campbell of Islay, and it had been repeated only yesterday by Mr. Carmichael. William Black and Mr. Munro confirm it, too, in their novels, and, in fact, it is only what one expects of Puritanism, whether in its dominating of the Scotch Presbyterian minister or of the Irish Catholic priest. The latter is to-day doing as much to kill the joy of life in Connacht as did even the minister of the Free Kirk yesterday on the Lews. It may have been partly to hide his identity that Sharp assumed what some thought an anti-Presbyterian attitude in his "Fiona Macleod" writing; it may have been the sympathy of the artist toward a church that has conserved art that led him to what some thought a pro-Catholic attitude; but scratch this gypsy artist and you find, surprising as it may be, a moral prejudice for Protestantism. Does he not admire Torcall Cameron and Archibald Ruthven, stern Calvinists both? **"The Fisher of Men,"** and **"The Last Supper"** have in them the austere beauty of the old morality plays, a beauty that is akin to the beauty of the Puritan imagination of Bunyan, and a tenderness that we may in vain look for there. They are written in all reverence and simplicity, and it is no wonder we find Mr. Yeats suggesting that "Fiona Macleod" turn them into plays for the Irish Theatre.

I do not care so much for **"The Birds of Emar,"** myths he has rewoven from the "Mabinogion" into Gaelic texture, or the series that purport to be collected among the Isles and are found to be very like certain well-known Greek legends. These, too, seem to me reweavings, and the **"Treud-nan-Ron"** and **"The Woman at the Crossways"**; and **"The Man on the Moor,"** though its origin is far from their origins, is also a reweaving. In certain of his writing of this time Sharp passes over virtually into criticism or comparative mythology, as in **"Queens of Beauty"** and **"Orpheus and Oisin,"** and in many of the papers of *Where the Forest Murmurs.* These all have interest; but some smell much of the lamp; and none of them are to be compared to the best of his "Seanchas," to **"The Harping of Cravetheen,"** or **"Enya of the Dark Eyes,"** or **"Silk o' the Kine,"** or **"Ula and Urla"**; or to his plays *The House of Usna* and *The Immortal Hour,* in which, for all the savagery, there is nobility, the nobility that was in the old legends themselves, that nobility that withstood even the hand of Macpherson, that nobility that has been reproduced most nobly of all in the "Deirdre" of Synge.

I am not so sure that the tone of these old myths is always distinctively Celtic, as it is undoubtedly in **"The Annir Choile,"** and in other "Seanchas" that reveal him at his best. There was viking blood in Sharp, and it comes out, I think, in such tales as **"The Song of the Sword."** How he came to write these barbaric tales I do not know, though I have sometimes thought that the "Dhoya" (1891) of Mr. Yeats may have suggested them, as the Hanrahan stories may have suggested certain of the more modern tales. But whatever their genesis, the heroes and heroines of the "Seanchas" seem to him like the heroes and heroines of Homer and the Greek tragedians; and his friend whom he thought inspired him to much of the "F. M." work stood, we must remember, as symbolical to him of the women of Greek as well as of Celtic legend.

There are many indications, in his last writing, not only in that unpublished book on "Greek Backgrounds" and in his articles in the magazines on Sicily, all by William Sharp, but in the "Fiona Macleod" work, that he would have come to write of Greek antiquity with an enthusiasm very like that with which he wrote of Gaelic antiquity. "W. S." is speaking with the voice of "F. M." when he says in a letter to Mrs. Sharp, dated Athens, January 29, 1904: "It is a marvelous homecoming feeling I have here. And I know a strange stirring, a kind of spiritual rebirth."

One reason, perhaps, that the best work of Sharp has come out of his consideration of the Celts of antiquity is that the stark stories he has to tell of them restrain his style, a style too flamboyant when there is in what he is writing a large opportunity for description of landscape or exhibition of great emotion in his characters. Another reason is, perhaps, that his tendency to introduce the supernatural is more in harmony with the subject material got out of antiquity than of the subject material got out of to-day. We can accept magic in these old tales, even to the incantations of Bobaran the White that swayed the waves of the sea so that Gaer, the son of Deirdre, was saved from the men of Lochlin. That is as it should be in druidic times. It is impossible, of course, that Bobaran had power over the waves, but in such a story such an episode seems more probable than the possible hypnotic suggestion of Gloom Achanna's pipe-playing that sent Manus MacOdrum to his death among the fighting seals, because to-day we do not often come upon such things. It is even less easy to ac-

cept the piping to madness of Alasdair in **"Alasdair the Proud."** Hypnotic suggestion may drive to death in the sea a man half fey because of sorrow long endured and the superstition that he is descended from seals, but pipe-playing cannot believably in modern tales drive a man insane, whatever it may do in the famous old "Pied Piper of Hamelin" or other folk-tales.

So, too, in the verse of Sharp, whether lyric or dramatic, it is the Celt that inspires him to his best work. Nowhere does his verse win so much of beauty and glamour as when his thought turns to the four cities of Murias and Finias and Falias and Glorias, or when it breaks into a chant on the lips of Etain, in *The Immortal Hour.*

Though there is less unevenness of technique, both in the style and in the unfolding of the story, in these "Seanchas" than elsewhere in his writing, the technique breaks down at times here, too, more usually through sins of omission than through sins of commission. Sharp realized the something wanting that so many find in much of his writing, even in much that is most beautiful, realized it so keenly that he felt called upon to explain. He explained not directly, it is true, as if in answer to criticism, but none the less definitely in thus affirming his attitude toward legends in the **"Sunset of Old Tales"**: "We owe a debt, indeed, to the few who are truly fit for the task [the collecting of tales from oral tradition], but there are some minds which care very little to hear about things when they can have the things themselves." This statement explains in part why it is that the life of the people, even that part of their life that fronts the past, has escaped him. He prefers his dream, thinking that it is their dream, or the dream of their ancestors. He has, indeed, the thing itself, the Highlander's dream, and when it is given to him to impart that dream fully we forgive him the proud words I have just quoted. The pity of it is he has not always so succeeded through the way he has chosen, and then it is, of course, that we condemn him for the lack of that humility the great dramatic artist must have whereby he must forget himself and so subordinate himself that tradition or life speaks through him.

It is not to be wondered, then, that there is little direct record of folk-lore of his own collecting in his writing, even when he is writing of folk-topics. There are borrowings in plenty, especially in *Where the Forest Murmurs,* and even when the collecting seems his own, as it does in **"Earth, Fire, and Water," "Children of Water,"** and **"Cuilidh Mhoire,"** it is diamond dust, not diamonds, to which he gives so beautiful setting. (pp. 282-89)

I have, I think, by this time made clear what to me is the great strength of William Sharp—his power to revisualize the Celtic past of Scotland and to imagine stories of that past that are as native to it as those handed down in Bardic legend or folk-lore. I have emphasized my belief that in other kinds of writing his attainment is less original, though often beautiful in its imitativeness, and this imitativeness I will explain as being due partly to that quality of the play-actor that was in him as in so many of Celtic blood, partly to his lack of time to hew out for himself a way of his own, and partly to his quick responsiveness to any new beauty pointed out by work that he admired. It was not altogether, however, lack of time that prevented his attainment of a larger originality, an originality in other sorts of writing than the "Seanchas." Sharp had an unfortunate disbelief in early life in the value of technique. In the preface to the **Romantic Ballads** (1888), for instance, he expressed the belief that "the supreme merit of a poem is not perfection of art, but the quality of the imagination which is the source of such real or approximate perfection." This, as I interpret it, means that a poem, when of perfect art, has back of that perfect art a high imaginative quality; but by his own practice Sharp knows that he thought the quality would suffice without the highest art in its expression. It was this belief that made him leave his work incomplete; he read his verses, no doubt, with the glow in which he wrote them recalled to memory, and without the realization that he had not got down on paper for others half of the creative force that was in him as he wrote.

I have found a reason for a lesser success than the early work of "Fiona Macleod" promised to him in his imitativeness, but in some ways he was handicapped, too, by lack of models to follow. Granted he could have blazed other ways for himself than that of the "Seanchas," he lessened the originality of his attainment by imitation, but if he could not have so blazed other ways he just as surely could have gone further had he had models, or rather good models, to follow, models, for instance, in novels of Highland life. The very fact of there being great realistic stories of Highland life might have made it possible for him to have written a Highland **Silence Farm.**

But enough of what might have been: what is is good enough, good enough at its best to treasure among those things that are a lasting part of our lives. However great may be the reaction against his work because of the nine days' wonder about the identity of its creator, certain parts of it, certain tales and certain verses and a play, will hold their own against the years. Through such tales as **"The Sad Queen,"** and such verses as **"The Dirge of the Four Cities,"** and **The House of Usna** even eyes of little vision may see "eternal beauty wandering on her way," leaving about them a glamour as recurrent to the mind as sunset to the skies. (pp. 294-96)

> *Cornelius Weygandt, "William Sharp ('Fiona Macleod')," in his* Irish Plays and Playwrights, *Houghton Mifflin Company, 1913, pp. 251-96.*

William Chislett, Jr. (essay date 1928)

[*In the following essay, Chislett counters Paul Elmer More's criticism of Sharp (see excerpt dated 1913) with an investigation into Sharp's role in the Celtic Renaissance.*]

"I cannot at all agree with Mr. Sharp's estimates of the works of Fiona Macleod," writes Mr. Paul Elmer More in *The Drift of Romanticism.*

> He apparently valued most the later writings in which the human motives disappear in a haze of disorganized symbolism, whereas the normal reader is likely to find his interest centering, with some minor exceptions, in the tales of **Pharais** and **The Mountain Lovers.** In these the discipline Sharp had acquired from long apprenticeship to the press kept him within the bounds of reason, while the new

freedom and the Celtic imagery added a note of strange and fascinating beauty.

To Mr. More, Fiona Macleod's symbolism is not impressive; his form and verse are often empty mouthings; he puts emotion above reason; he exalts revery; in a word, he is a Romanticist, which, to Mr. More, with all respect to his critical distinction, is enough said.

William Sharp was not a genius of the first water either as critic or creative artist; but many have liked his work, and some have "adored" it. Even Mr. More praises some of his things. On the whole, however, he prefers Lady Gregory and Synge, whose feet are on solid ground. We have seen that he also admires Lionel Johnson; but all schools find something to praise in that fine spirit.

I cannot write an impassioned defense of Fiona Macleod; but I am interested to note what he thought and said of the Celtic Renaissance and what he considered his own relation to it to be.

In **"The Shadowy Waters"** Sharp seems to speak directly to Mr. More. "To ignore now," he writes, "the Anglo-Celtic school—I prefer to say the Anglo-Celtic group—would be too parochial even for a London critic trained in the narrowest academical and literary conventions. One may ignore this or that writer; all cannot be ignored, for they are now many, and some have that distinction which rebukes the sullen." This is instructive when set beside Mr. More's contention that "in his inability to distinguish between an idea or even a genuine emotion and the fluttering of tired nerves Fiona Macleod fell again and again into meaningless rhetoric that makes the loosest vapourings of 'A. E.' or Mr. W. B. Yeats seem solid and compact of reason." How much truer criticism, really, is the following from Sharp's review of *The Four Winds of Eirinn:*

> Ethna Carbery's poems are the poems of the Irish heart, and Miss Hull's and Lady Gregory's re-told saga-tales are the mirror of the ancient Irish genius, as Mr. Yeats's poetry is preëminently the poetry of the Irish spirit: but the poems of "A. E." are the poems of a strayed visionary, of a visionary strayed into Ireland, and in love with that imagination and with that dream, but obviously in himself of no country set within known frontiers, of no land withheld by familiar shores. Surcharged with the intensest spirit of Ireland in the less mystical and poetic sense, is the slim volume of a handful of prose papers by Miss Ethel Goddard, entitled *Dreams for Ireland.* This book is uplifted with a radiant hope and with an ecstasy of spiritual conviction that make the heart young to contemplate: would God that its glad faith and untroubled prophecies could be fulfilled in our time, or that in our time even the shadows of the great things to come could lighten the twilight road.

Mr. More admits that Sharp did not "unite himself unreservedly with the so-called Celtic movement, and deprecated its too common hostility to prosaic sense and to everything Saxon." Yet, as we have seen, Mr. More believes he "frothed" more than the avowed adherents of the present Renaissance. But what Sharp really believed in was not Celticism but Anglo-Celticism, of which school he declares (**"For the Beauty of an Idea: Prelude"**) both Yeats and AE to be shining examples. In **"Celtic"** he shows that he himself is not so much seeking old Celtic enchantment as new enchantment comparable to the old. "The ideal of art," says he, "should be to represent beautiful life. . . . So far as I understand the 'Celtic movement,' it is a natural outcome, the natural expression of a freshly inspired spiritual and artistic energy. . . . There is no set law upon beauty. It has no geography. It is the domain of the spirit. . . . As for literature, there is, for us all, only English literature. All else is provincial or dialect."

In his Prologue to *The Sin-Eater,* however, he confesses to a closer relation to the movement.

> The beauty of the World, the pathos of Life, the gloom, the fatalism, the spiritual glamour—it is out of these, the inheritance of the Gael, that I have wrought these tales. Well do I know that they do not give "a rounded and complete portrait of the Celt." . . . Elsewhere I may give such delineation as I can, and is within my own knowledge of the manysidedness of the Celt, and even of the insular Gael. But in this book, as in *Pharais* and *The Mountain Lovers,* I give the life of the Gael in what is, to me, in accord with my own observation and experience, its most poignant characteristics—that is, of course, in certain circumstances, in a particular environment. . . . Some of my critics, heedless of the complex conditions which differentiate the Irish and the Scottish Celt, complain of the Celtic gloom that dusks the life of the men and women I have tried to draw. That may be just. I wish merely to say that I have not striven to depict the blither Irish Celt. I have sought mainly to express something of the "Celtic Gloom," which, to many Gaels if not to all, is so distinctive in the remote life of a doomed and passing race. . . . The Celt falls, but his spirit rises in the heart and the brain of the Anglo-Celtic peoples, with whom are the destinies of the generations to come.

Lionel Johnson wanted all literatures to come to Ireland and be made part of it; William Sharp desired Irish literature, and all other forms of the Celtic, to ally themselves with England and be content to be British. In this he resembled a whole group of writers; among them George Meredith, whom, by the way, he called "The Prince of Celtdom." (pp. 153-56)

> *William Chislett, Jr., "William Sharp on the Celtic Revival," in his* Moderns and Near-Moderns: Essays on Henry James, Stockton, Shaw, and Others, *1928. Reprint by Books for Libraries Press, Inc., 1967, pp. 153-56.*

Ifor Evans (essay date 1933)

[*Evans was an English novelist, educator, and critic who wrote primarily on English literature. In the following excerpt from his survey* English Poetry in the Later Nineteenth Century, *he points to Sharp's limitations as a poet.*]

Sharp's early verse in *The Human Inheritance* shows poetic ambition combined with unequal powers, and so it remained throughout his work. The title poem is a dim, visionary account of man's development, reminiscent of the early work of Bell Scott. Sharp created an atmosphere of diffused dreaminess which allowed a loose poetical texture:

> Below, the wide waste of the ocean lay.
> League upon league of moonled waters, spray

> And foam and salt sea-send: a world of sea
> By strong winds buffeted.

Much more concrete and effective is '**Motherhood,**' the first part of which, describing the birth-throes of a tigress, is Sharp's most decisive poetical composition. He used a Pre-Raphaelite detail for purposes of which the Pre-Raphaelites would not have approved. The detail, reminiscent at times of O'Shaughnessy, has gained from Sharp's own voyagings, and the grimness of the motive makes vivid contrast with his usual themes:

> Deep 'mid the rice-field's green-hued gloom
> A tigress lay with birth-throes ta'en;
> Her swaying tail swept o'er her womb
> As if to sweep away the pain
> That clutched her by the gold-barred thighs
> And shook her throat with snarling cries.

> Her white teeth tore the wild-rice stems;
> And as she moaned her green eyes grew
> Lurid like shining baleful gems
> With fires volcanic lighten'd through,
> While froth fell from her churning jaws
> Upon her skin-drawn gleaming claws.

Much of *Earth's Voices* he devoted to pastel studies of Nature, where the effect is usually marred by the diffuseness of the verse. In '**Sospitra,**' the outstanding poem in this volume, he returned to the metre of '**Motherhood,**' and to a narrative borrowed from Ouida. The poem has clarity, but it is infected with luxuriant and unnecessary epithets. As in the earlier volume he introduced a fresh, Australian background into a number of the poems. The *Romantic Ballads* (1888) were Sharp's attempt to free the ballad from the 'literary' qualities which Rossetti had fastened to it. His performance is unequal. In '**The Son of Allan**' he remains Rossetti's disciple in movement and refrain, while '**The Weird of Michael Scott**' gains simplicity only by a thinness in thought matched to a glib facility of movement. In 1891 *Sospiri di Roma* shows how Sharp's tendencies towards tenuity of thought were encouraged by irregular and rhymeless verse. Such patterns leave all the responsibility for control with the poet, and Sharp is unable to restrain the dreamy rhetoric which rose so easily within his mind.

Despite all discussions on dual personality and psychic memory, the 'Fiona' poems are, both in theme and vocabulary, merely Sharp's fuller exploitation of romantic inclinations apparent in his earlier work. These, it has been suggested, were strengthened by memories of stories told by his old Highland nurse, and they certainly gained further definition by the reading he had done in preparing his edition of Ossian (1896). Nor was 'Fiona' as a poet, particularly as a dramatic poet, without the help and encouragement of W. B. Yeats. The resulting verse suffered from diffuseness, but its dim, twilight colouring resuscitated the interest of earlier romanticism in ruins, legends, and far-off forgotten things, seen through a mist of vague but not unpleasant Ossianic rhetoric. The following, which is the opening passage from *The Immortal Hour,* shows how mechanical is Sharp's use of the adjective which suggests atmosphere, and how loose is the texture of the verse:

> By dim moon-glimmering coasts and dim grey wastes
> Of thistle-gathered shingle, and sea-murmuring woods
> Trod once but now untrod . . . under grey skies
> That had the grey wave sighing in their sails

And in their drooping sails the grey sea-ebb,
And with the grey wind wailing evermore
Blowing the dun leaf from the blackening trees,
I have travelled from one darkness to another.

He seems like a gleaner going through all the places where
romantic poetry has been harvested and gathering what
is left into his verses. *The Immortal Hour* had the good
fortune to attract Rutland Boughton as a possible libretto
for his music, and as a result it has had a successful stage
history. There is nothing in this play or in *The House of
Usna* to suggest that they would have sufficient strength
in themselves to survive as dramas.

The legend of Fiona Macleod gave the poetry of William
Sharp a temporary popularity disproportionate to its
merit. He never realized the distinction, essential in art,
between the reception of experiences or emotions and their
successful portrayal in an adequate medium. He is frequently content, as in **'Dreams within Dreams,'** to make
a rhetorical statement and feel that his duty as a poet is
at an end:

> I have gone out and seen the lands of Faery,
> And have found sorrow and peace and beauty there,
> And have not known one from the other, but found each
> Lovely and gracious alike, delicate and fair.

If this be poetry, then anyone who has stated that some
experience has moved him deeply is a poet. Similarly, he
relies on a small cohort of romantically coloured adjectives and nouns which he sends into his poems: 'dim' and
'grey' occur profusely, while the 'flittermice' that steal in
and out of the poems both of William Sharp and Fiona
Macleod serve as liaison officers between the dual personality. He had a poetic quality which appeared most clearly
when his verbal fluency could be restrained. It can be
found in his early poems, and recurs, less consistently, in
some of the short-line lyrics of the Fiona Macleod period,
as in **'The Vision:'**

> In a fair place
> Of whin and grass,
> I heard feet pass
> Where no one was.
>
> I saw a face
> Bloom like a flower—
> Nay, as the rain-bow shower
> Of a tempestuous hour.
>
> It was not man, nor woman:
> It was not human:
> But beautiful and wild
> Terribly undefiled,
> I knew an unborn child.

Encouraged at one period by Rossetti and at another by
Yeats, he had little of that passionate attachment to the
craftsmanship of verse which marked their work, but he
possessed a facile habit for refashioning the material from
which romantic poetry is made. (pp. 149-53)

> *Ifor Evans, "Minor Pre-Raphaelite Poets: Wil-
> liam Sharp (Fiona Macleod)," in his* English
> Poetry in the Later Nineteenth Century, *re-
> vised edition, Methuen & Co., Ltd., 1966, pp.
> 149-53.*

Hoxie Neale Fairchild   (essay date 1962)

[*Fairchild was an American educator and the author of
numerous essays and books on literary and religious
subjects. His major works include* The Noble Savage: A
Study in Romantic Naturalism *(1928), which is a
lengthy discussion of the depiction of unspoiled primitive
life in literature and its relationship to romantic naturalism, and the six-volume* Religious Trends in English
Poetry *(1939-68), which traces religious thought and
feeling in English poetry from the eighteenth to the twentieth century. In the following excerpt from the latter
work, Fairchild examines the spiritual aspects of Sharp's
poetry.*]

Everyone knows the strange story of "Fiona Macleod."
There is no need to interpret it in terms of dual personality. William Sharp was always William Sharp, but by 1893
he had convinced himself that the best excuse for writing
the strange misty stuff that he wanted to write was to pretend to be Fiona. Having a lively imagination and no sense
of reality, he was able to convince his readers and his
friends, and almost able to convince himself, of the phantom's actual existence.

What may be called his "pre-Fiona" poems are deservedly
almost unknown. They are indeed extremely different
from the poems of Fiona Macleod, but not so different that
we must postulate a miracle. Mr. Evans [see excerpt dated
1933] describes Sharp's entire career as moving from bad
Rossetti to very bad Yeats, but I see few if any signs of
Rossetti's influence in the first volume, *The Human Inheritance* (1882). Its most marked characteristic is Sharp's inability to find a balance between abstractly rhetorical
preachment and tersely objective rendering of sense impressions. His desire to do so is evidenced from the passage
from Whitman's "Starting from Paumanok" which provides his epigraph:

> I will make the poems of materials, for I think they are to
>   be the most spiritual poems;
> And I will make the poems of the body of mortality,
> For I think I shall then supply myself with the poems of
>   the soul, and of immortality.

But Sharp's "poems of the soul" prove to be stodgy, ver-
bose, pretentious philosophical essays. Their chief thesis
is that a belief in upward-spiralling metempsychosis is the
best means of reconciling ourselves to life's difficulties.
"The New Hope" lies in abandoning the old delusive quest
for permanence and learning instead to rejoice in "Eternal
change, no stagnant blissful dream!" Death means transition from a lower to a higher spiritual state. This process
will lead man

> Beyond himself, beyond the human soul,
> Farther than Christ or Christ's own farthest love.
>
>   · · · · ·
>
> Thus shall it be until the æons vast
> Draw man so nigh to God no human sight
> Can farther pierce th' ineffable great light.

At the other extreme, the "poems of materials" consist of
thirty little "Transcripts from Nature," all in a pattern
which, Sharp says, "is founded on the Tuscan *Rispetto*."
Their only purpose is to present a little picture with some
suggestion of mood but no conceptual thinking or "mes-

sage." Here Sharp is practicing a sort of imagism, although his impressions are not clear and hard enough to be authentically imagistic in the modern sense. **"Dream Land,"** belonging to neither type, is the sole faint adumbration of Fiona:

> Softly, hushfully,
> Silently flow
> Dim streams of sweetness
> Though lands of woe;
> Hushfully, hushfully
> Wash the cool waves
> Thro' intricate spaces
> Of wave-worn caves;
> And silently, suddenly
> Gather wan faces
> Long laid in graves.

Earth's Voices and Other Poems (1884) is "Dedicated in High Esteem and in Personal Regard to My Friend Walter H. Pater." Again the glad tidings of metempsychosis are preached, but not so persistently or long-windedly as in the earlier volume. A Rossetti influence now makes itself evident in an imitation medieval ballad and in a series of sonnets on paintings seen in Italy. On the other hand, the objectively descriptive element looms even larger than before. This time there are *two* groups of "Transcripts from Nature"; also five similar "Moonrise Sketches" and a series of quite hearty "Australian Sketches." On the whole, Sharp seems to be growing less prophetic and more aesthetic, but he has not yet found his own true—or untrue—voice. I have not read two other early volumes, *Romantic Ballads and Poems of Phantasy* (1888) and *Sospiri di Roma* (1891). The former title suggests further groping in the direction of Fiona.

In 1901 Yeats, still believing that she is a real though mysterious friend of Sharp's, thanks Fiona for *From the Hills of Dream*. "I never," he writes, "like your poetry as well as your prose, but here and always you are a wonderful writer of myths." In poetry, he prefers her when she is simplest and most objective, "for when you use elaborate words you invent with less conviction, with less precision, with less delicacy than when you forget everything but the myth." He recommends a style "that is like a tumbler of water rather than a cup of wine. . . . When you speak with the obvious personal voice in your verse, or in your essays, you are not that Fiona who has invented a new thing, a new literary method. You are that Fiona when the great myths speak through you." It is a little unfair of Yeats to object to that "cup of wine" style which Fiona had based upon his own early way of writing, a manner which in 1901 he had not decisively abandoned in favor of the "cup of water." He draws, however, a largely valid distinction between a subjectively "mystical" and a relatively objective element in the Fiona poems; and although the maturer Yeats would not praise the latter as highly as he does in 1901 it is certainly much more acceptable than the former. But the old inability to interfuse the visionary and the real which had beset Sharp in his pre-Fiona phase is still damagingly present. Too often he falsifies the impersonalities of Celtic tradition by trying to make them subserve the ends of his personal dream; at such times the motivation of the more objective poems becomes too transparently subjective. And when even this falsification will not give him what he wants, he flings the mask aside and permits the Ossianic bard to speak as a Victorian-

romantic reincarnation of James Macpherson. Unfortunately it is the poems in which this occurs, the poems of which Yeats rightly disapproves, that provide the clearest evidence of what Sharp desired to believe.

What he essentially wants is a kind of emotional experience in which everything is blissfully mixed up with everything else. He draws upon Macpherson and various other sources which encourage the romantic interfusion. The most debilitating qualities of the early Yeats are no doubt the strongest influence. Probably he also owes something to that fairy-loving Scot, George MacDonald. Perhaps he does not depend wholly on Yeats for the atmosphere of French Symbolism which is frequently felt. One of the epigraphs of *From the Hills of Dream* is the famous conclusion of *Axël*, where the heroine briefly shrinks from the suicide proposal, since "Là-bas, tout nous appelle. . . . Et, qui sait, tous les rêves à réaliser" ["There, everything calls to us . . . And, who knows, all the dreams to realize"], and Axël responds: "A quoi bon les réaliser? . . . ils sont si beaux!" ["What good is it to realize them? . . . They are so beautiful!"] It is axiomatic with Sharp, as with Villiers, that the surest way of destroying a value is to achieve it:

> I would not find;
> For when I find, I know
> I shall have claspt the wandering wind
> And built a house of snow.

After wondering whether his "poor little songs, children of sorrow," are leaves aimlessly stirred by the wind, he consoles himself by observing that

> The secret dews fall under the Evening-Star,
> And there is peace I know in the west: yet, if there be no
>   dawn,
> The secret dews fall under the Evening-Star.

Maeterlinck, whom Sharp must have admired, would appreciate the profundity of this sustaining thought.

Sharp also derived some encouragement from the occultism cultivated so assiduously by the French symbolists and their English admirers. Yeats found him remarkably susceptible "to symbolic [*i.e.,* magical] or telepathic influence, but . . . he never told one anything that was true; the facts of life disturbed him and were forgotten." Apparently Yeats believed that Sharp's mysterious friend was also interested in these arcana. From Paris in the spring of 1898 he writes Lady Gregory that he is living with the Rosicrucian mage MacGregor Mathers, "who spends most of his day in highland costume to the wonder of the neighbors." Maud Gonne, Yeats continues, "comes here to-morrow to see visions. Fiona Macleod (this is private as she is curiously secret about her movements) talks of coming here too, so we will have a great Celtic gathering." In this circle, to be "Celtic" was to see visions in a precise technical sense. Despite the attractions of Mathers' kilt, Fiona did not make her appearance; but perhaps Sharp is not *merely* plagiarizing Yeats in the Rosicrucian lines,

> Oh, fair immaculate rose of the world, rose of my dream,
>   my Rose!
> Beyond the ultimate gates of dream I have heard thy mystical call.

Sharp could easily have moved onward to this sort of occultism from his early belief in metempsychosis.

With such assistance, Celtic traditions could be interpreted as tangible embodiments of Sharp's intangible dream about being dreamy. In the dedication of *From the Hills of Dream,* "the old myth of Oengus of the White Birds and the Grey Shadows," whatever that may be, is cited as authority for the notion that love and death are the same thing. In **"The Crimson Moon,"** a feeble equivalent of Yeats's "Hosting of the Sidhe," it is prophesied that the fairy folk, the old gods from whom man has usurped the earth, shall arise and lay waste the anti-visionary civilization of these bad times:

> A day must surely come at last, and that day soon,
> When the Hidden People shall march out beneath the
>   Crimson Moon.

Pending the fulfillment of this prophecy we may leave Sharp at his devotions in "The Valley of Silence":

> In the dusk-grown heart of the valley
> An altar rises white;
> No rapt priest bends in awe
> Before its silent light:
> But sometimes a flight
> Of breathless words of prayer
> White-wing'd enclose the altar,
> Eddies of prayer.

(pp. 42-7)

Hoxie Neale Fairchild, "Slight Deviations," in his Religious Trends in English Poetry: Gods of a Changing Poetry, 1880-1920, Vol. V, *Columbia University Press, 1962, pp. 37-59.*

Flavia Alaya   (essay date 1970)

[*In the following conclusion to Alaya's biography of Sharp, the critic discusses the sense of place and cultural perspective in Sharp's works and places him in the tradition of spiritual exiles in literature.*]

It is impossible to pass final judgment on William Sharp's exploitation of his sense of place and to put it into historical perspective without first observing that a sympathetic response to the natural world is in some degree available as creative material to all artists. The power we all know in childhood of anthropomorphizing the external world and of seeing that world as an extension of what we only later and gradually come to know as our separate selves is, as one psychologist has pointed out, merely sustained longer by artists than by other men.

Yet all artistic sensibility to nature is not the same. If it were, there would be absolutely no validity to distinctions among various artistic eras, distinctions which, contrary to the antihistorical view of the psychologist, are the commonplaces of literary and artistic historiography. Every artist in every era may reverberate to his natural surroundings, but the shape and application he gives to that response define his philosophic fraternity with men of his time. "Windsor Forest" is a long way, philosophically as well as geographically, from the romantic Alps.

A distance less large, but a distance nonetheless, divides the nature sensibility of Wordsworth and of D. H. Lawrence. This is apparent. But what was the process by which this subtler distinction evolved? What did the Victorians contribute to the shape and application of the artistic response to nature that significantly altered it? As a Victorian in whose work and character was compressed every aspect of the nature sensibility and sense of place among his contemporaries, William Sharp may assist in determining and defining that evolutionary link.

Sharp's sense of place was in great part a legacy he owed to romanticism, a legacy of which not he alone but his entire generation were beneficiaries. Much more than those generic artists of whom the psychologist speaks, romantics seemed to receive more freely and to reverberate more liberally to the suggestions offered by the natural world. If the psychological premise devised to explain all such responses is correct, then the romantic distinguished himself by exceeding ordinary men—or indeed ordinary artists—in resisting the categorizing demanded by the adoption of a securely defined self. Perhaps his "agony" was the result of an unusually distasteful array of available roles in his society, none presenting him with an authentic and acceptable reflection of his own desires. Certainly the history coinciding with what we know in western culture as romanticism offers analogues for infinite dissatisfaction. Disruptions in religious, ethical, social, and political systems wrought their effect by making any thorough commitment to such systems less and less possible for the instinctively recalcitrant artist.

But such disruptions did not—could not—destroy the need for some such commitment, some such identification. The continuing need and the continuing search for identity characterize the romantic phase as much as does the generously sympathetic response to the outside world. The romantic could not disavow his instinctive psychological obligation to seek in some aspect of the reality around him a satisfactory reflection of himself. So demanding is this need that somewhere even the typical romantic conceded, if only partially or temporarily, and permitted a personal boundary to be drawn around him. The boundary was, more often than not, coterminous with the landscape on which he focused. Though Wordsworth's scenery may seem generically natural and his sensibility to nature broadly responsive, even he struck a limit. Partly it was a negative limit, antisocial in the simplest sense—a rejection of the city and its supposed obstacles to communion and self-reflection. But after the brief cosmopolitan excursions of his youth, Wordsworth drew an affirmative boundary too, which by and large described a particular half-gloomy, half-joyful English kind of landscape—watery, yet at its best not too sentimentally damp, variably cloudy, with a chance of sun, a chance of rain.

For a poet like Byron, the terrain might have been broader, but the climatic conditions were even more limited. Apart from the sunny divagations of his Don Juan, Byron's landscape was almost invariably cloudy and overcast, his moral horizon dark and befogged. And Shelley, though he renounced limits, in his very renunciation acknowledged their presence. He sought his volatile image in the wind, in a bird that was not a bird, in a man-god who was neither man nor god. Perhaps for this reason appreciation of Shelley is a touchstone of the romantic temperament. It is not surprising that Sharp preferred him to the other romantic poets: in the nearly quixotic attempt to push back limits he was thoroughly Shelley's successor. Wordsworth may, by contrast with Shelley, demonstrate the wisdom of taking a line of less resistance. In making his concession to a peculiarly English landscape of fact and feeling, he was implicitly conveying the knowledge that there is no total escape from identity, and the man who seeks it pays an enormous price, no matter how magniloquently his art may record the search.

In short, the romantic quest for freedom from traditionally imposed social roles was inevitably circumscribed. It became, in effect, a test of limits, regardless of how "illimitable" the seeker might try to make his vision. The Victorian period changed these conditions in only one significant respect, and that was but one of degree. To the concept of nation that had been formed a good deal earlier it gave a new and nearly overpowering emphasis as a boundary of man's cultural and emotional identity. The expansion that most characterized the epoch politically found its most sympathetic correspondence in the popular mind, but it was a source of "self" for many literary minds as well. It effected a cultural movement toward national identity that sustained itself practically unbroken until after the turn of the century. The subcurrent of reaction that steadily developed strength toward the end of the century did not fully establish itself until the First World War.

Sharp's life thoroughly described the locus of this cultural movement. He sought his personal identity in external nature by virtue of his romantic sympathy with it, but he also could not avoid the pressure to make such a search for personal identity a search for a correspondent configuration of race or nationality at a time when the external world itself was becoming increasingly categorized by nation and race. Modern history and political reality have, to a great extent, demanded the same of all men. For some, perhaps most, it is a demand that does not engage them in any visible conflicts. They accept their identity with their own familiar national society, as most Victorians did, without challenge or difficulty. But Sharp was one of those others whose dispositions respond to currents less obvious. He was a man made by nature extraordinarily sympathetic, and by history a striking exemplar of the continuing sense of displacement among modern artists, a displacement for which the exile has become the literary symbol, and for which nationalism may have been a necessary but nonetheless only temporary therapy. Urged by the circumstances of his early life, he uprooted himself from the natural and ordinary attachment to his own native place, his "home," an attachment that even at best could only have been half of an isotonic allegiance to Scottish culture and the English culture which had embraced it.

With an advancing technology of transportation conveniently assisting him in his flight, Sharp temporarily abandoned himself to a rebellious nomadism that negated his roots, and eventually made it impossible for him ever to restore a completely natural and comfortable identification with the home that ought to have been his. The society he encountered in London was itself artificial and rootless. It reflected an urbanization that was in great measure composed of the alienated poor, those who had deserted their identity with the soil to form a dispossessed class, and the alienated artists, those who had deserted their identity with English convention to form a bohemian coterie. Impelled by his own needs to espouse the city's muddled cosmopolitanism, Sharp was at the same time emotionally convulsed by the city's shapeless failure to provide a living community to which he could belong.

Given his own unsettled nature and the mistrust with which he regarded the settlements open to him, Sharp could find no satisfactory definition of himself. His quest thus remained a quest, episodic, filled with possibilities of pause, but no possibility of rest. The contrasts and oppositions of his experience provided a legitimate range within which to indulge the contrary impulses of his literary personality. His frustrated quest for limits ultimately represented itself as a quest for the illimitable; nothing less than that, or indeed more coherent than that, had revealed itself as an opportunity.

Sharp's sense of cultural exile was the expression, then, of a recalcitrant romanticism unwilling to commit itself to an English identity. But it was no isolated phenomenon. Some of the greatest writers of the period were spiritually or physically expatriated. Divided or uncertain loyalties informed their writing long before the crisis of the First World War liberated expatriates from their own diffusion and provided them with a rationale for fostering a community among themselves. Before exile was fashionable Victorians found means of revealing and disguising it at the same time.

Some of these emotional wanderers, like Samuel Butler, William Morris, and H. G. Wells, dreamed of utopias to satisfy their need for identity with place. Others, like Thomas Hardy and George Eliot, less optimistically visionary than the utopians, contracted their artistic sights and tended a small plot of earth where their belief in the basic interdependence of men could be dramatized on a microcosmic scale. Theirs was no mere regionalism or quest for local color, no simple social historian's concern with the curiosities of specific time and specific place. Rather they looked to these as reference points for all humanity. For them, as George Eliot put it, the "nightly heavens" of one's homestead were a means to "astronomy." Yeats was at one with her when he wrote that "all poetry should have a local habitation when at all possible," that "we should make poems on the familiar landscape we love," for he shared Eliot's sense of the ultimate purpose of that focus. "To the greatest poets," he said, "everything they see has its relation to the national life, and through that to the universal and divine life; nothing is an isolated artistic moment; everything fulfills a purpose that is not its own." The artist's object was to seize the particular and to transcend it by turning it into symbol.

Sharp's literary efforts combined both these impulses; he sought utopia and microcosm, and in combining these quests he demonstrated their intimate psychological unity. But often, too, his work found another, simpler metaphor for spiritual exile, in the dislocated wanderings of his characters. Through this metaphor he recorded a continuing emotional and psychological process of search, in which any focus upon a specific place was no more than an interpolated pause. This process is also to be found in the work of his greater contemporaries, who took up where Childe Harold and Don Juan had left off long before. The wanderings of Henry James's characters were the physical counterpart of their tortured spiritual explorations, and their search for identity was inextricably linked with concepts of national character. The same is true of the people in Conrad's novels. The English tongue may have adopted him, as he put it, but the English spirit did not. Proof lies in the very fragility of the sense of self possessed by his imperializing Englishmen—the inadequacy of their English character and rectitude to sustain an actual confrontation with man's interior jungle.

All of these writers shared with one another, as they shared with Sharp, a feeling that paradoxically yet inevitably grew side by side with Victorian nationalism, a sense of the deep interrelatedness of human experience. They shared what Conrad termed "the latent feeling of fellowship with all creation—the subtle but invincible conviction of solidarity . . . which binds men to each other and all mankind to the visible world."

Later Victorian fiction in general exhibits a strong tendency to express consciousness in terms of place and to endorse through that means a philosophy of cosmic solidarity and an ethic of cosmic sympathy. Such a development began early though tentatively in the Victorian novel and continued with increasing momentum over the course of the second half of the century. One may see this process of evolution by examining the novels of Dickens, for example, where the use of travel is not essentially grounded in cosmopolitanism and where travel may even tend to secure the national self-love of the English characters—as, for instance, the experience of Italy seems to do for Little Dorrit. Meredith represents a considerable step beyond this mode; even in so early a novel as *The Ordeal of Richard Feverel,* Richard is found undergoing his great epiphany in the Rhine country. Further, George Eliot, despite the essentially microcosmic impulse behind her use of place, writes a novel like *Daniel Deronda* with a wide European base, and elsewhere—everywhere—composes with a consciousness of place and movement. A similar balance prevails in Hardy, whose itineraries are usually circumspect in the extreme, but in whose work, indeed *because* he starts from such minuscule compass points, another village is virtually equivalent to another planet. There can be no doubt, at least, that divagation plays a considerable part in the moral experience of his characters; Angel Clare's voyage may be wide and Tess's wanderings narrow, but they are equally educative; and however much a treadmill may be the gypsy life of Jude and Sue in *Jude the Obscure,* it is still symbolic of the emotional locus of their lives.

These novelists thus go far to confirming Mary McCarthy's judgment that since the novel is rooted in the journalism of its epoch, the novelist shares the journalist's strong bias, in this period a bias toward tourism. As a corollary to this truth, one might observe that the cosmopolitan imagination is to some extent dependent upon the mobility of the writer himself. Characteristically well-traveled in life and literature are lesser fiction writers like Morris, Butler, Gissing, George Borrow, Kipling, Wells, and Stevenson, and larger ones like James and Conrad, in whom travel comes near to becoming what it distinctly *is* for Forster and Lawrence, the single most functional metaphor for consciousness.

But, to elucidate Sharp's position in this development, another point must be made. Conrad's "invincible conviction of solidarity" was a vision he reproduced through the exploitation of a stage both real and fabricated. It was real in the sense that the exotic and primitive world he used was actually there, and quite actually upon it were being played the dramas of national cupidity. Yet it was also a fantasy in the sense that it was so distant, so unfamiliar to the ordinary man who would read his novels, that it was quite fabricable, quite responsive to sensitive shaping to an artist's ends. "The problem was," he wrote in his preface to *Within the Tides,* "to make unfamiliar things credible." In doing so, he created an altar on which the Moloch of human division could himself be divided and sacrificed.

James did likewise. The drama of innocent America confronting a dissolute, if civil ancestry and attempting to resolve the discrepancy in its own moral identity was a drama that had not yet really happened—indeed may be said not yet to have happened—but it could be believed because it was so much hoped. So much hoped, in fact, that it is no surprise Sharp himself should have thought of America as an Eden where a new and believable community of men could be designed out of the materials that had seemed to decay in the old world.

If Sharp was like these men in seeking a foothold, a stage, upon which such symbolic dramas might be played, his failure to achieve like results is attributable to a less incisive sense of what gives literature its power. It is the result of his effort to fabricate a stage completely. The Celtic world—the only world he incorporated into his art to any significant extent—was, as he depicted it, virtually nonexistent. The drama of Druid against Christian might be capable of dimly reflecting more immediate cultural confrontations, but a dim reflection is after all nothing better than a dim reflection. Unlike his esthetic colleague William Morris, whose heroic fantasy *The Wood beyond the World* made the proximity of real and ideal geography a source of profound tension and artistic excitement, Sharp shunned any effects that might have turned his own fantasies into more vivid reflections of real life. In the process he rejected one of the principal opportunities lying open to the artist of his time. Shaping itself out of the chaos of conflict between country and city was a new kind of stage on which the old Celt of dreams and visions, the mythmaker of the past, was encountering "the plumber and the artificial gardener," the industrialist, the citymaker of the present, and attempting, though not always realizing, an adjustment to a new and irreversible truth.

In rejecting this encounter, Sharp flinched from a wonderful if perilous challenge, one which even his Celtic contemporary Yeats eventually faced and made vital. Hardy's ability to confront the same challenge helped to give his last novel, *Jude the Obscure,* its strange and staggering power, and made it an immensely courageous foray into a modern jungle few of his own epoch and experience had even the courage to visualize.

There is no way to avoid seeing this failure in Sharp as a failure of artistic vision, though there is a way of pardoning him for it. It is clear that before the deep crises that shook the world after the turn of the century, few artists were able to mount a valid protest against man's trend toward mechanized loneliness and isolation amid the turbulent, self-engrossed "national life at its center," and to brave the conventions and prejudices constraining the reproduction of their mood of defiance in art. Certainly, even though his own protest did not come to artistic life, Sharp must be credited with never faltering before the engagement with national pride. Whenever he had the opportunity and the strength, he continued to eschew the limitations with which he had to temporize and to search for a community ever more expressive of his deep and abiding universal sympathies, and of the variety and upheaval that characterized the shape of the inner man. In this experimental penetration of the facades of superficial allegiances and identities—and even of superficial cosmopolitanism itself—he helped to foster what were in his own day, for the most part, unconventional and unpopular truths.

Artists who survived Sharp to live through the First World War shuddered from its shocks to national allegiances, but they endured them, for they had been in a true sense prepared by the cosmopolitan sympathies of Sharp's generation. They found, as Sharp had not found, a genuine community of distempered idealism among their fellow writers and a growing community of misgiving among their audiences. Sharp is divided from these men by the quality and temper of the convictions he fundamentally shares with them, his groping and diffident, theirs strong and certain. Thus, where Sharp chafes quietly at the barriers to international communion, Joyce rages furiously at the slovenly compromises men make in the name of national dignity. Sharp's thin dream of a new and transcendent Celtic spirit is separated by thrust as well as genius from Joyce's promised forging of the "uncreated conscience" of his race. The same principle of energetic conviction divides the outcast night-wanderers of Sharp's London from the clanless tribesmen of Joyce's Dublin, the homelessness of Sharp's *Children of To-morrow* from the sense of exile, and the formless and ever-forming allegiances of the Jew Leopold Bloom. The psychic drama Sharp hoped for and tried to shape and the doggedness of his research into "the geography of the mind" are the seedling versions of Joyce's expert and intrepid psychological scrutiny of the inner man. The articulated consciousnesses of Joyce's characters are full of symbols Sharp would have enthusiastically ratified, because they unite men rather than divide them.

The exploration of the geography of the mind and imagination that characterizes Joyce has much in common with T. S. Eliot's exploration of the "wasteland." An expatriate himself, Eliot exemplifies in his early work the dilemma imposed by shattered bonds and toppled mechanistic, mercantilistic, and militaristic supports for the human identity. One source of the aridity in "Gerontion," and a key to the riddle of international perversion in *The Waste Land,* is the defeated hope of cultural intercommunion that Eliot felt as a young poet. To pursue Eliot through his later development is of course to trace a resurrection out of that despair and to discover a resolution that was hidden in the wasteland, waiting to be realized. Out of the broad catholicity of Eliot's cultural sympathies, the "fragments" from widely differing cultures which he "shored against his ruin," came the gradual fabrication of a new, transcendent community based upon a reconstituted Christian tradition.

Eliot's poetry is a body of work essentially dramatic, and it suggests the realization of Sharp's prophecy that modern literature would find its rejuvenation in a new kind of poetic drama. More than anything else, Sharp wanted the new drama to impose no obstacles to its universal reception, to be a stage from which a common idiom and vocabulary of truth might be spoken. That hopefully envisioned new stage was merely another symbolic expression of his desire for a place that could transcend all limits. Eliot's dramas do not entirely realize this hope, for they have a Christian boundary. But many of his poems are broadly and universally conceived peregrinations—with frequent use of geographical metaphor—through the geography of the soul.

Eliot's combination of the spirit of place with a sense of exile, and therefore with the compelling desire for a transcendent community, is only an extension of the combination that wholly characterized Sharp and partially characterized many writers of his generation, different as their work may otherwise be. That same combination provides a principle of unity among important later writers of extremely diverse philosophy and vision. D. H. Lawrence, whose own odyssey perhaps more closely than any other writer's resembles that of William Sharp, entitled the first chapter of his *Studies in Classic American Literature* "The Spirit of Place." Lawrence would have found Sharp incorrigibly "blue-eyed" and dream-minded, for Lawrence thought he could see through the clouds that enveloped the American "place" on which he chose to focus, and he debunked the myths with which Americans then surrounded and still surround themselves. Yet his vision shared a good deal with that of his less brilliant forerunner, and a few excerpts from Lawrence's book suggest the similarity of their intents. One can sense in Lawrence's tone that he had had and pushed away the same illusion that had moved Sharp, at least temporarily, to view America as a "fortunate Eden." Those who came to America, said Lawrence, "came largely to get away—that most simple of motives. To get away. Away from what? In the long run, away from themselves. Away from everything. That's why most people have come to America, and still do come. To get away from everything they are or have been. 'Henceforth be masterless.' " Had Sharp been more self-conscious a student of his own motives, these might have been his own words.

From the vantage point of a man who has had the true revelation, Lawrence spoke with authority of the same sense of place-identity that had obsessed Sharp:

> Every continent has its own great spirit of place. Every people is polarized in some particular locality, which is home, the homeland. Different places on the face of the earth have different vital effluence, different vibration, different chemical exhalation, different polarity with different stars: call it what you like. But the spirit of place is a great reality. The Nile Valley produced not only the corn, but the terrific religions of Egypt. China produces the Chinese, and will go on doing so. The Chinese in San Francisco will in time cease to be Chinese, for America is a great melting pot.

Lawrence's historical experience, which Sharp lacked, enabled him to build upon this view. With his infallible technique for making a new paragraph seem like a new chapter of Ecclesiastes, he turned his idea upon itself:

> There was a tremendous polarity in Italy. And this seems to have died. For even places die. The Island of Great Britain had a wonderful terrestrial magnetism or polarity of its own, which made the British people. For the moment, this polarity seems to be breaking. Can England die? And what if England dies?

A drawing of Sharp.

Lawrence's final statement needed this prologue, just as the "men" he envisioned in it had needed the prologue of William Sharp, perhaps countless William Sharps:

> Men are free when they are in a living homeland, not when they are straying and breaking away. Men are free when they are obeying some deep, inward voice of religious belief. Obeying from within. Men are free when they belong to a living, organic, *believing* community, active in fulfilling some unfulfilled, perhaps unrealized purpose . . . Men are free when they are most unconscious of freedom.

Though in other respects it is the antithesis of Lawrence's, the work of another novelist, E. M. Forster, shows how much the search for a new sense of "homeland" and a new "community of belief" invaded twentieth-century literature and how inevitably it accompanied the sense of place. Forster's *A Passage to India* suggests how the writer after the First World War could give the spirit of place a broader field of play than that to which novelists like George Eliot and Thomas Hardy were limited. He demonstrates that for the later writer such comprehensiveness was acceptable, a ground sufficiently responsive to general feeling to provide a legitimate artistic foothold and to require no exercise of caution. Forster treats with familiarity, in other words, the kind of place that for Conrad's first audiences would still have been distant, strange, and exotic. He can thus confront the topography of India with an aplomb belying any claims that land might have to being exotic and faraway. If it is exotic in Forster's vision, it is so mainly by virtue of the grotesque contrasts it expresses within

itself—only secondarily by virtue of the diehard associations of mystery that the word "India" trails with it still, part of the legacy that created innumerable Sharps lumping camelback through the wildernesses of distant places to bring their half-manufactured excitement to color- and travel-hungry Victorians.

Echoes of Sharp's technique in making symbolic use of place can readily be found in Forster's. That technique is thoroughly illustrated by the Marabar Caves, but its scope is no better demonstrated than in what for all purposes is the philosophical center of this symmetrical novel, Fielding's pause in Italy on his return trip to England. Forster describes Fielding's realization of this movement in these terms: "The Mediterranean is the human norm. When men leave that exquisite lake, through the Bosphorus or the Pillars of Hercules, they approach the monstrous and extraordinary." The philosophizing that accompanies Forster's place descriptions is as naturally their result as any conclusion drawn from inductive reasoning or speculation, for its basis is symbolic.

Forster's earlier novel, *Howards End*, contains very explicit contact with the cosmopolitanism of Sharp's generation, though that point of contact was one of reaction rather than support. Forster seems to have feared a movement that, at the turn of the century, even disturbed some cosmopolitans—what Ethel Goddard, in discussing Fiona Macleod's anti-nationalism in 1904, described as "that vulgar indolence of cosmopolitanism which excuses its ignorance of the traditions of any one country by an affectation of admiration for all countries" [see Further Reading]. This indolence, she assured her readers, was not Fiona Macleod's. But evidence that it existed in others is further provided by the animadversions in *Howards End* upon the leveling cosmopolitan spirit. Fear of such leveling was at the heart of Forster's assertion that Englishmen must return to being English, must look upon their land and love it, and not allow its distinctive character to be destroyed. Yet an examination of *Howards End* reveals Forster sharing another more essential mood of Sharp's cosmopolitanism, its transcendent nationalism. The cosmopolitanism Forster despised was represented for him by the same two forces for which Sharp had also found nothing but opprobrium: the spirit of urbanization and the spirit of imperialism. The "Imperial type," Forster wrote, "hopes to inherit the earth":

> It breeds as quickly as the yeoman and as soundly; strong is the temptation to acclaim it as a super-yeoman who carries his country's virtue overseas. But the Imperialist is not what he thinks or seems. He is a destroyer. He prepares the way for cosmopolitanism, and though his ambitions be fulfilled, the earth he inherits will be grey.

And the city?

> London was but a foretaste of this nomadic civilization which is altering human nature so profoundly, and throws upon personal relations a stress greater than they have ever borne before. Under cosmopolitanism, if it comes, we shall receive no help from the earth. Trees and meadows and mountains will only be a spectacle, and the binding force must be entrusted to Love alone. May Love be equal to the task.

Forster's similarity with Sharp at these points suggests

that in a deeper sense he was unjustified in calling these leveling forces "cosmopolitan." His real purpose in *Howards End* was not to propogate a narrow nativism, but to locate the "binding force" of which he spoke in a living community. His was a nationalism as transcendent as any of Yeats or Fiona Macleod. His England too was a melting pot; it absorbed, it did not exclude. It was an earth that even the exiled Schlegels, whose father had laid down the sword and sought refuge from an arrogant imperialism, could inherit.

Thus the miniature universe of *Howards End* has, like the panorama of western civilization in *A Passage to India,* a purpose in common with the big world beyond it. With a sense for the power of place to mold lives that had been exploited by the writers whom Sharp treated in *Literary Geography,* and by Sharp himself in *Silence Farm,* Forster went a step beyond them. He fabricated a community conceived not as a mold into which lives are behavioristically forced, but rather as a liberating spiritual force, one which challenges the best in man, commands, in a sense, the love out of him. Howards End is, as a true homeland ought to be, a positive agent, through which the spirit of the universe seeking to unite and not to divide might work its will. The distance between this and *A Passage to India* is not really great. In the later novel, Forster was only more courageously confronting the cosmopolitan challenge, in which "the binding force . . . must be entrusted to Love alone. May Love be equal to the task."

The unity the world seems to possess beneath its face of diversity has been arrived at by many different applications of the sense of symbolic place since William Sharp. Passage has been secured by means of Virginia Woolf's lighthouse—or better still, the quietly self-effacing house of Mrs. Ramsey, subtly reiterating its own image through Woolf's delicate novel. It has been achieved through the nature-mysticism of Katherine Mansfield, the Spain, the Italy, the Paris of Hemingway, or the Yoknapatawpha County of Faulkner.

All of these are indebted to the Victorian sense of place that gave to the romantic spirit new shape and concreteness. This process of translation found its quintessential expression in William Sharp. His work reveals, as though in summary of his era, that out of a sense of exile could emerge a dream of community, which, while borrowing partisan allegiances to place, did so only that it might go beyond them to contend the truth of the nonpartisanship of life. (pp. 196-209)

> *Flavia Alaya, in her* William Sharp—"Fiona Macleod": 1855-1905, *Cambridge, Mass.: Harvard University Press, 1970, 261 p.*

William F. Halloran (essay date 1972)

[*In the following excerpt, Halloran examines the development of various themes and techniques in Sharp's poetry, paying particular attention to the collection* From the Hills of Dream.]

Attempts to describe and evaluate the poetry of William Sharp (1855-1905) have been hampered by the division he imposed upon his writings by adopting, mid-way in his career, the pseudonym and authorial role of Fiona Macleod. Earlier critics tended to assert the superiority of the pseud-

onymous poems and ignore the others. More recent commentators have focused upon the experimental qualities of the early "William Sharp" poems. Neither approach is satisfactory, nor is the tendency to cast all the poetry under the banner of decadent romanticism and dismiss Sharp as a minor apostle of Rossetti. A careful reading of all the poems reveals a pattern of technical development, a consistency of subject matter, and a deeper sense of purpose than is apparent in a few poems by "William Sharp" or "Fiona Macleod."

Any study of Sharp's poetry must take account of the greater control of language, emotion, and ideas in the first volume of pseudonymous verse, *From the Hills of Dream* (1896). Since this improvement appears to have coincided with the pseudonym, it is commonly attributed to the assumption of a feminine persona. In a discussion of poets who have released their creative powers by stepping out of their ordinary selves, Raymond D. Havens expressed this theory as follows: "Fiona Macleod was much more than a pen-name. She was a personality created by Sharp in order that he might create" [see Further Reading]. Then, recognizing the incompleteness of that view, Professor Havens conceded that Sharp's "inner release" preceded the "creation of Fiona Macleod."

The feminine personality came to affect both the content and the style of the pseudonymous writings, but Fiona Macleod was initially a co-result rather than a cause of the change that came about in Sharp's work. The first Fiona Macleod book, a prose romance entitled *Pharais,* was nearly finished before Sharp decided, in the spring of 1894, to publish it under a feminine name. For the poetry, evidence is equally strong. Several poems in the first edition of *From the Hills of Dream* predate in manuscript the invention of Fiona Macleod. The basic difference between Sharp's early and later poetry is a difference in poetic method that resulted from a change in the circumstances of his personal life and a change in his thinking about the role of the poet. In the early nineties he abandoned the pose of a bardic recorder and assumed that of a poet-craftsman—a seer and a maker of verbal objects.

The first two volumes of poetry, *The Human Inheritance* (1882) and *Earth's Voices* (1884), while they reflect the influence of Rossetti's verbal pictures, demonstrate Sharp's greater interest in the natural world and his effort to attain a style more "natural," less artificial than that of Rossetti. An article Sharp wrote for the *Portfolio* in 1882, "D. G. Rossetti and Pictorialism in Verse," provides a useful key to his intentions during the eighties. After expressing admiration for Rossetti's accomplishment in poetry, Sharp took issue with 1) the excessive detail of his word pictures, 2) his artificial diction, and 3) his treatment of the natural world.

Arguing first that a poet should not attempt to describe a natural scene in all its details, Sharp advocated the creation of "a picture by some few salient lines, with or without an image, immediately bringing home to the reader the inner or true meaning of the thing represented." This descriptive technique is best illustrated by his "Transcripts from Nature," the short sketches modeled upon Italian *rispetti* which appeared in the two early volumes. One of these, **"A Crystal Forest,"** reads as follows:

> The air is blue and keen and cold,

With snow the roads and fields are white;
But here the forest's clothed with light
And in a shining sheath enrolled.
Each branch, each twig, each blade of grass,
Seems clad miraculously with glass:

Above the ice-bound streamlet bends
Each frozen fern with crystal ends.

The implicit personification (clothed forest) is not directed to any thematic purpose, and the selected details coalesce to convey a general impression of bright translucence. The "inner or true meaning" of the scene, to use Sharp's phrase, is no more or less than the feeling implicit in the juxtaposition of cold white snow and brilliantly shining ice. In such poems Sharp rejected the precise outlines of Rossetti for the subtler blending of light and forms on canvases by Turner, Whistler, and the early French Impressionists. In so doing, he moved away from Rossetti toward the style and manner of Mallarmé and the French Symbolists.

Secondly, Sharp assured readers of his 1882 article that if they tested the concluding lines of Rossetti's sonnet "Last Fire" against "some phrase of Chaucer, or Wordsworth, or Shelley, or Burns, on a summer day," they would find Rossetti's representation "literary, in contradistinction to directly natural." In "transcripts from nature in verse," he continued, "a direct simplicity is of much more importance than elaborate diction." Despite his theory and intention, Sharp could not decide in practice which artificialities to remove or where to place the limits on "naturalness." Overelaborate words and phrases often jar against a colloquial base in his first two volumes. Even the short "Transcripts from Nature" contain false embellishments and dead metaphors that interfere with direct and fresh apprehension. Sharp's effort to attain a natural and unobtrusive style is only occasionally successful in his early poems.

Thirdly, Sharp stated that Rossetti's poems lack a sense of the interplay between man and the natural world. He insisted that nature should be not merely a source of image and symbol but that it should be portrayed as a place for communion with one's self, one's ancestors, one's fellowman, and a transcendent spirit. In line with this theory, most poems in the first two volumes focus in one way or another upon the relationship between man and the natural world. Many describe scenes in terms of their associations with the past. The setting of **"Moonrise from Iona"** (1884), for instance, brings to mind the men and women who inhabited the island and observed the scene in ancient times. Others, such as **"The Last Aboriginal"** (1884), suggest that the experience of living close to nature unites men and women of different areas and stations in life. This notion is carried to an extreme of unintended irony in **"Motherhood"** (1882), where childbirth forms an emotional bond among a tiger, a primitive woman, and a Victorian lady.

Sharp's emphasis upon natural processes and interaction among human beings and nature rested upon a vague transcendentalism. In an 1879 letter to his friend, John Elder, he spoke of his faith in a "Power" who lets "the breath of His being blow through all created things . . . and whose message and revelation to man is shown forth in the myriad-paged volume of nature." But his faith collapsed easily: he continues,

Sometimes, I seem to waken into thought with a start, and to behold nothing but the blind tyranny of pure materialism, and the unutterable sorrow and hopelessness of life, and the bitter blackness of the end, which is annihilation. But such phases are generally transient, and, like a drowning man buffeting the overwhelming waves, I can often rise above them and behold the vastness and the Glory of the Light of Other Life.

The drowning man simile, which reappears at significant intervals in Sharp's writings, is an apt signal here of Sharp's uneasiness with his professed faith in the natural world as a source of spiritual enlightenment; and that uneasiness emerges frequently in his early poetry.

Belief in an amorphous and indistinct "power" proved to be an inadequate substitute for his childhood faith in a personal God. It seemed to disallow individual immortality and thus to cast doubt upon the integrity of the individual. Neither did it coincide with the distinct forms that appeared in his dreams and visions. "Whether with the Nirvana of the follower of Buddha, the absorption of the soul in the soul of God of the Deist and Theist, or with the loss of the individual in the whole of the Race of the Humanitarian," Sharp continued in the 1879 letter, "I cannot altogether agree. . . . I cannot embrace the belief in the extinction of the individual." In most of Sharp's early poems, however, individuality is suppressed as the poet subordinates a sense of his personal identity in mere records, transcriptions, of natural scenes or events.

Several poems in the 1884 volume reverse this direction and turn inward to portray visionary figures. **"Madonna Naturo,"** for instance, is a Swinburnian Earth Goddess. The feminine souls of **"During Music"** and **"Shadowed Souls"** have no apparent relationship with the natural world. Less visual, less precisely realized, and more ominous than those of Rossetti, these dream figures reflect Sharp's reluctance to accept the absorption of the individual into an amorphous universal power that animates man and nature. But such assertions of internal vision are rare in the early poems. Just as the many failures in execution indicate his inability to take full command of his poetic powers, so the tenuous impressionist method of the first two volumes reveals his uncertainty about his place in the universal scheme. The drowning man's attempts to rise above the waves are uncertain and unconvincing; the transcendental light succumbed too easily to the doubt and despair of materialism. The 1882 article on Rossetti—advocating impressionism, natural diction, and communion with nature—and the 1879 letter to Elder—which undermines its professed transcendentalism by asserting the power and immortality of the individual—define the two poles between which the poems in Sharp's 1882 and 1884 volumes move uncertainly.

For his third volume, *Romantic Ballads and Poems of Phantasy* (1888), Sharp wrote a rhapsodic preface which announced his intention to adopt a more forceful artistic role. Claiming a "Celtic passion for the weird and the supernatural, and for vividly romantic sentiment and action," he criticized "the most recent phase of . . . romantic sentiment, that mainly due to and greatly guided by Rossetti," as "too literary, not merely in expression, but inherently." Intent still upon avoiding artificiality in content and method, he declared his preference for "spontaneity," "directness of utterance," and "Romance." By the latter term he meant adventure and mystery, qualities, he said, that had descended from Coleridge and Keats through Rossetti and Morris before expiring during the past decade in the emphasis upon verse forms. Accordingly, the poems in the 1888 volume concentrate less upon nature and its manifestations of universal spirit and more upon the appearance of spirits in dreams and hallucinations. This emphasis anticipates the pseudonymous poetry, but here the spirits tend to be ominous and to lack a meaningful frame of reference. The production of gothic effects for their own sake and inattention to the details of composition undermine the quality of the volume. Even allowing for the Preface's assertion that poetry should be "spontaneous in its birth, free in its movement, impulsive in its spirit," the reader will be troubled by tonal inconsistencies and inappropriate or incoherent metaphors. In contrast to the assertive voice of the volume's preface, the speaker of the poems is a slightly frantic, but detached and impersonal painter of scenes and events.

The narratives in the first section contain rapid actions and mysterious apparitions. The most ambitious, and probably the best of these, **"The Weird of Michael Scott,"** attempts to portray the horror of psychic disintegration by means of a fiery doppelgänger that pursues and ultimately consumes its counterpart. The "Poems of Phantasy" in the second section are more compact. Like several lyrics in the 1884 volume, they describe visions or apparitions. The speaker in **"The Twin Soul,"** for example, relates a dream in which a "Spirit-Enchantress" called his soul out of his body to an "Unknown Goal." He does not understand the meaning of the event, and the poem, which seeks mainly to evoke a mood of terror, offers only a veiled hint of psychosexual disorder.

The last poem in the volume, **"The Death-Child,"** stands above the rest as a controlled and moving evocation of the darker side of Sharp's mind in 1888. It portrays, in a ballad stanza reminiscent of Keats's "La Belle Dame sans Merci," the "mortal child" of Death as a woman sitting beneath an elder tree by a dark pool and singing songs "sweet," "eerie," and "wild." Caught between the bloody stream of life and the mystery of death, she broods intensely before deciding to withhold her song until life's contradictions are resolved and its mysteries revealed at the end of time:

> And then she smiles a strange sad smile,
> And lets her harp lie long;
> The death-waves oft may rise the while,
> She greets them with no song.

The last poem in the 1888 volume thus implies that all song is futile in a world that is enigmatic and impermanent, an implication that contrasts strikingly with the exuberant and optimistic preface.

When Sharp published the "Poems of Phantasy" in America in 1892, he added a poem that recalls the drowning man metaphor in the letter of 1879:

"The Coves of Crail"

> The moon-white waters wash and leap,
> The dark tide floods the Coves of Crail;
> Sound, sound he lies in dreamless sleep,
> Nor hears the sea-wind wail.
>
> The pale gold of his oozy locks,

> Doth hither drift and thither wave;
> His thin hands plash against the rocks,
> His white lips nothing crave.
>
> Afar away she laughs and sings—
> A song he loved, a wild sea-strain—
> Of how the mermen weave their rings
> Upon the reef-set main.
>
> Sound, sound he lies in dreamless sleep,
> Nor hears the sea-winds wail,
> Though with the tide his white hands creep
> Amid the Coves of Crail.

Similar in mood and form to **"The Death-Child,"** this poem presents another instance of deception and defeat. Having been lured to adventure by the sea and to romance by the mermaid's "wild-sea-strain," the man has been caught by the merman's rings and drowned on the reefs. The natural world promises beauty and the fulfilment of desire, but delivers death. In reclaiming man to itself, nature's only gift is release from the dreams it inspired. Ironically, the sea that killed the man imparts the impression of life to his body (waving locks and creeping hands) which implies that natural life is only the movement of blind natural forces. The poem recalls the drowning man simile in Sharp's 1879 letter to John Elder and marks his continuing concern with the disparity between the reaches of spirit and the limitations of the material world.

"The Death-Child" and **"The Coves of Crail"** are important signposts in the development of Sharp's poetry. Dissatisfied with the artificiality of Rossetti's visionary poems and unhappy with his own reticent impressionism, Sharp was searching for a distinctive, more vital style. He found that style in these two poems, one of them asserting the futility of poetry and the other implying the inability of man to counter the powerful forces of the natural world. Paradoxically, he achieved firmer control of diction, rhythms, and imagery in describing himself as a victim of unintelligible powers beyond his control. The ballad stanza fostered understatement and discouraged sentimentality; and the focus upon the death-child and the thin white body enabled Sharp to express his own feelings and ideas convincingly by projecting them upon others. These two poems directly anticipate the form and substance of many Fiona Macleod poems and thus form a bridge between Sharp's poetry of the eighties and his later work.

Shortly after the 1888 volume appeared, Sharp wrote to a friend:

> I am tortured by the desire to create beauty, to sing something of "the impossible songs" I have heard, to utter something of the rhythm of life that has most touched me. The next volume of romantic poems will be daringly of the moment, vital with the life and passion of to-day (I speak hopefully, not with arrogant assurance, of course), yet not a whit less romantic than **"The Weird of Michael Scott"** or **"The Death-Child."**

He fulfilled that promise in 1891 with *Sospiri di Roma,* an exuberant celebration of the beauty of nature and the joy of life. Hastily written during the winter of 1890-91 and privately printed in Italy, the volume is excessively repetitious in form and content, but its imperfections tend to contribute to its intended effect of careless rapture.

Sharp described the most striking feature of the poems in

a letter to Bliss Carman on February 3, 1891: "Dealing entirely with certain impressions of Rome, the Sabine and Alban hill-country and the Campagna," the poems, he reported, are "all in irregular and unrhymed measures—a poetic 'species' in which I take great delight." For rhyme and regular stanzas, he substituted repetition, parallelism, and rolling cadences. Although the sospiri are word paintings intended primarily to render landscapes and moods, the poet sometimes imposes his thoughts, as well as his feelings, upon the scenes. By choosing and arranging images to encourage reflection, he transformed many of the landscapes into emblems.

"The Swimmer of Nemi," another poem describing a man in the water, illustrates the method:

> White through the azure,
> The purple blueness,
> Of Nemi's waters
> The swimmer goeth.
> Ivory-white, or wan white as roses
> Yellowed and tanned by the suns of the Orient,
> His strong limbs sever the violet hollows;
> A shimmer of white fantastic motions
> Wavering deep through the lake as he swimmeth.
> Like gorse in the sunlight the gold of his yellow hair,
> Yellow with sunshine and bright as with dew-drops,
> Spray of the waters flung back as he tosseth
> His head i' the sunlight in the midst of his laughter:
> Red o'er his body, blossom-white 'mid the blueness,
> And trailing behind him in glory of scarlet,
> A branch of the red-berried ash of the mountains.
> White as a moonbeam
> Drifting athwart
> The purple twilight,
> The swimmer goeth—
> Joyously laughing,
> With o'er his shoulders,
> Agleam in the sunshine
> The trailing branch
> With the scarlet berries.
> Green are the leaves, and scarlet the berries,
> White are the limbs of the swimmer beyond them,
> Blue the deep heart of the still, brooding lakelet,
> Pale-blue the hills in the haze of September,
> The high Alban hills in their silence and beauty,
> Purple the depths of the windless heaven
> Curv'd like a flower o'er the waters of Nemi.

The impressionistic description is carefully controlled to project meaning through the patterns of sound, color, and visual images. For twenty-seven lines the energetic swimmer is the center and crowning achievement of the natural scene. As our eyes are redirected in the final five lines from the lake to the hills to the deep "windless heaven / Curv'd like a flower" over the lake, the swimmer becomes less significant, the white receding center of the canvas. For all his beauty and power, he is a product and finally a captive of the natural world.

The pattern established by the poem's imagery is reaffirmed by myth and biography. As Edward Engleberg has noted, Sir James Frazer specified the northern shore of Nemi as "the site of the sacred grove where the priest protected the golden bough with his life" (*The Symbolist Poem*). Whether or not Sharp had read the first edition of *The Golden Bough* (1890), this swimmer in Nemi, golden-haired like Sharp himself, has captured in the red-berried ash branch the very symbol of dynamic life. With this association, the concluding lines become at once more omi-

nous and more significant. The prototype of all human energy and heroic action is, to be sure, the center of the natural flower, but he becomes a pitifully small center against the brooding lake, the silent hills, and the deep, windless heaven.

The biographical underpinnings of **"The Swimmer of Nemi"** augment its meanings and reveal its significance for Sharp. Although he did not have this poem in mind, Ernest Rhys has recalled [in his *Everyman Remembers*] Sharp's telling him that his first meeting with Fiona Macleod "was on the banks of Lake Nemi, when she was enjoying a sun-bath in what she deemed was a virgin solitude, after swimming the lake. 'That moment began,' he declared, 'my spiritual regeneration. I was a New Man, a mystic, where before I had been only a mechanic-in-art'." Although Rhys reproduced Sharp's words many years after he heard them and Sharp almost surely colored the story for Rhys, it has a basis in fact. As Rhys recognized, there was an "objective Fiona Macleod"; and "the passion she inspired gave him [Sharp] a new deliverance, a new impetus."

The Sharps arrived in Rome in late December, 1890, and Mrs. Sharp, in describing the friends they met there, states: "Mrs. Wingate Rinder joined us for three weeks, and with her my husband greatly enjoyed long walks over the Campagna and expeditions to the little neighboring hill towns" (*Memoir*). Mrs. Wingate Rinder was Edith Wingate Rinder who had come to Rome for the holidays with her husband's cousin, Mona Caird, a close friend of the Sharps. Although Sharp had certainly met Mrs. Rinder in London, they became well-acquainted during her stay in Rome, and Sharp began to think of her as an embodiment of his ideal of feminine beauty. It was she who provided the "new impetus" that produced *Sospiri di Roma.* She served as the inspiration of all the early Fiona Macleod writings and eventually became, in Rhys's words, the "objective Fiona Macleod."

We know from his diary that Sharp visited the Lake of Nemi on January 3, 1891 during the course of his first day-long excursion out of Rome with Edith Rinder. The lake, he says, "looked lovely in its grey-blue stillness, with all the sunlit but yet sombre winterliness around. Nemi, itself, lay apparently silent and lifeless, 'a city of dream,' on a height across the lake." **"The Swimmer of Nemi"** is almost certainly Sharp's idealized portrait of himself on that day at Nemi with Edith Rinder. The poem celebrates the sense of power and renewal that came upon him in her presence in that sunlit setting. Considering the public and personal confusion of identity several years later, it is significant that Fiona Macleod rather than Sharp was the swimmer in Nemi when Sharp told the story to Ernest Rhys. Apparently Sharp had transformed the golden-haired male of the poem, an idealized self-portrait, into a beautiful female clad in golden light, the ideal woman who figured so prominently in his life and art after 1892.

Sharp's feelings for Edith Rinder, his joy in the beauty of the warm Italian landscapes, and the pleasure he took in the pieces of classical sculpture in Rome and the surrounding country turned his earlier transcendentalism toward a more vigorous naturalism. The naked figures that populate *Sospiri di Roma* indicate an awakening of his interest in the human body and a desire to put aside his northern social inhibitions to recapture the frank sensuality of pagan Rome. He began to speak of himself as a pagan, embraced what he called the "new paganism," and produced in 1892 the first and only issue of *The Pagan Review,* a periodical which he edited and wrote under various pseudonyms. A married man of thirty-five in love with a beautiful twenty-six-year-old woman who was married to one of his friends, Sharp became alternately ecstatic and despondent with the realization that he had found too late the embodiment of his dreams. The celebration of life and love in *Sospiri di Roma* is less than complete. The nude figures are finally remote and static. The love goddess in **"Fior di Memoria,"** for example, is a statue that comes briefly to life only to return to stone in disgust with the hypocritical restraints of the modern world. The volume reflects its author's divided loyalties and the impossibility of realizing fully his love for Edith Rinder. It is very much a product of its time and the social circle in which the Sharps moved. The emancipation of women, which Mona Caird championed so vigorously, and the free expression of love without regard for social conventions and legal contracts were cherished ideals but not realities attained.

Sharp's speculation about an afterlife also took a new turn in *Sospiri di Roma.* As the speaker in **"High Noon at Midsummer on the Campagna"** contemplates evening and darkness, the past comes to life as a "low deep whisper from the ground," whereupon the speaker expresses his desire

> To be as the Night that dies not, but forever
> Weaves her immortal web of starry fires;
> To be as Time itself,
> Time, whose vast holocausts
> Lie here, deep buried from the ken of men,
> Here, where no breath of wind
> Ruffles the brooding heat,
> The breathless blazing heat
> Of Noon.

Absorption into Time, or a state of suspended animation, seemed at that moment a possible means of preserving the individual soul from annihilation. But the holocausts of the material world are a function of Time. Although the obvious presence of the ancient past in Italy represented a kind of immortality, the personified Time of **"High Noon"** was merely a substitute for the transcendental spirit of Sharp's early poems and the natural forces that killed and reanimated the body in **"The Coves of Crail."** Less frantic than the "Romantic Ballads" and less dark than the "Poems of Phantasy," *Sospiri di Roma*'s celebration of life contains an undercurrent of melancholy fed by the losses of the past, the limitations of the future, and the inevitability of death.

Yet the Italian volume is an exciting *tour de force,* a solid accomplishment in free verse that anticipates the general movement away from verse forms and rhyme a decade later, and a turning point in Sharp's own poetry. Focusing upon human energy, his own and others', Sharp grasped more firmly the possibilities of poetry. The bardic recorder of impressions gave way to the poet-creator, the conscious manipulator of sounds, images, and ideas. While maintaining his belief that the poet's main task is to record observable phenomena, Sharp became less reluctant to employ the artifice he condemned in Rossetti. Selecting and arranging images to convey ideas, he moved his impressionist method toward that of symbolism.

The descriptive technique of **"The Swimmer of Nemi"** is similar to that of **"The Coves of Crail,"** but the actions depicted in the two poems mark the break in Sharp's poetry. In contrast to the inert body in the water, the swimmer is a free agent who finds joy and fulfillment in asserting himself against natural limitations. With its carefully patterned imagery and its mythological and biographical overtones, the Nemi poem displays a similar assertiveness on the part of its author. In Italy during the winter of 1891 in the company of Edith Rinder, Sharp experienced the "inner release" that led to the writings of Fiona Macleod. Only a few poems in *Sospiri di Roma* exhibit the control and depth of the later work, but the volume projects a spirit of renewal that eventually made the difference.

Five years intervened between *Sospiri di Roma* and Sharp's next volume of poetry, Fiona Macleod's *From the Hills of Dream* (1896). Partly in response to the poor reception of the 1891 volume, Sharp attempted during these years to exert more control over his thoughts and emotions in a series of sonnets and formal love lyrics. His heightened concern with poetic craftsmanship may be illustrated by comparing the manuscript copies of two of these poems with their later published versions.

One manuscript sonnet, dated December 4, 1892, was originally the first of a three-sonnet sequence on an imaginary child:

> This child we shall not have, that yet doth live,
> Where doth it dwell, O blossom of our joy!
> Will that fair dream know all, and knowing forgive?
> Will rainbow-rapture never, never cloy?
> O exquisite dream, dear child of our desire,
> On mounting wings flitt'st thou afar from here?
> We cannot reach thee who dost never tire,—
> Sweet phantom of delight, appear, appear!
> How lovely must thou be wrought of her flesh,
> With eyes as proud as hers and face as fair,
> With voice like hers and as the dawn-wind fresh,
> And with the waving magic of her hair,
> And all the love and passion of thy sire
> With hers re-wed in thy white heart of fire!

More than a year before he invented Fiona Macleod, Sharp turned to the idea Lamb had immortalized in "Dream Children" and asserted the imaginative reality of the child he could not have with Edith Rinder. This new confidence in the validity of his imagination anticipates his invention of Fiona Macleod and his assertion of her reality on a much wider scale.

In this early version, however, distorted syntax and inflated diction limit the sonnet's effect. Sharp came to recognize the problem and moved to correct it. He made several improvements before publishing the sonnet as **"The Unborn Child"** in the 1896 Fiona Macleod volume. It appears there in a section entitled "The Love Songs of Ian Mor," an invention which enabled him to write as a man under the feminine pseudonym; and the sestet of the sonnet, which identifies the sex of the speaker, is essentially that of the 1892 manuscript.

When the poem appeared again, in the next edition of Fiona Macleod's *From the Hills of Dream* (1901), it was retitled **"An Immortal"** and shifted to a section called "From the Heart of a Woman." Sharp printed the 1896 octave, but in the process of changing the sex of the speaker transformed the sestet as follows:

> How lovely must thou be, wrought in strange fashion
> From out the very breath and soul of passion . . .
> With eyes as proud as his, my lover, thy sire,
> When seeking through the twilight of my hair
> He finds the suddenly secret flame deep hidden there,
> Twin torches flashing into fire.

Both endings use fire as a symbol of the passionate desire the child may inherit as life force or strength of spirit, but the early version makes only limited use of figurative language. The first two lines of the revision personify passion; the next three turn a simple comparison ("eyes as proud as his") into an extended figure by specifying when the lover's eyes are most proud; lines twelve and thirteen refer obliquely and with strong sexual overtones to the woman's eyes; and the last line contains a purposeful ambiguity: the "twin torches" are the two eyes of the man or the eyes of the two lovers which generate the creative fire of love. This more intricate handling of imagery transforms the 1892 and 1896 versions into a sonnet of some depth and power. The pattern of revision indicates that the higher quality of the Fiona Macleod poetry was not an immediate result of Sharp's invention of Fiona Macleod. In making **"An Immortal"** from **"The Unborn Child,"** Sharp shifted, to be sure, from a masculine to a feminine point of view; and this change of perspective undoubtedly affected the result. Whatever psychological complexities lay in the background, however, the comparative excellence of the final version came about by careful revision based on an increased awareness of the power of a central organizing symbol.

A similar pattern emerges when an early draft of a characteristic Fiona Macleod love lyric, which also predates Fiona Macleod, is compared to the printed version. In this case the significant change occurred in the first printing of the poem in the 1896 edition of **From the Hills of Dream** where it is entitled **"Shule, Shule, Shule, Agrah!"** [According to the critic, "Sharp appended the following note to this poem: 'I do not give the correct spelling of the Gaelic. The line signifies "Move, move, move to me, my Heart's Love!" ' "].

> His face was glad as dawn to me,
> His breath was sweet as dusk to me,
> His eyes were burning flames to me,
> Shule, Shule, Shule, agrah!
>
> The broad noon-day was night to me,
> The full-moon night was dark to me,
> The stars whirled and the poles span
> The hour God took him far from me.
>
> Perhaps he dreams in heaven now,
> Perhaps he doth in worship bow,
> A white flame round his foam-white brow
> Shule, Shule, Shule, agrah!
>
> I laugh to think of him like this,
> Who once found all his joy and bliss
> Against my heart, against my kiss,
> Shule, Shule, Shule, agrah!
>
> Star of my joy, art still the same
> Now thou hast gotten a new name?
> Pulse of my heart, my Blood, my Flame,
> Shule, Shule, Shule, agrah!

In the earlier version, the speaker had been a man, the dead lover a woman, and the first line of the last stanza read: "Thy sweet low laugh, is't still the same." The pattern of light imagery, which marks the speaker's changing emotions about the dead lover, is essentially unchanged. In the revised last stanza, however, the star that replaces the laugh functions as a symbol that transforms the poem. "Low laugh" conveys the speaker's inability to think of the dead person in other than physical terms. But the star, recalling the flames of stanza one, establishes the lover's remoteness while at the same time implying that he will continue to shed light and move the speaker's heart. With the symbol, the poem implies the power of the awakened imagination to revitalize the dead and dissolve the barrier between life and death. Indirectly and perhaps inadvertently, it celebrates the creative power that informs Sharp's later poetry.

The 1896 volume also exhibits a heightened concern with prosodic forms. The several translations and imitations of Celtic runes are Sharp's best efforts in free verse. When he reviewed **From the Hills of Dream,** Yeats stated his preference for "the poems in Rhyme and regular measure" and recognized with approval the formal intricacy of poems like **"The Vision"**:

> In a fair place
> Of whin and grass,
> I heard feet pass
> Where no one was.
>
> I saw a face
> Bloom like a flower—
> Nay, as the rainbow-shower
> Of a tempestuous hour.
>
> It was not man, nor woman:
> It was not human:
> But, beautiful and wild,
> Terribly undefiled,
> I knew an unborn child.

The structure of this poem is even more interesting than its possible psychological implications. Each stanza is a complete grammatical unit. The successively longer units (sixteen, twenty-three, and thirty syllables, or two additions of seven) heighten tension toward the final line which resolves the mystery. The abbb rhyme is broken in stanza three where the problem introduced by the new "a" rhyme-word is neatly solved by repeating it immediately in an extra line. That line ("It was not human") carries the central mystery, and it is heightened by its reduced length which breaks temporarily the crescendo effect. With such poems Sharp's complaint against excessive formalism in his 1888 preface is supplanted by his recognition of the power inherent in tight verbal structures and his own power to create them.

Along with the more expert use of figurative language and the greater concern with prosody, Sharp drew frequently upon myth in his later poetry. **"The Moon-Child"** combines all three qualities and presents an important insight into Sharp's later view of himself as a poet:

> A little lonely child am I
> That have not any soul:
> God made me as the homeless wave,
> That has no goal.
>
> A seal my father was, a seal
> That once was man:
> My mother loved him tho' he was

'Neath mortal ban.

He took a wave and drowned her,
She took a wave and lifted him:
And I was born where shadows are
In sea-depths dim.

All through the sunny blue-sweet hours
I swim and glide in waters green:
Never by day the mornful shores
By me are seen.

But when the gloom is on the wave
A shell unto the shore I bring:
And then upon the rocks I sit
And plaintive sing.

I have no playmate but the tide
The seaweed loves with dark brown eyes:
The night-waves have the stars for play,
For me but sighs.

This poem first appeared in a Fiona Macleod prose tale about Saint Columba, **"The Three Marvels of Hy,"** where the Moon-Child's father is a seal-man or, in Celtic legend, a man under spells, an exile from the community. Columba ostracizes the child, a little girl, because her father and her mother have been excommunicated. After hearing her song, this poem, Columba is moved to beg forgiveness, whereupon the child becomes a little boy, the Christ-Child, and the instrument of Columba's redemption.

It is useful to recognize the legendary significance of the seal and Sharp's initial conception of the child as a vehicle for redemption. Standing by itself in *From the Hills of Dream,* the poem is free of religious associations, and the child is simply the product of two antithetical environments, natural life represented by the seal and imaginative life represented by the maternal moon. After playing by day in the sea, he retreats at night to a lonely shore to sing the beautifully ordered and melancholy song. Neither bitter nor fearful, he is merely plaintive and resigned to the isolation of his double life.

The shell and the singing establish the child as a figure of the poet. Unlike the drowning man in Sharp's 1879 letter and the dead man in **"The Coves of Crail,"** the Moon-Child is not a mere pawn of natural forces. Unlike the swimmer of Nemi, he moves easily from physical activity in the water to creative activity on the land. Unlike the Death-Child of the 1888 volume, he does not allow the tragedy of natural life and the mystery of death to stop his singing. Rather he involves himself actively in the natural world by day and in imaginative life by night. At the close of the prose tale he is revealed as "shining with a light from within." His song is that light transformed into art. By 1896 Sharp had come to accept the imagination as a valid means of surmounting the limitations of human life. The renewal of body and spirit he experienced in Italy in 1891 and the continuing support of Edith Rinder bolstered his self-confidence. He no longer considered his imagination a mere source of illusions, but accepted it as a power through which he could perceive higher truth and communicate that truth to others. The prophetic strain that runs uneasily through Sharp's earlier writings becomes a dominant feature of the pseudonymous poetry and prose.

As he gained a firmer understanding of the interaction between outer and inner reality, between nature and the su-pernatural, Sharp worked harder to mold his insights into forms that embodied that interaction and were themselves beautiful. Here the influence of Yeats's early poetry and prose was crucial. When Sharp sent Yeats a copy of the 1901 edition of *From the Hills of Dream,* he mentioned changes that were "recreative—as, for example, in the instance of **'The Moon-Child,'** where one or two touches and an added quatrain have made a poem of what was merely poetic." Like Yeats, Sharp became intent upon making beautiful verbal objects that could move others to a deeper appreciation of the natural world and to a clearer perception of spiritual truth.

Sharp's experiments with impressionism in the eighties and early nineties deserve attention as a reaction against the precise detail and evocative diction of the Pre-Raphaelites and as an anticipation of Imagism, which came to fruition after the turn of the century when others attained the crisp, unembellished language that eluded Sharp. Despite the modernity of his early poems, Sharp became a better poet after 1891 when he turned to traditional forms and to direct projections of his thoughts, feelings, and dreams in personal lyrics and ballads. His later poems are more dramatic and immediate and alive; they employ figurative language more extensively and expertly; and they are more perfectly structured and highly finished. Alfred Kazin has spoken of the shift from the romantic concept of the *bard* whose revelations "were in line not only with their unconsciousness but with the moral order of the world," to the Symbolist cult of the *poet:* "The Symbolists . . . did not think of themselves as nature's priests but as nature's alchemists: they were fabricators rather than 'revealers'." Sharp's development illustrates this shift in viewpoint that French influences brought to England in the late eighties and early nineties.

Yet this shift and the resultant tightening of language and thought were not as sudden as the 1896 edition of *From the Hills of Dream* seems to imply. The 1888 volume is more compact and effective than those published in 1882 and 1884, and *Sospiri di Roma* is a transitional volume that contains several subtle and successful poems. Moreover, the second edition of *From the Hills of Dream* in 1901 is better than that of 1896, and the posthumous edition of 1907 contains further improvements and some excellent new poems. Once the appearance of double authorship is set aside and attention is paid to revisions, the development of Sharp's poetry comes into clearer focus.

In his 1902 essay on William Morris, "The Happiest of Poets," Yeats said of Rossetti: "One feels sometimes that he desired a world of essences, of unmixed powers, of impossible purities. . . . His genius like Shelley's can hardly stir but to the rejection of Nature, whose delight is profusion, but never intensity." It was precisely this "rejection of Nature" that Sharp criticized in his 1882 article on Rossetti and tried to counter in his poems of 1882 and 1884. Even in his turn toward the supernatural in the 1888 poems, the natural world maintains a central position. With *Sospiri di Roma* in 1891, Sharp set more clearly for himself the goal of intensity through involvement with nature; and in retrospect we see that goal as a unifying quality of his poetry. The Fiona Macleod poems are filled with dreams and visions, but their settings—real and imagined—are natural, just as their images and symbols are drawn from nature. "Green fire" becomes a recurrent symbol of the ideal union of nature and supernature, passionate intensity of body and soul. The poetry rejects city-life and the complexities of nineteenth-century society, just as it rejects the hyper-civilization that cultivates art and intellect for their own sake. Yeats said that Rossetti "would have prayed in old times in some chapel of the Star," whereas Morris "would have prayed under the shadow of the Green Tree, and the wet stones of the Well, among the worshippers of natural abundance." Although never content with mere abundance or "profusion," Sharp and others of the *fin de siècle* "Celtic Revival" prayed with Morris.

Another constant theme is the inevitability of loss and suffering. Sharp's failure to find divinity in nature during the eighties produced fear and despair. The Italian poems of 1891 affirm nature's beauty and the pleasure of life against a background of loss and death. The Fiona Macleod poetry faces the inevitability of defeat by trying to recapture the spirit of the simpler, more natural life of Gaelic Scotland, with the result that despair is replaced by melancholy. Some of the later poems sound a firmer note of loss without self-pity. The speaker in Fiona Macleod's **"The Lonely Hunter,"** for instance, imagines in the first two stanzas a natural bower which holds a dead lover without whom life is incomplete. These stanzas follow:

> Green wind from the green-gold branches, what is the
>   song you bring?
> What are all songs for me, now, who no more care to sing?
> Deep in the heart of Summer, sweet is life to me still,
> But my heart is a lonely hunter that hunts on a lonely hill.
>
> Green is that hill and lonely, set far in a shadowy place;
> White is the hunter's quarry, a lost-loved human face:
> O hunting heart, shall you find it, with arrow of failing
>   breath,
> Led o'er a green hill lonely by the shadowy hound of
>   Death?
>
> Green branches, green branches, you sing of a sorrow
>   olden,
> But now it is midsummer weather, earth-young, sunripe,
>   golden:
> Here I stand and I wait, here in the rowan-tree hollow,
> But never a green leaf whispers, "Follow, oh, Follow, Follow!"
>
> O never a green leaf whispers, where the green-gold
>   branches swing:
> O never a song I hear now, where one was wont to sing.
> Here in the heart of Summer, sweet is life to me still,
> But my heart is a lonely hunter that hunts on a lonely hill.

The hunter image combines constant striving with knowledge of defeat, while the beauty of nature and the sense of loss work against each other to produce a unique rhythm and a haunting mood.

Some of the latest Fiona Macleod poems move beyond melancholy regret and stoic resignation:

"The Mystic's Prayer"

> Lay me to sleep in sheltering flame
> O Master of the Hidden Fire!
> Wash pure my heart, and cleanse for me
> My soul's desire.
>
> In flame of sunrise bathe my mind,
> O Master of the Hidden Fire,
> That, when I wake, clear-eyed may be

My soul's desire.

Here there is none of the uncertainty and fear that pervaded Sharp's poems about death in the eighties. The afterlife will involve not a rejection of the natural world but an intenser life of mind and body combined with clarity of insight. Sharp's constant goal as a poet was to break out of the dualism that threatened to engulf the human in the natural. In the best of the pseudonymous poems he combined successfully the roles of poet, priest, and prophet by affirming the possibility of an ideal unity, natural life raised to a state of perfection and permanence. (pp. 57-78)

> *William F. Halloran, "William Sharp as Bard
> and Craftsman," in* Victorian Poetry, *Vol. 10,
> No. 1, Spring, 1972, pp. 57-78.*

Francis Russell Hart   (essay date 1978)

[*In the following excerpt, Hart discusses Sharp's fiction and defines the philosophy that arises out of his Celticism.*]

[William Sharp] is not a romantic transcendentalist, but a legendary moralist, and this crucial term of his—"legendary morality"—derives from his understanding of the late Victorian Celtic Revival, in which he played an influential role. To treat his Celticism as merely an aspect of later Victorian romanticism (hence of no real significance for the student of Scottish fiction) would be to beg important questions—for example, to what extent late Victorian romanticism is itself a product of the Celtic revival codified in the 1860s by Matthew Arnold. Sharp owed his entry into London literary circles largely to his friend Rossetti, and he became Rossetti's biographer and Pater's disciple. This was years before *Pharais* introduced the mysterious feminine alter ego Fiona Macleod. By the time of Fiona's appearance, Sharp was already heir to the Irish Renaissance of Yeats and AE.

A Yeatsian idea of Celticism appears in *For the Beauty of an Idea* and *Anima Celtica:* the Celticism of the Highlands and Islands is the bequest of a civilization doomed and mostly gone, but as idea it is a power incarnate in the spiritual history of man; a Celtic fiction contributes a fiction of idea to an ongoing spiritual evolution, by reawakening ancestral memories, primordial states and modes of expression. Hence, Fiona Macleod seeks to recreate the legendary, to rediscover a pre-Christian or "pagan" mythopoeic impulse in marking the historic end of the Gael's distinct destiny. This is a step beyond Arnold in the direction of Yeats.

In his 1897 essay "The Celtic Element in Literature," Yeats redefines Arnold's touchstones of the Celtic. Arnold, he says, did not understand "that our 'natural magic' is but the ancient religion of the world, the ancient worship of Nature and that troubled ecstasy before her, that certainty of all beautiful places being haunted, which it brought into men's minds." Substitute, then, for Arnold's "Celt" the "ancient hunters and fishers and . . . the ecstatic dancers among hills and woods." Modern Celticism becomes, for Yeats, an escape from "mere chronicle of circumstance, or passionless fantasies, and passionless meditations" through the flooding in of "the passions and beliefs of ancient times." The function of a Celtic movement is to open a "new fountain of legends"; "none can measure of how great importance it may be to coming times, for every new fountain of legends is a new intoxication for the imagination of the world," a new power for reacting against the rationalism of the eighteenth century and the materialism of the nineteenth.

In the essay **"Celtic,"** Fiona quotes Yeats's sentences with approval as giving the "inward sense and significance of the 'Celtic Movement,' " yet goes a step further. He speaks for a Celticism that is to give its spirituality to a potential greater "English" race to which, he believes, all British Celts actually belong. He writes against the irreconcilables, writes from a growing distrust of "pseudo-nationalism," from no great belief in " 'movements' and still less in 'renascences.' " He warns against the passion that the idea of Celtic nationality has awakened in Ireland, insists "there is no racial road to beauty, nor to any excellence," and becomes vehement against the new Celtophiles: "When I hear that 'only a Celt' could have written this or that passage of emotion or description, I am become impatient of these parrot-cries, for I remember that if all Celtic literature were to disappear, the world would not be so impoverished as by the loss of English literature, or French literature, or that of Rome or of Greece." These are surprising words coming from the most extravagant of Scottish Celtophiles. And it is noteworthy that such warnings against a narrow racialism come at the beginnings of a modern fiction for Gaelic Scotland.

Fiona shows earlier affinities as well. The prose poems called **Sospiri di Roma** recall the ornate dream-fugue impressionism of De Quincey. And Fiona's most provocative defense of the Celticism of his fiction comes in the dedication of **The Sin-Eater** volume to "George Meredith in gratitude and homage: and because he is prince of Celtdom." Fiona's Gael, he insists here, is not a "rounded and complete portrait of the Celt." He gives only "the life of the Gael in what is, to me, in accord with my own observation and experience, its most poignant characteristics." To those who "complain of the Celtic gloom that dusks the life of the men and women I have tried to draw," he argues that his doom and gloom heroes are true Celtic types, and that the gloom "to many Gaels if not to all, is so distinctive in the remote life of a doomed and passing race." Then follows shortly the most revealing statement of all:

> A doomed and passing race. Yes, but not wholly so. The Celt has at last reached his horizon. There is no shore beyond. He knows it. This has been the burden of his song since Malvina led the blind Oisin to his grave by the sea. "Even the Children of Light must go down into darkness." But this apparition of a passing race is no more than the fulfillment of a glorious resurrection before our very eyes. For the genius of the Celtic race stands out now with averted torch, and the light of it is a glory before the eyes, and the flame of it is blown into the hearts of the mightier conquering people. The Celt falls, but his spirit [the feminine—the *anima* Fiona] rises in the heart and the brain of the Anglo-Celtic peoples, with whom are the destinies of the generations to come.

It is the Arnold keynote of a triumphant defeatism, and a fit symbol for a fin de siècle world: "The sense of an abiding spiritual Presence, of a waning, a perishing World, and of the mystery and incommunicable destiny of Man." Such is the spiritual Celticism of "this book of interpreta-

tions." But it can be bestowed only if its own tragic and mythic possibilities are recovered from those that have sought to destroy them: "In Celtic Scotland, a passionate regret, a despairing love and longing, narrows yearly before a bastard utilitarianism which is almost as great a curse to our despoiled land as Calvinistic theology has been and is."

Fiona Macleod's intentions, then, are to remythologize a doomed Celticism into a spiritual bequest; to provide a fitting myth of life lived in the face of ceaseless change and mysterious destiny; to do this through interpretation as opposed to documentation of life; to renew a sense of life against the twin villainies of Calvinism and utilitarianism. Scholars of Celtic literature will find gross falsification in such a program. But John Kelleher's wise justification of literary Ireland's turn from the activism of Young Ireland to the Celticism of the fin de siècle may well apply. After many defeats and betrayals, he suggests, the hoary and stale assurances of a poetry of patriotic activism had little to offer. "A more subtle rationale than this was needed to hearten a nation that was now used to defeating itself. Poetry in Ireland would have to accept the atmosphere of defeat as its first ingredient; and out of defeat and melancholy it must somehow make the ultimate victory not only credible but expected."

For the Tauchnitz collection **Wind and Wave** (1902), Fiona selected representative tales divided "broadly into tales of 'The World That Was,' and 'The World That Is.' " The distinction is revealing: "The colour and background of the one series are of a day that is past, and past not for us only, but for the forgetting race itself: while the colour and background of the other, if interchangeable, is not of a past but only of a passing world." In either it would be pointless to expect from a Paterian impressionist a documentary naturalism. And behind Pater is Arnold's scorn for the claims of the "timely."

"The Dan-nan-Ron" illustrates the "World That Is." The heroine's tragedy turns on the archaic rivalry of her cousins and her suitor. They are descended, legend says, from the Sliochd nan Ron (People of the Seal). The cousins use the legend for their own selfish purposes, while the girl mocks such foolish, impossible tales of "the far-back forebears." One cousin is killed by the suitor; another, a flutist of hypnotic power, mysteriously survives. The young wife dies in childbirth; the husband, cursed and pursued by the wraithlike flutist, goes mad and swims to his death among a pack of seals. The story is based on a Hebridean superstition found also, Yeats reported, in the West of Ireland. Narrative description is vivid and terse; the violence is detailed in the simple basic colors of Morris's Pre-Raphaelite manner. There is neither languor nor "spirituality" here. Character is simply and elementally motivated: the husband is good, the wife is strong, determined, loyal, the brothers are selfish.

This, then, is "The World That Is," and the other tales are similar. In them, modern Highland character is conceived in terms of the interplay of elemental motive and legendary force, with periodic outbreaks of atavistic madness. Problems of communication and identity are linked to attitudes toward story and storytelling, to "that strange, obscure, secretive instinct which is also so characteristically Celtic, and often even prevents Gaels of far apart isles, or of different clans, from communicating to each other stories or legends of a peculiarly intimate kind." The seal-man motif signifies an atavistic force against the gray asceticism of conquering Christianity. The seals are enchanted pagans from the north, antisabbatarians with a penchant for Sunday frolicks on the shore. **"The Sea-Madness"** tells of "a man who keeps a little store in a village by one of the Lochs of Argyll . . . [he is] about fifty, is insignificant, commonplace, in his interests parochial, and on Sundays painful to see in his sleek respectability." Periodically he "is suddenly become what he was, or what some ancestor was, in unremembered days," and he disappears, goes to the shore, strips himself and sits on the rocks, or throws handfuls of water into the air while screaming strange Gaelic words.

"The Sin-Eater," the longer legendary tale not included in *Wind and Wave,* shows Macleod the potential novelist at his most economical. The setting on the wild Ross of Mull, the man Neil Ross walking alone from the west on his way back to Iona, the old woman who offers hospitality—all are done in a spare folk realism. Neil has come to curse an old man Adam Blair (a name from Lowland Covenanting history) who convinced Neil's father to break his troth to Neil's mother. Blair, cursed by all, has just died. The old woman recommends the destitute Neil as the sin-eater, the one who, in a ceremony all profess to find idle and obsolete, eats bread and drinks water from the corpse's chest and thus takes on his sins. Neil does the job for two half-crowns, just so that later he may throw off the sins and cause them to pursue the old man's soul in eternity. The narrator offers no critical view of such superstitions, but reports without comment the stages of Neil's ensuing madness. Neil tries in vain to throw the sins off into the sea, becomes fascinated and horrified by the sea, and dies strapped, drowning, to crossed spars. Having used the ritual as a means for personal revenge, he dies mad in an archetypal suicide.

The locality of this bare and impressive novella is essential yet muted, reminding us of what Fiona says at the opening of **"The Winged Destiny"**: "In tragic drama it is authenticity of emotion and not authenticity of episode that matters. It is of lesser moment whether the theme be imaginary, or historically of this country or that, or of this age or of another age." Had the story been expanded into a novel, the particulars of life on Mull and Iona would inevitably have been elaborated, and "facts and descriptions" have nothing to do with "spiritual history." "I have nothing to say of Iona's acreage, or fisheries, or pastures: nothing of how the islanders live. These things are the accidental. There is small difference in simple life anywhere." This is why Fiona's novel-length narratives are so few.

Pharais (1894) is called "a romance of the isles," but its affinities are rather with the prose poem of De Quincey. It purports to be "a story of alien life," but story is subordinate to vision. It is another tale of the working out of a hereditary curse of madness, filled with traditional Gaelic prayers and incantations and with experiences of The Sight. It is set in the same world as [William] Black's novels—the same steamer *Clansman* calls at the islands, and a professor of medicine must be consulted in Glasgow—and yet the image of island life is of a continuity from time immemorial. A young couple, about to have their first child, learns that the husband has the madness of his fathers and seeks to die. He finally succeeds: such is the plot.

Actions are ceremonial; emotions are simple, elemental passions—love, superstitious fear, devotion. Also pervasive is a neopagan Pre-Raphaelite ecstasy at the beauty of the body, the surreal violence of nature, the cold serenity of death, and the nearness of paradise (the title). There is no clear line between the human and the nonhuman, the subjective and objective, and we are in a world of symbolic romantic parable, or what Fiona came to call "legendary morality."

The Mountain Lovers (1895) is longer and better. In scope and mimetic complexity it comes closer to "novel." Sorcha and Alan are the children of old enemies—and old lovers. Sorcha's father, blind old Torcall, loved and then rejected Anabal, Alan's mother, who in anger married another. In lustful fury, Torcall seduced Anabal. Later, Torcall and Anabal feuded and banned the marriage of their children, Sorcha and Alan. Not caring, Sorcha and Alan live together in woods and caves, in a bliss of natural paganism and innocent sexuality. Their idyll is in extraordinary contrast with the major plot, the tragedy of Anabal and the doom of old Torcall. There is stylistic contrast as well: the children's love is given a vaguely mystical description, while the events of the tragedy are etched in horrible detail.

The events unfold gradually with forceful suspense. The effect depends on the use of innocent and devoted bystanders. Oona passes for Torcall's foster child, and Neil, who receives shelter and food from him, thinks of him vaguely as God or king. Their awarenesses provide narrative perspective, and the tragic meaning rests on their archetypal nature. Oona is like Pearl of Hawthorne's *Scarlet Letter,* a nature sprite, loving, innocent, yet mischievous and free. Neil is equally but differently "natural." He is an ugly misshapen elf-man, alleged to be a changeling, a child of a demon woman and a solitary shepherd. He is said to have no soul and spends much time in lamentation seeking one. Beside these four characters—the vengeful, mad old lovers, and their strange, natural watchers—the lovers themselves are thin and unimportant. Their love means little to the main story, until the birth of the child, Joy, and the serene death of Sorcha. Alan dedicates the child to the Lord, and it is suggested that he and the child and Oona will go away to some visionary far isles where Joy's ministry is to occur. This exile becomes meaningful in the historical context provided by the narrator:

> The tragic end of Anabal Gilchrist, the doom that had fulfilled itself for Torcall Cameron: what was either but a piece with the passing of the ancient language, though none wished it to go; with the exile of the sons, though they would fain live and die where their fathers wooed their mothers; with the coming of strangers, and strange ways, and a new bewildering death-cold spirit, that had no respect for the green graves, and jeered at ancient things and the wisdom of old—strangers whom none had sought, none wished, and whose coming meant the going of even the few hillfolk who prospered in the *machar,* the fertile meadows and pastures along the mountain bases? *It was to be: it would be.*

The child represents a break with the local past, with the old bitterness of anger, jealousy, and sorrow. The locale is poisoned by an ancient sin; providence will wreak its punishment through natural instruments, Oona and the dwarf. Together they represent a grotesque but innocent natural order. Sorcha cannot survive because she is the child of a marriage conceived without love; but Alan can survive—and with him Oona the half-sister to help foster the child Joy.

The term "legendary morality" is fitting. The figures are localized by name and language, by ceremony and superstition. They move in a world of local legend; yet they are elemental, too, archetypal creatures of ecstasy, of natural freedom, love, gloom, and anger. The combination of legendary and archetypal characterizes Macleod's fiction, and its intention is to contribute in a dual way to Celtic renaissance: to awaken the mythic consciousness of Europe by creating new symbols, and to create a Celticism of the spirit, archetypal, unlocalized, as part of a future Anglo-Celticism. The double purpose demands exclusion. The Celticism of legendary morality or spiritual history must be abstracted from cultural particularity. The realities of Highland life are no longer relevant; naturalistic environment has no place. Given such a program, Fiona Macleod could hardly find the form of the novel congenial. (pp. 340-47)

> *Francis Russell Hart, "Late Victorian Celticisms: Black, 'Fiona Macleod',"" in his* The Scottish Novel: From Smollett to Spark, *Cambridge, Mass.: Harvard University Press, 1978, pp. 336-47.*

Christine Lahey-Dolega (essay date 1980)

[*In the following excerpt, Lahey-Dolega examines Sharp's "sympathy for the feminine."*]

One can only explain the Fiona phenomenon in terms of [Sharp's] vast sympathy with the life of woman, which led him to an autopsychic identification with an imagined female self.

The creation of Fiona Macleod had been in the making long before the first book by Fiona was presented in 1894. The immediate catalyst for the use of the elaborate mask, according to Mrs. Sharp, was Sharp's trip to Italy in 1891. There he made the acquaintance of the Celtic enthusiast Mrs. Edith Wingate Rinder, who encouraged Sharp's studies in Gaelic mythology. His biographer [Flavia Alaya] speculates that the friendship was actually an affair, but there is little evidence to prove this was so. In any case, his meeting with Mrs. Rinder did coincide with a great burst of creative activity which culminated in the publication of a volume of very sensual *vers libre,* **Sospiri di Roma** (1891), and heralded his intense preoccupation with the feminine consciousness. This is not to suggest that the appearance of Fiona in the literary world was a sudden event, caused only by his new friendship or his delight in the Italian Campagna. As far back as the early London days, Sharp had told his future wife "that rarely a day passed in which [I] did not try to imagine [myself] living the life of a woman, to see through her eyes, and feel and view life from her standpoint, and so vividly that sometimes I forget I am not the woman I am trying to imagine." Mrs. Sharp opined, however, that in the busy, work-filled London days, he suppressed the "sensitive, delicate, feminine side" [see excerpt dated 1912], so that Fiona was held in abeyance.

This was the state of mind of the man who could request of his fiancée in 1880, over a decade before the sexual tension would be resolved and given formative conception: "Don't despise me when I say that in some things I am more a woman than a man". In Sharp's 1888 meeting with Yeats, Alaya conjectures that he discovered support for the creation of Fiona because he became familiar with Yeats's concept of the mask, which he appropriated for his own use. Alaya notes the appearance of the term in Sharp's 1890 essay on Browning in which he refers to the dramatic monologue as the perfect vehicle for "handling the 'masks' or postures of human variety," and further, emphasized the " 'autopsychic' nature of Browning's individuations of attitudes." Alaya justly remarks that on the basis of his acute observations on Browning alone does Sharp deserve praise. His belief that Browning was responsible for the dramatized self led him into a new exploration of pseudonymous writing. In 1892 Sharp put out single-handed one edition of **The Pagan Review,** a magazine in which he used no less than seven pseudonyms.

His growing interest in the "mask" as announced by **The Pagan Review** was further revealed in his little volume of "psychic dramas" entitled **Vistas.** These impressionistic dramas, resembling Yeats's *Shadowy Waters* and Wilde's *Salomé,* strip action to the minimum in order to dramatize psychological experience. In her essay, **"The Shadowy Waters"** (originally entitled "The Later Poetry of W. B. Yeats"), Fiona Macleod compared Yeats's poetic drama with Sharp's earlier dramatic dramas, referring to the latter as "dramas of the mind best seen against imagined tapestries, which reveal so much more to us than do the common or familiar tapestries, the dramas of the obvious, of merely spectator life." Sharp's "psychic episodes," as he calls them in the Dedication to **Vistas** (his "vistas into the inner life of the human soul"), represent a movement away from realistic drama and presage the general direction of modern dramaturgy toward the "autopsychical."

A few of the pieces collected in **Vistas** begin to indicate Sharp's surge of sympathy for the feminine. For example, **The Birth of a Soul,** a brief one-act play, takes place in the bedroom of a woman who is dying in childbirth. Her parting valediction states the theme of compassion for women's travails which Fiona would soon develop: "O God, may the child that is within me not be a woman-child, so that she may never know the bitterness of shame and all the heritage of woman's woe." And, in **A Northern Night,** the obstacle to true love is removed at the climax of the play when the lovers, Helda and Malcolm, who had been forced to resort to clandestine rendezvous, are told of the sudden death of the girl's aged suitor. The play closes with Helda's convulsive sobs as she realizes she has been released from marriage to an undesirable husband.

Fiona's **Runes of Women** (1896) also examines several aspects of what might be described as the pathos of womanhood. The volume of very poignant and powerful poems opens with a preface by "Anne Montgomerie," another female pseudonym Sharp adopted. The preface has this cryptic passage:

> Past all loving she *loved* the man. Past all understanding the poet *understood* the woman. Then she drew away the veil in which her heart was shrouded and by the revealing power of that love and that un-

derstanding *he translated* those characters into these Runes. [my italics]

Here is subtly inferred an explanation of the method of Sharp's poetic inspiration. The "man," Sharp, supplies the form (understanding) to the ideas which are translated from Fiona, the "woman" (love). The process is again explained by analogy in a letter written to Yeats in 1899, signed "Fiona Macleod," in which she states that

> . . . all the formative and expressional as well as nearly all the visionary power is my friend's . . . it is the allegory of the match, the wind, and the torch. Everything is in the torch in readiness, and, as you know, there is nothing in the match itself. But there is a mysterious latency of fire between them . . . the little torch of silent igneous potency at the end of the match . . . and all at once the flame is born. The torch says all is due to the match. The match knows the flame is not hers. But beyond both is the wind, the spiritual air. . . . The air that came at the union of both is sometimes Art, sometimes Genius, sometimes Imagination, sometimes Life, sometimes the Spirit. . . . But the torch is at once the passive, the formative, the mnemonic, and the artistically and imaginatively creative force.

The epigraph to the **Runes** is specifically directed to "women who bear in sorrow," but subjects other than childbirth are considered, all from a woman's point of view. **"The Prayer of Women"** is a plea to Christ to save women from the violations that men perform on them: "Save us from the desire of men's eyes, / And the cruel lust of them." **"The Rune of the Passion of Women"** treats of three kinds of sorrow: that of the lonely women, "When no man by the ingle sits, and in the cradle / No little flower-like faces flush with slumber; . . . " More bitter still is the sorrow "Of women who have known no love at all . . . / Who have lost their youth, their dreams, their fairness, / In a vain upgrowing to a light that comes not." But, "bitterer than either" unrequited love or barren love is love retreating:

> To have loved and been beloved with passion . . .
> To be a perfect woman with the full
> Sweet, wondrous, and consummate joy
> Of womanhood fulfilled to all desire—
> And then . . . oh then, to know the waning of the
>   vision . . .
> To seek blindly for the starry lamps of passion . . .
> O this the heaviest cross,
> O this the tree
> Whereon the woman hath her crucifixion.

The final poem, **"The Rune of Age,"** apostrophizes "What is that is already Has-Been," commanding this "Shadow" to "Breathe thy frosty breath upon my hair, for I am weary!" This Rune, in particular, evokes a pessimistic, narrow, self-limiting vision of women's lot, a lot which does not appear to be other than the traditional all-forbearing role assigned to the second sex. Why, one wonders, does not Fiona choose to incite rebellion, rather than champion resignation? Does she approve of the bondage so copiously portrayed in the **Runes?** Fiona's is a defeated, escapist attitude, archaic and reactionary when viewed in the context of the burgeoning women's rights groups of the crusading nineties. Nevertheless, Fiona's works attracted a large audience which seemed to be attuned to her perceptions. Alaya explains the paradox of Fiona's appeal through a consideration of her nature as mythical, symbolic woman. Far from attempting to be a representative woman of the age, intellectual and epicene, Fiona embodies the archetype of the numinous female, "de-intellectualized and re-natured." Thus, as Alaya observes, Fiona and her Celtic heroines hark back to a mythical past and anticipate the anti-intellectual portrayal, in the twentieth century, of women as Molly Blooms or Lady Chatterleys. (pp. 20-2)

> *Christine Lahey-Dolega, "Some Brief Observations on the Life and Work of William Sharp (Fiona Macleod)," in* Ball State University Forum, *Vol. XXI, No. 4, Autumn, 1980, pp. 18-26.*

FURTHER READING

"Celtic Glamour." *The Academy* 51, No. 1,302 (17 April 1897): 418-19.
   Asserts that "Fiona Macleod's" talents greatly exceed the limitations of the Celtic Renaissance.

Andrews, C. E., and Percival, M. O. Introduction to *Poetry of the Nineties,* edited by C. E. Andrews and M. O. Percival, pp. 3-52. New York: Harcourt, Brace and Co., 1926.
   Praises *Sospiri di Roma* as "pure color impressions of the quiet exquisite beauty of old Roman sunshine and warm Italian twilights." According to Andrews and Percival, Sharp's " 'Susurro' is so purely without any intrusion of the author's thought or feeling that its impressionism is as absolute as a painting of Monet. Sharp belongs with the twentieth century Imagists."

Balfour, Charlotte. "Fiona Macleod and Celtic Legends." *The Dublin Review* 149, No. 299 (October 1911): 329-40.
   Examines the Celtic and Christian legends present in "Fiona Macleod's" work, especially in *The Divine Adventure.*

Engelberg, Edward. Introduction to *The Symbolist Poem: The Development of the English Tradition,* edited by Edward Engelberg, pp. 17-49. New York: E. P. Dutton & Co., 1967.
   Identifies Sharp's poetry as "very *avant-garde,*" saying his "*vers libre* is among the first significant free verse in English poetry—that is, a free verse specifically designed to create the effects of image and symbol so characteristic of modern free verse."

Garbaty, Thomas Jay. "Fiona Macleod: Defence of Her Views and Her Identity." *Notes and Queries* 7, No. 12 (December 1960): 465-67.
   Utilizes letters by "Fiona Macleod" to illuminate Sharp's elaborate protection of her identity.

Goddard, Ethel. " 'The Winged Destiny' and Fiona Macleod." *Fortnightly* n.s. LXXVI (December 1904): 1037-44.
   Review of *The Winged Destiny.* Goddard observes that "Fiona Macleod's" Celtic vision includes universal themes.

Halloran, William F. "W. B. Yeats and William Sharp: The

Archer Vision." *English Language Notes* VI, No. 4 (June 1969): 273-80.
Examines the connection between "Fiona Macleod's" short story "The Archer" and W. B. Yeats's archer vision, as recorded in his autobiography and letters.

Havens, Raymond D. "Assumed Personality, Insanity, and Poetry." *The Review of English Studies* n.s. IV, No. 13 (January 1953): 26-37.
Includes Sharp in a survey of English poets who assumed markedly different personalities in their creative works.

Hoare, Dorothy M. "The Irish Movement: The Development of the Romantic Attitude to the Past—Fiona Macleod, Lady Gregory, Synge." In her *The Works of Morris and of Yeats in Relation to Early Saga Literature,* pp. 100-10. London: Cambridge University Press, 1937.
Considers *The Immortal Hour* "Fiona Macleod's" most typical work and finds that it expresses "the logical development of the Yeatsian romantic immersion in the past." According to Hoare, *The Immortal Hour* represents "the defects of vagueness, sentimentality, unreality more completely and more drastically than any other production of the Irish school."

Janvier, Catharine A. "Fiona Macleod and Her Creator William Sharp." *The North American Review* 184, No. 7 (15 April 1907): 718-32.
Biographical sketch written by an American friend of Sharp. The essay includes excerpts from several letters from Sharp to Janvier.

King, Georgiana Goddard. "Fiona Macleod." *Modern Language Notes* XXXIII, No. 6 (June 1918): 352-56.
Challenges the authenticity of Sharp's Celtic lore.

Le Gallienne, Richard. "The Mystery of Fiona Macleod." In his *Vanishing Roads, and Other Essays,* pp. 275-90. New York: Knickerbocker Press, 1915.
Biographical sketch of Sharp occasioned by the publication of Elizabeth Sharp's *Memoir.*

———. *The Romantic '90s.* Garden City, N.Y.: Doubleday, Page & Co., 1925, 162 p.
Includes personal recollections of Sharp. Le Gallienne acknowledges a difference in Sharp's writings after the adoption of the pseudonym "Fiona Macleod."

Murray, Isobel. "*Children of To-morrow:* A Sharp Inspiration for *Dorian Gray.*" *Durham University Journal* LXXX, No. 1 (December 1987): 69-76.
Suggests that Sharp influenced Oscar Wilde, despite the two men's rivalry.

Noble, James Ashcroft, "William Sharp." In *Poets and the Poetry of the Nineteenth Century: Robert Bridges and Contemporary Poets,* rev. ed., edited by Alfred H. Miles, pp. 455-58. New York: E. P. Dutton and Co., 1915.
Introduction to Sharp in a poetry anthology. Noble considers Sharp's poetry largely derivative, but nonetheless finds "an individuality of observation and emotion which forbids its classification among merely derivative work."

Noyes, Alfred. "Fiona Macleod." *The Bookman,* London XXIX, No. 172 (January 1906): 171-73.
Essay written on the occasion of Sharp's death. Noyes celebrates the passion and artfulness of Sharp's work, especially the short story "The Archer."

Parker, W. M. "Dreamer and Critic: William Sharp (Fiona Macleod)." In his *Modern Scottish Writers,* pp. 45-72. 1917. Reprint. Freeport, N.Y.: Books for Libraries Press, 1968.
Broad overview of Sharp's career.

Rea, Lilian. "Fiona Macleod." *The Critic* XLVIII, No. 5 (May 1906): 460-63.
Enthusiastic treatment of "Fiona Macleod's" literary career.

Rhys, Ernest. "William Sharp and 'Fiona Macleod'." *The Century Magazine* LXXIV, No. 1 (May 1907): 111-17.
Proposes to "call up from the reminiscences of a long friendship with [Sharp] some episodes which may, in passing, help to disclose the sources, mysterious and deliberately obscured, of the 'Fiona Macleod' tales and fantasies."

———. "William Sharp alias 'Fiona Macleod'." In his *Everyman Remembers,* pp. 79-83. New York: Cosmopolitan Book Corp., 1931.
Personal reminiscence of Sharp that recounts his involvement in the Canterbury Poets series and his introduction of "Fiona Macleod." Rhys asserts that many of Sharp's poems "do not stand the hard test, and in the end fall into that limbo where are hidden so many lost books of verse, so many romances that once delighted sentimental readers, and so many novels which had a month's run before they dropped into that cruel pit."

Rolt-Wheeler, Ethel. "Fiona Macleod—The Woman." *The Fortnightly Review* 112, No. DCXXXV (1 November 1919): 780-90.
Discusses possible causes and effects of Sharp's inspiration to write as a woman.

Sharp, R. Farquharson. "Fiona Macleod." *The Spectator* 157, No. 5,643 (21 August 1936): 312-13.
Defends Sharp's use of a pseudonym against Arthur Waugh's charge of deceit (below).

Stedman, Edmund Clarence. "Twelve Years Later: A Supplementary Review." In his *Victorian Poets,* rev. ed., pp. 415-84. New York: Houghton, Mifflin and Co., 1888.
Includes Sharp in a survey of Victorian poets.

Thompson, Francis. "Fiona Macleod on Mr. W. B. Yeats." In his *Literary Criticisms: Newly Discovered and Collected,* edited by Terence L. Connolly, S.J., pp. 373-76. New York: E. P. Dutton and Co., 1948.
Review that was originally published in the *Academy* in 1902, praising commentary by "Fiona Macleod" on Yeats's poetry.

Ward, Lauriston. "Miss Fiona Macleod and the Celtic Movement." *The Harvard Monthly* XXXV, No. 3 (December 1902): 123-35.
Calls "Fiona Macleod" the leading representative of the Celtic Renaissance, and details the narrative skill and poetic style of "Macleod's" works.

Waugh, Arthur. "Fiona Macleod: A Forgotten Mystery." *The Spectator* 157, No. 5,642 (14 August 1936): 279.
Condemns the "palpable tricks" Sharp used to sustain the mystery of "Fiona Macleod."

Williams, Harold. "New Forces in Poetry" and "Scotch

Novelists." In his *Modern English Writers: Being a Study of Imaginative Literature, 1890-1914,* pp. 19-53, pp. 346-354. London: Sidgwick & Jackson, 1918.

> Includes Sharp in one survey of poets and one survey of novelists. Williams points to Sharp's superficiality as a poet, specifically criticizing *From the Hills of Dream.* The critic's judgment of Sharp's novels is kinder, praising the beauty of his writing style.

Wyatt, Edith. "Nonsense about Women." In her *Great Companions,* pp. 265-72. New York: D. Appleton and Co., 1917.

> Disparages Sharp's efforts at writing "as a woman."

Angelos Sikelianos

1884-1951

Greek poet and dramatist.

A leading figure in twentieth-century Greek literature, Sikelianos is remembered chiefly for his poetry and dramas written in celebration of the intellectual, spiritual, and aesthetic ideals of Hellenism. Rich in imagery and symbolism, which are often drawn from the traditions of both Christianity and Greek mythology, Sikelianos's works convey their author's strong identification with nature and his desire to express universal human experiences.

The youngest of seven children, Sikelianos was born on the island of Levkas, reputedly the Ithaca of Homer's *Odyssey.* He studied law in Athens for two years, but abandoned his studies to join a theater group in 1902. Through his sister he met Eva Palmer, a wealthy American whom he married in 1907. After publishing some early poems in literary periodicals, Sikelianos established himself as one of the most important new poets in Greece with *Alafroiskiotos,* which has been described as the "spiritual autobiography" of his youth. A tour of the monasteries on Mount Athos and other historic sites with the novelist Nikos Kazantzakis in 1914 and 1915 instilled in Sikelianos an admiration for Greek history and culture that would eventually dominate his writings. Although their friendship eventually soured, Kazantzakis and Sikelianos both reported that they gained from their shared interests in philosophy, literature, and religion.

In 1927 and 1930, Sikelianos and his wife organized elaborate cultural festivals at Delphi that featured art exhibits, athletic competitions, and theatrical presentations. Based on his "Delphic idea," a vision of uniting humanity through a revitalized Hellenic culture, Sikelianos conceived of the festivals as a way to reclaim the ancient site of Delphi as an international cultural center. Although the performances of classical Greek dramas were widely praised, the festivals failed financially, exhausting his wife's fortune. She subsequently returned to the United States and the couple divorced. During World War II, the occupation of Greece by Italian and German forces aroused Sikelianos's patriotic spirit, and he responded by giving public readings of his nationalistic works denouncing tyranny. Following the war, he was elected president of the Society of Greek Writers. After suffering a debilitating stroke, Sikelianos died from accidentally ingesting Lysol.

Sikelianos's poetry has been praised for its rich lyricism and its sophisticated allusions to various philosophies and religious traditions of ancient Greece. In *Alafroiskiotos,* which symbolically presents the reawakening of the Hellenic spirit, Sikelianos celebrates the natural world and recasts Greek myth in personal terms. The five-volume *Prologhos sti zoi* is regarded as his most ambitious poetic work and the most complete expression of his philosophy. Dedicated to what Sikelianos perceived as the five components of experience—nature, race, love, religion, and the will to create—*Prologhos sti zoi* explores his conception of,

in Linos Politis's words, "a universal religious myth, which should unite the primitive matriarchal religions with the ancient Greek spirit, and this with the teaching of Orphism and the symbols of Christianity." The death of Sikelianos's sister inspired another important work, *Mitir Theou,* in which the central figure symbolizes both the Virgin Mary and the Greek goddess Demeter, a blending of sources which critics consider typical of his approach to poetry. As a dramatist, he is remembered primarily for the five tragedies he wrote between 1943 and 1954. These works, nationalistic in theme and lyrical in style, are best represented by *Sivilla,* which records Nero's journey to Delphi and his meeting with the Sibyl. Characterized by intricate symbolism and a lack of conventional dramatic tension, *Sivilla* and Sikelianos's other major dramas are considered better suited to reading than to performance.

Critics have noted similarities between Sikelianos's works and those of other Greek poets of the twentieth century, particularly George Seferis and Kostes Palamas. While Sikelianos shared an affinity for Greek mythology with Seferis and a sympathy for the Greek people with Palamas, his own poetry is distinguished by its incorporation of Christian themes. Additional critical inquiry into Sikelianos's work has focused on his patriotism, manifest in his use of Greek mythology and history and in his advocacy of Greek political liberation.

PRINCIPAL WORKS

Alafroiskiotos (poetry) 1909
*Prologhos sti zoi. 5 vols. (poetry) 1915-47
Mitir Theou (poetry) 1917; revised edition, 1944
To Pascha ton Ellinon (poetry) 1919; expanded edition, 1947
Dhelfikos loghos (poetry) 1927
   [*The Delphic Word,* 1928]
O dhithyramvos tou rodhou (drama) [first publication] 1932
   [*The Dithyramb of the Rose,* 1939]
Akritika (poetry) 1942
   [*Akritan Songs,* 1944]
O Dhedhalos stin Kriti (drama) [first publication] 1943
Sivilla (drama) [first publication] 1944
O Hristos sti Romi (drama) [first publication] 1946
Lyrikos vios. 3 vols. (poetry) 1946-47
O thanatos tou Dhiyieni (drama) [first publication] 1947
Asklipios (drama) [first publication] 1954
Apanta. 14 vols. (poetry and dramas) 1965-80
Selected Poems (poetry) 1979

*The five volumes are: *I sinidhisi tis yis mou,* 1915; *I sinidhisi tis fylis mou,* 1915; *I sinidhisi tis yinekas,* 1916; *I sinidhisi tis pistis,* 1917; and *I sinidhisi tis prosopikis dhimiouryias,* 1947.

Hero Pesopoulos (essay date 1945)

[*Pesopoulos was one of the founders and editors of the cultural review* Propylaia, *in which she published essays, literary reviews, and poetry. In the following excerpt, she characterizes Sikelianos's poetry and emphasizes his role in the revival of Greek culture.*]

Modern Greek Literature, which does not go farther back than the nineteenth century, shows the restless and questing vitality of a young and immature living creation, striving to discover its innate law and destiny.

If we consider the difficulties with which the Greek artist was faced from the very beginning—the overwhelming tradition of a 3,000-years' past on the one hand and the presence of a rich and already established European culture on the other—what Modern Greek Literature has achieved is indeed remarkable. (p. 101)

My purpose, however, is not to give a detailed account of modern Greek literature, or to attempt to show the various divergent currents which have struggled to prevail in the creation of a consistent tradition; but to introduce the greatest living Greek poet, who, in my opinion, embodies at this moment the most complete expression of the Hellenic spirit and ranks amongst the poets of international calibre: Angelos Sikelianos.

If his voice could be heard outside Greece, it would speak unfailingly of the unbroken continuity of Greek life and culture; because I feel, somehow, that in transitional periods like this, the convulsion of historical events which we are now witnessing, may sometimes conceal the full perspective of a nation's evolution. Whereas the creations of the human spirit cannot be easily violated, for a poem or a statue or a cathedral, which emerge like landmarks out of the perpetual flow of history, speak for themselves, and if their message is not understood to-day, it will be to-morrow. This applies to poetry perhaps more than to any other art. Because the real and great poet is both a seer and a teacher. Rooted in his race and his nation, he feeds with the people's dreams and secret yearnings the living tree of his imagination, which, like the sacred oak of Dodona, propounds immortal prophecies. The greater the vitality, the vigour and the creative impetus of the people, the truer and stronger the poet's oracle. His mission is to give form to, and project into our lives, like a tangible reality, the fluid dreams and aspirations which the people have striven from time immemorial to materialize in their actions. The great poet, always a forerunner, conquers with the "word" (logos) the undiscovered, virgin spaces of spirit, which at moments of supreme cultural achievement may be reached by the rest of humanity.

I should like to quote that well-known passage from Shelley's *Defence of Poetry:*

> Poetry is indeed something divine. It is at once the centre and the circumference of knowledge; it is that which comprehends all science and that to which all science must be referred. It is at the same time the root and the blossom of all other systems of thought; it is that from which all spring and that which adorns all; and that which, if blighted, denies the fruit and the seed and withholds from the barren world the nourishment of the scions of the tree of life.

Angelos Sikelianos is sixty years old now, a strong and most impressive personality. He was very young when he appeared on the literary scene and with his first great work, the **Alafroiskiotos,** he reached the peaks of poetic achievement. As was to be expected, he was not immediately recognized as a great poet. I do not mean, of course, by the large public which always awakes very slowly indeed to such peculiar phenomena as poets are, but even by the intellectual elite of the country, who did not seem to realize what a tremendous asset Sikelianos was for the cultural evolution of Greece. Even before I left Greece in 1939, very few people knew his work and fewer still really understood it and cared for it. They knew him, though, as the inspirer of the Delphic Festivals of 1927 and 1930. I shall not go into details about his very bold idea of making Delphi a centre of international culture. But to illustrate what a tremendous impression those performances of Aeschylus's *Prometheus Bound* and *The Suppliants* left behind, I shall mention this:—Romagnoli, the well-known Italian scholar who produced ancient Greek tragedies at Syracuse, was invited to Delphi among many other European celebrities. He came in a rather sneering mood to see what those "Greculi" would do. . . . Asked after the performances what he thought of them, he exclaimed: "A Syracuse c'est de l'archéologie, ici c'est de la religion."

It is really during the years of war and occupation, when individuals returned to their soul and tried to find their roots and strengthen them, that Sikelianos's activity increased and his influence spread, till he was acclaimed as our national poet.

Sikelianos marks the creative beginning of the Greek Renaissance. His powerful vision springs directly from the sources of eternal Greece, which is not a country, a nation or a state, but an Idea, embodying itself in ever new symbols and syntheses of universal value.

In an extremely fine essay Virginia Woolf, analysing the cause of that peculiar attraction which ancient Greece has had through the ages, says:

> . . . this is what draws us back and back to the Greeks: The stable, the permanent, the original human being is to be found there. The Greeks admit us to a vision of the earth unravaged, the sea unpolluted, the maturity, tried but unbroken, of mankind. Every word is reinforced by a vigour, which pours out of olive tree and temple and the bodies of the young.

And, further, discussing the power of Greek words she says:

> θάλασσα, θάνατος, ἀνθός, ἀστηρ . . . so clear, so hard, so intense that to speak plainly yet fittingly, without blurring the outlines or clouding the depths, Greek is the only expression. . . . Spare and bare as it is, no language can move more quickly, dancing, shaking, all alive but controlled.

The fascination that ancient Greece exercises on highly developed and sensitive minds who seek for a clear and true form of life, the nostalgia which flares up, aching for the unsurpassed perfection and mythical atmosphere of the Greek landscape, whenever the world gets sick of its own sickness and the dull and shallow pessimism, and all other -isms, go bankrupt—is a phenomenon so common to our European tradition that it needs no restating. Of course it is a quite different thing in what way that nostalgia will fertilize the imagination of the artists. Classicism, as John Lehmann pointed out, is a very dangerous word—a very dangerous tendency if we don't find a new content for it.

If I have referred to Virginia Woolf, it is because the poet I am writing about embodies the very characteristics she attributes to the ancient Greek world—characteristics which make it stubbornly endure the test of time. Indeed, if I had to sum up in a sentence the ultimate meaning of his poetry I would have said "He admits us to a vision of the earth unravaged, the sea unpolluted, the maturity, tried but unbroken, of mankind."

As I have pointed out, Sikelianos reached perfection with his very first poem, the *Alafroiskiotos.* Alafroiskiotos means literally the "light-shadowed," but it has a particular association in modern Greek folklore. Alafroiskiotos is somebody who lives in a world of his own and is endowed with the power to apprehend the mysteries of nature and sense the presence of the spirits of earth and ocean, such as the dryads, nereids and fawns, which stubbornly survive in Greek folklore. Sikelianos takes this modern Greek mythical figure and lifts it to the planes of the creative man who draws his powers from his secret kinship with nature, the eternal and perfect Greek nature. At this first stage of his evolution the poet recaptures the meaning of the Greek tradition and its bewilderingly multifarious landscapes through the medium of Greek nature.

Greek nature is "the moving immovable" in Greek history and has an artistic and formative value shaping all manifestations of Greek life. Alafroiskiotos symbolizes the return of the reincarnated Greek spirit to its native soil. As he emerges from the sacred sleep on the wide vastness of the beach, a perfect body, integrating harmoniously the highest spiritual, æsthetic and moral values and physical qualities, one feels: A new man has arisen for the world with new eyes, new senses, wide open to revelation, and new experiences which enlarge the vision and the achievement of the human race and forecast a new way of life— another step of man's ascension towards his "idea." With the *Alafroiskiotos,* Sikelianos threw a vivid patch of light to illuminate another stretch of that dark, unknown field which is man's destiny.

Thus, as the ancient Greeks created in their literature a form of life of universal value, Sikelianos started creating the modern Greek form of life, equally universal. For him poetry is an act of life—as life itself is an act of poetry. The poet has to discover and make accessible and habitable more and more landscapes. As Helios of the ancient myth sees the island of Rhodes hidden in the depths of the ocean, a plot which was destined to prove rich in substance for men and kindly for pasture, so did Sikelianos see Hellas, lying in the depths of history—the Hellas which all of us dreamt of—and brought her forth to light and gave her us, a new-born earth, glittering with all its riches and human beings.

He was then twenty-three years old. And he had already an astounding knowledge of the modern Greek language. His style is bold, his expression rich, and yet clear and restrained, his similes extremely powerful, of an almost homeric quality. He never uses in his images abstract notions or empty metaphors. His words are alive, producing unexpected repercussions, awakening reminiscences of all the great gestures that have ever arisen out of the Hellenic world, reflecting the life of the earth, the seas and the skies, the immense light-flooded skies of Greece.

A friend of mine to whom I read *Alafroiskiotos* exclaimed: "But it is ancient Greek!" meaning that Sikelianos had given again to our language the vigour, the newness, the directness and correctness of expression, the compactness of ancient Greek. Every single word of his has the unmistakable quality of the genuine inspiration and is saturated with that magic which only great poetry can create. And one has somehow the feeling that he never struggles for expression. It springs rich and spontaneous, and yet correct, never missing its aim. In the hands of Sikelianos modern Greek became a docile and extremely precise vehicle of poetic imagination.

Another thing which characterizes the poetry of Sikelianos is unity and continuity of vision. In *Alafroiskiotos* one finds already the seeds of his central ideas and the symbols which later on he will evolve and widen until they obtain full vigour and perfection.

The religious philosophies of the ancient Greek mysteries, the doctrines of Heraclitos, Empedocles, Pythagoras, Plato and the essence of Christianity, reveal to him the uninterrupted stream of the Hellenic heritage, and find a new synthesis in his poetry.

Sikelianos has had a prolific output. Among his great works in which he explores and integrates the Greek tradition are *The Prologue to Life* and the *Easter of the Greeks.*

The Prologue to Life consists of four long poems called consciousnesses—The Consciousness of my Earth, of my Race, of Woman, of Faith.

The *Easter of the Greeks* contains three odes: To Helen as the symbol of Beauty, to the Virgin Mary as the mother of God, and the song of the Argonauts.

Here is a translation of the introduction written by the poet to the **"Ode of the Virgin Mary"** which at the same time exemplifies Sikelianos's approach to his subject:

> The poet having heard on the slopes of Helicon those secret voices of Greece, which focus his soul as clearly to the Universe as the compass points unmistakably from North to South, and while, "a fighter, priest and seer," he is climbing the mountain, he suddenly hears the faint peal of a bell, which calls him—he thinks—to a distant village church to offer his worship to the Mother of Christ.

> So, in this most serene hour, before the single Law of Love, his Creed, manifested on those summits where the mind is frantic with inspiration "complete and initiated"—and Helicon is dressed from head to foot in golden corn—gushes out like a victorious pæan, and the legend of Christ that was lying in the depths of darkness is reborn and is crying out like the young bird that has fallen from its nest.

> And the poet's heart is filled with Pity, Strife's sister. He sets out again to climb steadily the steep path of the divine mountain and bring the reborn legend to the summit.

> And then the poet starts relating the Gospel, which is a part of his work, to the worthy fighters and the chosen few (for Art is not destined for the "learned masses" but for the few and for the Race, for Friendship and for Humanity) depicting as "simple, calm and happy" figures those personages which have been for centuries and will always be the secret mirror of our soul.

One of the most characteristic poems of his mature years is **"Daedalus,"** which when published in 1938 was acclaimed by those who had the country's culture at heart as a spiritual event. Sikelianos, in his interpretation of the ancient legend, makes Daedalus the symbol of the creative man, the undaunted and fearless fighter, who perpetually wrestling with his own bold visions, strives to free human destiny from the bondage of necessity and mould it after the image of the divine. Daedalus personifies the victory of the Will which can give man even wings, not alone to fly, but conquer death and desolation and fecundate the vast celestial spaces. But man will ascend to that supreme goal only through pain. He must sacrifice his earthly possessions, however precious, for the sake of humanity. He must labour and suffer alone, so that he may grasp in the fathomless depths of life the Law which surpasses death by the miracle of man's creative action.

The same spirit pervades the five great poems which Sikelianos published during the first terrible years of occupation. They are called *Akritica*—the songs of the guardians of the frontiers. Never before has his poetry reached such clarity and profundity of vision, such a sincere and

deep communion with its subject, as in some of these poems. (pp. 101-06)

> Hero Pesopoulos, "A Greek Poet: Angelos Sikelianos," in New Writing and Daylight, No. 6, 1945, pp. 101-07.

Henry Miller   (essay date 1946)

[*An American novelist, essayist, and critic, Miller was one of the most controversial authors of the twentieth century. The ribaldry and eroticism of such works as* The Tropic of Cancer *(1935) and* The Tropic of Capricorn *(1939) made him perhaps the most censored major writer of all time. Many of Miller's best known works are autobiographical and describe the author's quest for truth and freedom as well as his rejection of modern civilization. Miller called himself "a holy old Untouchable" and wrote, according to Kenneth Rexroth, for those "to whom the values, the achievements, and the classics of the dominant civilzation are meaningless and absurd." In the following essay, Miller affirms Sikelianos's philosophy and characterizes the role of the poet in modern culture.*]

For me Anghelos Sikelianos is one of those rare spirits whom one understands immediately or not at all. One does not approach his work through the intellect. To follow him in all his manifestations, and they are myriad, demands a collaboration of the whole being, which in turn implies a faith in the inscrutable continuity of life.

Coming at a time when the peoples of the earth seem more disunited than ever Sikelianos appears on the horizon like a re-born sun. We of this epoch have felt only the first slanting rays of this luminous orb. The thick dark folds of the past still envelope us; we are not yet aware that the herald of a new dawn is appealing to us, warning us with his oracular breath.

The failure of the Delphic Idea is only a seeming one. A seed was dropped which no power on earth can prevent unfolding. With the last oracle a curtain fell which obscured the true source of light and power. Since the days of ancient Greece man has known only a Purgatorial existence. The body, once radiant and part of a holy trinity, has wandered blindly through the labyrinth of the senses. Only when summoned to murder *en masse* has it recaptured any of its ancient splendour. It has not responded to love and worship; it has not been animated by the one and only source of life which is faith.

In every work of Sikelianos, whether prose or poetry, there recur certain words and phrases which distinguish him as an emissary of light. Even though only fragments of his writings were to remain, even though those were to come to us through some unfamiliar tongue such as Bantu, we could not fail to grasp the meaning and portent of his vision. As poet, prophet, visionary, he illumines for us not only the splendour and significance of the past but the splendour and significance contained in every passing moment. He stresses what is active, "overseeingly active." He revises the sense of drama which is rooted in pain, joy, mystery. He sees the earth as a vast experimental stage on which problems of super-cosmic dimension are foreshadowed. Only in the sense that he is concerned with the destiny of all mankind can Sikelianos be said to be a true Hellene. Greece alone cannot claim him. He begins where his ancient forebears left off. For the ancient Greeks were the true evangels of the Western world; it was only when they had turned their faces away from the light that they perished. To no other people on earth was there given such a glorious opportunity of illuminating the earth as to the ancient Greeks. Emerging at this darkest hour Sikelianos appears like a reincarnation not of any one particular illustrious spirit of the past but of the very effulgent substance of that luminous past. Of and by himself, like that mystic sword-blade he speaks of in *The Sibyl,* he opens Memory like a double wound deep within us.

As a poet Sikelianos ventures far beyond the poets of our time. To say that all his poems are poems of initiation is not enough; they are also poems of ordination. Whoever follows him in his empyrean flights must realise with a conviction never before vouchsafed that the true leaders of the world are the men of imagination, the seers. To unite man with man and peoples with peoples is not the work of politicians or of social reformers; men are united only through illumination. The true poet is an awakener; he does not promise bread and jobs. He knows that struggle and conflict are at the very core of life; he does not offer himself as a balm. All ideas of government fail in so far as they exclude the poet and the seer who are one. The democratic idea is operative only at the base of the pyramid; the pivotal, dynamic element is the aristocratic. They are not oppositional unless translated crudely. On the contrary they are complementary to one another. In his everyday social life man is essentially a democrat or else a clod or a buffoon; in his relation to the eternal man is an aristocrat, or else a renegade. The same gap, the same barriers, which exist between peoples or between classes exist within the soul of every man. We cannot advance with hearts shut and eyes closed; we cannot act without obedience to the law of spontaneity. To act without regard for the whole of life is to destroy all spontaneous impulse, all rhythm, all polarity. The egotist spreads chaos throughout the whole universe. It is not enough that men act in concert on the principle of the lowest common denominator: the quest of mass comfort, or of mass satisfaction, is just as capable of producing rivers of blood as are the mad dreams of the Caesars. Unison has the divine beat of the blood but the source of inspiration is above. In every land there are a chosen few who speak a universal language. Together throughout eternity they may be said to form a "river of luminous saintliness." Keep them apart and the earth itself will dry up. And that is what the temporising men of action endeavour to do. Under the spell of false prophets, false leaders, whole nations curl up and die— after orgiastic displays of pomp and power. Yesterday all the great nations of the earth were locked in combat. No man can say which one of them will be great or greatest to-morrow. But this much one can say—those which worshipped power, whether secretly or acknowledged, will perish. "Intelligence," says Sikelianos, "must enlarge and deepen the power of Love." The intelligence which spends itself in constructing engines of destruction, or in seeking to protect itself, is doomed. Intelligence has to transcend itself; it has to blossom forth with a solar radiance which will transfuse the activities of man with joyous significance. The supreme intelligence of the poet, who situates himself at the heart of the universe, has that beneficent, luminous quality. If he is mad then madness is the *sine qua non.* If he utters nonsense, then nonsense must be the

order of all our days. If he is to be rejected from the councils of men then let us reject all hope, all wisdom.

In urging "a return to our deepest historic self " Sikelianos sought to shift the attention of the Greek people from the pettifogging rivalries and ambitions of the other European peoples. Everything of value that is European stems from Greece. Why look to Europe where all has become confused? Look within yourselves, he pleaded. You have lost nothing; you have simply forgotten you have been asleep. Indeed, where else dare the people of Greece look today? To Russia? To America? To England? In her hour of greatest need Greece was betrayed by the great powers of the earth. What in fact can they supply her with, assuming they regain ascendency over the common enemy. Food, machinery, money perhaps. And distorted codes of justice, of education, of economy. And in return for these dubious gifts? In return they will ask, as all great powers have always asked, that Greece obediently play the role of cat's paw. Perhaps they will renew their archaeological burrowings, turn up new ruins, new evidences of ancient splendour. And they will weep copious crocodile tears over the things of the past while arming themselves to befoul the present beauties of the earth. They will encourage their heroic little ally to fight again with ancient ardour in the name of all that is un-Greek, un-Mediterranean. At the utmost they will only be able to teach the people of Greece how to become efficient soulless work dogs. Where in the Western world is there a nation which has any enthusiasm for life beyond the mere goal of preservation? Where is that superabundance of vitality, that excess of joy, that wisdom which exalts, such as was common to the man of ancient Greece? What faith was it that inspired the shambles of a Christian Europe? Who are the leaders in this hour of crisis? Do they resemble even remotely the lesser geniuses of the Hellenic world? Never was there such confusion, such disillusionment, such pitiful cringing and caterwauling. It is a disembodied world screaming in agony. It is the ghost fighting the ghost.

I believe that only those ideas which strike the prosaic rulers of the world as chimerical have validity. I believe that nothing works as easily, as smoothly, as perfectly as the miraculous. Ask men to surpass themselves and you liberate them. Ask them to be reasonable and you kill the springs of action. The sensible thing for a small nation like Greece would be to feather her nest. The sublime thing, and perhaps the only thing that will save Europe, would be for her to send forth her eagles. The nest which was plundered has become a rock whither in their restless flight the eagles come to alight. To right and left, to north and south, only quicksands are visible. A new species of bird seeks to dominate the airs. It is a soulless bird and its life will be of short duration. It seeks not to reach the sun but to spread desolation. It bears no message from gods or men; under its wings it carries only the promise of pain, terror, devastation.

Somewhere today on Greek soil there is an eagle who has shown himself capable of soaring above the highest flights of the new mechanical birds of the air. Time and again he has flown straight towards the sun, and his wings have not been melted nor his spirit quenched. Neither has he been proved insane. Nor accused of immunity to pain and suffering. He waits, he bides his time, like the great world actor which he is. When the smoke clears away, when the air ceases to be rent with the screams of bursting bombs, we shall be able perhaps to follow with reverence and understanding. (pp. 14-17)

> *Henry Miller, "Anghelos Sikelianos," in* The New Spirit, *edited by E. W. Martin, Dennis Dobson Ltd., 1946, pp. 14-17.*

Robert Liddell   (essay date 1950?)

[*Liddell is an English novelist, critic, and translator. In the following essay, he discusses prominent characteristics of Sikelianos's poetry, particularly noting the synthesis of Christian and ancient Greek traditions in his works.*]

Angelos Sikelianos first appeared as an important poet in 1907, with his first poem *Alafroiskiotos,* "the visionary." For years his work has been privately printed, circulated in small, uncommercial editions, hard to obtain and comparatively little known or appreciated. Nevertheless it has been known to those most concerned with Modern Greek literature, and it has been valued by them not as a private discovery or as the special preserve of a coterie—they have seen it as the work of a major poet. It was no cause for surprise to them that he should ascend the intellectual throne of Greece, left vacant in Palamas' old age; but the poems that have most truly made him a national poet, the poetry of the war in which perhaps its greatest suffering found expression, surprised as any tragic and original work must surprise.

Sikelianos was born in 1884 in Leucas, that island off the coast of Acarnania from whose cliffs Sappho is said to have leapt. To his island youth he owed a love of Greek landscape greater than that of any other Greek poet—he was also impressed (it is hard to say this as respectfully as one would wish) by his own Apollo-like physical beauty. It is necessary to add that biographical records and early photographs show this to have been very great. And in Leucas—which is the neighbour of Ithaca, and which may even have been the Ithaca of Odysseus—the mythological past was opened to him in a dramatic way: he saw the grave of a Homeric warrior being uncovered, and even saw the face, perfectly preserved, which almost instantaneously crumbled into dust after its exposure to the air.

Sikelianos went to Athens to study law, a common beginning to the literary life in Greece. But thereafter his life was very different from that of most other Greek intellectuals, and in particular from that of his great predecessor Palamas, who never left Greece, and rarely left his study in Athens. Sikelianos travelled; it was in the Libyan desert that he began to write *Alafroiskiotos.* He visited France and America—his first wife was the daughter of an American sociologist. And he knew intimately the islands and mountains of Greece, that country so unknown to many Athenians who are quite at home in Paris or London.

He and his wife were the inspiration behind the Delphic festivals of 1927 and 1930—those magnificent performances of the *Prometheus* and the *Supplicants* of Aeschylus in the ancient theatre of Delphi, and of Pyrrhic dances in the stadium. M. Octave Merlier, who had the good fortune to be present, has written of the sublimity of the occasion [in his *Le serment sur le Styx*]. The gigantic rocks above the Castalian spring, the Phaedriades, echoed the voice of the crucified demi-god, and the eagles of Parnassus hovered over his head. Those who were less fortunate can judge from photographs the extreme beauty of these performances, in which careful scholarship and exquisite taste were inspired by such a living love for Aeschylus and for Delphi that they were totally free from the cold antiquarianism that has characterized some other classical revivals.

For Sikelianos these festivals were, like those of the ancient Greek world, religious festivals—from this arose their peculiar and unique beauty. Not unnaturally they were a financial failure. Delphi is not very easily accessible; and of those who went there, not all were willing or able to make the necessary suspension of disbelief in the gods of Olympus—though this is never a difficult act of faith to make in Greece. Sikelianos had hoped for the continuation of the festivals and that Delphi, once a panhellenic centre, might become an international centre of peace and the arts, round Apollo's shrine and the fabled navel of the earth.

Sikelianos has been compared with Yeats. Yeats is a poet who can be admired by the English reader, and who probably should be presented to the admiration of the foreign reader, without much examination of his debt to hermetic philosophy. Similarly, in an elementary study of Sikelianos, it may be allowable to present a selection from that part of his work whose appeal is most direct—it may not be improper to omit any very close examination of the way in which he tries to achieve a harmony of the "two Ancient Testaments," that of Hebraism and that of Hellenism. It is perhaps enough to say that it is a more sympathetic harmony than that of Milton; it is more attractive a notion of Dionysos or Demeter to regard them as "types" or prophecies of Christ and the Virgin, than to place them in Pandemonium. We need not criticize the logic or the orthodoxy of Sikelianos' Christian Orphism. Such a poem as **"The Sacred Way"** speaks quite clearly for itself:

> By the new wound that Fate had opened in me
> I thought the setting sun entered my heart
> With such force, as when a wave
> Enters a slowly sinking ship
> By a sudden crack.
>
>   For that afternoon,
> Like a man long sick, who first goes out
> To suck life from the outer world, I was
> Walking solitary along the road
> That runs from Athens, having as its goal
> The sanctuary of Eleusis.
> And this road always was for me
> Like the path of the soul . . .
> It seemed like a great river, bearing
> Slow wagons drawn by oxen,
> Laden with logs or corn-sheaves, and other
> Carts that went quickly by me
> With men like shadows in them . . .
>
> But beyond, as if the world of men were gone
> And only Nature left, hour after hour
> Peace reigned. And the rock
> That I met, rooted at the road's edge,
> Seemed a throne destined for me
> Throughout all ages. And I clasped my hands
> On my knees as I sat, forgetting
> If I had set out that same day, or if it was
> In past ages I had taken that same road.

But suddenly in that peace, at the next turning
Appeared three shadows.
A Gipsy came towards me,
And after him there followed, drawn by chains,
Two slow-footed bears.
And soon, when they were in front of me,
And the Gipsy saw me, before I had the time
To look at him well, he took from his shoulder
The tambourine, and striking it with one hand,
With the other he pulled the chains with force.
Then the two bears stood up
Heavily upon their hind-legs . . . one
(It must have been the mother), the big one,
With all her forehead decked with plaited strings
Of blue beads, and a white charm on top,
Rose suddenly in majesty, as if she were
A primeval wooden image
Of the Great Goddess, the Eternal Mother,
The very same who, in her sacred grief,
Through time has taken on a human form,
And, weeping for her daughter, she was called
Demeter here—and, weeping for her son,
Alcmena she was there, or was Our Lady.
And the little bear-cub beside her,
Like a big toy, like a simple little child,
Rose also obediently, not yet guessing
The length of his pain and the bitterness
Of slavery, which his mother reflected
In her two fiery eyes that stared at him!
But when, in her weariness,
She was slow to dance, the Gipsy
With a cunning tug at the chain
In the cub's nostril, bleeding
Still from the ring with which a few days back
It seems that they had pierced it, suddenly
Forced her to her feet, bellowing with pain,
Turning her head to her cub, and dancing fiercely.

　　　And I, who watched, I passed
Out of time, far beyond time,
Free from the forms imprisoned
In time, in pictures and in images,
I was beyond, beyond time . . .
But by me, raised to her feet by the force
Of the ring, and of her ill-fated love,
I saw nothing but the majestic bear
With the blue beads on her head,
Prodigious symbol of the martyrdom
Of all the world, past and present,
Prodigious symbol of the primal pain
Of which the mortal ages have not yet
Paid the soul's dues . . . for she was still
And is in Hell.

　　　And for a time
I kept my head bent,
As I threw into the tambourine, I also
Slave of this world, a drachma . . .

　　　But at last
When the Gipsy withdrew, dragging
After him the two slow-footed bears again,
And vanished in the twilight, then my heart
Roused me to take again the road that ends
At the ruins of the Sanctuary of the Soul,
At Eleusis.
And my heart, as I was walking, groaned:
"Will there ever come, will there come an hour
When the soul of the bear and of the Gipsy
And my soul, which I call initiated,
Keep feast together?"

　　　And as I advanced,

And as night fell, I felt by that same wound
That Fate had opened in me, the darkness
Violently entering my heart, as when a wave
Enters a slowly sinking ship
By a sudden crack . . . And yet as if my heart
Thirsted for such a tide to sink in,
To be drowned utterly in the darkness,
And as it went down utterly in the darkness
A murmur spread around me,
A murmur,

　　　　　And it seemed to say:

　　　　　"It will come . . . "

The same synthesis of Our Lady and Demeter lies behind his earlier and longer poem **Mater Dei,** at the same time an elegy on the death of his sister, a hymn of resurrection, and a spring song; and this poem was in part inspired by the fact that the Greek Church keeps All Souls' Saturday just before Lent, and on Lenten Fridays sings the Salutations of Our Lady (the four parts of the great sixth-century Akathist Hymn): both are Spring festivals. This lovely poem—the most musical in Greek since the death of Solomos, the first and greatest lyric poet of Modern Greece—defies translation unless, like the able French version of M. Robert Levesque, it is offered as a key to a parallel text.

But Sikelianos also wrote poems on individual aspects of ancient or Christian Greece, without attempting a synthesis. The subjects that attracted him are more romantic than those chosen by Cavafy—and, even when the subject is one that Cavafy would not have disdained, the turn given to it is very different from that which he might have given. Such a poem is the sonnet on the elderly, childless Spartan, who in accordance with the laws of Lycurgus, chooses out a young man to beget an heir for him upon his wife, and lays an ambush to take him by force. Such a poem is that inspired by an incident related of Phidias by Plutarch, that the sculptor commemorated a boy athlete by writing "Pantarces is fair" on the foot of one of his statues. Cavafy might have made either subject into a Greek epigram—for what Sikelianos has made of them, we must go outside literature for an analogy, and compare them with low reliefs, or engraved jewels, or vase paintings.

Such a sonnet as **"Our Lady of Sparta"** might perhaps be compared with an ikon—it is certainly more that than the choral and orchestral work a Greek composer has made of it. But perhaps in this poem the process of synthesis is secretly at work: the ikon is on the Byzantine hill of Mistra, but the ancient name Sparta brings with it memories of Helen, as well as the ordinary associations of the word "Spartan" in modern speech:

Neither bronze pillar not Pentelic stone
Will I set Thy immortal picture on;
But on a column made of cypress wood,
World without end, my work shall so smell good! . . .
And on the hill that wears for coronal
The fort of the Venetians, I shall raise Thee
A mighty church, and therein I shall place Thee,
Shut with an iron door, immovable!
Bells, that shall echo with the lance's clang,
Or sword's against the breastplate, I shall hang
There—little bells above, as on a rattle!
The church's window panes, to give Thee shade,
Of deeply coloured crystal shall be made
—And every one a loophole on the battle!

On October, 28th 1940, Italy invaded Greece. A few days later Sikelianos gave a public reading of **The Sibyl,** a tragedy upon which he had been engaged during the summer of that year. He had decided to read it because of its relevance to the situation: had time allowed, one could have believed it written for the occasion. The tragedy had for its subject the visit of Nero to Greece, coming both as a tyrant and as a low comedian. The scene was laid at the sanctuary of Delphi. News was brought that Nero wished to be consecrated there as the reincarnation of Apollo. The Delphic sibyl led the people of Delphi in a heroic resistance, and they greeted the approach of the Roman soldiers with cries of "Let them come!" Sikelianos had become the spokesman of Greece, and the great ancient poet, Aeschylus, whom he so much loved, was to be associated with him in that office. With great courage the Royal Theatre had begun rehearsing the *Persians,* and two days after the Greek victory at Korytsa Athens heard the messenger's speech describing the battle of Salamis, and the voice that rose from the Greek fleet telling the Greeks that they were fighting for their altars, their homes and their all. It was also a joy to Sikelianos to see the Great Mother, under the title of Our Lady of Tinos, venerated as the supreme general and the protector of the Greek forces. For him, as for so many Hellenes and Philhellenes, all Greece, Ancient, Byzantine and Modern, became mysteriously unified and more vividly living in those days of hope and exaltation. It was in the terrible years of occupation and famine that followed that Sikelianos was to attain his highest stature as a great and tragic prophet.

In the winter of 1941-2, the period of his country's greatest suffering, Sikelianos wrote the five poems to which, as a collection, he gave the name **Acritica.** Smuggled out of Greece, they circulated in Egypt in photostat reproductions. A copy also reached M. Octave Merlier, the director of the Institut Français of Athens, then deported from his post and held under surveillance at Aurillac—he translated these poems for limited circulation among his friends, and they were the inspiration of those who were soon to be fighting in the *maquis* of the Auvergne.

Sikelianos had called his poems **Acritica,** and in every collection of Greek folk-poetry there will be found a section under this heading. They are poems inspired by the activities of Diyénis the Acrite, hero of the Byzantine epic which bears his name: the Acrites were the frontier guards of the Eastern Empire, who stood at the extreme limits of Christendom and civilization, and at this time Sikelianos could think of himself and of all his fellow-countrymen in that position.

There is a famous folk-song whose title might be translated as *Diyénis Agonistes:* in it the hero wrestles with Death:

> Charon we'll have a wrestling-bout on the bronze threshing-floor.
> And, Charon, if you conquer me, then you may take my soul:
> But, Charon, if I conquer you, then let the world be glad!
> They wrestled and they wrestled there—Charon it was that conquered.

To the Acrites of his own day Sikelianos swore, in **"The Oath by the Styx"**:

> But now I shall not leave you any more,
> Not for one instant do I seek to leave you,

> For I have made my heart,
> For you to dance, my lads, a threshing-floor.
> My eyelids closed, I see you here before me
> Enter the mysterious dancing-place of death,
> One after another, and holding hands.
> And with eyes closed I look at you,
> I never have enough, I never have enough of watching you,
> Immortal warriors, my brothers,
> Ceaselessly dancing the Syrtos and the Kleftic dance
> Upon my heart.

And these lines from **"Dionysos in the Crib"** are part of his Acrite's hymn, a psalm before sun-rise, *Deus, Deus meus, ad te de luce vigilo* addressed to Christ and Dionysos on the cruel Christmas Eve of 1941. It is dated "the Agrypnia of Christmas": the word means the watchnight service of the Greek Church.

> Sweet child, my Dionysos and my Christ:
> Young Titan come into the world to-day,
> You have no mother's arms to warm you . . .
> You are the son of this encircling night,
> Of this night, and of our unsleeping heart
> That, spark of light amid this frozen chaos,
> Wrestles this evening with death itself,
> Our own death, and the world's death!

The most remarkable of these poems is called **"Agraphon,"** literally **"Unwritten."** The title is perhaps best rendered in English, prosaically, as **"Oral Tradition"**—for it is a story of Christ not found in any gospel. It is the poem of an Acrite, for it is a cry of hope and courage from the extreme limits of suffering. Outside Hopkins there is perhaps no braver poem—as brave in world-anguish as he is in his personal anguish:

> They were walking outside the walls
> Of Sion, Jesus and his disciples,
> When, just before the sunset,
> They came without noticing to the place
> Where for years the city used to throw its refuse,
> Burnt mattresses of the sick, old rags,
> Broken pots, rubbish and filth.
>
> And there, on the top of the highest mound,
> Swollen, and with its feet turned up
> To the sky, a dead dog's corpse,
> Deserted by the crows that covered it
> Suddenly, when they heard footsteps . . .
> It gave forth such a stench that all
> The disciples drew back, as with a single movement,
> Holding their breath, with the hollow of the hand.
>
> But Jesus alone advancing
> Calmly to the mound, stood near
> And looked at the corpse. Then one of His disciples
> Could not control himself from crying out
> From far away: "Rabbi, how can you stand there?
> Surely you smell the horrible stench?"
>
> And He, without turning His head
> From the point He was looking at, made answer:
> "The horrible stench he whose breath is pure
> Smells also in the city that we came from.
> But now
> I marvel at that which comes out of the corruption
> With all my soul . . . Look
> How the teeth of this dog are shining
> In the sun, like hailstones, like lilies,
> Apart from the rot, a mighty promise,
> A reflection of the Eternal, but also,
> A harsh lightning-flash of hope and Justice!"

So He spoke; and if they understood or not
These words, the disciples together,
When He moved, followed Him again, in silence
Upon the way . . .

　　　　And now,
Surely the last, I turn my mind, O Lord,
Towards those words of Thine, and stand
Before Thee in this thought alone: Ah, grant!
Grant to me also, Lord, while I am walking
Ceaselessly outside the walls of the city of Sion—
And from one end to the other of the earth
All is in ruins, and all is refuse,
And all is bodies unburied that are choking
The holy spring of breath, in the city
Or out of the city—grant to me, O Lord,
In this horrible stench through which I am passing,
For one moment Thy holy calm—
That I may stand serenely in the midst

Of the dead corpses, that I too may seize
In my gaze somewhere upon some white point,
Like hailstones, or like lilies—
Something that flashes suddenly, and deep within me,
Out of the rot, apart from the rot
Of the world—like the teeth of that dog,
Which, O Lord, seeing them that afternoon,
Thou didst marvel at, a mighty promise,
A reflection of the Eternal, yes, and also
A harsh lightning-flash of hope and Justice!

　　　　　　　　　　　　　　(pp. 72-83)

Robert Liddell, "The Poetry of Angelos Sikelianos," in The Penguin New Writing, *No. 39, January, 1950, pp. 72-83.*

George Seferis　(essay date 1951)

[*Seferis was a Greek poet, translator, critic, and diplomat who was awarded the Nobel Prize in literature in 1963. Combining Greek mythology with modern poetic techniques in his works, Seferis greatly influenced the development of Greek poetry in the twentieth century. The following is an obituary tribute that was originally broadcast on BBC Radio in July 1951.*]

The death of the poet is the consummation of a birth. Angelos Sikelianos has passed away. Now his work, outside the shadow of this great man, rises up in its entirety, finding its realization in a light that is absolute,

　　Like an almond tree dressed only in its blossoms without
　　　a single leaf,
　　A white mass of flower going down to the depths of the
　　　mind, a silence all of flowers.

And so, as we measure the depth of the chasm left by the passing of Angelos Sikelianos, what I think of is this flowering silence of a birth. It is difficult to explain when one's emotion so presses upon one. Nevertheless, just as I try my best to grasp and keep his living human presence among us, I think again that it was he himself who put all the fervor of his soul into an effort to embrace life and death together. I can think of no other figure who awakes in the mind so many images of burial and of resurrection. Indeed, I would say that his work could be set in the frame of that loftiest form of springtime that I know—a Greek Passion Week.

As the years go by, and with the help of our poets, we, listening to the echoes of our tradition, begin to understand from what depths they proceed; gradually we sort out the qualities that distinguish us from the world around us. We see, sometimes, that our feelings when real, the symbols of our creed when the faith is real, and our instinctiveness because it has traveled into so many generations so far into time, and has roots not only among us but also far away— all these have a harmonious and extended wealth and a kind of tone that is sometimes extremely singular. How singular it can be can be seen by considering the great poets we have had in the last hundred and fifty years. If one imagines them as the cardinal points marking the horizon of an idea, the Greek idea, and if one tries to observe how peculiarly different they are from each other and at the same time how strikingly similar, one will perhaps have some notion of the extent and the pattern of our spiritual territory. We shall see something that is always true to itself, yet still mysterious, still antithetical, as are all things which pulsate with life.

Our tradition is full of contrasts. Only great men can bring them into harmony. In Greece there are the figures of Dionysus and of the Crucified Lord. But it needed the powerful pressure of the voice of Sikelianos to incarnate this word in our flesh:

　　Sweet child of mine, my Dionysus and my Christ.

It is in this way that I think of the image of the Mother of God, who is so close to him. And I think of dreams such as the following, which must have taken its color from the iconostasis of his childhood:

　　. . .I saw my father stretched out beside me,
　　pushing aside his winding sheet
　　to spring up stark naked before my eyes,
　　in greater beauty, greater maturity,
　　his flesh like rosebuds
　　full of light,
　　and say to me,
　　"My son, I have won freedom!"

And I try to survey the religious feeling of Sikelianos from its beginnings in his ancestral Christianity in Levkas, nurtured there by every breath from the soil of Greece, extending and assimilating myths which we were sure had been long dead, moving through Dionysus and Hades, who are one and the same, as Heraclitus has it, and always seeking for a resurrection, a rebirth: "High Greece."

In the years when Sikelianos was an adolescent, the whole of our intellectual world was quickened by the spur of this yearning.

　　In the mind of Greek youth
　　bathed in the new,
　　the rosy light deep down
　　is staged the drama
　　of the struggle of the young god,
　　the young Apollo
　　when he killed the Dragon.

This is the era of Palamas, but among the many expressions of this era I would refer only to the picture Sikelianos himself gives us of Pericles Yannopoulos [whom Seferis identifies in a footnote as a prose writer who comitted suicide in 1910 by riding on horseback into the sea.] He and Sikelianos are as alike as brothers.

　　And the love of the beautiful body and of the sun,

of the rhythmical strength which declares
beauty effortlessly,
with only a movement, with only
a quick smile, with only
a quick and limpid laughter
like a raven's cry in the abyss
of the sheen of these Attic skies
clean and unsponsored reborn to life
in his smile and in his movements.
O Attica! and no one breathed
that delicate fragrance of yours
with so lordly a feeling, no one so took
your unexpected colors
to hold within tight-pressed eyelids,
and take into his flesh your frugal spirit.
We know no one among us
so like your olive tree,
the blond ear of corn and again
your golden yellow marbles.

But Sikelianos was a much more powerful creator than Yannopoulos. He too felt that passionate and burning flame which devoured Yannopoulos and directed him to ride on horseback to his tomb beneath the sea, but he was also able, with the force of Dionysus running pure in his veins, to raise up a present, a contemporary life from the farthest and the most impenetrable sanctuaries of our tradition. At the sound of his voice a whole forgotten world rises from the tomb, like a Day of Judgment rooted in a Greek landscape, breathing with all the morning dew of the primeval vision, rooted in the senses of man. Sikelianos sees things without a break and with no refraction. And just as he refuses to separate death from the most fervent moment of life, just as he refuses to separate his own body from the body of his country, so he struggles to unite the world of the gods with the world of men. In Sikelianos there is an anthropism that is Hellenic and that is holy:

> . . . and we say that it is possible for earth
> to mingle with the stars, like a deep plow with a plowfield,
> and for the sky to nurse the ears of wheat. O Father,
> at times our hearts are burdened down and loaded
> with the bitterness of life and all its weight.

But I did not mean to go on talking about the poetry of Sikelianos. All I wanted to do was to remain a little longer with the friend whom we have lost.

I met him late in my life, and I feel that this was my own fault. What I think of as our first real meeting was after I first read the manuscript of **"The Sacred Way."**

> I felt the sun was pouring down into my heart
> through the new wound that fate had opened in me,
> so strong a setting, as when after a sudden split of timbers
> the waves rush in to the ship and force it down.

I remember gratefully the freshness of the emotion aroused in me by this tone of a strength somehow wounded, yet ripe and mature. Later, whenever I saw him in the country or heard the villagers speak of his walks over their fields, I always used to think of him with that monastic walking stick of his, a gift from Faneromeni, which was to help his steps, as he used to say, along this road of the soul, as he called the Sacred Way, which was also the last road taken by Yannopoulos. I liked to admire this lord of our language in the setting of our Greek landscape, a landscape which he enjoyed so intimately and which he touched with his own presence—marbles, hills, shores— just as a shepherd touches the familiar furniture of his hut.

I liked the way the simple people of the hills and plains called him Kyr Angelos. I was moved by this life of his which had achieved so rare a thing—a cleanliness and a purity in things both great and small.

So I felt about him too in the last years, whenever I was given the chance to see him in his long agony. Because the fate of this man, who said at the very beginning "The only method is death," was that he should live long on the threshold of the underworld. He lived through this period as he lived at all times, with the same noble-minded enjoyment, with the same air and grace with which he knew how to choose and give away a rose. I remember him one night in his house; he had been struck by a heavy blow which seemed the last deferred one upon this wounded lion. "I saw," he told me, "the absolute blackness. It was ineffably beautiful." I was starting on a long journey. I did not know whether I would see him again. I felt the wings of a great angel beating in the room. It was as if we were touched by the breath of things we had never seen, and yet we love them more than anything else in life—the air, the style of a Greece that all of us seek so passionately and which is attained by so very few.

On my way out I found myself whispering the last strophe of **"The Great Homecoming"**:

> Because I know it: in depths beyond the clustered light of
> stars,
> hidden and like an eagle
> there waits for me, where the divine darkness begins,
> the self-same, my first self.

I was looking at the resurrection of the stars. (pp. 15-21)

> *George Seferis, "Sikelianos," in his* On the Greek Style: Selected Essays in Poetry and Hellenism, *translated by Rex Warner and Th. D. Frangopoulos, The Bodley Head, 1967, pp. 13-21.*

Philip Sherrard   (essay date 1956)

[*Sherrard is an English poet, theologian, critic, and translator. In the following excerpt, he details Sikelianos's concept of Self.*]

There are two aspects to the poetry of Anghelos Sikelianos. On the one hand, there is the lyric assertion of the natural world, and of the human body as the perfection of this world. On the other hand, there is the austere vision of the seer who knows that the natural world is full of tragedy and suffering and that the true centre of man's life lies elsewhere. There is the refusal to shut the door on the senses, and the disavowal of all renunciation and asceticism; and there is the lifting up, as it were, into an intensity of contemplation in which all earth-life is forgotten. There is the celebration of, and the insistence on, the holiness of all life's spontaneous manifestations and anarchic energies; and there is the formal and hieratic sense that is aware of a divine order and that mankind's failure to realise this leads to calamity and downfall. Both aspects are integral to the total experience of the poetry, and any attempt to understand this experience must take account of how this comes about.

Sikelianos' first important poem, *The Visionary,* is an autobiographical poem, which describes, in lyrical terms, the poet's youth and early manhood on his native island, Leucada. It is simple, direct, unaffected. Things are seen with a clear eye, with clear senses, with feelings undulled by custom and fixed routine. There is an immediate and reciprocal relationship between the poet and the world he describes. Nature and natural events are felt as part of the poet's own subjective experience. The poet's life and the life of nature mingle:

> The lightning I encountered
> before it left the cloud. At the sound
> of the thunder-bolt echoed
> first the heart-beat of my joy;
> at light awakenings,
> at the sudden rustle of leaves,
> at the full peal of bells,
> at the night quietness of crickets,
> at the first talk in the road
> at morning, at the first windows
> of the fishermen opening, at the rising
> deep from the trees of many birds,
> at dawn scents,
> and at the sudden
> ring of the breeze which sounds
> in space, at the spring's gush
> which fills
> the golden pitcher of my love!

The Visionary represents a phase in the poet's growth to maturity. This growth is not that of the mind alone. It is much more organic than that. It is the growth of the whole person, body and soul together, instinct and mind together, an awakening and overflowing of an organic sense of life. The stream of life that runs through the poet's veins is one with that which runs through all nature. It is the same stream that shoots through stones and grass, through leaves and flowers. Man's body and blood are part of this same dance and rhythm of life. From direct, living, sensual contact with every living thing, man draws in the vital nourishment for his own life. This is the sap that feeds his growth, that stimulates new organs of perception. Intense physical delight turns to an illumination of the mind. The deeper the roots are sunk in the earth, the richer the springs that feed them, the stronger will be the powers of vision:

> Tighten well
> the girdle, that you grow
> light-footed, and all nature round you,
> luminous to your desire,
> will come with youthful vigour
> to attire your flesh;
> and the body will grow strong
> in thought, to live as it would throw
> itself into the fight,
> into the manly fight with death,
> testing with light heart
> all indurate opinion.
> And when your grasp is firm
> upon the sacred earth,
> in triumph and in deliverance
> will I forge wings for you
> which the sun cannot destroy,
> that you ascend and before it
> raise up my indomitable
> heart among the stars.

There is, implicit even in this early poetry, a mythological attitude to life. All in the beginning was part of one whole, of a primordial unity. The coming into being of time and place, of the natural world of multiplicity, is at once the spontaneous expression of this original oneness, an overflowing of its own nature into transient and perishable forms, and its division, its dismemberment. There is a double aspect of things. On the one hand, all natural forms are the manifestation of an original divine life, and are therefore holy. On the other hand, these same forms witness to the dismemberment of this original life. Earth and sky were once one. They can be one again. Earth can mix with the stars. The sky can harvest the wheat of earth. In these symbolical terms Sikelianos represents later the falling into disunity of things, the division of time from eternity, flesh from spirit, and the possibility of and need for their reconciliation if life is to be fulfilled. Man's task is to bring this reconciliation about. Through the attainment of spiritual vision, which is the realisation of his own nature, he also brings together the worlds which have fallen apart, he restores their original unity. But the impulsion for this act of creative understanding comes from participation in the life of the senses, in the life of the physical world. We are far from the cell and the scourge. Instead of imprisoning the forces of life in well-ordered channels, man lets them act through him, so that they reveal in his mind their true original nature. This does not mean that the source of intellectual wisdom is in the senses and in sensual experience. The source of intellectual wisdom is Eternal Wisdom. There is a descending and an ascending process. The process through which Eternal Wisdom enters into manifestation is one of descent. The process through which the individual so perfects his vision that it becomes one with Eternal Wisdom, and thus restores the original unity, is one of ascent. What provides the impulse for this ascent, Sikelianos would seem to imply, is the vitality of man's earthly life.

From where did Sikelianos derive this mythological attitude to life that is implicit even in such an early poem as *The Visionary?* The answer would seem to be that he derived it from the people of Greece and from their tradition. The lives of the Greek people during the long years of Turkish occupation may have been poor, squalid, constricted, harsh, and cruel, but they possessed a poetry, a vitality, a feeling of reverence and wonder before creation which elsewhere were rapidly being lost. For these people, the natural world was not an object suitable for experiment, analysis, and exploitation. It was not an object at all. It was alive with mysterious and powerful forces, and man's life still possessed a richness and a dignity which came from his sense of participation in the movement of these forces. Above all, the people of Greece had preserved through the centuries a wealth of song, legend, and dance in which were enshrined the perceptions and understandings, the qualities of thought and feeling, of a way of life whose roots went far back into the past. It is easy for those who do not possess a living tradition even of this nature—and most of us today do not—to romanticise it, to see it, uprooted from actuality, as something decorative and aesthetically pleasing, and to forget that, while it endures, it is the yeast which raises the individual and group life of a whole people from their earth towards the realm of imaginative freedom. What, indeed, is often preserved in such a tradition is far from merely decorative and charming, but is a genuine human and even superhuman wisdom, however unconscious, and however imperfect and fragmentary the form in which it is expressed. That the peasant himself may be unaware of the true nature of the doctrines and the symbols of which his lore is the repository, does not in the least effect their genuineness. When symbolic and doctrinal teaching has been broken at the higher levels—and this is what has happened or is still happening in most parts of the world—then it is precisely in the beliefs, art, and customs of the illiterate peasantry that may be found, in however adulterate a form, the material through which the wisdom of a former age can be recovered.

Participation in such a tradition is of the utmost value for the poet. Even if he is unaware of the true nature of the wisdom it preserves, his attitude to, and sense of, life will nevertheless be permeated by the qualities of this wisdom; his poetry, although unconsciously, will reflect it. This would seem to be what happened in Sikelianos' case. Sikelianos had the good fortune to be born into a Greece where the traditional memory was still alive, where the traditional pattern of life still flourished, and where he found an ancient soul and an ancient aura. Instinctively he turned towards it. He mixed his life with its life, his roots with the roots which nourished the lives of the people:

> And to the people I descended;
> and the doors of the houses
> opened so quietly
> as if the doors of a tomb.
> And it was as if they embraced me
> returning from the grave—
> thus
> the fates the thread had woven—
> or as if for me the dead
> had come alive again:
> so deep in the ground did our roots mingle,
> so were our branches raised
> into the heavens.

But it is one thing to write poetry which expresses subconsciously a mythological attitude to life. It is another to have full and conscious understanding of the principles upon which such an attitude depends. In *The Visionary* such an attitude is implicit. It had been given to the poet, one might almost say, by the gods themselves, as his birthright. It was the natural and unpremeditated outcome of the life which he had lived and of the influences which during childhood and adolescence he had received. This life and these influences had at a certain moment crystallised into a coherent whole. *The Visionary* marks the first stirring of the poet's energies, his first communion with life. But these energies and this communion would require for their full development the poet's creative co-operation on a deeper, more positive, and conscious level than had so far been the case. They would require an understanding of the true nature of the doctrines and the symbols which had been preserved, even though in a confused fashion, in the memory of the people. It would require the knowledge of the principles which were reflected, however inadequately, in the people's tradition. For these people are, as I said, often the direct heirs of the most ancient spiritual wisdom of mankind, the oral libraries, as [N. Kershaw Chadwick has put it in *Poetry and Prophesy*], of the world's ancient cultures. Their collective memory is often the repository of images and symbols of a most profound metaphysical tradition. Their beliefs are a relic of former knowledge.

Sikelianos had found such a people's tradition and such

a memory of images and symbols in the Greece into which he was born. He had been nurtured and nourished by this tradition and by this memory. They had become part of him to such an extent that simply by opening, as it were, the flood-gates of his subconscious being, he had, in *The Visionary,* given expression to the vision of life which they had generated in him. He had become their child and his responses and attitudes had to a large extent been determined by them. His task was now, working from these primary intimations which they had stimulated in him, to recover full conscious possession of that spiritual tradition from which they themselves were derived. "The problem was then for me," he writes of this stage of his development [in **"Prologue to Lyrical Life"**], "By what way and with what means could I achieve essential contact with and understanding of this tradition?" For it meant much more than being merely a student of "primitive" beliefs and "folk-lore" in the normal sense. If the fundamental sources of custom and belief, of the way of life of a people's tradition are the principles of a metaphysical tradition, it is presumption if whoever wishes to understand these sources is not himself at least something of a metaphysician.

Such metaphysical understanding does not involve anything abstract. It requires a direct experience of the spiritual realities, an actual participation in them. Just as Sikelianos had come to know the physical life of Greece by allowing each element of his own being to mingle and cohabit with its corresponding natural element, earth with earth, air with air, water with water, fire with fire, so now, to know the spiritual sources of his country's life, he had to allow his own spirit to penetrate into her spirit, had to allow his soul, freed as far as possible from all vain theory and supposition, to enter into the rich depths of the Greek soul, "to dig up again, from out of the earth of time, her most ancient universal historical foundations." In other words, there is again a double process. To understand the true nature of the doctrines and symbols of which the people's tradition was the residue, it was necessary to achieve a knowledge of the principles of the ancient spiritual tradition of which they were a part. This is an historical quest. But if knowledge of that ancient spiritual tradition was to be anything but exterior, the principles of that tradition had themselves to be experienced directly, subjectively. They had to be vital and dynamic in the poet's own inner world. This is a question of personal spiritual development. The historical quest is the external counterpart of this internal development. The recognition of such a counterpart Sikelianos regarded as indispensable for this development: "For as an eagle, each time it wishes to raise itself from earth, must first walk a certain specific distance, and if it does not have this requisite distance free before it, remains a prisoner of its own wings, in exactly the same way the spirit, . . . if it does not recognise a certain elevation of spiritual history to which it corresponds, is likewise in danger . . . of being trapped in precisely that world from which it continually aspires to save itself " [*The Delphic Union,* 1932].

In what, then, did Sikelianos recognise this ancient tradition of Greece of which the people's tradition was a survival and whose principles he sought to comprehend? He recognised it in the Greece of the pre-Socratics. It seemed to him that in that age, for perhaps the last time in Europe, the true nature of that mythological attitude to life implicit in *The Visionary* as in the art, beliefs, and customs of the Greek people, had been consciously understood. Orphism, the teachings of Pythagoras, the Mysteries of Eleusis, all bore witness to this. In these three, Sikelianos saw embodied what was essentially the same understanding of life, an understanding which transcended the limits of blood-groups and clans, which affirmed the brotherhood of man, and which preserved a sense of unity that embraced not only all mankind but all living things. All life is one. There is a unity of all creation. The human individual is the microcosm. All that is found in the universe is found also, actually or potentially, in the individual. The individual mirrors the whole in miniature, from the grain of sand to the highest level of reality. All grades and states of being have their meeting-place in man. The shifting, changing scenes of the visible world are the varying expressions of a deeper, underlying reality, of a universal order. The world is not simply the plaything of a blind and indiscriminate chance. It is the expression of an understandable process, though what this is, is often obscured for man by a defect in his own inner organisation. The emphasis is thus on inner organisation, not on external conduct. It is not morality which is important, but initiation. The individual has to pass through various stages of development until in his own depths he experiences the touch of divinity and is established in the life of the spirit. The seer is no longer distinguished from what is seen. He is one with the centre of his life which is the centre of all and is all. The supreme reality dwells in everything and moves everything. It is the green in leaves, it is the lark's song, the terror of the thunder-bolt and hurricane, the sunset's splendour and the remote epistle of the stars. It is formless, impersonal, pure, and passionless, and yet at the same time the warm, full-blooded life in the heart of man.

Sikelianos did not claim that this tradition of which Orphism, the teachings of Pythagoras, and the Eleusinian Mysteries were an expression, was of native Greek origin. He looked eastwards, to Asia, as the source of the deep religious currents of life that had penetrated westward and filtered into Europe, "the venerable Asia," as he calls her, "that beneath the obscure masks of her numberless civilisations seems to have preserved not only her own secret but also the secret of a brotherly relationship between us within a more ancient civilisation which has vanished." He was well aware of the Oriental background against which Greek culture arose, and he did not make that facile distinction between Hellenism and barbarism so dear even today to the classical scholar, for he understood that it was precisely from this so-called barbarian world that Greece drew the sustenance for her own creative life. In particular, Sikelianos looked to India, to the great teachings of the Vedas and the Upanishads for the source of that spiritual wisdom in which the ancient Greek tradition had participated.

It was, then, in this pre-Socratic tradition of Greece and in the principles which it embodied and to which poets like Pindar and Aeschylus had been the last to give full and conscious expression, that Sikelianos recognised the archetype of which the Greek people's tradition was the survival. It was in them that he found the historical counterpart to what had now become a personal understanding of life and its purpose. But this recognition of an historical counterpart was, it must be emphasised, but the reflection of the poet's own inner development. This development

was that which took place in the years after the writing of *The Visionary,* when the poet sought to penetrate to the sources of the vision of life which he expressed in his early poem—to penetrate, that is, into his own inner depths, since the vision of life which he expressed in *The Visionary* reflected his own primary intimations of the deeper sources of life within him. His search during those years was for the inner sources from which those intimations derived. But so completely were these intimations themselves the outcome of the quality of thought and feeling enshrined in the Greek people's tradition, that the search was at the same time for the principles from which this tradition derived. The two were one and the same thing. Moreover, this search was not, as I have said, merely abstract. It corresponded to the demand of the poet's awakening instincts and energies, it was a further stage of that development of which *The Visionary* had marked an earlier stage. It is from this point of view that Sikelianos may be said to have been simply obedient to the spontaneous demand of his own instinctive nature in his spiritual search. The impulsion of his own instincts and energies took him beyond the limits of the physical world, towards the sources of life, towards his own inner depths:

> Let desire's girdle be loosed around me,
> the secret course of my deliverance
> finds the magic thread, that girds me
> with delight as the sea the land;
>
> Surrounding life I now no longer search,
> but altogether, as root within the source,
> refresh myself within the ocean's depth,
> full of hidden sweetness and of silence! . . .

Thus Sikelianos writes in a short poem written at about this time. And another poem from the same period, **"Hymn of the Great Home-Coming,"** in which the poet celebrates the Dionysian erotic communion of his whole being with the rhythmic force of the nocturnal universe, with "the secret Dithyramb, which time no longer touches," concludes:

> Deep orgy! To your universal beat, in the new body I have
>   found,
> at your power's source most deeply I breathe with un-
>   heard of strength,
>
> And as, without my seeking it, Eros armed descends the
>   sky's
> depths before me, I leap and I dance with the mind's ar-
>   mour!
>
> Because I know: more deep than the thick starlight, like
>   an eagle hidden,
> awaits me, there where the sacred dark begins, *my original
>   self* . . .

For this journey towards the principles of life, this taking up by man in a responsible way of "some position before the demands of Eternity free from the spectre of time, a position unself-interested, proud, purely universal," is at once a liberation from the constricting categories of time and place, and a journey towards the depths of the human soul ["**Prologue to *Lyrical Life***"]. It is also no more and no less than the struggle of the poet to raise his consciousness to the level at which the principles and energies reflected in the spiritual tradition of ancient Greece, become the active, liberated, and determining principles and energies of his own being. It is, in other words, to recover the "original self" that is not merely the individual self of time and place, the selfhood or ego, but is the profound supra-individual self behind all tradition, behind all doctrine and symbol, the root of individual life as of cosmic life, the ultimate subjective ground of being and the rhythmic force which moves in all things. (pp. 125-35)

Sikelianos seems to have recognised at the centre of all life a single divine principle, what he calls, in [**"The Hymn of the Great Home-Coming"**], the "original self," and what we may call, for the sake of brevity, simply the Self. This Self is something different from the individual ego or selfhood. It might even be said to be opposed to the ego, though the relationship between the one and the other is perhaps not so easily reducible. It would be better to say that while the Self determines the centre of individuality—not only of man, but of all states of being—the individual, if isolated from its principle, has only a very partial, almost a fictional, existence. The individual derives its reality from the principle and therefore effectively possesses this reality only by participation in the principle. The Self is thus the permanent principle of which all individual states of being, each in its own domain, are modifications, transient, and contingent. It is the Universal Spirit, with the proviso that one must guard against falling into the dualist error which regards the spirit as something opposed to matter (matter, indeed, in the conventional dualist sense of the word, which is generally nowadays the only one understood, does not exist for Sikelianos). It permeates all things, all things are as it were its body, and yet it remains at the same time beyond all things. The individual and all manifested states exist only through the Self, and yet the Self transcends all manifestation. It is important to stress this point, for otherwise one is in danger of supposing that Sikelianos, in avoiding an erroneous dualism, has fallen into an equally erroneous pantheism. All manifestations are modalities of the Self. Everything exists in the Self, but the Self is not limited by things, which themselves, separated from their original source, have no real existence. The Self is a unity which includes multiplicity, standing in relation to multiplicity much as the sea stands in relation to the waves, the foam, the water-spouts, whirlpools, ripples, and so on, which are its various modifications but which do not affect its essential nature.

This Self Sikelianos also designates as Dionysus. Dionysus is the Lord of created beings, the great cosmic power, the great stream of life flowing through all, life itself in its dance and dizzying change from state to state, the heartbeat, the sap, the great tidal currents, winds of earth and the stars' measure. He is life in its flow and succession and ceaseless outpouring, in all its forms, with all its contradictions, in its joy and its suffering, its cataclysms and its splendours. But if Dionysus is the life of all created forms, he is not dependent on them. If he is the all in multiplicity, he is also the unity behind multiplicity. If he is the changing, destructible power divided out among beings, he is also the indestructible, immutable power, perfect and undivided consciousness. He is the inner harmony of life, that remains unchanged through all change. From this point of view, he appears as Apollo, the eye with which the universe beholds itself and knows itself divine, and the supreme organising power behind as well as within creation. Thirdly, Dionysus, or the Self, appears as Christ, as the supreme subjective source of individual life. Dionysus-Christ is the Word "in the beginning" of the individual,

revealed in the depths of the human soul. Then again, as another of the "personalities" which, depending on the aspect under which it is viewed, it has, the Self is Eros. Dionysus-Eros is the communicating energy between higher and lower states, between the divine and the natural world. It is the energy that descends from above into each individuality and is that which in each individuality aspires and inspires to union with the Self. Eros is of course intimately linked with sexual love, for the real object of sexual love, Sikelianos would seem to imply, and therefore of Eros in relationship to the individual, is to stimulate that desire for procreation which can only really be fulfilled with the individual's realisation of his total androgynous nature. Eros, then, in the individual, is the desire for that union with the Self in which the individual realises his complete and original nature.

Man's complete and original nature is, Sikelianos recognises, androgynous. The Self is androgynous. This brings us to a consideration of the feminine element or principle in Sikelianos' poetry. From one point of view, the Self would seem to be beyond any such division into masculine and feminine. It is only when it enters into creation that it polarises itself into a masculine spirit, Dionysus, and a feminine element or substance, for creation is the outcome of the "marriage" of these two. The feminine substance actualises itself under the inspiration of the active spirit. This substance is thus the "mother" of all that is created, the passive and infinitely caring support of nature, of everything that lives. She is the "natura naturans perpetuam divinitatem" who is the subject of Sikelianos' long poem, *The Mother of God"*:

> Ah, this warmth is deep; it is unlike, you feel, that
> where in the sun's spring-head like swans the lilies sail!
>
> This is the rose begun and which ever spreads
> on a silk embroidery needle-worked for years . . .
>
> And if I close my eyelids, then I see her: O how many
> around her sacred lamp are the tassels of the dark . . .
>
> As an eagle is she in the eagle's nest;
> from birth she rises up, and virginal is her womb.
>
> Motionless in her patience is she in her child-bed,
> clasping, as a lion-cub, her only-begotten child!

She is not herself nature, still less matter, in that profane sense in which these words are generally understood. Rather is she the passive root or ground of creation, a state of pure potentiality and receptivity, into which the spirit pours its fertilising seed. She is the human soul in its state of original purity, through which the forms and ideas of eternal Wisdom are born in man's mind. She is this eternal Wisdom itself, the divine Mother, or Mother Earth, from whose ever-virginal womb issues, after the penetration of the spirit, earth and everything that lives. It is this supernatural marriage of the spirit and the eternal feminine which was mirrored in the ritual of **"The Village Wedding"**; and elsewhere Sikelianos likens these two intercoursing powers of creation to two black pigeons:

> black like the Erebos of Orpheus, more black
> than the Night, one with the Holy of Holies
> of the uncreated dark—

locked in eternal embrace in the depths of the androgynous Self:

there where, in eternal copulation,
immortal pair of pigeons,
the Divinity itself, sleepless, multiplies,
in its most rich darkness, the Marriage!

And these lines, which speak of an "uncreated dark," give an indication of another aspect of the eternal feminine in Sikelianos' poetry, where it is not something contained within the Self and into which the Self divides on entering into creation, but where it is something beyond the Self altogether, a limitless world of unfathomed possibilities, of unfathomableness. It is something beyond all ideas of God or Being, a Divine Darkness that is absolutely infinite, the Nothing, Boehme's Ungrund or the Greek *apeiron,* an unformed Ocean or Inconscient Chaos in which Being itself lies hidden and unknown. It is important to remember this aspect if we are to understand the fulness of Sikelianos' vision.

Such then, briefly, are, from the universal point of view, the main principles of life as Sikelianos sees them. If we regard this universal order as the macrocosm, then the human individual is the microcosm; he contains, that is, these principles within him, either in a potential state or realised to the degree of his own realisation. The human individual is therefore both much more and much less than he is normally considered to be. He is much more, because he is not simply his corporeal self, but contains within himself the possibility of enormous development. He is much less, on the other hand, because he is only real in a relative way, in so far, that is, as he participates in or reflects something of the universal. He is as it were the image in the mirror, that only derives its reality from the object of which it is the reflection and that without the object does not have any existence—although it must be remembered that, according to the all-important paradox which lies at the heart of Sikelianos' teaching, this is a false analogy, and can only become more exact if we add its correlative, that, as the divine principle in man, the Self is "dismembered" until it is realised in the lives of individual men and women. The crucial reciprocity of this relationship is implicit throughout Sikelianos' work, and gives it, especially where the later poetry is concerned, its tragic tension.

The Self, then, dwells at the vital centre of every human being. It dwells there at first in a potential state, awaiting its deliverance [in *Dædalus in Crete*]:

From the beginning until the end who guesses
that the worm suddenly will put on wings?
Thus the soul of every man conceals complete
within it God, who should be delivered wholly . . .
And if man puts on wings, how will he not
even from the Sun's hands themselves take up the reins?

[The critic adds in a footnote that, "In all cases in which 'Sun' is capitalised, the reference is, of course, to the inward sun of which the outward sun is the visible image, Apollo as distinguished from Helios."] Thus imprisoned within the individual, captive in the largely false and wholly partial world of time and place to whose categories the individual is subject, the Self is as it were "crucified": it is nailed on the cross of the individual's egocentric ignorance and uncreativeness. Its deliverance, which is at the same time the deliverance of the individual from the same categories of the lower world, depends now on the individual's own creative effort and affirmation. It is here that can

be seen how Sikelianos' attitude to Christ differs from that of much "official" Christianity. Christ, as the Self, is "crucified" within the ignorance and uncreativeness of the individual, within the ignorance and uncreativeness of the world as a whole [in *The Sibyl*]:

South, North, East and West—
a great cross and upon it Man's
Spirit I see now nailed.

And again [in *Christ at Rome*]:

Desolate splinter of Divinity, the Word
hangs, alas, with hands punctured,
with his head lowered upon the breast,
like an eagle which as it flew an arrow
suddenly brought from the skies to the ground,
and the whiteness of his visage is before us
to light for us the whole abyss of suffering.

This crucified state of the Self is the responsibility of individual men and women, a consequence of their selfishness, narcosis, and uncreativeness. Sikelianos paraphrases the words of Isaiah:

I see him
suffer for us, groan for our error.
I see him, bitter, wounded, in despair,
because of our own sins drop blood,
lose his strength because of our own crime . . .

But the human individual, since he only achieves any very real existence through participation in the Self, condemns himself to virtual unreality and non-existence if he keeps the Self captive, crucified, within him, and refuses to make that creative effort on which the deliverance of the Self and, correspondingly, his own deliverance depends. Christ's crucifixion is the individual's lack of any real life. But Christ is, potentially, even when thus crucified, far more than the crucified one. He is the individual's possibility of full realisation of, and participation in, a higher order of life. He is, in his delivered state, this order itself:

For I am above my cross and above my nails,
like a great vine whose grape-clusters hang heavily
and wine of the most strong Intoxication will it give you.
With me if you are united, do you with all the world
unite . . .

It follows that for the human individual to worship the Christ crucified is to condemn himself to that virtual unreality and nonexistence which Christ's crucifixion within him signifies. It is to confuse the moon with the finger which points at the moon. For it is only through delivering the Self, through taking Christ off the cross of individual selfishness and ignorance and uncreativeness, and through the development of the sacred seed within from its potential to its fully realised state—it is only thus that the individual himself can partake of existence in a more than relative sense, and can free himself from the constricting categories of time and place and all the illusions and fevers that belong to them. And this deliverance requires not the individual's passive acquiescence in his own paltriness and ignorance; not, that is, the worship of the Christ crucified, but his creative co-operation in a process whereby, through a development of his own inner powers, he is able to confer on his life a fulness and splendour which he might well have imagined beyond his reach; a process which corresponds not only to the deliverance of Christ, the Self, from the cross, but also to the individual's becoming himself Christ, the realised and liberated Self. (pp. 160-66)

Just as the human individual must preserve [his] relationship with the feminine principle of life if he is to be creative and fruitful, so must society as a whole preserve it if it also is to be creative and fruitful; if, that is, it is in any way to reflect the universal order through which alone life can become something of value and beauty. It follows that ages which are creative, just as individuals who are creative, are those in which the human mind keeps, through contemplation, its contact with the ideas, or forms, of an Intelligence which is itself beyond the mind's natural reason. To exalt the reason at the expense of this Intelligence to the extent to which the West has done, is to invite destruction, since then society is swept along paths of meaningless blind activity which issues from minds divorced from the universal order and so completely unaware of the real causes of things and of the real consequences of what they do. There is a slope of descent away from reality which can be traced with an almost monotonous exactitude. In its creative phase, a society derives its vitality from, and reflects, the truths and ideas of a transcendent Intelligence, of that "Wisdom uncreate, the same now as it ever was, and the same to be for evermore" [St. Augustine, *Confessions*], which the human mind can, through contemplation, intuit, and in the light of which it can then give form and rhythm to every aspect of life. Sikelianos sometimes compares the relationship of the mind to this transcendent Wisdom to that of a child which draws milk from the breast of its mother. When this relationship is broken and the mind proclaims its own supremacy, denying its dependence on anything higher than itself, it at once becomes impossible for it to have any contact with reality in a living sense, just as the child cannot continue to draw milk from its mother's breast when taken from it. Instead, the mind seizes upon that knowledge which during the creative phase it has gained of reality, abstracts it from its living roots, and forms it into a system of mental concepts, which it then calls absolute truths and which, if it is allied to a desire for power and authority, it seeks to make everyone else call absolute truths, proclaiming them in dogma and embodying them in authoritarian institutions for which it pronounces divine sanction and to which it demands unconditional submission and obedience. Such a process of "materialisation" of the spirit continues with ever-increasing momentum until the point of maximum solidification and inertia is reached, when new forces, mounting unperceived from within and taking the form of natural cataclysms or wars or revolutions or other violence, destroy the whole fabric and a new phase of life is inaugurated.

It was this process of "materialisation" which Sikelianos saw mirrored in, for instance, the history of Delphi. According to his myth of Delphi, it was Orpheus who had delivered full knowledge of the divine mysteries to the priests of Delphi, that Delphi might become a centre of inspiration and wisdom for the whole people, leading them from the valleys of darkness up to the peaks of enlightenment. But with time the priests fall from their high task of keeping the sources of inspiration open, of keeping, that is, their mind wedded to that feminine "sensibility" through which alone, by direct perception, living contact, it can grasp truth. Instead, their thus dissociated mind forms that knowledge of the mysteries which it possesses

into a system, proclaims that system to be Truth and, exploiting the ignorance and superstition of the people [in *Dithyramb of the Rose*]:

> With word,
> with deed or other means to others closes
> the ways of the sacred ascent, where the pure
> soul of the higher world shines limitless . . .

Thus it is that tyrannies come into existence. Such tyrannies of course vary enormously. If they occur near the beginning of the descent, near the beginning of this process of "materialisation" of the spirit, the order which they seek to impose may embody concepts which reflect in an abstract and theoretic way principles of the universal order itself. This is so in the case of certain theocracies, like, for instance, that of Delphi. If they occur near the end of the descent, the order which they seek to impose may simply embody ideals of physical welfare and material prosperity and power, as is so in the case of certain modern State dictatorships. But in all cases a tyranny is the product of a mind which, divorced to a greater or lesser extent from the real sources of knowledge and wisdom, asserts its own supremacy and, allied to a desire for power and authority, seeks to impose its own distorted conception of truth on, and to stifle the sources of knowledge and wisdom in, others. (pp. 174-76)

The individual . . . in his process of realisation, must first attain that state of inner receptivity—ἀπάθεια—in which the truths of a universal order can again feed his life. The attaining of this state demands the realisation by man of a divine principle which Sikelianos represents as feminine, as the "eternal feminine." If man is to be entirely reflective of, if he is to participate entirely in, the universal; if, that is, he is fully to realise the Self, he must first realise this feminine aspect of the Divinity in its original purity; he must, that is, realise it in its universal state, as the pure receptive power. For . . . only in its universal state is this "eternal feminine" entirely receptive to the spirit. It follows thus that only when the individual has realised this universal femininity, that which "rises from the depths of the pre-ontological abyss as a power absolutely and substantially erotic and at the same time religious" ["**Prologue to *Lyrical Life***"], only when he has integrated it completely with his nature, will he too receive in its entirety and become wholly conditioned by, and expressive of, the spirit, the inmost Self; only then will he participate fully in the universal order. But . . . this eternal feminine in its universal aspect is prior to all manifestation, free from all differentiation and individuality, pure substance and pure potentiality. It follows that what prevents the individual from the realisation of this undifferentiated state in its universal aspect is all that part of himself which is manifested; is, in fact, his own individuality. The individual has, therefore, if he is to become one with the Self, to surpass his own individuality, and this is why it is said that the Self is in some way opposed to the individual. But here again is another difficulty. For it is only in so far as he is manifested, only in so far as he possesses individuality, that the individual, generally speaking, says that he possesses life, that he is alive. If, to realise the Self, he has to pass beyond all manifestation, all individuality, then he has to pass beyond what he calls life; he has, that is, to pass into that state which he calls death; he has to die. "The only method is death"! But seen in this light, death is not a limit or a cessation; it is on the contrary "the most deep and rich mystagogic starting place for the complete understanding and also realisation of the greatest and most inward demand of Life—the demand for the most perfect and 'religious' conscious participation of man, beyond phenomena, in the universal unfolding erotic breath and force of Creation." ["**Prologue to *Lyrical Life***"]. Death is in fact simply a cloud through which the individual must pass if he is to free the eternal feminine from the "cross" of his own individuality, and thus become totally ripe for union with the Self:

> For a cloud,
> a yellow cloud is death before me
> at this moment when, filling the sphere
> entirely of nostalgia for me,
> O great archetype of my passion,
> You call me beyond the written circle
> of History, further than the Word,
> to deliver, above the mystic silence
> of Your Cross, and from the darkness
> of the centuries, alone, Your Loveliness! . . .

The living soul must be stripped free of all manifested states, of all that belongs to time and place, must go out of its created nature. But it must also go out of its uncreated nature, "further than the Word," "forgetting the Word's ferment within me," for the divine Word is, as we have seen, the fruit, the Son, of the union of the passive substance, the Mother, with the spirit, the Father, and thus the Word is not this spirit, the Self, in its unity but still in its separation, still in some sense derivative. The divine Word is the image of the Self, what Meister Eckhart calls the soul's exemplar, going on to say that "the soul is conscious that what she seeks is neither her exemplar nor its nature, wherein this final attribute of divinity is multiplicity. And since the eternal nature (the Word) . . . is characterised by multiplicity—the Persons being in separation—therefore the soul breaks through her eternal exemplar to get to where God is a kingdom in unity." In other words, "No man cometh to the Father but through me." And thus it is in the last stages of initiation that the state of death, which seen from the point of view of individuality is all that lies beyond its created and uncreated nature, becomes the state where the sacred marriage of the living soul with the eternal feminine and through her with the Self in its essential unity takes place. This is the significance of the Heracleitan phrase, "Dionysus and Hades—one and the same," and why in the Eleusinian Initiation, Death and Eros "were the consubstantial power which orientate all phenomena beyond accident towards the eternal sphere of fulfilment and of creative Exaltation" ["**Prologue to *Lyrical Life***"]. For it is in the attainment of a state of total undifferentiation and absolute potentiality, beyond all manifestation, visible and invisible, beyond the image of the Self in the living soul, beyond the death of the individuality, in Hades—

> Ah, not even the Sulamite lay thus
> to give warmth to David's frozen limbs
> within the bed . . . as You close to me
> when my heart sunk down to Hades! . . .

—it is in the realisation of this primordial femininity that the initiate can become perfectly receptive to, can unite himself with and participate in, the life of the Self, of the universal spirit:

> that above the waves of time

> and above the closed Rhythms of creation
> flies rapidly, flies with power, like an arrow!

It is in this union with the universal spirit that the individual achieves his deliverance. He becomes integrated with the Self. He reflects and radiates all which is contained in the Self. He is illuminated by the splendour of the Self, shines with the light of perfect consciousness and fulfilment:

> It seems you are a life-kindling soul within
> the sun's depths, it seems you are within
> the sun, and the flames that light the other stars
> and light the world are outside you, are outside.
> You see the stars; these do not see you.
> You see the world; the world does not see you.
> You seem all hidden within your passion's
> sun, and from thence that you shoot
> there where do not yet rise
> creation's stubbornnesses! Study,
> study is this passion for you of death,
> and meditate upon it as is owing to the divine
> fire which is in you, which not as creature
> but as Creator you contain within your mind.

In this light the fulfilled person contemplates all things. He perceives the inner identity of all things, their participation in that life which is now his life. All has become one, the One has become all, in an all-embracing singleness; and man, in achieving his own unity, has become everything. (pp. 180-83)

> *Philip Sherrard, "Anghelos Sikelianos," in his* The Marble Threshing Floor: Studies in Modern Greek Poetry, *Vallentine, Mitchell & Co. Ltd., 1956, pp. 125-84.*

Linos Politis   (essay date 1973)

[*In the following excerpt, Politis presents a survey of Sikelianos's most important works.*]

Angelos Sikelianòs [was] the greatest poet of Greece proper since Palamàs. It is not without significance that he came from the Ionian Islands, or that his fatherland, Leucas, is very close to the rugged mainland opposite. The tradition of the Heptanesian school was still alive in him, and this no doubt accounts for the deep feeling for and knowledge of the popular language in all its purity that Sikelianòs possessed, and also his familiarity with other literature, particularly with that of Italy.

At the beginning of this century, when still very young, he started to publish poems in literary periodicals, with clear signs of the influence of late Parnassianism and Symbolism. These youthful efforts gave no promise of his later development—he himself omitted them from the three-volume *Lyric Life* (1946), the corpus of his work. His first real poetical appearance is his great composition *The Light-Shadowed* (the title is taken from the well-known line in Solomòs's *Free Besieged*), written in the spring of 1907 and issued (in a handsome uncommercial edition in large format) two years later.

The Light-Shadowed is like a lyrical autobiography of the young poet, a poem full of youthful sentiment and happiness, a wonderful outpouring of lyricism flowing unsullied from the purest and most secret sources. The poet has gathered up within himself a hoard of immediate experience, while he wandered in complete freedom in total accord with nature, by the olive groves and shores of his island home.

This youthful and happy identification of the poet with nature is what most attracts us in this early but already mature poem. The separate parts are loosely linked, the poetic process is not everywhere clear, but the lyric tone is always intense, and the language, a robust demotic, has a fullness and richness of expression hitherto unknown in modern Greek poetry. Nature, we feel, is not an objective phenomenon which the poet contemplates with admiration and worship, but there is a 'direct communication' between them, which, to use a phrase dear to Sikelianòs himself, has the character of a 'profound devotional exercise':

> . . . And I worshipped,
> And in my joy I cried:
> 'Go put your ear close to the ground.'
> And then I fancied the profound
> Heart of the earth replied.

Features which later become the distinguishing marks of his poetry, and what he and his critics consider most characteristic in it, are already found in this youthful poem; the ideas are still undeveloped, but receive perhaps a more genuine and more immediate expression.

That which appears unconsciously in *The Light-Shadowed,* the 'cosmic (or Orphic) expansion into the soul of life' or his 'exercise', was what he tried later to render more consciously. Immediately after the publication of the poem he began work on a vast composition, *Prologue to Life,* and in 1915-17 he brought out (in small volumes, again exquisitely printed) four parts, each entitled 'Consciousness'—the first of the earth, the second of the race, the third of woman, the fourth of faith (the fifth, the consciousness of the personal creativity, was first published much later). As he passed from youth to maturity he felt the need to 'take consciousness' of certain basic problems, which define his place in life—problems, which 'had been wrenched away from the primal core of his youthful entity'. He does not express himself clearly in his poetical compositions, and far less in his comments (especially the "Prologue to *Lyric Life*" of 1938). But his fundamental line is faith in the unity and roundness of the whole (the 'universal soul of the World') and in the coincidence of the 'feeling soul' (that of the poet) with the centre of the world. In the fragmented world of today, in its 'arbitrary, mechanical, mnemonic, distinguishing, and logocratic interpretation and ordering of life', he desires wholeness of the kind the ancients knew in myth (before the rationalism of the sophists), which secret cults and mysteries still preserved for them at a later date. Hence the poet's familiarity with the mystery religions, and above all with Orphism; hence too the deeper meaning that he sought in centres of ancient Greek religion, such as Eleusis, Olympia, and Delphi. He envisaged a universal religious myth, which should unite the primitive matriarchal religions with the ancient Greek spirit, and this with the teaching of Orphism and the symbols of Christianity. This is the reason for the frequent appearance of death in his poetry, in its ontological, existentialist aspect, and for the central place and the mission that the poet has as 'instructor of the whole of human life'. In all these there is sometimes an exaggerated and often tiresome egocentricity; perhaps, however, this living presence of the ego prevents these visions

from evaporating into 'philosophy', and preserves the biological urge, and the initiation and participation which is the inalienable contribution of the poetry of Sikelianòs.

In the *Prologue to Life,* the fragmentation of his youthful unity and the weakness of the composition are felt more. However, at the same time, Sikelianòs was writing perfect smaller poems, such as the series inspired by the Balkan wars (*Songs of Victory I*), a series of sonnets and some poems in the series *Aphrodite Urania:* the marvellous 'Pan' (where we seem to be living with immediacy at the moment of the birth of the myth) and the charming and much loved 'Thalerò', 'By the Cold Waters, by Pentavlì', 'John Keats', 'The Mother of Dante', and so on.

But the diffuse power of *The Light-Shadowed* finds maturity and completion in the relatively long poem, *Mother of God,* written in 1917, 'the most musical [poem written] in Greek since the death of Solomòs' [according to Robert Liddell; see excerpt dated 1950?]. It is not musical only because of the charm of the rhythm, and the fifteen-syllable couplets that remind us of *The Cretan*—which the poet prints separately, as if they were complete stanzas—but because in the free flow of the images one follows another like motifs in music. Three years previously Sikelianòs had lost his sister Penelope (wife of Raymond Duncan, brother of Isadora) and a new consciousness, that of death, led him deeper into 'experience of that Mystery working with uninterrupted energy around and below him'. For the Orthodox, the *Panagia* is more the sorrowful mother of Christ than the Virgin. The maternal or matriarchal divinity—as in the mother goddesses or mothers of the gods of the past—is the source of life, but also of death, in a mystical connection, as in March the cult makes an almost mystical connection between the Annunciation, the 'salutations' of Our Lady, and 'All Souls' Saturday' (the commemoration of the dead in the Greek Church). The poem moves musically, imperceptibly from the warmth of the first lines to the central idea of death; the pain of the dead sister and the sweet presence of the Mother of Christ are mystically united, welded (one might almost say) into an organic whole, one of the finest things in poetry. The language, perfectly wrought, exploits all that is best in Greek poetical tradition; it is rich, robust, and musical and gives birth to the loveliest fifteen-syllable lines ever written in Greek.

In the following years, 1918-19, the poet attempted a wider synthesis, a longer poem, divided into smaller parts (cantos), *The Easter of the Greeks.* It is an attempt to unite the symbols of ancient and modern religion, and to make poetic contact with the religious 'subconscious' expressed 'not in dogma or organization, but in the genuine myth of Christianity'. His purpose was high; it may be doubted if the poet managed to fulfil it. He printed a part of it in 1918, but did not put it into circulation, and from time to time he issued fragments of it. A whole note-book of his, he tells us, full of unpublished cantos was lost on a journey. Yet though the whole poem was not completed, this does not prevent parts of it from being among the most characteristic and the most perfect poems of Sikelianòs.

In 1927, twenty years after *The Light-Shadowed* and ten after *Mother of God,* Sikelianòs devoted himself to what he called the 'Delphic attempt', that is, an attempt to put his world theory into practice, that theory which he had expressed in his poetry. In the sanctuary of Delphi, which the ancients considered 'the navel of the earth', where the Greek spirit attempted the first synthesis of the Apollonian and Dionysiac elements, he dreamed of founding a new, world-wide, intellectual amphictyony, a 'Delphic union', and a 'Delphic university', whence might spring an intellectual independence and spiritual redemption of all peoples, and a unity beyond the fragmented individual of today, and above the ephemeral political creeds of our times. In May 1927 the first Delphic Festival was organized, with a performance of *Prometheus Bound* as its central feature, an exhibition of folk art, naked contests in the stadium, folk dances, and fairs. The Festival was repeated in 1930 with a performance of *The Suppliants* of Aeschylus. The soul of the whole enterprise was Sikelianòs's wife, Eva Palmer, an American by birth. She gave a more definite form to the poet's vaguer visions, and, initiated into the spirit of the dance by Isadora Duncan, she understood the inner connection between ancient tragedy, Byzantine music, and the folk culture of today, and she tried to make a synthesis of all these in her *mise en scène*. The music of the chorus was based on the modes of Byzantine melody, the costumes were woven by herself on popular models, and the movements of the chorus were inspired by the study of ancient monuments. It was the first serious attempt (and it was a revelation) to present tragedy in its home, the ancient theatre, with ancient equipment and a chorus that was really dancing.

The performances of Eva Sikelianòs were the one positive element in the Delphic Festivals. The other aims of the poet's 'Delphic attempt' were ultimately, and not surprisingly, unsuccessful. The Festivals were a complete financial failure. Eva went almost in voluntary exile to America, and only returned to Greece in 1952, when she died and was buried at Delphi.

Granted Sikelianòs's immediate way of feeling everything, it was natural that the erotic element should have a prime place in his work. He wanted this element to take its place in the universal vision of the world which his poetry expressed and to fulfil his need for 'a cosmic and integral participation of the whole of my being with the full erotic breath of the "god of the living" '. Already in his youthful **'Hymn of the Great Return'** he shows his nostalgia for a cosmic erotic integrity, where 'deeper than the dense starlight' his 'first self' awaits him. In his more mature poems (1936-9) he makes a more marked advance towards or search for the primal essence of the feminine and for an identification of body and soul, which should finally lead to a redemption and freedom that could conquer time and death (**'Study of Death'**). But, as usual in the work of Sikelianòs, he never passes the dangerous frontier where poetry slips into metaphysics. The impulse of life in his erotic poetry is so genuine and deep that it never loses its uninterpreted biological origins but vibrates with the purest poetical pulsation.

The poet gave the title *Orphic* to some of his second series of lyric poems written between 1927 and 1942, and this title is a clear commentary on them. Here is the famous **'Sacred Way'** (1935) with its rich symbolism, and the less well-known but equally fine poem **'Attic'** (1942). It is no coincidence that they are both set on the sacred road that leads to the most venerable ancient shrine of the mother goddess, Eleusis.

The *Songs of Victory II* are poems inspired by the Greco-Italian war of 1940-1 and the occupation. Most of them circulated secretly at that time, and were a form of resistance. They are not all on the same level. We may single out the enthusiastic **'Apology of Solon'** and **'The Unwritten'** (sc. Gospel), with its deep reflectiveness, issued at the beginning of the most terrible winter of the war in October 1941.

In the last decade of his life Sikelianòs turned towards the composition of tragedies. It was the natural reaction of a man who had lived intensely in the spirit of ancient tragedy, and had made the productions of Aeschylus' plays the centre of his Delphic attempt. In fact his first attempts towards tragedy began at the time of the Delphic Festivals, or soon after. But the composition of most of his tragedies dates from the war years and after, and they follow the same line as the *Songs of Victory.* In these years, moreover, Sikelianòs showed a strong interest in political and social engagement, and wished to popularize his message and bring it to the masses (though it remained aristocratic in essence).

The beginning, as we said, went further back. *The Last Orphic Dithyramb* or *The Dithyramb of the Rose* was printed in 1932, and was acted in the open air on the hill of Philopappos in April 1933. Like the ancient dithyramb it is not actually a tragedy; it is a dialogue between Orpheus and the two leaders of the chorus, which often turns into a monologue.

Even earlier Sikelianòs had begun a tragedy about Byron, and an *Asclepios* of which he published fragments in 1919. The work was perhaps never completed; an unfinished extract was published after his death. But the idea of tragedy was continually gestating in his mind, though his first completed tragedy, *The Sibyl,* was written shortly before 1940, and was publicly read by the poet a few days after the declaration of the Greco-Italian war. In this tragedy the Greek spirit clashes with that of Roman despotism, and the central episode is Nero's excursion to Delphi, and his conversation there with the Sibyl, who is in ecstasy. The work is genuinely inspired, but it is hard to call it a tragedy and still less is it a theatrical work (some of the stage directions are in fact interpretative glosses by the poet). Moreover, the language of Sikelianòs, always difficult to understand, and the symbols (such as the 'promanteia', the 'upright tune', the 'paean'), incomprehensible to most people, cannot easily reach the large public at which the theatre is directed. For this reason the one attempt to perform this work was not a success.

The subsequent tragedies are altogether lacking in tension. The basic theme is always the same, the clash of spirit and matter, in different circumstances: Daedalus and Minos in *Daedalus in Crete,* Nero and Christ in *Christ in Rome.* The theme gradually loses the high (if difficult) symbolism of *The Sibyl* and becomes an easier symbolism of social and political clashes (people and rulers). In *The Death of Digenis* (his last and feeblest tragedy, which has also the unwarranted title of *Christ Unbound*) Digenìs, leader of the Manichaean heretics, is a revolutionary against the emperor Basil, and the defender of the weak and poor against the rich and the rulers.

The tragedies (even *The Sibyl,* which is the best of them) do not show Sikelianòs at his best. The real Sikelianòs is the lyric poet, with his magnificent beginning with *The Light-Shadowed,* his full maturity in *Mother of God,* and in the erotic and Orphic poems of before the war. In 1938, when he meant to issue the collection of *Lyric Life,* he wrote a fine poem, which is a confession, and a worthy epilogue to his 'lyric life'. These are the first and the last lines:

> Because I deeply glorified and trusted in the earth
> Because I never opened out my mystic wings in flight
> But ever rooted deep in silence all my mind and spirit . . .
>
> . . . . .
>
> All that has been ephemeral has melted like a cloud,
> And here is the great Death, who has become to me a
>   brother.

(pp. 193-200)

> *Linos Politis, "Kavafis. Sikelianòs. Poetry up to 1930," in his* A History of Modern Greek Literature, *Oxford at the Clarendon Press, 1973, pp. 186-205.*

Edmund Keeley   (essay date 1979)

[*Keeley is an American novelist, translator, and critic. In the following essay, he discusses tragedy in Sikelianos's later work.*]

Readers of contemporary Western poetry in this country are usually familiar with the work of C. P. Cavafy and George Seferis to some degree, but few have read Angelos Sikelianos (1884-1951), the poet who was next in importance to Cavafy in establishing the demotic tradition during the first half of this century and who was considered by Seferis to be equivalent in stature within that tradition to Yeats within ours. My principal concern here is with Sikelianos's late and, to my mind, his best poems, but given our general lack of access to him in the original and the paucity of English translations, we can have little sense of the range of his career, and there may be point, therefore, in setting his late poems against the background out of which they emerged, that is, the sources that shaped him and the several early voices that were eventually transformed into the major voice that we hear at moments during the last two decades of his life.

Sikelianos is a traditional poet in both the craft and thought that he gave his art, even more so perhaps than Cavafy, who was twenty years his senior, and Seferis, who was fewer years his junior. And that aspect of the Greek tradition that nourished Sikelianos is rather different from what American readers of Cavafy and Seferis are likely to expect. Sikelianos's work is rooted neither in the Hellenistic world of the diaspora that provided the principal historical context for Cavafy's poetic myth, nor in the Homeric and Platonic worlds that sustained Seferis's imagination, among other sources. Sikelianos drew his inspiration primarily from the pre-Socratic tradition, with Orphism and the cult of Dionysus, the teaching of Pythagoras, the Mysteries of Eleusis, and the mantic center at Delphi four of the main influences from this tradition. As Philip Sherrard—my collaborator in the translated texts offered here—has pointed out (*Review of National Literatures,* Fall, 1974), in these sources Sikelianos found a shared perspective that proclaimed not only the brotherhood of all men but of all living creatures and that placed man as the channel of communication between higher and lower states of existence, between the visible and the invis-

ible. The pre-Socratic tradition also gave the poet his highest calling, that of inspired prophet and seer, of teacher and mystagogue, a calling that Sikelianos himself aspired to in modern Greece, as he believed Pindar and Aeschylus had in the Classical period and as perhaps Wallace Stevens, in our day, would have understood with the largest sympathy since he gave poets the title "priests of the invisible."

Sikelianos saw the poet exercising the role of priest and seer largely through the agency of myth, in the sense that Schelling defined the term, that is, myth not as a fabrication but as a revelation of divine truth, a revelation of what is universal and timeless, with gods seen not merely as symbols but as living beings. We have ample evidence of Sikelianos's preoccupation with myth in this sense from his earliest work through the late period that most interests us here; yet however much he may have been concerned with the representation of eternal mysteries, of a universe where the ancient gods still survived palpably, his starting point in the best of his early poems was the natural world around him and the life of the senses that nourished his humanity. The natural world was for him inevitably a Greek world, both in its physical configuration and in its embodiment of traditional folk elements. And the poet who brings the gods to life in this natural world is a man of flesh and blood with the rhetoric characteristic of his people when touched by that passionate sense of something deeply interfused that rolls through all things (as Wordsworth put it):

> The sun set over Acrocorinth
> burning the rock red. From the sea
> a fragrant smell of seaweed now began
> to intoxicate my slender stallion.
>
> Foam on the bit, the white of his eye
> bared fully, he struggled to break
> my grip, tight on the reins,
> to leap free into open space.
>
> Was it the hour? The rich odors?
> Was it the sea's deep saltiness?
> The forests's breathing far away?
>
> O had the meltemi held strong
> a little longer, I would have gripped
> the reins and flanks of mythic Pegasus!

("On Acrocorinth")

When Pan, in the early poem of that title, suddenly rises up over the burning heat of harsh pebbles on the shore opposite contemporary Salamis, the poet, in his easy passing between the world of flesh and the world of divinities, captures the god's vitality by focusing on the majesty of his goatish form:

> Then we saw the herd's lord and master, the he-goat
>   rise alone
> and move off, hoof-beats slow and heavy,
>   toward a rock
>
> wedged into the sea to shape a perfect lookout point;
>   there he stopped,
> on the very edge where spray dissolves,
>   and leaning motionless,
>
> upper lip pulled back so that his teeth shone,
>   he stood
> huge, erect, smelling the white-crested sea
>   until sunset.

420

Given Sikelianos's conception of the poet as seer, as agent for bringing into close communion the mortal and the divine, it is not surprising to find that his persona, the first-person voice which is the dominant one in his earlier poems, often seems larger than life, almost a force in nature that transcends humanity, anyway the voice for rhetoric that seems both inspired and, on occasion, grandiloquent. The persona sometimes actually assumes the identity and style of a self-ordained hierophant, an ascetic who has been initiated into the mysteries of both Dionysus and Christ, a voice that can directly address the gods and even their grand earthly habitations, as in the following excerpts from **"Hymn to Artemis Orthia"**:

> O Taygetus,
> bronze mountain,
> at last you receive me as an ascetic! . . .
>
> what new impulses
> nourished my untamable and silent strength,
>
> veil of the tumult on your five peaks
> where the snow was slowly thawing,
>
> aerial cataracts
> of the flowering oleander
> on the escarpments,
> dawning of the Doric Apollo
> before my eyes,
> O harsh sculptured form
> on the red unsoftened bronze!

This hierophantic, rhapsodic voice is the one least accessible to a contemporary Western sensibility, not only because that sensibility has been trained in our time to question rhetoric of almost any kind, but because the voice depends for credibility and vitality on the character of the language it offers, on the resonances and surprises that Sikelianos's creative—one could even say prototypical—use of demotic brings to the Greek reader. When the voice succeeds in the original (and it does not always), it is likely to fail in translation to some degree. The early voices of Sikelianos that are more accessible to the English-speaking reader, that better survive the dangerous crossing from one language to another, are those of the first person, sometimes overtly subjective persona celebrating the natural world around him and his union with it (as in **"The Return," "The First Rain,"** and **"Thalero"**) or the rituals of peasant life that still evoke a rich—if dying—folk tradition (as in **"The Village Wedding"**) and the poet's narrative voice telling the miracle of Dante's birth or of a Doric virgin's first embrace. But the greatest voice of all, to my mind, appears during the mid-thirties to mid-forties, beginning some fifteen years after the latest of the poems I have been quoting, a voice that brilliantly combines the subjective and the narrative in those late poems that reveal Sikelianos's sublime tragic vision.

There is evidence in the poems themselves that this vision of the immediately pre-World War II years was influenced by a personal crisis of some kind, one perhaps having to do in part with the death of Sikelianos's attempt to revive Delphi as a cultural and educational center and his increasing sense of alienation from his contemporaries, perhaps in part with his separation from his first wife (Eva Palmer) and eventually from his only son. It was in any case a crisis marked by suffering, and the subsequent catharsis seems to have brought the poet both a new humility and a renewed sense of mission. There is also implicit evidence that this personal catharsis in the years immediately before the war prepared Sikelianos to understand and to dramatize his country's cruel fate early in the German occupation—dramatize it with the kind of prophetic wisdom that makes **"Agraphon"** one of the major Greek poems of this century. But **"Daedalus"** is the poem that first gives us a clear insight into the poet's late tragic sense of life, and it is in this poem that we discover the particular voice he fashioned to express what he had come to understand. The narrative focuses on Daedalus—the great artificer, model for the poet—and Daedalus's persistence in the pursuit of a dream, that is, the creation of wings that will raise him "above the crowd, / above the waves that swallowed up his child, / above even the frontiers of lament, to save / with his own soul the soul of the world." It is a dream of creation that he holds to despite the misrepresentation, the condemnation, of "men untried by suffering" and "feeble and embittered women" who call him a "harsh father" for keeping to his fearful course in order to save his own pathetic life, though "his sun was near its setting." The narrative voice shifts to the subjective in the last stanza as the poet establishes his kinship with the tireless artificer and his noble search for the impossible, for that "awe-inspiring Art" which "the dull crowd" considers to be "the mere bauble of an idle mind":

> But you, great father, father of all of us
> who from our earliest years have seen that everything
> lies in the grave's shadow and who, with words
> or chisel, have struggled with all our spirit
> to rise above this flesh-consuming rhythm:
>
>   father,
> since for us too the earth and the heavens are one
> and our own thought is the world's hearth and center,
> since we also say that earth may mingle with the stars
> as a field's subsoil with its topsoil, so that the heavens too
> may bring forth wheat:
>
>   father, at those times
> when life's bitterness weighs with its full burden
> on our hearts, and our strength can be roused no more by
>   youth
> but only by the Will, that stands watchful
> even over the grave, because to It the sea
> which hugs the drowned remorselessly is itself shallow,
> and shallow too the earth where the dead sleep;
> in the dawn hours, as still we struggle on,
> while the living and the dead both lie in the same
> dreamless or dream-laden slumber, do not stop
> ascending in front of us, but climb always
> with slow even wings the heavens of our Thought,
> eternal Daedalus, Dawnstar of the Beyond.

The voice here, though essentially personal, is rather different from that of the rhapsodic first-person seer who inhabits much of Sikelianos's earlier verse. The poet is no longer the hierophant transmitting a godly message through priestly rhetoric; he allows the myth at the poem's center to have its own life through narrative exposition, then brings himself into the myth by analogy, sharing its significance, joining his own experience of suffering and commitment to its revelation, but holding his focus on what the myth has already established, so that the personal dimension does not overwhelm the metaphorical. As a result, the voice in this poem is both convincing and sublime, and it carries a new implication of humility.

A similar voice speaks in **"The Sacred Way,"** among the

very best of the pre-war poems. The subjective element is there from the start as the poet alludes rather more directly to the personal crisis that was only implicit in the previous poem: "Through the new wound that fate had opened in me . . . " and "like one long sick when he first ventures forth / to milk life from the outside world, I walked / alone at dusk. . . . " But he quickly establishes a mythological framework for this personal journey of the spirit by describing the sacred road to Eleusis that is its setting, a road he sees as a river bearing ox-drawn carts that are loaded with people who seem shades of the dead. And in this setting his journey merges with that of others taken centuries ago along the same road. Before the metaphor becomes uncomfortably labored, the poet moves on to his narrative about a gypsy and two dancing bears, and though there are further allusions to Demeter, Alcmene, and the Holy Virgin in support of the mythological framework, the tragic sense of life at the heart of the poem emerges most powerfully from the story that the poet tells of a mother bear rising up in pain out of an ill-fated tenderness to dance vigorously so that her innocent child will be spared a premature knowledge of the suffering that is his inevitable destiny.

> And then, as they drew near to me, the gypsy,
> before I'd really noticed him, saw me,
> took his tambourine down from his shoulder,
> struck it with one hand, and with the other tugged
> fiercely at the chains. And the two bears
> rose on their hind legs heavily.
>
> One of them,
> the larger—clearly she was the mother—
> her head adorned with tassels of blue beads
> crowned by a white amulet, towered up
> suddenly enormous, as if she were
> the primordial image of the Great Goddess,
> the Eternal Mother, sacred in her affliction,
> who, in human form, was called Demeter
> here at Eleusis, where she mourned her daughter,
> and elsewhere, where she mourned her son,
> was called Alcmene or the Holy Virgin.
> And the small bear at her side, like a big toy,
> like an innocent child, also rose up, submissive,
> not sensing yet the years of pain ahead
> or the bitterness of slavery mirrored
> in the burning eyes his mother turned on him.
> But because she, dead tired, was slow to dance,
> the gypsy, with a single dexterous jerk
> of the chain hanging from the young bear's nostril—
> bloody still from the ring that had pierced it
> perhaps a few days before—made the mother,
> groaning with pain, abruptly straighten up
> and then, her head turning toward her child,
> dance vigorously.

It is through this convincingly narrated action that the poet earns our assent to the mother bear's mythic role as "huge testifying symbol / of all primaeval suffering for which, / throughout the human centuries, the soul's / tax has still not been paid. Because the soul / has been and still is in Hell." And it is through the carefully plotted merging of the narrative and personal elements, of the mythical figure as eternal sufferer and the persona as "slave to this world," that the poet persuades us to accept both the tragic implications of the poem and the tentative resolution that concludes it:

> Then, as the gypsy
> at last went on his way, again dragging

> the slow-footed bears behind him, and vanished
> in the dusk, my heart prompted me once more
> to take the road that terminates among
> the ruins of the Soul's temple, at Eleusis.
> And as I walked my heart asked in anguish:
> "Will the time, the moment ever come when the bear's
>   soul
> and the gypsy's and my own, that I call initiated,
> will feast together?"
>
>   And as I moved on, night fell,
> and again through the wound that fate had opened in me
> I felt the darkness flood my heart as water
> pours through a hole in a sinking ship.
> Yet when—as though it has been thirsting for that flood—
> my heart sank down completly into the darkness,
> sank completely as though to drown in the darkness,
> a murmur spread through all the air above me,
> a murmur,
>
>   and it seemed to say:
>
>   "It will come."

The poem **"Agraphon,"** written during the devastating Athenium autumn of 1941 under the German Occupation, is the purest example of Sikelianos's late mode. Two-thirds of the poem consists of a narrated parable that is offered without introduction, except that which is implied by the title: a saying or tradition about Christ not recorded in the Gospels or capable of being traced to its original source. The parable tells a story of corruption outside the walls of Zion that Jesus, walking with his disciples, sees as a metaphor for corruption inside the city; but more important, He finds within the corruption, represented literally by a dog's stinking carcass, the glitter of white teeth "like hailstones, like a lily, beyond decay, / a great pledge, mirror of the Eternal, but also / the harsh lightning-flash, the hope of Justice." The parable is presented as straight narrative, then the personal voice is heard for the last third of the poem, not as a commentary on what has been presented but as an assimilation of it into the poet's immediate world, where the Zion of his time has become analogous to that corrupt city which Christ knew, and where the tragic circumstances enveloping the poet have brought him to that final knowledge and humility which the ancient poets tell us can come from intense suffering alone. The poet prays:

> And now, Lord, I,
> the very least of men, ponder your words,
> and filled with one thought, I stand before you:
> grant me, as now I walk outside this Zion,
> and the world from end to end is all ruins, garbage,
> all unburied corpses choking the sacred
> springs of breath, inside and outside the city:
> grant me, Lord, as I walk through this terrible stench,
> one single moment of Your holy calm,
> so that I, dispassionate, may also pause
> among this carrion and with my own eyes
> somewhere see a token, white as hailstones,
> as the lily—something glittering suddenly
> deep inside me, above the putrefaction,
> beyond the world's decay, like the dog's teeth
> at which that sunset You gazed, Lord, in wonder:
> a great pledge, mirror of the Eternal, but also
> the harsh lightning-flash, the hope of Justice!"

The voice in this poem moves us perhaps as no other in Sikelianos's verse not so much because the reality of that bitter 1941 season gives substance to his rhetoric, but because the poet's prayer comes to us after he has narrated a story, a myth in Schelling's sense, that provides both an objective and a generalized context for his personal, his national, predicament. Again, what there is of subjective rhetoric in the poem becomes transformed into the universal and the sublime.

During the period of the German Occupation, Sikelianos wrote a number of poems that were a direct, uncomplicated, unsubtle expression of his passionate concern for his country's fate, poems meant to rouse the spirit of resistance and to celebrate the heroic stance of his people. Overt rhetoric returned in the nation's service. Every Greek schoolchild of the period (including those of the Greek diaspora) still remembers the opening lines of the famous poem Sikelianos recited over the coffin of Kostis Palamas, his eminent predecessor, on February 28, 1943:

> Blow, bugles. . . . Thundering bells,
> shake the whole country, from end to end. . .

The recitation itself was an act of resistance, followed as it was by Sikelianos's booming voice rendering the forbidden Greek national anthem for the entertainment of the plain-clothed German occupiers who had come to mix, rather bewildered, with the huge crowd of mourners at Palamas's funeral. Now, thirty-five years after the fact, one perhaps sees those lines on Palamas's death and other patriotic poems of the time as the least satisfactory manifestation of Sikelianos's late voice—that is, viewed from a strictly literary perspective. But what I want to emphasize in conclusion is that Sikelianos did in fact write one poem that successfully projected, through the agency of myth, both his passionate feeling for his country's fate—that harsh lightning-flash hope of Justice—and his more universal tragic sense of life. There are lines in **"Agraphon"** that I believe will long survive as poetry both in and beyond the context of their historical occasion and specifically national impulse. That accomplishment by itself demonstrates why Sikelianos is one of the truly great masters in the modern Greek tradition. (pp. 73-81)

> *Edmund Keeley, "Angelos Sikelianos: The Sublime Voice," in* The Ontario Review, *No. 11, Fall-Winter, 1979-80, pp. 73-81.*

FURTHER READING

Bragdon, Claude. "The Delphic Movement." In his *Merely Players*, pp. 135-38. New York: Alfred A. Knopf, 1929.
    Equates Sikelianos and the The Delphic Movement with the poet A. E. and the Celtic Renaissance. Bragdon writes, "The Delphic Movement is different from the Celtic Renaissance only in so far as the spirit of Greece is different from the spirit of Ireland: both movements are concerned with the introduction of greater efficiency into agriculture, the revival of handicrafts, the reëstablishment of the drama as a force in human affairs—with the effort to restore the soul and not the stones."

Constantinidis, Stratos E. "The New Dionysus of Modern Greek Poetic Drama: Crucifix or Grapevine?" In *From the Bard to Broadway*, pp. 21-31. The University of Florida Department of Classics Comparative Drama Conference Papers, edited by Karelisa V. Hartigan, vol. VII. Lanham, Md.: University Press of America, 1987.
    Compares the treatment of Greek liberation in the dramas of Sikelianos, Nikos Kazantzakis, and Kostes Palamas.

Dimaras, C. Th. "The Work of Anghelos Sikelianos." *The Charioteer* I, No. 1 (Summer 1960): 65-9.
    Summary of Sikelianos's literary career.

Giannaris, George. "The Oratorio of Theodorakis." *Greek Report*, Nos. 14-15 (March-April 1970): 21-2.
    Relates how the composer Mikis Theodorakis adapted Sikelianos's poetry. The article serves as an introduction to Giannaris's translation of Sikelianos's "Pnevmatiko Emvatirio."

Keeley, Edmund. "Ancient Greek Myth in Angelos Sikelianos." *Byzantine and Modern Greek Studies* 7 (1981): 105-17.
    Examination of the role of ancient Greek mythology in Sikelianos's works.

Keeley, Edmund, and Sherrard, Philip. Introduction to *Angelos Sikelianos: Selected Poems,* translated by Edmund Keeley and Philip Sherrard, pp. xiii-xx. Princeton: Princeton University Press, 1979.
    Focuses on two prominent aspects of Sikelianos's poetry: his affirmation of the natural world and his conception of the poet as prophet.

Laourdas, Basil. "Ideas and Ideals in Contemporary Greek Literature." *Balkan Studies* 9, No. 1 (1968): 155-66.
    Includes Sikelianos in a survey of Greek literature. The critic compares Sikelianos's admiration of Classical antiquity to that of Shelley or Keats, but notes that for Sikelianos, "it was neither nostalgia nor pessimism which brought him to the Classics. It was the blessed and holy experience of a childhood spent on a lonely, beautiful Ionian island in the midst of people living their centuries old traditional life."

Prevelakis, Pandelis. "Kazantzakis-Sikelianos: The Chronicle of a Friendship." *Journal of the Hellenic Diaspora* X, No. 4 (Winter 1983): 5-20.
    Recounts the volatile friendship between Sikelianos and Nikos Kazantzakis.

Ricks, David. "A Greek Poet's Tribute to Keats." *Keats-Shelley Journal* XXXVII (1988): 35-42.
    Close study of Sikelianos's "Giannes Keats," a tribute to John Keats.

Sherrard, Philip. "Anghelos Sikelianos and His Vision of Greece." In his *The Wound of Greece: Studies in Neo-Hellenism*, pp. 72-93. New York: St. Martins Press, 1979.
    Discusses the ways in which Sikelianos incorporated his vision of ancient Greece into his concept of modern Greece.

Simon, John. "Traduttore, Traditore—or the Tradition of Traducing, II." *Poetry* CXXXVII, No. 4 (January 1981): 235-39.
    Negative review of Edmund Keeley and Philip Sherrard's translations of Sikelianos's poetry. Simon also disparages Sikelianos's contention that, in Simon's words, "the poet is a seer mediating between the visible and the invisible worlds, between the mortal and the divine." He

concludes: "if this sounds both somewhat vague and a trifle commonplace, so, I fear, is much of the poetry."

Hjalmar Söderberg

1869-1941

Swedish novelist, short story writer, dramatist, and essayist.

Regarded as one of the greatest fiction writers in twentieth-century Swedish literature, Söderberg wrote novels and short stories expressing the disillusionment that characterized the artistic and literary milieu of Europe at the turn of the century. Especially praised for their lucid, witty, and economical prose, his works often focus on the meaninglessness of life and the futility of the quest for love.

Söderberg was born in Stockholm to an upper middle-class family. He began work as a civil servant at the age of nineteen before turning his attention to journalism, writing reviews and a column for *Svenska dagbladet* and gaining recognition as an astute literary critic. Söderberg's first novel, *Förvillelser,* was published in 1895 and, while commercially successful, was attacked as immoral by critics who disapproved of the author's seemingly nonchalant treatment of his hero's sexual adventures. Released three years later, *Historietter,* Söderberg's first collection of short stories, was both a critical and popular success, and his later novels, notably *Martin Bircks ungdom* (*Martin Birck's Youth*), *Doktor Glas* (*Doctor Glas*), and *Den allvarsamma leken,* as well as his drama *Gertrud,* were also well received. After the First World War, Söderberg became increasingly interested in religion as a social phenomenon and focused his efforts on a historical analysis of Judeo-Christianity, which consisted of three major studies published over a fifteen-year period. Because these works and many of his short stories were considered "anti-Christian," Söderberg was compelled to respond to those who declared him "irreligious": "If there is such a thing as a 'religious sense,' then my lasting interest in religion shows that I have that sense—perhaps in greater measure than the countless people whose religiousness consists in believing what they were told in childhood and have never seriously questioned since." Söderberg concluded more than a half-century of literary effort by writing a series of articles, published in a Gothenburg newspaper, which voiced his strong opposition to totalitarianism and warned of the perils of Nazism, urging faith in democracy and emphasizing the need to fight for intellectual freedom. Söderberg died in 1941 at the age of seventy-two.

Söderberg's aim as a writer, as observed by Carl Lofmark, was to "seek after the truth, and to give people what he found or thought he had found of it." In his short stories, Söderberg's "truth" is often conveyed through the neutral observations of a first-person narrator, who comments objectively on the occurences which comprise the story, however cruel or otherwise disturbing they may be. "Pälsen" ("The Fur Coat"), one of Söderberg's best-known stories, describes a poor, sickly doctor whose troubles, including marital difficulties, are temporarily alleviated by the self-confidence he acquires while wearing a fur coat borrowed from a friend. His newfound hope for a better future is given credence upon his return home by the affec-

tionate embrace of his wife—until he realizes that she has mistaken him for the friend to whom the coat belongs. The disillusionment with which "The Fur Coat" ends is typical of Söderberg's stories, while the primary strength of these works, as noted by Lofmark, is that they "are concerned with things that do not change: the inner life of people, the real motives behind their actions, the reasons for cruelty and injustice, . . . and the meaning of life." Söderberg's novel *Martin Birck's Youth* traces the psychological development of its eponymous hero from childhood through middle age, examining his idealistic search for truth and subsequent disillusionment. Largely autobiographical, this work is also considered a reflection of the skepticism and cynicism of the fin-de-siècle period. Martin Birck typifies the Decadent character in whom, writes Tom Geddes, "intellectual activity predominates over the practical ability or desire to cope with everyday life, and who expresses this proclivity either in passive withdrawal or in an active rejection of accepted conventions." *Doctor Glas* describes the plight of a middle-aged doctor whose affection for Pastor Gregorius's wife, Helga, leads him to murder Gregorius in order to allow Helga to enjoy an uninhibited relationship with her lover, Klas Recke. Glas's action later proves futile when Helga is abandoned by Recke. At the conclusion of the novel, Glas does not seek involvement with Helga and rejects the advances of another woman, preferring instead to remain in melancholic isolation.

Söderberg has been praised for his vivid depiction of life in turn-of-the-century Stockholm, a city which, according to R. J. McClean, "was beginning to lose its provinciality and emerge as a European capital, and at the same time [was] typical of the pessimistic fin-de-siècle attitude." The artistry with which Söderberg expressed the attitudes and ideas of this period and his sincere effort to convey a realistic view of life have led to his reputation as one of the most important authors in modern Swedish literature.

PRINCIPAL WORKS

Förvillelser (novel) 1895
Historietter (short stories) 1898
Martin Bircks ungdom (novel) 1901
   [*Martin Birck's Youth,* 1930]
Doktor Glas (novel) 1905
   [*Doctor Glas,* 1963]
Gertrud (drama) 1906
Det mörknar öfver vägen (short stories) 1907
Den allvarsamma leken (novel) 1912
Jahves Eld (nonfiction) 1918
Jesus Barabbas (nonfiction) 1928
Den förvandlade Messias (nonfiction) 1932
Selected Short Stories (short stories) 1935

J. W. Glover (essay date 1930)

[*In the following excerpt, Glover favorably reviews the English translation of Söderberg's novel* Martin Birck's Youth.]

Martin Birck's Youth is not for a moment to be thought of as the usual tale of the dreamy child who wouldn't play with the rest, and the thwarted young man who couldn't disentangle art and sex. There is no false romanticising of the role of the misunderstood genius: rather, a calm, penetrating, often droll recapitulation of the many aspects of such a maladjustment.

With effortless felicity of expression and a sure, restrained touch, Söderberg ranges in this volume from childhood scenes of limpid beauty to poignant emotional crises of arresting power. Backing an extraordinary grasp of life as men live it, is the concentrated, distilled technique of a skilled craftsman. Consider the document of young Martin's long and heartbreaking struggle for understanding with a mother who agonizes over her strange son's defection from piety and the straight path of a good citizen. It comes at the end of an account of his humdrum day at the government office where fellow clerks add and check columns of figures—comes casually, and without warning: "It was after 3 o'clock; here and there the men were gathering up their papers and going off. Martin got up, took his coat and hat, put out his green lamp and departed. He had crape on his hat, for his mother was dead."

The sex problem, which bedevils Martin Birck throughout

the book, is not quite the problem of the young man of today; at least, in America. It grows directly out of the European plan of guarding and hoarding the virtue of gentlewomen for an economically sound marriage, while their impecunious male contemporaries are forced to waste their youth with prostitutes. The conclusion of the story of Martin leaves us wondering: the young poet and his mistress, a girl much like himself and, like him, self-supporting, face a world made utterly black for them because they feel they cannot marry. . . .

Unquestionably, in the present volume Söderberg reveals himself as in the line of the eminent skeptics. There are scattered lavishly through his pages passages that for hard clarity and penetrating irony rival alternately such contrasting figures as Francis Bacon and Voltaire. For him, the major human problems are still major and still unsolved: man and man, man and God, man and woman. His restatement of them, like that of every master of skepticism, at once strikes the universal chord. And in grasping the old horns of the old dilemmas, he has the impeccable taste, the perfection of style, the encyclopedia background of observation absolutely required of the man who would see for us and yet see nothing for us, convincingly. It is writing which will stand much re-reading.

> J. W. Glover, "The Story of a Creative Artist,"
> *in* New York Herald Tribune Books, *April 6,*
> *1930, p. 5.*

The New York Times (essay date 1930)

[*In the following excerpt, the critic contends that* Martin Birck's Youth *lacks the dramatic depth of works with similar themes.*]

[*Martin Birck's Youth*] is the usual story of intellectual compromise and spiritual imprisonment of those whose creative gifts lag far behind their horizons of desire.

Under a more masterful pen such a theme might not be without interest and emotional strength. Many of the world's finest books have been written about poets whose songs are sung only within the borders of their own hearts. This book, however, fails to come off as one of these. Strictly speaking, it is not fiction. It is a series of mood pictures, many of them touching and powerful, all of them sincere but lacking the magnetic spark of dramatic record. It succeeds in giving a picture of Mr. Söderberg's mind and an interesting one it is, but the portrayal of a novelist's mind should be secondary in importance to the tale he has to tell. That life is futile, that truth is rare, that happiness is an illusion are things over which sensitive adolescence breaks its heart and maturity accepts. It takes more than elaboration of these themes to make a story.

If one is willing to accept the book as a reflection of an embittered poet's mind it makes excellent reading. There is no doubt but that Mr. Söderberg has the gift of poetic prose. Martin's memories of early childhood succeed in bringing back to the reader moods of dimly remembered episodes of isolation and loneliness in his own life. Take this, for instance:

> But when the lamp was lighted and they sat around
> the table, each with his own work or book or paper,
> Martin went off and sat in a corner. For he had sud-

denly become sad without knowing why. There he sat in the dark, staring in at the circle of yellow light in which the others sat and talked while he felt himself outside, abandoned and forgotten.

This and the tears that follow without reason have the sharp clear ring of authenticity. For that matter the book as a whole gives the impression of truth and authenticity.

"A Book of Moods," in The New York Times, April 6, 1930, pp. 16, 19.

Charles Wharton Stork   (essay date 1930)

[*An American poet and critic, Stork is best known for his translations of Swedish literature. In the following excerpt, he commends the artistry with which Söderberg conveys his pessimistic vision of life.*]

It is a sad thought that everyone cannot enjoy Söderberg, that this master of delicate and incisive realism, this prince of humorists, is—for Anglo-Saxons, at least—an acquired taste. But it is well to face at the outset the fact that Söderberg is a European Continental, an Anatole France of Sweden. To those who believe that a man is unvirile or at least anœmic if he refuses to believe in human perfectibility this attitude toward life will seem barren and depressing, one to encourage discouragement. How much pleasanter to feel with Pippa, not only at 7 A.M. on a May morning, but at all hours and seasons, that "all's right with the world"! To insinuate the contrary is to give sanction to those doubts which, if they overtake even the most confident of us at unguarded moments, should all the more be repressed. What is culture if it is not sweetness and light? Listen to Söderberg: "Why all this optimism when not one of the old problems is solved?" And again, one of his characters affirms, "I believe in the lust of the flesh and the incurable loneliness of the soul."

We read fiction for pleasure. What does this new Swedish novelist offer in compensation for a somewhat despondent view of life? He himself rather hesitates to tell us and in this very hesitation we may, if the faculty be in us, discern one of his chief attractions. Söderberg is reticent because he wishes to present the truth as he sees it without exaggeration and without prejudice. He colors his picture neither with the golden glow of the untroubled believer nor with the red zeal of the revolutionary. He is honest to such a degree that he will not stress his own honesty. On the contrary, he doubts his very doubt: "How could I, a boy of sixteen, be right and all my elders and betters wrong?" And again in *Martin Birck,* "he was not quite certain that truth in itself could produce happiness, but history had taught him that illusion created unhappiness and crime." And yet all the more from this unobtrusiveness we divine the intellectual honesty of the skeptic, which bursts out only once in the present novel: "Would a man never come who did not sing, but spoke, and spoke plainly!" Such a man has the right to "paint the thing as he sees it," to re-value the time-honored beliefs and customs of the past in the light of his own experience.

We may, I think, trust in Söderberg's fidelity to his vision as in that of few living writers. He collects his data carefully and transmits them simply. In that there is always stimulus to a reader who appreciates how difficult it is to do.

But he might do all this and be no more than a good photographer.

As we follow the everyday run of events in *Martin Birck,* we may at first be impressed with their perfect verisimilitude and yet incline to class the author as unoriginal. In that respect, though probably in no other, the prose of Söderberg resembles the poetry of Wordsworth. Few readers will progress more than a page or two without that sense of the significant in the commonplace which is the very soul of originality. Söderberg has followed the famous counsel of Flaubert to De Maupassant: "Look at an object until you have seen in it everything that anyone else can see, and then look until you perceive what no one else has seen!" Rarely has any prose been fuller of implications—emotional, psychological, moral—than Söderberg's. To re-read him is invariably to be surprised at all one has missed before. One passes through life with him as one might walk through a meadow with a great naturalist or stroll through a city at night with Whistler. The trivial is clothed with meaning, the habitual is touched with magic. The world of Söderberg lives; it lives in beauty.

And as one grows more and more conscious of the author's pregnance in matter, one is equally delighted with the perfect consonance of his manner. He gives not only the thing in itself, but the feel of the thing, the overtone. His curious felicity is never startling or precious, it is simply adequate. How far this may be recaptured in translation may of course be an open question. Here at least is an attempt from the short story "Margot":

> It was a cool night in the early part of October. The moon was up; a cold, moist wind was blowing. The big buildings on Blasieholm formed a dark mass, whose broken and irregular edge seemed to be catching at the wisps of cloud that drove forward against a deep-blue background. The still, heavy water of Nybro Inlet mirrored a broad glittering moonpath in oily rings, and along the wharves the lumber sloops raised a thin and motionless forest of masts and tackle. In the upper air was haste and tumult; the clouds hunted each other from west to east, till over the woods of Djurgården they congested into a low black wall. It was as if Heaven were breaking camp for a journey, for a flight.

The reader of *Martin Birck* will find any number of similar passages, in description, character-drawing and the power of the author to express his own reactions on life and art. (pp. vii-xi)

The genius of Söderberg is inherent in the temperament of the man. In appearance he is homely, stoutish, and suave, a bit Bohemian but decidedly a gentleman. Quiet, observant, unpretentious, and rather indolent, he gives an impression of infinite leisure and tolerance which is largely borne out by his writing. His mind is a rich, seemingly passive soil, in which small events take root and grow, as it were, without an effort on his part. Therein lies the unique charm of his stories; their unforced, organic quality.

But in the simplicity of Söderberg there is infinite subtlety. He lets life speak through him because he realizes that in the last analysis nothing speaks as persuasively as life. In his presentation there is a skill beyond praise. With all his naturalism and tranquillity of style, he gives us great moments, moments of profound insight, of wistful loveliness, of quaint and surprising humor. After all, things do not choose themselves or arrange themselves in right relation on the canvas; they only seem to do so. Without obtruding his personality Söderberg speaks to the mind and emotions of his audience in no uncertain terms.

What does he give us finally? First, perhaps, the delight of seeing nature and humanity clearly and the greater delight of entering imaginatively into the essence of both. His truth has the beauty of understanding. We find that life does not need to be idealized to be beautiful; it needs only to be realized. And as a corollary he gives us a sympathy in this manifestation which is not unlike that of Whitman, for it is the sympathy of acceptance. There is a tone of sadness, sometimes of almost tragic depth, in the knowledge of "what man has made of man," and with it a smile of forgiveness. What we understand we pardon. Men and women are lovable in spite of, largely no doubt because of, their mistakes.

But also men and women are irresistibly funny. Söderberg has almost exactly the mood of Jaques in *As You Like It*. But whereas Jaques is dry, Söderberg is sly, with an ingenuous slyness that never, as with Sterne, slips off into a leer. How he enjoys letting his people amuse us, in watching with us their self-important gestures, the eternal passions that fade away in a month or a year, their curious delusions about fame and money and respectability! If these people could see themselves! And as we look, we may perhaps be a little mortified to see ourselves. How foolishly we have wasted our energies and annoyed those about us, for what? Perhaps we shall be a little more lenient to the faults of others from now on. The laughter which Söderberg evokes is thoughtful laughter.

Are we then given no positive impulse, is there no meaning in life, nothing worth striving for? "Perhaps not," says Söderberg. And yet, pessimist though he is, he has a reticent pride of his own. He cannot, we feel, tell a lie, cannot force anyone in his stories to do or think anything that is not in character. Furthermore, he adumbrates through the philosophy of Martin the ideal of writing "so that each and all who really cared to could understand him." And, like most of Söderberg's simple statements, that means considerably more than appears on the surface. (pp. xii-xv)

> *Charles Wharton Stork, in a preface to* Martin Birck's Youth, *by Hjalmar Söderberg, translated by Charles Wharton Stork, Harper & Brothers Publishers, 1930, pp. vii-xvi.*

Alrick Gustafson (essay date 1961)

[*Gustafson was an American critic who wrote extensively on Scandinavian literature. In the following excerpt, he comments on the strengths and weaknesses of Söderberg's works.*]

In Söderberg's novel *Martin Bircks ungdom* (*Martin Birck's Youth*) we have the classical Swedish literary incarnation of the melancholy *fin de siècle* mood. It contains the oft-told tale of man's frustrations and ultimate resignation amidst the petty limitations of existence. Its hero, whose life story we follow from early childhood to middle age, is sensitive, something of a poet, but will-less and helpless, a dreamer who must give up his early dreams of a successful career and a great passion. He settles finally

for the limited everyday existence of a clerical drudge in a government office and a pale erotic liaison with another creature whom life's ways have brought to a pass roughly identical with his own. Aside from the fascinating opening section on Martin Birck's childhood, this depressing tale holds our interest for two reasons: the exquisite sensitivity and economy of its prose style and the absolute authenticity with which it captures the local color of Stockholm in all its subtle gradations and moods. No Stockholm novel can approach Söderberg's in its miraculous evocation of the "poetry" of the city, its streets and squares, its waterways and building complexes, especially as these urban externals are caught up in dim lights and drifting mists and the unobtrusive fluctuations of the seasons. In Söderberg's work a sophisticated urban regionalism comes to replace the primitive provincial regionalism of the 1890's.

Neither Söderberg's total literary production nor his range of subject matter and mood was very large, chiefly because he was a stylistic perfectionist of the first order and because he refused to look upon life as anything more than a fatuous, highly delimited tragi-comedy. Wisdom to him consisted in demanding as little of life as possible. . . . In some ways his most mature works are the drama *Gertrud* and the novel *Den allvarsamma leken* (*The Serious Game*), both of which are profoundly tragic in their implications despite the arch urbanity of their dialogue and the sophisticated treatment of erotic themes. In *Martin Birck's Youth* love somehow asserted itself, and survived after a fashion, in a world otherwise strewn with the paltry flotsam of disillusionment. In *Gertrud* and *The Serious Game* love itself becomes an illusion, the last and most devastating in the experience of man and woman. "I believe," reads the title-page motto of *Gertrud*—"in the lust of the flesh and the incurable loneliness of the soul." The brilliant surface wit of Söderberg's work has often misled his readers into assuming that he is merely a scintillating cynic, a frivolous purveyor of elegantly salacious tidbits. *Gertrud* and *The Serious Game* should prove how wrong such assumptions are. Not far beneath the surface banter of Söderberg's accomplished prose style there lies a relentless effort to get at the truth about life. He is a satirist-moralist whose weapons are alternately the stinging rapier thrust and the deadly stiletto.

It is in his short stories that Söderberg's probing, fastidious, fabulously witty genius operates at its best. As "the Anatole France of Sweden" [see Stork essay above] he had a flair for penning naughty tales in a gay and elegant manner and mocking man's self-complacency and self-deceit with withering ironic turns of phrase. Among his favorite targets was the clergy, whose stupidity and hypocrisy he belabored with the savage joy of a Voltaire. In many of Söderberg's tales ("Pälsen" ["The Fur Coat"], "En herrelös hund" ["A Dog Without a Master"], "En kopp te" ["A Cup of Tea"], "Vox populi") the realism is unrelenting, merciless, sharply disillusioning. In other tales ("Blom," "Oskicket" ["Misbehavior"]) a kind of half-forgiving lyricism envelops the action, an element of warm human sympathy breaks through the harsh realities of scene and situation. In still others ("Sotarfrun" ["The Chimney Sweep's Wife"], "Historieläraren" ["The History Teacher"]) there is a note of genuine tragedy. In form the tales are usually very short, consisting in most cases merely of a highly charged episode, with implied meanings which open up large perspectives and provide by quiet indirection the author's usually caustic commentary on the human scene. They are essentially narrative *sketches*, depending for their effect more on economy of line and skillfully selected detail than on the element of narrative progression. In their kind they represent a perfect but limited form of the narrative art. Söderberg himself was aware of his strengths and limitations as a literary artist. "My ray of light (*stråle*)," he once said of his art, "is narrow but clear." He could not manage with complete mastery larger literary forms such as the novel and the drama, and he had little capacity for literary growth; but within the limits of his genius he produced work which in its kind has never been surpassed and seldom approximated by Swedish authors. (pp. 357-58)

> Alrik Gustafson, "Realism Renewed and Challenged," in his A History of Swedish Literature, *University of Minnesota Press, 1961, pp. 345-437.*

William Sansom   (essay date 1963)

[*Sansom is an English novelist and short story writer who is best known for his novel* The Body (1949), *a work reminiscent of Franz Kafka's fiction, and various collections of short stories and travel books. In the following excerpt, he comments on Söderberg's use of a narrative journal to convey the story of* Doctor Glas.]

[*Doctor Glas*] is the story of a mysteriously attractive woman married to an elderly clergyman with whom she is not in love, and therefore whose energetic sexual attentions amount, to her, to rape. She is not blameless, she is in love with another. As a girl she made her mistake in marrying the clergyman. Must she now pay forever for this innocent error? She appeals for help to the doctor Glas, who overrides his usually immaculate adherence to medical etiquette first by frightening the husband out of the marriage bed by fabricating for him a weak heart which the strain of sexual relations would break; and secondly, when this does not work, by contemplating the man's murder.

Strong meat. It would be wrong . . . to spoil the narrative value by disclosing the end of the matter, which is shadowed further by the fact that the lonely doctor, both enchanted and disillusioned with life, falls passionately but distantly in love with the unhappy Mrs. Gregorius. Strong meat, and meat that proved many a man's poison at the time of first publication in 1905, when it provoked a natural enough scandal by its obvious sympathy with ethical murder.

Strong art, too. When the book first came to me, I got again that marvellous rare feeling, after the first page or two, of being quite certain I was in the hands of a master, knowing that I could trust this book entirely—knowing that this intelligent and beautiful writer would make me both sit up startled by various excitements and at the same time lie back with wonderful relief to know I was securely protected against the second-rate in a book-long hammock of absolutely trustworthy, masterful stringing.

The book is written in the form of a journal, and in some of its introspective quality I have been told it is very, very Swedish indeed. I do not agree. There seems more to be a French feeling in it. Indeed, Söderberg was a devoted translator of Anatole France, and himself generally hailed as a kind of Swedish replica of France. And this journal plainly has a classic French economy, a well-chosen mingling of the oblique and the startlingly direct, the ability to be both clinically detached and emotionally involved in the right complementary doses and almost at the same time. Also, it is down to earth but not afraid of romantic histrionics where they are necessary. In fact, a little of everything making a much of all. Although it has always been true that a majority of Stockholm's citizens were and are very 'Swedish'—that is, formal and passionately melancholy, with bursts of joy—it was not true of Stockholm's artists. They often went French, and efficiently. The National Gallery there has many a Manet or Fantin-Latour well painted by a Swede. It is understandable enough that a northern people avaricious for the southern sun and southern flexibility should have developed the manner of their elected tastes. Not quite the Japanese of the North, but well on the way to this.

Söderberg—which translates simply as Southrock—comes up against an absurd but common prejudice in English hands, the fear of unfamiliar Swedish names and occasional Swedish words. Luckily, in Dr Glas there are very few of these. But it is the long truth that a kind of English reader who is used to Hebrew names in the Bible and the great confusion of Russians in Tolstoy or Dostoyevsky, still jibs at the less familiar Swedish, with its apparently most un-nerving ä-s and ö-s. I have seen a book of Scandinavian stories criticised pejoratively in a leading London literary paper for being spattered with names such as—well, Söderberg. Even these many decades of Ibsen and Strindberg do not seem to have bettered the distance and the nonsense. But the aeroplane will, and in the meantime we must adjust a stiff upper lip.

Dr Glas writes of his troubles in a private journal. The journal form has always the merit of an early suspense of disbelief: for a journal, if it really reads like a journal, easily gives the illusion of the real thing. But a journal has faults too, compared with a straight narrative—there is a tendency to private discursion, and in the lack of telling a straight tale the reader must supply many exits and entrances and provide for hops and jumps in space and time. Good, the latter—for far too much time has been spent in narrative fiction in getting in and out of trains and fiddling with door knobs. But with the former discursive tendencies, a fault may be found in Dr Glas's journal. It begins, perhaps, too slowly: although in the first breath the mention of Schopenhauer thumping a stranger over the head with his stick, simply because he disliked his face, shows that this book will be a lively and uncompromising affair. Also, in some parts, such as Glas's enquiry into the heavens and their stars, the ground seems too well-trammeled to travel over again. But such little *longueurs* must be excused as a whiff of the period when the book was written. Otherwise, in most of its writing and much of the frankness of its thought, it might have been written tomorrow.

The lonely and also celibate Doctor—whom one feels to be Söderberg himself, so wrapped in the writing is the personality—is a most human being, clearsighted and fogged, strong and weak, deliberating against hypocrisy and preaching a rational justice but at the same time himself a hypocrite in his own way and from the first irrationally unjust. To begin with, apart from any later questions of the ethical murder of the priest, he simply hates the man's face and physical textures. And he hates him for behaving with the traditionally accepted etiquette of many another Lutheran pastor. Yet he himself sticks to the letter of traditional medical etiquette. For instance, he refuses abortions when he suspects that his real duty is to perform them. Only, we feel, through his distant and romantic love for Mrs Gregorius does he finally take a step against the etiquette he normally questions yet obeys. He is a well-mixed-up human being, thinking the best, often doing the worst, and as we find him so, so do we sympathise with this lonely Stockholm doctor, so like the next thinking man; and finally—at least I speak for myself—we get jockeyed on to his side in the matter of the putative murder.

No place here to follow the plot, or divagate on the various characters or moods of moral. It may be right, though, to raise again the familiar question—what is a major, and what is a minor work of art? That this is a work of art and a masterpiece is to my mind unassailable. But because it is fairly short, and written in the oblique form of a journal—does that put it into the 'minor' masterpiece class? We live largely in a world where too often the greater canvases and rounder, all-life-embracing novels get the immediate applause of 'major'. I suspect, to use a theatrical term, Aunt Edna creeps in, the traditional all-round-slow-thinker who must be assuaged to fill the largest theatre. It has become a sort of habit to think a big thing great: though the conception of 'major' is often applied rightly to short lyric poems, singing of, say, one approach to love. I do not know that this small book should not be considered to rank for majoring—a double negative that many imply doubt, but suggests also, I hope, a hopeful suspicion.

Whatever—Dr Glas packs a lot of life into his singular tale. He is careful to furnish the anecdote with a selection of furnishings from his rooms and the streets of Stockholm—we get to know very well the view from his window, the curtain that was burned, the card-table his father left. Most important is how much he leaves out—so we see these few things, and whole rooms and streets where they existed, the more clearly. Also, he furnishes the narrative with sudden external unrelated thoughts that exactly by their unrelated quality add a note of greater reality to the story itself—as if one were watching, say, a street-fight and became involved with the phenomenon of an unconcerned cat passing by. Suddenly, for instance, he will ask point blank: 'By the way, why do the clergy always go into church by a back door?' He does not answer the question: he lets us think it out: and so the reader forms part of the mind of Dr Glas. He will be disarmingful and bitterly frank, as when he discusses going for a walk on a stifling Sunday morning when only the poorer sort are abroad, and 'the poor, alas, are not congenial'. And as a nature-crazy Swede, it is refreshing to find him utterly bored with Stockholm's great Archipelago, almost a holy word in Sweden. Again, though this is more related to his particular love-problem, he throws in a thought as to why throughout his life the women who had most attracted him never even noticed his existence. 'Why was that?' he asks. And this time supplies the possible and awful answer: 'I think I understand now. A woman in love has just that magic spell about her walk, her complexion, her whole being, which alone can hold me in thrall. And it was

always such women who awakened my desires. But naturally, being in love with other men, they did not see me.' And this momentary disclosure, with its appalling general hint of biological waste everywhere, is the reason why he is in love with Mrs Gregorius, because she is in love with someone else, hence a curious quadrilateral motive for deciding to kill the legal rapist or husband.

The book is well furnished with weather. How he evokes the sultry heat, or grey autumn winds of Stockholm! At every move, we are conscious of wind, rain, time, season, summer nights, autumn shadows. He never makes the mistake of *going on* about this: he only mentions it, enchanted within his disenchantment with life. We have the impression of real weather, which is one of the most important things in people's lives, as much for a townsman as a countryman: it is like being in one of those great theatrical productions of Chekov or Turgenev where as much attention, for once, is paid to the quality of daylight coming through the window as to the other dressings. The book, when all is over, even ends with weather, the hope for snow: 'Let it fall'.

However, these virtues are nothing to the mysterious qualities beyond analysis that make for genius. There is, in any work, so much that the writer himself does not know. The selection of what to say—and what to leave out—is a matter of unconscious taste and intuition. And from this suddenly, wonderfully, mysteriously, the great epiphany comes into play. Dr Glas is like an early Bloom pottering and plunging through the poetry of the streets of Stockholm. When I was talking of this mystery to the translator [of *Doktor Glas*], and had a certain passage in mind to illustrate what I meant by the extraordinary vision and wonder created in what seems a fairly ordinary situation, I was astonished that in agreement he quoted the exact passage I had in mind. It involves a simple moment when Glas and a friend are sitting drinking in a café. The lover of Mrs Gregorius walks by absently, knocks over a chair, passes on. The momentary episode is noted, but life must continue, for then:

> All around us the restaurant was empty. An autumn wind sighed in the trees. The dusk grew greyer, denser. Draped in our rugs like red mantles we sat on a long while, talking of matters both low and sublime; and Markel said things which are too true to be affixed with signs upon paper, and which I have forgotten.

And that is the end of that. I suppose you can say the strength of this passage is partly due to its painterly qualities—the two uses of colour—and to its plain statements of 'emptiness' and 'autumn wind sighing' and 'sat on a long while', and to the simplicity of the terse but beautiful surrender at the end. But it is the quantities of each of these that matter, and make the master's quality. (pp. 5-11)

William Sansom, in an introduction to Doctor Glas: A Novel, *by Hjalmar Söderberg, translated by Paul Britten Austin, Chatto & Windus, 1963, pp. 5-11.*

Reed Merrill (essay date 1979)

[In the following excerpt, Merrill examines the conflict between individual and social morality in Doctor Glas.*]*

The importance of [*Doctor Glas*] lies in its emphasis on ethics and in Söderberg's convincing defense of necessary murder, a traditionally indefensible moral, logical, or legal act. His hypothesis is constructed on the premise that in an extreme and ethically untenable situation, it is justifiable to destroy a person's life when that person has clearly demonstrated corruption and destructiveness which threaten the life of another. This idea might not seem unusual in the context of today's literature of license and amorality, because today's literature is not generally concerned with ethics.

Ethics insists upon the primacy of the individual, as Eliseo Vivas points out in his important work, *The Moral Life and the Ethical Life;* but a person who follows his self-created ethical theories often finds himself in conflict with status quo morality. More often than not, the individual whose aspiration is driven by his own ethical beliefs also discovers a kind of undiscovered territory where there are no precedents for his decision-making. This conflict and consequent collision, to use Hegel's term, is the matter of tragedy and of the tragic sensibility which expresses the clash of individual ethical values and collective dogmas. The literature of tragic sensibility has as its central theme the idea that individual imperatives transcend collective principles. This primacy of the individual indicates a belief in universal, human-made values which supersede previous absolute notions. These humanistic values tend to be anti-positivistic; as a matter of fact, humanists consistently have discovered it difficult if not impossible to maintain a delicate balance between orthodoxies and individual freedom. As a result, today's humanist tends to be most generally a sceptic, often an agnostic, frequently an atheist.

The conflict between moral orthodoxies and individual ethics remains a central issue in the modern novel of ideas, and it is the principal subject of *Doctor Glas.* The moral/ethical impasse seems to suggest that the terms "ethics" and "morals" are antithetical even though they tend to be used interchangeably. Traditionally, the tragic hero confronts a coalition of gods and men which he finds to be capricious and frequently irrational; he demonstrates his belief that his own ethical imperatives are more reasonable and human-oriented than established law or public convention. The resulting confrontations are classical paradigms of the conflict between absolutistic morality, in codified texts and systems, and individual ethics, in self-motivated actions directed toward humanistic ends.

In Nietzschean terms, laws are made to protect the weak, the poor in spirit, and the unhealthy; they control and restrict individual initiative for the collective protection. The tragic sensibility finds these restrictions destructive of human freedom and the inherent strength of the individual's "will to power"—self-assertion, positive determination, free action. The innovator-hero acts to assure future generations of self-aware men. Individual initiative and action is one alternative to reductivistic determinism of one sort or another (positivism, behaviorism, dogmatic religion, legalistic codifications, social contracts, various nihilisms). The other alternative seems to be relativity which in itself tends to be a kind of absolutism for its sheer lack of positive intention. In a world which seems to be consistently devoid of meaning, there is an ever-increasing number of writers whose subject is either total nihilism or unbounded relativism.

Doctor Glas is a modern example of the nihilism which grew from the romantic agony and its dissociation of sensibility: he is a split soul, but with a dramatic difference. Unlike his more dynamically willful predecessors such as Lermontov's Pechorin, Dostoevsky's Raskolnikov and Stavrogin, Turgenev's Bazarov, and a whole gallery of lesser negators, Doctor Glas's perspective has been filtered through Schopenhauerian fatalism and aestheticism. Glas is anti-Christian, especially anti-Lutheran; he accepts fate and naturalistic reality, yet he is ambivalent and troubled by his pessimism and tendency to withdraw from society. Glas is an ethical man, a healer of men whose hatred and disgust for mankind have forced him to a position of near total apathy and contempt. Man is at best in a decayed state of being: there seems no alternative to this pervasive naturalistic view, as Glas's life and profession have demonstrated. The world force is evil in transcendence: impenetrable, Manichaean, malevolent, grotesquely perverse and unpredictable in its menace. The somnolent world force parallels his despair. At the beginning of the diary-confession, he has withdrawn into himself to the point where his medical practice has considerably diminished. His only joy is a kind of stoic exaltation founded upon his pessimism, apathy, and solitude. However, his virtually monastic life was once disturbed by the most radical of acts, and this action constitutes the matter of his diary of the immediate past which Glas is rereading as his interior monologue begins.

Doctor Glas is a first-person confessional narrative in diary form. The diary, which is being read by Glas soon after the events described in it, is dated from June 12 to October 7 of the same year. Though it concerns the cause and effect of a single event, it is part of an ongoing diary Glas has been keeping for his personal edification. Unlike those of such famous fictional diarist prototypes as Dostoevsky's Underground Man, Lermontov's Pechorin, or Sartre's Roquentin, Doctor Glas's confessions have not been uncovered by an unsympathetic or disinterested editor whose purpose in publishing them is to expose their author's "vices" to future generations. Glas's diaries remain his secret, disclosing their contents to the reader only as Glas rereads them. For that reason, the diaries are hermetic and wholly interior—secret, yet open-ended in form and content. We are not given to know "how they turned out," although it is assumed that they never will be publicly revealed in Glas's lifetime. He notes with irony that he will hide his diaries within his medical journals and gynecological records, a darkly humorous reference to the gynecological roots of the crucial events of his narrative.

> But how am I to get rid of them? I know: I have a lot of cardboard boxes on my bookshelf, cases shaped like books, filled with scientific jottings and other old papers, carefully arranged in order and with labels on their backs. I'll have them in among my notes on gynaecology. And I can mingle them with sheets from my older diaries, for I have kept a diary before; never regularly, never for long, but periodically. . . . Anyhow, for the time being it's

all one. I shall always have time to burn them, if need be.

The beginning of the diaries clearly indicates a tone of Schopenhauerian pessimism, of Stoic apathy and autarky. Glas is a solitary; he compares himself and his life to that of Schopenhauer, another man who lived an interior existence, had few friends and withdrew into a self-contained realm, impervious to perturbation. Glas's only friends are casual: the worldly Martin Birck (the hero of Söderberg's most famous novel **Martin Birck's Youth**), and the cynical and world-weary Markel. At first, Glas seems to be a formula, typological Schopenhauerian. His life is purposeless and illusory, driven by blind and impenetrable cosmic will which can be only partially sublimated through the ego's self-created counter-illusions in a highly selective aestheticism. Like Schopenhauer, Glas is a romantic ironist who finds the world to be cruelly dualistic, ambivalent and inexplicable—a maddening mixture of illusion and reality. He represents, to quote Irwin Edman, "a romantic will which can never get what it wants and can never love what it gets" ["Introduction" to *The Philosophy of Schopenhauer* (1928)]. Emptiness and solitude dominate his diaries; yet, unlike his predecessor, Glas eventually will commit an act of free choice—a clear demonstration of his will—which will belie his inertia and cosmic fatalism. Unlike the typical romantic ironist who seldom has motives sufficient to instigate action in a world without meaning, Doctor Glas will act upon his ethical imperative by killing a priest. Yet when Glas reads through his record of events leading to the murder, he seems incredulous that he acted so resolutely since he has now returned to his original position of withdrawal and pessimism. Nevertheless, the diary reiterates the fact that he had acted for another human being in the face of blind and inscrutable universal will.

The diary begins on a dense and sultry June day. The oppressive atmosphere of Stockholm is reminiscent of St. Petersburg at the beginning of *Crime and Punishment*. Like Raskolnikov, Glas is walking the streets in a kind of daze when he is suddenly confronted by his *bête noir,* the Reverend Gregorius, whose repulsiveness reminds Glas of an anecdote about Schopenhauer. One day in a restaurant Schopenhauer came upon a person of "disagreeable mien." He began beating the man over the head with his cane "merely on account of his appearance." To Glas, Gregorius is a sordid blemish, a personification of the world's ugliness and bestiality. Glas is also reminded of an occasion when, in his early youth, he first saw Gregorius mounting the podium in church, saw his "odious physiognomy, like a nasty fungus, hop in the pulpit and heard him strike up his Abba Father. Same greyish pudgy face; same dirty yellow side-whiskers, now greying slightly, perhaps: and that same unfathomably mean look behind the spectacles."

Glas recalls a recent visit to his office by a troubled Helga Gregorius whose discomfort was so great she could not disclose the reason for her visit. Helga is less than half her husband's age; she is remarkably beautiful, and Glas is drawn to her exceptional beauty. The incongruity of her youth and radiance and her husband's age and ugliness stirs Glas's disgust, reviving his awareness of instability and inequity. Glas's peace is shriven; as he returns home that evening, he wonders why people like Gregorius must

exist. The surreal, animistic setting mirrors his troubled reflections.

> That there should be such people in the world! Who hasn't heard the old conundrum, so often debated when two or three poor devils are sitting around a cafe table: If, by pressing a button on the wall, or by a mere act of will, you could murder a Chinese mandarin and inherit his riches—would you do it? This problem I've never bothered my head to find an answer to, perhaps because I've never known the cruel misery of being really and truly poor. But if, by pressing a button in the wall, I could kill that clergyman, I do believe I should do it.
>
> As I went on homewards through pale unnatural twilight the heat seemed as oppressive as at high noon; and the red dust-clouds which lay in strata beyond Kungsholmen's factory chimneys, turning to darkness, resembled slumbering disasters.

Glas's reclusiveness, pessimism and disgust are again reinforced in a scene which is to have crucial significance in his later decision to activate his long-dormant desire to kill Gregorius. He recalls an incident which had occurred several years previously when an unmarried and pregnant girl came to his office seeking an abortion. He rejected the girl's request, partly as a result of his Hippocratic Oath, largely from indifference to her situation, concluding to himself: "respect for human life—what is it in my mouth but low hypocrisy." He had sent her away after her frustration had led to a tantrum. That same night Glas sat at his window contemplating the animated and troubling sounds of the night: "the blue night is awake beneath me; under the trees, rustlings and whisperings." His rejection of the girl is still on his mind the next morning when he sees a pregnant woman walking in the streets; his description of her is reminiscent of Schopenhauer's essay on women. She walks "as if she were carrying her stomach before her on a silver-plated salver." With distaste, he reflects on the birth process, its distortedness and ugliness: "A new-born child is loathsome. A deathbed rarely makes so horrible an impression as childbirth, that terrible symphony of screams and filth and blood." To Glas, sex, birth, death all functionally restate life's horror, corruption, and universal perversity.

> Why must the life of our species be preserved and our longing stilled by means of an organ we use several times a day as a drain for impurities; why couldn't it be done by means of some act composed of dignity and beauty, as well as of the highest voluptuousness? An action which could be carried out in church, before the eyes of all, just as well as in darkness and solitude? Or in a temple of roses, in the eye of the sun, to the chanting of choirs and a dance of wedding guests?

Mrs. Gregorius again visits Glas, finally confessing that she loathes her sexually voracious husband and is repulsed by his demands. She begs Glas to talk to her husband. Glas then informs Gregorius that because his wife has a disease of the womb, he must abstain from intercourse with her for at least six months. However, Glas does not realize that his admonition will only fire the minister's lust. During his interview with the priest Glas again compares Gregorius to his master, Martin Luther, whose lasciviousness was notable, but who was not a hypocrite about his sexual obsessions. One day later, Glas discovers that Helga has a lover, Klas Recke. As Glas reads his diary, he recalls how he envied Recke his conquest, his good looks, if not his trivial mind. For perhaps the first time in the diaries, a human event or relationship is not clothed by Glas in pessimistic irony. Helga and Recke seem to be chosen by nature for their liaison; they seem destined to live by instinct and passion and not man's laws made for self-protection, never for love. "Through the twilight I saw that look of hers, quenched in happiness. Yes, these two belong together, it's natural selection." Although Glas is drawn to Helga, it is difficult to believe that his admiration for her ability to love is anything but sincere. Although he has an obvious affection, even love, for Helga, life has passed him by. Glas exists after the fact and the possibility of an entangling relationship has no reality for him.

When Helga visits Glas's office several days later, it is to inform him that she has been raped by her husband. She ends the interview by saying: "I'm made to be trampled on." Forced to marry the priest, she is now being forced to satisfy his inflamed sexual desires. Glas is stirred by her anguish even though his common sense tells him that justice is impossible, that fate would divert any attempt to change matters. Yet against his nature Glas once again confronts Gregorius, telling him that he is suffering from acute heart disease which demands sexual abstinence. Upon this warning, the minister turns "green and mauve." On the following Sunday, a day again befuddled by the ominous atmosphere of oppressive humidity and dust-filled air, Glas experiences a dark night of the soul in which he feels, as he ironically phrases it, "the grandeur of true desolation." That night he dreams the first of two dreams which will foretell future happenings in the surreal stylization of the dream state. Unlike Raskolnikov, who also experiences a series of dreams but who until his final dream believes them to be illusory when they are prophetic revelations of reality, Glas accepts the future projections literally. In the dream he is operating on Gregorius' heart with a pen-knife while Helga sits in a corner playing a harmonium. The minister dies during the operation; Glas is led away by the police and as he is taken away he points to a window indicating an inferno outside.

> A red flash burst in through both the windows of the room; suddenly it was broad daylight, and a woman's voice that seemed to come from another room whined and whimpered: The world's on fire, the world's on fire!
>
> And I woke up.
>
> The morning sun was shining straight into the room.

The remainder of the diary is concerned with Glas's mounting resolution to eliminate Gregorius—the method and the consequences of the act. It is in this section that the ethical considerations of the murder are ruminated by Glas. After the first dream Glas seems totally committed to purging the world of Gregorius; however, it will be only after a series of fortuitous events that his resolutions will be complete. One day, seemingly accidentally, Glas discovers several potassium cyanide tablets which he had procured for "a day they may be needed"—for his own death. Perhaps necessity has provided them as well for Gregorius. The discovery triggers meditation about the ethics of self-annihilation, of euthanasia, of the "right to die," suggesting by inference the right to kill as well.

> The day will come, must come, when the right to die is recognized as far more important and inalienable a human right than the right to drop a voting ticket into a ballot box. And when that time is ripe, every incurably sick person—and every 'criminal' also—shall have the right to the doctor's help, if he wishes to be set free.

Though Gregorius is not specifically mentioned in this rumination, his case is clearly the one under consideration. Glas's commitment to destroy Gregorius, to cure him of his "incurable sickness," is reinforced when he discovers, again seemingly by chance, a note he had written several years previously in which he had stated: "Nothing so reduces and drags down a human being as the consciousness of not being loved." Although Glas *knows* he never will be loved, he discovers, much to his own incredulity, that he is not incapable of loving someone else intensely enough to act on her behalf. The murder will give Helga her freedom to love Recke and it will at least partially resolve one of the infinite, eternal, and grotesque paradoxes which describe the world's disorder and ambivalence. The real source and purpose of Gregorius' murder will never be divulged.

A few days later, as chance would have it, Glas is again called out in the night to attend the child of a woman whom he discovers to be the one he had earlier denied an abortion and who has since married. One of her children is ill. As Glas rushes through the streets, he is accompanied by the demonic furies of the night, a "cloud of drunken nightbirds and whores swarming about my coattails." In Olga's home he is stunned to find that her first child, the one she had begged to have aborted, is a mongolian idiot, "a monster." The child is a parody of good intention and Glas's oath, at the same time suggesting a possible future consequence of the Gregorius-Helga marriage; it is a brutal joke by ugly destiny on man's blindness and his stupid morality.

> Enormous ape-like cheekbones, a flattened cranium, little evil stupid eyes. It was obvious at first glance: an idiot.
>
> So—this was her first-born! It was him she was carrying under her heart, that time. This was the seed she begged him on her knees to free her from; and I answered with duty. Life, I don't understand you!

Helga's rape, the dream of cosmic fire, the discovery of the cyanide pills, the reflections of love, and, finally, Olga's idiot, all combine to strengthen Glas's resolve. He can no longer remain impervious to the cruel incongruities and perversities of fate. Circumstances force him to act on his newly-discovered ethical responsibility and in defiance of cosmic fatality. However, the murder will be strangely in congruence with his oath as a doctor.

The final spur to Glas's resolution to murder occurs when he meets with his sometime friends Birck and Markel in a neighborhood restaurant. During their conversation on happiness, Glas hears what others think of him and he is shocked. Birck is a total pessimist who is rancorous and bitter. Markel is a cynical epicurean hedonist whose contempt for the world matches Birck's, but whose consolation is purely sensualist aestheticism; he claims to be at one with himself yet drinks heavily. Birck and Markel are Glas's alter egos. Concerning happiness, Birck says "Haven't we all, always, a need to see ourselves and our efforts in the light of a certain ideality? Perhaps then the last resort, the deepest happiness lies in the illusion of not desiring happiness." Markel responds to the subject of happiness with indifference and uninterest in abstract ideas of the mob, a belief he finds common to Glas:

> —Such people don't seek happiness, only to get a little form and style into their unhappiness.
>
> And suddenly without warning, he added:
>
> —Glas is one of them.
>
> This last astounded me. I just sat there, without a word to reply. Right up to the moment I heard my own name uttered I thought he was speaking of himself. *And I still think so.* It was simply in order to conceal it that he pounced upon me. . . . Over the Mälaren lakes a violent red cloud sailed on its solitary way, detached from the others. (my italics)

After this encounter, Glas dreams again; the dream synthesizes his past and portends his future. Again he kills the minister. A disagreeable smell pervades the dream; it is a smell Glas had detected during the day, and it is an obvious symbol of Gregorius, but it disappears when Glas kills him. The Luther-Gregorius analogy again appears in the dream, and Glas awakens firmly resolved to kill Gregorius. Those who see their carnal desires as absolute manifest rights, and who behave contrary to their avowed principles, with imperviousness to the sufferings of others, must be punished. Gregorius must die and Glas is committed to the act. Glas will kill him to rid the world of this corrupt and immoral evil and to protect the vitality and beauty of natural passions and pagan instincts:

> I want to act. Life is action. When I see something that makes me indignant, I want to intervene. If I don't intervene every time I see a fly in a spider's web, this is because the world of flies and spiders is not mine, and I know one must limit oneself; and I don't like flies. But if I see a beautiful little insect with shimmering golden wings caught in a web, then I tear the web to pieces and kill the spider. I go walking in the forest; I hear a cry of distress; I run toward the cry and find a man about to rape a woman. . . . The law does not let me kill someone else to save my father or my son or my best friend, or to protect my beloved from violence, or rape. In a word, *the law is absurd; and no self-respecting person allows his actions to be determined by it.*
>
> But the unwritten law? Morality . . . ?
>
> Morality, the proverbial line chalked around a hen, binds those who believe in it. Morality, that's others' views of what is right. *But what was here in question was my view.* (my italics)

Conventional morality will not serve Glas's reasoning: "Morality's place is among household chattels, not among the gods. It is for our use, not our ruler. And it is to be used with discrimination, 'with a pinch of salt.' " Ethical action is finally dependent upon individual interpretation. The rejection of group concepts for higher principles, individually motivated, is Glas's restatement of the tragic concept that when an individual acts it is "as if he were a god." His will to action is reinforced by his remarkably Nietzschean version of the "Hippocratic Oath": "Your duty as a doctor is to help the person who can and should be helped, and cut away the rotten flesh which is spoiling the healthy." Glas clearly believes he has a moral responsibility to effect change. This belief is remarkably absent of self interest; rather it is altogether altruistic, since Helga is obviously indifferent to him but totally dependent upon him for her happiness. At the same time, Glas is fascinated with his new-found sense of responsibility; his normal course has been to watch the herd's struggle from a passive and ironic proper distance: "I who am a born looker-on, who want to sit comfortably in my box and see how people on the stage murder each other, while I myself have no business there. I want to stay outside."

On August 10, Glas suffers a final indecision, but two days later his mind is firmly resolved. He will consider every contingency: "Chance will make its changes, even so. One must rely to some small degree on one's powers of improvisation." The time and place of the murder will depend upon openly propitious circumstances for which he must be on constant alert. The cause-effect of the murder will forever be concealed, mediated only through the memory and reflection of Glas's own recording of the occasion. The act will be generated by the belief that one human being can twist circumstance to positive ends for another. The murder, if it is successful, will be a tacit challenge to the order of things which denies freedom and happiness and which exalts suffering and corruption. The act will be his challenge to destiny, universal will and public morality and, paradoxically, it will also be ethical. He has considered all possible contingencies *before* he kills Gregorius and he has already fully accepted the consequences of his action:

> Always, I have been rather solitary. My loneliness I have borne about with me through the crowd as a snail his house. For some individuals solitude isn't a circumstance they've tumbled into by chance, but a trait, of character. And this, I suppose, can only deepen my solitude. Whatever happens, whether things turn out well or ill—for me the 'punishment' can only be solitary confinement for life.

Schopenhauer symbolized the life of man as an expanding bubble soon to burst: all human effort is essentially insignificant. Acts have no rational ends, nor does the universe in which they occur. In spite of all the negative rejoinders, Glas's will drives him beyond futility and the ideal of the emptiness of all endeavor.

On August 22, Glas happens upon Gregorius at the refreshment stand in the market place. They drink Vichy water and Glas administers the cyanide, having seen his advantage while advising the minister at the same time that the pill will hinder " 'food fever,' the distress and palpitations that immediately follow a meal." Chance also aids Glas in his discovery and destruction of another pill which he had accidentally dropped to the ground. Gregorius dies almost instantly. Glas indicates stroke as the cause on the death certificate. At the funeral, Glas sardonically reflects on the death, parodying the notion of divine justice, saying to himself that "the Lord knew the fruit was ripe," but at the same time seriously speculating about the forces of necessity which contain all the essential secrets. The act is complete; Glas's pessimism is restored but in a condition of negative exultation. He now initiates an explanation of "unknowable reality and will," hypothesizing that his act might have been predestined, that it was inevitable; that it was outside the understanding of blind intellect, yet part of the eternal negative harmony.

> All I knew were a few of the most immediate reasons and circumstances, but behind these the long chain of causation lost itself in darkness. I felt my 'action' to be a link in a chain, a wave in a greater movement; a chain and a movement which had had their beginning long before my first thought, long before the day when my father first looked with desire upon my mother. I felt the law of *necessity:* felt it bodily, as a shiver passing through marrow and bone. I felt no guilt. There is no guilt. The shiver I felt was the same as I sometimes feel from great and serious music, or very solitary and elevated thoughts.

The ascetic Glas now speculates about his remaining days. How many more years will he be fated to "wander about at random in this world of enigmas and dreams and phenomena that elude interpretation"? He has reverted to his reflective stoic inwardness and fatalism: the conflict between blind will and cosmic forces will never be understood. All is illusion and vanity. The same evening, he attends a concert and, while listening to the overture to "Lohengrin," he once again meditates his act and his solitude. Necessity floods over him, filling mind and body in waves of musical confirmation. The music is like a nostalgic reflection; it suggests a temporary wholeness and at the same time an escape from suffering and disillusion. Music is the ultimate symbol of creativity and futility; it is man's attempt to transcend mere existence and constant change through artistic creation. When Edman describes Schopenhauer's idea of the power of music as an aesthetic metaphysic, he is describing Glas's beliefs as well:

> In the flow and movement of music the soul recognizes in the intimate and poignant stream and sound its own intimate and poignant life. If the plastic and the literary arts reveal the eternal forms of the world, it is in music that the will itself is immediately rendered. And so for Schopenhauer music is the most perfect and successful of the arts since it reveals the will with immediacy and urgency to itself.

While the music is playing, Glas concludes that any attempt to fathom the dark mysteries of human nature and the brute world force only lead to self-destruction. He abstracts himself from speculations and allows himself to merge completely with the music which "excites and strengthens, it heightens and confirms."

Early in September of the same year, Glas reexamines his diary, his act of murder, and the arguments of the now fictive and historical "interior voices" in his diary. He silently evaluates the entries. The rereading leads him to no new conclusions, only to a reinforcement of his belief that he acted correctly. He has returned to his quietistic former state; he is ascetic and withdrawn, a kind of stoic saint. The next entry, written nearly two weeks later, states explicitly what was implied in his earlier diaries—that his secret passion for Helga will never be expressed to her. Never again will Glas act for passion's sake, even though his act of murder was partially compelled by righteous indignation. Helga has now been abandoned by her empty-minded lover, but Glas has no intention of pursuing her.

> Never will she be mine; never. I never brought a flush to her cheek, and it is not I who now have made it so chalk-white. And never will she slip across the street in the night, with anxiety in her heart and a letter to me.

> Life has passed me by.

The entries end as Autumn arrives. Glas has installed white curtains in his celibate home; he anticipates the hermetic concealment of winter snow cover. An earlier statement, made before the murder, now seems a prophecy: "Whatever happens, whether things turn out well or ill— for me the 'punishment' can only be solitary confinement for life."

In seeking analogues to **Doctor Glas,** three other important works come immediately to mind: the biblical story of Abraham's "temptation" by God to murder his beloved son, Isaac (Genesis 22); Søren Kierkegaard's philosophical-theological justification of that story in *Fear and Trembling;* and Fyodor Dostoevsky's *Crime and Punishment* in which the young student radical, Raskolnikov, murders two women—one intentionally, the other accidentally—to prove his theory of the exceptional individual through "ethical" murder. All four works demonstrate the crucial confrontation of ethics and absolutes. All four works attempt resolution of the evident paradoxical meaning of the term "ethical murder" in strikingly dissimilar ways.

The biblical story of Abraham is the beginning of a theodicy; its message is unstinting subservience to the unwritten laws of an all-powerful, one might say savage, tribal God. Kierkegaard's "explanation" of the Abraham-Isaac story is modern-day absurdist. Kierkegaard maintains that faith is wholly individual and that the obvious paradox of God's request that Abraham murder his son can only be justified in terms of the impossibility to rationally, discursively, legalistically, or dogmatically explain the phenomenon of the "passionate certitude" of blind faith. For Kierkegaard, faith is a "one-to-one" relationship. There are no collective ideals of faith and it cannot be demonstrated; faith requires a "teleological suspension of the ethical," a belief in divine cosmic knowledge which exceeds the boundaries of the finite world.

Dostoevsky's Raskolnikov runs the gamut of ethical possibility as the result of his having put his theory to practice through murder. He begins as an arrogant *Übermensch,* insisting upon the verity of the individual's own self-created universal as a law unto itself. However, after the murders, a confrontation with "pure Christianity" in the form of Sonya the prostitute forces Raskolnikov to capitulate to absurdist belief in a Kierkegaardian "leap of faith," in the very last pages of the novel. It must be stated immediately, however, that Raskolnikov is not typical of Dostoevsky's intellectual heroes whose views are demonstrably humanistic and tragic in their ethical contemplation of the problem of good and evil.

Doctor Glas conceives of the world as being demonic and cruel, bent upon accentuating man's suffering and denying him his will and his intellectual powers. In terms of action, the difference between Glas and the classical tragic hero is only a matter of degree, but in repose Glas exhibits the kind of universal pessimism, inaction and despair that belies his counterparts who create through action. Yet Glas himself maintains a kind of "teleological suspension" in his acceptance of universal blind will which is strangely similar to Kierkegaard's demonstration of faith; their positions are essentially demonic or eudemonic, depending upon one's preference for negative or positive cosmic teleologies. Neither Kierkegaard's eternal optimism nor Söderberg's cosmic pessimism can be mediated by anything but faith and despair, or combinations of both. The tragic hero has the consolation of directing his actions towards universal, human-made values, while Kierkegaard's knight of faith and Söderberg's aesthetic pessimist must remain in a constant state of finite suspension, tension, and self-examination in a silent world, as Kierkegaard suggests:

> The tragic hero is soon ready and has soon finished the fight, he makes the infinite movement and then is secure in the universal. The knight of faith, on the other hand, is kept sleepless, for he is constantly tried, and every instant there is the possibility of being able to return repentently to the universal, and this possibility can just as well be a temptation as the truth.

It is heavily ironic that Doctor Glas's category of cosmic despair is similar to Kierkegaard's cosmic faith, since neither category has a demonstrable rationale. On the other hand, the effect of the tragic act is ethically demonstrative; it is the revelation of a previously-undisclosed contingency which can become an experimental universal value. Kierkegaard's discrimination between the tragic and the religious is the difference between concealment that is eventually exposed to the light of reason and experience, or concealment unresolved in infinite possibility—through faith in God's benevolence or in the malevolence of the gods:

> The tragic hero who is the favorite of ethics is the purely human, and him I can understand, and all he does is in the light of the revealed. If I go further, then I stumble upon the paradox, either the divine or the demoniac, for silence is both. Silence is the snare of the demon, and the more one keeps silent, the more terrifying the demon becomes; but silence is also the mutual understanding between the deity and individual.

Glas's silence bears ironic similarity to Kierkegaard's concept of silence. When Kierkegaard maintained that the tragic sensibility of the modern world would replace the conflict of cosmic fatalism and individual action, he did not anticipate a Doctor Glas:

> Modern drama has given up fate, has emancipated itself dramatically, sees with its eyes, scrutinizes itself, resolves fate in its dramatic consciousness. Concealment and revelation are in this case the hero's free act for which he is responsible.

The ironic pattern of tragedy, Kierkegaard maintains, is eventually reflected in an ethical explanation through revelation of previously-concealed cause-effect. It is doubtful, however, that tragic sensibility has changed as much as Kierkegaard maintains or that the actions and resolutions of tragic heroes do not continue to have the same functions and results. In any period, the tragic hero discovers at the end of his endeavors a kind of blind and irrational,

or at least sinisterly capricious, universal will or series of pluralistic forces which seem to have been all along militating against him. The modern hero of tragic sensibility does not act for solipsistic reasons, as Kierkegaard suggests, but with the same ethically-centered humanistic purposes of his predecessors. Glas's pessimism, however, is of a particular sort which might not seem as contemporary as various modes of Neo-Darwinian indeterminism or nihilistic naturalism. It is nevertheless a fact that he acts for all-too-human reasons in creating a pattern of ethical behaviour which was not there before. The consequent "terrible responsibility of solitude" is essentially the same problem as it always has been; only the terms have changed. (pp. 47-59)

> *Reed Merrill, "Ethical Murder and 'Doctor Glas'," in* Mosaic: A Journal for the Comparative Study of Literature and Ideas, *Vol. XII, No. 4, Summer, 1979, pp. 47-59.*

Carl Lofmark   (essay date 1987)

[In the following excerpt, Lofmark surveys Söderberg's short stories.]

[Söderberg's] early ambition had been to write 'a clear, cold prose with words like sharp teeth', and he made that dream come true. He combines brevity with power: the shortest of short stories can be full of significance and feeling, while his irony betrays the personal mood of a sceptic who has no time for romantic illusions. Though his medium is fiction, he is determined to avoid all that is false or pretentious; early in his career he declared his aim as a writer: 'to seek after the truth, and to give people what he found or thought he had found of it.' This passion for truth remained with him throughout his life.

His stories still make a strong impression today, because they treat basic questions in an honest way. They are concerned with things that do not change: the inner life of people, the real motives behind their actions, the reasons for cruelty and injustice, the nature of the world and the meaning of life in a modern, urban, post-Christian society. They seldom supply answers—for their author is a true sceptic—but they raise important questions and they provoke thought and reflection.

The question of the meaning of life is raised explicitly in **'The Sketch in Indian Ink'** and **'The Dream of Eternity.'** It was a critical question for Söderberg after he had lost the Christian faith in which he had been brought up. Religion was not only a great political and social force in his time, it was also a strong emotional support, which gave people a personal sense of purpose and belonging. When his critical consideration of the Christian teachings left him no honest option but to become a freethinker, Söderberg sustained a real loss; he could find no other emotional home, no other basis for morality and action which might replace it. His sense of loss is movingly expressed in **'A Dog Without a Master.'** A few years before his death Söderberg remarked: 'People have always been so fond of that story because they imagine it is about a dog.'

The sense of purpose and security that comes from knowing the meaning to one's life, however absurd that meaning may be, is recalled in **'The Dream of Eternity'** as something the narrator had possessed when he was young. But the story shows how he has come to abandon that childish fancy. The same is true in **'The Sketch in Indian Ink,'** where he disguises his personal emotion by assigning the painful episode to some time in the remote past (made more remote by the technique of the framework story) and by a studied nonchalance of style which treats the matter as no more important than the purchase of a cigar. Now, in the time of the framework story, the narrator has given up thinking about life's meaning. In a religious polemic of 1909 Söderberg wrote: 'What foolish conceit is it that makes people want their life to have a particular meaning, a meaning apart from life itself ? A different kind of meaning from the life of a flower, a tree or an animal?'

In **'The Dream of Eternity'** the narrator is shaken out of his faith in life's meaning and forced to contemplate time and eternity. He first sees time through images of old age and rotting wood and a tale of death, that greedy monster that will devour every one of us when our turn comes. But still more frightening are the sinister horrors of eternity, which come to the narrator when he is alone, at night, in the nightmarish dream of eternity.

Another aspect of time appears in **'The Burning Town.'** We cannot accept our own non-existence. If I think of the world with myself not in it, I must still assume myself as a spectator of that world. Our mental life depends on a body, and we see from the perspective of a self. Hence the persistence of human belief in a life after death: the self must continue to exist somewhere, somehow. The boy in the story cannot understand the problem, but he rebels instinctively at the absurd idea of a world without himself—that must be one of daddy's jokes.

Many of Söderberg's stories are constructed around the thoughts and feelings of a child, or else the narrator recalls events from his own childhood. He usually affects to be old and no longer troubled by the passions of long ago (though in fact the author was only in his twenties when the first eleven of these stories were published), but his opening words often contain some such phrase as 'in my childhood', 'when I was very young', 'many years ago'. The narrative style also is at times reminiscent of the nursery (as when he says he is going to tell us a story and asks us to pay attention), and many of the stories have something of the fairy tale about them. Critics have pointed out that, despite the 'old man' pose, there is something of the child in Söderberg's narrator: his constant asking of fundamental questions, the keen visual sense and alertness to detail, his interest in the thoughts and feelings of animals, especially dogs, the child's immediate and instinctive capacity for pity and sympathy, his quick sensitivity to any sign of falsehood or injustice.

That sensitivity shows in such stories as **'The Chimney Sweep's Wife'** or **'The Fur Coat.'** These tragic narratives have a realism that makes them immediately credible. The characters are typical, their thoughts—which are all revealed—are entirely in character, their conduct perfectly plausible: the whole course of events rings true. We cannot avoid recognizing that the world of these stories is our own world, their cruelty and injustice are real. The kind of behaviour we call inhuman is in fact only too human. Such stories imply their author's protest against a world order which he has to recognize but cannot with equanimity accept. **'The History Teacher'** exposes the agony of a man who, because he cannot inspire fear, is exposed to the

fiendish but natural cruelty of children; **'The Chinese,'** where dreamy speculations about the inhabitants of Mars gently hint at the inner strangeness of the alien, shows again the author's sympathy for the man who is different from the others and is consequently made to suffer. In every case it is the inner life of the character that interests Söderberg, he analyses motives, thoughts and feelings and tries to penetrate and understand the personality.

He also seeks to penetrate the inner life of animals. He is interested in the thoughts that pass through the mind of a dog (**'Vox populi'**, **'Killing'**, **'Rugg'**); he quite understands the beasts' point of view in **'The Parson's Cows,'** and in **'Killing'** he also enters, however briefly, into the life of a bird, a spider and a fox. The fox, who has been 'down town on business', resembles his author's dogs, who also have various matters of their own to attend to; but the dog, in addition to his mundane purposes, has a higher purpose to his life, a religion. That theme is most poignantly expressed in **'A Dog Without a Master,'** but occurs again in **'Rugg,'** together with further speculations about the nature and condition of dogs.

The dominant interest in Söderberg's life was religion. Though he always attacked the church and its teachings with great vigour, he denied being irreligious. 'You have never heard of an unmusical person with a lively interest in music, or an unmathematical person with a thorough knowledge of mathematics', he wrote. 'If there is such a thing as a "religious sense", then my lasting interest in religion shows that I have that sense—perhaps in greater measure than the countless people whose religiousness consists in believing what they were told in childhood and have never seriously questioned since.' The absurdity of the Bible's account of God's behaviour is pilloried in **'Drizzle,'** while religious faith is ridiculed in **'The Talented Dragon.'** Both stories show not only the folly, but also the cruelty of religion, and God noticeably lacks such human characteristics as sympathy or humour (in the latter story it is the ability to laugh that conclusively proves a man is not a god). Some readers may feel that these two stories go too far in their travesty of divine and human folly and become merely ridiculous; but the beliefs which Söderberg attacks are ridiculous beliefs (a God of mercy whose punishments are endless, whose infinite patience expires by the time of Noah, whose cure for human wickedness has conspicuously failed, who lovingly enjoys the spectacle of his own cruel justice: all these are solidly founded in holy writ). The idea that God amiably discusses problems of justice and world government with the Devil is derived from the 'Prologue in Heaven' of Goethe's *Faust;* in this Söderberg is ahead of Strindberg, who later copied the idea for the prologue to his *Dream Play* of 1902.

The story **'Patriarch Papinianus,'** which tackles the theme of divine justice, was inspired by the Dreyfus affair, which was becoming a great public issue just at the time of Söderberg's visit to Paris in November 1897. Dreyfus had been convicted of treason in 1894; the Senate Vice-President M. Scheurer-Kestner had in July 1896 received evidence of his innocence and tried to reopen the case, but the General Staff was attempting to suppress the evidence and silence the officer who had found it, while defending the real traitor, Esterhazy, and having documents forged to incriminate Dreyfus. The establishment, including the Church, vilified Dreyfus, but a handful of intellectuals, including

Zola and Clemenceau, leapt to his defence, and Söderberg joined them. This story, published in *Svenska Dagbladet* on 5 December 1897, contributed to the lively debate in the Swedish press.

Confronted by an evangelizing major in **'Satan, the Major and the Court Chaplain,'** the narrator stares deep into his glass of mineral water, watching bubbles rise up like souls of the blessed, and does his best to avoid being saved. The man is a religious fanatic, who takes very seriously his duty of saving souls; Söderberg is amused, yet at the same time he respects the sincerity of a man who genuinely believes and accepts the practical consequences. Very different is his attitude to the representative of the state church (in this case the court chaplain). Such men saw God as a benign Creator who shared their opinions and interests; they had exercised very great power for many centuries, and their rule had not been a blessing for mankind. He shows them, in **'Patriarch Papinianus'** and **'After Dinner,'** using their assumed authority to support the most foolish and outrageous moral principles. Söderberg's most sensational treatment of the type was his novel *Dr Glas* of 1905, where the calculated murder of a horrid but socially respectable priest is represented as the justified killing of a monster.

What particularly offends Söderberg about the clergyman is his dishonesty, which is practically a requirement of the profession; but dishonesty is a widespread human failing, by no means limited to the clergy. Söderberg is always quick to draw attention to insincerity and pretentiousness, wherever they may occur (for example in such stories as **'The Sixth Sense'** or **'The Consul General at the Palace Ball'**), while the common moral pretentions of his time, propagated by a mindless public opinion, are attacked in **'Vox populi,'** where an 'immoral' (but beautiful) work of art is condemned indignantly by two 'moral' (but ugly) old ladies, ably assisted by all the dogs of the neighbourhood. The story was part of a press controversy over the erection of Per Hasselberg's bronze 'Grandfather' (Farfadern) in Humlegård Park in 1896. Söderberg always expects a frank and unprejudiced openness in moral and political debate and a high degree of integrity in the pursuit of truth, both of which run counter to the entrenched interests of the established church.

Söderberg denied hating the clergy. It is foolish, he said, to hate collectively. And as an atheist he felt no more animosity towards Jesus than a Christian might feel towards Baldur or Osiris. He shows himself very capable of portraying individual representatives of the church sympathetically, in **'The Parson's Cows'** or **'The Sonata of Errors.'** Both of these stories show another kind of typical clergyman, kindly, sincere, conscientious, though very limited and conservative in his opinions. There is a generous humour about **'The Parson's Cows'** which allows human weaknesses and failings to be forgiven; in **'The Kiss'** even dishonesty, which comes to light as we enquire into the secret thoughts of two young people, appears to be forgiven as a result of the delightful humour with which their episode is treated (though the sceptical reader may doubt whether it is entirely forgiven). Another delightful piece is **'Churchyard Arabesque,'** written for a volume honouring his friend the writer Henning Berger upon his death in 1924, where, at the same time as creating a memorial to Berger, Söderberg amuses himself at the expense

of their common enemy the critic Böök (whom Söderberg had once alluded to as 'Löök', 'onion'). Söderberg is indeed a serious author, but he writes with a lively wit and good humour, and this, especially in the later works, preserves him from becoming gloomy and depressing.

Söderberg's quarrel with the Church arises not from any personal animosity, but from his compelling drive to discover the truth and publish what he finds. His stories are above all concerned with ideas. There is little action, but a good deal of thought and discussion. The stories centered on the Consul General are essentially discussions on questions of political, social or intellectual interest. The Church's view that suicide is immoral and should be punished had been ridiculed in **'Drizzle'** (1897); now, in **'After Dinner,'** the question is treated in the calmer, more rational atmosphere of a debate, though it is a debate that is still charged with emotion. Later, in **'The Sonata of Errors'** (1925), the debate is not even controversial, but an entirely friendly and constructive exchange of experiences between men who are animated by curiosity, but have no urge to prove themselves right or press their opinions upon others. One of these men is a kindly old priest.

The puzzle that arises in **'Archimedes' Point'** is one of physics: why can I not move myself forward by pushing myself in the back? The title refers to a legendary saying of the philosopher Archimedes (B.C. 287-212), who discovered the principles of dynamics: 'Give me a point on which to stand and I will move the earth!' But finding a firm point to stand on is easier said than done; and that is true in more fields than physics.

While the manner of reflection on all these ideas may seem appropriate to an elderly narrator, the questions considered are often of the speculative kind that more commonly fascinate us in youth. That is certainly true of the last story in this collection, **'The Stove That Wasn't Real'**: is the world real, or have I imagined it? There are, in fact, difficulties about arguing that the world exists only in my own imagination. For one thing, it means telling other people that they do not exist, and this tends to be not well received. For another thing, I must be remarkably well-informed, when I consult the encyclopaedia, to have imagined all the information it contains, and I must be a genius when I imagine Handel's 'Messiah'. Söderberg's story deals with another aspect of the problem: I may be surprised by things being not as I expected, and that suggests that my subjective idea has been corrected by an independent objective world which is no part of me.

The message of these stories is often a sombre one and their view of human nature is disturbing, yet they are told with a sense of humour which develops with the years. The first of them, taken from the early *Historietter,* are thoroughly pessimistic, but later, as in **'The Sixth Sense'** or **'The Talented Dragon,'** Söderberg's humour becomes so pervasive and cheerful that an inattentive reader might overlook the story's serious implications. Even in his gloomiest mood, Söderberg has time for fun and witty asides, while his most cheerful stories, like **'The Parson's Cows'** or **'The Kiss,'** are darkened at times by a touch of cynicism.

His concern for truth is not optimistic and positive, like that of the 18th century rationalist. He is aware that truth may cause pain and misery. That is recognized already by the boy in **'The Dream of Eternity'** who blames his friend for being glad to deny the soul's immortality, for reporting what he knows with joy, and not with despair. In his novel *Dr Glas* Söderberg similarly describes reason as an animal that will at first gladly devour the falsehood and nonsense you throw to it, but has a blind, voracious appetite, and will go on to consume all that you love and care for.

Early in life Söderberg's relentless search for truth had devoured not only the comfort and support of religion, but also the belief in free will. In the early autobiographical novel **Martin Birck's Youth** (1901) he plays with a puppet and imagines its thoughts and feelings:

> When you pull on the thread and he starts to play he thinks to himself, 'I am a being with free will, I play just as I want to play and entirely for my own pleasure. Oh what fun it is to play!' But when you stop pulling on the thread he feels tired and says to himself, 'I can't be bothered to play any more, the finest thing of all is to hang on a hook on the wall and relax completely.'

It is like that with Dr Henck in **'The Fur Coat'**: although his train of thought gives the impression of a rationally controlled life, his logic leads him to positive plans for the future only while he is wearing the fur coat; without the coat his logic leads just as surely to resignation and the reasoned conviction that he will shortly die.

The most important character in these stories is the narrator. Most of them are told in the first person and presented as personal reminiscences. This narrator, from whose memory the stories are drawn, appears to be a shrewd, honest observer of life, an educated man, now looking back with the detachment of age on events of long ago. His statements are qualified with doubts and reservations ('perhaps', 'in my opinion', 'I thought', 'it seemed', 'who knows?'), and these reveal his scrupulous objectivity; his only concern is to find and tell the truth. This narrator is, as has often been observed, a projection of Söderberg himself. His feeling that life is without purpose seems to have sapped his energy, so that he merely observes and comments on the follies and cruelties of life without feeling any impulse to participate and act. The characters, too, are generally passive, like Henck, or the history teacher, or Fredrik and Magda in **'The Chimney Sweep's Wife,'** or the apprentices who watch Magda's murder with silent curiosity and do not think to intervene. But the narrator's detachment from the events, his irony, his casual tone, his studied unconcern, mask an intense sensitivity, and while such techniques may protect the author, they do not save the reader from the strong emotions which many of the stories convey.

Söderberg's aim was to write clearly, and it is generally acknowledged that he achieved that aim. Every sentence is clearly intelligible, as with Kafka; and yet, as with Kafka, the meaning of the whole story is sometimes far from clear. The author does not always solve the problems he has raised; questions may be asked, or implied, but they are seldom answered. It then remains to the reader to reflect on the issues for himself. The fascination of such tales as **'Rugg,'** or **'The Chinese,'** derives precisely from their open-endedness. They are designed not to inform us, but rather to make us think. (pp. 2-11)

> *Carl Lofmark, in an introduction to* Short Stories, *by Hjalmar Söderberg, edited and translated by Carl Lofmark, Norvik Press, 1987, pp. 1-12.*

FURTHER READING

"The Quarter's History." *The American-Scandinavian Review* XXVII, No. 3 (September 1939): 260.
> Appreciation of Söderberg's works on the occasion of his seventieth birthday.

Geddes, Tom. "Swedish Fin-de-Siècle: Hjalmar Söderberg." In *Essays on Swedish Literature from 1880 to the Present Day,* edited by Irene Scobbie, pp. 60-81. n.p., n.d.
> Examines Söderberg's works as a reflection of attitudes and ideas prevailing in Europe at the turn of the century, focusing on themes of "melancholy, eroticism, and determinism."

McClean, R. J. "Some Modern Swedish Writers." *The Modern Language Review* XXXVIII, No. 3 (July 1943): 240-41.
> Overview of Söderberg's life and works.

Mitchell, Adrian. "A Gentle Murderer." *The New York Times Book Review* (24 May 1964): 41.
> Positive review of the English translation of *Doctor Glas.*

Söderberg, Eugénie. "Hjalmar Söderberg." *The American-Scandinavian Review* XXIX, No. 4 (December 1941): 334-37.
> Obituary tribute outlining Söderberg's literary career.

Stork, Charles Wharton. Preface to *Selected Short Stories,* by Hjalmar Söderberg, edited by Charles Wharton Stork, pp. vii-viii. Princeton, N.J.: Princeton University Press, 1935.
> Sketch of Söderberg's life and literary career.

"An Early Freudian." *The Times Literary Supplement,* No. 3217 (25 October 1963): 868.
> Descriptive review of *Doctor Glas,* calling the novel "a moving little book."

Topsöe-Jensen, H. G. "New Currents, 1900-1914: Sweden." In his *Scandinavian Literature: From Brandes to Our Day,* pp. 233-58. New York: W. W. Norton & Co., 1929.
> Overview of Söderberg's major works.

Twentieth-Century
Literary Criticism

Cumulative Indexes
Volumes 1-39

This Index Includes References
to Entries in These Gale Series

Contemporary Literary Criticism presents excerpts of criticism on the works of novelists, poets, dramatists, short story writers, scriptwriters, and other creative writers who are now living or who have died since 1960. Cumulative indexes to authors and nationalities are included, as well as an index to titles discussed in the individual volume.

Twentieth-Century Literary Criticism contains critical excerpts by the most significant commentators on poets, novelists, short story writers, dramatists, and philosophers who died between 1900 and 1960. Indexes to authors, nationalities, and titles discussed are included in each new volume.

Nineteenth-Century Literature Criticism offers significant passages from criticism on authors who died between 1800 and 1899. Indexes to authors, nationalities, and titles discussed are included in each new volume.

Literature Criticism from 1400 to 1800 compiles significant passages from the most noteworthy criticism on authors of the fifteenth through the eighteenth centuries. Cumulative indexes to authors, nationalities, and titles discussed are included in each new volume.

Classical and Medieval Literature Criticism offers excerpts of criticism on the works of world authors from classical antiquity through the fourteenth century. Cumulative indexes to authors, titles and critics are included in each volume.

Short Story Criticism combines excerpts of criticism on short fiction by writers of all eras and nationalities. Cumulative indexes to authors, nationalities, and titles discussed are included in each new volume.

Poetry Criticism presents excerpts of criticism on the works of poets from all eras, movements, and nationalities.

Children's Literature Review includes excerpts from reviews, criticism, and commentary on works of authors and illustrators who create books for children. Cumulative indexes to authors, nationalities, and titles discussed are included in each new volume.

Contemporary Authors Series encompasses five related series. *Contemporary Authors* provides biographical and bibliographical information on more than 92,000 writers of fiction, nonfiction, poetry, journalism, drama, film, and other related fields. Each new volume contains sketches on authors not previously covered in the series. *Contemporary Authors New Revision Series* provides completely updated information on active authors covered in previously published volumes of *CA*. Only entries requiring significant change are revised for *CA New Revision Series*. *Contemporary Authors Permanent Series* consists of updated listings for deceased and inactive authors removed from the original volumes 9-36 when those volumes were revised. *Contemporary Authors Autobiography Series* presents specially commissioned autobiographies by leading contemporary writers. *Contemporary Authors Bibliographical Series* contains primary and secondary bibliographies as well as analytical bibliographical essays by authorities on major modern authors.

Dictionary of Literary Biography encompasses three related series. *Dictionary of Literary Biography* furnishes illustrated overviews of authors' lives and works and places them in the larger perspective of literary history. *Dictionary of Literary Biography Documentary Series* illuminates the careers of major figures through a selection of literary documents, including letters, notebook and diary entries, interviews, book reviews, and photographs. *Dictionary of Literary Biography Yearbook* summarizes the past year's literary activity with articles on genres, major prizes, conferences, and other timely subjects and includes updated and new entries on individual authors. A cumulative index to authors and articles is included in each new volume. *Concise Dictionary of Literary Biography,* a six-volume series, collects revised and updated sketches on major American authors that were originally presented in *Dictionary of Literary Biography.*

Something about the Author Series encompasses three related series. *Something about the Author* contains heavily illustrated biographical sketches on authors and illustrators of juvenile and young adult literature from all eras. *Something about the Author Autobiography Series* presents specially commissioned autobiographies by prominent authors and illustrators of books for children and young adults. *Authors and Artists for Young Adults* provides high school and junior high school students with profiles of their favorite creative artists in the media of print, film, television, drama, song lyrics, and cartoons.

Yesterday's Authors of Books for Children contains heavily illustrated entries on children's writers who died before 1961. Complete in two volumes.

Literary Criticism Series
Cumulative Author Index

This index lists all author entries in the Gale Literary Criticism Series and includes cross-references to other Gale sources. References in the index are identified as follows:

AAYA: *Authors & Artists for Young Adults,* Volumes 1-3
CAAS: *Contemporary Authors Autobiography Series,* Volumes 1-11
CA: *Contemporary Authors* (original series), Volumes 1-131
CABS: *Contemporary Authors Bibliographical Series,* Volumes 1-3
CANR: *Contemporary Authors New Revision Series,* Volumes 1-29
CAP: *Contemporary Authors Permanent Series,* Volumes 1-2
CA-R: *Contemporary Authors* (revised editions), Volumes 1-44
CDALB: *Concise Dictionary of American Literary Biography,* Volumes 1-6
CLC: *Contemporary Literary Criticism,* Volumes 1-62
CLR: *Children's Literature Review,* Volumes 1-22
CMLC: *Classical and Medieval Literature Criticism,* Volumes 1-6
DC: *Drama Criticism,* Volume 1
DLB: *Dictionary of Literary Biography,* Volumes 1-101
DLB-DS: *Dictionary of Literary Biography Documentary Series,* Volumes 1-7
DLB-Y: *Dictionary of Literary Biography Yearbook,* Volumes 1980-1988
LC: *Literature Criticism from 1400 to 1800,* Volumes 1-14
NCLC: *Nineteenth-Century Literature Criticism,* Volumes 1-29
PC: *Poetry Criticism,* Volume 1
SAAS: *Something about the Author Autobiography Series,* Volumes 1-11
SATA: *Something about the Author,* Volumes 1-62
SSC: *Short Story Criticism,* Volumes 1-6
TCLC: *Twentieth-Century Literary Criticism,* Volumes 1-39
YABC: *Yesterday's Authors of Books for Children,* Volumes 1-2

Aiken, Conrad (Potter)
    1889-1973 . . . . **CLC 1, 3, 5, 10, 52**
    See also CANR 4; CA 5-8R;
        obituary CA 45-48; SATA 3, 30; DLB 9,
        45

Aiken, Joan (Delano) 1924- . . . . **CLC 35**
    See also CLR 1; CANR 4; CA 9-12R;
        SAAS 1; SATA 2, 30

Ainsworth, William Harrison
    1805-1882 . . . . **NCLC 13**
    See also SATA 24; DLB 21

Ajar, Emile 1914-1980
    See Gary, Romain

Akhmadulina, Bella (Akhatovna)
    1937- . . . . **CLC 53**
    See also CA 65-68

Akhmatova, Anna 1888-1966 . . . . **CLC 11, 25**
    See also CAP 1; CA 19-20;
        obituary CA 25-28R

Aksakov, Sergei Timofeyvich
    1791-1859 . . . . **NCLC 2**

Aksenov, Vassily (Pavlovich) 1932-
    See Aksyonov, Vasily (Pavlovich)

Aksyonov, Vasily (Pavlovich)
    1932- . . . . **CLC 22, 37**
    See also CANR 12; CA 53-56

Akutagawa Ryunosuke
    1892-1927 . . . . **TCLC 16**
    See also CA 117

Alain-Fournier 1886-1914 . . . . **TCLC 6**
    See also Fournier, Henri Alban
    See also DLB 65

Alarcon, Pedro Antonio de
    1833-1891 . . . . **NCLC 1**

Alas (y Urena), Leopoldo (Enrique Garcia)
    1852-1901 . . . . **TCLC 29**
    See also CA 113

Albee, Edward (Franklin III)
    1928- . . . **CLC 1, 2, 3, 5, 9, 11, 13, 25, 53**
    See also CANR 8; CA 5-8R; DLB 7;
        CDALB 1941-1968

Alberti, Rafael 1902- . . . . **CLC 7**
    See also CA 85-88

Alcott, Amos Bronson 1799-1888 . . **NCLC 1**
    See also DLB 1

Alcott, Louisa May 1832-1888 . . . . **NCLC 6**
    See also CLR 1; YABC 1; DLB 1, 42;
        CDALB 1865-1917

Aldanov, Mark 1887-1957 . . . . **TCLC 23**
    See also CA 118

Aldington, Richard 1892-1962 . . . . . . **CLC 49**
    See also CA 85-88; DLB 20, 36

Aldiss, Brian W(ilson)
    1925- . . . . **CLC 5, 14, 40**
    See also CAAS 2; CANR 5; CA 5-8R;
        SATA 34; DLB 14

Alegria, Fernando 1918- . . . . **CLC 57**
    See also CANR 5; CA 11-12R

Aleixandre, Vicente 1898-1984 . . . **CLC 9, 36**
    See also CANR 26; CA 85-88;
        obituary CA 114

Alepoudelis, Odysseus 1911-
    See Elytis, Odysseus

Aleshkovsky, Yuz 1929- . . . . **CLC 44**
    See also CA 121

Alexander, Lloyd (Chudley) 1924- . . **CLC 35**
    See also CLR 1, 5; CANR 1; CA 1-4R;
        SATA 3, 49; DLB 52

Alger, Horatio, Jr. 1832-1899 . . . . . **NCLC 8**
    See also SATA 16; DLB 42

Algren, Nelson 1909-1981 . . . . **CLC 4, 10, 33**
    See also CANR 20; CA 13-16R;
        obituary CA 103; DLB 9; DLB-Y 81, 82;
        CDALB 1941-1968

Alighieri, Dante 1265-1321 . . . . **CMLC 3**

Allard, Janet 1975- . . . . **CLC 59**

Allen, Edward 1948- . . . . **CLC 59**

Allen, Roland 1939-
    See Ayckbourn, Alan

Allen, Woody 1935- . . . . **CLC 16, 52**
    See also CANR 27; CA 33-36R; DLB 44

Allende, Isabel 1942- . . . . **CLC 39, 57**
    See also CA 125

Allingham, Margery (Louise)
    1904-1966 . . . . **CLC 19**
    See also CANR 4; CA 5-8R;
        obituary CA 25-28R

Allingham, William 1824-1889 . . . **NCLC 25**
    See also DLB 35

Allston, Washington 1779-1843 . . . . **NCLC 2**
    See also DLB 1

Almedingen, E. M. 1898-1971 . . . . . . **CLC 12**
    See also Almedingen, Martha Edith von
    See also SATA 3

Almedingen, Martha Edith von 1898-1971
    See Almedingen, E. M.
    See also CANR 1; CA 1-4R

Alonso, Damaso 1898- . . . . **CLC 14**
    See also CA 110

Alta 1942- . . . . **CLC 19**
    See also CA 57-60

Alter, Robert B(ernard) 1935- . . . . . . **CLC 34**
    See also CANR 1; CA 49-52

Alther, Lisa 1944- . . . . **CLC 7, 41**
    See also CANR 12; CA 65-68

Altman, Robert 1925- . . . . **CLC 16**
    See also CA 73-76

Alvarez, A(lfred) 1929- . . . . **CLC 5, 13**
    See also CANR 3; CA 1-4R; DLB 14, 40

Alvarez, Alejandro Rodriguez 1903-1965
    See Casona, Alejandro
    See also obituary CA 93-96

Amado, Jorge 1912- . . . . **CLC 13, 40**
    See also CA 77-80

Ambler, Eric 1909- . . . . **CLC 4, 6, 9**
    See also CANR 7; CA 9-12R

Amichai, Yehuda 1924- . . . . . . **CLC 9, 22, 57**
    See also CA 85-88

Amiel, Henri Frederic 1821-1881 . . **NCLC 4**

Amis, Kingsley (William)
    1922- . . . . . . **CLC 1, 2, 3, 5, 8, 13, 40, 44**
    See also CANR 8; CA 9-12R; DLB 15, 27

Amis, Martin 1949- . . . . **CLC 4, 9, 38, 62**
    See also CANR 8, 28; CA 65-68; DLB 14

Ammons, A(rchie) R(andolph)
    1926- . . . . **CLC 2, 3, 5, 8, 9, 25, 57**
    See also CANR 6; CA 9-12R; DLB 5

Anand, Mulk Raj 1905- . . . . **CLC 23**
    See also CA 65-68

Anaya, Rudolfo A(lfonso) 1937- . . . . **CLC 23**
    See also CAAS 4; CANR 1; CA 45-48

Andersen, Hans Christian
    1805-1875 . . . . **NCLC 7; SSC 6**
    See also CLR 6; YABC 1, 1

Anderson, Jessica (Margaret Queale)
    19??- . . . . **CLC 37**
    See also CANR 4; CA 9-12R

Anderson, Jon (Victor) 1940- . . . . . **CLC 9**
    See also CANR 20; CA 25-28R

Anderson, Lindsay 1923- . . . . **CLC 20**

Anderson, Maxwell 1888-1959 . . . . . **TCLC 2**
    See also CA 105; DLB 7

Anderson, Poul (William) 1926- . . . . **CLC 15**
    See also CAAS 2; CANR 2, 15; CA 1-4R;
        SATA 39; DLB 8

Anderson, Robert (Woodruff)
    1917- . . . . **CLC 23**
    See also CA 21-24R; DLB 7

Anderson, Roberta Joan 1943-
    See Mitchell, Joni

Anderson, Sherwood
    1876-1941 . . . . . . **TCLC 1, 10, 24; SSC 1**
    See also CAAS 3; CA 104, 121; DLB 4, 9;
        DLB-DS 1

Andrade, Carlos Drummond de
    1902-1987 . . . . **CLC 18**
    See also CA 123

Andrewes, Lancelot 1555-1626 . . . . . . **LC 5**

Andrews, Cicily Fairfield 1892-1983
    See West, Rebecca

Andreyev, Leonid (Nikolaevich)
    1871-1919 . . . . **TCLC 3**
    See also CA 104

Andrezel, Pierre 1885-1962
    See Dinesen, Isak; Blixen, Karen
        (Christentze Dinesen)

Andric, Ivo 1892-1975 . . . . **CLC 8**
    See also CA 81-84; obituary CA 57-60

Angelique, Pierre 1897-1962
    See Bataille, Georges

Angell, Roger 1920- . . . . **CLC 26**
    See also CANR 13; CA 57-60

Angelou, Maya 1928- . . . . **CLC 12, 35**
    See also CANR 19; CA 65-68; SATA 49;
        DLB 38

Annensky, Innokenty 1856-1909 . . . **TCLC 14**
    See also CA 110

Anouilh, Jean (Marie Lucien Pierre)
    1910-1987 . . . . . . **CLC 1, 3, 8, 13, 40, 50**
    See also CA 17-20R; obituary CA 123

Anthony, Florence 1947-
    See Ai

Anthony (Jacob), Piers 1934- . . . . . . **CLC 35**
    See also Jacob, Piers A(nthony)
        D(illingham)
    See also DLB 8

Antoninus, Brother 1912-
    See Everson, William (Oliver)

Antonioni, Michelangelo 1912- . . . . . **CLC 20**
    See also CA 73-76

Balmont, Konstantin Dmitriyevich
    1867-1943 .... TCLC **11**
    See also CA 109

Balzac, Honore de
    1799-1850 .... NCLC **5**; SSC **5**

Bambara, Toni Cade 1939- .... CLC **19**
    See also CA 29-32R; DLB 38

Bandanes, Jerome 1937- .... CLC **59**

Banim, John 1798-1842 .... NCLC **13**

Banim, Michael 1796-1874 ...... NCLC **13**

Banks, Iain 1954-................ CLC **34**
    See also CA 123

Banks, Lynne Reid 1929-.......... CLC **23**
    See also Reid Banks, Lynne

Banks, Russell 1940- .... CLC **37**
    See also CANR 19; CA 65-68

Banville, John 1945-.............. CLC **46**
    See also CA 117; DLB 14

Banville, Theodore (Faullain) de
    1832-1891 .... NCLC **9**

Baraka, Imamu Amiri
    1934- .... CLC **1, 2, 3, 5, 10, 14, 33**
    See also Jones, (Everett) LeRoi
    See also DLB 5, 7, 16, 38;
       CDALB 1941-1968

Barbellion, W. N. P. 1889-1919 ... TCLC **24**

Barbera, Jack 1945-.............. CLC **44**
    See also CA 110

Barbey d'Aurevilly, Jules Amedee
    1808-1889 .... NCLC **1**

Barbusse, Henri 1873-1935 .... TCLC **5**
    See also CA 105; DLB 65

Barea, Arturo 1897-1957 .... TCLC **14**
    See also CA 111

Barfoot, Joan 1946- .... CLC **18**
    See also CA 105

Baring, Maurice 1874-1945 .... TCLC **8**
    See also CA 105; DLB 34

Barker, Clive 1952- .... CLC **52**
    See also CA 121

Barker, George (Granville)
    1913- .... CLC **8, 48**
    See also CANR 7; CA 9-12R; DLB 20

Barker, Howard 1946-............. CLC **37**
    See also CA 102; DLB 13

Barker, Pat 1943-................. CLC **32**
    See also CA 117, 122

Barlow, Joel 1754-1812 .... NCLC **23**
    See also DLB 37

Barnard, Mary (Ethel) 1909-....... CLC **48**
    See also CAP 2; CA 21-22

Barnes, Djuna (Chappell)
    1892-1982 ... CLC **3, 4, 8, 11, 29**; SSC **3**
    See also CANR 16; CA 9-12R;
       obituary CA 107; DLB 4, 9, 45

Barnes, Julian 1946-.............. CLC **42**
    See also CANR 19; CA 102

Barnes, Peter 1931- .... CLC **5, 56**
    See also CA 65-68; DLB 13

Baroja (y Nessi), Pio 1872-1956 .... TCLC **8**
    See also CA 104

Barondess, Sue K(aufman) 1926-1977
    See Kaufman, Sue
    See also CANR 1; CA 1-4R;
       obituary CA 69-72

Barrett, (Roger) Syd 1946-
    See Pink Floyd

Barrett, William (Christopher)
    1913- .... CLC **27**
    See also CANR 11; CA 13-16R

Barrie, (Sir) J(ames) M(atthew)
    1860-1937 .... TCLC **2**
    See also CLR 16; YABC 1; CA 104;
       DLB 10

Barrol, Grady 1953-
    See Bograd, Larry

Barry, Philip (James Quinn)
    1896-1949 ....TCLC **11**
    See also CA 109; DLB 7

Barth, John (Simmons)
    1930- ...... CLC **1, 2, 3, 5, 7, 9, 10, 14,
                          27, 51**
    See also CANR 5, 23; CA 1-4R; CABS 1;
       DLB 2

Barthelme, Donald
    1931-1989 ..... CLC **1, 2, 3, 5, 6, 8, 13,
                          23, 46, 59**; SSC **2**
    See also CANR 20; CA 21-24R, 129;
       SATA 7; DLB 2; DLB-Y 80

Barthelme, Frederick 1943-........ CLC **36**
    See also CA 114, 122; DLB-Y 85

Barthes, Roland 1915-1980 .... CLC **24**
    See also obituary CA 97-100

Barzun, Jacques (Martin) 1907- .... CLC **51**
    See also CANR 22; CA 61-64

Bashkirtseff, Marie 1859-1884 ... NCLC **27**

Bassani, Giorgio 1916-............. CLC **9**
    See also CA 65-68

Bataille, Georges 1897-1962 .... CLC **29**
    See also CA 101; obituary CA 89-92

Bates, H(erbert) E(rnest)
    1905-1974 .... CLC **46**
    See also CA 93-96; obituary CA 45-48

Baudelaire, Charles
    1821-1867 .... NCLC **6, 29**; PC **1**

Baudrillard, Jean 1929-........... CLC **60**

Baum, L(yman) Frank 1856-1919 ... TCLC **7**
    See also CLR 15; CA 108; SATA 18;
       DLB 22

Baumbach, Jonathan 1933- ...... CLC **6, 23**
    See also CAAS 5; CANR 12; CA 13-16R;
       DLB-Y 80

Bausch, Richard (Carl) 1945- ...... CLC **51**
    See also CA 101

Baxter, Charles 1947-............. CLC **45**
    See also CA 57-60

Baxter, James K(eir) 1926-1972 .... CLC **14**
    See also CA 77-80

Bayer, Sylvia 1909-1981
    See Glassco, John

Beagle, Peter S(oyer) 1939-......... CLC **7**
    See also CANR 4; CA 9-12R; DLB-Y 80

Beard, Charles A(ustin)
    1874-1948 .... TCLC **15**
    See also CA 115; SATA 18; DLB 17

Beardsley, Aubrey 1872-1898 ..... NCLC **6**

Beattie, Ann 1947- .... CLC **8, 13, 18, 40**
    See also CA 81-84; DLB-Y 82

Beattie, James 1735-1803 .... NCLC **25**

**Beauvoir, Simone (Lucie Ernestine Marie
       Bertrand) de**
    1908-1986 ... CLC **1, 2, 4, 8, 14, 31, 44,
                          50**
    See also CA 9-12R; obituary CA 118;
       DLB 72; DLB-Y 86

Becker, Jurek 1937-............. CLC **7, 19**
    See also CA 85-88

Becker, Walter 1950-............. CLC **26**

Beckett, Samuel (Barclay)
    1906-1989 ..... CLC **1, 2, 3, 4, 6, 9, 10,
                          11, 14, 18, 29, 57, 59**
    See also CA 5-8R; DLB 13, 15

Beckford, William 1760-1844 .... NCLC **16**
    See also DLB 39

Beckman, Gunnel 1910-........... CLC **26**
    See also CANR 15; CA 33-36R; SATA 6

Becque, Henri 1837-1899........ NCLC **3**

Beddoes, Thomas Lovell
    1803-1849 .... NCLC **3**

Beecher, John 1904-1980.......... CLC **6**
    See also CANR 8; CA 5-8R;
       obituary CA 105

Beer, Johann 1655-1700.......... LC **5**

Beer, Patricia 1919?- .... CLC **58**
    See also CANR 13; CA 61-64; DLB 40

Beerbohm, (Sir Henry) Max(imilian)
    1872-1956 .... TCLC **1, 24**
    See also CA 104; DLB 34

Behan, Brendan
    1923-1964 .... CLC **1, 8, 11, 15**
    See also CA 73-76; DLB 13

Behn, Aphra 1640?-1689 .... LC **1**
    See also DLB 39

Behrman, S(amuel) N(athaniel)
    1893-1973 .... CLC **40**
    See also CAP 1; CA 15-16;
       obituary CA 45-48; DLB 7, 44

Beiswanger, George Edwin 1931-
    See Starbuck, George (Edwin)

Belasco, David 1853-1931 .... TCLC **3**
    See also CA 104; DLB 7

Belcheva, Elisaveta 1893-
    See Bagryana, Elisaveta

Belinski, Vissarion Grigoryevich
    1811-1848 .... NCLC **5**

Belitt, Ben 1911-................ CLC **22**
    See also CAAS 4; CANR 7; CA 13-16R;
       DLB 5

Bell, Acton 1820-1849
    See Bronte, Anne

Bell, Currer 1816-1855
    See Bronte, Charlotte

Bell, Madison Smartt 1957-........ CLC **41**
    See also CA 111

Bell, Marvin (Hartley) 1937-...... CLC **8, 31**
    See also CA 21-24R; DLB 5

Bellamy, Edward 1850-1898 ...... NCLC **4**
    See also DLB 12

Belloc, (Joseph) Hilaire (Pierre Sebastien Rene Swanton)
1870-1953 . . . . TCLC 7, 18
See also YABC 1; CA 106; DLB 19

Bellow, Saul
1915- . . . . . **CLC 1, 2, 3, 6, 8, 10, 13, 15, 25, 33, 34**
See also CA 5-8R; CABS 1; DLB 2, 28; DLB-Y 82; DLB-DS 3; CDALB 1941-1968

Belser, Reimond Karel Maria de   1929-
See Ruyslinck, Ward

Bely, Andrey   1880-1934. . . . . TCLC 7
See also CA 104

Benary-Isbert, Margot   1889-1979 . . . CLC 12
See also CLR 12; CANR 4; CA 5-8R; obituary CA 89-92; SATA 2; obituary SATA 21

Benavente (y Martinez), Jacinto
1866-1954 . . . . TCLC 3
See also CA 106

Benchley, Peter (Bradford)
1940- . . . . CLC 4, 8
See also CANR 12; CA 17-20R; SATA 3

Benchley, Robert   1889-1945 . . . . TCLC 1
See also CA 105; DLB 11

Benedikt, Michael   1935- . . . . CLC 4, 14
See also CANR 7; CA 13-16R; DLB 5

Benet, Juan   1927- . . . . CLC 28

Benet, Stephen Vincent
1898-1943 . . . . TCLC 7
See also YABC 1; CA 104; DLB 4, 48

Benet, William Rose   1886-1950 . . . TCLC 28
See also CA 118; DLB 45

Benford, Gregory (Albert)   1941- . . . . CLC 52
See also CANR 12, 24; CA 69-72; DLB-Y 82

Benjamin, Walter   1892-1940 . . . . . TCLC 39

Benn, Gottfried   1886-1956. . . . . TCLC 3
See also CA 106; DLB 56

Bennett, Alan   1934- . . . . CLC 45
See also CA 103

Bennett, (Enoch) Arnold
1867-1931 . . . . TCLC 5, 20
See also CA 106; DLB 10, 34

Bennett, George Harold   1930-
See Bennett, Hal
See also CA 97-100

Bennett, Hal   1930- . . . . CLC 5
See also Bennett, George Harold
See also DLB 33

Bennett, Jay   1912- . . . . CLC 35
See also CANR 11; CA 69-72; SAAS 4; SATA 27, 41

Bennett, Louise (Simone)   1919- . . . . . CLC 28
See also Bennett-Coverly, Louise Simone

Bennett-Coverly, Louise Simone   1919-
See Bennett, Louise (Simone)
See also CA 97-100

Benson, E(dward) F(rederic)
1867-1940 . . . . TCLC 27
See also CA 114

Benson, Jackson J.   1930-. . . . . CLC 34
See also CA 25-28R

Benson, Sally   1900-1972 . . . . CLC 17
See also CAP 1; CA 19-20; obituary CA 37-40R; SATA 1, 35; obituary SATA 27

Benson, Stella   1892-1933. . . . . TCLC 17
See also CA 117; DLB 36

Bentley, E(dmund) C(lerihew)
1875-1956 . . . . TCLC 12
See also CA 108; DLB 70

Bentley, Eric (Russell)   1916- . . . . CLC 24
See also CANR 6; CA 5-8R

Berger, John (Peter)   1926- . . . . . . CLC 2, 19
See also CA 81-84; DLB 14

Berger, Melvin (H.)   1927-. . . . . CLC 12
See also CANR 4; CA 5-8R; SAAS 2; SATA 5

Berger, Thomas (Louis)
1924- . . . . CLC 3, 5, 8, 11, 18, 38
See also CANR 5; CA 1-4R; DLB 2; DLB-Y 80

Bergman, (Ernst) Ingmar   1918-. . . . . CLC 16
See also CA 81-84

Bergson, Henri   1859-1941 . . . . TCLC 32

Bergstein, Eleanor   1938- . . . . CLC 4
See also CANR 5; CA 53-56

Berkoff, Steven   1937-. . . . . CLC 56
See also CA 104

Bermant, Chaim   1929- . . . . CLC 40
See also CANR 6; CA 57-60

Bernanos, (Paul Louis) Georges
1888-1948 . . . . TCLC 3
See also CA 104; DLB 72

Bernard, April   19??- . . . . CLC 59

Bernhard, Thomas
1931-1989 . . . . CLC 3, 32, 61
See also CA 85-88,; obituary CA 127; DLB 85

Berriault, Gina   1926- . . . . CLC 54
See also CA 116

Berrigan, Daniel J.   1921-. . . . . CLC 4
See also CAAS 1; CANR 11; CA 33-36R; DLB 5

Berrigan, Edmund Joseph Michael, Jr.
1934-1983
See Berrigan, Ted
See also CANR 14; CA 61-64; obituary CA 110

Berrigan, Ted   1934-1983 . . . . CLC 37
See also Berrigan, Edmund Joseph Michael, Jr.
See also DLB 5

Berry, Chuck   1926- . . . . CLC 17

Berry, Wendell (Erdman)
1934- . . . . CLC 4, 6, 8, 27, 46
See also CA 73-76; DLB 5, 6

Berryman, John
1914-1972 . . . . . CLC 1, 2, 3, 4, 6, 8, 10, 13, 25, 62
See also CAP 1; CA 15-16; obituary CA 33-36R; CABS 2; DLB 48; CDALB 1941-1968

Bertolucci, Bernardo   1940- . . . . CLC 16
See also CA 106

Bertran de Born   c. 1140-1215 . . . . . CMLC 5

Besant, Annie (Wood)   1847-1933 . . . TCLC 9
See also CA 105

Bessie, Alvah   1904-1985. . . . . CLC 23
See also CANR 2; CA 5-8R; obituary CA 116; DLB 26

Beti, Mongo   1932- . . . . CLC 27
See also Beyidi, Alexandre

Betjeman, (Sir) John
1906-1984 . . . . CLC 2, 6, 10, 34, 43
See also CA 9-12R; obituary CA 112; DLB 20; DLB-Y 84

Betti, Ugo   1892-1953 . . . . TCLC 5
See also CA 104

Betts, Doris (Waugh)   1932-. . . . CLC 3, 6, 28
See also CANR 9; CA 13-16R; DLB-Y 82

Bialik, Chaim Nachman
1873-1934 . . . . TCLC 25

Bidart, Frank   19??-. . . . . CLC 33

Bienek, Horst   1930-. . . . . CLC 7, 11
See also CA 73-76; DLB 75

Bierce, Ambrose (Gwinett)
1842-1914?. . . . . TCLC 1, 7
See also CA 104; DLB 11, 12, 23, 71, 74; CDALB 1865-1917

Billington, Rachel   1942-. . . . . CLC 43
See also CA 33-36R

Binyon, T(imothy) J(ohn)   1936- . . . . CLC 34
See also CA 111

Bioy Casares, Adolfo   1914-. . . . CLC 4, 8, 13
See also CANR 19; CA 29-32R

Bird, Robert Montgomery
1806-1854 . . . . NCLC 1

Birdwell, Cleo   1936-
See DeLillo, Don

Birney (Alfred) Earle
1904- . . . . CLC 1, 4, 6, 11
See also CANR 5, 20; CA 1-4R

Bishop, Elizabeth
1911-1979 . . . . . . CLC 1, 4, 9, 13, 15, 32
See also CANR 26; CA 5-8R; obituary CA 89-92; CABS 2; obituary SATA 24; DLB 5

Bishop, John   1935-. . . . . CLC 10
See also CA 105

Bissett, Bill   1939-. . . . . CLC 18
See also CANR 15; CA 69-72; DLB 53

Bitov, Andrei (Georgievich)   1937-. . . CLC 57

Biyidi, Alexandre   1932-
See Beti, Mongo
See also CA 114, 124

Bjornson, Bjornstjerne (Martinius)
1832-1910 . . . . TCLC 7, 37
See also CA 104

Blackburn, Paul   1926-1971 . . . . . . CLC 9, 43
See also CA 81-84; obituary CA 33-36R; DLB 16; DLB-Y 81

Black Elk   1863-1950 . . . . TCLC 33

Blackmore, R(ichard) D(oddridge)
1825-1900 . . . . TCLC 27
See also CA 120; DLB 18

Blackmur, R(ichard) P(almer)
1904-1965 . . . . CLC 2, 24
See also CAP 1; CA 11-12; obituary CA 25-28R; DLB 63

Carlyle, Thomas 1795-1881 ...... NCLC 22
See also DLB 55

Carman, (William) Bliss
1861-1929 .... TCLC 7
See also CA 104

Carpenter, Don(ald Richard)
1931- .... CLC 41
See also CANR 1; CA 45-48

Carpentier (y Valmont), Alejo
1904-1980 .... CLC 8, 11, 38
See also CANR 11; CA 65-68;
obituary CA 97-100

Carr, Emily 1871-1945 .... TCLC 32
See also DLB 68

Carr, John Dickson 1906-1977 ...... CLC 3
See also CANR 3; CA 49-52;
obituary CA 69-72

Carr, Virginia Spencer 1929- ...... CLC 34
See also CA 61-64

Carrier, Roch 1937- .... CLC 13
See also DLB 53

Carroll, James (P.) 1943- .... CLC 38
See also CA 81-84

Carroll, Jim 1951- .... CLC 35
See also CA 45-48

Carroll, Lewis 1832-1898 .... NCLC 2
See also Dodgson, Charles Lutwidge
See also CLR 2; DLB 18

Carroll, Paul Vincent 1900-1968 .... CLC 10
See also CA 9-12R; obituary CA 25-28R;
DLB 10

Carruth, Hayden 1921- .... CLC 4, 7, 10, 18
See also CANR 4; CA 9-12R; SATA 47;
DLB 5

Carter, Angela (Olive) 1940- ..... CLC 5, 41
See also CANR 12; CA 53-56; DLB 14

Carver, Raymond
1938-1988 .... CLC 22, 36, 53, 55
See also CANR 17; CA 33-36R;
obituary CA 126; DLB-Y 84, 88

Cary, (Arthur) Joyce (Lunel)
1888-1957 .... TCLC 1, 29
See also CA 104; DLB 15

Casanova de Seingalt, Giovanni Jacopo
1725-1798 .... LC 13

Casares, Adolfo Bioy 1914-
See Bioy Casares, Adolfo

Casely-Hayford, J(oseph) E(phraim)
1866-1930 .... TCLC 24
See also CA 123

Casey, John 1880-1964
See O'Casey, Sean

Casey, John 1939- .... CLC 59
See also CANR 23; CA 69-72

Casey, Michael 1947- .... CLC 2
See also CA 65-68; DLB 5

Casey, Warren 1935- .... CLC 12
See also Jacobs, Jim and Casey, Warren
See also CA 101

Casona, Alejandro 1903-1965 ...... CLC 49
See also Alvarez, Alejandro Rodriguez

Cassavetes, John 1929- .... CLC 20
See also CA 85-88

Cassill, R(onald) V(erlin) 1919- ... CLC 4, 23
See also CAAS 1; CANR 7; CA 9-12R;
DLB 6

Cassity, (Allen) Turner 1929- .... CLC 6, 42
See also CANR 11; CA 17-20R

Castaneda, Carlos 1935?- .... CLC 12
See also CA 25-28R

Castelvetro, Lodovico 1505-1571 ..... LC 12

Castiglione, Baldassare 1478-1529 ... LC 12

Castro, Rosalia de 1837-1885 ..... NCLC 3

Cather, Willa (Sibert)
1873-1947 ...... TCLC 1, 11, 31; SSC 2
See also CA 104; SATA 30; DLB 9, 54;
DLB-DS 1; CDALB 1865-1917

Catton, (Charles) Bruce
1899-1978 .... CLC 35
See also CANR 7; CA 5-8R;
obituary CA 81-84; SATA 2;
obituary SATA 24; DLB 17

Cauldwell, Frank 1923-
See King, Francis (Henry)

Caunitz, William 1935- .... CLC 34

Causley, Charles (Stanley) 1917- ..... CLC 7
See also CANR 5; CA 9-12R; SATA 3;
DLB 27

Caute, (John) David 1936- .... CLC 29
See also CAAS 4; CANR 1; CA 1-4R;
DLB 14

Cavafy, C(onstantine) P(eter)
1863-1933 .... TCLC 2, 7
See also CA 104

Cavanna, Betty 1909- .... CLC 12
See also CANR 6; CA 9-12R; SATA 1, 30

Cayrol, Jean 1911- .... CLC 11
See also CA 89-92

Cela, Camilo Jose 1916- ...... CLC 4, 13, 59
See also CAAS 10; CANR 21; CA 21-24R

Celan, Paul 1920-1970 ...... CLC 10, 19, 53
See also Antschel, Paul
See also DLB 69

Celine, Louis-Ferdinand
1894-1961 ..... CLC 1, 3, 4, 7, 9, 15, 47
See also Destouches,
Louis-Ferdinand-Auguste
See also DLB 72

Cellini, Benvenuto 1500-1571 .... LC 7

Cendrars, Blaise 1887-1961 .... CLC 18
See also Sauser-Hall, Frederic

Cernuda, Luis (y Bidon)
1902-1963 .... CLC 54
See also CA 89-92

Cervantes (Saavedra), Miguel de
1547-1616 .... LC 6

Cesaire, Aime (Fernand) 1913- .. CLC 19, 32
See also CANR 24; CA 65-68

Chabon, Michael 1965?- .... CLC 55

Chabrol, Claude 1930- .... CLC 16
See also CA 110

Challans, Mary 1905-1983
See Renault, Mary
See also CA 81-84; obituary CA 111;
SATA 23; obituary SATA 36

Chambers, Aidan 1934- .... CLC 35
See also CANR 12; CA 25-28R; SATA 1

Chambers, James 1948-
See Cliff, Jimmy

Chandler, Raymond 1888-1959 ... TCLC 1, 7
See also CA 104

Channing, William Ellery
1780-1842 .... NCLC 17
See also DLB 1, 59

Chaplin, Charles (Spencer)
1889-1977 .... CLC 16
See also CA 81-84; obituary CA 73-76;
DLB 44

Chapman, Graham 1941?- .... CLC 21
See also Monty Python
See also CA 116

Chapman, John Jay 1862-1933 ..... TCLC 7
See also CA 104

Chappell, Fred 1936- .... CLC 40
See also CAAS 4; CANR 8; CA 5-8R;
DLB 6

Char, Rene (Emile)
1907-1988 .... CLC 9, 11, 14, 55
See also CA 13-16R; obituary CA 124

Charles I 1600-1649 .... LC 13

Charyn, Jerome 1937- .... CLC 5, 8, 18
See also CAAS 1; CANR 7; CA 5-8R;
DLB-Y 83

Chase, Mary Ellen 1887-1973 .... CLC 2
See also CAP 1; CA 15-16;
obituary CA 41-44R; SATA 10

Chateaubriand, Francois Rene de
1768-1848 .... NCLC 3

Chatterji, Bankim Chandra
1838-1894 .... NCLC 19

Chatterji, Saratchandra
1876-1938 .... TCLC 13
See also CA 109

Chatterton, Thomas 1752-1770 .... LC 3

Chatwin, (Charles) Bruce
1940-1989 .... CLC 28, 57, 59
See also CA 85-88,; obituary CA 127

Chayefsky, Paddy 1923-1981 .... CLC 23
See also CA 9-12R; obituary CA 104;
DLB 7, 44; DLB-Y 81

Chayefsky, Sidney 1923-1981
See Chayefsky, Paddy
See also CANR 18

Chedid, Andree 1920- .... CLC 47

Cheever, John
1912-1982 ..... CLC 3, 7, 8, 11, 15, 25;
SSC 1
See also CANR 5; CA 5-8R;
obituary CA 106; CABS 1; DLB 2;
DLB-Y 80, 82; CDALB 1941-1968

Cheever, Susan 1943- .... CLC 18, 48
See also CA 103; DLB-Y 82

Chekhov, Anton (Pavlovich)
1860-1904 ...... TCLC 3, 10, 31; SSC 2
See also CA 104, 124

Chernyshevsky, Nikolay Gavrilovich
1828-1889 .... NCLC 1

Cherry, Caroline Janice 1942-
See Cherryh, C. J.

Cherryh, C. J. 1942- .... CLC 35
See also CANR 10; CA 65-68; DLB-Y 80

Dumas, Henry   1918-1968 . . . . CLC 62

Dumas, Henry (L.)   1934-1968 . . . . . . CLC 6
See also CA 85-88; DLB 41

Du Maurier, Daphne   1907- . . . CLC 6, 11, 59
See also CANR 6; CA 5-8R;
obituary CA 128; SATA 27

Dunbar, Paul Laurence
1872-1906 . . . . TCLC 2, 12
See also CA 104, 124; SATA 34; DLB 50,
54; CDALB 1865-1917

Duncan (Steinmetz Arquette), Lois
1934- . . . . CLC 26
See also Arquette, Lois S(teinmetz)
See also CANR 2; CA 1-4R; SAAS 2;
SATA 1, 36

Duncan, Robert (Edward)
1919-1988 . . . . CLC 1, 2, 4, 7, 15, 41, 55
See also CA 9-12R; obituary CA 124;
DLB 5, 16

Dunlap, William   1766-1839 . . . . NCLC 2
See also DLB 30, 37, 59

Dunn, Douglas (Eaglesham)
1942- . . . . CLC 6, 40
See also CANR 2; CA 45-48; DLB 40

Dunn, Elsie   1893-1963
See Scott, Evelyn

Dunn, Stephen   1939- . . . . CLC 36
See also CANR 12; CA 33-36R

Dunne, Finley Peter   1867-1936 . . . . TCLC 28
See also CA 108; DLB 11, 23

Dunne, John Gregory   1932- . . . . CLC 28
See also CANR 14; CA 25-28R; DLB-Y 80

Dunsany, Lord (Edward John Moreton Drax
Plunkett)   1878-1957 . . . . TCLC 2
See also CA 104; DLB 10

Durang, Christopher (Ferdinand)
1949- . . . . CLC 27, 38
See also CA 105

Duras, Marguerite
1914- . . . . CLC 3, 6, 11, 20, 34, 40
See also CA 25-28R

Durban, Pam   1947- . . . . CLC 39
See also CA 123

Durcan, Paul   1944- . . . . CLC 43

Durrell, Lawrence (George)
1912-1990 . . . . CLC 1, 4, 6, 8, 13, 27, 41
See also CA 9-12R; DLB 15, 27

Durrenmatt, Friedrich
1921- . . . . CLC 1, 4, 8, 11, 15, 43
See also Duerrenmatt, Friedrich
See also DLB 69

Dutt, Toru   1856-1877 . . . . NCLC 29

Dwight, Timothy   1752-1817 . . . . . . NCLC 13
See also DLB 37

Dworkin, Andrea   1946- . . . . CLC 43
See also CANR 16; CA 77-80

Dylan, Bob   1941- . . . . CLC 3, 4, 6, 12
See also CA 41-44R; DLB 16

East, Michael   1916-
See West, Morris L.

Eastlake, William (Derry)   1917- . . . . . CLC 8
See also CAAS 1; CANR 5; CA 5-8R;
DLB 6

Eberhart, Richard   1904- . . . CLC 3, 11, 19, 56
See also CANR 2; CA 1-4R; DLB 48;
CDALB 1941-1968

Eberstadt, Fernanda   1960- . . . . CLC 39

Echegaray (y Eizaguirre), Jose (Maria Waldo)
1832-1916 . . . . TCLC 4
See also CA 104

Echeverria, (Jose) Esteban (Antonino)
1805-1851 . . . . NCLC 18

Eckert, Allan W.   1931- . . . . CLC 17
See also CANR 14; CA 13-16R; SATA 27,
29

Eco, Umberto   1932- . . . . CLC 28, 60
See also CANR 12; CA 77-80

Eddison, E(ric) R(ucker)
1882-1945 . . . . TCLC 15
See also CA 109

Edel, Leon (Joseph)   1907- . . . . . . CLC 29, 34
See also CANR 1, 22; CA 1-4R

Eden, Emily   1797-1869 . . . . NCLC 10

Edgar, David   1948- . . . . CLC 42
See also CANR 12; CA 57-60; DLB 13

Edgerton, Clyde   1944- . . . . CLC 39
See also CA 118

Edgeworth, Maria   1767-1849 . . . . . . NCLC 1
See also SATA 21

Edmonds, Helen (Woods)   1904-1968
See Kavan, Anna
See also CA 5-8R; obituary CA 25-28R

Edmonds, Walter D(umaux)   1903- . . CLC 35
See also CANR 2; CA 5-8R; SAAS 4;
SATA 1, 27; DLB 9

Edson, Russell   1905- . . . . CLC 13
See also CA 33-36R

Edwards, G(erald) B(asil)
1899-1976 . . . . CLC 25
See also obituary CA 110

Edwards, Gus   1939- . . . . CLC 43
See also CA 108

Edwards, Jonathan   1703-1758 . . . . LC 7
See also DLB 24

Ehle, John (Marsden, Jr.)   1925- . . . . CLC 27
See also CA 9-12R

Ehrenburg, Ilya (Grigoryevich)
1891-1967 . . . . CLC 18, 34, 62
See also CA 102; obituary CA 25-28R

Eich, Guenter   1907-1971
See also CA 111; obituary CA 93-96

Eich, Gunter   1907-1971 . . . . CLC 15
See also Eich, Guenter
See also DLB 69

Eichendorff, Joseph Freiherr von
1788-1857 . . . . NCLC 8

Eigner, Larry   1927- . . . . CLC 9
See also Eigner, Laurence (Joel)
See also DLB 5

Eigner, Laurence (Joel)   1927-
See Eigner, Larry
See also CANR 6; CA 9-12R

Eiseley, Loren (Corey)   1907-1977 . . . . CLC 7
See also CANR 6; CA 1-4R;
obituary CA 73-76

Eisenstadt, Jill   1963- . . . . CLC 50

Ekeloef, Gunnar (Bengt)   1907-1968
See Ekelof, Gunnar (Bengt)
See also obituary CA 25-28R

Ekelof, Gunnar (Bengt)   1907-1968 . . CLC 27
See also Ekeloef, Gunnar (Bengt)

Ekwensi, Cyprian (Odiatu Duaka)
1921- . . . . CLC 4
See also CANR 18; CA 29-32R

Eliade, Mircea   1907-1986 . . . . CLC 19
See also CA 65-68; obituary CA 119

Eliot, George   1819-1880 . . . . NCLC 4, 13, 23
See also DLB 21, 35, 55

Eliot, John   1604-1690 . . . . LC 5
See also DLB 24

Eliot, T(homas) S(tearns)
1888-1965 . . . . CLC 1, 2, 3, 6, 9, 10, 13,
15, 24, 34, 41, 55, 57
See also CA 5-8R; obituary CA 25-28R;
DLB 7, 10, 45, 63; DLB-Y 88

Elkin, Stanley (Lawrence)
1930- . . . . CLC 4, 6, 9, 14, 27, 51
See also CANR 8; CA 9-12R; DLB 2, 28;
DLB-Y 80

Elledge, Scott   19??- . . . . CLC 34

Elliott, George P(aul)   1918-1980 . . . . . CLC 2
See also CANR 2; CA 1-4R;
obituary CA 97-100

Elliott, Janice   1931- . . . . CLC 47
See also CANR 8; CA 13-16R; DLB 14

Elliott, Sumner Locke   1917- . . . . CLC 38
See also CANR 2, 21; CA 5-8R

Ellis, A. E.   19??- . . . . CLC 7

Ellis, Alice Thomas   19??- . . . . CLC 40

Ellis, Bret Easton   1964- . . . . CLC 39
See also CA 118, 123

Ellis, (Henry) Havelock
1859-1939 . . . . TCLC 14
See also CA 109

Ellis, Trey   1964- . . . . CLC 55

Ellison, Harlan (Jay)   1934- . . . CLC 1, 13, 42
See also CANR 5; CA 5-8R; DLB 8

Ellison, Ralph (Waldo)
1914- . . . . CLC 1, 3, 11, 54
See also CANR 24; CA 9-12R; DLB 2;
CDALB 1941-1968

Ellmann, Lucy   1956- . . . . CLC 61
See also CA 128

Ellmann, Richard (David)
1918-1987 . . . . CLC 50
See also CANR 2; CA 1-4R;
obituary CA 122; DLB-Y 87

Elman, Richard   1934- . . . . CLC 19
See also CAAS 3; CA 17-20R

Eluard, Paul   1895-1952 . . . . TCLC 7
See also Grindel, Eugene

Elyot, (Sir) James   1490?-1546 . . . . . . LC 11

Elyot, (Sir) Thomas   1490?-1546 . . . . . LC 11

Elytis, Odysseus   1911- . . . . CLC 15, 49
See also CA 102

Emecheta, (Florence Onye) Buchi
1944- . . . . CLC 14, 48
See also CA 81-84

Finch, Robert (Duer Claydon)
1900- . . . . CLC 18
See also CANR 9, 24; CA 57-60

Findley, Timothy 1930- . . . . CLC 27
See also CANR 12; CA 25-28R; DLB 53

Fink, Janis 1951-
See Ian, Janis

Firbank, Louis 1944-
See Reed, Lou
See also CA 117

Firbank, (Arthur Annesley) Ronald
1886-1926 . . . . TCLC 1
See also CA 104; DLB 36

Fisher, Roy 1930- . . . . CLC 25
See also CANR 16; CA 81-84; DLB 40

Fisher, Rudolph 1897-1934 . . . . TCLC 11
See also CA 107; DLB 51

Fisher, Vardis (Alvero) 1895-1968. . . . CLC 7
See also CA 5-8R; obituary CA 25-28R;
DLB 9

FitzGerald, Edward 1809-1883 . . . . NCLC 9
See also DLB 32

Fitzgerald, F(rancis) Scott (Key)
1896-1940 . . . . TCLC 1, 6, 14, 28; SSC 6
See also CA 110, 123; DLB 4, 9, 86;
DLB-Y 81; DLB-DS 1;
CDALB 1917-1929

Fitzgerald, Penelope 1916-. . . CLC 19, 51, 61
See also CAAS 10; CA 85-88,; DLB 14

Fitzgerald, Robert (Stuart)
1910-1985 . . . . CLC 39
See also CANR 1; CA 2R;
obituary CA 114; DLB-Y 80

FitzGerald, Robert D(avid) 1902-. . . CLC 19
See also CA 17-20R

Flanagan, Thomas (James Bonner)
1923- . . . . CLC 25, 52
See also CA 108; DLB-Y 80

Flaubert, Gustave
1821-1880 . . . . NCLC 2, 10, 19

Fleming, Ian (Lancaster)
1908-1964 . . . . CLC 3, 30
See also CA 5-8R; SATA 9

Fleming, Thomas J(ames) 1927- . . . . CLC 37
See also CANR 10; CA 5-8R; SATA 8

Fletcher, John Gould 1886-1950. . . TCLC 35
See also CA 107; DLB 4, 45

Flieg, Hellmuth
See Heym, Stefan

Flying Officer X 1905-1974
See Bates, H(erbert) E(rnest)

Fo, Dario 1929-. . . . . CLC 32
See also CA 116

Follett, Ken(neth Martin) 1949- . . . . CLC 18
See also CANR 13; CA 81-84; DLB-Y 81

Fontane, Theodor 1819-1898 . . . . . NCLC 26

Foote, Horton 1916-. . . . . CLC 51
See also CA 73-76; DLB 26

Forbes, Esther 1891-1967. . . . . CLC 12
See also CAP 1; CA 13-14;
obituary CA 25-28R; SATA 2; DLB 22

Forche, Carolyn 1950- . . . . CLC 25
See also CA 109, 117; DLB 5

Ford, Ford Madox
1873-1939 . . . . TCLC 1, 15, 39
See also CA 104; DLB 34

Ford, John 1895-1973. . . . . CLC 16
See also obituary CA 45-48

Ford, Richard 1944-. . . . . CLC 46
See also CANR 11; CA 69-72

Foreman, Richard 1937-. . . . . CLC 50
See also CA 65-68

Forester, C(ecil) S(cott)
1899-1966 . . . . CLC 35
See also CA 73-76; obituary CA 25-28R;
SATA 13

Forman, James D(ouglas) 1932- . . . . CLC 21
See also CANR 4, 19; CA 9-12R; SATA 8,
21

Fornes, Maria Irene 1930-. . . . . . CLC 39, 61
See also CANR 28; CA 25-28R; DLB 7

Forrest, Leon 1937- . . . . CLC 4
See also CAAS 7; CA 89-92; DLB 33

Forster, E(dward) M(organ)
1879-1970 . . . . CLC 1, 2, 3, 4, 9, 10, 13,
15, 22, 45
See also CAP 1; CA 13-14;
obituary CA 25-28R; DLB 34

Forster, John 1812-1876 . . . . NCLC 11

Forsyth, Frederick 1938-. . . . . . CLC 2, 5, 36
See also CA 85-88

Forten (Grimke), Charlotte L(ottie)
1837-1914 . . . . TCLC 16
See also Grimke, Charlotte L(ottie) Forten
See also DLB 50

Foscolo, Ugo 1778-1827. . . . . NCLC 8

Fosse, Bob 1925-1987. . . . . CLC 20
See also Fosse, Robert Louis

Fosse, Robert Louis 1925-1987
See Bob Fosse
See also CA 110, 123

Foster, Stephen Collins
1826-1864 . . . . NCLC 26

Foucault, Michel 1926-1984 . . . . CLC 31, 34
See also CANR 23; CA 105;
obituary CA 113

Fouque, Friedrich (Heinrich Karl) de La
Motte 1777-1843 . . . . NCLC 2

Fournier, Henri Alban 1886-1914
See Alain-Fournier
See also CA 104

Fournier, Pierre 1916- . . . . CLC 11
See also Gascar, Pierre
See also CANR 16; CA 89-92

Fowles, John (Robert)
1926- . . . . CLC 1, 2, 3, 4, 6, 9, 10, 15, 33
See also CANR 25; CA 5-8R; SATA 22;
DLB 14

Fox, Paula 1923-. . . . . CLC 2, 8
See also CLR 1; CANR 20; CA 73-76;
SATA 17; DLB 52

Fox, William Price (Jr.) 1926- . . . . . CLC 22
See also CANR 11; CA 17-20R; DLB 2;
DLB-Y 81

Foxe, John 1516?-1587. . . . . LC 14

Frame (Clutha), Janet (Paterson)
1924- . . . . CLC 2, 3, 6, 22
See also Clutha, Janet Paterson Frame

France, Anatole 1844-1924 . . . . TCLC 9
See also Thibault, Jacques Anatole Francois

Francis, Claude 19??- . . . . CLC 50

Francis, Dick 1920- . . . . CLC 2, 22, 42
See also CANR 9; CA 5-8R

Francis, Robert (Churchill)
1901-1987 . . . . CLC 15
See also CANR 1; CA 1-4R;
obituary CA 123

Frank, Anne 1929-1945 . . . . TCLC 17
See also CA 113; SATA 42

Frank, Elizabeth 1945-. . . . . CLC 39
See also CA 121, 126

Franklin, (Stella Maria Sarah) Miles
1879-1954 . . . . TCLC 7
See also CA 104

Fraser, Antonia (Pakenham)
1932- . . . . CLC 32
See also CA 85-88; SATA 32

Fraser, George MacDonald 1925-. . . . CLC 7
See also CANR 2; CA 45-48

Frayn, Michael 1933-. . . . . . CLC 3, 7, 31, 47
See also CA 5-8R; DLB 13, 14

Fraze, Candida 19??- . . . . CLC 50
See also CA 125

Frazer, Sir James George
1854-1941 . . . . TCLC 32
See also CA 118

Frazier, Ian 1951-. . . . . CLC 46

Frederic, Harold 1856-1898. . . . . . NCLC 10
See also DLB 12, 23

Frederick the Great 1712-1786 . . . . . . LC 14

Fredman, Russell (Bruce) 1929-
See also CLR 20

Fredro, Aleksander 1793-1876. . . . . NCLC 8

Freeling, Nicolas 1927- . . . . CLC 38
See also CANR 1, 17; CA 49-52

Freeman, Douglas Southall
1886-1953 . . . . TCLC 11
See also CA 109; DLB 17

Freeman, Judith 1946-. . . . . CLC 55

Freeman, Mary (Eleanor) Wilkins
1852-1930 . . . . TCLC 9; SSC 1
See also CA 106; DLB 12

Freeman, R(ichard) Austin
1862-1943 . . . . TCLC 21
See also CA 113; DLB 70

French, Marilyn 1929-. . . . . . CLC 10, 18, 60
See also CANR 3; CA 69-72

Freneau, Philip Morin 1752-1832. . NCLC 1
See also DLB 37, 43

Friedman, B(ernard) H(arper)
1926- . . . . CLC 7
See also CANR 3; CA 1-4R

Friedman, Bruce Jay 1930-. . . . CLC 3, 5, 56
See also CANR 25; CA 9-12R; DLB 2, 28

Friel, Brian 1929-. . . . . CLC 5, 42, 59
See also CA 21-24R; DLB 13

Friis-Baastad, Babbis (Ellinor)
1921-1970 .... **CLC 12**
See also CA 17-20R; SATA 7

Frisch, Max (Rudolf)
1911- .... **CLC 3, 9, 14, 18, 32, 44**
See also CA 85-88; DLB 69

Fromentin, Eugene (Samuel Auguste)
1820-1876 .... **NCLC 10**

Frost, Robert (Lee)
1874-1963 ... **CLC 1, 3, 4, 9, 10, 13, 15,
26, 34, 44; PC 1**
See also CA 89-92; SATA 14; DLB 54;
DLB-DS 7; CDALB 1917-1929

Fry, Christopher 1907-....... **CLC 2, 10, 14**
See also CANR 9; CA 17-20R; DLB 13

Frye, (Herman) Northrop 1912-.... **CLC 24**
See also CANR 8; CA 5-8R

Fuchs, Daniel 1909-............ **CLC 8, 22**
See also CAAS 5; CA 81-84; DLB 9, 26, 28

Fuchs, Daniel 1934-.............. **CLC 34**
See also CANR 14; CA 37-40R

Fuentes, Carlos
1928-...... **CLC 3, 8, 10, 13, 22, 41, 60**
See also CANR 10; CA 69-72

Fugard, Athol 1932-... **CLC 5, 9, 14, 25, 40**
See also CA 85-88

Fugard, Sheila 1932- .... **CLC 48**
See also CA 125

Fuller, Charles (H., Jr.) 1939-...... **CLC 25**
See also CA 108, 112; DLB 38

Fuller, John (Leopold) 1937-....... **CLC 62**
See also CANR 9; CA 21-22R; DLB 40

Fuller, (Sarah) Margaret
1810-1850 .... **NCLC 5**
See also Ossoli, Sarah Margaret (Fuller
marchesa d')
See also DLB 1, 59, 73; CDALB 1640-1865

Fuller, Roy (Broadbent) 1912-.... **CLC 4, 28**
See also CA 5-8R; DLB 15, 20

Fulton, Alice 1952-.............. **CLC 52**
See also CA 116

Furphy, Joseph 1843-1912........ **TCLC 25**

Futrelle, Jacques 1875-1912 ...... **TCLC 19**
See also CA 113

Gaboriau, Emile 1835-1873 ...... **NCLC 14**

Gadda, Carlo Emilio 1893-1973 .... **CLC 11**
See also CA 89-92

Gaddis, William
1922- .... **CLC 1, 3, 6, 8, 10, 19, 43**
See also CAAS 4; CANR 21; CA 17-20R;
DLB 2

Gaines, Ernest J. 1933- ...... **CLC 3, 11, 18**
See also CANR 6, 24; CA 9-12R; DLB 2,
33; DLB-Y 80

Gale, Zona 1874-1938 .... **TCLC 7**
See also CA 105; DLB 9

Gallagher, Tess 1943-............. **CLC 18**
See also CA 106

Gallant, Mavis
1922-........... **CLC 7, 18, 38; SSC 5**
See also CA 69-72; DLB 53

Gallant, Roy A(rthur) 1924- .... **CLC 17**
See also CANR 4; CA 5-8R; SATA 4

Gallico, Paul (William) 1897-1976 ... **CLC 2**
See also CA 5-8R; obituary CA 69-72;
SATA 13; DLB 9

Galsworthy, John 1867-1933....... **TCLC 1**
See also CA 104; DLB 10, 34

Galt, John 1779-1839............ **NCLC 1**

Galvin, James 1951-.............. **CLC 38**
See also CANR 26; CA 108

Gamboa, Frederico 1864-1939..... **TCLC 36**

Gann, Ernest K(ellogg) 1910- ...... **CLC 23**
See also CANR 1; CA 1-4R

Garcia Lorca, Federico
1899-1936 .... **TCLC 1, 7**
See also CA 104

Garcia Marquez, Gabriel (Jose)
1928-.... **CLC 2, 3, 8, 10, 15, 27, 47, 55**
See also CANR 10; CA 33-36R

Gardam, Jane 1928-............... **CLC 43**
See also CLR 12; CANR 2, 18; CA 49-52;
SATA 28, 39; DLB 14

Gardner, Herb 1934- .... **CLC 44**

Gardner, John (Champlin, Jr.)
1933-1982 .... **CLC 2, 3, 5, 7, 8, 10, 18,
28, 34**
See also CA 65-68; obituary CA 107;
obituary SATA 31, 40; DLB 2; DLB-Y 82

Gardner, John (Edmund) 1926-..... **CLC 30**
See also CANR 15; CA 103

Garfield, Leon 1921-.............. **CLC 12**
See also CA 17-20R; SATA 1, 32

Garland, (Hannibal) Hamlin
1860-1940 .... **TCLC 3**
See also CA 104; DLB 12, 71

Garneau, Hector (de) Saint Denys
1912-1943 .... **TCLC 13**
See also CA 111

Garner, Alan 1935-............... **CLC 17**
See also CLR 20; CANR 15; CA 73-76;
SATA 18

Garner, Hugh 1913-1979 .... **CLC 13**
See also CA 69-72; DLB 68

Garnett, David 1892-1981 .... **CLC 3**
See also CANR 17; CA 5-8R;
obituary CA 103; DLB 34

Garrett, George (Palmer, Jr.)
1929-................. **CLC 3, 11, 51**
See also CAAS 5; CANR 1; CA 1-4R;
DLB 2, 5; DLB-Y 83

Garrigue, Jean 1914-1972 .... **CLC 2, 8**
See also CANR 20; CA 5-8R;
obituary CA 37-40R

Gary, Romain 1914-1980......... **CLC 25**
See also Kacew, Romain

Gascar, Pierre 1916-.............. **CLC 11**
See also Fournier, Pierre

Gascoyne, David (Emery) 1916- .... **CLC 45**
See also CANR 10; CA 65-68; DLB 20

Gaskell, Elizabeth Cleghorn
1810-1865 .... **NCLC 5**
See also DLB 21

Gass, William H(oward)
1924- .... **CLC 1, 2, 8, 11, 15, 39**
See also CA 17-20R; DLB 2

Gautier, Theophile 1811-1872 ..... **NCLC 1**

Gaye, Marvin (Pentz) 1939-1984 ... **CLC 26**
See also obituary CA 112

Gebler, Carlo (Ernest) 1954-....... **CLC 39**
See also CA 119

Gee, Maggie 19??- .... **CLC 57**

Gee, Maurice (Gough) 1931-....... **CLC 29**
See also CA 97-100; SATA 46

Gelbart, Larry 1923?-.......... **CLC 21, 61**
See also CA 73-76

Gelber, Jack 1932-........ **CLC 1, 6, 14, 60**
See also CANR 2; CA 1-4R; DLB 7

Gellhorn, Martha (Ellis) 1908- .. **CLC 14, 60**
See also CA 77-80; DLB-Y 82

Genet, Jean
1910-1986 ... **CLC 1, 2, 5, 10, 14, 44, 46**
See also CANR 18; CA 13-16R; DLB 72;
DLB-Y 86

Gent, Peter 1942-................ **CLC 29**
See also CA 89-92; DLB 72; DLB-Y 82

George, Jean Craighead 1919-...... **CLC 35**
See also CLR 1; CA 5-8R; SATA 2;
DLB 52

George, Stefan (Anton)
1868-1933 .... **TCLC 2, 14**
See also CA 104

Gerhardi, William (Alexander) 1895-1977
See Gerhardie, William (Alexander)

Gerhardie, William (Alexander)
1895-1977 .... **CLC 5**
See also CANR 18; CA 25-28R;
obituary CA 73-76; DLB 36

Gertler, T(rudy) 1946?- .... **CLC 34**
See also CA 116

Gessner, Friedrike Victoria 1910-1980
See Adamson, Joy(-Friederike Victoria)

Ghelderode, Michel de
1898-1962 .... **CLC 6, 11**
See also CA 85-88

Ghiselin, Brewster 1903- .... **CLC 23**
See also CANR 13; CA 13-16R

Ghose, Zulfikar 1935-............. **CLC 42**
See also CA 65-68

Ghosh, Amitav 1943- .... **CLC 44**

Giacosa, Giuseppe 1847-1906 ...... **TCLC 7**
See also CA 104

Gibbon, Lewis Grassic 1901-1935... **TCLC 4**
See also Mitchell, James Leslie

Gibbons, Kaye 1960- .... **CLC 50**

Gibran, (Gibran) Kahlil
1883-1931 .... **TCLC 1, 9**
See also CA 104

Gibson, William 1914-............ **CLC 23**
See also CANR 9; CA 9-12R; DLB 7

Gibson, William 1948-............ **CLC 39**
See also CA 126

Gide, Andre (Paul Guillaume)
1869-1951 .... **TCLC 5, 12, 36**
See also CA 104, 124; DLB 65

Gifford, Barry (Colby) 1946-....... **CLC 34**
See also CANR 9; CA 65-68

Gilbert, (Sir) W(illiam) S(chwenck)
1836-1911 .... **TCLC 3**
See also CA 104; SATA 36

Heifner, Jack 1946- .... **CLC 11**
See also CA 105

Heijermans, Herman 1864-1924 ... **TCLC 24**
See also CA 123

Heilbrun, Carolyn G(old) 1926- ..... **CLC 25**
See also CANR 1; CA 45-48

Heine, Harry 1797-1856
See Heine, Heinrich

Heine, Heinrich 1797-1856 .... **NCLC 4**

Heinemann, Larry C(urtiss) 1944- .. **CLC 50**
See also CA 110

Heiney, Donald (William) 1921-
See Harris, MacDonald
See also CANR 3; CA 1-4R

Heinlein, Robert A(nson)
1907-1988 ...... **CLC 1, 3, 8, 14, 26, 55**
See also CANR 1, 20; CA 1-4R;
obituary CA 125; SATA 9; DLB 8

Heller, Joseph
1923- .... **CLC 1, 3, 5, 8, 11, 36**
See also CANR 8; CA 5-8R; CABS 1;
DLB 2, 28; DLB-Y 80

Hellman, Lillian (Florence)
1905?-1984 ..... **CLC 2, 4, 8, 14, 18, 34,**
44, 52
See also CA 13-16R; obituary CA 112;
DLB 7; DLB-Y 84

Helprin, Mark 1947- ..... **CLC 7, 10, 22, 32**
See also CA 81-84; DLB-Y 85

Hemans, Felicia 1793-1835 ...... **NCLC 29**

Hemingway, Ernest (Miller)
1899-1961 ... **CLC 1, 3, 6, 8, 10, 13, 19,**
30, 34, 39, 41, 44, 50, 61; SSC 1
See also CA 77-80; DLB 4, 9; DLB-Y 81,
87; DLB-DS 1

Hempel, Amy 1951- .... **CLC 39**
See also CA 118

Henley, Beth 1952- .... **CLC 23**
See also Henley, Elizabeth Becker
See also DLB-Y 86

Henley, Elizabeth Becker 1952-
See Henley, Beth
See also CA 107

Henley, William Ernest
1849-1903 .... **TCLC 8**
See also CA 105; DLB 19

Hennissart, Martha
See Lathen, Emma
See also CA 85-88

Henry, O. 1862-1910 ... **TCLC 1, 19; SSC 5**
See also Porter, William Sydney
See also YABC 2; CA 104; DLB 12, 78, 79;
CDALB 1865-1917

Henry VIII 1491-1547 .... **LC 10**

Hentoff, Nat(han Irving) 1925- ..... **CLC 26**
See also CLR 1; CAAS 6; CANR 5;
CA 1-4R; SATA 27, 42

Heppenstall, (John) Rayner
1911-1981 .... **CLC 10**
See also CA 1-4R; obituary CA 103

Herbert, Frank (Patrick)
1920-1986 .... **CLC 12, 23, 35, 44**
See also CANR 5; CA 53-56;
obituary CA 118; SATA 9, 37, 47; DLB 8

Herbert, Zbigniew 1924- .... **CLC 9, 43**
See also CA 89-92

Herbst, Josephine 1897-1969 .... **CLC 34**
See also CA 5-8R; obituary CA 25-28R;
DLB 9

Herder, Johann Gottfried von
1744-1803 .... **NCLC 8**

Hergesheimer, Joseph
1880-1954 .... **TCLC 11**
See also CA 109; DLB 9

Herlagnez, Pablo de 1844-1896
See Verlaine, Paul (Marie)

Herlihy, James Leo 1927- .... **CLC 6**
See also CANR 2; CA 1-4R

Hermogenes fl.c. 175- .... **CMLC 6**

Hernandez, Jose 1834-1886 ...... **NCLC 17**

Herrick, Robert 1591-1674 .... **LC 13**

Herriot, James 1916- .... **CLC 12**
See also Wight, James Alfred

Herrmann, Dorothy 1941- .... **CLC 44**
See also CA 107

Hersey, John (Richard)
1914- .... **CLC 1, 2, 7, 9, 40**
See also CA 17-20R; SATA 25; DLB 6

Herzen, Aleksandr Ivanovich
1812-1870 .... **NCLC 10**

Herzl, Theodor 1860-1904 .... **TCLC 36**

Herzog, Werner 1942- .... **CLC 16**
See also CA 89-92

Hesiod c. 8th Century B.C.- ...... **CMLC 5**

Hesse, Hermann
1877-1962 .... **CLC 1, 2, 3, 6, 11, 17, 25**
See also CAP 2; CA 17-18; SATA 50;
DLB 66

Heyen, William 1940- .... **CLC 13, 18**
See also CA 33-36R; DLB 5

Heyerdahl, Thor 1914- .... **CLC 26**
See also CANR 5, 22; CA 5-8R; SATA 2,
52

Heym, Georg (Theodor Franz Arthur)
1887-1912 .... **TCLC 9**
See also CA 106

Heym, Stefan 1913- .... **CLC 41**
See also CANR 4; CA 9-12R; DLB 69

Heyse, Paul (Johann Ludwig von)
1830-1914 .... **TCLC 8**
See also CA 104

Hibbert, Eleanor (Burford) 1906- .... **CLC 7**
See also CANR 9; CA 17-20R; SATA 2

Higgins, George V(incent)
1939- .... **CLC 4, 7, 10, 18**
See also CAAS 5; CANR 17; CA 77-80;
DLB 2; DLB-Y 81

Higginson, Thomas Wentworth
1823-1911 .... **TCLC 36**
See also DLB 1, 64

Highsmith, (Mary) Patricia
1921- .... **CLC 2, 4, 14, 42**
See also CANR 1, 20; CA 1-4R

Highwater, Jamake 1942- .... **CLC 12**
See also CAAS 7; CANR 10; CA 65-68;
SATA 30, 32; DLB 52; DLB-Y 85

Hikmet (Ran), Nazim 1902-1963.... **CLC 40**
See also obituary CA 93-96

Hildesheimer, Wolfgang 1916- ..... **CLC 49**
See also CA 101; DLB 69

Hill, Geoffrey (William)
1932- .... **CLC 5, 8, 18, 45**
See also CANR 21; CA 81-84; DLB 40

Hill, George Roy 1922- .... **CLC 26**
See also CA 110

Hill, Susan B. 1942- .... **CLC 4**
See also CA 33-36R; DLB 14

Hillerman, Tony 1925- .... **CLC 62**
See also CANR 21; CA 29-32R; SATA 6

Hilliard, Noel (Harvey) 1929- ..... **CLC 15**
See also CANR 7; CA 9-12R

Hilton, James 1900-1954 .... **TCLC 21**
See also CA 108; SATA 34; DLB 34

Himes, Chester (Bomar)
1909-1984 .... **CLC 2, 4, 7, 18, 58**
See also CANR 22; CA 25-28R;
obituary CA 114; DLB 2, 76

Hinde, Thomas 1926- .... **CLC 6, 11**
See also Chitty, (Sir) Thomas Willes

Hine, (William) Daryl 1936- ...... **CLC 15**
See also CANR 1, 20; CA 1-4R; DLB 60

Hinton, S(usan) E(loise) 1950- ..... **CLC 30**
See also CLR 3; CA 81-84; SATA 19

Hippius (Merezhkovsky), Zinaida
(Nikolayevna) 1869-1945...... **TCLC 9**
See also Gippius, Zinaida (Nikolayevna)

Hiraoka, Kimitake 1925-1970
See Mishima, Yukio
See also CA 97-100; obituary CA 29-32R

Hirsch, Edward (Mark) 1950-... **CLC 31, 50**
See also CANR 20; CA 104

Hitchcock, (Sir) Alfred (Joseph)
1899-1980 .... **CLC 16**
See also obituary CA 97-100; SATA 27;
obituary SATA 24

Hoagland, Edward 1932- .... **CLC 28**
See also CANR 2; CA 1-4R; SATA 51;
DLB 6

Hoban, Russell C(onwell) 1925- .. **CLC 7, 25**
See also CLR 3; CANR 23; CA 5-8R;
SATA 1, 40; DLB 52

Hobson, Laura Z(ametkin)
1900-1986 .... **CLC 7, 25**
See also CA 17-20R; obituary CA 118;
SATA 52; DLB 28

Hochhuth, Rolf 1931- .... **CLC 4, 11, 18**
See also CA 5-8R

Hochman, Sandra 1936- .... **CLC 3, 8**
See also CA 5-8R; DLB 5

Hochwalder, Fritz 1911-1986 ...... **CLC 36**
See also CA 29-32R; obituary CA 120

Hocking, Mary (Eunice) 1921- ..... **CLC 13**
See also CANR 18; CA 101

Hodgins, Jack 1938- .... **CLC 23**
See also CA 93-96; DLB 60

Hodgson, William Hope
1877-1918 .... **TCLC 13**
See also CA 111; DLB 70

Hoffman, Alice 1952- .... **CLC 51**
See also CA 77-80

Hoffman, Daniel (Gerard)
    1923- .... **CLC 6, 13, 23**
    See also CANR 4; CA 1-4R; DLB 5

Hoffman, Stanley 1944- .... **CLC 5**
    See also CA 77-80

Hoffman, William M(oses) 1939- ... **CLC 40**
    See also CANR 11; CA 57-60

Hoffmann, Ernst Theodor Amadeus
    1776-1822 .... **NCLC 2**
    See also SATA 27

Hoffmann, Gert 1932- .... **CLC 54**

**Hofmannsthal, Hugo (Laurenz August
    Hofmann Edler) von**
    1874-1929 .... **TCLC 11**
    See also CA 106

Hogg, James 1770-1835 .... **NCLC 4**

Holbach, Paul Henri Thiry, Baron d'
    1723-1789 .... **LC 14**

Holberg, Ludvig 1684-1754 .... **LC 6**

Holden, Ursula 1921- .... **CLC 18**
    See also CANR 22; CA 101

Holderlin, (Johann Christian) Friedrich
    1770-1843 .... **NCLC 16**

Holdstock, Robert (P.) 1948- ...... **CLC 39**

Holland, Isabelle 1920- .... **CLC 21**
    See also CANR 10, 25; CA 21-24R;
    SATA 8

Holland, Marcus 1900-1985
    See Caldwell, (Janet Miriam) Taylor
    (Holland)

Hollander, John 1929- ...... **CLC 2, 5, 8, 14**
    See also CANR 1; CA 1-4R; SATA 13;
    DLB 5

Holleran, Andrew 1943?- .... **CLC 38**

Hollinghurst, Alan 1954- .... **CLC 55**
    See also CA 114

Hollis, Jim 1916-
    See Summers, Hollis (Spurgeon, Jr.)

Holmes, John Clellon 1926-1988 .... **CLC 56**
    See also CANR 4; CA 9-10R;
    obituary CA 125; DLB 16

Holmes, Oliver Wendell
    1809-1894 .... **NCLC 14**
    See also SATA 34; DLB 1;
    CDALB 1640-1865

Holt, Victoria 1906-
    See Hibbert, Eleanor (Burford)

Holub, Miroslav 1923- .... **CLC 4**
    See also CANR 10; CA 21-24R

Homer c. 8th century B.C.- .... **CMLC 1**

Honig, Edwin 1919- .... **CLC 33**
    See also CANR 4; CA 5-8R; DLB 5

Hood, Hugh (John Blagdon)
    1928- .... **CLC 15, 28**
    See also CANR 1; CA 49-52; DLB 53

Hood, Thomas 1799-1845 .... **NCLC 16**

Hooker, (Peter) Jeremy 1941- ...... **CLC 43**
    See also CANR 22; CA 77-80; DLB 40

Hope, A(lec) D(erwent) 1907- .... **CLC 3, 51**
    See also CA 21-24R

Hope, Christopher (David Tully)
    1944- .... **CLC 52**
    See also CA 106

Hopkins, Gerard Manley
    1844-1889 .... **NCLC 17**
    See also DLB 35, 57

Hopkins, John (Richard) 1931- ...... **CLC 4**
    See also CA 85-88

Hopkins, Pauline Elizabeth
    1859-1930 .... **TCLC 28**
    See also DLB 50

Horgan, Paul 1903- .... **CLC 9, 53**
    See also CANR 9; CA 13-16R; SATA 13;
    DLB-Y 85

Horovitz, Israel 1939- .... **CLC 56**
    See also CA 33-36R; DLB 7

Horwitz, Julius 1920-1986 .... **CLC 14**
    See also CANR 12; CA 9-12R;
    obituary CA 119

Hospital, Janette Turner 1942- ..... **CLC 42**
    See also CA 108

Hostos (y Bonilla), Eugenio Maria de
    1893-1903 .... **TCLC 24**
    See also CA 123

Hougan, Carolyn 19??- .... **CLC 34**

Household, Geoffrey (Edward West)
    1900-1988 .... **CLC 11**
    See also CA 77-80; obituary CA 126;
    SATA 14

Housman, A(lfred) E(dward)
    1859-1936 .... **TCLC 1, 10**
    See also CA 104, 125; DLB 19

Housman, Laurence 1865-1959 ..... **TCLC 7**
    See also CA 106; SATA 25; DLB 10

Howard, Elizabeth Jane 1923- ... **CLC 7, 29**
    See also CANR 8; CA 5-8R

Howard, Maureen 1930- ..... **CLC 5, 14, 46**
    See also CA 53-56; DLB-Y 83

Howard, Richard 1929- ... **CLC 7, 10, 47**
    See also CANR 25; CA 85-88; DLB 5

Howard, Robert E(rvin)
    1906-1936 .... **TCLC 8**
    See also CA 105

Howe, Fanny 1940- .... **CLC 47**
    See also CA 117; SATA 52

Howe, Julia Ward 1819-1910 ..... **TCLC 21**
    See also CA 117; DLB 1

Howe, Tina 1937- .... **CLC 48**
    See also CA 109

Howell, James 1594?-1666 .... **LC 13**

Howells, William Dean
    1837-1920 .... **TCLC 7, 17**
    See also CA 104; DLB 12, 64, 74;
    CDALB 1865-1917

Howes, Barbara 1914- .... **CLC 15**
    See also CAAS 3; CA 9-12R; SATA 5

Hrabal, Bohumil 1914- .... **CLC 13**
    See also CA 106

Hubbard, L(afayette) Ron(ald)
    1911-1986 .... **CLC 43**
    See also CANR 22; CA 77-80;
    obituary CA 118

Huch, Ricarda (Octavia)
    1864-1947 .... **TCLC 13**
    See also CA 111; DLB 66

Huddle, David 1942- .... **CLC 49**
    See also CA 57-60

Hudson, W(illiam) H(enry)
    1841-1922 .... **TCLC 29**
    See also CA 115; SATA 35

Hueffer, Ford Madox 1873-1939
    See Ford, Ford Madox

Hughart, Barry 1934- .... **CLC 39**

Hughes, David (John) 1930- ... **CLC 48**
    See also CA 116; DLB 14

Hughes, Edward James 1930-
    See Hughes, Ted

Hughes, (James) Langston
    1902-1967 .... **CLC 1, 5, 10, 15, 35, 44;
                                    PC 1; SSC 6**
    See also CLR 17; CANR 1; CA 1-4R;
    obituary CA 25-28R; SATA 4, 33;
    DLB 4, 7, 48, 51, 86; CDALB 1929-1941

Hughes, Richard (Arthur Warren)
    1900-1976 .... **CLC 1, 11**
    See also CANR 4; CA 5-8R;
    obituary CA 65-68; SATA 8;
    obituary SATA 25; DLB 15

Hughes, Ted 1930- ..... **CLC 2, 4, 9, 14, 37**
    See also CLR 3; CANR 1; CA 1-4R;
    SATA 27, 49; DLB 40

Hugo, Richard F(ranklin)
    1923-1982 .... **CLC 6, 18, 32**
    See also CANR 3; CA 49-52;
    obituary CA 108; DLB 5

Hugo, Victor Marie
    1802-1885 .... **NCLC 3, 10, 21**
    See also SATA 47

Huidobro, Vicente 1893-1948 ..... **TCLC 31**

Hulme, Keri 1947- .... **CLC 39**
    See also CA 123

Hulme, T(homas) E(rnest)
    1883-1917 .... **TCLC 21**
    See also CA 117; DLB 19

Hume, David 1711-1776 .... **LC 7**

Humphrey, William 1924- .... **CLC 45**
    See also CA 77-80; DLB 6

Humphreys, Emyr (Owen) 1919- .... **CLC 47**
    See also CANR 3, 24; CA 5-8R; DLB 15

Humphreys, Josephine 1945- .... **CLC 34, 57**
    See also CA 121, 127

Hunt, E(verette) Howard (Jr.)
    1918- .... **CLC 3**
    See also CANR 2; CA 45-48

Hunt, (James Henry) Leigh
    1784-1859 .... **NCLC 1**

Hunter, Evan 1926- .... **CLC 11, 31**
    See also CANR 5; CA 5-8R; SATA 25;
    DLB-Y 82

Hunter, Kristin (Eggleston) 1931- ... **CLC 35**
    See also CLR 3; CANR 13; CA 13-16R;
    SATA 12; DLB 33

Hunter, Mollie (Maureen McIlwraith)
    1922- .... **CLC 21**
    See also McIlwraith, Maureen Mollie
    Hunter

Hunter, Robert ?-1734 .... **LC 7**

Hurston, Zora Neale
    1891-1960 .... **CLC 7, 30, 61; SSC 4**
    See also CA 85-88; DLB 51, 86

Huston, John (Marcellus)
    1906-1987 .... CLC 20
    See also CA 73-76; obituary CA 123;
    DLB 26

Huxley, Aldous (Leonard)
    1894-1963 .. CLC 1, 3, 4, 5, 8, 11, 18, 35
    See also CA 85-88; DLB 36

Huysmans, Charles Marie Georges
    1848-1907
    See Huysmans, Joris-Karl
    See also CA 104

Huysmans, Joris-Karl 1848-1907 ... TCLC 7
    See also Huysmans, Charles Marie Georges

Hwang, David Henry 1957-........ CLC 55
    See also CA 127

Hyde, Anthony 1946?-............. CLC 42

Hyde, Margaret O(ldroyd) 1917- ... CLC 21
    See also CANR 1; CA 1-4R; SATA 1, 42

Ian, Janis 1951- .... CLC 21
    See also CA 105

Ibarguengoitia, Jorge 1928-1983.... CLC 37
    See also obituary CA 113, 124

Ibsen, Henrik (Johan)
    1828-1906 .... TCLC 2, 8, 16, 37
    See also CA 104

Ibuse, Masuji 1898-................ CLC 22

Ichikawa, Kon 1915-............... CLC 20
    See also CA 121

Idle, Eric 1943-
    See Monty Python
    See also CA 116

Ignatow, David 1914-...... CLC 4, 7, 14, 40
    See also CAAS 3; CA 9-12R; DLB 5

Ihimaera, Witi (Tame) 1944-....... CLC 46
    See also CA 77-80

Ilf, Ilya 1897-1937 .... TCLC 21

Immermann, Karl (Lebrecht)
    1796-1840 .... NCLC 4

Ingalls, Rachel 19??-.............. CLC 42
    See also CA 123

Ingamells, Rex 1913-1955 .... TCLC 35

Inge, William (Motter)
    1913-1973 .... CLC 1, 8, 19
    See also CA 9-12R; DLB 7;
    CDALB 1941-1968

Innaurato, Albert 1948-........ CLC 21, 60
    See also CA 115, 122

Innes, Michael 1906-
    See Stewart, J(ohn) I(nnes) M(ackintosh)

Ionesco, Eugene
    1912- .... CLC 1, 4, 6, 9, 11, 15, 41
    See also CA 9-12R; SATA 7

Iqbal, Muhammad 1877-1938 ..... TCLC 28

Irving, John (Winslow)
    1942-.................. CLC 13, 23, 38
    See also CA 25-28R; DLB 6; DLB-Y 82

Irving, Washington
    1783-1859 .... NCLC 2, 19; SSC 2
    See also YABC 2; DLB 3, 11, 30, 59, 73,
    74; CDALB 1640-1865

Isaacs, Susan 1943- .... CLC 32
    See also CANR 20; CA 89-92

Isherwood, Christopher (William Bradshaw)
    1904-1986 .... CLC 1, 9, 11, 14, 44
    See also CA 13-16R; obituary CA 117;
    DLB 15; DLB-Y 86

Ishiguro, Kazuo 1954-...... CLC 27, 56, 59
    See also CA 120

Ishikawa Takuboku 1885-1912 .... TCLC 15
    See also CA 113

Iskander, Fazil (Abdulovich)
    1929-....................... CLC 47
    See also CA 102

Ivanov, Vyacheslav (Ivanovich)
    1866-1949 .... TCLC 33
    See also CA 122

Ivask, Ivar (Vidrik) 1927-....... CLC 14
    See also CANR 24; CA 37-40R

Jackson, Jesse 1908-1983 .... CLC 12
    See also CA 25-28R; obituary CA 109;
    SATA 2, 29, 48

Jackson, Laura (Riding) 1901-
    See Riding, Laura
    See also CA 65-68; DLB 48

Jackson, Shirley 1919-1965..... CLC 11, 60
    See also CANR 4; CA 1-4R;
    obituary CA 25-28R; SATA 2; DLB 6;
    CDALB 1941-1968

Jacob, (Cyprien) Max 1876-1944 ... TCLC 6
    See also CA 104

Jacob, Piers A(nthony) D(illingham) 1934-
    See Anthony (Jacob), Piers
    See also CA 21-24R

Jacobs, Jim 1942- and **Casey, Warren**
    1942-....................... CLC 12

Jacobs, Jim 1942-
    See Jacobs, Jim and Casey, Warren
    See also CA 97-100

Jacobs, W(illiam) W(ymark)
    1863-1943 .... TCLC 22
    See also CA 121

Jacobsen, Josephine 1908-......... CLC 48
    See also CANR 23; CA 33-36R

Jacobson, Dan 1929- .... CLC 4, 14
    See also CANR 2, 25; CA 1-4R; DLB 14

Jagger, Mick 1944-................ CLC 17

Jakes, John (William) 1932-...... CLC 29
    See also CANR 10; CA 57-60; DLB-Y 83

James, C(yril) L(ionel) R(obert)
    1901-1989 .... CLC 33
    See also CA 117, 125

James, Daniel 1911-1988
    See Santiago, Danny
    See also obituary CA 125

James, Henry (Jr.)
    1843-1916 .... TCLC 2, 11, 24
    See also CA 104; DLB 12, 71, 74;
    CDALB 1865-1917

James, M(ontague) R(hodes)
    1862-1936 .... TCLC 6
    See also CA 104

James, P(hyllis) D(orothy)
    1920-..................... CLC 18, 46
    See also CANR 17; CA 21-24R

James, William 1842-1910..... TCLC 15, 32
    See also CA 109

Jami, Nur al-Din 'Abd al-Rahman
    1414-1492 .... LC 9

Jandl, Ernst 1925- .... CLC 34

Janowitz, Tama 1957- .... CLC 43
    See also CA 106

Jarrell, Randall
    1914-1965 .... CLC 1, 2, 6, 9, 13, 49
    See also CLR 6; CANR 6; CA 5-8R;
    obituary CA 25-28R; CABS 2; SATA 7;
    DLB 48, 52; CDALB 1941-1968

Jarry, Alfred 1873-1907........ TCLC 2, 14
    See also CA 104

Jeake, Samuel, Jr. 1889-1973
    See Aiken, Conrad

Jean Paul 1763-1825 .... NCLC 7

Jeffers, (John) Robinson
    1887-1962 .... CLC 2, 3, 11, 15, 54
    See also CA 85-88; DLB 45

Jefferson, Thomas 1743-1826 .... NCLC 11
    See also DLB 31; CDALB 1640-1865

Jellicoe, (Patricia) Ann 1927-...... CLC 27
    See also CA 85-88; DLB 13

Jenkins, (John) Robin 1912-....... CLC 52
    See also CANR 1; CA 4Rk; DLB 14

Jennings, Elizabeth (Joan)
    1926-..................... CLC 5, 14
    See also CAAS 5; CANR 8; CA 61-64;
    DLB 27

Jennings, Waylon 1937-........... CLC 21

Jensen, Laura (Linnea) 1948-...... CLC 37
    See also CA 103

Jerome, Jerome K. 1859-1927..... TCLC 23
    See also CA 119; DLB 10, 34

Jerrold, Douglas William
    1803-1857 .... NCLC 2

Jewett, (Theodora) Sarah Orne
    1849-1909 .... TCLC 1, 22; SSC 6
    See also CA 108, 127; SATA 15; DLB 12,
    74

Jewsbury, Geraldine (Endsor)
    1812-1880 .... NCLC 22
    See also DLB 21

Jhabvala, Ruth Prawer
    1927-.................. CLC 4, 8, 29
    See also CANR 2; CA 1-4R

Jiles, Paulette 1943-........... CLC 13, 58
    See also CA 101

Jimenez (Mantecon), Juan Ramon
    1881-1958 .... TCLC 4
    See also CA 104

Joel, Billy 1949-................ CLC 26
    See also Joel, William Martin

Joel, William Martin 1949-
    See Joel, Billy
    See also CA 108

Johnson, B(ryan) S(tanley William)
    1933-1973 .... CLC 6, 9
    See also CANR 9; CA 9-12R;
    obituary CA 53-56; DLB 14, 40

Johnson, Charles (Richard)
    1948- .... CLC 7, 51
    See also CA 116; DLB 33

Johnson, Denis 1949-............. CLC 52
    See also CA 117, 121

Johnson, Diane 1934-....... **CLC 5, 13, 48**
See also CANR 17; CA 41-44R; DLB-Y 80

Johnson, Eyvind (Olof Verner)
1900-1976 .... **CLC 14**
See also CA 73-76; obituary CA 69-72

Johnson, James Weldon
1871-1938 .... **TCLC 3, 19**
See also Johnson, James William
See also CA 104, 125; DLB 51

Johnson, James William 1871-1938
See Johnson, James Weldon
See also SATA 31

Johnson, Joyce 1935-............. **CLC 58**
See also CA 125

Johnson, Lionel (Pigot)
1867-1902 .... **TCLC 19**
See also CA 117; DLB 19

Johnson, Marguerita 1928-
See Angelou, Maya

Johnson, Pamela Hansford
1912-1981 .... **CLC 1, 7, 27**
See also CANR 2; CA 1-4R;
obituary CA 104; DLB 15

Johnson, Uwe
1934-1984 .... **CLC 5, 10, 15, 40**
See also CANR 1; CA 1-4R;
obituary CA 112; DLB 75

Johnston, George (Benson) 1913-... **CLC 51**
See also CANR 5, 20; CA 1-4R

Johnston, Jennifer 1930-.......... **CLC 7**
See also CA 85-88; DLB 14

Jolley, Elizabeth 1923-............ **CLC 46**

Jones, D(ouglas) G(ordon) 1929-.... **CLC 10**
See also CANR 13; CA 113; DLB 53

Jones, David
1895-1974 .... **CLC 2, 4, 7, 13, 42**
See also CA 9-12R; obituary CA 53-56;
DLB 20

Jones, David Robert 1947-
See Bowie, David
See also CA 103

Jones, Diana Wynne 1934- .... **CLC 26**
See also CANR 4; CA 49-52; SATA 9

Jones, Gayl 1949-............... **CLC 6, 9**
See also CA 77-80; DLB 33

Jones, James 1921-1977.... **CLC 1, 3, 10, 39**
See also CANR 6; CA 1-4R;
obituary CA 69-72; DLB 2

Jones, (Everett) LeRoi
1934- .... **CLC 1, 2, 3, 5, 10, 14, 33**
See also Baraka, Amiri; Baraka, Imamu
Amiri
See also CA 21-24R

Jones, Madison (Percy, Jr.) 1925- ... **CLC 4**
See also CANR 7; CA 13-16R

Jones, Mervyn 1922-.......... **CLC 10, 52**
See also CAAS 5; CANR 1; CA 45-48

Jones, Mick 1956?-
See The Clash

Jones, Nettie 19??-............... **CLC 34**

Jones, Preston 1936-1979 .... **CLC 10**
See also CA 73-76; obituary CA 89-92;
DLB 7

Jones, Robert F(rancis) 1934-....... **CLC 7**
See also CANR 2; CA 49-52

Jones, Rod 1953- .... **CLC 50**

Jones, Terry 1942?-
See Monty Python
See also CA 112, 116; SATA 51

Jong, Erica 1942-.......... **CLC 4, 6, 8, 18**
See also CANR 26; CA 73-76; DLB 2, 5, 28

Jonson, Ben(jamin) 1572-1637....... **LC 6**
See also DLB 62

Jordan, June 1936-.......... **CLC 5, 11, 23**
See also CLR 10; CANR 25; CA 33-36R;
SATA 4; DLB 38

Jordan, Pat(rick M.) 1941-........ **CLC 37**
See also CANR 25; CA 33-36R

Josipovici, Gabriel (David)
1940-...................... **CLC 6, 43**
See also CA 37-40R; DLB 14

Joubert, Joseph 1754-1824 .... **NCLC 9**

Jouve, Pierre Jean 1887-1976...... **CLC 47**
See also obituary CA 65-68

Joyce, James (Augustine Aloysius)
1882-1941 ...... **TCLC 3, 8, 16, 26, 35;**
SSC 3
See also CA 104, 126; DLB 10, 19, 36

Jozsef, Attila 1905-1937......... **TCLC 22**
See also CA 116

Juana Ines de la Cruz 1651?-1695 .... **LC 5**

Julian of Norwich 1342?-1416?....... **LC 6**

Just, Ward S(wift) 1935- .... **CLC 4, 27**
See also CA 25-28R

Justice, Donald (Rodney) 1925- .. **CLC 6, 19**
See also CANR 26; CA 5-8R; DLB-Y 83

Kacew, Romain 1914-1980
See Gary, Romain
See also CA 108; obituary CA 102

Kacewgary, Romain 1914-1980
See Gary, Romain

Kadare, Ismail 1936- .... **CLC 52**

Kadohata, Cynthia 19??- .... **CLC 59**

Kafka, Franz
1883-1924 .... **TCLC 2, 6, 13, 29; SSC 5**
See also CA 105, 126; DLB 81

Kahn, Roger 1927-............... **CLC 30**
See also CA 25-28R; SATA 37

Kaiser, (Friedrich Karl) Georg
1878-1945.................... **TCLC 9**
See also CA 106

Kaletski, Alexander 1946-......... **CLC 39**
See also CA 118

Kallman, Chester (Simon)
1921-1975 .... **CLC 2**
See also CANR 3; CA 45-48;
obituary CA 53-56

Kaminsky, Melvin 1926-
See Brooks, Mel
See also CANR 16; CA 65-68

Kaminsky, Stuart 1934-.......... **CLC 59**
See also CA 73-76

Kane, Paul 1941-
See Simon, Paul

Kanin, Garson 1912-.............. **CLC 22**
See also CANR 7; CA 5-8R; DLB 7

Kaniuk, Yoram 1930-............. **CLC 19**

Kant, Immanuel 1724-1804 ...... **NCLC 27**

Kantor, MacKinlay 1904-1977 ...... **CLC 7**
See also CA 61-64; obituary CA 73-76;
DLB 9

Kaplan, David Michael 1946- ...... **CLC 50**

Kaplan, James 19??-............. **CLC 59**

Karamzin, Nikolai Mikhailovich
1766-1826 .... **NCLC 3**

Karapanou, Margarita 1946-....... **CLC 13**
See also CA 101

Karl, Frederick R(obert) 1927- ..... **CLC 34**
See also CANR 3; CA 5-8R

Kassef, Romain 1914-1980
See Gary, Romain

Katz, Steve 1935-................. **CLC 47**
See also CANR 12; CA 25-28R; DLB-Y 83

Kauffman, Janet 1945-............. **CLC 42**
See also CA 117; DLB-Y 86

Kaufman, Bob (Garnell)
1925-1986 .... **CLC 49**
See also CANR 22; CA 41-44R;
obituary CA 118; DLB 16, 41

Kaufman, George S(imon)
1889-1961 .... **CLC 38**
See also CA 108; obituary CA 93-96; DLB 7

Kaufman, Sue 1926-1977......... **CLC 3, 8**
See also Barondess, Sue K(aufman)

Kavan, Anna 1904-1968.......... **CLC 5, 13**
See also Edmonds, Helen (Woods)
See also CANR 6; CA 5-8R

Kavanagh, Patrick (Joseph Gregory)
1905-1967 .... **CLC 22**
See also CA 123; obituary CA 25-28R;
DLB 15, 20

Kawabata, Yasunari
1899-1972 .... **CLC 2, 5, 9, 18**
See also CA 93-96; obituary CA 33-36R

Kaye, M(ary) M(argaret) 1909?-.... **CLC 28**
See also CANR 24; CA 89-92

Kaye, Mollie 1909?-
See Kaye, M(ary) M(argaret)

Kaye-Smith, Sheila 1887-1956..... **TCLC 20**
See also CA 118; DLB 36

Kazan, Elia 1909-.............. **CLC 6, 16**
See also CA 21-24R

Kazantzakis, Nikos
1885?-1957............. **TCLC 2, 5, 33**
See also CA 105

Kazin, Alfred 1915- .... **CLC 34, 38**
See also CAAS 7; CANR 1; CA 1-4R

Keane, Mary Nesta (Skrine) 1904-
See Keane, Molly
See also CA 108, 114

Keane, Molly 1904- .... **CLC 31**
See also Keane, Mary Nesta (Skrine)

Keates, Jonathan 19??-............ **CLC 34**

Keaton, Buster 1895-1966 .... **CLC 20**

Keaton, Joseph Francis 1895-1966
See Keaton, Buster

Keats, John 1795-1821...... **NCLC 8; PC 1**

Keene, Donald 1922- .... **CLC 34**
See also CANR 5; CA 1-4R

Laxness, Halldor (Kiljan) 1902- .... **CLC 25**
See also Gudjonsson, Halldor Kiljan

Laye, Camara 1928-1980 .... **CLC 4, 38**
See also CA 85-88; obituary CA 97-100

Layton, Irving (Peter) 1912- ..... **CLC 2, 15**
See also CANR 2; CA 1-4R

Lazarus, Emma 1849-1887........ **NCLC 8**

Leacock, Stephen (Butler)
1869-1944 .... **TCLC 2**
See also CA 104

Lear, Edward 1812-1888 .... **NCLC 3**
See also CLR 1; SATA 18; DLB 32

Lear, Norman (Milton) 1922- ...... **CLC 12**
See also CA 73-76

Leavis, F(rank) R(aymond)
1895-1978 .... **CLC 24**
See also CA 21-24R; obituary CA 77-80

Leavitt, David 1961?-............. **CLC 34**
See also CA 116, 122

Lebowitz, Fran(ces Ann)
1951?- .... **CLC 11, 36**
See also CANR 14; CA 81-84

Le Carre, John 1931-... **CLC 3, 5, 9, 15, 28**
See also Cornwell, David (John Moore)

Le Clezio, J(ean) M(arie) G(ustave)
1940- .... **CLC 31**
See also CA 116

Leconte de Lisle, Charles-Marie-Rene
1818-1894 .... **NCLC 29**

Leduc, Violette 1907-1972........ **CLC 22**
See also CAP 1; CA 13-14;
obituary CA 33-36R

Ledwidge, Francis 1887-1917...... **TCLC 23**
See also CA 123; DLB 20

Lee, Andrea 1953- .... **CLC 36**
See also CA 125

Lee, Andrew 1917-
See Auchincloss, Louis (Stanton)

Lee, Don L. 1942-................. **CLC 2**
See also Madhubuti, Haki R.
See also CA 73-76

Lee, George Washington
1894-1976 .... **CLC 52**
See also CA 125; DLB 51

Lee, (Nelle) Harper 1926- ...... **CLC 12, 60**
See also CA 13-16R; SATA 11; DLB 6;
CDALB 1941-1968

Lee, Lawrence 1903- .... **CLC 34**
See also CA 25-28R

Lee, Manfred B(ennington) 1905-1971
See Queen, Ellery
See also CANR 2; CA 1-4R, 11;
obituary CA 29-32R

Lee, Stan 1922-.................. **CLC 17**
See also CA 108, 111

Lee, Tanith 1947-................. **CLC 46**
See also CA 37-40R; SATA 8

Lee, Vernon 1856-1935 .... **TCLC 5**
See also Paget, Violet
See also DLB 57

Lee-Hamilton, Eugene (Jacob)
1845-1907 .... **TCLC 22**

Leet, Judith 1935- .... **CLC 11**

Le Fanu, Joseph Sheridan
1814-1873 .... **NCLC 9**
See also DLB 21, 70

Leffland, Ella 1931- .... **CLC 19**
See also CA 29-32R; DLB-Y 84

Leger, (Marie-Rene) Alexis Saint-Leger
1887-1975
See Perse, St.-John
See also CA 13-16R; obituary CA 61-64

Le Guin, Ursula K(roeber)
1929- ....**CLC 8, 13, 22, 45**
See also CLR 3; CANR 9; CA 21-24R;
SATA 4, 52; DLB 8, 52

Lehmann, Rosamond (Nina) 1901- ... **CLC 5**
See also CANR 8; CA 77-80; DLB 15

Leiber, Fritz (Reuter, Jr.) 1910-.... **CLC 25**
See also CANR 2; CA 45-48; SATA 45;
DLB 8

Leino, Eino 1878-1926 .... **TCLC 24**

Leiris, Michel 1901-............... **CLC 61**
See also CA 119, 128

Leithauser, Brad 1953-............ **CLC 27**
See also CA 107

Lelchuk, Alan 1938-.............. **CLC 5**
See also CANR 1; CA 45-48

Lem, Stanislaw 1921-........ **CLC 8, 15, 40**
See also CAAS 1; CA 105

Lemann, Nancy 1956-............ **CLC 39**
See also CA 118

Lemonnier, (Antoine Louis) Camille
1844-1913 .... **TCLC 22**

Lenau, Nikolaus 1802-1850...... **NCLC 16**

L'Engle, Madeleine 1918- .... **CLC 12**
See also CLR 1, 14; CANR 3, 21; CA 1-4R;
SATA 1, 27; DLB 52

Lengyel, Jozsef 1896-1975.......... **CLC 7**
See also CA 85-88; obituary CA 57-60

Lennon, John (Ono)
1940-1980 .... **CLC 12, 35**
See also CA 102

Lennon, John Winston 1940-1980
See Lennon, John (Ono)

Lennox, Charlotte Ramsay 1729 or
1730-1804 .... **NCLC 23**
See also DLB 39, 39

Lennox, Charlotte Ramsay
1729?-1804.................. **NCLC 23**
See also DLB 39

Lentricchia, Frank (Jr.) 1940-...... **CLC 34**
See also CANR 19; CA 25-28R

Lenz, Siegfried 1926-............. **CLC 27**
See also CA 89-92; DLB 75

Leonard, Elmore 1925-........ **CLC 28, 34**
See also CANR 12; CA 81-84

Leonard, Hugh 1926-............. **CLC 19**
See also Byrne, John Keyes
See also DLB 13

Leopardi, (Conte) Giacomo (Talegardo
Francesco di Sales Saverio Pietro)
1798-1837 .... **NCLC 22**

Lerman, Eleanor 1952-............. **CLC 9**
See also CA 85-88

Lerman, Rhoda 1936-............. **CLC 56**
See also CA 49-52

Lermontov, Mikhail Yuryevich
1814-1841 .... **NCLC 5**

Leroux, Gaston 1868-1927........ **TCLC 25**
See also CA 108

Lesage, Alain-Rene 1668-1747........ **LC 2**

Leskov, Nikolai (Semyonovich)
1831-1895 .... **NCLC 25**

Lessing, Doris (May)
1919- .... **CLC 1, 2, 3, 6, 10, 15, 22, 40;**
SSC 6
See also CA 9-12R; DLB 15; DLB-Y 85

Lessing, Gotthold Ephraim
1729-1781 .... **LC 8**

Lester, Richard 1932-............. **CLC 20**

Lever, Charles (James)
1806-1872 .... **NCLC 23**
See also DLB 21

Leverson, Ada 1865-1936........ **TCLC 18**
See also CA 117

Levertov, Denise
1923-......... **CLC 1, 2, 3, 5, 8, 15, 28**
See also CANR 3; CA 1-4R; DLB 5

Levi, Peter (Chad Tiger) 1931- ..... **CLC 41**
See also CA 5-8R; DLB 40

Levi, Primo 1919-1987........ **CLC 37, 50**
See also CANR 12; CA 13-16R;
obituary CA 122

Levin, Ira 1929- .... **CLC 3, 6**
See also CANR 17; CA 21-24R

Levin, Meyer 1905-1981 .... **CLC 7**
See also CANR 15; CA 9-12R;
obituary CA 104; SATA 21;
obituary SATA 27; DLB 9, 28; DLB-Y 81

Levine, Norman 1924-............. **CLC 54**
See also CANR 14; CA 73-76

Levine, Philip 1928-... **CLC 2, 4, 5, 9, 14, 33**
See also CANR 9; CA 9-12R; DLB 5

Levinson, Deirdre 1931-............ **CLC 49**
See also CA 73-76

Levi-Strauss, Claude 1908- .... **CLC 38**
See also CANR 6; CA 1-4R

Levitin, Sonia 1934-.............. **CLC 17**
See also CANR 14; CA 29-32R; SAAS 2;
SATA 4

Lewes, George Henry
1817-1878 .... **NCLC 25**
See also DLB 55

Lewis, Alun 1915-1944............ **TCLC 3**
See also CA 104; DLB 20

Lewis, C(ecil) Day 1904-1972
See Day Lewis, C(ecil)

Lewis, C(live) S(taples)
1898-1963 .... **CLC 1, 3, 6, 14, 27**
See also CLR 3; CA 81-84; SATA 13;
DLB 15

Lewis (Winters), Janet 1899-....... **CLC 41**
See also Winters, Janet Lewis
See also DLB-Y 87

Lewis, Matthew Gregory
1775-1818 .... **NCLC 11**
See also DLB 39

Mitchell (Marsh), Margaret (Munnerlyn)
1900-1949 .... TCLC 11
See also CA 109; DLB 9

Mitchell, S. Weir 1829-1914 ..... TCLC 36

Mitchell, W(illiam) O(rmond)
1914- .... CLC 25
See also CANR 15; CA 77-80

Mitford, Mary Russell 1787-1855.. NCLC 4

Mitford, Nancy 1904-1973......... CLC 44
See also CA 9-12R

Miyamoto Yuriko 1899-1951...... TCLC 37

Mo, Timothy 1950-............... CLC 46
See also CA 117

Modarressi, Taghi 1931- .... CLC 44
See also CA 121

Modiano, Patrick (Jean) 1945-..... CLC 18
See also CANR 17; CA 85-88

Mofolo, Thomas (Mokopu)
1876-1948 .... TCLC 22
See also CA 121

Mohr, Nicholasa 1935-............ CLC 12
See also CLR 22; CANR 1; CA 49-52;
SATA 8

Mojtabai, A(nn) G(race)
1938- .... CLC 5, 9, 15, 29
See also CA 85-88

Moliere 1622-1673 .... LC 10

Molnar, Ferenc 1878-1952....... TCLC 20
See also CA 109

Momaday, N(avarre) Scott
1934- .... CLC 2, 19
See also CANR 14; CA 25-28R; SATA 30,
48

Monroe, Harriet 1860-1936...... TCLC 12
See also CA 109; DLB 54

Montagu, Elizabeth 1720-1800 .... NCLC 7

Montagu, Lady Mary (Pierrepont) Wortley
1689-1762 .... LC 9

Montague, John (Patrick)
1929- .... CLC 13, 46
See also CANR 9; CA 9-12R; DLB 40

Montaigne, Michel (Eyquem) de
1533-1592 .... LC 8

Montale, Eugenio 1896-1981... CLC 7, 9, 18
See also CA 17-20R; obituary CA 104

Montgomery, Marion (H., Jr.)
1925- .... CLC 7
See also CANR 3; CA 1-4R; DLB 6

Montgomery, Robert Bruce 1921-1978
See Crispin, Edmund
See also CA 104

Montherlant, Henri (Milon) de
1896-1972 .... CLC 8, 19
See also CA 85-88; obituary CA 37-40R;
DLB 72

Montisquieu, Charles-Louis de Secondat
1689-1755 .... LC 7

Monty Python.................... CLC 21

Moodie, Susanna (Strickland)
1803-1885 .... NCLC 14

Mooney, Ted 1951-.............. CLC 25

Moorcock, Michael (John)
1939- .... CLC 5, 27, 58
See also CAAS 5; CANR 2, 17; CA 45-48;
DLB 14

Moore, Brian
1921- .... CLC 1, 3, 5, 7, 8, 19, 32
See also CANR 1; CA 1-4R

Moore, George (Augustus)
1852-1933 .... TCLC 7
See also CA 104; DLB 10, 18, 57

Moore, Lorrie 1957-........... CLC 39, 45
See also Moore, Marie Lorena

Moore, Marianne (Craig)
1887-1972 ... CLC 1, 2, 4, 8, 10, 13, 19,
47
See also CANR 3; CA 1-4R;
obituary CA 33-36R; SATA 20; DLB 45

Moore, Marie Lorena 1957-
See Moore, Lorrie
See also CA 116

Moore, Thomas 1779-1852....... NCLC 6

Morand, Paul 1888-1976.......... CLC 41
See also obituary CA 69-72; DLB 65

Morante, Elsa 1918-1985........ CLC 8, 47
See also CA 85-88; obituary CA 117

Moravia, Alberto
1907- .... CLC 2, 7, 11, 18, 27, 46
See also Pincherle, Alberto

More, Hannah 1745-1833 .... NCLC 27

More, Henry 1614-1687............. LC 9

More, Thomas 1478-1573........... LC 10

Moreas, Jean 1856-1910 .... TCLC 18

Morgan, Berry 1919-.............. CLC 6
See also CA 49-52; DLB 6

Morgan, Edwin (George) 1920-..... CLC 31
See also CANR 3; CA 7-8R; DLB 27

Morgan, (George) Frederick
1922- .... CLC 23
See also CANR 21; CA 17-20R

Morgan, Janet 1945- .... CLC 39
See also CA 65-68

Morgan, Lady 1776?-1859....... NCLC 29

Morgan, Robin 1941-............. CLC 2
See also CA 69-72

Morgenstern, Christian (Otto Josef Wolfgang)
1871-1914 .... TCLC 8
See also CA 105

Moricz, Zsigmond 1879-1942 ..... TCLC 33

Morike, Eduard (Friedrich)
1804-1875 .... NCLC 10

Mori Ogai 1862-1922........... TCLC 14
See also Mori Rintaro

Mori Rintaro 1862-1922
See Mori Ogai
See also CA 110

Moritz, Karl Philipp 1756-1793 ...... LC 2

Morris, Julian 1916-
See West, Morris L.

Morris, Steveland Judkins 1950-
See Wonder, Stevie
See also CA 111

Morris, William 1834-1896 .... NCLC 4
See also DLB 18, 35, 57

Morris, Wright (Marion)
1910- .... CLC 1, 3, 7, 18, 37
See also CA 9-12R; DLB 2; DLB-Y 81

Morrison, James Douglas 1943-1971
See Morrison, Jim
See also CA 73-76

Morrison, Jim 1943-1971......... CLC 17
See also Morrison, James Douglas

Morrison, Toni 1931-..... CLC 4, 10, 22, 55
See also CA 29-32R; DLB 6, 33; DLB-Y 81;
AAYA 1

Morrison, Van 1945- .... CLC 21
See also CA 116

Mortimer, John (Clifford)
1923- .... CLC 28, 43
See also CANR 21; CA 13-16R; DLB 13

Mortimer, Penelope (Ruth) 1918-.... CLC 5
See also CA 57-60

Mosher, Howard Frank 19??-...... CLC 62

Mosley, Nicholas 1923-........... CLC 43
See also CA 69-72; DLB 14

Moss, Howard
1922-1987 .... CLC 7, 14, 45, 50
See also CANR 1; CA 1-4R; DLB 5

Motion, Andrew (Peter) 1952-...... CLC 47
See also DLB 40

Motley, Willard (Francis)
1912-1965 .... CLC 18
See also CA 117; obituary CA 106

Mott, Michael (Charles Alston)
1930- .... CLC 15, 34
See also CAAS 7; CANR 7; CA 5-8R

Mowat, Farley (McGill) 1921- ..... CLC 26
See also CLR 20; CANR 4; CA 1-4R;
SATA 3; DLB 68

Mphahlele, Es'kia 1919-
See Mphahlele, Ezekiel

Mphahlele, Ezekiel 1919-......... CLC 25
See also CA 81-84

Mqhayi, S(amuel) E(dward) K(rune Loliwe)
1875-1945 .... TCLC 25

Mrozek, Slawomir 1930-........ CLC 3, 13
See also CA 13-16R

Mtwa, Percy 19??-............... CLC 47

Mueller, Lisel 1924-........... CLC 13, 51
See also CA 93-96

Muir, Edwin 1887-1959 .... TCLC 2
See also CA 104; DLB 20

Muir, John 1838-1914 .... TCLC 28

Mujica Lainez, Manuel
1910-1984 .... CLC 31
See also CA 81-84; obituary CA 112

Mukherjee, Bharati 1940-........ CLC 53
See also CA 107; DLB 60

Muldoon, Paul 1951-............ CLC 32
See also CA 113; DLB 40

Mulisch, Harry (Kurt Victor)
1927- .... CLC 42
See also CANR 6; CA 9-12R

Mull, Martin 1943-............... CLC 17
See also CA 105

Munford, Robert 1737?-1783........ LC 5
See also DLB 31

Munro, Alice (Laidlaw)
　1931- .... **CLC 6, 10, 19, 50; SSC 3**
　See also CA 33-36R; SATA 29; DLB 53

Munro, H(ector) H(ugh)　1870-1916
　See Saki
　See also CA 104; DLB 34

Murasaki, Lady　c. 11th century-... **CMLC 1**

Murdoch, (Jean) Iris
　1919- ...... **CLC 1, 2, 3, 4, 6, 8, 11, 15,
　　　　　　22, 31, 51**
　See also CANR 8; CA 13-16R; DLB 14

Murphy, Richard　1927- .... **CLC 41**
　See also CA 29-32R; DLB 40

Murphy, Sylvia　19??- .... **CLC 34**

Murphy, Thomas (Bernard)　1935-... **CLC 51**
　See also CA 101

Murray, Les(lie) A(llan)　1938- ..... **CLC 40**
　See also CANR 11; CA 21-24R

Murry, John Middleton
　1889-1957 .... **TCLC 16**
　See also CA 118

Musgrave, Susan　1951- .... **CLC 13, 54**
　See also CA 69-72

Musil, Robert (Edler von)
　1880-1942 .... **TCLC 12**
　See also CA 109

Musset, (Louis Charles) Alfred de
　1810-1857 .... **NCLC 7**

Myers, Walter Dean　1937- .... **CLC 35**
　See also CLR 4, 16; CANR 20; CA 33-36R;
　SAAS 2; SATA 27, 41; DLB 33

Nabokov, Vladimir (Vladimirovich)
　1899-1977 .... **CLC 1, 2, 3, 6, 8, 11, 15,
　　　　　　23, 44, 46**
　See also CANR 20; CA 5-8R;
　　obituary CA 69-72; DLB 2; DLB-Y 80;
　　DLB-DS 3; CDALB 1941-1968

Nagy, Laszlo　1925-1978 .... **CLC 7**
　See also obituary CA 112

Naipaul, Shiva(dhar Srinivasa)
　1945-1985 .... **CLC 32, 39**
　See also CA 110, 112; obituary CA 116;
　DLB-Y 85

Naipaul, V(idiadhar) S(urajprasad)
　1932- .... **CLC 4, 7, 9, 13, 18, 37**
　See also CANR 1; CA 1-4R; DLB-Y 85

Nakos, Ioulia　1899?-
　See Nakos, Lilika

Nakos, Lilika　1899?- .... **CLC 29**

Nakou, Lilika　1899?-
　See Nakos, Lilika

Narayan, R(asipuram) K(rishnaswami)
　1906- .... **CLC 7, 28, 47**
　See also CA 81-84

Nash, (Frediric) Ogden　1902-1971 .. **CLC 23**
　See also CAP 1; CA 13-14;
　　obituary CA 29-32R; SATA 2, 46;
　DLB 11

Nathan, George Jean　1882-1958 ... **TCLC 18**
　See also CA 114

Natsume, Kinnosuke　1867-1916
　See Natsume, Soseki
　See also CA 104

Natsume, Soseki　1867-1916 ..... **TCLC 2, 10**
　See also Natsume, Kinnosuke

Natti, (Mary) Lee　1919-
　See Kingman, (Mary) Lee
　See also CANR 2; CA 7-8R

Naylor, Gloria　1950- .... **CLC 28, 52**
　See also CANR 27; CA 107

Neff, Debra　1972- .... **CLC 59**

Neihardt, John G(neisenau)
　1881-1973 .... **CLC 32**
　See also CAP 1; CA 13-14; DLB 9, 54

Nekrasov, Nikolai Alekseevich
　1821-1878 .... **NCLC 11**

Nelligan, Emile　1879-1941 .... **TCLC 14**
　See also CA 114

Nelson, Willie　1933- .... **CLC 17**
　See also CA 107

Nemerov, Howard　1920- ... **CLC 2, 6, 9, 36**
　See also CANR 1; CA 1-4R; CABS 2;
　DLB 5, 6; DLB-Y 83

Neruda, Pablo
　1904-1973 ..... **CLC 1, 2, 5, 7, 9, 28, 62**
　See also CAP 2; CA 19-20;
　　obituary CA 45-48

Nerval, Gerard de　1808-1855 ...... **NCLC 1**

Nervo, (Jose) Amado (Ruiz de)
　1870-1919 .... **TCLC 11**
　See also CA 109

Neufeld, John (Arthur)　1938- ...... **CLC 17**
　See also CANR 11; CA 25-28R; SAAS 3;
　SATA 6

Neville, Emily Cheney　1919- .... **CLC 12**
　See also CANR 3; CA 5-8R; SAAS 2;
　SATA 1

Newbound, Bernard Slade　1930-
　See Slade, Bernard
　See also CA 81-84

Newby, P(ercy) H(oward)
　1918- .... **CLC 2, 13**
　See also CA 5-8R; DLB 15

Newlove, Donald　1928- .... **CLC 6**
　See also CANR 25; CA 29-32R

Newlove, John (Herbert)　1938- ..... **CLC 14**
　See also CANR 9, 25; CA 21-24R

Newman, Charles　1938- .... **CLC 2, 8**
　See also CA 21-24R

Newman, Edwin (Harold)　1919- .... **CLC 14**
　See also CANR 5; CA 69-72

Newton, Suzanne　1936- .... **CLC 35**
　See also CANR 14; CA 41-44R; SATA 5

Ngema, Mbongeni　1955- .... **CLC 57**

Ngugi, James (Thiong'o)
　1938- .... **CLC 3, 7, 13, 36**
　See also Ngugi wa Thiong'o; Wa Thiong'o,
　Ngugi
　See also CA 81-84

Ngugi wa Thiong'o　1938-... **CLC 3, 7, 13, 36**
　See also Ngugi, James (Thiong'o); Wa
　Thiong'o, Ngugi

Nichol, B(arrie) P(hillip)　1944- ..... **CLC 18**
　See also CA 53-56; DLB 53

Nichols, John (Treadwell)　1940-.... **CLC 38**
　See also CAAS 2; CANR 6; CA 9-12R;
　DLB-Y 82

Nichols, Peter (Richard)　1927-... **CLC 5, 36**
　See also CA 104; DLB 13

Nicolas, F.R.E.　1927-
　See Freeling, Nicolas

Niedecker, Lorine　1903-1970.... **CLC 10, 42**
　See also CAP 2; CA 25-28; DLB 48

Nietzsche, Friedrich (Wilhelm)
　1844-1900 .... **TCLC 10, 18**
　See also CA 107

Nievo, Ippolito　1831-1861 .... **NCLC 22**

Nightingale, Anne Redmon　1943-
　See Redmon (Nightingale), Anne
　See also CA 103

Nin, Anais
　1903-1977 ...... **CLC 1, 4, 8, 11, 14, 60**
　See also CANR 22; CA 13-16R;
　　obituary CA 69-72; DLB 2, 4

Nissenson, Hugh　1933-........... **CLC 4, 9**
　See also CA 17-20R; DLB 28

Niven, Larry　1938- .... **CLC 8**
　See also Niven, Laurence Van Cott
　See also DLB 8

Niven, Laurence Van Cott　1938-
　See Niven, Larry
　See also CANR 14; CA 21-24R

Nixon, Agnes Eckhardt　1927-...... **CLC 21**
　See also CA 110

Nkosi, Lewis　1936-.............. **CLC 45**
　See also CA 65-68

Nodier, (Jean) Charles (Emmanuel)
　1780-1844 .... **NCLC 19**

Nolan, Christopher　1965-.......... **CLC 58**
　See also CA 111

Nordhoff, Charles　1887-1947...... **TCLC 23**
　See also CA 108; SATA 23; DLB 9

Norman, Marsha　1947- .... **CLC 28**
　See also CA 105; DLB-Y 84

Norris, (Benjamin) Frank(lin)
　1870-1902 .... **TCLC 24**
　See also CA 110; DLB 12, 71;
　CDALB 1865-1917

Norris, Leslie　1921- .... **CLC 14**
　See also CANR 14; CAP 1; CA 11-12;
　DLB 27

North, Andrew　1912-
　See Norton, Andre

North, Christopher　1785-1854
　See Wilson, John

Norton, Alice Mary　1912-
　See Norton, Andre
　See also CANR 2; CA 1-4R; SATA 1, 43

Norton, Andre　1912- .... **CLC 12**
　See also Norton, Mary Alice
　See also DLB 8, 52

Norway, Nevil Shute　1899-1960
　See Shute (Norway), Nevil
　See also CA 102; obituary CA 93-96

Norwid, Cyprian Kamil
　1821-1883 .... **NCLC 17**

Nossack, Hans Erich　1901-1978 ..... **CLC 6**
　See also CA 93-96; obituary CA 85-88;
　DLB 69

Nova, Craig　1945-.............. **CLC 7, 31**
　See also CANR 2; CA 45-48

Pynchon, Thomas (Ruggles, Jr.)
1937- . . . . . **CLC 2, 3, 6, 9, 11, 18, 33, 62**
See also CANR 22; CA 17-20R; DLB 2

Quasimodo, Salvatore 1901-1968 . . . **CLC 10**
See also CAP 1; CA 15-16;
obituary CA 25-28R

Queen, Ellery 1905-1982 . . . . **CLC 3, 11**
See also Dannay, Frederic; Lee, Manfred
B(ennington)

Queneau, Raymond
1903-1976 . . . . **CLC 2, 5, 10, 42**
See also CA 77-80; obituary CA 69-72;
DLB 72

Quin, Ann (Marie) 1936-1973 . . . . . . **CLC 6**
See also CA 9-12R; obituary CA 45-48;
DLB 14

Quinn, Simon 1942-
See Smith, Martin Cruz
See also CANR 6, 23; CA 85-88

Quiroga, Horacio (Sylvestre)
1878-1937 . . . . **TCLC 20**
See also CA 117

Quoirez, Francoise 1935-
See Sagan, Francoise
See also CANR 6; CA 49-52

Rabe, David (William) 1940-. . . **CLC 4, 8, 33**
See also CA 85-88; DLB 7

Rabelais, Francois 1494?-1553 . . . . **LC 5**

Rabinovitch, Sholem 1859-1916
See Aleichem, Sholom
See also CA 104

Rachen, Kurt von 1911-1986
See Hubbard, L(afayette) Ron(ald)

Radcliffe, Ann (Ward) 1764-1823 . . **NCLC 6**
See also DLB 39

Radiguet, Raymond 1903-1923 . . . . **TCLC 29**

Radnoti, Miklos 1909-1944 . . . . . . **TCLC 16**
See also CA 118

Rado, James 1939-. . . . . **CLC 17**
See also CA 105

Radomski, James 1932-
See Rado, James

Radvanyi, Netty Reiling 1900-1983
See Seghers, Anna
See also CA 85-88; obituary CA 110

Rae, Ben 1935-
See Griffiths, Trevor

Raeburn, John 1941- . . . . **CLC 34**
See also CA 57-60

Ragni, Gerome 1942- . . . . **CLC 17**
See also CA 105

Rahv, Philip 1908-1973 . . . . **CLC 24**
See also Greenberg, Ivan

Raine, Craig 1944-. . . . . **CLC 32**
See also CA 108; DLB 40

Raine, Kathleen (Jessie) 1908- . . . **CLC 7, 45**
See also CA 85-88; DLB 20

Rainis, Janis 1865-1929. . . . . **TCLC 29**

Rakosi, Carl 1903- . . . . **CLC 47**
See also Rawley, Callman
See also CAAS 5

Ramos, Graciliano 1892-1953 . . . . . **TCLC 32**

Rampersad, Arnold 19??-. . . . . **CLC 44**

Ramuz, Charles-Ferdinand
1878-1947 . . . . **TCLC 33**

Rand, Ayn 1905-1982. . . . . . . **CLC 3, 30, 44**
See also CA 13-16R; obituary CA 105

Randall, Dudley (Felker) 1914-. . . . . . **CLC 1**
See also CANR 23; CA 25-28R; DLB 41

Ransom, John Crowe
1888-1974 . . . . **CLC 2, 4, 5, 11, 24**
See also CANR 6; CA 5-8R;
obituary CA 49-52; DLB 45, 63

Rao, Raja 1909- . . . . **CLC 25, 56**
See also CA 73-76

Raphael, Frederic (Michael)
1931- . . . . **CLC 2, 14**
See also CANR 1; CA 1-4R; DLB 14

Rathbone, Julian 1935- . . . . **CLC 41**
See also CA 101

Rattigan, Terence (Mervyn)
1911-1977 . . . . **CLC 7**
See also CA 85-88; obituary CA 73-76;
DLB 13

Ratushinskaya, Irina 1954- . . . . **CLC 54**

Raven, Simon (Arthur Noel)
1927- . . . . **CLC 14**
See also CA 81-84

Rawley, Callman 1903-
See Rakosi, Carl
See also CANR 12; CA 21-24R

Rawlings, Marjorie Kinnan
1896-1953 . . . . **TCLC 4**
See also YABC 1; CA 104; DLB 9, 22

Ray, Satyajit 1921-. . . . . **CLC 16**
See also CA 114

Read, Herbert (Edward) 1893-1968 . . **CLC 4**
See also CA 85-88; obituary CA 25-28R;
DLB 20

Read, Piers Paul 1941- . . . . . . **CLC 4, 10, 25**
See also CA 21-24R; SATA 21; DLB 14

Reade, Charles 1814-1884 . . . . **NCLC 2**
See also DLB 21

Reade, Hamish 1936-
See Gray, Simon (James Holliday)

Reading, Peter 1946- . . . . **CLC 47**
See also CA 103; DLB 40

Reaney, James 1926- . . . . **CLC 13**
See also CA 41-44R; SATA 43; DLB 68

Rebreanu, Liviu 1885-1944 . . . . **TCLC 28**

Rechy, John (Francisco)
1934- . . . . **CLC 1, 7, 14, 18**
See also CAAS 4; CANR 6; CA 5-8R;
DLB-Y 82

Redcam, Tom 1870-1933 . . . . **TCLC 25**

Redgrove, Peter (William)
1932- . . . . **CLC 6, 41**
See also CANR 3; CA 1-4R; DLB 40

Redmon (Nightingale), Anne
1943- . . . . **CLC 22**
See also Nightingale, Anne Redmon
See also DLB-Y 86

Reed, Ishmael
1938- . . . . **CLC 2, 3, 5, 6, 13, 32, 60**
See also CANR 25; CA 21-24R; DLB 2, 5,
33

Reed, John (Silas) 1887-1920 . . . . . . **TCLC 9**
See also CA 106

Reed, Lou 1944-. . . . . **CLC 21**

Reeve, Clara 1729-1807 . . . . **NCLC 19**
See also DLB 39

Reid, Christopher 1949-. . . . . **CLC 33**
See also DLB 40

Reid Banks, Lynne 1929-
See Banks, Lynne Reid
See also CANR 6, 22; CA 1-4R; SATA 22

Reiner, Max 1900-
See Caldwell, (Janet Miriam) Taylor
(Holland)

Reizenstein, Elmer Leopold 1892-1967
See Rice, Elmer

Remark, Erich Paul 1898-1970
See Remarque, Erich Maria

Remarque, Erich Maria
1898-1970 . . . . **CLC 21**
See also CA 77-80; obituary CA 29-32R;
DLB 56

Remizov, Alexey (Mikhailovich)
1877-1957 . . . . **TCLC 27**
See also CA 125

Renan, Joseph Ernest
1823-1892 . . . . **NCLC 26**

Renard, Jules 1864-1910 . . . . **TCLC 17**
See also CA 117

Renault, Mary 1905-1983 . . . . **CLC 3, 11, 17**
See also Challans, Mary
See also DLB-Y 83

Rendell, Ruth 1930-. . . . . **CLC 28, 48**
See also Vine, Barbara
See also CA 109

Renoir, Jean 1894-1979 . . . . **CLC 20**
See also obituary CA 85-88

Resnais, Alain 1922-. . . . . **CLC 16**

Reverdy, Pierre 1899-1960 . . . . **CLC 53**
See also CA 97 100; obituary CA 89-92

Rexroth, Kenneth
1905-1982 . . . . . . **CLC 1, 2, 6, 11, 22, 49**
See also CANR 14; CA 5-8R;
obituary CA 107; DLB 16, 48; DLB-Y 82;
CDALB 1941-1968

Reyes, Alfonso 1889-1959 . . . . **TCLC 33**

Reyes y Basoalto, Ricardo Eliecer Neftali
1904-1973
See Neruda, Pablo

Reymont, Wladyslaw Stanislaw
1867-1925 . . . . **TCLC 5**
See also CA 104

Reynolds, Jonathan 1942?- . . . . . . **CLC 6, 38**
See also CA 65-68

Reynolds, Michael (Shane) 1937- . . . **CLC 44**
See also CANR 9; CA 65-68

Reznikoff, Charles 1894-1976 . . . . **CLC 9**
See also CAP 2; CA 33-36;
obituary CA 61-64; DLB 28, 45

Rezzori, Gregor von 1914-. . . . . **CLC 25**
See also CA 122

Rhys, Jean
1890-1979 . . . . . . **CLC 2, 4, 6, 14, 19, 51**
See also CA 25-28R; obituary CA 85-88;
DLB 36

Author Index

Santos, Bienvenido N(uqui) 1911-... **CLC 22**
See also CANR 19; CA 101

Sappho c. 6th-century B.C.-....... **CMLC 3**

Sarduy, Severo 1937-.............. **CLC 6**
See also CA 89-92

Sargeson, Frank 1903-1982 .... **CLC 31**
See also CA 106, 25-28R; obituary CA 106

Sarmiento, Felix Ruben Garcia 1867-1916
See Dario, Ruben
See also CA 104

Saroyan, William
1908-1981 ..... **CLC 1, 8, 10, 29, 34, 56**
See also CA 5-8R; obituary CA 103;
SATA 23; obituary SATA 24; DLB 7, 9;
DLB-Y 81

Sarraute, Nathalie
1902- .... **CLC 1, 2, 4, 8, 10, 31**
See also CANR 23; CA 9-12R

Sarton, Eleanore Marie 1912-
See Sarton, (Eleanor) May

Sarton, (Eleanor) May
1912- .... **CLC 4, 14, 49**
See also CANR 1; CA 1-4R; SATA 36;
DLB 48; DLB-Y 81

Sartre, Jean-Paul (Charles Aymard)
1905-1980 ... **CLC 1, 4, 7, 9, 13, 18, 24,
44, 50, 52**
See also CANR 21; CA 9-12R;
obituary CA 97-100; DLB 72

Sassoon, Siegfried (Lorraine)
1886-1967 .... **CLC 36**
See also CA 104; obituary CA 25-28R;
DLB 20

Saul, John (W. III) 1942- .... **CLC 46**
See also CANR 16; CA 81-84

Saura, Carlos 1932- .... **CLC 20**
See also CA 114

Sauser-Hall, Frederic-Louis 1887-1961
See Cendrars, Blaise
See also CA 102; obituary CA 93-96

Savage, Thomas 1915- .... **CLC 40**

Savan, Glenn 19??-............... **CLC 50**

Sayers, Dorothy L(eigh)
1893-1957 .... **TCLC 2, 15**
See also CA 104, 119; DLB 10, 36

Sayers, Valerie 19??- .... **CLC 50**

Sayles, John (Thomas)
1950- .... **CLC 7, 10, 14**
See also CA 57-60; DLB 44

Scammell, Michael 19??-.......... **CLC 34**

Scannell, Vernon 1922- .... **CLC 49**
See also CANR 8; CA 5-8R; DLB 27

Schaeffer, Susan Fromberg
1941-.................. **CLC 6, 11, 22**
See also CANR 18; CA 49-52; SATA 22;
DLB 28

Schell, Jonathan 1943-............ **CLC 35**
See also CANR 12; CA 73-76

Scherer, Jean-Marie Maurice 1920-
See Rohmer, Eric
See also CA 110

Schevill, James (Erwin) 1920-....... **CLC 7**
See also CA 5-8R

Schisgal, Murray (Joseph) 1926-..... **CLC 6**
See also CA 21-24R

Schlee, Ann 1934-................ **CLC 35**
See also CA 101; SATA 36, 44

Schlegel, August Wilhelm von
1767-1845 .... **NCLC 15**

Schlegel, Johann Elias (von)
1719?-1749................... **LC 5**

Schmidt, Arno 1914-1979......... **CLC 56**
See also obituary CA 109; DLB 69

Schmitz, Ettore 1861-1928
See Svevo, Italo
See also CA 104, 122

Schnackenberg, Gjertrud 1953-..... **CLC 40**
See also CA 116

Schneider, Leonard Alfred 1925-1966
See Bruce, Lenny
See also CA 89-92

Schnitzler, Arthur 1862-1931 ...... **TCLC 4**
See also CA 104

Schorer, Mark 1908-1977 .... **CLC 9**
See also CANR 7; CA 5-8R;
obituary CA 73-76

Schrader, Paul (Joseph) 1946-...... **CLC 26**
See also CA 37-40R; DLB 44

Schreiner (Cronwright), Olive (Emilie
Albertina) 1855-1920......... **TCLC 9**
See also CA 105; DLB 18

Schulberg, Budd (Wilson)
1914- .... **CLC 7, 48**
See also CANR 19; CA 25-28R; DLB 6, 26,
28; DLB-Y 81

Schulz, Bruno 1892-1942.......... **TCLC 5**
See also CA 115, 123

Schulz, Charles M(onroe) 1922- .... **CLC 12**
See also CANR 6; CA 9-12R; SATA 10

Schuyler, James (Marcus)
1923- .... **CLC 5, 23**
See also CA 101; DLB 5

Schwartz, Delmore
1913-1966 .... **CLC 2, 4, 10, 45**
See also CAP 2; CA 17-18;
obituary CA 25-28R; DLB 28, 48

Schwartz, John Burnham 1925- .... **CLC 59**

Schwartz, Lynne Sharon 1939-..... **CLC 31**
See also CA 103

Schwarz-Bart, Andre 1928-....... **CLC 2, 4**
See also CA 89-92

Schwarz-Bart, Simone 1938-........ **CLC 7**
See also CA 97-100

Schwob, (Mayer Andre) Marcel
1867-1905 .... **TCLC 20**
See also CA 117

Sciascia, Leonardo
1921-1989 .... **CLC 8, 9, 41**
See also CA 85-88

Scoppettone, Sandra 1936-........ **CLC 26**
See also CA 5-8R; SATA 9

Scorsese, Martin 1942- .... **CLC 20**
See also CA 110, 114

Scotland, Jay 1932-
See Jakes, John (William)

Scott, Duncan Campbell
1862-1947 .... **TCLC 6**
See also CA 104

Scott, Evelyn 1893-1963.......... **CLC 43**
See also CA 104; obituary CA 112; DLB 9,
48

Scott, F(rancis) R(eginald)
1899-1985 .... **CLC 22**
See also CA 101; obituary CA 114

Scott, Joanna 19??-............... **CLC 50**
See also CA 126

Scott, Paul (Mark) 1920-1978.... **CLC 9, 60**
See also CA 81-84; obituary CA 77-80;
DLB 14

Scott, Sir Walter 1771-1832 ..... **NCLC 15**
See also YABC 2

Scribe, (Augustin) Eugene
1791-1861 .... **NCLC 16**

Scudery, Madeleine de 1607-1701..... **LC 2**

Sealy, I. Allan 1951- .... **CLC 55**

Seare, Nicholas 1925-
See Trevanian; Whitaker, Rodney

Sebestyen, Igen 1924-
See Sebestyen, Ouida

Sebestyen, Ouida 1924-........... **CLC 30**
See also CA 107; SATA 39

Sedgwick, Catharine Maria
1789-1867 .... **NCLC 19**
See also DLB 1

Seelye, John 1931-................ **CLC 7**
See also CA 97-100

Seferiades, Giorgos Stylianou 1900-1971
See Seferis, George
See also CANR 5; CA 5-8R;
obituary CA 33-36R

Seferis, George 1900-1971....... **CLC 5, 11**
See also Seferiades, Giorgos Stylianou

Segal, Erich (Wolf) 1937- .... **CLC 3, 10**
See also CANR 20; CA 25-28R; DLB-Y 86

Seger, Bob 1945-................. **CLC 35**

Seger, Robert Clark 1945-
See Seger, Bob

Seghers, Anna 1900-1983....... **CLC 7, 110**
See also Radvanyi, Netty Reiling
See also DLB 69

Seidel, Frederick (Lewis) 1936-..... **CLC 18**
See also CANR 8; CA 13-16R; DLB-Y 84

Seifert, Jaroslav 1901-1986..... **CLC 34, 44**

Sei Shonagon c. 966-1017?........ **CMLC 6**

Selby, Hubert, Jr. 1928- .....**CLC 1, 2, 4, 8**
See also CA 13-16R; DLB 2

Senacour, Etienne Pivert de
1770-1846 .... **NCLC 16**

Sender, Ramon (Jose) 1902-1982 .... **CLC 8**
See also CANR 8; CA 5-8R;
obituary CA 105

Seneca, Lucius Annaeus
4 B.C.-65 A.D. .... **CMLC 6**

Senghor, Léopold Sédar 1906-...... **CLC 54**
See also CA 116

Simon, Carly 1945-.............. CLC 26
See also CA 105

Simon, Claude (Henri Eugene)
1913-.................CLC 4, 9, 15, 39
See also CA 89-92

Simon, (Marvin) Neil
1927-............... CLC 6, 11, 31, 39
See also CA 21-24R; DLB 7

Simon, Paul 1941-............... CLC 17
See also CA 116

Simonon, Paul 1956?-
See The Clash

Simpson, Louis (Aston Marantz)
1923-.................CLC 4, 7, 9, 32
See also CAAS 4; CANR 1; CA 1-4R;
DLB 5

Simpson, Mona (Elizabeth) 1957-... CLC 44
See also CA 122

Simpson, N(orman) F(rederick)
1919-............................ CLC 29
See also CA 11-14R; DLB 13

Sinclair, Andrew (Annandale)
1935-...................... CLC 2, 14
See also CAAS 5; CANR 14; CA 9-12R;
DLB 14

Sinclair, Mary Amelia St. Clair 1865?-1946
See Sinclair, May
See also CA 104

Sinclair, May 1865?-1946 ...... TCLC 3, 11
See also Sinclair, Mary Amelia St. Clair
See also DLB 36

Sinclair, Upton (Beall)
1878-1968 .... CLC 1, 11, 15
See also CANR 7; CA 5-8R;
obituary CA 25-28R; SATA 9; DLB 9

Singer, Isaac Bashevis
1904-.... CLC 1, 3, 6, 9, 11, 15, 23, 38;
SSC 3
See also CLR 1; CANR 1; CA 1-4R;
SATA 3, 27; DLB 6, 28, 52;
CDALB 1941-1968

Singer, Israel Joshua 1893-1944 ... TCLC 33

Singh, Khushwant 1915-........... CLC 11
See also CANR 6; CA 9-12R

Sinyavsky, Andrei (Donatevich)
1925-............................ CLC 8
See also CA 85-88

Sirin, V.
See Nabokov, Vladimir (Vladimirovich)

Sissman, L(ouis) E(dward)
1928-1976 .... CLC 9, 18
See also CANR 13; CA 21-24R;
obituary CA 65-68; DLB 5

Sisson, C(harles) H(ubert) 1914-..... CLC 8
See also CAAS 3; CANR 3; CA 1-4R;
DLB 27

Sitwell, (Dame) Edith 1887-1964... CLC 2, 9
See also CA 9-12R; DLB 20

Sjoewall, Maj 1935-
See Wahloo, Per
See also CA 61-64, 65-68

Sjowall, Maj 1935-
See Wahloo, Per

Skelton, Robin 1925-............. CLC 13
See also CAAS 5; CA 5-8R; DLB 27, 53

Skolimowski, Jerzy 1938-......... CLC 20

Skolimowski, Yurek 1938-
See Skolimowski, Jerzy

Skram, Amalie (Bertha)
1847-1905 .... TCLC 25

Skrine, Mary Nesta 1904-
See Keane, Molly

Skvorecky, Josef (Vaclav)
1924-.................... CLC 15, 39
See also CAAS 1; CANR 10; CA 61-64

Slade, Bernard 1930-......... CLC 11, 46
See also Newbound, Bernard Slade
See also DLB 53

Slaughter, Carolyn 1946-.......... CLC 56
See also CA 85-88

Slaughter, Frank G(ill) 1908-...... CLC 29
See also CANR 5; CA 5-8R

Slavitt, David (R.) 1935-........ CLC 5, 14
See also CAAS 3; CA 21-24R; DLB 5, 6

Slesinger, Tess 1905-1945 .... TCLC 10
See also CA 107

Slessor, Kenneth 1901-1971....... CLC 14
See also CA 102; obituary CA 89-92

Slowacki, Juliusz 1809-1849 ..... NCLC 15

Smart, Christopher 1722-1771........ LC 3

Smart, Elizabeth 1913-1986........ CLC 54
See also CA 81-84; obituary CA 118

Smiley, Jane (Graves) 1949-....... CLC 53
See also CA 104

Smith, A(rthur) J(ames) M(arshall)
1902-1980 .... CLC 15
See also CANR 4; CA 1-4R;
obituary CA 102

Smith, Betty (Wehner) 1896-1972... CLC 19
See also CA 5-8R; obituary CA 33-36R;
SATA 6; DLB-Y 82

Smith, Cecil Lewis Troughton 1899-1966
See Forester, C(ecil) S(cott)

Smith, Charlotte (Turner)
1749-1806 .... NCLC 23
See also DLB 39

Smith, Clark Ashton 1893-1961 .... CLC 43

Smith, Dave 1942-............ CLC 22, 42
See also Smith, David (Jeddie)
See also CAAS 7; CANR 1; DLB 5

Smith, David (Jeddie) 1942-
See Smith, Dave
See also CANR 1; CA 49-52

Smith, Florence Margaret 1902-1971
See Smith, Stevie
See also CAP 2; CA 17-18;
obituary CA 29-32R

Smith, John 1580?-1631............. LC 9
See also DLB 24, 30

Smith, Lee 1944-.................. CLC 25
See also CA 114, 119; DLB-Y 83

Smith, Martin Cruz 1942-......... CLC 25
See also CANR 6; CA 85-88

Smith, Martin William 1942-
See Smith, Martin Cruz

Smith, Mary-Ann Tirone 1944-..... CLC 39
See also CA 118

Smith, Patti 1946- .... CLC 12
See also CA 93-96

Smith, Pauline (Urmson)
1882-1959 .... TCLC 25
See also CA 29-32R; SATA 27

Smith, Rosamond 1938-
See Oates, Joyce Carol

Smith, Sara Mahala Redway 1900-1972
See Benson, Sally

Smith, Stevie 1902-1971.... CLC 3, 8, 25, 44
See also Smith, Florence Margaret
See also DLB 20

Smith, Wilbur (Addison) 1933-..... CLC 33
See also CANR 7; CA 13-16R

Smith, William Jay 1918-.......... CLC 6
See also CA 5-8R; SATA 2; DLB 5

Smollett, Tobias (George) 1721-1771 .. LC 2
See also DLB 39

Snodgrass, W(illiam) D(e Witt)
1926-................CLC 2, 6, 10, 18
See also CANR 6; CA 1-4R; DLB 5

Snow, C(harles) P(ercy)
1905-1980 .... CLC 1, 4, 6, 9, 13, 19
See also CA 5-8R; obituary CA 101;
DLB 15

Snyder, Gary (Sherman)
1930-.............. CLC 1, 2, 5, 9, 32
See also CA 17-20R; DLB 5, 16

Snyder, Zilpha Keatley 1927-...... CLC 17
See also CA 9-12R; SAAS 2; SATA 1, 28

Sobol, Joshua 19??-.............. CLC 60

Soderberg. Hjalmar 1869-1941 .... TCLC 39

Sodergran, Edith 1892-1923...... TCLC 31

Sokolov, Raymond 1941-........... CLC 7
See also CA 85-88

Sologub, Fyodor 1863-1927........ TCLC 9
See also Teternikov, Fyodor Kuzmich
See also CA 104

Solomos, Dionysios 1798-1857 ... NCLC 15

Solwoska, Mara 1929-
See French, Marilyn
See also CANR 3; CA 69-72

Solzhenitsyn, Aleksandr I(sayevich)
1918-... CLC 1, 2, 4, 7, 9, 10, 18, 26, 34
See also CA 69-72

Somers, Jane 1919-
See Lessing, Doris (May)

Sommer, Scott 1951-.............. CLC 25
See also CA 106

Sondheim, Stephen (Joshua)
1930-...................... CLC 30, 39
See also CA 103

Sontag, Susan 1933-... CLC 1, 2, 10, 13, 31
See also CA 17-20R; DLB 2

Sophocles
c. 496? B.C.-c. 406? B.C...... CMLC 2

Sorrentino, Gilbert
1929-............ CLC 3, 7, 14, 22, 40
See also CANR 14; CA 77-80; DLB 5;
DLB-Y 80

Soto, Gary 1952-................. CLC 32
See also CA 119

Von Daniken, Erich 1935-......... CLC 30
   See also Von Daeniken, Erich

Vonnegut, Kurt, Jr.
   1922-...... **CLC 1, 2, 3, 4, 5, 8, 12, 22,**
                      40, 60
   See also CANR 1; CA 1-4R; DLB 2, 8;
     DLB-Y 80; DLB-DS 3;
     CDALB 1968-1987

Vorster, Gordon 1924-............ CLC 34

Voznesensky, Andrei 1933-... CLC 1, 15, 57
   See also CA 89-92

Waddington, Miriam 1917-........ CLC 28
   See also CANR 12; CA 21-24R

Wagman, Fredrica 1937-........... CLC 7
   See also CA 97-100

Wagner, Richard 1813-1883...... NCLC 9

Wagner-Martin, Linda 1936-...... CLC 50

Wagoner, David (Russell)
   1926-.................... CLC 3, 5, 15
   See also CAAS 3; CANR 2; CA 1-4R;
     SATA 14; DLB 5

Wah, Fred(erick James) 1939-...... CLC 44
   See also CA 107; DLB 60

Wahloo, Per 1926-1975............ CLC 7
   See also CA 61-64

Wahloo, Peter 1926-1975
   See Wahloo, Per

Wain, John (Barrington)
   1925-............... CLC 2, 11, 15, 46
   See also CAAS 4; CANR 23; CA 5-8R;
     DLB 15, 27

Wajda, Andrzej 1926-............. CLC 16
   See also CA 102

Wakefield, Dan 1932-............. CLC 7
   See also CAAS 7; CA 21-24R

Wakoski, Diane
   1937-........... CLC 2, 4, 7, 9, 11, 40
   See also CAAS 1; CANR 9; CA 13-16R;
     DLB 5

Walcott, Derek (Alton)
   1930-......... CLC 2, 4, 9, 14, 25, 42
   See also CANR 26; CA 89-92; DLB-Y 81

Waldman, Anne 1945-............. CLC 7
   See also CA 37-40R; DLB 16

Waldo, Edward Hamilton 1918-
   See Sturgeon, Theodore (Hamilton)

Walker, Alice
   1944-...... **CLC 5, 6, 9, 19, 27, 46, 58;**
                        SSC 5
   See also CANR 9, 27; CA 37-40R;
     SATA 31; DLB 6, 33; CDALB 1968-1988

Walker, David Harry 1911-........ CLC 14
   See also CANR 1; CA 1-4R; SATA 8

Walker, Edward Joseph 1934-
   See Walker, Ted
   See also CANR 12; CA 21-24R

Walker, George F. 1947-....... CLC 44, 61
   See also CANR 21; CA 103; DLB 60

Walker, Joseph A. 1935-.......... CLC 19
   See also CANR 26; CA 89-92; DLB 38

Walker, Margaret (Abigail)
   1915-..................... CLC 1, 6
   See also CANR 26; CA 73-76; DLB 76

Walker, Ted 1934-.............. CLC 13
   See also Walker, Edward Joseph
   See also DLB 40

Wallace, David Foster 1962-....... CLC 50

Wallace, Irving 1916-........... CLC 7, 13
   See also CAAS 1; CANR 1; CA 1-4R

Wallant, Edward Lewis
   1926-1962................. CLC 5, 10
   See also CANR 22; CA 1-4R; DLB 2, 28

Walpole, Horace 1717-1797......... LC 2
   See also DLB 39

Walpole, (Sir) Hugh (Seymour)
   1884-1941................... TCLC 5
   See also CA 104; DLB 34

Walser, Martin 1927-............. CLC 27
   See also CANR 8; CA 57-60; DLB 75

Walser, Robert 1878-1956........ TCLC 18
   See also CA 118; DLB 66

Walsh, Gillian Paton 1939-
   See Walsh, Jill Paton
   See also CA 37-40R; SATA 4

Walsh, Jill Paton 1939-........... CLC 35
   See also CLR 2; SAAS 3

Wambaugh, Joseph (Aloysius, Jr.)
   1937-..................... CLC 3, 18
   See also CA 33-36R; DLB 6; DLB-Y 83

Ward, Arthur Henry Sarsfield 1883-1959
   See Rohmer, Sax
   See also CA 108

Ward, Douglas Turner 1930-....... CLC 19
   See also CA 81-84; DLB 7, 38

Warhol, Andy 1928-1987.......... CLC 20
   See also CA 89-92; obituary CA 121

Warner, Francis (Robert le Plastrier)
   1937-...................... CLC 14
   See also CANR 11; CA 53-56

Warner, Marina 1946-............ CLC 59
   See also CANR 21; CA 65-68

Warner, Rex (Ernest) 1905-1986.... CLC 45
   See also CA 89-92; obituary CA 119;
     DLB 15

Warner, Sylvia Townsend
   1893-1978................. CLC 7, 19
   See also CANR 16; CA 61-64;
     obituary CA 77-80; DLB 34

Warren, Mercy Otis 1728-1814... NCLC 13
   See also DLB 31

Warren, Robert Penn
   1905-1989 ... **CLC 1, 4, 6, 8, 10, 13, 18,**
               39, 53, 59; SSC 4
   See also CANR 10; CA 13-16R. 129. 130;
     SATA 46; DLB 2, 48; DLB-Y 80;
     CDALB 1968-1987

Washington, Booker T(aliaferro)
   1856-1915 .... TCLC 10
   See also CA 114, 125; SATA 28

Wassermann, Jakob 1873-1934..... TCLC 6
   See also CA 104; DLB 66

Wasserstein, Wendy 1950-...... CLC 32, 59
   See also CA 121; CABS 3

Waterhouse, Keith (Spencer)
   1929-...................... CLC 47
   See also CA 5-8R; DLB 13, 15

Waters, Roger 1944-
   See Pink Floyd

Wa Thiong'o, Ngugi
   1938-................CLC 3, 7, 13, 36
   See also Ngugi, James (Thiong'o); Ngugi wa
     Thiong'o

Watkins, Paul 1964-.............. CLC 55

Watkins, Vernon (Phillips)
   1906-1967 .... CLC 43
   See also CAP 1; CA 9-10;
     obituary CA 25-28R; DLB 20

Waugh, Auberon (Alexander) 1939-... CLC 7
   See also CANR 6, 22; CA 45-48; DLB 14

Waugh, Evelyn (Arthur St. John)
   1903-1966 ... CLC 1, 3, 8, 13, 19, 27, 44
   See also CANR 22; CA 85-88;
     obituary CA 25-28R; DLB 15

Waugh, Harriet 1944-............. CLC 6
   See also CANR 22; CA 85-88

Webb, Beatrice (Potter)
   1858-1943 .... TCLC 22
   See also CA 117

Webb, Charles (Richard) 1939-...... CLC 7
   See also CA 25-28R

Webb, James H(enry), Jr. 1946-.... CLC 22
   See also CA 81-84

Webb, Mary (Gladys Meredith)
   1881-1927 .... TCLC 24
   See also CA 123; DLB 34

Webb, Phyllis 1927-.............. CLC 18
   See also CANR 23; CA 104; DLB 53

Webb, Sidney (James)
   1859-1947 .... TCLC 22
   See also CA 117

Webber, Andrew Lloyd 1948-...... CLC 21

Weber, Lenora Mattingly
   1895-1971 .... CLC 12
   See also CAP 1; CA 19-20;
     obituary CA 29-32R; SATA 2;
     obituary SATA 26

Wedekind, (Benjamin) Frank(lin)
   1864-1918 .... TCLC 7
   See also CA 104

Weidman, Jerome 1913-............ CLC 7
   See also CANR 1; CA 1-4R; DLB 28

Weil, Simone 1909-1943.......... TCLC 23
   See also CA 117

Weinstein, Nathan Wallenstein 1903?-1940
   See West, Nathanael
   See also CA 104

Weir, Peter 1944-................ CLC 20
   See also CA 113, 123

Weiss, Peter (Ulrich)
   1916-1982 .... CLC 3, 15, 51
   See also CANR 3; CA 45-48;
     obituary CA 106; DLB 69

Weiss, Theodore (Russell)
   1916-................... CLC 3, 8, 14
   See also CAAS 2; CA 9-12R; DLB 5

Welch, (Maurice) Denton
   1915-1948 .... TCLC 22
   See also CA 121

Welch, James 1940-......... CLC 6, 14, 52
   See also CA 85-88

Author Index

Literary Criticism Series
Cumulative Topic Index

This index lists all topic entries in the Gale Literary Criticism Series *Contemporary Literary Criticism, Literature Criticism from 1400 to 1800, Nineteenth-Century Literature Criticism,* and *Twentieth-Century Literary Criticism.*

TCLC Cumulative Nationality Index

AMERICAN

Adams, Henry 4
Agee, James 1, 19
Anderson, Maxwell 2
Anderson, Sherwood 1, 10, 24
Atherton, Gertrude 2
Austin, Mary 25
Barry, Philip 11
Baum, L. Frank 7
Beard, Charles A. 15
Belasco, David 3
Benchley, Robert 1
Benét, Stephen Vincent 7
Benét, William Rose 28
Bierce, Ambrose 1, 7
Black Elk 33
Bourne, Randolph S. 16
Bradford, Gamaliel 36
Bromfield, Louis 11
Burroughs, Edgar Rice 2, 32
Cabell, James Branch 6
Cable, George Washington 4
Cather, Willa 1, 11, 31
Chandler, Raymond 1, 7
Chapman, John Jay 7
Chesnutt, Charles Waddell 5, 39
Chopin, Kate 5, 14
Comstock, Anthony 13
Cotter, Joseph Seamon, Sr. 28
Crane, Hart 2, 5
Crane, Stephen 11, 17, 32
Crawford, F. Marion 10
Crothers, Rachel 19
Cullen, Countee 4, 37
Davis, Rebecca Harding 6
Davis, Richard Harding 24
Day, Clarence 25
DeVoto, Bernard 29
Dreiser, Theodore 10, 18, 35

Dunbar, Paul Laurence 2, 12
Dunne, Finley Peter 28
Fisher, Rudolph 11
Fitzgerald, F. Scott 1, 6, 14, 28
Fletcher, John Gould 35
Forten, Charlotte L. 16
Freeman, Douglas Southall 11
Freeman, Mary Wilkins 9
Futrelle, Jacques 19
Gale, Zona 7
Garland, Hamlin 3
Gilman, Charlotte Perkins 9, 37
Glasgow, Ellen 2, 7
Goldman, Emma 13
Grey, Zane 6
Hall, James Norman 23
Harper, Frances Ellen Watkins 14
Harris, Joel Chandler 2
Harte, Bret 1, 25
Hawthorne, Julian 25
Hearn, Lafcadio 9
Henry, O. 1, 19
Hergesheimer, Joseph 11
Higginson, Thomas Wentworth 36
Hopkins, Pauline Elizabeth 28
Howard, Robert E. 8
Howe, Julia Ward 21
Howells, William Dean 7, 17
James, Henry 2, 11, 24
James, William 15, 32
Jewett, Sarah Orne 1, 22
Johnson, James Weldon 3, 19
Kornbluth, C. M. 8
Kuttner, Henry 10
Lardner, Ring 2, 14
Lewis, Sinclair 4, 13, 23, 39
Lewisohn, Ludwig 19
Lindsay, Vachel 17
London, Jack 9, 15, 39

Lovecraft, H. P. 4, 22
Lowell, Amy 1, 8
Marquis, Don 7
Masters, Edgar Lee 2, 25
McCoy, Horace 28
McKay, Claude 7
Mencken, H. L. 13
Millay, Edna St. Vincent 4
Mitchell, Margaret 11
Mitchell, S. Weir 36
Monroe, Harriet 12
Muir, John 28
Nathan, George Jean 18
Nordhoff, Charles 23
Norris, Frank 24
O'Neill, Eugene 1, 6, 27
Oskison, John M. 35
Porter, Gene Stratton 21
Post, Melville 39
Rawlings, Marjorie Kinnan 4
Reed, John 9
Roberts, Kenneth 23
Robinson, Edwin Arlington 5
Rogers, Will 8
Rölvaag, O. E. 17
Rourke, Constance 12
Runyon, Damon 10
Saltus, Edgar 8
Sherwood, Robert E. 3
Slesinger, Tess 10
Steffens, Lincoln 20
Stein, Gertrude 1, 6, 28
Sterling, George 20
Stevens, Wallace 3, 12
Tarkington, Booth 9
Teasdale, Sara 4
Thurman, Wallace 6
Twain, Mark 6, 12, 19, 36
Van Dine, S. S. 23

Nationality Index

TCLC Cumulative Title Index

Title Index

"Bartek the Conqueror" (Sienkiewicz)　**3**:425, 427, 430

"Barter" (Teasdale)　**4**:428

The Bartered Bride (Tolstoy)　**18**:383

"Basantayapan" (Tagore)　**3**:496

Bashkir Folk Tales (Platonov)　**14**:420

Bashō zatsudan (*Chats on Bashō*) (Masaoka Shiki)　**18**:235

"Basilica" (Bierce)　**7**:97

"The Basket" (Lowell)　**1**:375; **8**:235

The Basket Woman (Austin)　**25**:31, 34, 38

"Basundhara" (Tagore)　**3**:496

"The Bat" (Pirandello)
　See "Il pipistrello"

The Bat Flies Low (Rohmer)　**28**:285

Bat Wing (Rohmer)　**28**:282

La bataille invisible (Leroux)　**25**:260

Les batailles (Péguy)　**10**:410-11

La batalla de los Arapiles (Pérez Galdós)　**27**:249, 287-88

"Batard" (London)　**9**:269

"Bateese de Lucky Man" (Drummond)　**25**:151

"The Bath" (Zoshchenko)　**15**:504

The Bathhouse (Mayakovsky)
　See *Banya*

"The Bathing Maids" (Leino)　**24**:376

Les bâtisseurs d'empire; ou, Le schmürz (*The Empire Builders*) (Vian)　**9**:529-35, 537

"The Battalion" (Devkota)
　See "Paltān"

"Batte botte" (Campana)　**20**:84

"Battle Ardour" (A.E.)　**10**:21

"The Battle Eucharist" (Howe)　**21**:113

The Battle-Ground (Glasgow)　**2**:176-77; **7**:333

"The Battle Hymn of the Republic" (Howe)　**21**:108-09, 113-14

The Battle of Cowpens: The Great Morale Builder (Roberts)　**23**:237-38

"The Battle of Grünwald" (Borowski)　**9**:22

"The Battle of Magnesia" (Cavafy)　**7**:157, 163

The Battle of Ravana and Jatayu (Devkota)
　See *Rāvan-Jatāyu-Yuddha*

"The Battle of the Century" (Lardner)　**14**:319-20

"Battledore" (Gray)　**19**:157

The Battleground: Syria and Palestine, the Seedbed of Religion (Belloc)　**18**:24, 45

Batum (Bulgakov)　**16**:86

"Der Bau des epischen Werks" (Döblin)　**13**:166

"Der Baum" (Heym)　**9**:142

Baumeister der Welt (*Master Builders*) (Zweig)　**17**:426, 448, 458

Bavarian Gentry (Lawrence)　**2**:367-68

"Baxter's Procrustes" (Chesnutt)　**39**:89-93

"Bay Rum" (Huidobro)　**31**:125

"The Bayaderes" (Leino)　**24**:370

"Bayn al-kharā'ib" (Gibran)　**9**:89

Bayou Folk (Chopin)　**5**:142, 144-46, 157; **14**:56, 58, 60, 63

Baza de espadas: El ruedo Ibérico III (*Military Tricks*) (Valle-Inclán)　**5**:487-88

Be Faithful unto Death (Móricz)
　See *Légy jó mindhalálig*

Be Good til You Die (Móricz)
　See *Légy jó mindhalálig*

"Be 'ir ha-haregah" ("In the City of Execution") (Bialik)　**25**:64

"Be Quiet, Wind" (Roberts)　**8**:321

The Beach (Pavese)

　See *La spiaggia*

The Beadle (Smith)　**25**:378-79, 381-82, 384-92, 394-404

Bealby (Wells)　**6**:528; **12**:494-95

Béâle-Gryne (Bosschère)　**19**:52,3, 55, 61-6

"Beale Street" (Dunbar)　**2**:128

"Beans and Rice and Mustard Greens" (Devkota)
　See "Dāl-Bhāt-Dukū"

"The Beanstalk" (Millay)　**4**:306, 309

The Bear (Chekhov)
　See *Medved*

Bear's Dance (József)　**22**:165

"The Beast in the Cave" (Lovecraft)　**22**:218

The Beast in the Jungle (James)　**2**:272

Beasts (Tozzi)
　See *Bestie*

Beasts and Super-Beasts (Saki)　**3**:363, 370, 373

The Beasts of Tarzan (Burroughs)　**32**:62, 79

"Beat the Ghost" (Devkota)
　See "Bhūtlāī jhatāro"

Beatrice (Haggard)　**11**:256

"Béatrice" (Schwob)　**20**:323

"Beatrice" (Teasdale)　**4**:424

Beatrix Randolph (Hawthorne)　**25**:238, 241, 249

"Beattock for Moffat" (Graham)　**19**:104, 112, 131

Beau Austin (Henley)　**8**:97, 99-100, 102, 107-08

Beauchamp's Career (Meredith)　**17**:269, 275-76, 278, 287-88, 290, 293

"La beauté" (Sully Prudhomme)　**31**:302

Beauté, mon beau souci (Larbaud)　**9**:196-97, 207

La beauté sur la terre (*Beauty on the Earth*) (Ramuz)　**33**:296, 302

"The Beauties of Nature" (Gray)　**19**:156

The Beautiful and Damned (Fitzgerald)　**1**:234-36, 242, 244-45, 247-48, 254, 258, 261, 264-67, 269-71; **6**:161, 167; **14**:148, 176, 183-84; **28**:86, 106, 110, 120

"The Beautiful City" (Trakl)　**5**:466

"Beautiful Lofty Things" (Yeats)　**1**.580; **18**:463

"Beautiful Rosalinda" (Herzl)　**36**:141

The Beautiful Summer (Pavese)
　See *La bella estate*

"Beauty" (Södergran)　**31**:286

"Beauty" (Thomas)　**10**:452, 463

"Beauty" (Wylie)　**8**:521

Beauty and Life (Scott)　**6**:386, 388, 394-95

"Beauty and Love" (Wen I-to)　**28**:416

"Beauty and the Barge" (Jacobs)　**22**:107

"Beauty and the Beast" (Kuttner)　**10**:268

"Beauty and the Commonplace" (Gale)　**7**:284

Beauty and the Jacobin (Tarkington)　**9**:460

Beauty on the Earth (Ramuz)
　See *La beauté sur la terre*

"Beauty Spots" (Kipling)　**8**:202

"Beauty That Is Never Old" (Johnson)　**3**:241

The Beaver Coat (Hauptmann)
　See *Der Biberpelz*

"Beaver Up" (Wylie)　**8**:522

"Bebka" ("Baby") (Remizov)　**27**:338, 340

"Because I Was Not Able to Restrain Your Hands" (Mandelstam)　**2**:407

"Because the Pleasure-Bird Whistles" (Thomas)
　See "January, 1939"

"Because . . . You Say" (Vilakazi)

　See "Ngoba . . . sewuthi"

"The Bed by the Window" (Benson)　**27**:17

The Bedbug, and Selected Poetry (Mayakovsky)
　See *Klop*

"Bedlam" (Dowson)　**4**:88

"Bedovaia dolia" ("A Disastrous Lot") (Remizov)　**27**:347

"Bedreigde stad" ("Threatened City") (Van Ostaijen)　**33**:418, 420-21

Bedtime Stories (Dazai)
　See *Otogi zōshi*

"Bedtime Story" (Molnár)　**20**:173

"Been There Before" (Paterson)　**32**:372

"Beethoven" (Gurney)　**33**:87

Beethoven (Rolland)　**23**:260, 262, 282

"Beethoven's Ninth Symphony and the King Cobra" (Masters)　**25**:316

Beffe della morte e della vita (Pirandello)　**4**:332

"Before a Crucifix" (Swinburne)　**8**:437; **36**:318

Before Adam (London)　**9**:261, 266, 283; **39**:270

Before Dawn (Hauptmann)
　See *Vor Sonnenaufgang*

"Before Easter" (Babits)　**14**:42

"Before Her Portrait in Youth" (Thompson)　**4**:440

"Before I Knocked and Flesh Let Enter" (Thomas)　**1**:471

Before Sunrise (Zoshchenko)
　See *Pered voskhodom solntsa*

"Before Tears" (Ledwidge)　**23**:119

"Before the Altar" (Lowell)　**8**:232, 235

"Before the Bookcase" (Bialik)
　See "Lifne'aron ha-sefarim"

"Before the Cloister" (Johnson)　**19**:244

Before the Dawn (Shimazaki)
　See *Yoaké maé*

Before the Face of the Almighty (Leino)
　See *Alla kasvon Kaikkivallan*

"Before the Mirror" (Khodasevich)　**15**:209

"Before the Mirror" (Swinburne)　**36**:315

"Before the Tears" (Ledwidge)　**23**:115

"Before the War of Cooley" (Ledwidge)　**23**:109, 116-17

Beg (*Flight*) (Bulgakov)　**16**:81-2, 94-5, 109-11

"Bega" (Pickthall)　**21**:245, 250-51, 257

"The Begetter" (Remizov)
　See "Rozhanitsa"

The Beggar (Devkota)
　See *Bhikhārī*

"Beggar and the Angel" (Scott)　**6**:394

Beggars (Davies)　**5**:206-07

Beggars (Dunsany)　**2**:143

"The Beggars" (Pavese)　**3**:340

"Beggars in Velvet" (Kuttner)　**10**:274

"Beggar's Soliloquy" (Meredith)　**17**:254

"Begin, Ephebe, by Perceiving" (Stevens)　**3**:448

Begin Here (Sayers)　**15**:374, 387

"The Beginning" (Brooke)　**2**:58

The Beginning of Wisdom (Benét)　**7**:69, 80

"Begone, Sweet Ghost" (Gogarty)　**15**:100, 103

Der Begrabene Leuchter (*The Buried Candelabrum*) (Zweig)　**17**:433, 457

The Begum's Fortune (Verne)
　See *Les cinq cents millions de la Begúm, suivi de les revoltés de la "Bounty"*

"The Beheaded Hen" (Quiroga)
　See "La gallina degollada"

Title Index

Title Index

Title Index

Title Index

Title Index

See "Elskovshvisken"
"Loveliest of Trees" (Housman)   10:250-51, 259
The Lovely Lady (Austin)   25:33
"The Lovely Lady" (Lawrence)   16:290
"A Lovely Woman" (Davies)   5:199
"A Lover" (Coppard)   5:179
The Lover (Martínez Sierra and Martínez Sierra)   6:279
Lover's Breast Knot (Tynan)   3:502, 506
"Lovers Embracing" (Fletcher)   35:95
Lovers of Louisiana (Cable)   4:25-6, 29
"The Lovers of Orelay" (Moore)   7:478, 487, 493
"The Lover's Song" (Yeats)   31:398
"Love's Apotheosis" (Dunbar)   12:122
Love's Comedy (Ibsen)
   See *Kjaerlighedens komedie*
"Love's Coming" (Davies)   5:201
Love's Cross-Currents (*A Year's Letters*) (Swinburne)   8:438-39, 441-43, 445
Love's Cruel Enigma (Bourget)
   See *Cruelle énigme*
Love's Dance of Death (Przybyszewski)   36:289
"Love's House" (Manning)   25:278
The Loves of Pelleas and Etarre (Gale)   7:277, 281-82
"The Loves of the Age of Stone" (Gray)   19:156
"Love's Phases" (Dunbar)   12:122
Love's Shadow (Leverson)   18:187-89, 194, 196, 202
"Love's Tangle" (Cotter)   28:43
"Love's Way" (Cullen)   37:167
"Lovets chelovekov" ("The Fisher of Men") (Zamyatin)   8:542, 544, 548, 552, 558-60; 37:419, 428, 431
"Low Tide" (Millay)   4:306
"Low Tide on Grand Pré" (Carman)   7:141, 146
Löwensköldska ringen (*The General's Ring*) (Lagerlöf)   4:235
The Lower Depths (Gorky)
   See *Na dne*
"The Loyal Minister of Art" (Wen I-to)   28:408, 415
"Loyalties" (Galsworthy)   1:294-95, 303
"Lucerne" (Tolstoy)   28:367
Luces de bohemia (*Lights of Bohemia*) (Valle-Inclán)   5:476-77, 480-83, 486
La lucha por la vida (Baroja)   8:52, 55, 61-2
Lucia in London (Benson)   27:9, 14
Lucian, Plato, and Greek Morals (Chapman)   7:189, 193
"Luciana" (Ramos)   32:431
Lucia's Progress (Benson)   27:9
Lucidor (Hofmannsthal)   11:302
La luciérnaga (Azuela)   3:75-6, 78, 80, 82-3
"Lucila Strindberg" (Quiroga)   20:213
"The Luck of Roaring Camp" (Harte)   25:189, 194, 197-98, 203-04, 207-08, 210, 212-14, 221-23
The Luck of Roaring Camp, and Other Sketches (Harte)   25:189, 197, 203-04, 207, 214-15
The Luck of the Strong (Hodgson)   13:237
The Luck of the Vails (Benson)   27:17-18
Luck, or Cunning, as the Main Means of Organic Modifications? (Butler)   1:133; 33:27, 29, 42, 50, 52, 53
Lucky Kristoffer (Hansen)

See *Lykkelige Kristoffer*
The Lucky One (Milne)   6:306, 308
Lucky Peter's Travels (Strindberg)
   See *Lycko-Pers resa*
"Lucrère" (Schwob)   20:323
"Lucubratio Ebria" (Butler)   33:35, 49, 65
"Lucy" (De la Mare)   4:78
Lucy Church, Amiably (Stein)   1:430; 28:315, 322, 324, 332-33
Lucy Gayheart (Cather)   1:154-55, 158, 163; 11:99, 107-09, 113-15
Les ludions (Fargue)   11:199-200
"Ludovitje" (Smith)   25:380, 384-85
"Luella Miller" (Freeman)   9:72
"The Luftbad" (Mansfield)   39:324
"Lui et elle" (Lawrence)   9:230
"Luis de Camões" (Campbell)   5:124
"Luis de Torres" (Ingamells)   35:137
"Luis G. Urbina" (Reyes)   33:318
Luisa (Giacosa)   7:305, 310, 313
"Luke Havergal" (Robinson)   5:418
"The Lull" (Saki)   3:372
"Lullaby" (Dunbar)   12:106
"Lullaby" (József)   22:165
"Lulú" (Valera)   10:504
Lulu (Wedekind)   7:576, 578, 582, 590
"Il lume dell'altra casa" (Pirandello)   29:292-93
Lumíe di Sicilia (*Sicilian Limes*) (Pirandello)   4:325; 29:297, 317
"Luminous Depths" (Čapek)   6:84; 37:51, 56
"Luna" ("The Moon") (Hippius)   9:161
Luna benamor (Blasco)   12:43
"Luna de los amores" (Lugones)   15:289
La luna e i falo (*The Moon and the Bonfires*) (Pavese)   3:336-38, 342-44
"La luna roja" ("The Red Moon") (Arlt)   29:44
Lunar Caustic (*The Last Address*) (Lowry)   6:240-41, 254
Lunario sentimental (Lugones)   15:287, 292
"Lundi rue Christine" (Apollinaire)   3:44
Lundy's Lane, and Other Poems (Scott)   6:386, 388, 394
"La lune de pluie" ("The Rainy Moon") (Colette)   16:128, 130-33
Lūnī (Devkota)   23:50
Lunnye muravyi (*The Moon Ants*) (Hippius)   9:161, 163
"Luojan leipa" ("The Lord's Bread") (Leino)   24:368, 376
La lupa. In portinaio. Cavalleria Rusticana. Drammi (Verga)   3:539, 545, 547
"The Lure" (Ledwidge)   23:116, 121
"Lure of Souls" (Rohmer)   28:277
"The Lurking Fear" (Lovecraft)   4:268, 271; 22:220
"The Lusitania" (Rosenberg)   12:301
"Lust" (Brooke)   2:55, 60
"Luste" (Valéry)   4:498
Luther (Huch)   13:247
Luthers Glaube: Briefe an einan Freud (Huch)   13:253
Le luthier de Crémone (Coppée)   25:119, 127
"La lutte contre la multitude" (Teilhard de Chardin)   9:492
"Lux in tenebris" (Tynan)   3:505
"Lux in tenebris lucet" (Sienkiewicz)   3:430
De Luxe (Bromfield)   11:78, 82
Le luxe des autre (Bourget)   12:67
"La lycanthropia" (Lugones)   15:293

Lycko-Pers resa (*Lucky Peter's Travels*) (Strindberg)   1:460; 8:407, 412
Lydia Bailey (Roberts)   23:234, 240
"Lydia und Mäxchen" (Döblin)   13:166
"Lying in the Grass" (Gosse)   28:132, 142
Den lykkelige alder (*The Happy Age*) (Undset)   3:516, 522
Lykkelige Kristoffer (*Lucky Kristoffer*) (Hansen)   32:248, 251, 256-60
"The Lynching" (McKay)   7:461
"The Lynching of Jube Benson" (Dunbar)   2:131; 12:108-09, 120
"The Lynn of Dreams" (Sharp)   39:374
"The Lyre Degenerate" (Campbell)   9:33
Lyric Life (Sikelianos)   39:417, 420
The Lyric Year (Millay)   4:305
Lyrical Dramas (Blok)
   See *Liricheskie dramy*
The Lyrical Poems of Hugo von Hofmannsthal (Hofmannsthal)   11:294
"Lyrics" (Roberts)   8:320-21
Lyrics of a Lowbrow (Service)   15:411
Lyrics of Love and Laughter (Dunbar)   2:131; 12:109, 124
Lyrics of Lowly Life (Dunbar)   12:106, 108-09, 121-22
Lyrics of Sunshine and Shadow (Dunbar)   12:109, 124
Lyrics of the Hearthside (Dunbar)   12:109, 122, 124
Le lys rouge (*The Red Lily*) (France)   9:41-2, 47, 53
Lysbeth (Haggard)   11:243, 246
Lyubasha's Tragedy (Gladkov)   27:91-3
Lyubov k blizhnemu (*Love of One's Neighbor*) (Andreyev)   3:22
"Lyubovnik yunony" ("Juno's Lover") (Khlebnikov)   20:130
Lyudi (Zoshchenko)   15:507-08
"Ma conversion" (Claudel)   10:130
Ma non è una cosa seria (*It Can't Be Serious*) (Pirandello)   29:282, 301, 318
Maaliskuun lauluja (*Songs of March*) (Leino)   24:373
"Ma'ame Pélagie" (Chopin)   14:61
Maan parhaat (*The Country's Best*) (Leino)   24:372
Der mabl (*The Deluge; In shturm*) (Sholom Aleichem)   35:306
Maboroshi no tate (*The Phantom Shield*) (Natsume Sōseki)   10:329
"Mac-American" (Reed)   9:383
Macaire (Henley)   8:98-100, 102, 107-08
MacDonough's Wife (Gregory)   1:332-33, 336-37
"Macedonian Sonnets" (Vazov)
   See "Makedonski soneti"
Der Mäcen (*The Maecenas*) (Liliencron)   18:210, 212, 216
The MacHaggis (Jerome)   23:82
The Machine (Heijermans)   24:293
"La machine à parler" (Schwob)   20:323
The Machine to Kill (Leroux)   25:258
The Machine-Wreckers (Toller)
   See *Die Maschinenstürmer*
Machines and Wolves (Pilnyak)
   See *Mashiny i volki*
Macht und Mensch (Mann)   9:329
"Macquarie Harbour" (Ingamells)   35:127
"Macquarie's Mate" (Lawson)   27:119, 129, 132
Mad (Symons)   11:437

"My Love's on a Faraway Island" (Anwar)
　See "Tjintaku djauh dipulau"
"My Lyre" (Södergran)
　See "Min lyra"
My Mark Twain (Howells)　7:370
"My Mate" (Service)　15:399
My Mortal Enemy (Cather)　1:154; 11:95,
　97-8, 101-02
"My Mother" (József)　22:164
"My Mother" (Ledwidge)　23:109
My Mother's House (Colette)
　See *La maison de Claudine*
"My Ninety Acres" (Bromfield)　11:86
"My Old Home" (Lu Hsün)
　See "Ku hsiang"
"My Old Man" (Lardner)　2:329
My Old Man (Runyon)　10:430, 435-36
"My Outdoor Study" (Higginson)　36:175
My Own Fairy Book (Lang)　16:264, 272
"My Pal" (Service)　15:412
"My Path" (Esenin)　4:115
My Poetic (Palamas)　5:385
"My Poetry" (Bialik)　25:65
"My Pushkin" (Tsvetaeva)
　See "Moj Puškin"
My Religion (Tolstoy)　4:450; 11:458
"My Religion" (Unamuno)
　See "Mi religión"
My Remarkable Uncle, and Other Sketches
　(Leacock)　2:378
My Road (Tolstoy)　18:371
"My Roomy" (Lardner)　2:338; 14:305, 318-
　20
My Son the Doctor (Sanchez)
　See *M'hijo el dotor*
"My Song" (Brooke)　2:58
"My Soul" (Roussel)
　See "Mon âme"
"My Soul" (Södergran)
　See "Min själ"
"My Standpoint" (Mori Ōgai)
　See "Yo ga tachiba"
"My Sunday at Home" (Kipling)　8:192, 202,
　204; 17:207
"My Table" (Yeats)　11:534-35; 18:459
My Ten Years in a Quandary, and How They
　Grew (Benchley)　1:77
My Universities (Gorky)
　See *Moi universitety*
"My Views on Anarchism" (Dagerman)
　17:93
"My Views on Chastity and Sutteeism" (Lu
　Hsün)　3:296
My Wife Ethel (Runyon)　10:436-37
"My Work on the Novel *Cement*" (Gladkov)
　27:93
My Youth in Vienna (Schnitzler)　4:401-02
Mys guron (Kuprin)　5:303
Myself Bettina (Crothers)　19:73
Myself When Young (Richardson)　4:374-75
Myshkina dudochka (*A Flute for Mice*)
　(Remizov)　27:349
Mysl (Andreyev)　3:17
Le mystère de la chambre jaune (*The Mystery*
　of the Yellow Room) (Leroux)　25:255-58,
　260
La mystère de la charité de Jeanne d'Arc (*The*
　Mystery of the Charity of Joan of Arc)
　(Péguy)　10:404-05, 408-09, 412-13, 416
Le mystère des saints innocents (*The Mystery of*
　the Holy Innocents) (Péguy)　10:405, 409,
　412

Mystères de Marseille (Zola)　6:567
Mysterier (*Mysteries*) (Hamsun)　2:202-04,
　206-08; 14:221, 227-28, 235, 237, 245, 247-
　48
Mysteries (Hamsun)
　See *Mysterier*
Mysteries Lyrical and Dramatic (Crowley)
　7:208
"Mysteriet" ("The Mystery") (Södergran)
　31:285, 294
"The Mysterious Case of My Friend Browne"
　(Hawthorne)　25:246
"The Mysterious Chamber" (Twain)　6:462
"The Mysterious Destruction of Mr. Ipple"
　(Bennett)　5:46
The Mysterious Island (Verne)
　See *L'ile mystérieuse*
"The Mysterious Rabbit" (Remizov)
　See "Tainstvennyi zaichik"
Mysterious Stories (Nervo)
　See *Místicas*
The Mysterious Stranger (Twain)　6:460, 466,
　486; 12:432, 434, 436-37, 442, 449; 19:387;
　36:361, 363-64, 378, 392, 399, 411
"The 'Mysterious Stranger' Defense" (Post)
　39:344
"Mystery" (A.E.)　10:26
"The Mystery" (Dunbar)　12:105
"The Mystery" (Södergran)
　See "Mysteriet"
"Mystery" (Sterling)　20:380
Mystery at Geneva (Macaulay)　7:427
The Mystery at the Blue Villa (Post)　39:339,
　343
Mystery-Bouffe (Mayakovsky)
　See *Misteria-Buff*
"The Mystery of a Derelict" (Hodgson)
　13:237
The Mystery of Angelina Frood (Freeman)
　21:58-9, 62
"The Mystery of Dave Regan" (Lawson)
　27:131
The Mystery of Dr. Fu Manchu (*The Insidious*
　Dr. Fu Manchu) (Rohmer)　28:276-77, 279-
　80, 288, 290, 293-94, 296, 298-99, 301
"A Mystery of Heroism" (Crane)　11:163
"The Mystery of Hoo Marsh" (Freeman)
　21:57
"The Mystery of Justice" (Maeterlinck)　3:326
Mystery of Mary Stuart (Lang)　16:270
The Mystery of the Charity of Joan of Arc
　(Péguy)
　See *La mystère de la charité de Jeanne d'Arc*
"The Mystery of the Four Husbands" (Leroux)
　25:260
The Mystery of the Holy Innocents (Péguy)
　See *Le mystère des saints innocents*
"The Mystery of the Paneled Room"
　(Rohmer)　28:283
The Mystery of the Yellow Room (Leroux)
　See *Le mystère de la chambre jaune*
The Mystery of Thirty-One New Inn (Freeman)
　21:43-5, 50-3, 56
"A Mystery Play" (Scott)　6:395
"Mystic and Cavalier" (Johnson)　19:244-45
"The Mystic Turned Radical" (Bourne)　16:60
"The Mystical Milieu" (Teilhard de Chardin)
　See "Le milieu mystique"
Mysticism at the Dawn of the Modern Age
　(Steiner)

See *Die Mystik im Aufgange des*
　neuzeitlichen Geisteslebens und ihr
　Vehältnis zu modernen Weltschauung
Mysticism in Relation to the Modern World-
　Conception (Steiner)　13:445
"Le mysticisme bien tempéré" (Gourmont)
　17:126
Mystics of the Renaissance and Their Relation
　to Modern Thought (Steiner)　13:436
"The Mystic's Prayer" (Sharp)　39:394
Die Mystik im Aufgange des neuzeitlichen
　Geisteslebens und ihr Vehältnis zu modernen
　Weltschauung (*Mysticism at the Dawn of the*
　Modern Age) (Steiner)　13:441, 448
A Myth of Shakespeare (Williams)　1:518
Myth, Ritual, and Religion (Lang)　16:260-61
"Die mythische Erbschaft der Dichtung"
　(Broch)　20:69
Mythologies (Yeats)　31:418
"The Mythologization of Reality" (Schulz)
　See "Mityzacja rzeczywistości"
"Mythos" (Van Ostaijen)　33:418-19
"Na arca" (Machado de Assis)　10:291
Na bolshoi doroge (*On the High Road*)
　(Chekhov)　31:80
Na dne (*The Lower Depths*) (Gorky)　8:70-1,
　78-9, 81, 88, 92
Na drogach duszy (Przybyszewski)　36:290
"Na Kamennyx otrogax Pierii" (Mandelstam)
　6:267
"Na krasnom kone" ("On a Red Steed")
　(Tsvetaeva)　7:560-62, 568; 35:386, 390-91,
　404, 410-11, 415-16
Na kulichkakh ("At the World's End"; "In the
　Backwoods") (Zamyatin)　8:546, 551, 557-
　58; 37:427, 430-31
Na polu chwały (*On the Field of Glory*)
　(Sienkiewicz)　3:427
"Na večernem asfal'te" (Bryusov)　10:92
"Na zare tumannoy yunosti" ("At the Hazy
　Dawn of Youth") (Platonov)　14:422, 425
Naamioita (*Masks*) (Leino)　24:371
"Naboth's Vineyard" (Benson)　27:17
"Naboth's Vineyard" (Post)　39:339
Naçulo konca (*The Fifth Seal*) (Aldanov)
　23:17, 22-3
"Nach dem Ball" (Liliencron)　18:208
"Nach der Lese" (George)　14:210
"Nachgelassene Gedichte" (Borchert)　5:109
"Nachmittag" (George)　14:210
"Ein Nachmittag" ("An Afternoon") (Heym)
　9:149
"Die Nacht" (Heym)　9:142
"Die Nacht" (Trakl)　5:457
Nachtasyl (*The Night Refuge*) (Gorky)　8:71
"Nächte" ("Nights") (Toller)　10:491
"Nachtergebung" (Trakl)　5:457
Nachts (*At Night*) (Kraus)　5:291
"Nachts schlafen die Ratten doch" (Borchert)
　5:109
"Nad ovragom" ("Over the Ravine") (Pilnyak)
　23:211, 213
Nada menos que todo un hombre (Unamuno)
　2:564; 9:511, 515, 517-19
Nada the Lily (Haggard)　11:241, 246, 257
Nadobnisie i koczkodany (*Dainty Shapes and*
　Hairy Apes) (Witkiewicz)　8:513
Nagelaten gedichten (Van Ostaijen)　33:414,
　416, 418
"Die Nähe" (Morgenstern)　8:306-07
La naissance du jour (*The Break of Day*)
　(Colette)　5:164-66; 16:125, 129, 133

Title Index

Title Index

Title Index

Title Index

Title Index

Title Index

Title Index

Title Index

Title Index

Title Index